AMERICAN LIBRARY ASSOCIATION HIGHLIGHTS AND ORGANIZATION

The American Library Association is the oldest and largest library association in the world. ALA was founded in 1876. The first meeting, organized by Melvil Dewey, was held in Philadelphia, October 4–6, and drew 103 librarians. Since its first meeting, ALA has grown in membership to more than 33,500.

The ALA COUNCIL is the governing body of the Association. It comprises 100 Councilors elected at large and Councilors representing each state, provincial, and territorial chapter. (See Council, ALA, p. 104). Council convenes at two meetings held each year: Midwinter (January) and Annual Conference (summer). The management arm of the Association is the EXECUTIVE BOARD, which comprises the officers of the Association, the immediate Past President, and eight members elected by Council from its membership.

PRESIDENT: Clara S. Jones, Director, Detroit Public Library (July 1976–June 1977)

VICE-PRESIDENT/PRESIDENT-ELECT: Eric Moon, President, Scarecrow Press

EXECUTIVE DIRECTOR: Robert Wedgeworth

MEMBERSHIP: 28,754 personal members; 4,762 organization members; total (August 31, 1976) 33,516

ANNUAL EXPENDITURES (August 31, 1976): $2,090,625, general fund; $2,851,541, publishing; $519,595, annual meetings; total: $5,461,761

ANNUAL CONFERENCES: Chicago July 18–24, 1976; Detroit June 17–23, 1977; Chicago June 25–July 1, 1978

The goal of the Association is the promotion of libraries and librarianship to assure the delivery of user-oriented library information service to all. Much of its work is done through ALA Committees.

ACTIVITIES of the Association include:
  Research on library problems
  Development of standards and guidelines
  Accreditation of library education programs
  Clarification of legislative issues
  Vigorous support of intellectual freedom
  Publishing
  Awards
  Leadership in national and international library cooperation

ALA UNITS

DIVISIONS of ALA are membership units which provide resources for special knowledge and for advancing knowledge and service through publications and professional programs: The Divisions are:

  American Association of School Librarians 17
  American Library Trustee Association 22
  Association of College and Research Libraries 30
  Association of State Library Agencies 34
  Children's Services Division 88
  Health and Rehabilitative Library Services Division 145
  Information Science and Automation Division 163
  Library Administration Division 189
  Library Education Division 191
  Public Library Association 259
  Reference and Adult Services Division 276
  Resources and Technical Services Division 290
  Young Adult Services Division 333

ROUND TABLES are membership units which deal with aspects of librarianship outside the scope of a Division:

  American Library History Round Table 20
  Exhibits Round Table 124
  Federal Librarians Round Table 125
  Government Documents Round Table 143
  Intellectual Freedom Round Table 171
  International Relations Round Table 180
  Junior Members Round Table 181
  Library Research Round Table 197
  Social Responsibilities Round Table 307
  Staff Organizations Round Table 311

ALA OFFICES are headquarters staff units which can address issues that affect the entire profession: Accreditation (7), Intellectual Freedom (167), Service to the Disadvantaged (110), Personnel (239), Research (285), and Legislation (183).

ALA AFFILIATES (1976) covered in text articles are: American Association of Law Libraries (16); American Library Society (20); American Society for Information Science (23); American Theological Library Association (24); Association of Research Libraries (33); Canadian Library Association (76); Catholic Library Association (79); Council on Library Technical Assistants (106); Medical Library Association (206); Music Library Association (210); REFORMA (National Association of Spanish-Speaking Librarians) (280); Sociedad de Bibliotecarios de Puerto Rico (307); and Theatre Library Association (317).

ALA CHAPTERS are covered under State Reports (pp. 349–418).

1977

The ALA Yearbook

A review of
library events 1976

American Library Association
Chicago, Illinois

ILLUSTRATION CREDITS

The ALA Centennial Celebration: xiv, xvi *American Libraries.* xvii (t.) Bruce Young, ACRL. xvii (b.) *American Libraries.* xviii Library of Congress. xix, xx *American Libraries.* xxi ACRL.

At the Hub: The British Library: xxii (t.) © British Museum; (b.) © British Library. xxv © British Museum. xxvii–xxix. © British Library.

The Centenary of a Giant of Librarianship: Louis Round Wilson: xxxii (t.l.) Catherine Carter; (b.r.) J. P. Frye, UNC News Bureau; (all others) Southern Historical Collection, University of North Carolina, Chapel Hill.

Telecommunications: xxxiv Sidney Harris.

Review of the Library Year: 2 Courtesy, R. D. Johnson. 3 Andrew Mueller, Courtesy, Lawrence University. 4 Victor's Photography, Courtesy, Rutgers University. 6 Connecticut College. 11 Dallas Public Library. 12 Memphis Press-Scimitar. 14 St. Louis Public Library. 15 Memphis Public Library and Information Center. 23 George R. Plosker from *American Libraries.* 25 Emory University. 27 Millicent Huff, Texas State Library, 29 U.S. Navy. 38, 39 Alabama Public Library Service. 40 Pearson, *Knickerbocker News* from Rothco. 41 *Texas Monthly.* 52 Rochester Institute of Technology. 54 (m.) Atheneum. 57 (b.) Danville, Va., *Register.* 62 (third from t.) Morton Apple. 65 (b.) E. H. Shepard, E. P. Dutton & Co., Inc. 66 *The Chicago Tribune* from *American Libraries.* 67 Dayton and Montgomery County Public Library. 71 (t.) Rich Stafford; (b.&l.) ALA LIbrary. 72 Pekin Public Library. 73 Marc Neuhof. 74 (t.& t.r.) Novato Branch Library; (m.l.) E. Alan McGee; (m.&m.r.) © Jonathon Green; (b.l.& b.r.) Rockford Road Branch Library. 81 The Children's Book Council. 82 Denver Public Library. 83 *Daily Local News* from *American Libraries.* 83 Public Library of Youngstown and Mahoning County. 84 Dallas Public Library. 85 Spokane Public Library. 86 Harper & Row, Publishers, Inc. 87 (l.) Atheneum; (m.t.) *The Guardian;* (m.b.) Jack Clayton; (r.) Archie Lieberman. 88 (t.) The Dial Press; (m.&b.) New York Zoological Society. 94 (t.) *American Libraries;* (b.) West Virginia Library Commission. 95 West Virginia Library Commission. 96 North Carolina State Library. 99 Ross from Rothco. 107, 108 Sidney Harris. 111 Frank Merrick, Free Library, Chester, Pa. 112 *Times Chronicle.* 118 Houston Public Library. 119 Institute of Texan Cultures. 120 Chicago Public Library. 126 West Virginia Library Commission. 127 © James Lott. 128 National Film Board of Canada. 129 Learning Corporation of America. 130 (b.) Sue Allison; (t.) © Walt Disney Productions. 131 Dallas Public Library. 132 Wisconsin State Library. 133 Vernon Matthews, *The Sun-Herald.* 135 (t.) Ken Ross, *Memphis Press Scimitar;* (b.l.) Chicago Public Library; (b.r.) Denver Public Library. 136 Toledo-Lucas County Public Library. 137 Dallas Public Library. 138 (l.) Multiplex Display Fixture Co.; (r.) Reflector Hardware Corp. 141 District of Columbia Public Library. 144 Wyoming State Library. 145 Louisiana State Library. 154 Newberry library. 157 Denver Public Library. 159 West Virginia Library Commission. 171 *American Libraries.* 172 Arthur Plotnik, *American Libraries.* 173 Millicent Huff, Texas State Library. 177 Fairfax County Public Library. 180 Christof Studios. 183 District of Columbia Public Library. 184 Bay St. Louis City-County Public Library, Miss. 189 Wisconsin Dept. of Public Instruction, Library Services. 195 *American Libraries.* 199 Public Library of Nashville and Davidson County, 205 *American Libraries.* 207 West Virginia Library Commission. 208 University of Wisconsin-Stout Library. 209 (t.) Massachusetts Institute of Technology; (b.) Louisiana Library Association. 216 NTIS. 225 Arthur Shay. 237 Inese Jansons. 240 Larry Fisher. 242 Memphis and Shelby County Library and Information Center. 247 Dallas Public Library. 248 Biblioteca Nacional, Madrid. 249 © James Austin. 250 Library of Congress. 251 ALA. 254 Russell Reif, Pictorial Parade. 255 Richard W. Payne. 258 (t.) Denver Public Library; (b.l.&r.) Public Library of Cincinnati and Hamilton County. 261 © Walt Disney Productions from ALA. 262 (t.l.) *American Libraries;* (t.r.) Public Library of Youngstown and Mahoning County. 264–266 ALA 267 (t.) Chicago Public Library; (b.) University of Chicago Press. 270 Sidney Harris, © 1974 *The New Yorker* Magazine, Inc. 271 Sidney Harris. 278 Arizona State Library. 293 David Ake. 294 Shawnee Mission School District #512. 297 UPI Compix. 298 The Haworth Press. 301 Library of Congress. 309 Stan Benham. 315 Millicent Huff, Texas State Library, 319 Lake Blackshear Regional Library. 331 (from t.) *Arizona Daily Star*/Scott Braucher, G. P. Putnam's Sons, Richard Eagan, Atheneum. 332 (t.&l.) Harper & Row, Publishers, Inc.; (m.r. & far.r.) James Heidish from Houghton Mifflin Company; (b.l. & far.l.) Delacorte Press; (b.r. & far.r.) Knopf.

020.62274 American Library Association—Yearbooks
    Library Associations—Yearbooks. Main entry: title
    [Publisher's cataloging].
LC 76-647548
ISBN 8389-0233-2

Copyright © 1977 by the American Library Association

All rights reserved. No part of this publication may be reproduced in any form without permission in writing from the publisher, except by a reviewer who may quote brief passages in a review.

Printed in the United States of America.

ENDINGS AND BEGINNINGS

"Be favorable to bold beginnings." — Virgil, *Georgics*

This *Yearbook* was born in a year of celebration and ceremonial, the year of our country's 200th birthday, the year when ALA became a centenarian. If we were late out of the starting gate, perhaps it was as well that we lagged behind our British friends. The Library Association, which celebrates its centennial this year in London, brought out the first volume of its *Year's Work in Librarianship* in 1929, a year of crash rather than creation in the U.S., of endings rather than beginnings. Dare we hope that *The ALA Yearbook*'s birth in a year of high notes is a symbolic indication of the beginning of a record which our colleagues in 2076 will be able to celebrate not just with pleasure but with untarnished pride?

Certainly we started right. The first President of our Association in its second century was our first Black President. That it took us a century to reach that point is shameful, but surely the calm grace, the warm wit, and intense commitment of Clara Jones made us all aware of what prejudice has cost both our nation and our profession. The tone of her year of office, we must hope, signals the beginning of a period during which we shall see the end of discrimination against minorities (and against the eternally underprivileged majority — women).

Dark clouds challenged the sunshine of our 1976 celebrations: economic crisis tearing at the fabric of some of our great cities; not so benign neglect in Washington undermining the social progress and programs of the 60's; and large-scale unemployment in a profession which not so long ago was claiming a librarian shortage of some 100,000 persons. But 1977 brings us, perhaps, another symbol of hope, another blow to prejudice: a President of the U.S. out of the Deep South. And not just that, but a man who speaks of libraries and education and open access to information as though he thought they were important. Jimmy Carter may be the most important event of 1977 for ALA and the library profession — but only if we work at it. We have to convince him and the Congress (and state legislators) that the direst enemy of progress is ignorance, and that libraries represent the cheapest, most efficent way of making information freely accessible to all the people of our nation.

As Samuel B. Gould said, in last year's *ALA Yearbook*: ". . . missing is an awareness that the library can, and perhaps will have to, be the focal point or rallying ground for coordinating the community's learning resources." If we do not, *now*, put everything we've got into the task of creating that awareness, we shall miss the first great opportunity of our second century.

It will take not just effort but political expertise and clout to pull it off, and we shall not achieve the necessary strength without greater unity in our ranks. We have a long way to go. As Ed Holley's "ALA at 100" in last year's *Yearbook* makes clear, we now have more staff at headquarters than there were librarians in the country in ALA's founding year of 1876. But we have not similarly strengthened our membership. While nearly half the nation's librarians attended the founding conference, today we are lucky to get ten percent; and less than one-third of the nation's librarians belong to ALA. We can no longer afford division, apathy, parochialism; participation, unity, real involvement and commitment are vital if we are to succeed.

Beyond ourselves, too, we need the strength that alliances can bring, alliances with other groups with related societal needs, related interests of one kind or another. We cannot hope, however, to garner their support unless we are prepared to offer ours to their causes and needs. And that means an end to the social noncommitment that has pervaded our meetings and deliberations for too many years. If libraries are a vital part of society, social concerns are *our* concerns. Neutrality in the provision of information is one thing; but if our profession is a neuter organization in society we are on the road to extinction.

Let us then, in 1977, move on from last year's celebrations to a determined, unified effort to create library services (and the support for them) which will give us far greater cause to celebrate—a year, or five years, or a decade from now—than the mere passage of time.

ERIC MOON

EDITOR'S INTRODUCTION

This is the second edition of *The ALA Yearbook*. It builds upon the initial success of the *Yearbook* as an authoritative and readable source of information about activities, events, and organizations that reflect the diverse interests of the American Library Association for the year ending December 31, 1976.

For readers to whom this is a new publication, *The ALA Yearbook 1977* brings together in alphabetical sequence an authoritative series of articles of varying lengths on topics of enduring as well as current interest. Included here are reports of the activities of units of the Association, e.g., the Children's Services Division; of the activities of ALA-affiliated organization, e.g., The Association of Research Libraries; on the activities of library-related organizations, e.g., the Council on Library Resources, Inc.; and of organizations with some library-related interests, e.g., the National Technical Information Service. In addition, there are broad articles on general topics. Many articles are illustrated. Others provide the latest statistical information.

The ALA Yearbook also includes correspondents' reports from state and regional library associations and from Canada and Great Britain. Several special reports that accompany the basic articles in the A-Z sequence highlight trends or note significant aspects of the subject. A directory of library-related organizations that provides information on purpose, officers, location, and membership is a useful reference feature. Obituaries, biographies, notable books, and an extensive section on awards complete the principal elements of the A-Z part of this volume.

The ALA Yearbook 1977 opens with a statement by Eric Moon, the ALA President-elect, 1976–77. Moon, who is well known as the former editor of *Library Journal* and as President of Scarecrow Press, provides insight to his leadership of the American Library Association in 1977–78.

The feature articles written for this edition include *The ALA Centennial Celebration*, by Peggy Sullivan, which captures the essence of the ALA Centennial Conference and reports on the historical celebration in Philadelphia on October 6, 1976.

Harry T. Hookway, Director of the British Library, describes the most dramatic national library development of our generation — the creation of the British Library. There have been references in the library literature to the separation of the British Library from the British Museum and the creation of the British Library Lending Division at Boston Spa, but Hookway's article is the first authoritative treatment of the new British Library in an American source.

Joseph Becker, international library consultant and member of the National Commission on Libraries and Information Science, has laid out a basic introduction in his feature article on *Telecommunications*. He covers the technology and explores implications for libraries of the future.

As competency-based examinations gain increasing numbers of adherents in North America, Norman Horrocks observes our British and Australian colleagues moving in the opposite direction. *Patterns of Education and Accreditation for Librarianship* compares the development of library education in Great Britain, Australia, and North America. Having taught on all three continents, Horrocks, who is presently Director of the School of Library Service at Dalhousie University, bases his comments both on current observations and on his own experience.

A special feature in this year's edition is a tribute—*Centenary of a Giant of Librarianship: Louis Round Wilson*. Edward G. Holley reminds us of the many outstanding contributions made by Dr. Wilson during his career as a library educator, as a university library director, and in other professional roles. On December 2, 1976, Wilson's many friends, former students, and colleagues gathered in Chapel Hill, North Carolina, to pay tribute to his brilliance and foresight—and to receive unexpectedly his forthright comments as to the accuracy and pertinence of their observations on his lengthy career.

The ALA Yearbook 1977 is to a student a text; to the practitioner, a handy reference source, and to the interested general reader a comprehensive overview of libraries and information services in 1976.

We note with appreciation the contributions of the Advisers for the *Yearbook*. Their recommendations concerning persons and topics to be covered aided in the general improvement of what they and the editors consider to be a strong new resource for library reference collections.

Finally, we acknowledge again with deep admiration the achievement of our authors and correspondents, who met the tight deadlines imposed by demanding *Yearbook* schedules. Their names, with the title of articles written and brief identification, appear in the list beginning on page ix.

ROBERT WEDGEWORTH
Editor in Chief

June 1977

EDITOR IN CHIEF
Robert Wedgeworth

MANAGING EDITOR
Richard Dell

PICTURE EDITOR
Nora Dell

CONTRIBUTING EDITORS
Ruth Tarbox, *Biographies*
Ruth Warncke, *Biographies*

LONDON CORRESPONDENTS
Stephanie Mullins, Dorothy Partington

CANADIAN CORRESPONDENT
R. B. Land

INDEXER
Roberta Parson

PROOFREADER
Robert Rauch

CONTRIBUTING RESEARCHERS
Paul DiMauro,
Hannah Silver,
Fred Tremper

LAYOUT ARTIST
Joseph Szwarek

THE AMERICAN LIBRARY ASSOCIATION

PRESIDENT
Clara Stanton Jones

VICE-PRESIDENT/PRESIDENT-ELECT
Eric Moon

TREASURER
William Chait

EXECUTIVE DIRECTOR
Robert Wedgeworth

DEPUTY EXECUTIVE DIRECTOR
Ruth R. Frame

ASSOCIATE EXECUTIVE DIRECTOR FOR PUBLISHING
Donald E. Stewart

ADVISERS

Warren B. Kuhn, *Chairperson,*
Dean, Library Services, Iowa State University Library, Ames, Iowa

Lillian Bradshaw, *Director,*
Public Library System, Dallas, Texas

Jack Dalton, *Director,*
Columbia University Library Development Center

William DeJohn, *Consultant,*
Illinois State Library Development Group, Springfield

Mary V. Gaver, *Director*
of Library Consulting Services, Bro-Dart, Inc.

Warren J. Haas, *Vice-President and University Librarian,*
Columbia University

Edward G. Holley, *Dean,*
School of Library Science, University of North Carolina

Clara Stanton Jones, *Director,*
Detroit Public Library System

E. J. Josey, *Chief,*
Bureau of Specialist Library Services, The State Education Department, The New York State Library

Paul Kitchen, *Executive Director,*
Canadian Library Association

Dan Lacy, *Senior Vice-President,*
McGraw-Hill Book Company

John G. Lorenz, *Executive Director,*
Association of Research Libraries

Helen H. Lyman, *Associate Professor,*
Library School, University of Wisconsin, Madison

Frank E. McKenna, *Executive Director,*
Special Libraries Association

Keyes D. Metcalf, *Library Consultant,*
Belmont, Massachusetts

R. Kathleen Molz, *Doctoral Candidate,*
School of Library Science, Columbia University

James Parton, *Assistant Librarian of Congress*
for Public Education

LuOuida Vinson Phillips, *Director of Instructional Resources,*
Dallas Independent School District

Alphonse F. Trezza, *Executive Director,*
National Commission on Libraries and Information Science

Helen Welch Tuttle, *Assistant University Librarian for*
Technical Services, Princeton University Library

Allen B. Veaner, *Assistant Director for Bibliographic*
Operations, Stanford University Libraries

Robert Vosper, *Director,*
Clark Library, University of California, Los Angeles

Leo M. Weins, *President,*
H. W. Wilson Company

Virginia P. Whitney, *Professor,*
Rutgers University Library

ABBREVIATIONS AND ACRONYMS

Following are selected abbreviations and acronyms used in *The ALA Yearbook*. For page references consult the *Index* under full names in the first edition (1976) and in this *Yearbook*.

AAAS American Association for the Advancement of Science
AACR Anglo-American Cataloging Rules
AAEA Appalachian Adult Education Center
AALC Asian American Librarian Caucus
AALL American Association of Law Libraries
AALS Association of American Library Schools
AAP Association of American Publishers
ABA American Booksellers Association
ABLISS Association of British Library and Information Science
ACLD Advisory Council on Library Development
ACNO Advisory Committee of National Organizations
ADPU Association of Public Data Users
AECT Association for Educational Communications and Technology
AFLS Armed Forces Librarians Section
AHEC Area Health Education Councils
AIRS Alliance of Information and Referral Services
ALHRT American Library History Round Table
ALS American Library Society
ALSA Area Library Service Authority
ALTA American Library Trustee Association
AMIGOS Southwestern states network
ANSI American National Standards Institute
ARAC Aerospace Research Application Center
ARL Association of Research Libraries
ARSC Association for Recorded Sound Collections
ASIDIC Association of Information and Dissemination Centers
ASIS American Society for Information Science
ASLA Association of State Library Agencies
ASTED L'Association pour l'avancement des sciences et des techniques de la documentation
ATLA American Theological Library Association
ATS Applications Technology Satellite
BALLOTS Bibliographic Automation of Large Library Operations Using a Time-Sharing System
BARC Bay Area Reference Center
BLLD British Library Lending Division
BNB British National Bibliography
BPA British Publishers' Association
BPDC Book and Periodical Development Council (Canada)
CACUL Canadian Association of College and University Libraries
CAIN Cataloging and Indexing
CALS Canadian Association of Library Schools
CAPL Canadian Association of Public Libraries
CARL Canadian Association of Research Libraries, a section of CACUL
CASLIS Canadian Association of Special Libraries and Information Services
CCTU Committee of Corporate Telephone Users
CE Continuing Education
CETA Comprehensive Employment and Training Act
CIA Computer Industry Association
CELS Continuing Education for Library Staffs in the Southwest
CIN Cooperative Information Network
CIP Cataloging in Publication
CISTI Canadian Institute for Scientific and Technical Information
CLA Canadian Library Association
CLA Catholic Library Association
CLASS California Library Authority for Systems and Service
CLENE Continuing Library Education Network and Exchange
CLEP College Level Examination Program
CLIP Coordinated Library Information Program
CLOUT Concerned Librarians Opposing Unprofessional Trends
CLR Council on Library Resources
CLTA Canadian Library Trustees' Association
COA Committee on Accreditation
COLA Cooperation in Library Automation
COLT Council on Library Technical Assistants
COM Computer Output Microform
COMARC Data base from pre-selected sources redistributed through MARC (LC)
CONSER CONversion of SERials
CONTU National Commission on New Technological Uses of Copyrighted Works
COPA Council on Postsecondary Education
COSLA Chief Officers of State Library Agencies
COMCAT Computer Output Microfilm Catalog
CR Classification Research
CRL Center for Research Libraries
CRS Congressional Research Service
CSAA Council of Specialized Accrediting Agencies
CSD Children's Services Division
CSLA Canadian School Library Association
CTS Communications Technology Satellite
CUNY City University of New York
DARE International Data Bank for Social Sciences (UNESCO)
DAVI Department of Audiovisual Instruction (of NEA)
DDC Defense Documentation Center
DISC Divisional Interests Special Committee
DLC District Library Center
DLS Division for Library Services
ERIC Educational Resources Information Center
ERT Exhibits Round Table
ESEA Elementary and Secondary Education Act
FID International Federation for Documentation
FIPS International Federation of Information Processing Societies
FLA Federal Librarians Association
FRACHE Federation of Regional Accrediting Commission of Higher Education
GAC Government Advisory Committee
I & R Information and Referral Services
IAML International Association of Music Libraries
IASA International Association of Sound Archives
IASL International Association of School Librarianship
IBBY International Board on Books for Young People
ICBD International Children's Book Day
IDS Interlibrary Delivery System
IFC Intellectual Freedom Committee
IFLA International Federation of Library Associations and Institutions
IIB International Bibliographic Institute
ILLINET Illinois Library and Information Network
ILRA Independent Research Library Association
ISAD Information Science and Automation Division
ISBDS International Standard Bibliographic Description for Serials
ISDS International Serials Data System
ISSN International Standard Serial Number
IUC Interuniversity Council
JCET Joint Council on Educational Telecommunications
JMRT Junior Members Round Table
JOLA Journal of Library Automation
JSCAACR Joint Steering Committee for Revision of AACR
LA Library Association (British)
LASER London and South Eastern Library Region
LEOMA Library Education Opportunities for Mid-America
LIAS Library Information Access System
LNR Louisiana Numerical Register
LOEX Library Orientation-Instruction Exchange
LRRT Library Research Round Table
LSCA Library Services and Construction Act
LUTFCUSTIC Librarians United to Fight Costly, Unnecessary Serial Title Changes (RTSD)
MARBI Representation in Machine-Readable Form of Bibliographic Information
MARC Machine-Readable Cataloging
MARS Machine-Assisted Reference Services
MCC Multicounty Cooperatives
MIDLNET Midwest Region Library Network
MLA Music Library Association
MLSA Metropolitan Library Service Agency
MRAP Management Review and Analysis Program (ARL)
NACAC National Ad Hoc Committee Against Censorship
NAL National Agricultural Library
NALGO National Association of Local Government Officials (British)
NASIC Northeast Academic Science Information Center
NCA National Commission on Accrediting
NCES National Center for Education Statistics
NCLIS National Commission on Libraries and Information Science
NCTM National Council of Teachers of Mathematics
NEA National Education Association
NEDCC New England Document Conservation Center
NEH National Endowment for the Humanities
NELB New England Library Board
NELINET New England Library Information Network
NFAIS National Federation of Abstracting and Indexing Services
NIAL National Institute of Arts and Letters
NIEA National Indian Education Association
NLM National Library of Medicine
NMA National Microfilm Association
NMA National Micrographics Association
NPR National Public Radio
NSDP National Serials Data Program
NTIS National Technical Information Service
OAS Organization of American States
OCLC Ohio College Library Center
OECD Organization for Economic Cooperation and Development
OLLR Office of Libraries and Learning Resources
OLPR Office for Library Personnel Resources
OLSD Office for Library Service to the Disadvantaged
OMS Office of University Library Management Studies
OSHA Occupational Safety and Health Agency
OSIS Office of Science Information Service
PALINET Pennsylvania Area Library Network
PASS Program for Achievement of State Standards
PBS Public Broadcasting Service
PISA Public Interest Satellite Association
PNBC Pacific Northwest Bibliographic Center
PRECIS Preserved Context Index System
PP & E Program Planning & Evaluation
PRS Public Relations Section
PSSC Public Service Satellite Consortium
RAILS Reference and Interlibrary Loan Service
RICE Regional Information and Community Exchange
RLG Research Libraries Group
SCAN Southern California Answering Network
SCAN State Controlled Area Network (Washington)
SDI Selective Dissemination of Information
SHARE Shared Area Resources Exchange
SIE Scientific Information Exchange
SLICE Southwestern Library Interstate Cooperative Endeavor
SOLINET Southeastern Library Network
STAR Serial Titles Automated Records
STC Short Title Catalog
TEC Committee for Technical and Comprehensive Education
TESLA Technical Standards for Library Automation
TLA Theatre Library Association
TWXIL TWX Interlibrary Loan Network
USBE Universal Serials and Book Exchange, Inc.
USOE U.S. Office of Education
WESTEX Western Continuing Education Exchange
WILCO Western Interstate Library Coordinating Organization (formerly WICHE—Western Interstate Commission for Higher Education)
WLN Washington Library Network
YASD Young Adult Services Division

CONTENTS

Features

xiv **The ALA Centennial Celebration**
PEGGY SULLIVAN, Director of Branches and Regional Libraries, Chicago Public Library

xxii **At the Hub: The British Library**
HARRY T. HOOKWAY, Chief Executive, The British Library Board

xxxiv **Telecommunications**
JOSEPH BECKER, President, Becker and Hayes, Inc., Los Angeles, California

xxxi **The Centenary of a Giant of Librarianship: Louis Round Wilson**
EDWARD G. HOLLEY, Dean, School of Library Science, University of North Carolina

xxxix **Patterns of Education and Accreditation for Librarianship: Canada, Great Britain, and Australia**
NORMAN HORROCKS, Director, School of Library Service, Dalhousie University, Halifax, Nova Scotia

Review of Library Events 1976

1 **Academic Libraries**
RICHARD D. JOHNSON, Director of Libraries, State University of New York, Oneonta

7 **Accreditation**
RUSSELL E. BIDLACK Dean, School of Library Science, University of Michigan, Ann Arbor

11 **Acquisitions**
J. MICHAEL BRUER, Associate University Librarian, New York University

13 **Adults, Library Services to**
MARGARET E. MONROE, Professor, University of Wisconsin Library School, Madison

16 **American Association of Law Libraries**
J. S. ELLENBERGER, Law Librarian, Covington and Burling, Washington, D.C.

17 **American Association of School Librarians**
ALICE FITE, Executive Secretary, AASL

19 **American Library History**
GEORGE S. BOBINSKI, Dean, School of Information and Library Studies, State University of New York, Amherst

20 **American Library History Round Table**
MARGARET F. MAXWELL, University of Arizona

20 **American Library Society**
JOHN B. HARLAN, President, American Library Society

22 **American Library Trustees Association**
ANDREW M. HANSEN, Executive Secretary, ALTA

23 **American Society for Information Science**
MARGARET T. FISCHER, Consultant, Greenwich, Connecticut

24 **American Theological Library Association**
THE REV. DAVID J. WARTLUFT, Executive Secretary, ATLA

26 **Anglo-American Cataloguing Rules**
PETER R. LEWIS, University of Sussex, Brighton, England

27 **Archives**
ANN MORGAN CAMPBELL, Executive Director, Society of American Archivists, Chicago, Illinois

28 **Armed Forces Libraries**
NATHALIE MCMAHON, Base Librarian, Fairchild AFB, Washington

30 **Association of College and Research Libraries**
BEVERLY P. LYNCH, University Librarian, University of Illinois at Chicago

33 **Association of Research Libraries**
SUZANNE FRANKIE, Associate Executive Director, Association of Research Libraries

34 **Association of State Library Agencies**
MARY R. POWER, Executive Secretary, ASLA

37 **Automation**
SUSAN K. MARTIN, Head, Library Systems Office, University of California, Berkeley

42 **Awards and Prizes**

50 **Beta Phi Mu**
JESSIE CARNEY SMITH, University Librarian, Fisk University, Nashville, Tennessee

50 **Bibliography and Indexes**
ROGER C. GREER, Professor, School of Library Science, Syracuse University

52 **Binding**
DUDLEY A. WEISS, Executive Director, Library Binding Institute, Boston, Massachusetts

53 **Biographies**

66 **Blind and Physically Handicapped, Library Services for the**
FRANK KURT CYLKE, Chief, Division for the Blind and Physically Handicapped, Library of Congress

67 **Bookselling**
ROBERT D. HALE, Hathaway House Bookshop, Wellesley, Massachusetts

68 **Budgeting, Accounting, and Cost Control**
ROBERT H. ROHLF, Director, Hennepin County Library, Edina, Minnesota

69 **Buildings**
RAYMOND M. HOLT, Consultant, Del Mar, California

76 **Canadian Library Association**
PAUL KITCHEN, Executive Director, Canadian Library Association

78 **Cataloging and Classification**
JANE ROSS MOORE, Professor and Chief Librarian, Graduate School and University Center, City University of New York

79 **Catholic Library Association**
MATTHEW R. WILT, Executive Director, CLA

80 **Children's Book Council**
JOHN DONOVAN, Executive Director, Children's Book Council, New York

82 **Children's Library Services**
PEGGY SULLIVAN, Director of Branches and Regional Libraries, Chicago Public Library

86 **Children's Literature**
ZENA SUTHERLAND, Lecturer, Graduate Library School, University of Chicago

88 **Children's Services Division**
MARY JANE ANDERSON, Executive Secretary, CSD

90 **Circulation Systems**
R. PATRICK MALLORY, Director of the Library, New Mexico Institute of Mining and Technology, Socorro, New Mexico

92 **Collection Development**
JEAN BOYER HAMLIN, Librarian, Dana Library, Rutgers University, Newark, New Jersey

93 **Community Delivery Services**
VIRGINIA L. OWENS, Associate Director for Planning and Research, Oklahoma Department of Libraries

95 **Continuing Professional Education**
JULIE VIRGO, Executive Secretary, ACRL

97 **CONTU**
ARTHUR J. LEVINE, Executive Director, CONTU, Washington, D.C.

98 **Copyright**
F. E. MCKENNA, Executive Director, Special Libraries Association

104 **Council, ALA**
PATRICIA R. HARRIS, Assistant to the Executive Director, ALA

106 **Council on Library Technical Assistants**
JOHN JOHNSON, Associate Dean of Learning Resources, Durham Technical Institute, North Carolina

107 **Data Bases, Computer-Readable**
MARTHA E. WILLIAMS, Research Professor, Coordinated Science Laboratory, University of Illinois Urbana

110 **Disadvantaged, Library Service to**
JEAN E. COLEMAN, Program Director, Office for Library Services for the Disadvantaged, American Library Assn.

112 **Education, Library**
A. VENABLE LAWSON, Director, Division of Librarianship, Emory University, Atlanta, Georgia

117 **Ethics**
SHIRLEY FITZGIBBONS, College of Library & Information Services, University of Maryland, College Park, Maryland

118 **Ethnic Groups, Library Service to Asian Americans**
LEO C. HO, Director, Learning Resources Center, Washtenaw Community College, Ann Arbor, Michigan
Blacks
JESSIE CARNEY SMITH, University Librarian, Fisk University, Nashville, Tennessee
Italian Americans
CARMINE M. DIODATI, JR., Supervising Librarian, New York Public Library, Wakefield Branch
Jewish Americans
MAX CELNIK and DAVID ARONOVITCH, Touro College, New York
Native Americans
CHERYL METOYER, Director, National Indian Education Association, Minneapolis, Minnesota
Polish Americans
VICTORIA M. GALA, President, Polish American Librarians Association, Hamtramck, Michigan

124 **Exhibits Round Table**
PAUL E. RAFFERTY, Field Enterprises, Chicago, Illinois

125 **Federal Librarians Round Table**
ROBERT B. LANE, Director, Air University Library, Maxwell A.F.B., Montgomery, Alabama

125 **Films**
IRENE WOOD, Editor, Nonprint Materials, *Booklist*

128 **Films, Children's**
MARILYN BERG IARUSSO, Assistant Coordinator, Children's Services, New York Public Library

130 **Filmstrips**
DIANA L. SPIRT, Professor, Palmer Graduate Library School, C. W. Post Center, Long Island University

130 **Financing the Public Library**
RODNEY P. LANE, Senior Associate, Government Studies and Systems, Philadelphia, Pennsylvania

132 **Foundations and Funding Agencies**
FOSTER E. MOHRHARDT, Consultant, Arlington, Virginia

134 **Freedom to Read Foundation**
RICHARD L. DARLING, Dean, School of Library Service, Columbia University

135 **Friends of Libraries**
LAURA SMITH SHELLEY, Director, Northland Public Library, Pittsburgh, Pennsylvania

136 **Furniture and Equipment**
WILLIAM S. PIERCE, Chief, Facilities Planning, Pennsylvania State University Library

140 **Gifts, Bequest, Endowments**
CLYDE C. WALTON, Director, University Libraries, Northern Illinois University, DeKalb.

143 **Government Documents Round Table**
NANCY CLINE, Documentary Librarian, Pennsylvania State University Library

144 **Government Publications and Depository System**
ARNE RICHARDS, Documentary Librarian, Farrell Library, State University, Manhattan, Kansas

145 **Health and Rehabilitative Library Services**
HARRIS C. MCCLASKEY, Associate Professor, Library School, University of Minnesota, Minneapolis

147 **Health and Rehabilitative Library Services Division**
MARY R. POWER, Executive Secretary, HRLSD

148 **IFLA**
MARGREET WIJNSTROOM, Secretary–General, IFLA, The Hague, Netherlands

153 **Independent Research Libraries**
LAWRENCE TOWNER, President and Librarian, Newberry Library, Chicago

156 **Independent Study in Public Libraries**
JOSEPH KIMBROUGH, Director, Public Library & Information Center Minneapolis

158 **Indexing and Abstracting Services**
TONI CARBO BEARMAN, Executive Director, National Federation of Abstracting and Indexing Services, Philadelphia

158 **Information and Referral Centers**
BRENDA DERVIN, Assistant Professor of Communications, School of Communications, University of Washington

160 **Information Industry**
CARLOS CUADRA, General Manager, SDC Search Service, System Development Corporation, Santa Monica, California

163 **Information Science and Automation Division**
DONALD P. HAMMER, Executive Secretary, ISAD

166 **Insurance for Libraries**
DONALD L. UNGARELLI, Director, B. Davis Schwartz Library, Long Island University

167 **Intellectual Freedom**
JUDITH F. KRUG, Director, Office for Intellectual Freedom, ALA

171 **Intellectual Freedom Round Table**
JOHN M. CARTER, Deputy State Librarian, Wyoming State Library

172 **Interlibrary Cooperation**
KEVIN FLAHERTY and JOSEPH SHUBERT, Librarian, State Library of Ohio

173 **International Board on Books for Youth**
JOHN DONOVAN, Children's Book Council, New York

174 **International Federation for Documentation FID**
KENNETH R. BROWN, Acting Secretary General, FID, The Hague, Netherlands

175 **International Relations**
JANE WILSON, International Relations Officer, ALA

180 **International Relations Round Table**
MOHAMMED M. AMAN, Dean, Palmer Graduate Library School, Long Island University,

180 **International School Librarianship**
JEAN LOWRIE, Director, School of Librarianship, Western Michigan University, Kalamazoo

181 **Junior Members Round Table**
MARILYN HINSHAW, Coordinator of Extension, Public Library, El Paso, Texas

182 **Labor Groups, Library Service to**
KATHLEEN IMHOFF, Director, Bureau of Public and Cooperative Library Services, Wisconsin Department of Public Instruction

183 **Law and Legislation**
ALEX LADENSON, Special Executive Assistant to Board of Directors, Chicago Public Library

185 **Law Libraries**
JULIUS J. MARKE, Professor of Law and Law Librarian, New York University School of Law

186 **Libraries and Learning Resources, Office of**
ROBERT KLASSEN, Chief, Program Development, Office of Libraries and Learning Resources, Washington, D.C.

189 **Library Administration Division**
DONALD P. HAMMER, Executive Secretary, LAD

191 **Library Education Division**
MARGARET MYERS, Executive Secretary, LED

192 **Library of Congress**
MARY C. LETHBRIDGE, Library of Congress

196 **Library Press**
ELIZABETH PRYSE MITCHELL, Assistant Editor, *American Libraries*

197 **Library Research Round Table**
GARY PURCELL, Director, Graduate School of Library and Information Science, University of Tennessee

198 **Literacy Programs, Library**
HELEN HUGUENOR LYMAN, Professor, Library School, University of Wisconsin–Madison

200 **Management, Library**
ROBERT ROHLF, Director, Hennepin County Library, Edina, Minnesota

201 **Measurement and Evaluation**
ELLEN ALTMAN, Graduate Library School, Indiana University, Bloomington

203 **Mediation, Arbitration, and Inquiry**
RUTH R. FRAME, Deputy Director, ALA

204 **Medical Libraries**
ESTELLE BRODMAN, Librarian and Professor of Medical History, Washington University School of Medicine, St. Louis, Missouri

206 **Medical Library Association**
JOHN S. LOSASSO, Executive Director, MLA

207 **Micrographics**
HOWARD WHITE, Editor, *Library Technology Reports*

208 **Multimedia Materials**
RICHARD L. DUCOTE, Dean of Learning Resources, College of DuPage, Glen Ellyn, Illinois

210 **Music Library Association**
DENA J. EPSTEIN, Assistant Music Librarian, University of Chicago Library

210 **National Agricultural Library**
RICHARD A. FARLEY, Director, National Agricultural Library

211 **National Commission on Libraries and Information Science**
FREDERICK BURKHARDT, Chairman, NCLIS

213 **National Endowment for the Humanities**
GLORIA WEISSMAN, Assistant to the Deputy Chairman, NEH

214 **National Library of Medicine**
MELVIN S. DAY, Deputy Director, NLM

214 **National Micrographics Association**
DON M. AVEDON, Technical Director, NMA

215 **National Technical Information Service**
TED RYERSON, Assistant to Assistant Director, Production, NTIS

216 **Networks**
ALPHONSE F. TREZZA, Executive Director, NCLIS

220 **Notable Books**

221 **Obituaries**

225 **Older Adults, Library Services to**
JOHN B. BALKEMA, Librarian, National Council on Aging

225 **Organization of American States**
MARIETTA DANIELS SHEPARD, Chief, Library and Archives Development Program, OAS

226 **Organizations and Associations**

237 **Personnel and Employment: Affirmative Action**
ELIZABETH DICKINSON, Head, Book Catalog Editing Section, Hennepin County Library, Edina, Minnesota

239 **Personnel and Employment: Performance Appraisal**
NEAL K. KASKE, Associate Librarian, Library Systems Office, University of California, Berkeley

240 **Personnel and Employment: Staff Development**
NANCY I. ZEIDNER and DUANE E. WEBSTER, Library Manager, Association of Research Libraries, Office of University Library Management Studies

243 **Personnel and Employment: Job Market**
BARRY SIMON, Attorney-at-Law, Wheeling, Illinois

245 **Preservation of Library Materials**
GEORGE M. CUNHA, Director, New England Document Conservation Center, North Andover, Massachusetts

248 **Principal Libraries of the World**
NANCY H. KNIGHT Freelance Librarian, Springfield, Virginia

252 **Processing Centers**
DALLAS R. SHAWKEY, Coordinator of Cataloging, Brooklyn Public Library

253 **Public Libraries**
C. LAMAR WALLIS, Director of Libraries, Memphis, Tennessee

259 **Public Library Association**
MARY JO LYNCH, Associate Executive Secretary, PLA

260 **Public Relations**
PEGGY BARBER, Director, Public Information Office, ALA

263 **Publishing, ALA**
DONALD E. STEWART, Associate Executive Director for Publishing, ALA

267 **Publishing, Book**
American Association of Publishers

269 **Publishing, Magazine**
BILL KATZ, Professor, Library School, State University of New York at Albany

271 **Publishing, Newspaper**
CURTIS D. MAC DOUGALL, Professor Emeritus, Northwestern (in part)

274 **Realia**
THOMAS BROWNFIELD, Director, Canal Fulton Public Library, Ohio

274 **Recordings, Sound**
GORDON STEVENSON, Associate Professor, State University of New York at Albany

276 **Reference and Adult Services Division**
ANDREW M. HANSEN, Executive Secretary, RASD

277 **Reference Services**
GILBERT MCNAMEE, Director, Bay Area Reference Center, San Francisco Public Library

280 **REFORMA**
JOSÉ TAYLOR, President, REFORMA; Los Angeles Public Library

281 **Regional Library Associations**
CHARLES BOLLES, Mountain Plains; FLORENCE M. FRAY, Pacific Northwest; J. B. HOWELL, Southeastern; HEARTSILL H. YOUNG, Southwestern

285 **Research**
BARBARA O. SLANKER, Director, Office for Research, ALA

290 **Resources and Technical Services Division**
PAUL J. FASANA, Technical Services Librarian, Research Libraries, New York Public Library

291 **School Libraries and Media Centers**
ELIZABETH T. FAST, School Media Specialist, Groton Public Schools, Groton, Connecticut

296 **Science Information, Division of**
LEE G. BURCHINAL, Director, DSI, National Science Foundation

297 **Security Systems**
NANCY H. KNIGHT, Freelance Librarian, Springfield, Virginia

300 **Serials**
WILLIAN H. HUFF, Serials Librarian, University of Illinois Library, Urbana

303 **Social Responsibilities**
E. J. JOSEY, Chief, Bureau of Specialist Library Services, State Education Department, New York State Library

307 **Social Responsibilities Round Table**
NANCY KELLUM-ROSE, Branch Librarian San Francisco Public Library

307 **Sociedad de Bibliotecarios de Puerto Rico**
ARTURO FERNÁNDEZ-ORTIZ, University of Puerto Rico

308 **Special Libraries**
MIRIAM TEES, Chief Librarian, The Royal Bank of Canada, Montreal

311 **Staff Organizations Round Table**
PATRICK ASHLEY, Head, Search Department, Northwestern University Library

311 **Standards**
JERROLD ORNE, Professor Emeritus, School of Library Science, University of North Carolina

314 **State Library Agencies**
ROGER H. MCDONOUGH, New Jersey State Librarian Emeritus

316 **Telecommunication and Public Broadcasting**
FRANK W. NORWOOD, Executive Director, Joint Council on Educational Telecommunications

317 **Theatre Library Association**
RICHARD M. BUCK, Performing Arts Research Center, New York Public Library at Lincoln Center

318 **Toys and Games**
FAITH H. HEKTOEN, Consultant, Connecticut State Library

319 **Trustees**
ALICE B. IHRIG, Consultant and Speaker on Library Affairs

322 **UNESCO**
I. BETTEMBOURG, UNESCO, Paris

324 **Universal Bibliographic Control**
DOROTHY ANDERSON, Director, IFLA UBC Office

324 **Universal Serials and Book Exchange, Inc.**
ALICE D. BALL, Executive Director, USBE

325 **Washington Report**
SARA CASE, Associate Director, Washington Office, ALA

327 **White House Conference**
EILEEN D. COOKE, Director, Washington Office, ALA

328 **Women in Librarianship, Status of**
KATHLEEN WEIBEL, University of Wisconsin—Extension Library School, Madison

329 **Young Adult Library Services**
CAROL STARR, Coordinator of Young Adult Services, Alameda County Library, California

331 **Young Adult Literature**
PATRICIA J. CAMPBELL, Assistant Coordinator of Youth Adult Services, Los Angeles Public Library

333 **Young Adult Services Division**
EVELYN SHAEVEL, Executive Secretary, YASD

Special Reports

114 **Library Education and Placement Problems**
DORALYN J. HICKEY, Director, School of Library Science, University of Wisconsin, Milwaukee

149 **The New Constitution of IFLA**
MARGREET WIJNSTROOM, Secretary-General, IFLA

151 **IFLA—Fifty Years of Service to International Librarianship**
PETER HAVARD-WILLIAMS, Department of Library and Information Studies, University of Technology, Leicestershire

177 **International Guests: ALA Centennial Conference**

217 **National Library Resource Centers**
GORDON R. WILLIAMS, Director, The Center for Research Libraries, Chicago, Illinois

256 **Urban Library Services**
KEITH DOMS, Director, The Free Library of Philadelphia

298 **Disasters**
BILL COHEN, The Haworth Press; JAN REBER, security consultant

335 **Canadian Report**
R. BRIAN LAND, Professor, Faculty of Library Science, University of Toronto

341 **Women in Canadian Librarianship**
SHERRILL CHEDA, Campus Librarian, Learning Resource Centre, Seneca College of Applied Arts and Technology, Ontario

342 **London Report**

State Reports—349

Alabama. PAUL H. SPENCE, University Librarian, University of Alabama, Birmingham

Alaska. MARY MATTHEWS, Regional Coordinator, Alaska State Library, Fairbanks

Arizona. HELEN GOTHBERG, Assistant Professor, Graduate Library School, University of Arizona

Arkansas. ALICE GRAY, Director, Central Arkansas Library System, Little Rock

California. WILLIAM L. EMERSON, Playa Del Rey, California

Colorado. ANNE MARIE FALSONE, Assistant Commissioner, Office of Library Services, Colorado State Library

Connecticut. MEREDITH BLOSS, City Librarian, New Haven Free Public Library

Delaware. HELEN H. BENNETT, Retired, State Department of Public Instruction, Delaware

District of Columbia. DARRELL LEMKE, Coordinator of Library Programs, Washington, D.C.

Florida. BARRATT WILKINS, Acting State Librarian

Georgia. JOHN CLEMONS, Associate Professor, Emory University

Hawaii. ROSE MYERS, Librarian, West Oahu College, Honolulu

Idaho. JEANNE GOODRICH, Idaho Falls Public Library

Illinois. SYLVIA G. FAIBISOFF, Professor, University of Arizona Library School, Tucson

Indiana. EDWARD N. HOWARD, Director, Vigo County Public Library, Terre Haute

Iowa. REBECCA CHRISTIAN and GAYLE BURDICK, Editor, Iowa Library Association, Des Moines

Kansas. MARY ANNE CRABB, Public Information Officer, Hutchinson Public Library, Kansas

Kentucky. BARBARA S. MILLER, Coordinator of Children's Services, Louisville Free Public Library

Louisiana. VIVIAN CAZAYOUX, Associate State Librarian for Library Development, Baton Rouge

Maine. FREDERICK VON LANG, Director, Auburn Public Library, Maine

Maryland. LANCE C. FINNEY, President, Maryland State Department of Education, Division of Library Development, Baltimore

Massachusetts. MARY A. HENEGHAN, Regional Administrator, Eastern Massachusetts Regional Library System, Boston

Michigan. ELIZABETH HAYDEN, Supervisor of Extension Department, Lansing Public Library

Minnesota. ALICE WILCOX, Director, University of Minnesota Library, Minneapolis

Mississippi. GEORGE R. LEWIS, Director of Libraries, Mississippi State University Library

Missouri. MADELINE MATSON, Missouri State Library, Jefferson, Missouri

Montana. ALICE MC CLAIN, Director of Libraries, Montana State University, Bozeman

Nebraska. VIVIAN A. PETERSON, Concordia Teachers College, Seward, Nebraska

Nevada. THOMASINE KLEFFEN, Librarian, Municipal Library, North Las Vegas

New Hampshire. STANLEY W. BROWN, Chief, Public Services, Dartmouth College Library

New Jersey. SCHUYLER MOTT, Director, Ocean County Library, Toms River, New Jersey

New Mexico. PAUL A. AGRIESTI, Deputy State Librarian, New Mexico State Library, Santa Fe

New York. MICHAEL G. DE RUVO, School Media Specialist, Roslyn Junior High School, New York

North Carolina. DAVID P. JENSEN, Director of Library Services, Greensboro College

North Dakota. PATRICIA SCHOMMER, Acquisitions Librarian, State University Library, Fargo

Ohio. JOHN S. WALLACH, Director, Green County District Library, Xenia, Ohio

Oklahoma. IRMA R. TOMBERLIN, Professor of Library Science, School of Library Science, University of Oklahoma, Norman

Oregon. RICHARD MOORE and MARY DOWNEY, Branch Librarian, Multnomah County Library, Portland

Pennsylvania. PAT REDMOND, Chester County Library Westchester, Pennsylvania

Rhode Island. EMIL A. CIALLELLA, JR., Director, Central Falls Public Library, Rhode Island

South Carolina. CARL STONE, Anderson County Library, South Carolina

South Dakota. EMILY K. GUHIN, Alexander Mitchell Library, Aberdeen

Tennessee. ROBERT F. PLOTZKE, Director of Library Services, Mayne Williams Public Library, Johnson City

Texas. MARY POUND, Publications Coordinator, General Libraries, University of Texas at Austin

Utah. IDA-MARIE JENSEN, Associate Librarian, Associate Professor, Utah State University

Vermont. JOSETTE ANNE BOISSE, Librarian, Spaulding High School, Barre, Vermont

Virginia. WILLIAM L. WHITESIDES, Director of Libraries, Fairfax County Public Library, Springfield, Virginia

Washington. DOROTHY CUTLER, Chief, Library Development, Washington State Library, Olympia

West Virginia. LUELLA I. DYE, Director, Craft Memorial Library, Bluefield, West Virginia

Wisconsin. CHARLES A. BUNGE, Director, Library School, University of Wisconsin, Madison, Wisconsin

Wyoming. JOHN M. CARTER, Deputy State Librarian, Wyoming State Library, Cheyenne

Index
419

Feature Articles

The ALA Centennial Celebration

Peggy Sullivan

ALA Councilors prepare for photograph in Chicago's Grant Park during the Centennial Conference in July.

The celebration of the United States Centennial in 1876 was the occasion for the start of organizations such as the American Library Association. The ALA held its first Conference in Philadelphia, where those attending were also able to enjoy the pleasures of the great Centennial exhibition while participating in the founding of the new library association. When the time came for the celebration of ALA's Centennial year in 1976, the nation's celebration had become more diffuse and, according to some critics, too commercial. The parade of tall ships in New York on July 4 provided a memorable central focus for the nation's birthday and a refreshing change from many less appropriate events. Some years earlier, as a committee to plan ALA's Centennial observance was getting into its work, Philadelphia had been abandoned as the site for the Centennial Conference, and Chicago, headquarters for the Association for more than half its existence, was chosen. It offered the convention space, the central location, and the know-how in conference management that have become important factors in recent ALA Conferences, which attract registrants in the thousands.

The charge of the committee which planned ALA's Centennial celebration was manifold. It was to recommend Conference activities, seek recognition from other groups wishing to salute ALA on its Centennial, and recommend publications and other activities related to the observance. The long-range mission of the committee was accomplished in spite of delays and numerous changes of personnel. Alice Ihrig, onetime chairman of the committee, provided a necessary link with the committees and staff responsible for the many aspects of planning and conducting the celebration of ALA's hundredth birthday. While much of the excitement of the celebration was generated from the Association's headquarters and centered around its Annual Conference, there were other recognitions that added much to the historic year's activities and to its significant and enduring memories.

THE CHICAGO CENTENNIAL
CONFERENCE

Almost from the minute of her election to the office of ALA Vice-President and President-elect in 1974, Allie Beth Martin focused on the plans for the Chicago Conference in 1976. She appointed the necessary committees, visited with staff and membership groups, wrote to representatives of other groups to seek advice and assistance, and planned her own inaugural address to the Association to be a stimulus for the interest necessary to make the Annual Conference what she and others wanted it to be. There was to be a festive air throughout the week, time allowed from board meetings and other necessary business to permit lively participation in the events planned to call ALA to the attention of the city and a larger community, and emphasis on the future and its promise as well as on the past.

Fortunate timing of ALA presidential succession allowed Edward G. Holley, scholarly library historian, to precede Allie Beth Martin as President. Under his leadership and at the instigation of Kathleen Molz in a discussion of possible events for the San Francisco Conference of 1975, the Life of the Mind lectures were arranged. Funded by the remaining portion of the grant made by several library publishers to David H. Clift on the occasion of his retirement as Executive Director of ALA, the lecture series consisted of six presentations at ALA conferences, three made in 1975 and three in 1976. Dan Lacy, John Hope Franklin, and Kathleen Molz were the lecturers in San Francisco. Their emphasis was chiefly on the historical background of librarianship in the U.S. Molz was concerned with relationships between librarianship and library associations on the one hand and the federal government on the other. Franklin explored the extent of the tradition of fullness of access for all groups and individuals seeking to use the libraries of the country throughout a long history and found the record, on the whole, offering shame as well as success. Lacy viewed the tradition of open access from the perspective of present achievement and future promise in terms of more and better technology, information storage, and cooperative efforts among libraries.

1976 Lectures. The 1976 lectures in the Life of the Mind series were more individually distinctive. The stage had been set by the first group, and President Martin sought in the speakers variety of topics as well as of treatments. Harriet Pilpel related libraries to the First Amendment of the Constitution and the concept of freedom in this country, while Herman Liebaers reminisced about his own growing knowledge of American librarianship, obtained as visitor and colleague of many American libraries and librarians. He stressed the contributions the American Library Association has made to international librarianship, the International Federation of Library Associations, UNESCO, and other international library programs. But he was sure enough of his own views and of his audience's reactions to venture some caustic criticisms of some of those programs and to raise some questions about the nature of the U.S. library presence abroad.

A lesser man than Daniel J. Boorstin might have been nonplussed or upstaged by the introductory remarks at his lecture, when Keyes Metcalf shared his memories of the men who have served as Librarian of Congress in his years of professional activity. The period spanned almost half of ALA's own history, and his warmly personal comments brought the era to life again for others. Boorstin, who had first declined to participate in the lecture series because he said he intended to take seriously the library profession's comments about the great task of being Librarian of Congress (a part of the 1975 organized resistance to his appointment), spoke chiefly about public libraries and their American tradition. He touched also on problems of the future that are likely to develop unless technology can be more of an ally than a competitor to library development and service.

The Life of the Mind lectures are to be published by the American Library Association as a monograph. Publication is likely to call attention to the criticisms and recommendations which each speaker offered to American librarianship and libraries, and which add an important dimension to what might have been merely lyrical encomiums for the ALA Centennial. Spread as they were through the conference week each year, they may also have set a pattern for more such formal presentations as part of ALA Conferences.

Allie Beth Martin. In a way, there was a marked difference between the general

ALA Centennial Celebration

xv

ALA Centennial Celebration

(Below) Conference participants in Chicago visit the Newberry Library and (below right) the Art Institute's exhibit on the Age of Franklin and Jefferson.

tone of celebration sought throughout most of the Conference and the thoughtful mood of the Life of the Mind lectures. This was intentional, for a landmark in time brings out many moods. President Martin wanted all of them to have a place in the Conference, but in her early planning, she could not have anticipated the shadow that marked some of the events, as those who planned them and those who participated in them said often, wistfully, "Wouldn't Allie Beth have loved *this*!" Her death in April 1976 meant that Clara Jones, who had been elected First Vice-President of the Association in 1975, presided at most of the Centennial Conference sessions. At one of those general sessions, Allie Beth Martin was honored, and a Centennial citation was accepted by her sister.

Celebrate a Century. The festive events of the Conference had practical reasons for being. Sunday nights in conference cities have often been disaster times for newly arrived participants searching for restaurants for dinner. The Celebrate a Century evening was planned to make the opening dinner a part of conference events. The Art Institute of Chicago, exhibiting a collection of memorabilia honoring the nation's Bicentennial in the Age of Franklin and Jefferson, provided special opening times for ALA conferees. Buffet dinners at the Art Institute and at the Conrad Hilton, a major conference hotel, followed.

Librarians at Large. Tuesday, July 20, of Conference week, was Librarians at Large Day, the occasion for almost 300 librarians to work in libraries and information centers of the Chicago area. Logistics for this major undertaking included plans for appropriate placement, sometimes based on providing an entirely different kind of experience, assistance with transportation, and an evaluation of the effort. This activity had been suggested by the ALA Centennial Committee, and it was hoped that the event might become a part of other ALA Conferences. Offering the opportunity first in Chicago made available a wide variety of special libraries, many of them easily accessible for persons in the downtown area. Chicago Public Library and other public libraries of the area, academic libraries, and school libraries welcomed librarians for a day and provided opportunities for participants to work at reference desks, tell stories to preschool children, use information retrieval technology with which they had had no experience, and to find out something about the priorities and policies of libraries other than their own. Unexpected interests were shown in the advance registrations, when a few potential Librarians at Large said they would like to work with members of the ALA staff for the day. These, too, were accommodated by the committee chaired by Beth Hamilton, Director of the Illinois Regional Library Council, who used many of the IRLC's resources in the great logistical enterprise.

Fair in the Park. The Fair in the Park grew out of a desire to show, in some public place, librarians at leisure and at work. Held on Wednesday evening, it was an outside event in Grant Park, for which good weather was essential. The dull skies of the morning cleared to provide a beautiful early evening for the event. The variety of programming, considerably strengthened by the booths and other activities sponsored by ALA membership units, library school alumni reunions, and other groups, included chalk talks by chil-

dren's book illustrators, a pie-throwing booth where academic library directors took their chances as targets for anyone strong enough to hit the bell on a carnival test-of-strength machine, a staged debate about the famous proposed "mud catalogue" of the past century, and several places where materials about special library activities were exhibited and distributed.

The planners of this event invited a number of performers to participate, so clown routines, dance troupes, and musicians moved among the some 3,000 persons attending and performed along the open cement strip which provided a kind of main runway for the event. One of the reasons for having an event of this kind, to which participants could come and go fairly casually, was to provide a free event of interest to a broad range of ages and an opportunity for those attending the Conference to relax, chat with friends, and enjoy the many activities going on simultaneously.

Wednesday evening is traditionally the Grant Park concert performance in Chicago, and after the Fair in the Park, the free concert was dedicated to the American Library Association. Many who had attended the Fair in the Park stayed for this musical evening, which also introduced ALA to the many Chicagoans and others who arrived for the concert.

Inaugural Dinner. The off-again-on-again tradition of ALA inaugural dinners was on for the Centennial Conference. On Friday evening Clara Jones was inaugurated President of the Association which she had already served in an interim capacity. The theme, after a week of memorialization of the past, was the future, ALA's second century. Gwendolyn Brooks, Chicago's Pulitzer-Prize-winning poet, read a poem she had written for the occasion, honoring ALA and its new President. There was a special drama in this, as the Black poet saluted ALA's first Black President.

Throughout the week, many of ALA's Past Presidents, some of them returning after periods of inaction in the Association, had been arriving in Chicago, and they were honored at the inaugural banquet as Ken Swanson of the local committee read a sometimes-playful, sometimes-serious, always wittily appropriate review of their major contributions as Presidents.

The Fair in the Park, sponsored by ALA membership units, library school alumni, and other groups, was followed by a Grant Park concert dedicated to the ALA.

The two-tiered head table seemed to overflow with the Past Presidents, the winners of major awards, the donors of the awards, members of the Executive Board, representatives of the Local Arrangements Committee, and other guests.

Capsulizing Clara Jones's inaugural speech, *Library Journal* reporters noted:

> The message seemed clear. More response to membership needs and demands. More connections with the society libraries serve, and ". . . it is extremely important to gain more conscious public recognition of the magnitude of libraries and library work . . . to achieve our goals in state and national legislation, improve the position of libraries in budget allocations and in planning for national library and information service. . . ." We can think of no better person to deliver that message to America than Clara Jones [" 'Centering Down': ALA's Centennial Conference," *Library Journal* (September 1, 1976), 1715].

The final flourish of the celebratory mood came as President Jones concluded her speech by inviting everyone to join her in stepping into the second century of ALA, and swept down the hall to lead a grand march which surprised the audience into participating. Placards for all the states appeared, as the marchers linked arms, pulled friends into the march, circled back for another round, and finally stopped in some disarray as another evening of dancing and visiting began.

President Clara Jones receives gavel from former President Edward Holley at the ALA Inaugural dinner during the Centennial Conference.

ALA Centennial Celebration

This account has been limited to the Centennial events planned as a part of ALA's general conference activities. There were others, of course, as membership units like the Resources and Technical Services Division observed the centenary of Melvil Dewey's decimal classification system, and the American Library History Round Table presented talks by Howard W. Winger and George Bobinski on two major historical publications they had edited in the Year of the Centennial.

DEDICATION AT LIBRARY OF CONGRESS

The Library of Congress Thomas Jefferson Building was dedicated in a formal ceremony on Tuesday, September 21, 1976. The American Library Association was honored by the Library of Congress at this dedication, with Librarian of Congress Boorstin offering a tribute to ALA and Clara Jones responding for the Association. The outdoor ceremony went on in spite of a drizzle that turned into a steady rain and prompted, from speakers and audience, a patter of plays on words about ALA and the Library as fair-weather friends and ALA as an umbrella organization.

An afternoon symposium on Thomas Jefferson was held in the Coolidge Auditorium of the library, with Dumas Malone, noted Jefferson scholar, presiding. Frederick R. Goff spoke on Jefferson's library, and Merrill D. Peterson compared Emerson and Jefferson as different types of American scholars.

LIBRARY HISTORY SEMINAR V

October was the month when the first ALA Conference was convened in 1876, and, appropriately enough, it was the library historians who commemorated that event in Philadelphia. The Fifth Library History Seminar was held at the Philadelphia Hilton Hotel October 3 through 6, 1976. Sponsors were Beta Phi Mu, the library honor society and the *Journal of Library History*; ALA's American Library History Round Table assisted. The pattern of the Seminar consisted of speeches on historical topics (personalities, e.g., Herbert Putnam; the impact of events, e.g., Dewey's introduction of women into the forefront of American librarianship; and a group of papers on public library development in individual states) with reactors responding formally to the papers. Special features were three evening speeches, Dan Lacy on "Liberty and Knowledge—Then and Now," Edward G. Holley on "Scholars, Gentleladies, and Entrepreneurs: American Library Leaders," and David Kaser on "Coffee House to Stock Exchange: Natural History of the Reading Room." Doris C. Dale and Frederick H. Jurgemeyer presented "The Sights and Sounds of ALA, 1876–1976" in audiovisual form at the final session of the Seminar.

Approximately 50 persons participated in the Seminar, including several library school students who were awarded scholarships to attend. The proceedings are to be published. The American Library Association was host at a reception at the conclusion of the Seminar; participants

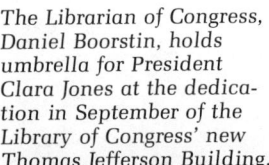

The Librarian of Congress, Daniel Boorstin, holds umbrella for President Clara Jones at the dedication in September of the Library of Congress' new Thomas Jefferson Building.

were joined by ALA officers and guests from the Philadelphia area for a festive commemorative session.

ALA'S OWN PROMOTION

The ALA Centennial occasioned many recognitions from other national library associations and libraries, but much of the stimulus for celebration of the Centennial was generated by the Association itself as a means of calling attention to libraries and their contributions to society. A line of souvenir items was introduced by ALA in 1975. The "ALA 100" logo was made available to publishers and other suppliers to the library market to encourage them to use the design in their promotional materials, and the logo was also featured in ALA's Centennial bookmarks and paperweights. One popular sales item was a sweat shirt featuring Melvil Dewey and bearing the caption, "Dewey? Sure we do!"

The New York Times for Sunday, October 3, featured a 16-page advertising supplement edited by Arthur Plotnik with consultation from the Public Relations Board. Titled "The Great American Library Success Story & Your Information Investment," the supplement mixed pictures and text to provide a view of what libraries in the U.S. are doing in the ALA Centennial year. The need for better financial support, the relationship of libraries to all information needs, and ALA's own role in library development were mentioned in brief stories. The publication was a first of its kind for ALA, but response suggests that it may have established a precedent to be followed.

Publication of the first ALA Yearbook was another special event of the Centennial year. Robert L. Wedgeworth, Executive Director of ALA, served as editor of this illustrated publication, initiated as an annual. Articles included yearly reviews of library developments in a variety of areas, directory information on ALA membership units, state and regional library associations, and several feature articles, exploring in depth such topics as microforms.

A novelty book produced by ALA for 1976 was the ALA datebook which appeared late in 1975. Its format was that of a small desk-size appointment calendar, and its illustrations were taken from a variety of historical photographs of Association activities.

Publications. Compilation of a complete bibliography of publications relating to the ALA Centennial will have to wait for a latter-day scholar or enthusiast. There were the usual news stories in the library press about events which have been described here, and such publications as the January 1, 1976, issue of Library Journal, titled "The Need to Know." The July issue of Library Trends, edited by Howard W.

(Above) The ALA Executive Board in session during the 1976 Conference: President-elect Eric Moon (center) is flanked by Executive Director Robert Wedgeworth (left) and past President Edward Holley. (Top left) Alice Hogemeyer (center) proposes a round table for services to the deaf at the meeting. (Left) New Board members Kathleen Molz and Thomas Galvin.

Georgia State Senator Julian Bond giving autograph after his Conference address sponsored by ACRL.

Winger, featured essays on many aspects of librarianship, their historical development, and their possible impact on the future. The celebration of *Library Journal*'s own centennial was the occasion for the publication of its special issue, and both of these issues are mentioned here without having individual articles included in the following bibliography. Three major publications scheduled for publication during the ALA Centennial year did not appear in time, but are expected for 1977. Dennis Thomison's history of the American Library Association and Sidney Jackson's *A Century of Service. . .* , both to be published by ALA, are among these, and the *Dictionary of American Library Biography*, scheduled for publication by Libraries Unlimited, is another major publication in library history which will touch in many ways on ALA history.

The year before the Centennial, *American Libraries* began publication of a series of ALA Centennial Vignettes. In order of appearance, these were:

John Y. Cole, "Wordy Outlets for Impracticables and Pretenders: The Librarian of Congress Balks at Attending ALA 1876," *American Libraries* VI (May 1975), 283.

Evelyn Geller, "Tessa Kelso: Unfinished Hero of Library Herstory," *American Libraries* VI (June 1975), 347.

Michael H. Harris, "Charles Coffin Jewett's 1845 Overture to the Librarian's Creed," *American Libraries* VI (July–August, 1975), 404.

Peter T. Conmy, "William Howard Brett: Apostle of Good Faith in Public Librarianship," *American Libraries* VI (September 1975), 465.

"Copper Queen Saga: How Lynching Led to a Library: Or, a True Story of Badmen and Books in the Old West," based on a report of Roma Sachs Freedman, *American Libraries* VI (October 1975), 539.

George S. Bobinski, "Quiet Power Behind the Throne: The Secretary Who Made the Decision," *American Libraries* VI (November 1975), 592.

"Twelve-Year-Old Edison Rides Rails to Library: Inventor on Track of Early Experiments," based on a report by Ralph A. Uleveling, *American Libraries* VI (December 1975), 637.

"A Civil War General Surveys the Library Field in 1876, Creates a Corps of Librarians from Scattered Troops," based on a report by Elizabeth M. Corbett, *American Libraries* VII (January, 1976), 21.

Edwin S. Gleaves, "An Association of Librar-

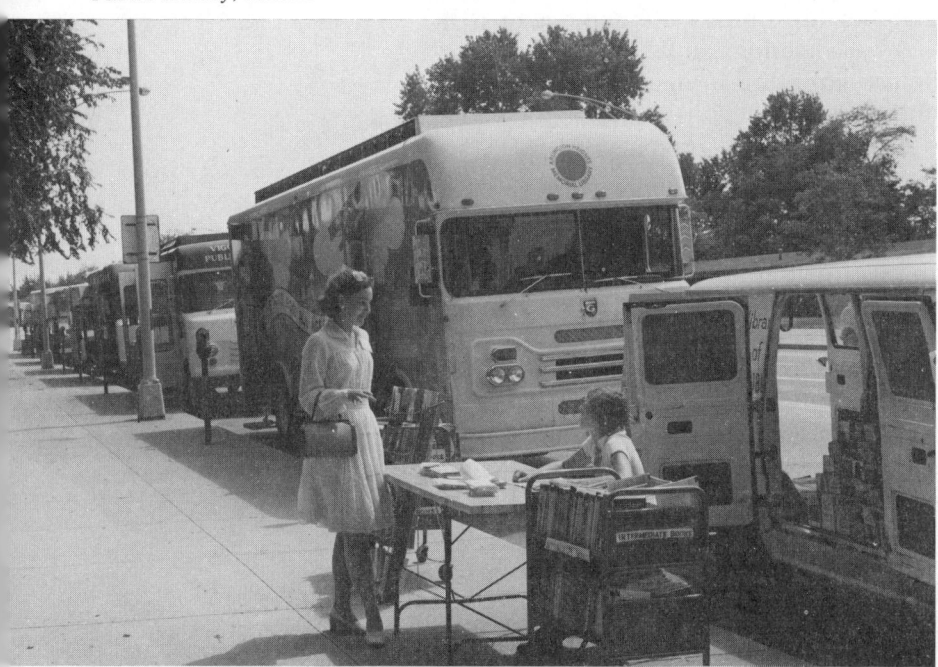

Bookmobile Round-Up at the July Conference. Participating was Mary E. Clark (standing) of the Aurora Public Library, Illinois

Conference registrants collecting materials in the exhibit area.

During a boat trip on Lake Michigan members of the ACRL Art Section view the Chicago skyline in a break from Centennial Conference business.

ians Who Were 'Nevertheless Human': Turn-of-the-Century Bibliosmiles Meet for the Grand Ha-Ha," *American Libraries* VII (February 1976), 79.

"Covering the Library Beat from West Baden to Great Britain: The One and Only Editor of *Public Libraries* Magazine," based on an account by Doris Cruger Dale, *American Libraries* VII (March 1976), 124.

"The Lady Was a Tramp Steamer: The Good Ship ALA," *American Libraries* VII (April 1976), 193.

John Wilkins, "Blue's 'Colored' Branch: A 'Second Plan' That Became a First in Librarianship," *American Libraries* VII (May 1976), 256–257.

In the January issue of *College and Research Libraries*, Richard D. Johnson, the editor, announced plans for the year. *CRL* was to present a series of articles in which major themes in the past century of American academic librarianship were to be explored. Included in the series were articles on specific kinds of services, cooperative efforts, and buildings.

Other ALA Divisions, in addition to the Association of College and Research Libraries, observed notable anniversaries of their own. The Children's Services Division traced its history back to 1901, and the American Association of School Librarians commemorated its 25 years of existence with a continuing series of articles on major events and trends of that period and of the earlier history of school librarianship. The divisional journals, *Top of the News* (for the Children's Services Division and the Young Adult Services Division) and *School Media Quarterly* (for the American Association of School Librarians) reported these commemorations.

One monograph appearing in 1976 provided a partial history of the American Library Association and a biography of the man who was its executive for a longer period than any other individual. Peggy Sullivan's *Carl H. Milam and the American Library Association* was published by H. W. Wilson in June. Milam was Secretary and Executive Secretary of ALA from 1920 to 1948, and was known as "Mr. ALA."

"ALA at 100," Edward G. Holley's review of the Association's history and its present position, was a feature article in the *ALA Yearbook* and was distributed separately to persons attending Library History Seminar V.

The items included in this final listing are not all about ALA, nor is the listing complete, as noted above, but the historical interest stimulated by celebration of the Centennial is reflected in some. Others offer a part of the story of the Association in its first hundred years:

"ALA Pictorial Scrapbook," *American Libraries* VII (January 1976), 42–47.

Peter T. Conmy, "Centennial of American Library Association and Togetherness," *Catholic Library World* XLVI (March 1975), 338–341.

Eugene Garfield, "A Memorable Day with Henry E. Bliss," *Wilson Library Bulletin* XLIX (December 1974), 288–292.

Larry K. Hanson, "The Dewey Decimal: A Nostalgic Tribute and Remembrance," *American Libraries* VI (April 1975), 228–229.

Edward G. Holley, "Celebration of the ALA Centennial," *American Libraries* VI (February 1975), 114–115.

Edward G. Holley, "Who We Were: Profile of the American Librarian at the Birth of the Professional Association, 1876," *American Libraries* VII (June 1976), 323–326.

Ravindra N. Sharma, "Winsor: The Quintessential Librarian," *Wilson Library Bulletin* LI (September 1976), 48–52.

Dennis Thomison, "The A.L.A. and Its Missing Presidents," *Journal of Library History* IX (October 1974), 362–366.

Dennis Thomison, "David and Goliath: the ALA vs. the American Library Association," *Library Journal* C (June 15, 1975), 1606–1607.

At the Hub: The British Library

Harry T. Hookway

(Right) Circular reading room of the British Library designed by Panizzi and completed in 1857 inside the quadrangle of the main building of the British Museum (above).

In library history one of the most exciting developments of the 20th Century has been the formation in July 1973 of the British Library, when a great new national library for the United Kingdom began its operations. Why was it needed and what does it do?

BACKGROUND

Before the creation of the British Library in 1973, the complex, rich, and diverse structure of academic, specialist, and public libraries in the United Kingdom had been supported by a few national institutions and related services. Of these, the most important were the British Museum Library, including the National Reference Library of Science and Invention; the National Lending Library for Science and Technology; the National Central Library; the British National Bibliography; and the Office for Scientific and Technical Information. Before describing the new organization, it may be helpful to provide a brief summary of the main characteristics of these institutions, while noting that the National Libraries of Scotland and Wales provided—and still provide—distinctive services principally directed toward meeting the special requirements of Scotland and Wales.

The British Museum Library needs little introduction, for it was famous throughout the world. As the name implies, it formed part of the British Museum, an organization set up by Act of Parliament in 1753. The primary function of the library had been to provide a comprehensive national reference collection of books, manuscripts, maps, music, and stamps. It enjoyed from the 18th Century a statutory right to receive one copy of every book, journal, newspaper, map, and piece of music published in the United Kingdom. As a consequence, the British Museum Library held by far the greatest general collection of material printed in the English language. The range of foreign books and periodicals, thanks to the initiatives of that "Prince of Librarians," Sir Antonio Panizzi (1797–1879), was also exceptionally extensive by any standards. However, for a long time there was relatively little contact, or cooperation, with the network of libraries that was evolving throughout the country in a haphazard fashion. The result was that a number of other institutions were created to fill the growing gaps in provision of facilities at the national level.

The National Central Library was one such institution. It was founded in 1916 as the Central Library for Students when its primary purpose was to lend books to adult class students who had no other sources for borrowing. It was incorporated by Royal Charter in 1931 as the National Central Library and developed to provide lending services for the humanities and the social sciences partly through its own collections but mainly by means of its union catalogues, as well as continuing the original role of assisting adult class students. The Library also assisted interlibrary cooperation by arranging the interchange of surplus and duplicate library material nationally and internationally through the British National Book Centre. The main users were public libraries and universities.

The British National Bibliography was set up in 1949 following the recommendations of a Committee of the (British) Library Association which had been considering the lack of adequate provision for centralized cataloguing and bibliographical services. The British National Bibliography's functions were "to carry on the business of compiling, editing and publishing in appropriate bibliographic form lists of books, pamphlets and other recorded material of whatever nature published in Great Britain, the Dominions [sic] and Colonies and/or foreign countries, together with such annotations or further information as may be desirable for the use of librarians, bibliographers and others." In practice, the organization concentrated on British publications and provided a range of services including the weekly National Bibliography and a printed card service. Roughly 90 percent of the public libraries, over half the university libraries, half the college and school libraries, and a significant proportion of special libraries subscribed to the current book list services, and extensive use was also made of the catalogue card service. With the support of the Office for Scientific and Technical Information the British National Bibliography developed computer-aided techniques for production of the national bibliography and started a MARC tape service.

The National Lending Library for Science and Technology became fully operational in 1962 following a recommendation of the Government's Advisory Council on Scientific Policy that a new lending library for science and technology should be set up with the specific function of providing a rapid central postal loans service from stock to meet the needs of research workers in industry and elsewhere. The Library was planned on the basis of providing a stock that fitted demand as closely as possible, whereas such central loan collections as already existed consisted mostly of material that few or no other libraries possessed. Use of the service grew rapidly, with most demands for loans or photocopies falling in the category of recent serial publications. The largest single group of users came from industry.

The National Reference Library of Science and Invention grew out of the Patent Office Library, which had been founded in 1885 as a public reference library of the physical sciences and their related technologies. It was not restricted to meeting

British Library

the patent needs of industry, but developed a general scientific collection. The Government's Advisory Council on Scientific Policy, which had recommended that the National Lending Library for Science and Technology should be set up, also recommended that the Patent Office Library should be developed as the National Reference Library of Science and Invention. The British Museum was given responsibility for the library on the basis that the British Museum Library's collections of scientific and technical literature, including copyright deposit material in these fields, could then be made available to the reconstituted organization. From 1960 onward the new library aimed to provide all literature of current value in every language covering the whole of the natural sciences and technology, with special coverage in the field of invention. Much of the material was on open access so that users could search for and find the information required very quickly. By far the largest single group of users were patent workers and industrial information officers.

The Office for Scientific and Technical Information was the youngest of the institutions supporting the library structure of the country. Its origins are also to be found in a report of the Advisory Council for Scientific Policy, which recommended that serious research into the problem of collation and dissemination of scientific information should be undertaken. In the event, OSTI was set up in 1965 with wide terms of reference, including responsibility for promoting and sponsoring research leading to the development of new techniques and systems, improved information services and experiments with new ones. The intention was that OSTI should not become responsible for operating services unless no other suitable organization existed.

A NEW DIMENSION

By 1968 it had become clear that although the national institutions referred to above were intended to complement the country's library structure by providing services which for economic or administrative reasons could not be justified on a regional or local scale, their activities were not closely articulated, each institution enjoying either complete or a very considerable degree of independence from the others. As a consequence there had grown up confused, wasteful, and overlapping arrangements for provision of services at the national level. In view of the great and increasing importance of library and information services for the prosperity and cultural life of the country, the Government set up a National Libraries Committee to consider whether in the interests of efficiency and economy those facilities should be brought into a unified framework. The Committee reported in 1969. Its principal recommendation was that the administration of the national library institutions described earlier here should become the responsibility of a new statutory and independent public body. In 1971 the Government of the day issued a White Paper announcing their intention to set up the British Library as an independent corporate body under the control of a board of management to be called the British Library Board. The Government accepted the main thrust of the National Libraries Committee's principal recommendation and, having consulted the Governing bodies of the institutions concerned, announced that the British Museum Library, the National Reference Library of Science and Invention, the National Central Library, the National Lending Library for Science and Technology and the Office for Scientific and Technical Information would be transferred to the new organization. The Government argued that effective articulation of the activities of the national library institutions would have a profound influence on the future efficiency of the country's li-

Structure of The British Library

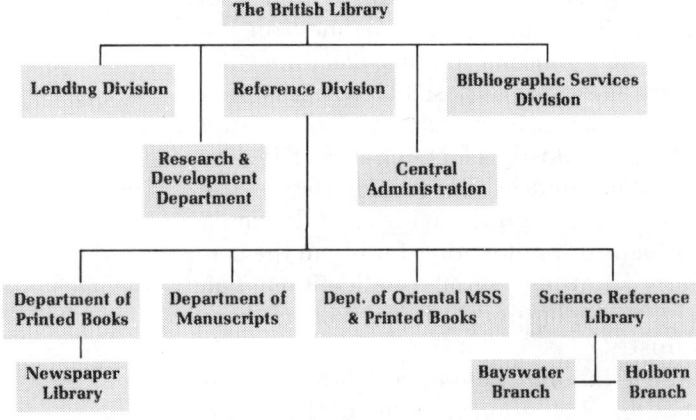

Organization of the new British Library.

brary structure, and concluded that central planning and management so that unnecessary duplication could be avoided, new techniques more effectively employed, resources better allocated, and the full benefits obtained of working on a truly national scale could only be achieved if the institutions concerned were brought together in one organization, centrally financed and directed. Events moved at a very rapid pace following publication of the White Paper: an organizing committee for the new library started its work in 1971; by 1972 the British Library Act had become law, having received a welcome from all parties in both Houses of Parliament; and the British Library Board was set up in April 1973, followed by the progressive transfer of staff, functions, and collections to form the British Library from July of that year onward, the process being completed in August 1974.

The British Library Act is characterized by its brevity and nonspecific enabling character. The position of the British Library and its Board of Management is formally defined in paragraphs 1–3 of Section 1 of the Act, which run as follows:

(1) This Act shall have effect with a view to the establishment for the United Kingdom of a national library, to be known as "The British Library," consisting of a comprehensive collection of books, manuscripts, periodicals, films and other recorded matter, whether printed or otherwise.

(2) The British Library shall be under the control and management of a public authority, to be known as "The British Library Board," whose duty it shall be to manage the Library as a national centre for reference, study, and bibliographical and other information services, in relation both to scientific and technological matters and to the humanities.

(3) The Board shall make the services of the British Library available in particular to institutions of education and learning, other libraries and industry; and (a) it shall be within the functions of the Board, so far as they think it expedient for achieving the objects of this Act and generally for contributing to the efficient management of other libraries and information services, to carry out and sponsor research; and the Board may contribute to the expenses of library authorities within the meaning of the Public Libraries and Museums Act 1964, or of any other person providing library facilities whether for members of the public or otherwise.

STRUCTURE OF THE LIBRARY

The principal activities of the British Library are grouped into three operational divisions—Reference, Lending, and Bibliographic Services. Of these, the Reference Division is formed from the former British Museum Library and the National Reference Library of Science and Invention; the Lending Division combines the functions of the National Central Library and the National Lending Library for Science and Technology; and the Bibliographic Services Division is based essentially on the functions of the former British National Bibliography together with the Copyright Receipt Office. The organizational structure of the Library is shown in the accompanying chart, and it can be seen that in addition to the operational divisions there is a Research and Development Department, which is based on the functions of the former Office for Scientific and Technical Information suitably expanded to cover the promotion and sponsorship of research and development related to library and information operations in all subject fields. There is also a Central Administration which, as its name implies, provides the overall financial, personnel, and management services required by any large and complex organization.

All these activities are under the control of the British Library Board, which is made up of a Chairman serving part-time; a full-time Chief Executive who is also Deputy Chairman; three other full-time members who have charge, as executives responsible to the Chief Executive, for the three main operational areas; and, in addition, nine part-time members chosen for their breadth of experience and ability to evaluate the policies and performance of the Library. The Board receives a Grant in Aid from the Government, but it is not part of the Civil Service, nor are its employees, and it has a large measure of autonomy as may be judged from paragraph 11 (1) of the Schedule to the British Library Act, which specifies that "it shall be within the capacity of the Board as a statutory corporation to do all such things, and enter into all such transactions, as are incidental or conducive to the discharge of its functions."

Harry T. Hookway, Deputy Chairman and Chief Executive of the British Library Board.

British Library

AT THE HUB

At the time this article was written the British Library had been fully operational for roughly two and a half years. During that time the prime objectives of the Board have been to develop a range of central services in such a way that public, university, polytechnic, industrial, specialist, and other libraries who use the services can make better use of their own resources in directions of particular interest to themselves and their users. Thus the reference facilities are being planned so as to provide all the essential central reference services around which other libraries can build up their own collections and services. Particular attention is being paid to improving the use and accessibility of the stock through new information services.

The central lending services are intended to complement local lending collections, partly by acquiring items in heavy demand when the pressure on local resources exceeds supply; partly by acquiring little used (and often expensive) items when it makes sense for the item to be available centrally thus optimizing the resources locally available; partly by retaining items for loan after the period of intensive demand has passed so that libraries may adopt a more rational discarding policy, utilizing the space available to them, in the knowledge that the item will still be available if required.

The bibliographic services are organized to make the most effective use of centralized cataloguing facilities. All major cataloguing and indexing activities within the library are now computer based, with the result that much improved information services can be provided for those readers who wish to consult books and periodicals acquired since the middle of 1975. A great advantage of the new techniques is that the same catalogue record, in the case of books published in Britain, is used for the production of the weekly British National Bibliography whose coverage has been broadened substantially. In addition the computer system provides an extensive range of local cataloguing services to libraries in Britain.

By developing its wide range of services in these directions the Board is planning the Library to be at the center—the hub, as it were—rather than the apex of the library services of the United Kingdom.

FACTS AND FIGURES

From what has gone before, it will be appreciated that the British Library is a substantial institution, whose activities require substantial resources in staff and finance. For the current year the Library's expenditure is projected to be £21,600,000 ($37,000,000), of which £2,500,000 ($4,300,000) is expected as income from services for which a charge is made. Expenditure by the Reference Division will be £9,900,000 ($16,900,000); by the Lending Division, £5,560,000 ($9,500,000); and by the Bibliographic Services Division £1,710,000 ($2,920,000). There are 2,150 employees, of whom 1,100 are in the Reference Division, 160 in the Bibliographic Services Division, 690 in the Lending Division and the remaining 200 in Central Administration and the Research and Development Department.

Apart from the Lending Division whose activities are centered in Boston Spa, the remaining operations of the Library are scattered among 17 different locations in London. This unwelcome situation must continue until a sorely needed new building is provided. The Board has accepted the Government's proposal that the building should be constructed on a site of 9½ acres next to St. Pancras railway station, and that construction should start in 1979 if economic conditions at that time permit. Detailed planning of the library building with the object of making a start in 1979 is now under way. Meanwhile, for some time to come, the Library must make the best use it can of existing accommodation, seeking to ensure that book stock and services do not deteriorate and that the staff has adequate working conditions.

The Reference Division of the Library is divided into four departments: Printed Books, Manuscripts, Oriental Manuscripts and Printed Books, and the Science Reference Library. The first three departments are still housed within the British Museum building and readers still consult books in the famous circular reading room designed by Panizzi. The Science Reference Library is spread between five locations in central London, of which the Holborn Branch next to the British Patent Office is the most intensively used.

The Department of Printed Books has in excess of 8,000,000 items in its collections with nearly a million recorded uses every year. There are over 30,000 current readers tickets on issue, but only 800 reader seats. About one third of the Department's on-site users are from overseas, many of them from the United States. In addition to the main collections of printed books, the Department has one of the largest and finest collections of music scores in the world, a Map Library with a complete set of Ordnance Survey material, and an extensive collection of early maps and topographical material (including some of special importance concerned with prerevolutionary America) and a philatelic collection which is preeminent among the world's historical collections of postage stamps. Although a new building is urgently required if major improvements are to be effected, none the less a number of important developments will take place in the next decade which may well change fundamentally the role of the Department in relation to other parts of the British Library, to the library services of the United Kingdom, and to the public. One significant step along the road was the inauguration in 1975 of a new series of computer-based catalogues using AACR and MARC for author/title productions and on the PRECIS system for the subject catalogues. These replace the British Museum General Catalogue and the British Museum Subject Index in respect to material published from 1975 onward. The products of the new system will generally be in microfilm, and the main use to begin with will be by users who come to consult the Department's collections on site. Later on, however, the library community as a whole and the public will benefit from the new possibilities for producing quickly, conveniently, and relatively inexpensively a range of up-to-date information about the holdings of the Department.

The Science Reference Library is the principal reference library in the United Kingdom for contemporary literature of science, technology, and invention. By contrast with the other departments of the Reference Division, no readers ticket is required, and about half the stock is on open access. There are over 750,000 volumes, 30,000 current periodicals, a very large quantity of trade literature, and some 17,000,000 patent specifications. The Science Reference Library plays an active role in assisting the dissemination of scientific and technical information, and provides facilities for readers access to all the major on-line computer based bibliographic services. Some 40 data bases can be accessed, including Medline; the European Space Agency Recon facilities at Frascati, Italy; and the Lockheed Dialog bases via the Tymshare network. Catalogue records of all new material are held in the British Library's computer data base and the catalogues are produced as microfiche. The library has two distinct but interrelated roles: the traditional role of a research library of last resort and that of a special library of first resort for multidisciplinary studies particularly related to industry and industrial property.

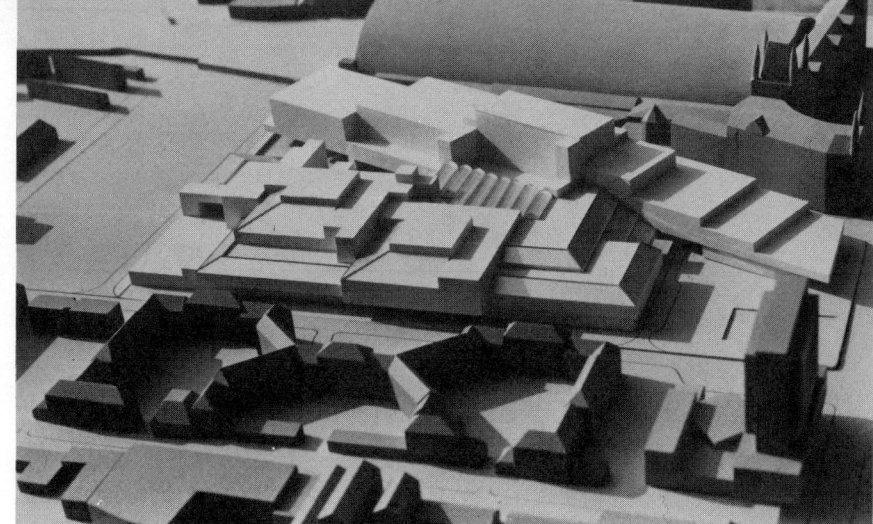

Model of proposed new building of the British Library to be begun in 1979.

The Departments of Manuscripts and of Oriental Manuscripts and Printed Books have outstanding collections the equal of any in the world, but space does not permit an extended discussion of their work. Both departments are extensively used and both are taking steps to make their collections more readily accessible by improving the facilities available to readers.

The Lending Division of the British Library provides a comprehensive document supply service, mainly from its own stock, but also supplementing them by the resources of other libraries. Two basic principles govern the Division's acquisition policy. First, it purchases all material for which a significant demand is expressed, and if the demand is sufficiently intense, additional copies are bought. Second, material is acquired for which there may be little demand but when there is small chance of its being available elsewhere. The Division therefore covers all subject fields, acquires all significant serial publications—over 47,000 current titles are received—and all English language monographs of a type and level likely to be required on interlibrary loan. In addi-

xxvii

(Top) Some 40 data bases can be accessed using terminals in the Science Reference Library. (Above) Crowded space in the Reference Division of the Library, which includes historical and literary collections and the National Science Library.

tion, it acquires comprehensively conference proceedings, report literature, music scores, dissertations produced in the U.S. and the United Kingdom, and scientific books in Slavonic languages. The main categories of material not acquired comprehensively are foreign language monographs and foreign official publications. The amount of such material published is very large, and the demand in the United Kingdom is small and unpredictable. However, foreign language monographs that are requested from the Lending Division and are not readily available from elsewhere in Britain are usually bought if in print. The demand for the Lending Division's services is striking.

About 2,500,000 requests a year are received at present, and demand is still increasing. There are 5,100 registered user libraries in the United Kingdom, and this must include all but a very few libraries in the country. The Division handles nearly 80 percent of British interlibrary loan traffic, and an estimated one-third of the world's traffic. Some 45 percent of demand is generated by industrial, commercial, government, and other specialist libraries, 38 percent is from academic institutions, 9 percent from overseas and 8 percent from public libraries.

Speed of response is very important if local resources are to be supplemented effectively, and at present the Divison is able to send out by first class mail about 80 percent of items that are in stock the same day as the requests are received. Photocopying is used as extensively as permissible within the terms of the Copyright Act since this is often more convenient for the users and increases the availability of the stock.

The proportion of requests satisfied varies considerably between different categories of material. At one extreme, the Lending Division can supply 93 percent of English language serials from stock, and, at the other, only 26 percent of requests for foreign language monographs can be supplied from stock. However, the overall satisfaction rate for all categories of material is 84 percent from the Division's own stock, and 93 percent when supplemented by the resources of its supporting libraries, including the Reference Division.

A striking feature of the use made of the Lending Division's services has been the growth of requests from overseas for loans and photocopies. Some 286,000 photocopy requests a year are being received from overseas, and the demand is still growing. Nearly half of all overseas requests are from Western Europe and, outside Europe, the greatest number come from the United States. The biggest users are the Center for Research Libraries in Chicago (about 1,500 requests a month) and the National Library of Medicine (1,200 a month): both these organizations act as agents for individual libraries. A considerable and increasing number of overseas requests now arrive by telex, and at present some 105 institutions in 31 countries take advantage of the overseas telex service, thus reducing substantially the time taken overall to satisfy a request. Heavy users of the lending service are becoming interested in the transmission of requests directly by computer, and this method is already used by the Center for Research Libraries and the National Library of Medicine. In addition to its main function as a central service for the supply of loans and photocopies, the Division carries out a number of other activities, including operation of the MEDLARS center in the United Kingdom.

The Bibliographic Services Division has as its main purpose the integration of the internal processing operations of the British Library with the external services required by the library community in the country so that the necessary cataloguing, indexing, and classification activities need only be carried out once and the records are then capable of use for any required purpose. In practice this results in the Division's having two important responsibilities, of which one is to produce the bibliographic records for the Reference Division of the British Library, catalogued according to AACR standards and using the PRECIS indexing system. However, the larger concern is with the needs of library and information services throughout the country. The Division also cooperates closely with national bibliographic services overseas. The most important operational service of the Division is still the authoritative record of British books published each year, the British National Bibliography: probably no single work is more frequently consulted by British librarians. Each book is catalogued, indexed, classified in the Dewey and Library of Congress systems, and given Library of Congress subject headings. Since 1971 the bibliography has been computer produced. The source of the intake for the British National Bibliography is the Copyright Receipt Office, where British publishers must by law deposit a copy of each publication within one month of issue. Aside from a yearly intake of around 35,000 books, at present the Office receives about 150,000 newspaper issues, 100,000 periodical parts, 12,000 maps, and 4,000 items of music. These are not yet included in the bibliography.

Both the current and the retrospective records of the British National Bibliography back to its creation in 1950 are now in machine readable form in the British Library's MARC data base, as are all Library of Congress current records and its retrospective records from 1968. In the foreseeable future records from other national bibliographic centers that are in MARC compatible machine readable form will also be added as a result of the international agreements the British Library has concluded for the exchange of magnetic tapes. Already the data base contains over one million records and is increasing at the rate of about 3,000 records per week. Users can take these records, or a selection from them, on magnetic tape and transfer the records to their own computer. As an alternative they can purchase a full catalogue service from the Division using the British Library's facilities and software to prepare computer output microfilm catalogues. In addition to these services, the Division produces a number of special publications such as *Books in English* (in ultramicrofiche) and the *British Education Index*.

Supporting the main operational services are a number of special offices, including the United Kingdom National Serials Data Centre, the Cataloguing-in-Publication Office, the Bibliographic Standards Office, and the Subject Systems Office.

The Division is implementing a three-phase development of the British Library's computer based services. The first phase, involving the transfer of all major cataloguing activities within the Library to a batch processing system developed for the British National Bibliography, is now complete. Systems design, programming, and planning are now proceeding on the second and third phases of the program, which will see the progressive introduction of on-line operations based on an ICL 2900 series computer. Meanwhile, an interim on-line facility based on an IBM 370 series computer will be available from April 1977.

PLANNING FOR THE FUTURE

The Research and Development Department promotes and sponsors research and development related to library and information operations in all subject fields. Its work is directed to the benefit of library and information services as a whole and it is able to award research grants and contracts to outside bodies. During the year 1975–76 the Department made 96 awards for new projects and extensions or supplements to existing projects with a total value of £1,110,000 ($1,900,000). Resources are devoted to key areas such as studies of how reference material is used, users' needs and user education, assessment of the value of on-line computer based information retrieval systems, primary communications, and experimental information services in special fields such as education.

Research is also sponsored that will lead to a clearer understanding of the policy issues facing the library services of the country. Three such issues from recent years are library automation, interlibrary loans, and library management.

With library automation the main policy requirement in UK, as in other countries, has been to determine the role of local, cooperative, and national organizations in the handling of monograph (including cataloguing) and serial records.

The Lending Division's building complex houses a comprehensive document supply service.

The projects supported by OSTI and, later, the British Library besides building up expertise, demonstrating operational systems, providing economic assessments and furthering a cost-conscious approach to automation, have created a wide interest in the main policy issues. A large number of librarians have been involved, either as heads of projects or as members of advisory groups or of discussion groups related to the projects. The Library itself could not have embarked with confidence on its own automation program without the benefit of this research.

An important policy interest in the field of interlibrary loans centers on the most economical and effective ways of transporting material on loan. A preliminary study financed by the Library suggests that significant improvements might be made by adopting a national transport scheme, independent of the Post Office and involving carriage by rail between Boston Spa and regional centers and carriage by vans within the regions. The potential value of, and possible ways of organizing and financing, such a scheme are being investigated further in two pilot studies, one in the Northwest Region — which is producing encouraging results — and one in London, due to begin soon.

Much research in library management suggests only ways of improving the domestic operations of a library. In the past it has tended to involve collection of management data or the evaluation of management techniques rather than the solution of specific, widely occurring problems. But there are signs of a change in approach, which the Library is encouraging in various ways. The change results, to a large extent, from the growing interest in problems of resource allocation, and it is reasonable to hope that in future research can be conducted on problems such as the relative value of different library services, the relationship between resource allocation and specific policies (e.g., loan policy), the effect of pooling resources (e.g., manpower and specific book stocks) in certain geographical areas, and the allocation of resources between local, regional and national library services. Many of these problems are essential to national library policy and research on them, if properly conceived, conducted, and monitored, can greatly help in the making of policy.

CONSULTATION

Since the British Library's central reference, lending, bibliographic, and research services require substantial resources and could have a profound effect on the future development of all parts of the library system, they are being developed in full consultation with the principal user and institutional interests. The Board has created wide-ranging consultative machinery, formal and informal, to ensure that planning and performance are responsive to the needs of users. An Advisory Council has been set up under Section 2(3) of the British Library Act to advise on the Library's relations with other libraries, and on the character and balance of the central services to be offered. Members are drawn from nominees of the organizations and institutions representing the main categories of users. In addition, advisory committees of experts have been set up to provide the advice and assistance needed for the principal operations of the Library. At present there are advisory committees for the Lending Division, Bibliographic Services Division, Reference Division (Bloomsbury), Science Reference Library, and the Research and Development Department.

INTERNATIONAL OUTLOOK

In the brief compass of this article it has not been possible to do more than give an overview of the British Library and its role at the hub of the library services of the United Kingdom. Of course, the Library is more than the national library for the United Kingdom — it is international in scope and outlook as is evidenced by its support of the IFLA Office for Universal Bibliographical Control, the Office for International Lending (in the Lending Division), and the International Serials Data System. The Library has many bilateral arrangements with other National Libraries and links with the major research libraries of the United States are close, in particular with the Library of Congress.

The British Library is still at an early stage of development, but it is clear that it has had, and will continue to have, a major role to play in seeking to ensure that the best possible use is made of the library resources of the United Kingdom.

The Centenary of a Giant of Librarianship: Louis Round Wilson

Edward G. Holley

In the same year that ALA was founded, one of the giants of the library profession, Louis Round Wilson, was born in the small village of Lenoir, North Carolina. Throughout his long career as a university librarian, library educator, author, lecturer, and association official, Wilson has contributed significantly to the library profession and to ALA. Equally significant have been his contributions to his state, his university, and his native region. To celebrate his approaching birthday, the University of North Carolina at Chapel Hill declared December 2, 1976, LOUIS ROUND WILSON CENTENNIAL DAY. About 400 friends and colleagues from throughout the country went to Chapel Hill for two symposia on library education and library administration, a reception by the School of Library Science Alumni Association, and an invitational banquet by Chancellor Ferebee Taylor at which three national associations paid tribute to Wilson's contributions to their work. The Wilson Library mounted an exhibit of documents from the Louis Round Wilson papers in the Southern Historical Collection.

Wilson Day began with a symposium on "Library Education in the Southeast since World War II." A major paper was delivered by Jack Dalton, formerly Librarian of the University of Virginia, former Director of the ALA International Relations Office, and former Dean of the Columbia University School of Library Service. Responding to Dalton's paper were Virginia Lacy Jones, Dean of the Atlanta University School of Library Service, and Mary Edna Anders, Interim Executive Director of the Southeastern Library Association and author of the recently published *Libraries and Library Services in the Southeast*.

The afternoon symposium, "University Libraries and Change," featured a paper by Herman H. Fussler, former Director of Libraries and now Martin A. Ryerson Distinguished Service Professor at the University of Chicago. Panelists included Robert B. Downs, Dean of Library Administration Emeritus, University of Illinois; Guy R. Lyle, Director of Libraries Emeritus, Emory University; and Stephen A. McCarthy, former Director of Libraries, Cornell University, and former Executive Director, Association of Research Libraries. As a further recognition of Wilson's Centenary, the University will publish the two papers and the reactions to them early in 1977.

Chancellor Taylor's banquet in honor of Dean Wilson featured presentations from five groups. James Govan, University Librarian, presented Wilson with a bound volume of letters from colleagues and friends. The UNC General Alumni Association named him one of Carolina's "Priceless Gems," an honor usually reserved for those associated with the University's athletic programs. The Association for State and Local History and the American Association of University Presses both gave him an award of merit, and Clara Stanton Jones, President of the American Library Association, presented Wilson with the Association's Melvil Dewey Award for 1976. Ms. Jones also announced that the Edmonds Foundation had established a $1,000 Louis Round Wilson Scholarship for the School of Library Science and Vice Chancellor William Little announced that a bronze bust of Dean Wilson had been commissioned for the Louis Round Wilson Library. The 450 guests for the banquet received a copy of Maurice F. Tauber's biographical sketch of Wilson (1956) supplemented by Frances A. Weaver's "Louis R. Wilson, The Years Since 1955." Dean Wilson responded briefly to each presentation, and, afterwards, greeted his many friends and former students personally.

100 PRODUCTIVE YEARS

Louis Round Wilson was born on December 27, 1876. He attended Haverford College but later transferred to UNC, where he received an A.B. degree in 1899. He received the A.M. and Ph.D. degrees from UNC in 1902 and 1905. Wilson became University Librarian at Chapel Hill

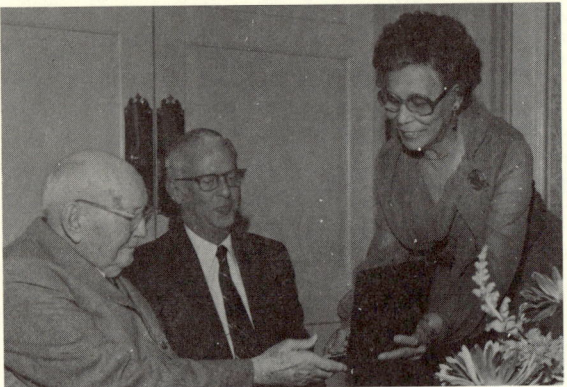
(From left) Louis R. Wilson, University of North Carolina Chancellor Ferebee Taylor, and ALA President Clara Jones at banquet in December marking Wilson's 100th birthday.

Wilson at Haverford College, about 1896.

Wilson with daughter Elizabeth in 1912 in front of his East Rosemary Street house in Chapel Hill.

Wilson (far left) aboard the ship Bremen returning from Europe in 1935 with author Thomas Wolfe (far right).

Haverford College classmates and Wilson (far left) in 1896.

Wilson (center) on the occasion of the naming of North Carolina University Library in his honor in 1956. (Left) University Chancellor Robert B. House and (right) the University's President, William Friday.

Wilson in front of one of nine display cases featuring aspects of his life and work exhibited in the Louis Round Wilson Library.

in 1901. During the next 31 years he was a major figure in the expansion and development of the University as well as the University Library. At various periods, in addition to his post as University Librarian, Wilson promoted and served as Director of University Extension, founded and directed the UNC Press, served as a fund raiser, and edited the *Alumni Review.* In the Library he established the North Carolina, Southern Historical, and Rare Book Collections, all nationally recognized as distinguished library collections. During his period of service the University erected two library buildings, one in 1907 and another in 1929. The latter building was named the Louis Round Wilson Library in 1956.

Wilson was also early interested in the training of librarians. He began summer courses to train county and town librarians in 1904 and later expanded the courses to the regular year so that they were available not only to library student assistants but also to liberal arts students. He planned for the creation of a library school which was assured in 1929 when the Carnegie Corporation announced a grant of $100,000 for that purpose. The School of Library Science opened in 1931 with Wilson as its first Director.

In whatever activities he engaged, Louis Round Wilson was aware of the importance of books and libraries. He was one of the founders of the North Carolina Library Association in 1904, he persuaded the ALA to hold its annual conference in Asheville, North Carolina, in 1907, he promoted the establishment of the North Carolina Library Commission, and served as its first Chairman, 1909–16, and he worked diligently with the Southern Association of Colleges and Secondary Schools in the development of library standards. He was a founder of the Southeastern Library Association and served as its President, 1924–26.

After three decades of phenomenal achievement, Wilson accepted the invitation of Robert Maynard Hutchins to become Dean of the Graduate Library School of the University of Chicago. That School, established with a million-dollar grant from the Carnegie Corporation in 1926, had not made much progress during its first half dozen years. However, the decade of Wilson's deanship at Chicago, 1932–42, proved to be a golden age for library education. The Graduate Library School became a beehive of activity as Wilson, his faculty, and his doctoral students probed into various facets of librarianship, wrote articles and books, and came to dominate the profession intellectually.

Active in the American Library Association, Dean Wilson accepted membership on the Board of Education for Librarianship during its second year and served from 1925 to 1932. He was the ALA President, 1935–36, and was one of the ALA officials chiefly interested in federal support for libraries. In 1951 ALA presented Wilson its highest award, Honorary Membership.

Wilson's publication record, already extensive at Chicago where he wrote his landmark book, *The Geography of Reading,* and served as General Editor of the 26-volume University of Chicago Studies in Library Science, continued after his retirement to Chapel Hill in 1942. He undertook the editorship of the 18-volume Sesquicentennial History of the University of North Carolina, was the co-author with Maurice F. Tauber of another landmark work, *The University Library,* and wrote three volumes of UNC history. He taught part-time in the School of Library Science until 1959 and served as an adviser to President William C. Friday until 1969. He also conducted numerous university library surveys, as well as a survey of the region, *Libraries of the Southeast,* the latter with Marion A. Milczewski. Few individuals in any discipline have accomplished so much during their period of retirement. He marked the centenary of his birth with publication of a new book, *Louis Round Wilson's Historical Sketches,* issued a month before the celebration in Chapel Hill.

Dean Wilson continues a lively interest in the library profession, in the University, and in Chapel Hill and North Carolina. He lives in the house on Rosemary Street which he had built in 1912.

BIBLIOGRAPHICAL NOTE

In addition to the forthcoming symposia proceedings, two items were published for the Louis Round Wilson Centennial: *Louis Round Wilson Bibliography: A Chronological List of Works and Editorial Activities* and *Louis Round Wilson: The Years since 1955* by Frances A. Weaver, issued as a supplement to Maurice F. Tauber's *Louis R. Wilson: A Biographical Sketch* (1956).

Louis Round Wilson

Telecommunications
Joseph Becker

Telecommunications may be simply defined as the "exchange of information by electrical transmission over great distances." As greater emphasis is placed on the development of statewide, regional, and national library networks to facilitate interinstitutional services, a concomitant requirement emerges to understand and apply telecommunications technology. A great variety of telecommunications methods have been used for interlibrary communications in the past, ranging from the simplest use of the telephone, the teletype, the radio, and even experiments with microwave telefacsimile transmission. Although the advantages of telecommunications have been known to libraries for many years, their utilization has been retarded by problems of cost and systems planning. In recent years, however, as libraries have made greater use of computers and as they have moved toward new programs of interlibrary cooperation and resource sharing, interest in telecommunications in general has grown.

TRANSMISSION TECHNOLOGY

Telecommunications systems are designed to carry three principal types of signals: (1) voice—originating as human speech or recorded tones; (2) digital—originating with computers or other machines in which data is encoded in the binary language; and (3) video—originating with TV recorders, facsimile scanners, or other devices that change light particles into electrical energy in the form of small, discrete bits of information. Each of the three types of telecommunication signals is associated with a telecommunications channel that can carry it most efficiently.

Voice can be efficiently transmitted over telephone lines, but data, like the digital language of the computer or the video language of the television camera and facsimile scanner, needs a broader band-width for efficient transmission than the narrow-band-width telephone line can provide. Band-width is a measure of the signal-carrying capacity of a communications channel in cycles per second. It is the numerical difference between the highest frequency and the lowest frequency handled by a communications channel. The broader the band, the greater the signal transmission rate. The tens of thousands of bits which make up a computer message or TV picture, if sent by telephone, have to be squeezed through the narrow line over a longer period of time to transmit a given message. This consumes telephone capacity that would normally be used to carry other conversations. A good example of the problem can be illustrated with the "picture-phone." This is the telephone company service which permits a caller to see and hear the other person at the distant end. The two-way picture part of this dialogue requires more than 100 times more telephone transmission capacity than the voice portion. There are 100,000,000 telephones in the U.S. today. Thus, if only 1% of the subscribers had picture-phones we would theoretically exhaust our national telephone capacity for any other use.

Wider-Band-Width Use. Digital and video signals are carried over the wider-band-width channels because of the great number of bits that must be accommodated per unit of time. Sending computer data or pictures over telephone lines is possible if data phones are used; they convert digital and video data to their tone equivalents at the transmission end and reconvert them at the receiving end. This is, however, a very slow process and from a communications viewpoint most inefficient. A reference to "slow-scan television" means that the video signal is being carried over a telephone line. Library experimentation with telefacsimile has by and large been restricted to transmission of the facsimile signals over telephone lines. An 8" × 10" page carried by telephone lines takes about three minutes, as compared to 30 seconds when sent over a broad-band-width channel.

A telecommunications system used for library purposes will eventually need to integrate audio, digital, and video signals into a single system. The idea of an "integrated telecommunications system" became practical only during the past ten years, and commercial and governmental efforts are under way to provide these technically sophisticated and unified facilities as rapidly as possible.

TRANSMISSION SYSTEMS

Technically speaking, there are five means by which voice, digital, and video signals may be carried to their destination: by telephone line, by radio, by coaxial cable, by microwave relays, and by communications satellite. An explanation of each is given below presented in ascending order of their band-width capacity.

Telephone Lines. The telephone as a means of communication is beyond comparison. It is simple, quick, reliable, accurate, and provides great geographic flexibility. Quite often the telephone can supply all the communications capability required by a library, especially when it is coupled with the teletypewriter.

Radio Broadcasting. As the word "broadcasting" implies, signals are radiated in all directions and the omnidirectional antennas which are used in radio broadcasting are designed to have this effect. Frequencies used are 500 to 1,500 kilocycles for AM (amplitude modulation), and 88 to 108 megacycles for FM (frequency modulation). In low-frequency systems the signals are propagated close to the ground and the effective radius of reception is small. With ultrahigh frequency, vast distances can be covered by striking upper layers of the atmosphere and having the signal deflected to earth. High-frequency systems, however, are subject to atmospheric interference.

Coaxial Cable (and CATV). A remarkable extension of the carrier art was provided by the development of the coaxial cable. Within the sheath of most coaxial cables are a number of copper tubes. Within each tube is a copper wire, supported by insulating disks spaced one inch apart. The name coaxial reflects the fact that both the wire and the tube have the same axis.

Coaxial cables can carry many times the voice capacity of telephone lines and are

Telecommunications

thus considered to be broad-band-width carriers able to accommodate digital and video data with equal efficiency. The coaxial cable has the additional advantage that the electrical energy confined within the tube can be guided directly to its destination, instead of spreading in all directions as is the case in radio broadcasting.

Many libraries planning new buildings are including special ducts to accommodate known or potential requirements for coaxial cable between computer units, terminals, and dial access stations.

The technology of Community Antenna Television (CATV) incorporates extensive use of coaxial cables. CATV operates very similarly to the way a closed circuit television system works. CATV stations by law are required to make available to subscribers at least one channel for "public service" and "educational" purposes. Local requirements are generally a matter of opinion and vary from community to community.

It is hardly possible to predict what effect CATV and its coaxial cables will have on libraries. It is clear, however, that many libraries will soon have coaxial cables as well as telephone lines, and this implies a new capability for bi-directional broad-band-width information exchange. Attachment of a coaxial cable from a CATV trunk station to a library provides an electronic pathway 300 megacycles wide. The telephone line is only 4,000 cycles wide. Since a megacycle is one million cycles, the relative practical difference in an operational environment is in the order of 50,000:1. It is this significant difference that causes some people to suggest that advanced telecommunications will someday bring newspapers and books into the library by electronic facsimile, along with computer information from data banks, individualized instruction from schools, and a much greater variety of educational materials.

Microwave. The term microwave applies to those systems in which the transmitting and receiving antennas are in view of each other. The word is not very definitive but generally describes systems with frequencies extending up to 15,000 megacycles. Microwave is, therefore, one of the larger broad-band-width carriers. Microwave telecommunication systems are used to transmit data and multi-channel telephone or video signals. Since microwaves do not bend, transcontinental microwave telecommunication systems consist of relay towers spaced at approximately 30-mile, line-of-sight intervals across the country. Because of the earth's curvature, transoceanic microwave systems are not feasible. It is this limitation which helped give rise to the development of the communications satellite.

Communications Satellites. The newest and most promising telecommunication development is the communications satellite. A communications satellite is placed in orbit above the earth to receive and retransmit signals received from different points on earth. The satellite's orbital velocity is synchronized with the speed of the earth's rotation. Thus a satellite in synchronous equatorial orbit with the earth appears to remain in a fixed position in space. The enormous band-width capacity which satellites possess makes them very attractive channels for two-way voice and picture applications for education, business, and libraries.

Laser Potential. New channels of communication are being opened that will provide capacity for even broader bandwidth. The new technology of laser communications, for example, stands in the wings with a long-range answer. The word Laser stands for Light Amplification by Stimulated Emission of Radiation. This strange kind of light remains sharp and coherent over great distances and can therefore be used as a reliable channel or pipe for telecommunications. All other long-distance transmission systems tend to spread or disperse their signals, but laser beams provide a tight, confined highway over which signals can travel back and forth.

Fiber Optics. Another recent technology called "fiber optics" is also destined to have a major impact on telecommunications. These threads of glass act as conduits for light energy and, as such, they enable more signals to make the trip per unit of time than is possible over conventional copper wire circuits. These remarkable fibers can be handled like wire—they bend, they twist, they coil, and they connect—they may seem fragile but are not. As part of a vast technological upgrading program, telephone companies are replacing copper wires with fiber optic pathways—as action tantamount to increasing the capacity of the nationwide telecommunications system many times over.

ARPANET AND THE FUTURE

As these new arteries connect more and more libraries and information centers, the prospect of creating a network of information resources becomes a tangible telecommunications reality. In fact, an example of a far-flung, operating network of computer telecommunications facilities already exists. It is called ARPANET, and was designed five years ago by the Advanced Research Projects Agency of the U.S. Department of Defense. ARPANET stretches all the way from Hawaii to England and Norway. At last count ARPANET consisted of 123 main computers of 16 different types; it connected 72 computing centers in 45 cities and 3 countries, covering 10,000 miles and serving 2,000 terminals. At present a family of minicomputers controls the network's telecommunications subsystem.

Packet Switching. ARPANET employs a revolutionary technique called "packet switching" to increase the efficiency and cost effectiveness of its telecommunications system. Any communications line, to be used cost effectively, must carry its maximum messages per unit of time. A family of minicomputers in ARPANET's telecommunications system makes sure this will happen. ARPANET employs 64 store-and-forward computers that handle 1,000 words of text a second with no more than a half second delay in point-to-point communications.

Packet switching consists of breaking each message up into small packets and then switching each and every packet along the quickest communications path available at any given instant. Thus the individual packets which constitute a message may travel over different paths to reach the same final destination. This means that part of a message from a library in Los Angeles to a library in Washington, D.C., could go by way of Montana, and part of it through Texas. Since each packet is properly tagged with its own identifier, the total message can be reassembled by the receiving minicomputer in the same order in which the packets were sent.

ARPANET's minicomputers are programmed to monitor telecommunication line utilization every two-thirds of a second, to find out instantly which lines are open, to select the least-used line, and to relay packets from minicomputer to minicomputer in a way which maximizes line utilization. ARPANET telecommunications, therefore, cost less than would otherwise be the case if single, unmonitored communication channels existed between each of its computers.

Packet switching, as used in ARPANET, is far superior to the standard method of communicating messages. In fact the technology has been so successful and the cost benefits have been so real that commercial data communication companies in the U.S. are beginning to market packet-switching telecommunication systems to the public. An experimental packet-switching system is now in operation at the British Post Office, connecting three or more cities of the United Kingdom.

Teleconferencing Benefits. One of the great accomplishments of ARPANET and one that was not anticipated in the original design is the social accomplishment of integrating the contributions of the people affiliated with the network. Teleconferencing is an ARPANET term to describe the use of the telecommunications network for personal communications among widely separated individuals. ARPANET users regularly employ the network as an electronic mailbox. They use it to send messages to one another, to comment on each other's work, sometimes to gripe, and often to collaborate on-line. The social interaction thus achieved by ARPANET has turned out to be an unexpected benefit and a powerful capability. "Teleconferencing" is the means by which the human element in ARPANET expresses itself and promotes the network in mutual self-interest.

ARPANET has little to do with libraries now, but the technical features which it contains are likely to be incorporated into the design of library and information networks of the future. The stockpiling of machine-readable bibliographic records and their subsequent distribution through computers and communications is already revolutionizing library practice in technologically advanced countries.

Until recently, the idea of tying libraries together through a telecommunications network was considered a costly objective. However, new developments in communications technology portend lower communication costs. Numerous communication satellites have been launched and major strides have been

Telecommunications

made to increase communications capacity throughout the world by constructing more microwave stations and installing complementary coaxial terrestial communication and other systems.

NEW DEVELOPMENTS

At home another development, called the direct broadcast communication satellite, has attracted the attention of librarians. A direct broadcast satellite is one capable of communicating printed and audiovisual information between two or more institutions without using intermediate land lines. An ordinary rabbit ears antenna enables the institution to receive signals directly from the satellite. This means that, in time, every library will have its own TV number just as it now has its own telephone number.

Current Experiments. The National Library of Medicine has experimented with direct broadcast satellites between NLM's main building in Bethesda, Maryland, and library centers in Alaska. And the Joint Federal Librarians Round Table/Armed Forces Section of the American Library Association is sponsoring a "Satellite Opportunities Project" to test and evaluate the use of satellites for the delivery of library services and materials. This project is under the direction of Joan M. Maier, Chief of Library Services of the National Oceanic and Atmospheric Administration.

The American Library Association also takes an active role in official telecommunications matters. It is, for example, a member of the Joint Council on Educational Telecommunications (JCET), an organization representing the entire spectrum of educational users concerned with national communication issues and regulations. And it is also a member of the Public Service Satellite Consortium composed of public broadcasters and large medical and educational institutions having a common interest in telecommunications.

A new organization called Public Interest Satellite Association seeks to safeguard the public interest in communication satellite development. PISA believes that national satellite policy and technological developments, now pending, can and must be influenced.

Government Agencies. Three agencies of the federal government are involved in matters relating to telecommunications:

(1) The Office of Telecommunications Policy in the White House provides guidance to the President and the Congress on national telecommunications policy issues affecting public and private interests; (2) The Federal Communications Commission is a regulatory agency currently reviewing the overall question of telecommunications cost for voice and data communication and is also investigating the regulatory implications raised by the growing interdependence of computers and communications; and (3) The General Service Administration operates the Federal Telecommunications System connecting all federal offices in the country over a special telephone network leased from the commercial carriers.

NCLIS. The National Commission of Libraries and Information Science, in its *Goals for Action,* urged librarians seriously to consider new forms of telecommunications technology in the planning of networks:

> Since the main purpose of a nationwide network is to place the user in contact with his materials, ways of speeding up the delivery of information constitutes one of the more important aspects of the network concept. A nationwide network must incorporate appropriate means of communicating rapidly and effectively with the facility at which the desired material is located. It is in regard to the techniques which allow optimal interconnection between user and resource that the greatest change in current thinking and practices will be required.

It did, however, sound a note of caution where telecommunications costs are concerned, favoring the use of the Federal Telecommunications System at reduced rates, or obtaining a regulatory exception that would stimulate telecommunication among libraries:

> Although distribution of documents from, say, holographic or microform collections through electrical channels to individual libraries or even directly to the user will soon be technically feasible, the bulk of information will, most probably for a long time to come, be transmitted over regular communication channels such as mail, parcel service, Greyhound Bus, rail, bookmobile and other means. Even though at the present time many commercial telecommunication companies are upgrading their lines, it would appear that the regular costs for library and information telecommunications would still be too high, and that an exception to the federal telecommunications regulations may be needed to guarantee reasonable rates for interstate information exchange.

Patterns of Education and Accreditation for Librarianship: Canada, Great Britain, and Australia

Norman Horrocks

Accreditation is a well-established procedure in U.S. educational circles. In certain subject fields the U.S. accrediting agency has extended its services to Canada upon invitation from the Canadian institutions concerned. Geographical proximity, the ease with which Canadian and U.S. citizens could obtain jobs in the other's country, and, in librarianship, the initial absence of any clearly established agency able to carry out domestic accreditation were major contributing factors. For Canadian librarianship, as in other disciplines in the early years of professional education, there were also advantages in being able to have U.S. standards to meet and, from a practical viewpoint, to show to university administrations. In recent years in some disciplines, a Canadian body now handles the accreditation of Canadian schools, e.g., for social work. For librarianship the Canadian Library Association (CLA), established in 1946, has arranged with the American Library Association (ALA) for its Committee on Accreditation (COA) to accredit programs in Canadian library schools. It is now customary to have a Canadian member on the COA as well as Canadian representation on site-visit teams. In all such cases the Canadians act as members of ALA, however. In addition the CLA may send, at its own expense, an observer when Canadian schools are being visited.

In Summer 1976 the COA completed its site visits and had voted on all schools with programs accredited under the 1951 Standards and which had asked to be revisited under the 1972 Standards. COA is now in the process of evaluating its experience with these new Standards by soliciting opinions from the schools visited and from the members of the site-visit teams. Concurrently, but quite independently, the Association of American Library Schools (AALS), whose institutional members all offer graduate degrees, is also carrying out its own evaluation of the accreditation process. It hopes to report its findings to the January 1978 Annual Meeting of the Association. AALS is also concerned with programs beyond the master's level, such as the "sixth-year program" and doctoral degrees offered by some of its members. The COA is concerned only with the first professional degree, i.e., the master's degree. It is authorized to handle accreditation on behalf of ALA by the Council on Postsecondary Accreditation (COPA), and ALA is recognized by COPA as being the agency to accredit library science programs. In this sense ALA represents the whole spectrum of the library profession. Other associations and groups in addition to AALS however, have expressed concern and interest in accreditation. For example, the American Society for Information Science (ASIS), the Special Libraries Association (SLA), and the Medical Library Association (MLA) want to see their subject interests reflected in library school curricula. Spanish-speaking librarians in the U.S. gained ALA Council approval in January 1977 for their needs to be brought to the attention of library schools. The Canadian Library Association also displays periodic interest in library education matters by passing Resolutions at its Annual General Meeting; e.g., at the 1976 Halifax Conference it was

> Resolved that CLA requests all Canadian schools of library science to include in their curricula instruction on multilingual and multicultural library service.

Against this background of what is a continuing and healthy examination and concern for library education in North America, it may be of interest to look at recent developments in two other predominantly English speaking countries, the United Kingdom and Australia. In the U.K., as in the U.S., there is a long established central organization—the Library Association (LA) was established in 1877, the year after ALA. The Library Association of Australia (LAA) is a more recent creation, as is CLA, having been established in 1937 as the Australian Institute for Librarians. The change of name came in 1963 with the granting of a Royal

Patterns of Education

Charter by Queen Elizabeth. The LA received its Royal Charter from Queen Victoria in 1898.

The significance of the Royal Charters is that they provide the authority to the two Associations to grant recognition to those persons whom they consider to be eligible to be entered on their Registers as professionally qualified librarians. There are two categories of recognition; as an Associate (A.L.A. or A.L.A.A.) or the higher form, the Fellowship (F.L.A. or F.L.A.A.). In neither Association is possession of a university bachelor's degree required for admission to the Register as an Associate, or later, as a Fellow, although increasingly more librarians in both countries do in fact have an undergraduate degree for reasons to be explored further here. Additionally it has to be remembered that full-time schools for library education are comparatively recent developments in both countries. Apart from the School at London University, which began in 1920 but had only small enrolments until the suspension of its program on the outbreak of war in 1939, it was not until 1945 that full-time schools of librarianship began to be established in the U.K. This was a major breakthrough for librarianship in Britain. They were designed originally for ex-service men and women but were continued and grew in numbers and strength until today virtually all students seeking their first professional qualification attend full time. The first full-time library school in Australia came in 1960, and since then there has also been an increase in the number of such schools. Before the establishment of full-time schools those seeking admission to either Association's Register as a professional librarian had to complete successfully centrally administered examinations and meet certain additional requirements concerning age and service in an approved library under professional supervision. Preparation for the examinations was by attendance at part-time classes, generally held only in towns with sizeable populations, by correspondence courses, or by attending short summer or weekend courses, often residential.

In the U.K., the establishment of the postwar schools in 1945 took place in colleges which were not degree-awarding institutions. Students enrolled in these programs were prepared for the Library Association's centrally administered examinations, held twice a year. Several events combined in the mid-1960's to bring about the next radical changes in library education. These were internal examining, a new LA syllabus, university schools of librarianship, and the British Government's establishment of the Council for National Academic Awards (CNAA). In some of these developments the LA was an active force for change and in others it was carried along by events.

The educational difficulties associated with preparing students for examinations conducted by an outside agency were soon apparent to those in the new full-time schools. In practice the examinations were set and graded by busy practicing librarians. After much discussion between the LA and the schools it was agreed that after a site visit by LA representatives who looked at staffing, accommodation, and service, schools might be allowed to conduct their own examinations with the stated proviso that this was on behalf of the LA. Although the North American term of accreditation was not used in this context there are some obvious similarities.

In 1964 the LA changed its syllabus to reflect more accurately the needs of the profession as expressed by practicing librarians and library educators. The new syllabus called for a doubling of the time needed from one to two years of full-time study. It also recognized the Associateship as the basic professional qualification with the Fellowship now to be obtained by thesis rather than by examination. The increased number of students enrolled in the two-year program plus the LA's requirement that for internal examining to be approved there had to be a one-to-ten staff-student ratio led to great expansions in the schools. Also in 1964 Sheffield University began its School, which on the North American pattern admitted only those with bachelor's degrees. In the same year the College of Librarianship, Wales, opened as an institution devoted solely to library education and in Belfast, Northern Ireland, Queen's University opened its School.

Most of the non-degree-awarding library schools in the colleges now found their institutions reorganized as Polytechnics. In these larger, strengthened educational bodies the expanded library schools were thus well equipped to present their case for recognition to the Council on National Academic Awards. The CNAA had been given power by the central Government to approve the awarding of degrees to individual programs which met certain criteria. The schools were quick to take advantage of this situation, and in 1968 the Leeds School gained recognition for its B.A. in library studies and its B.Sc. in information studies.

Seventeen schools in the U.K. now offer what seems to many a bewildering array of programs leading to a variety of qualifications at diploma, bachelor's, master's and doctoral level together still with preparation for the two-year syllabus of the LA. In addition, schools are offering or planning facilities for those who have a basic professional qualification—generally the A.L.A. or a bachelor's degree in librarianship—and who now wish to study for a higher qualification. This is either by assistance with the preparation of the thesis for the F.L.A. or more commonly for a degree. In a large number of these instances part-time study facilities are being sought.

The present unifying factor in this confused situation is the LA. It still controls the Register of Chartered Librarians, i.e., those it recognizes as professionally qualified by virtue of its Royal Charter. The CNAA has its own Librarianship Board, which validates degrees and higher degrees in librarianship in the non-university Schools. Holders of degrees, whether through the CNAA or from University Schools, are eligible along with those who take the LA's own examinations to become A.L.A.'s after two years of approved service in a library under the supervision of a professionally qualified librarian. The LA recognizes or—in North American terms—accredits all 17 schools. (Since the 1968 Government *Report on the Supply and Training of Librarians* there seems little likelihood of there being an increase in the number of schools in the U.K.)

For many years the library profession in the U.K. has debated whether or not it should become a fully graduate profession. With the advent of the university schools and the CNAA awards what once seemed a pipe dream is fast approaching reality. The correspondence pages of the *Library Association Record* and the *Assistant Librarian* for the past decade have been full of letters debating this issue. The LA is accused of "selling out" those who possess the A.L.A., the recognized professional qualification, but no degree. The LA argues that given the existence of the degree programs in universities and through the CNAA it should encourage and facilitate the means whereby the present nongraduate A.L.A's can obtain degrees. In fact it would seem that the schools have already decided the issue for the profession by gradually phasing out the nongraduate courses.

The as yet unresolved factor is the likely impact of the future all-graduate profession on the LA itself. It comes as a shock to many North American librarians to learn that membership in the LA is required to sit for its examinations, whereby one becomes eventually an A.L.A., and also that continued annual payment of dues is needed to retain one's place on the Register of Chartered Librarians. The same is true for those who obtain degrees in librarianship from a university or through the CNAA. If they wish to be additionally designated as an A.L.A., they must pay and maintain annual dues. To date it would seem that most have done so but it also seems clear that this could change in the future if librarians feel that they do not need to belong to the LA. It would seem to be almost ironic that the LA having finally come to terms with the desirability of a graduate profession should find itself implicitly threatened by those qualifying with degrees in librarianship not seeking membership in the Association itself. It will be one of the major challenges facing the LA as it moves into its second century.

Two other areas of concern to the LA might be identified. With the acceptance of the A.L.A. as the basic professional qualification awarded by the Association there has been a steady decline in those qualifying for the Fellowship by submitting a thesis. The F.L.A. is recognized in Britain as being a first-degree equivalent and was a means of gaining admission to a master's degree program at library schools, notably the London and Queen's University Schools. There are now other routes available to those with the A.L.A. It may be that the Fellowship, once the highest professional qualification available to British librarians, will lose its significance for all practical purposes. On another side of the coin, the LA has remained aloof from technician training which, insofar as it has been organized in the U.K., has been through the Library

Patterns of Education

Assistants Certificate program of the City and Guilds Institute of London. There are some clear limitations to this program, and the time could well be right for the LA to take a more active part in this activity now that its involvement with professional education has been reduced.

Formal library education came to Australia much later than to the U.S., Canada, and the U.K. The centrally administered examination system of the LAA began in 1944. Short courses had been offered prior to this time by large library systems, but they were virtually in-service training sessions. Australians seeking formal library qualifications had to go to North American schools or sit as external candidates for the examinations of the British Library Association. (One of the consequences of the changes in the LA syllabus discussed above was that overseas candidates were effectively prevented from sitting for the LA examinations. The establishment of library schools in Australia and in African countries in particular, has led to the development of more effective indigenous library education programs.)

By 1956 courses were offered in all major towns to prepare students for the centrally administered examinations of the LAA. The situation was akin to that in the U.K. before the establishment of the full-time schools after 1945. However, the general Australian educational pattern provided more university graduates for the library profession, as in other fields, than was the case in the U.K. As early as 1961 the LAA announced that it would at some future date require a university degree for all those seeking professional recognition on its Register. At this time it was thought that Australia would eventually follow the North American pattern of an undergraduate degree followed by a professional qualification. As events have transpired, however, Australia has, like the U.K., added first degrees in librarianship to the list of acceptable professional qualifications.

The first full-time School of Librarianship in Australia began at the University of New South Wales in 1960. It was a graduate program on North American lines. The second school, at the Royal Melbourne Institute of Technology, in 1963, was more akin to a nonuniversity school in the U.K. There was then a lag until 1970 when schools were established in each state and the Australian Capital Territory. The 1976 *Handbook* of the LAA lists 15 schools offering programs above the library technician level. Three are university schools with the remainder in other institutions of tertiary education, generally Colleges of Advanced Education or Institutes of Technology. As in the U.K., a wide variety of credentials is offered.

The LAA has been much concerned with the proliferation of schools and programs in a country that, although geographically large, has a population of only 13,000,000. It has attempted to lay down standards for school library education in its *Statement on Courses in School Librarianship*. It has also issued its general standards for accreditation of programs in its *Statement on the Recognition of Courses in Librarianship*. Although many of the points in the *Statement* deal with similar matters to the ALA's COA Standards there are some differences, e.g., the COA eschews quantitative measures.

As in the U.K., the Australian nonuniversity schools can now offer degrees validated by a central government agency. The Australian counterpart to the U.K. Council on National Academic Awards is the Australian Council on Awards in Advanced Education. Whereas in the U.K. the CNAA and the LA are concerned with the recognition or accreditation of these programs, in Australia the individual State or Territories Accreditation Committee is also involved. The LAA also controls, however, the Register of those it regards as professionally qualified and to whom it awards the A.L.A.A. From July 1976 the A.L.A.A. was to be awarded only to those who have a university degree or comparable award plus a professional library qualification. The awards from accredited programs which include a major in librarianship are regarded as meeting the requirement for the A.L.A.A. Again, as in the U.K., payment of annual dues is necessary for the retention of the Associateship and inclusion on the Register.

It must be beyond their wildest dreams for the treasurers of the American Library Association and the Canadian Library Association ever to have thought of compulsory membership in their associations. It will be interesting to watch how the Library Association (U.K.) and the Library Association of Australia develop plans for membership recruitment and involvement under changed circumstances.

Review of
the Library Year

Academic Libraries

Academic libraries in the United States continue to suffer from the same economic depression and inflationary influences as do their parent institutions, and 1976 was a year filled with examples of college and university libraries coping in a variety of ways with these and other problems.

The most dramatic example of such problems was in the experience of the City University of New York (CUNY) when, lacking funds for continued operations, schools of that university closed their doors for a two-week period from May 28 to June 14. This was a particularly difficult time of the year as students were preparing for final examinations and commencement ceremonies. When the university did resume operations in June, staff attempted to put the pieces together. Library staff returned to their assignments to find periodicals and shipments of books stored at various places on campus, and circulation records were in complete disarray as many students and faculty had already left the community. But such problems were minor, compared to the tremendous loss in morale among students, faculty, and staff. Although the schools were again open, there was no assurance of any improved financial support, and for the libraries further cutbacks in acquisitions, services, and staff continued.

ECONOMIC ADVERSITY

Problems so dramatically presented in CUNY were repeated in various ways in other colleges and universities. As librarians attempted to find solutions to the library component of this problem, they also wrote journal articles or gathered together to discuss ways in which they could best manage library affairs.

The Eastern New York State Chapter of the Association of College and Research Libraries (ACRL) held a November 1975 meeting in Albany in which several speakers addressed "Retrenchment in Higher Education: Implications for Libraries." [Lynn Barber supplied a summary of the conference in *College & Research Libraries News* 37:6–7 (January 1976).] The proceedings of the conference were "published" via video tape and thus made available to a broader audience in 1976.

Reporting on her Council on Library Resources fellowship, Marion T. Reid shared her summary report on how a number of libraries which she had visited handled financial problems [Marion T. Reid, "Coping with Budget Adversity: The Impact of the Financial Squeeze on Acquisitions," *College & Research Libraries* 37:266–72 (May 1976)].

In June 1976 Stanford University hosted a conference on "Managing Under Adversity," and a broad range of speakers, primarily representing privately supported academic libraries, reported on experiences in each of their institutions when funds were cut. (The summary proceedings of this conference, edited by John C. Heyeck, were published by the Stanford University Libraries in the autumn 1976.) In October 1976 Indiana State University, Terre Haute, sponsored a conference on the same general subject, "No-Growth Budget: Implications for Academic Libraries."

There were no standard procedures any institution could follow, and each library improvised as it coped with its own particular needs. Two libraries reported financial contributions from their own staffs. The University of Cincinnati announced the establishment of an endowment for library support by the library staff, with 97 percent of the staff making initial contributions totaling $40,000. At Oberlin College, Eileen Thornton, librarian emerita, presented her home to the college in the form of a trust, with the eventual income to benefit the college library.

RESOURCES

While library budgets remained steady or declined, book and periodical prices continued their inflationary spiral. To maintain the integrity of needed periodical and serial holdings, some libraries devoted increasingly smaller portions of their acquisitions budgets to the purchase of monographs and other nonserial materials.

Herbert S. White looked at this particular problem in a journal article, drawing upon the major study he and Bernard M. Fry had undertaken with a grant from the National Science Foundation. White was pessimistic as to a solution for this problem, short of a federal subsidy. [Herbert S. White, "Publishers, Libraries, and Costs of Journal Subscriptions in Times of Funding Retrenchment," *Library Quarterly* 46: 359–77 (Oct. 1976).]

The Andrew W. Mellon Foundation made a grant of $110,000 to the Office of University Library Management Studies (OMS) of the Association of Research Libraries to study library collections, designing and testing a procedure for the analysis of acquisition, retention, and preservation policies in university libraries. Possibly this study might propose some additional solutions to resource problems. Looking to a program similar to the National Lending Library in England, a joint committee of the Association of Research Libraries and the Center for Research Libraries recommended that CRL is "the most appropriate agency to undertake the development of a national periodicals lending library" as one element in a national periodicals system.

As networks and other cooperative programs grew, emphasis remained strong on the sharing of resources. A major forum during the year on this subject was the Pittsburgh confer-

See also
London and Canadian Correspondents' Reports

Academic Libraries

ence at the end of September on "Resource Sharing in Libraries." An initial report appeared in *Library Journal*. [Karl Nyren, "Conference Report: Resource Sharing in Libraries," *Library Journal* 101:2336–39 (Nov. 15, 1976). See also the two-page feature in *Journal of Academic Librarianship* 2:246–47 (Nov. 1976).] At that conference William Welsh, Library of Congress, underscored the need for interdependence and a rejection of the hierarchical approach: "we have come to realize that the great, self-sufficient research library was a castle in the sand. . . . We also know now that libraries cannot be organized in a hierarchy in which one institution becomes the 'library of last resort,' because information doesn't behave that way and people don't act that way. We. . .must each share the burden of being a library of first resort for the other." Published proceedings of the conference will be an important publication in 1977 as was the publication in 1976 of *Farewell to Alexandria*, edited by Daniel Gore (Westport, Conn.: Greenwood Press, 1976), which included the major papers from the 1975 conference, "Touching Bottom in the Bottomless Pit," sponsored by the Associated Colleges of the Midwest.

Although resource sharing was a major topic, academic libraries also reported in the pages of *College & Research Libraries News* their various specialized acquisitions throughout the year. Separate attention may be directed to major acquisitions of two academic libraries.

In each case one institution surrendered a collection to another, either because its educational program changed or because it lacked financial support to continue. The Hartford Seminary Foundation sold its 240,000-volume collection to Emory University in Atlanta, Georgia, for its Candler School of Theology Library. Emory undertook a special program to renovate library facilities there to house this major new resource adequately.

In the second case, the American Geographical Society in New York City, facing deficits in its own program for several years and obliged to curtail its library operations, initiated the transfer of its collection to the University of Wisconsin at Milwaukee. At year's end there remained several legal obstacles to the completion of this move, but the university proposes to provide suitable housing for the collection, a major map resource for that institution, and adequate funding so that it may be maintained and developed.

COOPERATIVE PROGRAMS

The program for a California Library Authority for Systems and Service (CLASS), first announced in 1975 as a major cooperative program for public and academic libraries, came closer to operational status in 1976 with the appointment of Ronald Miller, Executive Director of the New England Library Network (NELINET), as its first Director.

A new cooperative program among Chicago academic libraries, the Chicago Academic Library Council, got underway in 1976 with eight institutional members. Its first program was to institute a program of direct borrowing among six of the participants.

The Research Libraries Group (RLG) of the New York, Columbia, Yale, and Harvard libraries received a grant of $197,200 from the National Endowment for the Humanities, matching an earlier grant from the Carnegie Corporation, to be employed to develop a computer-based cataloging system among the

McHenry Library, University of California, Santa Cruz, completed in 1976.

members. Through the use of the United Parcel Service, RLG facilitated the delivery of materials from one member to another. When a UPS strike disrupted this service, the group initiated its own delivery system.

Just as the Research Libraries Group was developed among several of the major research institutions on the east coast, a similar program came into being on the west coast between Stanford University and the University of California, Berkeley. Supported by grants for a three-year period totaling $580,000 from the Alfred P. Sloan and Andrew W. Mellon Foundations, these two university libraries began a program of cooperation that would involve coordinated acquisitions, direct borrowing privileges, as well as the intercampus movement of people and books.

BIBLIOGRAPHIC NETWORKS

The W. K. Kellogg Foundation provided a major impetus to the expansion of bibliographic networks with a series of grants totaling $4,250,000. First, there was a grant of $1,500,000 to develop in Michigan a statewide computer-based information library network; second, a grant of $339,319 to the Ohio College Library Center (OCLC) to strengthen its own network informational services; and, third, grants totaling $2,400,000 to 300 small private liberal arts colleges to participate in such informational networks. Most of these small institutions employed their grants to participate in the OCLC network.

With a total of more than 800 institutions now participating in its network, OCLC established a regional service center in Claremont, California, in order to serve its new Pacific coast members better. OCLC terminals were now located as well in test or pilot operations in several of the campuses of the University of California and of the California State University and Colleges.

Barbara Markuson's major review of OCLC operations appeared as the principal feature in the January 1976 issue of *Library Technology Reports* [Barbara Evans Markuson, "The Ohio College Library Center: A Study of the Factors Affecting the Adaptation of Libraries to On-Line Networks," *Library Technology Reports* 12:11–132 (Jan. 1976)], and *American Libraries* published its own "Primer on OCLC for All Librarians" (*American Libraries* 7:258–75 (May 1976)).

Library Catalogs. Although some critics of computer-based bibliographic networks expressed concern at the lack of standards and the multiplicity of rules employed by participating libraries, one major library did recognize its need to standardize. The Harvard College Library decided to adopt Library of Congress cataloging practices in the summer of 1976.

As the nation began its third century, it ap-

peared that a principal feature in libraries of the nation's second century, the familiar card catalog, was slowly on its way to extinction. Among the first to take this major step was the University of Toronto which closed its card catalog. Alternatives to the 3" × 5" card included use of computer output microform (COM) and on-line computer terminals. (*See also* Canadian Report.)

SERVICES

Bibliographic Instruction. Emphasis on the need for formal bibliographic instruction in college and university libraries is the dominant feature in academic library service programs. Within the American Library Association interest was so high that a group of academic and public librarians petitioned to set up an association-wide library instruction round table thus permitting greater participation by librarians in discussions on this subject. Earlier ACRL had formed an ad hoc Bibliographic Instruction Task Force to look into this matter, and the task force issued "Draft Guidelines for Bibliographic Instruction in Academic Libraries" (*College & Research Libraries News* 37:301 (December 1976)) for consideration at the ALA Midwinter Meeting in January 1977. At that meeting the task force was to recommend establishment of a permanent section within ACRL on bibliographic instruction.

Bibliographic Data Bases. A second major feature was the introduction into a larger number of academic libraries of on-line computer access to various bibliographic data bases. To provide a guide, David M. Wax produced *A Handbook for the Introduction of On-Line Bibliographic Search Services into Academic Libraries* (Washington, D.C.: Association of Research Libraries, 1976), based on the experiences of the Northeast Academic Science Information Center (NASIC) over the past three years.

Payment for Services. Should such new and novel services be provided free of charge, or should users be asked to make some form of payment? Indications were that after a test period in a library users will be requested to pay

The Seeley G. Mudd Library, Lawrence University, Appleton, Wisconsin, dedicated in May 1976, houses more than 200,000 volumes.

The Mabel Smith Douglass Library, Rutgers, State University of New Jersey, was completed in 1976 at a cost of $3,000,000 and doubled the size of the previous facility.

at least a token sum. Some libraries are questioning if they should charge for lending books to other libraries. A survey undertaken among the 105 members of the Association of Research Libraries in 1976 indicated that eight of the member libraries charge for interlibrary loan. In addition, four impose charges for commercial borrowers only. The practice of charging noncommercial borrowers is relatively new among these libraries, and it may be premature to state that this is a pattern for other libraries to follow.

Library Automation. More and more, academic libraries are no longer designing and installing their own automated systems but are purchasing ready-made products, with such primary examples as cataloging, serials, and circulation systems. Various commercial vendors have introduced attractive circulation control systems, generally involving use of a bar-coded label in the book and a light pen to "read" and record this information in a minicomputer in the library.

Library Enhancement. The National Endowment for the Humanities and the Council on Library Resources continued their series of grants under their College Library Program. The Johnson C. Smith University in Charlotte, North Carolina, was the 24th institution receiving such a grant to enable it to become "fundamentally a teaching facility of the institution." The Council on Library Resources also announced the first recipients of grants under its new Library Service Enhancement Program. With more than 200 applicants, the Council made awards to 12 institutions. A librarian in each was thus freed from normal duties for the course of an academic year to develop a program to further enhance the role of the library in that school.

Princeton University received grants of $190,000 from the Andrew W. Mellon Foundation and $75,000 from the Xerox Foundation for a program extending over several years to upgrade access to the library's collections, both through improving the condition of the book stack area and through use of a newly installed automated circulation system. In addition, Princeton also received a $10,000 grant from the Council on Library Resources as partial support for a program to improve services in the microform area, the grant funds to be employed to train staff and orient faculty and students in the better utilization of microforms.

LIBRARY SECURITY

Although it is difficult to make any definite statements, the general impression from academic librarians is that book losses through theft and mutilation are on the increase throughout the nation. Reporter Gael M. O'Brien presented an informal survey of this situation in college and university libraries in his article "'National Crime Wave' Plagues University Libraries" (*Chronicle of Higher Education*, Aug. 9, 1976). A number of commercial vendors have available detection systems so that materials cannot be removed from a library without an alarm being sounded unless the item is properly charged out; and academic libraries are seriously considering whether such systems, expensive to install and maintain, can be cost effective for their particular institutions. *Library Technology Reports* provided a new survey of the systems presently available [Nancy H. Knight, "Theft Detection Systems for Libraries: A Survey," *Library Technology Reports* 12:575–690 (Nov. 1976)]. (*See also* Security Systems.)

At the July ALA Conference the ACRL Rare Books and Manuscripts Section presented a program on the security of library materials, "Stealing the American Heritage: The Theft of Manuscripts from Libraries and Archives," at which time a new security program of the Society of American Archivists was introduced. (Papers from this program are to be published in *College & Research Libraries* in 1977.) Several individual institutions reported major thefts during the year, but the loss that a number of academic libraries suffered in common was the systematic mutilation of some 19th-century American periodicals and the removal of prints by the artist Winslow Homer. In this particular case a published bibliography that had been intended to reveal for scholars the artwork of Winslow Homer served as a shopping list for a thief.

LIBRARY MANAGEMENT

MRAP and ALDP. The Association of Research Libraries Management Review and Analysis Program (MRAP) was now several years old, and the Council on Library Resources provided a grant to two faculty members at Pennsylvania State University to study its effectiveness. A similar program for smaller academic libraries, the Academic Library Development Program (ALDP), continued in test form at the University of North Carolina at Charlotte, and P. Grady Morein, project coordinator, and other major participants in it gave a progress report in July at the ALA Conference (a summary of which appeared in *College & Research Libraries* 38:37–45, January 1977).

Library Statistics. There remained a considerable time lag in the publication of academic library statistics, but for a first time early in 1976 the National Center for Education Statistics released summary figures from its fall 1975 survey of academic libraries. New questions and different ways of reporting information occur each year in the forms received by libraries from Washington. A major change is in the increased number of questions on services given. The fall 1976 questionnaire asked academic libraries for a first time to give information on number of reference and directional questions handled during an average week.

Working on his own statistical study of library acquisitions among academic libraries, with grants from the National Science Foundation and the National Endowment for the Humanities, economist Fritz Machlup expressed his concern in an autumn article at the inability of academic libraries to give him detailed information on their holdings or expenditures over a period of years, both in quantity as well as by form or subject. He questioned what he termed the "ignorance is bliss" management techniques of academic library administrators. This may have been adequate for an era of plenty, he maintained, but when funds are scarce library decision makers will require better information systems in order to make wise buying decisions. [Fritz Machlup, "Our Libraries: Can We Measure Their Holdings and Acquisitions," *AAUP Bulletin* 62: 303–307 (Oct. 1976).]

Salaries. The major report on the condition of the profession was the ACRL survey, *Salary Structures of Librarians in Higher Education for the Academic Year 1975–76* (1976). This new survey under the direction of Richard J. Talbot and Ann von der Lippe, University of Massachusetts, Amherst, continues the earlier series of surveys conducted for the Council on Library Resources by Donald F. Cameron and Peggy Heim. Once again the Council on Library Resources provided support and assistance for the survey.

The new survey, however, had a much broader base. Reports were received from 1,208 institutions (including 356 two-year colleges not covered in the earlier surveys) and reported salaries for 13,507 professional library staff members. The survey indicated that women comprise 61.5 percent of the library staffs in U.S. institutions of higher education and fill the majority of every library position, except for the principal administrative roles of director, associate director, and assistant director. The survey also revealed that at every level and for every position category men earn more than women. Minority librarians constituted 9.6 percent of the survey population; the pattern repeats itself with minority men earning more than minority women.

Certain comparisons with earlier surveys are difficult because of the inclusion in the new report of two-year colleges, but the survey did point out that in only three years since the last study the percentage of academic librarians with less than five years of experience has decreased by one-half, which the authors attribute to a decline in the employment of beginning professionals.

The survey is essentially a pessimistic report and repeats that the unattractive salary structures for librarians previously reported by Cameron and Heim continues in aggravated form. Librarians' salaries have failed to rise significantly since 1972–73, and the pyramidal structure of librarians' salaries in universities and five-year institutions remains a pronounced feature of the salary structure.

Unions. On the collective bargaining front the one major conflict reported was a strike of non-professional staff in the Brown University Library. Now that unions are in academic libraries, attention is focused on where professional and non-professional library staff members belong when unionization occurs. C. James Schmidt, Chairperson of the ACRL Academic Status Committee, provided a short but valuable report on the position of librarians in institutions that fall under the jurisdiction of the National Labor Relations Board in his article, "Collective Bargaining and Academic Librarians: A Review of the Decisions of the NLRB" [*College & Research Libraries News* 37: 1–3 (January 1976)]. A survey by Margaret Chaplan and Charles Maxey, "The Scope of Faculty Bargaining: Implications for Academic Librarians," [*Library Quarterly* 46:231–47 (July 1976)], indicates the strong likelihood that if collective bargaining does occur on a campus librarians will be included in the same unit with the formal teaching faculty.

At year's end a more complete account appeared of the impact of unionization on college and university libraries with the publication of *John W. Weatherford's Collective Bargaining and the Academic Librarian* [Metuchen, N.J. (Scarecrow, 1976)] which the author prepared not only "to challenge the assumptions of enthusiasts" but also to provide "an academic librarians' primer of collective bargaining" (p. 108).

Staff Development. The Council on Library Resources announced 16 librarians in its eighth class of CLR Fellows and made its first awards under a new Advanced Study Program of Librarians in granting fellowships to five academic librarians to pursue advanced degrees in subject fields.

The CLR management intern program con-

The new Connecticut College Library, New London, completed in 1976 at a cost of $6,217,000.

tinued, and five librarians were presented these awards. The Andrew W. Mellon Foundation made its third annual grant to ACRL to support four administrators from predominantly Black college and university libraries by providing them experience in some of the nation's major academic libraries.

To enable librarians to improve their writing skills, CLR also made a grant to the University of Connecticut to form a New England Academic Librarians' Writing Seminar under the direction of Norman D. Stevens at that institution. (See also Personnel and Employment: Salaries.)

LIBRARY BUILDINGS

Jerrold Orne and Jean O. Gosling's 1976 report on academic library construction presents as well a summary of all construction for the preceding 10-year period ["Academic Library Building in 1976," Library Journal 101: 2435–39 (Dec. 1, 1976)]. The authors report the decade was "a period of remarkable growth in academic libraries," during which 647 new library projects were reported. More than two-thirds of the projects were completed during the first half of the decade with federal funding the principal source of support. During the second half of the decade sources for support were primarily from local public or private funds. The annual number of projects reported each year continues to decrease, with 36 libraries included in the 1976 report. The total funds expended were at their lowest for the past four years but with the highest square-foot cost in the decade ($39.22). Viewing the decade's record, Orne and Gosling concluded that the great support given by the federal government at first encouraged academic administrators to continue their support of library building and that larger institutions were continuing to build necessary libraries. At year's end Stanford University added its own substantiation to their conclusion when it finally gave the go-ahead to construction of a major addition to its 1919 main library building.

The same issue of Library Journal, reporting the annual record of academic library building, also included a useful 10-year summary from Joleen Bock of libraries in two-year colleges ["Two-Year College Learning Resources Center Building," Library Journal 101: 2452–55 (Dec. 1, 1976)]. Her survey indicated the provision of 325 new library/learning resource centers during the decade, and as with the report from Orne and Gosling she reported a gradual decline in recent years, with 36 buildings reported in the most recent year. Increasingly, Bock reported, these libraries included production facilities for a variety of media (e.g., audio/video, graphic/photographic), learning laboratories, and career information centers.

LEGISLATION

Copyright. The single piece of legislation which academic librarians followed with greatest interest throughout the year was the revision of the copyright law. In 1975 academic librarians wondered, in reading the Senate version of a copyright bill, what was the significance for them of the words in section 108(g)(2) "systematic reproduction." In 1976 the House Judiciary Subcommittee on Courts, Civil Liberties, and the Administration of Justice, considering the bill, amended this section with words that recognized the legitimacy of interlibrary loan programs. But with their amendment, academic librarians now wondered what was meant by the qualification that materials could be provided under such programs so long as they were not "in such aggregate quantities as to substitute for a subscription to or purchase of such work."

In the concluding days of the 94th Congress new copyright legislation was finally enacted (PL. 94-553), and during 1977 academic librarians would have the opportunity to acquaint themselves with their rights as well as obligations under the law which will go into effect in

1978. [There was a brief summary of sections of the act relevant to librarians in *American Libraries* 7:610–11 (Nov. 1976), and Hardy Carroll provided a short article with "Primary Sources for Understanding the New Copyright Law" in *College & Research Libraries News* 38:1–2 (January 1977).] (See also Copyright.)

Research Libraries. Another piece of legislation enacted in the closing days of the 94th Congress was the revision of the Higher Education Act (P.L. 94-482), providing a new Title II-C, "Strengthening Research Library Resources," the purpose of which is "to promote research and education of higher quality throughout the United States by providing financial assistance to major research libraries." Although no funds were tied to this legislation, the opportunity was now present for aid to research libraries that are not formally linked to institutions of higher education but which perform a major role in the furtherance of education and research.

APPOINTMENTS

Three of the Midwest's Big Ten schools received new library directors during the year: Hugh C. Atkinson moved from Ohio State to the University of Illinois at Urbana-Champaign; William J. Studer replaced Atkinson at Ohio State; and Eldred R. Smith assumed the directorship at Minnesota. Also in America's heartland Kenneth G. Peterson assumed the position as Dean of Library Affairs at Southern Illinois University at Carbondale, Donald R. Hunt became Director at the University of Tennessee-Knoxville, and John H. Gribbin became Director at the University of Missouri in Columbia. Beverly P. Lynch, Executive Secretary of ACRL, announced her resignation, effective in January 1977; she became Director of the Library at the University of Illinois at Chicago Circle.

On the east coast Carlton C. Rochell was selected to head the New York University Library, Charles R. Andrews at Hofstra University, Nina T. Cohen at Wesleyan University, and Ina C. Brownridge at the State University of New York at Binghamton.

In the west Allene F. Schnaitter became Library Director at Washington State University and Peter Spyers-Duran at California State University, Long Beach. In the University of California new directors were appointed for two of the five southern campuses: Millicent D. Abell at San Diego and Eleanor A. Montague at Riverside.

John P. McDonald returned to his post as Director at the University of Connecticut, following a tour of duty as Executive Director of the Association of Research Libraries. John G. Lorenz succeeded him at the ARL.

As the year concluded, librarians gathered for a very special occasion on December 2 in Chapel Hill, North Carolina: the observance of the 100th birthday in December of Louis Round Wilson. (*See* feature article by Edward G. Holley in preliminary pages of this *Yearbook*.)

RICHARD D. JOHNSON

Accreditation

The 1976 ALA Conference marked an important milestone in the Association's half-century of accrediting programs in library education. By the end of the Conference, 57 of the 58 programs previously accredited under the 1951 *Standards for Accreditation* had been examined and evaluated by ALA's Committee on Accreditation (COA) under the new Standards adopted by Council in 1972. One Canadian school had requested that it be removed from the accredited list until its new two-year program could be evaluated. Three previously accredited programs were denied reaccreditation. In addition to those 54 reaccredited programs (48 in the United States and six in Canada), ten programs in the United States had been accredited for the first time, for a total of 64.

Between November 1973 and April 1976 a total of 101 individuals participated in the 67 site visits that led to these decisions. What many had believed to be an impossible timetable for COA had been met.

One library school whose program was denied reaccreditation exercised its right of appeal to ALA's Executive Board. The Board announced during the 1976 Conference that COA's decision in the case had been upheld. Under its *Manual of Procedures*, COA is committed to "consider without prejudice a request for another evaluation visit at a later date, normally not less than two years from the date of the COA action," of any program that has been denied reaccreditation.

Of the ten newly accredited programs, six are in the Southeast, two in the Northeast, one in the Midwest, and one in the Southwest. The parent institutions included the University of Alabama, Alabama A&M University, the University of Arizona, Clarion State College, North Carolina Central University, St. John's University, the University of South Carolina, the University of South Florida, the University of Tennessee, and the University of Wisconsin–Milwaukee.

ALA accreditation of programs in library education is part of a nationwide system of postsecondary educational accreditation that evolved late in the 19th century. Voluntary and nongovernmental, it is unique to the United States, although in some fields, such as library education, Canadian professional associations have chosen to be part of the American system. Accreditation developed because, unlike nearly every other nation, the United States has no federal ministry of education to

See also
London and Canadian Correspondents' Report

Accreditation

control the conduct of educational institutions—although in recent years there has been a growing concern that, with the constraints accompanying federal aid to higher education, HEW and the Justice Department are moving in that direction. Individual states have tended to exercise only limited control of colleges and universities, especially those in the private sector. While this lack of governmental control has been hailed as a primary strength of the U.S. educational system, it was recognized a century ago that not only do prospective students and faculty require some means for identifying the quality of an institution's educational programs, but also that the public must be protected against incompetent or poorly trained professionals. Accreditation was designed to meet this need.

What is Accreditation? No better answer can be found than that provided by the Council on Postsecondary Accreditation in its 1976 annual report called *The Balance Wheel for Accreditation:*

> Accreditation in postsecondary education is a self-improvement, self-regulating process. It includes an in-depth self-analysis by an institution or program to evaluate its compliance with mutually agreed-to criteria, followed by an on-site examination by third-party peers to verify whether the institution or program has perceived itself correctly.
>
> The granting of accreditation status signifies that an institution or program meets or exceeds a level of educational quality believed to be necessary for that particular institution or program to achieve its stated purposes and, thereby, meet its responsibility to all its publics.

The Council on Postsecondary Accreditation (COPA), to which ALA pays an annual membership fee of $500, is a national, nonprofit organization, with headquarters in Washington, D.C. Its purpose is "to support, coordinate, and improve all nongovernmental accrediting activities conducted in the United States at the postsecondary level." It serves as a "balance wheel" in relationship to the approximately 50 regional and national accrediting bodies (of which ALA is one) and the nearly 4,000 accredited institutions and programs throughout the United States. COPA provides order and value to the accreditation process through its regular review of the practices of its recognized accrediting bodies "to assure the integrity and consistency of their policies and procedures." In effect, it is COPA that "accredits" COA. The accreditation authority of ALA through COA is also recognized by the Office of the U.S. Commissioner of Education.

ALA delegates to the Committee on Accreditation responsibility for the execution of the accreditation program of the Association and for the development and formulation of standards of education for librarianship. These standards, of which there have been four versions (1925, 1933, 1951 and 1972), are subject to the approval of the ALA Council.

Graduate Library School Programs Accredited by the American Library Association (January 1977)

NORTHEAST

[1]**Catholic University of America,** *Master of Science in Library and Information Science*
Graduate Department of Library Science, Washington, D.C. 20064. Elizabeth W. Stone, Chairman

Clarion State College, *Master of Science In Library Science*
School of Library Media and Information Science, Clarion, Pennsylvania 16214. Elizabeth A. Rupert, Dean

[1,2]**Columbia University,** *Master of Science*
School of Library Service, New York, New York 10027. Richard L. Darling, Dean

[2]**Drexel University,** *Master of Science,*
Graduate School of Library Science, Philadelphia, Pennsylvania 19104. Guy Garrison, Dean

Long Island University, C. W. Post Center, *Master of Science*
Palmer Graduate Library School, Greenvale, New York 11548. Mohammed M. Aman, Dean

[2]**University of Maryland,** *Master of Library Science*
College of Library and Information Services, College Park, Maryland 20742. J.S. Kidd, Acting Dean.

State University of New York, Albany, *Master of Library Science*
School of Library and Information Science, Albany, New York 12222. John J. Farley, Dean

State University of New York at Buffalo, *Master of Library Science*
School of Information and Library Studies, Buffalo, New York 14260. George S. Bobinski, Dean

[1]**State University of New York, College of Arts and Science, Geneseo,** *Master of Library Science*
School of Library and Information Science, S.U.N.Y., Geneseo, New York 14454. Ivan L. Kaldor, Dean

[1,2]**University of Pittsburgh,** *Master of Library Science*
Graduate School of Library and Information Sciences, Pittsburgh, Pennsylvania 15260. Thomas J. Galvin, Dean

[1]**Pratt Institute,** *Master of Library Science*
Graduate School of Library and Information Science, Brooklyn, New York 11205. Nasser Sharify, Dean

[1]**Queens College, City University of New York,** *Master of Library Science*
Department of Library Science, Flushing, New York 11367. Richard H. Logsdon, Chairman

[1,2]**Rutgers University,** *Master of Library Service*
Graduate School of Library Service, New Brunswick, New Jersey 08903. Thomas H. Mott, Jr., Dean

[1]**St. John's University,** *Master of Library Science*
Division of Library and Information Science, Jamaica, New York 11439. Rev. Jovian P. Lang, Acting Director

[2]**Simmons College,** *Master of Science*
School of Library Science, Boston, Massachusetts 02115. Robert D. Stueart, Dean

Southern Connecticut State College, *Master of Science*
Division of Library Science and Instructional Technology, New Haven, Connecticut 06515. Emanuel T. Prostano, Director

[1,2]**Syracuse University,** *Master of Science in Library Science*
School of Information Studies, Syracuse, New York 13210. Robert S. Taylor, Dean

SOUTHEAST

University of Alabama, *Master of Library Service*
Graduate School of Library Service, University, Alabama 35486. James D. Ramer, Dean

[3]**Alabama Agricultural and Mechanical University,** *Master of Science in Library Media*
School of Library Media, Normal, Alabama 35762. Dorothy M. Haith, Dean

[1]**Atlanta University,** *Master of Science in Library Service*
School of Library Service, Atlanta, Georgia 30314. Virginia Lacy Jones, Dean

[1]**Emory University,** *Master of Arts; Master of Librarianship*
Division of Librarianship, Atlanta, Georgia

30322. A. Venable Lawson, Director

[1,2]**Florida State University,** *Master of Science; Master of Arts*
School of Library Science, Tallahassee, Florida 32306. Harold Goldstein, Dean

University of Kentucky, *Master of Science in Library Science; Master of Arts*
College of Library Science, Lexington, Kentucky 40506. Thomas J. Waldhart, Acting Dean

[2]**University of North Carolina,** *Master of Science in Library Science*
School of Library Science, Chapel Hill, North Carolina 27514. Edward G. Holley, Dean

North Carolina Central University, *Master of Library Science*
School of Library Science, Durham, North Carolina 27707. Annette L. Phinazee, Dean

[1]**George Peabody College for Teachers,** *Master of Library Science*
School of Library Science, Nashville, Tennessee 37203. Edwin S. Gleaves, Director

University of South Carolina, *Master of Librarianship*
College of Librarianship, Columbia, South Carolina 29208. F. William Summers, Dean

University of South Florida, *Master of Arts*
Graduate Department of Library Science/Audiovisual, Tampa, Florida 33620. Fred C. Pfister, Chairman

University of Tennessee, Knoxville, *Master of Science in Library Science*
Graduate School of Library and Information Science, Knoxville, Tennessee 37916. Gary R. Purcell, Director

MIDWEST

[1,2]**Case Western Reserve University,** *Master of Science in Library Science*
School of Library Science, Cleveland, Ohio 44106. William Goffman, Dean

[1,2]**University of Chicago,** *Master of Arts*
Graduate Library School, Chicago, Illinois 60637. Howard W. Winger, Dean

Emporia Kansas State College, *Master of Librarianship*
School of Library Science, Emporia, Kansas 66801. Sarah R. Reed, Director

[1,2]**University of Illinois,** *Master of Science*
Graduate School of Library Science, Urbana, Illinois 61801. Herbert Goldhor, Director

[2]**Indiana University,** *Master of Library Science*
Graduate Library School, Bloomington, Indiana 47401. Bernard M. Fry, Dean

University of Iowa, *Master of Arts*
School of Library Science, Iowa City, Iowa 52242. Frederick Wezeman, Director

[1]**Kent State University,** *Master of Library Science*
School of Library Science, Kent, Ohio 44242. Guy A. Marco, Dean

[2]**University of Michigan,** *Master of Arts in Library Science*
School of Library Science, Ann Arbor, Michigan 48109. Russell E. Bidlack, Dean

[1,2]**University of Minnesota,** *Master of Arts*
Library School, Minneapolis, Minnesota 55455. Wesley Simonton, Director

University of Missouri, Columbia, *Master of Arts*
School of Library and Informational Science, Columbia, Missouri 65201. Edward P. Miller, Dean

Northern Illinois University, *Master of Arts*
Department of Library Science, DeKalb, Illinois 60115. Lewis F. Stieg, Chairman

[1]**Rosary College,** *Master of Arts in Library Science*
Graduate School of Library Science, River Forest, Illinois 60305. Sister M. Lauretta McCusker, O.P., Dean

[1]**Wayne State University,** *Master of Science in Library Science*
Division of Library Science, Detroit, Michigan 48202. Robert E. Booth, Director

[1]**Western Michigan University,** *Master of Science in Librarianship*
School of Librarianship, Kalamazoo, Michigan 49008. Jean Lowrie, Director

[1,2]**University of Wisconsin-Madison,** *Master of Arts*
Library School, Madison, Wisconsin 53706. Charles A. Bunge, Director

University of Wisconsin-Milwaukee, *Master of Arts in Library Science*
School of Library Science, Milwaukee, Wisconsin 53201. Doralyn J. Hickey, Dean

SOUTHWEST

University of Arizona, *Master of Library Science*
Graduate Library School, Tucson, Arizona 85719. Donald C. Dickinson, Director

Louisiana State University, *Master of Library Science*
Graduate School of Library Science, Baton Rouge, Louisiana 70803. Donald D. Foos, Dean

[1,2]**North Texas State University,** *Master of Library Science*
School of Library and Information Sciences, Denton, Texas 76203. Dewey E. Carroll, Dean

[1,2]**University of Texas at Austin,** *Master of Library Science*
Graduate School of Library Science, Austin, Texas 78712. C. G. Sparks, Dean

[1,2]**Texas Woman's University,** *Master of Arts; Master of Library Science*
School of Library Science, Denton, Texas 76204. Frank L. Turner, Acting Director

WEST

Brigham Young University, *Master of Library Science*
School of Library and Information Sciences, Provo, Utah 84602. Maurice P. Marchant, Director

[1,2]**University of California,** *Master of Library Science*
School of Library and Information Studies, Berkeley, California 94720. Michael K. Buckland, Dean

[1,2]**University of California, Los Angeles,** *Master of Library Science*
Graduate School of Library and Information Science, Los Angeles, California 90024. Robert M. Hayes, Dean

[1]**University of Denver,** *Master of Arts in Librarianship*
Graduate School of Librarianship, Denver, Colorado 80210. Margaret Knox Goggin, Dean

University of Hawaii, *Master of Library Studies*
Graduate School of Library Studies, Honolulu, Hawaii 96822. Ira W. Harris, Dean

University of Oregon, *Master of Library Science*
School of Librarianship, Eugene, Oregon 97403. Herman L. Totten, Dean

[2]**University of Southern California,** *Master of Science in Library Science*
School of Library Science, University Park, Los Angeles, California 90007. Martha Boaz, Dean

University of Washington, *Master of Librarianship; Master of Law Librarianship*
School of Librarianship, Seattle, Washington 98195. Peter Hiatt, Director

CANADA

University of British Columbia, *Master of Library Science*
School of Librarianship, Vancouver, B.C. V6T 1W5. Roy B. Stokes, Director

Dalhousie University, *Master of Library Service*
School of Library Service, Halifax, Nova Scotia B3H 4H8. Norman Horrocks, Director

McGill University, *Master of Library Science*
Graduate School of Library Science, Montreal, Quebec H3A 1Y1. Vivian Sessions, Director

Universite de Montreal, *Maîtrise en bibliothéconomie*
École de bibliothéconomie, Montréal, Québec H3C 3J7. Georges Cartier, directeur

[2]**University of Toronto,** *Master of Library Science*
Faculty of Library Science, Toronto, Ontario M5S 1A1. Francess G. Halpenny, Dean

[2]**University of Western Ontario,** *Master of Library Science*
School of Library and Information Science, London, Ontario N6A 5B9. William J. Cameron, Dean

[1]Offers post-Master's specialist or certificate program. (The ALA does not accredit post-Master's specialist or certificate programs.)
[2]Offers program for Doctoral degree. (The ALA does not accredit programs leading to the Doctoral degree.)
[3]Single specialization program in school library media.
*American Libraries 3:653–657 (June 1972), 889 (September 1972).

Accreditation

See also Patterns of Education and Accreditation for Librarianship: Introductory Pages

Only the program leading to the first professional degree in librarianship (*i.e.*, the master's degree) is subject to accreditation. An undergraduate program, a sixth-year certification program, or a doctoral program in a library school is considered by COA only to the extent that it strengthens or weakens the school's master's degree program.

COA Changes and Organization. The Committee on Accreditation has doubled in size, and its responsibilities have increased dramatically since the first of 14 programs in library education was accredited in 1926. Called the Board of Education for Librarianship until 1956, when it became the Committee on Accreditation, it comprised five members. In 1965 the Committee's membership was increased to seven, and in 1970 the membership was further increased to ten. A total of 84 individuals have served on the Committee since its predecessor, the Board of Education for Librarianship, was created in 1924.

COA members are appointed for two years with the possibility of reappointment for one additional term. Two veteran members, John T. Eastlick and Carrie C. Robinson, left the committee following the 1976 Conference. Their replacements are Charles D. Churchwell and Jane H. Morgan. After two years as the Committee's Chairperson, Russell E. Bidlack stepped down from that responsibility following the 1976 Conference, and Lucille Whalen took his place. The remaining six members of the Committee for 1976–77 are Susanna Alexander, Alex P. Allain, Bernard M. Fry, Irene B. Hoadley, Bruce Peel, and Patricia B. Pond.

Appointments to COA and the designation of the Chairperson are made by the ALA Executive Board upon the recommendation of ALA's President-elect. Effort is made to have both library practitioners and library educators representing various aspects of library service on the Committee. All should have a demonstrated interest in the trends, issues, and problems of library education, with a sensitivity for how these may vary in different geographical areas. Because the Canadian Library Association has delegated to ALA responsibility for the accreditation of library education programs in Canada, the Committee membership includes a Canadian, Bruce Peel. In recent years, as part of their concern for the interests of the educational consumer, accrediting bodies have endeavored to include public representation. Alex P. Allain, a lawyer and library trustee, presently fills that role on COA.

Secretariat services for COA are provided by the Accreditation Officer, a post filled by Elinor Yungmeyer from August 1975. The Accreditation Officer, with a staff of one administrative assistant and one administrative secretary, serves as the main liaison of COA services through ALA Headquarters, providing information and assistance not only for committee members and library schools, but also for the library community generally throughout the United States and Canada.

What Accreditation Cannot Do. Much of the Accreditation Officer's time is spent in explaining to the library community the role of COA in library education. Frequently the response to questions must take the form of what accreditation *cannot* do. ALA's purpose in accreditation is to improve the quality of library education. Because educational accreditation is voluntary and nongovernmental, COA renders a judgment regarding the quality of a program *only* when invited to do so by the president of the institution of which that program is a part. COA cannot solicit a request from an institution for an initial accreditation visit.

Because accreditation, through the exercise of peer judgment, is limited to an evaluation of educational quality, COA cannot respond to the job market nor to geographical demands for more or fewer library schools. Accreditation is *not* an instrument for the control of the number of library school graduates nor the geographical distribution of library schools. Neither COA nor its parent body, the ALA, determines whether a graduate of an unaccredited program may or may not be employed by a library.

Curriculum Considerations. The Accreditation Officer and COA members are frequently urged to require that the curriculum of every library school include certain specific courses. Examples have been: intellectual freedom, Latin American bibliography, the cataloging of serials, bibliographic instruction, archival managment, the organization of picture collections, literature for young people, and Library of Congress classification. The 1972 Standards, like the current standards of nearly every other accrediting group, are indicative rather than prescriptive; they are qualitative, not quantitative. While the 1972 Standards require that every library school's curriculum provide for "the study of general professional principles and procedures . . . reflect the findings of basic and applied research . . . [and] respond to current trends in library development and professional education," not a single course is identified as indispensable.

In determining that a program is accreditable, COA certifies that it meets the Standards. While some accredited programs meet the Standards at a higher level than others, COA does not rank them. The Accreditation Officer cannot advise a prospective student that one program is superior to another. COA is able to respond, however, to prospective students' queries regarding the location of accredited programs and the persons in those schools who can provide information on such matters as the subject specializations available, tuition costs, entrance requirements, and related information.

Not "Pro Status Quo." On some occasions alleged accreditation requirements have been used by institutions and educational programs as an excuse to avoid experimentation and innovation. A reading of the 1972 Standards should provide convincing evidence that the opposite is true for library education. While the Standards require that library schools formulate and publish goals and program objectives, and that the curriculum and faculty expertise reflect those goals and objectives, the Standards emphasize that "the curriculum should be continually under review and revision, and should be receptive to innovation." A key provision under the standard on faculty is that "the school should demonstrate the high priority it attaches to good teaching by its appointments and promotions, by its receptivity to innovation in methodology and educational technology, by its provision of a suitable learning environment, and by its solicitation of student reactions to faculty performance."

Affirmative Action. A question that has been debated among educators in recent years has been the degree to which affirmative action should be a factor in the accreditation process. The Committee on Accreditation has taken the view that the goals of affirmative action regarding both students and faculty are implicit in the 1972 Standards. During the site visit, COA teams have regularly included the institution's affirmative action officer among officials of the central administration to be interviewed. Teams have also examined with some care the diversity of both faculty and student body as well as questions of equity in faculty salaries, work load, and fringe benefits. Prior to each Midwinter Meeting, COA's Chairperson prepares for Council a report on the Committee's efforts to implement affirmative action in keeping with the provisions of the 1972 Standards.

Visit Schedule. While the "first round" of accreditation and reaccreditation visits under the 1972 Standards had been completed by 1976, COA's schedule remains heavy. In order to retain accredited status, library schools are required to submit annual reports that respond to COA's recommendations at the time of the accreditation decision and also provide data on financial support and enrollment along with information regarding curriculum, faculty, and administrative changes. The Committee's fall meeting is regularly devoted to reviewing those reports. Furthermore, schools with accredited programs are normally revisited every four to six years. The "second round" of visits under the 1972 Standards will thus begin in the fall of 1978 and will continue through the spring of 1983.

Before commencing the new round of site visits, COA will have revised and shared with all library schools its *Manual of Procedures for Evaluation Visits . . .* and its *Self-Study: A Guide to the Process and to Preparation of a Report for the Committee on Accreditation.* The Committee is also seeking in-depth evaluations of its work during the past three years. The results of questionnaires mailed to each of the 67 schools that have been visited under the 1972 Standards and to the chairperson of each visiting team are being given serious consideration by the Committee. Just as it requires a library school seeking to maintain accreditation for its program regularly to review its curriculum as well as its goals and program objectives, so does COA seek to learn from its past experience and to improve its policies and procedures. — RUSSELL E. BIDLACK

Acquisitions

The acquisitions picture in 1976 continued to be mostly grim and bleak. Federal aid for educational purposes was problematic as always, and the inverse relationship between increasing postal rates and book prices on the one hand, and decreasing library budgets on the other, was unchanged. There is hope for the future, however, because of the prospect of sharing resources through library networks, but, one must admit, they present their own special kinds of problems. Publishers and other information disseminators remain unconvinced that the objective of networking is not to reduce the amount of resources actually acquired by a given institution, but rather to maximize the availability of materials required by the clientele being served. The impact on future acquisitions practice and procedure is certain to be extensive, but library

This photo of a Dallas policeman is among the 75,000 photographs and negatives depicting Dallas history from 1929 to the present in a collection purchased by the Dallas Public Library in 1976.

Acquisitions

Oral history tapes of prominent Black Memphis educators and businessmen were donated to the Memphis/Shelby County Public Library and Information Center by Memphis Links, Inc., in 1976. Left, retired High School Principal Blair T. Hunt during a taping session.

networks have been growing too rapidly since 1970 to permit specific, long-range predictions.

FEDERAL APPROPRIATIONS

Early indications were that funding for the Higher Education Act (HEA) and the Library Services and Construction Act (LSCA) would, at best, remain at the 1974 level. In fact, President Ford's election year education budget called for a one-billion-dollar reduction in education expenditures below the level of appropriations approved by Congress for fiscal 1976. Moreover, the President's fiscal 1977 budget proposed a consolidation of 27 (later reduced to 24) federal aid programs in education into one block grant of $3,300,000,000. Very little was earmarked for libraries and no funds at all were requested for HEA (college library resources) and LSCA (public library programs).

In the final analysis, after a great deal of maneuvering for position, and perhaps with an eye on the voters, Congress recommended substantial increases in LSCA funding as well as an extension of the Higher Education Act. The general expectation was that Ford would veto the appropriation and that Congress would be forced to override with every hope of ultimate success. But there was no opportunity for final action in the Congress in 1976 because of the early recess for elections. (See also Law and Legislation; Washington Report.)

LIBRARY BUDGETS

Despite continuing efforts by Congress to renew or maintain federal support for libraries, and despite, or perhaps because of, various experimental programs such as revenue sharing and other programmatic tinkering, the literature was filled with reports of budgetary cutbacks and general austerity. On the other hand, in perhaps an optimistic sign, a large number of libraries appeared to be experiencing a very high level of support. News headlines such as "legislature doubles state appropriations" and "per capita aid is increased" were not at all uncommon. But it was interesting, and for some depressing, to observe that almost all of the tales of disaster were from states outside the Sun Belt, which in turn reported more than half of the economic gains. Whether this reflects the beginning of a general upswing in library fortunes, or whether it represents a phenomenon peculiar to conditions in the South and Southwest, remains to be seen.

Postal Rates. The crisis in many library budgets for acquisitions continued to be exacerbated by the unremitting pressure for increased postal rates. For several years running, there has been no relief in sight. Special fourth-class rates were scheduled in 1976 to go up 80 percent over the following four years. And the fourth-class rate for library material loaned or exchanged was expected to increase 350 percent. Late in the year, however, a bill (S.2844) designed to provide $1,000,000,000 annually to the Postal Service as a subsidy for the next two years cleared a House-Senate conference. At the same time, long-term prospects remained that rates would trend upward rather than downward.

Procedures. Research reported in the field of library acquisitions showed a heavy emphasis on ordering systems and procedures. One contribution described a key-word-in-context index to the on-order file and a method of payment for material by means of a blank check, the objective being to cut staff costs and increase efficiency. Other reports in this vein included the description of a central purchasing agency for school libraries, the potential

A rare copy of Prose and Poetry of the Live Stock Industry of the United States, *the one-millionth acquisition of the Texas A & M University Library, was placed on display in 1976 by Irene B. Hoadley, Director of the University Libraries.*

benefits of a wholesaler's microfiche ordering system for libraries, research in experimental computer-to-computer ordering by means of ISBN (international standard book number), and the development of an ordering system by a jobber utilizing ISBN on magnetic tape.

In the area of gifts and exchanges appeared a detailed analysis of national exchange centers and the efficiency of international exchange of publications; and another report offered suggestions for improving the exchange of publications with developing countries.

Other topics which received attention included the principles and procedures of book selection, a system designed to improve the economic handling of duplicate periodical issues, acquisitions methods and funding in the field of art, and a procedure for optimal allocation of resources among the processes of a library system leading to a formula approach to budgeting.

Book Trade. Analysis and criticism of the state of the book publishing industry continued to be issued by John Dessauer and others, many of whom have suggested that conditions seem to call for industry-wide cooperative action. Perhaps in consequence of these recommendations, the Book Industry Study Group was formed to conduct market and related research on behalf of the entire industry. For its first project, the Group contracted with John P. Dessauer, Inc., to conduct a survey of the various industry sectors in order to identify needs and priorities and to recommend a long-range plan of action.

Many signs pointed to the gravity of the situation. For example, although book publishers' sales rose to $3,810,000,000 in 1975, representing a 7.8 percent increase, the growth rate had clearly slowed down from 1974. Profit margins were meagre at best, and many smaller publishers were operating in the red. There was cause for concern in that paperbacks were outselling hardbacks and many independent publishers were being taken over by conglomerates. One observer asserted that fully 60 percent of the population are not buying books at all.

These and other factors seemed to suggest that book prices could go up by as much as 50 to 60 percent by 1980. Thus, no one was surprised to learn in 1976 that average prices for U.S. hardcover trade and technical books in 1975 increased to $16.19, up from $14.09 in 1974, according to *The Bowker Annual* (1976, p. 206). At the same time, average prices of U.S. periodicals and serial services continued their inexorable rise, reaching $19.94 and $118.03, respectively (p. 204–205).

COPYRIGHT

The first new comprehensive copyright law since 1909, signed by President Ford on October 20, will become effective on January 1, 1978 (*see* Copyright). The extended lead time was intended to allow the Copyright Office to revise regulations, forms, and publications, and to permit the President to appoint the Copyright Royalty Commission as required by the law. Of particular interest to acquisitions librarians is the new law's attempt to clarify the doctrine of fair use. Specifically, it prohibits "systematic" photocopying of copyrighted materials but permits interlibrary arrangements "that do not have, as their purpose or effect, that the library or archives receiving such copies or phonorecords for distribution does so in such aggregate quantities as to substitute for a subscription to or purchase of such work." Guidelines which generally define "aggregate quantities" are contained in an appendix to the bill which constitutes a joint explanatory statement developed by the Committee of Conference. The statement followed the guidelines of the National Commission on New Technological Uses of Copyrighted Words (CONTU), which permit libraries to request no more than five copies of separate parts of publications under certain limitations and during any given year. (*See also* CONTU.)

Government Publications. The apparent failure of the Government Publications Office (GPO) to resolve long-standing production and distribution problems was the object of continued criticism in many quarters. The GPO established an Advisory Council on Printing and Publications Service, composed of GPO customers, to focus on problems and recommend changes.

Prices of government publications have risen 70 percent since 1972, and the GPO announced in 1976 that it was considering another round of across the board hikes. But a pricing study ordered by the Public Printer resulted in 13 recommendations and hope was expressed that some of them might permit selected price reductions.   J. MICHAEL BRUER

Administration

See *Management, Library*

Adults, Library Services to

Several major social forces had direct impact upon public library services to adults in 1976. The economic recession continued to draw tighter limits to service programs; copyright legislation of 1976 promised to challenge easy information duplication in some respects; sensitivity to the rights of patrons to protection under the Privacy Act of 1974 increased; the issuance of the National Commission of Libraries and Information Sciences's *Goals for Action* stimulated adult services librarians to new perspectives on service; and the general move toward public accountability has sus-

(Above) Reading and Literature programs for veterans were offered in 1976 by the St. Louis Public Schools at the Cabanne Branch of the St. Louis Public Library. "Live and Learn" programs for adults at the St. Louis Library (right) utilized video cassettes for both high school and college-level courses previously offered on educational television.

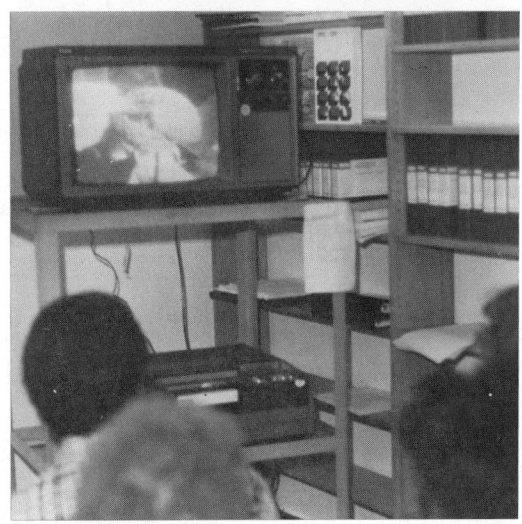

tained an emphasis in public libraries on evaluation of services and, hence, on review of goals and objectives for such service.

Budget Limitations. Major metropolitan library systems have been meeting severe budget cuts for the last four years, and continued cuts for 1976 tended to be absorbed by cutting staff, shortening hours of service, closing branch units, dropping acquisitions. Each public library's pattern has been individual, however, with some refusing to cut staff, developing job-sharing plans, or relying on attrition to meet the quota. The need to establish clearer priorities under the pressure is universal; Baltimore County Public Library consulted its community in making the choices, with Sunday hours, media, adult group programs, bookmobiles (all adult services designed to meet needs of special groups) the top targets for elimination. On the other hand, some public libraries have been highly successful in winning major new funding on the basis of urgent need, and the Cleveland Public Library in 1976 won a referendum increasing library support $4,100,000 a year for the next five years. Other libraries, whose priorities fell within specific federal fund priorities, were able to sustain growth through grants for specific adult services, such as Houston Public Library's $11,259 from the Law Enforcement Assistance Administration for audiovisual materials in the Harris County Juvenile Detention Center.

Adult service librarians have been ingenious in their use of volunteers to sustain and expand service even under budget limitations. Detroit Public Library recruited retired persons (including retired librarians), women, and young people to carry on outreach services in hospitals, nursing homes, and service to shut-ins. The complexities of use of volunteers have been recognized, but the desire of communities to keep libraries effective, as well as libraries' desire to sustain important services to special publics, makes use of volunteers a continuing solution. CETA-funded positions made possible short-term staffing for new library services such as Information and Referral Service (q.v.).

The growth of use of fees for selective adult services was a trend. Those services most costly and newest in development tended to be those to which fees were attached: rentals for audiovisual equipment and materials, rental of bestsellers; in-depth reference services for a fee; fees for use of computerized data bases. While establishing fees for service is challenged as contrary to the tradition of "free" public library service or as discriminatory against those who cannot afford the fee, the practice went on in 1976 much as it did in the mid-1930's Depression.

Federal Legislation and Leadership. Passed late in 1976, the new copyright legislation has just begun to be interpreted for its meaning to library practice. It is relatively clear, however, that in-library photocopying for service to the individual adult will not undergo major policy change at this time; networks and systems photocopying limitations offer greater threat to adult services in the coming years. Adult service librarians will spend time in 1977 redesigning service patterns to make easy a compliance with the new law which becomes effective in 1978.

While the Privacy Act of 1974 safeguards individual privacy from misuse of federal records, librarians outside federal libraries will increasingly be ethically held to similar standards of client protection. Adult service librarians in 1976 became aware of the need for review of traditional practice in the light of the new law.

Late in 1975 the National Commission on Libraries and Information Science released its report; *Toward a National Program for Library and Information Services: Goals for Action,* with an emphasis on resource sharing and building national and regional networks of libraries for information service. While the need of "all" citizens for information is acknowledged, and the need for study of the information needs of the deprived and the library nonuser is identified, the commitment of national resources is more clearly given to service of specialized information to experts in economic, scientific, and social sciences. Published late in the same year, the working papers for the 1973 NCLIS-sponsored conference, *Library and Information Service Needs of the Nation,* shared this client-oriented approach to library planning but gave more nearly equal attention to homemakers, children, and aging, those in rural areas, institutionalized, handicapped, and economically deprived. The adult services librarians' struggle to maintain cultural, recreational, and other broadly educational services under the impact of rapid elaboration of the more strictly information-oriented services in the context of financial stringency was clearly significant in 1976, as Karl Nyren's sensitive report of the 1976 Pittsburgh Conference on Resource Sharing in Libraries well documented.[1]

Goals and Objectives. The "public library goals and objectives movement," enunciated by Larry Earl Bone in 1975,[2] became in 1976 the pivotal point on which public library service standards will be developed.[3] Measurable objectives, in a client-service context, tied to clearly stated goals for which priorities have been consciously established, provide the framework within which public library adult services were beginning to envision the future in 1976.

A promising event of 1976 was the announcement of the formation of a consortium of 10 innovating public libraries committed to the development of adult educational services. Stemming from their cooperative work under the College Entrance Examination Board's Office of Library Independent Study, the public library staffs are committed to adult services programs strengthened by program planning, staff training, and evaluation.[4]

Adult Service Activities. During the year 1976, emphasis on adult service activities of independent study, information and referral services, outreach, service to aging, mass media, and literacy continued in a soft spotlight. American Library Association leadership promised to provide a major thrust to public library literacy programs through a developmental program related to the publication of Helen H. Lyman's manual on literacy. Service to ethnic minorities continues but with less fanfare.

Bicentennial celebrations inspired adult programs' use of books, art, music, and the spoken word to celebrate the country's history. Mass media were used in Mississippi to "explore the American Dream;" the *Adams Chronicles* became the focus for reading lists, discussion guides, and study guides in a variety of libraries. Cultural programs stimulated by the grants to Boston and Chicago public libraries by the National Endowment for the Humanities seemed, in 1976, to provide a small renaissance in lectures, displays, programs of cultural orientation.[5] A familiar role was revived in 1976.   MARGARET E. MONROE

The Memphis and Shelby County Public Library conducted a free volunteer income tax assistance program one day a week from February 1 to April 15, 1976.

Adults, Library Services to

REFERENCES
1. Karl Nyren, "Resource Sharing in Libraries," *Library Journal,* 101 (November 15, 1976), 2339.
2. Larry Earl Bone, "The Public Library Goals and Objectives Movement: Death Gasp or Renaissance?" *Library Journal,* 100 (July 1975), 1283–1286.
3. Meredith Bloss, "Standards for Public Library Service—Quo Vadis?" *Library Journal,* 101 (June 1, 1976), 1259–1262.
4. "New Consortium to Run Independent Study Project," *Library Journal,* 101 (May 1, 1976), 1069.
5. Barbara Jacobs, "Libraries and Their Users Take Advantage as the NEH Warms to Library Projects," *American Libraries,* vol. 7 (April 1976), p. 213–214.

The Chicago Public Library Cultural Center began its second annual "Writing in Chicago" program with this 1976 performance of "Spoon River and Beyond" by the Gallery Theatre Company.

American Association of Law Libraries

Aging Library Service to
See *Older Adults*, Library Service to.

American Association of Law Libraries

The American Association of Law Libraries (AALL) was founded in 1906. According to its constitution, the Association "is established for educational and scientific purposes . . . to promote librarianship, to develop and increase the usefulness of law libraries, to cultivate the science of law librarianship and to foster a spirit of cooperation among the members of the profession." The Association is presently established around 13 regional geographic chapters, each of which has considerable autonomy in its direction and financial management. Following debate at the Association's 1975 and 1976 conventions, an internal reorganization was approved under a new bylaw which provides for creation of new Special Interest Sections by the AALL Executive Board. These Sections initially will be project-oriented, for example, for convention program planning and publishing, and should derive their direction from what are now several large committees. Since 1965 the Association has maintained a headquarters office in Chicago.

Activities. During 1976 the Association began a legislative program that could more systematically monitor federal and state legislation affecting its interests. A reorganized Legislation and Legal Developments Committee with a wide geographic membership basis began a review of all federal programs and pending legislation in such areas as postal rates (applicable to mailing of legal publishing), appellate court records depository status, revision of the copyright law, and other topics. The AALL Copyright Committee has been actively interested in the course of revising this law for many years and recently has taken an important role in the development of acceptable legislation providing for library photocopying reproduction and distribution procedures. For several years, Professor Julius J. Marke, Law Librarian, New York University School of Law, has directed this Committee.

Based upon a 1975 questionnaire to the membership, the AALL Education Committee continues to define the purposes and scope of the Association's educational programs. Important among these, with the completion of the annual rotating educational institute programs in June 1975, is a plan to present somewhat more advanced continuing education for law librarians beginning with a June 1977 preconvention institute at McGill University in Montreal that will feature "Civil Law Sources for Common Law Trained Librarians." Three shorter educational workshop programs will follow the convention in Toronto. A curriculum and course of study for elementary training in legal bibliography and law librarianship was in preparation in 1976. This program, with frequent revisions, will be presented at the chapter level, at which such training is usually most important. For at least 10 years, the Association has offered a variety of mostly privately funded academic scholarship assistance for the study of library science or law to qualified persons interested in a career in law librarianship.

For several years, the Association has maintained a committee on Law Library Service to Prisoners. It periodically compiles checklists of recommended legal materials for correctional facility libraries and lists of law libraries and consultants available for advice to correctional institutions.

AALL's Placement Committee completed a major reorganization of its records for better service to respondents and employers. The Committee cooperates in the placement program of the Association of American Law Schools.

Publications. *Law Library Journal*, published quarterly by AALL, includes transcripts of the substantive programs of the annual meeting (usually in the November issue) and the proceedings of the business meetings. It also includes reports on statistics for various types of law libraries (collected with the aid of a grant from the Council of Library Resources) and other substantial papers relating to law librarianship. Another Association committee advises the H.W. Wilson Company on indexing and editorial policy for the *Index to Legal Periodicals* and AALL publishes the *Index to Foreign Legal Periodicals*. A biographical directory of the membership was underway in 1976 and scheduled for publication in the spring of 1977. The AALL *Recruitment Checklist* was revised in 1974. The *Directory of Law Libraries* (geographic) was published in 1976; it is issued biennially in even-numbered years.

Membership. Membership is divided into several classes with variations in annual dues: institutional, open to any law library ($60 minimum, $30 for each professional staff member); active individual, open to any person connected with a law library, state library, or with a general library having a separately maintained law section ($30); individual associate, for a person not connected with a law library, upon approval by the Membership Committee ($30); institutional associate, for any company or institution other than a law library, upon approval by the Membership Committee ($75); life members, for those retired from active library work (no dues); student, for students in either law or library school ($10).

Total membership, including persons designated as members under institutional memberships, exceeded 2,500 in 1976.

Expenditures for the fiscal year ending May 31, 1976, were $149,110; $60,453 was spent on the *Law Library Journal* and the *Index to Foreign Legal Periodicals*.

Annual Meeting. The 1976 annual meeting in Boston registered a record 990. It concluded with a three-day educational institute at the Harvard Law School on the topic of American legal history. The 70th annual meeting, scheduled for June 25–29, 1977, in Toronto, Canada, was to address topics concerned with developments in American and Canadian law and legal bibliography. — J.S. ELLENBERGER

AALL Officers

PRESIDENT (June 1976–June 1977):
Jack S. Ellenberger, Covington and Burling, Washington, D.C.

VICE-PRESIDENT/PRESIDENT-ELECT
Alfred J. Coco, Law Library, University of Denver, Colorado

ADMINISTRATIVE SECRETARY:
Antonette Russo

Headquarters: 53 W. Jackson Blvd., Chicago, Illinois 60614

American Association of School Librarians

The American Association of School Librarians (AASL), a Division of the American Library Association, represents elementary and secondary library media specialists in the schools of the nation through an expressed commitment for the continuous improvement of quality media programs in the schools. It provides its membership and the public with current information regarding the status of the profession of school librarianship. It prepares position statements to support the role of the library media professional and the need for the maintenance of that professional in the local school district. It contributes to the development of guidelines which substantiate and delineate the criteria for personnel, materials, and facilities for the school media program in the school building and on the district level.

The goals and objectives of the Association are identified, reviewed, and established by the Board of Directors who are elected by the AASL membership through a national election held in the spring of each year. The total governing body of 14 people, the officers and regional directors, determines the policies of the Association, which are implemented and supervised by the professional staff of an Executive Secretary and a Professional Assistant. These policies are translated into action through the many visible activities of the AASL committee structure which is designed and organized for the purpose of developing materials and programs in areas of crucial concern to the school media specialist.

Affiliation. A *Plan for Affiliation with the AASL*, written by a special committee of the AASL Board and staff, was unanimously approved by the AASL Board at the 1976 ALA Midwinter Meeting on January 22. The *Plan* permits statewide, territorial, District of Columbia, or regional organizations to affiliate with the American Association of School Librarians. Associations desiring affiliation must have purposes that are compatible with those of AASL, hold regular meetings, and have a systematic channel of communication. For the organization to attain governance status, at least 25 members including the President must be personal members of AASL.

Full implementation of the *Plan* began with the affirmative vote of the AASL membership at the ALA Annual Conference on July 20. Following the affirmative membership vote for the AASL *Plan for Affiliation*, the AASL Board approved a plan for charter affiliation which calls for the acceptance of affiliate applications during the fall and winter months. All library/media associations received a formal application for affiliation with the American Association of School Librarians in September. The last date for the acceptance of charter affiliates was December 31, 1976.

The purpose of the *Plan* is to strengthen the national voice of the media profession through a network of state and regional media associations affiliating with the national association. AASL affiliates will have governance in the national association through a delegate assembly which will elect three representatives to serve on the AASL Board of Directors. Improved communications, a national resource for media information, sharing of services, and better coordination of mutual goals and objectives are some of the advantages indicated in the rationale for affiliation with the American Association of School Librarians.

Twenty-nine associations requested affiliate status with AASL and were granted charter status according to the policy determined by the AASL Board of Directors.

Certification Model. AASL's project to develop a national certification model for media personnel culminated with the publication *Certification Model for Professional School Media Personnel*. The model identifies competencies necessary to guarantee accountable performance in the school library/media field. Seven are required for the media professional. These competencies should serve as a model to state departments of education. They in no way inhibit the expansion of the major competencies into a more inclusive coverage. The competencies delineated are: (1) Relation of Media to Instructional Systems, (2) Administration of Media Programs, (3) Selection of Media, (4) Utilization of Media, (5) Production of Media, (6) Research and Evaluation, and (7) Leadership and Professionalism.

Selection. AASL had been asked by the

American Association of School Librarians

school library/media professional, teachers, principals, and administrators to provide guidance in matters pertaining to the censorship of instructional materials. Committed to the philosophy that the selection of quality instructional materials is one of the most important and controversial tasks performed by school personnel, the AASL Board of Directors approved *Policies and Procedures for Selection of Instructional Materials* on August 15, 1976. A revision of the 1970 publication, it contains a model for the selection process. The Board also moved to endorse the *Library Bill of Rights of the American Library Association.* In this endorsement AASL resolved that these rights are fundamental to the philosophy of school media programs as stated in *Media Programs: District and School* (1975).

Programs. An air of celebration surrounded program activities during the ALA Centennial Conference as AASL marked 25 years of professional support for the library/media professional. The AASL Silver Anniversary Program, which featured highlights of the history of the association, was narrated by AASL President Judith G. Letsinger and supported by a cast of the "who's who" of school librarianship, including Frances Henne and Mary V. Gaver. The program provided insights into the events of importance which have marked the development of a national professional organization. A film production prepared by Weston Woods Studios climaxed the event. An original work of art with color lithographs by Steven Kellogg was a souvenir of the special program.

Joining in this recognition of service to the profession, the ALA Council on July 19 adopted a resolution marking the AASL's 25th anniversary. In referring to AASL, the resolution, submitted by Edward G. Holley, stated that AASL "has tirelessly supported the improvement and extension of library media services for children and young people. The Division has provided the Association with leaders whose names are known to librarians and educators across the country for their pioneering efforts in promoting higher standards of excellence and professional development."

"Increasing State and Local Commitment to Support of Media Programs: What You Can Do" was the theme of the Legislation Workshop sponsored by AASL at the Chicago Conference. Ruth W. Waldrop, Chairperson of the AASL Legislation Committee, presided at the first session; Alice Ihrig spoke on "General Principles for Developing Commitment and Support." Individual state legislation efforts for the support of increased instructional materials and facilities were reviewed by representatives from North Carolina and Washington. *Simple Steps for Successful Legislation,* an AASL handbook prepared for the workshop, was distributed to those in attendance. The morning session was followed by the address of Wilmer S. Cody, Superintendent of the Birmingham (Alabama) City School System. Cody was primarily responsible for the successful passage in April 1975 of a five-mill property tax. The passage of that tax is making possible the accreditation of the system's 78 elementary schools and the subsequent upgrading and establishment of elementary school libraries.

"Children and Television" was the title of a preconference sponsored by AASL on July 16–17. The two-day preconference, chaired by Leonard Freiser of the AASL Video Communications Committee, focused on the effects of television on behavior, learning, and creativity. Other program highlights viewed the child as consumer, violence and stereotypes, and

See ALA Highlights in Introductory pages for Organization of the American Library Association

---

Charter AASL Affiliates

Region I: New England, D. Philip Baker, Regional Director
  Connecticut Educational Media Association
  New England Educational Media Association
Region II: Middle Atlantic, Johanna Wood, Regional Director
  Delaware Learning Resources Association
  District of Columbia Association of School Librarians
  Educational Media Association of Maryland
  New Jersey School Media Association
  Pennsylvania School Librarians Association
  School Library Media Section - New York Library Association
Region III: Midwest, Robert Graham, Regional Director
  Illinois Association of School Librarians
  Indiana School Librarians Association
  Iowa Educational Media Association
  Michigan Association for Media in Education
  Minnesota Educational Media Organization
  Ohio Educational Library Media Association
  Wisconsin School Library Media Association
Region IV: Central, Agnes Milstead, Regional Director
  Kansas Association of School Librarians
Region V: Southeast, Dorothy W. Blake, Regional Director
  Florida Association for Media in Education, Inc.
  Kentucky School Media Association
  North Carolina Association of School Libraries
  School and Children's Section of the Southeastern Library Association
  Virginia Educational Media Association
  Georgia Library Media Department
Region VI: Southwest, Cathryne Franklin, Regional Director
  School Libraries Division/Arkansas Library Association
  Oklahoma Association of School Library Media Specialists
  School Libraries Division/Arizona State Library Association
  Texas Association of School Librarians
Region VII: West, Joan Griffis, Regional Director
  Oregon Educational Media Association
  Washington State Association of School Librarians
  Hawaii Association for School Librarians

school use of television. Robert M. Liebert, Professor of Psychology, SUNY, StonyBrook, addressed the preconference on "Television, the Anonymous Teacher." "Childism in TV: A Basic Oppression" was discussed by Chester M. Pierce, Professor of Education and Psychiatry, Harvard University.

Publications. The *Certification Model for Professional School Media Personnel*, cited previously, was released through the American Library Association Publishing Services. This AASL committee activity was chaired by David R. Bender and funded by a grant from the J. Morris Jones/World Book Encyclopedia/ALA Goals Award.

Policies and Procedures for the Selection of Instructional Materials, also cited above, was revised (August 1976) by the AASL Intellectual Freedom Representation and Information Committee. The revised publication contains appendices with checklists for requests for reconsideration of instructional materials to be used by a complainant and a media advisory committee. Joy Terhune serves as Chairperson of the AASL Intellectual Freedom Representation and Information Committee.

Simple Steps to Successful Legislation was prepared by the AASL Legislation Committee (Ruth W. Waldrop, Chairperson). The publication is addressed to the individual practitioner in the library/media profession as a guide in the development of a campaign for the improvement of learning opportunities for students through increased public support for school library/media programs.

Awards. The 1976 Distinguished Library Service Award for School Administrators was awarded to Wilmer Cody, Superintendent of the Birmingham (Alabama) City School System. The annual citation is presented to a person directly responsible for the administration of a school or group of schools who has made a unique and sustained contribution toward furthering the role of the library and its development in elementary and/or secondary education. Since assuming the Birmingham superintendency in 1973, the number of professional librarians has been increased from 18 to 83 and a coordinator of media services hired to coordinate the work of the school librarians.

Donald C. Adcock was chairperson of the AASL Jury during 1976. Members included Frances Fleming, Joy Terhune, Mary Choncoff, Edith Briles, Bernice Yesner, and Anne Marie Falsone.

Littleton Public Schools in Colorado won the $5,000 School Library Media Program of the Year Award sponsored by the American Association of School Librarians and the Encyclopaedia Britannica Companies for achievement in providing exemplary library media programs at the elementary level. The system was commended for its realization of long-range goals since 1966 when only one of the system's elementary buildings had a library media facility. National Finalist citations were presented to three other nominees: Chula Vista (California) City School District, St. Helena (California) Unified School District, and Stamford (Connecticut) Public Schools. Presentations of citations to all national award winners was made by AASL and Britannica officials at ceremonies in the four school communities.

ALICE FITE

AASL Officers

PRESIDENT (July 1976–June 1977):
Peggy L. Pfeiffer, Jefferson High School, Lafayette, Indiana

VICE-PRESIDENT/PRESIDENT-ELECT:
Frances C. Dean, Montgomery County Public Schools, Rockville, Maryland

EXECUTIVE SECRETARY:
Alice E. Fite

PROFESSIONAL ASSISTANT
Babetta Jimpie

Membership (August 31, 1976): 6,181 (4,061 personal and 2,120 organizational)

American Library History

American library history received much recognition and tribute during 1976 because of the celebration and activities associated with the Centennial of the American Library Association and the Bicentennial of the nation. Sales of Melvil Dewey T-shirts and ALA commemorative mugs, paperweights, and bookends continued into 1977. The ALA Annual Conference held in Chicago, July 18–24, provided numerous sessions with a historical theme. Among them were "The Service Ethos in American Libraries, 1876–1976," sponsored by the Library Administration Division Circulation Services Section; "Audiovisual in Libraries—Past, Present, Future," sponsored by the Audiovisual Section of the Information Science and Automation Division; "Library Buildings Out of the Past and Into the Future," sponsored by LAD's Buildings and Equipment Section; and Librarian of Congress Daniel Boorstin's historical survey of American public libraries at the Third General Session in his address on "The Indivisible Community." The American Association of School Librarians also celebrated a silver anniversary at the same conference with a special program of memorabilia and song.

On October 3–6, Library History Seminar V took place in Philadelphia, the site of the first ALA Conference in 1876 on approximately the same dates. This conference, consisting of scholarly presentations, was sponsored by the *Journal of Library History* with co-sponsorship and assistance from Beta Phi Mu, the American Library History Round Table, and the Drex-

American Library History Round Table

el University Graduate School of Library Science.

Many library professional journals featured special issues or sections dealing with library history. Among them were *American Libraries* with its Great American Library Cover Series and its ALA Centennial Vignette Series, *Library Trends* with its special July, 1976 issue (the largest ever in size) on "American Library History, 1876-1976," and *College and Research Libraries* with numerous articles throughout the year dealing with historical aspects of academic libraries and librarianship.

The ownership of the *Journal of Library History* changed hands from the Florida State University School of Library Science to the University of Texas Graduate School of Library Science. The *Journal* had been established by the FSU library school in 1966. The new editor is Donald Davis of the University of Texas Graduate School of Library Science faculty.

There was an upsurge of monograph publications with an American library history theme during 1976. A selection of these included *The Happy Bookers* by Richard W. Armour (McGraw Hill), *The Eighteen Editions of the Dewey Decimal Classification* by John P. Comaromi (Forest Press), *Carl H. Milam and the United Nations Library* edited by Doris Dale (Scarecrow), *The Librarian: Selections From the Column of That Name by Edmund L. Pearson* edited by Jane B. Durnell and Norman D. Stevens (Scarecrow), *Landmarks of Library Literature, 1876-1976* edited by Dianne J. Ellsworth and Norman D. Stevens (Scarecrow), *ALA at 100*, a pamphlet written by Edward Holley that originally appeared in *The ALA Yearbook* for 1976 (ALA), *Essays in Honor of American Librarianship*, edited by Sidney Jackson (ALA), *Carl Milam and the American Library Association* by Peggy Sullivan (H. W. Wilson), *A Historical Introduction to Library Education: Problems and Progress to 1951* by Carl M. White (Scarecrow) and a third edition of *Libraries in the Western World* by Elmer Johnson and Michael Harris (Scarecrow).

GEORGE S. BOBINSKI

American Library History Round Table

1976, ALA's Centennial year, was a year of growth for the American Library History Round Table. Renewed interest in American library history was reflected in an increase in membership, up from 305 the previous year to 343 members. Round Table activities during the year were in keeping with its stated goals: the encouragement of research and interest in American library history. These were reflected in programs sponsored and assisted by ALHRT during the Annual ALA Conference held in Chicago. The ALHRT program meeting addressed itself to problems and pleasures of historical writing, with George S. Bobinski, Dean, School of Information and Library Studies, State University of New York, Buffalo, and Howard W. Winger, Dean, Graduate Library School, University of Chicago, as speakers. Since Bobinski is editor of the soon to be published *Dictionary of American Library Biography*, and Winger served as editor of the July 1976 issue of *Library Trends* devoted to library history, they were able to relate from firsthand experience some of the trials as well as the rewards of such publication. ALHRT also co-sponsored a lively meeting with the LAD Circulation Services Division entitled "The Service Ethos in American Libraries, 1876-1976." The Round Table financed the production of a slide-tape presentation on ALA history by Robert Starring of the University of Michigan Library which was presented as a part of this program.

The Round Table assisted as one of the sponsors of Library History Seminar V, October 3-6, 1976 at the Philadelphia Hilton Hotel. Dates of the Seminar were chosen to coincide with the founding of the American Library Association on October 6, 1876; a reception sponsored by the President and Executive Board of the American Library Association celebrating the Centennial of the founding was held on October 6, one hundred years later, at the Historical Society of Pennsylvania in Philadelphia. The reception was preceded by three and a half days of seminar meetings, speakers, and panel discussions on various aspects of American library history. Proceedings of the Seminar are to be published.

MARGARET F. MAXWELL

ALHRT Officers

CHAIRPERSON (July 1976-June 1977):
Margaret F. Maxwell, University of Arizona, Tucson

CHAIRPERSON ELECT:
Budd Gambee, University of North Carolina, Chapel Hill

SECRETARY-TREASURER:
Susan Thompson, Columbia University, New York

Membership (August 31, 1976): 343

American Library Society

The American Library Society (ALS) was founded in 1970 "to promote the advancement of the library and information sciences; to aid the library and information professions in achieving their goal of providing the best possible in library and information service for the people of the United States of America; and to protect the freedoms of access to information, the press, and speech." It remained in 1976 one of the world's smallest organizations interested in library and information services.

Ethics Statement. The ad hoc Committee on Ethics, chaired by Jay E. Daily of the University of Pittsburgh's Graduate School of Library and Information Science, was, for the second consecutive year, a center of ALS activity during 1976. Created in 1974, the ad hoc Committee was assigned its charge to review activity in the field of professional ethics and intellectual freedom with the purpose of recommending to the membership ways in which ALS could involve itself effectively with reasonable hope of making significant contributions in the field but without duplicating the efforts of other organizations. In accordance with that charge, Daily and committee members William Z. Nasri, of the University of Pittsburgh's Graduate School of Library and Information Science, and the Reverend Chalmers Coe, Minister of the First Congregational Church of Columbus, Ohio, spent 18 months preparing a statement of ethics, the text of which is reprinted in full below:

ETHICS OF LIBRARY SCIENCE

General. The librarian offers access to knowledge on the basis of need rather than privilege. He assists any who request help to find the information sources they wish without offering opinions of those sources or of the individual's wish for them. When asked his opinion of information sources, he answers on the basis of objective evaluation, his own and others, rather than prejudice. Where subjective judgment is inevitable, he admits it and states his bias.

Employment. Accepting employment in a library assumes that the librarian will give the work his best efforts for a period at least of a year. A librarian will not accept employment if he believes that he cannot agree in good conscience with the work of the parent authority in which the library is located or if he cannot approve of the actions of his superiors.

A librarian will not carry out work that is in conflict with his own ethics. His principles are superior to the work asked of him and he will resign rather than compromise his ethics.

Reference Services. Aside from day-to-day work providing reference services, a librarian will follow the literature devoted to those services and will carefully review all possible works for his collection.

In providing reference services, the librarian will preserve the collection from theft or vandalism, but he will not make any work inaccessible because of its contents. If he judges a book to be particularly vulnerable to theft or vandalism, he will arrange for adequate supervision of its use.

Cataloging. A librarian will catalog and classify information sources according to their usefulness in the collection for which they are intended. He will never use the subject heading list or the classification schedules for the purposes of expressing his own opinion of the work.

Administration. A librarian who administers a library will treat all his co-workers fairly, regarding himself as their servant as well as their leader. He will take those steps that will enable all his co-workers to contribute their best efforts to the work at hand. He will reward effort and will not practice favoritism in the assignment of duties or in furthering the careers of his co-workers.

Professional. A librarian is obliged to fight efforts that would limit intellectual freedom and restrict the development of information sources and their free use. He is obliged to protect the confidentiality of his records against invasions of privacy.

A librarian is obliged to work to further the profession in the way that makes best use of his talents and preferences: by contributing to professional journals, by membership and participation in professional societies, by encouraging those in search of a career to consider librarianship, and by making the work of the librarian known and respected in his society.

A librarian is obliged to work openly and deal honestly with everyone. He would refuse a gift from a dealer if it is meant to gain preference for the dealer's product on any basis but its superiority. He will not engage in illegal activities in the library nor permit others to do so.

Librarians participate to the extent they wish in the political and social life of their community, and if they are so inclined, practice the religion of their choice. However, while at their work, they will be guided as far as possible by objective considerations in the development of the collection, in organizing it for use, and in making it accessible to the public they serve. In no case will their personal political, social, and religious ideas take precedence over what is objectively the best way of providing library service in their community and in their library.

The statement was presented to the membership at the seventh annual meeting on July 21 and was adopted by acclamation. The committee was then charged with the task of developing a plan for implementation of the statement. Its report was expected by mid-1977.

Publications. Publishing continued to be the principal activity of ALS in 1976. *Concerning Libraries*, the quarterly journal of the American Library Society, completed its seventh year of publication in 1976 while the publication of the second edition of the *Handbook of the American Library Society* was postponed until 1977 to allow the inclusion of updated data resulting from the mid-1976 revamping of the ALS membership roster. Meanwhile plans progressed for the *Occasional Papers of the American Library Society*, the first number of which was scheduled to appear in mid-1977.

Annual Meeting. The seventh annual meeting was held at the Art Institute of Chicago July 21 during the week of the ALA Centennial Conference. Norman Horrocks, Director of Dalhousie University's School of Library Service, spoke on differing methods of library school accreditation around the world following the membership's adoption of the code of ethics. Other speakers at ALS meetings included Robert Wedgeworth, ALA Executive Director, Jean E. Lowrie, Director of Western Michigan University's School of Librarianship and ALA Past President, and Marcelle Foote, Director of the Indiana State Library.

The eighth annual meeting was scheduled for August 1977, in Plymouth, Indiana, in conjunction with the completion of the new Plymouth Public Library building.

American Library Society

For ALA statement on Ethics, see also Ethics

American Library Trustee Association

Membership continues to be open to any individual or organization showing a sincere interest in the purposes of ALS. Both individual and organizational members receive the publications of the Society, but only individual members may vote and hold office. Dues are $1 for individuals and $3 for organizations. In 1976 the combined membership totaled 60.

JOHN B. HARLAN

ALS Officers

PRESIDENT (July 1976–July 1978):
John B. Harlan

VICE-PRESIDENT:
Donna B. Harlan, Indiana University at South Bend

SECRETARY/TREASURER:
Kathryn A. Whitman, Indiana University at South Bend

Headquarters: 1013 S. 21st St., South Bend, Indiana 46615

American Library Trustee Association

The American Library Trustee Association (ALTA), a Division of the American Library Association, placed a priority on being involved at the state and regional levels in 1976. The Regional Vice Presidents (increased in number from seven to ten during the year) and members of the ALTA Speakers Bureau participated actively at numerous workshops and conferences to assist library trustees to become more knowledgeable about their responsibilities and how to meet them. Various reprints from *The Public Library Trustee* were distributed widely at these meetings. Program planners called on the ALTA secretariat to provide suggestions for speakers for information on packaged program materials. Information and ideas were also provided to state library agencies and state associations for developing library trustee manuals.

For his 1975–76 year as ALTA President, John T. Short emphasized the need for raising the knowledge and concern levels of library trustees about the millions of adults and teenagers in America who cannot read. Short stated that the ALTA response to the problem should be "to enhance the *awareness* of the problem by the trustee and to encourage new priorities by individual boards."

ALTA was strongly represented among the participants in ALA's 1976 Legislation Day in Washington, D.C., on April 6. ALTA's Legislation Committee was expanded in an effort to secure trustee representation from each state for the development of a legislative network.

"What to Do Before the Consultant Comes," prepared by the ALTA Task Force for Evaluation of Consultant Studies, was published in *The Public Library Trustee* (November 1976). It outlines tasks for the library board and staff to perform before a consultant is employed and a procedure for hiring a consultant.

Honor Award. The ALTA Honor Award was established in 1976 for presentation annually beginning in 1977 to give recognition to public library benefactors. Policies governing the selection to recipients of the citations provide that nominations of those making major gifts to libraries may be made by any person or persons, institution, agency, or organization other than the proposed nominee. The significance of the gift will be measured from the point of view of the library receiving the gift, not by size alone. Considerable weight is to be given to innovation and imagination on the part of the donor. Benefits may be in the form of money, real or personal property, negotiable paper or other tangible contributions. Although recognition will not be confined to gifts made at any particular time, recent support will be given priority. All nominations must be endorsed by the board of trustees of the library involved.

Citations. The 1975 ALTA trustee citations for distinguished service to library development were presented at the ALA Centennial Conference in Chicago. One was awarded to Elizabeth A. Ruffner of Prescott, Arizona, in recognition of "enthusiastic leadership in her home community . . . as Board Member and President of the Prescott Public Library." She organized the Friends of the Prescott County Library System and co-chaired a Library Development Committee which brought about the State Library Plan including the formation of six regional libraries in the State of Arizona. Another citation, presented to James A. Hess, commended him "for his incessant labors in the past two decades toward excellence in library service for the people of East Brunswick and South Middlesex County, New Jersey . . . for his promotion of networking through the organization of libraries of South Middlesex, for his advocacy of a formal federation of libraries in that county, and for his many contributions to ALTA." Hess serves as an ALTA Regional Vice President.

Programs. Featured ALTA programs during the ALA Centennial Conference included a panel presentation on The Library Trustee's Role in Library Finance and a talk by Richard Armour, author of *The Happy Bookers*. Workshops at the 1976 Conference highlighted library funding, the trustee as lobbyist, negotiation and unionization, automated and computerized information services for libraries, the trustee's role in the preservation of intellectual freedom, evaluating library services and personnel, and a manual for library publicity.

Membership promotion activities included a mailing to directors of public libraries in the Midwestern states encouraging them to enlist their libraries' trustees as members of ALTA. A

See also
Trustees

new membership promotion brochure was also prepared and distributed.

In her inaugural speech, incoming President Maxine Scoville expressed her "firm conviction that ALTA should be involved in a continuous program of education for local trustees, thereby creating an awareness of the many responsibilities and opportunities the position presents." She called on ALTA to "contribute a positive, well-informed lay leadership to work in cooperation with the professional leadership in the American Library Association to meet the tremendous challenge of providing the citizenry the very best in libraries and library services."

ANDREW M. HANSEN

ALTA Officers

PRESIDENT (July 1976 – June 1977):
Maxine Scoville

FIRST VICE PRESIDENT/PRESIDENT-ELECT:
Donald Earnshaw

EXECUTIVE SECRETARY:
Andrew M. Hansen

ASSOCIATE EXECUTIVE SECRETARY:
Mary Jo Lynch

Membership (August 31, 1976): 2,539 (1,476 personal and 1,063 organizational)

American Society for Information Science

The American Society for Information Science (ASIS) was founded on March 13, 1937, as the American Documentation Institute (ADI). The initial interest was in the development of microfilm as an aid to learning. With the increasing awareness of the potential of automatic devices for literature searching and for information storage and retrieval in the 1950's and 1960's, information science emerged as an identifiable configuration of disciplines. The membership voted to change the name to ASIS in 1968.

ASIS became a leading and the most widely representative national professional association for those concerned with designing, managing, and using information systems and technology. ASIS provides a forum for the discussion, publication, and critical analysis of work dealing with the theory and practice of all elements involved in the communication of information. The Society acts as a bridge between research and development and the requirements of diverse types of information systems.

One regular Chapter and two Student Chapters were chartered by the ASIS Council in 1976 to bring the total number of Chapters to 28 and of Student Chapters to 17. The new regular Chapter is the Southern Chapter (Arkansas, Mississippi, Alabama, and western

Tennessee); the new Student Chapters are Central New York and Los Angeles Area.

One new Special Interest Group (SIG) was also established by ASIS: Community Information Services (CIS), to bring the total number to 23.

The membership grew by nearly 14 percent in 1976, bringing it to 4,391. Membership in ASIS is available to any interested person. Annual dues are $45. No formal educational qualifications for membership exist. Other types of membership include: student ($15), available for not more than three years to persons regularly enrolled as full-time students at a college or university in courses of training or study for which degree credits are given; retired ($22.50), available on request to any member who has been a member for five years or more and has retired from active work; affiliate status ($20), available for one year with limited benefits; and institutional memberships, available to any organization, firm, association, or other institution interested in forwarding the purpose and programs of ASIS.

Events in 1976. ASIS introduced a Jobline ("Job Hotline"), a special telephone service that gives brief announcements of current job openings 24 hours a day, 7 days a week. The telephone number is (202) 659-8132. ASIS also issued a 12-page booklet entitled "Looking for an Exciting Career in a Wide-Open Field? How About Considering Information Science?" In October ASIS launched a new looseleaf subscription update service on data bases entitled "Computer-Readable Bibliographic Data Bases: A Directory and Data Sourcebook." Subscribers are kept up to date on more than 300 data bases in the United States and Europe and are kept informed on new data bases that have been created (See also Data Bases, Computer-Readable). As part of its continuing education program, ASIS sponsored with The Catholic University of America a home-study course for library and information science professionals on Management and Technology in Libraries and Information Centers. The first course offered in the series is entitled "Motivation: A Vital Force in the Organization."

Meetings. The 39th Annual Meeting in San Francisco in October attracted more than 1,500

(Above) U.S. Representative Charlie Rose (Dem.-N.C.) giving the keynote address at the 1976 ASIS annual meeting in San Francisco. (Top) Outgoing ASIS President Melvin Day and incoming President Margaret Fischer at Council meeting with Managing Director Sam Beatty. ASIS financial problems and its future direction were the major topics.

attendees and 84 exhibitors. The theme was "Information * Politics": the asterisk in the title focused on the number of political connections of information and politics, information v. politics, and politics with information. The keynote address was given by Congressman Charlie Rose; the plenary session speakers were Aaron Wildavsky (University of California, Berkeley), Quincy Rodgers (Domestic Council, Committee on the Right of Privacy), John C. Gray (The British Library), and Alphonse Trezza (National Commission on Libraries and Information Science). ASIS's effort to reach out was well evidenced with 14 other groups or associations conducting sessions or meetings, including a special preconference institute sponsored by the Library of Congress on the impact of LC's major programs on the needs of the nation, as well as on the needs of Congress.

The fifth Mid-Year Meeting was held at Vanderbilt University, Nashville, in May; the theme was "Information Interaction." The keynote address by Arthur Miller of the Harvard University Law School launched a program that focused attention on the users of information and on the concepts of communication and information transfer as the process by which information ultimately becomes useful.

"America in the Information Age" was the theme for the ASIS Bicentennial Conference in Washington, D.C., in April. The conference attempted to assess the critical role of information in national policy formulation, governmental management, and planning for the future. Certified as an official Bicentennial event by the American Revolution Bicentennial Administration, the conference featured talk shows, artifacts displays, career counseling, a monologue by Hugh Sidey, a debate between Joseph Califano and James J. Kilpatrick, and a mock Congressional hearing. Hubert Humphrey and Edward Kennedy spoke. There was an on-line information center. SYNCON—a dynamic, democratic conference technique—brought together 11 groups of selected individuals for spontaneous discussion and idea sharing.

For 1977, ASIS planned two major national meetings: the sixth Mid-Year Meeting, May 19-21, Syracuse University, on the topic "The Value of Information"; and the 40th Annual Meeting, September 26 to October 1, in Chicago, on "Information Management for the 1980's."

Publications. Publications issued in 1976 included: *Journal of the American Society for Information Science*, vol. 27, no. 1-6; *Bulletin of the American Society for Information Science*, vol. 2, no. 6-10 and vol. 3, no. 1-2; *Annual Review of Information Science and Technology*, vol. 11 (1976); *Information * Politics: Proceedings of the ASIS Annual Meeting*, vol. 13 (1976); *Cumulative Index to the Annual Review of Information Science and Technology*, vol. 1-10 (1966-1975); and *ASIS Special Interest Group Technical Publication Series: SIG on Computerized Retrieval Services*, no. CRS-1, (June 1976).

Awards. ASIS presented its 1976 Award of Merit to Laurence B. Heilprin (University of Maryland) for his work in developing the foundations of information science, especially in relation to the application of cybernetics. The first Watson Davis Awards, in commemoration of the Society's founder and to honor members for continuous dedicated service to ASIS, were presented to Gerald J. Sophar (National Agricultural Library), Herbert S. White (Indiana University), Laurence B. Heilprin, Lois F. Lunin (Baltimore), and James M. Cretsos (Merrell-National Laboratories).

MARGARET T. FISCHER

ASIS Officers

PRESIDENT (October 1976-October 1977):
Margaret T. Fischer, Greenwich, Connecticut

PRESIDENT-ELECT:
Audrey N. Grosch, University of Minnesota, Minneapolis, Minnesota

PAST PRESIDENT:
Melvin S. Day, National Library of Medicine, Bethesda, Maryland

TREASURER:
Douglas S. Price, National Commission on Libraries and Information Science, Washington, D.C.

MANAGING DIRECTOR:
Samuel B. Beatty

Headquarters: 1155 16th St., N.W., Washington, D.C. 20036

American Theological Library Association

As an outgrowth of the Religious Books Round Table of the American Library Association and with the impetus of the American Association of Theological Schools (subsequently renamed the Association of Theological Schools in the United States and Canada), the American Theological Library Association (ATLA) was organized at Louisville, Kentucky, in 1947. Its purpose is to bring members into closer working relationships with each other, to support theological and religious librarianship, to improve theological libraries, and to interpret the role of such libraries in theological education in the United States and Canada.

Under the theme "Update" the 30th annual conference was held at Calvin Seminary, Grand Rapids, Michigan, June 21-25. It featured a continuing education workshop format of four full-day offerings and four half-day options. The workshop on cataloging and classification was coordinated by Doralyn Hickey,

Dean of the School of Librarianship, University of Wisconsin at Milwaukee. Paul Winkler, Chief Descriptive Cataloger at the Library of Congress and coeditor of the revised AACR cataloging rules, discussed developments in the code revision. Margaret Beckman, Librarian of the University of Guelph, led a workshop on library architecture. Theological library implications for Doctor of Ministry programs were explored in a workshop headed by John B. Trotti, Librarian of Union Theological Seminary, Richmond, Virginia. A workshop probing the future of "ATLA's Needs" was coordinated by John D. Batsel, Past President of ATLA and Librarian of Garrett-Evangelical Seminary, and R. Grant Bracewell, Librarian, Emmanuel College, University of Toronto. Half day offerings included the present status of "Copyright and Photocopying" by F. E. McKenna, "Library Systems" by Herman Miller, Inc., and views of religious publishing by the Grand Rapids-based religious publishers Eerdmans and Zondervans.

The 1977 conference was scheduled for the Vancouver School of Theology, Vancouver, British Columbia, June 20-24, with Gunther Strothotte as local host.

New Officers. Erich R. W. Schultz, Librarian of Wilfrid Laurier University, Waterloo, Ontario, assumed his term as President, having served previously in that capacity for nine months after the resignation of the former President. Elected Vice-President and President-elect was John B. Trotti. Doralyn Hickey and Donald Dayton, Librarian of North Park Theological Seminary, Chicago, were elected to the Board of Directors.

Under the ATLA Board of Microtext, Charles Willard, Executive Secretary and Librarian of Princeton Seminary, the feasibility of a cooperative theological microfilm library was investigated. A prospectus and invitation were prepared for release early in 1977. For a uniform charge of $250 annually members will be able to borrow any titles in the program and purchase any titles in the program at a 30 percent discount. Significant participation will allow a mass assault on the vast amount of theological literature published on rapidly disintegrating paper.

ATLA's Board of Indexing, publisher of the *Index for Religious Periodical Literature*, is making plans to index/abstract materials published in religious *Festschriften* and other occasional publications. The *Index* continues its biannual computer-produced index combining traditional subject indexing with brief abstracts as well as an index to book reviews. Under its editor, G. Fay Dickerson, the *Index* conducted a user survey during 1976 to ascertain how patrons search for information and to solicit suggestions for index terms and cross-reference needs. Upon compilation the data will be used to reflect actual user needs in format and terminology.

A new edition of *Aids to a Theological Library*, a compilation of reference tools in religious research, edited by John B. Trotti, has been published by ATLA. The original publication was edited by Raymond P. Morris and published by ATS.

A workshop on the problems of subject cataloging in theological libraries was held at St. Joseph's Priory, Washington, D.C., September 15–18. In addition to a tour of the Library of Congress Processing Department and discussions with Edward Blume, Chief of the Subject Cataloging Division of LC and Warren Kissinger, Subject Cataloger for Philosophy and Religion, participants heard a paper on "An Alternative Approach to Subject Cataloging in Theological Libraries," by Stephen L. Peterson, Librarian of Yale Divinity School. A substantive report of the workshop was published

American Theological Library Association

Dedication ceremony of the Pitts Theology Library, Candler School of Theology at Emory University, Atlanta, Georgia, in November 1976. It was formerly the Durham Chapel. The renovation enabled the library to house the 220,000-volume Hartford Seminary Library Collection purchased for $1,750,000.

in the ATLA November *Newsletter.*

On March 26 the Tennessee Theological Library Association held its organizational meeting at the United Methodist Publishing House in Nashville, Tennessee. Frank W. Robart, Director of the Divinity Library, Joint University Libraries in Nashville, was elected President. Although not officially affiliated with ATLA, the TTLA represents another local gathering of theological librarians of which nearly a dozen groups exist across the U.S. The ATLA Board of Directors is actively considering a structure which would constitute chapter status for such groups.

Membership in ATLA is open to all interested parties, but only professionals working in the field at the postbaccalaureate level are eligible for full membership status. And only accredited institutions at the postbaccalaureate level are eligible for institutional membership. Personal dues range from $10 to $30 based on salary and institutional dues from $30 to $65 based upon total operating expenditure. Membership increased by 4.5 percent during 1976 to a total of 585 in all categories.

Headquarters of ATLA are housed at the Lutheran Theological Seminary at Philadelphia. Its Executive Secretary, the Rev. David J. Wartluft, also serves as Assistant Librarian.

DAVID J. WARTLUFT

Anglo-American Cataloguing Rules

At the end of December 1976, the full draft text of a new edition of the *Anglo-American Cataloguing Rules* (AACR) was completed by the editors for final review before simultaneous publication by the American Library Association, the Canadian Library Association, and the (British) Library Association.

Two representatives from each of these associations and of the Library of Congress and the British Library met with the editors in Chicago in January 1975 as the Joint Steering Committee for Revision of AACR (JSCAACR) to commence work on a two-year project, funded by the Council on Library Resources and by the five organizations themselves. The object was to bring up to date what had quickly become established upon its publication in 1967 as probably the most widely used code of uniform practice for the creation of bibliographical records in the world. The widest possible participation in the project was sought by the setting up of associated national committees in each of the three participant countries, to examine rules and review editorial proposals with representative groups and teams of practising catalogers and catalog users; these committees sent their views and submissions to JSCAACR, which took them into consideration in advising and instructing the editors on the policies, shape, and form of the new edition.

In the United States, the major coordinating and investigative role was played by the Catalog Code Revision Committee (CCRC) of ALA/RTSD, which set up a number of Teams to share the task of scrutinizing the whole *North American Text* of AACR 1967, and consulted numerous other bodies related to ALA; the Library of Congress, as well as discussing common positions with CCRC, made a number of proposals on its own account. The Canadian Committee on Cataloguing combined the interests of the library associations and the National Library of Canada; and in Great Britain, a joint committee of the Library Association and the British Library acted similarly, watching especially over the interests represented by the separately published *British Text* of 1967.

Cataloging agencies in other parts of the world were also given an opportunity to comment on AACR as input to the project. Though the new edition still has the primary aim of meeting the needs of libraries and bibliographic agencies in North America and Great Britain, recent developments in international standardization and the potential of AACR as a basis for future development in other countries made it a matter of mutual interest that this dimension be taken into account.

Why do we need a new edition in 1977? First, experience with AACR over the last 10 years has revealed that, in spite of its general excellence, it has still a number of ambiguities and blemishes that need correction. Second, the full impact of catalog mechanization had not been felt before 1967; and its effects in recent years on the organization and services of bibliographic agencies, catalog departments, shared cataloging, and exchange of records have been so rapid and far-reaching that a new appraisal of AACR's effectiveness was urgently called for. In this environment, reconciliation of the two texts was one key factor; and a new approach was demanded both in relation to MARC-based systems and to the recent development of International Standards of Bibliographical Description (ISBD) to facilitate exchange and comprehension of bibliographic records. Third, the arrival in these same years of an extended range and volume of new nonbook materials and media into libraries of all kinds called for more comprehensive and up-to-date coverage of that field.

The draft text released for review in 1977, therefore, contained some extensive reorganization and some significant new rules and changes. But it maintained the basic principles and practices of AACR: this is to be a new edition, not a new code.

PETER R. LEWIS

ANSI

See *Standards; Organizations*

Archives

Public interest in the documents of the American heritage reached unprecedented levels in the Bicentennial year. Although it covered the whole span of American history from Thomas Jefferson to Richard Nixon, much attention was devoted to records of the period of the American Revolution. The number of individuals viewing the Declaration of Independence at the National Archives increased sharply from 5,000 a day in 1975 to about 25,000 a day in 1976. The Bicentennial celebration was also marked by the international exchange of a number of extraordinary documents. As its birthday gift to the United States, the United Kingdom loaned one of the four surviving copies of the Magna Carta, which was installed for the year in the Capitol Building. King Juan Carlos of Spain was the courier for a number of Spanish documents loaned to the Smithsonian Institution.

Response to interest in colonial documents approached the ridiculous. Entrepreneurs reprinted the Declaration of Independence on everything from placemats to simulated parchment. One startling Bicentennial surprise came from a New York Company. It offered for $15 a copy of the Declaration emblazoned on a bone vinyl shower curtain! The advertisement noted that "1776 showers later, you'll still get a kick reading the Declaration of Independence complete with signatures in flowing brown script." One historian dubbed commercialism of that sort "bicentennial schlock."

Nixon Case. The constitutionality of the 1974 law which placed former President Nixon's papers and tapes in government custody was upheld in a January 7, 1976, ruling by a three-judge panel of the U.S. District Court. The opinion of the Court affirmed the importance of preserving the basic record of the Nixon presidency, noting that "the temptation to distort or destroy the historical records might be thought by Congress to be less resistible in the event that the materials provided some foundation for allegations that misconduct took place." The 106-page court opinion stated that the review of presidential materials "requires both enormous expertise and enormous manpower," and that there was "adequate justification for the congressional decision to entrust custody of the documents and the responsibility to GSA (the National Archives) rather than Mr. Nixon. Chief executives are not by nature professional archivists, and they lack expertise as to what materials may prove to be of historical value." The panel did not dismiss lightly Nixon's claims of privacy. Instead, the decision pointed out that the record of archivists "for discretion in handling confidential materials is unblemished." Nixon's appeal of the decision to the Supreme Court was still pending at the end of the year.

Texas history dominates the lobby of the Lorenzo de Zavala State Archives and Library Building, Austin, Texas. The Bicentennial year brought increased public interest in American historical documents.

Ford and Carter Papers. Litigation over the Nixon materials created new interest in the status of the papers of other recent political figures. A special election year study made by the *SAA Newsletter* found that Gerald R. Ford was the first United States president who had made arrangements for the archival administration of his papers prior to assuming office. The Michigan Historical Collections of the University of Michigan began to actively collect Ford papers in 1963. With the exception of scrapbooks, however, no Ford materials were open for research in 1976. The papers of Jimmy Carter were far more accessible, with more than two-thirds of Carter's gubernatorial papers open for research at the Georgia Department of Archives and History. Only a small portion of the total volume of the Carter papers carried access restrictions.

An agreement reached in December 1976 between Ford, the University of Michigan, and the National Archives provided for continuous Federal custody of Ford's presidential materials. They, along with papers documenting his earlier career, will be administered by the National Archives in a Ford Library on the Ann Arbor campus.

Federal Officials. The 17-member National Study Commission on the Records and Documents of Federal Officials, created by Congress to make recommendations concerning the appropriate handling of the documents of all federal officials, held its first meeting in December 1975. The year 1976 was spent gathering data through studies conducted by consultants and members of the Commission staff, directed by Robert Brookhart. The Commission held public hearings in November and December 1976. The panel's recommendations to Congress and the White House were due in March 1977.

Archival Projects. Many archival projects were underway in 1976 to facilitate access to the records of the nation. The Social Welfare History Archives at the University of Minnesota, for example, was conducting a nationwide survey of more than 9,000 archives and manuscript repositories for sources documenting the history of women in the United States from the colonial period to the present. The results of the survey will be published as a multivolume guide designed to serve scholars in a variety of fields in the humanities and social sciences.

As one of its major Bicentennial projects, the Center for the Documentary Study of the American Revolution of the National Archives was preparing a detailed computer-assisted subject and name index and a descriptive chronological listing of the Papers of the Continental Congress. These papers, comprising some 200,000 pages of documentation, have been described as "one of the most precious bodies of records possessed by any government."

More than 10,000 institutions and organizations throughout the country were contacted during the year by the National Historical Publications and Records Commission as the first step toward the production of a directory of repositories of historical records. The guide, which will provide summary information on historical records of all types in as many repositories as possible as well as other basic information about each repository, is expected to include many more institutions than any prior publication in this field.

Funding. A coalition of archivists, librarians, historians, and others mounted a successful effort in 1976 to get Congress to provide financial assistance in fiscal year 1977 for the new records grant program of the National Historical Publications and Records Commission. Although the original budget submitted by the administration had not included the funding, Congress appropriated $1,000,000 for the records program which had been in existence for over a year with minimal funding.

In recognition of the increasing importance of outside funding for archival projects, the Society of American Archivists (SAA), with the support of the National Endowment for the Humanities (NEH), scheduled a conference to explore archival priorities on the campus of the University of Illinois at Chicago Circle in January 1977.

Conferences. A second NEH-funded conference was sponsored by the Joint AHA/OAH/SAA Committee on Historians and Archives in October 1976 in New Harmony, Indiana. Conferees directed their attention to three major themes: What are the rules governing access to the papers of public figures? How are they administered? What changes are needed? Alonzo Hamby, Ohio University, and Philip P. Mason, Wayne State University, delivered the keynote statements. Among the resolutions adopted by the conference group was one calling for the autonomy of the National Archives.

The largest gathering of professional archivists and manuscript curators in history was held in Washington, D.C., September 27–October 1, 1976, when approximately 900 members of the Society of American Archivists met concurrently with almost 600 delegates to the International Congress on Archives. The occasion marked the 40th anniversary meeting of the SAA and the 8th International Congress. ICA sessions, which were translated simultaneously into five languages, revolved around the theme "The Archival Revolution of Our Time." At the close of the ICA meeting, U.S.S.R. Archivist F. I. Dolgikh relinquished the President's gavel to Archivist of the United States James B. Rhoads. SAA's 1975–76 President, Elizabeth Hamer Kegan, of the Library of Congress, turned over her responsibilities to Robert M. Warner, University of Michigan.

During its Washington meeting, the International Congress on Archives approved the formation of an International Federation of Archival Associations as an ICA Section. The new Section will represent over 60 archival associations which now exist in some 25 countries. Helmut Dahm, President of the Association of German Archivists, led a meeting of association representatives which voted to ask for ICA recognition. A seven-nation steering committee was named to coordinate the organizational efforts of the new federation. Represented will be Poland, the Federal Republic of Germany, Brazil, Israel, Great Britain, the United States, and the Netherlands, where the world's oldest archival association was founded in 1891.

Theft. The problem of theft from archives continued to concern the profession in 1976 as it had in 1975. Positive steps were recorded in recovering stolen archival materials and in prosecuting thieves. Perhaps the most noteworthy event was the establishment by SAA of the National Register of Lost or Stolen Archival Materials, a list of items found to be missing since 1955. The Register is published bimonthly and sent to hundreds of manuscript dealers and libraries. In addition, Alex Ladenson, legal counsel for the SAA Archival Security Program, drafted model state legislation for the protection of library and archival property (*See also* Security Systems.)

ANN MORGAN CAMPBELL

Armed Forces Libraries

Navy Libraries. In 1976 the Naval General Library Program for the Navy and Marine Corps included 224 libraries ashore and 538 shipboard libraries. Management of resources and services underwent intensive study and review during the year. Newly constructed library buildings were occupied at the Naval Station, Pearl Harbor, the Naval Communication Station, Diego Garcia Island, and plans were developed for the library building at the new Naval Submarine Base, Bangor, Washington. Testing and validation were begun on a sound/slide library attendant training package for ships' libraries and small shore station libraries. Marine Corps libraries were heavily funded to provide library materials, including microforms, in support of off-duty education programs.

Army Libraries. More than 600 worldwide libraries served the needs of Department of Army personnel during 1976. These included 110 library systems that provide general service (public, college, and special) to military personnel, dependents, and civilians at Army installations and hospitals in the U.S. and overseas; 64 medical libraries; 73 technical libraries serving scientists, engineers, and other specialists, 26 academic libraries serving the military training schools/colleges (e.g., United States Military Academy at West Point and the Army War College); 266 law libraries and other special libraries (e.g., the Military History Research collection and the General Reference Library at the Pentagon). A formal career program insuring opportunities for training, development, and assignment exists for the 500 professional librarians working in the various Army libraries. A comprehensive study of the total Army Library community was completed in July 1976. Accepted study recommendations were to be implemented in 1977.

Air Force Libraries. The Air Force provides

The largest of the U.S. Navy's 538 floating libraries on board the nuclear powered aircraft carrier USS Nimitz.

unified library service under a central point of control in the Military Personnel Center, Randolph Air Force Base, Texas; the purpose is to prevent unnecessary duplication of materials and services. The Air Force library mission during 1976 provided a comprehensive program to meet both Air Force official needs and leisure-time reading requirements of its personnel. Three categories of libraries—base, technical, and academic—served personnel. Base libraries were provided at each base and consisted of a single library or library system composed of main, branch, and field libraries. Technical libraries met specialized requirements at the Air Force Accounting and Finance Center, Military Airlift Command, Air Force Systems Command, and the USAF Security Service. Air Force academic libraries are at the Air University, Alabama; the Air Force Institute of Technology, Ohio; the Air Force Academy, Colorado; and the School of Health Care Sciences.

AFLS. The Armed Forces Librarians Section of the American Library Association held its second annual preconference workshop in July 1976 in Chicago. Sponsored jointly with FLIRT (Federal Librarians Round Table), the workshops were well attended by federal librarians concerned with such aspects of federal library management as "Resource Allocation," conducted by Gordon Randall, Manager, IBM Research Division Library, and "Libraries, Unions, and the Legal Picture Today," conducted by Kevin Keaney of the National Agricultural Library. Officials who assumed office in July 1976 were Arlene Luster, President; Helen McClaughry, Vice-President, President-elect; Nathalie McMahon, Secretary; Nina Jacobs, Director-at-Large, and Bernard Strong, Army Representative. NATHALIE MCMAHON

Association of College and Research Libraries

The Association of College and Research Libraries (ACRL) is the Division of the American Library Association representing the libraries in those institutions supporting formal education above the secondary school level. ACRL also has the responsibility for librarianship as practiced in independent and other research libraries and specialized libraries.

Goals. ACRL promotes academic librarianship through its programs of identification and evaluation of book and non-book materials for academic libraries, its activities related to the bibliography, compilation, study and review of professional literature, its statements on library standards, and its concern for the role, function, and status of the academic librarian. Eleven sections (Agriculture and Biological Sciences, Anthropology, Art, Asian and African, College Libraries, Community and Junior College Libraries, Education and Behavioral Sciences, Law and Political Science, Rare Books and Manuscripts, Slavic and East European, and University Libraries), 75 committees, 2 discussion groups and 14 chapters provide the opportunity and the means by which the ACRL members develop policies and programs to further the provision of excellent library and information services to the postsecondary education, higher education, and the research library communities.

A committee of ACRL members under the direction of Le Moyne W. Anderson, Colorado State University, was reviewing ACRL's goals, priorities, and structures in 1976. A report on the survey of the ACRL membership, taken by the committee in order to help it formulate its recommendations on issues and the organizational structures of the Division, was published in May. The profile of the membership emerging from the survey is that about 60 percent of the membership is female, more than half of the members are under the age of 45, with the overwhelmingly largest group working in university libraries. The largest single category of ACRL members are in administrative posts, and the largest bloc of members lives in the New York/Pennsylvania/Delaware zip code areas. The committee will make its final report to the Board of Directors at the 1977 Annual ALA Conference.

Following much discussion over the goals and structures of bibliographic instruction within ACRL, the Ad Hoc Task Force on Bibliographic Instruction recommended that ACRL establish a section on bibliographic instruction. The matter will be acted upon by the ACRL Board of Directors at the 1977 Midwinter Meeting.

Academic Library Standards. In 1976 ACRL received a Bailey K. Howard/World Book Encyclopedia/ALA Goals Award to support the work of the Joint Committee on University Library Standards (Association of Research Libraries/Association of College and Research Libraries). Under the direction of Eldred Smith, University of Minnesota, the committee planned to complete its work on a statement of standards to be used by university libraries in 1977.

The American Historical Association became the first society based upon a learned discipline to endorse the *Joint Statement on Faculty Status for College and University Librarians,* when the Executive Committee of its Council approved in 1976 the resolution on the status of librarians.

Academic Library Collections. The bibliography of vocational-technical periodicals prepared by the Community and Junior College Libraries Section and published in *Choice* was reprinted in 1976 as No. 4 of the *Choice Bibliographical Essay Series. Vocational-Technical Periodicals for Community College Libraries* is designed to help librarians select periodicals to support vocational and technical programs in community and junior colleges.

The 10-year cumulated edition of *Choice* was published. The edition is a subject arrangement of all *Choice* reviews published in the first 10 years of the magazine.

In 1976 ACRL adopted a revision of the policy *Statement on Access to Original Research Materials in Libraries, Archives, and Manuscript Repositories,* first adopted in 1974, and the policy *Statement on the Reproduction of Manuscripts and Archives for Noncommercial Purposes.* Also prepared in 1976 was the final statement in the series of policy statements relating to manuscript and archival materials;

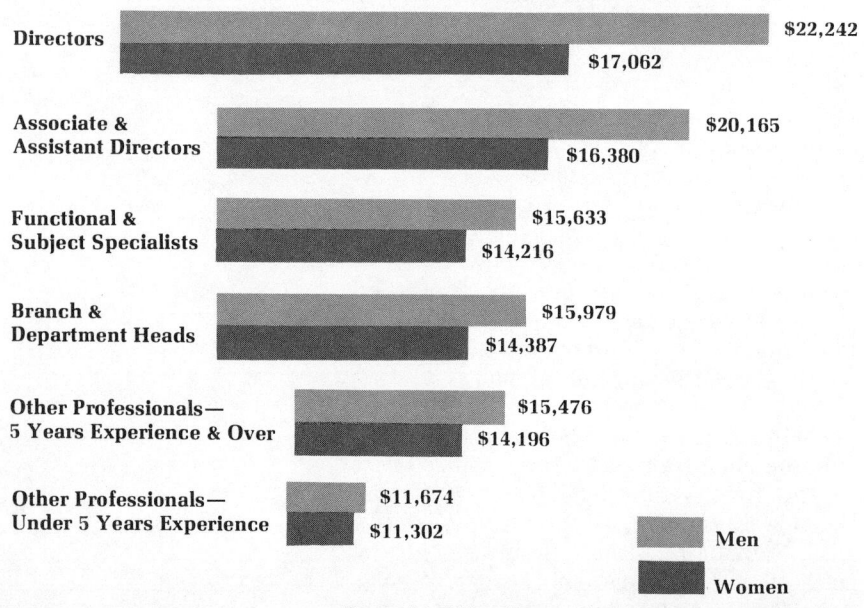

A Comparison Between the Average Salaries of Men and Women Professional Library Staff, 1975-76

- Directors: Men $22,242; Women $17,062
- Associate & Assistant Directors: Men $20,165; Women $16,380
- Functional & Subject Specialists: Men $15,633; Women $14,216
- Branch & Department Heads: Men $15,979; Women $14,387
- Other Professionals—5 Years Experience & Over: Men $15,476; Women $14,196
- Other Professionals—Under 5 Years Experience: Men $11,674; Women $11,302

Source: *C & RL News* (Oct. 1976)

the draft "Statement on the Reproduction of Manuscripts and Archives for Commercial Purposes" appears in the November 1976 issue of *College & Research Libraries News*. ACRL continues to work with the Association of Research Libraries and the Society of American Archivists to seek agreement on access policies.

Compensation Structures. ACRL continued its long-standing interest in the welfare and status of the academic librarian. (*Budget Classification and Compensation Plans for University and College Librarians* was published in 1929.) Under the direction of Richard Talbot, University of Massachusetts, and with the financial support of the Council on Library Resources, ACRL conducted a survey of academic library salaries. The results were published by ACRL in *Salary Structures of Librarians in Higher Education for the Academic Year 1975–76*. The survey showed that the salaries of librarians had not changed significantly since 1972-73, the pyramidal structure of salaries continues, and at every level the average salaries of women were less than men (Figure 1) although women comprise 61.5 percent of academic librarians.

In 1975/76 the average combined salary of all academic librarians was $14,207 (Table 1) although the average salaries varied according to the type of institution and affiliation (Tables 1 and 2). The ACRL survey found that, on the average, few librarians were paid as well as professors. As in earlier surveys, the 1975/76 salaries of academic librarians compared generally with those of assistant professors (Table 3).

Publications. As part of ACRL's program of making available to librarians and educators audiovisual presentations on topics of interest to the profession, ACRL distributed a video cassette of a panel discussion on "Problems with Evaluating Library Instruction," one of the programs that were a part of the Sixth Annual Conference on Library Orientation for Academic Libraries.

In 1976 ACRL established a new audiovisual publications series which will identify systematically and make available the audiovisual materials useful to the academic library community. An editor of the series and an editorial board will be appointed early in 1977.

Mary Frances Collins, Editor of *College & Research Libraries News* since January 1975, resigned effective with the January 1977 issue. John Crowley, State University College in Oneonta, New York, was appointed to succeed her.

The proceedings of two ACRL preconferences were published in 1976. *Collective Bargaining in Higher Education; Its Implication for Governance and the Faculty Status for Librarians,* edited by Millicent Abell, State University of New York at Buffalo, and published as No. 38 in the *ACRL Publications in Librarianship* series, contains the proceedings of the preconference on collective bargaining sponsored in 1975 by the Academic Status Committee.

Eighteenth-Century English Books, edited by Hendrick Edelman, Cornell University, pre-

Association of College and Research Libraries

Table 1: Average Salaries for Professional Library Staff Members by Type of Institution and by Affiliation, 1975–76*

Type of Institution	All Combined	Public	Independent	Chruch-Related
All combined	$14,207	$14,927	$13,104	$11,555
Type I: universities	14,036	14,428	13,523	12,086
Type II: five-year colleges	14,213	15,029	11,934	11,315
Type III: four-year colleges	12,479	14,710	11,286	11,186
Type IV: two-year colleges	17,130	17,331	10,970	10,826

*These data include salaries of 10,817 professional library staff members and exclude 2,240 head librarians, associate and assistant directors, and medical and law branch librarians.

Table 2: Average Salaries of Professional Library Staff Members by Type of Institution, Affiliation, and Position, 1975–76

Position	All Combined	Public	Private Independent	Church-Related
All combined				
Director	$20,387	$22,878	$19,522	$15,741
Associate/Assistant director	18,528	19,684	18,405	13,035
Specialist	14,992	15,469	13,920	12,392
Branch and department head	14,915	15,956	13,918	11,780
Other professional: five years and over	14,560	15,114	13,352	11,574
Other professional: under five years	11,408	11,801	10,824	10,018
Type I: universities				
Director	$27,966	$29,844	$27,166	$21,703
Associate/Assistant director	21,381	21,757	21,447	17,461
Specialist	14,883	15,077	14,530	13,277
Branch and department head	15,461	16,006	14,955	13,068
Other professional: five years and over	14,065	14,425	13,529	11,619
Other professional: under five years	11,224	11,470	10,942	10,249
Type II: five-year colleges				
Director	$21,347	$23,991	$19,250	$17,229
Associate/Assistant director	17,774	19,323	14,660	11,946
Specialist	14,520	15,231	11,813	11,835
Branch and department head	14,405	15,519	12,359	11,475
Other professional: five years and over	15,297	15,805	12,151	11,380
Other professional: under five years	11,628	12,070	10,198	9,607
Type III: four-year colleges				
Director	$16,104	$19,826	$15,626	$14,965
Associate/Assistant director	12,781	16,308	12,350	11,564
Specialist	13,214	15,406	10,933	11,841
Branch and department head	12,300	14,607	11,515	11,222
Other professional: five years and over	13,968	15,721	11,621	11,578
Other professional: under five years	10,703	11,968	10,290	9,641
Type IV: two-year colleges				
Director	$18,680	$19,958	$12,464	$11,148
Associate/Assistant director	15,368	15,682	*	*
Specialist	17,648	17,735	*	*
Branch and department head	16,916	17,142	11,403	10,674
Other professional: five years and over	19,056	19,219	*	*
Other professional: under five years	14,092	14,319	*	*

*Sample too small to be meaningful

Association of College and Research Libraries

sented the papers of the 1975 Rare Books and Manuscripts Section's preconference held in San Francisco.

Various chapters of ACRL issued audio and video tapes of chapter program meetings and reported on these sponsored programs. *Retrenchment in Higher Education*, available from the Film Library of the State University of New York at Albany, presents a discussion held during a meeting of ACRL's Eastern New York Chapter on the issues facing libraries in the time of shrinking budgets.

The ALA Executive Board accepted unanimously the report of the Ad Hoc Committee on *Choice*, chaired by Thomas J. Galvin. The Committee, charged to study the management and fiscal issues relative to *Choice*, included in its recommendations that ALA reaffirm that *Choice* is a publication of ACRL and that ACRL be assigned managerial, fiscal, and editorial responsibility for the magazine.

At the end of 1976 Richard Gardner announced his resignation as Editor of *Choice*, effective June 1977, to accept a professorship in the Graduate School of Libraries and Information Science, UCLA.

Internship Program. The Andrew W. Mellon Foundation extended its support of the Academic Library Internship Program to December 1978. In addition to the four librarians participating in the program in 1976, funds were available to support up to six more interns in 1977–78.

Programs and Institutions. At the invitation of ACRL's New England Chapter, the ACRL Board of Directors voted to hold the first national ACRL Conference in Boston, November 8-11, 1978. The conference will be devoted solely to programs of interest to academic librarians. George Parks, University of Rhode Island, will be conference chairman. Richard D. Johnson, State University College at Oneonta, New York, chairs the program committee. Carol Ishimoto, Harvard University, chairs the local arrangements committee, and Willis Bridgegam, Amherst College, is conference treasurer. The New England Chapter and the

Table 3: Percentage Distribution of Faculty and Professional Library Staff Members and Their Average Salaries by Type of Institution, Affiliation, and Position, 1975–76 (Standard Academic Year of Nine Months for Faculty, Twelve Months for Librarians)*

Position	Percent of Staff	All Combined	Public	Private Independent	Church-Related
Type I: universities					
Director	2.9%	$27,966	$29,844	$27,166	$21,703
Associate/Assistant director	5.8	21,381	21,757	21,447	17,461
Specialist	14.0	14,883	15,077	14,530	13,277
Branch and department head	29.1	15,461	16,006	14,955	13,068
Other professional: five years and over	29.0	14,065	14,425	13,529	11,619
Other professional: under five years	19.3	11,224	11,470	10,942	10,249
AAUP category I: universities					
Professor	34.9%	$24,590	$24,150	$26,540	$22,220
Associate professor	27.4	18,060	18,010	18,550	17,230
Assistant professor	29.3	14,670	14,690	14,740	14,150
Instructor and lecturer	8.4	11,540	11,510	11,750	11,600
Type II: five-year colleges					
Director	9.6%	$21,347	$23,991	$19,250	$17,229
Associate/Assistant director	7.5	17,774	19,323	14,660	11,946
Specialist	9.6	14,520	15,231	11,813	11,835
Branch and department head	41.6	14,405	15,519	12,359	11,475
Other professional: five years and over	19.3	15,297	15,805	12,151	11,380
Other professional: under five years	12.3	11,628	12,070	10,198	9,607
AAUP category IIA: five-year colleges					
Professor	25.4%	$22,010	$22,500	$21,010	$19,490
Associate professor	29.8	17,340	17,680	16,700	15,650
Assistant professor	34.3	14,320	14,570	13,800	13,130
Instructor and lecturer	10.5	11,730	11,950	11,360	10,690
Type III: four-year colleges					
Director	24.0%	$16,104	$19,826	$15,626	$14,965
Associate/Assistant director	9.1	12,781	16,308	12,350	11,564
Specialist	7.1	13,214	15,406	10,933	11,841
Branch and department head	44.5	12,300	14,607	11,515	11,222
Other professional: five years and over	9.1	13,968	15,721	11,621	11,578
Other professional: under five years	6.1	10,703	11,968	10,290	9,641
AAUP category IIB: four-year colleges					
Professor	22.7%	$19,270	$21,460	$20,430	$17,640
Associate professor	26.9	15,300	17,340	15,570	14,160
Assistant professor	36.9	12,930	14,350	13,020	12,100
Instructor and lecturer	13.4	10,820	11,740	10,900	10,180

*Faculty salary data is from Table 3 of the 1975–1976 AAUP Salary Survey.

ACRL Officers

PRESIDENT (July 1976–June 1977):
Connie R. Dunlap, University Librarian, Duke University, Durham, North Carolina.

VICE-PRESIDENT/PRESIDENT-ELECT:
Eldred R. Smith, Director of Libraries, University of Minnesota, Minneapolis, Minnesota.

IMMEDIATE PAST PRESIDENT:
Louise Giles, Dean of Learning Resources, Macomb County Community College, Warren, Michigan (Died December 31, 1976.)

EXECUTIVE SECRETARY:
Beverly P. Lynch, 1972–1976
(Resigned January 1, 1977.)

Membership (August 31, 1976): 8,473
   Section Membership (August 31, 1976)
   Agriculture & Biological Sciences   947
   Art   1,027
   Law & Political Science   1,087
   Slavic & East European   695
   Education & Behavioral Sciences   1,424
   Asian & African   824
   Anthropology   777
   Community & Jr. College Libraries   1,608
   University Libraries   4,068
   College Libraries   2,800
   Rare Books & Manuscripts   1,580

other ACRL chapters have pledged their cooperation in this endeavor. The proposed conference will be the first national meeting ACRL has held outside the scheduled meetings of ALA.

The 1976 Rare Books and Manuscripts Section preconference met in Ann Arbor and addressed the theme of "Maps and Atlases: A New World in Rare Book and Manuscript Collections." Conference proceedings will be issued early in 1977.

At the ALA Centennial Conference, Julian Bond addressed the membership of ACRL on the subject of ethnicity. Other ACRL programs at the conference were papers by Nettie Lee Benson and Edwin Wolf on "The Development of Ethnic Collections of Rare Books and Manuscripts," a discussion on "The Theft of Manuscripts from Libraries and Archives," and a consideration of "Urban University Libraries in Crisis."—BEVERLY P. LYNCH

Association of Research Libraries

1976 was a year of growth and change for the Association of Research Libraries in a number of areas.

In May John G. Lorenz, former Deputy Librarian of Congress, became the ARL Executive Director, succeeding John P. McDonald. In July Suzanne Frankie was promoted to Associate Executive Director, and in September, James L. Beattie joined the staff as ARL Research Specialist.

During the year the number of members in the ARL increased from 101 to 105, including 94 university libraries and 11 nonuniversity libraries. The number of Canadian members increased from 5 to 8.

Because of the number and types of institutions seeking membership in the Association and the changing scene in higher education, the Association membership in October voted to establish a Task Force to review the criteria for ARL membership, with the specific objectives of achieving an appropriate balance between quantitative and qualitative factors applicable to research services and collections in both academic and non-academic libraries. Pending recommendations from this Task Force, a moratorium was declared on the admission of new members. The work of the Task Force on ARL Membership will be coordinated with that of the ARL/ACRL Committee on University Library Standards, which will issue draft standards in 1977.

As the result of an assessment of the role of the ARL Board, Commissions, Committees, Task Forces, and Office Staff, the five Commissions of the Association were dissolved. The ARL Board assumed Commission responsibilities for considering the role, objectives, and future programs of the ARL in the context of emerging issues facing research libraries. At a special meeting in September the Board considered a number of program priority areas: (1) establishment of a national periodicals lending library; (2) library service and user access to library resources; (3) financial concerns of research libraries; (4) preservation of library materials; (5) role of the research library in the

Association of Research Libraries

Table 1: ARL Membership Criteria for University Libraries, 1976

Categories	Median 1975–1976	Percentage	Required Minimum
Volumes in library	1,592,582	50	774,795
Volumes added—gross	78,085	50	38,980
Number of professional staff (FTE)	59	50	31
Number of total staff (FTE)	226	50	115
Expenditures for library materials and binding	1,268,788	50	$ 82,540
Expenditures for salaries and wages	2,007,356	50	$ 956,703
Total operating expenditures	3,490,754	50	$ 1,683,349
Number of current periodicals	18,876	50	9,379

Table 2: Collections and Interlibrary Loans, ARL Members, 1975–1976

	University Libraries[1]	Nonuniversity Libraries[2]
Volumes in library	193,530,258	37,171,252
Volumes added (net)	8,237,834	1,156,553
Total microform units in library	87,592,794	9,054,102
Interlibrary loans		
Loaned	1,910,439	1,260,439
Borrowed	495,793	76,214
Current serials	2,362,260	376,544

[1] 88 members of ARL   [2] 11 members of ARL

Table 3: Expenditures, ARL Members, 1975–1976

	University Libraries[1]	Nonuniversity Libraries[2]
Library materials and binding	$125,940,270	$ 12,549,811
Salaries and wages (excluding fringe benefits)	$243,412,175	$108,315,972
Other operating expenditures	$ 35,985,590	$ 51,944,247
Total operating expenditures	**$415,772,233**	**$174,730,868**

[1] 88 members of ARL   [2] 11 members of ARL

Table 4: Personnel, ARL Members, 1974–75

	University Libraries[1]	Nonuniversity Libraries[2]
Professional staff (full-time equivalent)	6,946	4,121
Nonprofessional staff (FTE)	13,920	3,247
Student assistants (FTE)	5,188	316
Total staff (FTE)	**26,054**	**7,684**

[1] 88 members of ARL   [2] 11 members of ARL

Source: *ARL Statistics 1975–76. A Compilation of Statistics from the Ninety-nine Members of the Association of Research Libraries.* Compiled by Suzanne Frankie.

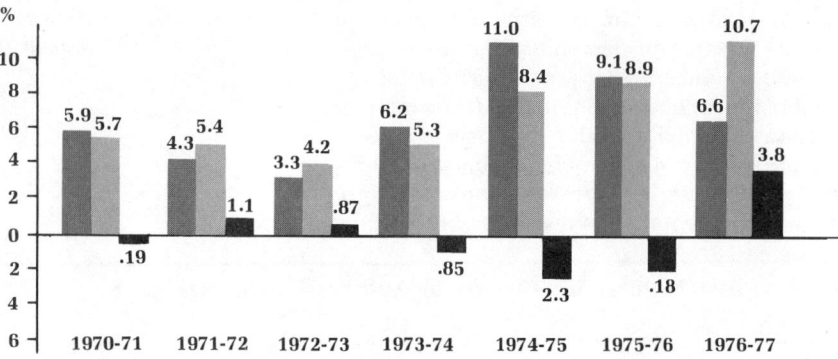

UNIVERSITY LIBRARY SALARIES AND THE COST OF LIVING
(Yearly increases in median salary as compared with increases in the consumer price index)

■ % Increase in Real Salary   ■ % Increase in CPI   ■ % Increase in Median Salary

Source: ARL Salary Survey, 1975–76

ing 1976 to support the work of the ARL Center for Chinese Research Materials in providing resources and bibliographic services for studies of contemporary China.

In addition the ARL Office of University Library Management Studies received a grant from the Mellon Foundation to conduct an analysis of collection development in research libraries. — SUZANNE FRANKIE

ARL Officers

PRESIDENT (October 1976–October 1977):
Edward C. Lathem

VICE PRESIDENT/PRESIDENT-ELECT
Ray Frantz, Jr.

EXECUTIVE DIRECTOR:
John G. Lorenz

ASSOCIATE EXECUTIVE DIRECTOR:
Suzanne Frankie

Headquarters: 1527 New Hampshire Ave., NW, Washington, D.C., 20036

---

national information system; (6) use of microforms; (7) networking; and (8) application of technology in research libraries. Program statements will be developed for each of these areas.

The ARL Committee on Interlibrary Loan conducted a survey late in 1976 to solicit information on the current policies and plans of ARL libraries regarding the charging of fees for interlibrary loan services. The results will be published in 1977.

Other membership activity included the establishment of a Task Force on ARL Statistics and a Task Force on National Library Network Development.

Many years of Association work in two legislative areas culminated in 1976 in the passage of the Copyright Revision Act and the Higher Education Act, which includes an amended Title II-C aimed at strengthening the resources of the major research libraries.

The theme of the membership meeting in May 1976 was "Research Libraries and Cooperative Systems." Trends in network development, national planning, network costs, management, and impact on research libraries were among the topics discussed.

In observance of America's Bicentennial, the October membership meeting was the occasion for the opening of "76 United Statesiana," a special exhibition of 76 works of American scholarship relating to America. A special catalog was published to commemorate the exhibition. It was anticipated that ARL libraries and others would replicate the exhibition in their own institutions. The program for the meeting included keynote speeches on American scholarship and the heritage of research libraries by Louis Wright, of the Council on Library Resources, and Gordon N. Ray, President of the John Simon Guggenheim Memorial Foundation.

Grants from NEH, the Mellon Foundation, and the State Department were received dur-

Association of State Library Agencies

Multitype library cooperation dominated the concerns of the Association of State Library Agencies (ASLA) in 1976. Recognition of the role of the state library agency in facilitating and coordinating interlibrary cooperation is reflected in every facet of the Division's activity. A nationwide survey of interlibrary cooperation activities was conducted and published; a review of the 1970 standards was started; a state aid study committee was organized; a continuing education program for personnel interchanges in all types of libraries was successfully launched; studies were begun on the relationship between the state library agencies and health information libraries as well as of state administration of library service to the blind and physically handicapped. Altogether it was an active and productive year for ASLA and its growing membership.

Priorities Identified. At Midwinter the ASLA Board of Directors identified five major priorities for the Division. For the purposes of immediate and future planning, issue statements were formulated on each of the priorities to serve as guidelines for the Officers and Directors in evaluating the ASLA program. They are:

Interlibrary Cooperation-Issue: To what extent can ASLA serve as the ALA "home" for all persons concerned with multitype library cooperation and activities?

Continuing Education-Issue: How can ASLA meet the continuing education needs of its members? (e.g., staff exchange program, preconference and conference programs, etc.)

Clearinghouse Functions-Issue: How can ASLA best offer its members an opportunity for interchange of ideas and information?

New Program Directions-Issue: How can the members best input their ideas for new ASLA leadership and carry out such programs? (e.g., model studies, policy statements, library funding, role of state agencies.

Membership Promotion-Issue: How can ASLA best expand its membership base to insure its continuation within ALA without losing its focus on the concerns of state library agencies?

A brief questionnaire was developed to enable the ASLA membership to rank the priorities and to suggest other concerns for the Board to consider. This questionnaire was distributed with the March issue of the *ASLA President's Newsletter* and is sent to each new member of the Division. Response has been high, providing the Division with an ongoing mechanism to review the interests and needs of the members and allowing members to take an active role in setting policy.

Within the priorities established for ASLA, interlibrary cooperation has generated great interest. *The ASLA Report on Interlibrary Cooperation*, published in June, was based on results from a survey conducted by a Subcommittee of the Interlibrary Cooperation Committee in the Spring of 1976. This comprehensive survey marks the first attempt to identify and document interlibrary cooperative activities in each of the 50 states and U.S. Territories. The Report is arranged by state and territory and contains information on state level organizations responsible for interlibrary cooperation activities as well as single and multitype library systems, networks, and consortia. Also included is information on funding patterns by state and territorial library agencies for interlibrary cooperation functions; communication devices and network hardware; machine readable information data bases; interlibrary services to special user groups; and legal bases and barriers for multitype library cooperation. A matrix showing the number of U.S. libraries by type appears in the appendices. The ASLA Report is designed to complement another ongoing ASLA survey, *The State Library Agencies: A Survey Project Report*, compiled and edited by Donald B. Simpson (Chicago: The Association of State Library Agencies, 1975; third edition now in progress and scheduled for distribution in May 1977).

At the Annual Conference the ASLA Planning Committee was charged by the Board of Directors to develop a Position Statement on Interlibrary Cooperation. This statement will constitute the Division's testimony at the 1977 Midwinter Hearing of the ALA Committee on Organization which will consider a "home" for Intertype Library Cooperation within the American Library Association. Unanimously adopted by the ASLA Board of Directors on December 13, the ASLA Position Statement asserts that the Division "is the unit within the American Library Association best able to promote and represent the interests and activities of libraries involved in statewide coordination, interlibrary cooperation, and networking," by documenting that "ASLA represents the responsibilities and activities of statewide planning, coordination, and development, emphasizing the interdependence of all types of libraries."

A new Standards Review Committee, chaired by W. Lyle Eberhart, State Librarian, Wisconsin, was established to consider the revision of *The Standards for the Library Functions at the State Level* (Chicago: ALA, 1970). Using the 1970 Standards as a point of departure, this committee determined that the development of state and multistate networks, and the priority on network development in the NCLIS National Program, indicate that expanded emphasis should be given in the Standards to networking and multitype cooperative activities. A publication target date has been set for 1979.

LPI Program. The Library Personnel Interchange (LPI) program was developed and tested in the New England states by a joint committee of ASLA and the Regional Planning Committee of the New England Library Association (NELA). Designed to provide library personnel at any level to gain experience in a different work situation by observing new practices, comparing techniques, and generally broadening horizons, the LPI is an exciting new dimension in staff development. The goal of the LPI program is "to share human and information resources among all types of libraries."

Program objectives are:

To provide a fresh perspective on library problems and their possible solutions.

To enrich the programs of the library and its services to all types of users.

To familiarize librarians with specialized resources in the field.

To stimulate, promote, and demonstrate the advantages of interlibrary cooperative activities and networking.

To improve library operations.

To afford opportunities for mutually beneficial exchanges of skills and experiences between host and visiting participant.

To foster and improve job satisfaction and staff morale.

To provide a basis for the evaluation of training and orientation procedures.

The New England Library Board serves as the coordinating agency for the New England states. ASLA is facilitating the development of the program in other areas as interest is generated.

The Committee for Comparative Study of the Administrative Processes in State Library Agencies selected the budgetary process as the first administrative area to examine. A survey

Association of State Library Agencies

instrument was developed and sent to each state library agency and U.S. Territory in December. The Committee will analyze and edit the survey results at the 1977 Midwinter Meeting, working toward the publication of a special report.

Because of the increasing interest in information concerning state aid, the Division established a State Aid Study Committee to: (1) collect information about existing state aid programs; (2) collect information about proposed changes or developments in state aid programs; (3) identify published sources of information about state aid and state aid programs; (4) establish a clearinghouse for information about state aid programs; and (5) disseminate information about state aid programs through the publication of a special report.

Because of the strong response to the Committee Volunteer forms developed for the membership in 1976, the ASLA Board of Directors sanctioned the formation of four new discussion groups. They are Continuing Education, General Consultants, Interlibrary Cooperation, and State Library Agencies Fiscal Management.

The ASLA Program for the Centennial Conference was entitled "Information Delivery Systems in the Next Century" featuring futurist and University of Minnesota professor, Arthur M. Harkins. This program was videotaped and is available to interested persons through the ASLA office for a postage and handling charge of $10.

COSLA Activities. The ASLA leadership and staff cooperate with the Chief Officers of State Library Agencies (COSLA), organized in 1974 as an independent organization of 50 men and women who head state agencies responsible for library development. Its membership consists solely of those top library officers of the 50 states, variously designated as state librarian, director, commissioner, or executive secretary. ASLA program concerns in several fields are broader than those of COSLA and most chief officers are also ASLA members; therefore, communication is maintained between the two organizations at several levels. Specific results of cooperation between the two organizations are the *State Library Agencies: A Survey Project Report*, the sharing of directory and statistical information and plans for coordination of such data gathering, and discussion of legislative issues. As a means of assuring communication and reciprocity between ASLA and COSLA the President and Executive Secretary of each organization meet regularly with the board of the other organization.

Merger Proposed. It is significant that ASLA is one of only three ALA divisions to increase in personal members during 1976. This can be directly correlated to the development and refinement of program priorities established by the membership and Board of Directors and the resultant activity generated. However, despite the ASLA growth in membership, ASLA is still the smallest division within ALA. Because of the mandate to become a self-supporting unit by August, 1977, as stipulated in the Dues Schedule Transition document, the Boards of ASLA and the Health and Rehabilitative Library Services Division appointed a joint committee of their Boards to explore their commonalities of interests. This Committee met in Chicago on November 30–December 1. After carefully reviewing alternatives to division status within ALA, it was the unanimous decision of the Joint Committee that they recommend to their respective Boards a proposal for a merged division representing the interests and concerns of both groups. This proposal was unanimously adopted by both Boards on December 13 and will be submitted to the ALA Council at the 1977 Midwinter Meeting.

The *ASLA President's Newsletter*, under the editorship of Irma R. Bostian, Illinois State Library, has developed over the last several years into a valuable desk reference tool. Directories of the Chief Officers of State Library Agencies, Specialized Consultant Staff, Salary Data, COSLA Minutes, and other features appear regularly in the publication. In 1976, the Newsletter included signed articles for the first time.

The ASLA Executive Office provides a variety of information services for ASLA and ALA members, ALA staff, and others interested in and involved with the work of state library agencies and intertype library cooperation. The Executive Secretary coordinates the work of the Division and facilitates the clearinghouse function.   MARY R. POWER

ASLA Officers

PRESIDENT: (July 1976–June 1977)
Barratt Wilkins, Assistant Director, State Library of Florida, R. A. Gray Building, Tallahassee, Florida 32304

VICE-PRESIDENT/PRESIDENT-ELECT:
Donald B. Simpson, Director, Bibliographical Center for Research, 1357 Broadway, Denver, Colorado 80203

EXECUTIVE SECRETARY:
Mary R. Power, Executive Secretary, ASLA, American Library Association, 50 East Huron Street, Chicago Illinois 60611

Membership (August 31, 1976): 1,240 (385 personal and 855 organizational)

Audiovisual Media

See *Films; Filmstrips; Multimedia Materials; Recordings, Sound.*

Automation

In contrast to 1975, which had seen relatively few major developments but rather continued slow and steady growth, library automation in 1976 moved forward several steps in a number of areas, particularly in interface between the public and private sectors of the information community. Virtually all the projects initiated in 1975 or described in last year's *ALA Yearbook* continued to grow at a healthy pace. The newly appointed Librarian of Congress, Daniel Boorstin, began his tenure at the Library of Congress (LC) at the end of 1975; in early 1976, it was clear that he planned to make a number of major changes in the organization of LC as an institution. Some changes affected those departments of the Library of Congress that have been most heavily involved in the specification and production of automated tools for the library community. Probably the most unusual news about automation in 1976 was that events tended to focus on institutions other than libraries—commercial organizations, networks, or consortia which provide services or products for libraries. In addition to the Library of Congress, 1976 activities are reviewed here under machine-based reference services, circulation systems, library networks, and news.

LIBRARY OF CONGRESS

Henriette Avram, who had been Chief of the MARC Development Office since its inception, was made Special Assistant to the Librarian of Congress for Networking. By the end of the calendar year, the post of Head of the MARC Development Office had still not been filled. Since a task force had been assigned to study the organization of the Library of Congress, one can assume that it is possible that no permanent assignment will be made until the task force has made its recommendations; however, Avram's move to the Office of the Librarian makes it a distinct possibility that the MARC Development Office will become an operational data processing office rather than fill the role of an operations as well as a development unit as it has in the past.

MARC Expansion. The expansion of the MARC distribution service to cover western European languages continued in 1976. By the end of 1976, all western European languages were being covered by the distribution service and plans called for all nonideographic languages to be included in the service by 1980.[1] The experimental project involving on-line exchange of data between the Library of Congress and the Research Libraries Group was funded for its first 18-month phase early in 1976, and was proceeding smoothly. The first goal of this project would allow the RLG computer to search for and retrieve data from the Library of Congress computer. For users within the Library of Congress itself, terminals were made available for accessibility to the MARC data base. The terminals are in the LC reading rooms together with instructions on use; users of the Library are able to go to the terminals and search the data base by any of several access points.

Despite the extremely slow start of the CONSER project (CONversion of SERials), sponsored by the Council on Library Resources, input of serials data into the OCLC data base was proceeding by the middle of the year, and in June the Library of Congress began to authenticate the bibliographic records for serials within its purview and prepare them for distribution through the regular MARC serials distribution service. As of the middle of the year, approximately 125,000 titles were available for authentication. The initial intent of the CONSER project was to create a serials data base of approximately 200,000 titles for United States and Canadian libraries. With the

---

Selected personnel changes in automation, 1976

This person	left	to go to
Henriette Avram	MARC Development Office, LC	Librarian's Office, LC
C. David Batty	McGill University	University of Maryland
Dennis Beaumont	CLSI	Information Design, Inc.
Grover Burgis	CAPTAIN network	
Charles Davis	University of Michigan	University of Alberta
Maryann Duggan	WICHE	Veteran's Administration, Idaho
Ralph Franklin	Washington Library Network	Nonlibrary career
Margaret Johnson	University of California	Ohio College Library Center
Ronald Miller	NELINET	California Library Authority for Systems and Services (CLASS)
Eleanor Montague	WICHE	University of California, Riverside
Elizabeth Pan	Catholic University	U.S. Patent Office
Karl Pearson	System Development Corporation	WICHE
Joseph Price	National Serials Data Program	LC Serial Records Division
John Rather	Library of Congress	retirement
Lucia Rather	LC MARC Development Office	LC Processing Division
David Remington	LC Processing Division	LC Catalog Distribution Division
William Scholz	New Mexico State Library	Consulting
Joshua Smith	American Society for Information Science	Herner & Co.
Fran Spigai	Oregon State System of Higher Education	Lockheed Information Systems
Madeleine Stovel	BALLOTS (Stanford)	
Ruth Tighe	NELINET	NCLIS
Sue Tyner	University of Cincinnati	University of California

Automation

progress of the project, the Council on Library Resources announced that it would fund the Library of Congress to take over administration of the CONSER project as of 1977.

COMARC Project. In another cooperative data base building effort, COMARC, the Library of Congress is accepting machine-readable records based on Library of Congress catalog card data from certain preselected libraries, and authenticating these records for redistribution through the MARC service. In 1976 the institutions participating in this program were Northwestern University Library, the Washington Library Network, and the Information Dynamics Corporation. Review of the machine-readable records created by several other institutions was in progress in order to determine their suitability for inclusion in the COMARC program.

RAL. In another team effort of the Library of Congress and the Council on Library Resources, the consulting firm of R & D Consultants has been retained to study the expansion of the Register of Additional Locations (RAL) data base by cooperative means involving the identification of machine-readable data bases from which location reports could be obtained for the Library of Congress. A survey of potential sources of machine-readable data bases was to be conducted, followed by on-site interviews with the most likely prospects for these data bases. The results of the study were to assist the Library in expanding the RAL file as rapidly as possible by capitalizing on existing machine-readable data bases. The greatly enlarged RAL file would then be the foundation upon which an interlibrary loan network in the U.S. could be based. A related study involves a survey for a microform edition of the Register of Additional Locations. By using computer output microform technology, LC anticipated being able to distribute this publication on a much more timely basis than has been possible in the past. The 1976 survey was to assist the Library in determining the desired frequency of the microform edition, the need for printed RAL with its present scope and cumulation pattern, and the requirements of the institutions using the RAL.

In 1976, the Information Science and Automation Division cosponsored with the Library of Congress two institutes on the topic of processing and automation at the Library of Congress. They were very well attended, and it was apparent that follow-ups would be called for in the future.

MACHINE-BASED REFERENCE SERVICE

In 1975 it was observed that libraries were adopting machine-based reference services somewhat late and rather slowly. In 1976 the trend toward use of such services has taken on

(Right) Alphonse Trezza, Executive Director of NCLIS, speaking at the "Automation for Libraries" conference sponsored by the Alabama Library Association, the Montgomery Public Library, and the Alabama Public Library Service. (Above) Conference participants included, from left, Montgomery Councilman Larry Dixon, Alabama Public Library Service Director Anthony Miele, and Lt. Col. Thomas Bennett of the Air Force Data Automation Agency.

greater speed and enthusiasm. Despite the high cost of providing the services, libraries of all types are becoming anxious to determine how best to incorporate this type of information use into their services. The cost of the NSF-funded DIALIB project in northern California has been described in an article by Cooper and DeWath indicating that a cost of a search, exclusive of communication and equipment cost, might be somewhere in the area of $25 to $30 per search, certainly a formidable cost for most libraries.[2] For that reason, most libraries adopting machine-based reference services have found it necessary to pass on at least some, if not all, of the cost to their users. The principle of charging for access to information is not easy for many librarians to accept. The issue of fees for information was argued in 1976 just as vehemently as the copyright question; however, an informal survey taken at a meeting of the ARL librarians in May 1976 indicated that at least 75 percent of the libraries give their users access to one or more of the on-line reference data base services.[3]

SUNY-Albany was for years the location of a second operational unit of the MEDLINE system, backing up the National Library of Medicine in its access to medical literature. In 1976 the SUNY-Albany center for MEDLINE service disbanded, and the computer programs and people involved in the MEDLINE service reorganized themselves into a not-for-profit company called Bibliographic Retrieval Service (BRS), intended to compete with System Development Corporation and Lockheed to offer on-line data bases searching in all subject areas to any library. The company was not to start operation until January 1977, and spent the

last half of 1976 gathering commitments for services from libraries. They intended to offer the same data bases as those offered by SDC and Lockheed at cheaper rates and for telecommunications costs of $3 an hour.

Professional Activities. More than any other evidence, the professional activities of the American Library Association, the Special Libraries Association, and the American Society for Information Science were an indication of the greatly expanded interest in machine-readable reference data bases. Two major conferences on machine-readable reference services took place at the ALA Centennial Conference in July 1976: (1) an all-day pre-conference workshop, sponsored by the Reference and Adult Services Division on Machine-Readable Reference Service and (2) a program sponsored by the Information Science and Automation Division and Reference and Adult Services Division. At year's end it seemed probable that the Reference and Adult Services Division would have a discussion group called Machine Assisted Reference Services (MARS) by 1977. Apparently libraries are finding it possible to reallocate funds within their budgets to allow use of these data bases, and the users themselves, when user fees are charged, are able to justify the expense.

CIRCULATION SYSTEMS

Commercial Systems. For several years, on-line minicomputer circulation systems have been of great interest to all kinds of libraries. Until 1975, the only company able to produce a circulation system for the library market was CLSI of Newtonville, Massachusetts (see *News* below), which had made some 100 installations throughout North America by 1976. Several other systems reached the market. At the ALA Midwinter Meeting in January 1976, the 3M Company announced its minicomputer-based circulation system, radically revised from the Check-A-Book system, which it had purchased from another company. In its design 3M incorporated features such as call number search, fine processing and reserve processing, which the CLSI system could not accommodate. For the first installation, at Princeton University, the equipment was accepted, and Princeton expected to be circulating materials as of winter 1977.

When the San Jose Public Library planned a circulation system, it went out to bid and accepted, according to its specifications, the low bidder, Systems Control Incorporated of Palo Alto, California. The Systems Control design accommodates up to 32 terminals, written in the BASIC programming language, incorporating a wide variety of custom built features for the San Jose Public Library. Although SCI indicated that it does not intend to market the system widely, the system is of sufficient sophistication to warrant careful observation as it is installed and implemented at the San Jose Public Library.

Two other commercially available systems exist—one offered by the Gaylord Company and one by Checkpoint Plessey. Both systems contain processors which gather data within the local library, to be processed remotely. The Gaylord data are processed in Syracuse at Gaylord's major computer facility, and the Checkpoint Plessey data are processed at the user library's computer facility. Both these systems have the advantage of being inexpensive and the disadvantage of some lack of sophistication. The Gaylord system has been installed in the Liverpool, New York, Library. The Checkpoint Plessey system is in use in over 200 libraries in Great Britain.

Academic Library Systems. In the category of homegrown circulation systems, three academic libraries made news during 1976. The University of Chicago circulation system, under development for several years, was available for demonstration at the ALA Midwinter Meeting in January 1976. The University staff had determined that the undergraduate reserve collection should initially use the circulation system in order to test it strenuously.

At the Virginia Polytechnic Institute, a combined effort of the Library, the computing center and the Hewlett-Packard Company has created a circulation system on a HP-3000 minicomputer which incorporates most of the features desired by a medium-sized or large academic library and for a cost that is reportedly less than that offered by any commercially available system at the time. Finally, the University of Texas at Dallas has contracted with Innovative Systems Incorporated to design and implement a circulation system combined with a book security system, also on a Hewlett-Packard minicomputer.

Automation

39

Automation

Trends. All the systems described above use bar-coded labels for book and borrower identification. Reading of the bar code is done with a light pen. Bibliographic data are brief, sometimes but not always linked to a full bibliographic file. Future evolution of these systems, however, will probably incorporate the optical scanning type font used commonly by banks, replacing the bar code, which cannot be read by human eye. With the burgeoning of these systems, it was becoming increasingly apparent to librarians in the mid-1970's that the major network systems such as OCLC or BALLOTS will not provide the circulation services that had originally been anticipated. Instead, effort will have to be devoted to linking the inventory circulation system with bibliographic systems a regional or nationwide level.[4]

NETWORKS

Networks have been top library news for the past five years or so, but 1976 was the year in which the national library network garnered much attention. Groups have been formed by the Library of Congress, the Council of Computerized Library Networks, National Science Foundation, the Council of Library Resources, the National Commission of Library and Information Science, the Association of Research Libraries, and other groups to design the configuration of a national library network. Redundancy and duplication in such efforts are distressing. Without a clear centralization of authority, there will be no centralization of effort in the immediate future. Certainly the reorganization at the Library of Congress and the increased funding for NCLIS have been key events in mobilizing forces toward the development of the national library network. At the end of 1976, it was not clear how long the effort would take, nor was it clear how many iterations of designs and how much participation would be required before a firm path were chosen.

The existing library network organizations are maturing, and with the component effort toward building a national library network organization shuffling has taken place in 1976. In New Jersey, the CAPTAIN network, which had finally hired an executive director and apparently was on its way to pursuing some of its stated programs, received no funding in 1976 from the New Jersey State Legislature, and subsequently the executive director resigned. While the CAPTAIN network still exists, Rutgers University is the only institution using its computer facilities. Coordination is being handled on an acting basis by a member of the library staff at Rutgers, and at year's end, the future of the network was unclear.

Since its inception, the Southeastern Library Network (SOLINET) has been officially associated with the Southern Regional Educational Board (SREB), which has taken a considerable interest in the library automation and networking activities of the southern part of the country. During the year, SREB broke off its affiliation with SOLINET and hired a consultant to study the library needs and requirements of the southeastern portion of the country and to recommend the next best steps to take. Acknowledging that the break with SREB has taken place, SOLINET continues to be the coordinating office for southern and southeastern libraries in their use of the OCLC system. Meanwhile, the OCLC governing board, also concerned about the role of OCLC in the forthcoming national library network, created a separate advisory board and let a Request for Proposal for a study to determine the role of OCLC within the United States. The successful bidder, the Arthur D. Little Company, would embark on the project in January 1977.

A relative newcomer to the networking world, the Bibliographic Center for Research in Denver, offers a variety of services including access to both technical processing and reference data bases. Its Biblio program provides links with OCLC and BALLOTS, and the Metro service provides members with access to the data bases of Lockheed, SDC, and the New York Times. BCR is a network with no specified geographic region for membership. Another new network, MIDLNET, is also active in the central part of the country. As each of these networks takes on new members in different states, they find that they are stepping on each other's toes or jockeying for position in one state or another. This phenomenon is a recent occurrence in automated networks, but there is no doubt that, at least for network organizations, overlap will exist in certain parts of the country. There are no contractual boundaries to indicate where each of the networks must or should operate, and that organization which is able to offer and provide services to libraries more easily or for a better price than other networks may very easily become the more widely used network.

Finally, the Research Libraries Group, which was formed specifically to bring together libraries with problems typical of large research libraries, is beginning to communicate with other research libraries on the topic of joining with RLG in its network effort.

The funding agencies, including some that are unfamiliar to libraries, are apparently impressed with the potential of library networks and are injecting new money into the effort of specific networks to spread computerized services and add capabilities to their systems. The Kellogg Foundation of Battle Creek, Michigan, has granted over $4,000,000 in a variety of areas to perform these tasks. Of this total, $2,000,000 will go to approximately 300 small, private liberal arts colleges to enable their libraries to join OCLC. Each library will

"I have one that does math. I need one that spells and reads."

receive $8,000 to cover the cost of terminals, training and transitional operating expenses. Another $1,500,000 will go to the state of Michigan to create a computer-based library network including 24 regional library systems, and 448 private and academic libraries in Michigan were eligible for grants to enable them to obtain the necessary computer equipment and training. Finally, $300,000 will go to OCLC for an 18-month experiment to develop the software and hardware necessary to link its on-line computer system with other citation retrieval systems such as those of Lockheed and SDC.

In November, the Stanford University Libraries announced that together the Sloan and Mellon Foundations awarded a grant of $581,000 over a period of three years to the Stanford University Libraries and the University of California, Berkeley, General Library to enable the two institutions to devise cooperative collection development procedures, make use of the BALLOTS on-line technical processing system, and add to the capabilities of the computer system. Among the specific functions addressed in the grant proposal was authority control.

NEWS IN BRIEF

The ALA/ISAD Telecommunications Committee, after working for several years on specifications for protocols for computer communications, in 1976 presented its final proposal to the Division.[5] Based on this work, a committee is being formed by the Library of Congress, the National Commission on Libraries and Information Sciences, and the American National Standards Institute to further develop and refine these specifications and to propose specific means of implementing the proposal in library communications systems.

The National Commission on Libraries and Information Science produced a position paper on machine-readable bibliographic control of nonprint media that was disseminated in 1976 for discussion purposes at meetings. It will continue to be disseminated in 1977 for maximum response from the user community before the machine-readable bibliographic format for nonprint is made final.

Several library automation vendors entered uncertain or transitional stages during 1976. Information Dynamics Corporation, which for a decade or so produced the Micrographic Catalog Retrieval System (MCRS) and tried to market an on-line bibliographic service called BIBNET, went into receivership. The MCRS portion of the company was bought late in the year by 3-M, and, it was reported, would continue to be marketed by the 3-M Company. The data base upon which BIBNET was built was residing in the files of the System Development Corporation, and it was unclear by the end of 1976 what the status of the BIBNET data base would be.

Following months of rumors of financial distress, CLSI announced that it would auction all its assets. Its major creditor had called in its loans, and in June all of the firm's assets were sold in public auction. The Xerox Corporation, which owned 25 percent of the preferred stock, continued to lend money to CLSI prior to the auction, ultimately bringing its investment to $2,100,000. At the auction, the company was bought for $1,500,000 by CL Systems Incorporated, a new company financed by the management that had already been managing CLSI. Xerox no longer owns any part of the company. The company said it planned to speed up the development program that had been delayed for lack of capital. In 1976 it signed a master agreement with the University of California and had installed a system at UCLA and the University of California at Davis.

The Inovar Corporation, founded by H. Spiwack, to provide catalog conversions and produce book and microform catalogs for libraries, was bought by Brodart early in the year, and its founder announced his intention of leaving the company completely as of early 1977.

Issues. A number of issues of the mid- and late-1970's touch library automation application. The copyright bill, once signed, will have implications for individual libraries and networks. Library automation applications will be examined carefully in the light of their effect on copyright, cooperative purchasing and photocopying of materials.

The question of public/private interface is perhaps one that can never be resolved. Several libraries in 1976 joined not-for-profit networks, although they were from profit-making corporations. The Internal Revenue Service had ruled that the not-for-profit networks could accommodate these special libraries and not lose their tax-exempt status. The developments, however, are just the tip of the iceberg; additional problems and issues will continue to arise as the information dependence of one type of institution on another becomes more and more involved. SUSAN K. MARTIN

A programmed Language Community Access Tool (APL/CAT) instituted in 1976 in the Dallas Public Library provides community service information in response to telephone queries to the computerized CAT.

REFERENCES
1. Association of Research Libraries, *The Future of Card Catalogs* (Washington, D.C.: ARL, 1975).
2. Michael Cooper and Nancy DeWath, "Cost of On-line Bibliographic Searching," *Journal of Library Automation* 9:195-209 (September 1976).
3. Association of Research Libraries, 88th Meeting, Seattle, 1976, *Proceedings* (Washington, D.C.: ARL, 1976).
4. Susan K. Martin, *Library Networks, 1976–77* (White Plains, N.Y.: Knowledge Industry Publications, 1976).
5. "Protocol for Computer-to-Computer Communication," *Journal of Library Automation* 9:167–171 (June 1976).

Awards and Prizes

ALA AWARDS

Through its national awards program, the American Library Association seeks to honor those who have rendered distinguished service to libraries and librarianship. Such recognition is made for individual achievement of a high order in some area of librarianship, for effective participation in library affairs, and for writings and illustrations which enrich our collections. In addition, recognition and assistance are given to individuals and groups selected to conduct special studies, and scholarships are awarded to promising candidates seeking to enter the profession or for advanced study. The winners of the ALA awards for individual achievement constitute a Hall of Fame for librarianship. The juries and committees making the selections are charged with the responsibility of maintaining the high standards established by their predecessors in selecting individuals who have furthered to a notable degree the purposes for which libraries were created.

The following are ALA awards for 1976.

ALA Goal Award

Established in 1960, the J. Morris Jones—Bailey K. Howard—World Book Encyclopedia—ALA Goal Awards (under the jurisdiction of the Executive Board) is an annual grant of to a maximum $10,000 made by the Field Enterprises Educational Corporation, Inc., to encourage and advance the development of public and/or school library service and librarianship through recognition and support of programs which implement the Goals and Objectives of ALA.

RECIPIENTS: ALA Publishing Committee and the Association of College and Research Libraries.

ALTA Honor Award

Announced in 1976 for award in 1977, this is an annual award consisting of a citation to recognize benefactors to public libraries. The recipient may be any person or persons, institutions, agency, or organization. The significance of the gift will be measured from the point of view of the recipient library.

Armed Forces Librarians Achievement Citation

Established in 1964, this is an annual citation presented to members of the Armed Forces Librarians Section, Public Library Association, who have made significant contributions to the development of armed forces library service, and to organizations encouraging an interest in libraries and reading. It is donated and administered by the Armed Forces Libraries Section, Public Library Association.

RECIPIENT: Mariana J. Thurber.

Beta Phi Mu Award

Established in 1954, this is an annual award consisting of $500 and a citation of achievement, presented to a library school faculty member or to an individual for distinguished service to education for librarianship. Donated by Beta Phi Mu, a national honorary library science fraternity, it is administered by the Library Education Division.

RECIPIENT: Carolyn Whitenback.

Charles Scribner's Sons Award

Established in 1970, this comprises four $250 cash awards presented annually to two school librarians and two public library librarians to enable them to attend the ALA's Annual Conference. Winners must be members of the Children's Services Division, with one to five years of library experience, and never have attended an ALA conference. It is donated by Charles Scribner's and administered by the Children's Services Division.

RECIPIENTS: Michele Gendron, Evelyn C. Minick, John J. Burroughs, Jr., and Alys Carrasco.

Dartmouth Medal

Established in 1974, this is presented to honor achievement in creating reference works outstanding in quality and significance. Creating reference works may include, but not be limited to, writing, compiling, editing, or publishing books or the provision of information in other forms for reference use, e.g., a data bank. Bestowal of the award is normally related to works which have been published or otherwise made available for the first time during the calendar year preceding the presentation. Donated by Dartmouth College, Hanover, New Hampshire, it is administered by the Reference and Adult Services Division.

(No award given)

David H. Clift Scholarship

Approved by the ALA Council in 1969, this scholarship provides an annual grant of $3,000 to worthy students to begin and/or further their library education at the graduate level without regard to race, creed, color, national origin, or sex. It is administered by the ALA Awards Committee and the Library Education Division.

RECIPIENTS: Nancy Ann Reed and Linda Griffin.

Distinguished Library Service Award for School Administrators

Established in 1967, this is an annual citation presented to a person directly responsible for the administration of a school or group of schools who has made a unique and sustained contribution toward furthering the role of the library and its development in elementary and/or secondary education. Two meritorious school administrators may be cited each year.

RECIPIENT: Wilmer Cody.

Esther J. Piercy Award

Established in 1968, this is an annual citation presented in recognition of a contribution to librarianship in the field of technical services to a librarian with not more than 10 years of professional experience. It is donated and administered by the Resources and Technical Services Division.

RECIPIENT: Ruth L. Tighe.

Eunice Rockwell Oberly Memorial Award

Established in 1923, this is a biennial award given in odd-numbered years, and comprises a citation and a cash award from the income of the Oberly Memorial Fund, presented to an American citizen who compiles the best bibliography in the field of agriculture or a related science in the two-year period preceding the year in which the award is made. It is administered by the Association of College and Research Libraries, Agriculture and Biological Sciences Section.

(No award given)

Francis Joseph Campbell Citation

Established in 1965, this consists of a citation and a medal, presented annually to a person who has made an outstanding contribution to the advancement of library service for the blind. It is donated and administered by the Section on Library Service to the Blind and Physically Handicapped of the HRLS.

RECIPIENT: Charles Gallozzi.

Frederic G. Melcher Scholarship

This annual $4,000 scholarship was established in 1956 by the Children's Services Division to encourage young people to enter the field of library service to children.

RECIPIENT: Nancy Snyder.

Grolier Foundation Award

Established in 1953, this is an annual award, consisting of $1,000 and a citation of achievement presented to a librarian in a community or in a school who has made an unusual contribution to the stimulation and guidance of reading by children and young people. Donated by the Grolier Foundation, it is administered by the ALA Awards Committee.

RECIPIENT: Virginia Haviland.

Grolier National Library Week Grant

This is an annual $1000 cash award presented to the state library association that submits the best plan for a public relations program to be conducted in the year in which the grant is presented. Donated by the Grolier Educational Corporation, it is administered by the National Library Week Committee of the American Library Association.

RECIPIENT: Illinois Library Association.

H. W. Wilson Library Periodical Award

Established in 1960, this consists of $250 and a certificate, presented annually to a periodical published by a local, state, or regional library, library group, or library association in the United States or Canada which has made an outstanding contribution to librarianship. (This excludes publications of ALA, CLA, and their divisions.) Donated by the H. W. Wilson Company, it is administered by the ALA Awards Committee.

RECIPIENT: *Hennepin County Library Cataloging Bulletin*, Sanford Berman, Editor.

Hammond Incorporated Library Award

Established in 1962, this consists of $500 and a citation, presented annually to a librarian or library in a community or school for making an unusual contribution through either continued service or a single contribution of lasting value, to effective use of or increased interest in maps, atlases, and globes by children and young people through high school age. Donated by Hammond, Incorporated, it is administered by the ALA Awards Committee.

RECIPIENT: Gail Borden Public Library District, Elgin, Ill.

Health and Rehabilitative Library Services Exceptional Service Award

Established in 1957, this is a citation presented to a member of the HRLS Division in recognition of exceptional service to HRLS or any of its component areas of service. It is donated and administered by the HRLS Division.

RECIPIENT: Earl C. Graham.

Herbert Putnam Honor Fund Award

Established in 1939, this is presented at intervals as a $500 grant-in-aid to an American librarian of outstanding ability for travel, writing, or other use that might improve his or her service to the library profession or to society. Presented when the income from the Herbert W. Putnam Honor Fund accumulates to $500, it is expected to be next presented in 1980. It is administered by the ALA Awards Committee which servs as the jury.

(No award given)

Isadore Gilbert Mudge Citation

Established in 1958, this is given at the annual conference of the ALA to a person who has made a distinguished contribution to reference librarianship. It is donated and administered by the Reference and Adult Services Division.

RECIPIENT: John Neal Waddell (posthumously).

James Bennett Childs Award

An annual award consisting of a medal, presented to a librarian or other individual for distinguished contributions to documents librarianship. Donated by the Government Documents Round Table. Administered by the Government Documents Round Table. The award was announced in 1976 for presentation at the annual ALA conference in 1977.

JMRT 3M Company Professional Development Grant

Annual cash awards are presented to librarians to attend an annual conference of the ALA. The recipients must be members of the ALA and the Junior Members Round Table. Administered by the Junior Members Round Table, the award was donated by the 3M Company.

RECIPIENTS: June Kay Breland, Janis H. Bruwelheide, Susan G. Broomall, Leslie C. Burk, Lafaye Cobb, Kristen M. Dahlen, Janis J. Dickens, H. Dale Montieth, Sharon Lee Stewart, Joyce A. Wyngaarden.

John Cotton Dana Public Relations Awards Contest

Established in 1942, this is an annual citation made to libraries or library organizations of all types submitting materials representing the year's public relations program. It is donated by the H. W. Wilson Company in a contest sponsored jointly with the Public Relations Section of the Library Administration Division.

RECIPIENTS

Public Libraries

Pomona, California, Public Library: Award for executing a wide-variety of community interest programs with the aid of strong graphics and other promotional channels.

Sacramento, California, Public Library: Honorable Mention for conducting a professional and effective public relations program by making optimum use of media to involve public support for needed enrichment without additional fiscal burden to the community.

Cortez, Colorado, Public Library: Honorable Mention for a fine example of how a small library and a staff of three people served a population of 6,300 by presenting a full range of library programs and services for all ages.

Pueblo Regional Library District, Pueblo, Colorado: Honorable Mention for a videotape presentation which is a visual scrapbook of an outstanding multi-media public relations program.

Perry County Public Library, Hazard, Kentucky: Honorable Mention for the articulation of "Celebration of Talents," a remarkable facet of a program overflowing with ideas and activities, providing the community with the finest of inspirational goals.

Clark County Library District, Las Vegas, Nevada: Honorable Mention to Friends of the Library for development of a 60-second television public service announcement which captured the techniques of "hard sell" commercials on television's amazing offers and applied them to books.

Buffalo and Erie County Public Library, Buffalo, New York: Honorable Mention for an outstanding videotape venture involving local audiovisual students and a local television station.

Public Library of Charlotte and Mecklenburg County, Charlotte, North Carolina: Honorable Mention for expanding programs of the library by spearheading civic drives, such as registering voters, and thereby accentuating library services.

Beaver County Federated Library System, Monaca, Pennsylvania: Honorable Mention for effectively supporting its member libraries by dynamic programs offering a wide range of skills and techniques for improved services to the public.

Salt Lake County Library System, Salt Lake City, Utah: Honorable Mention for an imaginative television spot announcement promoting the services of a county library system.

Long Beach, California, Public Library: Special Award for a dramatic multimedia presentation motivating parents and teachers to share books with children, particularly in low income and ethnic groups.

Los Angeles, California, Public Library: Special Award for its novel summer reading program featuring a "Monster Reading Rally" and a "Children's Dinner Theatre" in the library atmosphere.

Santiago Library System, Orange, California: Special Award for a splendid public relations effort which reached a new audience by providing captioned films for the deaf and promoting the program to the users.

South Pasadena, California, Public Library: Special Award for implementing a supportive library friends group to significantly contribute to successful library programming.

Evergreen, Colorado, Regional Library: Special Award for an enterprising public relations program based on audience identification and community involvement.

Danbury, Connecticut, Public Library: Special Award for an outstanding treatment of "Xenophobia"! This library's series of science fiction and monster movies was imaginatively publicized through a videotape which captured the "spirit" of the film programs through special video effects and clever copy.

Broward County Library System, Ft. Lauderdale, Florida: Special Award for an imaginative children's program utilizing a variety of media which achieved excellent newspaper coverage.

Orlando, Florida, Public Library: Special Award for spectacular television public service announcements, cleverly conceived and excellently produced, promoting its "Razzle Dazzle Summer Program" and its books by mail service.

Atlanta, Georgia, Public Library: Special Award for an exemplary Friends of the Library organized bond campaign for a new central building which utilized the talents of community leaders in sophisticated opinion forming techniques.

Scott Candler Library, Decatur, Georgia: Special Award for revitalizing the library by making it more visible to the community and more responsive to the community needs.

Iberville Parish Library, Plaquemine, Louisiana: Special Award for a top quality slide tape presentation on the history and contemporary life of its community. This presentation reached general audiences and was effective in gaining library support from government and industry.

Cambridge, Massachusetts, Public Library: Special Award for implementing a state aided program to create an awareness of the value of the library to the Portuguese community.

Concord, Massachusetts, Free Public Library: Special Award for providing a variety of activities to the community, thereby dispelling an "intellectuals only" attitude.

Watertown, Massachusetts, Free Public Library: Special Award for an imaginative Bicentennial project which involved the community and reached citizens of all ages including the blind through Braille materials.

Detroit, Michigan, Public Library: Special Award for a well-organized promotion of a special program which involved a community in a Family Book Fair.

Mideastern Michigan Library Cooperative, Flint, Michigan: Special Award for an effective presentation of a new service for the blind and physically handicapped and for the recruitment and recognition of volunteers who assisted.

Pike-Amite Library System, McComb, Mississippi: Special Award to "Scooter Mouse" for an imaginative approach which changed the image of the Public Library from a formal adult institution to an exciting educational and recreational center.

Madison, New Jersey, Public Library: Special Award for innovative activities which focused on the library's 75th anniversary.

Public Library of Youngstown and Mahoning County, Youngstown, Ohio: Special Award for outstanding cooperation between public and school libraries to promote a Bicentennial project which encouraged community pride and resulted in permanent murals depicting local history for each library agency.

Pioneer Multi-County Library, Norman, Oklahoma: Special Award for a cassette-slide presentation, well-organized and professionally produced, which effectively oriented staff as well as informed parents concerning services for children.

Fulton County Library Project, McConnellsburg, Pennsylvania: Special Award for devising a vigorous public relations program aimed at the establishment of an adequate facility to serve people desperately in need of resources and services.

Montgomery County-Norristown Public Library, Norristown, Pennsylvania: Special Award for a public relations program involving individual patrons.

Greenville, South Carolina, County Library: Special Award for an effective 7-county cooperative promotion of the library as "The Information Place." The campaign included billboards, book bags and television plus targeted public relations efforts.

Fairfax County Public Library, Springfield, Virginia: Special Award for a training program demonstrating that staff attitudes and internal communications are basic to the public relations process.

Timberland Regional Library, Lacy, Washington: Special Award for an innovative public service radio spot series which cleverly highlighted library resources. Designed for one local station, these were so appealing that 16 stations now air them.

Brown County Library, Green Bay, Wisconsin: Special Award for a well conceived, coordinated, and publicized Bicentennial Summer Reading Theme series of programs offering a wide choice of activities for children.

Madison, Wisconsin, Public Library: Special Award for celebrating their centennial by using a variety of approaches to strengthen and refresh the image of the library.

Bankstown, Australia, Municipal Library: Special Award for making the library a "New Multi-Cultural Center" in a "New Multi-Cultural Environment" by the issuance of *Passport to the World* booklists focusing on immigrants.

Dartmouth Regional Library, Nova Scotia, Canada: Special Award for addressing "International Women's Year" by organizing mature programs which were designed to enhance knowledge and discussion on this vital topic.

State Libraries

West Virginia Library Commission: Honorable Mention for the West Virginia Library Commission's "Exposure," a public relations service for librarians.

Special Libraries

State Prison of Southern Michigan, Jackson, Michigan: Award for outstanding efforts to up-grade the quality of a prison library which made changes visible to the users.

Orange County Law Library, Santa Ana, California: Special Award for an outstanding effort by a law library to promote its collection by designing its services to meet the needs of its users.

Maryland State Department of Education, Division of Instructional Television: Special Award for a top quality video presentation introducing four new instructional television reading series productions for grades Pre K-8.

Seneca County Library Council, Tiffin, Ohio: Special Award for increasing public awareness of the special resources and services of its libraries in a program designed to enhance information transfer.

College and University Libraries

West Point Academy Library, New York: Award for a total public relations program, which anticipated a changing clientele and met broadening needs with new services which publicized the library's role in the institution.

Salem State College Library, Massachusetts: Honorable Mention for a promotional effort highlighting the services and resources of their *Library of Social Alternatives*, an innovative, student-oriented agency.

University of Denver Library, Colorado: Special Award for a well-executed public relations program, with unique graphics, promoting a library sponsored exhibit of the North American Indian.

Allegany Community College Library, Cumberland, Maryland: Special Award for using displays, demonstrations, news releases and special services to present cleverly executed themes which promoted interest in the library.

Hampshire College Library Center, Amherst, Massachusetts: Special Award for an offbeat television production on library orientation which was created by student talent.

University of Wisconsin-Parkside Library,

Kenosha, Wisconsin: Special Award for effective use of graphics and displays in communicating library services and resources.

School Libraries

Greenwich, Connnecticut, Public Schools: Award for achieving full integration of media and print material to promote the school's goals through the library media program.

Monroe Junior High School Library, Columbus, Ohio: Honorable Mention for a student-produced slide-tape program to motivate student use of the library and acquaint parents with library resources.

Azalea Middle School, St. Petersburg, Florida: Special Award for a lively slide-tape presentation depicting the flexibility and warmth of the media center to stimulate use by students and teachers.

Board of Education of Baltimore County, Towson, Maryland: Special Award for an outstanding promotion at local, state, and national levels of a federal film project which stimulated reading of children's literature.

Rocky Hill School Library, Knoxville, Tennessee: Special Award for a fine public relations program conducted with a minimum of material and human resources. The result was increased participation and good will.

Service Libraries

Yongsan Library, U. S. Army Recreation Services Agency, Korea: Award for an imaginative and comprehensive program which stressed ethnic correlation and unusually perceptive responsiveness to special needs and community affairs.

Barksdale Air Force Base Library, Louisiana: Honorable Mention for providing an extra touch for a great variety of patrons by conducting a dynamic people-oriented and activity-related program.

Travis Air Force Base Library, California: Special Award for the extension of library resources and services, marked by the theme, "Getting Us Out Into The Community", a superior achievement in a stated public relations program.

K. I. Sawyer Air Force Base Library, Michigan: Special Award for superior ability in promoting library resources and services by "Piggy Banking" subjects that are of current importance and special events.

Columbus Air Force Base Library, Mississippi: Special Award for relating to slow readers by imaginative approaches bringing diverse interests into the library, for example, model airplanes, and Indian artifacts, and by widely promoting library publicity outside the confines of the library.

Minot Air Force Base Library, North Dakota: Special Award for a planned, purposeful public relations program with stated goals and objectives accompanied by a step by step action plan.

John Newbery Medal

Established in 1921, this is presented annually to the author of the most distinguished contribution to American Literature for children published in the U.S. in the preceding year. The recipient must be a citizen or resident of the U.S. Donated by Daniel Melcher, it is administered by the Children's Services Division.

RECIPIENT: Susan Cooper for *The Grey King*.

John R. Rowe Memorial Award (until 1965 Exhibits Round Table Award)

Established in 1965, this is an annual award of $500 made to an individual or group to aid or improve some particular aspect of librarianship or library service on the basis of need in the profession or in the operation of professional library associations. It is donated and administered by the Exhibits Round Table.

(No award given)

Joseph W. Lippincott Award

Established in 1937, this comprises $1,000, an engraved medal, and a citation of achievement, and is presented annually to a librarian for distinguished service in the profession of librarianship. Donated by Joseph W. Lippincott, it is administered by the ALA Awards Committee.

RECIPIENT: Lester Asheim.

Kohlstedt Exhibit Award

Established in 1972, this was formerly known as the Melvil Dewey Exhibit Award. It is a citation given each year at the Exhibits Round Table Banquet recognizing the best single and multiple booth displays at the conference. The award citation, named after Donald W. Kohlstedt in recognition of his hard work for better library conference exhibits, is administered by the Kohlstedt Committee of the Exhibits Round Table.

RECIPIENTS:

Multiple Booth Award: Doubleday and Company, New York

Single Booth Award: Harlin Quist, New York

Special Bicentennial Award: Ellsworth Magazine Service, Chicago, Illinois.

Laura Ingalls Wilder Medal

Established in 1954, this is made to an author or illustrator whose books, published in the U.S., have, over a period of years, made a substantial and lasting contribution to children's literature. Presented every five years, it is donated and administered by the Children's Services Division.

(No award given)

Library Buildings Award Program

This is a biennial award established in 1962 by the American Institute of Architects, the American Library Association, and the National Book Committee to encourage excellence in the architectural design and planning of libraries. Citations are presented to the winning architectural firms and to libraries, a building plaque is also presented to each library winning an Honor Award. ALA participation authorized by Council in 1962.

RECIPIENTS:

Honor Award Winners: Pekin, Illinois, Public Library and Everett McKinley Dirksen Congressional Leadership Research Center, Pekin, Ill. Bates College Library, Bates College, Lewiston, Maine.

Jefferson Market Branch Library, New York Public Library, New York.

Merit Winners: Hapeville Public Library, Hapeville, Georgia.

Randall Memorial Library, Stow, Massachusetts.

Rockford Road Branch, Hennepin County Library, Crystal, Minnesota.

Marin County Library, Novato, Calif.

Stephen B. Luce Library at Fort Schuyler, State University of New York Maritime College, Bronx, New York.

Corning Public Library and Southern Tier Library System, Corning, New York.

Lineberger Memorial Library, Lutheran Theological Southern Seminary, Colombia, South Carolina.

Nathan Marsh Pusey Library, Harvard University, Cambridge, Massachusetts.

Joseph Mark Lauinger Memorial Library, Georgetown University, Washington, D.C.

Library Research Round Table Research Award

This was established in 1975 by the Library Research Round Table to encourage excellence in library research. No more than two awards of $400 each are presented annually to the persons submitting the best completed research reports. Research papers completed in the pursuit of an academic degree are not eligible.

RECIPIENTS: James C. Baughamm; Ruth W. Wender, Missi Fruehauf, Marilyn Vent, and Connie Wilson.

Margaret Mann Citation

Established in 1950, this is given annually to a cataloger or classifier, not necessarily an American, for outstanding professional achievement in the areas of cataloging or classification, either through publication of significant professional literature, participation in professional cataloging associations, introduction of new techniques of recognized importance, or outstanding work in the area of teaching within the past five years. It is donated and adminis-

tered by the Cataloging and Classification Section, Resources and Technical Services Division.
RECIPIENT: Eva Verona.

Melvil Dewey Medal

Established in 1952, this comprises an engraved medal and a citation presented annually to an individual or a group for recent creative professional achievement of a high order, particularly in those fields in which Melvil Dewey was actively interested: notably, library management, library training, cataloging and classification, and the tools and techniques of librarianship. Donated by the Forest Press, Inc., it is administered by the ALA Awards Committee.
RECIPIENT: Louis R. Wilson.

Mildred L. Batchelder Award

Established in 1966, this is a citation presented annually to an American publisher for a children's book considered to be the most outstanding book originally published in a foreign language in a foreign country, and subsequently published in English in the U.S. during the preceding calendar year. It is donated and administered by the Children's Services Division.
RECIPIENT: Henry Z. Walck, Publisher for *The Cat and Mouse Who Shared a House* by Ruth Hurlimann, translated by Anthea Bell.

Minority Scholarship

Established in 1972 by the ALA Council, this scholarship is a cash award of $4,500 made to worthy students who are also members of principal minority groups. Recipients must enter formal programs of graduate study leading to master's degrees or advanced certificates at ALA-accredited library schools. It is administered by the ALA Awards Committee and the Library Education Division.
(No award given)

Randolph J. Caldecott Medal

Established in 1937, this is presented annually to the illustrator of the most distinguished American picture book for children published in the U.S. in the preceding year. The recipient must be a citizen or resident of the U.S. Donated by Daniel Melcher, it is administered by the Children's Services Division.
RECIPIENTS: Leo and Diane Dillon for *Why Mosquitoes Buzz in People's Ears: A West African Tale.*

Ralph R. Shaw Award for Library Literature

An award, consisting of $500 and a citation, presented to an American librarian to recognize an outstanding contribution to library literature issued during the three years preceding the presentation. The award will be given only when a title merits such recognition. Donated by the Scarecrow Press. Administered by the ALA Awards Committee.
RECIPIENT: Herman Fussler.

Resources and Technical Services Division Resources Scholarship Award

Established in 1975, this consists of a citation and a $1,000 scholarship grant. The citation is presented annually to the author or authors of an outstanding monograph, published article, or original paper on acquisitions pertaining to college or university libraries. The scholarship grant is given to the library school of the winners' choice. Donated by Makely, Inc., it is administered by the RTSD Resources Section.
RECIPIENTS: Hendrick Edelman, Carol Nemeyer, Sandra Paul, for "The Library Market: A Special Publishers Weekly Survey."

Shirley Olofson Memorial Award

An annual cash award made to individuals to attend their second annual conference of ALA. The recipients must be members of ALA and be potential or current members of the Junior Members Round Table. Donor: Junior Members Round Table. Administered by the Junior Members Round Table.
RECIPIENTS: Celesta M. Busch, Patricia B. Devlin, Barbara J. Ford, Susan A. Galligan, Jean H. Michie, Helen R. Morgan, Katherine E. Runyon-Lancaster, Jon F. Scheer, Elizabeth L. Schulz.

Trustee Citations

Established in 1941, these are presented to two outstanding trustees, in actual service during part of the calendar year preceding the presentation, for distinguished service to library development whether on the local, state, or national level. They are donated by ALA and administered by the American Library Trustee Association.
RECIPIENTS: James A. Hess and Elizabeth F. Ruffner.

Other Prizes and Awards

The following are selected prizes awarded in 1976 unless otherwise indicated.

Albert J. Beveridge Award

Administered by the American Historical Association, this was offered biennially from 1939 to 1945 and since given annually. It comprises $5,000 drawn from the Albert J. Beveridge Fund for the best book on English or American History.
RECIPIENT: Edmund S. Morgan for *American Slavery, American Freedom: The Ordeal of Colonial Virginia.*

Amelia Frances Howard-Gibbon Medal

This has been given annually by the Canadian Library Association to the most outstanding Canadian illustrator of children's books.
RECIPIENT: William Hurelek *A Prairie Boy's Summer.*

Bancroft Prizes

Established in 1948 under the will of Frederic Bancroft and presented by Columbia University, these comprise three annual prizes of $4,000 for distinguished works on (a) American history (including biography), (b) American diplomacy, and (c) international relations.
RECIPIENTS: *The Problem of Slavery in the Age of Revolution: 1770–1823* by David Brion Davis and *Edith Wharton: A Biography* by R.W.B. Lewis.

Besterman Medal

This has been given annually by the Library Association in London since 1970 for an outstanding bibliography or guide to literature published in the United Kingdom the preceding year.
RECIPIENT: *Printed Maps of Victorian London, 1851–1900,* by Ralph Hyde.

Booker Prize for Fiction

This has been awarded annually since 1969 by the National Book League, England, for the best novel published in English in the British Commonwealth, Ireland, or South Africa. The prize is £5,000 plus a trophy.
RECIPIENT: David Storey for *Saville* (Cape).

Boston Globe—Horn Book Awards

These consist of three $200 prizes given annually since 1967, one for the best work of fiction for children, one for the best illustrated children's book, and one for the best nonfiction work for children.
RECIPIENTS:
Fiction: *Unleaving* by Jill Patton Walsh.
Illustration: *For Thirteen* by Remy Charlip and Jerry Joyner.
Nonfiction: *Voyaging to Cathay: Americans in the China Trade* by Alfred Tamarin and Shirley Glubok.

Bratislava International Biennial (BIB) of Illustrations

Awards are presented for children's book illustrations. Gold, silver, and bronze plaques are awarded.

RECIPIENTS: (1975) BIB Grand Prize to Nikojac Popov for his illustrated edition of *Robinson Crusoe*, published in the USSR; Susan Jeffers, illustrator of *Three Jovial Huntsmen*, was the first American to win a Golden Apple, one of five 1975 honor BIB awards.

Campion Award

Established in 1955, this is administered by the Catholic Book Club and is given annually to an author for long and distinguished service in the cause of Christian letters. It comprises a medallion that honors Blessed Edmund Campion, the martyr.
RECIPIENT: John J. Delaney.

Canadian Library Association's Book of the Year for Children Medal

This has been given annually since 1947 for the best children's book published in Canada. A French-language award was also established in 1950.
RECIPIENT: Mordecai Richler for *Jacob Two-Two Meets the Hooded Fang*.

Carey-Thomas Award

This is a citation given annually since 1943 by *Publishers Weekly* for a "a distinguished project of creative publishing." Candidates are nominated by the Bowker book review staff.
RECIPIENT: Morgan Library/David R. Godine, Publisher, *Early Children's Books and Their Illustration* by Gerald Gottlieb.

Carnegie Medal

This has been awarded annually since 1937 by the British Library Association for the most outstanding children's book published in Great Britain.
RECIPIENT: (1975 medal) Robert Westall for *The Machine-Gunners* (Macmillan).

Carter G. Woodson Book Award

Established in 1973 and administered by the National Council for the Social Studies, this is awarded annually to encourage the writing of sensitive and realistic social science books for children on topics related to ethnic minorities.
RECIPIENT: Laurence Yep for *Dragonwings*.

Child Study Association of America/Wel-Met Children's Book Award

This has been given annually since 1944 for the children's book that treats problems of young people realistically.
RECIPIENT: Carol Farley for *The Garden Is Doing Fine*.

Christian Gauss Award

Established in 1950 by the Phi Beta Kappa Senate, this is a $2,500 annual award for the best book of literary scholarship or criticism published in the U.S.
RECIPIENT: Elizabeth Schneider for *T.S. Eliot: The Pattern on the Carpet*.

Constance Lindsay Skinner Award

This has been given annually since 1940 by the Women's National Book Association to a bookwoman who is resident in the U.S. for a sustained contribution to the world of books over a period of time or for a single achievement. It comprises a bronze plaque.
RECIPIENTS: Barbara Ringer, Helen Meyer, and Frances Cheney.

Copernicus Award

Given annually to a poet over 45, this award recognizes the complete work of the poet and his contribution to poetry as a cultural force. It is a cash prize of $1000.
RECIPIENT: Robert Penn Warren for "Or Else: Poem/Poems 1968–1972."

Coretta Scott King Award

Established in 1969, this is presented annually at the ALA Annual Conference for a book written in the spirit of the life and work of Martin Luther King. It consists of $250, a plaque, and a set of *Encyclopaedia Britannica*, 15th edition.
RECIPIENT: Pearl Bailey for *Duey's Tale*.

Distinguished Achievement Award

This is a citation awarded annually since 1959 by the Executive Board of the Library School Alumni Association to a person who has made a substantial contribution to the development of librarianship as a profession. It is sponsored by the Drexel University Graduate School of Library Science.
RECIPIENT: Daniel Boorstin.

Dorothy Canfield Fisher Memorial Children's Book Award

Established in 1957, this is an illuminated scroll given annually by the Vermont Department of Libraries and the Vermont Congress of Parents and Teachers to the author of a book chosen from a select list by Vermont schoolchildren in grades four through eight.
RECIPIENT: Jean Merrill for *The Toothpaste Millionaire*.

Edgar Allen Poe Awards

These were established in 1945 by the Mystery Writers of America to "recognize outstanding contributions to various categories of mystery, crime and suspense writing." Categories also include best mystery motion picture and best mystery television program.
RECIPIENTS:
Best Novel: Brian Garfield for *Hop-Scotch*.
First Novel: Rex Burns for *The Alvarez Journal*.
Fact Crime Book: Tom Wicker for *A Time to Die*.
Juvenile: Robert C. O'Brien for *Z for Zachariah*.
Paperback Novel: John R. Feegel for *Autopsy*.
Grand Master Award: Graham Greene.

Eleanor Farjeon Award

This has been given annually since 1967 by the Children's Book Circle (England) to an individual for "distinguished services to children's books."
RECIPIENT: (1975) Naomi Lewis.

Francis Parkman Prize

Offered annually by the Society of American Historians since 1957, this comprises $500 and a bronze medal for the book on American history or biography which best epitomizes Parkman's literary and scholarly approach.
RECIPIENT: Edmund S. Morgan for *American Slavery, American Freedom: The Ordeal of Colonial Virginia*.

Frederic G. Melcher Book Award

Presented annually since 1964 by the Unitarian Universalist Association, this comprises $1,000 plus a medallion for a book published in the U.S. that has made a significant contribution to liberal religion.
RECIPIENT: Joseph Campbell for *The Mythic Image*.

Gavel Award

Inaugurated by the American Bar Association in 1958, this is a gavel presented annually to recognize an outstanding media contribution "to public understanding of American legal and judicial systems." Awards for the literary category began in 1964.
RECIPIENT: Yale University Press, Chester Kerr—Director, *The Morality of Consent* by Alexander Bickel.

Hans Christian Andersen International Children's Book Medals

These are given biennially by the International Board on Books for Young People to a living author (since 1956) and an illustrator (since 1966) for distinguished contributions to children's literature.
RECIPIENTS: Cecil Bødker for writing and Tatjana Mawrina for illustration.

Haskins Medal

Established in 1940 by the Mediaeval Academy of America, this honors Charles Homer Haskins and is given annually for a distinguished publication in the field of medieval studies.

RECIPIENT: Robert I. Burns for *Islam under the Crusaders: Colonial Survival in the Thirteenth Century Kingdom of Valencia.*

Herbert Baxter Adams Prize

This is an award of $300 offered biennially since 1938 by the American Historical Association for the best book on European history by an American author.

RECIPIENT: *The Just War in the Middle Ages* by Frederick H. Russell.

Howells Medal

This was established in 1921 by the American Academy of Arts and Letters to honor William Dean Howells and is given every five years to the author of the most distinguished work of American fiction published during the preceding five years.

RECIPIENT: (1975) Thomas Pynchon for *Gravity's Rainbow.*

International Reading Association Children's Book Award

Established in 1974, this is a $1,000 prize given for a children's book whose author shows unusual promise.

RECIPIENT: Laurence Yep for *Dragonwings.*

James A. Hamilton—Hospital Administrator's Award

This is offered annually by the American College of Hospital Administrators for a book that has made a valuable contribution to the literature of hospital administration.

RECIPIENT: Robert N. Anthony and Reginia Herzlinger for *Management Control in Nonprofit Organizations.*

James Russell Lowell Prize

Established in 1968 by the Modern Language Association of America, this is a $1,000 prize for an outstanding literary or linguistic study.

RECIPIENT: Jonathan Culler for *Structuralist Poetics.*

Jane Addams Children's Book Award

This is a hand-illuminated certificate given annually since 1953 to a worthy author by the Women's International League for Peace and Freedom, to encourage the publication of children's books of literary merit with constructive themes.

RECIPIENT: Eloise Greenfield for *Paul Robeson.*

John Burroughs Medal

This has been offered annually since 1926 by the John Burroughs Memorial Association at the American Museum of Natural History for the foremost literary work in the field of nature.

RECIPIENT: Ann Haymond Zwinger for *Run, River, Run.*

John Gilmary Shea Prize

Inaugurated in 1944 by the American Catholic Historical Association, this award of $300 is for an outstanding work on the history of the Catholic Church.

RECIPIENT: Emmet Larkin for *The Roman Catholic Church and the Creation of a Modern Irish State, 1878–1886.*

Joseph L. Andrews Bibliographical Award

Established in 1967, this citation is presented annually by the American Association of Law Libraries for the most significant contribution to legal bibliographical literature.

RECIPIENT: Fannie J. Klein for *The Administration of Justice in the Courts: A Selected Annotated Bibliography.*

Kate Greenaway Medal

This has been given annually since 1956 by the British Library Association for the best illustrated book for children published in Great Britain.

RECIPIENT: (1975) Victor Ambrus for *Horses in Battle* and *Mishka* (Oxford University Press).

Marcia C. Noyes Award

Established in 1948 by the Medical Library Association, this is an engraved silver tray presented irregularly to recognize an outstanding medical librarian.

RECIPIENT: Mildred C. Langer.

McColvin Medal

This is an annual award given since 1970 by the British Library Association to the author or compiler of an outstanding reference book published in Great Britain.

RECIPIENT: (1975) *Folksongs of Britain and Ireland*, edited by Peter Kennedy.

National Book Awards

Administered since 1950 by the National Book Committee and since 1975 by the National Institute of Arts and Letters, these recognize the most distinguished books in 10 categories. Cash awards of $1,000 are presented to the winners.

RECIPIENTS:
Arts and Letters: Paul Fussell for *The Great War and Modern Memory.*
Children's Literature: Walter D. Edmonds for *Bert Breen's Barn.*
Contemporary Affairs: Michael J. Arlen, *Passage to Ararat.*
Fiction: William Gaddis for *JR.*
History and Biography: David Brion Davis for *The Problem of Slavery in the Age of Revolution: 1770–1823.*
Poetry: John Ashbery for *Self-Portrait in a Convex Mirror.*

National Medal for Literature

This was established in 1964 by the National Book Committee in memory of Harold K. Guinzburg. The award has been administered since 1975 by the National Institute of Arts and Letters. It consists of $5,000 and a bronze medal and is made to a living author in American literature.

RECIPIENT: Allen Tate.

Nobel Prize for Literature

One of five prizes (the others are for physics, chemistry, medicine, and peace), it was established by Alfred Bernhard Nobel (1833–96), first offered in 1901. It is administered by the Swedish Academy in Stockholm and is made to an author for his total literary output. It consists of a gold medal and a sum of money (about $143,000 in 1975).

RECIPIENT: Saul Bellow.

Otto Kinkeldey Award

Established in 1967 and presented by the American Musicological Society, this comprises $400 and a scroll and is given annually to a U.S. or Canadian author who has published a notable full-length study in musicology the previous year.

RECIPIENT: 1976, David P. McKay and Richard Crawford for *William Billings of Boston: Eighteenth-Century Composer.*

P.E.N. Translation Prize

Established in 1962 by the P.E.N. American Center, this is an annual prize of $1,000 donated by the Book-of-the-Month Club and awarded for the best translation of a book into English from any language.

RECIPIENT: Richard Howard for his translation of *A Short History of Decay* by E.M. Cioran from the French.

Phi Beta Kappa Award in Science

Established in 1958, this is a $2,500 cash award for the best book about the sciences written by a scientist.

RECIPIENT: William W. Warner for *Beautiful Swimmers.*

Phi Beta Kappa Ralph Waldo Emerson Award

Established in 1959, this is a $2,500 cash

award which recognizes an interpretive, historical, philosophical, and religious study written in the tradition of humane learning.

RECIPIENT: Paul Fussell for *The Great War and Modern Memory*.

Pulitzer Prizes

These were instituted in 1917 under the terms of the will of Joseph Pulitzer (1847–1911). A number of prizes, currently $500 each, are awarded annually in various categories. The following are of special interest to librarians.

RECIPIENTS:

Biography: R.W.B. Lewis for *Edith Wharton: A Biography*.

Drama: Michael Bennett, James Kirkwood, Nicholas Dante, Marvin Hamlisch, Edward Kieban, "A Chorus Line."

History: Paul Horgan for *Lamy of Santa Fe*.

Letters (nonfiction): Robert N. Butler for *Why Survive? Being Old in America*.

Letters (fiction): Saul Bellow for *Humbolt's Gift*.

Music: Ned Rorem for "Air Music."

Poetry: John Ashbery for *Self-Portrait in a Convex Mirror*.

Ranganathan Award for Classification Research

Established in 1976 by the International Federation for Documentation, this is a certificate of merit to persons recognized for their outstanding contribution in classification research in recent years. Awarded to honor the late Dr. S. R. Ranganathan.

RECIPIENT: Derek Austin, British Library.

Regina Medal

This has been given annually since 1959 by the Catholic Library Association to an author, publisher, editor, illustrator, etc., for dedication to children's literature, irrespective of religion or race.

RECIPIENT: Virginia Haviland.

School Library Media Award

Established in 1962, this is sponsored annually by Encyclopaedia Britannica Companies and the American Association of School Librarians. It is given for outstanding achievement in providing elementary school library media centers and comprises a cash prize of $5,000 and plaques to top judged schools.

RECIPIENT: The Littleton Public Schools, Littleton, Colorado.

Rheta A. Clark Award

This has been awarded annually since 1958 by the faculty of the Department of Library Science and Technology, Southern Connecticut State College, New Haven.

RECIPIENT: Catherine Wiatrowski.

Rheta A. Clark Award of Merit

Established in 1973 and sponsored by the Connecticut School Library Association (now the Connecticut Educational Media Association), this is given to a librarian for "outstanding librarianship and devotion to the profession."

RECIPIENT: John Crawford.

Scribes Award

Established in 1960, this is a citation presented at the annual meeting of the American Bar Association for a book written either by a lawyer or a layman which best conveys the true spirit and meaning of the legal profession.

RECIPIENT: Richard Kluger for *Simple Justice*.

Special Libraries Association Hall of Fame

This is an award consisting of an engraved medallion and a certificate, given to recognize persons who over a period of years have made outstanding contributions to the Special Libraries Association.

RECIPIENTS: Phoebe Hayes and Ruth M. Nielander.

Special Libraries Association Professional Award

Established in 1949, this award recognizes notable professional achievement in the field of special librarianship.

RECIPIENT: Jacqueline Sisson.

W. H. Smith & Son Literary Award

Established in 1959, this is a £1,000 award offered annually by the London bookseller W. H. Smith to an author of the British Commonwealth who has made a significant contribution to English literature.

RECIPIENT: Seamus Heaney for *North*.

Western Heritage Awards

Established in 1960 by the National Cowboy Hall of Fame in Oklahoma City, these are given annually for various media categories that preserve the image of the American West. They comprise bronze statues of "The Horse Wrangler." Only book prizes are noted here.

RECIPIENTS:

Nonfiction: Jeff C. Dykes for *Fifty Great Western Illustrators*.

Turbese Lummis Fisk and Keith Lummis for *Charles F. Lummis: The Man and His West*.

Don James for *Butte's Memory Book*.

Juvenile Book: Natachee Scott Momaday for *Owl in the Cedar Tree*.

Wheatley Medal

This has been awarded annually since 1962 by the British Library Association for an outstanding index published in the United Kingdom during the preceding three years.

RECIPIENT: (1975) Mrs. M. D. Anderson for index to *Copy-editing* by J. Butcher (Cambridge University Press).

William H. Welch Medal

Established in 1949, this is presented (usually annually) by the American Association for the History of Medicine to recognize "particular contributions of outstanding scholarly merit in the field of medical history published during the preceding five years."

RECIPIENT: Lelland J. Rather.

Woodrow Wilson Foundation Award

Established in 1947 and recommended by a committee of the American Political Science Association, this comprises $1,000 for the "best book of the year in the field of government and democracy."

RECIPIENT: Robert R. Alford for *Health Care Politics*.

Centennial Awards

For recipients of Special Centennial Citations, see under BIOGRAPHIES: Anderson, Florence; Greenaway, Emerson; Haycraft, Howard; Henne, Frances; McKenna, F. E.; Stevenson, Grace; Thorpe, Frederick; Van Jackson, Wallace; and Waller, Theodore.

For Honorary Members of ALA, named in 1976, see under BIOGRAPHIES: Downs, Robert; Gaver, Mary; Jones, Virginia Lacy; Liebaers, Herman; Melcher, Daniel; and Shera, Jesse. See also Rothrock, Mary U., under OBITUARIES. Allie Beth Martin (d. April 11, 1976) was also named Honorary Member (see 1976 *Yearbook*, p. vi).

Beta Phi Mu

Beta Phi Mu was founded almost 30 years ago at the University of Illinois by a group of leading librarians and library educators who recognized the notable achievements of honor societies for other professions and who also recognized the need for such a society for librarianship and library education. Beta Phi Mu was born with the idea of encouraging high scholarship among library school students. That such scholarship might be more useful to the library profession, Beta Phi Mu encouraged excellent preparation for the profession through distinguished educational institutions that promote good teaching.

Beta Phi Mu has continued its activities to recognize distinguished service and to recruit potential scholars by offering awards, scholarships, and acknowledgment to those who fit the bill. And many did so in 1976. Patricia Ann Hooten was one of them. She received the $500 Continuing Education Scholarship for 1976–77. Agnes Denise Farraguia and Robert Blintz each received a $1,000 tuition scholarship for 1976–77 ($500 each semester) for study at the University of Michigan School of Library Science and in the Department of Library Science, Queens College, respectively.

Having already distinguished himself in library education, Miles M. Jackson of the Graduate School of Library Studies, University of Hawaii at Manoa, developed a proposal for travel to mainland China and won the first Harold Lancour Scholarship Award for foreign study to help him along the way. Results of the trip will be reported.

Library educators fared well during 1976 in the recognition that was bestowed upon them. Carolyn Whitenack of Purdue University received the Beta Phi Mu Award for distinguished contributions to education for librarianship. Elizabeth W. Stone, noted library educator at Catholic University, has been recognized increasingly by the profession for her promotion of library education activities. As the result of her work in developing the Continuing Library Education Network (CLENE), Stone was awarded a certificate of distinction by Beta Phi Mu.

The Society's interest in library education takes many forms. One is the sponsorship of conferences which may be joint ventures with undergraduate library clubs and various organizations. An example was Library History Seminar V, October 3–6 at Philadelphia's Hilton Hotel, made possible by a grant from Beta Phi Mu to the *Journal of Library History* and assisted by the American Library History Round Table of ALA. Some 50 persons attended to hear some of the profession's most distinguished lecturers discuss various phases of American library history. On the final day participants toured historic libraries. The concluding session, a commemorative one planned by ALA, was held at the Historical Society of Pennsylvania, the place where the original meeting was held a century before. Proceedings of the Seminar were being edited at year's end in preparation for publication, which should contribute significantly to the literature of library history.

Further support for the Seminar came in the form of $200 travel grants, provided by Beta Phi Mu to eight persons to help defray expenses to the sessions. Recipients were Dennis Reynolds, Reva Joanne Brick, Roger Michener, and Gordon B. Neavill, Chicago; Philip Allen Metzger and Marie Shultz, Austin, Texas; Kenneth Tracy, Stillwater, Oklahoma, and Robert Williams, Madison, Wisconsin.

Beta Phi Mu's interest in intellectual freedom was expressed through its $12,000 gift to the ALA Intellectual Freedom Committee as a contribution to its First Amendment film project, a joint venture with the Freedom to Read Committee of the Association of American Publishers. The film will illustrate both the current and the historical functions of the U.S. First Amendment. (*See also* Intellectual Freedom.)

When the chapter rolls are called, the Beta XI Chapter at North Carolina Central University and Beta Mu Chapter, Palmer Graduate Library School, Long Island University, will answer as new members for 1976, as will their initiates who received the Beta Phi Mu honor in October and November, respectively.

Directing all Beta Phi Mu activities for the year were President Jessie Carney Smith, Vice President/President-elect Howard W. Winger, Past President David Kaser, Treasurer Marilyn P. Whitmore, Executive Secretary Frank B. Sessa, Administrative Secretary Mary Y. Tomaino, and the Board of Directors: Rose Vainstein, Edward C. Sayre, Josephine McSweeney, Hester B. Slocum, Mary Alice Hunt, and Herman L. Totten.

JESSIE CARNEY SMITH

Bibliography and Indexes

The total number of published bibliographies and indexes listed in the monthly issues of *American Book Publishing Record (BPR)* increased slightly (513) over the number (501) listed in 1975.

Table 1 shows the broad subject distribution of titles listed in *BPR* for the years 1974–76 with the differences in numbers indicated.

VARIATIONS IN KIND

While the total of bibliographies listed in *BPR* is greater than in 1975, further examination suggests that overall subject bibliographic control may not have improved. For example, the social sciences show a significant increase in the number of bibliographies published dur-

Table 1. Bibliographies and Indexes in BPR, 1974–76*

Subject	Category	1974	1975	Change from 1974	1976	Change from 1975
000	General	90	77	−13	54	−23
100	Philosophy, Psychology	7	9	+ 2	6	− 3
200	Religion	13	9	− 4	12	+ 3
300	Social Sciences, Education	105	156	+51	230	+74
400	Language	5	14	+ 9	6	− 8
500	Pure Science	24	16	− 8	14	− 2
600	Applied Science	41	32	− 9	29	− 3
700	Fine Arts	62	51	− 9	34	−17
800	Literature	129	80	−49	66	−14
900	Travel, History, other	84	57	−27	62	+ 5
	Total	560	501	−59	513	+12

*Because of the unavailability of December figures for 1976, extrapolations were made from December 1975 figures.

ing the year. Closer analysis indicates, however, that this comparatively high increase is due mainly to the efforts of one source with a high volume of output of bibliographies ranging from 7 to 35 pages in length. When the social sciences are excluded from the total count for each of the three years indicated in Table 1, the picture becomes intriguing, if not alarming:

Year	1974	1975	1976
Total (excluding 300's)	455	345	293

Thus the number of bibliographies and indexes listed in BPR (excluding the social sciences) has declined by 46% since 1974. The specific subject categories most affected by this decline appear to be the Pure Sciences (500's) 42%; Applied Sciences (600's) 30%; Fine Arts (700's) 42%; Literature (800's) 50%; and Travel, History, Geography, and Biography (900's) 26%. By themselves, these figures are rather startling with respect to the implications for subject bibliographic control in these categories. However, caution is necessary in drawing any but the broadest conclusions from these data. The number of significant variables unaccounted for in these figures inhibits any generalization about the current state of subject bibliographic control. The number of entries represented in the published bibliographies, for example, must be analyzed; the number of bibliographies produced in formats not represented in BPR listings, such as report literature, serials, government publications, theses and on-line data bases must be accounted for in any in-depth analysis.

Nevertheless, the evidence presented in Table 1 suggests enough questions to warrant a serious investigation to determine the quality of subject bibliographic control in the various disciplines. It may be that retrospective book bibliographies are no longer necessary. On the other hand, it may be that a limited market, combined with rising costs, has made bibliographic publications a high-risk product for the average trade publisher. The library profession needs to know more about the compilers of these bibliographies: are they subject specialists or librarians; individuals or groups;

Table 2. Comparison of Bibliography and Book Publishing: 1972–76

	1972	1973	1974	1975	1976
Bibliographies	416	519	568	501	513
Total New Books	38,654	39,951	40,846	39,372	N. A.
Percentage of Bibliographies to Total New Books	1.1	1.3	1.4	1.3	N. A.

N. A. = Not available as of December 1976.

researchers or students? A major question emerges regarding user behavior—that is, where are users going for subject access to materials, especially in those disciplines for which bibliography in monographic form has been the traditional pattern of control? Is it possible that the NUC Subject Catalog and Cumulative Book Index are also serving scholars as subject bibliographies in addition to their function as components of the general U.S. national bibliography? Given the general lack of overall planning and coordination of current efforts in bibliographic compilation, plus the possibility that current production figures presented in Table 1 are indeed indicative of a trend, the need for more reliable and complete information about the current state of bibliographic control is urgent.

Table 2 compares bibliographic production to total book output during the period 1972–76. The proportion of bibliographies to total book production remains fairly consistent with the previous two years. The general decline in book production beginning in 1975 appears to reflect a trend continued in 1976.

There were no significant developments in planning and development of mechanisms for achieving better bibliographic control by means of a national bibliography. A two-day seminar on the Prospects for Change in Bibliographic Control was held at the University of Chicago in November. Preliminary reports (Library Journal, January 1, 1977, pp. 22–23) indicated that the focus of that conference was on improved access to material already collected by libraries. Thus networking efforts continue to occupy attention as the primary objective in achieving bibliographic control of material.

ROGER C. GREER

Binding

American libraries have experienced a tremendous expansion in collections in the past several years. They are now faced with the problem of preservation of their materials or, put somewhat differently, maintaining them for optimum reader usability. In 1976 several steps were taken by the Library Binding Institute (LBI) to assist librarians in this task.

Class A library binding for many years has been and still is the standard for most library materials (rebinding of used volumes, prebinding of new volumes, and initial hardcover binding of periodicals). Libraries have many different kinds of materials and their end use determines how they are to be bound. The result is that there are several different kinds of binding available. But no reliable data have been available to determine the relationship of end use and type of binding, except for Class A volumes. In addition, for many years LBI has promoted the development of new materials and methods, but lacked facilities to evaluate library books and the materials and methods used in binding such books.

To cope with these problems LBI funded at the Rochester Institute of Technology School of Printing the first laboratory primarily concerned with the physical book and, in particular, library books. The Laboratory, independent of LBI, is owned and administered by RIT under the direction of Werner Rebsamen. Dedicated September 20, 1976, it will train graphic arts students and others in the requirements of book construction and binding, with special reference to factors peculiar to library use. It will conduct programs involving research and development of materials and methods and the testing of various types of volumes.

The Laboratory is administering LBI's Free Examination Service for libraries under which libraries may send volumes to be examined to determine compliance with contract specifications. Use of the Laboratory will be incorporated into LBI's educational programs for bindery employees, librarians, and others concerned with the physical book.

The Laboratory is the first of a series of three projects planned by LBI. The second and third consist of establishing a library of books and materials relating to library binding and the physical book which will be available generally to book binders, students, and researchers, and establishing an annual lecture series on significant developments in the preservation of the physical book and library materials.

While the establishment of the Laboratory is the most important development in 1976, three others merit comment. The first of a series of informal workshops sponsored by LBI and a library association was held in California. Judith Hoffberg of ARLIS (Art Libraries Society of North America) helped plan the event which was held in the Kater-Crafts Bindery and was attended by librarians from diverse types of libraries. The discussions covered many of the various problems encountered in maintaining collections and is the prototype for other similar meetings now scheduled or planned for 1977, one of which was scheduled to be held at the LBI Laboratory.

A new movie on how volumes are processed in a bindery was completed in December and is available for rental or acquisition by library science schools and associations or through Certified Library Binders.

The third significant achievement was the final laboratory testing of cover materials intended for library use prior to an in-field testing program in 1977. This is the first phase of LBI's program to develop performance specifications for component materials and methods used in library binding. (See also Preservation of Library Materials.) — DUDLEY A. WEISS

Professor Werner Rebsamen, Director of the Library Binding Institute's Book Testing Laboratory, at work in the facility dedicated in 1976 at the Rochester Institute of Technology.

Biographies

ANDERSON, FLORENCE, Secretary of the Carnegie Corporation, 1954–74, was awarded a Special Centennial Citation by ALA in 1976.

Born in Brooklyn, New York, on October 29, 1910, Anderson received an A.B. degree from Mount Holyoke College in Massachusetts in 1931. She was a special student at the New School of Social Research and New York University, and received honorary degrees from Western College for Women in 1964, and from Mt. Holyoke College in 1972. She was elected to Phi Beta Kappa.

Anderson joined the staff of the Carnegie Corporation in 1934. She advanced from Administrative Assistant to Assistant Secretary, to Associate Secretary, and to Secretary in 1954. Concurrently, she served as Secretary to the Carnegie Foundation for the Advancement of Teaching from 1955 to 1974.

Anderson was an officer and Captain in the U.S. Marine Corps, serving as Assistant Adjutant of the Marine Corps School from 1943 to 1945. She is a Director of the National Information Bureau and a trustee of the Virginia Gildersleeve International Fund for University Women.

In *Carnegie Corporation Library Programs, 1911–1961,* Anderson wrote the history of the Carnegie Corporation's role in library development. In her role as Secretary she was instrumental in providing grants for all types of libraries, for library education, library organizations, and library research.

Her Citation reads, "in her quiet and modest manner [she] has played a major role in the strong support given by the Carnegie Corporation to library projects."

ASHEIM, LESTER EUGENE, the William Rand Kenan, Jr., Professor at the School of Library Science, University of North Carolina, received the J. W. Lippincott Award for distinguished service in the profession of librarianship in 1976.

Born in Spokane, Washington, on January 22, 1914, Asheim received B.A., B.A.L.S., and M.A. degrees from the University of Washington. He became Librarian of the U.S. Federal Penitentiary at McNeil Island, Washington, in 1941 and, after service in the U.S. Army, Regional Librarian for the U.S. Public Housing Authority in Seattle in 1946. In 1948 he was appointed Assistant Professor in the Graduate Library School at the University of Chicago. He received the Ph.D (L.S.) from the University of Chicago in 1949. In 1951 he became Dean of Students and from 1952 to 1961 served as Dean and Associate Professor.

Asheim was Director of the International Relations Office of ALA from 1961 to 1966, traveling widely, especially in the newly developing countries. He returned to his primary field as Director of ALA's Office for Library Education in 1966. In 1971 he joined the Graduate Library School of the University of Chicago as Professor until 1974, when he was appointed to his position at the University of North Carolina.

A diligent researcher and able writer, Asheim has published a number of significant books on library education, in the Public Library Inquiry series, on the book, mass communication, issues in librarianship, international librarianship, and library manpower. He received the Scarecrow Press Award for *Libraries in Developing Countries* in 1968. His article "Not Censorship but Selection," in the *Wilson Library Bulletin* (September 1953), is regarded as a classic on the subject.

As Director of the ALA Office for Library Education, Asheim developed the policy statement on Library Education and Manpower (now Library Education and Personnel Utilization) approved by the ALA Council in 1970. Arousing persistent controversy, the policy has nevertheless been widely followed. During the storm, Asheim, a lucid and witty speaker, appeared on many programs in effective defense of the statement.

Asheim received the Beta Phi Mu Award for Distinguished Service to Education for Librarianship in 1973. In 1976 he became President of the Library Education Division of ALA.

BAER, MARK H., Director of Libraries, Hewlett Packard, Palo Alto, California, was elected President of the Special Libraries Association for 1976–77. He had held various San Francisco Bay Region Chapter and Association level offices and committee appointments, including SLA director. He was named Distinguished Alumnus of 1976 by the School of Librarianship, the University of Washington in Seattle.

Mark Baer holds B.A. and M.L.S. degrees from the University of Washington. From 1956 to 1957 he was chemistry/chemical engineering librarian at the University of Washington. From 1957 to 1959 he served as engineering and technology librarian at Oregon State University, and from 1959 to 1966 he was director of technical information services of the Ampex Corporation in Redwood City, California.

Florence Anderson

Lester Asheim

Mark H. Baer

Biographies

Among a number of academic assignments, he taught a course on selection, evaluation and acquisition of the literature of science and technology at the University of California in the Graduate School of Librarianship, where he served from 1966 to 1970 as lecturer on organization, administration, and services of the industrial research library. He was appointed as Conference Cochair for the Pan Pacific Conference of the Special Libraries Association and Special Libraries Association Japan, 1973–79.

CHENEY, FRANCES NEEL, librarian and educator and author, was presented a 1976 Constance Lindsay Skinner Award by the Woman's National Book Association during the Centennial Conference of the American Library Association in Chicago for "outstanding contribution to the world of books."

Born in Washington, D.C., August 19, 1906, she received a B.A. from Vanderbilt University in 1928, B.S. in L.S. from Peabody Library School in 1934, M.S. from Columbia University in 1940, and an honorary Litt. D. from Marquette University, Milwaukee, in 1966. She began her library career as Librarian of the Chemistry Library at Vanderbilt University, 1928–29, became Circulation Assistant, 1929–30, Reference Librarian, 1930–37, Reference Librarian for the Joint University Libraries, 1937–43, and Head of the Reference Department, 1945–46. From 1943 to 1944 she worked at the Library of Congress in Washington, D.C., as Assistant to the Chair of Poetry and as a bibliographer in the General Reference Division.

In 1946 she joined the faculty of Peabody Library School as Assistant Professor, becoming Associate Professor in 1949, Professor in 1967, and Professor Emeritus in 1975. During a number of those years she was also Associate Director and Acting Director. She was a visiting faculty member to the Japan Library School, Tokyo, 1951–52.

Cheney has been active throughout her career in professional organizations. She was a member of the American Library Association Executive Board, 1956–61, and chaired the ALA Subscription Books Committee, 1962–63. She is a Past President of the Association of American Library Schools, the ALA Reference Services Division, and the ALA Library Education Division. She has also served as President of the Southeastern Library Association and of the Tennessee Library Association.

Readers of the *Wilson Library Bulletin* depended upon her reviews and comments in the section "Current Reference Books," which she edited for many years, ending in June 1972. She edited the *Tennessee Librarian*, 1949–51 and 1953–55. Published bibliographies include *Sixty American Poets*, an annotated bibliography (1944), and *An Annotated List of Selected Japanese Reference Materials*, 1952. *Fundamental Reference Sources* (ALA, 1971) is a textbook for students of reference. She has contributed numerous articles to professional publications.

Her awards include the Beta Phi Mu Award for Good Teaching in 1959 and the Mudge Award for Reference Service in 1962.

COLE, FRED CARRINGTON, President of the Council on Library Resources, was awarded a Special Centennial Citation by ALA in 1976. He was hailed for his "considerable skill in making Ford Foundation dollars for libraries achieve maximum impact."

Cole was born in Franklin, Texas, on April 12, 1912. He earned A.B. (1934) A.M. (1936) and Ph.D. (1941) degrees at Louisiana State University. Combining interests in editorship and history, Cole held editorial posts on the *Journal of Southern History* from 1936 to 1942. He was Coeditor of the *Southern Biography Series*, 1938 to 1945, History Editor of the Louisiana State University Press, 1938 to 1942, and Associate Editor, *Mississippi Valley Historical Review*, 1946 to 1953.

Cole's academic career began at Tulane University, where he joined the faculty in 1946. From 1947 to 1955 he was Dean of the College of Arts and Sciences, and from 1954 to 1959 was Academic Vice-President. When he was appointed to President of CLR in 1967, he had been President of Washington and Lee University since 1959.

As adviser and consultant in education, research, and manpower, Cole served the Ford Foundation, the U.S. Department of Health, Education and Welfare, the National Science Foundation, the Surgeon General, and the Department of the Army. He was on active duty in the U.S. Navy from 1942 to 1946. He received a special commendation from the Surgeon General, U.S. Navy, and the Outstanding Service Award from the Department of the Army.

Cole was instrumental in setting up the Council on Library Resources when he served as a consultant to the Ford Foundation. The projects funded by CLR under his direction have been in cataloging, bibliography, automation, college library programs, library management, and the upgrading of the skills of librarians. His Citation records: "His quiet manner and self-effacing personality belie a progressive attitude and serious concern with the library's role in the future of American Society."

Frances Neel Cheney

Fred C. Cole

Susan Cooper

COOPER, SUSAN, was awarded the Newbery Medal in 1976 for the most distinguished contribution to American literature for children published in 1975 for *The Grey King,* a compelling narrative that is the fourth in a sequence of five books.

The five-volume sequence draws on major English and Celtic myths for a story of the endless battle between good and evil, moving between various modern English settings, involving both modern children and figures from myth. Titles preceding *The Grey King* are *Over Sea, Under Stone, The Dark Is Rising, Greenwitch.* The *Dark Is Rising* was the only Honor Book for the 1974 Newbery Award.

Born in Burnham, Buckinghamshire, England, on May 23, 1935, Susan Cooper went to the United States in 1963 when she married Nicholas J. Grant, an American scientist. She lives near Boston. After receiving an M.A. degree from Somerville College, Oxford, in 1956, she worked as a reporter and feature writer for the *Sunday Times* in London until her marriage.

Susan Cooper has also written an adult science fiction novel, *Mandrake;* a biography, *J. B. Priestley;* and a study of the United States, *Behind the Golden Curtain.*

DAY, MELVIN S., Deputy Director of the National Library of Medicine, was President of the American Society for Information Science from October 1975 through October 1976.

Melvin Day was born in Lewiston, Maine, on January 22, 1923. He attended Bates College and received a B.S. in 1943. He did graduate work at the University of Tennessee in industrial management, 1956–58.

He worked as a chemist with Metal Hydrides Inc., Beverly, Massachusetts, 1943–44, and on the Manhattan Project from 1944 to 1946 while in the U.S. Army Corps of Engineers, Oak Ridge, Tennessee. From 1948 to 1960 he held various positions with the Atomic Energy Commission, Oak Ridge, Tennessee, including Director of the Division of Technical Information. In 1960 he was appointed Deputy Director, Office of Technical Information and Educational Programs, NASA Headquarters, and in 1962 he became Director of the Office of Scientific and Technical Information. In 1966 he was named Deputy Assistant Administrator for Technology Utilization, NASA. From 1971 to 1972 he served as Head of the Office of Science, Information Service, of the National Science Foundation.

Day served on numerous committees, frequently chairing them and including the ASIS International Relations Committee and the UNESCO International Advisory Committee on Documentation and Libraries. He received the Public Health Service Superior Service Award, the NASA Exceptional Service Medal, and the AEC Sustained Superior Performance Award.

DILLON, LEO AND DIANE, won the 1976 Caldecott Medal for their illustrations in *Why Mosquitoes Buzz in People's Ears: A West African Tale* retold by Verna Ardema. They are unique among illustrators. Married for 20 years, their two identities have become intertwined in their art, as in their lives, with highly successful results. When working together on a book they completely blend their individual styles until neither can tell exactly how they divided the work.

They were born just eleven days apart in March 1933, Leo in Brooklyn, New York, Diane in Glendale, California, but with quite different backgrounds. Leo's parents went to the United States from Trinidad as adults, were successful in their work, did not understand discrimination or recognize the problems children can encounter because of race. They were proud of their son's talent and encouraged him, although they thought of his art as an avocation only. For Leo, art was not only a source of pleasure but became an outlet for his feelings and saw him through difficult situations.

Diane always knew she wanted to be an artist, drawing all the time. Her father, a high school teacher, and mother, a pianist and organist, encouraged her artistic talent but did not consider it important to pursue a career.

Leo had four excellent years at the School of Industrial Arts in Manhattan, now called the High School of Art and Design, where he was taught by Benjamin Clements: ". . . a great teacher . . . he shaped my life." Then he joined the Navy. After the Navy years he worked with his father for a while before enrolling in Parsons School of Design.

Diane attended Los Angeles City College for two years as an art major, later moving to New York to live with relatives who sent her to Skidmore College. After three semesters there she transferred to the Parsons School of Design.

Leo and Diane, two highly talented students, met and were in school together at Parsons for three years. Diane went away from New York briefly after leaving school, but returned to marry Leo in 1957.

They decided to do free-lance work together, and the Leo and Diane Dillon collaboration, which continued through 20 years, began. (A son, Lee, was born in 1965.)

Biographies

Melvin S. Day

Leo Dillon

Diane Dillon

Biographies

Earlier books that have been honored include *Behind the Back of the Mountain: Black Folktales from Southern Africa*, an ALA Notable Children's Book (1973); Children's Books Showcase (1974); Society of Illustrators Citation of Merit (1974); and AIGA Children's Book Show (1973–74). *The Ring in the Prairie: A Shawnee Legend* was a Child Study Association Book of the Year (1970).

Both the Dillons have taught at the School of Visual Arts and have shown their work at various galleries and societies.

DOWNS, ROBERT BINGHAM, library administrator, educator, and writer, was cited as "a notable example of the scholar-librarian" when an Honorary Membership was conferred upon him by ALA in 1976.

Born in Lemoir, North Carolina, on May 25, 1903, Downs received the A.B. degree at the University of North Carolina, and the L.S.B.S. and M.S. from the Columbia School of Library Service in 1929. After holding posts in public, college, and university libraries, he became Director of the Libraries and the Library School of the University of Illinois in 1943. From 1958 to his retirement in 1971, he served as Dean of Library Administration. Downs in 1976 continued his research, writing, and consultant activities.

Downs served as adviser to universities and governments of Japan, Mexico, Turkey, Brazil, Afganistan, Tunisia, and Puerto Rico. From 1952 to 1953 he was President of ALA, from which he received the Clarence Day, the Lippincott, and the Melvil Dewey Awards. He was awarded six honorary degrees and the University of Syracuse Centennial Medal.

In honor of Downs's national leadership in intellectual freedom, the Illinois Library School established the Robert B. Downs Intellectual Freedom Award in 1968, recognizing the single most signal contribution to the cause.

Among Downs's many books, those on the resources of American and British libraries are notable in the profession. *Books That Changed the World* and six other titles on the impact of books and reading on society are widely read beyond the profession.

A man of dignified and reserved mien, Downs can combine fun and scholarship. In a speech on "Southern Political Folklore and Humor" (*Southeastern Librarian*, Spring 1971), he quotes Artemus Ward and Petroleum V. Nasby with relish, but characteristically closes with a quotation from Jefferson on the power of the people and the need "to inform their discretion" by education.

ELLENBERGER, JACK S., Librarian with Covington & Burling, Washington, D.C., was President of the American Association of Law Libraries, 1976–77. All of his professional service has been with law libraries.

Jack Ellenberger was born in Lamar, Colorado, on September 5, 1930. He attended Georgetown University, School of Foreign Service, and received a B.S.F.S. with a major in international relations in 1957. He received his M.S.L.S. in 1959 from the School of Library Service of Columbia University.

He was Librarian for Carter, Ledyard & Milburn, New York City, 1957–60, and for Jones, Day, Reavis & Pogue, Cleveland, Ohio, 1960–61. He became Librarian for the Bar Association of the District of Columbia, 1961–63.

From 1962 he was an instructor in law librarianship at the U.S. Department of Agriculture Graduate School. He has also been a consultant for law libraries.

He was an active member of the American Association of Law Libraries from 1957. He chaired several committees of that association, including the Committee on the *Law Library Journal*. He has also been active since 1960 in the Law Librarians' Society of Washington, D.C., the local chapter of the AALL. From 1957 a member of the Special Libraries Association, he chaired the SLA Copyright Committee from 1971. He is also a member of ALA and the District of Columbia Library Association.

Ellenberger is coauthor of an 11-volume work—*Legislative History of the Securities Act of 1933 and the Securities Exchange Act of 1934* (1973).

FRITZ, JEAN (GUTTERY), author of historical biographies and fiction for young readers, delivered the 1976 May Hill Arbuthnot Honor Lecture April 9 at the University of Southern California, Los Angeles.

Born in Hankow, China, of missionary parents November 16, 1915, she went to the U.S. for a one-year furlough at the age of six and returned to the country as a permanent resident when she was thirteen. After high school in West Hartford, Connecticut, she attended Wheaton College in Norton, Massachusetts, receiving a B.A. degree in 1937.

In New York City she worked in the research-service department of a textbook publisher, later doing some free-lance ghost writing for another publisher. In 1941, shortly before Pearl Harbor, she was married to Michael Fritz. They spent the war years on the West Coast, in San Francisco and

Robert Bingham Downs

Jack S. Ellenberger

Jean (Guttery) Fritz

then Fort Lewis, Washington, where he was stationed. During those years she did book reviewing for newspapers.

After the war they returned to New York, moving to Dobbs Ferry in 1951. When she learned that the library there had no children's department Jean Fritz, as a volunteer, began a storytelling hour and then organized a children's room. In 1954 her writing began to be published. She is particularly interested in American history of the colonial and revolutionary periods, as the titles of some of her best-known books indicate: *And then what happened, Paul Revere?*, *Where was Patrick Henry on the 29th of May?*, *Why don't you get a horse, Sam Adams?*, *Will you sign here, John Hancock?*, *What's the big idea, Benjamin Franklin?* Her books have been praised by reviewers, recommended by and listed in approved buying guides, and some are on the ALA Notable Children's Books list for the year of publication.

"The Education of an American," her Arbuthnot Honor Lecture, was particularly appropriate for the Bicentennial Year, and developed a theme that closed with: "But to give them an ever larger sense of community, we must also, I believe, give them a sense of history. . . . And I am persuaded that if our children can feel themselves a part of this arduous, continuing adventure we call history, they will find the courage and, I hope, the creativity to save their future."

FUSSLER, HERMAN HOWE, Martin A. Ryerson Distinguished Service Professor at the Graduate Library School, the University of Chicago, was presented the Ralph R. Shaw Award for library literature 1976 for *Research Libraries and Technology*. In 1954 he was awarded the Melvil Dewey Medal by the American Library Association.

He was born in Philadelphia on May 15, 1914. He received an A.B. in mathematics in 1935 and an A.B. in library science in 1936 from the University of North Carolina and an M.A. in 1941 and a Ph.D. in 1948 from the University of Chicago, Graduate Library School.

His professional areas of major interest and his contributions to librarianship have been in college, university, and research libraries; library buildings; library resources, management, and other concerns of large libraries; library-related technologies; and bibliographical control.

Fussler began his library career as a library assistant with the New York Public Library, Science and Technology Division, in 1936. From April to December 1937, he was Head, Demonstration of Microphotography, sponsored by the Rockefeller Foundation and ALA, at the Paris International Exposition. He was Head of the Department of Photographic Reproduction at the University of Chicago Library, 1936–46. He served as Assistant Director of the Information Division and Librarian of the Metallurgical Laboratory of the Manhattan Project, 1942–45. He was Science Librarian of the University of Chicago Library, 1943–47.

In 1947 Fussler was appointed Assistant Director, then Associate Director, and in 1948, Director of the University of Chicago Library, and he served as Director until 1971. During his service as Director, the Joseph Regenstein Library was built under his supervision.

He served the Graduate Library School at Chicago from 1938 as Lecturer, later as Instructor and Assistant Professor, and from 1948 as Professor. From 1961 to 1963 he was Acting Dean.

He edited *Management Education: Implications for Libraries and Library Schools* (1973) and was co-author of *Patterns in the Use of Books in Large Libraries* (1969, revised edition), and has written extensively on other library subjects.

Fussler served on the Science Information Council of the National Science Foundation, 1970–74, on the National Advisory Commission on Libraries, 1966–67, and other national advisory bodies. For the Association of Research Libraries he contributed to the work of various committees, 1953–72, and he was on the Council of the American Library Association, 1956–59. His service also includes work for the American Council of Learned Societies and the American Association for the Advancement of Science.

GAVER, MARY VIRGINIA, librarian, educator, researcher, editor, writer, and publisher, was presented the highest award of the American Library Association, Honorary Membership, during the 1976 Centennial Conference. The Citation recognizes her contributions "to the growth and development of the school media center; to the fields of education and publishing as well as to the library profession; to promoting school librarianship in other lands." She was commended also for outstanding service to the profession through its associations and for her "remarkable record as a champion of excellence in library service. . . ."

Born in Washington, D.C., December 10, 1906, she received an A.B. degree from Randolph-Macon Women's College, Lynchburg, Virginia, in 1927, where she also received the Phi Beta Kappa key. She earned a B.S. in Library Science from the School of Library Service, Columbia University, in 1932 and an M.S. in L.S. from that institution in 1938. She was a Carnegie Fellow in 1937. She continued graduate study at Teachers College, Columbia, 1947–50.

During years as Librarian in the high school at Danville, Virginia (1927–37), as Technical Director, State-Wide Library Project, W.P.A. of Virginia (1938–39), and as high school Librarian, Scarsdale, New York (1939–42), she developed programs of service remarkably in advance of those usually found during that period.

In 1942 Mary Gaver became Librarian and Associate Professor of Library Service at the New Jersey State Teachers College in Trenton, a position she held until 1954. Between 1934 and 1942 she was a Visiting Instructor at the University of Virginia and at Emory University.

In 1954 she joined the faculty of the Graduate School of Library Service at Rutgers University, where she was an Associate Professor, 1954–60, and Professor, 1960–71. She became Professor Emeritus in 1971.

She joined Bro-Dart, Inc., as Consultant for Library and Publisher Relations in 1971, and was named a Vice-President of the firm in 1973. She was General Editor of *The Elementary School Library Collection*, 1st through 8th editions, published by the Bro-Dart Foundation (1965–73).

Active in professional organizations, Mary Gaver served as President of the American Library Association, 1966–67; President of the Library Education Division of ALA, 1949–50; and President of the American Association of

Biographies

Herman Fussler

Mary Virginia Gaver

Biographies

School Librarians, 1957–58. She chaired the Knapp School Libraries Project Advisory Committee, 1963–65. She was National President of Woman's National Book Association, 1974–76, and President of the New Jersey Library Association, 1954–55.

Her publications include *Effectiveness of Centralized School Library Services (Phase I)*, a Research Project sponsored by U.S. Office of Education, a Cooperative Research Program, January 1, 1959–June 30, 1960 (2nd ed., Rutgers University Press, 1963); *Patterns of Development of Elementary School Libraries Today*, 3rd ed., a five-year report on emerging media centers (Encyclopaedia Britannica, 1969); *Services of Secondary School Media Centers* (ALA, 1970); *A Survey of the educational media services of Calgary Public Schools* (with others) (Edmonton, University of Alberta, School of Library Science, June, 1971).

Special awards presented to Mary Gaver during her exceptional career recognize specific and general competencies: Rutgers Research Council Award, 1962; Herbert Putnam Honor Award by ALA, 1963; Beta Phi Mu Award for Good Teaching, 1964; Constance Lindsay Skinner Award of the Woman's National Book Association, 1973; and research grants from the Rutgers University Research Council in 1968–69 and 1969–70.

C. W. Post College, Long Island, awarded her an honorary LL.D. degree in 1967, and Mount Holyoke College one in 1968. She was given honorary life memberships in the New Jersey Library Association, the New Jersey School Library Association, the Virginia Library Association, and the Virginia Educational Media Association.

She "made a most distinguished contribution to the world of books, and to society through books," according to the Constance Lindsay Skinner Award Citation.

GREENAWAY, EMERSON, public librarian, was awarded a Special Centennial Citation by the American Library Association during the ALA Centennial Conference for his contribution to librarianship. The Citation reads in part: "The name of Emerson Greenaway will be forever etched in library literature because of his authorship of the Greenaway Plan, a pioneering venture to improve the selection and rapid acquisition of current trade books by public libraries. The landmark Greenaway Plan was only one of many efforts Emerson Greenaway made to promote the value of libraries to a free society. As a public librarian . . . he worked to extend library service to all members of the community. . . ."

Emerson Greenaway was born in Springfield, Massachusetts, on May 25, 1906. He received a B.S. from the University of Massachusetts in 1927 and an A.B. in L.S. from the University of North Carolina in 1935. He received honorary degrees from Western Maryland College, University of Massachusetts, Temple University, Drexel Institute of Technology, and Wheaton College.

He began his career as a Reference Assistant for the City Library Association, Springfield, Massachusetts, 1928–30. In 1930–1934 and 1936 he was Assistant Librarian and Supervisor of Branches for the Hartford Public Library in Connecticut. In 1935 he served as Special Assistant to the Director of the Enoch Pratt Free Library, Baltimore. He was the Librarian at the Fitchburg Public Library in Massachusetts, 1937–40, and at the Worcester Free Public Library, also in Massachusetts, 1940–45. He was Director of the Enoch Pratt Free Library, Baltimore, 1945–51, and the Free Library of Philadelphia, 1951–69.

He lectured at the School of Library Science, Simmons College, 1940–45, the School of Library Service, Columbia University, 1963–64; and the School of Library Science at Drexel Institute of Technology, 1965.

Greenaway was President of ALA, 1958–59, and chaired the ALA Legislation Committee, 1960–66. He chaired the ALA International Relations Committee, 1968–73. He surveyed libraries abroad for UNESCO and in the U.S. launched the first National Library Week.

He received several awards and honors, among them the Lippincott Award of the American Library Association, 1955; Distinguished Service Award of the Pennsylvania Library Association, 1960; and the Distinguished Achievement Award by Alumni of the Graduate School of Library Science, Drexel Institute, 1965.

HAVILAND, VIRGINIA, Chief Librarian, of the Children's Book Section of the Library of Congress, received the 1976 Grolier Foundation Award for "unusual contributions to the stimulation and guidance of reading by children and young people."

Born in Rochester, New York, on May 21, 1911, she received a B.A. degree from Cornell University in 1933. She worked in the Boston Public Library from 1934 to 1963, holding the position of reader's adviser for children, 1952–63. In 1963 she went to the Library of Congress to become the first Librarian of the newly established Children's Book Section.

She lectured on children's library services at Simmons College School of Library Service in Boston, 1957–63, and on children's literature at Trinity College in Washington, D.C., from 1969. Since 1952 she has been a professional reviewer of children's books for *Horn Book*. She served on numerous special book award committees, including the Newbery-Caldecott Committee (Chair, 1953–54), New York *Herald Tribune* Spring Book Festival Awards (1955, 1957), and National Book Awards for Children's Books (1969).

In international children's book service, she was a member of the jury selecting the Hans Christian Andersen international book awards, 1959-68, and President of the Jury, 1971–74. She was frequently the official representative of ALA/CSD to European conferences of the International Board on Books for Young People (IBBY) and of the International Federation of Library Associations (IFLA). She is the first Chairperson of Friends of IBBY, U.S. National Section, a group organized in 1976.

She has written books for children, including the popular *Favorite Fairy Tales* series, *Favorite Fairy Tales Told in England* (1959), and other from various countries. The series was extended by regular travel abroad where she found help from librarians, storytellers, and writers.

She edited the basic bibliography *Children's Literature: A Guide to Reference Sources*, published by the Library of Congress in 1966, Supplement in 1972. Special publications of the Library of Congress edited or compiled by her include *Children and Poetry*, (with William Smith) (1969); *Americana in Children's Books* (1974); and *Yankee Doodle's Literary Sampler* (with Margaret N. Doughlan) (1975).

Emerson Greenaway

Virginia Haviland

In 1976 she received the 18th Regina Medal, awarded by the Children's Section of the Catholic Library Association, for "Continued distinguished contribution to children's literature." Research and writing have filled her life.

HAYCRAFT, HOWARD, publisher and author, received a Special Centennial Citation from the American Library Association during its 1976 Centennial Conference for "his many contributions to the world of books and libraries and his support of the library profession."

Born in Madelia, Minnesota, July 24, 1905, he received an A.B. from the University of Minnesota in 1928. After a year on the staff at the University of Minnesota Press, he went to the H. W. Wilson Company in 1929. He became Vice-President in 1940, President in 1953, and Chairman of the Board in 1967. He was a director of Forest Press, 1951–68, serving as President, 1961–62. From 1942 to 1946 he was in the U.S. Army Service Forces, with the rank of Captain, then Major. He served as a member of the President's Committee for Employment of the Handicapped from 1963 to 1974.

In 1954 he received the University of Minnesota's Outstanding Achievement Award and in 1966 the first Francis Joseph Campbell Citation "for outstanding contributions to library service to the blind" from the ALA. Gustavus Adolphus College (Minnesota) awarded him an L.H.D. in 1975.

Publications of which he is author, editor, or joint editor include works familiar in library reference: *Authors Today and Yesterday* (1933), *Junior Book of Authors* (1934), *American Authors 1600–1900* (1938), *Twentieth Century Authors* (1942), and *British Authors before 1800* (1952)

He has a special interest in mystery and detective stories and has published numerous books in this field, including *Murder for Pleasure: The Life and Times of the Detective Story* (1941); *The Art of the Mystery Story* (1946); *Ten Great Mysteries* (1959); *Three Times Three: Mystery Omnibus* (1964), and *Sherlock Holmes' Greatest Cases* (1967).

He was President of the Mystery Writers of America in 1963, and received that group's Edgar Allen Poe Award for criticism.

Books for the Blind: A Postscript and An Appreciation, published in 1972, is another of his publications. Active for many years in the Round Table on Library Service to the Blind of the American Library Association, he chaired it from 1968 to 1969.

The breadth and variety of Haycraft's interests and competencies in areas relating to books and libraries earned him a special place of honor in the library community.

HENNE, FRANCES ELIZABETH, librarian, educator, and scholar, was presented a special Centennial citation by the American Library Association during its Centennial Conference in Chicago. Throughout her career she has directed her energies and incisive intellect to literature for the young, its evaluation and dissemination, and its study as a scholarly discipline, and she has provided gifted leadership in school librarianship.

Born in Springfield, Illinois, October 11, 1906, she received an A.B. from the University of Illinois in 1929, a M.A. in 1934, a B.S. from the School of Library Service, Columbia University, in 1935, and a Ph.D. from the University of Chicago Graduate Library School in 1949.

Her experience in libraries included positions in the Springfield (Illinois) Public Library, 1930–34; New York State College for Teachers, Albany, 1935–38, as Reference and Circulation Librarian; and Librarian, University High School, University of Chicago, 1939–42. Beginning her work in library education on a part-time basis in 1937, she joined the faculty of the Graduate Library School of the University of Chicago as a full-time instructor in 1942. She held positions as Assistant Professor, Associate Dean and Dean of Students, Acting Dean, and Associate Professor at that school until 1954. She went to the School of Library Service, Columbia University, as Visiting Associate Professor in 1954, becoming Associate Professor in 1955, Professor in 1961, and Professor Emeritus in 1975. In 1950 she was a Visiting Faculty Member at the University of Minnesota Library School and in 1954 at Rutgers University.

Henne's contribution to local, state, and national professional associations are too numerous to name in full. ALA committees on which she served include ALA/Textbook Publishers Institute Liaison, 1956–62, New York World's Fair Advisory, 1963–66, and Commission on a National Plan for Library Education, 1962–67. She was a member of ALA Council, 1965–69.

President of the American Association of School Librarians, 1948–49, and a member of that Board, 1945–47, she had a major role in the preparation of *School Libraries for Today and Tomorrow, Functions and Standards,* published by ALA in 1945. She was Co-chair (1954–60) of the National Standards Revision Committee that prepared *Standards for School Library Programs* (ALA, 1960), and Chair (1965–69) of the Standards Revision Committee and the Joint AASL-DAVI Committee that prepared *Standards for School Media Programs* (ALA and NEA, 1969). She was a member of the Knapp School Library Development Project Advisory board, 1960–62.

From 1965 to 1974 she was a member of the New York Regents Advisory Council on Libraries. She frequently served as a consultant or in an advisory capacity for the U.S. Office of Education and the New York State Education Department. From 1968 to 1973 she was an adviser to the Educational Media Selection Centers Project, a joint program of U.S.O.E. and the National Book Committee.

She contributed numerous articles to library and education periodicals and general magazines and is a frequent and popular lecturer to library groups. She was a joint author of *Youth, Communication and Libraries* (1949) and *Planning Guide for the High School Library Program* (1951), both published by ALA.

Special awards include a Carnegie Fellowship 1938–39, the Lippincott Award from ALA in 1963, and a special honorary award from the American Association of School Librarians in 1968.

She is regarded by many as the dean of American school librarians. Through her teaching she has been an inspiration to a generation of librarians.

JONES, VIRGINIA LACY, Dean of the School of Library Service, Atlanta University, was made an Honorary Member of ALA in 1976.

Virginia Jones was born in Cincinnati, Ohio, on June 25, 1912. She received a B.S. degree from Hampton Institute in 1936, B.L.S. from the University of Illinois Library School in 1938, and Ph.D. from the Graduate Library School, University of Chicago, in 1945.

Howard Haycraft

Frances E. Henne

Virginia Lacy Jones

Biographies

After six years on the staff of the Louisville Municipal College Library, Jones went to the Library of Atlanta University in 1939. In 1941 she became an instructor in the School of Library Service, and since 1945 has been Dean and Professor.

She served as an ALA Councilor from 1946 to 1950, 1955 to 1959, and 1967 to 1969, and as a member of the Executive Board from 1970 to 1976. She also was a member of the Board of Directors of the Library Education Division and a member of various committees of the Association of College and Research Libraries. In 1967 she served as President of the Association of American Library Schools. President Lyndon Johnson appointed her to the President's Advisory Committee on Library Research and Training Projects, 1967 to 1970.

A writer on many library topics, Jones has served on the Editorial Board of *Phylon*, the Atlanta University review of race and culture, since 1947. Among her honors are two Fellowship Awards from the General Education Board, the Hampton Institute Alumni Achievement Award in 1956, and the Atlanta Bronze Woman of the Year Award in 1959. She was given the Melvil Dewey Award from ALA in 1973.

The Citation for Jones's Honorary Membership reads in part, "In your pursuit of excellence for librarianship you have conducted institutes, persuaded foundation officials, pressured state library associations to drop discriminatory practices, and insisted that your students demonstrate both commitment and scholarship. Your graduates have reflected that same dedication to equal access to libraries, integrity in behavior, belief in the dignity and worth of librarianship, high standards of performance, and perseverence which have been hallmarks of your own distinguished career."

Ann Elizabeth Kerker

Judith Krug

Herman Liebaers

KERKER, ANN ELIZABETH, Professor of Library Science and Veterinary Medical Librarian, Purdue University, was elected President of the Medical Library Association for 1976–77, the first academic veterinary medical librarian to be elected to that office.

Born in Butte, Montana, on May 19, 1912, she received a B.S. in bacteriology from Purdue University in 1937. Before attending the University of Illinois Library School (M.S. in library science in 1959), she worked as a medical technologist for the Arnett Clinic, Lafayette, Indiana, 1933–45. In 1945 she became a medical technologist for affiliate and associate companies of Standard Oil Company (N.J.) in foreign service in South America, Saudi Arabia, and Aruba. In 1955 she returned to Indiana and from 1956 to 1959 worked as a Life Science Library Assistant at Purdue. When the Purdue School of Veterinary Medicine opened in 1959, she became the school's first medical librarian. She was promoted in the academic ranks from instructor until she was appointed full professor in 1970.

She was active in the American Library Association and the Special Libraries Association as well as the Medical Library Association. She was MLA Treasurer, and chaired its Finance Committee. She served on its Board of Directors, 1968–70.

In 1975 she spent three months in Brasilia as a consultant on a program sponsored by Purdue University's International Programs in Agriculture.

Kerker received the Eunice Rockwell Oberly Award for her *Comparative and Veterinary Medicine: a Guide to the Resource Literature* (1973).

KRUG, JUDITH FINGERET, Director of the Office for Intellectual Freedom of the American Library Association from 1967, received the Irita Van Doren Book Award from the American Booksellers Association in 1976 "for many contributions to the cause of the book as an instrument of culture in American Life."

Born in Pittsburgh, March 15, 1940, she received a B.A. from the University of Pittsburgh in 1961 (political theory) and an M.A. from the University of Chicago in 1964 (library science). She continued graduate study in political theory.

She was a Reference Librarian at the John Crerar Library, Chicago, 1962–63; Head Cataloger at Northwestern University Dental School, 1963–65; and a Research Analyst at the American Library Association, 1965–67.

Krug is Executive Director of the Freedom to Read Foundation, established in 1970 as a separate corporation working in close liaison with the American Library Association "to promote and protect freedom of speech and freedom of press. . . ."

Her publications include articles in library and education journals, and she is coeditor of the *Newsletter of Intellectual Freedom* and the *Freedom to Read Foundation News*. From 1975 she served on the American Civil Liberties Union Board of Directors, Illinois Division.

LIEBAERS, HERMAN, Librarian of the Royal Library of Belgium, 1943–54, and Director of the Royal Library, 1956–73, was awarded Honorary Membership at the ALA Centennial Conference in 1976. As one of the speakers in the series of lectures on Libraries and the Life of the Mind, he spoke at the Conference on "The Impact of American and European Librarianship upon Each Other."

Born at Tienen, Belgium, on February 1, 1919, he attended school in Brussels, received an M.A. degree from Ghent University in 1942, an M.A. in library science from the State Jury, Brussels, in 1944, and a Ph.D. from Ghent University in 1955.

Liebaers was President of IFLA from 1969 to 1974. His interest in international librarianship led him to visit most of the countries of the world. He was Librarian of the European Council for Nuclear Research, 1954, and Assistant Secretary of the Belgian American Educational Foundation, 1954–56.

He served as Associate Professor at Brussels University from 1970; consultant on the Council of Library Resources from 1973 and was Grand Marshal of the Court from 1974.

He has written number of articles that have been published in Belgian and in other languages, periodicals on library science, typography, Dutch literature and general cultural issues.

He has been named Fellow of the United States Educational Foundation, 1950; Fellow of the Belgian American Educational Foundation, 1950; and Laureate of the Koninklijke Academie voor Nederlandse Taal-en Letterkunde, Ghent, 1956. He also was awarded honorary membership in the International Association of Bibliophiles, Paris, 1971. The degree of Doctor Honoris Causa was conferred by the University of Liverpool in 1971.

MCKENNA, F(RANK) E(UGENE), Executive Director of the Special Libraries Association, was awarded a Special Centennial Citation by the ALA during the Centennial Conference. The Citation reads in part: "Frank McKenna has energetically promoted cooperative efforts between the ALA and the SLA. He has made major contributions to U.S. copyright negotiations, has provided leadership as the senior library association official in this country, and served as a distinguished special librarian."

McKenna was born in Globe, Arizona, July 29, 1921. He received a B.S. in chemistry from the University of California at Berkeley in 1941 and a Ph.D. in physical chemistry from the University of Washington in Seattle (1944). He worked as Columbia University Research Chemist for SAM Laboratories (Manhattan Project., 1944–45, and was a Research Supervisor at SAM Laboratories for Carbide & Carbon Chemicals Corp., 1945–46. After a postdoctoral Research Fellowship at the University of Chicago's Institute for Nuclear Studies, 1946–47, he held positions from 1948 to 1967 as Senior Chemist, Senior Information Specialist, and, from 1953, Supervisor of the Information Center for the Air Reduction Company, Under his leadership the Airco Information Center expanded its resources and services and became a model of "putting knowledge to work."

He was President of the Special Libraries Association, 1966–67, Editor of *Special Libraries* and Manager of the Publications Department, 1968–70, and in 1970 he became Executive Director.

He contributed frequently to *Special Libraries* and to scholarly journals in technical fields. In November 1972 he was Visiting Professor at the University of Tokyo, University of Kyoto, and the National College of Librarianship in Japan.

McKenna, noted for his dry wit as well as for his relentless pursuit of excellence, once described the ideal information specialist as "intelligently adventurous but not rash."

MELCHER, DANIEL, publisher, author, library trustee, donor of the Newbery and Caldecott Medals, received the highest award of the American Library Association, Honorary Membership, during the 1976 Centennial Conference.

Born in Newton Center, Massachusetts, July 10, 1912, he received a B.A. degree from Harvard in 1934. He began his publishing career as a publicity assistant at George Allen & Unwin, London (1934–35), studying publishing methods in London and Leipzig during 1935. Returning to the United States he worked in various capacities for several publishers: Henry Holt and Company, 1936; Oxford University Press, 1937–39; Alliance Book Corporation, 1939–40; Viking Press 1940–42. He spent the war years in Washington, D.C., as a publishing consultant, War Finance Division, U.S. Treasury Department, 1942–43, as National Director, Education Section, War Finance Division, 1943–45, and as Director of the National Commission on Atomic Information, 1946.

Back in New York he joined R. R. Bowker Company, holding positions of General Manager, Director, Vice-President, 1959–63, and President 1963–68. He was Chairman of the Board from 1968 until he resigned in 1969. During his tenure there he initiated the publication of what are now standard reference tools for librarians and booksellers, among them *Books in Print, Subject Guide to Books in Print,* and *Forthcoming Books.*

He chaired the Board of Gale Research Company, 1971–73, and served as a Trustee of the Montclair (New Jersey) Public Library, 1972–73, and a member of the Council of the American Library Association, 1972–74. He served also on the Board of Directors of the Institutes for Achievement of Human Potential (Philadelphia) from 1969.

The son of Frederic G. Melcher, who died in 1963, Dan Melcher continued the tradition begun by his father, donating the Newbery (since 1922) and Caldecott (since 1938) Medals, presented annually by the ALA Children's Services Division.

Melcher wrote *The Printing and Promotion Handbook* (1949, 1956, 1967), *Melcher on Acquisition* (with Margaret Saul) (1971), and numerous articles in library and book trade publications.

METCALF, KEYES DEWITT, Librarian of Harvard College and Director of the Harvard University Library, 1937–55, was honored by the Buildings for College and University Libraries Committee of the Building and Equipment Section of the Library Administration Division at the Centennial Conference in 1976 for his work as a building planner and consultant.

Metcalf was born in Elyria, Ohio, on April 3, 1889. He received a B.A. degree from Oberlin College in 1911, and a certificate and diploma from the Library School of the New York Public Library in 1914. His tenure as Director of Libraries at Harvard (ten years of which he was also Professor of Bibliography) was preceded by service at the Oberlin College from his students days and New York Public Libraries, 1913–37, and followed by the appointment as Adjunct Professor of the Rutgers Graduate School of Library Science, 1955–58.

An expert on buildings and administrative problem solving, Metcalf filled 600 consultant assignments, taking him to Europe, Africa, Asia, Australia, Latin America, and Canada, as well as to 46 states in the U.S.

Active in ACRL and other units of ALA, he served as President of ALA in 1942–43. He was also President and a founding member of the American Document Institute (now the American Society for Information Science). Thirteen universities awarded him honorary degrees. In May 1961 the New York Public Library's 50th Anniversary Awards were given to the Library of Congress, the British Museum, the Bibliothèque Nationale, and Keyes D. Metcalf for "his creative contributions to research librarianship."

Among Metcalf's many publications on buildings are *Planning Academic and Research Libraries* (1965) and *Library Lighting* (1970).

He traveled the equivalent of 60 times around the earth at the equator. In the mid-1970's Metcalf had lost none of his enthusiasm for libraries, nor his skill in problem solving. At the ALA Centennial Conference he addressed the third General Session with candid reminiscences of the last four Librarians of Congress, all of whom he knew. His speech was regarded by all who heard it as a highlight of the Conference. In his 87th year in 1976, Metcalf continued his work as consultant and author.

MEYER, HELEN HONIG, head of Dell Publishing Company, was a cowinner of the 1976 Constance Lindsay Skinner Award, pre-

F. E. McKenna

Daniel Melcher

Keyes Metcalf

Helen Honig Meyer

Eric Moon

Harriet F. Pilpel

Anne B. Piternick

Jesse Shera

sented by the Women's National Book Association for outstanding contributions by women to the world of books. The other recipients of the award in 1976, in an unusual triple tie in the voting, were Frances Cheney (q.v.) and Barbara Ringer (see Biographies in 1976 *Yearbook*).

Born in Brooklyn, New York, December 4, 1907, Helen Honig went to work at an early age at Dell as the first assistant to George T. Delacorte. At that time, in the early 1920's, the company had a small staff and published two magazines. Helen Honig Meyer (she was married to Abraham J. Meyer, a New York broker) saw the firm grow to a staff of more than 900 producing an annual volume of 100,000,000 books and magazines each year. She participated in that growth by steadily taking on more and more executive responsibility. By 1942 she was Executive Vice-President. In 1957 she became President of Dell Publishing Company and various enterprises associated with it.

She became a director of the American Association of Publishers, and she chaired the Department of State Government Advisory Committee on International Book and Library Programs for two years, serving as a member in 1976.

MOON, ERIC EDWARD, President of Scarecrow Press, was elected first Vice-President and President-elect of ALA in 1976. He was nominated by petition. ALA Councilor from 1965 to 1972, Moon has held a number of other posts in the Association.

Born in Yeovil, in the county of Somerset, England, March 6, 1923, Moon attended the School of Librarianship of Loughborough College of Further Education. He became a Fellow of the Library Association in 1950. From 1938 to 1958 he held positions in various public libraries in England and was active in the Library Association, serving on its Council from 1955 to 1958, and as Examiner from 1956 to 1958. After a year and a half as Provincial Director of Libraries in St. John's, Newfoundland, he went to the United States. He was Editor of *Library Journal* from 1959 to 1968 when he became Director of Educational Development for the R. R. Bowker Company. In 1969 Moon became Executive Officer of the Scarecrow Press and shortly therafter President.

Moon wrote *Book Selection and Censorship in the Sixties* (1969) and with Karl Nyren edited *Library Issues: The Sixties* (1970). In 1966 he was awarded the Savannah State College Library Award for Distinguished Service to Librarianship.

As editor, author, speaker, and Councilor, Moon has been both one of ALA's most vigilant critics and a rigorous supporter. Writing of the Association in 1972 (*American Libraries*, April 1972), he said, "But if it is all a mess, it is a healthy one." He became a spokesman in the 1960's for those who wished to make ALA more immediately responsive to individual members' rights and concerns and less involved in the maintenance of the status quo.

PILPEL, HARRIET FLEISCHL, attorney and senior partner in the New York City law firm of Greenbaum, Wolff & Ernst, delivered a lecture on "Libraries and First Amendment Rights" in the Life of the Mind Series at the ALA's 1976 Annual Conference in Chicago.

A graduate of Vassar College and the Columbia Law School, she was admitted to the New York bar in 1936. In a career devoted to civil liberties, freedom of the press, and the legal problems of authors, she has served on numerous governmental committees and national boards. She has been Vice-Chairperson of the National Board of Directors of the American Civil Liberties Union and Chairperson of its Communications Media Committee, a member of the Panel of Experts of the U.S. Government Copyright Office, a Trustee of the Copyright Society of the U.S.A., and a member of the Executive Committee of the National Book Committee. She was the author (with Theodora Zavin) of *Rights and Writers* (1960) and (with Morton David Goldberg. of *A Copyright Guide* (1960). She has written frequently on law and intellectual property in *Publishers Weekly*.

In recognition of her many contributions to the causes of sex education and planned parenthood, she was given the Annual SIECUS (Sex Information and Education Council of the U.S.) Award (1973) and the Margaret Sanger Award (1974).

PITERNICK, ANNE B., library educator, became President of the Canadian Library Association for 1976–77.

Born in Blackburn, England, she received a B.A. from the University of Manchester in 1948 and later an A.L.A. After service as a Research Librarian from 1951 to 1956, she joined, at the University of British Columbia, the Library Reference Division. In 1960 she became Head of the Science Division.

From 1961 to 1964 she served as Information Officer of the Canadian Uranium Research Foundation, and in 1964 she returned to the University of British Columbia in a joint appointment in the Metallurgy Department and Library and as Head of the Social Science Division of the Library. She served the University of British Columbia, in the School of Librarianship, as part-time lecturer from 1961 to 1966, and in 1966 she was appointed to a full-time position on the faculty. In 1973 she was promoted to Associate Professor. She has contributed many articles on library subjects. Her special interests are in reference and information service, library use, and information systems.

She was President of the Canadian Association of Special Libraries and Information Sciences, 1969–70, and Vice-President and President-elect, 1975–76.

SHERA, JESSE HAUK, library educator and author, was presented with an Honorary Membership in ALA at the Centennial Conference in 1976. The Citation addresses him as "scholar, intellectual, pioneer in documentation and information science, lecturer, and teacher."

Shera was born in Oxford, Ohio, on December 8, 1903. His A.B. degree was conferred by Miami University in Oxford in 1925, A.M. by Yale in 1927, and Ph.D. by the Graduate Library School of the University of Chicago in 1944. After service in the Library of Miami University, the Library of Congress, the U.S. Office of Strategic Services, and the Library of the University of Chicago, he became Associate Professor in the Graduate Library School. In 1952 he was appointed Dean of the School of Library Science, Western Reserve University (later Case Western Reserve). When he retired as Dean in 1970, he continued as Professor until 1972, when he was made Dean Emeritus.

Among the ten books Shera has written, *Foundations of the Public Library* (1949), a revision of his Ph.D. thesis, is regarded as a classic in the field. Others, such as *The Compleat Librarian* (1970) and *Foundations of Education for Librarianship* (1972), given a Scarecrow Press Award, have also earned professional praise. Many of his articles and speeches have raised storms of controversy and ventilated important issues throughout his career.

Shera's establishment of the Center for Documentation and Communication Research at the Case Western Reserve School of Library Science in 1955 was a landmark accomplishment, recognizing the technology of information retrieval as an integral part of librarianship. Recognition of this contribution came in invitations to Shera to lecture and participate in documentation conferences in France, England, Brazil, and India, as well as all over the United States. He has received the Melvil Dewey, Lippincott, Beta Phi Mu, and other awards in honor of the breadth of his contributions.

A scholar with critical spirit, Shera continued in 1976 to lecture and write, refusing to let his colleagues settle down in comfort while libraries remain imperfect and discoveries are still to be made.

STEVENSON, GRACE THOMAS, Associate and Deputy Executive Director of ALA, 1952–65, was awarded a Special Centennial Citation at the 1976 Conference.

Born in Morgansfield, Kentucky, January 27, 1900, Grace Stevenson attended St. Joseph's College in Owensboro, Kentucky. Following her graduation she taught in settlement schools in the mountains of Kentucky, a contrast to her work as head of the personnel department of a San Francisco shipyard in World War II.

Stevenson worked in public libraries in Indiana and California before she went to the Seattle Public Library, where in 1945 she became head of the Adult Education and Film Department. While there Stevenson chaired adult education units in the Public Library Division, ALA, and in the Pacific Northwest Library Association. She chaired the committee that produced the American Heritage Film List for ALA's 75th Anniversary in 1951. In that year, Stevenson became Director of the American Heritage Project at ALA.

In 1952, she became Associate (later Deputy) Executive Director of ALA, a post she held until her retirement in 1965. Concurrently, until 1960, she was Director of the Office for Adult Education, supervising a series of projects financed by the Fund for Adult Education of the Ford Foundation.

Stevenson became the first woman President of the Adult Education Association of the United States in 1957.

After her retirement in 1965, Stevenson was active in library development, particularly in the Southwest. A colleague said of Grace Stevenson, "She has done more for library development in the ten years of her retirement than many have done in their whole careers." In 1968 her work resulted in *Arizona Library Survey*, in 1969 in *Library Services Across the Border: Idaho, Oregon, and Washington: A Study*, and in 1971 *Chapter Relationships, National, Regional and State* for ALA.

The Centennial Citation honors Grace Stevenson "for her dedicated service to the American Library Association and her unflagging leadership during the Association's first century."

STONE, ELIZABETH W., Professor and Chairperson of the Graduate Department of Library Science at Catholic University of America and Executive Director of CLENE (the Continuing Library Education Network and Exchange), was presented a Certificate of Distinction by the ALA Library Education Division during the 1976 ALA Centennial Conference in Chicago. The Certificate cites "her work, dedication and enthusiasm for continuing education as represented in her development of CLENE."

She was born on June 21, 1918, in Dayton, Ohio, and attended Stanford University. She received A.B. and M.A. degrees there and a secondary teaching credential. She received an M.S. in Library Science from the Catholic University of America and Ph.D. from American University.

From July 1973 to May 1974 Elizabeth Stone served as Project Director of the Continuing Education Study sponsored by the National Commission on Libraries and Information Science. The final report, *Continuing Library and Information Science Education*, published in 1974, recommended the formation of a new CLENE organization to act as a special service and resources facility that makes continuing education opportunities available to all library, information, and media personnel at all levels of service in all locales.

Prior to her work with CLENE, she served as Associate Director for a research project sponsored by Title II of the Higher Education Act which investigated job dimensions and continuing education needs of personnel in federal libraries and information centers. As part of Phase II of that project she was coauthor of *Human Resources in the Library System* (3 volumes).

She served as President of the American Association of Library Schools, the District of Columbia Chapter of the Special Libraries Association, and the District of Columbia Library Association.

THORPE, FREDERICK A., British publisher, known around the world as "Mr. Large Print," was awarded a Special Centennial Citation by the American Library Association at the 1976 Centennial Conference. The Citation reads in part: "In his tireless efforts to convince the public of the need for reading matter in large print, he has travelled throughout the English-speaking world, calling attention to the needs of the visually handicapped." As head of Ulverscroft Large Print Books Ltd., he directed publication of its thousandth title in 1976, Tolstoy's *War and Peace* in five volumes.

In 1964, at the age of 50, he retired from a large publishing business intending to take life easy. He took up the challenge of producing Large Print books for the elderly, a pioneering enterprise that became known as the Ulverscroft Large Print Series. His program made it possible for many visually handicapped persons to enjoy books previously available only in small print. He developed paper and ink suitable for the special processes required in Large Print production.

In 1969 he received the O. B. E. (Order of the British Empire) and in June 1972 the Francis Joseph Campbell Award (ALA). When he began to devote his time and energy to the problems of the visually handicapped, the need for special

Grace T. Stevenson

Elizabeth W. Stone

Frederick A. Thorpe

Wallace Van Jackson

Theodore Waller

Carolyn I. Whitenack

service was not as clearly perceived as it was to become 12 years later, after the dedicated work of Frederick Thorpe. Thorpe established the Ulverscroft Foundation; profits that may accrue from Large Print books are placed in the Foundation. Its primary purpose is to offer assistance in all types of eyesight problems, including the placing of optical equipment in English hospitals.

VAN JACKSON, WALLACE, was presented a Special Centennial Citation during the American Library Association's Centennial Conference in 1976 for "leadership in the development of Black academic libraries in the United States, in library education, and in the development of library service in Africa."

He was born on May 6, 1900, in Richmond, Virginia. He received a B.A. from Virginia Union University in 1934 and a B.L.S. from the Hampton Institute in 1934. In 1935 he received an A.M.L.S. from the University of Michigan. He studied at the University of Chicago Graduate Library School from 1939 to 1941.

Before undertaking library work he was a teacher, a school principal, and the editor of the *Richmond Voice* (Virginia), 1925-27. From 1927 to 1939 he served as Librarian of Virginia Union University. He was a consultant to librarians of Black colleges throughout the south and worked with deans of southern graduate schools to improve library resources for professional education. In 1941 when the Atlanta University School of Library Service was opened he was a member of the faculty and played a vital role in the beginning of the school. He was a member of the Editorial Board of *Phylon* magazine, 1942-47, and served as Librarian of Atlanta University (1941-47). He later worked at Texas Southern University (1949-54), Virginia State College (1954-62, 1963-68), Mary Holmes College (1968-69), and Assistant to the Librarian at the Hampton Institute (1969-70).

He has also held library positions in Liberia, Swaziland, Nigeria, Botswana and Lesotho. He inspired many Black Americans and Africans to enter the library profession.

WALLER, THEODORE, President of the Grolier Educational Corporation, received a Special Centennial Citation from ALA in 1976. Part of the Citation reads, "In the last two decades, one man who has worked hardest to achieve better communication and understanding between the library community and publishers is Theodore Waller."

Born in Oakland, California, April 25, 1916, Waller, after attending the University of Chicago from 1933 to 1937, joined the staff of the National Youth Administration in San Francisco. During World War II he worked with the War Relocation Authority, and from 1946 to 1947 was Executive Officer and Chief of the UNRRA Mission to Byelorussia. He represented the United World Federalists in Washington, 1948-49.

Waller's career in publishing began in 1950 when he joined the American Book Publishing Company. Subsequently he held executive positions with the New American Library of World Literature, Inc., Franklin Watts, Inc., and the Teaching Materials Corporation, divisions of Grolier. In 1966 he became President of the Grolier Educational Corporation.

From 1953 to 1956, Waller was a member of the ALA Committee on Intellectual Freedom, and from 1956 to 1962 of the International Relations Committee. In 1966 he was appointed to the National Advisory Commission on Libraries. The recommendations of that Commission led to the establishment of the National Commission on Libraries and Information Science in 1970.

As Executive Secretary to the American Book Publishers Council's Committee on Reading Development, Waller promoted the formation of the National Book Committee, which instituted the National Book Awards and National Library Week. He was a strong and active member of the Steering Committee for NLW.

In 1972 Waller served as Co-chairman of the U.S. Ad Hoc Committee for International Book Year. He is a member of the International Book Committee of UNESCO. ALA honored him for "his support of books, reading, libraries, and the library profession."

WHITENACK, CAROLYN I., Chairperson of Media Sciences in the Department of Education at Purdue University, received the 1976 Beta Phi Mu Award for Good Teaching during the Centennial Conference of the American Library Association for "creative leadership and distinguished national and international contributions in the field of education for librarianship, educational media, and school librarianship."

Born in Mercer County, Kentucky, April 20, 1916, she began her education at Georgetown College (1932-34). She received a B.A. from the University of Kentucky in 1948 and an M.S. from the University of Illinois, Graduate School of Library Science, in 1956.

After teaching in elementary schools of Mercer County and Versailles, Kentucky, she became instructor and librarian, Department of Library Science, University of Kentucky, in 1947 and went to the Louisville Public Schools as head of the cataloging department and school library services in 1950. She moved to Indiana in 1953. She was Director, Division of School Libraries and Teacher Materials, Indiana Department of Public Instruction, until 1956 when she went to Purdue University to chair School Library and Audiovisual Education in the Department of Education. She became Professor and Chairperson of Media Sciences there.

Active in professional associations, she was the first school librarian to be nominated for President of the American Library Association, serving as Second Vice-President, 1960-61. A member of ALA Council, 1955-60, she served on various ALA committees including the Audiovisual Committee, 1970-73. She was President of the American Association of School Librarians, 1968; Joint Chairman, Standards for School Media Programs Committee, 1967-69; and Chairman, AASL/AECT Joint Editorial Committee, *Media Programs: District and Schools* (published 1975). On the Board of Directors, AASL, 1955-60, Whitenack has also been active in the National Education Association, the Association for Supervision and Curriculum Development, Association for Educational Communications and Technology, and National Council of Teachers of English. She served as President of the Kentucky and Indiana School Library Associations. She has been a delegate to International Conferences of the World Confederation of the Teaching Professions (1962, 1967, 1968,

1974); to the UNESCO Bibliographic Control of Nonprint Materials Conference (1968); and to the International Federation of Libraries (1962, 1970, 1974).

The Citation reads in part: "Her unique approach to library/media education can be amply illustrated by the media science curriculum at Purdue University in its effective assimilation of media into library service education."

WHITNEY, VIRGINIA P., Librarian of Rutgers University, was President of the Association of Research Libraries, 1975–76.

She was born in Medford, Massachusetts, on December 1, 1914. She received a B.S. in political science from Middlebury College in 1936 and a M.L.S. from Rutgers University in 1962.

Virginia Whitney became a Library Assistant at the East Orange (N.J.) Public Library in 1955 after working as a secretary for Socony-Vacuum Oil Company. In 1962 she joined Rutgers University Library as Urban Centers Librarian and served the University in various library capacities until she was named University Librarian in 1971. She held a joint appointment from 1965 to 1970 as a librarian and as a Lecturer in the Rutgers University Graduate School of Library Science.

She contributed to many university programs as a member of various committees at Rutgers and has also been active in professional associations. She was elected a member at large of the ALA Council, 1974–78 and to the Budget Assembly, 1976–77, and served on the Board of Directors of the ARL, 1973–77. She is on the Advisory Council of the Princeton University Library. She was appointed to the Visiting Committee for Libraries, Massachusetts Institute of Technology Corporation, 1973–76, and reappointed in 1976 to serve until 1979. From 1976 she served as an adviser to the editors of this *Yearbook*.

WIJNSTROOM, MARGREET, Secretary-General of IFLA, is a leader in Dutch public librarianship and international library cooperation.

Margreet Wijnstroom was born on August 26, 1922, at Bloemendaal in North Holland (Netherlands). She earned diplomas for Assistant Librarian (1943) and Library Director (1946) and a law degree (Amsterdam University, 1953). While studying law, she worked part-time in various libraries, and from 1954 to 1957 she was head of the Department of Public Relations of the Public Library of Amsterdam. In the Netherlands she became a member of various advisory committees for library legislation and standardization and Vice-Chairman of the Dutch Association of Librarians. In 1976 she held seats on the Library Council and the Board of the National Library Center.

From 1958 to 1971 Wijnstroom served as General Secretary of the Central Association of Public Libraries, The Hague, and as Director of the Central Association's office. She also represented Dutch public librarianship at IFLA Conferences. From 1971 she held the post of Secretary-General of IFLA (International Federation of Library Associations and Institutions).

Her publications include *De openbare bibliotheek in Europa* ("The Public Library in Europe"; 1976) and many articles in Dutch and other periodicals on copyright, library standards, legislation, IFLA, and other professional interests.

WINNIE-THE-POOH, created by A. A. Milne, celebrated his 50th birthday in 1976. Asked to tell about himself, he wrote: "I was born in London in 1921, but I didn't become Winnie-the-Pooh until five years later. What actually happened was that for a few weeks I led an anonymous existence as a nameless teddy bear, golden tan, eighteen inches high, in Harrod's department store in London, and when I was beginning to despair of finding a real home I was picked up and taken to the house of A. A. Milne, who lived in nearby Chelsea. There I discovered I was a birthday present to Christopher Robin Milne, an only child, on the occasion of his first birthday. It was only when I took my place in the Milne nursery that I really began to come to life, and almost at once I became Christopher's inseparable companion.

"Unbeknown to me, while I thought that only Christopher Robin was aware of my existence, Christopher's father and mother were taking the keenest interest in the way their son enjoyed playing with us, and his father, the popular author and playwright, fell into the habit of devising amusing situations in which we were all involved. He would make up little stories and relate them to his son with such happy results that Mrs. Milne urged that he put them down on paper. Accordingly he dictated his stories to her, and when they appeared in print in 1926 with *Winnie-the-Pooh*, the name which Christopher had given me, on the cover of the book, their appeal was so great that a second collection called *The House at Pooh Corner* appeared by popular demand two years later.

"Pooh Corner was the area near Cotchford Farm, the Milne country house in Sussex where I spent the seven happiest years of my life. Piglet's house was there, and Kanga's, and Rabbit's. Even Christopher Robin had a house, not far from Eeyore's gloomy place, and on the map in *Winnie-the-Pooh* you can see Owl's house and my own Pooh Bear house. Of course the 100 aker wood is on this map, which was drawn by Christopher Robin, even though he admitted that "Mr Shepard helpd." All my best adventures took place in this wonderful setting, and I shall always consider myself fortunate for having experienced them!

"It all ended when Christopher Robin went off to school, and then I languished in a cupboard with Eeyore, Tigger, Piglet, and Kanga until one day Mr. Milne's American publisher appeared and offered to take us on a tour of the United States. In no time at all we found ourselves traveling through every state in the Union and making new friends in every important city in a country which we all loved so much that we became American citizens in 1957.

"I have been back to England only twice since 1947: to help honor E. H. Shepard (he drew the pictures of me in the books) when he was feted on his 90th birthday at London's Victoria and Albert Museum in 1970, and again in 1976 to celebrate my own 50th birthday. Incidentally, my birthday activities in New York were so strenuous (they included a two-day party at the Bronx Zoo) that for at least a year I shall be content to remain quietly at home in the reception room of the offices of E. P. Dutton in New York City."

POOH'S AUTOBIOGRAPHY
REPRINTED COURTESY OF
ELLIOTT GRAHAM,
E. P. DUTTON & CO, INC.

Virginia P. Whitney

Margreet Wijnstroom

WINNIE-THE-POOH

Blind and Physically Handicapped, Library Services for the

Blacks and Libraries

See *Ethnic Groups, Library Service to.*

Blind and Physically Handicapped, Library Services for the

During 1976 the Division for the Blind and Physically Handicapped of the Library of Congress continued to place emphasis on improving and expanding services for its readership. Nearly 13,400,000 books and magazines in special formats were circulated by the division and its network of affiliated libraries throughout the United States.

Service in 1976 was extended by the addition of regional libraries in Alaska and Vermont and five subregional libraries in the states of Georgia, Illinois, and Kansas to the network of nearly 150 libraries. Regional li-

Groundbreaking ceremonies for the Illinois Regional Library for the Blind and Physically Handicapped in Chicago, March 12. From left, architect Stanley Tigerman, Chicago Library Board Vice President Louis A. Lerner, CPL President Ralph G. Newman, the late Chicago Mayor, Richard J. Daley, and CPL Director, David L. Reich.

braries in Arkansas and Virginia added braille materials to their collections of recorded books. The first overseas deposit collection was opened at the U.S. Army Hospital in Berlin, West Germany.

As part of cooperative efforts of network libraries, the Southern Conference of Regional Librarians for the Blind and Physically Handicapped began publication of the quarterly DIKTA. DIKTA is a forum for ideas, opinions, and articles on innovative practices of interest to librarians serving the blind and physically handicapped.

Regional libraries in Los Angeles, Austin, Cleveland, Cincinnati, Philadelphia, and Daytona Beach, among others, shared in the development of automated circulation systems that save time and labor in selecting books and processing reader requests. The systems have been designed to generate address labels for mailing books to patrons and to store reader records.

Network library collections were expanded by the addition of approximately 1,000 commercially produced talking-book and 300 press-braille titles. More than 50 braille magazines were produced for distribution to the readers; and of 50 magazines recorded on flexible disc were made available by circulation directly to users. In the last few years, the division has made increasing use of the flexible disc as a fast, cost-effective means of satisfying the demand for popular materials. Plans have been drafted to add more flexible disc magazines for direct circulation from producers to readers.

Production of a braille edition of the *New York Times Large Type Weekly* marked expansion of service to braille readers. For the first time in the history of the program, a national circulation newspaper is being brailled regularly and distributed nationally to blind readers. Issues of the embossed edition were mailed directly to more than 2,500 readers.

In connection with technical improvements in reading equipment for program users, the division began developing a combination cassette and phonograph machine. The combination machine will play 1-7/8 and 15/16 ips cassettes as well as 33-1/3, 16-2/3, and 8-1/3 rpm discs. Using the built-in speed control, readers will be able to skim their talking books, or if they want they can listen to them at normal speeds.

Under contract to the division, Mitre Corporation began testing "Telebook," an experimental concept in talking-book service. If the service proves its worth, readers will have instantaneous access to reading materials merely by dialing a central, toll free telephone number and requesting that talking books or magazines be played via telephone or special FM-radio receivers.

The recent development of the Visitoner and Kurzweil reading machines has stimulated interest in seeking new devices and unconventional methods for translating printed material into braille and other formats usable by blind readers. Kurzweil Computer Products, Inc., completed initial development of a high performance reading machine featuring multi-font character recognition. Designed specifically as an aid for blind people, the Kurzweil machine will "read" a wide variety of printed matter—books, magazines, typewritten letters—and yield output in the form of full-word English speech. The speech rate may be varied by the user up to the normal speech rate of approximately 200 words per minute. The reading machine will also have an alternate "spelled-speech" mode to allow a user to hear his material spelled out letter by letter. Work is in progress to develop a braille output capability.

FRANK KURT CYLKE

Bookmobile

See *Community Delivery Service*

Bookselling

Bookselling continues to be one of the most satisfying if not most remunerative of professions. There is nothing more rewarding for a bookseller than placing the one book in a person's hand that was desired above all others, whether it be a title from some bestseller list or one that required research and a search service.

As with other aspects of life in the U.S. in the 1970's, retail bookselling is going through a period of stress and self-examination from which some believe will emerge a new "golden era" for all persons involved with books, from writers to readers. The trade was hard pressed at the end of 1976 by diminishing profits, a pressure that has been increasing over a period of several years, forcing it to find new ways to maintain standards.

Solutions must be found to the problem of costs that continue to spiral, sending book prices beyond the reach of many readers, and to problems of a technology that seems at times to master rather than serve us.

New Markets. Chains continued in 1976 creating new book buyers each week by opening shops where there had never been real bookstores before, exposing to a virgin audience the potential of books. Moving right along beside the chains are hundreds of small personal bookshops opened by practical idealists. The times are not receptive to dilletantism. Eager neophytes learn quickly, if they do not know before, that one has to know bookkeeping as well as books if bookselling is going to thrive.

Established stores retrenched in 1976, many cutting waste wherever it was found, and sometimes reducing services. Doing so was recognized by most as a step backward, one that will be reversed as soon as possible by providing increased services to make up for the temporary inconvenience.

Thus major chains created a demand, much of which they continued to meet, while sending off to other stores those customers who wanted to go beyond the fast turnover and current titles so efficiently stocked by the chains. Bookstores, large or small, locally owned and managed can maintain backlists and afford to specialize in areas that would not be profitable for the larger corporate operations.

Discounts. 1976 was the year of the big discount. Attempting, and appearing to succeed, to merchandise books in the same way appliances, clothing, and almost everything else seems to be merchandised in the U.S., discount bookstores lured people looking primarily for bargains regardless of what the bargain was. The up-front bait was discounted bestseller list titles on a massive base of remainders, reprints, imports, hurt books, and used books.

Heavy promotion created a stir among the nonreading public and among confirmed book buyers. The rush was on and book sales soared. Final results are not yet in, but it would appear that once again a combination of things which chilled the hearts of established booksellers may have created a whole new group of book buyers who will fan out across all retail bookselling.

Promotion. Trade associations, recognizing the need for developing new markets, launched their own promotions. The Association of American Publishers sponsored television spots—"A Book Is a Loving Gift"—in New York and Minneapolis. The American Booksellers Association underwrote a nationwide radio campaign urging listeners to "find

The annual surplus book sale of the Dayton and Montgomery County (Ohio) Public Library in June brought over 2,000 customers.

a friend in a book" in a bookstore. Both projects were aimed at those who have not yet realized the value of books in their lives.

The American Booksellers Association (ABA) continued its training programs for booksellers, holding one-day workshops in Minneapolis, Dallas, Atlanta, and Washington, as well as conducting workshops at meetings on both coasts. A two-day seminar for potential booksellers was planned to precede the regular Booksellers Schools to be held in Boston in February 1977 and in Colorado Springs in March 1977. ABA publications such as *Trends* and the weekly *Newswire* kept booksellers informed of what was happening and about to happen.

Booksellers' eagerness to know, and to participate in exchange of, information was made evident by record attendance of 9,000 at the ABA Convention in Chicago in June 1976, and at ABA regional meetings in Los Angeles and St. Petersburg, Florida, and by high attendance at locally organized meetings in New England and the northwest.

An air of cautious optimism prevailed in spite of demands which made the possibility of failure an ever-present threat. The year was not a banner one for business by any criterion. Yet it brought out authors of every view, traveling coast to coast to help sell books; they appeared not only on television and radio but also in bookstores, where they met and talked to their readers. Poets read to small but rapt audiences in corners of bookstores. Children sat on floors on Saturday mornings to listen to writers and illustrators tell how they create books. Bringing writers and readers together is a growing part of bookselling.

Once again, many thought, bookstores were becoming community centers. A return to an adaption of the ancient tradition of storytelling is part of the bookseller's dream. It takes one away for a moment from accounts and accounting, making the demands of reality worthwhile. That the dream is good business only adds to its pleasure. Even the most accountant-controlled bookseller is aware that a good bookstore's contribution to its community is different from that of any other retail store. It is that realization and that contribution that gave bookselling its real purpose in 1976 and will in all the years to come.

ROBERT D. HALE

Budgeting, Accounting, and Cost Control

Using the words of the stock market analyst, "1976 was a mixed year in budget growth with many more losers than gainers, and overall budget growth on the down side." The general state of the economy, stabilizing—and in some cases declining—student population, and increasing tax pressures on cities and on the property tax in general throughout the country resulted in a fairly negative picture regarding library budget growth in 1976. Among the losers of budget battles, receiving in some cases even less money for 1976 than they had received in 1975, and in all cases receiving significantly less funds than they had requested for 1976, were such diverse libraries as Trenton State College, American Geological Society, Buffalo and Erie County Library, City University of New York, Nassau County, Phoenix Public Library, and the Colorado State Library. New York City libraries, both the University and Public, once again received significant budget cuts resulting in reduced hours and the elimination of positions. New York Public Library closed eight more branches.

The picture was not bleak throughout the entire country, however. Certain libraries did receive increases—some of them quite significant. Among the gainers in 1976 were Monroe County (Michigan) Library, whose book budget was increased by 25 percent, Hennepin County Library in Minnesota, the Alabama State Library, the Cumberland County (North Carolina) Library, the Oklahoma City and County Libraries, and the Rhode Island State Library.

One of the most significant developments in 1976 was a new role that the state of Michigan will play in funding the Detroit Public Library. It was the first time that a state had taken over a significant portion of the direct funding of a city public library and perhaps is an indication of future trends in at least the larger older cities of the country. (*See further* Michigan State Report.)

CETA Funding. The emergence of the Comprehensive Employment Training Act, providing millions of dollars in federal funds for emergency and theoretically temporary employment, became an essential funding element for many city public libraries in 1976. Some libraries in 1976 seemed to have become dangerously dependent upon CETA funds for the staffing of their public services. An example of this dependency was the Detroit Public Library, which at one time during the year had 108 employees hired through CETA funds. In view of the undependability of such funds, subject to decrease or elimination by the federal Congress and to apportionment by local City Councils or Boards, reliance upon them becomes dangerous and also removes some control over local decisions on staffing.

The year 1976 found the Urban Libraries Council and the American Library Association agreeing on a new Title V for the Library Services and Construction Act. The new Title V proposes significant federal grants to large urban public libraries serving 100,000 people or more. Several problems remain to be resolved regarding the Title V proposal concerning separation of populations of the central city from suburban or county populations served by these same city libraries.

Academic libraries continued to retrench across the country in the face of stabilizing and in some cases declining student populations, coupled with budget increases which barely kept up with inflation and in some cases were actually below 1975 funding. Pressure on academic libraries to enter into cooperative ventures, collection pooling, and greater reliance on shared technical services and materials exchange became even greater in 1976; battles continued within institutions for additional funds and among institutions in each state for legislative appropriations.

School libraries and media centers continued to grow in some areas in 1976, but in some parts of the country, school libraries were starved almost to the point of extinction as student enrollment declined, particularly in older suburbs and in central cities, creating severe budget restrictions in school districts in general. As is too often the case, when school budgets are under severe scrutiny, the school libraries and media centers are often cut out of proportion to other departments or activities. There remained several bright spots in the newer and still expanding suburban areas where quality school support and education remained paramount in the interests of voters. The overall picture, however, was uneven throughout the country.

The increasing need for realistic and understandable performance measures and budget reporting was facilitated in 1976 with the production of "Data Gathering and Instruction Manual for Performance Measures in Public Libraries." This manual was published as a result of the interest in the 1973 Public Library Association publication "Performance Measures for Public Libraries."

Project Survival. The Public Library Association at the American Library Association Conference in July 1976 began "Project Survival." As reported in the September issue of *American Libraries*, PLA plans a series of spring strategy sessions pointing out to the public that libraries are important and that they are having trouble surviving. While sponsored by PLA, "Project Survival" hopes to deal with the financial decline of all types of libraries.

The year 1976, in conclusion, was essentially a mixed year in budgeting and financial growth, and in areas in which growth and significant budget increases were achieved, it seemed to be based primarily on local political and even personality considerations without any direct relationship to the state of the local economy versus the state of the national economy. Perhaps it can be pointed out that 1976 found librarians more acutely aware of their own need to develop adequate reporting and measurement of their services so that they can deal more directly and intelligently and less emotionally with the budgeting process and the constant quest for new funds.

ROBERT H. ROHLF

Buildings

Although overshadowed by other events during the Bicentennial year, library building projects continued to play a significant role. In at least one community, Chula Vista, California, a major public library was dedicated on the nation's birthday as a fitting symbol of the freedoms commemorated by the 200-year celebration. A number of the nation's foremost architects included library buildings in their lists of "America's Proudest Architectural Achievements."[1] These included the New York Public Library, the Boston Public Library, the Beinecke Rare Book and Manuscript Library at Yale, the Phillips Exeter Academy Library in New Hampshire, the Folger Shakespeare Library in Washington, D.C., and the Thomas Crane Public Library, Quincy, Massachusetts.

Construction Rate. The rate of construction of public library buildings increased in 1976, while academic and other types of libraries seemed to continue at the level established for the past few years. In large measure, this disparity is probably due to the availability of federal funds for public library building projects, particularly federal revenue sharing funds. More than half of the public library building projects completed during the year were supported in part by federal funds. Of the nearly 300 building projects reported for public libraries, most were either branch libraries or main libraries for smaller communities. Unfortunately, without a national census of library space needs, it is impossible to judge how well the current construction rate is keeping pace with demand for more room in libraries having to cope with expanding collections, augmented services, increasingly sophisticated operations, computerization of procedures and services, and system and network requirements.

Academic library building projects were completed in about half of the 50 states during the year. They included renovation projects, additions, and new libraries of nearly 300,000 square feet.

The construction of new, remodeled, and/or extended learning resource centers for two-year colleges continued apace. In what may prove to be the cutting edge of library organization, increasing numbers of the learning resource centers are combining the traditional library with such elements as audiovisual centers, graphic production facilities, audio video production, reprographic production, audio and video learning centers, and other elements designed to assist the individual learner. In many areas of the nation, the community college learning resource center represents the most advanced delivery of library services and materials.

From available records it would appear that the construction of new school media centers has fallen sharply. This is due to a number of factors, including the stabilization or decline in enrollment occurring throughout the nation and the lack of funds. Where new schools are still being built, the media center concept continues to exert a profound influence on school architecture and often serves as the hub around which classroom activities occur.

AIA-ALA LIBRARY BUILDINGS AWARDS

Three libraries were recipients of the First

Buildings

Honor Award, and nine received Awards of Merit under the 1976 awards program. All libraries designed by registered architects in the United States and completed after January 1, 1965, were eligible. Nearly 200 entries were received for jurying, which was conducted by a panel of jurors at AIA headquarters in Washington, D.C., in January.

Winners of the First Honor Award for Distinguished Accomplishments in Architecture were the Bates College Library, Lewiston, Maine; the Pekin, Illinois, Public Library; and the Jefferson Market Branch of the New York Public Library.

Four academic and five public library buildings were recipients of the Award of Merit in Architecture.

The jury notes provide an interesting commentary on the award recipients. The Pekin Public Library was honored for the way in which the architects had combined under one roof the Everett McKinley Dirksen Congressional Leadership Research Center with the main library. Renovation of the Jefferson Market Branch of the New York Public Library in Greenwich Village earned accolades for introducing contemporary library function into a century-old structure while adhering to the highest professional standards of both eras. Bates College Library was cited as "an elegant and straightforward structure which harmonizes with the neighboring buildings without compromising the clarity and economy of a thoroughly contemporary structure while taking advantage of a difficult site."

Another renovation and expansion project, the Randall Memorial Library in Stow, Massachusetts, was praised as a "strong architectural statement on the part of both the 19th and 20th centuries, neither of which has been relegated to a subordinate position." For the 18,000-volume Hapeville Public Library, the smallest honored in the 1976 awards program, came these words of praise: "a small, immaculately planned and detailed library illustrating the power which can be evoked by a beautifully machined object in a sylvan setting."

Effective use of earth berms to block street noise and a plan which "responds frankly to the realities of an automobile-dominated environment" was partly responsible for the Merit Award given the Novato Branch of the Marin County Library (California). The commentary further noted that the earth berms "provide a humane and sensible solution to acoustic and climatic problems too often overlooked in contemporary architecture."

The diagonal separation of public areas from staff and work spaces in an essentially square building won praise for the Rockford Road Branch of the Hennepin County Library in Minnesota. The jury found that this novel division "adds excitement and utility . . ."

With a skylight running the length of a rather long and narrow structure, the Corning Public Library houses public library services and activities as well as the headquarters for the Southern Tier Library System. This building was found by the jury to strike "a nice balance between seriousness of purpose and contemporary exuberance" with its overall form responding well "to a downtown plan which recognizes the potential importance of the library as part of a functioning urban center which will generate street life and traffic beyond normal commercial office hours."

Conversion of a portion of Fort Schuyler, in the Bronx (New York), into a library for the Maritime College of the State University of New York was recognized as a very sensitive reconstruction. While "interior partitions, plumbing, and lighting were demolished, removed or rearranged, bare granite walls and columns, exposed brick arches, apertures for muskets and cannon were all retained. . . . the exterior design remained unchanged. Inside . . . is a fully modern college library."

As the last major building to be constructed on the campus, the Lineberger Memorial Library at the Luthern Theological Southern Seminary in Columbia, South Carolina, had to relate to a variety of existing structures and circulation patterns. The jury noted that a variety of spaces had been created to meet the special needs of their users.

Built into a bluff overlooking the Potomac River, the Joseph Mark Lauinger Memorial Library at Georgetown University manages to blend with the character and scale of nearby buildings and the Georgetown skyline in spite of its size (175,000 square feet). In its comments the jury stated that "a less sensitive solution would have destroyed one of the most picturesque urban landscapes remaining on the banks of the Potomac."

Members of the jury included John F. Hartray, Jr., Chicago, Chairman; John S. Bolles, FAIA, San Francisco; Judith Edelman, AIA, New York City; Raymond M. Holt, Library Consultant, Del Mar, California; and Roscoe Rouse, Director, Oklahoma State University Library, Stillwater, Oklahoma.

In summarizing its review of submittals to the 1976 awards program, the jury made a number of comments worthy of quoting here:[2]

The design of libraries, like everything else, was easier for our grandparents. Like the church, the courthouse, and the railroad station, the library provided each community with a vital linkage to the world at large. Library architecture was, therefore, taken seriously. The finest historic styles which were adapted and the quality of construction was the best attainable. Today these structures form one of our great unrenewable architectural assets.

The architectural excellence of our historic libraries was, however, not usually reflected in the quality of their planning. This is not surprising. The collections were small and their growth

Buildings

Nathan Marsh Pusey Library, Harvard University, Cambridge, Massachusetts.

rates were not clearly perceived. Staff salaries and other operating costs were relatively insignificant in comparison to initial construction costs. Form, therefore, could afford to ignore function and follow historic symbolism.

The forces which shape the contemporary library are completely different. The cost of operations has increased much more rapidly than that of construction. Collections grow at accelerating rates; so does the variety of services which libraries are expected to offer. From the projects submitted in this awards program it appears that library planners and consultants have a strong grasp of these new realities. Architects, however, are only beginning to understand them.

The sheer bulk of library buildings even in small communities has become a major problem for architects. The designers of many of the projects submitted sought to reduce the apparent size of their buildings with applied decoration, making promises on the facade that were not kept in the interior. The best of the entries achieved a humane and understandable scale through the spacial and structural expression of the real and permanent functional differences suggested by the consultant's program.

The need for control with a minimum of staff presents the unique difficulty. Visitors to a modern library usually must be brought from the edge of the building to a point somewhere near its center before being allowed to proceed to the various departments. This trip can be a terrible bore. Many of the winning designs solved this problem by allowing a wedge of exterior space to penetrate to the center of the building. Less obvious strategies had to be employed where a tight site or existing structures constrained the plan. But the problem was faced and solved in some way by all of the successful designers.

The desire to recognize the symbolic importance of the library appears to have stimulated both the best and the worst of the solutions presented in this program. Success or failure depended on whether or not the form chosen reflected an important and permanent function within the floor plan. Some projects displayed what seemed acres of uniformly lighted acoustical ceilings under which stacks, tables, and card catalogs were distributed at random. These terrifying environments were not improved by the addition of an unrelated dome, mansard, skylight, or clerestory which only amplified the visual anarchy at eye level.

Stephen B. Luce Library, State University of New York Maritime College, Fort Schuyler, New York.

Buildings

BUILDING ACTIVITY

The Public Library of Houston, Texas (240,000 square feet), was by far the largest of the new public library buildings to open its doors in 1976. A good deal is expected to be heard about this functional library in the years ahead. Largest of the academic libraries was the Library of the University of Arizona at Tucson, which was completed but remained unoccupied at year-end pending the funding of furnishings. The library for the Northern Illinois University at DeKalb was almost as large with 292,323 square feet. A 225,000-square-foot addition was completed for Brigham Young University Library at Provo, Utah.

Mississippi continued to lead in public library building activity; California was a fairly close second with buildings tending to be somewhat larger in size. State library periodicals and newsletters recorded the completion of many projects and the beginnings of many others, both public and academic.

The Library of Congress The battle to repulse congressional leaders wishing to convert substantial portions of the new Madison Annex into office space was won in 1976. This attempt, which began in 1974, had grown to a full scale assault by late 1975. Mounting opposition from librarians, legislators, and others across the nation was rallied to turn the tide in January 1976. The Madison Annex was secured for its intended purposes as a much needed part of the growing Library of Congress complex. Meanwhile, the shell of the new Madison Annex was completed and work on the interior begun. Costs have exceeded the original amount of $90,000,000 and another $30,000,000 was the estimated price for finishing the structure.

ALA BUILDING INSTITUTE AND PROGRAMS

More than 350 librarians, trustees, architects and others registered for the 1976 LAD Buildings and Equipment Section (BES) Pre-Conference Institute, "Meeting Library Building Space Needs." An intensive workshop was divided into eight major sessions with speakers tackling such topics as "Calculating Space Requirements for the Next Decade of Growth in Your Library;" "Impact of Nonbook Media on Library Space Requirements;" "The Effect of Library Systems and Networks on Space Requirements;" "Interior Design;" "Fundamentals of Implementing Space Requirement Solutions;" and "Effect of Technological Developments on Space Utilization." A tour of Chicago's Furniture Mart was featured.

Nearly 50 speakers and panelists made presentations concerning the planning of adequate library buildings. That library facilities must be prepared for accelerated change caused by a variety of reasons was generally conceded. Close cooperation of the planning team was emphasized, beginning with the building program and continuing to completion of construction. The role of the interior designer on the building team was lucidly explained and illustrated by a slide presentation on the Chula Vista Public Library (California). Librarians were urged to give more thought to how nonprint media materials should be handled—whether through centralization or by integration into the print collections. Several speakers called attention to the growing impact of various technologies affecting libraries, among them microform, automation, video tape, cassettes, and other forms.

In addition to the Pre-Conference Institute on Library Buildings, the three program meetings sponsored by the Buildings and Equipment Section during the Annual ALA Conference were also well attended. The first of these was in honor of ALA's Centennial and featured illustrated presentations on the history of library buildings. A standing-room-only crowd

Pekin Public Library, Illinois.

of nearly 400 saw a four-part program that included academic libraries, public libraries, and library interiors; it concluded with observations by John F. Hartray, AIA, on contemporary library design derived from his analysis of projects submitted for the 1976 AIA/ALA Library Buildings Awards program of which he chaired the jury. His commentary was followed by a presentation of awards to the librarians representing the 12 winning buildings.

A second Conference program was a salute to Keyes D. Metcalf (see Biographies) for his contribution as a library consultant to academic libraries around the world. Architects and librarians who had worked with Metcalf were on hand to pay tribute and describe their asso-

ciation with him on a host of projects.

The third program, "Taking a Critical Look at Your Library Building Plans," featured a plan review session at which an architect, interior designer, and library consultant described their approach to plan review. It was followed by an actual review of plans for a major public library building. During the remainder of the morning, the audience broke into group sessions to participate in the review of plans for more than a dozen library buildings currently on the drawing boards.

FUNDING LIBRARY CONSTRUCTION

The availability of federal revenue sharing funds spurred public library construction in numerous U.S. cities, towns, and villages. Congressional approval of an extension of the State and Local Fiscal Assistance Act (PL 94-488) through October 1, 1980, carried with it an authorization of $25,600,000,000 of federal reserve sharing funds to be divided between state and local governments in the next three and three-quarter years. With the deletion of former restrictions, however, libraries could expect increased competition for such grants. More than one-third of the money used by public libraries for construction of new and remodeled buildings in 1976 was from this source, and these funds were involved in over half the public library projects. As local governmental agencies complete other projects or as the public library otherwise improves its place on the list of local priorities, an increasing number of public library building projects can be expected to be funded in whole or in part from this source.

Another source of federal funds, the Public Works and Employment Law (PL 94-447), was enacted too late in the year to have a visible impact on public library projects. The requirement for beginning construction within 90 days of project approval placed this source outside the reach of most libraries since they were without current programs and architectural plans which could be immediately activated. Some of the smaller communities may find it possible to meet the deadline and will move to do so successfully. They will be reported in another year.

National economic conditions, high unemployment, and the election of a Democratic administration heightened speculation that Title II of the LSCA Act might be funded in 1977 since there was ample evidence of the high degree of success it attained during its brief period of activity. Similarly, construction funds might be made a part of legislation related to both higher education and to the elementary and secondary schools.

LAD/BES ACTIVITIES

Committees of the Buildings and Equipment Section of the Library Administration Division

Jefferson Market Branch, New York Public Library.

Buildings

Novato Branch Library, Marin County, San Rafael, California.

Hapeville Branch Library, Hapeville, Georgia.

Randall Memorial Library, Stow, Massachusetts (above and left).

Rockford Road Branch Library, Hennepin County Library, Crystal, Minnesota.

of ALA were very much involved in the Conference programs as well as in other activities. A new library building consultant list was compiled from responses of those presently active in this field. It is now available through the LAD office and replaces a list several years old. All committees worked on the updating of building programs, slides, bibliographies, and other materials on library buildings available for loan through the LAD office.

Several new committees were formed by the Section, including a Library Buildings Awards Committee and a Community College Learning Resources Centers Facility Committee. Two other committees on school media centers and institutional libraries, respectively, were in the process of formation. The Library Buildings Awards Committee has been charged with the responsibility for reviewing the current AIA/ALA Library Buildings Awards program and making recommendations for its future. The Community College Learning Resources Centers Facilities Committee produced a much needed bibliography on the "Two-Year Learning Resources Center Building" as its first project.

The proceedings of the 1974 Library Buildings Pre-Conference Institute were published by ALA under the title *An Architectural Strategy for Change*. Following the keynote address by Allie Beth Martin, chapters dealt with the remodeling and expanding of libraries, advice from a panel of architects, consultants, and engineers, and critiques of a number of library buildings. The reproduction of architectural drawings, photographs, and building data

AIA–ALA Library Buildings Awards 1976

Library	Jurisdiction	Architect	Gross Square Footage	Approximate Volume Capacity	Year Completed
First Honor Awards					
Bates College	Bates College Lewiston, Maine	The Architects Collaborative, Cambridge, Massachusetts	101,676	420,000	1973
Jefferson Market Branch	New York Public Library	Giorgio Cavaglieri, New York	24,000	33,000	1967
Pekin Public Library	Pekin, Illinois	John Hackler and Co., Architects, Peoria, Illinois	34,073	65,000	1975
Merit Award Winners (Academic Libraries):					
Joseph Mark Lauinger Memorial Library	Georgetown University, Washington, D.C.	John Carl Warnecke & Associates, Washington, D.C.	175,000	1,400,000	1970
Stephen B. Luce Library	State University of New York Maritime College, Fort Schuyler, Bronx, New York	William A. Hall and Associates, New York	27,490	90,000	1966
Nathan Marsh Pusey Library	Harvard University, Cambridge, Massachusetts	Hugh Stubbins and Associates, Cambridge, Massachusetts	87,000	1,000,000	1975
Lineberger Memorial Library	Lutheran Theological Southern Seminary, Columbia, South Carolina	Walter Dodd Ramberg, Sparks, Maryland	25,000	100,000	1975
Merit Award Winners (Public Libraries):					
Corning Public Library	Corning, New York	RTKL Associates, Inc., Baltimore, Maryland	40,000	110,000	1975
Hapeville Public Library	Hapeville, Georgia	Stevens & Wilkinson, Atlanta, Georgia	5,000	18,000	1974
Novato Branch Novato, California	Marin County Library, San Rafael, California	Marquis Associates, Vallejo, California	11,000	65,000	1971
Randall Memorial Library	Stow, Massachusetts	Finegold & Bullis, Boston, Massachusetts	8,500	32,000	1974
Rockford Road Branch Library, Crystal, Minnesota	Hennepin County Library, Southdale, Minnesota	Parker Klein Associates, Architects, Inc., Minneapolis, Minnesota	15,450	50,000	1972

sheets should be helpful to those concerned with library building projects of all kinds. This volume takes its place alongside previous proceedings as a vital part of the literature on the subject.

Mention should also be made of the attractive covers *American Libraries* used on the January through May issues commemorating "Great American Libraries." Included in the series were the Redwood Library and Athenaeum, Newport, Rhode Island, oldest library structure in the nation; the Old Rotunda Library of the University of Virginia, Charlottesville, Virginia, designed by Thomas Jefferson; the Carnegie Free Library of Allegheny, Pittsburgh, Pennsylvania—the first of Carnegie's 2,509 libraries in America; the Henry E. Huntington Library in San Marino, California; and the Library of Congress, Washington, D.C. Each cover was produced by a different artist, providing an unusual visual treat—a worthy contribution to the ALA Centennial year.

RAYMOND M. HOLT

REFERENCES
1. "Highlights of American Architecture, 1776-1976," *AIA Journal* (July 1976), pp. 88–150.
2. AIA News Release, "Report of the Jury," 1976 Library Buildings Award Program (March 27, 1976).

Cable TV

See *Telecommunications and Public Broadcasting*.

Canadian Library Association

Founded in Hamilton, Ontario, in 1946, the Canadian Library Association (CLA) is a national organization whose objectives are to develop high standards of librarianship and library and information services. The Association is grouped into five divisions, each called an association and each having its own constitution. None of the divisional constitutions is permitted to be in conflict with the constitution of the parent body. The divisions are: Canadian Association of Public Libraries, Canadian Association of College and University Libraries, Canadian Association of Special Libraries and Information Services, Canadian Library Trustees' Association, and Canadian School Library Association.

1976 Issues. Faced with rapidly rising costs of supplies and services over the year, and the aftereffects of a national postal strike at the end of 1975, the Canadian Library Association was forced in 1976 to curtail some of its programs, such as divisional publications and meetings of some of its executive bodies and committees. In his presidential address at the annual conference, Brian Land pointed out that there are 94 library or library-related associations in Canada and suggested that a fresh look at the feasibility of a national federation of library associations in which membership services and activities could be better rationalized might be worthwhile. A Presidential Task Force on the Future of CLA, appointed by the 1976–77 CLA President, Anne Piternick, has, among other things, followed up on this suggestion by making overtures to the provincial and regional associations on this possibility. The initial reaction of these bodies, some of which pre-date CLA by many years, was not enthusiastic, their view being that critically important provincial/regional needs are best served by independent provincial/regional associations. Input into national association planning, it should be noted, is available to provincial/regional organizations through their representation on CLA Council.

Presentations to Government. CLA made some significant representations to government in 1976. In May, led by President Land, the Association submitted a brief to, and appeared before, the Standing Joint Committee of the Senate and the House of Commons of Canada on Regulations and Other Statutory Instruments, which was examining the question of public access to government information. The main thrusts of the brief were to recommend ways in which the government publishing and distribution system should be improved, and ways of making unpublished information and data more easily and widely accessible through greater utilization of the government's own library facilities and professional library expertise.

In March the Association presented a brief outlining proposals for federal funding of interlibrary lending in Canada to the Secretary of State and the Minister-designate for the National Research Council, the ministers responsible for the National Library and the Canada Institute for Scientific and Technical Information, respectively. Prepared by then First Vice-President Piternick, the brief was inspired by a situation whereby certain large university libraries, which serve unofficially as regional resource centers, were forced to introduce charges to cover the costs of lending their materials. The brief contended that these charges are to the detriment of equitable library service across the country but also recognized that the resource libraries have been bearing an undue financial burden by serving in this capacity. In response to the brief, the ministers created an interdepartmental committee (under the chairmanship of the National Librarian) to examine the question.

Public Lending Right. The Association also came to grips with the so-called "Public Lending Right" issue. CLA Council, the policy-making body of the Association, called a special hearing on the subject at its mid-winter meeting where representatives of the publishing community, and the Canadian Copyright Institute, along with writers, including novelist Marion Engel, argued in favor of a system by which authors would be compensated for library lending of their works. Weighing these views against those of Samuel Rothstein of the School of Librarianship, University of British Columbia, who spoke against the implementation of a PLR system, Council decided to recommend to the membership that it support, through other means, the principles of adequate recompense for authors and stimulation of Canadian writing. At its June conference, the Association passed a resolution supporting the use of library holdings data in the development of a system of increased financial rewards to writers which it urges the federal government to undertake and fund, not because of any legal entitlement to recompense for library use, but in recognition of the cultural contribution of Canadian writers. The Association communicated its position to the Secretary of State in June.

During the year, the Council approved a statement prepared by President-Elect Piternick on *Goals and Objectives for CLA,* which elaborates on the goals and objectives set forth in the Constitution and By-laws. Council also approved a *Code of Ethics,* which was endorsed by the membership at the annual meeting, and Guidelines for Employment Practices, which outlines the responsibilities of library employers and employees.

Division Activities. CLA's five divisions made significant advances in their respective spheres of interest. The Canadian Association of College and University Libraries adopted a set of guidelines on academic status for university librarians; it shared authorship with the Canadian Association of University Teachers. The guidelines, which assert that professional librarians play an integral role in the pursuit, dissemination and structuring of knowledge and understanding in the university, cover appointments, dismissal procedures, grievance procedures in cases not involving permanent appointments or dismissal, salaries and benefits, and library governance.

The most noteworthy activity of the Canadian Association of Public Libraries was its pursuance of Project: Progress, a comprehensive survey of the state of public libraries in Canada. In August the public libraries division received from the Centre for Research in Librarianship, University of Toronto, a 211-page research design made possible by a $15,000 contract between the Centre and CLA. The design brings together the efforts of a team of experts from Canada, Great Britain and the United States to set out a method for analyzing and justifying the role of the public library in Canada to the year 2000. The Project: Progress Steering Committee began a major campaign to fund the $400,000 survey proper by canvassing all public libraries across the country, asking that they contribute one-tenth of one percent of their current annual budget each year for three years. The Committee also began planning an approach to funding agencies.

The Canadian Association of Special Libraries and Information Services, the only division to be organized into local chapters, continued to concentrate its efforts on local programming in Edmonton, Ottawa, and Toronto. The division established a Calgary chapter in September. The Canadian Library Trustees' Association concentrated its efforts on internal administrative procedures and membership recruitment.

Other Activities. Revenue from the publishing program of the Canadian Library Association represents nearly fifty percent of total income. In April the Association received an $88,000 grant from the Canada Council to automate and expand the *Canadian Periodical Index.* As the cornerstone of the publishing program, the *Index* increased its coverage of periodicals from 88 to 97 titles in 1976. CLA began implementation of an automated production system for the Index which will shorten the gap between preparation and production of monthly issues and will greatly reduce the length of time needed to produce the annual cumulation.

In September the Association received a grant of $19,875, also from the Canada Council, in support of *Canadian Materials.* Conceived by the Canadian School Library Association, this publication is a thrice yearly periodical devoted to critical reviews of Canadian print and nonprint materials for schools and libraries.

The Association published five major professional and reference monographs in 1976. It publishes a bimonthly professional journal, the *Canadian Library Journal,* operates a microfilming program, and serves as the North American distributor for publications of the Universal Bibliographic Control Section of IFLA.

CLA held its 31st annual conference in Halifax, Nova Scotia, June 10–16, 1976, attracting 1,020 delegates to a varied program, the central theme of which was "Libraries in the Canadian Mosaic," an examination of ways in which libraries can meet the needs of a multicultural society.

Membership. As of June 30, 1976, CLA membership totaled 4,075 of which 3,135 were personal members and 940 institutional. Members join the parent organization and are entitled to select membership in any or all divisions for a $10 fee, with the first divisional choice being free. Basic personal membership fees range from $5 to $50 depending on status and salary while institutional fees are calculated according to annual budget, the minimum being $30 and the maximum $2,500.

PAUL KITCHEN

Canadian Library Association

See also
Canadian Correspondent's Report

During the year, the Council approved a statement prepared by President-elect Piternick on *Goals and Objectives for CLA,* which elaborates on the goals and objectives set forth in the Constitution and Bylaws. Council also approved a *Code of Ethics,* which was endorsed by the membership at the annual meeting, and *Guidelines for Employment Practices,* which outlines the responsibilities of library employers and employees.

REFERENCES
Canadian Library Association, *Annual Report 1975–76* (1976).
Feliciter (from January 1976 monthly tabloid newspaper amalgamating all divisional material).

CLA Officers

PRESIDENT (June 1976–June 1977):
Anne Piternick, University of British Columbia, Vancouver, British Columbia

FIRST VICE-PRESIDENT/PRESIDENT-ELECT:
Ken Haycock, Vancouver School Board, Vancouver, British Columbia

SECOND VICE-PRESIDENT:
Flora E. Patterson, National Library, Ottawa, Ontario

TREASURER:
Bruce Cossar, Trent University Library Peterborough, Ontario

EXECUTIVE DIRECTOR:
Paul Kitchen

Headquarters: 151 Sparks Street, Ottawa, Ontario. K1P 5E3

Cataloging and Classification

1976 marked the centennial of three major events in American librarianship, all of particular and continuing significance for cataloging and classification. In 1876 the American Library Association was founded, and the first editions of both Charles Ammi Cutter's *Rules for a Printed Dictionary Catalogue* and the Dewey Decimal Classification (DDC) were published—events celebrated at the 1976 Annual Conference of ALA. DDC also celebrated its 100th birthday with the issuance of the facsimile reprint of the first edition (44 pages) while work on the multi-volumed 19th edition, scheduled for publication in 1979, continued. Conferences marking the DDC centenary were held in England, Brazil, and Belgium, emphasizing the universality of this classification system now used in 134 countries and translated into more than 19 languages.

PRECIS Interest. The year 1976 also saw increasing interest in the United States in PRECIS (PReserved Context Index System), another and entirely new approach to the subject indexing of books and other documents, combining human indexing with computer-aided construction of index terms. Used in the *British National Bibliography* since 1971, the first workshop of its kind about PRECIS in the United States was held at the University of Maryland in October.

The Cataloging Distribution Service (CDS) of the Library of Congress celebrated its 75th anniversary. In 1901 the first catalog cards from LC became available and established the uniform size catalog card as well as communicating the work of LC catalogers throughout the world. In fiscal year 1976 CDS distributed over 82,000,000 cards, tens of thousands of publications and MARC (MAchine-Readable Cataloging) records. *Library of Congress Subject Headings (LCSH)* became available in microform produced by a COM (Computer-Output-Microform) process as well as in machine-readable form, with tape services for other authority records scheduled to follow. The microform edition of *LCSH* is issued quarterly, and each issue cumulates in one alphabet the subject authority information from the eighth edition of *LCSH* and all subsequent quarterly supplements, giving subscribers a complete new edition of *LCSH* every three months.

The Cataloging in Publication (CIP) program of the Library of Congress, operational for five years, provided data for approximately 24,000 titles in fiscal year 1976, an increase of nearly 6,000 titles over the previous year. Over 1,080 publishers are submitting a combined weekly average of 460 titles.

OCLC Expansion. OCLC (Ohio College Library Center) marked the fifth anniversary of its on-line shared cataloging system in August. There are now over 845 libraries at participating institutions in 39 states and the District of Columbia. Participating libraries are cataloging about 25,000 books a day and are finding existing records already in the system for 91 percent of the books cataloged, compared with 84.7 percent found in the previous year. OCLC is producing over 160,000 catalog cards daily and its on-line union catalog contains more than 2,400,000 bibliographic records and about 12,000,000 location listings. The W. K. Kellogg Foundation offered grants enabling small private liberal arts colleges throughout the country to join OCLC.

A grant from the Carnegie Corporation of New York to the Research Libraries Group, Inc. (RLG), a consortium of the libraries of Columbia, Harvard, and Yale universities and the New York Public Library Research Libraries, will be used to develop a computer-based cataloging system in conjunction with the Library of Congress. When completed, this will mark the first time a library network has remote access, on-line, directly into LC's MARC data base.

Work continued on the revision of the *Anglo-American Cataloging Rules* by ALA, the Library of Congress, the Library Association, the British Library, and the Canadian Committee on Cataloging. At the end of the year, the Joint Steering Committee for Revision of the *Anglo-American Cataloging Rules* decided that the text of this second edition in its advanced state of preparation should be reviewed by all the bodies which have contributed to the extensive revision effort, and the bodies concerned agreed to participate in such a review. The review was scheduled for early 1977, with publication anticipated later in the year.

The Margaret Mann Citation in Cataloging and Classification was awarded to Eva Verona of Zagreb, Yugoslavia, in recognition of her definitive work *Corporate Headings: Their Use in Library Catalogues and National Bibliographies* and her continuing outstanding leadership toward the realization of universal bibliographic control of library materials through international standardization of cataloging principles and practices.

The emphasis in this review, as in last year's, is the movement toward universal bibliographic control of library materials and the development of cooperative national and international bibliographic networks. Indeed, these are the prevailing trends in cataloging and classification. That they raise certain questions for American public and other non-research oriented libraries should not pass unnoticed, however, and the problems were well described in Maurice Freedman's much discussed article, "Processing for the People" *(Library Journal 101* [January 1, 1976] 189–97).

That the need for change and upgrading in current methods of bibliographic control is becoming more and more apparent was one of the themes at the 38th Annual Conference of the Graduate Library School of the University of Chicago whose topic was "Prospects for Change in Bibliographic Control." "Processing and Automation at the Library of Congress," an institute cosponsored by the Information Science and Automation Division of ALA and the Library of Congress, was held in the spring and, because of demand, again in the fall. The institute sessions described both present activities of the Processing Department of LC and future plans, including those for the national bibliographic service.

Other Involvements. Matters of a more traditional nature also received attention in 1976. Meeting topics and subjects of journal articles included: the form of the catalog—card, book, or microformat, divided or dictionary; the matter of norms for cataloging operations; the use of the *National Union Catalog* as a cataloging tool; classification and subject headings for non-book materials; the completeness of the cataloging record and subject headings appropriate for children's materials; the question of racism and sexism in subject headings and classification; bibliographic control of microforms; form of subject headings; catalog maintenance in general and especially in terms of changing subject headings. The Library of Congress continued its Cataloging in Person Program at the ALA Midwinter and Annual Conferences, giving catalogers an opportunity to discuss their problems with LC staff members. LC *Cataloging Service* published comprehensive information about LC practices and decisions in subject and descriptive cataloging, including interpretations of rules, and also reprinted or printed the currently valid romanization tables.

For cataloging and classification, then, 1976 was a year of celebration of significant anniversaries, of development of the trends reported in the 1975 *ALA Yearbook*, and of continuing attention to the nature of the catalog, the cataloging process, the catalog/bibliographic record, and the organization of bibliographic materials.

JANE ROSS MOORE

Catholic Library Association

Responding to the demands imposed by the development of Religious Education Centers, the Catholic Library Association (CLA) published a 200-title annotated bibliography, *Books for Religious Education* ($3). The bibliography includes recommended titles for children, young adults, and adults. A second edition, in preparation in 1976, will take account of the growing demands for recommended print materials since bibliographies available from other sources are devoted exclusively to nonprint materials.

CLA was an active participant in the Eucharistic Congress held in Philadelphia during August. A sample library of titles in *Books for Religious Education* formed the CLA booth display at the Congress Exhibition. Publishers supplied copies of the recommended books.

CLA published *Periodicals for Religious Education Centers and Parish Libraries*, an evaluation of 106 magazines, newspapers and newsletters with signed recommendations of periodical sources useful in the selection of media for religious education.

Continuing Education. With continuing education occupying much attention in the library profession, CLA has inaugurated preconvention institute to meet the interest. A needs assessment questionnaire was circulated among CLA members to give direction for future institute and convention planning. As a result of the 1976 institutes, a booklet, first in a series, "Studies in Librarianship," was published. The booklet, a collection of papers delivered at the CLA Institute on Librarian-Educator Interdependence, explores the interdependence that should exist between the teacher and the librarian, between librarian and librarian, publishers, manufacturers, and producers, all of whom influence the media of educational technology.

Children's Book Council

NCEA. Continuing its joint convention arrangement with the National Catholic Educational Association (NCEA), CLA has taken an active role in satisfying the demands of library publishers and suppliers who find it financially impossible to continue to support the many conferences and conventions of librarians. Efforts at cooperation with educators are gradually raising the image of the librarians within the educational scene. Through CLA Headquarters, the services of members have been volunteered for committee assignments within the National Catholic Educational Association to demonstrate the principle that "librarians are educators, too."

Service Themes. *Catholic Library World*, official journal of the Association, devoted its pages in 1976 to specialized themes, including, "Library Service to the Poor," "Library Volunteers," "Media Management," "Library Standards/Programs," and "Media Review, 1976." Volume 18 (1975–76) of the *Catholic Periodical and Literature Index* was completed in 1976. The two-year cumulation adds additional comprehensive coverage of Catholic periodicals and books to the *Index*, which began in 1930, and to the former *Guide to Catholic Literature* from 1888.

Membership in CLA is open to all persons, institutions, and organizations interested in the purpose of the Association, "the promotion of Catholic principles by the improvement of library resources and services through cooperation, publication, education and information". The annual dues are $15 for personal members. Higher categories are Contributing, $100; Sustaining, $250; and Supporting, $500. Membership year: July to June. Membership as of December 1976 was 3,081.

MATTHEW R. WILT

CLA Officers

PRESIDENT (April 1975–April, 1977):
James C. Cox, Loyola University Medical Center Library, Maywood, Illinois

VICE-PRESIDENT/PRESIDENT-ELECT:
Sister Mary Arthur Hoagland, I. H. M., Philadelphia Diocesan School Libraries

EXECUTIVE DIRECTOR:
Matthew R. Wilt

Headquarters: 461 W. Lancaster Avenue, Haverford, Pennsylvania 19041

Censorship

See *Intellectual Freedom*.

Children's Book Council

In 1976 Children's Book Council membership numbered approximately 60 publishers. New members joining during the year were Bantam Books, Inc., and Bonim Books, a Division of Hebrew Publishing Co. Abelard-Schuman, Hawthorn Books, and Scroll Press resigned in 1976.

The Council's interests are in promoting greater use and enjoyment of children's trade books, and in sponsoring events and celebrations covering both contemporary and classic children's literature. The most notable of these celebrations is National Children's Book Week, initiated in 1919 and celebrated annually ever since. Book Week was the first institutionalized "week" of any sort created anywhere, and a model for other various "weeks," ranging in scope from observances of significant contributions to services, the arts, health and welfare, to occasions when entrepreneurs exploit the public's interest in finding something to celebrate. Book Week, observed November 8–14 in 1976, had as its theme "Bookmagic." A great variety of display and activity materials were prepared by artists and offered to the public by CBC to encourage enthusiastic observances of Book Week. In 1976 the honor of preparing the materials was shared by Caldecott Medalist Uri Shulevitz (the annual poster, perhaps the item with which Book Week is most associated); British illustrator John Goodall (mini-frieze); streamer artists Ron Barrett, Harold Berson, and Jacqueline Chwast; Stan Mack (mobile); and, as a special contributor, Natalie Babbitt, who wrote and illustrated "A Puzzling Story for Book Week," a pamphlet that delighted many thousands of children throughout the fall of the year. The 1976 Book Week poet was Mary Ann Hoberman.

Another major promotional effort made by CBC in 1976 was to encourage greater interest in poetry among children, and adults working with children. The Council assembled a talented group of poets to write special poems for this effort. They were Robert Froman, Nikki Giovanni, X.J. Kennedy, and Eve Merriam, whose poems appeared on bookmarks illustrated, respectively, by Ray Barber, Steven Kellogg, Leonard Lubin, and Ron Himler. At the same time, attractive display materials featuring poetry—a poster by Janina Domanska and a streamer by Robert Andrew Parker—were designed to become permanent promotional items for libraries and schools. Robert Quackenbush prepared an illustrated folder in which children write their own poems or the names of favorites. Accompanying these materials was a useful folder with practical suggestions on promoting poetry and poetry programs in schools and libraries.

Other CBC materials prepared in 1976 were for summer reading programs, and new or revised bookmarks on dogs, growing things, and the Newbery and Caldecott Medals. The Council continued publication of *The Calendar*, well received by thousands of readers.

1976 marked the fifth CBC Showcase, a selection of 28 books published in 1975 that

Promotion materials portraying the "Book Magic" theme of Children's Book Week in 1976 included: Streamer by Ron Barrett.

Mobile by Stan Mack.

Streamers by Harold Berson (left) and Jacqueline Chwast (right).

Poster by Uri Shulevitz.

Mini-frieze by John S. Goodall.

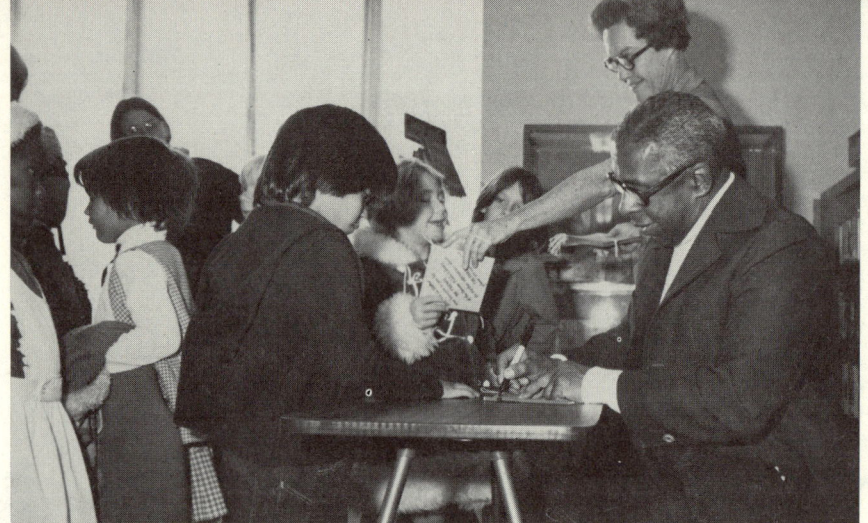

The 1976 Children's Book Week at the Denver Public Library opened with the "Family Travels with the Storyteller" program featuring Spencer G. Shaw, who later signed autographs for members of his audience.

the judges, Irene Haas, Janet Halverson, Una Johnson and Joseph Low, considered especially distinguished for graphic and bookmaking excellence. Showcases based on CBC's catalog are mounted in hundreds of communities throughout the country.

Growing out of a need the Council identified for in-service and pre-service materials on children's books, CBC in 1975 had introduced a series of mini-seminars in the form of half-hour taped sessions by expert teachers and established professionals. Titled *Prelude,* the first series led to a second series offered in 1976. The second included sessions on "Children's Response to Books" by Charlotte S. Huck; "Encouraging Families to Read Together" by Lavinia Russ; "Enjoying Poetry With Children" by Leland B. Jacobs; "Fantasy and the Human Condition" by Lloyd Alexander; "Good Science Teaching Develops the Whole Child" by Roma Gans; and "Using Folklore As an Introduction to Other Cultures" by Anne Pellowski.

CBC works closely with other groups through a number of joint committees that develop programs and conferences on the subject of children's books. In the case of three of the committees, subcommittees excluding CBC representatives have substantial annual booklisting projects designed to introduce new books to teachers in various disciplines. For 1976, a subcommittee of the National Science Teachers Association–CBC Committee selected outstanding 1975 children's science books that appeared in the March 1976 issue of *Science and Children.* The April 1976 issue of *Social Education* included an annotated listing of notable 1975 children's books for social studies educators, prepared by members of the National Council for the Social Studies. And nationwide selection teams selected "Classroom Choices for 1975," an annotated listing to which children had contributed; this list appeared in the October 1976 issue of the International Reading Association's *Reading Teacher.* The Council's other joint committees are with the National Council of Teachers of English; the Association for Childhood Education International; and the American Library Association. This last committee sponsored an especially notable day-long program during ALA's Centennial Conference on "Art in Children's Books," co-chaired by Susan Collier for ALA and Suzanne Glazer for CBC.

The Council's 1976 President was James Giblin, Vice President of Seabury Press and Editorial Director of Clarion Books. In addition to Giblin, fourteen other publishers sat on CBC's Board. Diane Majer, of William Morrow & Co., chaired the 1976 Book Week Committee. Patricia Ross of Alfred A. Knopf, Inc., chaired CBC's Poetry Committee.

The Children's Book Council was founded in 1945 and is an association of children's trade book publishers. Its administrative office is at 67 Irving Place, New York, NY 10003.

JOHN DONOVAN

Children's Book Week

See *Children's Book Council.*

Children's Library Services

Probably the most difficult task in reviewing a single year of library service is the identification of new trends. It may well be that in a number of libraries serving children there are new programs being tested or planned, but they may not yet have been reported widely enough to be identifiable as significant in library service to children. At the other end of the spectrum of programs and services are those so widely accepted and practiced that they may easily escape mention. Library instruction programs in both public and elementary school libraries and storytelling programs are examples of these. The recent trend in the latter, however, continues: it is much more common for such programs in public libraries to be directed toward preschool or primary-grade children than it is for them to be conducted for an audience of middle- and upper-grade children, who were once the mainstays of such programs. There are many reasons for this, and they are the same reasons that cause many of the changes and trends in library service to children. A note on them should be of interest.

Librarians have still not decided what the effects of television are on children, but it is often suggested that children who watch it regularly (and that is certainly most children) want fast, clear action in other media, may have shorter attention spans than they otherwise might have, and have limited time for other activities. Without the encouragement of children seeking storytelling programs, librarians have lost some of their own interest, especially when day-care centers and nursery schools have been clamoring for more library visits and with elementary schools more likely to have school librarians of their own so that class visits to public libraries are rarely planned. The pattern of use in public libraries' children's rooms has become almost the reverse of what it was, say, 20 years ago: the daytime group use consists largely of young children, and the after-school crowd is likely to be composed of the more motivated users rather than those seeking such group experiences as story hours.

School libraries have responded by incorporating stories into planned class visits or other library activities, and public libraries have considerably expanded their range of programs to include occasional puppet shows, regular craft classes, areas for games, and film programs. One regrettable result, however, is that probably a smaller percentage of librarians working with children are skilled as storytellers, partly because they have neither the need nor the energy to conduct regular programs. Interestingly enough, this also means that respect for storytelling may become even greater. There was an air of "old believer" reverence in a group which gathered at a Chicago Public Library branch Saturday, May 8, to hear some of their colleagues tell stories and to participate in the program of the Alice Liddell Theatre Company. The same enjoyment for a tradition that is certainly ailing if not dying can be observed frequently in similar in-service programs or demonstrations.

Bicentennial. One observance clearly associated distinctively with 1976 was that of the nation's Bicentennial. It may safely be estimated that more summer reading clubs were based on themes of the Bicentennial than any other single theme. Enthusiasm for the Bicentennial may have been somewhat higher along the east coast, where local observances often featured local events that occurred in the era of the American Revolution, and, in general, children often maintained greater interest in the historical observance than did their parents and other adults, who deplored the commercial nature of many of the programs. The July 4 parade of the Tall Ships, seen on national television and the followup visits of many of the ships to other cities certainly captured the imaginations of all ages. Demands for reading about the ships themselves will undoubtedly be felt for a long time to come in libraries.

Crafts. The increasing importance of crafts as a library activity was dramatized in some library Bicentennial events. Exhibits often featured items of everyday living in earlier eras, and heirloom patchwork quilts or farm implements stimulated speculation about what life was like for an earlier generation. The prevalent counter reaction to problems of urban living and the need for many families to curtail expenses because of feared or actual unemployment or because of limited buying power

Children's Library Services

A two-week clinic to detect "Lazy Eye," a serious visual condition if undetected, was sponsored by the Chester, Pennsylvania, Public Library and the local Lions Club.

caused by inflation worked together to arouse interest in simple crafts. In some communities, such projects as a patchwork quilt prepared from the individual patches contributed by individuals provided children and adults with the satisfaction of doing highly individual work that was enhanced when it became a part of a finished product that represented beauty and accomplishment, with the individual contributions still clearly identifiable. One such quilt, displayed at the Vineyard Haven (Massachusetts) Public Library depicted events and places of local historical interest and, although the Bicentennial was the stimulus for the project, the depictions were not limited to one historical period.

Craft programs for children in libraries are becoming more numerous, but there is some question about whether they are also becoming of better quality. The cost of materials and the need to find projects that can be completed in a fairly short period of time often lead to selection of projects in which children are kept busy without being encouraged to create for themselves. Increased skills and improved tastes may lead to more carefully chosen projects and products which provide satisfactions in their making as well as in their completion. One of the problems may lie in the library media themselves: books and other media which show how to make things abound, but there is less guidance for the planner of craft programs who wants to encourage creativity among a group of children and to allow them to have the satisfaction of completing something of interest. And the need to do all of this

Patrons of the Public Library of Youngstown and Mahoning County, Ohio, elect to do their reading tepee style.

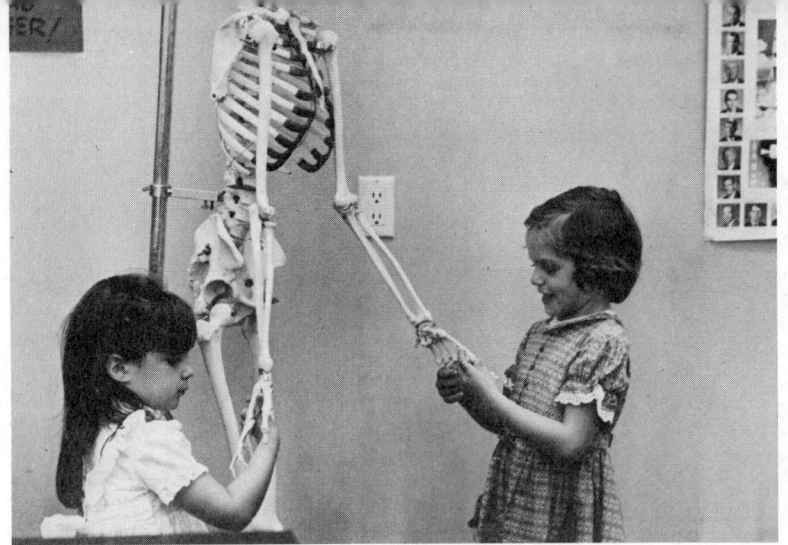

Children's library services at the Dallas Public Library in 1976 included a cooperative program with the Museum of Natural History featuring skeletons, minerals, and live snakes as well as field trips to a local produce market.

on a more limited budget than might have been in effect before the crafts program even began adds a serious complication.

Budgets. There seems to have been less comment on budget cuts for libraries in 1976, but that may have been because they had become common and therefore less newsworthy, or because the major cuts had already been made. It was still true that library service to children would be likely to suffer most in overall cuts, such as the closing of small branches of public libraries or the curtailment of personnel in school media programs. However, in most communities where the number of children under 12 continued to drop or at least stabilize, there was recognition that programs were more likely to be curtailed or consolidated than to be instigated.

Appointments. Some new appointments in public library children's services programs gave hope for strong leadership for the future. Amy Kellman's appointment as Coordinator of Children's Work at the Carnegie Library of Pittsburgh gave assurance that this early pioneer library in the provision of service to children was going to strengthen its traditional program, and the naming of Charlotte Szabo as successor to Anne Izard in the post of Children's Consultant for the Westchester Library System offered the same kind of assurance. People watchers who had been distressed at the lessened importance of some children's consultant or supervisory posts in public libraries were heartened by these and other developments. In a way, library service to children was paying once more the price for its success, as in a county library system where the director commented that since the best program people there were children's librarians, he was going to give them general responsibilities so that their philosophy of service would spread to others.

Outreach. Various kinds of outreach programs continued in school and public libraries, with many of them directed toward children. In Gloucester City, New Jersey, public library storytellers continued a program of telling stories to handicapped children in their homes, begun in October 1975 with funds from Title I of the Library Services and Construction Act. In the one-to-one storytelling, the same storyteller visited the same child over a period of time, and some 30 children were benefitting from the program.

The starting of new dial-a-story services from public libraries was less likely to be newsworthy in 1976, since the program had been tested in various areas and had proved popular, but there were indications that the service, providing short storytelling by demand telephoning, was spreading also. Perhaps the best news about this was that it showed that library programs did not have to be measured by how many people they attracted through the library doors in order to be considered successful.

Gentle Nudge Program. A program combining some elements of outreach, emphasis on the preschool child and his parents, and the value of incentive grants is Gentle Nudge, an $18,500 project of the Oklahoma State Library, planned and directed by Mary Ann Wentroth, the state's Consultant on Children's Library Service. Lectures, workshops, and discussions focusing on early childhood education and development for parents are aspects of this program, in which seven libraries in the state received $1,500 each in addition to earlier grants under the Library Services and Construction Act, and eight public libraries received $1,000 each as initial grants. In this program, as in several others, use and lending of toys were important elements, and much of the informational material directed toward parents consists of making them aware of safety problems with toys as well as of the most effective ways for them to be used by children in a way that is educational as well as recreational.

A controversy may be developing as librarians who work with children are extending programs directly to parents and other adults. Storytelling clinics or workshops, parent education programs conducted jointly with preschool story hours, and such varied programs as Gentle Nudge are examples of this kind of

Children's Library Services

Children from day-care centers attending a morning puppet show at the Spokane Public Library in the fall of 1976.

service extended to parents. Librarians who are adult service specialists are, in some instances, looking questioningly at such developments and wondering where responsibilities recognized by them and by children's librarians really overlap, merge, or end. One outcome of this may be a lessening of distinctions between departments or divisions of library service.

Volunteers. One group of adults who seem to be better utilized in school and public libraries than they have been for some time are volunteers. Work with children is often especially appealing to them. Since many elementary libraries owe their existence to parent volunteers who recognized their value but who have often been replaced by—or have themselves become—regularly employed and qualified librarians, the tradition of volunteers is strong. But in the transition from full staffing by volunteers to employment of library personnel, there was often strong feeling against use of volunteers in any way. There has also been some of this resistance in public libraries, but the trend seems to be changing. Emphasis on the need for more individual work with children in reading guidance, crafts programs, or other activities creates a demand for more people, and with prospects for additional staff indeed dim, use of volunteers tends to become more acceptable. The professional journals have reflected this trend, and that undoubtedly will lead to more extensive use of them in effective ways.

The increasing number of elderly people in the country and their continued good health in long years of retirement, during which they often live far removed from younger members of their family, are reasons for further utilization of this pool of often willing and able volunteers. While most library programs directed toward them still emphasize taking services to them or attracting them to the library to make use of its resources, they are often sought as volunteers in programs like the one the Tulsa City-County Library System initiated several years ago. The curricular emphases on local history and identity in several senses—racial, sexual, ethnic, for example—may lead to more recognition of the community resource which elderly people are and to more opportunity for them to share their knowledge and experience with others. When students in a storytelling class of the Graduate Library School of the University of Chicago made it a practice to tell stories to various gatherings of elderly residents in the community, they discovered not only receptive and appreciative audiences but also individuals who remembered other versions of traditional stories and who wanted an opportunity to tell stories of their own, based on newspaper clippings or on their own lives. They requested a field trip to the storytelling class at some future date so that they could reciprocate by telling stories there, as well as by enjoying the stories told. The therapeutic value of such programs for the elderly is surely great, but the programs are few and the value difficult to measure. It may be that the library will become the community agency best able to achieve the link between the old and the young which society has lamented having lost.

Censorship. A continuing problem in library service to children is that of censorship of materials. The difficulties of selection of all kinds of controversial topics in media are heightened in selection for children, since parental views are often firm about what should be permitted. Nevertheless, the trend toward openness continues, with many public libraries allowing for use of the children's borrower's card in all parts of the library, and with some intershelving of children's and adult nonfiction. This is more practicable in smaller library agencies and usually proves to be as helpful for adults who want introductory treatments of some topics as for children who want to read more advanced material.

While major controversies in intellectual freedom raged in school systems in 1976, the problem areas tended to be junior high or high schools. One reason that elementary schools and children's rooms in public libraries have escaped major publicity could be that they continue the practice noted long ago by Marjorie Fiske—buying in the "safer" areas and pleading the limitations of budget (and very real limitations they are) or the strong plea that "this book is obviously *not* a children's book." There is probably greater need than ever for item-by-item selection and more willingness to express and defend strong individual opinion and taste than was ever before true.

Interlibrary Loan. Organization of the collection and integration of children's library service into networks of cooperation presented special problems in 1976. As several major public libraries move or plan to move into Library of Congress classification plans for more efficient use of such cataloging resources as the Ohio College Library Center program, the collection of children's media presents special problems, and is often excluded from the contemplated change. As multitype library networks spread further, the role of elementary school libraries in them is far from clear, and the networks are often less effective in dealing with the many small, fairly similar units and collections which are the pattern among elementary schools than they are with larger library agencies. As reported at the major conference on resource sharing held at the Graduate School of Library and Information Sciences at the University of Pittsburgh in the autumn of 1976, the question of interlibrary services for children still brings more silence than response. An interesting sidelight is that, as scholars use collections of children's media to get a sense of what life was like in other times or what standards of conduct were promulgated, they are becoming strong advocates for better interlibrary loan procedures for children's materials. All such arbitrary rules as a maximum number of loans per child, refusal to reserve materials for children (or children's materials for anyone), and refusal to provide children's media on interlibrary loan are being questioned more thoughtfully. Implications of such changes are being investigated more carefully than they have for some time, and the controversy is recognized as one in which sides shift, with librarians who work with children often divided in their views of what is appropriate. This is certainly a major area for future watching. PEGGY SULLIVAN

Children's Literature

What may be the best stimulus to book sales in a long time is the "Give-a-Book Certificate(s)" plan proposed by the Children's Book Council, and agreed to by the American Booksellers Association and the National Association of College Stores. Because of legal complications, the program will probably not go into effect until the spring of 1977. It is modeled on the highly successful British scheme of book tokens, which have spurred the sales of children's books through the use of widely accepted gift certificates for books.

Publishing Activities. Production figures in the children's book world have changed little since 1975, with continuing decimation of back list titles of hardcover books and increasing activity among paperback publishers. One factor that may affect paperback editions as well as translated editions is the new British process called "Quad Retone," which cuts costs of resizing color illustrations. Bantam has launched a paperback line for children; it made a guaranteed bid of $175,000 for the reprint rights to Paul Zindel's *Pardon Me, You're Stepping on My Eyeball!* (Harper & Row, 1976). With the merger of The Viking Press and Penguin Books, the Seafarer line, paperback reprints of Viking hardcover children's books, will be reprinted under the Puffin imprint. Viking will also expand its publication to include 24 titles yearly in addition to Seafarer conversions and will concentrate on books for younger children.

Franklin Watts, who left the company of that name (which he founded in 1942) to establish Franklin Watts Ltd. in London in 1969, returned to the United States to publish again under the rubric of the Frank Book Corporation. Perhaps the gayest event of the publishing year was the celebration of the 50th birthday of Winnie-the-Pooh. The animals that were Christopher Milne's childhood toys are in a glass case at Dutton & Co. in New York,

Paul Zindel's Pardon Me, You're Stepping on My Eyeball, *published by Harper & Row, will be included in Bantam's new children's paperback series. Paperback rights were sold for $175,000 in 1976.*

Susan Cooper's The Grey King won the 1976 John Newbery Medal.

Robert Westall, winner of Great Britain's Carnegie Award for the Machine-Gunner.

Bruno Bettelheim, author of The Uses of Enchantment, published in 1976.

Mordecai Richler, author of Jacob Two-Two Meets the Hooded Fang, chosen by the Canadian Library Association as the best written children's book of 1976.

and the American publishers gave a splendid party at the Tavern on the Green in Central Park. A. A. Milne's son, a bookseller who does not enjoy publicity, did not attend the English gala, a luncheon held at Cotchford Farm, the Milne family's former home in Sussex.

Of the many books about children's literature published in 1976, two received special attention. Bruno Bettelheim's *The Uses of Enchantment* (Knopf) was perhaps best pinpointed by the reviewer in the *Times Literary Supplement* of October 1, 1976 as "Freud Among the Fairies." And a massive, witty, and profusely illustrated book by Barbara Bader, *American Picturebooks from Noah's Ark to the Beast Within* (Macmillan), has won praise as a signal contribution to the literature even from those who find it less than perfect.

Exhibits, Meetings. In Montreal there were special exhibits and speakers about books for children at the Second International Book Fair. At the Bologna Children's Book Fair the attendance was bigger and the trading more brisk than ever before, with almost 20 editors at the U.S. Combined Exhibit. For the first time one of the large exhibit halls was devoted to comics. Among the major international meetings of the year were the Conference in Södertälje, Sweden, in August of the International Research Society for Children's Literature, and the Congress of the International Board on Books for Young People, in Athens, Greece, in September. Twenty-five registrants were from the United States; one of the speakers was Mary Jane Anderson, the Executive Secretary of the Children's Services Division of ALA.

1976 also saw the first meeting of the United States affiliate, The Friends of IBBY, at the Midwinter meeting in Chicago, an event attended by both the past and present Presidents of IBBY, Niilo Visapää and Hans Halbey. (*See also* International Board on Books for Young People.)

The Children's Book Council, in addition to its many established programs devoted to the publicizing of children's books, added a new one for poetry, with bookmarks, posters, a pamphlet, and a bibliography. CBC also announced that since the first series of taped talks in the "Prelude" series (CBC Mini-Seminars on Using Books Creatively) had been so successful, a second series of six talks would be prepared. (*See also* Children's Book Council.)

The 7th Annual May Hill Arbuthnot Honor Lecture, funded by Scott, Foresman (Mrs. Arbuthnot's publisher) and organized by the Children's Services Division, was given by Jean Fritz at the University of Southern California, an event in which 13 other institutions in Southern California participated.

Awards. The Randolph Caldecott Medal for the most distinguished illustration of the year in a book for children was awarded to Leo and Diane Dillon for their pictures in *Why Mosquitoes Buzz in People's Ears* (Dial), a West African tale retold by Verna Aardema. Winner of the John Newbery Medal for the year's most distinguished contribution to children's literature was Susan Cooper, for *The Grey King* (Atheneum), the fourth book in a five-volume fantasy (*See* Biographies). Honor books for the

Children's Services Division

The 1976 Caldecott Medal was awarded to Leo and Diane Dillon for illustrating Why Mosquitoes Buzz in People's Ears.

Winnie-the-Pooh's 100th birthday celebration at New York's Bronx Zoo was sponsored by E. P. Dutton Company with costumes courtesy of Sears Roebuck. The two-day event in October 1976 featured Pooh puppet shows, a parade, and (below) a folk sing-along from the Pooh Songbook.

Caldecott Award were *Strega Nona* (Prentice-Hall) by Tomie de Paola and *The Desert is Theirs* (Scribners), written by Byrd Baylor and illustrated by Peter Parnall. The Newbery Honor Books were *The Hundred Penny Box* (Viking) by Sharon Bell Mathis and *Dragon-Wings* (Harper & Row) by Laurence Yep.

Walter Edmonds won the National Book Award with *Bert Breen's Barn* (Little, Brown). Finalists in the National Book Award competition were Eleanor Cameron, *To the Green Mountains* (Dutton); Norma Farber, *As I Was Crossing Boston Common* (Dutton); Isabelle Holland, *Of Love and Death and Other Journeys* (Lippincott); David McCord, *The Star in the Pail* (Little, Brown); Nicholasa Mohr, *El Bronx Remembered* (Harper & Row), and Brenda Wilkinson, *Ludell* (Harper & Row). The Hans Christian Andersen Medal for literature, given for the body of an author's work, was awarded to Cecil Bødker of Denmark and the companion award for illustration went to Tatyana Mavrina of the Soviet Union. The two authors whose work was "highly commended" were E. B. White of the U.S.A. and Agnya Barto of the U.S.S.R. and the highly commended artists were Ludovit Fulla of Czechoslovakia and Otto S. Svend of Denmark.

In Britain, the Carnegie Award for literature was given to Robert Westall for *The Machine-Gunners* (Macmillan) and the Greenaway Award for illustration to Victor Ambrus for *Horses in Battle* and *Mishka* (both published by Oxford). The awards are chosen by the Library Association of the United Kingdom. The Canadian Library Association chose Mordecai Richler's *Jacob Two-Two Meets the Hooded Fang* (Knopf) as the best written children's book of the year, and the Howard-Gibbon Medal for illustration went to William Kurelek for *A Prairie Boy's Summer* (Tundra), which was also a runner-up for the literary award.

The 1976 Mildred Batchelder Award for translation went to Henry Z. Walck for the translation by Anthea Bell of the Grimm brothers' story *The Cat and Mouse Who Shared a House* by Ruth Hürlimann. Eloise Greenfield received the Jane Addams Children's Book Award for her biography *Paul Robeson* (Crowell), and a former Newbery Award book, Jean George's *Julie of the Wolves* (Harper & Row), won the Silver Slate Pencil Award, the highest honor given by the Netherlands to a non-Dutch book.

Authors and illustrators of children's books who died in 1976 include Paul Gallico, Berta Hader, Margaretha Shemin, and Ernest Shepard.

ZENA SUTHERLAND

Children's Services Division

The major goal of ALA's Children's Services Division (CSD) is the improvement and extension of library service to children (preschool through grade eight) in all types of libraries. CSD is specifically charged by ALA Council with responsibility for evaluation and selection of media for children and improvement of techniques of library service to children. To facilitate the achievement of these goals, the Division's committees are organized into five priority areas: Child Advocacy; Evaluation of Media; People Power; Social Responsibilities; and Planning, Research and Development.

Projects. In 1976 CSD members continued ongoing projects: preparing bibliographies for the Boy Scouts of America; sending representatives to meetings of and maintaining liaison with other national organizations serving children; selecting and awarding the annual Mildred L. Batchelder citation and the Newbery and Caldecott medals; selecting *Notable Children's Films of 1974* and *Notable Children's Books of 1975*; preparing bibliographies for use in conjunction with television viewing, preparing selective bibliographies of prints and posters, toys and games; selecting the Frederic G. Melcher Scholarship recipient and the four CSD members who would attend ALA's Annual Conference for the first time aided by cash grants from Charles Scribner's Sons; selecting *U.S. Children's Books of International Interest* for use by teachers and researchers abroad as well as to encourage their translation; preparing selective bibliographies of foreign children's books for periodic publication in *Booklist*.

In partnership with the Children's Book Council, CSD members continued their active participation in the U.S. National Section of the International Board on Books for Young People (IBBY). Thirty U.S. Section members and friends attended IBBY's Biennial Congress held from September 27 to October 3, 1976, in Athens.

New Committees. A joint committee with the U.S. National Park Service was established to review and evaluate park-produced materials for children. A committee established to promote CSD membership produced a handsome brochure (designed by children's book illustrator Ellen Raskin) and began distribution of it through a nation-wide task force network. During the summer conference new committees were formed: to establish criteria and procedures for Board evaluation of the executive secretary; to develop a new publication for storytellers; to study the criteria and procedure for selection of the Mildred L. Batchelder Award. A joint CSD/YASD committee began revision of *Selecting Materials for Children and Young Adults* (ALA, 1967).

Programs. Ceremonies announcing Henry Z. Walck Publishers, Inc., as the 1976 Mildred L. Batchelder winner were held April 2, 1976, at the UNICEF Children's Cultures Center in New York City and in six selected cooperating institutions throughout the nation.

The Arbuthnot Honor Lecture, sponsored annually by the CSD with the assistance of Scott Foresman and Company, was presented April 9 in Los Angeles. Jean Fritz, author of children's historical fiction, lectured on "The Education of an American."

CSD's Committee on National Planning of Special Collections in cooperation with the Simmons School of Library Science presented a symposium, "Research, Social History, and Children's Literature," in Boston on May 14–15.

At ALA's Centennial Conference CSD's program on "Service to Children: Issues and Options" featured viewpoint presentations by Harold R. Jenkins (Kansas City Public Library), Mary Frances K. Johnson (University of North Carolina at Greensboro), and Roderick G. Schwartz (Washington State Library). At the CSD Intellectual Freedom Committee's program, "Intellectual Freedom and Children: 1876–1976," Mary Cable, a social historian, and Margaret Coughlan, a children's literature specialist at the Library of Congress, presented complementary papers on changing attitudes toward children as reflected in the changing world of books for children. The Film Evaluation Committee, cooperatively with PLA, offered a film showing from the Notable Children's Film selections. And CSD's Library Service to Children with Special Needs Committee cooperated with HRLSD and others in a preconference, "Mainstreaming the Exceptional Child in the Library." A special exhibition, mounted in the exhibit area by the Selection of Foreign Children's Books Committee, drew attention to titles that had appeared on their selective lists during the year. The 1976 Newbery-Caldecott banquet featured speeches by medal winners Susan Cooper and Leo and Diane Dillon. Past presidents and executive secretaries of the Division were guests of honor at this Centennial Conference banquet and at other CSD events during the week.

A regional institute, "The Early Years: Public and School Libraries Reach Out to Preschool Children and Parents," sponsored by CSD and directed by its Preschool Services and Parent Education Committee, was held October 3–6 at Bergamo Center in Dayton, Ohio.

Publications. Publications included: *Newbery and Caldecott Award: Authorization and Terms—1976* and *Choosing the Newbery and Caldecott Winners*, by Bette Peltola (reprinted from *Top of the News*, April 1976); *Active Heroines in Folktales for Children*, compiled by the CSD Discussion Group on Sexism in Library Materials for Children; *Start Early for an Early Start*, edited by Ferne Johnson for the Preschool Services and Parent Education Committee; and *Opening Doors for Preschool Children and Their Parents*, by the Preschool Services and Parent Education Committee; the annual brochures are *Newbery Medal Books, Caldecott Medal Books, Notable Children's Books* (1975). A revision of the *CSD Organization Manual* was completed. A CSD/YASD/AASL Committee completed evaluation of Girl Scout materials and the manuscript for a catalog of these materials for librarians, which was published by the Girl Scouts of America in April. — MARY JANE ANDERSON

CSD Officers

PRESIDENT (July 1976–June 1977):
Peggy Sullivan, University of Chicago

FIRST VICE-PRESIDENT/PRESIDENT-ELECT:
Barbara Miller, Louisville Public Library, Kentucky

SECOND VICE-PRESIDENT:
Helen Mullen, Free Library of Philadelphia, Pennsylvania

EXECUTIVE SECRETARY:
Mary Jane Anderson

Membership (August 31, 1976): 4,599 (2,846 personal and 1,753 organizational).

Circulation Systems

Circulation, which implies motion and movement, has been adopted by librarians to describe the flow of library materials from storage to user possession—usually for a controlled time period. As libraries try harder to make resources available at the user's convenience, the importance of circulation control becomes more apparent. Traditionally, circulation control has been confined to some type of control of the inventory charged out of the library. As automated record keeping becomes more available and prices per data record decrease, total inventory control is becoming more feasible. In the traditional schemes, total inventory control is implied by the assumption that what is not charged out is in the library. This assumption is not logical as it fails to take into account that material which is neither checked out nor in the library and which may have been ripped off.

Manual Systems. Many methods of circulation control are being practiced in the libraries of the world. All methods can be classified as manual or automated. The manual systems in many instances still prove superior to available automated systems. One type of manual system in widespread use in the mid-1970's relies upon the use of a book card. The card, usually prepared with the class number and the author's name or title of the book or both, has spaces for the borrower to sign and for an indication of date out, the date due, or both. The cards are signed at the time the material is checked out and a due date is then usually stamped or written in the book. Frequently the cards are tabbed or color coded with plastic jackets to indicate the due date and then are filed either by author or by class number. Advantages of this method include a legible (usually typed) filing key, a ready indicator of the use of each individual item, and quick scanning for overdues. Disadvantages include a traceable record of who is using what materials, the general tendency for signatures to be illegible, the cost of book cards, and the time required for the user to sign individual book cards. Both Gaylord and Bro-Dart attempted to overcome the problems of illegibility and speed through the use of charging machines they offer. Gaylord's earlier machine required the use of a special borrower's card which has the raised negative image of a number, considered to be the unique number for a particular borrower. When inserted in the machine with a book card, it prints the borrower's number and the selected due date. A newer Gaylord machine allows the use of an embossed ID card which has up to four lines of information. The machine is designed to clip the edge of the card in order to assure advancing of lines for each transaction. The design eliminates the anonymity of the earlier version since borrowers' names now appear on the charge card.

The Sysdac system, offered by Bro-Dart, utilizes an embossed ID card and a charging machine that generates a tape-type label and attaches this label to the book card usually with a stub indicating date due to be attached to the book. The borrower's name is printed onto the tape which is attached to the book card. This assures a legible recording of the borrower. The tapes do not have the same permanence as the handwritten or Gaylord imprinted cards.

Call Slip Procedures. Call slips may be used instead of book cards. The borrower fills out the class number, author, title and other pertinent information on a slip. In closed stack libraries the slip is then used to indicate the item which is to be retrieved. In open stack libraries, the slip serves as a scratch ticket and ultimately as the charge-out record. Since a call slip has a life of one transaction, it can be more easily designed for use with embossed borrowers' cards and imprinting machines. As with the book card systems, the call slips can be tabbed, color coded, or marked in other ways to indicate date due. An effective variation of the call slip design has been implemented in some large libraries through the use of McBee Key-Sort cards that are predrilled along the edges and can then be punched for sorting with a rod. All those which are punched in certain areas will drop off of the rod while those not punched remain on the rod. This modification can make a call slip retrievable on several factors rather than restricting it to only one place in the file. Advantages of a call slip system include the destructibility of borrower records for completed transactions, the flexibility of design of the call slip format, and a greater ease in use of embossed borrowers' cards. Disadvantages include the frequent illegibility of class number or other filing data, and the generally high waste of call slips used for scratch. Both the book card and the call slip systems provide a readily accessed file of information on all materials checked out.

Exception Systems. Some libraries operate on the assumption that if something is not in the library, it is out and will come back, and therefore they require only a record of those items which do not come back on time. Such circulation control is based on an exception system. One of the most common assigns a sequential, unique transaction number to each checkout transaction. The transaction number is frequently printed or stamped on a card which is reproduced photographically or by thermograph along with the book title or book information and the borrower's identification card. The due date is then generally indicated on the transaction card, which is placed with the material as it goes out. Upon return of the material the transaction cards are collected and collated in sequence. If photographic recording is used, at the end of the reel the film is developed and stored for later reference. When the appropriate time has elapsed to consider overdues, the transaction cards are reviewed and only those numbers which are missing are flagged. Information for the missing numbers is then retrieved from the film record and the appropriate notices sent out. Advantages of this system include legible and accurate recording of both borrower and transaction information, speedy checkout procedure, and speedy return procedure. Disadvantages include the implication of a permanent record of transactions, the labor involved in collation of return transaction cards, the need to process photographic film, and the inability to identify the whereabouts of a particular item which has been recently charged out.

COMPUTERIZATION

For more than a decade libraries have been looking to the use of computerized data manipulation as a tool to overcome many of the problems inherent in circulation control. In fewer than ten years the automated circulation systems have evolved from individual, unique, home-brew systems which were the creation of analysts and programmers who were either on the library's staff or who volunteered their services to the library, to the present few vendors of versatile, packaged circulation systems. The advent and adoption of bar-coded labels in the 1970's marked a breakthrough in automated circulation systems. With the bar-coded label, item identification data could be read directly from the item rather than from a data card or other form which must be removed from the item for reading. Furthermore, it was no longer necessary to keyboard item identification information as the bar-coded labels were designed to withstand mistreatment.

LIBS 100 System. One of the early entries into turnkey circulation systems was made by CLSI (Computer Library Services, Inc.) with the LIBS 100 system. This system, which had been in development for nearly four years and in actual operation since September 1974, features flexibility for individual customers. Each library may tailor the input and output products to local needs. In the early part of 1974, CLSI was already talking about utilizing the LIBS 100 system for a network circulation control, the central processor being maintained at network headquarters and the various network members having only data entry and output terminals. Such services facilitate expanded access for users to the total resources held by all network members. CLSI applied this concept in 1976 with the implementation by the state of Illinois of ILLINET, utilizing the LIBS 100 Circulation Control System.

The LIBS 100 system utilizes bar-coded labels for both the borrower ID and the item identifier. The basic terminal consists of a light pen and a console with various function keys. A cathode-ray tube (CRT) terminal with keyboard is also used as a system controller and for entry of data when the bar-coded labels are not available. In 1976 the maximum number of circulation terminals which could be associated with any one LIBS 100 system was limited to about 75. The major drawback of this circulation system is the absence of a receipt or ticket to indicate the item that is checked out. Without such a receipt, it is necessary that the circulation terminal be operated by a member of the library staff. The CLSI Circulation Control System, in use in a variety of libraries for three years, benefited from responsive and efficient maintenance offered by the company.

Gaylord System. The Gaylord Circulation Control System has been designed to utilize a centrally operated computer in Syracuse, New York, and minicomputers at the library or system using the service. The circulation input/output terminals are connected to the local minicomputer and the day's transactions are recorded locally. The system is designed to require the central host computer to contact the local minicomputers each night by dial-up telephone and update all files. The system requires the use of a microfiche record of the local holdings; a unique item identifier is assigned by Gaylord at the time that holdings are recorded to the system. It also uses paper printouts to serve as exception, overdue, and hold files. These printouts, produced weekly in Syracuse, are mailed to the local customer. Like the other systems on the market, this system produces a variety of statistical and management reports. Gaylord points out that this system can be incorporated easily into network or multilibrary circulation control systems.

Cincinnati Electronics. The Cincinnati Electronics Corporation produced a terminal redesigned from specifications drawn up at the University of Chicago. In 1976 they were designing software for circulation control utilizing a minicomputer, storage peripherals, and their JRL-1000 circulation terminal. They reported that the software would be completed and available for marketing in 1977. The terminal upon which this system is based adds to the light pen a printer programmed to produce a receipt to show the item checked out. The terminal also contains interfaces and logic and is plug-compatible with a keyboard CRT. The manufacturer is also marketing two bar-code label printers—one computer driven and the other with a keyboard. The Circulation Control System is based upon total inventory control, and, according to the design in 1976, will identify in on-line storage every item in the library or system. The company's plans called for the option of supplying a total turn-key system including computer or the option of licensing the software for installation on an existing locally available computer, an option that may prove attractive to libraries which serve institutions that already operate large computer installations. The software is expected to be written in a common programming language, and maintenance will be provided by Cincinnati Electronics as part of the licensing package. Since this system offers a receipt printer as an integral part of its design, it can be easily installed and adapted to a self-service mode of circulation control.

Automation Advantages. General advantages of automated circulation control systems include the increased capacity to manipulate and extract information from the files, the ability to establish a total inventory control system, improved management information, better control of holds, reserves, and delinquent or skipped borrowers. Disadvantages may include the initial and ongoing cost, the turnaround time for information, particularly if the system does not make provision for on-line file updates, and the requirements for backup so that circulation data can continue to be captured even when the power is out or the computer is not operating. The cost factor may be particularly noticeable in the smaller libraries; a group of such libraries may wish to consider the advantages of a network of automated circulation control. This approach would provide for a sharing of the initial cost and of the ongoing operational cost and would provide additional advantages, which may include network-wide borrowers' cards and facilitated regional cooperation. The ideal system would contain an on-line file of all holdings of all network participants and an on-line file of all eligible borrowers. It would read a label permanently affixed to the material being loaned and would provide a total inventory record of all resources within the network. It would include the foresight to provide for the destruction of completed charge-out records so that users' reading preferences could not be traced and it would provide statistical information for management use in planning for improved collection development and service patterns.

R. PATRICK MALLORY

Collection Development

A number of conditions noted in 1975 continued to be evident in 1976: a slowing in the growth rate of many library collections due to reduced funding, continuing inflation in book and journal prices, increased emphasis on resource sharing, and concern over the preservation of collections both from physical deterioration and from losses through theft and mutilation. One effect of these conditions particularly evident in 1976 was a mounting awareness on the part of librarians of the need to know more about their collections in order to plan wisely and to allocate resources effectively. Librarians were becoming increasingly cost conscious, and many procedures and assumptions were being questioned or studied for validity.

Added impetus to these studies could be expected from a new project announced by the Association of Research Libraries Office of Management Studies in October 1976. Under a grant from the Mellon Foundation the Office will undertake a one-year Collection Analysis Project, applying contemporary management methods to the identification and investigation of key issues related to collection development, such as characteristics of effective collection development policies, requirements for decision-making processes regarding collection development in a period of economic retrenchment, the reconciliation of steady-state or reduced budgets to the increased costs of acquiring needed collections. All of these were matters of acute concern to collection development personnel in most libraries in 1976.

Studies Under Way. Studies were being conducted in 1976 not only by librarians but by others outside the profession who have a concern with the availability of materials. Examples of such studies are the National Enquiry into the Production and Dissemination of Scholarly Knowledge, a three-year study being conducted by the American Council of Learned Societies, which is addressing the proliferation of scholarly journals, pressure on scholars to publish, and the rapidly growing costs of library services; a survey of publishing and library services by Fritz Machlup of New York University, who hoped to obtain data on the size of library holdings, annual acquisition rates in various fields, and the costs of acquiring various kinds of materials, and with this information hoped to determine whether in a period of retrenchment some fields were being given preferred treatment to the detriment of others.

Gifts. In line with analysis of other aspects of collection development there has been concern over the effectiveness and economics of gift and exchange programs as a means of acquiring materials for library collections. At the request of UCLA Libraries, the Systems and Procedures Exchange Center of ARL/OMS undertook a survey of gift and exchange functions in ARL libraries in spring 1976. The SPEC flyer describing the results discusses the various organizational configurations of gift and exchange functions and the major considerations in operating these activities. It points out that there was some concern on the part of respondents over the cost-effectiveness of such operations and a need for some definition of the level and type of activities which attract useful materials and limit receipt of the less useful. At the 1976 ALA Annual Conference the Acquisition of Library Materials Discussion Group of RTSD/Resources Section devoted its meeting to gifts and exchanges, and found considerable interest in a continuation of such discussions in the future. Still a matter of concern to libraries is the decrease in valuable donations of personal papers by authors, composers, and others who were denied tax deductions for such gifts by the Tax Reform Act of 1969. New legislation passed in September 1976 unfortunately did not restore tax deductions for such gifts. (See also Law and Legislation; Gifts, Bequests, and Endowments.)

HEA: Title II-C. There was, however, some good news for research libraries in the 1976 amendment to the Higher Education Act, with the inclusion of a new Title II-C, "Strengthening Research Library Resources," which authorized grants totalling $45,000,000 for three years to assist major research libraries in developing resources. It was uncertain at year's end when funds would become available; they were not appropriated at the time the legislation was passed.

Copyright Bill. Another piece of library legislation of significance for library collections is the new Copyright Bill signed in 1976, which will come into effect in January 1978. It specifically provides that libraries may not rely on photocopying through interlibrary loan in lieu of purchase or maintenance of a journal subscription, but permits limited photocopying under certain conditions. (See further Copyright.)

Journal Costs. The problem of journal price increases and their absorption of increasing amounts of library materials budgets continues. Since the condition has prevailed for several years, most libraries have done all they can to eliminate unnecessary or borderline titles, and now if cuts must be made they must cancel needed journal titles or transfer even more money from the monograph budget. Two studies by Bernard F. Fry of Indiana University will explore this issue further: one will examine the impact of foreign journal costs on U.S. libraries and examine library decision making on journal subscriptions; the other will explore the effects of such decision making on the future of humanities publications.

Other Developments. Some progress was reported during 1976 toward the creation of a national periodical resource. A joint committee of the Association of Research Libraries and the Center for Research Libraries, created to consider the major issues relating to the establishment of such a resource, was at work in parallel with a National Commission on Libraries and Information Science Task Force. An announcement in October from NCLIS indicated that the Task Force was considering a three-level system, with the primary immediate emphasis on a document delivery system.

Plans called for system organization by 1977 with service to begin in 1978.

No fewer than 10 programs at the 1976 ALA Annual Conference were related directly or indirectly to the development and preservation of collections. They ranged from a preconference on maps and atlases, through programs on ethnic collections, audiovisual materials, material for schools, and the international flow of books, to a program on reviews for library selection purposes. Specifically addressing the topic of loss and mutilation was the program "Stealing the American heritage. . ." sponsored by the Association of College and Research Libraries Rare Books and Manuscripts Section. Two separate sessions of small concurrent collection development discussion groups were held at the Conference, one dealing with publishing and the book trade in selected geographical areas, the other with the selection of materials from various geographical areas. As in previous years, these proved to be a successful way of bringing people with similar interests together to share their problems and their solutions.

JEAN W. BOYER

Community Delivery Services

During 1976 public libraries continued the search for alternative methods of delivering services outside the central library's service area, and to new user groups. A study in the State of Washington sought reliable cost figures for three alternative methods of extending services, MOD (mail-order-delivery), bookmobiles, and branch libraries. The study did not attempt to achieve comparable cost-benefit ratios for these three unlike services, but to arrive at realistic cost figures for each which would be translatable to other areas and useful to library planners in projecting development costs. For example, a mail-order delivery book service serving 20,000 families with eight circulations a year could cost $17,894 plus staff salaries and books. Building a 2,500-square-foot prefabricated branch library could require a capital outlay of $67,000, and annual operation of a bookmobile manned by a professional librarian and two other staff persons could cost $28,791, exclusive of amortization, overhead, books, and home base space.

Bookmobiles. On the road at last count, as reported by all states, were 1,495 bookmobiles. Kentucky led the list with 110 vehicles. Other states with over 50 each were Georgia, California, Ohio, North Carolina, Texas, and Indiana. The U.S. Office of Libraries and Learning Resources reported that federal funds under LSA and LSCA funded 804 vehicles over a 20-year period (1956–76).

Librarians having already outfitted and equipped the bookmobile for every conceivable library program and potential user, no

Bookmobile rally at the September 1976 conference of the New England Library Association.

startling innovations in use appeared in 1976. The Bicentennial Bookmobile, however, was a concept visible during the year in several states, including Ohio, and ALA's Centennial Conference featured a bookmobile roundup of visiting mobile units.

Oklahoma County Libraries reported the successful conversion of the materials collections of their five vehicles to paperbacks in an effort to reduce operating costs, after an initial pilot study. Daniel Boone Regional Library at Columbia, Missouri, operated a media mobile as an LSCA project considered sufficiently worthy of replication to be listed in the USOE publication *Library Programs Worth Knowing About.*

The project featured daytime use of the vehicle for work with disadvantaged children and their parents, and evening service to undereducated adults in rural areas. Included were giveaway easy books for children, plus visuals, toys and instruction game kits, and adult basic education materials designed for class use. Evaluators claimed that the addition of special media increased circulation on the bookmobile an average of 40 percent per stop.

For librarians who found inflation threatening to phase out their bookmobile programs, the Mid-Mississippi Regional Library at Kosciusko reported economy and efficiency in a modified motor home, locally designed, selling for under $20,000.

The year was also noteworthy for the most objectionable television commercial of library import yet devised. It featured a bookmobile librarian dispensing advice and a well known laxative. And a contest of sorts for the "oldest bookmobile" brought Mary Ryan of the Clackamas County Public Library (Oregon) a flood of mail and a list of oldsters still traveling the roads.

Books-by-mail. More libraries began mail-order delivery of books during the year, either as a replacement for more expensive services or a supplementary service designed to reach unserved groups. Such programs exploited the increased popularity of paperbacks among the reading public, and the techniques of the mail-order catalog retail merchandisers added a new dimension to library service. Carefully planned and well promoted programs seemed to be the most successful. *Library Journal* reported that many programs were proving too expensive and that a survey of libraries found that half "are having trouble getting mailbook operations off the ground."

A particularly successful program was reported by the North Central Regional Library, Wenatchee, Washington, and other libraries described such innovations as serving the inmates of jails with books by mail. The Mohawk Valley Library Association (New York) extended its successful rural mail book service to urban patrons.

Home Delivery. Delivery services to the homebound were tried and tested, and proved rewarding particularly when combined with volunteer services. The Tri-City (Illinois) Homebound Library Service was sponsored by the St. Charles, Geneva, and Batavia Public Libraries. Coordinated by a professional librarian who acted as personal librarian to the residents of five institutions serving the elderly or the handicapped, the service involved loading the trunk of the librarian's car with books which she personally selected for her readers.

Facilities Other Than Branches. Alternatives to full-fledged branch libraries in 1976 included fixed facilities such as reading centers and deposit stations. The Choctaw Nation Library System at McAlester, Oklahoma, and the Cumberland Trail Library System, Flora, Illinois, were among those which proposed to establish community reading centers as economy moves. Baltimore County, Maryland, proposed to erect prefabricated buildings which could be quickly assembled, staffed completely by volunteers, and provide circulation services only, leaving reference and information services to other components of the library system. These kinds of facilities offering circulation services represented the other side of the coin from the neighborhood information and

West Virginia's Alpha Regional Bookmobile serves five rural counties in pursuit of its motto on the van — "Free Library Service for Everyone."

referral centers which provide the interpretation of information sources to their patrons. These are the services which Clara Jones has called offerings at the 'gut level,' help that reaches people where they are."

More Alternatives. Some mention should be made of outreach in reverse, that is, services which attempt to bring the patron to the library, especially the patron who would not otherwise have access to it. Morton Grove, Illinois, maintained a "Maxiwagon" service during 1976 with the object of transporting village residents to and from the library on a regular schedule, as well as taking library materials to those who because of age or illness could not get to the library. In addition to people, the Maxiwagon carried books and serves as a minibookmobile.

Drive-in services (Oklahoma County Libraries, Oklahoma City, and the St. Louis Public Library, Missouri) were provided in 1976 to make it possible for readers to place orders for materials ahead of time and call for them later in the day. These moves bolstered the urban libraries' services to patrons who live in the outlying areas.

Still farther out on the fringe of possibilities for libraries to extend their services is cable television. An article by Denis J. LaComb in the *Library Journal* (October 1) outlines the Kern County Library (California) proposal to reach its patrons who cannot come to the library by utilizing the local cable system. Direct programming by the library will make it possible to deliver its services inside the living room of the potential library user. This is library service on the frontier and provides a clue to the possibilities of the new video technology.   VIRGINIA L. OWENS

REFERENCES

Norman E. Green, Michael P. Lynch, and C. B. Millham, "Present Costs of Several Modes of Delivery of Library Services," *PNLA Quarterly* 41, no. 1:(Fall 1976), pp. 10–13.

Helaine MacKeigan, comp. *1974–75 American Library Directory* (New York & London: R. R. Bowker Company, 1974).

Paul Little, "Converting Bookmobiles to Paperbacks," *Library Journal* 101, no. 7 (April 1, 1976), pp. 867–871.

Gene Martin, "Media Mobile," in U.S. Office of Education, *Library Programs Worth Knowing About* (San Francisco: Far West Laboratory for Education Research and Development, 1974), pp. 30–31.

Mary Ryan, "Special Report: Vintage Bookmobiles," *Wilson Library Bulletin* 50, no. 7 (March 1976), pp. 540–541.

Karl Nyren, "Community Information and Reading," *Library Journal* 101, no. 8 (April 15, 1976), p. 941.

Denis J. LaComb, "Video Technology: Its Future in Libraries," *Library Journal* 101, no. 17 (October 1, 1976), pp. 2003–2009.

Conferences

See State Reports.

Continuing Professional Education

The year 1976 in continuing professional education could be called the "Year of Coordination" insofar as it relates to the library profession. As awareness of the value of continuing education and the priority placed on it by the library profession has grown, individuals and organizations have sought ways to most effectively utilize and develop continuing education resources.

There has been increasing realization that the development of continuing education programs is the responsibility of a variety of organizations and not limited only to library schools, professional associations, state library agencies, or individual libraries. Excellent programs may also be developed by community colleges, nonlibrary professional associations, and academic institutions, as well as commercial organizations. In order to publicize and coordinate this variety of resources, in the past year an emphasis has been placed on the publication of newsletters and providing clearinghouses of continuing education opportunities.

The third annual Library Skills Seminar held in May 1976 at Marshall University offered a two-week seminar of nutshell courses under the sponsorship of the West Virginia Library Commission.

Continuing Library Education Network and Exchange. As described in last year's edition, CLENE was established in 1975. The year 1976 saw further growth in CLENE's membership and activities. As of December 31, 15 national and regional library associations had joined CLENE. There were also 15 state library agency members, 18 libraries and library and information science schools, and more than 500 individual members.

A yearlong institute was funded by USOE to be conducted by CLENE. The "Training Institute for State Library Agency Personnel Involved in Continuing Education" began in November with a Workshop for State Library

Continuing Professional Education

Three workshops funded by LSCA for approximately 120 librarians were sponsored by the North Carolina Library Association Committee on Continuing Education and the North Carolina State Library. The 1976 "Reference Tools and Techniques" workshops included videotape instruction (left) and other nonprint media.

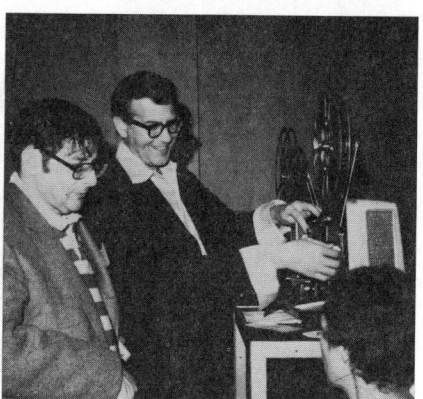

Agency Personnel to Strengthen Statewide Systems of Continuing Education. Twenty-four state library agencies were involved.

A second USOE-funded project was begun during 1976. The goal of the project is to develop a prototype system for recognition of those in library/media/information sciences who are involved in professional development. An important part of the project is the development of a prototype home study course. Its purpose is to demonstrate that geographical location need not be a barrier to continuing education involvement.

Two CLENE membership assembly meetings were held during 1976. In January the theme of the Assembly was "Self-Assessment in Continuing Education," and in July the theme was "Updating and Skills for Ourselves." In January, 1977, the Assembly addressed the closely related topics of continuing education and in-service training.

A Directory of CLENE members, resembling a "Who's Who in Continuing Library Education," was published. It listed not only names, addresses, and biographical data, but also contained publications and areas of competence and research interest.

The *Directory of Continuing Education Opportunities*, based on programs submitted by sponsoring organizations, was published for the first time, with a new edition scheduled for publication in early 1977. The *CLENExchange*, issued quarterly, continued to list publications and events of interest to those involved with staff development and continuing library education.

Activities. Coordination was the keyword in describing activities elsewhere in the field. *American Libraries* listed continuing education activities in its *Datebook* section. Other national library associations such as the Medical Library Association continued to publish similar listings. Regional library organizations including the Southwest Library Association CELS Project and the New England Library Board operated similar clearinghouses, and 13 of the 24 state library agencies represented at the USOE/CLENE training institute (described earlier) were producing publications which list continuing education activities.

The Special Libraries Association approved, but did not fund, the establishment of a paid staff position (similar to that within the Medical Library Association) to support education activities. The American Society for Information Science's efforts focused on assisting local chapters and special interest groups in continuing education activities, and coordinating and publicizing programs rather than developing them at a staff level.

A significant research study in the area of continuing library education was released at the end of 1976. Conducted by the Medical Library Association and funded by the National Library of Medicine, *Continuing Education for Health Sciences Library Personnel* reports results of a two-year study. The purpose of the project was "to assess and identify the needs for continuing education for health sciences library personnel and to design, implement, and to evaluate some components of a program which would be responsive to these needs."

Continuing education needs were assessed using several different approaches. A less traditional approach to assessing continuing education needs of a profession was taken in an attempt to provide objective data which would support the perceived subjective needs of health sciences library staffs. The contents of the published journal literature at the time the study was undertaken were compared with the literature five and ten years previously to document changes in the field. The results of continuing education needs studies conducted by other library groups and organizations were analyzed and compared with the results obtained in the present study.

Despite differences in types of library staffs surveyed (all types of librarians, information scientists, special librarians) the needs identified were very similar: Administration, Audiovisuals, Reference tools and services (including on-line systems), Budgeting. The study analyzed these needs by types of health sciences library staffs but found that the perceived needs were the same, although the settings might require different approaches to the materials.

One of the most significant findings from this phase of the study was the fact the library staffs had such difficulty in articulating what specific continuing education needs they had, and at what level. This pointed to the need for the development of task analysis data from which assessment tests could be developed.

Studies Outlined. At the same time that an inventory of needs was being developed, data from a one-year time period were collected on continuing education opportunities that were already available. More than 1,000 organizations that might be offering continuing education activities relevant to health sciences library staffs were solicited for information about their programs. Information about the location, subject matter, cost, length, target population, and type of sponsoring organization was analyzed for 264 courses sponsored by 205 organizations.

A study was made of the organizational constraints and supports given to library staffs for their continuing education activities. The results showed that continuing education is primarily a self-directed activity. The most significant response from this phase of the study was the number of respondents who indicated that their most immediate superior "accepts my decision with regard to my continuing education needs." This response was checked more frequently than any other question regarding support on the questionnaire. It points to the motivation of the individual as an important factor in continuing education.

Another significant finding was that employers are more supportive of employees attending professional meetings than independent continuing education courses. This supports the view that for some people who are able to get release time and/or expenses paid for professional meetings, conducting continuing education courses in conjunction with professional meetings is important. Two-thirds of the respondents had no in-service training available to them in their employing institutions. These people must look to outside organizations and their professional associations to provide continuing education.

The most meaningful professional learning experience reported by the largest number of respondents was an on-the-job challenge. The category was checked by twice as many people as the next highest ranked category. This finding again points to the needs of the individual and to his/her responsibility to respond to the need at an individually motivated level. It also supports the need for information about what continuing education opportunities are available so that the individual can tap into them.

In order to learn more about continuing education programming both in librarianship and in other professions, library organizations and organizations in professions known to be active in continuing education programming were surveyed. A surprising finding was that some of the national library associations seem consistently less interested in supporting or sponsoring continuing education programs than any of the other groups surveyed. For example, 3 of the 11 national library associations felt no responsibility for providing continuing education programs for any levels of their membership. National library associations ranked highest of all groups in their perceived "lack of membership interest" as a reason for not providing continuing education, and they ranked lowest in the percentage of associations planning to offer continuing education programming in the next two years although they were the group with the second greatest potential for growth.

A model continuing education program for health sciences library staffs was developed based on the information gathered in the project. Some options were considered, but discarded as not being economically feasible or not appropriate to the environments in which the target library staffs function, e.g., educational television, telephone lecture networks.

The final model addressed eight areas: Optimal allocation of available resources, The target audience, Needs assessment, Formats for delivering continuing education, Methods for developing programs, Identifying, training, and evaluating instructors, The mechanics of conducting programs, and Quality control.

One of continuing professional education's most effective and loyal spokesmen, Allie Beth Martin, died this past year. While she will be missed, she will not be forgotten. An Allie Beth Martin Memorial Lecture Fund has been established by CLENE to cover expenses for a speaker as part of semiannual CLENE Assembly programs. JULIE VIRGO

REFERENCES

Robert Berk. *Continuing Education Needs of Health Sciences Librarians as Reflected by Changes in the Published Literature.* ERIC Document ED 110 004.

Alan Knox. *Helping Adults to Learn.* (Washington, DC: Continuing Library Education Network and Exchange, 1976).

James Nelson. *A Directory of Human Resources for Continuing Library Education in Kentucky.* (Lexington, KY: College of Library Science, University of Kentucky, 1976).

Ruth Patrick. *An Annotated Bibliography of Recent Continuing Education Literature.* (Washington, DC: CLENE, 1976).

Julie Virgo. *Continuing Education for Health Sciences Library Personnel.* (Chicago, IL: Medical Library Association, 1976).

Ruth Warncke. *Planning Library Workshops and Institutes.* (Chicago, IL: American Library Association, 1976).

CONTU

The National Commission on New Technological Uses of Copyrighted Works (CONTU) is a Presidential commission established under Title II of Public Law 93-573, December 31, 1974. The 12 presidential appointees are Judge Stanley H. Fuld, Chair, Melville B. Nimmer, Vice Chair, George D. Cary, William S. Dix, John Hersey, Rhoda H. Karpatkin, Dan Lacy, Arthur R. Miller, E. Gabriel Perle, Hershel B. Sarbin, Robert Wedgeworth, and Alice E. Wilcox. Two ex officio members are the Register of Copyrights and the Librarian of Congress. The mandate of the Commission is to research and study the copyright implications of advances in both the computer and photocopying technologies, and make recommendations for necessary legislative and administrative action to recognize the rights of copyright owners while, at the same time, preserving public access to such works.

Activities in 1976. Meetings four through ten were held during 1976 to conclude the background briefing of the Commissioners and to begin formal hearings on the issues. The February meeting concentrated on the status of the data base industry. That meeting was held in part at the National Library of Medicine, where the Commission was briefed on the information services of the library—both on-line computer-based services and the supplying of information by photocopying. The Commissioners also heard presentations on several automated information systems.

In New York City in April the Commissioners were briefed on the information activities of the New York Times Company, including its Information Bank, and heard presentations from representatives of the Information Industry Association, who emphasized that new methods of storing, retrieving, and printing data were making traditional publishing obsolete. CONTU also heard a summary of related projects under way under the sponsorship of the National Science Foundation.

At the April meeting the Commissioners adopted a research plan outlining the areas of investigation and the procedures to be followed throughout the rest of the Commission term. Four areas of concern regarding the application of copyright to new technological processes and uses of works of authorship were identified: (1) computer software, (2) data bases, (3) new works created by computer and (4) photocopying. The Commissioners passed a resolution offering the Commission's good offices to assist the Congress in developing guidelines relating to photocopying practices covered by the proviso to section 108(g) (2) in the general revision copyright bill. The offer was accepted and the CONTU guidelines agreed to by the parties became part of the Congressional Conference Report on the new copyright law, P.L. 94-553.

According to the research plan, the first issue to be explored in depth was that of computer programs or software. Accordingly, the May and June Commission meetings were devoted to hearing testimony from software developers, users, and other interested parties. Among the organizations represented during the four days of hearings were the Computer and Business Equipment Manufacturers Association (CBEMA), the Computer Industry Association (CIA), the American Federation of Information Processing Societies (AFIPS), the General Services Administration (GSA), and EDUCOM. At the close of the June meeting, a subcommittee of Commissioners was appointed to analyze the testimony and written submissions in order to report recommendations to the full Commission. Subcommittees were also appointed to deal with each of the other three areas.

In addition to the meetings, the Commission has been collecting existing reports and research information on the areas of concern and further has contracted, along with NCLIS, for a research study on photocopying practices. The study will analyze the volume and distribution of library photocopying, and design and test the feasibility of a transaction-based mechanism for the payment of royalties on library photocopying of copyrighted serial publications. Results of the study were to be submitted to the Commission in May 1977.

The September meeting of the Commission was held in Los Angeles. It concentrated on the issues relating to data bases, and testimony was heard from users, brokers, and operators. The question was how to weigh the need to disseminate information against the various methods of protecting the rights of copyright holders. An introduction to the new works topic was also presented at that meeting.

In October the Commission invited witnesses to present factual data relevant to machine reproduction of copyrighted works. Among those appearing were Maurice Line, the Director of the British Library Lending Division; Thomas D. Gillies, Director of the Linda Hall Library in Kansas City, Missouri, and Gordon Williams, Director of the Center for Research Libraries in Chicago. The Commissioners decided to devote the tenth meeting to subcommittee reports and a discussion of the work remaining.

A preliminary report to the President and Congress was filed October 8, 1976, describing the first year of the Commission and its accomplishments and activities over that year. The final report and recommendations were to be completed in 1977. ARTHUR J. LEVINE

Cooperative Library Systems
See *Interlibrary Cooperation*.

Copyright

A new U.S. copyright law was finally enacted by Congress and was signed by President Ford on October 19, 1976 (Public Law 94-553, Title 17 of the United States Code). The effective date of the new law is January 1, 1978, with the exception of a few provisions (which are not related to library photocopying activities).

The Senate bill S.22 was unanimously approved by a vote of 97-0 in February 1976. S.22 had been slightly revised by the McClellan Subcommittee (that is the Subcommittee on Patents, Trademarks and Copyrights of the Senate Committee on the Judiciary).

The Kastenmaier House Subcommittee decided not to continue consideration of House bill HR 2223 but rather to consider S.22 and its accompanying Senate Report No. 94-473. The formal name of the Kastenmaier Subcommittee is the Subcommittee on Courts, Civil Liberties, and the Administration of Justice of the House Committee on the Judiciary.

Sessions for the markup of S.22 by the House Subcommittee were originally scheduled to begin in February and to be completed in April 1976. The markup soon fell behind schedule and continued thru the summer and early fall. Markup was interrupted by recesses of Congress for both the Democratic National Convention and the Republican National Convention. Further, Congressional leaders had decided that the 94th Congress should adjourn (rather than recess) on October 2 because of the Presidential election in November.

Omnibus Package. The copyright revision law was an omnibus document which includes, for example: definitions, exclusive rights, fair use, reproductions by libraries and archives, sound recordings, secondary transmissions, ephemeral recordings, pictorial, graphic and sculptural works, nondramatic musical works, performance rights, use in conjunction with computers, and noncommercial broadcasting. In some cases there were three or four interested parties. As a result, numerous documents were submitted to the Kastenmaier Subcommittee during the period of its markup sessions. It is therefore not surprising that the House Report (HR 94-1476) has 368 pages of which 46 pages are the bill itself.

The Subcommittee reported its marked up bill to the House Committee on the Judiciary on August 3; and on September 3 the Judiciary Committee reported the bill to the House. The bill was approved by the House of Representatives on September 22 by a vote of 316 to 7.

Because the House bill now differed materially from the bill approved by the Senate, it was necessary that the two versions be made mutually acceptable by a Joint Senate-House Conference Committee.

House-Senate Conference. The Conference Committee members were those of the House and Senate Subcommittees. The Conference Committee Report (HR 94-1733) recommended to both houses of Congress that the Senate recede from its disagreement and accept the House version in all major points. One notable exception was that the Conference Committee version adhered to the Senate version of Section 105—so that a limited term of copyright (five years) was *not* granted to publications of the National Technical Information Service. The Senate adopted the Conference Committee's version of the bill with its report on September 30. The House approved the bill, on October 1.

Because the 94th Congress, 2nd Session, adjourned on October 2, it was necessary that

"What about the copyright?"

President Ford sign the bill within ten business days after the bill reached his desk. It has been reported that the President signed the bill into law only two hours before a "pocket veto" would have occurred.

COMPLEX PROVISIONS

The new U.S. copyright law and its three accompanying reports are complex because of the many types of materials subject to copyright and copyright regulations. Library photocopying is only a small part of the total copyright law. The new law, as enacted, represents a collection of compromises between the numerous parties with contending interests in each area. During debates on the floor of the House, Representative Tom Railsback of Illinois said: "There is no way to satisfy all parties who have an interest in this legislation. A good compromise is probably one that satisfies no one, but is acceptable to everyone, and it has been said this bill is a compromise of compromises."

During the markup by the House Subcommittee, the six major U.S. library associations continued their unified efforts to attain equitable treatment of libraries of all types (AALL, ALA, ARL, Medical LA, Music LA and SLA).

Guidelines. Three sets of "Guidelines" were evolved that relate to different aspects of photocopying activities:

(1) Guidelines for the Proviso of Subsection 108(g)(2) Relating to *Inter*-Library Photocopying Activities (these so-called CONTU Guidelines[1] are in the Conference Committee Report, HR 94-1733) *Note:* There is *no* reference to *intra*-library photocopying activities in the new law or in the reports.

(2) Guidelines for Classroom Copying in Not-for-Profit Educational Institutions. (The so-called educational fair use guidelines[2] under Section 107 are in House Report 94-1476)

(3) Guidelines for Educational Uses of Music[3] (Section 107) are in House Report 94-1476.

Caution. Sections of the law itself and sections

Guidelines: New Copyright Law

Photocopying—Interlibrary Arrangements

Subsection 108(g)(2) of the bill deals, among other things, with limits on interlibrary arrangements for photocopying. It prohibits systematic photocopying of copyrighted materials but permits interlibrary arrangements "that do not have, as their purpose or effect, that the library or archives receiving such copies or phonorecords for distribution does so in such aggregate quantities as to substitute for a subscription to or purchase of such work."

The National Commission on New Technological Uses of Copyrighted Works offered its good offices to the House and Senate subcommittees in bringing the interested parties together to see if agreement could be reached on what a realistic definition would be of "such aggregate quantities." The Commission consulted with the parties and suggested the interpretation which follows, on which there has been substantial agreement by the principal library, publisher, and author organizations. The Commission considers the guidelines which follow to be a workable and fair interpretation of the intent of the proviso portion of subsection 108(g)(2).

These guidelines are intended to provide guidance in the application of section 108 to the most frequently encountered interlibrary case: a library's obtaining from another library, in lieu of interlibrary loan, copies of articles from relatively recent issues of periodicals—those published within five years prior to the date of the request. The guidelines do not specify what aggregate quantity of copies of an article or articles published in a periodical, the issue date of which is more than five years prior to the date when the request for the copy thereof is made, constitutes a substitute for a subscription to such periodical. The meaning of the proviso to subsection 108(g)(2) in such case is left to future interpretation.

The point has been made that the present practice on interlibrary loans and use of photocopies in lieu of loans may be supplemented or even largely replaced by a system in which one or more agencies or institutions, public or private, exist for the specific purpose of providing a central source for photocopies. Of course, these guidelines would not apply to such a situation.

Guidelines for Subsection 108(g)(2)

1. As used in the proviso of subsection 108(g)(2), the words ". . . such aggregate quantities as to substitute for a subscription to or purchase of such work" shall mean:

(a) with respect to any given periodical (as opposed to any given issue of a periodical), filled requests of a library or archives (a "requesting entity") within any calendar year for a total of six or more copies of an article or articles published in such periodical within five years prior to the date of the request. These guidelines specifically shall not apply, directly or indirectly, to any request of a requesting entity for a copy or copies of an article or articles published in any issue of a periodical, the publication date of which is more than five years prior to the date when the request is made. These guidelines do not define the meaning, with respect to such a request, of ". . . such aggregate quantities as to substitute for a subscription to [such periodical] ".

(b) With respect to any other material described in subsection 108(d), (including fiction and poetry), filled requests of a requesting entity within any calendar year for a total of six or more copies or phonorecords of or from any given work (including a collective work) during the entire period when such material shall be protected by copyright.

2. In the event that a requesting entity—

(a) shall have in force or shall have entered an order for a subscription to a periodical, or

(b) has within its collection, or shall have entered an order for, a copy or phonorecord of any other copyrighted work,

material from either category of which it desires to obtain by copy from another library or archives (the "supplying entity"), because the material to be copied is not reasonably available for use by the requesting entity itself, then the fulfillment of such request shall be treated as though the requesting entity made such copy from its own collection. A library or archives may request a copy or phonorecord from a supplying entity only under those circumstances where the requesting entity would have been able, under the other provisions of section 108, to supply such copy from materials in its own collection.

3. No request for a copy or phonorecord of any material to which these guidelines apply may be fulfilled by the supplying entity unless such request is accompanied by a representation by the requesting entity that the request was made in conformity with these guidelines.

4. The requesting entity shall maintain records of all requests made by it for copies or phonorecords of any materials to which these guidelines apply and shall maintain records of the fulfillment of such requests, which records shall be retained until the end of the third complete calendar year after the end of the calendar year in which the respective request shall have been made.

5. As part of the review provided for in subsection 108(i), these guidelines shall be reviewed not later than five years from the effective date of this bill.

The conference committee is aware that an issue has arisen as to the meaning of the phrase "audiovisual news program" in section 108(f)(3). The conferees believe that, under the provision as adopted in the conference substitute, a library or archives qualifying under section 108(a) would be free, without regard to the archival activities of the Library of Congress of any other organization, to reproduce, on videotape or any other medium of fixation or reproduction, local, regional, or network newscasts, interviews concerning current news events, and on-the-spot coverage of news events, and to distribute a limited number of reproductions of such a program on a loan basis.

Another point of interpretation involves the meaning of "indirect commercial advantage," as used in section 108(a)(1), in the case of libraries or archival collections within industrial, profit-making, or proprietary institutions. As long as the library or archives meets the criteria in section 108(a) and the other requirements of the section, including the prohibitions against multiple and systematic copying in subsection (g), the conferees consider that the isolated, spontaneous making of single photocopies by a library or archives in a for-profit organization without any commercial motivation, or participation by such a library or archives in interlibrary arrangements, would come within the scope of section 108.

Classroom Copying

The purpose of the following guidelines is to state the minimum standards of educational fair use under Section 107 of H.R. 2223. The parties agree that the conditions determining the extent of permissible copying for educational purposes may change in the future; that certain types of copying permitted under these guidelines may not be permissible in the future; and conversely that in the future other types of copying not permitted under these guidelines may be permissible under revised guidelines.

Moreover, the following statement of guidelines is not intended to limit the types of copying permitted under the standards of fair use under judicial decision and which are stated in Section 107 of the Copyright Revision Bill. There may be instances in which copying which does not fall within the guidelines stated below may nonetheless be permitted under the criteria of fair use.

Guidelines for Classroom Copying in Not-For-Profit Educational Institutions

I. *Single Copying for Teachers*

A single copy may be made of any of the following by or for a teacher at his or her individual request for his or her scholarly research or use in teaching or preparation to teach a class:

A. A chapter from a book;
B. An article from a periodical or newspaper;
C. A short story, short essay or short poem, whether or not from a collective work;
D. A chart, graph, diagram, drawing, cartoon or picture from a book, periodical, or newspaper;

II. *Multiple Copies for Classroom Use*

Multiple copies (not to exceed in any event more than one copy per pupil in a course) may be made by or for the teacher giving the course for classroom use or discussion; *provided that:*

A. The copying meets the tests of brevity and spontaneity as defined below; *and,*
B. Meets the cumulative effect test as defined below; *and,*
C. Each copy includes a notice of copyright

Definitions

Brevity

(i) Poetry: (a) A complete poem if less than 250 words and if printed on not more than two pages or, (b) from a longer poem, an excerpt of not more than 250 words.

(ii) Prose: (a) Either a complete article, story or essay of less than 2,500 words, or (b) an excerpt from any prose work of not more than 1,000 words or 10% of the work, whichever is less, but in any event a minimum of 500 words.

[Each of the numerical limits stated in "i" and "ii" above may be expanded to permit the completion of an unfinished line of a poem or of an unfinished prose paragraph.]

(iii) Illustration: One chart, graph, diagram, drawing, cartoon or picture per book or per periodical issue.

(iv) "Special" works: Certain works in poetry, prose or in "poetic prose" which often combine language with illustrations and which are intended sometimes for children and at other times for a more general audience fall short of 2,500 words in their entirety. Paragraph "ii" above notwithstanding such "special works" may not be reproduced in their entirety; however, an excerpt comprising not more than two of the published pages of such special work and containing not more than 10% of the words found in the text thereof, may be reproduced.

Spontaneity

(i) The copying is at the instance and inspiration of the individual teacher, and

(ii) The inspiration and decision to use the work and the moment of its use for maximum teaching effectiveness are so close in time that it would be unreasonable to expect a timely reply to a request for permission.

Cumulative Effect

(i) The copying of the material is for only one course in the school in which the copies are made.

(ii) Not more than one short poem, article, story, essay or two excerpts may be copied from the same author, nor more than three from the same collective work or periodical volume during one class term.

(iii) There shall not be more than nine instances of such multiple copying for one course during one class term.

[The limitations stated in "i" and "iii" above shall not apply to current news periodicals and newspapers and current news sections of other periodicals.]

III. *Prohibitions as to I and II Above*

Notwithstanding any of the above, the following shall be prohibited:

(A) Copying shall not be used

of the Reports and the "Guidelines" should not be read as independent documents. For a complete understanding the reader must move back and forth between the law and the reports.

Because the "Guidelines" may not be easily interpreted in certain situations, it is hoped that the "Guidelines" can be restated in such a way that they can be more readily understood by librarians responsible for photocopying activities. So as to remain within the limits of "fair use" as stated in the "Guidelines," it will be necessary for libraries to maintain records so that each library will know whether it has reached the upper limit of "fair use" as stated in the "Guidelines." Libraries in educational institutions will probably have to establish separate records for each instructor and may have to keep records for each class conducted by each instructor.

Photocopying Record Keeping. The new law specifies that the provisions regarding library photocopying shall be reviewed five years after the effective date of the law and every five years thereafter. Because of this provision (Section 108i) as well as the "Guidelines," it is important that libraries prepare to keep more complete records of their photocopying activity than may have been the practice in the past under previous laws.

Numerous regulations must be issued by the Copyright Office to meet requirements of the new law.

Highlights. A *Special Issue of the ALA Washington Newsletter* on *New Copyright Law* was published in November. It contains brief highlights of the new law; succinct summaries of sections relating to photocopying; recommended preparations for compliance on January 1, 1978, and for mandated review in 1982; a legislative history; excerpts from P.L. 94-553 and its Reports, including the three sets of "Guidelines."[4]

Five Copying Points. It is difficult to select matters of particular importance in the new law. Five items must be mentioned because of

---

to create or to replace or substitute for anthologies, compilations or collective works. Such replacement or substitution may occur whether copies of various works or excerpts therefrom are accumulated or reproduced and used separately.

(B) There shall be no copying of or from works intended to be "consumable" in the course of study or of teaching. These include workbooks, exercises, standardized tests and test booklets and like consumable material.

(C) Copying shall not:
   (a) substitute for the purchase of books, publishers' reprints or periodicals;
   (b) be directed by higher authority;
   (c) be repeated with respect to the same item by the same teacher from term to term.

(D) No charge shall be made to the student beyond the actual cost of the photocopying.

Agreed March 19, 1976.

Ad Hoc Committee on Copyright Law Revision:
  By Sheldon Elliott Steinbach.
Author-Publisher Group:
  Authors League of America:
    By Irwin Karp, *Counsel.*
  Association of American Publishers, Inc.:
    By Alexander C. Hoffman, *Chairman, Copyright Committee.*

Music

In a joint letter dated April 30, 1976, representatives of the Music Publishers' Association of the United States, Inc., the National Music Publishers' Association, Inc., the Music Teachers National Association, the Music Educators National Conference, the National Association of Schools of Music, and the Ad Hoc Committee on Copyright Law Revision, wrote to Chairman Kastenmeier as follows:

During the hearings on H.R. 2223 in June 1975, you and several of your subcommittee members suggested that concerned groups should work together in developing guidelines which would be helpful to clarify Section 107 of the bill.

Representatives of music educators and music publishers delayed their meetings until guidelines had been developed relative to books and periodicals. Shortly after that work was completed and those guidelines were forwarded to your subcommittee, representatives of the undersigned music organizations met together with representatives of the Ad Hoc Committee on Copyright Law Revision to draft guidelines relative to music.

We are very pleased to inform you that the discussions thus have been fruitful on the guidelines which have been developed. Since private music teachers are an important factor in music education, due consideration has been given to the concerns of that group.

We trust that this will be helpful in the report on the bill to clarify Fair Use as it applies to music.

The text of the guidelines accompanying this letter is as follows:

Guidelines for Educational Uses of Music

The purpose of the following guidelines is to state the minimum and not the maximum standards of educational fair use under Section 107 of HR 2223. The parties agree that the conditions determining the extent of permissible copying for educational purposes may change in the future; that certain types of copying permitted under these guidelines may not be permissible in the future, and conversely that in the future other types of copying not permitted under these guidelines may be permissible under revised guidelines.

Moreover, the following statement of guidelines is not intended to limit the types of

on-going activities of certain copyright proprietors or their organized groups:
(1) The law does not mention royalty payments for photocopying.
(2) The law does not mention *intra*-library photocopying.
(3) The "Guidelines" for the proviso of Subsection 108(g)(2) "are for *inter*-library photocopying. The burden of compliance is on the *requesting* library, *not* on the *supplying* library.
(4) The so-called "for-profit" special libraries (whose parent organizations have profit motives) are *not* treated differently from any other library provided that their collections are: (a) open to the public *or* (b) available to other persons doing research in a specialized field.
(5) No distinction is made in the law or in the "Guidelines" that photocopying publications in certain subject areas are specifically regulated (subject areas such as science, technology, medicine).

Problems. Almost before the new law was signed and continuing on into 1977, some copyright proprietors have issued misleading advertising with the implication that the new law is already in effect in 1977, and/or that the supplying library has the burden for compliance—even when the requesting library has not reached the limit of five times per title during the past five years (as allowed by the "Guidelines"). Further, associations of copyright proprietors and other groups with apparent profit motives have made presentations to CONTU that continue their efforts to concentrate only on science-technology-medicine, or to suggest that activities by special librarians in corporations are different from those of other libraries.

Special and Public Interests. In the relatively short debate of the bill on the floor of the House, the bill was described by Representative Kastenmaier of Wisconsin as "basically economic legislation which affects a variety of industries and interest groups."

---

copying permitted under the standards of fair use under judicial decision and which are stated in Section 107 of the Copyright Revision Bill. There may be instances in which copying which does not fall within the guidelines stated below may nonetheless be permitted under the criteria of fair use.

A. Permissible Uses

1. Emergency copying to replace purchased copies which for any reason are not available for an imminent performance provided purchased replacement copies shall be substituted in due course.

2. (a) For academic purposes other than performance, multiple copies of excerpts of works may be made, provided that the excerpts do not comprise a part of the whole which would constitute a performable unit such as a section, movement or aria, but in no case more than 10% of the whole work. The number of copies shall not exceed one copy per pupil.

(b) For academic purposes other than performance, a single copy of an entire performable unit (section, movement aria, etc.) that is, (1) confirmed by the copyright proprietor to be out of print or (2) unavailable except in a larger work, may be made by or for a teacher solely for the purpose of his or her scholarly research or in preparation to teach a class.

3. Printed copies which have been purchased may be edited or simplified provided that the fundamental character of the work is not distorted or the lyrics, if any, altered or lyrics added if none exist.

4. A single copy of recordings of performances by students may be made for evaluation or rehearsal purposes and may be retained by the educational institution or individual teacher.

5. A single copy of a sound recording (such as a tape, disc or cassette) of copyrighted music may be made from sound recordings owned by an educational institution or an individual teacher for the purpose of constructing aural exercises or examinations and may be retained by the educational institution or individual teacher. (This pertains only to the copyright of the music itself and not to any copyright which may exist in the sound recording.)

B. Prohibitions

1. Copying to create or replace or substitute for anthologies, compilations or collective works.

2. Copying of or from works intended to be "consumable" in the course of study or of teaching such as workbooks, exercises, standardized tests and answer sheets and like material.

3. Copying for the purpose of performance, except as in A (1) above.

4. Copying for the purpose of substituting for the purchase of music, except as in A (1) and A (2) above.

5. Copying without inclusion of the copyright notice which appears on the printed copy.

Representative Railback also stated on the House floor: "This legislation is unlike any processed by the Judiciary Committee. It involves money, big money; it involves special interests, many special interests; and most importantly it involves the public interest." If one reviews the many aspects of the new U.S. copyright law, it is more than apparent that Railsback's comment was very accurate. With one notable exception, each interested party in each aspect expected important benefits. Only libraries and their users would not benefit monetarily. In the library photocopying aspects, the public interest and right to information are certainly "involved" but only at the added cost of the royalty payments that are anxiously desired by the copyright proprietors—and which would have to come from library budgets and thus must come from the parent body of the library, be it public, academic, special or school library.

Enactment of the new law does not end concerns for librarians, libraries, and library users.
F. E. MCKENNA

REFERENCES
1. CONTU Guidelines: By agreement of representatives of the 6 major library associations, Authors League of America, and Association of American Publishers with the assistance of CONTU.
2. Educational Fair Use Guidelines: By agreement of the Ad Hoc Committee of Educational Institutions and Organizations on Copyright Law Revision, Authors League of America, and Association of American Publishers.
3. Guidelines for Educational Uses of Music: By agreement of the Music Publishers Association of the United States, National Music Publishers Association, Music Teachers National Association, Music Educators National Conference, National Association of Schools of Music, and the Ad Hoc Committee on Copyright Law Revision.
4. *ALA Washington Newsletter: Special Issue on New Copyright Law* 28: no. 13 (November 15, 1976), available from ALA, 50 E. Huron Street, Chicago, $2: Highlights, summaries, excerpts from PL 94-533 and Reports and "Guidelines."

Council, ALA

The Centennial theme "Celebrate!" permeated every aspect of ALA's life during 1976, and even the Council—the Association's governing body—was stung by the Centennial spirit. In honor of ALA's 100th anniversary, Council presented Centennial Citations to 10 persons. A special award to honor individuals who had made outstanding contributions to librarianship and the ALA during the Association's first century, Centennial Citations were presented to Florence Anderson, Secretary, Carnegie Corporation; Fred Carrington Cole, President, Council on Library Resources; Emerson Greenaway, Librarian Emeritus, Philadelphia Free Public Library; Howard Haycraft, Publisher, H. W. Wilson Company; Frances Henne, educator, author, librarian; Frank McKenna, Executive Director, Special Libraries Association; Grace T. Stevenson, Deputy Executive Director Emeritus, American Library Association; Frederic A. Thorpe, Publisher, Ulverscroft Large Print Books; Wallace Van Jackson, Librarian Emeritus, Virginia State College, and Theodore Waller, President, Grolier Educational Corporation. (*See* Biographies.)

Meetings and Issues. The 150 representatives on Council met for over nine hours of meetings, in addition to orientation and information sessions. Council's mood during 1976 expressed a willingness to act, mixed with a reluctance to promise more than the Association could realistically deliver. With very little debate, a Resolution requesting that ALA Headquarters be moved to Washington, D.C., was defeated, with none of the time-consuming rhetoric that has surrounded earlier debate on this issue. A Resolution calling for direct representation of ALA Divisions and Round Tables on Council was defeated with the recommendation that a future Council information meeting be devoted to discussion of this question. It was clear that Council was not about to undo quickly the work of the late 1960's Activities Committee on New Directions and ANACONDA. Council also considered a recommendation from the Committee on Organization requesting the establishment of a Library Instruction Round Table to provide a forum for discussion of activities, programs and problems of instruction in the use of libraries. Council postponed action on this recommendation, pending a report of the Ad Hoc Committee on the Future Structure of ALA. Council was reluctant to change the status quo without serious consideration and deliberate review of the consequences.

Dues and Finances. Since the adoption of a new dues scale in 1974, there has been the growing feeling that all of the Association's membership units should contribute to the fiscal resources of the Association. At the Midwinter Meeting, Council accepted a report of the Special Committee on Round Tables, outlining the function and policy authority of Round Tables. Council referred to COPES, however, the portion of the report that described Round Tables' fiscal relationship to ALA. The report recommended that ALA's 11 Round Tables contribute an unspecified amount annually (which each Round Table would decide) to the ALA General Fund to offset those costs which ALA assumes to maintain a Round Table. COPES returned with the recommendation that the Round Tables be assessed annually 10 percent of dues income. In turn, the Executive Board presented a counterproposal—that all Round Tables be asked to make a voluntary contribution of up to 10 percent of dues income. Council amended that recommendation and voted to assess Round Tables a charge ranging from a low of 5 percent to a maximum of 10 percent of dues income. It was clear that Council's spirit was that Round Tables, like the Divisions, will have to be accountable to a limited extent for the services they receive from ALA Headquarters.

Procedures. Council has been concerned for some time with the problem of how it goes about its business. Council continued its orientation sessions for newly elected and returning Councilors. At the Midwinter Meeting the orientation meeting included a review of how Council works—its organization, its role within ALA, and its authority as a policy maker within the Association—and discussion on three issues of timely importance: a critique of the NCLIS Report and prospects for implementation; getting membership input in the ALA policy-making process; and getting citizen input into library planning through the White House Conference. During 1976 Council acted on a number of Resolutions that will expedite Council's work and clarify its responsibilities. To speed the mechanics of Council business, the size of the Council Resolutions Committee was increased from 7 to 12 members and the Council Resolutions Committee was asked to develop guidelines for the preparation of Resolutions for Council consideration. Foremost on Council's Agenda was the vexing question of Council's and Membership's authority to act on matters affecting Association policy. In 1975 a Council Committee on the Relationship between Membership and Council on Policy Issues was appointed to develop a solution to this source of tension. Reporting at the Midwinter Meeting, the Council recommended that the Council Committee on Resolutions be charged with the responsibility for determining the policy nature of all Resolutions to be presented to Council. It was further recommended that the Council Committee on Resolutions review all Resolutions passed by Membership, to determine if they involve policy, and that they then be forwarded to Council for action. If there were any disagreement with the Committee on Resolutions' decision, the matter would be voted on by Council. Debate on this proposal was complex and lengthy. A motion to table and a motion to refer to Committee were defeated. Finally, Jane Anne Hannigan, Chairperson of the Committee presenting the Resolution, told the Council that the recommendation presented was the best solution the Committee could offer. Past-President Edward G. Holley asked Council, "Do you want or do you not want to adopt this as a trial way of trying to get around this difficult issue?" Council voted in the affirmative. In a related move, Council recommended that an Ad Hoc Committee be appointed to reorganize and recodify the *ALA Policy Manual.*

Too often Council has been criticized for its inability to follow up on actions taken. Council, at the Annual Conference meeting, passed a Resolution committing the Executive Board or its delegate to report to Council "on the status of implementation of motions and Resolutions passed by Council during the preceding year." This is the first step in assuring that Council's words are translated into action.

There has been a growing sense that Council should be more representative of the feelings of ALA members and more in touch with issues that are important to librarianship. At the 1976 Midwinter Meeting Council acted to recommend that Councilors "work together wherever possible to establish library issue caucuses . . . with the goal of identifying, developing information and communicating recommendations on library issues to ALA Council. . . ." A network of library issue caucuses might indeed be an effective vehicle for bringing important issues before the Council.

Race and Sexism Issues. One of the most interesting aspects of reviewing Council action is to see what themes persist from year to year. One is the issue of racism and sexism. At the 1976 Annual Meeting, Council again passed a Resolution on this topic. The Resolution came to Council from the membership; and it commits the Association to combatting sexism and racism. The Resolution is not aimed at eliminating sexist and racist references in library material, but at building better awareness of racism and sexism among those persons who select and create materials. The Resolution, as approved by Council, calls on the involvement of many Association units: ALA is directed to survey library schools to determine if awareness training is a part of the curricula—if it is not, ALA will urge that it be included; the LAD Personnel Administration Section is to develop a model in-service program of racism and sexism awareness training; the Public Library, School Librarians, Children's Services, Reference and Adult Services, and College and Research Library Divisions are urged to develop a program on the awareness of library users to problems of racism and sexism; the Resources and Technical Services Division is to develop a coordinated plan for the reform of cataloging practices. This is not the first time that the ALA has gone on record as opposing racism and sexism—at least five policy statements adopted within the last 15 years touch on these issues. What makes the 1976 Resolution unusual is that it directs that specific action be taken by a number of ALA units. The earlier resolutions, though well intentioned, are characterized by a vagueness that would make implementation difficult. At the 1977 Annual Conference, Council is to receive a progress report on implementation of the 1976 Resolution.

Council took two other actions during 1976 which related to this issue. At the Midwinter Meeting, Council approved a Resolution presented by the SRRT Task Force on Women, directing that ALA prepare guidelines for editing ALA publications to eliminate sexist terminology. This Resolution was in response to 1975 National Library Week materials which the Task Force felt were demeaning to women. At the Centennial Annual Conference, Council approved the establishment of a standing Committee on the Status of Women in Librarianship. The Committee was "to officially represent the diversity of women's interest within ALA."

Expanding Service. An interest in making library service more responsive to all people was reflected in a Resolution endorsed by REFORMA calling for graduate library education programs to "take immediate steps to expand their curricula with courses taught by bilingual/bicultural faculty," reflecting the cultural heritage and needs of the 10,600,000 Spanish-speaking people of the United States. This spirit also motivated adoption of a Resolution introduced by Zoia Horn that ALA encourage public libraries and systems to provide library service in jails and local detention facilities and that the Health and Rehabilitative Library Services Division, the Public Library Association, and the American Library Trustee Association and other interested groups work together "to design a plan to assist public libraries in extending their services."

Presidential Resolutions. Responding to the high political spirit of a U. S. Presidential election year Council sent Resolutions of appreciation and commendation to candidates Jimmy Carter and Gerald R. Ford. To President Ford, Council expressed the ALA's gratitude for his sponsorship of the White House Conference on Library and Information Services and pledged the Association's support in its implementation. In a letter to ALA President Clara Jones, Jimmy Carter congratulated the ALA on its centenary and expressed his commitment to the support of libraries and information services. The ALA's Resolution in response commended Carter for "his recognition of the services provided by libraries" and offered ALA's full cooperation in informing the American people of "the national need for support of libraries."

On the international scene, Council urged the U. S. delegation to the UNESCO General Conference at Nairobi to support the proposed protocol to the Florence Agreement on the Importation of Educational, Scientific and Cultural Materials.

The Council's 1976 meeting closed on a positive note with the initiation of a new Council action: presentation of Certificates of Commendation to retiring Councilors for service to the Association. It was well-deserved recognition that capped a progressive Centennial year. — PATRICIA R. HARRIS

Council on Library Resources

See *Foundations and Funding Agencies*.

Council on Library Technical Assistants

The Council on Library Technical Assistants (COLT) was founded in 1967 by people involved in two-year associate degree programs for the training of library technical assistants and graduates of those programs. From the beginning COLT has had as its goal the recognition and acceptance of the LTA as a member of the library team.

The Council provides a clearinghouse for all information relating to library paraprofessionals. It works to advance the status of paraprofessionals and promote the acceptance of that status. COLT works to initiate employment, placement, and certification activities of paraprofessionals. The organization provides channels of communication between library educational programs and paraprofessionals. COLT encourages appropriate standards for education institutions offering programs for library, media, and information workers. The Council works in close cooperation with other library related organizations. The membership is made up of persons involved in two-year associate degree programs for the training of library technical assistants and graduates of those programs. The total membership includes deans, librarians, directors, instructors, employers, and library technical assistants.

The year 1976 was one of growth for the Council. Growth was seen in membership, organization, and philosophy. Affiliation with ALA brought not only recognition but also a sense of accomplishment. ALA affiliation also provided a larger audience as it was decided by the COLT Executive Board to hold either a conference, workshop, institute or seminar in conjunction with the ALA Annual Conference.

During previous years COLT placed emphasis on the role, the training, job description, and job prospects of Library Technical Assistants. At the ALA Conference in San Francisco in 1975, the Council adopted a theme for 1976, that of Continuing Education both for the professionals and paraprofessionals. It was felt that each should know the role of the other if they were to function as members of a team.

Objectives and Program. COLT also broadened its objectives and philosophy to include not only the various types of libraries, media centers, and information centers but also library related support staff such as aides, clerks, and audiovisual technicians.

Early in the year the COLT Executive Board decided that 1976 was the year to create a new and more energetic organization. The Council has worked to get more of its membership involved with the operation of the organization and in support of goals of the organization.

Meetings were planned in different geographical areas near a school with a LTA program. Each of the meetings was structured so that LTA students, COLT members, and Board members had a chance to talk and discuss informally various problems. One problem that kept recurring was job placement.

Beginning with the January 1976 issue, the *COLT Newsletter* took on a journal format and a new editor. Richard Taylor of Wilbur Wright College in Chicago initiated changes and sought to get articles and ideas not only from the membership but from anyone who might want to contribute to the newsletter.

A COLT sponsored preconference in Chicago during the 1976 ALA Conference had as its theme "Work Roles of Nonprofessionals and Professionals." The meeting was attended by over 100 persons; Barbara Conroy of CLENE spoke on "Continuing Education for Library Personnel."

Directory. During mid-year COLT published a new edition of the *Directory of Institutions Offering or Planning Programs for the Training of Library Technical Assistants,* edited by Richard L. Taylor. The new *Directory* contains data from 157 schools in the United States and Canada. It is useful for directors of library training programs, students of librarianship, employers of library paraprofessionals, and, most of all, for potential library technology students and their advisers.

Organizational Changes. At the July meeting, the President of COLT, Betty Duvall, of Florissant Valley Community College in Saint Louis, Missouri, announced her resignation and the Vice-President/President-elect, Margaret Barron of Cuyahoga Community College in Cleveland, Ohio, assumed the office.

James O. Wallace of San Antonio College and the LTAs there welcomed the COLT Executive Board in October. COLT Board members and students in the program participated in an open discussion on what COLT could do for them and they in turn could do for COLT.

During the year, it was decided that the organization needed a permanent address for mail and inquiries. After a careful search, the decision was made to locate in Westerville, Ohio, at the School Management Institute.

Committees. Alice Naylor, University of Toledo Community and Technical College, Toledo, Ohio, Chairperson of the Publicity and Public Relations Committee, printed and distributed at each meeting a COLT button and brochure. The Membership Committee, chaired by Linda Joachim, Indiana University, Bloomington, increased membership in COLT to 315 members representing most of the 50 states and including Canada, Brazil, Australia and Yugoslavia, giving COLT an international membership. Sue Gill, Florissant Valley Community College, Chairperson of the Education and Research Committee, updated the bibliography on LTAs in the May 1976 issue of the *COLT Newsletter.* COLT planned to publish a revised edition. The Organizational and Liaison Committee continued the working relationship with related organizations.

JOHN JOHNSON

COLT Officers

PRESIDENT (July 1976–June 1977):
Margaret Barron, Cuyahoga Community College, Cleveland, Ohio

VICE-PRESIDENT/PRESIDENT-ELECT:
John Johnson, Durham Technical Institute, Durham, North Carolina

EXECUTIVE SECRETARY:
Dorothy Smith, Community College of Philadelphia, Pennsylvania

---

Data Bases, Computer-Readable

Data bases were much in the news in the information science and library science communities during 1976. A number of new data bases were made available to the public and many data bases were added to the list of "on-line data bases." The number of training programs, courses and workshops—dealing with data bases, search strategy formulation, and on-line use of systems—increased in 1976. Many of these were attended by university and public librarians. In the past it has been largely the special librarians and information scientists who have been heavily involved in data base use. It appears that public librarians and academic libraries (outside the medical field which is already highly involved) are preparing for on-line services. Several data base and on-line publications were introduced in 1976 and a new on-line vendor announced services to be introduced in 1977.

New Data Bases. The number of new data bases that appeared in 1976 is too large to enumerate here. They cover areas of science, technology, business, humanities, current research, and advertising. The Technotec, service of CDC (Control Data Corporation), provides on-line advertisements for customers of that service. Fortunately for library and infor-

"It hasn't helped their reading, but they've become very proficient with computer hardware."

Data Bases, Computer-Readable

"I sit here and solve mathematical problems, program electronic music, analyze architectural possiblities . . . but somehow being a Renaissance man isn't what it used to be."

mation science, two major secondary sources in the field announced conversion of their records to computer-readable form. Too long have the shoemaker's children gone without shoes. The British *Library and Information Science Abstracts* (LISA) was computerized in 1976, and the U.S. publication *Information Science Abstracts* initiated its conversion in 1976. LISA will be made available on-line through one of the major on-line vendors in 1977. The addition of these two data bases complements the currently used data base sources for information and library science information— INSPEC, ERIC, BIOSIS, CACondensates, NTIS, *Social Science Citation Index* and MEDLINE.

On-Line Vendors. A major change in the on-line vendor market in 1976 was the development of a new company, Bibliographic Retrieval Service (BRS), that announced services to be provided from eight of the most popular data bases beginning in January 1977. BRS will provide more competition in the market place that is now dominated by Lockheed Retrieval Service (LRS) and System Development Corporation (SDC) in the for-profit sector and by the National Library of Medicine in the government sector. BRS claims to be "unbundling" in the sense that they have disclosed the components of the prices charged for data-base search services. They charge the same connect time rate for use of all data bases and add to that the data base vendor's royalty charge for use of each of the specific data bases.

The communication network charges of TELENET are based on an hourly rate, and the rate depends on the traffic load at the node used. Print charges are added on top of search charges, as is true with LRS and SDC. BRS has announced group discount rates dependent on a schedule of numbers of hours of use guaranteed by the customer. In November and December both Lockheed and SDC announced group discount rates for their data-base services. It is interesting to note that the guaranteed minimum number of hours of use, or guaranteed dollars approach, is one that had been tried by both SDC and LRS several years ago. At that time it was a deterrent to data base use. Subsequently, SDC and LRS sold on-line services on a basis that committed the user to paying for only the number of minutes or hours used with no guaranteed minimums. This tack has worked well for both organizations. If the guaranteed minimum approach works in 1977, it will be largely because the market has been opened up by Lockheed and SDC making an approach that was unpalatable in the early 70's acceptable in the late 70's. Potential users are more familiar with the capabilities of on-line search services than they were four or five years ago. They have lost their skepticism. They no longer view on-line searching as a "flash in the pan," but see it as an effective, economic, and necessary method of information retrieval.

It remains to be seen whether or not BRS will open up a relatively untapped portion of the data-base market—the academic and public library sector—or whether the advent of a new vendor will fragment the existing market to the detriment of all.

Copyright. While the topic of copyright is covered elsewhere in this *Yearbook*, a precedent that may affect the data-base publishers took place in 1976. In the case of *Wainwright v. Wall Street Transcripts*, the U.S. District Court found for Wainwright. Wall Street Transcripts republished abstracts prepared by Wainwright, making only slight changes and adding no new material. This practice of reusing abstracts, which has been used within the information world for many years, may be challenged again on the basis of this precedent. (*See also* Copyright.)

Publications. Two new journals that will deal with on-line use of data bases were announced in the summer of 1976. They are *Online* and *On-Line Review*. *Online* will be published in the U.S. by Jeff Pemberton and *On-Line Review*, an international journal with both American and European editors, will be published by Learned Information in England. Both serials were scheduled at year's end to begin publication in the first quarter of 1977. That two separate publishers in different parts of the world conceived of journals covering the same general area at the same time indicates the impact the on-line use of data bases has made in the information world.

An SDC study, "Impact of On-Line Retrieval Services—A Survey of Users, 1974–75," by Wanger, Cuadra and Fishburn, published in 1976, provides many interesting statistics that help characterize the on-line community in terms of service units, searchers, and users or clients. Much of the data substantiate the opinions of many professionals in the field.

Directory and Data Sourcebook. Data-base directories were published both in Europe and the United States. *Data Bases in Europe,* edited by Alex Tomberg, was published by EUSIDIC and Aslib in November 1976. A 58-page document, it contains information about 337 bibliographic data bases and 149 data banks (numerical data bases), and it indicates which organizations process those data bases. *Computer-Readable Bibliographic Data Bases — A Directory and Data Sourcebook,* compiled and edited by Martha E. Williams and Sandra H. Rouse, was published by the American Society for Information Science in October 1976. This 814-page *Directory* contains information on 301 publicly available bibliographic data bases produced in the United States and Europe. The directory contains four indexes, a Subject Category Index, a Name/Acronym/Synonym Index, a Producer Index, and a Processor Index. The subject category index aids users who have difficulty remembering correct names and acronyms of data bases. This index is especially useful for accessing multiple data bases that have similar acronyms or when the name of the data base bears no resemblance to the subject matter contained in it. The name, acronym, synonym index is needed because many authors of papers and centers providing data-base services refer to data bases by names that they assign to the data base rather than by the name the data-base-producing organization gives to its own data base. Names of hard copy publications that correspond to data bases are also included as access points to data-base names.

Data Bases and Data-Base Records On-Line. Although, in terms of numbers, only about one-third of the currently maintained data bases listed in the *Directory* are available on-line either in the U.S. or Europe, the majority of the records are on-line. That is, of 277 data bases, 107 are on-line. The 277 data bases contain approximately 52,000,000 records and of these 33,000,000 are on-line. Thus the majority of publicly available machine-readable bibliographic records can be searched and retrieved on-line.

There are still many abstracting and indexing publications that have not been converted to computer-readable form but it is likely that most of the popular ones will be converted in the next few years. Many of the computer-readable data bases that are not yet on-line are vying for space in the computer files of the major on-line vendors.

Numbers of Data Bases and Machine-Readable Records. Based on data obtained for *Computer-Readable Data Bases* the distribution of data bases and of data-base records (which for the most part corresponds to bibliographic references) split up between U.S. producers and non-U.S. producers as shown in the table.

Numbers and Percentages of Data Bases and Records Generated in the U.S. and Elsewhere

	No. DB's	% DB's	No. Records (in millions)	% Records
U.S.	160	58%	46.3	89%
Non-U.S.	117	42%	5.7	11%
Total	277	100%	52.0	100%

The figure of 52,000,000 records is based on those 277 data bases for which relevant file size data were available. The total number of machine-readable data-base records may really be somewhat larger than 52,000,000 because data regarding the file size and growth rate were not available for all data bases. Most of the data bases for which file size data were not available are the less familiar and smaller data bases. These figures relate to those data bases listed in the *Directory* that are currently maintained. Twenty-four of the 301 in the *Directory* were not maintained *per se* with the same name after 1975. Some were merged into other data bases, changed names, or were terminated.

Although these figures do not include all data-base-producing community into two seg- more publicly available bibliographic or bibliographic-related data bases than those listed in the *Directory;* however, most of the additional data bases would not add significantly to the number of records. The additional records would very likely be offset by the duplication of records that exists in the 52,000,000, *i.e.*, some data bases include records selected from other data bases. The TOXLINE file, for example, contains records taken from CBAC and several other files.

Data-Base Production — Government and Private Sector. Based on analysis of data contained in the *Directory,* one finds that the U.S. government is no longer the principal data-base producer in this country. Dividing the data-base-producing community into two segments — government and private — one finds that the government sector produces 41 percent of the computer-readable bibliographic and bibliographic-related data bases and the private sector 59 percent. The private sector can be broken further into the "for-profit" and "not-for-profit" groups, with the "for profits" producing 31 percent and the "not-for-profits" producing 28 percent of the data bases. The data-base production activity can also be looked at from the view of the number of records contained in the files. When broken down this way, the government (federal and state) is the producer for 25 percent of the records, and the private sector is responsible for 75 percent — the "for-profit" component of the private sector producing 35 percent and "not-for-profit" 40 percent.

These data are applicable to the 160 currently maintained U.S. data bases described in the *Directory*. The result does not include the 24 data bases in the *Directory* that did not add new records in 1975. Some of these discontinued data bases are still available for search even though they are not being updated; some have been added to other files which are continuing files. The Bibliography of Agriculture, for example, is a data base that is no longer maintained but the same material is currently put into the AGRICOLA data base.

Education and Training for Data-Base Use. More training sessions, workshops, and courses dealing with data bases and techniques for making the best use of data bases and search systems were offered and attended in 1976 than ever before. It is good that the demand and interest in data-base training are high, but the quality of training provided has been uneven. The vehicles for education and training include university courses, short courses, workshops, seminars, CAI, continuing education programs, and various training packages for individual learning.

One of the problem areas is that distinctions between education, training, and marketing are often not understood. Attendees at sessions where on-line demonstrations are provided often think that they have had training for on-line searching when they have not. There is definitely a need for education in foundations and principles relating to information science to be provided in schools of library and information science and there is also a need for practical training in the use of data bases and systems within the schools. Unfortunately, there is a dearth of good training packages. There are not enough faculty members in the schools with adequate preparation to provide the education and training, and few schools allocate or can afford to allocate sufficient funds for hands-on experience with on-line systems.

Another problem is that a number of entrepreneurs who are not familiar with the history, needs, and the development of the data-base field have appeared. Entrepreneurs with solid technical credentials and a proper understanding of information needs have done much to further data-base use. Those with only a profit motive and insufficient technical understanding tend to reinvent the wheel and invent new terminology, thereby misinforming or confusing newcomers.

Positive Trends. On the positive side 1976 saw the on-line vendors providing discount rates for data-base use to schools of library and information science. The rates may not be as low as the schools would like but it was a move in the right direction. Cooperation has increased among data-base producers and between the producers and the processors of the data bases. In fact joint workshops between producers or between producers and processors were held. The producers have become more seriously involved in education and training and are committing more resources to that end. They are providing more training and better training aids. Overall, the growth of data-base use via on-line systems has continued. The number of searches conducted on-line in 1976 was approximately 1,200,000, an increase of 200,000 over 1975. Though the increase was not as steep as the increase from 1974 to 1975, the real numbers are significant.

MARTHA E. WILLIAMS

REFERENCES
1. Alex Tomberg, *Data Bases in Europe*, 2nd ed., European User Series 1 (EUSIDIC and Aslib: London, 1976) 58 pp.
2. Judith Wanger, Carlos A. Cuadra, and Mary Fishburn, *Impact of On-Line Retrieval Services—A Survey of Users 1974–75*, (System Development Corporation, 1976).
3. Martha E. Williams and Sandra H. Rouse, *Computer-Readable Bibliographic Data Bases—A Directory and Data Sourcebook*, (Washington, D.C.: American Society for Information Science, October 1976), 814 pp.
4. For all statistics presented in the above article, see Martha E. Williams, "Data about Data Bases," *Bulletin of American Society for Information Science* (vol. 3, no. 2, 1976).

Depository Library System

See *Government Publications and Depository System*

Disadvantaged, Library Service to

What is the best way of describing the "state" of library service to the poor during 1976? To use the vernacular—it looked both good and bad.

The Bad News. It looked bad when talk was heard throughout the U.S. library world of the "death" of the public library and with it, or preceding it, the demise of services aimed at special groups which include the poor, educationally disadvantaged, the traditional "non-user." Some public librarians now turn away from outreach activities, condemning these actions as "missionary" and nonproductive. However, the community people to whom outreach services are aimed will not disappear because funding is scarce. Poor people are taxpayers (directly or indirectly). Turning away, dropping library service to the poor, does not mean that their service needs have disappeared and are no longer felt.

Things looked bad when libraries such as the Buffalo and Erie County Public were required to curtail any library service not directly related to keeping open the main building. Things looked bleak when state librarians were reported discussing the "dilemma" of which segment of the community should be served (*LJ/SLJ Hotline*, December 13, 1976,

vol. V, no. 41, p. 2). The pendulum swings toward a slightly more positive view of state library activities when articles report one state's consistent development of services to reach the poor (Callaham, Betty E. "South Carolina Libraries: Reaching Out." *Catholic Library World*, vol. 47, no. 8, March 1976, p. 322–325).

The Good News. Library service to the poor looked encouraging when a community such as Tulsa voted for allocating an increase in revenue from property taxes to the public library or when Wake County provided matching funds after the public library system received Title XX money to provide Information & Referral services (*LS/SLJ Hotline*, December 29, 1976, vol. V, no. 42). Innovative Tulsa Public Library launched a basic literacy program in addition to a system-wide information and referral service. (Tulsa is also experimenting with the Lockheed Information System for those who can afford to pay.) The Peninsula Library System of San Mateo County, California, developed a computerized community information file on services offered by the county government (Blake, F.M., and Irby, J. "The Selling of the Public Library." *Drexel Library Quarterly*, January–April 1976, vol. 12, nos. 1 & 2, p. 149–158).

I & R is only one service method for reaching the poor, although it is one of the most crucial. Neal H. Hurwitz of the Institute for Urban and Minority Education, claims ". . . Researchers have found that the poor live in a communications environment devoid of meaningful information—or the presence of misinformation . . . the condition of powerlessness [paralyzes] individual and group initiative, and [blocks] self interested organization within disfranchised groups. . . ." ("Communications Networks and the Urban Poor," prepared for the ERIC Clearinghouse on Urban Education, Teachers College, Columbia University. *Equal Opportunity Review*, May 1975, p. 2.)

Responsibility to the Poor. As government (a primary generator of information) becomes more complex, the needs of the poor to obtain, interpret, and use information significant to their lives becomes essential. The poor have to rely on free, easily accessible information. If the public library does not provide easily accessible information then it is revamping its role and giving only lip service to the democratic functioning of public libraries. New York State Senator Major Owens (who is also a librarian) explains: "The failure of libraries to serve the poor is symptomatic of the failure to fill the information gap in general. . . ." ("Relevant Library Services for the Poor Mean Better Library Service for All." *Catholic Library World*, vol. 47, no 8, March 1976, p. 320.)

Another significant service that libraries can provide is programming for the development of basic literacy skills by disadvantaged, out-of-school adults—16 years old and up. It is encouraging to know that over 40 state, regional, and local library agencies or systems have made inquiries to the Literacy Volunteers of America (Syracuse, New York) regarding information and training in order to establish library literacy programs using volunteer tutors. LVA is already involved with 10 East Coast public libraries (including Brooklyn Public Library) in similar programs. The Los Angeles County Public Library system is launching a bilingual reading project called LIBRE. The American Library Association's book entitled "Literacy and the Nation's Libraries" will be available by June 1977. This book was written as a result of an ALA project on literacy which was funded by the Office of Education in 1975.

Sarah Rebecca Reed, Dean of the School of Library Science at Emporia Kansas State Teachers College, invited the director of OLSD to conduct three one-day workshops on the "Role of Libraries in Literacy and Lifetime Learning" in Kansas during December. The workshops were part of Helen Strader's course

The Crozer Branch Library, Chester, Pennsylvania, developed a children's summer program in 1976 which brought inner city youngsters to the library's West End branch for puppet shows (left) and an African music and dance session.

Education, Library

on Library Service to the Disadvantaged.

The active recognition that other professional organizations are giving to librarians constitutes encouragement. Recognition of libraries comes in the form of library participation or representation on the national programs of a variety of organizations and in the interpretation funding regulations for accepting proposals for demonstration projects. The Alliance for Information and Referral Services (AIRS); the National Community Education Association (NCEA); and the National Association for Public and Continuing Adult Education (NAPCAE) during 1976 invited librarians to speak at their associations' annual conference programs. Miles Martin, Toledo, Ohio, conducted a workshop on training for offering information and referral services at the AIRS conference. Lois D. Fleming, Florida State Library, moderated a panel discussion on the topic "The Public Library: Your Community Education Center." The panel was a mixture of educators and librarians. The librarians were: Phyllis Gray, Miami Beach; Shirley Aaron, Tallahassee; John Axam, Philadelphia; Donald Foos, Baton Rouge; and Edward Sintz, Miami-Dade. At NAPCAE's conference, Brooklyn Public Library staff members discussed their work in BPL's independent learner program.

Federal regulations for awarding funds to demonstration programs/projects under Community Education and Consumers Education are being interpreted to include proposals from public libraries. Although the amount of funds to flow to libraries from these sources may be limited it is a welcomed trend.

The Office for Library Services to the Disadvantaged is sponsoring a publication entitled *American Indian Libraries Newsletter*. The newsletter is edited by Cheryl Metoyer (Cherokee), a PhD graduate of the library school at Indiana University. Additional current publications include *The Directory of Ethnic Librarians* and the *Directory of Ethnic Publishers and Resource Organizations*. Both directories were compiled by Beth Shapiro.

OLSD has cooperated with an ad hoc committee of the Asian-American Librarians Caucus in conducting a limited survey on the availability of public library services for Asian Americans in areas where the U.S. Census figures have indicated significant Asian American populations. Results of the survey will be presented by Tze-Chung Li, Rosary College, at the 1977 ALA annual conference in Detroit. OLSD has a new subcommittee, currently chaired by Susan Schmidt (Ohio) on library service to rural and Appalachian People.

Helen Modra of Victoria, Australia, visited several locations in the United States where she spoke to librarians and educators about public library literacy programs. Modra is in charge of library service to the disadvantaged in Victoria.

JEAN E. COLEMAN

The 1976 "Backyard Library" program of the Montgomery County-Norristown Public Library's Outreach Program in cooperation with the Abington Free Library, Crestmont, Pennsylvania, enabled neighborhood children to browse and borrow every week in an outdoor setting close to home.

Document Preservation

See *Preservation of Library Materials*

Education, Library

During 1976 the first round of accreditation visits under the 1972 Standards for Accreditation were completed by the ALA Committee on Accreditation. The appropriate organizational structure for library education within the professional associations proved to be an item of continued debate with no resolution agreed upon. The Continuing Library Education Network and Exchange (CLENE), having been officially incorporated, elected officers and succeeded in obtaining federal support for two of its projects. The labor market for new graduates of library education programs continued tight; however, new programs in library education continued to appear.

Accreditation. Graduate library school programs holding accreditation under the 1951 ALA Standards for Accreditation to maintain accreditation had to be reaccredited under the 1972 Standards by June 30, 1976. The following 32 schools succeeded in meeting that deadline in 1976: Brigham Young, British Columbia, Buffalo, California (Berkeley), Case Western, Columbia, Emporia, Dalhousie, Florida State, Indiana, Kent, Kentucky, Long Island, Maryland, Missouri, Montreal, North Carolina, North Texas, Oregon, Peabody, Pittsburgh, Pratt, Queens, Simmons, Southern California, Southern Connecticut, Syracuse, Texas, Texas Woman's, Washington, Wayne State, and Western Ontario. Clarion State, St. John's, and Wisconsin-Milwaukee received their initial accreditation during the year. The total number of programs accredited under the new standards was brought to 64, including six in Canada. Only one school, Alabama A & M, received accreditation as a single specialization program in school library media, the new accreditation status permitted under the 1972 Standards.

With the completion of the first cycle of accreditation visits, the ALA Committee on Accreditation planned to conduct an evaluation of the accreditation process and revise its *Manual of Procedures for Evaluation Visits Under Standards for Accreditation, 1972*. Suggestions and comments are being sought from schools accredited under the 1972 Standards, from individuals who chaired site visits, and from other concerned groups. The evaluation was not expected to be completed until September 1977.

The Executive Board of the Association of American Library Schools, also concerned about accreditation, appointed a task force to study the process, including attention to the accreditation of advanced degree programs as well as the first professional degree and to the certification needs and requirements for subject specialists within librarianship. (*See also* Accreditation.)

Advanced Programs. Of the 64 schools now offering ALA accredited programs, 22 also offer doctoral programs, and 26 a formal sixth-year program in librarianship. Though no new doctoral programs were introduced in 1976, new sixth-year programs were offered at Queens and Rosary, indicating a continued interest in the development of this intermediary program between the master's and doctoral study which serves to meet the continuing education and professional needs of the library practitioner.

Undergraduate Programs. The 1976 *Directory of Institutions Offering or Planning Programs for the Training of Library Technical Assistants,* published by the Council on Library Technical Assistants, lists 157 schools in the United States and Canada concerned with instructional programs for LTA's. This is an increase of 23 schools over those listed in the previous edition of the directory, indicating the continued interest in the development of educational programs for LTA's. However, the diminishing job market for school media librarians and the trend toward increasing certification requirements were affecting the enrollment in some undergraduate programs which provide minimum certification, and some colleges were abandoning these programs. (*See also* Council on Library Technical Assistants.)

OTHER CONCERNS

Organization Activities. Though the officers of the ALA Library Education Division have tried to alert the profession to the fiscal crisis created by the failure of both practitioners and educators to join the Division in sufficient number to support an active program, there has been limited enlistment of new members as a result of these efforts. In a questionnaire distributed through *American Libraries,* the *LED Newsletter,* and at the July membership meeting, twice as many non-members of the Division responded than Division members. The majority of the respondents favored Round Table status within ALA if LED had to discontinue as a Division and agreed that Division status should be abandoned if LED were unable to support itself through membership dues. Some members, however, strongly maintained that there should be no change and that ALA should continue to subsidize the Division if necessary. A matter of even greater concern to those required to project the future of library education within ALA was the seeming apathy to the problem among Association members in general as indicated by the small return received on the questionnaire.

The officers of the Division consider it essential that ALA have a means "to speak out at the national and international levels on matters related to the preparation of library personnel, and in a voice that reflects the needs, interests, and concerns of all kinds of librarians and all levels of library staff." To meet this need they have prepared a proposal for presentation to the ALA Council recommending the establishment of a Council Standing Committee on Library Education, the employment of a Library Education Officer to provide staff liaison and support to the Standing Committee, the encouragement of Association Divisions and other units to appoint committees on library education, and the creation of a Library Education Assembly composed of representatives from each of these committees on library education to serve as a liaison for membership with the Standing Committee.

Although the Association of American Library Schools (AALS) and the Library Education Division maintained communication through their official representatives, there was little effort to treat the future of LED as a common problem. The AALS Board approved the establishment of a Task Force on Organizational Alignment in 1975, but it was still to be established and given its charge by the end of 1976. AALS did give attention to fiscal matters during the year, increasing institutional and associate institutional members annual dues $25 and agreeing to present a recommendation for an increase in personal membership dues at the January 1977 business meeting.

The AALS Council of Deans and Directors approved more formal structure through which to function. The Council met with a group of personnel directors of large research libraries during the ALA Chicago conference to discuss areas of mutual concern. For the first time regional meetings were held by the Council in conjunction with the Southeastern Library Association meeting and the joint meeting of the Southwestern and Mountain Plains Library Associations.

The library science librarians, having been organized as a Discussion Group within the Library Education Division for some time, became more visible through their publication of the *Directory of Library Science Libraries* in 1975 and the beginning of a *Newsletter* in 1976.

Continuing Education. Emphasis on continuing education remains a focal point in librarianship. Staff development programs by individual libraries and state agencies; institutes and workshops by educational agencies, private enterprise, and professional associations; and the development of correspondence courses tailored for continuing education were all evident during the year.

The Continuing Library Education Network and Exchange increased its credibility as a focal point for continuing education efforts for the profession. CLENE elected officers and Ruth Patrick became its first elected president.

Education, Library

Education, Library

CLENE was awarded two grants from the U.S. Office of Education; one grant supports the development of a model for a continuing education recognition system for librarianship with Dorothy Deininger, Rutgers, serving as the principal investigator for the project. To obtain information from the profession for this project, CLENE members are being asked to organize local meetings of practitioners to discuss the need for the development of a recognition system for continuing education in librarianship and to suggest criteria for effectively evaluating continuing education programs and for determining a viable recognition or reward system. The second grant is in support of an institute for state library personnel, including the development of an evaluation instrument for continuing education programs which it is hoped can be adapted for use in other situations.

CLENE published *Continuing Education Courses and Programs for Library, Information, and Media Personnel* at the first of the year, and plans to up-date the publication annually. It also published the *Proceedings* of its two Assemblies, a membership directory, and two papers: *Developing CE Learning Materials* and *A Guide to Planning and Teaching CE Courses*. (See further Continuing Professional Education.)

Grants and Federal Support. The Department of Health, Education and Welfare awarded approximately $1,000,000 dollars under Title II-B of the Higher Education Act for 19 projects related to library research, demonstration projects, and design of information service for certain target groups. Eleven of the grants were awarded to library schools and institutions of higher education and eight to nonacademic agencies.

During the year the Wyoming State Library sponsored a ten-week HEA Title II-B Institute for the Education of Prospective State Library Agency Professional Personnel. A detailed curriculum related to preparation of state library agency personnel was developed by Jane Robbins and Anne Powell through the means of the institute for the use of library schools nationwide. This document may encourage library schools to give greater attention in the

---

Library Education and Placement Problems

When asked about future job prospects in librarianship, many librarians and library educators are at a loss to answer. The common reply may be simply, "It depends. . . ." Most prospective students come, however, with a set of expectations about the job market, and the answer which seems wishy washy is likely to be brushed aside.

The "it depends" response can hardly be definitive for a young person with a liberal arts background looking for a profession that will be both humanizing and profitable, but the responsibility of librarians and library educators to try to explain the parameters is unavoidable. What then are the desirable characteristics for today's library/information job market?

Talent. Included in this category are the intellectual and learning facilities of the recruit. New librarians who are not bright and alert, who are not able to generate interest in the activities of a prospective employing institution, or who are slow on the uptake are going to have a harder time writing good resumes, devising successful strategies for locating job opportunities, and impressing an employer during an interview. Thus if the recruits are coming to librarianship because they were not talented enough to be successful in another field, then it is important that they understand their own abilities well and recognize whether they are appropriate to librarianship. People who "hated math," dislike the idea of machines, do not want to have to work with complex systems, and have trouble expressing themselves orally or in writing are very likely to have difficulty in finding a suitable job in the library field today.

Flexibility. This facet involves the ability to make career adjustments based on the prospective job market at the time of graduation. There is no way that the library field can forecast precisely its dimensions for the years ahead or even for just one year. Those who prepare to be school media specialists may discover that the available jobs are in special libraries associated with business and industry instead of a school system. They may also find that the positions are in some other part of the country rather than close at hand. In order to take advantage of real opportunities (as opposed to fantasized ones), a new librarian must have the capacity to adjust mentally and emotionally. Further, the person must be ready to learn new skills and absorb new knowledge even during the summer or the term following graduation. "Continuing education" may start before the diploma comes, especially if media specialists are needed instead of academic reference staff this year.

Personability. Few librarians are expected to be "personality kids," but an ability to project a positive, friendly self is necessary to compete successfully in a sluggish job market. People usually know whether they are sufficiently assertive, in a pleasing way, to make colleagues notice them and want to have them around. If a student's personality is brittle, then the other characteristics need to be overarchingly superior to compensate. Even then, interview experiences may never be very satisfying.

Knowledge. In this category the responsibility falls equally upon the library school and the student. A student who fails to absorb what is provided through the educational program, or

future to the training needs of librarians serving at the state level.

Wilson Fund. The H. W. Wilson Foundation announced in November that it would continue the H. W. Wilson Scholarships for a sixth program covering the years 1977–1981, providing during the five-year period a $3,000 scholarship grant to each of the 64 American and Canadian ALA accredited library schools.

Statistics. The continuing tight labor market for librarians and the rising cost of graduate study seemed to be having an impact on the number of graduates of fifth year programs. In 1975, for the first time in many years, there was a reduction in the number of master's degrees awarded by the accredited schools over previous years. The 1976 Learmont and Darling report covering the year 1975 indicated 6,010 master's degrees were awarded by the 51 reporting schools, a drop of 360 or approximately 5 percent over the previous year. Of those graduates, 58 percent were identified as employed, which was the percentage reported for the prior year; the employment status of 30 percent of the graduates was unknown to the reporting schools and 11 percent of those employed were in nonprofessional positions. Though the number of graduates seemed to exceed the market need for librarians, the reported median salary of $10,000 for new graduates was $362 over the 1974 median.

Faculties and Salaries. The average number of full-time faculty for the 1975–76 school year was 11.24 for the 62 ALA accredited schools included in the Bidlack study of faculty salaries. Of the total 697 full-time faculty members employed in the reporting schools, 408 or 58 percent were men, and 289 or 41.5 percent were women. Average salaries for the academic year ranged from $23,632 for professors to $13,027 for instructors.

APPOINTMENTS, MILESTONES, HONORS

Appointments. New deans or directors appointed during the year included Richard Logsdon at Queens, Vivian Sessions at McGill, Dorothy Haith at Alabama A & M, Mohammed M. Aman at Long Island, William Summers at South Carolina, Fred Pfister at South Florida, and Maurice Marchant at Brigham Young.

---

whose library school experiences were inadequate, can be very quickly outclassed in a competitive situation. Although talent, personality, and flexibility will help to create the opportunity to interview for a position, a recognizable lack of knowledge can bring a quick end to the discussion. Readiness to acquire new knowledge is also often expected by employers.

Dedication. This old fashioned virtue is still sometimes the deciding factor in the selection of a new employee for library or information service. A willingness to work hard and devote extra energies to the job is a characteristic that somehow seems to differentiate the ordinary candidate from the superior one. It is often hard to spot in advance of employment, however, and the student may wish to demonstrate this quality in connection with library school courses so that it will receive comment in recommendations provided by the faculty.

As many librarians and educators know, librarianship does not always attract recruits who are fully talented, flexible, personable, knowledgeable, and dedicated. There is, then, a further question as to whether those who can be expected to be seriously deficient in one of these qualities should be encouraged—or even permitted—to attend library school. Because Americans pride themselves on offering educational opportunities for those with the intellectual capabilities appropriate to the field of study, not simply to those for whom a job can be "guaranteed," it would appear that students should be admitted to library schools when (1) they meet the admission standards specified by the institution, (2) there is adequate room for them in the program, and (3) they have received as accurate information as possible about the obligations which the institution is willing to assume for placement. Because library education has something of value to offer as a "discipline" for some students who are not expecting to seek a position in the field, it is probably not desirable to restrict library school enrollments simply on the basis of expected job market characteristics. Librarians and library educators must, however, work especially hard to make sure that new students do not seek admission on the false assumption that the library job situation is wide open when it is not. The obligation to make realistic information available to prospective recruits is indisputable; thus copies of articles on trends in librarianship, analyses of employment prospects, and statements about placement services available to graduates should be put—or even forced—into the hands of prospective and newly enrolled library students.

The irony of the library job situation is that there is no shortage of work to be done in library and information services, but there are, from time to time, shortages of funds with which to support the services. If and when the economy reopens, a new lack of qualified librarians may emerge, similar to the one which faced the post-World War II society. It would be indeed tragic if good prospects were turned away from library education simply because today's librarians and library educators had not been able to anticipate economic changes. — DORALYN J. HICKEY

Vacancies existed in the dean or director position at Kentucky, Maryland, St. John's, and Texas Woman's.

Retirements. Library educators who retired during the year included Periam Danton at Berkeley, Jerrold Orne at North Carolina, Eleanor Ahlers at Washington, Sara Srygley at Florida State, and Morris Gelfand at Queens.

Deaths. Death claimed three outstanding library educators: Carlyle Frarey, Columbia; John Phillip Immroth, Pittsburgh; and Carl T. Cox, Tennessee. (See Obituaries.)

Honors. Library educators continued to be honored by the profession. Four of the eight individuals receiving the Centennial Conference special award of Honorary Memberships in ALA were associated with library education: Robert B. Downs, Illinois; Mary V. Gaver, Rutgers; Virginia L. Jones, Atlanta; and Jesse Shera, Case Western. Lester Asheim, North Carolina, received the J.W. Lippincott Award for distinguished service in librarianship. Carolyn Whitenack, Purdue, received the Beta Phi Mu Award for contributions to education for librarianship, and Elizabeth Stone, Catholic, the Beta Phi Mu Certificate of Distinction for the development of the Continuing Library Education Network and Exchange. (See Biographies.)

Summary. The year seemed much like any other for library education. Practitioners continued their traditional use of library education as the profession's scapegoat, pointing out the failure of the library schools to prepare students adequately in media, automation, cataloging, and management, its incapability of meeting the full spectrum of continuing education needs felt by the practitioner, and its resistance to providing more library education in every community in the country. Library educators, however, moved ahead with healthy egos. They sensed that never before had students been recruited with higher motivation for library service or with a greater capability for initiating and coping with change. Woman's liberation and the tight labor market seemed to be joining forces to create a new seriousness on the part of those entering the profession and a career consciousness that had been less evident when jobs were plentiful and library schools had served as an entree for "acceptable employment" prior to marriage and children.   A. VENABLE LAWSON

REFERENCES

Russell E. Bidlack, "Faculty Salaries of 62 Library Schools, 1975–76," *Journal of Education for Librarianship* 16:258–70 (Spring 1976).

Carol L. Learmont and Richard L. Darling, "Placements and Salaries 1975," *Library Journal* 101: 1487–93 (July 1976).

Employment Practices:

See *Personnel and Employment.*

Equipment

See *Furniture and Equipment.*

Ethics

The ALA special Code of Ethics Committee worked long (approximately four years) and openly (seeking advice of Division Presidents, special groups within the ALA organization, and staff members, as well as holding two open hearings during the New York Conference in 1974). Critics have held that there never was a thorough airing of issues important to various interest groups within the ALA community, however, and that the 1975 approved Statement on Professional Ethics does not reflect the profession's contemporary concerns and issues. This article summarizes criticisms in 1975 and 1976 and suggests points for consideration toward a new statement.

Criticisms. Perhaps the most disturbing aspect after the approval of the Statement by the ALA Council in January 1975 was the lack of reaction among membership. Is it a general symptom of malaise that the membership was not concerned that the profession's concerns and philosophy were not reflected in the new statement? Or, rather, could it be that the lack of substance in the statement could elicit no reaction? The general blandness and the lack of specifics reflected in the statement could have caused this lack of response.

The decision of the Committee to have as a goal the "briefest, possible statement" that would "meet with general acceptance among librarians whatever their affiliation" was perhaps the first mistake. Simplicity can easily become nothingness; the complexity and changing quality of the library/information profession cannot be reflected simply or without a discussion and review of the goals of the profession, its values, and important issues for the 1970's and beyond, critics pointed out.

The American Library Association with its 13 Divisions, 10 Round Tables, and 13 affiliated organizations is a pluralistic organization with great diversity of concerns among its membership. It was argued that all of these concerns must be reflected in a code of ethics that members will respect and identify with.

An important aspect of professionalization is the area of a professional culture which includes a professional organization and professional standards or norms that are usually expressed in a code of ethics. These should establish the rules for professionals to follow in their relationships with their clients and among themselves. As William J. Goode said in 1961, in reaction to the 1938 ALA Code of Ethics:

> A code reflects the particular genius of the profession that writes it. How lacking in this code is any sense of drama, of moral urgency! How absent is a sturdy awareness that the profession

has a task, a destiny, a set of issues about which it is concerned. [*Library Quarterly* 31 (October 1961), pp. 306–20].

This criticism is applicable again in reaction to the 1975 statement. In neither the introduction nor the statement itself is there an expression of the *importance* of the work of those in the field to society, nor of a concept considered by many to be essential to the profession—service.

The struggle which the Committee has had, and also a major problem of the profession, could be due to a lack of a clear, philosophical base including values, beliefs, and goals of the profession. These important aspects need to be discussed again, by each Division and Round Table individually and then as representatives to a hearing, before a new code is accepted.

Issues for a New Statement. During a search of library literature covering the period from 1960 through 1976, several important statements concerning the ethics issue were included in articles by Goode (1961), Anderson (1966), Bogie (1967), Rothstein (1968), Bundy and Wasserman (1968), Moon (1968 editorial), Fetros (1971), and Vavrek (1972). Some of the important issues raised during that time period are valid for an ethics statement today and will be summarized briefly.

Though a code of ethics should be idealistic and broad in framework, it should focus on individual members of the profession rather than on the institutional setting. It should not set up a series of constraints but rather allow for individual freedom and autonomy of the professional. For the library code to have validity, incorporation of a definition of a professional is essential, establishing its identity within the profession and within society at large. The broad goals of the profession in relationship to its unique service contribution to society need to be enunciated.

Within the statement itself, three major relationships need to be clarified:

(1) Relationship with clients, including the right of privacy and confidentiality of the client; the right of the client for accurate information; and the right of equal access of all clients.
(2) Relationship with the employing institution, including the relationship between the governing board, the chief librarian and the professional staff (especially in decision making), and the rights of employees (the issue of the right to organize, strike, etc.).
(3) Relationship with the profession, including responsibility to the professional group (for example, the issue of participation during work time); those with colleagues; and participation in recruitment of the best candidates to the field.

The following items also should be considered for inclusion: the educational process, including continuing education—both formal and informal; and possible conflicts of interest such as the consulting roles, the right to strike, and the intellectual freedom principle vs. self-censorship. The current most important documents in the field should be referred to, including (but not restricted to) the ALA Bill of Rights and the Freedom to Read Statement, and at least reference should be made to the essential documents developed by the various Divisions, for example, RASD's "A Commitment to Information Services: Developmental Guidelines" and AASL's guidelines for school media centers. The Committee felt that "much of what is generally dealt with in a code was already to be found in statements adopted by Council through the years," but they should not have ignored these basic documents, it was argued.

The question of enforcement of a code of ethics is an important one, and should also be addressed. The Council Committee on Professional Ethics, a standing committee, has an important task ahead—to stimulate each Division and Round Table of ALA in expressing their needs, concerns, and beliefs, which should then be reflected in a revised code of ethics with standards of professional practice delineated. —SHIRLEY FITZGIBBONS

Statement on Professional Ethics
Approved by ALA Council, January 1975

INTRODUCTION

The American Library Association has a special concern for the free flow of information and ideas. Its views have been set forth in such policy statements as the Library Bill of Rights and the Freedom to Read Statement where it has said clearly that in addition to the generally accepted legal and ethical principles and the respect for intellectual freedom which should guide the action of every citizen, membership in the library profession carries with it special obligations and responsibilities.

Every citizen has the right as an individual to take part in public debate or to engage in social and political activity. The only restrictions on these activities are those imposed by specific and well-publicized laws and regulations which are generally applicable. However, since personal views and activities may be interpreted as representative of the institution in which a librarian is employed, proper precaution should be taken to distinguish between private actions and those one is authorized to take in the name of an institution.

The statement which follows sets forth certain ethical norms which, while not exclusive to, are basic to librarianship. *It will be augmented by explanatory interpretations and additional statements as they may be needed.*

STATEMENT

A librarian

- has a special responsibility to maintain the principles of the Library Bill of Rights.

- should learn and faithfully execute the policies of the institution of which one is a part and should endeavor to change those which conflict with the spirit of the Library Bill of Rights.

- must protect the essential confidential relationship which exists between a library user and the library.

- must avoid any possibility of personal financial gain at the expense of the employing institution.

- has an obligation to insure equality of opportunity and fair judgment of competence in actions dealing with staff appointments, retentions, and promotions.

- has an obligation when making appraisals of the qualifications of any individual to report the facts clearly, accurately, and without prejudice, according to generally accepted guidelines concerning the disclosing of personal information.

Ethnic Groups, Library Service to

The subject of ethnic-group use of library resources was a comparatively new concern of organized librarianship in the mid-1970's. Librarians were becoming aware of the need for specialized knowledge and techniques for serving patrons who had not previously expressed a desire for specifically ethnic-oriented materials. Americans of diverse origins also became more vocal in their requests for library services that would provide information regarding all areas of their ethnic heritage.

ASIAN AMERICANS

The Asian American Librarian Caucus (AALC) entered its second year in 1976. It had been established at the ALA Conference in San Francisco in 1975. The purpose of this organizations is to: (1) provide a forum of discussion of problems and concerns of Asian American librarians; (2) provide a forum for the exchange of ideas by Asian American librarians and other librarians; (3) support and encourage a library service to the Asian American communities; (4) recruit Asian Americans into the library/information science professions; and (5) seek funding for scholarships in library/information science schools for Asian Americans.

Janet Suzuki was the first Chairperson, and under her leadership several projects were accomplished or in progress.

Affirmative Action Program. The Affirmative Action Program Conference was held in Chicago at the 1976 ALA meetings with attendance of more than 100 Asian librarians. The opening speaker was Elmer W. McLain, Regional Director, Chicago Region, Equal Employment Opportunity Commission. Members of the panel were Margaret Yee, Asian Affairs Office, HEW, Chicago Region; Chandra Vaidyanath, Librarian, Milwaukee Public Library; Affirmative Action Committee; and Errol Lam, Librarian, Bowling Green State University. McLain spoke on affirmative action and the laws related to its enforcement. Chandra Vaidyanath discussed the problems of librarian prejudice against Asians promotion and application for employment. Lam spoke on the need for constant work toward Asian American visibility.

Survey of Library Service to Asians. At the Midwinter AALC meetings in January, the Board approved and accepted a proposal by T. C. Li of Rosary College calling for a survey on librarian service to Asians. The survey will attempt to discover whether such services are available in libraries and how needed they are. By year's end the first part of the library questionnaire had been sent to 50 libraries with large concentrations of Asian Americans. The questionnaire was developed by the eight-member ad hoc committee organized since Midwinter in conjunction with ALA's office under member Jean Coleman. The second part of the survey will question Asian Americans in the Chicago area. Final recommendations were to be made at the ALA Conference in Detroit.

Bibliography. Members of the Bibliography Committee, headed by Elsie Wong, produced a bibliography scheduled to be published by ALA in 1977.

Members. The Caucus at the end of 1976 had 120 members. Recruiting new members will be of top priority in 1977. A major problem faced by AALC in 1975 was communication, and during 1976 a revised AALC bylaws major amendment supported the establishment of regional chapters of AALC. It was hoped they would help remedy problems of communication for a national organization covering a large geographical area.

Leo C. Ho, Chairperson during 1976, appointed five regional coordinators. They were Stella Chang, Utah; John Clen, Alabama; Raymond Lum, Maryland; Philip Wei, Minnesota; and Irene Yeh, California.

The Caucus publishes four newsletters annually.

Officers (1976–77) are Leo C. Ho, Chairperson; Vivian Kobayashi, Vice-Chairperson/Chairperson-elect; Miles Hamada, Secretary; and Tamiye Trejo, Treasurer. Standing committee Chairpersons are Affirmative Action, Errol Lam; Liason, Irene Yeh; Recruitment and Scholarship, Don Robertson; Membership, Roy Chang; Publicity, David Tsuneishi; and Program, Vivian Kobayashi. LEO C. HO

BLACKS

1976 was a good year—indeed a very good year—for Blacks and libraries. Alex Haley's 12-year research project which took him to Africa and to Europe, to libraries and to archives, and led to his notable work, *Roots* (published by Doubleday in 1976), empha-

Houston's Japanese-American Society sponsored a "Living Arts of Japan" exhibit featuring Kabuki dancing, Origami, flower arranging, and tea ceremonies in November 1976 at the Houston Central Library.

sizes the importance of recording the past. It is also toward this end that *The ALA Yearbook* is directed.

The nation's Bicentennial celebration and ALA's Centennial activities have special meaning for Blacks and libraries. These celebrations tell us that the roots of Black people, too, can be traced through the history of the nation and through the history of ALA. For Blacks and libraries, the year was filled with recognition and honor, assessment of progress and identification with accomplishments, notable events, and outstanding leadership, and, indeed, a new chapter in the history of ALA and in the history of Black people—one for which the nation can be proud.

ALA celebrations for the year cast spotlights on many important events of its history, and Blacks and librarians rejoiced that finally the library profession had its first Black President, Clara Stanton Jones. The grace, poise, charm, wisdom, scholarship, and leadership which she brought to office were equal to the honor which the profession bestowed upon her through her election.

The awards, honors, and prizes Black librarians received in 1976 attracted wide attention. As ALA awarded honorary memberships to eight persons and gave Special Centennial Citations to 10 others in recognition of outstanding contributions to the library profession, two notable Black librarians were among those counted. Virginia Lacy Jones, Professor and Dean, School of Library Service, Atlanta University, received Honorary Membership, while Wallace Van Jackson, notable in the development of Black academic libraries in the United States and an accomplished leader in providing library service in Africa, received a Special Centennial Citation. The work of these two leaders had long been recognized among Blacks in the profession.

The Joneses—Clara Stanton and Virginia Lacy—are unrelated, yet they are intimately related professionally to the ideals of ALA, Blacks, and libraries. The honors which they received increased, as ALA President Jones addressed the ALA Black Caucus, praised it for its dedication and empathy in librarianship, and graciously accepted the Trailblazer Award of the Caucus for her significant achievement in the field. The Caucus continued to make itself heard, as it told the profession, "Yes, ALA, there is a Virginia," and as it acknowledged Jones as "mentor" of some 1,366 graduates of the Atlanta University School of Library Service during her 37 years there.

Black writers, including writer-librarians, were counted among the prizewinners of the year. Sharon Bell Mathis, elementary school librarian from Washington, D.C., and author of *The Hundred Penny Box* (Viking), walked off with one of the two Newbery Honor Book citations for her work. Leo Dillon (and wife Diane)

The Northeast Texas Library System borrowed "The Negro Texan" exhibit created by the Institute of Texan Cultures for a full year and arranged for its display in 11 systems libraries throughout 1976.

not only illustrated the Newbery Honor Book by Mathis but also won the Caldecott Medal for the nation's outstanding children's picture book of 1975, *Why Mosquitoes Buzz in People's Ears: A West African Tale* (retold by Verna Aardema and published by Dial).

Firsts. Black librarians managed a number of firsts during the year. Andre Carl Whisenton, graduate of Atlanta University School of Library Service, became the first Black to head a departmental library of the federal government when he accepted directorship of the U.S. Department of Labor Library. Ella G. Yates, also an Atlanta graduate, became the first Black to head the Atlanta Public Library.

ALA's Centennial celebration found expression in a variety of ways including the recognition given to librarians in the June issue of *American Libraries*. Devoted to the theme "Who We Are," the issue portrays the librarian in diverse roles and concludes with a section on "Who We Will Be," in which four library school students look into their future. Though not exclusive to Black themes, the issue clearly illustrates the variety of positions now available to Black librarians. Among the portraits shown are James F. Williams II, medical librarian, Willye Dennis, Chief of Children's Services at Duval County Library System, Jacksonville, Florida, and Jennifer L. Taylor, student in the School of Information and Library Studies, State University of New York at Buffalo.

ALA's Centennial celebration acknowledged further the roots of Blacks and libraries as John Wilkins' article entitled "Blue's Colored Branch" portrayed the imprint of Thomas Fountain Blue of the Louisville Public Library on the cultural landscape of American libraries and on the training of Black librarians. *American Libraries* further highlighted Blacks and libraries over the last century as it cap-

Ethnic Groups, Library Service to

"The Rise of Chicago Black Writing" workshop series conducted by George Kent of the University of Chicago faculty (standing at right) at the Woodson Regional Library was so successful it was extended for an additional two months in 1976.

suled the plight of Blacks against discrimination and underscored the work of early giants Edward Christopher Williams, Librarian at Western Reserve from 1894 through 1909, Eliza Atkins Gleason, first Black holder of a doctorate in library science whose 1941 dissertation on "The Southern Negro and the Public Library" became a landmark in library history, and, more recently, Virginia Lacy Jones and Mollie Houston Lee, leader in library service and in collecting Black literature in North Carolina.

Deans of three library schools were instrumental in making workshops of varied nature available to the library profession, each making a noticeable imprint on scholarship, culture, and the Black experience in 1976. During the Annual Conference, Herman L. Totten, Dean, School of Librarianship, University of Oregon, directed a conference on "Bibliographical Control of Afro-American Literature" supported under Title II-B, Higher Education Act. The state-of-the-art conference brought together representative librarians from across the nation to react to position papers on various themes relating to the topic which seasoned scholars had prepared in advance. Papers of the conference will significantly add to the body of Black literature.

In October, Annette Phinazee, Dean, School of Library Science, North Carolina Central University, directed a colloquium on "The Southeastern Black Librarian" in celebration of the school's 37th anniversary. The conference brought together librarians from the Southeast and elsewhere who aimed to honor and to recognize the contributions of Blacks to librarianship. In addition to providing several papers on Black librarians, lectures on similar themes, and group discussions, the University awarded an honorary degree to President Jones of the ALA. The establishment of a Beta Phi Mu chapter at the time of the conference helped to provide a capstone for the important contributions of the school and of Southeastern Black librarians. Virginia Lacy Jones was responsible for the Lawrence Livermore On-Line Information Retrieval Workshop, jointly sponsored by Lawrence Livermore Laboratory and Atlanta University School of Library Service in September. The workshop aimed to promote on-line information retrieval in Black libraries and provided the base for further development in this area.

One wonders if the contributions of Blacks to librarianship in 1976 can be condensed. Consider, for example, the ALA office holders who were in service when the gong was sounded to ring in 1976. At that time, Spencer Shaw headed the Children's Services Division and Louise Giles was at the helm of the Association of College and Research Libraries. Then there were the grant recipients. North Carolina Agricultural and Technical State University received the only Council on Library Resources Library Enhancement Program award given to a Black library, and Stanton Biddle, Associate Director for Research and Planning, Howard University, became an intern in CLR's Academic Library Management Program. Four additional librarians, Claude Greene, Reta J. Lacy, Alberta J. Mayberry and Brenda D. Sloan, became participants in the nine-month ACRL internship program for administrators of predominantly Black academic libraries.

Thus, the roots of Blacks and libraries in 1976 were firmly planted. This brief history serves as a source for the recent past and indicates stepping stones for moving into another good year for ALA, Blacks, and libraries.

JESSIE CARNEY SMITH

ITALIAN-AMERICANS

There were 8,800,000 persons living in the United States in March 1972 who claimed that they were of Italian origin, by U.S. Bureau of Census figures. These persons comprised 4 percent of the total population of the United States. This figure doubled the count of first generation Italian-Americans in the 1970 census but could by definition include the total number of generations of Italian-Americans in the country.

Table 1. Summary Characteristics of Persons of Italian Origin

	Total	Male	Female
Number (in thousands)	8,764	4,432	4,333
Percent under 14 years old	24.2	24.3	24.0

Source: U.S. Bureau of the Census, *Current Population Reports*, "Population Characteristics," Part 20, Number 249 (1973).

Table 2. Summary Characteristics of Persons of Italian Origin

	Total	Male	Female
Percent High School Graduation			
25 to 34 years old	80.4	79.9	81.2
35 years old and over	44.0	47.6	40.5
Employed (in thousands)	3,674	2,420	1,254
Professional	12.3	12.7	11.6
Managerial	11.5	14.5	5.7

Source: *Ibid.*, U.S. Bureau of the Census (1973).

Table 3. Italian-American Employment Patterns (Percent)

	Male	Female
Professional	13	12
Managerial	14	6
Clerical and Sales	15	46
Craftsmen	22	1
Operatives	16	18
Laborers	9	1
Service Workers	10	15
Private Household Workers	0	2

Source: *Ibid.*, U.S. Bureau of the Census, 1973.

Underrepresentation. Italian-Americans constitute the largest minority in the United States today. Yet, as well as can be ascertained, though highly educated when compared with those of other ethnic backgrounds, they are underrepresented in the real politics of institutions and systems in the United States.

In the Library Systems throughout the United States Italian-Americans constitute less than 1 percent of the total managerial population, according to a survey by the Italian-American Librarians Caucus of ALA ("A Survey of Library Directories, 1976–77," New York).

Of the eight language groups listed as "Mother Tongue" in the 1970 Census, Italian was the second language group after English in 10 states, except in Connecticut—there it was the first largest mother tongue. Italian as a mother tongue ranked third in eight states and fourth in 11.

Trends. In order to provide librarians with a vehicle for integrating Italian-American materials and personnel in a professional manner into the Library Systems of the United States and to encourage librarians to use their native talents, the Italian-American Librarians Caucus was formed in 1975 under the Office of Library Services for the Disadvantaged of the American Library Association.

The Caucus's Bibliography, *Writings on Italian-Americans* (Italian-American Center for Urban Affairs, 1975) has become a model of its kind. The 50 members of the Caucus organized on a regional basis have served as consultants for television and ethnic heritage projects: NBC's "Italian-American Conversations," 1976, the Pennsylvania Ethnic Heritage Dissemination Project, and the Kent State Ethnic Library and Museum Directory. They have been members of educational committees such as the Committee for the Italian-American Foundation, a national clearinghouse on Italian-American Studies in Washington, D.C., and the National Italian-American Historical Association. The Caucus encouraged the work of Michael C. DeMarco in New York, who will build a library and print a catalog of copyrighted manuscripts. The need to collect materials from changing Italian-American communities throughout the nation is necessary for the future study of the 1970's. And grassroots directories and guides for the more than 20,000 Italian-Americans entering the country each year would encourage institutional use by this readership.

Carmine Michael Diodati, Jr., founder of the Italian American Librarians Caucus.

Publications. Two new monthlies, based in New York City, but national in scope and devoted to Italian-American life and culture, are *Identity*, edited by Raffaele Donato, a former public television producer, and *I AM*, by Ron de Paola, formerly with *Life*. Regional newspapers interested in library materials are biweekly publications: *The Florida Bulletin*, published by Ven Sequenzia, Hollywood, Florida, and *The Connecticut Italian Review* and *The Italian Review*, published by Frank Piturro, Bronx, New York.

A list of materials in ERIC may be ordered from the Italian-American Librarians Caucus (50 E. Huron Street, Chicago, Illinois 60611).

A finders' list of dissertations on Italian-American interests is available through the National Italian-American Historical Association in New York.

CARMINE M. DIODATI, JR.

JEWISH AMERICANS

The combined holdings of the major Judaica research collections comprise almost 2,000,000 books, pamphlets, and other printed materials. Some of the most prominent of the research collections are the seminary libraries, including the Hebrew Union College–Jewish Institute of Religion with approximately 250,000 volumes as well as about 2,000 manuscripts, the Jewish Theological Seminary with over 200,000 volumes and over 600 manuscripts, and Yeshiva University with over 100,000 volumes of Judaica in addition to a manuscript collection.

The New York Public Library and the Library of Congress also have extensive collections of Judaica—respectively, 135,000 and 150,000 books as well as manuscripts. University libraries with large Judaica collections include Harvard with 150,000 volumes and manuscripts and the University of California at Los Angeles with 90,000. In addition a number of large Judaica libraries specialize in certain areas of Judaica studies. Most significant of these institutions is the Yivo Institute for Jewish Research, New York City, which specializes in the history and culture of East European Jewry and Holocaust studies with 200,000 volumes; it has in total, including records and manuscripts, some 10,000,000 items. Also of importance is the Leo Baeck Institute, New York City, which specializes in the history and culture of the German-speaking communities of Central Europe. It has approximately 40,000 volumes as well as an extensive manuscript collection. Still another Judaica library of importance is that of the American Jewish Historical Society, which specializes in the history and culture of the Jews of North and South America. Housed since 1968 on the campus of Brandeis University, Waltham, Massachusetts, it holds approximately 50,000 volumes and owns about 4,000,000 items altogether including a large number of manuscripts.[1]

Associations. Three Jewish bodies of note are involved with librarianship. The Association of Jewish Libraries is concerned with filling the needs of Jewish libraries and librarians. Approximately 400 are presently affiliated as members in two divisions: the Research and Special Library Division, which represents University and Research libraries, and the Synagogue School and Center Library Division, which serves the smaller, more popular library.

The Committee for Archives and Research Libraries in Jewish Studies is currently assuming significant responsibility in regard to Judaica libraries. It was originally founded (1973) as a funding agency. In 1976 it was becoming important in coordinating the efforts of some 25 organizations for the encouragement, support, and further development of the archives and research libraries that are relevent to Jewish studies. It tries at the same time through its auspices to advance understanding and support by Jewish and general communities for efforts relating to library and archival fields.

The Jewish Caucus of the American Library Association is especially geared to promoting under its direction ideas of concern to Jewish librarians and to the general Jewish public.

It recruits its membership from librarians of Jewish background from across the United States and has a membership of around 200. The Caucus issues a newsletter, published quarterly, that gives information about Jewish bibliographies, films, new subject headings, and other matters.

Community Libraries. Of increasing importance in the Jewish community of the United States today are the libraries that have been set up for communal use in Jewish community centers and synagogues. The program has gained great momentum in the last few years, particularly under the impetus of the Federation of Jewish Philanthropies of New York, which serves a network of Young Men's and Young Women's Hebrew Association buildings and also serves other community centers. In the Greater New York area in 1976 there were combined holdings of from 75,000 to 100,000 volumes. In other parts of the country, major Jewish centers were rapidly acquiring communal collections of note.

Jewish Library Workshops. Important workshops and courses of an experimental nature have been given in different aspects of Jewish librarianship. They include the training of Judaica librarians and the promotion of new procedures of intrinsic value to Judaica works such as new cataloging and classification schemes, acquisition procedures, and bibliographies. Courses have been given in different aspects of Jewish librarianship, including Jewish Bibliography and Reference, the Classification and Cataloging of Judaica materials as well as the deciphering of manuscripts. Such contributions have been undertaken under the auspices of the Federation of Jewish Philanthropies, the Association of Jewish Librarians, the Jewish Theological Seminary, and the Jewish Book Council.

Jewish Book Council. The Jewish Book Council of the National Jewish Welfare Board promotes Jewish creativity in Yiddish, Hebrew, and English by presenting a number of annual awards. The Council, which had been giving awards since 1948 (total, 140), gives $500 for each award to the writer of a work of Judaica which is considered of high literary merit. Currently eight awards are given in the following areas: fiction, Jewish thought, poetry, juvenile literature, the Holocaust, Jewish history, Israel and Zionism, and translation of a Jewish classic. Another award from the Jewish Book Council is given to various libraries for attaining standards of excellence. In 1976 six such awards were given to various libraries in the United States. In addition, the Jewish Book Council is involved in other promotions of Jewish literary interest. It promotes

Jewish Book Month programming and publishes the *Jewish Book Annual,* which has bibliographies and essays of importance to Jewish literature, as well as *Jewish Bookland,* which presents book reviews by authorities in various fields.

Nobel and Pulitzer Prize Winners. Many Jewish writers have been recognized as significant contributors to the general world of literature. In the past decade a few of these writers have received the world's top literary awards for their works. In 1976 Saul Bellow won the Nobel Prize for Literature; in 1966 Shmuel Yosef Agnon and Nelly Sachs had received that award. The Pulitzer Prize was won in 1967 by Bernard Malamud and in 1952 by Herman Wouk.

MAX CELNIK;
DAVID ARONOVITCH

REFERENCES
1. Charles Berlin, "Library Resources for Jewish Studies in the United States," *American Jewish Year Book 1975–76.* vol. 75, pp. 3–53 (American Jewish Committee, New York, 1974).
2. Phillip P. Mason, Editor, *Directory of Jewish Archival Institutions* (Wayne State University Press, Detroit, 1975).
3. Menahem Binyamin Siberfeld, "Libraries," *Encyclopedia Judaica,* vol. 11. pp. 191–192 (Keter Publishing House Ltd., Jerusalem, 1971).

NATIVE AMERICANS

An overview of the current status of library service for American Indian people reveals two major trends: an increasing awareness of the informational needs of American Indians demonstrated through appropriate publications and the planning of American Indian library services at the state and national level.

Newsletter. The joint efforts of the American Library Association and the National Indian Education Association were successful in creating the *American Indian Libraries Newsletter.* Published periodically by the ALA Office of Library Service to the Disadvantaged, Committee on Library Service for American Indian People, the *Newsletter* serves as a communication link among American Indian librarians, professional organizations, and other individuals interested in exploring the informational needs of American Indian people. This is the first newsletter designed especially for consideration of American Indian library services. Primarily, the *American Indian Libraries Newsletter* seeks to increase the library profession's awareness of the informational needs of American Indians. The newsletter acts as a forum for the exchange of ideas among those individuals and organizations who are willing to share information concerning library programs, resources, and services relating to American Indian communities.

State Planning. Project ILSTAC (Indian Library Services Technical Assistance Center) funded by the U. S. Office of Education, Office of Library and Learning Resources, is concerned with developing statewide plans for library services to the American Indian communities in North Carolina, New Mexico, Minnesota, and Washington. ILSTAC, a project of the National Indian Education Association (Minneapolis) provides technical assistance to those individuals and organizations concerned with American Indian library services. Information relating to the planning and development of American Indian library programs and resources is disseminated as the third function of the project.

National Planning. To encourage long-range planning in the area of library services in American Indian schools and communities. the Bureau of Indian Affairs sponsored a Library Workshop in Albuquerque, New Mexico, July 13–14. The workshop sought to provide initial input into the design of a plan for the improvement of American Indian School libraries. A draft of the document was to be presented to the National Commission on Libraries and Information Science. It was hoped at year's end that the BIA plan would be included in the national library plan.

The Indian Libraries Task Force of the National Commission on Libraries and Information Science continues to study the national conditions of library services for Indians.

A potential source for the national improvement and support of library services for American Indian people will be the White House Conference on Library and Information Services. The Conference offers American Indian people, librarians, educators and other interested individuals the opportunity to submit recommendations for the examination and betterment of every aspect of American Indian

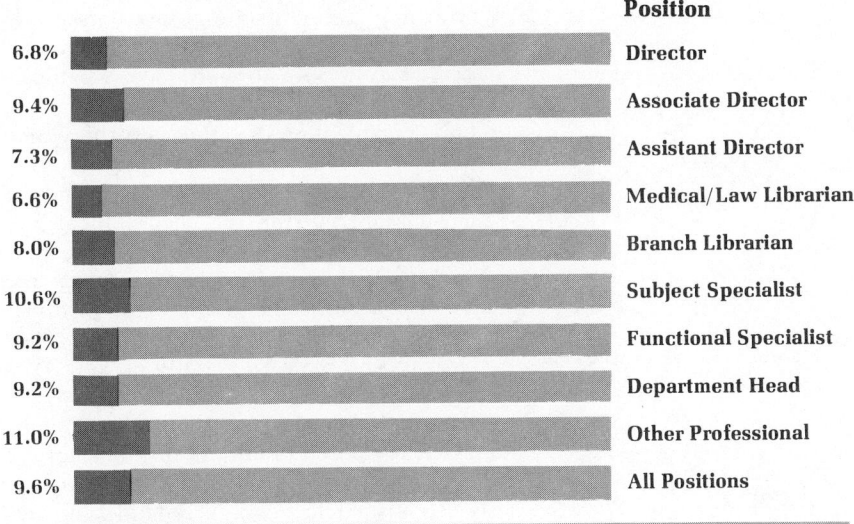

Distribution of Minority Professional Library Staff, 1975-76

Percentage	Position
6.8%	Director
9.4%	Associate Director
7.3%	Assistant Director
6.6%	Medical/Law Librarian
8.0%	Branch Librarian
10.6%	Subject Specialist
9.2%	Functional Specialist
9.2%	Department Head
11.0%	Other Professional
9.6%	All Positions

Source: ACRL Salary Survey, 1975–76

library service. An American Indian Library Services preconference would provide a means of increasing participation from the American Indian communities, allowing American Indian people to express their views concerning their unique informational needs.

Awareness and planning are the key in the development of library services for American Indian people. Rural, urban, and reservation communities have benefitted and will continue to profit, it is hoped, from focusing on state and national library planning which emphasizes their contributions. CHERYL METOYER

POLISH AMERICANS

One of the visible results of this new interest in heritage in 1976 was the formation of the Polish American Librarians Association (PALA). The first meeting of the Association was held in February 1976, and as of November 1976 there were more than 100 members nationwide. In addition, PALA had at that time approximately 300 correspondents including Canadians and Poles in Poland who were interested and supported the Association.

PALA continues to conduct a general survey of the availability of Polish and Polish-American-oriented materials in school and public libraries. The results indicated a shocking paucity of material on the large group. Except for specialized university collections serving their Slavic departments, and a few large public libraries, very little is available to those desiring such material—not because materials do not exist but because they are not acquired. Many reference sources may be consulted for those wanting to know what is available regarding Polish/Polish-American publications and audiovisual materials.

Collections. Considerable collections are housed in selected public libraries in large urban centers in the U.S., including Detroit, Chicago, New York, and Cleveland. Private collections are widespread in the U.S. Two significant private collections open to researchers are in the Polish Museum in Chicago and at St. Mary's College in Orchard Lake, Michigan. Smaller collections are maintained in most Polonia organization headquarters of which there are several thousand in the nation. (Polonia is the collective term for all persons of Polish descent outside the geographical borders of Poland.) Some of the largest Slavic collections in university libraries are at the University of California, Berkeley; the University of Chicago; Columbia University; Yale University, and State University of New York at Buffalo.

Historical Note. In 1535 the first municipal library (as opposed to church or monastery libraries in existence since c.1000 in Poland) was established in Poznan, Poland. The second, founded in 1594 in Torun, served as a school workshop as well as a public library, and the third opened in Gdansk in 1596 (*New Polish Publications*. no. 6, June 1976, pp. 13–14). Today libraries and Book and Press Clubs (a unique Polish institution) flourish in Poland. The Poles' love affair with libraries has a long history, perpetuated in the U.S.

With typical Slavic hospitality and respect for academic achievement, Poles and Polish Americans willingly share their accumulated library resources with their fellow Americans and the world. Unfortunately, because of the "melting pot theory and local attitudes toward various ethnic groups, libraries in the U.S. have not, generally speaking encouraged ethnic collections. This attitude is slowly changing and can only result in enriching our population and in improving the quality of life for all. VICTORIA M. GALA

Exhibits Round Table

1976 was an active year for Exhibits Round Table (ERT). In addition to the regular services provided for exhibitors and librarians, ERT co-sponsored the publication of an orientation handbook advising librarians how to visit exhibits; surveyed state and regional conferences; and began preparations for publication of an Exhibit Procedures Manual.

Together with Junior Members Round Table (JMRT), ERT co-sponsored publication of a booklet on how to get the most out of conference exhibits. The booklet, originally published in 1964, features illustrations by cartoonist Roy McKie and design by two-time Caldecott medalist Nonny Hogrogrian. Virginia Amos, JMRT/ERT liaison, was in charge of revising the booklet, which was included in information packets distributed to new JMRT members at the ALA Annual Conference.

At year's end a committee was formed to revise the Exhibit Procedures Manual. The committee, under the direction of Mary Daume, Monroe County, Michigan, surveyed various state library association conference and exhibits chairpersons to determine what use is made of the Manual. From this survey it was determined that the previous edition, published in 1964, contained some valuable advice, but that much of the material was outdated or unnecessary. The committee planned to publish a new edition in 1977.

The ERT Standards Committee, chaired by Jean Mester of the H. W. Wilson Company, surveyed library and educational association conventions and rated the exhibits. The ratings, including such items as exhibit facilities, exhibitor services, amount of traffic and hotel facilities were passed on to the respective exhibit chairpersons who, it is hoped, will use these exhibitor comments as a guideline in future exhibit planning.

Awards. ERT continued in 1976 to award those exhibits judged most outstanding at the Annual Conference. The Donald W. Kohlstedt award for outstanding multiple booth went to Doubleday. The best single booth was Harlin Quist Publishing Company. A special award was given to Ellsworth Subscription Service for best typifying the theme of the Centennial year's exhibits, "Celebrate a Century."

PAUL E. RAFFERTY

ERT Officers

CHAIRPERSON (July 1976–June 1977):
Paul E. Rafferty, Field Enterprises Educational Corporation

CO-VICE-CHAIRPERSONS:
Joe Everly, Demco Educational Corporation
Teresa Mitchem, Chilton Book Company

SECRETARY:
Jane Burke, CLSI

TREASURER:
Ernest DiMattia

Membership (August 31, 1976): 168

Federal Librarians Round Table

The year 1976 was one of affirmation and achievement for the Federal Librarians Round Table (FLIRT). As the year 1976 began, FLIRT's officers adopted a three-part program of action. They would: (1) publish a newsletter with news for, by, and about federal librarians; (2) plan a militant Conference program for the 1976 ALA Centennial that would alert the profession to the scope and excellence of federal library and information programs; and (3) provide an opportunity for all federal librarians to participate in a dynamic sub-group of the nation's largest professional library association.

In fulfillment of this program, FLIRT published four issues of the FLIRT Newsletter during the membership year. Each number featured an editorial on a topic of interest to federal librarians, reports on continuing education activities, news of appointments, transfers, and retirements, listings with full bibliographic data of new reports and documents, and other items of special relevance for federal librarians. In addition to regular membership mailings, over 4,000 promotional copies of each newsletter issue were distributed to all addressees on the mailing list of the Federal Library Committee.

FLIRT also delivered on its promise to provide useful conference programming. A two-part program, co-sponsored by the Government Documents Round Table (GODORT), and entitled, "The Dynamics of Federal Information: A Bicentennial Update," dealt with National Resources and Services on Sunday, July 18, and with National Documentation and Control on Monday, July 19. Speakers on the first day's program were: Henriette Avram, Special Assistant for Network Development, the Library of Congress; Martin M. Cummings, Director, National Library of Medicine; Richard A. Farley, Director, National Agricultural Library; and Lee J. Burchinal, Chief, Office of Science Information, National Science Foundation. Speakers for the second day were: William Knox, Director, National Technical Information Service; Hubert Sauter, Administrator, Defense Documentation Center; John Livsey, Government Printing Office; and Kevin Flood, National Audiovisual Center. Over 700 librarians attended the sessions.

Other Centennial Conference programming included a preconference on Federal Library Management, co-sponsored by the Armed Forces Librarians Section of the Public Library Association. One hundred federal librarians participated in five workshop sessions dealing with (1) resource allocation, (2) public relations, (3) management analysis, (4) patron-oriented services, and (5) libraries and unions. Workshop presentations were made by Gordon Randall (IBM Corporation), Peggy Barber (ALA), Duane Webster (Association of Research Libraries), Marvin Scilken (Orange, New Jersey, Public Library), and Kevin Keaney of the National Agricultural Library. Keaney also served as workshop coordinator and moderator.

As the year ended, FLIRT membership was nearing 500 for the first time. Catherine Zealberg, Director, Army War College Library, was elected to lead FLIRT into its sixth year of successful operations. Her goal is to foster the growth and responsiveness of FLIRT as a vehicle for the aspirations as well as the frustrations of the total federal library community within the framework of the American Library Association.

ROBERT B. LANE

FLIRT Officers

PRESIDENT (July 1976–June 1977):
Catherine Zealberg, Army War College Library, Carlise Barracks, Pennsylvania

VICE PRESIDENT/PRESIDENT-ELECT:
Dr. Joan Maier, Chief, Library Services, NOAA, Boulder, Colorado

SECRETARY:
Normand Varieur, Chief, Scientific and Technical Information Division, Picatinny Arsenal, Dover, New Jersey

Membership (August 31, 1976): 498

FID

See *International Federation for Documentation*.

Films

Although nontheatrical films of a broadly educational or a curriculum-related nature contin-

Films

ued to be a significant informational resource in school, college, and public libraries during 1976, there was a decrease in the sales of such films, reflecting a lack of funding for special educational and library projects and the general cut-back in library budgets. According to statistics from the Association of Media Producers, the tightening of the market felt by all individuals involved with 16mm films is substantiated in the trends during 1976. Indications from 29 16mm film and prerecorded videotape distribution companies indicated an approximate 7% drop in sales in the first three quarters of 1976 as compared to the same period in 1975.

A sizable number of 16mm films remained on the market and were being introduced during 1976, most likely the result of previous productions being made available or, as seen in numerous cases, recycled educational releases of documentaries and entertainment features originally produced for and broadcast on television. In spite of the disheartening trends felt by many, a great deal of interest and activity surrounds 16mm films on the part of filmmakers, librarians, educators, and distributors.

Midwest Film Conference. The Midwest Film Conference grew to prominence during its eighth annual meeting February 20 to 22 in Chicago. Previously held in companionable but inadequate quarters, the Conference was moved in 1976 to a larger, more convenient hotel, which was also more accessible to the considerable number of out-of-state participants.

The 1,200 librarians, teachers, film students, filmmakers, and distributors in attendance were treated to a non-competitive array of documentaries, features, and short films during the weekend event. Rather than being arranged into topical categories, the 150 films, ranging in subject matter and film technique and offering something of interest to everyone, were somewhat randomly arranged into three programs screened simultaneously from 8 a.m. to 1 a.m. so that participants could wander from one program or scheduled film of particular interest to another.

In addition to the laudable number and variety of films presented, the Conference, dedicated to "the creative use of film in education," impressively featured significant personalities in the field of film and some informative seminars and workshops. Frederick Wiseman, in the opening evening program, discussed his approach to filmmaking, which has focused on starkly realistic and dramatic documentaries about American institutions (*Law and Order, Basic Training, Primate,* and *Welfare*). Charles Braverman, whose original documentary technique of the split-second animation of stills was made famous in *An American Time Capsule* and *The Sixties,* talked of his new films the following night. Ante Zaninovic of Zagreb Films in Yugoslavia, Kathleen Shannon and Hannah Fisher of the National Film Board of Canada, and Anne Hersey, an independent producer from San Francisco, were other filmmakers who commented on their work, screened some of the films, and answered questions from interested Conference attendees during the weekend. A lecture on laser holography, a seminar on the feature film in the classroom, an examination of how film is being taught in high school and college, and a distributors' panel discussion rounded out the heavily scheduled weekend program of the Film Conference.

American Film Festival. As in previous years, the American Film Festival, sponsored by the Educational Film Library Association May 31 to June 5 in New York City, was a significant and stimulating showcase of new nontheatrical 16mm films for filmmakers, distributors, and library and classroom selectors. The Festival featured four days of competitive film screenings, juried by subject, film, and utilization specialists who viewed nearly 400 films selected as finalists from more than 700 entries released during the preceding year. The 40 categories in which the finalists were screened covered social and human issues, education and information, art and culture, environment and nature, and feature-length documentaries.

Promotional material highlighting the 1976 program of the Film Services division of the West Virginia Library Commission. More than 1,500 16mm films were offered free to all West Virginia public libraries.

A new category was added for films loosely dealing with the U.S. Bicentennial celebration. In addition, a new out-of-competition screening offered recent documentaries that were too long to be featured in regular competition and some older documentaries which were of special merit. Two evening screenings of the popular Film as Art program, an out-of-competition showcase of highly personal experimental and avante-garde films, were introduced by Amos Vogel, who selected the 11 films and discussed this film genre.

Robert Radnitz, producer of the films *And Now Miguel, Island of the Blue Dolphins* and the feature film *Part 2 Sounder*, was the speaker at the EFLA and New York Film Council luncheon. In warmly informal comments, he expressed his belief in "family films" and spoke eloquently about the movie industry's rating system, noting examples of its hypocritical inconsistencies.

An exhibit area attracted some 75 exhibitors representing film producers and distributors, equipment manufacturers, and reviewing media. An afternoon panel discussion between filmmaker/distributors and film buyers provided an opportunity for an exchange of comments between the two groups on such subjects as film previewing and video copying of prints. Cecile Starr's retrospective examination of the documentary films of Helen Grayson during the 1940's and 1950's vied for the attention of Festival registrants during the same time slot as the filmmakers' and film buyers' panel.

Awards. At the Awards Banquet on Friday night, a special citation of recognition was presented by EFLA to Rohama Lee, editor/publisher of *Film News* for 30 years. John Culkin, of the Center for Understanding Media, announced the Blue and Red Ribbon winners for the categories screened during the previous week. In addition, winners were announced for the two special Festival Awards. The 1976 John Grierson Award, given for the work of a new filmmaker of social documentary, was a tie between Richard Brick for *Last Stand Farmer* and Daniel Keller for *Lovejoy's Nuclear War*. *The Gentleman Tramp*, a portrait of Charlie Chaplin, won the 1976 Emi-

ly Award, presented to the film earning the highest score in the Festival. The 1976 18th annual American Film Festival wound down the following day with screenings of all the award-winning films, which then began a country-wide circuit of screenings.

Other EFLA Events. The Educational Film Library Association also sponsored two smaller events during 1976. The Distribution Conference, held in New York City during February, focused on marketing of 16mm educational films, a meeting in which both large distribution companies and independent filmmakers/distributors discussed their experiences and viewpoints on distribution. The four-day Film Library Administration Institute, held in Kansas City, Missouri, in October, turned its attention to a different area of the educational film field. Seminars, panel discussions, and presentations dealing with management, operations, and programming in film libraries were designed for film librarians and media personnel in public, school, and university libraries, museums, and other community and professional organizations.

Annual Conference. As in previous years, the ALA Annual Conference provided a showcase for films of interest to librarians. Sponsored by the PLA–Audiovisual Committee, "Films for Libraries," a five-day screening of a wide variety of films was held at the Centenni-

(Top left) EFLA Executive Director Nadine Covert with 1976 Grierson Award winners Richard Brick, center, and Daniel Keller. (Center) Amos Vogel at the festival's "Film As Art" program. (Right) EFLA Board President Stephen C. Johnson presenting special citation to Rohama Lee, editor and publisher of Film News.

Films, Children's

The International Animation Film Festival held in August 1976 paid special tribute to Lotte Reiniger (below) for her film "Aucassin and Nicolette" (scenes pictured) and for her 60 years of contributions to the art of animation.

al Conference in Chicago, July 18–22. Eighty-nine films selected from 600 entries submitted by 53 film distributors were chosen to represent various subject areas and different visual techniques of the art of nontheatrical 16mm films. The films were screened in subject categories including Americana, children's films, creative short films, metrication, and social/political issues, so that viewers could pick and choose the subjects and films of particular interest to them. "Cinema Nitecap," another PLA Audiovisual Committee event, presented a calvalcade of short, entertaining, animated and live-action films shown to an appreciative capacity audience. Two PLA–Audiovisual Committee co-sponsored film events were also on the Centennial Conference program. "Notable Films for Children" highlighted the Children's Services Division selection of outstanding 1974 films for children. Screenings of selected titles from this list were followed by discussion of the films by members of the Children's Services Division Film Evaluation Committee. "Sampling of 1976 Selected Films for Young Adults" featured five films from the annual listing selected by the Young Adult Services Division Media Selection and Usage Committee. Panel reaction from members of the YASD Committee followed the screenings in this program.

While the incoming statistics from film producers and distributors and from library budgets did not augur well for the growth of the 16mm film market, the various film events throughout the year indicated continuing interest in and commitment to the place of film in libraries. —IRENE WOOD

REFERENCES
Nadine Covert, "16mm Distribution Conference Report," *Sightlines* 9, no. 3:5 (Spring 1976).
Nadine Covert and James L. Limbacher, "1976 Festival Report," *Sightlines* 9, no. 4:4–5 (Summer 1976).
"Shorts, Docu Distribs Convene," *Variety* 282, no. 6:34 (March 17, 1976).

Films, Children's

Encouraging signs of increased attention on the part of film associations to the problem of improving the quality of children's films were evident in 1976. In May the New York Film Council presented a forum on the topic "Children's Films—Orphans of the Industry." Later in the year this topic was the theme of a full volume of *Film Library Quarterly* (Volume 9, Number 3), published by the Film Library Information Council. *Sightlines*, published by the Educational Film Library Association (EFLA), also devoted its fall issue to children's films.

The 18th American Film Festival, held in New York under the auspices of the Educational Film Library Association, honored a number of films for children.

Children's Films
  Blue Ribbon—*Angel and Big Joe*
    (Learning Corporation)
  Red Ribbon—*The Beast of Monsieur Racine*
    (Weston Woods), an animated film based on the children's book by Tomi Ungerer (Farrar, Straus & Giroux)
Curriculum Films: Elementary/Junior High
  Blue Ribbon—*Learning About Air*
    (A.C.I.)
  Red Ribbon—*Show Biz: A Job Well Done*
    (Barr)

In the following additional categories films for children were award winners: Fiction Films: *The Shopping Bag Lady* (Learning Corporation)—Red Ribbon. Guidance Films: *Rookie of the Year* (Time-Life)—Blue Ribbon. Consumer Education: *Soopergoop* (Churchill)—Blue Ribbon. Religion and Society: *The Story of Christmas* (Films, Inc.)—Blue Ribbon.

Robert Radnitz, a film producer who specializes in the "family film," was the speaker at the luncheon given jointly by EFLA and the New York Film Council. A sneak preview of his most recent film, *Part 2 Sounder*, marked the opening day of the Festival.

In June 1976 the Film Evaluation Committee of the Children's Services Division of ALA released its list of 21 Notable Films for Children copyrighted or released in the United States in 1974. The selections were:

All at Sea	Sterling
Animation Pie	Film Wright
The Beast of Monsieur Racine	Weston Woods
The Bronze Zoo	Texture
The Case of the Elevator Duck	Learning Corporation
Cecily	Learning Corporation
The Fable of He and She	Learning Corporation
Flight of Icarus	ACI
Free to be . . . You and Me	McGraw-Hill
Hank the Cave Peanut	Yellow Bison
Harold's Fairy Tale	Weston Woods
The Highwayman	Eccentric Circle
I'm Feeling Alone	Churchill
Legend of John Henry	Pyramid
Me and You Kangaroo	Learning Corporation
The Mole as Painter	Phoenix
My World . . . Water	Churchill
A Round Feeling	Eccentric Circle
The Story of Christmas	Films Incorporated
The Swineherd	Weston Woods
Wild Green Things in the City	ACI

An ALA Conference program cosponsored by the CSD Film Evaluation Committee and

Films, Children's

Scene from the "The Shopping Bag Lady," winner of the red ribbon for children's fiction films at the 1976 American Film Festival.

the PLA Audiovisual Committee highlighted the Notable Films List at the Annual Conference. The CSD Committee endorsed two feature films released in 1976 for commercial distribution: *The Blue Bird* (20th Century/Fox), *Part 2, Sounder* (20th Century/Fox).

The International Animation Film Festival '76, held August 10–15 at the National Arts Centre, Ottawa, and hosted by the Canadian Film Institute, was the scene of a special tribute given to animation pioneer Lotte Reiniger for her film *Aucassin and Nicolette* (NFBC) and for her outstanding contributions to the art of animation during the last 60 years. Reiniger's numerous films of classic fairy tales are in the collections of many libraries.

In March the Academy Award for the outstanding production of 1975 among all short live-action motion pictures was presented to *Angel and Big Joe* (Learning Corporation), a film starring Paul Sorvino and Dadi Pinero portraying the friendship of a telephone lineman and a young migrant worker. The film is already widely used in school and public libraries.

The 4th Birmingham International Education Film Festival, devoted to recognition of excellence in films for classroom use, honored a number of films. The "Electra" Statuette Award for Best of the Festival was given to *The Shopping Bag Lady* (Learning Corporation).

Cine (The Council on International Nontheatrical Events) presented Golden Eagle Awards to children's films as part of its screening process to select the best U.S. non-feature films to represent the country at overseas festivals. The choices included the following titles:

Beep Beep	Churchill
My Dad's a Cop	William Brose Productions
Nicky: One of My Best Friends	Togg Films
Rikki-Tikki-Tavi	Xerox
Taleb and His Lamb	Barr
The Superlative Horse	Phoenix
Whazzat?	Encyclopaedia Britanica Educational Corporation
The Magic Rolling Board	Pyramid

The Sixth International Children's Film Festival was presented on weekends from February 21 to March 28 by the Center of Films for Children at the Los Angeles County Museum of Art. Features and shorts from the United States and other countries were screened for children and their families.

Film collections for children continued to profit from the television market in 1976. A number of live-action films, produced for *ABC After School Specials*, were made available for school and library purchase from Time-Life Multimedia.

MARILYN BERG IARUSSO

Scene from "Angel and Big Joe," winner of the blue ribbon at the 18th American Film Festival.

Filmstrips

One of the most significant and potentially far-reaching developments in filmstrips during the mid-1970's has been a dramatic change in packaging: from typical box-like containers in conventional sizes to various book-like containers in various sizes that can be shelved in a library collection for easy access by users. It seems to be the trend. Whether the easily accessible container has one or more strip films does not seem to affect this change in packaging; the commitment on the part of the company is all that is required. Several years ago a few farsighted producers and distributors responded to the logical extension of the idea behind a unified or integrated media collection by designing containers that are similar to books both in size and in ease of opening. Today many producers and distributors are following suit, and the list continues to grow. One of the oldest of the "newer media" is now coming full circle into libraries with integrated collections, both on the cards or pages of interfiled catalogs and at long last on the shelves for public use intershelved with other library materials.

Current Subjects. Filmstrip titles cover, as they have in the past, many different areas. They reflect the continuing interest of the public with careers, health, and safety. It is noteworthy that the concentration among these three areas is heavily weighted toward children. Titles on language arts and adaptations to film of juvenile books are still popular; the latter category was a trend setter about ten years ago. Science and social studies with their continuous replenishment on traditional topics and reassessment of approaches, e.g., the energy crisis and the Middle East and Arab world command a sizeable share of titles. Over the year 1976 filmstrip titles on women's issues decreased sharply, while those on home economics increased. An analysis of the relationship, if any, of filmstrip titles and topics to current political and economic trends and future school curricula might be revealing.

Although 1976 was disappointing for both buyers and sellers, the filmstrip market has managed to survive better than most. Multimedia kits continued to show the largest dollar gain. However, it is important to remember that filmstrips are inevitably the basic audiovisual ingredient in these packages. Sound filmstrips, generally cassette, account for the lion's share of the audiovisual sales together with kits and 16mm film. According to a report from the Association of Media Producers, this group accounts for 89 percent of the total industry sales.[1] Tom Hope's Table of Sales by Product Format covering the years 1966 to 1974 concurs and also indicates the competitive place of filmstrips as one of the big three in sales for almost a decade.[2]

Preschoolers at the Olympia, Washington, Public Library followed up a showing of the filmstrip "Stone Soup" by concocting their own recipe.

"VD-Attack Plan" filmstrip set by Walt Disney Educational Media Company presented Shame, Fear and Ignorance as the trio preventing young people from learning the facts about venereal diseases.

One of the encouraging signs of the times was the formation in January of a new professional trade association—the Association of Media Producers—whose members represent a majority of the leading companies in the field, i.e., those who issue several or more new products a year. A primary goal of the Association is to promote the creation of the highest quality learning materials. Together with their counterpart in the publishing industry—the Association of American Publishers—and the ALA's Resources and Technical Services Division and Association of American School Librarians, they are presently surveying school media centers to obtain marketing, selection, and acquisition information from the field in order to make effective economic decisions.

In a time of inflation, high unemployment, and restrictive federal funding for materials and equipment, filmstrips will continue to be the dray horse of the industry. They are neither new nor glamorous, but they are easy to use, adaptable for individual or group use, and lend visual excitement to the process of learning.

DIANA L. SPIRT

REFERENCES
1. *Annual Survey,* 1975 (1976 in prep), Association of Media Producers, 1707 L St., N.W., Suite 515, Washington, D.C. 20036
2. Tom Hope, "1976: The Year in Media Materials and Equipment," in James W. Brown, ed. *Educational Media Yearbook* 1977–1978 (New York: Bowker, 1976), p. 108.

Financing the Public Library

The summary of 1975 events relating to public library finance began and ended with reader's-choice optional interpretations.[1] Observers with a penchant for pessimism could easily interpret 1975 developments as anxiety producing. Those optimistically oriented, perhaps with a little more stretched justification, could view 1975 developments as anticipatory of better things to come. No one could say, however, that the millennium in public library financial support had arrived.

Events in 1976, on balance, provide increased justification for a more optimistic view—at least as grounds for anticipating further developments to strengthen and stabilize the fiscal support system underpinning public libraries. A summary of key events inducing some degree of optimism about the future includes the following:

- The Library Services and Construction Act (LSCA), scheduled to terminate in mid-1976, was automatically extended for one additional year when it was funded for FY 1977. The level of funding for FY 1977 is $60,200,000, 17 percent above the FY 1976 level.
- General Revenue Sharing, viewed by some as a substitute for LSCA, was also reenacted and continued until 1980. The distribution of such funds remained about the same as under the 1972 enactment except that designation of priority expenditures (which included public libraries) to guide local utilization of GRS funds was eliminated in the new act.
- The National Commission on Libraries and Information Science (NCLIS) (q.v.) continued its difficult task of weaving together the strands of library and information services into a coherent national program. The NCLIS Report, *Toward a National Program for Libraries and Information Services: Goals for Action*, has been widely distributed and discussed. The call in that *Report* for a balanced intergovernmental funding system to support public library development gained increased credibility as a priority objective to which all members of the library community could subscribe.
- A report, completed during the year under NCLIS aegis, evaluated the effectiveness of federal funding of the public library and called for a revised and strengthened funding measure to replace LSCA.[2] The study also stressed the need for improving state-aid systems designed to develop and maintain upgraded public library and information services.
- The Urban Library Council undertook a study to test whether public libraries should be considered as an integral part of the states' mandate to provide public education services.[3] The study, scheduled for release in early 1977, demonstrated functional, legal, and organizational relationships between public libraries and public education. The analysis also highlighted the gross disparities in method and level of funding of these related services and provided a stimulus and strategy for improving state-aid systems for public libraries.
- Finally, momentum and preliminary planning for a White House Conference on Libraries and Information Services (q.v.) increased under the enabling statute (PL 93-568). The national conference is to be preceded by preparatory conferences in each state. Funding was expected to be available in early 1977 to assist states in planning and conducting these conferences. This activity can be expected to provide consensus-building forums in which public library financing will be a high priority topic.

NCES Study. The year 1976 was also marked by the compilation and availability of updated and new definitive findings essential to understanding public library financing issues and to planning effective strategies for their resolution. Early in the year the National Center for Educational Statistics (NCES) served up preliminary findings from the 1974 library survey. NCES counted slightly more than 8,300 public libraries, excluding branches, served by some 86,000 full time professionals, with total expenditures in 1974 of $1,100,000,000.[4] The survey also indicated the existence of gross disparities among libraries in expenditures per capita. Such disparities were particularly discernible between libraries located within Standard Metropolitan Statistical Areas and those serving jurisdictions outside SMSA's.

The NCLIS study of Federal funding disclosed that libraries were continuing to lose ground when their total expenditures were compared to expenditures of other essential local services including schools, police, hospitals, and even recreation activities. Public library costs represented only 1.3 percent of the total expenditures for this group of services in 1967 and the percentage dropped to 1.2 percent in 1975. The Urban Library Council study revealed that expenditures for public libraries represented in 1975 only a minuscule percentage (1.8 percent) of public school expenditures and that state subsidy mechanisms for public libraries are far less efficient than state school aid formulas in meeting standards of stability and equalization.[5]

NCLIS Study. New and more definitive information is also now available on the amount and source of funds in state-aid systems for public libraries. A questionnaire completed by Chief State Library Officers as a part of the NCLIS study[6] provided data for measuring state-aid amounts per capita. In 1975, the average state aid per capita for the nation was a mere $.68, and the median for 45 reporting states was $.53. Only six predominantly industrial states, led by New York at $1.65, had per capita local library aid of $1 or more. The second ranking state in per capita public library aid was Georgia (at $1.56), the home state of President Jimmy Carter. Twenty-five of the states reporting (45) were below the average per capita aid level of $.53, ranging as low as $.06 in one state. Many states rely exclusively, or heavily, on federal funds to finance their state-aid systems. In 1975, about 27 percent of the total dollars distributed through state-aid

Fee punch cards introduced by the Dallas Public Library in January 1976 charge non-city residents for checkout privileges. The $8.50 fee for 50 transactions was based on the average city resident's tax support allocated to city libraries.

See also
London and
Canadian
Correspondents'
Reports

The Southwest Wisconsin Library System headquarters building at Fennimore was the first library building in the nation to be financed by a Farmers Home Administration loan.

systems were federal funds. Clearly, in the context of a balanced intergovernmental funding system, the states have a long way to go in improving their state-aid systems.

GRS Impact. One other new piece of definitive information should be reported. The extent to which general revenue sharing (GRS) funds have represented a substantial aid to local level financing of public libraries has long been debated. The NCLIS study also provided a means for a rather precise measuring of GRS impact on local library funding. The conclusion of this research was that no more than one-third to one-half of the GRS funds allocated by municipalities and counties to local libraries resulted in any increase in library expenditure. A total of $76,000,000 in GRS funds was allocated by municipalities and counties to public libraries in 1973–74. The conclusion means that much of this money was used to substitute for local tax dollars which otherwise would have been required to maintain existing service levels. Thus, while local library officers should make every effort to capture GRS funds, the track record on gaining new money through this source is not good.

There is reason, however, to echo the hopeful note sounded at the outset of this summary. The year 1976 produced some new developments and provided much new information that can be used strategically in efforts to achieve a balanced intergovernmental funding system for the public library. While much work needs to be done, the targets of needed change and improvement are in clearer focus. Newly available information can be used in the attainment of more clearly defined goals. It remains for the entire library community to build a firm, but malleable, consensus of support around strategic efforts to improve the public library funding system as an integral part of a total system of libraries and information services. In this way, the promise that can be read into 1976 events can be converted into a higher degree of reality in 1977. (See also Foundations and Funding Agencies; Gifts, Bequests, and Endowments; Public Libraries.)

RODNEY P. LANE

REFERENCES
1. *The ALA Yearbook: A Review of Library Events 1975.* American Library Association, Chicago, Illinois, 1976 Centennial Edition, p. 278.
2. *Evaluation of the Effectiveness of Federal Funding of Public Libraries,* submitted to the National Commission on Libraries and Information Science by Government Studies and Systems, Philadelphia, Pennsylvania, December 1976, p. 115.
3. *Legal, Functional and Fiscal Support Relationships Between Public Libraries and Public Education,* prepared for the Urban Libraries Council by Government Studies & Systems, Philadelphia, Pennsylvania, January, 1977.
4. *1974 Survey of Public Libraries,* Preliminary Release, National Center for Educational Statistics, January 28, 1976.
5. Urban Libraries Council, *op. cit.,* p. 39.
6. National Commission on Libraries and Information Science, *op. cit.,* p. 56.

Foundations and Funding Agencies

Information about grants to libraries is incomplete. Many grants to individuals, small grants to libraries, general contributions that may include some library aid, and numerous local private contributions are not included in available reports. It is encouraging to find that more and more information becomes available each year, and this review represents the bulk of grants in the library field.

Three categories of grants to libraries are considered in this report covering 1976: private foundations; Council on Library Resources; and federal agencies. An extended look at the Council on Library Resources is taken since CLR in 1976 reached its 20th anniversary.

PRIVATE FOUNDATIONS

The Foundation Center provides summaries of data gathered on foundation grants to libraries. Although this is the most comprehensive information available, it should be pointed out that it covers only those foundations reporting to the Foundation Center and lists only grants of $5,000 or more.

Grants to individual librarians are not included. Support of this type is important to professional development. It would be useful if some unit of the American Library Association could compile information on professional support provided to librarians through Guggenheim, Fulbright, CLR, and similar organizations.

A summary of data from the Foundation Center for 1974–75 and 1975–76 is given in Table 1.

Analysis for 1975–76. In comparing the data for 1975 and 1976, it is clearly hazardous to try to identify trends in donations to libraries. The most useful information is obtained from examining individual agencies. The establishment of a large, new foundation, the liquidation of another, or a major change in a foundation's area of interest can have marked effects in any single year.

It is significant that a new organization—the W. R. Hewlett Foundation—is a major library donor. Ten grants of $500,000 or more were made during the year. Six of those were for library buildings. Grants to libraries in 1976 indicate a smaller percentage was designated for buildings, while increased interest was shown in computerization, microforms, and audiovisual fields.

A breakdown showing the distribution of grants on a geographical basis indicates that 90 percent of the money was distributed to U.S. libraries, with 10 percent granted to libraries in other countries.

Within the U.S. almost 75 percent of the funding went to 11 states: California, New York, Illinois, District of Columbia, Pennsylvania, New Jersey, Michigan, Texas, Georgia, Massachusetts, and Connecticut. About 80 percent of the grants to libraries came from foundations in three states: New York, California, and Michigan, and in the District of Columbia.

The largest single grant listed was by the W. R. Hewlett Foundation to Stanford University for $5,024,229. It included professorships and fellowships as well as library support. Stanford University, Princeton University, and the New York Public Library led as recipients of donations.

A random sample of subjects covered by the 1976 grants includes Adult Education, Black Oral History, Computerized Services, Film Arts, Health Sciences, Indian Law, Jewish Archives, Middle East, Microfilming, Music Collections, Parent Training, Prison Bookmobiles, Transportation Library, Urban Research, and Women's History Library.

COUNCIL ON LIBRARY RESOURCES

The Council on Library Resources is unique in the history of librarianship as the only major foundation devoted specifically to supporting

Table 1: Foundations Making Grants of $400,000 or More to Libraries

Foundation Name	Amount	Grants
*Hewlett (W. R.) Foundation	$5,274,000	2
Ford Foundation	3,565,000	40
Council on Library Resources	3,190,000	45
Mellon (Andrew W.) Foundation	2,632,000	17
Mudd (Seeley G.) Fund	2,525,000	2
Irvine (James) Foundation	2,475,000	6
Kresge Foundation	2,470,000	21
Lilly Endowment	1,171,000	10
Astor (Vincent) Foundation	1,110,000	4
Rockefeller Foundation	990,000	18
Fuld (Helene) Health Trust	862,000	21
Campbell (John Bulow) Foundation	610,000	3
Cowell (S. H.) Foundation	550,000	2
Northeast Area Foundation	488,000	3
Fleischmann (Max C.) Foundation	485,000	7
Jerome Foundation	468,000	2
Houston Endowment	450,000	3
Gannett (Frank E.) Newspaper Foundation	415,000	5
Cary (Mary Flagler) Charitable Trust	401,000	8
Davis (Arthur Vining) Foundations	400,000	6

*Includes professorships, fellowships, and the library.

Other Foundations Making Five or More Grants

Clark Foundation	10
Penn (William) Foundation	10
Surdna Foundation	10
Southern Education Foundation	9
Cleveland Foundation	6
Corning Glass Works Foundation	6
Reynolds (Z. Smith) Foundation	6
Benedum (Claude Worthington) Foundation	5
Biddle (Mary Duke) Foundation	5
Hartford Foundation	5
Hayden (Charles) Foundation	5
Rhode Island Foundation	5
Rubinstein (Helena) Foundation	5
Tinker Foundation	5

Table 2: Grants to Libraries by Private Foundations

Year	No. of Grants	Total	Average per Grant
1974–75	518	$47,937,793	$92,365
1975–76	481	38,469,048	79,977

Proportion of Library Grants to Total Foundation Grants

Year	Library Grants	Total Grants	Percent
1974–75	518 grants	19,797 Grants	2.6
	$47,937,793	$1,358,218,624	3.5
1975–76	481 grants	22,897 grants	2.1
	$38,469,048	$1,455,000,000	2.6

The first permanent free public library in Mississippi, a cottage built in 1830, is now surrounded by the million-dollar library and culture center dedicated in October in Biloxi. The center was funded by city capital improvement bonds and state revenue sharing funds from the Mississippi Library Commission.

Table 3: Summary of LSCA, ESEA and HEA Appropriations

	Obligations FY 1974	Obligations FY 1975	Obligations FY 1976	TQ*	Appropriated FY 1977
LSCA					
Title I	$44,155,500	$49,155,000	$49,155,000 (approp)	$12,289,000 (approp)	$56,900,000
Title II	10,786,985	4,363,051			
Title III	2,593,500	2,594,000	2,594,000 (approp)	648,000 (approp)	3,337,000
ESEA					
IV-B**			147,330,000 (approp)		154,330,000
HEA					
Title II-A	9,960,200	9,975,000	9,958,000		***
Title II-B (research)	1,418,433	999,338	999,918		
Title II-B (training)	2,845,394	2,000,000	500,000 (approp)		
Title VI-A		7,492,324	7,480,000		

*Transitional Quarter
**Advance funded
***A continuing (H. J. Res. 1105) provides appropriations at present levels through March 31, 1977, pending further Congressional action in 1977.

library projects. Established by the Ford Foundation in 1956, it has supported significant efforts in Bibliographic Access, Preservation, Micrographics, Library Technology, Library Management, Automation, National and International Library Services, Networks, Standards, Services to Users, Resource Development, and Professional Development for Librarians.

Direct grants have been made to institutions and individuals. Cooperative programs have been worked out with private foundations and federal bodies. Programs may be supported for operation by libraries, or may be operated by CLR. The history of this foundation shows remarkable flexibility, a concern for libraries, and major interest in assisting librarians in their personal development.

In its report for 1975–76, CLR summarized its current target areas under four headings: Automation and National Library Services, Professional Development, Libraries and Their Users, Library Management, Preservation and Micrographics, and International Library Cooperation. The report points out that 45 percent of its funds in the past five years have been spent on automation, national library services, networking, and standardization — all parts of a national system.

FEDERAL FUNDING AGENCIES

U.S. Office of Education. The summary given in Table 2 is augmented this year by listing appropriations for two additional categories — Elementary and Secondary Education Act (ESEA) and Title VI-A of the Higher Education Act (HEA). Corrections are shown in the 1974 and 1975 obligations for HEA II-B Research.

National Endowment for the Humanities. For significant library programs, see National Endowment for the Humanities.

FOSTER E. MOHRHARDT

REFERENCE
The Council on Library Resources, *Twentieth Annual Report* (1976), covers recent developments. Free on request.

Freedom to Read Foundation

In 1976 the prolonged litigation of *Moore* v. *Younger*, which the Foundation began in 1972 in an attempt to have the California Harmful Matters Statute declared unconstitutional, was finally drawing to a close. The Foundation had filed an appeal in May 1975 in the California Court of Appeal, Second District, in order to extend the favorable ruling of Judge Schifferman of the Los Angeles Superior Court, which was binding only in Los Angeles County.

In a hearing on a motion to dismiss filed by California Attorney General Evelle Younger, the judges of the Appellate Court declared that the plaintiffs had received all of the relief to which they were entitled, but more importantly, ordered the Superior Court opinion to be published, which the Foundation interprets to mean that it is binding throughout California. As far as court action is concerned, therefore, *Moore* v. *Younger* has been successfully completed. There remained only to secure the opinion of the California Attorney General that he now construes libraries, librarians, and library employees to be exempt from the liabilities of the Harmful Matters Statute. At the end of 1976, the opinion had not yet been issued.

Smith v. United States. The second major litigation in which the Foundation was involved in 1976 was the case of *Smith* v. *United States*. Jerry Lee Smith, an Iowa publisher and bookseller, was convicted in Federal District Court for violating provisions of the federal postal law prohibiting the mailing of obscene materials. Smith had mailed his publication only within Iowa, which had repealed all portions of its obscenity laws pertaining to adults. Since Iowa, therefore, had declared that no materials distributed to adults within Iowa were legally obscene, the prosecution appeared to be applying a national standard for obscenity in apparent violation of the 1973 *Miller* decision of the U.S. Supreme Court. The case seemed to offer the possibility, through appeal, of seeking reconsideration and correction of the contradictions of the *Miller* decision.

The Foundation supported Smith's appeal and filed an *amicus* brief in the U.S. Court of Appeals for the Eighth Circuit. A three-judge panel, which heard the case on January 28, upheld the District Court decision. Despite the unfavorable decision, the possibility of securing a rehearing of the issues and problems posed by *Miller* encouraged the Foundation to proceed with an appeal to the U.S. Supreme Court. Since Smith lacked the funds for an appeal, the Foundation decided to finance Smith's appeal. A petition for a Writ of Certiorari was filed on April 10 in the U.S. Supreme Court. Despite the Court's reluctance and refusal to accept several recent obscenity cases, it granted certiorari and agreed to hear *Smith v. U.S.*

Both Smith's brief and the *amici curiae* brief prepared by the Foundation in the names of the American Library Association and the Iowa Library Association were filed in early September. The hearing was scheduled for December. The case represents the first time that the Foundation has taken a case before the U.S. Supreme Court. This opportunity to present the American Library Association point of view could be an important milestone in the work of the Freedom to Read Foundation. (See also Intellectual Freedom, Intellectual Freedom Round Table.) RICHARD L. DARLING

Friends of Libraries

Friends of Libraries (with a capital F and L) are organized groups of people whose purpose is to support the library, morally and financially. Group effort for founding and maintaining libraries came early in the history of libraries. In the 1700's and early 1800's, before the time of tax-supported libraries in America, many citizens banded together to organize and establish libraries in their communities. It was not until the 20th century that these lay groups came to be known as Friends of the Library, and were organized with the purpose of aiding libraries. The Friends movement has continued to grow until there are now Friends Groups assisting public, academic, school, and special libraries as well as some statewide Friends Groups which serve as central clearinghouses for the individual Friends Groups. The American Library Association recognizes the value of these lay groups through the activities of its Friends of Libraries Committee (chaired in 1976–77 by Henry Alsmeyer of Texas A & M University). The Committee is part of the Public Relations Section (PRS) of the Library Administration Division (LAD).

At the Annual Conference in 1976 in Chicago, several programs included Friends. In a preconference sponsored by LAD-PRS entitled "Public Relations Panorama—A Preconference on Making Libraries Visible," the Friends Committee was represented by Laura Shelley, Northland Public Library, Pittsburgh, in an afternoon panel presentation: "The Library in the Community." Shirley Stearns, Friends of California Libraries, Montebello, California, directed an evening "Swap 'n Shop." During the Conference, the Friends Committee spon-

sored an informal exchange program called "Friends Groups—Information and Problem Solving." Sue Fontaine, University of Missouri, Columbia, presented a slide-tape show highlighting activities of Friends Groups around the country. The Friends Committee also co-sponsored with the American Library Trustee Association (ALTA) a luncheon with John D. MacDonald, noted mystery writer, as guest speaker.

The Friends Committee is continuing to work on revising *Friends of Libraries* (ALA, 1962). The old edition, though outdated and out of print, is still one of the few items dealing strictly with Friends Groups and it has served as a valuable resource for many people throughout the country. Sarah Leslie Wallace (Library of Congress) was the editor of the 1962 edition and has agreed to act as editor for the newly revised and updated edition. A publication date has not yet been set.

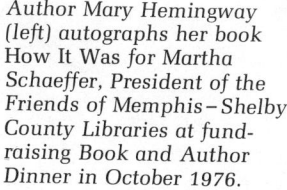

Author Mary Hemingway (left) autographs her book How It Was *for Martha Schaeffer, President of the Friends of Memphis—Shelby County Libraries at fund-raising Book and Author Dinner in October 1976.*

(Left) Friends of the Chicago Public Library member Fanny Bokum, center, with Chicago PL's Jody Weisman and Stephen Kochoff at the second annual "Wild Onion Festival" which began the library's Culture Center's annual "Writing in Chicago" Program. (Below) Friends of the Denver Public Library netted $4,000 for audiovisual equipment at a one-day book sale in September 1976.

Friends of the Toledo–Lucas County Public Library sponsored an "Auction on the Lawn" to benefit the library in 1976.

The Friends Committee during 1976 continued efforts to produce a nationwide directory of Friends Groups. The directory, to be arranged by state, will include academic, public, statewide and other Friends Groups. Don Hammer, LAD Executive Secretary at ALA Headquarters, is directing the project.

Many other efforts not under the auspices of ALA helped to spread information about Friends of Libraries during 1976. The Friends of California Libraries, an active statewide Friends Group, produced a kit which includes practical information on starting a Friends Group, sample by-laws, bond issues, and other pertinent information. It is available for a small charge. *Tips from CLIP,* the Coordinated Library Information Program, Inc., Madison, Wisconsin, in its May-June 1976 issue carried an article of interest to Friends Groups; the Pennsylvania Library Association included a special Friends program at the annual convention in September in Pittsburgh. The Friends of Tompkins County Public Library, Ithaca, New York, reported that people from their group led a panel discussion on the "Role Friends Can Play in Library Fund Raising, Programming, and Running a Book Sale" at the North Country 3-"R" Council Meeting in Massena, New York. An infrequent nationwide Friends newsletter published by Northland Public Library, Pittsburgh, carries news and articles of specific interest on Friends. Plans are for this small scale publishing venture to continue on an experimental basis until it has been determined whether there is a real demand for a Friends of Libraries newsletter.

LAURA SHELLEY

Furniture and Equipment

Notwithstanding taxpayers' revolts and tight municipal budgets that have affected many public libraries and "zero" budgets and projections of declining enrollment which bode ill for many educational institutions, the number of library building projects continues to be significant. That there continues to be great interest in new building projects and reasonable prospects of their completion is attested to by the more than 500 attendees at the Library Buildings and Equipment Institute sponsored by the Library Administration Division's Building and Equipment Section before last summer's American Library Association Convention. Of course, not all of these projects involve entirely new buildings; a significant number involve additions to existing structures or renovation of existing space or both. But whether the space provided is entirely new or at least partly incremental, in nearly every case there is a requirement for new furniture and equipment. Reviewed here are the current state of the library furniture industry and new products, systems, and materials available to librarians planning for new or additional library space.

The industry that supplies furniture and equipment to libraries continues in a state of instability, with some firms no longer in business and replaced by new, untested manufacturers. There have been few really new products or concepts, nor have there been many new lines of wood library furniture.

THE INDUSTRY

Most of the manufacturers whose names are familiar to librarians continue in business, although there are exceptions. Virginia Metal Products, a long established manufacturer of steel library shelving, has gone out of business. There were rumors in 1976 that others with familiar names were having problems and it was certainly true that some manufacturers were much less active than they once were in bidding what work was available. Sjostrom, now a part of Gunlocke (a manufacturer of quality seating), seemed to be on its way back. Worden, a familiar name for some years, seemed to have upgraded its product and was attempting to make its presence felt in the high-quality market. Risom, at one time a significant factor in the industry but lately inactive, seemed to be ready to reenter competition effectively with new ownership. Hallowell, a respected fabricator of steel, began to manufacture the well known Ames line on the east coast and may well become a factor in the steel shelving industry. Fancher is a new manufacturer of what seems to be good quality wood library furniture. Another new manufacturer of wood technical furniture is Magna Design of Lynnwood, Washington. But the most interesting story is that of Library Bureau, the pioneer firm in the manufacture of library furniture and equipment, which seemed to be having a rebirth at age 100.

The Library Bureau. The Library Bureau was established in 1876 by some of the founding librarians at the first meeting of the American Library Association. The lack of a con-

Furniture and Equipment

sistent supply of suitable "library fittings" encouraged those gentlemen to organize a firm to make available such furniture, equipment, and supplies to libraries and call it the Library Bureau. In 1925 the Library Bureau merged with Rand Kardex, which in turn merged with Remington Typewriter Company in 1927, bringing about the establishment of Remington-Rand, Inc. In 1955 Remington-Rand and Sperry-Gyroscope combined into Sperry-Rand, the corporation of which Library Bureau until recently was a part. As the conglomerate became larger and more complex, Library Bureau became a proportionately less important segment of it. Librarians familiar with the Library Bureau situation during the 60's and early 70's could not help being concerned about the way this large multinational corporation was operating Library Bureau. For, although many excellent firms compete for the business of libraries throughout the country, Library Bureau had a unique position because of its longevity and stability as well as by virtue of its being the firm that offered, in the view of many, the most nearly complete line of library furniture and equipment.

Throughout this period many who were interested in the fortunes of Library Bureau became more and more concerned about its inability to develop new products and market them as effectively as it was capable of doing. It became apparent that the strictures of corporate management and finance precluded the continuing development of the firm.

There were rumors of Library Bureau's being sold off, and on at least one occasion LB executives and others attempted to purchase the firm from Sperry-Rand. But on March 29, 1976, Sperry-Rand "exploded a bombshell" in the Mohawk Valley, where Library Bureau's Herkimer, New York, plant is located when it announced that the firm was closing down Library Bureau. The Mohawk Valley was already suffering an unemployment rate of 13.7 percent of the labor force compared to the national rate of 7 percent. The addition of 270 Library Bureau employees would have made that appalling figure even worse. From the standpoint of librarians who purchase furniture and equipment, the loss of Library Bureau with its wide and varied line of dependable products would have caused a considerable problem. This is especially true for those librarians who own substantial amounts of Library Bureau furniture and equipment that need to be matched in the future. Further, the library furniture and equipment industry is not large enough nor stable enough to suffer the loss of such an important component. The presence in the industry of a firm such as Library Bureau encourages other firms to maintain standards of manufacturing quality and marketing expertise that might otherwise not be necessary. Even competing firms generally agree that the loss of Library Bureau to the industry would not be good even though it might offer them a temporary sales and financial advantage.

The employees and executives of Library Bureau, along with a number of prominent citizens in the Mohawk Valley, decided that Library Bureau could not be permitted to die without a fight. The community was quickly organized, and Sperry-Rand was approached about a possible selling price. After some persuasion, Sperry-Rand set a sale price for the Division which the community then set out to meet. Leadership came from many sources. Initially, Congressman Don Mitchell of the 31st District contacted Richard Rifenburgh, a Herkimer-based corporate executive who became the prime mover in the campaign. Rifenburgh, 44, is a self-made millionaire who looks more like a professional football player than a business executive and had been to a large extent responsible for the early success of Mohawk Data Science Corporation, an important manufacturer of computer equipment. Rifenburgh, along with Library Bureau executives and employees and local officials, immediately began to put together a package from a number of sources that would enable them to purchase the company. The financial plan arrived at involved a $2,000,000 loan from the Federal Economic Development Administration, $2,000,000 in loans from local banks, and at least $1,500,000 through sales of common stock of Library Bureau. First, it was necessary to raise enough funds to pay for the initial cost of the campaign; $16,000 was quickly raised locally to pay for the cost of printing and mailing and other minor expenses.

The campaign began July 1. The corporate entity founded to raise the public equity funds, Mohawk Valley Community Corporation, was empowered to sell up to 905,000 shares of common stock at $2 a share. If MVCC met its minimum requirement by August 16, it would have the necessary equity to raise $4,000,000 in debt funds. The campaign was staffed by Library Bureau employees and other volunteers and all segments of the community joined in the effort. Local media cooperated fully with considerable coverage of the cam-

Children enjoying the modern furniture at the new Fretz Park Branch of the Dallas Public Library.

(Above) Lobby display panels by Multiplex Display Fixture Company use burlap over pegboard for displaying heavy items. (Right) Graphics displayer by Reflector Hardware Corporation has swinging panels with protective plastic for wall or upright mounting.

paign and a good deal of TV and radio time was made available. Library Bureau employees and local citizens canvassed door to door asking Mohawk Valley citizens to buy stock in the new company. Lt. Gov. Mary Ann Krupsak made a special trip from Albany to appear on a TV talk show concerning the campaign, and she also purchased stock for children in her family. Senators Jacob Javits and James Buckley worked hard in public support of the campaign. As the campaign neared its end the group was still short with one day left to raise the money. On that final day, more than $500,000 came in, raising the total support to more than $100,000 over what was needed. "Community support approached a religious fervor," said Rifenburgh. "It's the first time I ever saw the entire Mohawk Valley band together from Utica all the way down to Little Falls for one common project." Although most of the 3,500 stockholders came from within the Mohawk Valley, there were many from various other parts of the state. There was not a single large investor. Library Bureau employees, almost without exception, invested their own dollars in the campaign and now own approximately 30 percent of the company.

As a result of this successful stock sale and the bank loans that were provided on the basis of this equity investment, Library Bureau is no longer a part of its former parent corporation, Sperry-Rand. It is in a position to set its own destiny and can continue to be a significant factor in the library furniture industry.

Rest of the Industry. The Library Bureau is not the only major supplier of the library furniture industry. Sjostrom, another mainstay in the industry for many years, went through three changes of ownership within ten years and its stability, and indeed continued existence, has been questioned. There have even been problems at times in maintaining its well known high standards of quality. The Gunlocke Chair Co. of Wayland, New York, an old line manufacturer of high quality seating, acquired Sjostrom several years ago to form a new combination. However, the vicissitudes of opening a new factory for the Sjostrom line, along with a new management, combined to produce serious problems for the continued operation of the company and the manufacture of library furniture of high quality. Finally, however, many of these difficulties seem now to have been overcome and at year's end most observers were optimistic about the future of Sjostrom/Gunlocke.

A less happy story was that of Virginia Metal Products, a long time manufacturer of steel library shelving. For many years this company had been known for building fine quality steel library shelving. However, in 1976 the firm was phased out by the conglomerate that owned it. The number of firms who make steel library shelving of the highest quality was reduced.

Another interesting case is that of Risom, Inc. For many years a well-known firm manufacturing high quality commercial seating, desks and other case goods, Risom during the 60's, began to manufacture a quite handsome line of durable library furniture. It was successful in providing a number of libraries with installations of high quality furniture. In the early 70's, however, the company experienced management problems. In 1976 some of the executives of the company and two of its affiliated concerns banded together and bought Risom from the conglomerate that owned it. They appear to be operating the firm with renewed vigor and capital and new ideas. It appears that Risom may again become a significant factor in the library furniture industry.

Worden, of Holland, Michigan, is another name familiar to librarians as a manufacturer of library furniture. They generally have been considered to offer a line that aims for the middle portion of the library market rather than the higher priced, quality market. They recently seemed to have made strenuous efforts to upgrade the product and at the year's end seemed to be changing their marketing approach to match it. Worden's new Addenda 2000 line is unusual. Four complete sublines, each with slightly different characteristics but utilizing many common components, are offered to suit the aesthetic concerns of different architects and designers.

Other manufacturers, including Library Bureau, also offered new lines with solid end panels, primarily in oak. Such solid end panels should be used with some caution. Careless maintainence personnel and users are likely to cause damage that is painfully obvious on such panels.

OTHER TRENDS,
SYSTEMS, AND PRODUCTS

The trend of 1975, noted in the article in the previous edition of this *Yearbook*, toward increasing use of art, decorative objects, and living plants in libraries, continued in 1976. An example of a library that makes heavy and effective use of this approach is the Canadian Institute for Scientific and Technical Information (Canada's national science library) in Ottawa. It utilized such treatment as enormous mobiles; one wall covered by an enormous quilt; two other walls that are made up of fluorescent tubes that light in interesting patterns; another wall that contains a number of artifacts, such as items of clothing, firearms, pictures, dried vegetables, and other artifacts; and finally, the *pièce de résistance,* a display wall with tiny lights that are activated by the green plants growing beneath. Another fine example, the new Seeley G. Mudd Learning Center at Oberlin College (Ohio), utilizes super graphics; a great variety of very attractive soft seating of various kinds; a plywood frame, carpet-covered artifical boulder for students to lie around on; a seminar room with one wall completely covered by a glossy photograph of motorcyclists; and a number of other interesting decorative features. Many other libraries are brightening their interiors with equally attractive decorative approaches. Users have reacted favorably to these interesting environments and it is certain that new libraries yet to be furnished will use some of the same or other techniques to achieve equally interesting results.

Functioning library furniture cannot be too wild or far out or it will not perform the function for which it is purchased. Card catalogs, for instance, must be able to hold cards effectively and economically and be accessible to users. Any design of card catalogs must take these considerations into account or the unit produced will be a failure. This is equally true of reader tables and chairs that are to be used by the great mass of persons using any library. There are opportunities, however, for innovation and advanced design in some of the peripheral items of library furnishings. Lounge seating is certainly the most obvious possibility for variation. Display devices that show special groups of library materials and direct users around the library offer considerable possibilities for variation and design. Gaylord, a supplier of library accessories and supplies, has begun marketing attractive and imaginative display devices that house current periodicals, paperback books, cassettes, phonorecords, and other materials. New exhibit and display systems such as the Scandinavian Library Center systems by Library Bureau offer possibilities for vitalizing the presentation of displays of library materials.

There continued to be great concern among librarians about the security of library materials. For some years a number of companies have offered systems that attempt to prevent the unauthorized removal of materials, and they have met with varying degrees of success. The problem of materials losses has become so serious for many librarians that the sales of such systems have increased markedly. Several new firms have entered the business along with the more established firms that have been offering such systems for several years. *Library Technology Reports* (November issue) published a comprehensive examination and analysis of these systems along with results of their operation in libraries who own them. Libraries are also becoming concerned with other aspects of library security and are increasingly utilizing sophisticated exit alarm systems, TV surveillance systems and similar devices to safeguard the property and safety of libraries and their users. (*See also* Security Systems.)

Furniture and Equipment

Sales of library exit alarm systems, such as this Checkpoint MK II installation, increased markedly in 1976.

Gifts, Bequests, Endowments

There do not seem to have been any astonishing developments in the area of nonprint hardware in 1976. The industry was going through a time of refinement and improvement of existing products rather than evolving new ones. The trend continued toward reducing the kinds of hardware in use with concentration on the more flexible kinds of hardware which have great amounts of software available. One new interesting development in this area is the recent availability of the Mini-Max Video Cassette System by Sony which utilizes 1/2 inch tape rather than the present standard 3/4 inch size. Both cassette player and video cassettes are much smaller and less expensive than those using 3/4 inch tape. If this format becomes the new standard size, it will reduce the storage requirement for both hardware and software.

For years many librarians searched vainly for a roll microfilm reader to replace the simple, inexpensive Recordak MPE-1 that Eastman Kodak formerly made. Bell and Howell's new 16.35, shown in prototype in 1976 and now in production, looks as if it may fill the bill. It seems to be simply constructed, relatively inexpensive, and easy to operate. Its screen will show the image of an entire newspaper page.   WILLIAM S. PIERCE

Gifts, Bequests, Endowments

By far the most important gift in 1976 was made by former President Gerald R. Ford. In a letter dated December 13, 1976, he donated his papers, related historical materials, and memorabilia to the National Archives and Records Service. The gift consists of his "papers, documents, correspondence, notes, books and other publications, photographs, films, recordings, works of art and similar historical materials" from the time he first ran for Congress in 1948 until his Presidential term ended January 20, 1977. Excluded are certain personal papers, mainly of family origin. It is expected that the gift will total some 11,300 cubic feet, some 10,500 of which came from his presidential years. The deed of gift provides that although the NARS will own and administer these materials, the papers are to be located in a Gerald Ford Library in Ann Arbor, constructed and owned by the University of Michigan, and the memorabilia will be in a museum to be erected by an "appropriate organization" in or near Grand Rapids.

Standards of access developed by the Society of American Archivists in 1973 will govern administration of the papers and unless specific items are protected by law, executive order or by the responsible librarian, restriction on access will not exceed thirteen years.

Ford became the first American President to make a gift of his presidential papers and memorabilia while still in office.

Many important gifts were made to libraries in the Bicentennial Year. Perhaps the most appropriate came from Rea E. Hooper of Los Angeles, a descendant of George Mason, who presented one of two known copies (the other is in England) of the broadside known as the Virginia Convention Resolution and Association to the University of Virginia. It was printed by Clementina Rind in Williamsburg in August 1774, and "committed Virginians to bring economic pressure on Great Britain for the repeal of acts passed by Parliament to punish Massachusetts for the Boston Tea Party."

Two libraries received gifts as their collections reached the 500,000-volume level. Friends of the library and alumni provided funds to purchase a copy of the very rare first edition of Hawthorne's *Fanshawe* for Bowdoin College, while the Friends of the University of California, Santa Cruz, presented a copy of Francisco Palou's rare *Relacion Historica de la Vida y Apostolicas Tareas del Venerable Padre Fray Junipero Serra . . .*, Mexico, 1787, to the library of that institution.

Grants. The New York Public Library, which received a grant of $1,000,000 from the Vincent Astor Foundation in 1975, with the income to be used to "support staff requirements and on-going library programs," accepted $50,000 in 1976 from the Charles E. Merrill Trust for "general support of the library's collections" and $100,000 (over four years) from the Pope Foundation for preservation of the newspaper *Il Progresso Italo-Americano*.

The William Penn Foundation gave $100,000 to the University of Pennsylvania Library's capital development program, largely to endow both general and special collections, while Dr. and Mrs. Joe Potash of Cazenovia, N.Y., gave more than 500 items to the Syracuse University Library Associates to be sold at their antiquarian book auction. Included were two letters written by Abraham Lincoln, as well as letters signed by three other presidents, and others prominent in the decade of the 1860's.

A grant of $176,000 given jointly by the National Endowment for the Humanities and the Council on Library Resources to Barrow Preservation Research, Inc., of Richmond, Virginia, may produce results beneficial to all libraries. The grant was to "support a large scale test of the morpholine vapor deacidification process for preserving books" using a processor able to hold 50 to 100 volumes at a time.

Manuscripts and Archives. A number of important gifts of manuscripts and archives were made in 1976, and among them were the archives of the American Political Science Association, "amounting to more than 200,000 items covering over sixty years," to the Georgetown University Library; the archives of the late Avery Brundage, Chicago businessman and President of the U.S. Olympic Committee, President of the International Olympic Committee, and seven times President of the AAU, to the University of Illinois. This collection consisted of "correspondence, manuscripts, official papers, decorations, awards, and trophies" concerning national and international athletics, assembled by Brundage over a 45-year period.

Additional gifts of manuscripts were the Congressional papers and related materials consisting of over 200,000 items gathered over 30 years of service in the Congress by Robert L. Jones, to the University of Alabama, Huntsville; the business records (1830–1960) of the St. John d'el Ray Mining Company of Cleveland, Ohio, which operates mines in Brazil, to the Netti Lee Benson Latin American Collection, University of Texas; the correspondence (c.1850–1875) of William Chapman Ralston, founder of the Bank of California, to the Bancroft Library of the University of California, Berkeley; and a collection of about 2,000 manuscript items dealing with antislavery and reform from the family records of Isaac Post (1798–1872), given by Mrs. Ruden W. Post, Rochester, N.Y., to the University of Rochester.

The Universalist Historical Society presented its library to the Andover-Harvard Theological Library. It consisted of 5,000 books, 2,220 bound periodicals, 672 volumes of manuscripts, 1,600 pamphlets, pictures, slides, scrapbooks, oral history tapes, biographical files on members, and files about churches. Combined with other holdings, Andover-Harvard now has the "richest collection available of Unitarian Universalist historical archives."

Helen Galston Tibbe of Menlo Park, California, gave the Galston-Busoni Archives and the Galston Music Collection "2,000 pieces of music for piano, mss, letters and memorabilia" associated with the lives of composer-conductor Ferrucio Busoni and concert pianist Gottfried Galston, to the University of Tennessee Library, Knoxville; a distinguished southwest architect, John Gaw Meem, placed his archives and library in the Zimmerman Library of the University of New Mexico. A complementary gift by Meem and his wife consists of the papers of William R. Buckley; Jean Gould, noted biographer, presented many of her papers to the University of Toledo; the Canadian Consulate General in cooperation with the Canadian Broadcasting Corporation, donated a "sound archive" consisting of more than 1,000 "recordings of music and the spoken word of Canada in English, French and Spanish" to the New York Public Library; and the Jules C. Alciatore family gave 373 Beyle manuscripts (1618–1913), 600 volumes of editions of Beyle's works and about 2,300 volumes about Beyle and "related literary subjects" to Tulane University Library.

Betty Ford presents Hardy Franklin, Public Library Director, Washington, D.C., with gift books during visit to the Martin Luther King Memorial Library in January.

Other Gifts. Among the many reported in 1976 was a gift of "95 volumes of letterbooks and financial records of the Astor family," 1807–1918, by the New York Historical Society. The Society also received one of eight known copies of Reynard and Lodowick's *Journal of the Late Actions of the French at Canada . . .*, London, 1693, which concerns the battle for the Mohawk Valley in the King William's War.

A collection titled the "Madison People's Poster and Propaganda Collection," of some 25,000 pieces of student activism ephemera, was presented to the State Historical Society of Wisconsin; the late James A. Healy gave more than 1,000 books and periodicals and some 3,200 manuscripts dealing with the Irish literary movement to the Stanford University Libraries. The Reverend Paul C. Richards, "semi-retired antiquarian books and autograph dealer," presented a major collection of Theodore Roosevelt material to the Mugar Memorial Library of Boston University. Included were more than 100 original Roosevelt manuscripts, almost 700 unpublished letters, as well as photographs, campaign items, and other memorabilia.

Other gifts of subject interest include, from Ring Lardner, Jr., a gift of letters and other items, including his father's first publication, *Zanzibar* (of which only one other copy is known), to the Lardner collection at the Newberry Library, Chicago. The John M. Shaw gift to Florida State University of 200 volumes expanded a special collection designed "to honor the Scottish folk who conquered the wilderness of Northwest Florida". John W. Shleppey gave his American Indian collection to the University of Tulsa. Shleppey, a Seattle collector and dealer over a 40-year period, had put together a collection of some 6,000 bibliographic items (not counting manuscripts, photos, and documents) which was unusually

Gifts, Bequests, Endowments

strong in materials about Indian law. Henry C. Crapo donated to the University of Waterloo Library more than 200 volumes concerning the dance and the opera. In the collection are Antonius Arena's *Basses Dances* (Lyon, 1535); Negri's *Nuove Inventioni di Balli* (Milan, 1604); and Caroso's *Nobilita di Dance* (Venice, 1605). Several unusual 18th century manuscripts also are in the collection. Dr. and Mrs. Nathan S. Kolins of Tucson, Arizona, presented the library of the late G. Ernest Wright, a Harvard professor, to the University of Arizona. This 700-volume library "contains virtually all theological commentaries on the Hebrew bible that were published in English, French, German and other languages between 1930 and 1974." The late Alberta Hirshheimer Burke left about 1,000 volumes by and relating to Jane Austen, "one of the largest collections of Austen memorabilia in the United States," to the Goucher College Library, Towson, Maryland; Mr. and Mrs. David Mills gave an "important and comprehensive collection of John Masefield books and manuscripts" to Bryn Mawr College. In the collection were autographed manuscripts of *Jim Davis* and *The Past of Holy Peter*, typed manuscripts of *Reynard the Fox*, *Son of Adam* and *Minnie Maylow's Story*, autograph letters of Mayfield, and "an impressive collection of *Reynard the Fox* imprints." Aaron M. Orange gave to the Library of the City College, City University of New York, an important collection of books and memorabilia concerning the pioneer anthropologist Lewis Henry Morgan, which included first editions of all of his works, biographical material and assorted pamphlets.

The Stony Brook Foundation presented a collection of more than 5,000 photographs and other memorabilia of the Long Island Railroad to the library of SUNY, Stony Brook. The collection, which had been assembled by Robert Emery, retired Long Island Railroad conductor, has rare photos, unusual maps, scale drawings, crew sheets, track diagrams and timetables, 1885–1968. Joao R. Rocha, editor-publisher of the Portugese language *Diaro de Noticas* (New Bedford), presented a complete file of that newspaper to Southwestern Massachusetts University Library.

Bucknell University accepted more than 900 items from the library of the late LaFayette Butler of Hazleton. The University was allowed to choose 2,500 volumes from Butler's library, and among those selected were a group of Aldine press books, first and second Shakespeare folios, a 1676 *Hamlet*, as well as letters and manuscripts of D. H. Lawrence, George Moore, and Norman Douglas. The late Charles Midlow, New Orleans, left Tulane University Library a collection which had more than 11,000 bookplates, 400 volumes about bookplates, and "related graphic arts," and about 800 color transparencies.

Mrs. Henry W. Bopp, Terre Haute, Indiana, presented bibles and medieval books to Trinity College Library, Hartford, Connecticut. Among the books received were a Venice, 1483 Vulgate, a 1560 Geneva "Breeches" bible, and the three editions of the Sauer *Bible* (Germantown, 1743, 1763, 1776), as well as a 1568 Vesalius *De humani corporis fabrica*.

Herman Lande of New York City gave Elmira College a collection of rare books and other items, including first editions, first issues of *On the Origin of Species . . .* (1859), *An Essay Concerning Human Understanding* (1690), and Blake's Illustrations to the *Book of Job* (1826). Americana included a fine copy of Franklin's *Poor Richard Improved* (1766) and *Proceedings of a Board of General Officer's . . . Respecting Major John Andre* (September 29, 1780). With these came autograph letters of each member of the Board, including Generals Van Steuben, Greene, and LaFayette.

William N. Eisendrath, Jr., presented a collection consisting of 700 art books and monographs, 2,770 major exhibit catalogs, and 1,800 minor catalogs and pamphlets, to the University of Missouri, St. Louis. The collection is particularly strong in "modern and contemporary art and contains numerous exhibit catalogs of minor artists."

Henry A. Kissinger presented his papers to the Library of Congress on November 12, 1976. The gift includes his personal papers, copies of government papers on which he had worked, and transcripts of his office telephone conversations. The papers are closed for 25 years or until his death, whichever is later, although under certain circumstances earlier access will be permitted.

The Andrew W. Mellon Foundation gave $190,000 to Princeton University to improve user access to the collection through use of the library's new automated circulation system.

The late Frederich W. Hilles established an endowed chair in English, a publication fund and funds for the library, as well as leaving his personal collection to Yale University. His library consists of 6,000 volumes, some 2,000 rare books and 1,500 manuscript items, including letters by Sir Walter Scott, James Boswell, Thomas Carlyle, Edmund Burke, and Lord Chesterfield.

William P. Wadsworth of Geneseo presented the "Homestead Papers" to the Milne Library, SUNY, Geneseo. These papers, which date from the late 18th century through 1915, require 90 feet of shelving, and constitute "an invaluable source record for more than a century of history in the Genesee Valley."

NEH. The National Endowment for the Humanities awarded $104,207 to the American Antiquarian Society to organize and prepare for publication a catalog of the more than 500,000 manuscripts in the Society's collections which relate to the United States, 1621 to the early 20th century. The Newberry Library of Chicago will produce an *Atlas of Great Lakes Indian History* for the Great Lakes-Ohio Valley, 1615–1871, aided by an NEH grant of $173,642 and a gifts and matching grant of an additional $180,000.

NEH also made a challenge grant offer to the New York Public Library which could reach $3,000,000. NEH will match funds raised as follows: on a 1 to 1 basis for the first $500,000, 1 to 2 on the second $500,000 and 1 to 3 on the 3rd $500,000 (for each of two years). Since 1972, NEH has supported the development of NYPL research facilities with gifts and matching grants totalling $3,500,000. NEH, in addition, gave $100,000 and the National Science Foundation $39,000 to Ignace J. Gelb of the University of Chicago, "to compile a source book on the social and economic history of the ancient Near East." The book "demonstrates the wide range of sources available" and contain illustrations of original documents with English translations. — CLYDE C. WALTON

Government Documents Round Table

The Government Documents Round Table is an active membership unit of the American Library Association. Working through its various task forces, GODORT provides a centralized forum for the discussion of concerns and the exchange of ideas in the documents field. The individual task forces of GODORT were created to deal with specific types of documents (state, local, federal, and international) or to address specific interest areas in which documents librarians experience some unique problems (microforms, organization and administration, education, and machine-readable data files). The Government Documents Round Table provides a force for initiating and supporting programs designed to increase the availability, use, and bibliographic control of documents.

Since its founding in 1972, GODORT has produced a bimonthly newsletter, *Documents to the People*, and work was underway in 1976 to produce an index to this newsletter. *Documents to the People* reports on current developments, government programs, state and local workshops, and legislative activity affecting documents librarianship. In 1976 considerable coverage was given to the federal copyright law revision, the Freedom of Information Act and the Privacy Act, and "government in the sunshine" legislation which calls for more open meetings of government agencies.

GODORT serves as a continuing information exchange and also as a liaison between documents librarians and other interest units within ALA. At the 1976 Annual Conference in Chicago, GODORT and the Federal Librarians Round Table co-sponsored a major program, "The Dynamics of Federal Information: A Bicentennial Update" covering national documentation and control, and national resources and services. GODORT has also sent a representative to the meetings of the Catalog Code Revision Committee to provide information on the specific needs of documents librarians.

In an effort to improve the access to government documents and promote their widest possible use, GODORT task forces have provided advice to the federal depository library program and various operations of the U.S. Government Printing Office, have developed guidelines and standards for servicing of state documents, and have established a clearinghouse for the exchange of state documents classification schemes. GODORT developed the ALA resolution enforcing the principle that publications produced with public monies should remain free of copyright constraints. The production of a bibliographic guide to municipal publications was explored by the Local Documents Task Force during the year, and the International Documents Task Force plans to compile a directory of collections of foreign documents within the U.S.

GODORT seeks members from all types of libraries and encourages its members to participate actively in state and international associations. The Round Table encourages research relating to government publications and promotes workshops, seminars, and training programs for documents. As recognition of the importance of documents librarianship, the Government Documents Round Table has established two awards. In 1975 it created the James Bennett Childs Award for outstanding contribution to the field of documents librarianship and the first award was officially presented in August 1976 to Childs himself in a ceremony held at the Library of Congress. In July a second award, the CIS/GODORT/ALA "Documents to the People" Award, was established to honor the individual and/or library that has most effectively encouraged the use of federal documents in support of library services. This award includes a grant of $1,000 "to promote professional advancement in the field of documents librarianship."

GODORT is recognized as a respected representative able to speak for the problems, needs, and goals of documents librarians.

— NANCY CLINE

GODORT Officers

COORDINATOR (July 1976–June 1977):
Nancy Cline, Pennsylvania State University

ASSISTANT COORDINATOR:
Lois Mills, Western Illinois University

SECRETARY:
Robert Schaaf, Library of Congress

Membership (August 31, 1976): 1,114

Staff member Marta Velasquez finds shelving space a problem in the government publications section of the Wyoming State Library.

Government Publications and Depository System

U.S. Government documents remain a rich and varied body of material. The Government Printing Office, headed by the Public Printer, Thomas F. McCormick, played a key role in 1976 as it maintained a great flow of information perhaps unique in the world, through its printing, sale, and other distribution of documents. Direct sale of publications, according to an estimate by McCormick, accounted for some 81,000,000 publications in Fiscal Year 1975, 84,000,000 in FY 1976, and 87,000,000 in FY 1977. Perhaps an even more significant outlet for a substantial portion of this massive flow of material from the government to the people was the distribution of documents to some 1,200 designated deposit libraries, where nearly all the material is retained and made freely available to the public. (For a brief history of the depository system and pertinent legislation, see *The ALA Yearbook*, 1976 edition, p. 177.)

While there were 1,183 deposit libraries by the end of 1975, additional designations brought the total to 1,201 by October 19, 1976.

By October there were 40 states served by regional depositories—libraries agreeing to receive all depository material—and one more regional designation (the University of Georgia) was pending.

Increased Distribution to Deposit Libraries. The Superintendent of Documents, through its Library and Statutory Distribution Service, distributed about 13,000,000 documents to deposit libraries in FY 1976, about 3,250,000 in the transition period July–September 1976, and was expecting to distribute about 13,400,000 in FY 1977. This may be compared with 10,600,000 in 1974 and 11,800,000 in FY 1975. To handle the deposit distribution efficiently, the GPO completed the centralizing and semi-automation of the system, using rented warehouse space in the Eisenhower complex, Alexandria, Virginia.

ALA Commendation. The Government Documents Round Table and its Federal Documents Task Force in a resolution passed at the 1976 ALA Conference formally commended the work of the Library and Statutory Distribution Service and its Director, John D. (Jim) Livsey. This action represented something of a departure, as GODORT in its four-year existence had often been critical of the performance of the GPO and its components.

Inspection Program. By October 1976 a total of 703 libraries had been inspected by Superintendent of Documents representatives. A major purpose of the program was to help the depository libraries and their librarians carry out most effectively the mission of the depository program—to bring public documents to the public. Prior to 1975, when the inspections began, the Government relied on a biennial questionnaire sent to all deposit libraries.

Microfiche Program. A pilot program involving the distribution of a microfiche edition of *Code of Federal Regulations* to selected libraries began in November 1975 (see *The ALA Yearbook*, 1976 edition, pp. 71–72). By March a complete microfiche edition of *CFR 1975* was made available to project libraries. An evaluation report dated June 30 was prepared and submitted to the Joint Committee on Printing, with GPO's recommendations to expand the microform program for deposit documents.

In mid-October the GPO received the Joint Committee on Printing's authorization to continue the *CFR*, on microfiche, as an option to deposit libraries, but not for sale. As of February 22, 1977, the Library and Statutory Distribution Service announced that the JCP had NOT authorized "microform activity for Depository distribution." In effect, the microfiche program was stalled again.

IMPROVED COMMUNICATIONS

The semiannual meetings with the Depository Library Council continued to be an important means of exchanging information with the library community.

Publications. A wide variety of publications enhanced communication with the GPO's public and promoted better knowledge and utilization of documents. These included the following: (1) A drastically expanded and refined *Monthly Catalog of U. S. Government Publications*, effective with the July issue, the first issue for Fiscal Year 1977; (2) a monthly annotated list of GPO publications for sale, *Selected United States Government Publications*, mailed free to nearly a million recipients; (3) a bimonthly newsletter, in its second year, *Public Documents Highlights*, prepared by the Superintendent of Documents' Library and Statutory Distribution Service, which provides a useful exchange and sharing of information, primarily for librarians at the some 1200 depository libraries; (4) *Subject Bibliographies (SB's)*, succeeding the *Price Lists* formerly published by the Superintendent of Documents; the *SB's* are mainly subject or agency lists of publications in stock at the GPO, with more specific headings than the *Price Lists*; (5) the bimonthly *GPO Newsletter*, issued by the Office of the Public Printer as a medium of information for the myriad of federal agencies the GPO serves as printer and distributor; (6) a new edition (scheduled for issuance in spring 1977) of the invaluable *List of Classes of U. S. Government Publications Available for Selection by Depository Libraries*, as of March 1977; (7) a helpful new tool for the use of depository libraries, *Inactive or Discontinued Items from the 1950 Revision of the Classified List*, revised August 1976; (8) a *GPO*

Publications Reference File, distributed initially to the 48 regional deposit libraries and other selected depositories in each state. This reference file, previously an "in-house" tool for the GPO, is an in-print list on 48X microfiche of all GPO sales publications, to be updated monthly; (9) numerous announcements published on the GPO's *Daily Depository Shipping List,* received by some 1,200 deposit libraries with shipments of documents; and (10) a five-year plan for Fiscal Years 1978–1982 was under review by McCormick early in 1977.

Relocation. In December 1976 it was announced that the National Capital Planning Commission had approved the relocation of the GPO and its nearly 8,000 employees from its present location on North Capitol Street to a site about a mile away, in the Brentwood section of Washington.

ARNE H. RICHARDS

REFERENCES

U.S. House of Representatives, Committee on Appropriations, Subcommittee on Legislative Branch Appropriations, *Legislative Branch Appropriations for 1977, Hearings...* (94th Congress, 2d Session, esp. pp. 497–553).

LeRoy C. Schwarzkopf, "Fall 1976 Meeting of Depository Library Council to the Public Printer," in *Documents to the People,* v. 5, no. 1 (January 1977), pp. 6–13.

Public Documents Highlights (all issues), published by Superintendent of Documents, Library and Statutory Distribution Service.

Health and Rehabilitative Library Services

Library services for the exceptional person include those provided for the gifted, and persons impaired because of sensory deviations, motor disturbances, disorders of speech and language, mental retardation, and personality and character disorders. Such service has been marked by a continuum beginning with segregation and restriction of resources, extending to provision of resources required for physical existence, and is now leading to their incorporation into existing dominant social systems. Recognition of the members of society who are also persons with special needs brings both identification and labeling problems. The process in itself may create a handicap and exacerbate conditions as individuals so marked are treated differently from others. Ironically, this very process of identification has enabled increasing numbers of people to receive library services, often in institutions, more recently in the community. It can contribute to segregation in adult years.

Attempts by librarians to overcome homogeneity in the perception of exceptional people is central to "mainstreaming." Mainstreaming, concerned with efforts to incorporate the exceptional into the dominant social system, was realized in 1976 in legislation, policies, and changes in basic social attitudes as planning and programming moved toward innovation. The idea of making the full range of library services available to the general public equally available to the exceptional, however, is a product of many decades.

Legislation. Action in the areas of health and rehabilitative library services in 1976 were marked by changes in law and personal commitment. The Education of All Handicapped Children Act of 1975 (Public Law 94-142) was intended to assure that every child categorized as "handicapped" had access to free appropriate public education. Passed in November 1975, this legislation requires that from 1978 all states must locate and provide tangible programs and authorizes federal financing at an eventual level of 40 percent of the excess cost of education of handicapped students. It was estimated that this will eventually provide up to one billion dollars a year in federal funds for special education. Action at the national, state, and local levels in 1976 was moving this promise forward to meet the needs of individual children through evaluation and updating of existing policies as well as the creation of new policies. The legislation goes farther than any other in prescribing the direction of federal education policy establishing priorities to serve children currently unserved and to serve children with the most severe handicaps who are inadequately served. A deadline of September 1, 1978, was set for all states to provide programs for all handicapped children between the ages of 3 and 18; a second deadline, September 1, 1980, extends the maximum age to 21. Unless those requirements are met, and following reasonable notice and opportunity for hearing, funding must be withheld from the school district or state involved. Specifically, the act requires that each handicapped child have an individualized, written program designed in consultation with parents, the teacher, and, if appropriate, the child, to be reviewed and revised at least annually.

Basic to realization of this legislation are changes in the ways in which the exceptional are coming to perceive themselves and their relationship to society. Concern with living, working, transportation, education, and rehabilitation environments was seen at the state

A new jukebox adds sparkle and sound to the library of the Leesville State School in Louisiana.

Health and Rehabilitative Library Services

level in 1976 during meetings and conferences held in anticipation of the 1977 White House Conference on Handicapped Individuals. The state and regional meetings generated data that will serve as a statement of rights for the exceptional and enable national and state legislators to introduce legislation to meet the special requirements and address major problems confronting disabled citizens. The ALA Council has requested consideration of library services within the national conference and librarians contributed to state and regional meetings.

Support Services. The year 1976 also brought a restructured program of media and materials support services by the U. S. Bureau of Education for the Handicapped, H.E.W., Learning Resources Branch (BEH/LRB). The National Center on Educational Media and Materials for the Handicapped (NCEMMH) became a centralized unit, at Ohio State University, supported by four specialized offices and 13 learning resource centers. This program, designed to interface with state and local media-materials programs, provides services where appropriate materials do not exist, where users of materials are not aware of existing materials, where users know about the availability of existing materials but do not have physical access, and where materials are accessible but the user does not know how to use them effectively. The Center, established by the U.S. Congress through Public Law 91-61, is providing leadership, needs analysis, instructional resource development, information and delivery systems, and enhancement of teacher competencies.

Expanding Programs. Librarians' advocacy of legislation, conferences, and experimentation have become interdisciplinary, and local support, now tangibly translated to state and national levels, is resulting in widened attention to the needs of all library users. In 1976 the ALA Health and Rehabilitative Library Services Division (HRLSD, formerly the Association of Hospital and Institution Libraries) actively expanded its responsibilities to include new service areas and programs. With emphasis on change in purpose and organizational structure, HRLSD selected five priority objectives in support of major ALA goals: (1) development of conference programs, (2) expansion and improvement of publications, (3) development of chapter relations, (4) programs of continuing education, and (5) increased involvement with all facets of the library community. (*See further* Health and Rehabilitative Library Services Division.)

Programs included strengthened liaison with the International Federation of Library Associations; close cooperation with the President's Committee on Employment of the Handicapped, especially in areas of physical access and personnel standards; development of library standards for those with visual and hearing impairments; finalization of new *Standards for Juvenile Correctional Institutions* and the soon to be published *Standards for Library Services for Adult Correctional Institutions*; development of guidelines for patient health education; creation of a Bibliotherapy Discussion Group; completion of a study on Vocational Materials for the Physically Handicapped conducted by the Section on Library Services to the Blind and Physically Handicapped.

Conference Program. The American Library Association's Centennial Conference included a three-day Preconference Institute, "Mainstreaming the Exceptional Child in the Library," co-sponsored with the American Association of School Librarians, the Children's Services Division, and the Public Library Association. A major workshop program emphasizing the special needs of the aging was co-sponsored with the American Library Trustee Association, the Association of State Library Agencies, the Public Library Association, the Reference and Adult Services Division, and the Library Services to the Disadvantaged Advisory Committee. The HRLSD Awards Luncheon honored Charles Gallozzi, recipient of the Francis Joseph Campbell Citation, and Earl C. Graham, recipient of the 1976 Exceptional Service Award. Dr. Walter Menninger of the Menninger Foundation, keynote speaker, addressed the topics of health education and consumerism. The Conference closed with creation of a new Section on Library Services to Prisoners.

Technological Developments. Technological development increased the potential for librarians in meeting the needs of the exceptional. Examples include the Opticon reader, a compact device which allows the user to move an optical scanner across a printed page and to receive tactile impressions representative of the printed letters on the index finger of one hand; the Talking Calculator, which communicates with the user when buttons are depressed, providing both audio and visual output facilitating complex mathematical calculations; the Vocoder, which translates auditory signals into actual impressions for use by those with hearing and other sensory limitations; and the Optiscope Enlarger, for rapid enlargement of print. In addition, continuing research and experimentation with microfiche readers, computers, and specialized media opened possibilities for improved services.

Marked by the nation's Bicentennial and the American Library Association's Centennial, 1976 strengthened the commitment of librarians both ready and increasingly able to meet the demanding requirements of the needs of exceptional people, requirements dependent upon both skills and informed concern. (*See also* Blind and the Physically Handicapped, Library Service for the.) HARRIS C. MC CLASKEY

Health and Rehabilitative Library Services Division

The Health and Rehabilitative Library Services Division (HRLSD) completed its second full year as a division within the American Library Association in 1976. This newly formed division is an outgrowth of the old Association for Hospital and Institution Libraries (AHIL) and the Round Table for Library Service to the Blind. As national concern and awareness for integrating individuals who have exceptional or special needs into society at-large has increased, so has the activity of HRLSD. The primary purpose and concerns of this newly created division are:

> ... the educational, recreational, cultural, and rehabilitative development of persons needing library materials and services of a unique nature because of visual, physical, health, and/or behavioral problems, and the professional development of those providing these materials and services.

Responsibilities Outlined. Within the American Library Association, the Health and Rehabilitative Library Services Division has specific responsibility for:

1. Developing and implementing standards for library materials, services, and personnel, and fostering study and research.
2. Stimulating the professional growth and training of personnel.
3. Coordinating with all units of ALA, especially those programs and activities which relate to the concerns of this division.
4. Cooperating with governmental agencies, private organizations, and professional associations in interpreting and stimulating library services to these special groups.
5. Identifying the interests and needs of present and potential users and encouraging them to take advantage of the availability of these special library materials and services.
6. Enlisting assistance and support of civic groups, volunteers, news media, etc., in publicizing services.
7. Granting recognition for outstanding special library service.

Toward meeting the Division's stated purpose and responsibility to the library profession, and in addition to the on-going work of its committees, HRLSD sponsored two significant programs during the ALA Centennial Conference in Chicago. Developed and managed by HRLSD, a preconference institute, "*Mainstreaming the Exceptional Child in the Library*," was a highly successful program. Co-sponsored by the American Association of School Librarians (AASL), the Children's Services Division (CSD), and the Public Library Association (PLA), the goal of this program was to look at the library needs of children instead of applying the clinical or diagnostic labels as "mentally handicapped," "learning disabled," "physically handicapped," "hearing or vision impaired." The objectives of the 3-day preconference were "to understand exceptionality and attitudes within the library community" and "to develop skills, based upon present knowledge and experience, which can be used effectively in meeting the needs of each child." Moya M. Duplica, Associate Professor of Social Welfare, University of Washington School of Social Work, served as the Institute Coordinator. Burton Blatt, Director of the Division of Special Education and Rehabilitation, Syracuse University, and President-Elect of the American Association on Mental Deficiency, was the keynote speaker. HRLSD members served as resource specialists for the program. A workshop, entitled "Communicating with the Elderly," was an equally successful program for HRLSD during the Centennial Conference. Richard Calabrese, Department of Communication, Rosary College, was the workshop coordinator.

Regular publications of the Division include the *HRLSD Journal*, published semi-annually in the spring and the fall, and the *HRLSD Newsletter*, published irregularly. The theme of the spring issue of the journal focused on "Information Needs of the Hearing Impaired." Lee Putnam of Gallaudet College served as guest editor. Eunice Lovejoy, State Library of Ohio, was the guest editor for the fall issue which centered on "Library Services for the Blind and Physically Handicapped." At the Centennial Conference Robert Ensley was selected as the new editor of the *Journal*. The *Newsletter*, prepared in the HRLSD Office, helps to keep members advised about activities taking place in the field as well as to keep the membership informed about Divisional activities.

Through its Exceptional Service Award, HRLSD recognizes service of its members to the Division or to any of its component areas of service, namely services to clientele and professional and non-professional staff in hospitals, institutions, communities, health, rehabilitative, and special education agencies as well as the homebound. Earl C. Graham was the recipient of this award in 1976.

New Section Formed. In 1976, a new Section for Library Service to Prisoners (LSPS) was organized. The purpose of this Section is:

> To raise the consciousness level of people within the library and correctional communities regarding the urgent and particular library and information needs of all prisoners; to encourage and assist librarians to begin, expand, and improve library service to prisoners and correctional staff; to serve as a clearinghouse for information, ideas, materials, programs, and human resources for correctional library services; to contribute to and promote cooperation among the library communities and correctional agencies and

organizations; to initiate and support pertinent legislation; and to contribute to and promote the adoption and improvement of standards for correctional library service.

The Bylaws of the LSPS will come before the HRLSD Board of Directors at the 1977 Midwinter Meeting and will be voted on by the Membership at the Annual Conference in Detroit.

The HRLSD Section for Library Service to the Blind and Physically Handicapped serves librarians working with and interested in library service to the blind and physically handicapped. The purpose of the Section is:

> To extend and improve library service to those unable to read or use standard printed materials because of physical limitations; to provide a symposium for the exchange of ideas and personnel; to acquaint all librarians whose service communities may include blind and physically handicapped readers with the Section and to enlist their cooperation in meeting those objectives.

The LSBPH Section recognizes and honors librarians who have made outstanding contributions in the field for the advancement of library service to the blind with the Francis Joseph Campbell Award. This award was established in 1965 and was formerly administered by the Round Table on Library Service to the Blind. Charles Galozzi was the 1976 recipient of the Francis Joseph Campbell Award.

New Committees established in HRLSD in 1976 include Library Service to the Impaired Elderly, Standards for Libraries for the Mentally Retarded, and Standards for Library Service to the Blind and Physically Handicapped. In addition, Discussion Groups for Bibliotherapy and Library Service to the Hearing Impaired were organized.

Merger Planned. HRLSD, one of only three ALA divisions to increase in personal members and recognizing the need to become a self-supporting unit within ALA, jointly formed with the Association of State Library Agencies a Committee of their respective Boards to consider their commonalities of interests and possible solutions to the divisional status problem. This Committee met in Chicago on November 30–December 1. After carefully reviewing alternatives to division status within ALA, it was the unanimous decision of the Joint Committee that they recommend to their respective Boards a proposal for a merged division representing the interests and concerns of both groups. This proposal was unanimously adopted by both Boards on December 13 and will be submitted to the ALA Council at the 1977 Midwinter Meeting.

The HRLSD Office continues to provide a variety of information services. In addition to coordinating the many activities of the Division, it serves as a clearinghouse and referral agency for the HRLSD membership, other ALA units, and for outside organizations seeking information and assistance. MARY R. POWER

History

See *American Library History Round Table; American Library History.*

IFLA

The year 1976—the 49th year of the International Federation of Library Associations and Institutions (IFLA)—marked the beginning of a new IFLA era. At the 42nd General Council meeting, August 23–28 in Lausanne, Switzerland, members adopted unanimously new statutes and bylaws which provide a legal basis for a significant restructure of international library cooperation represented by IFLA. The change in name (the words "and Institutions" were added) reflects the fact that the emphasis on library associations has gradually been replaced by a joint responsibility for IFLA work by associations and institutions (primarily libraries and library schools alike). By October 1 IFLA membership encompassed 16 International Association Members, 124 National Association Members, 539 Institutional Members and Affiliates, and approximately 50 Personal Affiliates in 101 countries. The latter category is new for IFLA.

Organization. The coordination and execution of the professional work will in future be guided by a Professional Board. The Chairman of the Professional Board is an ex *officio* member of the Executive Board. The professional activities are concentrated in 24 sections for type of library and type of library activity. Each of these sections has a registered membership. The members of a section nominate and elect a standing committee: a core of experts guaranteeing the continuous progress of the work. The sections are coordinated by divisions. The Division for Regional Activities is an example of IFLA's movement into regional development programs. Planning has been made for South East Asia, Latin America and the Caribbean, and Africa. Regional offices have been set up in Kuala Lumpur, Malaysia,

---

HRLSD Officers

PRESIDENT:
Lethene Parks, Pierce County Library, Tacoma, Washington

VICE-PRESIDENT/PRESIDENT-ELECT:
Susan M. Haskin, Bureau of Library Services, Michigan Department of Education, Lansing, Michigan

EXECUTIVE SECRETARY:
Mary R. Power

Membership (August 31, 1976): 1,566 (548 personal and 1,018 organizational)

The New Constitution of IFLA

Below is an outline of the new structure highlighting the main changes and comparing them with former usage; it is hoped this presentation will make possible a better understanding of the cool and unexciting legal language in which the statutes are couched.

Name (Article 1). The name is expanded so as to include libraries and library schools which play an increasingly important role in IFLA. The name adopted is: International Federation of Library Associations *and Institutions*, to be designated by the acronym IFLA. This acronym will be the same for all languages.

Purposes (Article 2). In the old statutes, the object of the Federation was defined as follows: "to promote cooperation in the field of librarianship and bibliography, and particularly to carry out investigations and make propositions concerning the international regulations between libraries, library associations, bibliographers and other organized groups." The newly-defined purposes reflect the widening of IFLA's professional scope: "to promote international understanding, cooperation, discussion, research and development in all fields of library activity, including bibliography, information sciences, and the education of personnel, and to provide a body through which librarianship can be represented in matters of international interest." The second paragraph of Article 2 adds further that IFLA will cooperate with other international organizations in the information field and will set up offices to carry out specific tasks.

Membership, affiliation, and voting rights (Articles 3 and 12). Here a departure from past practice is evident. IFLA previously had two categories of Members: "Full (association) Members" with voting rights (one vote each) and "Associate Members (institutions)" without voting rights. IFLA will now consist of Association Members and Institutional Members, both categories with "voting rights in all meetings, and on all matters" (Article 12.1). In meetings other than Council meetings (for instance, meetings of Sections), each Member will have one vote, whether he is an Association Member or an Institutional Member. However, in Council meetings, Association Members have a number of votes determined by a classification into groups which is based on the amount of IFLA membership dues. In accordance with a rule of procedure adopted in Lausanne, there are four such groups, with 5, 10, 15, and 20 votes respectively. These votes are allotted to the total number of library associations in a given country (some countries have more than one library association which is an IFLA member. An example may prove useful here: the six Association Members from the Federal Republic of Germany will have to divide 20 votes between themselves. The Rules of Procedure ensure that Association Members will not be outvoted by Institutional Members in a Council meeting: Association Members must always have at least 51% of the total number of possible votes.

A new phenomenon is the "personal affiliate" without voting rights. For the first time, individuals can join IFLA if they wish to show their interest in and support of the Federation's goals.

Consultative Status (Article 4). Another new feature is the possible granting of consultative status to (i) international and multi-national library associations (upon appropriate application from the association); (ii) other international organizations (upon invitation by IFLA). In fact, international library associations now have a choice between Association membership and Consultative Status.

The Council (Articles 10 and 11). The Council is, of course, still the highest organ of the Federation, although formerly its title was "General Council." Voting by proxy is introduced in a minimal way in the new statutes. Article 11.5 allows a Member to be represented at a Council meeting by another Member of the same membership category, although it should be carefully noted that "no Member shall hold more than one proxy."

The Executive Board (Articles 14–16). The Executive Board of IFLA currently consists of one President and six Vice-Presidents. As of September 1977 the Executive Board will consist of one President, a first and a second Vice-President, a Treasurer, and 2–4 other members and, as an *ex officio* member, the Chairman of the Professional Board. A new Executive Board will be elected (President and 5 members of the Board) on September 3, 1977, at Brussels. During the anniversary meeting (5–10 September 1977), the old Board will continue to function.

The Professional Board (Articles 17–19). A fundamental difference between the old and the new statutes is to be noted in the creation of a Professional Board with extensive responsibilities and powers. The trend which was noticeable when the Programme Development Group was initiated in 1969, namely to shift the responsibility for professional planning and programming from the Executive Board to a body which would be better equipped to deal with IFLA's professional work, has now been institutionalized. The Professional Board will not be elected directly by the membership at large, but rather will consist of the chairmen of Divisions and chairmen of the Steering Committees of professional units, so as to ensure that professional matters are dealt with by those who are most competent. As eight Divisions and two professional units are currently foreseen, the first full Professional Board will consist of approximately 10 persons. For a transitional period (up to and including the Brussels meeting), a provisional Professional Board has been set up.

Divisions and Sections (Articles 20 and 21). Perhaps the most significant change in the organization of IFLA is the initiation of Sections (roughly comparable with the former Sections and Committees) which are grouped together in Divisions by type of library or by type of library activity. The statutes name only one Division specifically, the Division for Regional Activities. Other Divisions and Sections will be created upon recommendations of the Professional Board. For the time being, 24 Sections have been established, grouped in 8 Divisions (for further details, see "Draft Regulations for Divisions and Sections", Working Document IV for the Lausanne Council Meeting). The centre of the new structure will be at the sectional level, where—contrary to past practice—there will be fixed memberships (consisting of Members and Affiliates who register formally) and elected Standing Committees. The latter are to be elected by postal vote. To be placed on the ballot, a candidate must be nominated by at least three Members, irrespective of the type of Member or the country in which the Member is located. The intent of this procedure is clear: Members must feel a responsibility towards IFLA's professional work and support their representatives accordingly. Moreover, continuity in attendance at Section meetings might thereby be improved, although Section meetings will, of course, still remain open to all interested persons. The core of attendees will, however, consist of a distinctive group of experts. In the new structure of IFLA's professional work, Members will, it is hoped, truly have a feeling of belonging to the Federation, and their involvement in sectional work will strengthen this feeling.

A Division is the sum of the Sections belonging to it, and has a coordinating role. The management of a Division is entrusted to a Coordinating Board, consisting of the Chairmen and Secretaries of the Sections belonging to the particular Division. An example: the Division of Libraries Serving the General Public is composed of 4 Sections: Public Libraries, Children's Libraries, School Libraries, and Hospital Libraries. In this way, it is hoped that sound programming and efficient cooperation can be achieved and duplication of effort avoided.

Round Tables (Article 22). The possibility for setting up Round Tables, thereby enabling small groups of persons with similar professional background and a set of common problems to meet and exchange ideas, is yet another new feature of the constitution. Such Round Tables may be set up by Divisions or Sections, subject to the approval of the Professional Board. In Lausanne, one Round Table was in fact established, a Round Table of librarians representing centres of research and documentation in children's literature.

Transitional Period. During the transitional period, from the present up to and including the anniversary meeting in Brussels (September 1977), the officers of the Federation will carry on their various duties....

Dues. The present basis for the establishment of the dues of Association Members will be continued until December 31, 1979. The present basis is 0.1% of a country's annual Unesco assessment. These basic dues need to be paid jointly by the Association Members of a given country. During 1977, it will still be permissible for Association Members of a given country to deduct from that country's assessment the fees paid by their country's Institutional Members. As from January 1, 1978, this possibility will cease to exist.

At its 1977 meeting, the Council will decide on the amount of dues to be paid by Institutional Members and Affiliates in 1978. The Council will also set the maximum number of sectional registrations allowable for each category of membership, as well as the fee for additional registrations (which will come into effect in 1978).

Conclusion. The various main changes in the IFLA structure are justified by the need to give Institutional Members a say in the Federation's affairs and consequently to attract more Members to IFLA and give current Members the feeling that they truly belong, especially to specific Sections. Such a feeling will enhance the quality and the continuity of future professional work. The importance accorded to professional work is also evident from the creation of a Professional Board which is to give leadership in all professional matters. In short, IFLA has now moved towards a policy of stimulating its membership into active participation in all Federation affairs. MARGREET WIJNSTROOM,

Reprinted by courtesy of *IFLA Journal* (2-1976-4), pp. 224–227.

IFLA—Fifty Years of Service to International Librarianship

IFLA in 1977 celebrates its golden jubilee. But it might have been celebrating its centenary in 1976 with the ALA or in 1977 with the Library Association of the United Kingdom if the intentions of librarians at early meetings could have been realized. The first meeting in London was in fact called "the First International Conference of Librarians." In 1897 the ALA and the LA (UK) together organized the Second International Conference, which also attracted delegates from many countries, and a further Congress was held in Paris in 1900. Organized international cooperation was also discussed at meetings in St. Louis in 1904 and in Brussels in 1910. It was not until 1926, however, that further progress was made. At the "Congress international des Bbliothécaires et des Amis du Livres" held in Prague in 1926, Gabriel Henriot, President of the French Library Association, proposed the establishment of an Executive Committee made up of a delegate for each library association. This Committee was to work out a timetable for conferences, establish relations with the Institute for International Intellectual Cooperation of the League of Nations, formulate a scale of membership fees for member associations, defend library interests in the international field, organize international bibliographies, investigate relations between archivists and librarians, and, finally, examine various problems of interest to all members.

The Beginnings. This surely was to form the blueprint for future international activity and, if we read UNESCO for the IIIC, it is a summary in very broad outline of the work of what was to become IFLA over the years. In 1926, at the ALA jubilee conference in Atlantic City, major proposals were accepted in principle, but were referred to the various associations for consideration. In Edinburgh, the next year, the Section for International Library Cooperation of the Library Association once again considered the problems of an international organization. By this time, the lines of discussion had been clarified: there were three possibilities: (1) an organization based on the International Institute for Intellectual Co-operation; (2) a permanent office base in Paris, but independent of the IIIC; and (3) an organizing committee for conferences. The third proposition was accepted, probably from a desire to remain independent of an officially sponsored organization, and the realization that funds were not likely to be forthcoming for a permanent secretariat. The International Library and Bibliographical Committee was thus extablished in 1927—considered now IFLA's year of birth.

In 1928 delegates from 11 countries (including the United States) began planning in Rome for the first major conference to be held in that city the following year. The Committee also set up six subcommittees: classification schemes; cataloguing rules; bibliographies and an international code; international fellowships and exchanges; education for librarianship; and bylaws. In a further meeting in 1929, by which time 22 associations had joined, the name of the Committee was changed to the International Federation of Library Associations, the title only recently changed by the addition of "and institutions." The executive committee was called the "International Library Committee." The secretary was to be T. P. Sevensma, Librarian of the League of Nations. This pattern was to be followed for a number of years, continuity in particular being provided by Sevensma, to whom IFLA owes an immense debt. The International Library Committee's task was in fact to organize five yearly conferences, and to develop programs out of the conferences' discussions. The scale of meetings during this period was very small. In 1930, the year after the first congress, the attendance was 38 delegates with a total attendance of under 50. By this time there were 24 member associations representing 20 countries.

Early Development. The 1930 meeting at Stockholm provided the pattern of meetings during the period of Sevensma's tenure as Secretary: report of the Secretary; discussions of meetings raised by the Congress or the Committee, reports of subcommittees, reports from other organizations, discussion on future meetings, and national reports. Some of these proposals were followed up and some were not. However, it is interesting to note how proposals revive in the most unlikely places. In the last few years, a consistent proposal of the Section of Library Schools has been an International Library School, the practical result of which was a summer school held at Sheffield in 1975. (In 1930 Henriot had proposed an "Institut International des Bibliothécaires," for the advanced education for librarians from various countries, with a full-time course, and six months' summer courses.)

In 1932 the Secretary also proposed the standardization of national reports (a matter under discussion in the late 1970's by the Publication Committee). More important was the implementation of the International Loan Scheme, which ensured that books and journals could be lent freely from country to country. The achievement of IFLA in the years 1930–40 was indeed considerable, given the difficulties of international work, the lack of money, the lack of a permanent staff and the limited travel.

A second International Congress was organized in Madrid in 1935. The third congress would have been held in Germany had not the war broken out. In 1946 the Federation took up its international existence once more. In 1939 it had met (ironically) in a room at the Peace Palace. In 1947 it met at the Nobel Institute in Oslo, for the installation of the new President, W. Munthe, Director of the Oslo University Library. He succeeded Marcel Godet of Switzerland, who had been President since 1936 and who had kept IFLA alive during the war years.

Post-World War II Problems. The demands made upon libraries as the result of war conditions had increased; international loan had to be restored; stocks and libraries rebuilt; microfilm to be encouraged. Library associations had to be reformed, and international collaboration had to be effective. There were problems of advancing library relations with Eastern Europe (and Russia in particular) and the developing countries. There were questions concerning relations with FID—Godet had been concerned with relations between librarians and documentalists before the war—and with the newly formed UNESCO. Godet had a clear perception of these issues.

The continuing development of the organization was taken up by President Pierre Bourgeois, the Swiss National Librarian, in his first presidential address in Copenhagen in 1952, in the 25th year of the Federation's existence. Bourgeois recognized that the work of IFLA had become complex. Instead of a handful of academic librarians, there was need for specialists to cope with the great variety of problems raised in more than a dozen subcommittees. Further, IFLA should extend its territory: it had at first been primarily European and North American. It did not have the means to extend its work in all the regions of the world. His vision was of regional congresses—and how long he would have to wait!

The gradual increase in effectiveness of IFLA has not depended on ideas—these were there in the beginning. Godet very early saw the function of international meetings and the importance of treating international questions or problems of general application.

Postwar Growth. Indeed the reorganization in 1952 opened a floodgate of activity. Anthony Thompson started as the first Secretary-General in 1962, transferring to London, when Sir Frank Francis became President in 1964. Further evidence of IFLA's progress was to be found in the fact that the 1960 council topped the 100 mark for the first time. In 1964 at Rome there were 300, an unprecedented number, and by the end of the decade, the numbers were approaching 1,000. The work of sections and groups has developed out of all recognition in the 1960's and 70's, partly because of the effective efforts of IFLA to become a world federation—bringing in first Eastern Europe under Sir Frank and then the Third World under Herman Liebaers, who saw the importance of developing Universal Bibliographical Control as a continuing activity. Liebaers encouraged the Tashkent seminar in 1970, which effectively brought librarians from the developing countries into real IFLA life. This was followed up by a "pre-council" seminar for English-speaking developing countries in 1971 at Liverpool, for French-speaking countries in 1973 at Grenoble, and for Spanish-speaking countries in 1975 at Washington. From 1971 to 1976, membership rose from less than 350 to more than 700. Council of Library Resources grants made UBC and permanent secretariat maintenance possible in the mid-1970's. The accompanying article covers current publications and other programs.

Organizational Revisions. The increase in attendance at Council and the increase in overall membership, with the resultant problems of organization, led Herman Liebaers to recommend to the Board a further revision of statutes. The revised statutes, agreed to in principle in Lausanne in 1976, to be confirmed at Brussels at the World Congress in 1977, will make a new IFLA. (See accompanying summary of the statutes and their potential significance for wider participation.)

Future. IFLA has appeared to complete major work in 12-year cycles—1952, 1964, now 1976. What will the effect of the next statutes be? As in the earlier revisions, they will undoubtedly release great professional energies, harnessed for the benefit of libraries and related institutions the world over. With the development of international technology, the role of IFLA has become of intimate concern to the individual library. Universal Bibliography Control needs forward planning and world cooperation; so does Universal Availability of Publications (UAP).

The time for the relevance of IFLA to the world has arrived. The Executive Board and the Professional Board through the expanded secretariat must persuade librarians to participate in international librarianship. And librarians should appreciate the immediate relevance to them of the world studies now in progress, for it is in professional activity related ultimately to the needs of the individual library that the importance of IFLA lies.

PETER HAVARD-WILLIAMS

Mexico City, and Dakar, Senegal. These regional groups initiated projects ranging from training of personnel to standardized cataloging procedures. The program was made possible by a grant from the Canadian International Development Agency.

Credit must be given to the first IFLA meeting ever organized in a developing country: the IFLA World Wide Seminar held in Seoul, South Korea, May 31–June 5. Theme of the seminar, attended by 416 delegates from 28 countries, was Library Resources and National Development: Use and Control of Eastern Publications by East and West.

The coordination and stimulation of professional programs receive high priority within IFLA. For this purpose a coordinator of the professional work was appointed at IFLA Headquarters, The Hague. The appointment was made possible by a grant from the Council on Library Resources, Washington, D.C.

UBC and UAP Programs. Two major objectives within IFLA in 1976 concerned the programs for Universal Bibliographic Control (UBC) and Universal Availability of Publications (UAP). UAP is, like UBC, a concept, a system, and an objective which derives naturally from work that has been carried on for a long time in individual countries, in IFLA organs and elsewhere, and which brings together a variety of activities and plans. The older program of UBC has the aim of ensuring that bibliographical records, in standard form, are provided for publications in countries all over the world. (See also Universal Bibliographic Control.)

The IFLA International Office for UBC in London recently completed surveys on the use of ISBNs (International Standard Book Numbers) in libraries and on cataloging-in-publication. Working groups have completed drafts for various ISBDs (International Standard Bibliographic Descriptions), such as ISBD (Cartographic Materials), ISBD (Non-Book Materials) and ISBD (Music). The UBC Office also prepared the working documents for the UNESCO/IFLA Conference on National Bibliographies, scheduled for Paris, September 12–15, 1977.

International Activities. The IFLA Office for International Lending, Boston Spa, England, worked out a draft program of action for UAP presented at the Seoul meeting. The office continues its work on an international loan request form. Comments on an experimental form are being monitored. By July 1976, 19 countries were using the form and by that time 25,000 forms had been sold. The Office was also gathering information on barriers to international lending such as difficulties with customs and developments in legislation on photocopying.

UNESCO sponsors both UBC and UAP programs. In 1976 IFLA executed several contracts with UNESCO in these areas. Relations with other major international organizations in the information field were strengthened during the IFLA Council in Lausanne, where the IFLA Executive Board met with representatives of FID (International Federation for Documentation), ICA (International Council on Archives), ISO (International Standards Organization) and ICSU (International Council of Scientific Unions). IFLA's policy is directed at close cooperation with related organizations with the aim of reaching a more efficient program and of avoiding duplication of efforts.

Publications. Among the 13 books published in 1976 were *National and International Library Planning*, edited by R. Vosper and L. I. Newkirk; *Reading in a Changing World*, edited by F. E. Mohrhardt; *Corporate Headings: Their Use in Library Catalogues and National Bibliographies*, a comparative and critical study by Eva Verona; *World Directory of Administrative Libraries*, edited by O. Simmler; and *World Directory of Map Collections*, edited by W. W. Ristow.

Brussels Congress. The IFLA Secretariat was occupied during 1976 in planning its 50th Anniversary Congress at Brussels, Belgium, in September 1977. King Baudouin accepted the High Patronage of the Congress. Some 3,000 librarians from all over the world were expected to gather at the third World Congress of Librarians as a true manifestation of the profession. The Programme Planning Committee, headed by Robert Vesper of the U.S., developed a series of theme meetings under the general title: Libraries for All: One World of Information, Culture and Learning. Among the speakers expected at year's end were Daniel Boorstin, USA, Chief Adebo, Nigeria, A. M'Bow, UNESCO, Roger Caillois, France, Ludmilla Teresjkova, USSR, C.N. Parkinson, UK, and the authors C.P. Snow and Angus Wilson. The ALA planned a charter flight to Brussels, where many Americans would join their colleagues from, it was hoped, all 100 countries where IFLA membership live and work.

MARGREET WIJNSTROOM

REFERENCES
Annual Bibliography on the History of the Printed Book and Libraries.
For surveys of IFLA work in various sections, see *IFLA Journal* and *IFLA Annual*.
IFLA Directory lists annually the sections and officers and IFLA membership.
International Cataloguing is a quarterly, continued in 1976.
"Standards for Library Schools" in *IFLA Journal*, vol. 2, no. 4 (1976).

Independent Research Libraries

During 1976 there appeared to be an emerging awareness of the peculiar role and special importance of independent research libraries as a subspecies of research libraries in general.

Independent Research Libraries

The first *ALA Yearbook* (1976) on the year 1975 inaugurated this particular section with an article and statistics, both compiled by this contributor. More important, in library literature, was the splendid survey by William S. Budington, Executive Director of the John Crerar Library of Chicago, "'To Enlarge the Sphere of Human Knowledge': The Role of The Independent Research Library," which appeared in *College and Research Libraries* (July 1976, p. 299–315). That article ends with a statement that bears repeating:

> By their distinctive modes of formation, support, and collections "built to strength" rather than curricula, the independent research libraries attract the best of scholarship. In doing so, they supplement academic library resources in unique and unmatchable dimensions. In truth, to quote again from the objective set by Isaiah Thomas in 1882 for the American Antiquarian Society, . . . they "have a tendency to enlarge the sphere of human knowledge, aid the progress of science, to perpetuate the history of moral and political events, and to improve and instruct posterity."

Finally, at year's end, the Independent Research Libraries Association (IRLA), comprising 15 such libraries, issued a descriptive brochure entitled *Independent Research Libraries Association,* with a summary introduction and a statement describing each of its member institutions (available for $1 at the Newberry Library, 60 West Walton Street, Chicago, Illinois 60610).

Government Efforts. Even more significant than these modest "literary" efforts was the response of the federal government to the growing awareness of the independent research library. As was reported in 1975, because of legislative oversight, it was not until recently that the independents stopped falling between the two stools of the Library Services and Construction Act (for public libraries) and Title II of the Higher Education Act of 1965 (for academic libraries). That remedied (too late for truly significant help under present funding), the Congress in 1976 specifically wrote into new legislation the words "independent research libraries," making them eligible for grants under Title II-C of the amended Higher Education Act and the $15,000,000 authorized (but not appropriated in 1976). Depending on guidelines yet to be established, and the priorities therein, this provision could be of major significance in helping independent research libraries make up for years of great neglect in the late 1960's and early 1970's.

Legislation amending the authorization for the National Foundation for the Arts and Humanities appears to make the clients of both Endowments eligible for grants, at a ratio of $3 (private) for $1 (public) for operations. Again, authorization was not followed by appropriation in 1976. Nonetheless, the chances seem good, and independent research libraries should benefit in 1977 and thereafter.

NEH Grants. Meanwhile, the National Endowment for the Humanities made three, three-year experimental pilot grants for library operations at varying levels and with varying gift ratio requirements. The recipient institutions were the Massachusetts Historical Society, the Maryland Historical Society, and the Newberry Library (two being IRLA libraries). The distinctive feature of these grants is that they are for library operations, not for "add-on" research programs, and they thus recognize the need for direct institutional support.

Newberry Library Board Chairman Edward Blettner (left) shows a map to Mayor Richard Daley of Chicago in the Atlas of Early American History: The Revolutionary Era 1760–1790, produced by the Newberry under grants from the National Endowment for the Humanities. Newberry Librarian Lawrence W. Towner (far left) and the book's editor, Lester J. Cappon, far right, were at the City Hall presentation in December.

Independent Research Libraries Association Statistics (Fiscal Year Ending in 1975)

	Material Acquisitions	Binding and Conserv. Cost	Binding and Conserv. Salaries	Total Acquisitions	Physical Maintenance	Maintenance Salaries	Total Other Salaries
American Antiquarian Society	$ 60,196	$ 1,235	$ 10,258	$ 71,689	$ 37,731	$ 19,964	$ 185,338
American Philosophical Society	$ 47,353	$ 7,937	$ 25,000	$ 55,290	$ 68,717	$ 9,000	$ 144,547
The John Crerar Library	$ 244,565	$ 13,238	$ 31,260	$ 257,803	$210,635		$ 813,147
The Folger Shakespeare Library	$ 112,788	$ 2,212	$ 21,621	$ 136,621	$ 92,386	$169,551	$ 545,400
Linda Hall Library	$ 377,323	$ 31,000	$ 23,200	$ 431,523	$ 57,238	$ 38,200	$ 361,683
Henry E. Huntington Library	$ 291,631	$ 5,502		$ 297,133	$ 65,818	$ 91,942	$ 433,963
The Library Company of Philadelphia	$ 17,242		$ 25,000	$ 32,242	$ 48,495	$ 15,600	$ 91,279
Massachusetts Historical Society	$ 6,000	$ 2,525	$ 6,952	$ 62,525	$ 52,235	$ 17,710	$ 126,860
The Pierpont Morgan Library	$ 28,353	$277,725	$ 47,000	$ 316,988	$ 41,746	$ 62,957	$ 611,181
The Newberry Library	$ 221,880	$ 11,332	$ 96,656	$ 329,868	$162,208	$ 84,429	$ 518,523
The New York Academy of Medicine	$ 196,001	$ 27,174		$ 223,175	$213,797	$114,709	$ 798,243
The New-York Historical Society	$ 54,857	$ 7,481		$ 62,338	$206,243	$233,959	$ 389,898
The New York Public Library	$1,854,000	$298,000	$416,000	$2,568,000	$226,000	$950,000	$8,667,000
Pennsylvania Historical Society	$ 13,058	$ 2,827	$ 7,400	$ 15,885	$ 23,808	$ 26,400	$ 156,117
Virginia Historical Society	$ 17,384	$ 8,777		$ 26,151	$ 45,416	$ 63,119	$ 174,765

	Total Fringe Benefits	Benefits % of Salaries	Other Operational Expenditures	Total Library Expenditures	Research and Education Programs	Grand Total Operations
American Antiquarian Society	$ 33,852	15.7 %	$ 85,923	$ 489,553	$ 96,022	$ 585,673
American Philosophical Society	$ 25,905	14 %	$ 41,963	$ 327,789	$ 18,264	$ 346,053
The John Crerar Library	$ 71,211	9.1 %	$ 351,429	$ 1,704,246		$ 1,704,246
The Folger Shakespeare Library	$ 58,008	0.08 %	$ 590,034	$ 1,592,000	$223,000	$ 1,815,000
Linda Hall Library	$ 38,696	9 %	$ 48,815	$ 974,155		$ 974,155
Henry E. Huntington Library	$ 77,833	16.14 %			$103,876	
The Library Company of Philadelphia	$ 14,104			$ 226,112		$ 226,112
Massachusetts Historical Society	$ 35,842	23 %	$ 21,005	$ 295,172		$ 295,172
The Pierpont Morgan Library	$ 91,994	14 %	$ 222,331	$ 1,124,866		$ 1,347,197
The Newberry Library	$ 97,009	13.86 %	$ 261,564	$ 1,453,601	$945,775	$ 2,400,376
The New York Academy of Medicine	$ 195,577	21.3 %	$ 619,700	$ 2,166,201		$ 2,166,201
The New-York Historical Society	$ 98,022	15.5 %	$ 393,296	$ 990,460		$ 990,460
The New York Public Library	$2,475,000	25 %	$1,577,000	$16,463,000		$16,463,000
Pennsylvania Historical Society	$ 29,680	0.015%	$ 93,070	$ 251,890		$ 344,960
Virginia Historical Society	$ 29,366	12.3 %	$ 71,977	$ 410,794		$ 410,794

	Total Endowment	Gifts and Grants for Endowment	Endowment Income	Operations Income	Gifts for Current Use	Grants for Current Use
American Antiquarian Society	$ 3,673,370	$ 52,590	$ 247,014	$ 40,950	$ 43,852	$ 67,112
American Philosophical Society	$21,398,247	$ 51,453	$1,063,245	$ 4,003	–	$ 12,057
The John Crerar Library	$ 6,769,854	–	$ 505,390	$ 696,714	$ 191,226	–
The Folger Shakespeare Library	$22,799,234	–	$ 999,000*	$ 358,000	$ 55,000	–
Linda Hall Library	$25,000,000	–	$1,550,000	$ 120,000	–	–
Henry E. Huntington Library	$32,109,877	$380,506	$2,113,281	$ 255,348	$ 373,853	$ 34,210
The Library Company of Philadelphia	$ 4,200,000	–	$ 240,514	$ 16,995	$ 26,755	$ 17,000
Massachusetts Historical Society	$ 6,635,609	$373,141	$ 296,434	–	$ 13,000	$ 2,500
The Pierpont Morgan Library	$13,697,025	–	$ 565,986	–	$ 57,094	$ 5,000
The Newberry Library	$20,086,059	$613,487	$ 856,453	$ 99,572	$ 46,106	$538,745
The New York Academy of Medicine	$30,203,376	–	$1,323,597	$ 552,431		
The New-York Historical Society	$15,879,167	$ 21,500	$ 648,583	$ 105,622	$ 179,441	$ 88,000
The New York Public Library	$70,034,000	$581,000	$3,309,000	$1,072,000	$2,277,000	$525,000
Pennsylvania Historical Society	$ 3,219,278	$ 500	$ 242,161	$ 100,572	–	$ 4,296
Virginia Historical Society	$ 3,928,772	$ 60,000	$ 280,184	$ 81,554	$ 44,881	$ 97,473

*available for operations

	Total Operating Income	Total Volumes	Total Microform Units	Total Manuscripts	Volumes Added	Professional Staff	Non-Professional Staff
American Antiquarian Society	$ 499,286	612,500	85,635	3,500	3,320	11	18
American Philosophical Society	–	143,135	29,736	7,000 running ft.	1,665	7	7
The John Crerar Library	$ 1,706,791	1,154,863	406,422		19,294	28	55
The Folger Shakespeare Library	$ 1,651,000	212,830	100,000	40,000	2,502	40	28
Linda Hall Library	$ 1,670,000	412,283	490,739		10,532	15	30
Henry E. Huntington Library	$ 2,510,461	533,394		5,000,000	9,118	22.6	28.5
The Library Company of Philadelphia	$ 43,755	400,000				5	11
Massachusetts Historical Society	$ 311,934	320,532	52,750	4,890 running ft.	1,532	6	8
The Pierpont Morgan Library	$ 645,030	66,859			1,240	17	33
The Newberry Library	$ 1,540,876	1,282,206	92,325		11,358	33	9
The New York Academy of Medicine	$ 2,182,559	607,174	504	2,221	7,207	19	37
The New-York Historical Society	$ 288,941	605,000	47,350	1,500,000	1,500	6	18
The New York Public Library	$12,967,000	4,573,636	1,208,040	10,744,958	92,461	178.5	283.0
Pennsylvania Historical Society	$ 347,029	210,000	11,350	14,000,000		10	10
Virginia Historical Society	$ 564,092	261,500	2,100	4,046,000	1,308	8	18

Note: In the cases of the New York Ac. of Med., the Am. Phil. Soc., and the Huntington, both income and costs include other than library activities.

Donors must include 10 percent of each library's readers, a useful inducement to heighten reader awareness that services provided free cost something and are worth supporting. (*See also* National Endowment for the Humanities.)

This pattern of government response comes none too soon. Figures for the fiscal year ending in 1975 (the latest available) for the IRLA libraries, when compared with the like figures for the year ending in 1973, show the impact of the Nixon recession and inflation (not to mention the general educational depression) on those libraries. Already in trouble in 1973, they were in worse shape in 1975. Total operations expenses were up 7.9 percent, while total income was up only 3.6 percent. Worrisome for the future was the 47.7 percent decline in gifts and grants for *endowment*. Other aspects of the pattern seem to be clear: while the sizes of the staffs were down (14 percent decline in professional staff, 34 percent in non-professional), total salary costs were up. Even more worrisome, acquisition expenditures were down 17.8 percent, for a drop of nearly 20,000 volumes a year.

In short, it may be asked that, if the possibility of federal support has come none too soon, will it prove in 1977 and 1978 to have come too little and too late? Contemplating that question, one is fortunate to be able to say that, in this pluralistic society, we do not rely upon the federal government alone to sustain our culture. Individuals, corporations, and foundations can also be reached successfully. The trustees and staffs and readers at independent research libraries are confident that the response of all elements of the community will be there, if the question can only be well put. But time is not on the side of the angels in this instance. The future is very close upon us.

LAWRENCE W. TOWNER

Independent Study in Public Libraries

By far the most significant development in the area of independent study in public libraries during 1976 was the publication of the two-part *Final Report: The Role of the Public Libraries in Adult Independent Learning*, by Anne S. Mavor, Jose Orlando Toro, and Ernest R. DeProspo for the College Entrance Examination Board. The study covers activities coordinated by the CEEB's Office of Library Independent Study and Guidance Projects (Jose Orlando Toro, Director) from 1972 to 1976. The work was funded by the Council on Library Resources, the National Endowment for the Humanities, and the United States Office of Education, Office of Library Research and Demonstration, and was assisted by the efforts of nine public libraries throughout the nation: Atlanta, Denver, Enoch Pratt (Baltimore), Miami-Dade, Portland (Me.), Salt Lake City, St. Louis, Tulsa (City-County), and Woodbridge (N.J.). Also assisting was the state of New York, which developed a statewide program under the direction of the New York State Library.

Considerable interest has been generated in this project since its inception. A comprehensive summary of the study appeared in *RQ*, Summer, 1976.

Statistical Summary. Some statistics of interest gleaned from the *Final Report* from data entered on 934 learners with 969 projects:

(1) Male learners   38%
    Female learners 62%
(2) Homemakers comprised 21% of the learners.
(3) 76% of the learners were 44 years of age or younger.
(4) The two educational groupings with the most learners were high school graduates (30%) and those with some college education (32%).
(5) 26% of the learners were light (less than once a year) or new library users.
(6) The highest percentage of learners had educational credit goals (34%), followed by goals of increasing knowledge (28%) and job change (20%).
(7) The two highest interest categories were the Social Sciences (29%) and Technology and Applied Science (25%).
(8) Most of the learners preferred books (67%) to other media when choosing a learning method.
(9) Most of the learners preferred to study at home (62%) as opposed to the Library (22%) or the classroom (16%).
(10) Most learners were satisfied with the service: 91% indicated overall satisfaction, 92% would use the service again, and 98% would recommend it to a friend.

During the last six months of the project (January–June 1976) the nine participating libraries focused attention on the question of continuity after the project was ended: Should action be taken to form a network of experimental public libraries? As one of the library directors put it, "We now have the expertise, talents, and resources to become a national network, capable of providing consulting, planning, training, information sharing, and other support services that meet expressed needs. . . ."

Consortium. In June of 1976, the nine libraries and the Minneapolis Public Library established themselves as the Consortium for Public

Independent Study in Public Libraries

Library Innovation. Briefly summarized, the Consortium has committed itself to the following major activities:
- Overall improvement of the Learners Advisory Service through systematic research, experimentation and dissemination.
- Research on library service and management problems and the implication of these requirements for library school curriculum modification.
- Development of a prototype evaluation and data system for planning, monitoring, and managing the various functions of public libraries.
- Sharing of planning, training, and evaluation talent with other libraries.
- Dissemination and expansion of the results of consortium activities and research.

Various audiences will be interested in the results obtained from the experimental work of the Consortium and the findings will be specifically directed to directors of public libraries, librarians providing in-depth service, professors of library science and researchers, and policy makers in local governments and community agencies.

It would be unfair to suggest that the only work being done in the field is that of the Learners Advisory Service, although that is the most conspicuous and documented.

The University of Pittsburgh's Graduate School of Library and Information Science, which in 1975 sponsored a three-week Institute in self-directed study in libraries, received a survey research grant from the U. S. Office of Education, HEW, to conduct a study of self-learning patterns of persons who use a wide range of community resources in independent learning projects. The Director of the project is Professor Patrick R. Penland, who states, "Support for this research demonstrates the need of a behavioral foundation for the helping services of the media, library and information profession. The findings of this study remove the limitations of previous approaches that have largely ignored the human components in systems design."

Other Activities. In Chicago, at Northeastern Illinois University's Department of Instructional Media, Jane A. Reilly worked during 1976 on a research project on library-based independent learning programs under the auspices of the Goodwin Watson Institute for Research & Program Development. Libraries which have not received one of Reilly's questionnaires and would like to participate in her study are invited to contact her.

A new support service for independent learners surfaced with an impressive monthly publication in January 1976. "The National Center for Educational Brokering is a clearinghouse of information on referral, advisement and assessment services for adults," according to the Center's Director, Francis U. Macy. The Center is at 405 Oak Street, Syracuse, N.Y. 13203.

Exhibit for the "On Your Own" program at the Denver Public Library, which provides a multimedia self-study approach to learning about man and his history.

The Public Library Association of ALA established a new Section on Alternative Education Programs at the 1976 Chicago Conference. Travis Tyer, Library Development Group, Illinois State Library, and Patricia Gaven, Chairperson of the PLA Adult Literacy and Learning Committee, are working with PLA Executive Secretary Andrew Hansen in the formative stages of the new Section. Persons interested in this activity are invited to participate. The only requirement is membership in PLA.

Interest in library-based independent learning programs spans the Atlantic. Judith Bowen, Research Associate of the Leeds Polytechnic's Department of Librarianship, and Ronald G. Surridge of London's Bromley Public Library attended the 1976 Chicago ALA Conference to meet with participants in the Learners Advisory Service of the Consortium for Public Library Innovation. They were particularly interested in U. S. experience in planning and evaluation and management by objectives.

Finally, of interest to libraries with independent learning programs, or those who would like to start them, is new legislation enacted in 1976 known variously as the Lifelong Learning Bill, the Mondale Bill, and Title I-B of the Higher Education Act. Authorized funding for this program is $20,000,000 in 1977, $30,000,000 in 1978, and $40,000,000 in 1979. Objectives of the program are to improve coordination of federal support for lifetime learning opportunities available through a number of different organizations, including libraries.

157

Indexing and Abstracting Services

The National Commission on Libraries and Information Science is specifically mentioned in the law as one of the federal agencies to be consulted in the implementation of the new lifelong learning program.

JOSEPH KIMBROUGH

REFERENCES

Anne S. Mavor, Jose Orlando Toro, and Ernest DeProspo. *Final Report; Part 1: The Role of the Public Libraries in Adult Independent Learning.* New York, College Entrance Examination Board (January 1976). 160 p. Appendices.

———. *Final Report; Part II: The Role of the Public Libraries in Adult Independent Learning.* New York, College Entrance Examination Board (September, 1976). 77 p. Appendices.

———. "An overview of the National Adult Independent *Learning* Project," *RQ*, v. 15, no.4 (Summer, 1976) pp. 293–308.

Indexing and Abstracting Services

Abstracting and indexing (A&I) services provide bibliographic aids in the form of references, subject terms, and brief descriptions in order to identify, find, and obtain access to published or unpublished documents or non-bibliographic sources. The published documents, often referred to as the primary literature, include books, journals, monographic series, plays, newspapers, broadsides, music, and any other form of published works. Unpublished documents are usually technical reports, whether preliminary or final, correspondence, manuscripts, and other material not formally published. Non-bibliographic sources include such material as foundations or other organizations, numeric data, works of art, and other material not in bibliographic form.

Abstracting services include an abstract or brief summary of each item indexed. Indexing services, including abstracting services, identify data such as author, title, and place of publication to identify uniquely the item indexed so that it can be located. Indexing services usually provide subject access to the document through the use of subject headings or key words.

In 1976 approximately 2,500 A&I services on all subjects were published. Over 300 of these were available in machine-readable form (*see also* Data Bases). Coverage of the primary literature grew by approximately 10 percent over the previous years. More than 52,000,000 documents were available for search on-line at the end of 1976.

Current Trends. Current trends in A&T services are emerging in eight areas: (1) special current awareness services; among them are *Standard Profiles* (BIOSIS), *CA Selects* (Chemical Abstracts Service) *ASCA Topics* (Institute for Scientific Information), *Key Abstracts* (INSPEC), *Published Searches* (National Technical Information Service and Engineering Index, Inc.) and *Macroprofiles* (United Kingdom Chemical Information Service); (2) increased on-line interactive searching; (3) continued research on data tagging and flagging (the National Science Foundation and the National Library of Medicine are supporting projects in these areas; among organizations doing research are the American Institute of Physics, Chemical Abstracts Service, Engineering Index, and the National Aeronautics and Space Administration); (4) changing formats of primary publications to provide the user with access routes to such non-traditional primary sources as deposited papers, microform publications, audio tapes, video tapes and computer files; (5) full-text searching to utilize computer-readable records of full documents for purposes other than typesetting, such as fully automatic or machine-aided creation of abstracts (extracts) and of indexes; (6) increased cooperation among A&I services. Among examples of cooperative projects are the interchange of abstracts on tape between the American Institute of Physics (AIP) and the Energy and Research Development Agency (ERDA) and between AIP and Engineering Index, Inc., the composition by Chemical Abstracts Service of BIOSIS and *Information Science Abstracts*, the NFAIS Overlap Study, and international classification scheme for physics; (7) expansion of user education programs. Among the many examples of these programs are the new user manual *PsycINFO Users Reference Manual* issued by the American Psychological Association, the BIOSIS/CAS Workshop, the NFAIS seminar program, and the extensive educational activities of the many data base producers and dissemination centers; and (8) progress in standards activities, specifically the publication of the ANSI Z39 bibliographic references standard, including work on bibliographic descriptions for data bases. Among emerging problems are the need for even more educational programs, the difficulty of maintaining precision of output as the data bases expand rapidly, and the ever-present problem of providing access to the many documents indexed by the A&I services.

TONI CARBO BEARMAN

Information and Referral Centers

It is difficult to outline clearly the history of the I and R movement in the United States. Centers appear and disappear. Support comes and goes. Sponsorship changes. Most observers generally agree, however, that the concept emerged in the charity organization emphasis of the late 1800's. The emphasis then was not on facilitating citizen access but on preventing duplication in the relief rolls. The trend soon faded.

The next important appearance of I and R in

Information and Referral Centers

An exaggerated advertising approach was used to introduce in a lighthearted fashion the new terminal computer link to three national information centers installed in the Reference Library of the West Virginia Library Commission during 1976.

the U.S. followed World War II. The Department of Labor established some 3,000 community advisory centers to assist veterans by providing complete and accurate information on all government and community services for veterans and to make referrals for those needing further help. Most of the centers died out by 1949. With their death, the I and R concept lay virtually buried until the mid-1960's when a spontaneous eruption saw the concept come alive in a variety of private and public social agencies.

No precise figures were available on how many I and R agencies existed in the mid-1970's. The difficulty of counting is illustrated by a recent study which indicated that some 45 percent of the 1,000 social service agencies operating in a major U.S. city had some sort of I and R function. In the late 1960's, the National Easter Seal Society adopted I and R as a basic program. In 1972 the United Way of America operated 60 I and R centers in North America. In addition such services as those styled "Call for Action" or "Action Line" in mass media have become well known in many metropolitan areas.

Public libraries have become increasingly concerned about providing services for the average urban citizen. No count is available on how many public libraries are operating formalized I and R programs. It is generally expected that librarianship's involvement in the I and R movement will increase, particularly as citizen demand and needs increase. In 1976 five model neighborhood information centers, backed by federal funding, were being administered by public libraries in five large metropolitan cities. Librarianship's involvement is further confirmed by the recent goals and guidelines statement of the Public Library Association suggesting that public libraries could usefully serve as the coordinating agencies for the information services in their communities.

A Prototype. No discussion of I and R is complete without reference to the CAB's (Citizen Advice Bureaux) of England, agencies which many consider to be the prototype of I and R. Some 450 CAB's operate in communities answering about one million inquiries a year. The CAB's are officially mandated to make available accurate information and skilled advice on everyday problems, to explain legislation, and to help the citizen use wisely the services provided by the state. The CAB's were created at the outbreak of World War II to help Britons through the confusion and hardship of war. Since their founding, the CAB's have been partially financed by government grants but run by local committees of citizens and representatives of public and voluntary agencies.

I and R Functions. Although the I and R center serves in some way as an information manager or helper for the average citizen, how that user is best served is a subject of some dispute. Existing agencies vary along several lines. Some are multi-topic agencies that deal with virtually any topic a citizen might present. Others are highly specialized, handling only inquiries in specific areas. Some are highly centralized and impersonalized. Still others are highly individualized and neighborhood-based. Some are extremely sophisticated and dependent on computerized data banks. Others are extremely simple, relying primarily on the distribution of prepared leaflets.

Patterns. In the midst of this diversity, patterns emerge. I and R services seem to be predominantly conceived as individualized servers of citizen needs. Thus it is expected that a citizen will present the center with his unique requirements and that the center will respond to them appropriately. Existing I and R agencies offer a variety of individualized services to clients. A center offering the gamut of services may be involved in information giving (answering specific inquiries from citizens); advising (providing individualized interpretation); steering (suggesting that the citizen make use of a particular social agency); referring (making contact for the citizen with a particular social agency); supporting (providing emotional support and a listening ear); escorting (actually physically accompanying the citizen); advocating (helping a citizen maneuver through the system); and accounting (following up to make sure the citizen is helped).

Backing up these individualized services are a variety of other roles. These include mainly creating and maintaining resource files; researching community needs; and serving as a human-service delivery clearinghouse. In addition, some existing I and R agencies serve functions that are really by-products of the primary focus on individualized client service. They include acting as a public resource during community emergencies; advocating new service programs to meet citizen needs; launching community education programs; and making human service more accountable.

BRENDA DERVIN

REFERENCES

Miriam Braverman, editor, "Information and Referral Services in the Public Library." *Drexel Library Quarterly*, vol. 12, no. 1 & 2 (January–April 1976), entire issue.

Alfred J. Kahn et al., *Neighborhood Information Centers: A Study and Some Proposals* (New York: Columbia University School of Social Work, 1966).

Manfred Kochen and Joseph Donohue, editors, *Information for the Community* (ALA, 1976). See especially Chapter 4, "Information and Referral Services: A Short History and Some Recommendations" by Nicholas Long, and Chapter 2, "The Everyday Information Needs of the Average Citizen: A Taxonomy for Analysis," by Brenda Dervin.

Information Industry

In the second half of the 20th century, there has been a gradual but nonetheless dramatic change in the U.S. economy. Whereas manufacturing and, before that, agriculture once dominated the economy, the production and distribution of knowledge are now the dominant activities, involving about 50 percent of the labor force (*Publishers Weekly*, June 7, 1976). The U.S. has become the world's first "information society." Information activities are estimated to be growing at about 10 percent a year, roughly double that of the economy as a whole.[1] It is clear that access to relevant information is an increasingly vital requirement for our economic well-being, as well as for our efforts to improve the quality of life.

Many different organizations are engaged in the production and distribution of knowledge. In the broadest sense, they include educational institutions, research and development firms, and the organizations engaged in publishing, computer services, data communications, and various kinds of library and information services. The "information industry" is a subset of this larger group, consisting of those organizations that are in the business of producing and distributing information products and services.

Historically, the first organizations to be involved in the information industry were publishing companies, which receive the intellectual output of authors, "package" it, and help to announce and disseminate it to the interested publics. Some publishers produce indexes, abstracts, and other summaries of the basic material. These "secondary" services help users to identify the "primary" (books or periodical) publications of potential interest.

GROWTH OF THE INFORMATION MARKETPLACE

Both primary and secondary information services exist in a large and growing number of forms. As more importance is placed on immediate access to information, more and more companies, agencies, and organizations dealing with information as their basic commodity—publishers, micropublishers, abstracting and indexing services, and other information dissemination organizations—are entering the information marketplace and competing for the attention of potential users. As a result, both the variety and quality of information products, systems, and services have been increasing steadily.

On-Line Reference Services. The most dramatic development in library and information services in the past decade has been the on-line reference services. These services, which developed at a spectacular rate during the early 1970's, are now in use in thousands of special libraries, academic libraries, and technical information centers in the U.S. and other countries. During 1976 the number of on-line data bases available through these services almost doubled and, although precise data are lacking, it seems likely that the number of users of these data bases grew from 30 to 40 percent. A major survey of the use of on-line services, published in 1976, showed a high degree of usefulness and user acceptance.[2]

On-line reference services are helping information-on-demand companies to establish an important role as information retailers. Such companies provide "one-stop" access to a wide variety of information and research services, including computer-based bibliographic retrieval. They are particularly useful to clients who do not have corporate libraries or whose needs for data-base reference service do not warrant their having their own terminals and trained searchers. Increasingly, information-on-demand companies are also helping to satisfy the demands of their clients for copies of individual journal articles and reports. The Information Industry Association (IIA) estimates (IIA Friday Memo, October 22, 1976) that in 1975 approximately 250,000 copies of journal articles were provided to end users by about 12 document fulfillment services. This is just the beginning of a major "after-market" for periodical and report literature.

Although on-line reference services compete, in some respects, with the printed products of abstracting and indexing services, they also stimulate interest in these products and provide additional income to the publishers, to offset some of the increasing costs of acquiring, screening, indexing and abstracting the primary material. The term "publisher" here includes the U.S. federal government, which generates and distributes a great deal of information in printed, microform, tape, and electronic formats, for fees ranging from a few hundred dollars to $50,000 or more.

International Activities. Just as information is basically interdisciplinary, so is it international. 1976 saw many U.S. information industry companies working to expand the use of their products and services overseas. Some information firms derive as much as half of their income from overseas sales. The increasing overseas use of U.S.-based information services has helped to stimulate and accelerate development of similar services in other countries. During 1976, for example, there was continued development of EURONET, a cooperative, multinational communications activity of the European Economic Community aimed in part at facilitating intra-European access to data-base services established in the member nations. It is not yet clear whether the emergence of EURONET as an operational entity will be accompanied by pricing agreements and subsidies aimed at reducing the influence of non-European information services.

The U.S. government has continued to foster international exchange of scientific and technical information and assistance to the less-developed countries in using U.S. information resources. During 1976 the United Nations adopted a resolution based on a U.S. proposal to create an international technical information center and, early in 1977, the U.S. Information Agency inaugurated INFO/Speed, a series of demonstrations of computer-based information services to key information leaders in Africa, Asia, and South America.

The Information Industry Association. The Information Industry Association was formed in 1969 to promote the development of private enterprise in the information field and gain recognition of information as a commodity, as well as a resource. In 1976 membership in the Association grew to over 100 corporate and 20 associate members.

To reflect the increasing growth and diversity of the industry, the board of directors of IIA was expanded during 1976 from 12 to 15 members The current officers are:

Chairman: Herbert R. Brinberg, American Can Co.
Vice Chairman: Jerome D. Luntz, Newsweek, Inc.
Treasurer: Robert H. Riley, Chase Manhattan Bank, NA
Secretary: Haines B. Gaffner, Consultant
Past Chairman: Harold T. Redding, Dun & Bradstreet, Inc.

Board Members:
James B. Adler, Congressional Information Service, Inc.
Robert F. Asleson, R. R. Bowker Co.
Isaac L. Auerbach, Auerbach Publishing Corp.
Earl M. Coleman, Plenum Publishing Corp.
Carlos A. Cuadra, System Development Corp.
Thomas Grogan, McGraw-Hill, Inc.
Edward M. Lee, Information Handling Services, Inc.
John Rothman, The New York Times Co.
Roger K. Summit, Lockheed Information Systems
Loene Trubkin, Data Courier, Inc.
President: Paul G. Zurkowski

The Association publishes Information/ACTION, a bi-monthly member services bulletin, as well as a weekly industry update sent to active IIA voting representatives. In 1976 the "Information Sources Directory," the first compilation of all the products and services offered by IIA member companies, was issued and quickly sold out its first run.

Three major committees and their related task forces cover the interest areas of Association members.

COMMITTES AND TASK FORCES

Education & Marketing Committee
Task Forces
Library Relations
Training Clearinghouse
Public Relations
Publications
Meetings and Workshops

Government Relations Committee
Task Forces
Procurement
Fair Competition
Micropublishing

Information Industry

Privacy and Freedom of Information
State and Local Government Relations
National Congressional Relations

Proprietary Rights Committee
    Task Forces
Copyright Clearinghouse
Education
CONTU/Copyright Regulations
Primary Publications
Government Copyright
Data Bases
Software
Microforms

Other Standing Committees of IIA
Standards
Membership
Committee on National Information
  Policy

The Association works with related trade and professional associations on matters of mutual concern, including copyright, government micropublishing efforts, depository library legislation and privacy matters. Several IIA committees work together to sponsor the National Information Conference and Exposition (NICE), held annually in Washington, D.C., in the spring.

Awards. Each year the Association presents two industry awards to honor the contributions of information industry firms and leaders. The 1976 "Information Product of the Year Award" was presented to Congressional Information Service, Inc., Washington, D.C., for their *American Statistics Index*. Eugene B. Power, founder of University Microfilms, received the "Hall of Fame" Award.

CONCERNS OF THE INFORMATION INDUSTRY

Commercial firms that create or distribute information products or services for a fee operate in a highly competitive environment in which success depends in large part on being able to recognize user needs and to provide needed products and services at competitive prices. As a matter of both principle and economic survival, these firms believe in the need for a marketplace that can be freely entered and that does not have either unfair barriers to participation or a price structure that is distorted by subsidies. Such barriers or distortions can arise when the government elects to use its taxation and regulatory powers to develop and sell products and services in competition with other sectors of the economy.

Growing Government Involvement. The information industry has been highly vocal in expressing its concerns about the growing involvement of the government in information distribution functions, such as micropublishing and on-line retrieval services. This kind of concern, however, has been expressed by others. For example, late in 1976, the Assistant Attorney General in the Department of Justice's Antitrust Division, testifying before the National Commission on Electronic Fund Transfers, stated that the very presence of the government, with its potential for subsidizing its services, may deter the entry by some private firms into some fields. "As long as the government continues to provide services without charge, private incentives to develop alternatives will necessarily be chilled and economic resources inefficiently allocated."[3]

In 1976 one U.S. information company found it necessary to withdraw on-line retrieval service on a major international biomedical data base because the company could not compete effectively with a similar, highly subsidized service operated by the U.S. government. In this case, the government service had been in operation before the commercial information service, but there have been instances in which government institutions have initiated or expanded tax-supported information services in areas where there already existed one or more user-supported information services.

Policy and Rules. Although the information industry would like to see greater restraint on the part of the government in its information-service activities, leaders believe that it is equally important that there be some kind of national information policy that sets forth, for the benefit of the government, the private sector, and the users they serve, a set of policies, principles, and ground rules. Such rules should help each sector to identify for itself an appropriate role that will contribute to the common goal of improving our information standard of living.

Recognition of the need for national information policy continued to grow during 1976. In July, the National Commission on Libraries and Information Science (NCLIS) sponsored a meeting to assist the White House Domestic Council's Committee on the Right of Privacy to develop recommendations on national information policy. The principal recommendation made by the Committee in their report to the President was to establish in the White House an Office of Information Policy parallel to the Office of Management and Budget (OMB). While OMB itself attempts to exercise some policy control over the other federal agencies in the information area, its concern is primarily budgetary. The extent of OMB information policy control, therefore, has been very limited, and, in the absence of national information policy review at the highest levels of government, each federal agency has tended to make its own information policy.

During 1976 the information industry continued its interest and involvement in copyright issues, as well as in broader problems of reconciling the needs of society for access to information with the need to protect individuals against the unwarranted dissemination of inaccurate, misleading, or strictly personal information.

Copyright Concerns. The long-awaited passage of the Copyright Revision Bill by Congress cleared the decks for serious consideration of the application of copyright protection to data bases, software, microforms, and other information products and tools. Work in this direction picked up sharply in 1976, under CONTU (National Commission on New Technological Uses of Copyrighted Works) (q.v.). CONTU plans to devote its energies and resources in 1977 to the development of recommendations on data bases, clearinghouses, and related matters.

IIA-NTIS Conflict. During 1976, a proposal by the National Technical Information Service (NTIS) of the Department of Commerce drew sharp attention in the information industry. NTIS, which has heretofore acted as distributor of public domain reports, proposed that copyright protection should be granted for its publications. The Information Industry Association is opposing this change in the long-standing public-domain policy. In a letter to the Judiciary Committee, the IIA stated that NTIS can make no claim of authorship of publications created by other federal agencies and that granting copyright protection to NTIS "would curtail the number of channels through which government documents can reach the people . . . ." They suggested that NTIS be granted a "format copyright" on their microform publications, while keeping the original publications in the public domain.

Later in 1976 NTIS announced another new plan, under which NTIS would accept orders from the general public for paper reprints from any journal published by a select group of publishers. For a fee, NTIS will fill these orders by utilizing one or more reprint facilities, including the British Lending Library Division. The NTIS plan to enter this area, as a broker for nongovernment documents, is sure to generate a great deal of controversy, not only because it raises questions about the proper function of government vis-a-vis the private sector, but because other agencies and groups have been developing plans along other lines. For example, a special Task Force of the National Commission on Libraries and Information Science has been addressing the problem throughout much of 1976. The Task Force, composed primarily of librarians but including some industry representation, will issue a report early in 1977 that recommends a three-tier system in which the Library of Congress plays a central role. In parallel with NCLIS's work, a committee of the IIA has been working to design a document provision service to meet the expressed needs of libraries and technical information centers within the private sector and within the framework of the new copyright legislation.

Whatever the outcome of the NTIS plan, or the NCLIS recommendations, or the information industry effort, these activities underscore the need for a national information policy of adequate scope and depth. One can only hope that it begins to emerge in 1977.

CARLOS CUADRA

REFERENCES
1. Edwin B. Parker, "Information and Society," in *Library and Information Service Needs of the Nation: Proceedings of a Conference on the Needs of Occupational, Ethnic, and other Groups in the United States* (Washington, D.C.: U.S. National Commission on Libraries and Information Science, 1975).
2. Judith Wanger, Carlos A. Cuadra, and Mary Fishburn, *Impact of On-Line Retrieval Services: A Survey of Users, 1974–75* (Santa Monica, California: System Development Corporation, 1976).
3. Donald I. Baker, "Statement before the Providers Committee of the National Commission on Electronic Fund Transfers, November 12, 1976" (Washington, D.C., U.S. Department of Justice).

Information Science

See *Automation; Data Bases, Computer-Readable; Serials; Networks; Processing Centers; Circulation Systems.*
See also *American Society for Information Science* and *National Commission on Libraries and Information Science.*

Information Science and Automation Division

As a result of the New ALA dues structure, under which the Divisions of ALA are responsible for their own finances, the Information Science and Automation Division (ISAD) has been very much concerned with its future status within the Association. ISAD began the 1975–76 budget year with an ALA subsidy of $11,272. ISAD saw an increase in membership of 226 members by the end of the fiscal year (August 31, 1976) over the previous year, and with frugal spending, the Division ended the year requiring no subsidy and had a surplus of $5,449.

Along the way to eliminating the subsidy, ISAD carried out a number of activities intended to attract new members and hold the present members. A new recruitment brochure, used for the first time at the ALA Annual Conference in Chicago, was later used at state association conferences and ISAD institutes. The ISAD Board of Directors established an ad hoc membership task force that was to draw up a membership recruitment plan. That task force concluded that ALA and ISAD membership information was not accessible to most non-

Information Science and Automation Division

members and that the ALA Membership Task Force should distribute membership materials more readily. The ISAD Task Force also reported that ISAD's goals and functions should be reevaluated, its charge strengthened and clarified, and recruitment objectives defined. Strategies could then be developed to reach specific potential membership groups. The group also recommended that an ISAD Member Services Committee should be established which would help to provide "ongoing support, and review, to ISAD's recruitment efforts and member needs."

Reorganization Recommendations. The Bylaws and Organization Committee reported to the ISAD Board recommendations for the reorganization of ISAD. Some members felt that in order for the Division to be responsive to the needs of the profession it must change its aims and programs to meet the changing needs of its members. The Committee's recommendations were that:

(1) The name of the Division and its function statement be changed to reflect the current activities and the current and projected areas of interest of the division. It would appear that the Division is moving toward something like a technology utilization division.

(2) Sections of the Division should be constituted to encompass a broad type of technology, including, audiovisual technology, computing technology, and video cable technology. Two other areas that seem appropriate are reprographic technology and preservation of library materials technology.

(3) These broader concerns should be addressed by the ISAD board and by the sectional executive committees at the Midwinter 1977 Conference in Washington, and that the proposed reorganization be discussed by and voted upon by the membership of the Division at the 1977 Conference at Detroit.

Activities. As important as organization concerns are, they did not divert the Division from its usual active schedule of meetings and programs at the ALA Centennial Conference in Chicago. ISAD sponsored nine programs, co-sponsored three others, and held 23 committee, board and other meetings. Additionally its Video and Cable Communications Section held two showings on the Conference hotels' closed circuit systems of library produced video programs. The programs, called *Video Visions: Programming for the 20th Century*, were practical demonstrations of telecommunications for improving library and information services.

The Division's programs included an introduction to library automation co-sponsored with the Junior Members Round Table as part of JMRT's orientation program, a look at information retrieval systems and current data bases, an open forum on the standardization of bar codes, and a program on the past, present, and future of audiovisual activities in libraries.

As a response to the ALA Council requirement that all documents avoid sexist terminology, the Bylaws and Organization Committee revised the Division's bylaws and the bylaws of both sections. The bylaws were published in the March 1976 issue of the *Journal of Library Automation* and later approved by the membership.

During 1976 the ISAD Telecommunications Committee worked on the problem of computer-to-computer protocol for data interchange. This work is of tremendous importance to the development of networks and to communications among them. The project's importance was recognized by the National Commission on Libraries and Information Science, which decided to combine forces with the Institute for Computer Sciences and Technology of the National Bureau of Standards to expedite the development of a protocol. Some of the members of the ISAD Committee, including the Chairperson, Philip Long, were to serve on the NCLIS/NBS task force.

Other committees in ISAD were also active during the year. The Program Planning Committee, in addition to sponsoring some of the Division's Conference programs and coordinating other programs held by the other units of ISAD, sponsored two institutes during the year. Both institutes, one in March and the other in October, were co-sponsored by the Library of Congress and both were on Processing and Automation at the Library of Congress.

Four institutes were planned for 1977: an institute on The National Bibliographic Network in Chicago February 24–25; in New York City in April; and in Los Angeles in May institutes on the future of the catalog will be sponsored, and an institute on circulation systems was considered for September.

The ISAD/LED Committee on Education for Information Science and Automation planned a one-day institute on April 25, at the University of New York at Albany to deal with strategies for change within a library school environment.

Standards. The Technical Standards for Library Automation Committee (TESLA) has been considering several proposals for ANSI standards. A proposed standard for patron identification, a standard account number, and a standard for sound levels in libraries are being studied. A procedure for the assignment and maintenance of library identification codes is also being discussed.

The ISAD Editorial Board has been concerned for some time about the failure of advertising in the *Journal of Library Automation* (JOLA) to produce more income for the publication. For 1975–76, it was estimated that JOLA advertising would produce a gross income of $3,300. It actually produced $1,946. In the hope of revitalizing JOLA advertising, the

ISAD Board of Directors proposed an 18-month experiment under which the Editorial Board would appoint an advertising editor and JOLA would handle its own advertising. At the end of that time, the situation will again be evaluated.

The new Audiovisual Section adopted a set of bylaws designed specifically for its needs, and its Executive Committee passed a motion that ISAD consider changing its name to the Information Technology Division. The section sponsored two programs at the ALA Annual Conference. One was on AV in libraries, the other on non-print media data bases. Plans were underway for a preconference prior to the 1977 Detroit ALA Conference on the subject of New Technologies and the Impact on Libraries.

The Video and Cable Communications Section was extremely active with a broad range of projects. Six committees have been established and were operational by the end of 1976.

Distribution and Exchange Committee. This Committee, chaired by Lynne Bradley, identifies and evaluates bibliographic standards for video and identifies problem areas in elements of cataloging description. It also identifies and evaluates models of library video programming procurement, exchange, and distribution. The Committee has established two subcommittees to carry on its work. One subcommittee, under Bradley, is charged with the responsibility of gathering information on video software cataloging and of providing that data to the RTSD Catalog Code Revision Committee.

The second subcommittee, under Marilyn Rehnberg, is to survey the nation's libraries to determine which libraries are using videotapes, what equipment they use, what cataloging is done, and what services are provided, among other things. A questionnaire will be distributed through the newsletter *Cable Libraries*. The results will be tabulated and published.

Legislation and Regulation Committee. Under the chair of Margaret Cleland, this committee monitors federal agencies, copyright legislation, funding legislation in support of telecommunications, and all cable related developments in executive agencies and the Congress.

Through Larry Molumby, the committee testified in July before the U.S. Legislative Subcommittee on Cable Communications on behalf of libraries and their use of cable communications. The testimony included a description of the services provided by libraries, the investment in staff and funds made by libraries, the need for public access, and the need for financial support.

Another item for concern was the Public Broadcasting Service's (PBS) recent issuance of rules for off-air taping of some of its programs. Libraries have been excluded by the rule that allows "formal curriculum use" only. The Committee is attempting to have this rule altered to allow public libraries to tape programs and retain them for seven days.

Technological Developments Committee. Under Robert Boese, this committee investigates the current status and use of video and cable technology for library services, and monitors technical developments of video and cable and related technologies significant to library application. An investigation is being made to determine what action the Public Service Satellite Consortium is taking in the matter of commercial monopolization of the satellite channels. Two other projects include the compilation of a standard terminology list and a directory of technical experts.

Video and Cable Utilization Committee. John Goodell is Chairperson of this committee, which investigates, analyzes and disseminates information about the methods and practices of video and cable utilization by libraries. The Committee in 1976 was compiling video service policy statements used by libraries. Such policy statements include on-site taping, in-library viewing, taping with/for community groups, utilization of broadcast television, and other areas. The responses will be analyzed for similarities and differences and a report will be made to the Section.

Another project is that of the creation of a statement of responsibility for libraries that would encourage correct previewing and purchase procedures so that video distributors could have confidence in those libraries subscribing to the statement that they would not take advantage of the preview period to copy the preview print illegally.

Two other committees newly established in VCCS are Membership Special Committee and Publications Special Committee. Membership, chaired by Leslie Burk, is exploring potential

---

ISAD Officers

PRESIDENT (July 1976 – July 1977):
Joseph A. Rosenthal, University of California, Berkeley, California

VICE-PRESIDENT/PRESIDENT-ELECT:
Maurice Freedman, The Branch Libraries, New York Public Library

PAST PRESIDENT:
Henriette Avram, Special Assistant for Network Development, Library of Congress, Washington, D.C.

EXECUTIVE SECRETARY:
Donald P. Hammer

Membership (August 31, 1976): 3,456 (1,800 personal and 1,656 organizational)

membership areas, a promotional campaign, and membership information dissemination opportunities. Publications, under Roberto Esteves, was organized to investigate the best way to meet the informational needs of VCCS members, to solicit articles for the *Journal of Library Automation,* and to coordinate activities with the newsletter *CableLibraries.*

VCCS has carried out other activities during the year, three of which are a "single-issue newsletter" that was sent to every member summarizing the section's planning and activities, the sponsorship of *Video Visions* closed-circuit demonstration of library produced video tapes, plus a Conference program on Video Programs and Their Problems.

DONALD P. HAMMER

See also *Automation; Networks;* and *Data Bases, Computer-Readable.*

Insurance for Libraries

Each year millions of homeowners, business concerns, schools, and other institutions experience devastating losses by a fire. The National Fire Protection Association estimated that in 1975, 3,105,200 fires caused an approximate loss value of $4,170,600,000. Practically every 10 seconds of every day, fire strikes somewhere in the United States. Usually, insurance is the best method to safeguard the buildings and contents against financial loss. Selecting the right policy and coverage is protection against the ever-present, destructive nature of fires. However, Charles F. Gosnell adeptly stated, in an article in the *Encyclopedia of Library and Information Science:*

> ... it is well to recognize and remember that all losses, whatever the intermediate arrangement for compensation or spreading the risk, are losses to society as a whole and are eventually paid for by the public at large. Insurance is a fine device for softening the blows of loss, but is not in itself productive. Productivity occurs when the losses are prevented, and society is therefore so much the richer.[1]

Fire, in a library, is probably the single most menacing threat because of the contents of the building. Yet many library fiscal managers appear to lack the knowledge to obtain adequate and proper insurance coverage. Although the ultimate responsibility for proper insurance coverage rests with the library board and the insurance manager, the librarian's role is vitally important. As part of the job of managing the business affairs of the library, the librarian should help to determine the risks of loss that should be protected and those that should be self-insured. This is the concept of risk management, but the librarian's role should not cease after the insurance has been obtained. The librarian should develop a program to train staff in life-safety and fire prevention methods.

Misconceptions. Bruce Harvey, in an article in *Library Security Newsletter,*[2] suggests that misconceptions about fire hazards in libraries include the view that "fires in libraries are rare" and that "libraries can be made virtually fireproof by construction, the use of special materials and furnishings, and the provision of security patrols." A survey cited by Harvey—*National Survey on Library Security*—indicated that 87 percent of the 255 participating institutions did not have sprinklers or automatic suppression systems, 60 percent did not have fire alarms, 50 percent had no guards, no burglary or fire alarms, and two out of three libraries rated fire prevention equipment as the lowest of 11 security improvements. Information about fire prevention training programs and automatic fire prevention systems is sorely lacking in the literature.

USEFUL GUIDE

A succinctly written book—*Managing the Library Fire Risk* by John Morris—is a useful guidebook to make librarians and library boards more aware of the ever-present danger of fire and of fire prevention systems and programs. The first four chapters analyze several fires. The last four chapters are especially useful as a guide for staff awareness on fire prevention. They cover (1) Alternatives for protecting the library, (2) Disaster preparedness and fire prevention, (3) Salvage of wet books, and (4) Automatic fire protection systems. The book discusses early-warning fire detection systems, Halon 1301, automatic sprinkler systems, fire-resistant materials, and automatic-closing fire doors, from the viewpoint of a fire engineer's recommendations and from systems in actual operation. Written emergency guidelines should be prepared and the staff should be thoroughly familiar with the plans discussed in the chapter on disaster preparedness and fire prevention. The chapter on salvage of wet books outlines two techniques: freeze-drying and the heated vacuum process as well as the need to include an emergency plan for the restoration of wet books. The book notes that automatic fire protection systems are functionally divided into two types. They are (1) automatic detection systems and (2) extinguishing systems. Also included are drawings, descriptions and comments on such systems as automatic sprinklers—wet-pipe system, dry-pipe system and pre-action system; pre-action fire cycle system; aquamatic sprinklers (on-off); Halon 1301, and automatic detection systems.

To safeguard the library building and contents against financial loss, a combination of adequate insurance coverage, automatic fire protection systems, and fire prevention programs or guidelines should be high priorities for library fiscal managers.

(*See also* Security Systems.)

DONALD L. UNGARELLI

REFERENCES

1. Charles F. Gosnell, "Insurance, Library," in *Encyclopedia of Library and Information Science*, v. 12 (New York: Marcel Dekker, Inc., 1974).
2. Bruce Harvey, "Fire Hazards in Libraries," *Library Security Newsletter* 1, no. 1: 1 + (January 1975).
3. John Morris, *Managing the Library Fire Risk* (California: University of California, 1975).

See also *Security Systems*.

Intellectual Freedom

"It was the best of times, it was the worst of times, it was the age of wisdom, it was the age of foolishness. . . ." With these words, Charles Dickens began *A Tale of Two Cities*. Well over 100 years later, the words serve once again to illuminate a period of time. The year 1976 was the Bicentennial birthday of the United States, as well as the Centennial birthday of the American Library Association. In the nation as a whole, during that landmark year, intellectual freedom fared no better, but no worse, than in the preceding year. Within the library profession, however, it fared somewhat better.

HISTORICAL PERSPECTIVE

There is no doubt, from a historical perspective, that these are the best of times. Citizens of the United States have more freedom to speak their minds, to write their thoughts, than ever before in our history, perhaps in the history of civilization. And yet, these are, or have the potential of becoming, the worst of times. The adversaries of intellectual freedom are not only becoming more sophisticated and subtle, but have at their disposal more money than the defenders can hope to accumulate in the foreseeable future. Still, the proponents of intellectual freedom, spearheaded by the American Library Association's intellectual freedom program, continue to hold their own.

NATIONAL PROGRAMS

ALA Honors. The contributions of ALA's intellectual freedom program were recognized in two separate awards presented during 1976. In June Judith F. Krug, Director of the Office for Intellectual Freedom (OIF), received the 1976 Irita Van Doren Award. Sponsored by the American Booksellers Association, the Publishers' Ad Club, and the Publishers' Publicity Association, the Award is presented in memory of Irita Van Doren, literary editor of the *New York Herald Tribune* for 37 years. The citation, engraved on a silver bowl, reads: "Irita Van Doren Award, 1976, to Judith F. Krug for her many contributions to the cause of the book as an instrument of culture in American life."

In December the Office for Intellectual Freedom received the Harry Kalven Freedom of Expression Award, sponsored by the Illinois Division of the American Civil Liberties Union. Harry Kalven was Professor of Law at the University of Chicago from 1945 until his death in 1974. The award has been given annually since 1974 both to honor Kalven for his achievements in the area of First Amendment law and to honor the recipients who have carried on his work. The citation reads: "Their dedicated efforts on behalf of free expression and the unfettered flow of ideas have reached across the nation: they continue to provide the First Amendment with the ceaseless, relentless defense it requires."

But while the work of the intellectual freedom program received growing recognition, it was no secret that it could not alone tackle every injustice that comes to its attention or fight every battle through to its conclusion. Nevertheless, the alarms are sounded, and slowly, but surely, other groups are joining in the fight.

NCTE Committee. 1976 saw the establishment of an anti-censorship committee by the National Council of Teachers of English (NCTE). The purpose is to inform NCTE members of agencies and organizations which may be of assistance during a censorship controversy; serve as a resource on current patterns of censorship; and offer advice on strategies for dealing with censorship threats. This new group held its organizing meeting in November, during the annual conference of NCTE.

National Coalition. Also in 1976, the National Ad Hoc Committee Against Censorship, determined to present a more permanent image to the world, renamed itself the National Coalition Against Censorship. Organized as a result of the First Amendment cases [*Miller v. California*, 413 U.S. 15 (1973); *Paris Adult Theatre I v. Slaton*, 413 U.S. 49 (1973); *Kaplan v. California*, 413 U.S. 115 (1973)] decided by the U.S. Supreme Court in June 1973, the Coalition is informally structured, composed of representatives from 23 national organizations, and guided by an eight-member steering committee, on which ALA holds a seat. The primary purpose of the Coalition is to educate the memberships of its constituent organizations to the importance of the First Amendment. In partial accomplishment of this goal, the Coalition's New York coordinator wrote articles during the year for journals of the members' organizations. Several newspaper articles were developed using the files of both the Coalition and the OIF. A second-level education effort is the responsibility of OIF and entails the development of state level groups to effect grass-roots education programs. The Coalition, unfortunately, has continuing monetary problems, resulting in a large part of the New York staff's time being devoted to seeking funds rather than to promoting the First Amendment.

Intellectual Freedom

Despite its funding difficulties, the Coalition held three plenary sessions during 1976, focusing on such topics as the pros and cons of the Federal Communications Commission's "Fairness Doctrine"; the repressive nature of the espionage section of S.1, the proposed codification of the federal criminal code; and film censorship.

IFC. Many of the issues of general interest to the National Coalition Against Censorship and its constituent organizations were of specific concern to the ALA Intellectual Freedom Committee (IFC). In some instances, the IFC dealt with the issues because of the far-reaching implications they had for the library profession as a whole. In other instances, the Committee was requested by other groups affected by the issues to study these concerns and arrive at a position. The FCC Fairness Doctrine was in the former category, the problems experienced by the Tricontinental Film Center in the latter.

FCC FAIRNESS DOCTRINE

The Fairness Doctrine of the Federal Communications Commission became an issue of concern for the IFC when two bills were introduced in the 94th Congress to repeal it. S.2, sponsored by Sen. William Proxmire (D. Wisc.), was entitled the First Amendment Clarification Act of 1975; H.R. 2189, under the sponsorship of Rep. Robert Drinan (D. Mass.), was entitled the First Amendment Implementation Act of 1975. From the titles of the bills, it was obvious that the sponsors believed the Fairness Doctrine inhibited First Amendment guarantees, particularly those relating to freedom of speech. The bills were brought before the IFC at the 1975 Annual Conference, not because their passage seemed imminent, but because the issues directly related to the Association's interpretation of intellectual freedom.

The Fairness Doctrine, enacted into law by Congress in 1959, was ostensibly designed to resolve controversies stemming from the limited number of broadcast channels and to insure persons and organizations attacked or criticized on radio and television broadcasts a fair opportunity to reply. The opponents of the Fairness Doctrine hold that it inhibits discussions of controversial issues because broadcasters, especially small ones, are deemed to be forced to spend significant financial resources and time to satisfy the FCC that they provided a "fair" coverage of controversial issues on which they air programs. The opponents of the Fairness Doctrine believe that this results in a shying away from controversial issues by radio and television stations, with a net loss to the American public of information on major topics of importance.

Because of the complexity of the issues involved, the Committee did not deal with the matter during the 1975 Conference. A subcommittee was appointed to study the Fairness Doctrine and the two bills, and to report to the Committee at its next session.

The report presented by the subcommittee at the 1976 Midwinter Meeting was of interest for its lack of unanimity. It raised many questions, but answered few. For instance, in order to be consistent with ALA's traditional interpretation of the First Amendment, could the IFC endorse any restrictions on open, free, and robust debate, including those restrictions of the Fairness Doctrine? Could the IFC, in this instance, favor the restrictions of the Fairness Doctrine, because, given a limited number of radio and television broadcast channels, the question of access becomes an economic one? Individuals and groups who have the resources to "buy time" will be the ones who can make their views well known, while those who lack such resources will not be able to compete in the marketplace of views and ideas.

Divided in their answers to these questions and unable to reach a consensus, IFC members sent the issue back to the subcommittee for further study and analysis. The Fairness Doctrine debate continued at the Intellectual Freedom Committee's 1976 Annual Conference sessions. Major points of discussion included whether or not the Fairness Doctrine inhibited or enhanced controversial programming, and whether or not cable television would provide individuals and groups unable to buy access to network channels an opportunity to more readily air their own points of view. By the time of the Annual Conference, however, it was quite apparent that S.2 and H.R. 2189 would not pass during the 94th Congress and, indeed, they died with the adjournment of Congress in October. Nevertheless, in the belief that the issues remain important to the future of the IFC and the library profession's intellectual freedom position, the Committee will continue its debate at future meetings.

TRICONTINENTAL FILM CENTER

In April the Tricontinental Film Center requested the IFC's help in its efforts to resist an order from the U.S. Department of Justice that the Center register as a "foreign agent" under the Foreign Agents Registration Act. A distributor of third-world films, Tricontinental sells mainly to libraries and there are far-ranging implications with regard to libraries' tax-exempt status if Tricon were to adhere to the Justice Department's order. The Foreign Agents Registration Act requires that all individuals and groups in the employ of a foreign agent must so designate their status by registering. Once registered, any materials distributed by such "agents" must carry a label identifying their source. The implications for libraries which buy such materials are obvious.

First, there is a question of whether such a requirement constitutes labeling, an activity long opposed by ALA because it predisposes the user of materials so inscribed. Second is the implication for libraries' tax-exempt status. As publicly supported institutions, libraries may not "propagandize" on behalf of or against any particular organization, individual, or point of view. Their role is to provide, in a neutral setting, materials representing all points of view concerning questions and issues of import in the hope that the user will come to his own conclusions without the library subtly or obviously influencing such conclusions. Tricontinental Film Center contends that it distributes films from all third-world countries and that it enters into a contract with each producer whose work it handles. Furthermore, Tricontinental contends that being forced to register as a foreign agent would effectively force it out of business.

To help resolve the issue, the Intellectual Freedom Committee recommended that ALA counsel be requested to write to the Justice Department, asking for clarification of the consequences for the tax-exempt status of libraries if Tricontinental were to register as a foreign agent. A second letter was sent following the 1976 Annual Conference. In late summer, a response received from the Justice Department indicated that it was reviewing its request that Tricontinental register as a foreign agent.

FIRST AMENDMENT FILM

Beyond the IFC's involvement with the difficulties experienced by the Tricontinental Film Center, the film medium played a priority role in IFC activities during 1976, as its First Amendment film project took shape. During the spring OIF staff interviewed 16 producers and compiled a selective list from which the IFC's film subcommittee could make a final choice. In early summer the Committee named Lee Bobker, President of Vision Associates of New York, as the film producer.

Funding the project was another hurdle. At the spring meeting of the ALA Executive Board, the IFC proposed to fund the film partially through advance, pre-release orders. The Executive Board approved the film project, pending the Committee's ability to arrange appropriate funding. By July, when ALA held its Centennial celebration in Chicago, 99 prepaid film orders had been received. During the Annual Conference, Beta Phi Mu, the international library science honorary society, contributed a $12,000 grant to the Intellectual Freedom Committee toward the completion of the film. Finally, the Association entered a joint venture agreement with the producer.

During the fall, content of the film was determined and by December, the shooting script was completed. Photography began in early January. Tentatively titled *Days in the Death of Freedom*, the film is scheduled for release in April 1977.

The film focuses on the everyday potential for bit-by-bit erosion of the First Amendment rights enjoyed by U.S. citizens. The solution to such chipping away of our most basic freedoms is not only "eternal vigilance," but a continuing education of the populace. Each child born represents a new audience which must be educated and reeducated throughout a lifetime.

FEDERAL LEGISLATION

S.1. Indeed, it was only through education that individuals and organizations of every persuasion throughout the land were able to beat back the passage of S.1, the bill designed to "codify, revise, and reform" the Federal Criminal Code. A complex 750-page bill, S.1 was a residual of the Nixon administration. It went far beyond its description and proposed a number of far-reaching changes that raised very real threats to the civil liberties of American citizens. Of particular concern to the American Library Association were the sections on espionage and obscenity. So intense was the opposition to S.1 that toward the end of 1975, H.R. 10850 was introduced in the House by Representatives Robert Kastenmeier (D. Wisc.), Don Edwards (D. Calif.), and Abner Mikva (D. Ill). The House bill revised most of the glaring civil liberties problems in S.1, and eliminated entirely the repressive sections on obscenity and espionage. H.R. 10850 underwent two major revisions and added several more sponsors during 1976, but like S.1, the bill died with the adjournment of the 94th Congress.

Percy Bill. A second federal legislative action affecting intellectual freedom during the year was an extension of Senator Charles Percy's (R. Ill.) endeavor to mandate, through his previously introduced Senate Bill 1338, the use of federal funds for the acquisition of non-sex-biased materials. S. 1338, introduced in March 1975, included provisions to amend the Elementary and Secondary Education Act of 1965 by stipulating that five percent of federal funds be used on "a priority basis" in the acquisition of non-sex-biased library resources. In the summer of 1975, President Allie Beth Martin wrote to each sponsor of S. 1338 in order to make public ALA's objections to federal requirements that libraries purchase materials promoting specific points of view.

Since the bill did not appear to be moving toward passage, it was generally forgotten. In the last days of the 94th Congress, however, an amendment (2220) to Section 328 of S. 2657 was added on the floor of the Senate that

Intellectual Freedom

would have included in Title IV-B (School Libraries and Learning Resources) of the Elementary and Secondary Education Act a requirement that the funds appropriated for Title IV-B be used " . . . for the acquisition of school non-sex-biased library resources, textbooks, and other printed and published instructional materials. . . ."

ALA Position. The Office for Intellectual Freedom and the ALA Washington Office presented ALA's view that such an amendment would be contrary to Section 432 of the General Education Provisions Act, which states that education laws cannot be construed to authorize any U.S. department, agency, or officer to exercise control or direction over the selection of library resources and instructional materials by any educational institution or school system. It was pointed out that the Department of Health, Education and Welfare itself had stated, in issuing Title IX regulations, that in its opinion specific regulatory provisions in the area of educational materials would raise grave constitutional problems concerning the right of free speech under the First Amendment.

ALA held that, as a matter of principle, the content of library collections must be determined, ultimately, by the needs and desires of library patrons who, as individuals, retain the right of freedom of speech. Furthermore, the Association again stated its belief that the First Amendment prohibits federal governmental regulation of the content of school library resources.

The language concerning non-sex-biased materials was removed by the conference committee. Senate conferees said that although they agreed with its "intent," they believed it would violate the First Amendment.

INTERNATIONAL PROBLEMS

Hugo Blanco Incident. Federal legislation was not the only area in which ALA's intellectual freedom principles met head on with approved or proposed government policy. Another area concerned international problems with intellectual freedom overtones and, in accordance with ALA policy, the International Relations Committee (IRC) worked with the IFC in handling the matters. At the 1976 Midwinter Meeting, the two committees reviewed the U.S. Department of State's refusal to grant Peruvian author Hugo Blanco a visa to visit the United States for a lecture tour. Two issues were involved: the denial of Mr. Blanco's rights under Article 19 of the UN Universal Declaration of Human Rights and the denial of the rights of U.S. citizens to hear Mr. Blanco. The two committees prepared a resolution which was approved by Council on January 23 and sent to the U.S. Department of State. In early July, it was learned that the State Department had decided to grant Hugo Blanco the visa he desired but that the Justice Department had blocked his admission to the country.

Israel–UNESCO Issue. Another matter of import to the IRC and the IFC began in late 1974 when the UNESCO General Conference denied Israel permission to affiliate with UNESCO's European Regional Group. The matter was initially discussed by the two committees at the 1975 Midwinter Meeting. The committees brought to Council a resolution, which was subsequently approved, not only condemning UNESCO's action, but requesting that the U.S. government withhold funding from UNESCO until the exclusion of Israel was rectified. In the fall of 1976, the matter of Israel's affiliation with the European Regional Group appeared on the agenda of the 19th UNESCO General Conference held, in late October, in Nairobi, Kenya. The Conference, by a vote of 70 to 0 with 17 abstentions, recommended that Israel's request for affiliation with the European Regional Group be allowed.

USSR Censorship Ploy. Another item on the agenda for that General Conference of UNESCO appeared rather suddenly. It was an attempt by the USSR and various developing nations to force the General Conference to adopt a resolution granting to each sovereign nation the authority to control the news media within its borders. Such an action would have severely hampered newspaper reporters and broadcast journalists from providing any information except that which a particular government wished to have made available. The United States took the lead in a successful fight against the proposed resolution, and the resolution was sent back to committee for a total rewrite.

U.S. SCHOOL LIBRARIES

The simultanteous potential of becoming the worst of times still continues unabated. The rumblings that were heard in Kanawha County, West Virginia, in 1974 and gained strength in 1975, found new adherents and stronger voices in 1976. The strength of the voices continued to be felt in classrooms and school libraries around the country where taxpayers, particularly parents, continued to demand an involvement with school classroom and library materials selection.

As the strength of parental involvement grows within the various school systems, the classroom materials begin to reflect the values and principles held by these adults. Libraries, particularly those in schools, also feel the pressures. Some parents want materials removed that focus on sex; others are concerned with those which portray communism; and still others abhor materials that discuss drugs, abortion, single-parent families, and other matters. Women's groups may want materials removed that do not portray women as being equal to men in almost every way, and other groups wish to remove materials that they consider to have a racist bias. Some wish to add materials that reflect society as they see it, to the exclusion of how others see it. One ploy used frequently in 1976 was to attempt to keep a school or a library from buying all materials by a particular publisher who has issued one book with which the complainants disagree. It was in order to combat this kind of ploy, as well as to reiterate the importance of the principles of intellectual freedom, that the Association of American Publishers published the pamphlet "Books and the Young Reader."

Ohio Decision. In the midst of the pressures, one positive note appeared in the fall, when the Sixth Circuit Court of Appeals handed down a decision growing out of a case in Strongsville, Ohio *(Minarcini, et al. v. Strongsville City School District, et al.)*. The school board of that community had banned from the curriculum and from the school library *Cat's Cradle* and *Good Morning, Mr. Rosewater*, both by Kurt Vonnegut, and *Catch-22* by Joseph Heller. The ban was challenged by the Ohio Civil Liberties Union and the result was a favorable decision for libraries. In its opinion, the Sixth Circuit Court stated:

> A library is a storehouse of knowledge. When created for a public school it is an important privilege created by the state for the benefit of the students in the school. That privilege is not subject to being withdrawn by succeeding school boards whose members might desire to "winnow" the library for books the content of which occasioned their displeasure or disapproval....
>
> A public school library is also a valuable adjunct to classroom discussion. If one of the English teachers considered Joseph Heller's *Catch-22* to be one of the more important modern American novels (as, indeed, at least one did), we assume that no one would dispute that the First Amendment's protection of academic freedom would protect both his right to say so in class and his students' right to hear him and to find and read the book. Obviously, the students' success in this last endeavor would be greatly hindered by the fact that the book sought had been removed from the school library. The removal of books from a school library is a much more serious burden upon freedom of classroom discussion than the action found unconstitutional in *Tinker v. Des Moines Independent Community School District*, 393 U.S. 503 (1969).
>
> Further, we do not think this burden is minimized by the availability of the disputed book in sources outside the school. Restraint on expression may not generally be justified by the fact that there may be other times, places, or circumstances available for such expression....
>
> A library is a mighty resource in the free marketplace of ideas. It is specially dedicated to broad dissemination of ideas. It is a forum for silent speech.... [*Minarcini v. Strongsville*, No. 75-1467-69 (6th Cir. August 30, 1976), p. 6, 7, 9, 10]

If it is not overturned, the Sixth Circuit Court's decision will become a landmark for libraries.

As was shown in "Freedom in America: The Two-Century Record," the Intellectual Freedom Committee's 1976 Centennial Conference program, freedom in America is sustained by what occasionally seems to be a very slender thread. Our best hope for maintenance of our freedoms—and perhaps the only one—is constant education and reeducation to their importance. For while it is true that we live in the best of times, the elements to make them the worst of times thrive, and only the continued vigilance of librarians and libraries will keep our freedoms secure. —JUDITH F. KRUG

Intellectual Freedom Round Table

One of the highlights of the ALA Centennial Conference was an IFRT sponsored speech by I. F. Stone, for many years the controversial editor, publisher and author of *I. F. Stone's Weekly*. The speech, one of the best attended in ALA history, was only one of many contributions made during the year to the profession by the Intellectual Freedom Round Table. They included financial donations to the Office of Intellectual Freedom and the Freedom to Read Foundation of $500 to each.

IFRT continued to attempt to define its role in relation to the Freedom to Read Foundation, the Office of Intellectual Freedom, and the Intellectual Freedom Committee. An Ad Hoc Committee on Priorities submitted a report which was approved by the IFRT Membership; major recommendations included the following:

(1) IFRT shall develop and implement action programs which support, inform, educate and involve the librarian at the local level in intellectual freedom matters.

(2) IFRT shall serve as a forum for discussion of activities, programs and problems in intellectual freedom of libraries and librarians.

(3) IFRT shall offer greater opportunity for involvement among members of ALA in defense of intellectual freedom.

IFRT Officers

CHAIRPERSON (July 1976–June 1977):
John M. Carter, Wyoming State Library
Cheyenne, Wyoming

VICE-CHAIRPERSON/CHAIRPERSON-ELECT:
Karl Weiner, Skokie Public Library,
Skokie, Illinois

SECRETARY:
Ione Pierron, Eugene, Oregon

TREASURER:
Ella Gaines Yates, Atlanta Public Library,
Atlanta, Georgia

Membership: (August 31, 1976): 930

I. F. Stone receives congratulations following his IFRT address at the 1976 ALA Centennial Conference.

Interlibrary Cooperation

In an attempt to keep open the lines of communication between itself and similar segments of ALA, the IFRT established two new offices which provided for liaison persons to the Intellectual Freedom Committee and the Freedom to Read Foundation.

Another major action of IFRT was the establishment of the "John Phillip Immroth Memorial Award for Outstanding Contributions to Intellectual Freedom." This award was named after the late founder and original Chairperson of IFRT who died in 1976 (see Obituaries). (See also Intellectual Freedom, Freedom to Read Foundation.)   JOHN M. CARTER

Interlibrary Cooperation

The trend toward multitype interlibrary cooperation noted in last year's article seemed to accelerate in 1976. The *ASLA Report on Interlibrary Cooperation* (Association of State Library Agencies, 1976) identified single and multitype library systems, networks, and consortia in all 50 states. Multitype operations were reported by 37 states. At year's end it seemed hardly possible that a library in the nation had not considered linking with at least one cooperative undertaking, whether an informal, loose-knit consortium or a huge organization extending over a wide region and involving every type of library.

Conferences. Conferences examined aspects of interlibrary cooperation and at year's end many librarians awaited published proceedings of two particularly significant meetings. The first was a four-hour meeting, "Opportunities in Multitype Interlibrary Cooperation," sponsored by several ALA divisions at the ALA Centennial Conference July 22. Roderick G. Swartz, Washington State Librarian, and Sylvia Faibisoff of the University of Arizona examined respectively the ways interlibrary cooperation is used to respond to user needs and the planning, governance, and funding of cooperative programs. A series of speakers examined urban/rural cooperatives, special problems by types of libraries, cooperative services, and state and federal roles.

The other was the "Pittsburgh Conference on Resource Sharing in Libraries," September 29–October 1, to which the University of Pittsburgh School of Library and Information Science drew some 350 library people for three days of high-powered discussion of the "explosive . . . dizzying" growth of networks.

State library agencies seemed to be taking the lead in advancing development of intra- and inter-state multitype cooperatives, partly in response to the program proposed by the National Commission on Libraries and Information Science (NCLIS). In several states state library agency participation and support enabled libraries of all types to participate in OCLC and in shared data-bank programs. The Denver-based Bibliographic Center for Research (BCR) extended shared use of data-banks to all types of libraries in Colorado, Utah, Wyoming, Kansas, Iowa, and South Dakota.

Support from state library agencies in Michigan, Minnesota, and Wisconsin enabled MIDLNET to get off the ground. By year's end MIDLNET had made OCLC membership available to libraries in Iowa and Missouri and was developing data-bank access in six states.

In a November meeting in Atlanta, state librarians from the SOLINET region reviewed interrelationships between state plans for interlibrary cooperation, SOLINET development, and interlibrary cooperation opportunities made possible by the creation of the first full-time Executive Director for the Southeastern Library Association (SELA).

Multitype Systems. Statewide planning for interlibrary cooperation generally was marked by greater participation on the part of academic libraries in 1976. In Wisconsin, for instance, a 45-member Task Force on Interlibrary Cooperation and Resource Sharing worked for some 12 months with Sally Drew, examining barriers as well as potential for interlibrary cooperation and formulating alternatives for further development (*Wisconsin Plan for Interlibrary Cooperation*, ed. S. Drew, Madison, Division for Library Services, 1976).

By year's end this theme of converting regional library systems from public library-based operations to multitype systems was evident in many states. Illinois took a major step in this direction by funding an interlibrary cooperation coordinator position for each of its 18 systems. Ohio was moving to implement a November 1975 state law authorizing multitype Metropolitan Library Systems, and the first of these, the Cleveland Area Metropolitan Library System (CAMLS), was off to a good start under the leadership of Dorothy Sinclair.

Some states had yet to decide the locus or nature of authority for multitype library system development. Early in 1976 nine states reported the absence of specific authority for multitype library cooperative development, but others cited "joint exercise of powers," contract, or other broad authority for action in this area of interlibrary cooperation.

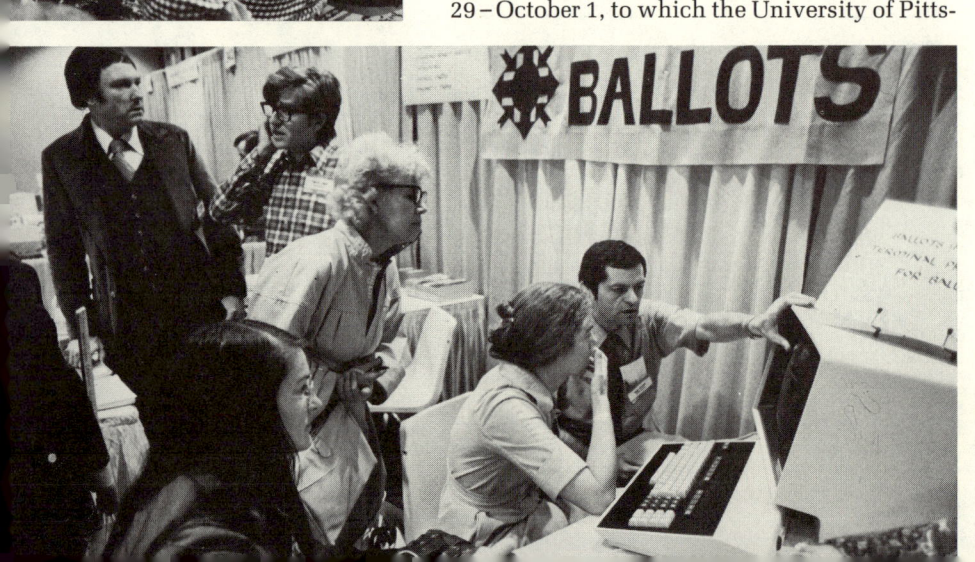

Manned exhibits explaining Stanford's BALLOTS and Ohio colleges' OCLC on-line bibliographic data bases drew attention from the participants at the California Library Association's meeting in December 1976.

Broadened state library agency advisory councils, consortia of university libraries expanded to include more than academic libraries, and new committees provided mechanisms for broader participation in planning interlibrary cooperation. For example, Minnesota reorganized its state library agency advisory council; the Michigan Library Consortium continued its expansion from a committee of university libraries—the Detroit Public Library, and the Michigan State Library—to a wider multitype library group; and the Ohio Multitype Interlibrary Cooperation Committee was formed by seven statewide organizations working with the State Library to develop a statewide networking plan for the end of 1977. Connecticut organized a 15-member Cooperating Library Service Units Review Board under a 1975 statute.

Established statewide networks were developing and changing. The Indiana State Library, which had pioneered INDIRS and INCOLSA, commissioned another statewide 12-month study of interlibrary cooperation, undertaken by Harold E. Baker of Indiana State University. On the west coast the Washington Library Network gained further impetus from the direction of State Librarian Rod Swartz, and CLASS (California Library Authority for Systems and Services) was gearing up for development under its newly appointed director, Ron Miller, formerly of NELINET.

Expanding Networks. Burgeoning networks, however, were by no means restricted by state boundaries. Those covering several states and acting as service brokers (such as AMIGOS, NELINET, SOLINET, and BCR) expanded. Stanford's BALLOTS extended its services to libraries beyond California, and the Washington Library Network was preparing to extend beyond Washington State in 1977.

Responding to November 1975 membership action asking OCLC to investigate the possibility of extending voting privileges to libraries outside Ohio, OCLC established a nationally representative committee to advise on the development of alternatives to the existing governance structure. OCLC continued to expand its service capacity by adding a third on-line computer enabling it to reduce response time significantly. Kellogg Foundation grants to colleges in 39 states permitted several hundred small academic libraries to use OCLC.

The Library of Congress substantially strengthened these aspects of interlibrary cooperation in 1976 by creating the office of Special Assistant for Network Development. LC convened three meetings of policy makers of network-related organizations and funding agencies, expected to result in the development of a major position paper. Particular interest focuses on a pilot study initiated by the Research Libraries Group (Harvard, New York Public, Columbia, and Yale) to work with LC on computer-to-computer dialog for resource sharing. NCLIS commissioned a study of the role of the Library of Congress in the emerging national network, and this report is expected in early 1977.

Some Negatives. While the trend toward increased interlibrary cooperation clearly continued to gain momentum in 1976, the movement was not without its critics. Perhaps the first signs of a potential backlash began to appear, as librarians from large university and research libraries in particular found themselves spending sizable sums of their scarce funds to serve patrons for whom they were not primarily responsible. As fees for interlibrary loan and photocopying became more common, a standing ovation was given a librarian at a resource sharing meeting who protested the burdens being placed on the "net lenders" by "outsiders." Other problems loomed in the path of network growth: uncertainties of the new copyright law, the deteriorating quality of the postal service, and the potentially crippling effects of strikes like the one that grounded UPS for a part of 1976.

Creativity of staff members, and person-to-person contact determines the extent to which these efforts improve service to the people libraries serve. Interlibrary cooperation begins with discussion and imagination. Ideas for interlibrary cooperation requiring no new legislation, funds, or organization are not exhausted. Some in the area of school-public library cooperation in behalf of children were set out in the handbook/game, "The Cooperation Game" (Columbus, The Ohio Library Association, 1976).

JOSEPH F. SHUBERT;
KEVIN FLAHERTY

Public library interlibrary loan requests are handled at a TWX machine by the Texas Library Communications Network at the Texas State Library, Austin.

International Board on Books for Young People

The central event in the calendar of the International Board on Books for Young People (IBBY) is its biennial Congresses and 1976 was a year in which a Congress took place. Representatives from the approximately 40 National Sections of IBBY gathered in Athens, Greece, from September 28 through October 2. The Congress was the 15th in a series that goes back to the early fifties, when the late Jella Lepman convened an international gathering of children's book figures who determined that similar meetings should take place on a regular basis. In order to provide a focus for such gatherings, IBBY was established. It was soon identified as a unique body, one of the few international literary and service organizations whose membership represents many different disciplines. Each National Section is formed in ways that seem most suitable to it. In the U.S., for example, the National Section is made up of the membership of the Children's Services Division (CSD) of ALA and the membership of the Children's Book Council (CBC). The governing body, there, includes the Presidents of both CSD and CBC and various other persons with official responsibilities toward their respective organizations or toward IBBY. In some countries, the National Section may be composed of an authors' group working closely with persons in education; in other countries, particularly in Eastern Europe, the National Section is a quasi-official governmental group. The mixture, especially on the occasions of IBBY's Congresses, is surprisingly diverse, and serves to dramatize national differences, while at the same time pointing out, as well, that children's books can serve to unite those who might otherwise be incompatible.

The theme of the 1976 Congress, selected by the hosts, the Circle of Greek Children's Books, in cooperation with the Greek National Ministry of Civilization and Sciences, was fairy tales and poetry. Numerous papers on these subjects were presented over several days. The American delegation—the largest on hand, apart from people from Greece—was represented with two contributions. Virginia Haviland of the Library of Congress spoke on "Fairy Tales in an Age of Technocracy" and Mary Jane Anderson of CSD spoke on "The Poetry of Early Childhood." Other presentations included those by Hans Halbey, Director of the Klingspor Museum in Offenbach, Germany, on "Maurice Sendak's 'In the Night Kitchen': Analysis and Research of Children's Reception"; Bettina Hürlimann, the critic and former Swiss publisher on "Are Illustrations to Fairy Tales a Necessity?"; and Israeli author Uriel Ofek on "The Role of Poetry in the Life of a Modern Child." Many of the papers will appear in due course in *Bookbird*, the quarterly periodical of the International Institute of Children's Literature in Vienna, one function of which is to publicize the activities of IBBY.

Awards. The highlight of the Congresses is customarily the presentation of the Hans Christian Andersen Medals, given every two years to an author and an illustrator for the entire body of their work for children. The 1976 recipients were the writer Cecil Bødker of Denmark and the illustrator Tatyana Mavrina of the U.S.S.R. Cecil Bødker's only book published in the U.S. as of the time of the award was *The Leopard* (Atheneum, 1975), but several of her books were to appear under the Seymour Lawrence/Delacorte Press imprint. Ms. Mavrina's work appears not to have been published outside of Eastern Europe; she works in basic colors, has a heavy line, and is a mistress of traditional peasant art that is an integral part of much of Eastern European children's books; her work would remind one, perhaps, of early work, here, of the Petershams, or perhaps Willy Pogany. One U.S. author, E.B. White, was Highly Commended in this competition. The 1976 IBBY Honor Books, recommended as especially notable and worthy of publication internationally, were *M.C. Higgins, the Great* by Virginia Hamilton (Macmillan, 1974) and *Dawn* by Uri Shulevitz (Farrar, Straus & Giroux, 1974). The President of the Hans Christian Andersen Jury, reelected to preside over the 1978 Jury, as well, was Lucia Binder of Austria. Zena Sutherland of the University of Chicago served on the 1976 Jury.

Officers. Hans Halbey of the German Federal Republic was reelected President of IBBY for a second and final term during the Congress. Reelected to the IBBY Executive Committee were Ann Beneduce (U.S.A.), Knud Hauberg-Tychsen (Denmark), Lily Ayman (Iran) and Lise Lebel (France). Newly elected members are Shigeo Watanabe (Japan), Sergeij Alexejev (U.S.S.R.), Regina Werneck (Brazil) and Assen Bossev (Bulgaria). The Executive Committee customarily meets two times during the year, and governs IBBY's activities between Congresses. Currently, IBBY is developing cooperative programs with both UNESCO and UNICEF; IBBY's representative to UNICEF is Augusta Baker of the United States. IBBY expects to have a significant role in the International Year of the Child, as 1979 has been designated.

Friends of IBBY. The main activity of the U.S. National Section of IBBY has been its development as a membership organization, Friends of IBBY. At the end of 1976, approximately 200 Americans had joined the organization, whose purpose is to support IBBY's goals and IBBY itself and to encourage interest in both international children's literature and translated children's books. Friends has an annual meeting, usually associated with ALA's Midwinter, and issues a semi-annual Newsletter. Virginia Haviland of the Library of Congress is Chairperson of Friends. Its first annual meeting, in 1976, was significant in two ways: substantial papers on both French and English language Canadian children's literature were presented by two prominent librarians—Irène Aubrey of the National Library in Ottawa and Irma McDonough of the Provincial Library Service in Toronto—and the current and immediate past Presidents of IBBY— Hans Halbey and Niilo Visapaä of Finland— made special trips to America to extend greetings and good wishes from IBBY colleagues worldwide.

JOHN DONOVAN

International Federation for Documentation (FID)

The International Federation for Documentation (FID) held its 38th Conference and Congress in Mexico City in September 1976. Theme for the meeting was Information and Development.

The General Assembly met during the Conference with representatives from 36 of the 63 national members present. The most important business handled by the General Assembly was the election of new officers and councillors, the approval of a new dues structure, and the approval of annual budgets for 1977 and 1978. The budgets are approximately $275,000 for each of the years based on monies from dues and sales of publications as well as small subsidies from UNESCO. The General Assembly assigned the Council the task of developing a revised FID program with greater professional orientation which is to be structured around specific activities. This program will be presented to the 39th Conference and Congress in 1978. The national memberships of Greece, New Zealand and Iraq were ratified at the Mexico meeting.

The FID Regional Commission for Latin America (FID/CLA) held its 15th General Assembly meeting in conjunction with the FID Conference. As a result of a recommendation made during the meeting, FID/CLA will launch a project to analyze and evaluate libraries, documentation centers, networks, and information systems in Latin America.

In October the Regional Commission for Asia and Oceania (FID/CAO) held its 4th General Assembly in Bangkok.

In addition to its own meetings, FID officers and staff participated in the various meetings of UNESCO, IFLA, the International Organization for Standardization (ISO), and FID was represented at some 30 other international, regional, and national meetings in its field.

FID Committees carried out numerous tasks in 1976. FID/CR (Classification Research) published the proceedings of its 1975 Conference, "Ordering Systems for Global Information Networks"; published volume 16 in its report series *Classification Research (Argentina)* and awarded the first "Ranganathan Award for Classification Research" to Derek Austin of the British Library for his work on PRECIS (Preserved Context Index System). FID/DT (Terminology of Information and Documentation) published "Informatika. Tom 1: Terminologiya Informatikii (Bibliograficheskij Ukazatel' Rabot)," containing some 1,700 references. FID/ET (Education and Training), jointly with FID/DC, Asociación Latinoamericana de Escuelas de Bibliotecología y Ciencias de la Información (ALEBCI), and UNESCO, sponsored a seminar on the "Role of education and training of information specialists on development" in September in Mexico. FID/RI (Research on the Theoretical Basis of Information) published *Quantitative und Qualitative Analyse der wissenschaftlich-technischen periodischen Weltliteratur* (FID 545). FID/LD (Linguistics in Documentation) sponsored a workshop on linguistics and information science in May in Stockholm.

FID/CCC (Central Classification Committee) sponsored a symposium, "General classification systems in a changing world," in Brussels in November to commemorate the Dewey Decimal Classification centenary.

A new Committee, FID/PD (Patent Information and Documentation), was established in 1976, with the purpose of serving the needs of users of patent information.

VINITI (Vsesojuznyi Institut Naučno-tehničeskoi Informacii) completed the publication of the first volume of the FID journal *International Forum on Information and Documentation* (IFID).

The FID Secretariat, in addition to the News bulletin, published the bimonthly *R & D Projects in Documentation and Librarianship*, *Extensions and Corrections to the UDC, Series 9, No. 2*, and *Information Systems Design for Socio-economic Development* and *Retrospect and Prospect* (FID 542), the proceedings of a 1975 symposium held in Brussels.

KENNETH R. BROWN

International Relations

Jane Wilson joined the ALA staff January 15 as the new International Relations Officer to serve as the liaison for international relations within the ALA and with other national, regional, and local library associations. For the first time since 1972 the Association has a staff position concerned with international library relations. The International Relations Officer also coordinates ALA's international relations activities and interests with IFLA and other international organizations, with the State Department and its associated agencies, with such organizations as the OAS, and with related library organizations.

Centennial Conference. Approximately 86 librarians from around the world joined in the celebration of ALA's 100th Anniversary in July. The largest delegation was from Australia and numbered 21 while the next largest groups were from Japan (12) and the United Kingdom (9). Other countries represented by one or more librarians were: Belgium, Chile, Colombia, Denmark, Egypt, France, Iceland, Iran, Israel, Kuwait, Mexico, Netherlands, New Zealand, Nicaragua, Nigeria, Norway, Pakistan, Philippines, Republic of China, Sweden, Switzerland, Thailand, Togo, Trinidad, and the U.S.S.R. The international guests were feted at a reception sponsored by the International Relations Round Table, and Chicago's famous Museum of Science and Industry hosted a luncheon and tour. During the Conference, the ALA International Relations Committee sponsored a program meeting, "World Library Update," which featured talks by D. J. Foskett (Institute of Education, University of London, England), Valeri Korin (All Union Library of Foreign Literature, U.S.S.R.), Marina Restrepo

International Relations

(Escuela Interamericana de Bibliotecologia, Universidad de Antioquia, Colombia), Hakim Mohammed Said (Society for the Promotion and Improvement of Libraries, Pakistan), Mahin Tafazzoli (Teheran Book Processing Center, Iran) and Masao Yoshida (National Diet Library, Japan) on recent developments in librarianship within their countries.

Two other Conference program meetings were concerned with international matters. The first of the 1976 lectures in "Libraries and the Life of the Mind in America" series featured Herman Liebaers, Grand Marshal to the Court of Belgium and former president of IFLA, who spoke on "The Impact of American and European Librarianship Upon Each Other." At this same meeting, J. Melsens, the Canadian Consul General in Chicago, and Brian Land, past president of the Canadian Library Association, formally presented copies of Canada's Bicentennial gift to the American people, *Between Friends/Entre Amis*, to ALA officials. At a meeting on International Documents sponsored by the GODORT International Documents Task Force, Herbert Leader, Director of Publishing, Her Majesty's Stationery Office, London, spoke on the work of his organization.

Book Week in Nigeria. At the November 22, 1974, meeting of the Government Advisory Committee on International Book and Library Programs (GAC), the International Trade Committee of the American Association of Publishers issued an invitation to the American Booksellers Association, the American Library Association, and the Association of American University Presses to join in the sponsorship of a special book exhibit with a concurrent three-part seminar to be held in Nigeria and to be known as "Book Week USA." The organizations involved accepted the invitation and the ALA appointed Esther J. Walls as the Chairperson to coordinate the library part of the program. This was to be the first time these four organizations had worked together on any project in the United States, much less on the international scene, and neither, it developed later, had Nigerian bookseller, library, and publishing associations been involved in international projects.

Thus, after many months of planning, "Book Week," a combination conference and series of workshops for publishers, librarians, and booksellers took place in Ibadan, Nigeria, January 19–25. The theme of the Conference, "The Role of the Book in Education," seemed most appropriate since in 1976 the Nigerian government began to implement the Universal Primary Education Program which requires that all children complete the sixth grade.

Attending the Conference were 156 representatives including 16 guests from the U.S. and four from England. The ALA delegation included Esther J. Walls, Associate Director of Libraries, State University of New York at Stony Brook; Jean Lowrie, Director, School of Librarianship, Western Michigan University, Kalamazoo; and Irving Lieberman, Professor of Librarianship, University of Washington. Those librarians who participated from Nigeria varied in level of experience from the Director of the National Library, the Director of the Library School at the University of Ibadan, special librarians, head and staff of university libraries, college librarians, to library school students.

Overviews of publishing, bookselling, and librarianship in the two countries were presented in plenary sessions by both Nigerian and American speakers. Another such session was concerned with interrelationships between librarians and the publishing and bookselling community. In addition, the library team participated in workshops on the goals and philosophy of librarianship; specific problem areas in librarianship; audiovisual sources; and computer applications in librarianship.

Many positive conclusions resulted from the historic meeting. It was noted that there is a definite role for U.S. librarians in encouraging the Nigerian government to continue to give high priority to the development of library services. Further encouragement is needed to help Nigerians in the development of national standards, national resources, bibliographical tools and standardized cataloging formats. The Nigerian librarians pleaded for better relationships with the Nigerian publishers and booksellers, and communication was begun at the Conference. U.S. and Nigerian librarians, booksellers, and publishers were unanimous in wanting another conference in 1978. Jean Lowrie, as the ALA Representative on GAC, will represent the ALA on a joint U.S. committee which will explore the follow-up to "Book Week."

IFLA. The ALA continued its active participation in IFLA affairs. As in Oslo in 1975, the August IFLA General Council meeting in Lausanne, Switzerland, was concerned with the restructuring of the organization. ALA Executive Director Robert Wedgeworth was the official delegate of the Association. He delivered a statement on the occasion of the ALA's 100th Anniversary followed by a slide presentation giving an impressionistic view of the history of library services in the United States. Margreet Wijnstroom, Secretary-General of IFLA, and Peter Havard-Williams, IFLA Vice-President, had represented IFLA at the ALA Centennial celebration.

As a result of the reorganization of IFLA, it was necessary for the seven member associations within the United States to establish a U.S. IFLA Committee in order to apportion both the national dues and the IFLA Council votes. The first meeting of the group was held in New York in early November. The ALA was represented by Wedgeworth and Jane Wilson.

UNESCO. Since the founding of UNESCO in 1948, the ALA has had a continuing interest in its library and book programs. Recently, because of the politicization of UNESCO and its stand on Israel, the United States has been withholding its full dues assessment pending the resolution of this matter. As a result, there had been great concern that the United States might lose its vote at the 19th UNESCO General Conference in October and November in Nairobi. On July 14, just prior to the ALA Annual Conference, the U.S. Congress approved a $3,500,000 appropriation for FY 1975, the minimum amount necessary to maintain the U.S. vote at the forthcoming Conference. A resolution on UNESCO, initiated by members of the International Relations Committee, was adopted by the ALA Council on July 23, which commended the Congress for this action and further resolved that the Association reaffirmed its belief in universal membership and full participation in UNESCO. The resolution also urged the American government to continue its vigorous support of the free flow of information and international cultural exchange.

In recent years there has been great concern in many quarters, including the ALA, with the development within UNESCO of two separate programs in the field of information and library services, NATIS (National Information Systems) and UNISIST (World Science Information System). The promotion of NATIS has been the responsibility of the Department of Documentation, Libraries and Archives, while the responsibility for UNISIST has fallen within the Division of Scientific and Technological Documentation and Information. It was understood that the Director-General of UNESCO would present a resolution designed to establish a unified information program within UNESCO at the 19th General Conference; however, the exact nature of the proposal was unknown until just before the Conference. In October immediately following U.S. Senate approval of the U.S. Delegation members to the Nairobi Conference, the Association wrote Delegates informing them of the ALA endorsement of such a unified information program. Only a few days later, the Association received UNESCO Document 19 C/43 (which contained two alternate proposals for establishing such a unified information program) and an invitation from the Department of State to participate in a meeting of the Ad Hoc Panel on UNESCO's Information Programs to prepare a common position paper for submission to the UNESCO General Conference. Jane Wilson and Eileen Cooke, Washington Office, represented the Association at this meeting. At Nairobi, the

Guests from the Japan Library Association met with personnel of the Fairfax County Public Library, Springfield, Virginia, on a tour of the U.S. to study American Public libraries.

International Guests

Following are guests from countries outside the U.S. and Canada who attended the ALA Centennial Conference in 1976:

Maria Cornejo Acosta, Jefe, Centro de Documentacion, Pedagogica, Superintendencia de Educacion Publica, Santiago, Chile

Ekoue-Degblon Amah, Director, University of Benin Library, Lome, Togo

Julian Behrstock, Director, Division of Free Flow of Information and Book Development, UNESCO, Paris, France

Judith Bowen, Research Associate, Leeds Polytechnic School of Librarianship, Leeds, England

Joan Brewer, Senior Lecturer, Adelaide College of Advanced Education, Adelaide, Australia

George Buick, Director, Murdock University Library, Murdock, Australia

Luisa Cardenas, Directora, Projecto Bibliotecas, Ministerio de Educacion Publica, Managua, Nicaragua

Maria Teresa Chavez, Directora, Biblioteca de Mexico, Mexico D.F., Mexico

Nancy Ou-Lan Chou, Director, Tamang College of Arts and Sciences Library, Taipei, Taiwan

Johan Cornelissen, Director, Stedelgke Openbare Bibliotheek, Renaix, Belgium

Owen Davies, London, England

Therese Delanty, Research Librarian, State Library of New South Wales, Sydney, Australia

James Dwyer, State Supervisor of School Libraries, South Australia, Adelaide, Australia

Lirlyn Elliott, University of the West Indies Library, St. Augustine, Trinidad

Eva Engberg, International Reading Association, European Office, Paris, France

Joseph Olatunji Fadero, Principal Librarian, Ministry of Education, Lagos, Nigeria

Dawn Fishburn, Senior Librarian, Bankstown Municipal Library, Sydney, Australia

D. J. Foskett, Librarian, University of London Institute of Education, London, England

Edward Fox, Director, Birmingham School of Librarianship, Birmingham, England

Margaret Fung, Associate Professor, National Taiwan Normal University, Taipei, Taiwan

Carmen E. de Garcia-Moreno, Director, Universidad Ibero-Americana Library, Mexico D.F., Mexico

Betty Goodger, Cataloger, State Library of New South Wales, Sydney, Australia

Michael Gorman, Head Bibliographical Standards Office, British Library, London, England

Martha M. Gorman de Alzate, Assistant Director, University of the Andes Library, Bogota, Colombia

Pensri Guaysuwan, Reference Librarian, Thammasat University Library, Bangkok, Thailand

Ali Haidar, Director of School Libraries, Ministry of Education, Kuwait, Kuwait

Indridi Hallgrimsson, Reference Librarian, University of Iceland Library, Reykjavik, Iceland

Eugenie Marie Halls, Senior

International Relations

Librarian, Education Resource Center, Melbourne, Australia

Sigrun Hannesdottier, University of Iceland Library, Reykjavik, Iceland

Peter Havard-Williams, Head, Department of Library and Information Studies, Loughborough University, Loughborough, England

Peggy Heeks, Assistant County Librarian, Berkshire County Library, England

Janet Hine, Head Cataloger, State Library of New South Wales, Sydney, Australia

Julialba Hurtado, Asesora O.E.A., Ministerio de Educación, Managua, Nicaragua

Atsuko Imamura, Translator, Kaiseisha Publishing Company, Tokyo, Japan

Kiyomichi Kai, Librarian, Tokyo Metropolitan Yashio High School Library, Tokyo, Japan

Madeleine Kinebanian, Head Librarian, Ecole de Traduction et d'Interprétation de l'Université de Genève, Genève, Switzerland

Yohko Kohno, Chief Librarian, ToYo Women's Junior College, Tokyo, Japan

Valeri J. Kozin, Head, Automation Department, All-Union State Library of Foreign Literature, Moscow, USSR

Herbert Leader, Director of Publishing, Her Majesty's Stationery Office, London, England

Lucy Te-Chu Lee, Associate Professor, Tamkang College of Arts & Sciences, Hsingtien Taiwan

Herman Liebaers, Grand Marshal to the Court of Belgium, Brussels, Belgium

Henk M. Lucas, Associate Director, Agricultural University Library, Wageningen, The Netherlands

Josephine McGovern, Librarian, Parliament of Victoria, Melbourne, Australia

Carmel Maguire, Senior Lecturer, School of Librarianship, University of New South Wales, Sydney, Australia

Barbara Manton, Librarian, Nunawading High School Resource Center, Melbourne, Australia

Elizabeth C. Miller, Young People's Librarian, Invercargill, New Zealand

Junkichi Morikawa, Kōsei Gakuen High School Library, Tokyo, Japan

Miyoko Murano, Musashino Municipal Obnode, Elementary School Library, Tokyo, Japan

Mieko Nagakura, Librarian, National Institute for Educational Research, Tokyo, Japan

Margot Nilson, Vice President, International Association of School Librarianship, Göteborg, Sweden

Jeanne Carol Owen, Head, Department of Librarianship, Queensland Institute of Technology, Brisbane, Australia

Valerie Packer, Media Consultant, Northern District's Education Centre, Cheltenlam, Australia

Ann Parry, Deputy Head, Library Services, New South Wales Department of Education, North Sydney, Australia

Aksel Petersen, Inspector of School Libraries, Odense, Denmark

Marie-Thérèse Pouillias, Service des Bibliothèques, Paris, France

Naimuddin Qureshi, Head, Science Division, University of Karachi, Karachi, Pakistan

Neil Radford, Associate Librarian, University of Sydney, Sydney, Australia

Marina Restrepo, Directora, Escuela Interamericana de Bibliotecología, Universidad de Antioquia, Medellin, Colombia

Denis Richardson, University Librarian, Melbourne University, Melbourne, Australia

Maxine Rochester, Lecturer, Canberra College of Advanced Education, Canberra, Australia

Margaret Rossiter, School Library Association, Canberra, Australia

Hakim Mohammed Said, President, Society for the Promotion and Improvement of Libraries, Karachi, Pakistan

Farkhondeh Saidi, Department of Library Science, University of Tehran, Tehran, Iran

Frederick H. Schaeffer, Australian National University Library, Canberra, Australia

Patricia Shoyinka, Chief Cataloger, University of Ibadan Library, Ibadan, Nigeria

Georg Simon, Royal Danish School of Librarianship, Copenhagen, Denmark

Ralph C. Simon, Director of Libraries, Technion City, Haifa, Israel

Makoto Sugiura, Manager, Information Center, Institute of Business Administration and Management, Tokyo, Japan

Isabel S. Sunio, Chairman, Library and Library Science Department, Philippine Normal College, Manila, Philippines

Ronald Surridge, Deputy Director, Bromley Public Library, London, England

Mahin Tafazzoli, Director, Teheran Book Processing Center, Teheran, Iran

Mitsuo Takamori, Editorial Director, Kaiseisha Publishing Company, Tokyo, Japan

Maya Thee, University of Bergen Library, Bergen, Norway

Narcisa Tioco, Chief Librarian, University of the East Library, Manila, Philippines

Margaret Trask, Head, Department of Library and Information Studies, Kuring-Gai College of Advanced Education, Sydney, Australia

Yoichi Utsumi, Director, Fukuoka Junior College of Social Welfare Library, Tagawa, Japan

Dia Van Vliet-Posthuma, Head, Administrative Department, International Federation of Library Associations, The Hague, Netherlands

Margreet Wijnstroom, Secretary General, International Federation of Library Associations, The Hague, Netherlands

Setsuko Yamada, Musashino Municipal Kyonan, Elementary School Library, Tokyo, Japan

Keiko Yamazaki, Tokyo Metropolitan Kudan High School Library, Tokyo, Japan

Masao Yoshida, Chief, Branch Libraries Section, National Diet Library, Tokyo, Japan

Veronica Young, Chief Librarian, Randwick Municipal Library, Sydney, Australia

Laurence Zaky, Head of Public Services, American University in Cairo, Cairo, Egypt

Mohamed H. Zehery, Kuwait Institute for Scientific Research, Kuwait, Kuwait

This list was compiled primarily from information supplied on advance registration forms and thus some attendees' names may not be included. Library school students and exhibitors are excluded.

UNESCO General Conference approved the concept of a unified information program within UNESCO.

U.S.S.R. Visit. A delegation of U.S. librarians headed by ALA Executive Director Wedgeworth visited the U.S.S.R. from November 14 to 27 under the auspices of the Department of State's Bureau of Educational and Cultural Affairs. The Ministry of Culture of the Soviet Union served as host to the Delegation. This mission resulted from contacts initiated at the 1973 IFLA meeting in Grenoble by the Soviet librarians with Wedgeworth. The late ALA President Allie Beth Martin followed up on this matter when visiting Moscow after the 1975 IFLA meeting in Oslo. The primary purpose of the visit was to explore the possibility of negotiating a series of exchange programs on a broad range of topics and in different institutional settings between Soviet and U.S. librarians. It is envisioned that librarians and institutions within the United States representing such interests as library service to children, library statistics and standards, and the application of technology to library education will be involved in the implementation of such an exchange program. Other members of the Delegation were: Nathalie Delougaz, Chief, Shared Cataloging Division, Library of Congress, and Susan K. Martin, Head, Systems Office, University of California, Berkeley. During 1977 the ALA International Relations Committee will be studying the report of the mission and exploring means of following up on the recommendations.

Divisional Activities. Various international activities are carried out within the divisions of ALA. In the area of cataloging, the RTSD Cataloging Code Revision Committee (CCRC) is concerned with the current revision of the Anglo-American Cataloging Rules (AACR) which is in itself an international activity devoted to the development of a single code to be used by Canada, the United Kingdom, and the United States. At the same time it is anticipated that the code will be used in other English-speaking areas as well as in many non-English-speaking countries; hence, it may serve as a beginning in the development of an international cataloging code. During 1976 the Committee considered the provisional drafts of ISBD(NBM), ISBD(G) and ISBD(S), and John D. Bryum, Jr., Chairperson of the CCRC and ALA Representative on the Joint Steering Committee for Revision of the AACR, represented the Division at the IFLA General Council Meeting in Lausanne. At its 1976 Midwinter Meeting, the RTSD Board of Directors voted to establish an ad hoc committee "to study issues involved in the development of international cataloging policies of international organizations and to propose methods to ensure adequate consultation with the appropriate library organizations and individuals in the United States."

CSD continued its active involvement in international library affairs by supporting the participation of three delegates to the IBBY Biannual Conference in Athens; presenting the 1976 Mildred L. Batchelder Citation for an outstanding children's book translated into English; selecting U.S. nominees for the Hans Christian Andersen medal and supporting the participation of an American juror (Zena Sutherland); and selecting "U.S. Children's Book of International Interest" for use by teachers, researchers, and publishers in other countries.

The International Relations Committee AASL completed a file of exemplary school media centers in the United States and Canada for use by the AASL Office in recommending schools for international librarians and educators to visit when coming to the United States. During the ALA Centennial Conference, members of the Committee planned various special activities for visiting international school librarians including a tour of the Center for Children's Books, the Laboratory High School Library, and the Regenstein Library, all at the University of Chicago. The Committee also assisted in planning the program for the International Association of School Librarianship's (IASL) 5th Annual Conference which was held in Annapolis Junction, Maryland.

In October the International Library Education Committee's (LED) latest revision of "Notes on Professional Education for Librarianship in the United States" was issued for use in answering the many queries on this topic received from abroad. A French language edition is also now available.

The ACRL Community Colleges Libraries Section worked closely with a delegation of junior college librarians from the Japan Library Association who attended the Centennial Conference. Earlier in the year, the HRLSD's International Relations Committee solicited information on specialized services from U.S. state library agencies as part of an IFLA survey.

International Representatives. ALA is represented in the following international units: Joint Steering Committee for Revision of the Anglo-American Cataloging Rules, John D. Byrum, Jr., and Frances Hinton, Deputy; the U.S. Mission to the United Nations, Jack Dalton; the United Nations Non-Governmental Organizations Section/Office of Public Information, Donald Jay; the U.S. National Commission for UNESCO, Esther J. Walls (who also serves as a member of its Executive Committee); the Government Advisory Committee on International Book and Library Programs, Jean Lowrie and David Donovan (until September 1976), while Jane Wilson serves as the ALA official observer; International Board on Books for Young People, U.S. Section, Peggy Sullivan, Amy Kellman, Paul Heins, Mary Jane Anderson. (see IFLA; UNESCO; FID.)

JANE WILSON

Mohammed Aman (lower, right) of IRRT and William Bennett of U.S.I.A. at the 1976 reception for foreign librarians held at the Newberry Library in Chicago (top).

International Relations Round Table

The International Relations Round Table (IRRT) was established by the ALA Council in 1949 as the Round Table on Library Service Abroad. In 1956 the name was changed to International Relations Round Table. The purpose of the IRRT, according to the by-laws, has been "to develop the interests of libraries in activities and problems in the field of international library relations, to serve as a channel of communication and counsel between the International Relations Community and the members of the Association and to provide hospitality and information to visitors from abroad."

The Executive Committee of the IRRT is responsible for implementing its goals and objectives. The Committee includes the Chairperson; Vice Chairperson/Chairperson-elect; Secretary/Treasurer; two members at large; the Editor of *Leads,* and the past Chairperson. In addition, two Committee Chairpersons are appointed by the IRRT Chairperson for the Membership and Nominating Committees. Individual chairpersons are also appointed for Africa; East Asia; Latin America; Middle East and North Africa; Southeast Asia; East and West Europe and International organizations.

IRRT has representation on the Freedom to Read Foundation and the ALA Membership Promotion Task Force. IRRT and the International Relations Committee (IRC) maintain close working relationships. The IRRT Chairperson attends meetings of the IRC as an observer; the IRC Chairperson attends the meetings of the IRRT Executive Board as a non voting member.

One of the significant events of the ALA Annual Conference is the IRRT Reception for Foreign Librarians. It is a professional and social occasion during which U.S. librarians establish or renew contacts with their colleagues from overseas who are attending the ALA Conference. In 1976 the Reception was at the Newberry Library in Chicago. More than 500 guests, including representatives of IFLA, national libraries, and ALA, and ALA honorary members, attended the Reception.

Another important feature of the ALA Annual Conference is the IRRT's Hospitality Booth. The booth is staffed by IRRT volunteers and library science students from the hosting city. They provide assistance to foreign visitors, answer questions about the ALA and its activities, arrange visits to libraries, and distribute invitations to the Reception.

Since 1957 IRRT has published *Leads,* a quarterly journal which is available to members of IRRT. In 1976 *Leads* became available to non-members for a $10 annual subscription. *Leads* contains articles on library development in various countries; area reports; news from international library organizations; people in the international library news; general news items of interest to the membership; and meetings of IRRT and IRC and ALA international activities. It is indexed in *Library Literature.*

To celebrate the ALA's Centennial and the U.S. Bicentennial in July 1976, IRRT co-sponsored a program on the International Flow of Books with the Resources and Technical Services Division (RTSD), the Association of College and Research Libraries (ACRL), and other ALA groups.

For the 1977 Conference in Detroit, IRRT planned a conference on "ALA and International Library Organizations—A Look at the Next Decade." The conference will examine, among other matters, the new structure of IFLA and the role ALA is expected to play in IFLA, UNESCO, and other international organizations.

Any member of the ALA may elect membership in IRRT upon payment of the $5 additional dues required for membership.

MOHAMMED M. AMAN

IRRT Officers

CHAIRPERSON (July 1976–June 1977):
Mohammed Aman, Palmer Graduate Library School, Long Island University, Greenvale, New York

VICE-CHAIRPERSON:
David Donovan, Agency for International Development, U.S. Department of State, Washington, D.C.

SECRETARY-TREASURER:
Tze-Chung Li, Graduate School of Library Science, Rosary College, River Forest, Illinois

Membership (August 31, 1976): 634

International School Librarianship

The growth of school libraries as a key element in today's educational program around the world is a mark of the 1970's. This is evident in individual countries and in the development of international school library groups. In 1971 the ad hoc international committee on school librarianship of the World Confederation of Organizations of the Teaching Profession (WCOTP), which had functioned for four years, was incorporated as the International Association of School Librarianship with the objective of promoting development of and understanding about school library services and programs around the world.

IASL. In 1976 IASL had a membership of 446 members representing 39 countries and 12 school library associations. It published a quarterly *Newsletter* and *Proceedings* of its annual conferences. It has held meetings around the world, is affiliated with WCOTP and International Federation of Library Association (IFLA), and works with the International Reading Association, International Board on

Books for Young People, Organization of American States (OAS), and UNESCO and supports a research and survey program. For the 1976 conference, held in the United States, the program was developed by the American Association of School Librarians and the Canadian School Library Association. Presentations on the theme "Crucial Issues in School Library Development" were made by outstanding school library educators, administrators of media systems, and school superintendents. In attendance were 137 participants from 14 countries. Displays of photographs, booklists, publications, slides and other audiovisual materials, and equipment were arranged by England, Denmark, Australia, Canada, Japan, and the United States. Officers in 1976 were President, Jean Lowrie, United States; Vicepresident, Axel Peterson, Denmark; Treasurer, Mildred Winslow, United States. Directors were Michael Cooke, Wales; Joseph Fadero, Nigeria; Joyce Fardell, Australia; Doris Fennell, Canada; Ursula Picache, Philippines; Amy Robertson, Jamaica; with Kenneth Vance, liaison to the School Library Planning Group, IFLA. IASL planned to publish a new edition of "Persons to Contact" and directory of School Library Associations during 1977. The 1977 Conference was scheduled to be held in Ibadan, Nigeria, on the theme "School Libraries and Cultural Involvement."

IFLA. In 1973 IFLA agreed to the establishment of a Planning Group for School Library Work. A part of the Children's Library section of the Public Library Division, it had representatives from 12 countries and is chaired by F. Laverne Carroll, U.S.A. It presented its first program at the IFLA Conference in Lausanne in 1976. The papers, representing France, Yugoslavia, and the U.S., covered developments in school library programs. With the adoption of new statutes at Lausanne, IFLA recognized school libraries as a separate section within Libraries Serving the General Public—an acknowledgment of the growth and effectiveness of national and international school library programs and associations.

Publications. Regular publication of information about school libraries gathered by school librarian/media specialists from around the world is now available. The IASL *Newsletter* by year's end had a corps of reporters from 19 countries regularly reporting on activities in school systems, legislation, publications information, research, book exhibits, and conferences, all of which is significant for the development of school libraries internationally. Likewise, the IFLA *Journal* now includes a précis on school library developments. The establishment of regular communication channels through the printed word as well as through conferences (regional and international) adds support to the efforts of the developing countries.

Activities. Following are typical activities on the international level.

The school library section of the Singapore Library Association held a special series of courses in cataloging and produced a handbook on "Cataloging School Library Collections."

National legislation has been passed in Denmark and Iceland legislating the development of school library programs in every school.

A series of one-day seminars in Queensland, planned by the Brisbane Branch of the School Library Association of Queensland for teachers of middle primary grades, covered effective library usage, the value of literature, and strategies of teaching and learning, especially through the use of books and non-book materials.

In Nigeria and Zambia, where new compulsory primary education laws were recently passed, the development of school library programs is receiving some recognition. A School Library Association for Lagos State, Nigeria, was established. In East Central State, a similar association has existed for several years; it produces an excellent *Newsletter*.

A grant from UNESCO supported a regional conference in Perth, West Australia, for representatives from the Asian and Pacific area on "Planning and Development of School Library Services." Thirteen countries participated, represented by 43 individuals, a unique comparative accounting of school libraries in the region.

The IASL UNESCO Gift coupon program for school library books in Africa and Asia now includes Latin America. Coupons valued at $6,000 have been distributed since the inception of this particular gift program. The Netherlands is the largest contributor, followed by Canada.

It is evident that school libraries which contain all types of media are now seen as a basic component in the educational scheme, that basic text materials are not considered sufficient, and that international understanding as well as personal development can be fostered through the school library programs at all levels.

JEAN LOWRIE

Junior Members Round Table

Originally organized because new and young librarians wanted to share the common experiences of the neophyte professional, the Junior Members Round Table (JMRT), one of the first Round Tables organized in the American Library Association, continues to provide its members with the opportunity to satisfy that need. Over the years JMRT's goals have broadened to include active involvement in professional associations, professional development opportunities for individual members, and, frequently, service projects that benefit the JMRT membership as well as the Association.

The national JMRT organization was restructured in 1974, to provide support for the development of affiliated chapters. The Affiliates Council, the result of the 1974 reorganization, is a body of representatives from state and regional affiliates. It functions as a coordinating and communications mechanism on the national level.

The Round Table proved more vital and lively in the decade of the 70's than in most other times in its existence. It is one of the largest in total personal membership, now numbering nearly 1,000. Recent years have brought increasing numbers of affiliate chapters on regional and state levels, where young and new librarians are even more accessible. Typically, these affiliates have grown up from the need the new professionals in the state or region have to feel useful and fully contributing to their chosen profession and its associations. Ann Scott and Rheda Epstein, as President and Vice-President of the Council, led its activities in 1975–76. The Council did not gain significant membership during the year, but it continues to gain strength and direction while promoting the interests of JMRT's local units.

3M Grant. With the help of 3M, JMRT was able to do something specific in 1976 to aid the professional orientation and development of ten members of the organization. The Minnesota Company provided a $5,000 grant which allowed JMRT to award each of the ten new librarians an expense-paid trip to the Chicago Centennial Conference. During the course of the Conference, the recipients received background information on the American Library Association and attended meetings of key groups within the Association as well as those which were of individual interest. Lamar Veatch and Patty Landers headed the committee which successfully developed the 1976 project.

Olafson Memorial Award. Another JMRT award project honors Shirley Olafson, a former JMRT President who died in 1971 during her term of office. The Olafson Memorial Award, which pays Conference Registration costs, is made to JMRT members who are attending their second ALA Conference. During 1975–76 the Olafson Awards Committee presented ten awards. The committee was chaired by Jacqueline McGirt. JMRT's interest in the participation and professional development of its members is further supported by its Continuing Education efforts at Annual Conferences. At the 1976 Chicago Conference, JMRT co-sponsored workshops with both the Library Administration Division's Personnel Administration Section and the Information Science and Automation Division.

A third major area of emphasis for JMRT is the preparation of Annual Conference programs aimed at JMRT's attending membership. Featured programs of the 1976 Conference included an orientation for new Conference attendees, a reception for library school students, and an excellent membership program on the theme of career development as experienced by several well known professionals.

JMRT also maintains an active involvement in the work of several other units of the Association, with liaison positions to the Membership Committee, Exhibits Round Table, the Freedom to Read Foundation, Continuing Library Education Network Exchange (CLENE), as well as the work with ISAD and LAD. This continuous contact and cooperative effort adds to JMRT's participation in the Association as an organization. A further contribution to that effort is the daily Conference newsletter, *Cognotes*, which JMRT edits and publishes at each Annual Conference. — MARILYN HINSHAW

JMRT Officers

CHAIRPERSON (July 1976–June 1977):
Nancy Doyle, Forsyth County Library, Winston-Salem, North Carolina

VICE-CHAIRPERSON:
Marilyn Hinshaw, Pecos Library System, El Paso, Texas

SECRETARY-TREASURER:
Dale Manning, Joint University Libraries, Nashville, Tennessee

Membership (August 31, 1976): 1152

Labor Groups, Library Service to

The AFL/CIO–ALA Joint Committee on Library Service to Labor Groups, Reference and Adult Services Division, surveyed all public libraries in communities over 10,000 with a central labor council in 1976 to ascertain the status of existing labor collections and services. The information produced by this survey will fulfill many purposes: (1) it will provide information to those libraries that want to improve their service to labor groups, or begin such services; (2) it identifies and updates information about existing labor services in libraries; (3) it should stimulate interest in public libraries to provide library services to labor groups, and (4) it will provide labor groups (i.e., education committees of central labor councils) with information about what help and information librarians would like to have from labor groups.

The survey, to be published in the Spring of 1977, will update and expand information available in the 1963 *Library Service to Labor*.

The Joint Committee worked throughout the year developing and conducting the survey. A significant 53.2 percent response was reported.

There appears to be a renewed interest in library services to labor groups. Many visitors attended the meetings of the Joint Committee. The Committee is also investigating coordinating future programs with the SRRT Task Force on Farm Labor. The National Archives is engaged in locating archival materials on labor unions and members of the Joint Committee are advising it.

A reunion dinner was held in Chicago at the ALA Conference for all of the previous and present members of the Joint Committee; many persons involved in the 31-year history of the Committee attended. KATHLEEN IMHOFF

Law and Legislation

The Bicentennial year began rather inauspiciously for library legislation at the federal level. The budget presented by President Ford for fiscal year 1977 contained no funds for the Library Services and Construction Act, nor for the Higher Education Act. Moreover, the President recommended the consolidation of these programs into one block grant as proposed in a new Financial Assistance for Elementary and Secondary Education Act.

As the year unfolded, however, the legislative picture became somewhat brighter. In March President Ford reversed himself by revising the FY 1977 budget to include funding for LSCA and HEA. His proposal to consolidate the latter two programs into a block grant for elementary and secondary education encountered Congressional opposition, and consequently was shelved.

Federal Legislation. Since LSCA was scheduled to expire on June 30, 1976, Rep. John Brademas of Indiana supported by other members of the House introduced a bill (H.R. 11233) to extend the authorizations of appropriations for the Library Services and Construction Act for the five-year period 1977 through 1981. The bill was quickly passed in the House by an overwhelming vote of 378-7. The authorizations provided in the bill were slightly lower than those for the previous period but substantially larger than the amounts actually appropriated in the preceding years. For Titles I and III, specific dollar amounts were provided for the first three years and "such sums as necessary" for the last two. For Titles II and IV no specific amounts were provided, only "such sums as necessary." The Senate failed to act on the Brademas bill, however, which means that a new authorization bill for LSCA would have to be introduced early in the first session of the 95th Congress. In the interim, the FY 1977 appropriations for LSCA were approved by Congress under a continuing resolution. Although President Ford vetoed the HEW appropriations bill which included funds for LSCA, Congress promptly overrode the veto. The amount appropriated for LSCA in the bill is larger than that of the previous year.

The District of Columbia Public Library bookmobile with its "Read Your Way Up" motto was on display on Capitol Hill on Legislation Day during 1976's National Library Week.

The Urban Libraries Council initiated a proposal to amend LSCA by adding a new Title V to provide a program of federal aid to large urban public libraries serving cities of over 100,000 population. The proposed bill provides for an authorization of $60,000,000 for FY 1978 to be used for the purchase of library materials. In the same vein, the ALA Council at its annual meeting in July approved a resolution urging Congress to amend LSCA "to provide financial assistance to large urban public libraries in cities of over 100,000 population."

The library programs under the Higher Education Act expired in 1975 and were continued through 1976 under the one-year extension authority of the General Education Provisions Act. Congress enacted a bill (S. 2657) which extended HEA programs through 1979. The former Part C of Title II, the National Program for Acquisition and Cataloging, was repealed since the Library of Congress has undertaken to fund the program under its own authorization. A new Part C of Title II was adopted by Congress which authorizes grants for library resources to major research libraries. A major research library is defined as a public or private non-profit institution whose library collections are available to qualified users, and which: (1) make a contribution to higher education and research; (2) have national or international significance for scholarly research; and (3) are of a unique nature. Under the Act, no more than 150 research libraries are eligible for grants under this program, and the criteria for eligibility is to be determined by the Commissioner of Education. The grants will be processed directly from HEW to the research libraries. The latter, however, are required to notify the state library agency "of its activities under this part."

Several attempts to amend Title IV-B of the Elementary and Secondary Education Act

Law and Legislation

President Gerald Ford campaigns on the steps of the City-County Public Library, Bay St. Louis, Mississippi, in 1976. The library was funded by LSCA funds.

failed to materialize. A bill in the House, authorizing the states to retain up to two percent of their funds for school libraries and learning resources to be used for guidance and school counselling activities, was defeated. Similarly a Senate bill, requiring that a certain percentage of the purchases of library resources be for non-sex-biased materials, failed to pass.

White House Conference. President Ford requested Congress on August 30, 1976, to enact a supplemental appropriation in the amount of $3,500,000 for the White House Conference on Library and Information Services which failed to be considered before Congress adjourned. The President as 1976 ended had yet to name his appointees to the 28-member advisory committee as required by PL 93-568. (See White House Conference.)

OTHER ISSUES

Copyright. The copyright revision bill (S. 22) was at long last enacted into law and goes into effect on January 1, 1978. The new Act provides that a copyright endures for a term consisting of the life of the author and 50 years after the author's death. With reference to the controversial provision relating to "systematic reproduction," the final version reads as follows:

> The rights of reproduction . . . do not extend to cases where the library or archives or its employee . . . engages in the systematic reproduction or distribution of single or multiple copies or phonorecords of material described in subsection (d): *Provided,* That nothing in this clause prevents a library or archives from participating in interlibrary arrangements that do not have, as their purpose or effect, that the library or archives receiving such copies or phonorecords for distribution does so in such aggregate quantities as to substitute for a subscription to or purchase of such work. (See Copyright.)

Public Works. The Local Public Works Capital Development and Investment Act of 1976 was signed into law by the President on October 1. Administered by the Economic Development Administration of the Commerce Department, the new law provides $2 billion for public works construction projects including renovation, repair and improvement. The federal share is 100 percent of the cost of the project. States and all local governmental units are eligible to apply for direct grants from EDA. The Federal Register dated August 23, 1976, contains the rules and regulations covering this program on pp. 35669–74.

Revenue Sharing. A bill to extend the revenue sharing program (H.R. 13367) was enacted into law. Congress authorized a total of $24.6 billion for a four-year period, expiring September 30, 1980. The existing eight priority expenditure categories which included libraries have been eliminated in the new Act. This does not mean, however, that libraries are no longer eligible for revenue sharing funds. But it does mean that whatever special status they might have formerly enjoyed no longer exists. With the priority categories removed, the competition for revenue sharing funds will undoubtedly become much keener.

STATE ACTIVITIES

Arizona. With 42 state legislatures in session during 1976, there was considerable legislative activity involving libraries. In Arizona, the state library, archives and public records division was restructured. It was removed from the department of administration and reorganized as a separate department under the jurisdiction of the legislature. A board consisting of four members of the legislature, including the President of the Senate and the Speaker of the House, was created to exercise general supervision over this newly established department. This represents a radical departure in state government, granting the legislature executive authority over an administrative function.

Michigan. Another event of considerable significance occurred in Michigan with the passage of a bill in which the state undertook the funding of the Detroit Public Library on a regular annual basis, thus relieving the beleaguered city administration from levying taxes for the same purposes. This measure constitutes a recognition of the principle that the funding of public libraries is a state governmental obligation which may well serve as a strong precedent for other states to follow.

Networks and Systems. Legislation relating to networks and systems was strengthened.

South Dakota. South Dakota started the year with a completely revised state library act. The new law extends and clarifies the scope of service that the state library is required to provide. Whereas formerly its principal function was to promote public library service, it is now charged with the responsibility for the extension and development of multi-type library services throughout the state. Specifically it is mandated to provide "a network and system whereby the resources of libraries in this state are made available to the citizens of the state."

Oregon. Oregon has also revised its state library act in which it provides that the library resources in the state are to be made available "to all of the people of this state under reasonable conditions and subject to appropriate compensation to libraries providing library services to persons beyond their primary clientele."

Washington. The state of Washington passed a new law establishing the Washington Library Network to be administered by the state library. It provides for the operation of computer, telecommunication, interlibrary loan, and reference and referral systems.

Illinois. In Illinois the formula for the state

funding of library systems was increased from 70 cents to $1 per capita and from $25 to $35 per square mile, effective July 1, 1977. New York state has pumped an additional $4,000,000 into its library systems.

California. A new agency under the name California Library Authority for Systems and Services (CLASS) was established under the California Joint Exercise of Powers Act for the purpose of providing a statewide system of library development and resource sharing. The parties to the agreement creating this cooperative legal entity are the California State Library, the University of California, California State University and Colleges, City of Los Angeles, County of Santa Clara and Grossmont Community College District. In addition, any library, public or private including those of other states, may become a member. It is expected that CLASS will operate a computerized listing of books in California libraries for cataloging and interlibrary loan purposes. Other suggested cooperative activities are a periodical lending bank, last copy book storage, and a delivery service.

Court Cases. The Los Angeles Superior Court ruled that the Los Angeles County Library committed an act of reverse discrimination when it promoted a Black and Chicano ahead of the seven plaintiffs (six white and one Japanese-American) who had scored higher grades on a civil service examination. The court ordered the library to rescind the appointments.

A labor union representing employees of the Palos Verdes Library District filed a suit in the Los Angeles Superior Court to compel the library board to restore longevity pay increases and other fringe benefits eliminated by the board. The attorney for the plaintiffs based their claim on the contract theory. The court, however, ruled against them, stating that there was nothing to prevent the board from taking "legislative" action to change its policies.

The U.S. Circuit Court of Appeals sitting in Cincinnati reversed a decision of the District Court, and held that school officials cannot arbitrarily remove books from library shelves that they find offensive. In its unanimous opinion, the court declared:

> A library is a storehouse of knowledge. When created for a public school, it is an important privilege created by the state for the benefit of the students in the school. That privilege is not subject to being withdrawn by succeeding school boards whose members might desire to winnow the library for books the content of which occasioned their displeasure or disapproval.

When the Detroit Public Library attempted to use funds under the Comprehensive Employment and Training Act to rehire a number of former employees who had been laid off because of a forced reduction in staff, it ran into a legal technicality. One of the requirements of the Act is that "in any given city, no more than 10 percent of municipal workers paid from CETA funds can consist of rehired employees." The city contested this provision before a Federal District Court and won a favorable ruling. It should also be noted at this point that CETA was extended by Congress through fiscal 1977 on an expanded level beyond that of the previous year.

Local Communities. Atlanta adopted a referendum for the construction of a new central library building at a cost of $19,000,000. The library bond issue was the only one passed by Atlanta voters; three others for a variety of municipal services were defeated. Present plans call for a modern structure designed by Marcel Breuer. Referenda in Vicksburg, Mississippi, and Ouachita Parish, Louisiana, for library building projects were also successful. Columbus, Ohio, passed an important referendum providing for a new property tax levy for library operating purposes in addition to the existing intangible tax levy. At the U. S. Conference of Mayors held in Milwaukee, a resolution was adopted urging financial assistance to public libraries in cities of over 100,000 population for the purchase of library materials and for the construction of library buildings.

ALEX LADENSON

Law Libraries

Law Librarians' activities during 1976 reflected their sensitivity and concern for the need to pool law library resources, as well as a sense of social responsibility.

Law Library Network. An ad hoc group of about 60 law librarians decided in 1976, after a number of meetings, that a law library network or consortium to develop a cooperative bibliographic data base and service mechanism for law libraries was highly necessary and desirable and would also serve a significant social purpose. Study papers were prepared and reviewed on "Services and Needs"; "Data Base Components and Standards"; "Membership and Organization"; and "Administration and Financing." A Committee on Source of Data and Systems Support submitted a detailed statement on several potential support organizations. This ad hoc group was encouraged to continue its efforts by experts in the field. It is presently seeking expert assistance in formulating the best possible plan for meeting the bibliographic needs of law libraries.

Funding for the preliminary study from outside sources appears to be assured. The Executive Committee of the American Association of Law Libraries (AALL) created a Special Committee on Law Library Network Activities for a term of two years, beginning January 1, 1977, to study the problems involved and to prepare specifications for the independent study required. The Committee will also prepare a grant application and seek funding for this purpose. The AALL Executive Committee has committed the Association to support the study from its own funds to the extent of $5,000, provided at least twice that sum is secured from outside sources.

Service to Prisoners. As brought out in AALL President Jack Ellenberger's Report on the Association's activities, the Association has maintained a Committee on Law Library Service to Prisoners with the purpose of offering prisoners bibliographic control of recommended legal materials and of advising on administration of Prison Law Libraries. The Committee plans a national network of volunteer law librarians to consult with prison library personnel and offer professional help in collection development, library administration, and reference. Volunteers will eventually be listed in a "Directory of Law Library Consultants to Correctional Institutions."

Advertising of Law Books. The Federal Trade Commission *Guides for the Law Book Industry* (August 8, 1975) invites submission of complaints to the FTC for review, about book publishers' and dealers' violations of the *Guides*. The FTC was only interested at the end of 1976 in receiving complaints about violations specifically banned by the *Guides*. The AALL Committee on Relations with Publishers and Dealers, however, believes that the FTC should be notified about other violations as well, so that it can be made aware of the deficiencies in the *Guides*. With that purpose, and also to facilitate the making of proper complaints to the FTC, the Committee designed and distributed a complaint form in 1976 for the use of AALL membership.

Bibliographic Award. At the closing banquet of the 1976 AALL meeting, the Joseph Andrews Bibliographic Award was presented to Fannie J. Klein, former Associate Director of the Institute of Judicial Administration at New York University School of Law, in recognition of her bibliography on the *Administration of Justice in the Courts*, published by Oceana Publications in 1976. (*See also* American Association of Law Libraries.)   JULIUS J. MARKE

Learned Society Libraries

See *Independent Research Libraries*

Legislative Activities, Federal

See *Washington Report; Law and Legislation; Copyright.*

Legislative Service

See *Library of Congress.*

Libraries and Learning Resources, Office of

Within a year of the establishment of the Office of Libraries and Learning Resources (January 1975), the Associate Commissioner/Director Dick Hays announced the appointment of Malcolm Davis as Director of its Division of Educational Technology and Paul Janaske as Acting Director of the Division of Library Programs. Under their leadership, a total of 10 authorized programs totaling $237,554,000 were administered by the Office in fiscal year 1976 (July 1, 1975 to June 30, 1976). A transitional quarter (July 1 to September 30, 1976), made necessary when the U.S. government switched to a new fiscal year (September 30, 1976–October 1, 1977), provided an additional $12,937,000 for operation of the public library programs. Recent Congressional approval of the FY 77 OLLR budget provided funding for public library programs at a level of $60,237,000; school libraries and learning resources, $154,330,000; educational broadcasting facilities, $14,000,000; and educational television and radio programming support, $7,000,000. Although a new authorization for the Higher Education Act programs was passed October 12, adjournment of the 94th Congress postponed consideration for funding until the 95th session of Congress in 1977.

PROGRAM SUMMARY

Public Library Services. (Library Services and Construction Act, Title I) FY 76, $49,155,000; TQ, $12,289,000; FY 77, $56,900,000. More than 93,000,000 Americans were served in 1976 by projects involving LSCA monies. These services reach 29,000,000 classified as disadvantaged clientele, 7,500,000 elderly persons, 800,000 state institutionalized persons, and 480,000 blind and physically handicapped individuals. The percentage of expenditures for services to the disadvantaged, metropolitan libraries and resources centers, physically handicapped, state institutionalized bilingual education, right-to-read, aged, early childhood education, career education, environmental education, and drug abuse has increased from 24 percent in FY 71 to 66 percent of all LSCA expenditure in FY 76.

The present objectives continue to be to extend and promote public library services in areas without such services or which have inadequate services; to support promising exemplary outreach projects for disadvantaged clientele; and to strengthen state library administrative agencies and metropolitan libraries which serve as regional and national resource centers.

Even though 96 percent of the U.S. population has access to public library service, 83 percent of the population has inadequate library services according to the states' adopted standards. During the 20 years of existence of federal support programs for public libraries, the number of persons without access to library services has been reduced from 26,000,000 to 9,000,000. However, the number of persons with inadequate services increased by 48,000,000 because of the 52,000,000 increase in the total population. Such inadequacies and unevenness among the states in the quality of public library services offered will require the continued attention of LSCA.

One successful project, conducted by the Green Gold Library System, reaches over eight Louisiana parishes to assist those persons in severe economic straits. Among its diverse offerings are adult literacy classes, a job information center, live theatre for children, concerts for the elderly, and special services to local prisons, state hospitals, and Head Start centers. In Arizona, a statewide project concerned with minority needs set two priorities: services to Mexican-American communities that include the acquisition of bilingual materials and the initiation of activities for adults and a service to Indians that is primarily for the establishment and further development of reservation libraries. In the Wasatch Front area of Utah, service to the blind and physically handicapped members of the community has been greatly enhanced with the initiation of Title I, LSCA-funded radio reading, which is broadcast daily via a closed-circuit system.

Public Library Construction. (LSCA, Title II) In FY 76 only non-LSCA Federal funds were available for public library construction projects administered under LSCA authority providing $1,600,000 obligated for 11 projects. Seven of these projects received $1,029,678 in federal funds from the Appalachian Regional Development Act. Three projects were funded for $546,000 under the Job Opportunities Program, Title X, Public Works and Economic Development Act, and one project received $30,000 in Federal funds from the Urban Growth and New Community Development Act program. A total of $938,203 in local and State funds was allotted for these construction projects.

Interlibrary Cooperative Services. (LSCA, Title III) FY 76, $2,594,000; TQ, $648,000; FY 77, $3,337,000. This program coordinates the resources of at least two or more different types of libraries (public, school, academic, and special libraries and information centers). Approximately 7,500 libraries are involved in 130 Title III projects which include such cooperative efforts as telecommunication networks to provide information and bibliographic services and interlibrary loan capability; centralized acquisition and processing centers for materials; planning activities to develop comprehensive statewide library networks; and administrative training for managers of interlibrary cooperative projects. These efforts now involve approximately 7 percent of the nation's libraries.

The projects may take the form of regional cooperatives, like one in Virginia which enables six public and seven academic libraries to have access to the information bank of a large metropolitan newspaper. Libraries may also cooperate across State lines. In the St. Louis, Missouri, metropolitan area, for example, four libraries became members of the Ohio College Library Center, a principal center for bibliographic information. Or, a project may be as simple as strengthening interlibrary communication through a TWX (teletypewriter exchange) network.

School Libraries and Learning Resources. (Elementary and Secondary Education Act, Title IV, Part B) FY 76, $147,330,000; FY 77, $154,330,000. With the end of school year 1976/76, ESEA Title IV, Part-B, purposes are no longer identified as categorical pieces of legislation, but are now part of a package from which local education agencies choose among: (1) purchasing school library resources, textbooks, and other instructional materials; (2) providing funding for testing, counseling, guidance; or (3) strengthening instruction through the purchase of school equipment.

One of the exemplary projects is in the District of Columbia's Region Two. A new project called CIRT (Career Interests, Region Two) will be set up to strengthen counseling and guidance services in selected public and nonpublic elementary and secondary schools. CIRT emphasizes building career awareness, developing wholesome attitudes toward school, and improving the self-concept of the participating students. School counselors, librarians, teachers, administrators, and parents all had a hand in planning the program, which calls for a functional career interest station to be housed in the library of each project school, each station to be supplied with appropriate printed and audiovisual materials and equipment. Library staff members and parents are expected to attend training seminars for the career program.

The librarians and counselors will team up with the Region Two Career Education Coordinator to develop techniques for evaluating the program's effectiveness in improving school attendance, increasing students' self-confidence, and improving awareness of the types of careers which are available and what it takes to gain entry into them. Of evaluative interest also are the amount and kinds of uses made of project materials and community resources. CIRT offers an example of multiple benefits—materials, equipment, and guidance—brought to bear under the authority of one law on the specific needs of individual public and nonpublic pupils.

Libraries and Learning Resources, Office of

College Library Resources. (Higher Education Act, Title II-A) FY 76 $9,975,000. Once again the appropriation for the HEA Title II-A program in FY 76 provided for the minimal Basic grant amounting to $3,930 awarded to 2,560 institutions of higher education and other public and private nonprofit library institutions whose primary function is to serve institutions of higher education. Approximately 75 percent of these monies was used to purchase printed library materials and remaining amount for the acquisition of audiovisual materials and microforms.

With the Education Amendments of 1976, passed October 12, a new authorization was created for the strengthening of research libraries under HEA Title II-C. If funded in 1977 grantees under II-C would not be eligible for the smaller HEA Title II-A Basic grant program. The II-C program, however, would limit the number of recipients to "not more than 150 institutions."

Library Career Training. (HEA, Title II-B) FY 76 $500,000. With diminishing funds, the program supported 51 fellowships and traineeships at 12 training institutions. The program also supported retraining institutes for 120 participants at five training sites. The focus of the fellowship program continues to remain with the recruitment of minorities, which in FY 76 amounted to 72.5 percent of the awards made. The Office has continued to contribute significantly through these programs to the number of American Indians, Spanish-speaking Americans, and Blacks entering paraprofessional and professional positions in librarianship.

(1) Catholic University: Training State Library Personnel to Implement and/or Strengthen Statewide Systems of Continuing Education for Library, Information and Media Personnel, June 15, 1976–June 30, 1977 (Part-time).

(2) Coahoma Junior College, Clarksdale, Mississippi: Library Improvement Through Skill Training, July 1, 1976–June 30, 1977.

(3) SUNY at Buffalo: Women in Library Management, June 6–10, 1977.

(4) Oklahoma City University: Paraprofessional Training for American Indian Information Centers, July 6, 1976–March 31, 1977 (Part-time).

(5) Pennsylvania School Libraries Association: Evaluation Techniques for School Library/Media Programs, July 26–30, 1976.

Library Demonstrations. (HEA, Title II-B) FY 76 $1,000,000. Over the past nine years the Library Research and Demonstration program has developed nationally applicable models of alternative ways to best meet library and information needs. Funding is authorized for projects to develop new techniques and systems for processing, storing, and distributing information, for the dissemination of information derived from such projects, and for the improvement of education and training of library and information personnel. The aim is to stimulate developments that can be replicated. Some 260 projects have been supported by these programs at a federal cost of $22,400,000 over these years.

Priority was accorded to demonstration projects in FY 76 which were designed to (1) improve the efficiency in library systems through changes in processing, reader services, etc. (6 projects); (2) improve training for library and information careers (6 projects); (3) promote institutional cooperation in serving special target groups (4 projects); (4) improve planning and development of better library and information services, e.g., information needs assessments for various community settings (3 projects).

College Instructional Equipment. (HEA, Title VI-A) FY 76 $7,500,000. In FY 76 776 grants were made by State Commissions to institutions for the purchase of instructional equipment (including closed-circuit television) and attendant minor remodeling. These grants were made from State allocations determined by a formula based on higher education enrollment and per capita income. State Commissions rank applications according to state plans and recommend to OLLR the Federal share which, except in certain instances, cannot exceed 50 percent of the total project cost. Over 200 grants averaging $7,121 per grantee were made to academic institutions for closed-circuit television equipment. The other instructional equipment grants averaged $10,567 per grantee.

Educational Broadcasting Facilities. (Communications Act of 1934, Part IV of Title III, as amended by P.L. 94-309) FY 76, $12,982,575 (includes $482,575 of prior year funds); FY 77, $15,000,000 (includes $1,000,000 in demonstrations administered by the office of the secretary, HEW). On June 5 Congress passed a one-year authorization (P.L. 94-309) providing again for the development of additional noncommercial radio and television broadcasting facilities under Part IV of Title III, Communication Act of 1934. The intent is to extend and improve coverage of noncommercial educational telecommunications systems through the award of grants for the acquisition and installation of transmission and reception facilities.

The program has fostered responsible planning and created a partnership among Federal, State, local, and private interests. Grants have been made to 50 States, the District of Columbia, Puerto Rico, Guam, Virgin Islands, and American Samoa. The $106,583,000 federal investment during the life of the program has stimulated more than $41,000,000 in nonfederal matching money for educational television and radio equipment. Including broadcast costs not eligible for federal participation (land, buildings, operation of station, etc.), it is estimated that each federal dollar has stimulated $11 in local, state, and private funds. The 556 grants awarded to date made possible the creation of a real-time national network with live interconnected program service available to 65 percent of the population. Since 1963 the number of noncommercial television stations in operation has increased from 76 to 246, utilizing approximately one-third of the channel assignments reserved by the FCC. Federal assistance was first made available to radio stations in 1967. Only 67 full-service radio stations were on the air at that time. By the end of 1976 166 full-service radio stations were serving their communities; but more than 30 major population centers were still without such service.

Educational Television and Radio Programming. (Special Projects Act, P.L. 93-380) FY 76, $7,000,000; FY 77, $7,000,000. This activity supports a range of projects from creative development to installation and evaluation of radio and television programs which have clear potential for helping children, youth, and adults to learn. In FY 76 Children's Television Workshop, producers of "Sesame Street" and "The Electric Company," received $5,400,000. This funding represented partial support of the eighth season of "Sesame Street," which consists of 130 hour-long color television programs, and the fifth season of "The Electric Company", which consists of 130 half-hour color programs.

In FY 76 a contract was also awarded for the initial production of 20 half-hour television shows and accompanying materials to help new and prospective parents become more effective as "first teachers" of their children. Other projects include (1) a contract to produce 10 half-hour television programs entitled "Music Is . . ." for students in grades 4–6; (2) a project to complete publication of curriculum materials and teacher guides for two alcohol education film series recently produced under a previous Office of Education contract; and (3) contract for the production of a film produced by Smithsonian Institution entitled, "Black Presence in the American Revolution" for the use in schools, prisons, literacy programs, and community centers.

ROBERT KLASSEN

REFERENCES
1. "Federal Funds: Selected Library Programs," *American Education*, 12:31–32, November 1976.
2. *Annual Report of the Commissioner of Education, Fiscal Year 1975.*

Library Administration Division

The Library Administration Division, along with most of the other Divisions in the American Library Association, has been greatly concerned about its financial future within the Association. After much debate and effort during 1976, the Division believes that it has been able to stabilize its financial situation at the level at which it has been operating for the last few years and will be able to build its program from that point. The Division had a balanced budget for the 1975-76 budget year and did not need an ALA subsidy for 1976-77. The budget projected for 1976-77 was predicated on the expectation that the Division would not lose membership, however. The fragility of its situation was dramatically illustrated by the fact that its 1975-76 fiscal year ended with only a modest $328 surplus.

The Division has been active in many areas and contemplates greatly increased planning and development for the future. It established, for example, a Special Committee on Division Development, with Donald E. Wright as Chairperson, to study six areas of divisional interest and make recommendations to the LAD Board of Directors. The areas are:

"Libraries and Unions" was the topic of the first conference of the newly formed Library Administration Forum of the Wisconsin Library Association. The conference took place in October.

1. Budget and other fiscal matters: Joseph Kimbrough, Chairperson
2. Membership potential and growth: Mary A. Heneghan, Chairperson
3. Publishing activities: Raymond M. Holt, Chairperson
4. Staff services: Herbert F. Mutschler, Chairperson
5. Interrelationships among the Division's units: Dale Canelas, Chairperson
6. Division programs: Elizabeth T. Fast, Chairperson

This special committee is expected to present a preliminary report to the LAD Board at the 1977 Midwinter Meeting and a complete report by the 1977 annual Conference.

Additionally, the Division has established a Committee on Common Concerns chaired by Herbert F. Mutschler. That Committee will explore the relationships of LAD with other divisions within ALA. The Committee will identify interdivisional problems, possible cooperative activities, and other potential rela-

Library Administration Division

tionships, and explore the alternatives and solutions to those concerns.

AIA/ALA Building Awards Program. The 1976 AIA/ALA Building Awards Program jury awarded three honor awards and nine merit awards to outstanding library buildings in the U.S. The winning buildings represented various building situations—alterations, additions to very old buildings, and new structures among them. They ranged from old Victorian buildings loaded with gingerbread to an underground library at Harvard University.

The jurors of the 1976 awards program were John F. Hartray, Jr., architect, Chicago; John S. Bolles, architect, San Francisco; Judith Edelman, architect, New York City; Raymond M. Holt, library consultant, Del Mar, California; and Dr. Roscoe Rouse, Director, Oklahoma State University Library, Stillwater, Oklahoma. (See Buildings.)

Buildings and Equipment Section. The Buildings and Equipment Section has revised the Library Buildings Consultants' list. Now containing information on 55 consultants, it is available free from the LAD office at ALA Headquarters.

The Section established four new committees and a discussion group in 1976. The committees are Community College Learning Resources; School Library/Media Facilities; Buildings for Hospital, Institutional and Special Libraries; and Library Buildings Awards, which is to study and make recommendations for the improvement of the AIA/ALA Library Buildings Awards Program. BES set up the Library Buildings and Equipment Problems Discussion Group to provide a forum for architects, equipment manufacturers, and vendors to discuss their problems, new ventures, and other matters, and to make direct contacts with librarians interested in the same areas. The Section has also drawn up bylaws expected to be implemented sometime within the year 1977.

Membership Recruitment and Activities. The Division activities during the year designed to increase membership included production of a new brochure explaining the activities and interests of the Division, advertisements in several professional journals, announcements at meetings, letters mailed to individuals who did not continue their membership in 1976, and greetings to new members of the Division. A campaign was also run asking each present member of LAD to recruit another member and materials were supplied for that purpose. The Division increased its membership slightly by the end of the year.

Conference Activities and Preconference Institutes. At the 1976 Centennial Conference in Chicago the Division sponsored 11 programs and two preconferences. The programs ranged from a series of whole-day hearings held by the Circulation Services Section—Fines and Penalties Committee that were aimed at collecting information concerning the effect of fines and other penalties on library service and public relations to "A Salute to Keyes Metcalf, Library Building Consultant Extraordinaire." Additional programs included the John Cotton Dana Public Relations awards; the Friends of Library Committee luncheon at which mystery story writer John D. MacDonald spoke, and a Circulation Services Section program, "The Service Ethos of American Libraries, 1876–1976," among many others.

One of the preconference institutes, a "Public Relations Panorama," was sponsored by the LAD Public Relations Section. The other preconference sponsored by the Buildings and Equipment Section was on "Meeting Library Building Space Needs."

Library Organization and Management Section. The Committee on Comparative Organization during 1976 was conducting a survey among 3,200 academic libraries to determine the current changes in library administration. The committee achieved a return of 2,000 questionnaires and at year's end was compiling the data for publication.

The Statistics Committee for Reference Services published the proceedings of their 1974 "Symposium on Measurement of Reference." That Committee is now seeking funds for a research project on devising a national model for measurement of reference services by statistical means. The Committee is also interested in a cooperative project with CLENE (Continuing Library Education Network and Exchange) on developing a "transportable learning laboratory" on reference measurement.

The Statistics Coordinating Committee and the officers of LOMS are planning an informal liasion between the various LOMS statistics committees and the ALA Divisions or other units to which they relate. The Committee was also studying the array of statistics committees with a view to consolidating the many committees into one principal unit.

The Insurance for Libraries Committee has worked with the author of "An Insurance Manual for Public Libraries in Illinois" in order to broaden the subject of that pamphlet so that it will be useful to libraries all over the country concerned with insurance problems. That manual will probably be published in 1977.

The Budgeting, Accounting and Costs Committee has completed a project to make the budgetary documents of 94 public and state libraries available on microfilm to other libraries. Microfilm records of the budgets and explanatory documents of 56 public and 38 state libraries are availiable on interlibrary loan from the ALA Headquarters Library.

Public Relations Section. The Public Relations Section awarded a certificate at the Annual Conference to the H. W. Wilson Company in appreciation for its sponsorship for 31 years of the John Cotton Dana Public Relations Awards.

The Section set up a new Committee on Workshops and Continuing Education to devise "packaged workshops" that can be used in various places around the country for training purposes in the use of public relations methods and materials.

The Publications Committee of PRS in 1976 was revising the public relations leaflets that LAD had distributed for many years.

The Friends of the Libraries Committee was revising its 1962 pamphlet, "Friends of the Libraries, Organization and Activities," and was also compiling a directory of Friends groups throughout the country.

Other Activities The Circulation Services Section is sponsoring the ad hoc Committee on Fines and Penalties. That committee produced working papers on the effects of fines and other penalties on academic, public, and school libraries and held hearings on the three areas in order to collect data. The Committee was expected to make its final report at the 1977 ALA Midwinter Meeting. The Staff Development Committee of the Personnel Administration Section sponsored its annual workshop at the ALA Conference. The ad hoc Committee to Revise the ALA Personnel Organization and Procedures Manual completed its work by the end of the Centennial Conference.

Publications. In addition to the publications previously mentioned, the Division has published, through ALA Publishing Services, the proceedings of the 1974 buildings preconference, *An Architectural Strategy for Change*. Raymond M. Holt was editor.

The Small Libraries Publications Series was being revised and three of the manuscripts were near completion at the end of 1976.

The proceedings of the 1975 buildings preconference institute, "Running Out of Space — What Are the Alternatives?" was in manuscript form at year's end and was expected to be published sometime during the year 1977. Gloria J. Novak was editor.

DONALD P. HAMMER

LAD Officers

PRESIDENT (July 1976 – June 1977):
Ernest A. DiMattia, Jr., Ferguson Library, Stamford, Connecticut

VICE-PRESIDENT/PRESIDENT-ELECT:
Richard L. Waters, Dallas Public Library

EXECUTIVE SECRETARY:
Donald P. Hammer

Membership (August 31, 1976): 4,002 (2,242 personal and 1,760 organizational)

Library Education Division

Although the Library Education Division (LED) of ALA celebrated its 30th anniversary in 1976, there were serious discussions as to the future of the Division. Because the new ALA dues schedule has mandated that Divisions will no longer receive a subsidy from ALA general funds and must be self-supporting by the end of the 1976–77 fiscal year, it was necessary for the LED Board and membership to consider possible options and alternatives.

The LED Organization and Activities Committee prepared an article for *American Libraries* (May 1976): "A Threatened Division Plans for its Survival" outlined the issues and included a chance for the ALA membership to voice opinions on the role of the association in library education.

Former LED President Melvin J. Voight retired in September 1976 as Librarian of the University of California, San Diego. Voight was a member of ALA Council and a pioneer in the field of library data processing.

At the LED business meeting during the Annual Conference, further membership input was received; the Board then voted to develop a proposal for presentation to the ALA Executive Board and Council in 1977 which would call for continued involvement of ALA in library education in addition to its accreditation function. The proposal suggests that instead of Divisional status, this involvement would be carried out through a Standing Committee, Education Assembly, with education committees in other ALA units, plus staff support.

Activities and Programs. "New Sciences, New Technologies, New Media: Their Impact on Education for Librarianship" constituted the theme for the 1976 LED conference program. Moderated by Thomas J. Galvin, LED President, the session consisted of a paper on "Information Science" by Allen Kent, University of Pittsburgh, and one on "Media" by Jane Anne Hannigan, Columbia University.

Two LED groups also sponsored Conference discussion programs: the RTSD/LED Education for Resources and Technical Services Committee explored training for serials librarians while the LED Teachers of Children's Literature and Related Courses Discussion Group considered teaching related to informational children's books. An informal discussion was also held between deans and directors of library school programs and personnel officers of large academic and research libraries in an effort to explore mutual concerns about new graduates entering the job market.

LED committees and discussion groups were active in 1976 with a variety of continuing projects related to specific areas of library education concerns. New projects included exploration of the feasibility of supporting a library school in Tanzania by the International Library Education Committee and the ALA International Relations Committee. Subcommittees on the library technical assistant and library associate categories were established by the Training of Library Supportive Staff Committee. The Teachers Section was abolished by a vote of the membership at the Annual Conference.

In addition to work on a union list of library science serials and establishment of contacts with libraries maintaining professional collections in state library agencies, the Librarians of Library Science Collections Discussion Group developed a proposal for an institute on the role of the library school library in continuing education.

The LED Board granted a two-year extension and an increase in membership to the YASD/LED Education for Service to Young Adults at the Pre-service Level Committee as they began work on a position paper outlining the need for training in services to young adults, including adolescent psychology sociology background.

Endorsement was given by the LED Board for a 1977 symposium on Education for Information Science to be sponsored by the ISAD/LED Committee on Education for Information Science and Automation. Support was also given for a change in name from the HRLSD/LED Committee on Education for Hospital and Institution Librarianship to the Committee on Education for Health and Rehabilitative Library Services.

Encouragement was also given by the LED Board for continuation of an informal network of library school deans and directors to respond quickly when legislation relating to library education matters comes before Congress.

Publications. The annual LED directory *Financial Assistance for Library Education* was published with the assistance of an H.W. Wilson Foundation grant. The "Availability of Media in Library Schools" was compiled by the LED Media Research Committee.

Updating of several LED handouts resulted in new revisions of "Correspondence and Home Study Courses in Librarianship," "Doctoral Programs in Library and Information Science," "Notes on Professional Education for Librarianship" (compiled by the International Library Education Committee) and "Directory of Library Science Libraries" (compiled by the Librarians of Library Science Collections Discussion Group). In cooperation with the Office for Library Personnel resources, LED staff compiled the monthly listing of continuing education opportunities for "Datebook" in *American Libraries*.

The LED staff also continues the editing of the quarterly *LED Newsletter*. It gives advisory service and answers correspondence relating to such matters as library education statistics, foreign equivalencies, continuing education, scholarships, and information for prospective library school students.

Awards. Carolyn Whitenack, Media Sciences, Department of Education, Purdue University, received the 1976 Beta Phi Mu citation and $500 award for distinguished leadership in library education. In addition, a special certificate of distinction went to Elizabeth W. Stone, Graduate Department of Library Science, Catholic University of America, for her work in continuing education as represented by the development of CLENE (the Continuing Library Education Network and Exchange). (*See* Biographies.)

For 1976, the ALA David H. Clift Scholarship (administered by the ALA Awards Committee and LED) went to Nancy Reed and Linda Griffen, who began the master's program in library education at the University of Denver and University of Missouri, respectively.

Administered by the LED Grants Committee, a $3,000 grant from the Asia Foundation provided travel awards for five Asian students in U.S. library schools to attend the ALA Annual Conference. In addition, six students attended state and regional library association conferences in 1976 and 42 Asian librarians received ALA membership with this grant.

MARGARET MYERS

LED Officers

PRESIDENT (July 1976–June 1977):
Lester E. Asheim, School of Library Science, University of North Carolina, Chapel Hill

VICE-PRESIDENT/PRESIDENT-ELECT:
Robert D. Stueart, School of Library Science, Simmons College, Boston, Massachusetts

EXECUTIVE SECRETARY:
Margaret Myers

Membership (August 31, 1976): 1,757 (605 personal and 1,152 organizational)

Library of Congress

The year 1976 saw organization and personnel changes at the Library of Congress, the most far-reaching to take place in many years. Daniel J. Boorstin, who took the office of Librarian of Congress in November 1975, appointed a deputy and an assistant early in 1976 to share with him in the general management of the Library. William J. Welsh, formerly director of the Processing Department, became the Deputy Librarian of Congress, and Donald C. Curran, formerly financial management officer, became the Assistant Librarian of Congress. Other responsibilities were divided: Elizabeth Hamer Kegan became Assistant Librarian for American and Library Studies, directing the activities of the American Revolution Bicentennial Office and providing coordination and support to the American Folklife Center, the Oliver Wendell Holmes Devise, and the National Commission on New Technological Uses of Copyrighted Works. James Parton, who came to the Library from the world of publishing, assumed, as Assistant Librarian for Public Education, responsibility for exhibits, publications, and information programs of the Library.

Departmental Reorganization. Two departments were created from the former Reference Department, a Reader Services Department consisting of the General Reference and Bibliography, Stack and Reader, Loan, Serial, Science and Technology, Blind and Physically Handicapped, and Federal Research Divisions, and a Research Department, containing the Music, Geography and Map, Manuscript, Prints and Photographs, Rare Book and Special Collections, Slavic, Orientalia, and Latin American, Portuguese, and Spanish Divisions.

Other organization changes were foreshadowed with the creation in January of a Task Force on Goals, Organization, and Planning to assist the Librarian of Congress in a full scale review of the Library and its activities. The review, which the Librarian said he hoped would be the most comprehensive in the history of the Library, was carried on during the whole of 1976, the Task Force soliciting suggestions for improving the Library and its services from Library of Congress employees, from librarians generally, and from all of the Library's constituencies through advisory groups representing the media, libraries, the humanities, publishing, law, science and technology, the arts, and the social sciences. As the year ended the Task Force was readying its report for submission to the Librarian on January 28 with recommendations regarding the Library's goals and objectives; the legislative, national, and international roles of the institution; services to users; collection development; the cultural role of the Library; management, planning, and organization development; and personnel and staff development.

Problems of Space. Space continued to be one of the major problems of the Library this year as in years past. The Library Environment Resources Office, a new office now responsible for the assignment of space in existing buildings as well as for the coordination of planning efforts for the James Madison Memorial Building, had to move some units of the Library from buildings on Capitol Hill to locations elsewhere and to move some of the lesser-used parts of the Library's collections to new rental space in nearby Maryland. A proposal to cease further appropriations for construction of the Madison Building as a library building and to revise the plans to create an office building for the House of Representatives did not win support in Congress, and a contract was signed in March for the fourth and final phase of building construction. In spite of the delays in appropriations and contract award, completion of the building is expected in 1979. Bids were opened late in the year for the compact motorized bookstacks intended for the new building, and specifications were developed for the necessary conventional bookstacks, card catalogs, carpeting, and furniture items.

The American Library Association, marking its centennial year, participated in ceremonies in September renaming one the Library's existing buildings, the former Annex, the Thomas Jefferson Building, a change enacted by Public Law 94-264 to recognize the statesman and bookman whose private library formed the nucleus of the national collections. At the same time the 1897 building, called the Main Building since completion of the second building, was named the Library of Congress Building.

Copyright. Efforts to modernize the copyright law of the United States, which began in 1924 and in the Congress of the United States in 1955, finally bore fruit with the signing on October 19 of Public Law 94-553, the first comprehensive revision of the statute in 67 years. Among the significant provisions of interest to librarians is the section on fair use generally and in particular that provision expressly intended to mark out the permissible limits of library and archival reproduction of copyrighted works. Under terms of Section 108 libraries and archives can make and supply single copies of specified kinds of materials under fairly simple safeguards and conditions as long as the activity does not involve multiple copying or "systematic" arrangements. The Register of Copyrights is required to make reports with possible recommendations to Congress at five-year intervals on how section 108 is working. The section further provides that in the interlibrary loan context activities are not systematic as long as the library receiving the reproductions does not do so in such "aggregate" quantities as to substitute for a subscription to or purchase of a work. (See further Copyright.)

The National Commission on New Technological Uses of Copyrighted Works, established on the last day of 1974, submitted a preliminary report on its first full year of existence to Congress and the President on October 8. In

Library of Congress

addition to continuing research, investigation, and analysis in the areas of computer software, automated data bases, new works created by computer, and photocopying, the Commission helped to develop the language and guidelines relating to library photocopying that were printed in the conference report accompanying the copyright bill.

With certain exceptions the revised statute will not come into effect until January 1, 1978, but the Copyright Office has already begun the reorganization necessary for its implementation and to assist in the program of education of the public at large, of special constituencies concerned with copyright, and of the Copyright Bar.

TV-Radio Archives. The Library also has under study the impact of another provision of the copyright legislation, that creating a television and radio archives in the Library of Congress. In order to "preserve a permanent record of the television and radio programs which are the heritage of the people of the United States and to provide access to such programs to historians and scholars without encouraging or causing copyright infringement," Congress included in the copyright legislation the first statutory attempt to develop a national repository of all types of television and radio programming, including but not limited to news.

The commitment of the Library of Congress to a leadership role in coordination with other network-related organizations in the design and development of the library component of the national library and information services network was emphasized by the creation of a Network Development Office within the Office of the Librarian of Congress, headed by the special assistant for network development, Henriette D. Avram. The office organized three meetings in 1976 of policymakers of network-related organizations and funding agencies, meetings that resulted in the compilation of a major position paper tentatively entitled "Toward a National Library and Information Services Network: the Library Component." After the advisory group studying it has made its revisions, it will be issued in the spring of 1977 to the library and information science communities.

Other LC Projects. Ongoing are other studies involving the Network Development Office and the Processing Department: an 18-month pilot project with the Research Libraries Group to provide on-line access to the LC MARC data base through a connection with a computer facility at the New York Public Library; the development of the methodology for a project to determine the role of authority files in the evolving national library network; indentification of the major characteristics of existing or planned networks so that the major missing components can be determined (this study was nearing completion at the end of 1976); building on the experience of the operational CONSER (CONversion of SERials) project now creating a national serials data base through the cooperation of 14 institutions or organizations, including LC, a study to determine the resources required for the Library to assume CONSER's management and operation; the COMARC (COoperative MARC) project in which machine-readable records are transmitted from the originating institution on magnetic tape; and two studies involving the *Register of Additional Locations*, one to identify other machine-readable bases from which to obtain location data and the other to provide the Library of Congress with user reaction to the printed and microform editions of *RAL*.

International cooperation was forwarded in November when representatives of the British Library, the National Library of Australia, the National Library of Canada, and the Library of Congress met to discuss various problems relating to the sharing of cataloging responsibility for the imprints of their respective countries. Steps were taken toward the long-term goal of cataloging uniformity among the national libraries in the Anglo-American group in order that the cataloging data they exchange can be used with the least possible modification of the cataloging done by the originating library. In this first meeting the four libraries agreed on a common strategy and timetable for adoption of the second edition of the *Anglo-American Cataloging Rules* and the 19th edition of the *Dewey Decimal Classification*.

The Reader Services Department began a nationwide "court of last resort" toll-free service in which library networks can refer reference questions beyond their resource capabilities to the Library of Congress for reply. The pilot project involved the Research Libraries Group Bibliographic Center, Georgia Library Information Network (GLIN), Indiana State Library, the Bibliographical Center for Research, Rocky Mountain Region, at the Denver Public Library, Southern California Answering Network (SCAN) at the Los Angeles Public Library, Bay Area Reference Center (BARC) at the San Francisco Public Library, Illinois State Library, New Jersey State Library, North Carolina State Library, and the University of Texas.

Goodby 94th, Hello 95th. The Congressional Research Service said goodby to the 94th Congress, which had set a new record in requests for research and reference, and began to prepare for the arrival of the 95th. Kits with practical background information on such topics as Congressional organization and the legislative process, how to set up a Congressional office, aids for services to constituents, and other materials were prepared and distributed to freshman Congressmen and Senators. Papers on issues in public policy were prepared for background study on substantive matters,

Library of Congress

The Librarian of Congress, Daniel Boorstin (right), ALA President Clara Stanton Jones, and Charles Churchwell of Brown University talk at the ALA Centennial Conference.

and two major seminars were planned for new members. Shortly after the end of the year, Gilbert Gude, a former member of both the Maryland state and the national legislatures, assumed the directorship of the Service.

SCORPIO, the Library's information retrieval program, was installed this year in the computer center of the U.S. Senate. With the full MARC file available to SCORPIO users, members of the Congress can now access the Library's information systems directly from their own computers during an 85-hour week—or longer when either house is in session. The Reader Services Department has also expanded the terminal facilities available to patrons of the Library's reading rooms, and the use of the Library's systems has been demonstrated at a number of scholarly meetings and conferences, most recently at the Washington meeting of the American Historical Association.

Given responsibility for directing a National Program of Preservation and Restoration, Frazer Poole, assistant director for preservation, brought together in December 60 persons interested in conservation to help in the planning of a national program. Although the conference did not develop a formal resolution, it indicated a clear consensus that a national program is critically needed and that the Library of Congress is the appropriate agency to initiate action.

Folklife Center. The act creating the American Folklife Center in the Library of Congress provided for the appointment of 12 members, four by the President of the United States, four by the Speaker of the House of Representatives, and four by the President pro tempore of the U.S. Senate. The act in addition named to the board the Librarian of Congress, the Secretary of the Smithsonian Institution, the Chairman of the National Endowment for the Arts, the Chairman of the National Endowment for the Humanities, and the Director of the Center. With the naming of the Presidential appointees in June, the board was complete and able to begin to carry out the purposes of the legislation: to preserve and disseminate American folklife through a broad range of activities, including research, performance, exhibition, workshops, publications, archives, and recording. Alan Jabbour, appointed director of the Center, worked with the board during its first six months on building the Center staff and developing its resources. Planned for early 1977 was an event intended to further several of the Center's purposes, a conference on "Ethnic Recordings in America, a Neglected Heritage."

On May 6 and 7, the fifth and concluding symposium in a series on the American Revolution was held, The American Revolution: A Continuing Commitment. Unlike the earlier symposia in the series, which dealt with the period of the Revolution, this final one examined contemporary problems which are, in a broad sense, legacies of the struggle. The proceedings of the symposium were published in December. In September the Library published the results of a study, made possible by a grant from the Ford Foundation, of 17 of the 21 extant copies of John Dunlap's printing of the Declaration of Independence. And although the Bicentennial year has come to a close, the Library's Bicentennial program which began in 1968 continues with three volumes of a major work, *Letters of Delegates to Congress, 1774–1789*, in press and 10 additional volumes in the 15-record *Folk Music in America* to come.

LC and the Arts. An active concert season included performances by the Library's resident ensemble, the Juilliard String Quartet, and there were two performances of the first American ballad opera, *The Disappointment* by Andrew Barton. Tapes of Library performances were made available to 36 radio stations through the Katie and Walter Louchheim Fund in the Library of Congress. Robert Hayden, the Library's Consultant in Poetry for 1976–77, took over from the departing consultant, Stanley Kunitz, and shared the stage of the Coolidge Auditorium with a number of poets and lecturers, including Nicolas Barker, who delivered in 1976 the first of the Engelhard Lectures on the Book, a series established by Mrs. Charles Engelhard in memory of her husband, the financier-industrialist.

Important additions to the collections during 1976 included the papers of Nannie Helen Burroughs, the records of Moral Re-Armament, Inc., the large collection of cartoon and caricature drawings from the estate of Erwin Swann (to be exhibited at the Library of Congress in 1977), about 3,800 original negatives made by the late master photographer Paul Strand, videotapes of the Columbia Broadcasting System's news broadcasts, and, at very end of the year, the papers of Henry Kissinger, which join the papers of 27 earlier Secretaries of State at the Library of Congress. MARY C. LETHBRIDGE

Library Press

1976 was a Centennial year for the library press as well as for librarianship. It was the hundredth anniversary of one of the major organs of library journalism, *Library Journal*, whose ancestor, the *American Library Journal*, made its debut in 1876 with Melvil Dewey as editor.

Centennial Tributes. *Library Journal* celebrated its first century with a 292-page special issue (January 1, 1976) on "The Need to Know." Twenty-four experts contributed essays on their fields of specialization. Their topics provide a fairly thorough list of the most-written-about subjects throughout the year: urban libraries, the future of government library support, financial crises, copyright, library education, social responsibility, intellectual freedom, automation, information science, networking, problems in school librarianship, the future of ALA, and women in librarianship.

For its ALA Centennial issue (June 1976), *American Libraries* focused on "Who We Are: A National Profile of the American Librarian." Following cameos of leading librarians in 1876 and a statistical description of today's 115,000 librarians, interviews with 29 contemporary library workers captured the diversity and the human element in the field today. Among those interviewed: librarians whose work involves information and referral, young adult and children's services, prison work, library education, the Congressional Research Service, automated systems, rare books, and service to the deaf; law, military, medical, and art librarians; and several nonprofessionals, unemployed librarians, and library school students.

More Centennial coverage came on October 3, when the Sunday *New York Times* carried to its 4,500,000 readers a 16-page supplement, "The Great American Library Success Story: Your Information Investment." Financed almost entirely by advertising, this special insert was prepared by the ALA under the editorship of Arthur Plotnik, Editor of *American Libraries*.

Numerous other library publications produced Centennial tributes, such as a special *Library Trends* issue (v. 25, no. 1, July 1976) on "American Library History: 1876–1976," edited by Howard Winger, Dean of the Graduate Library School at the University of Chicago.

The Field. In its second year as a separate publication, R.R. Bowker's *School Library Journal* continued to lead the library press in circulation statistics. As of October 1976, figures on average "paid circulation for the year" as reported to the U.S. Post Office, were as follows:

School Library Journal	40,440
American Libraries	36,366
Library Journal	34,590
Wilson Library Bulletin	30,665

The trend toward specialization in the profession is reflected in the proliferation of journals and newsletters on specialized topics.

An important appointment in the library press during 1976 was the naming of Lois R. Pearson as the first Associate Editor of *American Libraries* since Plotnik took over that magazine's editorship in 1975. Pearson, a reference librarian at New York University for the last five years, came to librarianship after a long career at *Newsweek Magazine*, where she moved from clip desk to researcher, reporter, assistant editor, and, finally, associate editor in the International Department. She took her library degree from the University of Texas (Austin) and studied journalism at New York University.

A noteworthy change was the return of *CALL (Current Awareness—Library Literature)*, edited and published by Samuel Goldstein, a Simmons School of Library Science faculty member. This bimonthly compendium of articles, abstracts, reviews, and hundreds of library journal and newsletter tables of contents provides a unique updating service. After a hiatus since v. 3, no. 4–5 (coverage through October 1974), *CALL* was back on schedule as of v. 5, no. 4, July–August, 1976. Vowing, "I am born stubborn and optimistic enough to give it one more whirl," Goldstein announced plans to fill the gaps as soon as possible.

Awards. The 1976 winner of the H.W. Wilson Library Periodical Award was the *Hennepin County Library Cataloging Bulletin*, Sanford Berman, Editor.

A grant of $12,500 was awarded to the ALA Publishing Committee for an *American Libraries* prize competition to stimulate articles of outstanding value to librarianship. Contributed by the Field Enterprises Educational Corporation, this award represents part of the 1976 J. Morris Jones and Bailey K. Howard–World Book Encyclopedia–ALA Goals Award. Winning articles will be published in *American Libraries* over a two-year period beginning 1977.   ELIZABETH PRYSE MITCHELL

Library Research Round Table

The Library Research Round Table (LRRT) was established in 1968 to promote and improve research in library and information science. The ALA Conference programs of the Round Table during 1976 were directed toward meeting that purpose. At its major Conference program in 1976, attended by about 500 persons, Manfred Kochen of the University of Michigan Mental Health Research Institute, spoke on "Information Systems to Help Plan for the Growth of Knowledge."

Another component of the LRRT conference program was the Research Forum Series, which consisted of five programs on various research topics. Research Forum I featured three papers which reported on applications of operations research techniques to library circulation and user studies. The moderator was Michael Buckland, University of California, Berkeley, and the speakers were John J. Regazzi of the Foundation Center, New York; Robert L. Burr, College of William and Mary; and William E. McGrath, Southeastern Louisiana University. Forum II was titled "The Impact of Networks on Libraries—Directions for Future Research" and consisted of papers presented by Joe Hewitt, University of North Carolina; Linda Lucas, University of Illinois; and Barbara E. Markuson, Indiana State Library. The moderator was Mary Jane Reed. Forum III was moderated by Marianna T. Choldin and addressed the topic "Books and Empires: The Rise of Bibliography in 19th-Century Russia, Germany and England." Papers were presented by Robert E. Cazden, University of Kentucky, W. Boyd Rayward, University of Chicago, and Donald W. Krummel, University of Illinois. Forum IV, titled "SPSS as a Library Research Tool," was presented by Maurice P. Marchant, Nathan Smith, and Keith Stirling from Brigham Young University.

Forum V was moderated by Phyllis Dain of Columbia University. It featured papers by Phyllis Dain, Kathleen Molz, Columbia University, and Peggy Sullivan, University of Chicago. The forum was titled "Style and Sustenance in American Librarianship: Case Studies of 20th-Century Leadership Roles." The entire Research Forum Series was chaired by Robert B. Burns, Colorado State University.

The Library Research Round Table was cosponsor with the LAD/LOMS Statistics for Reference Services Committee and RASD of a program on the purposes of reference measurement. Among other topics, the program dealt with the definitions proposed for reference statistics for use in the National Center for Educational Statistics Library General Information Survey.

A regular component of the LRRT Conference program is the Research Information Exchange Suite. It provides an opportunity for persons with a research interest to discuss their interests or projects in an informal setting.

Two papers were selected as winners in the Annual Research Competition. In its second

---

LRRT Officers

CHAIRPERSON (July 1976–June 1977):
Gary R. Purcell, University of Tennessee, Knoxville

VICE-CHAIRPERSON/CHAIRPERSON-ELECT:
Jane B. Robbins, Wyoming State Library, Cheyenne

SECRETARY-TREASURER:
James D. Sodt, University of Kentucky Lexington

Membership (August 31, 1976): 679

year in 1976, the competition is designed to stimulate research activity in the profession. The winners of the 1976 competition were James C. Baughman, Simmons College ("Toward a Structural Approach to Collection Development) and Ruth Wender, Esther Fruehauf, Marilyn Vent and Connie Wilson of the Regional Library Services, Oklahoma City ("The Determination of Clinician Needs From a Literature Search Study"). GARY PURCELL

Library Science

See Management, Library; Automation; Cataloging and Classification; Education, Library; Furniture and Equipment; Research; Reference Services; School Libraries and Media Centers; Standards; Serials; and Continuing Professional Education. Consult Index for specific topics.

Literacy Programs, Library

In 1976 events of 1975 and cumulative effects of government education and social agencies in the literacy effort in the nation and in library programs came to some fruition. New knowledge from recent research and studies, and growth of literacy programs and service in libraries throughout the country, were reflected in broader concepts and practices of librarians as well as in increased awareness, deeper understanding, and a broader recognition of the role of all types of libraries in the literacy effort. More materials for adult basic education, particularly at the beginning level of learning, became available. More bibliographies and guides for program administrators, teachers, tutors, and librarians were developed. A decade of experience in adult education and reading development programs, information and materials services, much trial and error, demonstrations and experimentation has produced actual data and some guides for direction in the future.

What Is Literacy? The concept of what literacy is continues to expand. Literacy is not merely learning to read and write, but a contribution to the liberation of man and to fulfillment and control of one's own life. Literacy can be defined only in relation to the social, cultural, and economic environment. The measurement of literacy is the extent of comprehension in context of experience and use. To be literate can mean that a person has the ability to use communication skills and knowledge about the subject and information needed in order to do the things he or she needs and wants to do. Literacy makes it possible to perform daily tasks, meet work requirements, understand new techniques, and gain pleasure and satisfaction in life.

Adult Performance Level (APL) is the most recent measurement for literacy. A University of Texas study, *Adult Functional Competency* (Northcutt, 1975) identifies skills and knowledge that are needed for meeting the requirements of adult living. The skills include those for communication (reading, writing, speaking, and listening), computation, problem solving, and interpersonal relations. Such skills are applied in everyday life. In measuring functional competency "performance" describes or replaces "coping" and "survival" in a definition of literacy needs and attainment. The Human Resources Research Organization (HumRRO) research emphasizes that people want job-related skills and knowledge (Sticht and others, 1974). The need for follow-on reading and efficient delivery system indicates that in these areas library resources, networks, and staff could have a critical role.

Statistics. The dimension of the need for achieving greater literacy among the U.S. population is awesome. Although the United States has a highly literate population, it is estimated that in 1976 28,500,000 people needed basic literacy training. Projections for 1980 are that more than 27,000,000 workers 16 years of age and over will have fewer than 12 years of schooling.

In 1975, 57,000,000 adults 16 years of age or older and not enrolled in school had not completed high school. The APL national survey on functional competency reported that consumer economics is an area of greatest difficulty for adult Americans. Although occupational knowledge is an area in which half of population is proficient, about one in five adults have difficulty.

Lifetime Learning. Lifetime learning is essential in today's society. More and more emphasis is placed on individualized learning and different, less traditional avenues of learning, such as the open university. Individual, self-paced learning can lead to meeting credential requirements and to qualification for occupational changes or advancement. Developmental literacy programs range from sixth grade through college and beyond. Basic education includes all ages. Alternatives to traditional formal learning expand and part-time students in higher education account for approximately half of the students in collegiate institutions.

PLA. Interest was high in 1976 in the Public Library Association's projected section on Alternative Education Programs (APES); interest was expressed by 700 members who signed up in advance. Patricia Gaven, Chairperson of the Steering Committee, said, "the vigorous support for the petition for section development . . . indicates the field librarians' intense interest in alternative education programs, of which literacy is an essential part. The section provides an umbrella for all learning programs as librarians affirm and assert their educational role."

National Programs and ALA. The American Library Association in a joint project of all membership Divisions launched a nationwide effort to focus librarians' attention on their active commitment to the achievement of national literacy. An important manual for librarians, *Literacy and the Nation's Libraries,* was in press at year's end for publication in 1977 by ALA. Librarians working with adult educators have defined the library functions and responsibility. The educational function, a part of historical and traditional function of libraries, is reaffirmed.

Libraries of the country are increasingly involved in continuing education through literacy programs for clientele from pre-school child to adults of all ages. Specific attention is being given to communication skills, reading behavior, and subject content for literacy. Media centers, learning resource centers, older established library systems, and new regional systems and networks are focusing resources on literacy.

A significant number of libraries and librarians are active in literacy services. They have deep commitment to the goals of literacy programs. They take part in and carry out staff development and training programs for professionals and volunteers. They work together in formal and informal literacy systems, they provide advisory and tutorial assistance service for learners, and teach when it is necessary. They develop coordinated delivery systems and use available resources in the community. They collaborate with adult basic education programs of the schools, the Right to Read Academies, the numerous volunteer programs of churches, community organizations, and such organized efforts as Lauback International and Literacy Volunteers of America. Many reach out to unserved groups in the community and set literacy as a priority.

Perhaps no program provided more practical results, materials, and leadership to the profession that the Library Adult Basic Education Project out of the Appalachian Adult Education Center of Morehead State University in Kentucky. The AAEC worked with more than 70 library systems [see "Access to Print," *The ALA Yearbook* (1976), p. 220-221] Its discontinuance is a great loss to the field of adult education.

More than 30 libraries (generally systems including many units) responded to the ALA Literacy Manual project for reports on literacy or learning programs. The libraries represent programs ranging from periods of 30 to 2 years. The program profiles show various administrative arrangements, a range of cooperating agencies—social and educational agencies, ethnic organization, government programs, and volunteer groups and individuals. Teaching, which has been not only controversial but also ignored, is often perceived as a necessary part of library service. Older reading development programs in the public libraries of Brooklyn and Philadelphia continue to offer leadership through bibliographies and advice. Strong programs with librarians serving as learners' advisers and with rich material resources are found in Dallas, Tulsa, Denver, Bay County, and Sante Fe (Florida), Mountain View (California), and Janesville and Beloit (Wisconsin). The Chicago Public Library has a Study Unlimited program that provides opportunities for anyone to prepare for a general educational development test (GED) or high school equivalency or college level examination program (CLEP) for credit through examination. Independent literacy and learning programs are conducted in public libraries of Salt Lake City, Mount Vernon, and Tarrytown (New York), in Washington, D.C., and at Illinois Central College. City departments in San Francisco will cooperate with schools and public libraries through an education redesign plan for the San Francisco Unified School districts to assist functionally illiterate and non-English-speaking or foreign-born adults and children in becoming literate. A major goal of media centers in the Cleveland Public Schools is the development of student competency in reading.

Cooperation and collaboration among various agencies is a major component of existing library literacy programs. The Appalachian school programs in adult basic education and public libraries continue. The Literacy Volunteers of America, Inc., of Syracuse (New York) are training library professional staff and community volunteers in conjunction with library-sponsored literacy programs in New York, Maine, Vermont, New Hampshire, Connecticut, Massachusetts, Iowa, Maryland, Illinois, California, and other states. Public libraries in Baltimore, Brooklyn, and Queens are

Participants in the Nashville & Davidson County Public Library's "English as a Second Language Program" utilize learning centers formed to aid library patrons who have difficulty speaking and understanding English.

initiating services. R.E.A.D. and Right To Read assist and support literacy programs in communities of all sizes and for various age groups.

In such programs librarians select and organize materials for use by individuals, teachers, tutors, classes, and groups in informal and formal learning situations. They advise and diagnose and instruct learners and users. All types of libraries, school, public, academic, and special, extend the reach of their professional skills and information resources. Existing library programs show that libraries have many and varied responsibilities. They can serve as information sources about learning opportunities, develop referral service, and collaborate with other agencies. Librarians can provide advice and counsel to individual learners and other agencies. They can be resource centers for materials, recruit participants, suggest alternative activities, and provide space and physical facilities. They can provide information about opportunities and materials and study programs, sponsor and conduct training opportunities, serve as liaison between literacy programs and the library, and work with teachers and administrators. Every library, it would seem, has an obligation to take part in the national effort to break the barriers of illiteracy. HELEN HUGUENOR LYMAN

REFERENCES
Norvell Northcutt and others, *Adult Functional Competency: A Summary* (Austin: The University of Texas at Austin, Division of Extension, March, 1975).
Herbert Kohl, *Reading, How To* (New York: Bantam, 1974).
Helen Huguenor Lyman, *Literacy and the Nation's Libraries* (Chicago: American Library Association, 1977).
Thomas G. Sticht, ed., *Reading for Working: A Functional Literacy Anthology* (Alexandria, Va.: Human Resources Research Organization, 1975).
Wilson Library Bulletin (Special Issue), "Libraries and the First R," 50, no. 9 (May 1976), pp. 704–741.

Management, Library

Effectiveness and efficiency were the key library management concerns in 1976. The conflict between efficiency, related primarily to profit-making organizations, and effectiveness, which as Peter Drucker points out should be related primarily to service organizations, continued to puzzle library administrators during the year. Continuing budgetary problems and declining incomes and purchasing power together with increasing staff discontent and unrest tested library administrative skills to their utmost. Library administrators, who for decades had been coping with growth both in students or populations served and in budgets, were faced in 1976 with severe limitations on budget growth and, in many cases, on declining or at least plateauing service populations. Managers had to learn how to deal with nongrowth in 1976. In many instances they were finding that managing in a period of decline—or at best, status quo—called for a great deal more imagination, initiative, and effort than managing during periods of rapid growth and expansion.

The abilities of managers to deal with this new library situation was viewed quite pessimistically from many quarters and the library press (particularly the *Library Journal*) seemed embarked on a series of articles dealing with the growing distress of library administrators in general and dismay with the apparent lack of new administrative leaders in the library field. Several articles and speeches appeared declaiming a general ineffectiveness of library administrative leadership and deploring the bureaucratization of library administration.

Seemingly as an indication of some abdication of administrative leadership, but with a gesture at least toward opening up the entire administrative process, participatory management became increasingly popular in 1976. The Toronto Public Library, after a decision in 1975, embarked on a new administrative organization and decision-making process based almost entirely on staff councils for decision making. The staff councils were dispersed throughout the library at several levels of management and related directly to committees of the library board. The unique feature of this procedure was the direct board relationship with staff committees and the corollary decline in the unilateral decision-making process of the director. This approach was being watched carefully by other library administrators and boards to determine if the staff could respond to a challenge of direct role in administration and how the staff, the board, and administrative officers of the library can effectively share responsibility or effect direct and timely administrative decisions.

Evaluation and Measurement. Evaluation and measurement became even more important in library management in 1976. The publication of *A Data Gathering and Instructional Manual for Performance Measures in Public Libraries* (Chicago, Celadon Press) provided a new tool to assist library managers in evaluation. The manual grew out of the favorable response to *Performance Measures for Public Libraries* published by ALA in 1973. The need for effective evaluation and measurement became increasingly obvious in 1976 as budget officers, city managers, and university presidents insisted more and more on relevant figures relating to effectiveness or efficiency when discussing library budget needs and programs. This emphasis was readily apparent by the standing-room-only crowds that attended the Public Library Association's "Ideas Exchange Program" on measurement and effectiveness at the Centennial ALA Conference in Chicago. The interest and concern of the attendees indicated management by objectives was still growing and being adopted by more and more public agencies in the United States. (*See also* Measurement and Evaluation.)

Management Training. Management training grew by leaps and bounds in 1976. More library schools provided either seminars or special short courses for library administrators and middle managers. Library schools which had been providing such courses in the past, such as those at the University of Maryland and the University of Pittsburgh, increased their efforts in providing training ranging from several-day short courses to institutes of several weeks.

Library administrators found 1976 developing even more formalized personnel plans within their parent organizations, and library staffs and managers becoming more extensively involved in overall personnel plans regulated outside the library. In effect, civil service plans were adopted by an increasing number of smaller jurisdictions which heretofore had informal procedures. In conjunction with this, unionization became an issue in many libraries, and library unions were asking for, and in some cases receiving, an expanding role in library decision making. Particularly active library unions in San Francisco and Los Angeles had seemingly direct effect on library administrative decisions and on hiring and assignment practices. The increasing militancy of library unions seems to indicate a trend and library administrators must learn to cope with unions and deal effectively and positively with them. The militant library unions stood in contrast to semipassive staff associations which have been prominent in the history of libraries in the United States.

Paraprofessionals. The growing use of paraprofessionals for what were formerly professional positions in libraries was another feature of 1976. More and more libraries were accepting as professionals those without graduate library school degrees. Sacramento Public Library, for example, continued to recruit people without library school degrees for positions formerly professional. The Cleveland Public Library implemented a plan to promote staff clerical people to paraprofessional and professional jobs through a certification program under which experience and efficiency are treated as equivalent competencies associated with a library school degree.

Paraprofessionals in libraries also became more militant, and the Council of Library Technicians (*q.v.*) (COLT) became increasingly active on the national scene and became a part of the American Library Association Conference. Librarians' concern with the growing use of paraprofessionals and the hiring of nongraduate-degree individuals into formerly professional positions was indicated by California Librarians uniting in an organization called "Concerned Librarians Opposing Unprofessional Trends." CLOUT expressed its concern over the role of paraprofessionals in administrative positions and the increasing use of clerical workers and even volunteers to take over tasks formerly assigned those holding graduate degrees. CLOUT members expressed fears that attempts to save money during budget crises would have disastrous long-range implications for public service and for librarians throughout the country.

Other Problems. In addition to pressures from budget officers for management effectiveness, from unions for increasing salaries and benefits, and from professional staff for greater participation in the management process, library administrators in 1976 were also faced with the problems of dealing increasingly with connective organizations, and the administration and management of their own library in relation to other network libraries. Network systems impose certain restrictions and requirements on library services, and library administrators must cope with the impact of the system on their own library and the impact that any administrative decision within their own library may have on the network or networks to which they belong.

Library management in 1976 faced increasing pressures from budget cutting, increased staff agitation, and a general disillusionment with the level of library management in general. The years ahead forecast increasing concerns for library managers who must learn to deal effectively and crisply with their problems. And library leaders are continuing to point out the increasing need for formal training in management for those who wish to be responsible for library administration.

ROBERT ROHLF

Measurement and Evaluation

Economic stringency continued to be a major problem for libraries in 1976 as it has for most of the decade. Considering the state of the national economy and the pessimistic prognostications for full recovery to a buoyant economy in the immediate future, it appeared likely at the end of 1976 that pressure for "accountability" to justify ever increasing costs of library service would only increase.

If the federal government institutes zero-based budgeting, a virtual certainty, state and municipal governments are sure to follow in the same direction. As a result, technocrats in budget offices will require more hard evidence that benefits of programs justify costs.

Since libraries do not provide vital public services like health or safety, they will be hard put to defend adequate or increased levels of financial support without some concrete data

Measurement and Evaluation

by which the value of their service can be evaluated.

The methodological and validity problems surrounding measurement and evaluation are really too complex and too time consuming for the administrator who must be concerned primarily with the press of day-to-day operations. The issues of measurement and evaluation must be resolved by the profession at the national level to provide not only a sound method which can be used by administrators in their own institutions but also to insure a measure of uniformity for aggregate comparison. Some steps in this direction have begun.

In 1971 the Public Library Association sponsored a study to measure the effectiveness of public library service. The results of the research conducted in 23 libraries on which the study was based was published by the Association in 1973 under the title *Performance Measures for Public Libraries*.[1] The utilization of performance measures in individual city libraries and in state-wide studies in Illinois and New Jersey was reported by Ernest DeProspo in *The ALA Yearbook* (1976).

Since 1973 the study team has received many inquiries from libraries in the U.S. and Canada asking how they might apply performance measures in their own institutions. These inquiries stimulated a new publication during 1976. *A Data Gathering and Instruction Manual for Performance Measures in Public Libraries*.[2] This manual is a modification and refinement of the original data collection method. It describes in step-by-step detail how to collect performance measures data for collections, use of facilities and equipment, and use of materials and reference service, how to score findings, and how to analyze the results. The original performance measures study was limited to analyzing a single library unit. The revised manual incorporates system-wide analysis of nearly all of the performance measures.

The importance of measurement and evaluation as essential elements in setting standards for library service was officially recognized by the PLA Goals, Guidelines and Standards Committee. The Committee's position represents a fundamental change from the traditional method since the 1930's of establishing standards based on the opinions of committee members about what constituted "good library service." The Committee in 1976 endorsed a proposal to develop standards which are to be performance oriented and which "will be developed as a tool for library and municipal management to be useful in determining adequacy of library and information service at the community level. . . ."[3] The proposal was subsequently approved by the ALA Executive Board, which authorized the Association to seek funds for implementation.

Monitoring the accessibilty and availability of collections has become relatively common over the past 10 years. One of the most lucid of these studies was written by Paul B. Kantor in 1976. He goes beyond the users' ability to obtain materials to "integrate two important measures of performance"—"exposure time" and "satisfaction level." Together, they are factors in an overall measure of performance, "Total Contact Time per Potential User."[4] The contact time approach builds on previous work by Meier and Hamburg. However, Kantor's method of estimating the time appears more accurate than the earlier works. The satisfaction level is computed for the users locating a desired item based on four "parameters"—acquisition, circulation, other library procedures and the users' own ability to use the system. The parameters can be independently measured and can be combined "multiplicatively to yield the probability of satisfaction."

Problems and Goals. The issues of measurement and evaluation have attracted the interest of a number of highly competent individuals in the past few years. Many of these people have been engaged in assessing the quality of some aspect of library service or library operation. Although the quality of much of this work has been good, the problem remains that impact on individual libraries throughout North America has been minimal. The research front itself is fragmented and uncoordinated. Some individuals have been able to secure federal funding for small projects to measure one or two services. Lack of coordination in appropriating funds, however, has caused duplication of effort in analyzing some operations such as book availability while totally ignoring other services such as reference. Cumulation of effort by building on previous research as in physical sciences is almost totally absent. At the present time the profession needs to develop valid methodologies to measure and evaluate library operations and services. This will require leadership at the national level not only to coordinate and fund the basic methodological research needed but also to educate librarians in the application of these methods to the libraries in their own communities.

ELLEN ALTMAN

REFERENCES
1. Ernest R. Deprospo and others, *Performance Measures For Public Libraries* (Chicago: American Library Association, 1973).
2. Ellen Altman and others, *A Data Gathering and Instructional Manual for Performance Measures in Public Libraries* (Chicago: Celadon Press, 1976).
3. Meredith Bloss, "Standards for Public Library Service—Quo Vadis?" *Library Journal* 101: (June 1, 1976), 1259–1262.
4. Paul B. Kantor, "The Library as an Information Utility in the University Context: Evaluation and Measurement of Service," *Journal of the American Society for Information Science* 27 (March 1976), 100–112.

Media Centers

See *School Libraries and Media Centers.* Consult Index for specific topics.

Mediation, Arbitration, and Inquiry

In 1976 the Staff Committee on Mediation, Arbitration and Inquiry received 19 Requests for Action, the highest number filed with the Committee in one year since its formation in 1971. The complaints in the requests included unethical behavior by a librarian, lack of due process in appraisals and dismissals, censorship of materials, unfair salary practices, unfair tenure practices, and unfair employment practices. The institutions involved in these cases were eight public libraries, seven academic libraries, three school libraries, and one regional library system.

Case Investigations. In action on several of these cases, the Committee investigated the allegations of the request and made recommendations for feasible resolution of the major aspects of the problem; in one case, it directed the complainant to other agencies. In an instance in which the request alleged censorship of the *Advocate* through its removal from an academic library, the problems were resolved locally by a review of the need for the newspaper and purchase of a subscription and back issues in microfilm. The identification of the employer was the major aspect of another case in which the complainant charged that he had been dismissed unfairly while employed in one agency with his salary provided by another agency. The Committee's primary effort in this case was to direct the complainant to agencies which had the legal authority to redress his grievance.

Two of the cases on which the Committee worked in 1976 were related to legal defenses for actions performed by librarians while on duty. In one instance a suit was initiated by the librarian and the program of action assisted in paying legal costs. In view of the court's dismissal of this suit, it did not appear that any further action would be feasible. In the other request for action involving a legal defense, the Committee advised the complainant regarding his request to the employer for payment of legal costs.

The year was the first in which a complaint was received alleging unethical behavior by a librarian who was not a staff member of the institution involved. The complaint centered on alleged unfair review or inaccurate statements regarding the library and the librarian made by another librarian. The complainant was advised by the Committee regarding methods, procedures, and techniques for rebutting incorrect or unsubstantiated statements and reports pertaining to this matter.

Several of the cases involved problems of contract renewal and due process in determining contract renewal. In one instance the employee charged that her contract had been renewed orally, but that the employer had reneged on his earlier agreement and had employed another person without proper notice to the complainant. Two other librarians alleged salary discrimination in comparing salaries paid to them and to a newly appointed librarian.

Contract Cases. Those cases involving questions of contract renewal and due process in contract renewals in academic libraries generally included problems of faculty status and tenure for librarians. In the instances of public librarians who lodged complaints about contracts, the major problems were the issue of the existence of written contracts, the length of probationary periods, and the determination of continuing employment after the probationary period had been completed.

At least two of the cases received in 1976 involved questions regarding union representation of librarians within the union contract. The emphasis in one of these cases was upon job assignment, scheduling, and location of the authority to make changes in the utilization of personnel. The emphasis in the second case was on representation of the library staff by the union in settling grievances and in determining proper salaries in accordance with contract terms.

One of the unusual complaints included in four of the Requests for Action filed in 1976 was harassment of staff and unethical behavior by the library administrator.

Three of the Requests for Action related to reorganization of library structure and reassignment of job duties and responsibilities, though the fact of reorganization was not identified by any complainant as the focal point of a request.

In one of the cases received in 1976, investigation indicated that the employee had been dismissed with due process within the library's probationary period, and the Committee was unable to recommend any actions to assist in this matter. In another case, the complainant entered a higher step in the local grievance procedure and SCMAI was unable to take further action in the case.

At the time of the preparation of this report (December 1976), one case had progressed to the stage of formal inquiry. One 1976 request was in legal suit brought by the complainant. All other cases were in the process of investigation and mediation or awaited some determination by the complainant.

Reports Published. In 1976 two inquiry reports on cases received in 1975 were published in *American Libraries:* the Boutwell case (see *American Libraries,* July–August 1976, p. 446–449) and the Harris case (see *American Libraries,* October 1976, p. 574–

577, and November 1976, p. 616). In each instance, the library Board of Trustees was censured for its failure to develop and implement policies and procedures that would provide reasonable security of employment and fair employment practices consistent with the ALA Policy 106.1, Security of Employment in Libraries.

In the Wendell Boutwell case, one of the most pertinent facts was the practice of the Mt. Vernon Public Library (Illinois) to rehire (or not rehire) every employee every year. With neither a standard probationary period nor a provision for permanent employment of any type, every employee was, in effect, on perpetual probation.

In the Anita Harris case, the Committee found that the absence of written policies and procedures with regard to all aspects of personnel administration in the Bryan-Bennett Library (Salem, Illinois) contributed to events leading to Harris's dismissal in a manner which did not afford her due process. The entire texts of these reports are available in the *American Libraries* issues noted above.

Policy Lack. The Committee's investigations in 1976 indicated that many libraries (public, school, academic, and library systems responsible for work with a variety of types of libraries) do not have well defined policies and clear procedures regarding terms of employment, performance appraisals, warnings and notices, length of probation, contract periods and renewals. These investigations also revealed that many libraries do not have detailed, or inclusive, written job descriptions for many positions, and that they lack clear channels of authority for resolving operational and personnel problems.

There were also many indications from the 1976 investigations that librarians do not always understand the changes in their own status which occur with structural reorganization or new contractual patterns in the institution. The lack of clear understanding about how such changes affect their positions, and how problems or grievances must be addressed and resolved, creates serious personnel problems for both the individual librarian and the institution.

It was distressing to the Committee that requests for assistance continued to be filed after the time when any mediation or arbitration could be effective. Many Requests for Action addressed to the ALA revolved around problems which could have been handled satisfactorily at a local level in the early stages of the problem if the institutions in question had adopted the Library Bill of Rights and fair employment policies and had followed their adopted policies and procedures.

The Staff Committee on Mediation, Arbitration and Inquiry has reiterated many times the need for libraries, library organizations, trustee organizations, and library schools to expand and assure the orientation, training, education, and continuing education of all concerned persons in areas of library personnel administration and welfare.

Requests for information about the ALA Program of Action should be sent to Robert Wedgeworth, Executive Director, ALA, 50 E. Huron St., Chicago, Illinois 60611.

RUTH R. FRAME

Medical Libraries

Because the National Library of Medicine is so important in the day-to-day operations of medical libraries in the United States, if not in the entire world, several actions taken by the body in 1976 took on great significance. Among them were NLM's leadership in breaking the impasse on the proposed copyright bill; its attempt to rethink its positions on fees to be charged those who use its products and services; and its study of the muddled basis for the Regional Medical Library program under the Medical Library Assistance Act. Two other matters, not so closely related to work at NLM but with impacts on medical libraries, were the foundation of an OCLC Medical Users Group and the problem of upward mobility of medical librarians, which resulted in vacancies in high level positions throughout the field occurring simultaneously.

Copyright. The passage by the U.S. Senate of S22 on a vote of 97 to 0 shocked the many medical librarians, whose increasing use of photocopying for provision of articles in journals to health professionals at a distance from centers of library excellence was tied in substantially with the provisions of the Medical Library Assistance Act. The intent under that Act was to serve patients everywhere by providing the same quality of medical information to health practitioners in smaller towns and rural areas as that provided to those in sophisticated medical centers, so that they in turn could provide a high level of care to patients wherever they lived. It seemed inconsistent for the Congress to approve this goal without also approving the means by which it was to be carried out. The size of the vote and the apparent lack of interest of the White House in medical library affairs (no presidential appointments have been made to the National Library of Medicine's Board of Regents for two years) made it appear unlikely that changes would occur in the final version of the proposed law.

Spurred by this, the library profession as a whole and medical libraries in particular began a campaign to persuade the members of the pertinent House of Representatives Committee (Committee on the Judiciary, Subcommittee on Courts, Civil Liberties and the Administration of Justice) to modify the language of the House bill so that such things as interlibrary loans, copies for class use, or single copies of articles for health professionals far from a library would be allowed. Meetings of faculties of medical and allied health sciences schools and professionals in hospitals, clinics, and other facilities, were held and follow-up letters were sent to members of the Subcommittee in the House by these groups. In addition several library organizations, among them the Association for Research Libraries, the Medical Library Association, and the Special Libraries Association, banded together to try to work out substitute language acceptable to the Congressional groups as well as library users. Here the staff of the National Library of Medicine, because of their interest in the Medical Library Assistance Act and because of their greater expertise in governmental methods, were particularly helpful. (See further Copyright).

it that the cost of obtaining information from the large number of biomedical data bases (almost 20 by the end of 1976) was kept so low most medical libraries could afford to procure such services. They could then, in turn, make them available at so small a cost that it was not worth the while of entrepreneurs to enter the market. A discussion on the theory of this pricing structure was held at a meeting of the NLM's Board of Regents in the summer of 1976, after a report by NLM staff and a subcommittee had been received. As a result, the Board restated its approval of this policy, so NLM data bases will continue to be available on a marginal cost basis. (See also Data Bases.)

OCLC Users Group. Since the days of John Shaw Billings and the founding of the Surgeon-General's Library, medical libraries have tended to go their own way, outside the general purview of other types of libraries—some-

Medical Libraries

Fee for Service. Medical libraries, like many other cultural organizations within American society, among them zoos and museums, have not ordinarily charged fees for the services they provide. With the advent of automated data bases, however, the out-of-pocket costs for providing information to any one user became substantial. As a result a number of libraries began to levy charges to recover at least part of their costs (usually money laid out). Another phenomenon that grew out of the costs of such services was the springing up of commercial "brokers" to perform searches on a variety of automated data bases for clients at a fee which was more than just out-of-pocket costs; indeed, in some scientific fields these firms were using the resources of local libraries and not themselves investing the sums necessary to obtain the data bases or the reference tools used with them. By the end of 1976, the issue was not a problem among health scientists, and again the National Library of Medicine helped here. By charging for the marginal costs of the data bases, rather than either the full-recovery costs or a profit, NLM had seen to

times even those within their own institutions. The large number of medical libraries, for example, who report to a dean of a health sciences school or a vice-chancellor for health affairs in a university as compared to the comparatively small number who report to their university librarian is a case in point. Most medical libraries use a medical, rather than a universal, classification system; shelve their journals by title, rather than by corporate author; and provide more services to health professionals not part of their institutions than to non-professionals. Similarly, most medical libraries looked to the NLM rather than to the Library of Congress for cataloging aid, and had that not faltered in the past decade, might still be true. If so, the increasing numbers of medical libraries cooperating within the general framework of the Ohio College Library Center (OCLC) cataloging-bibliographical orbit would not have come about.

Once within the OCLC, however, medical librarians found that the general rules laid down for the whole group ran counter to their traditions and needs. As soon as a large num-

The new Augustus Long Health Sciences Library of Columbia University occupies four floors of the 20-story Health Sciences Center and accommodates 750 users.

Medical Library Association

ber of such libraries were in OCLC, therefore, they began first to complain and then to put pressure on OCLC to allow them the ease and flexibility of their own systems. A users group met several times with officials at OCLC; the decision of NLM to transform and transfer its own recent cataloging to the OCLC store of information portends either (1) loss of medical library singularity, (2) "bending" of OCLC rules to accommodate medical libraries easily, or (3) the formation of a medical "OCLC" under some outside auspices.

Mobility. Health and disease are emotionally loaded words, and the feeling of the U.S. public that more health care workers must be trained and allowed to practice their profession has made health care the second largest national product in the United States. Findings of the Carnegie Foundation (Kerr study) that a sufficient number of physicians are being produced and no new medical schools are necessary may, of course, change this picture. But in the present expanding universe, health sciences libraries have burgeoned and larger numbers of people have become engaged in them. While it is still comparatively easy to find beginning health sciences librarians, it is more difficult (partly because of this very instability of the market) to find those with background and experience to be the chief librarians in new installations. As a result, a game of "musical chairs" has come about, with everyone at the top taking one side step whenever a chief position becomes vacant. In the late summer of 1976 no fewer than 11 major medical libraries were seeking head librarians; they included such prestigious places as Harvard, Yale, California, Arizona, New Mexico, Connecticut, and Maryland. So desperate have some institutions become that a really good chief librarian may be importuned by several places to become a candidate for their job; or institutions may even look with favor on a woman, breaking at last with past proclivities, or one with experience in nonmedical libraries. For the most part, however, nonlibrarians have generally not been appointed. Whether the contracting economic situation for health institutions will change this personnel picture remains to be seen. (*See also* National Library of Medicine.)   ESTELLE BRODMAN

Medical Library Association

The Medical Library Association, founded in 1898, states as its major purposes the fostering of medical and allied scientific libraries and the exchange of medical literature among its members. The Association's first program, the MLA Exchange, was established in 1898 and continues to provide institutional members with a valuable means for collection development. Libraries can exchange duplicate materials for the cost of postage. About 330,000 titles are relocated annually.

The MLA continuing education program offers a well-developed series of one- and two-day courses. In 1976 over 700 members enrolled in 36 courses held in 20 geographic locations. In addition, registration for the 24 courses at the 1976 Annual Meeting totaled 930.

Activities. The Division of Education in August conducted a three-day program, "Institute on Management for Librarians," in Asilomar, California, the third management program sponsored by MLA during 1975/1976.

Fifteen geographic groups and 14 special interest groups are affiliated with the Association and hold meetings at least once a year. The groups sponsor activities and programs for those interested in participating in local affairs or specific areas of health sciences librarianship.

MLA members participated in several programs of national interest in 1976, including support of the library community's position on photocopying of copyrighted material and the Continuing Library Education Network and Exchange (CLENE).

Publications. The Association's publications program provides to the membership the *Bulletin of the Medical Library Association*—($30 for subscription), MLA *News* ($10 for subscription), and *Directory* of the Medical Library Association—($15 for nonmembers). Other publications include *Vital Notes on Medical Periodicals, Current Catalog Proof Sheets, Medical Reference Works and Supplements, Handbook of Medical Library Practice,* and *Careers in Health Sciences Librarianship.*

Membership. The individual membership categories and dues are: Regular Members, persons engaged in the health sciences libraries field, $45; Emeritus Members, retired persons who have been members 10 consecutive years, $15; Associate Members, persons, organizations or institutions interested in medical libraries, $45; Student Members, persons enrolled in accredited library programs, $10; and Life Members, persons eligible to be Regular Members, $900. Institutional dues are based on the number of periodical subscriptions:

MLA Officers

PRESIDENT (June 1976–1977):
Ann E. Kerker, School of Veterinary Medicine, Purdue University, Lafayette, Indiana

PRESIDENT-ELECT:
Gilbert J. Clausman, New York University Medical Center

EXECUTIVE DIRECTOR:
John S. LoSasso

Headquarters: 919 N. Michigan Ave., Chicago, Illinois 60611

they range from $75 for up to 199 to $175 for more than 1,000. As of December 31, 1976, the Association had 2,970 individual members and 1,125 institutional members, a total of 4,095 compared with 1975 membership of 3,884.

The 75th annual meeting was held June 12-17 in Minneapolis, attended by 1,430. The 1977 Annual Meeting was scheduled for June 12-16 in Seattle. — JOHN S. LOSASSO

Micrographics

No one event in micrographics stands out for the year 1976. Perhaps most important was the fact that libraries of many types and sizes turned to micrographics to solve specific problems both administrative and bibliographic, thus signaling further acceptance of this medium as a viable library tool.

Libraries, for example, continued to increase their collections of microform files of newspapers, periodicals, and other library materials in the interest of economy, security, and ease of handling. The most noteworthy recent developments in library micrographics, however, have been in the use of micrographics in combination with automation rather than as a space-saving and storage medium.

COM. Computer Output Microfilm (COM), which enables the computer to spew forth its information in microform at speeds far exceeding that of paper printouts with savings in time, materials, and handling, has shown great promise for libraries. This technology received a boost in libraries with the introduction of two special purpose microfilm reader systems—the Information Design ROM III and the Auto-graphics LCR 1100 Library Catalog Reader. Although both machines were introduced a year or two earlier, 1976 was the year that saw the actual use of these systems in a rapidly growing number of libraries both large and small. From the user's viewpoint, the systems are similar. The public catalog is produced by computer on a roll of 16mm film at a reduction of 42X, enabling a storage density of approximately 40 catalog entries per inch of film. The roll of film, from 750 to 1,200 feet long, is contained in the microfilm readers, which have high speed film transport systems and an index indicator on the front. By operating very simple controls, the average user can probably look up an entry in about the same amount of time it would take using a conventional card catalog or a printed book catalog.

COM catalogs are a natural outgrowth of computer generated book catalogs which have proved to be so practical in libraries forced to maintain many public catalogs at different locations. Just as computer generated book catalogs have proved to be more economical than card catalogs in certain situations, so have COM catalogs proved to be even more economical than book catalogs. Thus far they have found their greatest acceptance in public libraries, with large systems such as Baltimore, Los Angeles County, and Fairfax County, Virginia, leading the way. Among academic libraries, the University of Toronto Library with 1,250,000 catalog records was the most noteworthy institution to convert to a COM catalog system in 1976 (see further Canadian Report: Academic Libraries).

Other library uses of COM during the year included the publication on microfiche of the periodical lists of large library collections, most notably those of the University of Colorado and the University of California at Berkeley. The University of California, Los Angeles, started offering its new acquisitions list on COM fiche, and the Library of Congress announced that it would issue a cumulative microform edition of the Register of Additional Locations. The Register is a bibliographic companion to the National Union Catalog (NUC) and contains locations for titles with imprints from 1956 to the present that were not included in the NUC. The present machine-readable file contains approximately 1,620,000 location reports with an average of 12.4 locations per title. It is used primarily for interlibrary loan information, and is particularly useful for those works not cataloged by LC.

Dartmouth Demonstration Project. Another example of the combination of automation and micrographics is a demonstration project at Dartmouth College funded by a grant from the Exxon Corporation. The project, headed by Arthur W. Luehrmann, Jr., involves the development of a computer-based system for retrieving and displaying visual information contained on color microfiches. A control unit to link an Image Systems microfiche storage system and a computer terminal will be developed for this project. It is anticipated that over 65,000 visuals will be available in the system, including works of art, photographs, maps, and anatomical drawings. Each picture will be described by approximately 15 to 20 attributes. Through a multiple variable search program based on logical connections the user will be able to request any of the visuals in the system. The computer will interact with the control unit and effect the retrieval of the requested microfiche frames.

GPO. During 1976, for a while at least, it appeared that the U.S. Government Printing Office might finally become a large scale micropublisher. A pilot project begun in the last quarter of 1975 was completed in 1976. For this project, 33 of the 1,200 depository libraries were supplied with the Code of Federal Regulations on microfiche filmed at a reduction ratio of 24:1 from the source documents. The results of the pilot project were generally considered to be favorable both economically

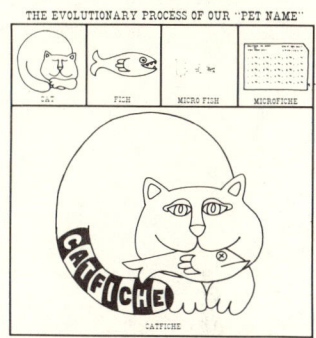

Six years of planning by the West Virginia Library Commission resulted in this 1976 "Catfiche Conference" held by its Technical Services Division. The system has cataloged the holdings of all West Virginia academic, public, and special collections in microfiche.

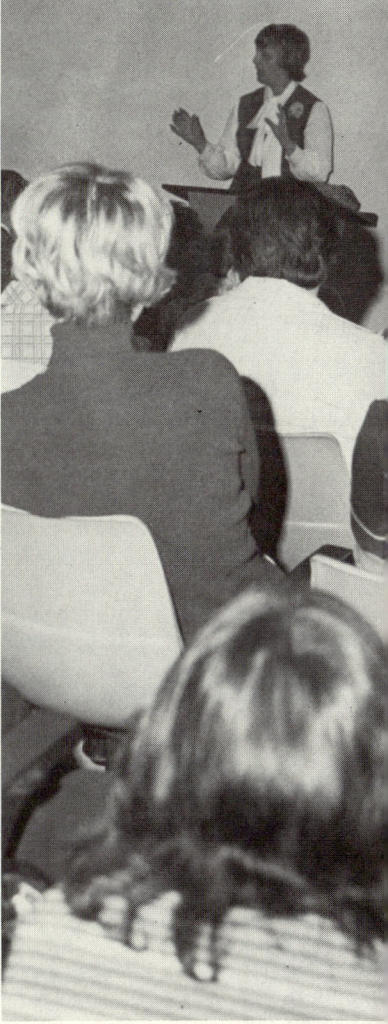

Multimedia Materials

and in terms of acceptance by the participating libraries. A report recommending the increased use of micropublishing techniques was submitted to the Congressional Joint Committee on Printing, but as of the end of the year the Joint Committee had only given GPO the green light to continue publishing the Code of Federal Regulations in microform, making it available, however, to any depository library requesting it in microform.

A dramatic demonstration by GPO of the efficiency and utility of micropublishing came during 1976. When the U.S. Postal Service received permission for a postage rate hike, it was necessary to publish and to distribute to all 1,200 depository libraries a 20,000-page document entitled "Changes in Rate of Postage and Fees Before the Postal Rate Commission." The Government Printing Office was given ten days to print and distribute that document. (The Postal Service would lose an estimated $3,000,000 a day in lost revenue if that time limit were not met.) The 20,000 pages, which occupied 9 feet of shelf space, were reduced to 228 microfiches that required approximately 2 inches of space and were distributed through the mail. The time limit was met.

Other Activities. Early in 1976 ALA brought forth its first major micropublishing project with the publication of *The Sourcebook of Library Technology: A Cumulative Edition of Library Technology Reports 1965–1975*. Contained on 30 microfiches, *The Sourcebook* replaced the hard-copy backfile of *Library Technology Reports* which had grown to 11 binders of looseleaf reports.

Microform Review, a reviewing medium for library micropublications, launched a new publication, *Microform Equipment Review*, which joined *Library Technology Reports* and National Reprographics Centre for documentation in publishing evaluations of microform equipment. Edited by William R. Hawken, the new publication was aimed primarily at the library market.

In October *Microform Review* and the Resources and Technical Services Division (RTSD) of ALA cosponsored the Second Annual Library Microform Conference. Held in Atlanta, the conference attracted librarians from as far away as Hawaii and New England for two days of lectures and exhibits.

Among other significant activities for the year were the publication of the *American National Standard for the Advertising of Micropublications (Z39.26, 1975)* and a progress report on work on a standard for nonsilver types of microfilm stock such as diazo and vesicular. ALA reaffirmed its position that until such time that this work is completed and a standard adopted, only silver halide type film manufactured in conformity with the *American National Standard Specifications for Photographic Film for Archival Records, Silver-Gelatin Type, on Cellulose Base (PH1.28, 1969)* should be used for archival micropublications. — HOWARD S. WHITE

Multimedia Materials

Since statistics on expenditures for nonprint materials later than those reported in the 1976 Centennial edition of *The ALA Yearbook* were not available at the end of 1976, it was impossible to determine if the growth in the support of multimedia materials had been felt. One could probably speculate that dwindling budgets and the continued loss of federal aid has caused little growth.

Carter G. Woodson Regional Library. One new public library trend overshadowed most others in 1976 with the development of a new kind of public library service. The Carter G. Woodson Regional Library of the Chicago Public Libarary, which opened late in 1975, provided an example of Chicago's regional library concept. In addition, it offered exciting architecture and one of the world's great collections of Afro-American history and literature in the Vivian G. Harsh Collection. Two multimedia elements may set the pace for future public library services. The whole range of multimedia materials is an integral part of the regional library concept. However, the Media Center and the Independent Study Program are highlights of the Chicago program.

CPL makes the following statement about the regional library Media Center:

> The availability of new audiovisual formats for recreation, information, and educational development is expected to accelerate in years to come, and the Woodson Regional Library has a highly sophisticated Media Center that can keep pace with this trend. Its substantial holdings of films, audio- and videocassettes, slides, slide films, and records have been indexed in the main card catalog.
> Records—from classical music through pop chart hits to sound effects and speeches—are stored in easy-to-use browsing bins, and there are turntables and headphones for in-library use. The collection of 16 mm and 8 mm films is particularly strong, including such diverse forms as personality profiles, news footage, feature films (notably, rare silents from motion pictures' early years), and documentaries. World events; how-to instructions for sports, home and auto repair, and arts and crafts; drama; analyses of contemporary urban and national problems; and courses in social sciences are only a partial listing of the subjects explored in sight and sound in The Media Center.

The Woodson Regional Library probably represents one of the most progressive approaches by public libraries to multimedia. There is contined hope that public libraries will fill the final gap by assuming a role as a community resource center for the production of original audiovisual materials.

The Independent Study Program of the Woodson Regional Library identifies the role of its Independent Study Program:

The University of Wisconsin Stout Library's 6,000-page public catalog has been reduced to 21 pieces of microfiche which can be carried in a pocket.

Materials for three Independent Study Programs are housed in their related departments. Study Unlimited provides courses of City Colleges of Chicago on videotape for personal enrichment or college credit. The College Level Examination Program (CLEP) assists in preparation for college entrance above the freshman level, and the General Educational Development program (GED) offers preparation for the high school equivalency diploma examination.

In the mid-1970's this trend is developing in several dozen public libraries in the United States. The necessary multimedia support of such independent study programs will require far-reaching library commitment.

Academic Libraries. The growth of multimedia collections in academic libraries highlights several issues for college and universities as they go about modifying their services and procedures to accommodate the new formats. The age-old question of whether book materials and audiovisual materials should be combined or separate was still being debated in 1976. Many academic libraries have integrated these collections and services. Separate book and nonbook collections and facilities, in the view of many librarians, can only cause frustration and lack of use and understanding by both students and faculty. Though integrating collections may cause packaging problems, or shelving problems, the needs of users remain paramount.

Bibliographic Control. Another issue is the bibliographic control of nonbook collections. The question of how to catalog anything that is not a book continues to plague libraries. New cataloging rules and handbooks anticipated the addition of nonbook materials to OCLC, and the increasing number of associations and conferences dealing with this issue promised to make it easier for librarians to recognize that bibliographic control for all formats is easier to approach as one problem rather than a dozen isolated problems.

School Libraries. A number of identifiable trends in school libraries emerged in 1976. The continued financial crunch on school libraries is causing a new look at the sharing of multimedia resources. Schools have not been noted for the extent of their interlibrary loan activities. But increases in interlibrary loans are causing more school libraries to share their resources.

The use of video communications in schools has been addressed by the American Association of School Libraries. A new committee of AASL planned to look into the psychological ramifications of using more video programming in schools.

Though schools have been in the vanguard of developing the use of educational technology, they have not felt the need until comparatively recently to explore more sophisticated computerized bibliographic control. This will be an ongoing trend among school libraries in the late 1970's.

The American Association of School Libraries and the American Vocational Association in a joint effort will evaluate school library resources and services in support of vocational education. There is a need for bibliographies of multimedia vocational resources. Schools need to identify exemplary programs—where are they and why are they effective? Demonstration centers might be beneficial in program development.

Schools are taking a new look at how their library and media center resources can better serve the gifted child. A preliminary study of the use of multimedia materials in serving students with special learning needs indicated a scarcity of materials. The requirements of those students must be met if the role of the school library media program is to reach its maximum potential.   RICHARD L. DUCOTE

The newly renovated Louis Skidmore Room houses the 140,000 photographs and slides of the Rotch Library Visual Collection at the Massachusetts Institute of Technology.

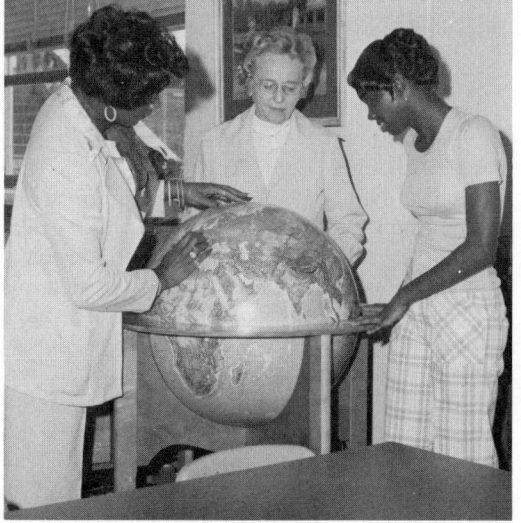

Audiovisual librarians and student (right) in the Byrd High School Library, Shreveport, Louisiana, which won the 1976 Modisette Award for high schools.

Music Library Association

During 1976 the Music Library Association responded to the report of its Goals and Objectives Committee. In February the Board of Directors met in Seattle in open session with the membership to discuss recommendations on the operation and program of the Association. In September the Board's response was published in the Association's journal, Notes, 33 (September, 1976) 45–50; some suggestions were implemented, some rejected, and others deferred pending the reorganization and relocation of the Association's business office.

Concurrent with ALA's Annual Conference, MLA met in Chicago in July, a meeting notable for several innovations: the first open Board meeting, the first joint meeting with ALA-ACRL Art Section to consider common concerns, and the inauguration of a Publications Council comprising the chairperson of the Publications Committee, the editors of all ongoing publications, the treasurer, the business manager, and executive officers.

While the internal condition of the Association continued healthy and productive, significant progress was made in cooperative projects with other groups. Membership in the International Federation of Library Associations, assumed in 1975, became increasingly important as IFLA considered formats for music [ISBD (M)] and nonbook materials including sound recordings [ISBD (NBM)]. MLA had participated in the formulation of ISBD(M) through a special committee set up by the International Association of Music Libraries, but no similar vehicle has been available for nonbook materials. Comments are being channeled through the chairperson of MLA's Automation Committee. The effectiveness of earlier MLA activity in this area was noted in the Introduction to Music: A MARC Format, issued by the MARC Development Office at the Library of Congress, singling out the Music Library Association, "particularly its MLA/MARC Committee" as having "contributed significantly to the development of the format."

Other cooperative activities included participation in the revision of the Anglo-American Cataloging Rules through an official representative, continued participation in the International Association of Music Libraries, the Council of National Library Associations, and joint committees with the American Musicological Society, the Music Publishers' Association, and the National Association of Schools of Music. Effective working relations have been developed with the Ohio College Library Center and the Library of Congress. OCLC has requested MLA to establish a task force of music librarians from subscriber libraries to advise the Center during the implementation of the MARC music format, a pioneer effort in this field. The seven outside libraries selected by MLA to contribute card copy to Music, Books on Music and Sound Recordings, issued as part of the National Union Catalog, were increased to nine in 1976 by the addition of Harvard University and the University of Illinois. This addition provided not only greater coverage but special experience in the fields of automation and ethnomusicology. The program of contributed cataloging has steadily improved due to the cooperation between the outside libraries and the two sections at the Library of Congress that are directly involved: the catalog publication division and the music section of the processing department.

DENA J. EPSTEIN

MLA Officers

PRESIDENT (February 1975–February 1977):
Clara Steuermann, California State University, Los Angeles

SECRETARY:
Geraldine Ostrove, New England Conservatory of Music, Boston, Massachusetts

TREASURER:
Shirley P. Emanuel, Library of Congress, Washington, D.C.

BUSINESS MANAGER:
Nina N. Romani

Headquarters: 343 S. Main St., Ann Arbor, Michigan 48104

National Agricultural Library

The bibliographic data bases in machine readable form created by the National Agricultural Library (NAL) for controlling documents received were named AGRICOLA July 1976. AGRICOLA (AGRICultural OnLine Access) is an umbrella for a family of data bases providing for the information needs of NAL clientele. The major data base, CAIN (CAtaloging and INdexing), constitutes the bulk of the AGRICOLA file and includes bibliographic information on agricultural and related scientific documents acquired worldwide. The AGricultural ECONomics (AG ECON) data base is on agricultural marketing policies, program policies, program products, demand, supplies and prices. The Food and Nutrition Information and Educational Materials Center (FNIC) data base is a machine readable cumulation of citations to journal articles, monographs, and audiovisual materials in applied human nutrition, food service sanitation and safety, volume food storage and preparation, and administrative management. NAL is developing and soliciting additional data bases that fall within the scope of AGRICOLA. (See also Data Bases.)

Cooperative Projects. The first step was undertaken in 1976 in the proposed microfilming of all land-grant college research documents. The agricultural research publications of six New England states were microfilmed under a federal-state agreement coordinated by the New England Board of Education. An agreement was also negotiated with Utah State University Library and with the Southeastern land-grant libraries for the microfilming of their own state agricultural experiment and extension service publications.

Another cooperative project involves the use of AID (Agency for International Development) funds to provide library and information service to land-grant sorghum researchers and graduate students on four land-grant campuses: Nebraska, Puerto Rico, Purdue, and Texas.

National Programs. The National Agricultural Library and Cornell University Libraries signed a cooperative agreement for the addition of bibliographic records of agricultural serials and journals to the CONSER (Conversion of Serials) data base. Cornell and NAL hold extensive collections of agricultural serials and share many titles in common. This cooperative effort will result in improved access to this important body of literature and avoid duplication of effort for libraries throughout the country.

Since 1974 NAL has been linked with the Ohio College Library Center (OCLC). During the period July 1975 through June 1976 more than 1,000 cataloging records were processed each month through OCLC. About 56 percent of these were "full" records, that is, original cataloging or Library of Congress cataloging from sources other than OCLC. The remaining 44 percent were records found in the OCLC data base which were accepted or modified for NAL use. NAL has begun a project to input preliminary records for use with the serials check-in component. As designed, the Serial Control Subsystem of OCLC will provide an on-line inventory control of serial publications.

Gifts and Publications. The Library has been enriched through the transfer of historical and archival records from several institutions. Records for 1964–70 were received from the American Agricultural Editors Association, and the Graduate School, USDA, deposited its archives.

A number of bibliographic publications were issued by the Library: *The Prince Family Manuscript Collection; Serials Currently Received by the National Agricultural Library 1975, a Keyword Index; Dairy Technology and Production, a List of Serials.* A reprinting of *Agricultural/Biological Vocabulary,* three volumes, was issued in response to requests from researchers and librarians. The Library also resumed issuance of an official *Annual Report* after a hiatus of many years.

Bicentennial Observance. The Associates NAL, Inc., in cooperation with the Graduate School, USDA, published the papers of its Bicentennial symposium "Agricultural Literature—Proud Heritage, Future Promise," held September 24–26, 1975. A further salute to the Bicentennial was a symposium on "Heritage of Agriculture in Maryland, 1776–1976, held July 30, 1976. The papers of this symposium were published in the Associates NAL, Inc., quarterly journal for October 1976.

RICHARD A. FARLEY

NAL Officers

DIRECTOR:
Richard A. Farley

ASSOCIATE DIRECTOR:
Samuel T. Waters

DEPUTY DIRECTOR FOR RESOURCE DEVELOPMENT:
Jeanne M. Holmes

DEPUTY DIRECTOR FOR LIBRARY SERVICES:
Wallace C. Olsen

EXECUTIVE OFFICER:
Gerald J. Sophar

Headquarters: National Agricultural Library 10301 Baltimore Blvd., Beltsville, Maryland 20705

National Commission on Libraries and Information Science

During 1976 the National Commission on Libraries and Information Science expanded its efforts to collect data necessary for decision making and to initiate implementation activities. These efforts had gained major impetus from the June 1975 publication of the Commission's National Program Document, *Toward a National Program for Library and Information Services: Goals for Action,* and from its almost immediate endorsement—in principle and concept—by the major professional library and information science associations—the American Library Association, the Association of Research Libraries, the Special Libraries Association, the American Society for Information Science, the Medical Library Association, American Association of Law Libraries, and the National Federation of Abstracting and Indexing Services. With a framework established and community support ensured, the Commission could begin implementation activities or, where necessary, begin acquiring hard, current information needed to begin implementation.

CLENE. The earliest implementation activity of the Commission was CLENE (the Continuing Library Education Network and Exchange), the outgrowth of an NCLIS-commissioned report and two NCLIS-sponsored conferences. CLENE, in 1976, became a fully operational independent activity, with a full range of activities in the development of operational mechanisms underway, including a survey and analysis to develop lists of needs and

National Commission on Libraries and Information Science

priorities; the acquisition of literature of continuing education and the design of a data base; the publication of proceedings, directories, bibliography, and indexes; and an intensive public information program, which includes newsletters, presentations, and feature articles.

Computer Communication. The Commission continued its cooperative support (with the National Science Foundation and the Council on Library Resources) of the Committee on the Coordination of National Bibliographic Control (CoCoNaBiC), formerly the Advisory Group on National Bibliographic Control, but, recognizing that standards for bibliographic records are of limited value unless these records can be transferred between different computers and systems, NCLIS entered into a cooperative arrangement with the Institute for Computer Sciences and Technology (ICST) of the National Bureau of Standards to sponsor a task force charged with developing computer-to-computer communications protocols.

The basic problem stems from the fact that different types of computers—and even some systems on the same computer type—"speak different languages," and to date, message standards have been generally limited to one-on-one situations. For an efficient national network means must be provided that will permit terminals connected to one computer to access data from another computer, and online exchange of data records among computers. The means should also be transparent to the user; that is, it should not require him to cope with the dozens of different terminal interfaces and coding schemes currently extant or even be aware of the fact that he is communicating with a different kind of computer. Nor can it be tied to a particular character framing (for example, 8-bit characters) or necessarily a particular communications medium or network (for example, Tymshare, Telenet, AT&T), or even limited to character representation.

The task force will base its efforts on the preliminary work done by the Telecommunications Committee of the Information Science and Automation Division of the American Library Association; but because its efforts will be concentrated, it will complete the task more quickly than would be possible with the Telecommunications Committee's twice-a-year meeting schedule. The task force's recommendations will be forwarded to the American National Standards Institute, to ALA, and to the American Society for Information Science. It is hoped that the recommendations can serve as a basis for developing a standard.

National Periodicals System. In January the Commission convened a task force charged with developing recommendations for the design of a National Periodicals System to provide prompt access to copies of articles from scholarly journals. The task force established specific goals, including improved access and delivery, reduction of burden on large net lenders, and more effective use of library funds. The group established service requirements including comprehensive coverage, value of content, rather than language, as a selection criterion, the use of all available means of communication and transmission, and flexibility to develop new services in response to changing requirements and technology. They have also enumerated criteria for evaluating various alternatives, including acceptability to the library and information community, legal bases, governance, and performance.

Applying these criteria to a variety of proposed mechanisms, the task force has concluded that a hierarchical system of three levels will best meet the needs of the library community. Initial services will come at the state and regional levels. It is estimated that between 75 to 80 percent of the requests can be filled at this level. The resources of last resort for little-used titles will be a combination of existing strong collections (the Library of Congress and major research libraries, for example) with a bibliographic system such as CONSER (CONversion of SERials) to provide location data. It is estimated that between 5 to 8 percent of the requests will be filled at this level. The middle level, between the state and regional level and the level of last resort, will be a dedicated National Periodicals Center managed by the Library of Congress, probably initially located in rented quarters in the Washington, D.C., area and consisting of 45,000 titles. This level is expected to fill approximately 20 percent of the needs. The Center would be phased in over a period of time, with the assembly of dedicated collections starting on a given date and service starting approximately one year later. Within five years, this system will effectively remove most of the burden from the heavy net lenders, leaving them free to cope more efficiently with requests for the more esoteric and little-used materials.

AECT Project. Somewhat later in 1976, NCLIS took a further step toward improving the identification for the provision of bibliographic resources by commissioning the Association for Educational Communications and Technology to develop goals, objectives, and functional specifications for bibliographic control of nonprint media, as well as an inventory of existing bibliographic data bases for nonprint media. This project is being extensively coordinated with ALA, ASIS, and other concerned associations and individuals. The draft material has been circulated, and a coordination and feedback session was held at the ASIS Annual Meeting in October. Similar sessions were to be held at the ALA Midwinter

Meeting in January 1977 and at the AECT meeting in May. With the information from this project, realistic plans for improving both bibliographic control of and access to nonprint media can be more readily developed.

Library of Congress. The Library of Congress is an acknowledged keystone in the National Program and NCLIS has two studies underway in conjunction with LC. One will examine the near-term (five to seven years) role of the Library itself and another will examine the role and structure of authority files in the national network. Cooperative efforts with other agencies have been a hallmark of 1976 projects.

Photocopying. In addition to the projects with the Library of Congress and the National Bureau of Standards already noted, NCLIS is jointly funding with the National Science Foundation and CONTU (q.v.) (the Commission on New Technological Uses of Copyrighted Works) a study of the volume and patterns of library photocopying in the United States, including the design and feasibility assessment of a royalty payment mechanism. In July NCLIS sponsored a conference designed to provide input from a broad cross-section of the community to the study of emerging issues of national information policy which the Committee on the Right of Privacy of the Domestic Council had been directed to prepare for the President.

Other Projects. Other projects underway in 1976 and scheduled for completion in 1977 include an updated National Inventory of Library Needs and a series of seminars to update the chiefs and senior personnel of state library agencies on developments in library management and planning and evaluation techniques. Completed at year's end was a study of the "Effectiveness of Federal Funding Programs for Public Libraries." It includes data never before assembled in a coherent fashion and confirms the need for a coordinated rational—and much more substantial—federal presence in the funding of public libraries. It is anticipated that the report will have a significant impact on future library legislation.

White House Conference. Perhaps the most exciting event for NCLIS in 1976 was the issuance by the President at the ALA Centennial Conference of the long-awaited "call" for the White House Conference on Library and Information Services. This conference, which is to be preceded by state and territorial conferences, will be invaluable in providing grass roots input to implementation of the National Program and enabling each state to assess its own needs, resources, and priorities as well as articulating their role in a national library and information network. A major portion of the funding for the White House Conference is allocated to support the state conferences on a grant basis, and as the year ended, the funding request had been included in the first supplemental appropriations bill for fiscal 1977.

During 1976 the Commission's program of implementation passed through the start-up stage and began gathering momentum. This is expected to continue through 1977, gaining additional impetus from the planning for the White House Conference, and, as the state and territorial conferences are held, from the heightened awareness on the part of the entire community which these conferences will engender. Many years will be required to begin approaching the ideal of equal opportunity of access. However, a substantial start has been made, and NCLIS looks for deliberate, measured, but continuous progress. Close cooperation and coordination with library associations, library and information centers, and governmental agencies is essential if successful implementation is to become a reality.

FREDERICK BURKHARDT

National Endowment for the Humanities

The National Endowment for the Humanities is an independent federal agency which supports projects of research, education, and public activity in the humanities. According to the Act which established the Endowment, the humanities include history, philosophy, languages, literature, linguistics, archeology, jurisprudence, history and criticism of the arts, ethics, comparative religion, and those aspects of the social sciences employing historical or philosophical approaches. The Endowment's grant-making programs are administered by four major divisions—Public Programs, Education Programs, Research Grants, and Fellowships—and by the Office of Planning and Analysis. All of the Endowment's Divisions supported library projects in 1976.

Grants for libraries are available from all divisions of NEH.

Division of Education Programs. The College Library Program jointly sponsored by the Council on Library Resources and NEH encourages programs at accredited four-year colleges and universities that are intended to promote relationships between library services and academic programs. The program administered 18 active grants in 1976.

Research Grants Division. One program focusing on libraries and archives is included in the Centers of Research Programs Section, providing "grants to libraries for organizing, cataloguing, and improving access to research materials in the humanities. The program also supports microfilming of materials in foreign repositories, limited microfilming for preservation, oral history to supplement collections of written materials, and the development of automated data processing systems to improve bibliographic control of collections of research resources of all kinds." The Collections Program administered some 130 active grants in 1976.

Fellowships Division. This program provides fellowships for study and research in the humanities to independent centers for advanced study, in order to increase opportunities for the interchange of ideas among scholars. In 1976 awards were made to the American Antiquarian Society, the Folger Library, the Hoover Institution, and the Huntington and the Newberry Libraries.

Public Programs. The Division makes a limited number of grants to test ways in which public libraries and library-related organizations can better use their humanities holdings to meet the needs and interests of the adult nonstudent population. Five library grants were made in 1975, and 11 in 1976. Grantees included, among others, the Prince George's County Memorial Library System (Maryland), Indiana Library Association, Toledo-Lucas County Public Library, Graduate Library School of the University of North Carolina, and Tri-County Library System, in Rome, Georgia.

Office of Planning and Analysis. Two library-related grants were made in 1976 by the Office of Planning and Analysis. Virginia Mathews was awarded a grant to organize a conference on the role of the humanities in libraries. The Indiana University Graduate Library School received support for the planning phase of an analytical study of library decision making as it relates to the acquisition of periodicals and books in the humanities. Two other grants on the production and dissemination of scholarly knowledge—to New York University and to the American Council of Learned Societies—contain a component of research into the role of libraries.

GLORIA WEISSMAN

National Libraries
See *Principal Libraries of the World*.

National Library of Medicine

In 1976 the National Library of Medicine received a special appropriation of $26,000,000 for construction of the Lister Hill Center building. This is a landmark in the Library's history for it will combine under one roof the talents of a wide range of health professionals, information scientists, computer experts, educators, and specialists in the most modern audiovisual techniques. The new building, to be adjacent to the present Library, will be completed in late 1979.

A "Colloquium on the Bicentennial of Medicine in the United States" was sponsored at the National Institutes of Health on May 6 and 7, 1976, by the Library and the Josiah Macy, Jr., Foundation. Several hundred distinguished physicians, scientists, and educators gathered to discuss a series of topics related to U.S. medicine. The essays presented at the Colloquium have been published in a two-volume *Festschrift*.

Two new on-line data bases made their appearance in 1976, joining MEDLINE (MEDLARS On-Line) and the other retrieval services reported last year. They are CANCERPROJ (ongoing cancer research projects and clinical trials), a cooperative effort between the Library and the National Cancer Institute, and EPILEPSYLINE (citations and abstracts relating to epilepsy), in cooperation with the National Institute of Neurological and Communicative Disorders and Stroke.

Three more countries have entered into partnership arrangements with NLM for MEDLARS/MEDLINE cooperation: Iran, Mexico, and South Africa. They join eight other NLM partners: Australia, Canada, France, Germany, Japan, Sweden, the United Kingdom, and the World Health Organization. Under the agreements, the foreign partners provide indexed citations for NLM's MEDLARS data base; in return they receive the MEDLARS computer tapes or direct on-line access to the Library's computers in Bethesda.

Beginning in January 1976, the Library's bibliographic publications and MEDLARS data bases carried a notice of copyright protection outside the U.S. A new quarterly periodical *Toxicology Research Projects Directory*, started publication during the year. Selected congresses, symposia, proceedings, and monographs with multiple authorship are now being indexed and entered into *Index Medicus* and MEDLINE. Previous coverage had been restricted almost entirely to journal articles.

MELVIN S. DAY

National Library Week
See *Public Relations, Library*.

National Micrographics Association

The National Micrographics Association, headquartered in Silver Spring, Maryland, is a professional organization serving 8,000 individuals and 250 trade member companies. 1976 was another successful year for NMA with increased distribution of publications, several new titles published, much activity in standards development, and some new educational programs.

Publications produced during 1976 include the *1976 Annual Conference Proceedings*, the 1976 edition of the *Buyer's Guide to Micrographic Equipment, Products and Services*, a supplement to the *Micrographics Index* and a supplement to the *Guide to Micrographic Equipment*. In addition, two new publications were introduced, *COM and Its Applications*, a compendium of articles on COM (computer output microfilm) which have appeared in NMA's *Journal of Micrographics* and *Micrographic Retrieval—Computer Interface,* a special interest package consisting of a 24-page text and 37 related articles on microfiche. NMA's third audiovisual presentation, *COM: Systems and Applications,* was also introduced.

NMA's standards activities continued to thrive. The U.S. Department of Defense adopted eight NMA standards for use in the microform program of the Army, Navy, and Air Force. NMA standards covering formats of computer output microfilm and microfiche of documents were approved as American National Standards. A revised edition of *Basic U.S. Government Micrographic Standards and Specifications* was updated. All of NMA's standards committees continued their work in establishing standards for the micrographic industry. Two new committees were established during the year—the Microfiche Cartridge Committee, responsible for investigating the need for a standard microfiche cartridge, and the Metric Committee, which will prepare a "white paper" recommending an orderly plan for the conversion of the micrographic industry to a metric system of weights and measures.

In the area of education, NMA conducted seminars on the day before their two major meetings. Seminar subjects included Fundamentals of Micrographics, Computer Output Microfilm, Retrieval and Systems Design, Inspection and Quality Control, and Basic Data Processing. A new venture for NMA in its continuing philosophy of educating people about micrographics was the introduction of the *Micrographics Lecture Kit.* The kit is designed to aid an instructor teaching micrographics.

The 25th Annual NMA Conference and Exposition was held in Chicago in April with 9,000 in attendance. The NMA Mid-Year Meeting was held in Denver in October with a record-breaking membership attendance of nearly 500.   DON M. AVEDON

NMA Officers

PRESIDENT (1976–77):
Thomas P. Anderson

VICE-PRESIDENT:
Richard J. Conners

TREASURER:
Louis J. Zeh, Jr.

EXECUTIVE DIRECTOR:
O. Gordon Banks

TECHNICAL DIRECTOR:
Don M. Avedon

Headquarters: 8728 Colesville Road,
Silver Spring, Maryland 20910

NATIS

See *UNESCO*.

National Technical Information Service

The United States has no national scientific and technical information system; it has a plurality of products and services offered by government and private sources. The National Technical Information Service (NTIS), however, offers the broadest range and also in-depth coverage by products and services across the entire spectrum of science and technology. New reports are added to the system at increasing annual rates; growth progressed from 46,000 reports in 1971 to over 65,000 reports in 1976, about twice the number of new books produced by all U.S. publishers each year. The reports describe the results of the U.S. Government's entire research, development, testing and evaluation program or over 50 percent of the total research and development expenditures for both the public and private sector. The total data base now includes some 1,000,000 items—with more than 500,000 records in machine readable form.

Weekly Government Abstracts (WGA), a series issued to attract new customers, includes 26 different subject categories. Additions were "Health Planning" (late 1975) and "Problem-Solving Information for State and Local Governments" (January 1976). Subscriptions in fiscal year 1976 totaled 30,000, compared with 25,800 a year earlier. The items in the NTIS system are potentially exposed to 12,000,000 referrals each year through the WGA series.

In 1975 emphasis was placed on a new Published Search (bibliographies developed online) program. More than 1,000 Published Searches were developed on topics that appeared to be of considerable public interest. In 1976 NTIS and Engineering Index (Ei) worked together to offer their customers a series of NTIS/Ei Published Searches on specific topics covered by both data bases. Ei draws on resources worldwide—professional and industrial journals and proceedings, transactions, and special publications of engineering societies, associations, universities, and research institutions. NTIS contributes up-to-date technical reports and analyses resulting from federally sponsored research.

A major developmental area for NTIS in 1976 was computer-based data files produced by federal agencies and the computer programs for manipulating the files. These files are listed in the *Directory of Computerized Data Files, Software, & Related Technical Reports.* In addition, the General Services Administration (GSA) selected NTIS to organize and manage a Federal Software Exchange Center. Federal Property Management Regulations require all agencies, other than Depart-

In 1976 NTIS used computer-based data files produced by federal agencies to service other agencies and for sales to the public with the approval of the General Services Commission.

ment of Defense, to report all common-use software to the exchange. Although the primary GSA market is other federal agencies, NTIS will also sell copies to the public, with GSA permission.

During 1976 NTIS emphasized user education programs. Seminars and workshops conducted nationally and internationally, described the NTIS Bibliographic Data File, content, subject analysis, products and services, information retrieval, and ordering techniques. Working toward improved document delivery services, NTIS offers three ordering options for its customers: rush handling, premium service, and regular service.

The thrust of 1977 developmental programs will continue to be in technical information services for state and local governments, increased field technical assistance to business and industry, improved access to demographic and socio-economic information, and an expanded foreign market program. TED RYERSON

Networks

The previous article on networks in this *Yearbook* (1976) defined a network as: "two or more libraries and/or other organizations engaged in a common pattern of information exchange, through communication, for some functional purpose." This article uses the same broad definition.

The previous article attempted to put the concept of library networking in context in terms of the "environmental" factors affecting the development of the networking phenomenon—i.e., that the proliferation of published data and the increased demand upon information sources in combination with a straitened economy have resulted in an increased acceptance of the merits of resource sharing, through networking, as a means of resolution of current library problems. In addition, the growth of coherent library networking is being promulgated by the National Commission on Libraries and Information Science as the most effective device for providing equal opportunity of access to information to every U.S. resident—the Commission's idealized ultimate goal. The general range of concerns affecting national development was also addressed in the previous article: overcoming the fear of loss of autonomy on the part of network members; devising sufficient and equitable funding mechanisms; determining the most appropriate form of legal and administrative organization; developing criteria for the evaluation of network performance. In this report, an attempt will be made to describe some of the various types of networks, highlight significant developments of 1976, and comment on the literature.

Types. In faithful adherence to an old adage, "birds of a feather flock together," the more traditional cooperative (network) activities were among like types of libraries. With the passage of LSCA (Library Services and Construction Act), Title III, and HEA (Higher Education Act), Title II-B—which provided funds specifically in LSCA and permissively in HEA for intertype library cooperation—networking among different types of libraries received long overdue stimulus. While this intertype cooperation seems to have occurred largely between public libraries and academic libraries, some experimentation in school-public library cooperation has also been undertaken. An example is provided by a policy statement issued by Wisconsin's Council on Library Development and Department of Public Instruction—which "puts on record the Division for Library Services' strong support for the development of effective formal and informal cooperative arrangements through which public libraries and school media programs share their strengths with each other and with other types of libraries to gain for their users comprehensive access to needed information" (*LJ*, September 1, 1976). Interestingly, the account reports that the Division of Library Services, while endorsing cooperation, does not support consolidation of the two types of libraries. Illinois is the only state in the U.S. that has a full multi-type statewide library network. The Illinois Library and Information Network (ILLINET) is composed of local public, academic, special and school libraries, 18 library systems, 4 research and reference centers, and 2 special resource centers of last resort.

Networking, then, can occur either as a multi-type or as a single-type library phenomenon. Functionally, library networks are formed to provide either a single function, such as interlibrary loan, or a varying combination of functions, such as cooperative purchasing, collection building, and storage. The ultimate network envisioned by NCLIS has been termed a "full-service" network, wherein the network provides a full range of cooperative activity designed to meet the information needs of the individual citizen. Another axis along which a

National Library Resource Centers

It is increasingly apparent to library patrons, to librarians, and to library or university trustees that no library can possibly afford to buy all of the books, periodicals, and other library materials that its patrons from time to time need to consult. It is also apparent that no library can continue to grow in size endlessly, building an ever larger building every decade or so, in order to accommodate its steady accumulation of even that small portion of the total that it can afford to buy annually. There are only two possible solutions to these problems. One is to restrict access to information to that limited portion that each patron's own primary library can provide from its own shelves, with a consequent slowing of research and the useful applications of research. The other is to develop a more efficient system for interlibrary sharing of more publications. The first alternative — limitation of access only to what each patron's own primary library can provide from its own shelves — is clearly contrary to everyone's interest. Present interlibrary borrowing alleviates the problem somewhat, but for a number of reasons it is basically inadequate to the need.

The basic inadequacies in interlibrary borrowing and lending between colleague libraries include the failure to fill about 30 percent of the requests and a slow response time for those that are filled. These difficulties are inherent in a system that relies only on other collections that are themselves intended primarily to serve a limited group of users such as a city, county, state, university or college campus, government agency, or research facility. None of these libraries will have, or keep, the more infrequently used materials. Many that the library does have it is unwilling to lend because of the disadvantage to its own patrons for whom it acquired them. Response time is slow because every library intended primarily to serve local patrons in person is quite properly organized to do this job most efficiently. It is not organized to fill interlibrary loans quickly and cheaply. Some groups of libraries have developed cooperative acquisitions programs, but experience has shown that even a region that includes several states is often not large enough to support the comprehensive acquisitions required to satisfy the needs of the region, and a great many needed titles remain inaccessible. In addition, the problem of slow response time usually remains because the lending libraries are primarily serving their own patrons. Finally, such arrangements provide no solution to the need for more space to house the growing collections in the participating libraries.

National Library Resource Center. Such experience, compared with the experience of more comprehensive and faster access that can be provided by broadly based and dedicated library resource centers as the British Library Lending Division (BLLD) in Boston Spa, England, and The Center for Research Libraries (CRL) in Chicago and the knowledge of patterns of use of library materials have persuaded most librarians that the only solution adequate to the need, and affordable, requires the establishment of a national library resource center, or centers, for the United States. This solution is supported by the conclusions of the Task Force on a National Periodicals System for the U.S., established by the National Commission on Libraries and Information Science (NCLIS). The Task Force had not completed its work in 1976, but its progress report stated that it had concluded that a three-level system is best suited to meet the anticipated future needs for access to periodical materials in the U.S. The three levels would consist of (1) improved local, state, and regional capacities to meet a substantial portion of routine needs for periodical literature; (2) a major comprehensive periodical collection with the sole purpose of meeting the full range of national needs; and (3) continued capability to tap the unique resources of national and other major research libraries. It is the second level in this tri-partite system as outlined by the NCLIS Task Force that is fundamentally new and that would require the establishment of a national library resource center.

Center's Needed Characteristics. Although the first and third levels in that system are essential, they are clearly not sufficient even with the improvement anticipated. The success of the total system in providing the comprehensiveness and speed of access to information that the nation's research and educational needs require, and in solving the increasingly urgent space problems of every library, will depend primarily upon the characteristics of the national library resource center at the second level. Such a center must have the following characteristics.

(1) It must be comprehensive in coverage, *e.g.*, it must be receive at least one copy of every periodical currently being published anywhere in the world that is significant for present or future research, and it must be prepared to expand to equally comprehensive coverage of other materials when feasible.

(2) It must be capable of accepting from other library collections their infrequently used backfiles of periodicals and other materials important to research, when not already in the resource center's own collection, in order to alleviate total library space problems while assuring the continued preservation and accessibility of the material when needed.

(3) Its collections, physical facilities, and staff must be organized to provide maximum speed and economy in filling requests for loans or photocopies from other libraries. Bibliographically correct and complete requests for any item in the center's collection should normally be filled and the material on its way to the requesting library the same day, or if received late, the next.

(4) It must not have a primary responsibility to serve the needs of any one institution, organization, or group of pa-

trons to insure that the priority of those needs would never interfere with or inhibit the speed and surety of access to its collections by any other library.

(5) In order to insure that the national resource center's budget is not given second priority to what the controlling library might regard as its primary responsibility, its budget must be separate from and not under the control of any library with primary responsibility to serve the library needs of some one institution's or organization's patrons.

(6) It must have a governing and policy controlling body representing the user libraries to insure its continued responsiveness and responsibility to those it is intended to serve.

(7) It should be located with maximum centrality to U.S. libraries in order to insure minimum delivery times and communication costs.

GORDON R. WILLIAMS

---

matrix of network types can be drawn is the utilization of computer telecommunication, or teleprocessing. Many networks use telephones and teletype. The use of computers in the process is a relatively recent development.

Topography: Local. The geographic size and political components of library networks are yet another aspect of the topography of networks. It is probably safe to say that the largest number of networks today are substate in scope. They center around a local public library, a cluster of academic libraries, or an arbitrary grouping originally tied together through personal contacts among staff. BARC, the Bay Area Reference Center in the San Francisco area, is an example of this; the Worcester Area Cooperating Libraries (WACL), composed of public, private and public academic and special libraries (i.e., the American Antiquarian Society Library), is another. WACL provides a variety of services to its members, including document delivery in support of interlibrary loan. Yet another example is FAUL (Five Associated University Libraries) in central New York State, which also offers a broad variety of services to its members.

Statewide. The next readily identifiable level of organization is on a statewide basis—where library activities within the entire state have been coordinated to form a network. Nor are these always coordinated through the state library agencies. Some states have established separate bodies, outside the state library agencies, for the development of other statewide networks. InCoLSA (Indiana Cooperative Library Services Authority) reflects this approach; the newly formed CLASS (California Library Authority for Systems and Services), which appointed its first director late in 1976, is the most recent case in point. State networks centered in the office of the state library agencies are typified by those in the states of Illinois, Maryland, Massachusetts, Michigan, and Washington. The Illinois and Washington State networks are multi-type and utilize computers; the Maryland, Massachusetts, and Michigan networks are, as yet, single-type and not automated.

Regional. Beyond the state level the picture gets somewhat muddled, for there are both multistate and regional networks. The difference lies in the membership criteria: in the case of the regions, membership is by individual library, and SOLINET (Southeastern Library Information Network), AMIGOS (a network in the Southwest), and the Bibliographic Center for Research (BCR) are typical of these (though, to confuse the picture further, BCR does have some state entities as members). NELINET (the New England Library Information Network) and WILCO (Western Interstate Library Cooperative) are multistate networks. In the case of the former, the organization is not through the respective state library agencies but NELINET does observe state (or rather, New England) boundaries. WILCO, on the other hand, operates through the state library agency heads. Perhaps one of the most intriguing statements regarding this muddle was attributed to Don Simpson, Executive Director of BCR, by the newsletter *Advanced Technology/Libraries* (September 1976): "Territoriality of networking is one item that is still up for discussion. To my knowledge there's no law or statute that says a network must begin here or end there."

Terminology. Obviously, the precision of the terminology leaves much to be desired. An attempt to provide conceptual clarity was provided in a discussion paper generated by WILCO in which a distinction among the different computer-based networks was made in terms of bibliographic utilities versus service centers. According to this concept, a bibliographic utility generates and distributes a product, of which OCLC (the Ohio College Library Center) is the most noteworthy example; service centers provide services based upon the product distributed by the utility, and examples of this are the OCLC "regions"—among them NELINET, FAUL, SOLINET, and ILLINET.

Another step in clarification of terminology may well be provided by the survey launched in 1976 by the National Center for Education Statistics (NCES) in its attempt to gather statistics on the extent of cooperative activity in U.S. libraries for its LIBGIS (Library General Information Survey) data base. For the purpose of data collection, it was felt that, however arbitrary, a distinction be made by the respondents as to whether they considered themselves cooperatives, consortia, or networks. A draft of the survey instrument defined the terms as follows:

> *Cooperative:* . . . a group of independent and autonomous libraries banded together by informal or formal agreements or contracts which stipulate the common services to be planned and coordinated by the directors of the cooperative systems.
> *Consortium:* . . . a formal arrangement of two or more libraries not under the same institutional control for joint activities to improve the library service of the participants by cooperation extending beyond traditional interlibrary loan as defined in the National Interlibrary Loan Code of 1968.
> *Network:* . . . a formal organization among libraries for cooperation and sharing of resources, usually with an explicitly hierarchical structure, in which the group as a whole is organized into subgroups with the expectation that most of the needs of a library will be satisfied within the subgroups of which it is a member.

Whether these terms will prove viable and thus gain acceptance, bringing yet another ray of clarity to the situation, remains to be seen. Some consideration, it is expected, will be given to the possibility of deriving definitions inductively on the basis of the data collected in the survey.

TRENDS FOR THE FUTURE

Library of Congress. An event of even greater significance to the network scene that occurred in 1976 was the establishment in the Library of Congress of the Office of Special Assistant to the Librarian for Networks and Planning. The implication was clear: network development had achieved sufficient momentum to merit attention from the Library of Congress at the highest level. Since the establishment of the Office, a Network Advisory Group has been formed consisting, at the moment, of representatives of operating networks, the Council on Library Resources, and the National Commission on Libraries and Information Science. This group, in its capacity as advisory to the new Office, met three times in 1976, concentrating its efforts on identifying those activities which can be undertaken now to ensure and promote coherent network development on a national scale. Among the problems with which the group is wrestling are the identification, role, and function of the network components, the relationship of the components to LC, the responsibility of LC in the national network, the configuration and the architecture of a national network and its governance, and, of course, funding. Primary emphasis is initially being given to the computerized aspects of a national bibliographic network (*i.e.*, relating to printed material and its description, distribution of that data, and further uses derivable from access to such data) since this seems to be the area of greatest immediate concern on a national level. The technology is available to interconnect computer-based networks nationally and while, admittedly, even more sophisticated and yet undeveloped technology is bound to alter present techniques, the computer-based networks, in their zeal not to be overlooked, are pressing for implementation of the national network now. The broader network view has not, however, been totally ignored; the advisory group has recognized that the computer-based bibliographic service to libraries is but one part of a true national network, and they have thus, somewhat euphemistically, described their present emphasis as the "library bibliographic component" of a "national library and information services network." Furthermore, subcommittees of the group have been appointed to address the issues of governance and the design of the ultimate overarching national network entity with which librarians must deal.

Issues. Issues appearing in 1976 which may (or may not) affect the appearance of the eventual national network include: an interest by law libraries in developing their own network along lines similar to that of the National Library of Medicine; the potential for obtaining different services from different developing utilities, as the Washington Library Network and BALLOTS (Bibliographic Automation of Large Library Operations using a Time-sharing System) at Stanford University approach fully operational status beyond the confines of their initial base; and the implications of the President's notice of intent to call a White House Conference on Library and Information Services issued during the celebration of ALA's Centennial in Chicago in July. Utilization of minicomputers to support localized circulation and, in some cases, cooperative acquisitions and interlibrary loan, were also expected to show an increase. The quandary as to what library functions can be rationally supported on a national scale, and which should be retained on a subnational or individual institution basis could also prove less of a quandary in 1977.

Literature. The literature of networking (especially in its broadest sense) is scattered and elusive. Reports of progress on a state level can be found in the state library publications. Both the Illinois and Michigan library publications devoted an entire issue to networking in 1976. CLR's annual reports carry some data on progress in network activity funded by that organization. *JOLA* (the *Journal of Library Automation*) carries occasional articles relating to automated networks. Knowledge Industry, Inc., published a second edition of its monograph on the same subject (*Networks 75–76* by Susan K. Martin). *Library Journal* carries a running account of cooperative ventures reported by individual libraries.

ALPHONSE F. TREZZA

Notable Books

Following are titles on the ALA 1976 list of *Notable Books*. [Titles that appeared in the period 1944–75 and were on the annual ALA *Notable Books* list or its predecessors were published in a consolidated list in the first edition of this *Yearbook* (1976), pages 466–478.] For prizewinning children's books, see Awards and Prizes.

Compiled for use by the general reader and by librarians, the titles on the *Notable Books* list are selected for their significant contribution to the widening of knowledge or for the pleasure they can provide to adult readers. Criteria include wide general appeal and literary merit.

The Notable Books Council of 1976 included: Jerome K. Corrigan, Prince George's County Memorial Library (Oxon Hill, Maryland); Kay Ann Cassell, Bethlehem Public Library (Delmar, New York); Robert Cayton, Marietta College Library (Marietta, Ohio); Robert Donahugh, the Public Library of Youngstown & Mahoning County (Youngstown, Ohio); Elizabeth Egan, Helen M. Plum Memorial Library (Lombard, Illinois); Lyn Hart, Enoch Pratt Free Library (Baltimore, Maryland); Jane K. Hirsch, Montgomery County Public Library (Rockville, Maryland); Joan Hoagland, Cleveland Public Library (Cleveland, Ohio); Martha Reynolds, Frederick County Public Libraries (Frederick, Maryland); Ross Stephen, William Rainey Harper College (Palatine, Illinois); and Dorothy Snowden, consultant, *The Booklist*.

The list below is available, in brochure form with annotations, from the Order Department, ALA.

Lisa Alther
   Kinflicks (Knopf)
Michael J. Arlen
   The View From Highway 1: Essays on Television (Farrar)
W. H. Auden
   Collected Poems, edited by Edward Mendelson (Random)
John Baskin
   New Burlington: The Life and Death of an American Village (Norton)
Jack Bass and Walter de Vries
   The Transformation of Southern Politics: Social Change and Political Consequence Since 1945 (Basic Books)
Bruno Bettelheim
   The Uses of Enchantment: The Meaning and Importance of Fairy Tales (Knopf)
Elisabeth Mann Borgese
   Drama of the Oceans (Abrams)
Rosellen Brown
   The Autobiography of My Mother (Doubleday)
C. D. B. Bryan
   Friendly Fire (Putnam)
Henry Caudill
   Watches of the Night (Atlantic-Little)
Ann Cornelisen
   Women of the Shadows (Atlantic-Little)
George Dangerfield
   The Damnable Question (Atlantic-Little)
Robertson Davies
   World of Wonders (Viking)
Terrence Des Pres
   The Survivor: An Anatomy of Life in the Death Camps (Oxford University Press)
Oriana Fallaci
   Interview with History (Liveright)
Jack Fincher
   Human Intelligence (Putnam)
Carlos Fuentes
   Terra Nostra (Farrar)
Gabriel Gárcia Márquez
   Autumn of the Patriarch (Harper)
John Gardner
   October Light (Knopf)
Ronald Glasser
   The Body Is the Hero (Random)
Sanche de Gramont
   The Strong Brown God: The Story of the Niger River (Houghton)
Martin Green
   Children of the Sun: A Narrative of "Decadence" in England after 1918 (Basic Books)
Judith Guest
   Ordinary People (Viking)
Herbert Gutman
   The Black Family in Slavery and Freedom, 1750–1925 (Pantheon)
Alex Haley
   Roots: The Saga of an American Family (Doubleday)
Edward T. Hall
   Beyond Culture (Anchor)
Richard Harris
   Freedom Spent (Little)
Irving Howe
   World of Our Fathers (Harcourt)
Ruth Jhabvala
   Heat and Dust (Harper)
Mark and Dan Jury
   Gramp (Grossman)
John Keegan
   Face of Battle (Viking)
Maxine Kingston
   The Woman Warrior: Memoirs of a Girlhood Among Ghosts (Knopf)
Ron Kovic
   Born on the Fourth of July (McGraw)
J. Anthony Lukas
   Nightmare: The Underside of the Nixon Years (Viking)
William H. McNeill
   Plagues and Peoples (Anchor)
Richard Price
   Blood Brothers (Houghton)
Muriel Rukeyser
   The Gates (McGraw)
Gail Sheehy
   Passages: Predictable Crises of Adult Life (Dutton)
Agnes Smedley
   Portraits of Chinese Women in Revolution (Feminist Press)
Hedrick Smith
   The Russians (Quadrangle)
Muriel Spark
   The Takeover (Viking)
John Toland
   Adolf Hitler (Doubleday)
William Trevor
   Angels at the Ritz, and Other Stories (Viking)
Anne Tyler
   Searching for Caleb (Knopf)
John Updike
   Marry Me: a Romance (Knopf)
Gore Vidal
   1876, a Novel (Random)
William Warner
   Beautiful Swimmers (Atlantic)
E. B. White
   Letters of E. B. White, collected and edited by Dorothy Lobrano Guth (Harper)
Richard Yates
   Easter Parade (Delacorte)
Helen Yglesias
   Family Feeling (Dial)

Obituaries

ALEXANDER, MARY LOUISE (1896–1976), Librarian of the Ferguson Library (Stamford, Connecticut) for more than two decades, was named to the Special Libraries Association Hall of Fame in 1966. She had served as President of SLA for two terms in the early 1930's and had played a key role in organizing SLA's group concerned with advertising and marketing. Before directing the Ferguson Library, she worked as a special librarian for New York advertising agencies, including the J. Walter Thompson agency and the one later known as Batten, Barton, Durstine & Osborne.

Born in Iowa in 1896, she attended the University of Wisconsin and the University of Missouri.

During World War II she served as special assistant to Eleanor Roosevelt in the Office of Civilian Defense. She later was Librarian in the Office of Price Administration.

Under her direction the Ferguson Library added a wing and vastly improved its resources and services. She has been credited with initiating the first film lending library in New England.

COX, CARL RAYMOND (1920–1976), Professor and Chief Librarian of Herbert H. Lehman College of the City of New York, the Bronx, was killed in an automobile accident on May 20, 1976.

Born in Illinois, September 16, 1920, he attended Central YMCA College (B.A.) in Chicago and Columbia (M.S. in L.S., 1949). He was a cryptographer for the U.S. Army Corps (1942–45), a library assistant for *The Chicago Sun* (1945–47), and a subject cataloger for the Library of Congress (1949–51) and New York Public Library (1951–53). From 1953 to 1958 he was principal librarian for technical services, California State Library, and from 1958 to 1965 Assistant Director of Technical Services, the University of Maryland. He later served at SUNY (Albany) as Associate Director for Library Systems.

COX, CARL THOMAS (1929–1976), library educator and specialist on reference and nonprint materials, was Professor of Library Science at the Graduate School of Library and Information Science of the University of Tennessee.

Born in Knoxville, Tennessee, June 21, 1929, he earned degrees at Carson-Newman College (B.A.), Jefferson City, Tennessee, and Peabody College (M.A. and Ed.D.). He served in the U.S. Army, 1952–54, and was visiting Professor at Peabody Library School, Nashville, during the summers of 1958–60 and 1964. He joined the faculty of the University of Tennessee, Knoxville, in 1965. He died on September 1.

For ALA, he chaired the RASD Outstanding Reference Books Committee and served on its Reference and Subscription Books Review Committee. He edited the research column of *School Media Quarterly*.

FONTAINE, EVERETT O. (1892–1976), member of the American Library Association Staff for more than 25 years, died in New York City August 6, 1976, at the age of 84.

Born in Momence, Illinois, October 26, 1892, he received an A.B. degree from the University of Illinois in 1915 and later studied at Northwestern University. He joined the U.S. Army in 1918 and served as Librarian at the U. S. Naval Air Station in Pensacola, Florida, 1919–20. After World War I, returning to Chicago, he worked in sales promotion and publicity for the Ontario Company and the American Medical Association, 1921–24.

In 1924 he joined the staff of the American Library Association. He was Sales and Advertising Manager for ALA, 1924–35, and Chief of the Publishing Department, 1936–51. He went to P. F. Collier & Sons, New York City, as Director of Publishing in 1951, becoming Editorial Director for *Collier's Encyclopedia* in 1952.

During his years at ALA he initiated programs that continue today, including developing the Conference Exhibit Program. In 1949, on recognition of his 25th anniversary with ALA, many tributes were received. Among them were: "the association has made during those years a distinguished contribution to the literature of librarianship through its publishing efforts, largely through your efforts"; the President of ALA said: ". . . glad they are celebrating your first quarter Century of Progress for it is closely tied to the program of ALA"; and he received "Congratulations on this anniversary of publishing books that have shaped the world of libraries and librarians."

FRAREY, CARLYLE JAMES (1918–1976), cataloger, library educator, and editor, was Assistant to the Dean of the Columbia University School of Library Service. Born in Springwater, New York on April 1, 1918, he attended Oberlin College, Ohio, where he worked in the catalog department and took his A.B. degree in 1942. He was a sergeant in the U.S. Air Force Weather Service from 1942 to 1946.

Frarey later worked at the City College of New York and Duke

Carl R. Cox (1920–1976)

Everett O. Fontaine (1892–1976)

Carlyle J. Frarey (1918–1976)

University libraries before going to the University of North Carolina School of Library Science as an Associate Professor in 1954. He served as Acting Dean from 1960 to 1964 when he joined the Columbia University Faculty.

Frarey was a member of the ALA Council from 1953 to 1957, and was a director of the American Association of Library Schools in 1962. From 1953 to 1960 he was Managing Editor of the *Journal of Cataloging and Classification*, later *Library Resources and Technical Services*. In addition to editing books and writing articles on technical services, he served as a consultant in the field, and was a member of the Decimal Classification Editorial Policy Committee of the Lake Placid Foundation and of the Committee on the Universal Decimal Classification, U.S. National Commissions/International Federation of Documentation.

Beginning in 1966 and continuing until 1975, Frarey made an annual survey of the placement of the year's library school graduates in the United States. The results, organized by salary, type of library and position, and geography, with interpretation of trends, were published in *Library Journal* and reprinted in *The Bowker Annual*. Frarey died on March 13, 1976.

GILES, LOUISE (JONES)

(1930–1976), library administrator and educator, was a nationally recognized authority in community college education and collective bargaining in two-year colleges. She was President of the Association of College and Research Libraries (1975–76).

Born in Aragon, Georgia, on April 20, 1930, she earned a B.A. degree in modern languages from the University of Akron in 1952, and a master's in library science degree from Drexel University in 1953. She was an exchange fellow for independent study in Honduras during 1953–54 and at the time of her death was a doctoral candidate at the University of Michigan.

Her professional career began at the Detroit Public Library in 1953. There she had many varied positions including Administrator of the foreign language collection from 1959 to 1960 and First Assistant from 1960 to 1965. Her academic library career and interest in community colleges began when she accepted an appointment to Oakland Community College. She developed the learning resources center concept for that institution while serving as Librarian and Dean from 1965 to 1970. Giles served as Dean of Learning Resources at Macomb County Community College, 1970 to 1976.

Her leadership, dedication and commitment to higher education, librarianship and to the equality and dignity of humanity was well known. She served on many accreditation teams and was a consultant on the management of learning resources centers.

As an active member of ALA Louise Giles served on ALA Council (1972–76), and as Chairperson of the Community and Junior College Libraries Section of ACRL (1973–74). She was selected for membership on and chaired numerous specialized committees, including the ALA Audiovisual Committee, the 1974 New York Conference Program Planning Committee, the ISAD Discussion Group on Information Technology, and the 1976 Chicago Conference ACRL Program Planning Committee. A recent assignment was service on the Executive Board's ad hoc committee on *Choice*. She also was at one time the ACRL representative to the Joint Committee on Two-year College Learning Resources Programs (AACJC/AECT/ACRL-ALA). She was active in the American Association of Community and Junior Colleges and the ALA Black Caucus.

Louise Giles died in a fire in her home on December 31, 1976. Also killed in the fire was her husband, Edwin, a school principal in Detroit. As a tribute to her contributions to the library profession and to the Association, the ALA Minority Scholarship Fund was renamed the Louise Giles Minority Scholarship Fund.

JO ELLEN FLAGG

Louise Giles (1930–1976)

IMMROTH, JOHN PHILLIP

(1936–1976), author, university educator, faculty member at the University of Pittsburgh Graduate School of Library and Information Sciences, was a noted authority on cataloging, classification, and bibliography, and an outstanding proponent of intellectual freedom. Born in La Junta, Colorado, on September 30, 1936, he attended the University of Colorado, from which he received two degrees—B.A. in Speech and Dramatics (1959) and M.A. in English Literature (1962). In 1965 he received his M.A. in Library Science from the University of Denver. During the next three years he held teaching and library positions in Colorado and was active in the Colorado Library Association.

Joining the faculty of the University of Pittsburgh in 1968, Immroth earned a Ph.D. from that institution in 1970. He was author or co-author of seven major books and dozens of scholarly articles and reports. His latest publication was the fifth edition of an *Introduction to Cataloging and Classification*, written with Bohdan Wynar and issued in 1976. At the time of his death, he was revising the ALA *Glossary of Library Terms* and was the newly appointed editor of the *PLA Bulletin*. In 1971 the ALA Resources and Technical Services Division awarded Immroth the Esther J. Piercy Award in recognition of his contributions in the area of technical services.

Immroth was an active member of the American Library Association, particularly in the area of intellectual freedom. He was a charter member of the Freedom to Read Foundation and a member of the ALA Intellectual Freedom Committee from 1972 to 1974. He was instrumental in the organization of the Intellectual Freedom Round Table in 1973 and served

John Phillip Immroth (1936–1976)

as the Round Table's first Chairperson. Under his leadership, the Round Table became one of the most active in ALA.

Immroth died of accidental asphyxiation on April 2 while attending a library meeting in Scranton, Pennsylvania. A scholarship fund was established at the University of Pittsburgh in Immroth's memory. —REBECCA S. MUELLER

LIPPINCOTT, JOSEPH WHARTON (1887–1976), author and publisher, was President of the publishing house of J. B. Lippincott, 1927–48, and Chairman, 1948–58. He donated the ALA award named after him which, in most years since 1938, has been presented to a librarian for distinguished service.

He was born in Philadelphia, the headquarters of J. B. Lippincott Company, on February 28, 1887. Eventually the third member of his family to head that firm, he joined the family business in 1908 after graduation from the Wharton School of Finance and Commerce (University of Pennsylvania).

Lippincott wrote 17 children's books, among them *Wilderness Champion: The Story of a Great Hound* (1944), reflecting his interest in natural science.

RANSOM, HARRY HUNTT (1908–1976), Chancellor of the University of Texas, 1961–71 was styled by colleagues as "the grand acquisitor" as a tribute to his commitment toward building great rare-book, manuscript, and other collections for the University libraries.

He joined the Texas faculty in 1935. He was Dean of the College of Arts and Sciences, 1954–57, and President, 1960–61, when he was named Chancellor of the University of Texas System. He became Chancellor Emeritus in 1971.

Ransom was born in Galveston, Texas, on November 22, 1908. He received an A.B. from the University of the South in 1928 and an A.M. (1930) and Ph.D (1938) from Yale. He taught English and other subjects at State Teachers College, Valley City, North Dakota, 1930–32, and Colorado State College, 1934–35. During World War II he served as a major in the Army Air Forces.

He was an innovator. He founded the *Texas Quarterly,* which he edited from 1958, supported new ventures in teaching and in liberal education, and was the principal force behind the establishment of the Humanities Research Center at Texas. The holdings at the libraries at Texas total about 3,000,000 books and manuscripts, including 250,000 rare books, valued at $50,000,000.

He was working on a history of the University Library at the time of his death in Dripping Springs, Texas, on April 19.

Ransom wrote *Bibliography of English Copyright History* (1948), *Notes of a Texas Book Collector* (1950) and *The First Copyright Statute.*

He edited, with J. Frank Dobie and M. C. Boatright, "Texas Folklore Publications."

REESE, ERNEST J. (1881–1976), administrator, library educator, and editor, was respected by generations of librarians as a pioneer educator who stressed the intellectual context of librarianship. Born in Cleveland, Ohio, on November 4, 1881, he earned a certificate in the first class of the School of Library Science at Western Reserve University in 1905. He completed his Ph.B. at Western Reserve in 1906, and from 1906 to 1908 studied theology at Oberlin College. After serving in the Library at the Punshaw School in Honolulu, Hawaii, for three years, he joined the faculty of the University of Illinois School of Library Science in 1912. While at the University of Illinois, he studied political science at the graduate level.

In 1917 Reese became the Principal of the New York Public Library Training School. When that institution was merged with the New York State Library School at Albany in 1926, to form the School of Library Service of Columbia University, he became an Associate Professor. In 1935 he was made a Professor, and in 1935, the Mevil Dewey Professor, the first occupant of the first endowed chair in an American Library School. Reese served as Assistant Dean of the School from 1944 until 1948, when he became Professor Emeritus.

In an extension of his career, he served as Assistant and Acting Librarian at the Dayton, Ohio, Public Library in 1950, visiting professor at the School of Library Science, University of Illinois, and Acting Director, 1952–53.

Reese was Managing Editor of *College and Research Libraries,* 1944–45, and of *Library Trends,* 1952–53.

A prolific writer with an exceptionally analytic mind and an articulate style, Reese was best known for two landmark books, *Curriculum in Library Schools* (1936) and *Program for Library Schools* (1943). He was awarded the Beta Phi Mu Award by ALA's Library Education Division in 1963. He died on March 12, 1976.

ROSSELL, BEATRICE SAWYER (1896–1976), librarian, editor, and writer, died December 20, 1976, in Phoenix, Arizona, where she had lived during her retirement years.

Obituaries

Joseph W. Lippincott (1887–1976)

Ernest J. Reese (1881–1976)

Beatrice S. Rossell (1896–1976)

Obituaries

Born in Elizabeth, New Jersey, July 17, 1896, she attended the New York State Library School in Albany, 1923–27. She was an assistant in the Albany Public Library, 1923–27, and publicity assistant there, 1927–29. In 1929 she joined the Headquarters Staff of the American Library Association as publicity assistant and Editor of the *ALA Bulletin*. Leaving that position in 1940, she was head of the music and art department, Evanston Public Library (Illinois), 1940–41. In 1941 she became Director of Educational Service for the Quarrie Corporation, later Field Enterprises Educational Corporation. In 1949 she became Director of Childcraft School and Library Service, Field Enterprises Educational Corporation, leaving that position in 1954 to become Head Librarian of the Perrysbury (Ohio) Public Library.

Throughout her career she was recognized for her creative leadership, her integrity, her concern for the extension and improvement of library services, and the promotion of library causes through legislative activities.

She was well known as an effective speaker. She wrote many articles for professional magazines, and librarians are familiar with her *Public Libraries in the Life of the Nation*, published by ALA (1943); *Working with a Legislature* (1948); and "How to Start A Public Library" in *Wonderful World of Books* (1952).

ROTHROCK, MARY U. (TOPEY) (1890–1976), known for her pioneering work in regional library development for the Tennessee Library Authority, had a long career in the libraries of the Southeast.

Born in Trenton, Tennessee, on September 19, 1890, Rothrock received B.S. and M.S. degrees from Vanderbilt University. She attended the New York State Library School at Albany from 1912 to 1914, and was awarded a B.L.S. degree in 1922.

After a brief interlude at New York Public Library, Rothrock returned to Tennessee, where she served first in the Cossett Library in Memphis, then as Librarian of the Lawson McGhee Library in Knoxville from 1916 to 1934. After her career with TVA, she became Librarian of the Knox County Library from 1949 until her retirement in 1954.

While Mary Rothrock was Supervisor for Library Services for TVA, from 1934 to 1938, she was instrumental in achieving the first comprehensive survey of libraries in the Southeast as a basis for future planning. The survey was a cooperative endeavor of TVA and the Southeastern Library association, of which Rothrock was a founder. When she completed her term as Supervisor, she continued to serve as Library Consultant to TVA until 1951.

Rothrock served on ALA's Council and Executive Board. In 1938 ALA honored her with the first Lippincott Award, and elected her President for the 1947–48 term. In 1948 the University of Chattanooga awarded her an honorary degree.

A member of the Advisory Commission on Libraries to the U.S. Office of Education, Rothrock also served as an advisor to the Public Library Inquiry from 1947 to 1950. She was active in historical associations, and wrote and edited several books and many articles on Tennessee history.

Mary Rothrock was affectionately known to many as Topey. The ALA Council had voted to award her its highest honor, Honorary Membership, in January 1976. She died on January 30, 1976. The Citation prepared for presentation at the Centennial Conference reads in part, "As a leader of the TVA regional library development, you set the example for the systemization of libraries throughout the nation. You sowed the seeds of new public libraries in the rural South and nurtured them by serving as a catalyst in the promotion of library legislation to provide for their support . . . you are truly a woman for all seasons. . . ."

Mary U. Rothrock (1890–1976)

OCLC

See *Cataloging and Classification; Networks; Automation.*
See also various State Reports.

Older Adults, Library Services to

It is only within the past few years that library service to older adults has been thought about, written about, and put into practice. Two ALA-related activities demonstrate clearly that librarians everywhere are initiating programs for seniors, strengthening existing programs, and working in liaison with other community service agencies to effect a better life for older Americans.

The first of these ALA efforts is the "Older Americans Program Idea Exchange." This project of the RASD Committee on Library Services to an Aging Population collects information on currently active library programs for seniors. The collection will be offered to state and regional associations for use at conventions, and information from the collection will be available to libraries for program ideas. Nearly 200 libraries have responded with detailed information about their programs. These responses display great variety in type and scope of activity.

The second ALA project, again through the RASD Committee on Library Services to an Aging Population, was in conjunction with Operation Independence, an official Bicentennial program of the National Voluntary Organizations for Independent Living for the Aging (NVOILA). Some 175 localities cooperated in this project wherein community organizations worked together to develop a program to help keep the frail elderly in their own homes. The Committee contacted the librarians in all of these communities, explained Operation Independence to them, and gave them the name of the community coordinator or lead agency. They also contacted all lead agencies, described the advantages of including the library in the community coalition, and gave the name of the public librarian in their community. The response to this effort was overwhelming. Libraries, because of this solicitation, sent materials to the Idea Exchange, and many of them joined forces with other community organizations in developing coordinated services for the elderly. On November 4 ALA received a citation from NVOILA in recognition of this contribution.

At the annual convention of ALA in Chicago in July, HRLSD sponsored a well-attended general session on "Communicating with the Elderly." Richard Calabrese conducted a training session on communication. In small workshop groups the participants investigated the myths of aging which stand in the way of communication. Grace Stevenson, Deputy Executive Director of ALA, Emeritus, gave an emotionally charged address on fact and fantasy for the retired librarian.

At the same convention HRLSD created a new Committee on Library Services to the Impaired Elderly. The committee was formed to coordinate service delivery to a large group of patrons and potential patrons not directly addressed by any other committee or section of ALA. The short-term goal for the first year is to identify existing programs and leaders in the field.

The University of Wisconsin has received a grant from the Administration on Aging to offer scholarships to librarians for a new interdisciplinary course in gerontology. Designed for working practitioners, the course is given in clusters of three sessions, five times during the semester, so that it does not interfere unduly with the workweek. JOHN B. BALKEMA

Organization of American States

Developing an inter-American network for transmitting bibliographic information was the principal goal of the Library and Archives Development Program of the Organization of American States in 1976. Integrating national information systems of libraries, documentation and archives also received OAS attention.

A provisional Spanish MARC format, produced by Maria and Stephen Faunce under an OAS contract with the University of Puerto Rico, was issued during the year. Specialists in MARC-based systems, centralized cataloging and library networking from the United States, Canada and Spain, collaborated with the OAS in the following meetings with librarians from Latin America and the Caribbean: (1) in Chicago in January, cosponsored by the Seminars on the Acquisition of Latin American Library Materials (SALALM), to discuss planning centralized cataloging services for an inter-American network; (2) on the MARCAL format at the Library of Congress in February; (3) at the University of Costa Rica in June on establishing centralized cataloging services for Central America; (4) in Mexico in October, with collaboration from the Consejo Nacional de Ciencia y Tecnologia (CONACYT), to approve the MARCAL manual and the OAS network plan; and (5) in Washington in the fall for a Regional Seminar on archives.

Recommendations of these meetings covered acceptance of the Anglo-American Cataloging Rules and the Universal Bibliographic Control principles; the planned expansion of the Rovira subject heading lists, with developing equivalency lists in English and Spanish for subject and author headings leading to computer-based authority files; and collaboration with the AMIGOS Bibliographical Council to participate in OCLC services.

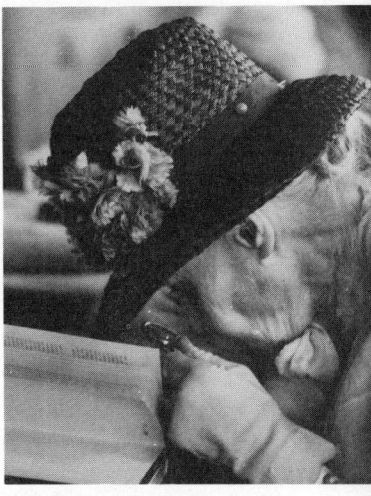

Patron at the Chicago Public Library. A librarian at CPL with special knowledge of gerontology was appointed to coordinate programs for older adults in branches, housing projects, and nursing homes.

Organizations and Associations

Some 27 projects were approved for execution in 1976/77 for technical assistance and training, including assistance to Costa Rica for centralized cataloging, to Nicaragua for a national cataloging center, to Colombia to develop an expanded subject heading list and to create cooperative cataloging. To further planning for automation of these projects and for accessing OCLC, assistance was planned to CONACYT in Mexico for an automated subject approach to scientific library holdings to prepare it to serve as a multinational center on MARCAL and library automation.

To form an integrated national system of libraries, documentation and archives, technical assistance and training programs were carried out at Member States' request: (1) national courses for personnel, multinational specialized courses in school and university library systems and post-graduate courses in the Inter-American Library School in Colombia; (2) for in-service training and observation, including travel grants to participate in the International Association of School Librarians meeting; and (3) fellowships for advanced training of library school teachers and school and university library systems directors. Such projects included teaching contracts, fellowships for study, equipment and library materials, and some publication funds.

Travel grants were given for the Costa Rican cataloging service director and for subject specialists for Mexico's Centro de Información Científica y Técnica (CICH) to visit cataloging and information centers in the United States and Puerto Rico, for the Nicaraguan school library system director to observe the Venezuelan school library systems, and Paraguayan library school teachers to observe library schools in Brazil and Colombia.

Technical assistance was given for school library systems in Chile, Costa Rica, Nicaragua and Peru, for the Municipal Public Library of Guayaquil, Ecuador, for centralized cataloging in Costa Rica, archives development in Bolivia, documents restoration in Costa Rica, modernizing and equipping the Archivo General of Perú, and for publishing the *Boletín Interamericano de Archivos* in Argentina.

To form a single coordinated information system through integrating libraries, documentation centers and archives, a 1976 program similar to library development provided technical assistance in archives. Training was given at the Centro Interamericano de Archivos in Cordoba, Argentina, and in a new OAS regional laboratory for preserving and microfilming documents in the Dominican Republic. National courses were given in Bolivia and Peru. Seven professors were contracted for archives and seven for library training.

Advisory services were provided by OAS staff to Member States, for the Dewey Spanish translation, to the Books for the People Fund, Inc., for Project LEER and for the children's book production center planned for Mexico.

Grants were received from the Council on Library Resources, Inc., for the MARCAL meeting in Mexico, and from the Tinker Foundation for the archives seminar in Washington, D.C. — MARIETTA DANIELS SHEPARD

REFERENCES

Marietta Daniels Shepard, "Information Technology Applied by the OAS to Developing an Inter-American Network for Transmitting Bibliographic Information," submitted to 38 FID Congress, Mexico, 27 Sept.–1 Oct. 1976 5p.

MARCAL: Manual de Catalogación Mecanizada para América Latina. Edición preliminar por Stephen S. A. Faunce y María Casas de Faunce. (Rio Piedras, Puerto Rico, y Washington, D.C., Organización de los Estados Americanos, 1976) (Manuales de bibliotecario, no. 9).

Centralized Cataloging in Latin America: Part I. Centralized Cataloging and the Feasibility of an Inter-American Network for the Transmission of Bibliographic Information Utilizing New Information Technology, by Marietta Daniels Shepard. Part II. Planning for Centralized Cataloging Services in Latin America, Minutes of the 19 January 1976 Meeting, by Sammy Kinard, submitted for the Twenty-first Seminar on the Acquisition of Latin American Library Materials, University of Indiana, Bloomington, Indiana, May 2–6, 1976. (Amherst, Mass., SALALM Secretariat, University of Massachusetts, 1976).

Report of the Mid-Project Meeting on the MARCAL Format (I MARCAL), Washington, D.C., 2–6 February 1976. Rev. 1, 9 June 1976. Typescript. (Washington, D.C., Library and Archives Development Program, Organization of American States, 1976).

Draft Conclusions of ATRIBAL (Reunión de Análisis del Formato MARC para la Transferencia de Información Bibliográfica en América Latina—ATRIBAL—II MARCAL, México, D. F., 4 al 6 de Octubre de 1976), from notes taken by Marietta Daniels Shepard.

Reunión de Estudio Centro Catalográfico Centroamericano, Universidad de Costa Rica, Ciudad Universitaria "Rodrigo Facio," San Pedro de Montes de Oca, Costa Rica, *Informe final.* Organizado por la Organización de los Estados Americanos y la Univeersidad de Costa Rica. 1976, 2 vols.

Boletín Interamericano de Archivos (Cordoba, Argentina, Centro Interamericano de Formación de Archiveros, Escuela de Archiveros de la Universidad Nacional de Córdoba, Argentina), 1974+.

Organizations and Associations

The American Library Association has a special relationship with organizations and associations cited here. All data given are as of the end of 1976 unless otherwise indicated. (The asterisk denotes ALA membership in the organization.)

Adult Education Association of the United States of America*

(founded 1951).

PURPOSE: "To further the concept of education as a continuing process throughout life." The Association makes available knowledge about adult continuing education, alerts key leadership and the general public to the need for lifelong learning, and provides an organizational framework for persons who make adult education their professional commitment. The Association works with program development, legislation at the federal and state levels, and seeks to stimulate local, state and regional adult education activities. Special interest sections, councils and commissions are created to advance theory and research, and translate into practice educational or social concerns of the adult learner.

MEMBERS/SUBSCRIBERS: 5,547.
PRESIDENT: Rosalind K. Loring, (November 1976 – November 1977).
PRESIDENT-ELECT: Huey B. Long.
EXECUTIVE DIRECTOR: Linda S. Hartsock.
ANNUAL CONFERENCE: November 18 – 22, 1976, New York, New York.
PUBLICATIONS: *Adult Leadership* (10 issues a year); *Adult Education* (quarterly); *Dateline* (10 issues a year).
HEADQUARTERS: 810 18th Street, N.W., Washington, D.C., 20006.

Alliance of Associations for the Advancement of Education*
(founded 1970).
PURPOSE: "To improve the quality of education in America through promoting cooperation among member associations in the exchange of information, in the conduct of research, in the issuance of substantive statements on crucial issues in education, in the development of projects which are of concern to member organizations and in the provision of special services to association operations."
MEMBERSHIP: 9; *Annual Expenditure:* $6,000.
PRESIDENT: William Work (July 1, 1976 – June 30, 1977).
VICE-PRESIDENT/PRESIDENT-ELECT: Alberta L. Meyer.
EXECUTIVE SECRETARY: Elvie Lou Luetge.
EVENTS: Quarterly Round Table Meetings.
PUBLICATIONS: Annual compilation of articles.
HEADQUARTERS: 3615 Wisconsin Avenue, N.W., Washington, D.C., 20016.

American Association for Gifted Children
(founded 1945).
PURPOSE: To recognize and stimulate creative work among gifted children, to foster appreciation of their capabilities, to promote plans to further their interests, to encourage public sentiment in support of early recognition of gifted children and their welfare, and to publish supporting materials.
MEMBERSHIP: 200; *Annual Expenditure:* $25,000.
PRESIDENT: Anne Impellizzeri (1976 – 77).
VICE-PRESIDENT AND EXECUTIVE DIRECTOR: Marjorie L. Craig.
PUBLICATIONS: *Guideposts; The Gifted Child* (as needed).
HEADQUARTERS: 15 Gramercy Park, New York, New York, 10003.
ALA REPRESENTATIVE: Naomi Noyes, Children's Services Division (1976 – 77).

American Association for the Advancement of Science
(founded 1848).
PURPOSE: "To further the work of scientists, to facilitate cooperation among them, to improve the effectiveness of science in the promotion of human welfare, and to increase public understanding and appreciation of the importance and promise of the methods of science in human progress."
MEMBERSHIP: 115,000; *Annual Expenditure:* $7,585,579 (1974).
PRESIDENT: William D. McElroy (January 1976 – December 1976).
VICE-PRESIDENT/PRESIDENT-ELECT: Emilio Q. Daddario.
EXECUTIVE SECRETARY: William D. Carey.
ANNUAL CONVENTION: February 18 – 24, 1976, Boston, Massachusetts.
PUBLICATIONS: *Science* (weekly); *Science Books* (quarterly).
HEADQUARTERS: 1515 Massachusetts Avenue, N.W., Washington, D.C., 20005.
ALA REPRESENTATIVE: Russell Shank, Association of College and Research Libraries (1975 – 76).

American Association of Community and Junior Colleges
(founded 1920 as American Association of Junior Colleges).
PURPOSE: "To provide national direction and leadership and promote the development of community and junior colleges in America and internationally."
MEMBERSHIP: 900.
CHAIRPERSON: Richard H. Hagemeyer (July 1976 – July 1977).
VICE-CHAIRPERSON: Lee G. Henderson.
PRESIDENT (executive officer): Edmund J. Gleazer, Jr.
ANNUAL CONVENTION: March 17 – 19, 1976, Washington, D.C.
PUBLICATIONS: *Community and Junior College Journal* (8 issues a year); *Community, Junior and Technical College Directory* (annually).
HEADQUARTERS: National Center for Higher Education, One Dupont Circle, N.W., Washington, D.C., 20036.
ALA AFFILIATION: Joint Committee on Learning Resources Programs, Association for College and Research Libraries; chairperson, William J. Hoffman (1975 – 76).

American Association of University Professors
(founded 1915).
PURPOSE: Organization of college and university teachers, research scholars, and academic librarians for the promotion of professional and educational interests.
MEMBERSHIP: 86,000.
PRESIDENT: Peter O. Steiner (through June 1978).
VICE-PRESIDENT: Martha Friedman.
GENERAL SECRETARY: Joseph Duffy.
ANNUAL CONVENTION: June 6 – 7, 1975, Washington, D.C.
PUBLICATIONS: *Academe* (quarterly); *AAUP Bulletin* (quarterly).
HEADQUARTERS: One Dupont Circle, Washington, D.C., 20036.

American Booksellers Association (ABA)
(founded 1900).
PURPOSE: The ABA strives to create and maintain favorable trade conditions and foster good bookseller-publisher relations. To increase the sale of books of all types, the association assists its members in dealing with operational and public relations problems.
MEMBERSHIP: 3,800; *Annual Expenditure:* $863,000.
PRESIDENT: Robert D. Hale.
VICE-PRESIDENT: Robert Dike Blair.
EXECUTIVE DIRECTOR: G. Roysce Smith.
ANNUAL MEETING: June 1976, Chicago, Illinois.
PUBLICATIONS: *Newswire, Basic Book List, Book Buyers Handbook,* and *Sidelines Directory.*
HEADQUARTERS: 800 Second Ave., New York, New York, 10017.

American Civil Liberties Union*
(founded 1920).
PURPOSE: "Defense of civil liberties; freedom of in-

quiry and expression; due process of law; equal protection of the laws, and privacy."
MEMBERSHIP: 275,000; Annual Expenditure: $8,000,000.
CHAIRPERSON: Edward J. Ennis (1976–1977).
EXECUTIVE DIRECTOR: Aryeh Neier.
BIENNIAL CONFERENCE COMMITTEE MEETING: June 10–13, 1976, Philadelphia, Pennsylvania.
PUBLICATIONS: *Civil Liberties* (quarterly); *Privacy Report* (monthly); *First Principles* (monthly).
HEADQUARTERS: 22 East 40th Street, New York, New York, 10016.

American Correctional Association
(founded 1870 as the National Prison Association).
PURPOSE: "To strengthen and increase recognition of corrections as a profession and contribute to the professionalization of correctional personnel."
MEMBERSHIP: 10,000; *Annual Expenditure*: $320,000 (December 31, 1976).
PRESIDENT: William D. Leeke (August 1976–July 1978).
VICE-PRESIDENT: Katherine Gable-Strickland.
EXECUTIVE DIRECTOR: Anthony P. Travisono.
MEETING: Annual Congress of Correction, August 22–26, 1976, Denver, Colorado.
PUBLICATION: *American Journal of Correction* (bimonthly).
HEADQUARTERS: 4321 Hartwick Road, Suite L-208, College Park, Maryland, 20740.
ALA AFFILIATION: Joint Committee on Institutional Libraries, Health and Rehabilitative Library Services· chairperson, Barratt Wilkins (1976–78).

American Council on Education
(founded 1918).
PURPOSE: Composed of institutions of postsecondary education and national and regional educational associations, the Council provides through voluntary and cooperative action, "comprehensive leadership for improving educational standards, policies, and procedures."
MEMBERSHIP: 1,599; Annual Expenditure: $7,000,000.
PRESIDENT: Roger W. Heyns (permanent).
CHAIRPERSON, BOARD OF DIRECTORS: William J. McGill.
EXECUTIVE SECRETARY: Richard A. Humphrey.
ANNUAL MEETING: October 6–8, 1976, New Orleans, Louisiana.
PUBLICATIONS: *Educational Record* (quarterly); *Higher Education and National Affairs* (weekly).
HEADQUARTERS: One Dupont Circle, Washington, D.C., 20036.
ALA REPRESENTATIVE: Louise Giles, Association of College and Research Libraries (1975–76).

American Federation of Labor/Congress of Industrial Organizations – ALA, Library Service to Labor Groups
(founded 1945).
PURPOSE: To promote library service to labor groups through the ALA and the AFL-CIO.
MEMBERSHIP: 15; *Annual Expenditure*: $200.
ALA COCHAIRPERSON: Demarest L. Polacheck.
HEADQUARTERS: c/o Reference and Adult Services Division, ALA, 50 E. Huron Street, Chicago, Illinois, 60611.
ALA AFFILIATION: Joint Committee on Library Service to Labor Groups, Reference and Adult Services Division.

American National Red Cross
(founded 1881).
PURPOSE: In accordance with its Federal Charter, the Red Cross is committed to voluntary action to aid human suffering and to a nationwide system of emergency preparedness. Special emphasis is placed on disaster relief, services to the armed forces and veterans, and to public health and safety programs. It participates in the international family of the Red Cross.
MEMBERSHIP: 30,044,842 (June 30, 1976, estimate); Annual Expenditure: $276,401,400 (June 30, 1976).
CHAIRMAN: Frank Stanton.
PRESIDENT (executive officer): George M. Elsey.
NATIONAL CONVENTION: May 9–12, 1976, Portland, Oregon.
PUBLICATION: *The Good Neighbor* (bimonthly).
HEADQUARTERS: 17th & D Streets, N.W., Washington, D.C., 20006.
ALA LIAISON WITH RED CROSS YOUTH: Elizabeth Murphy, Children's Services Division (1975–76).

American National Standards Institute; Sectional Committee on Computers and Information Processing (X 3)
(founded 1960).
PURPOSE: "To identify and develop data processing standards necessary to achieve: efficient and economic interchange of data and compter programs within and between present and projected information processing systems; and to enhance the national and international marketability, utilization, and life expectancy of data processing equipment and systems."
MEMBERSHIP: 49.
CHAIRPERSON: John F. Auwaerter (October 1976–October 1979).
VICE-CHAIRPERSON: Robert M. Brown.
EXECUTIVE SECRETARY: William F. Hanrahan.
HEADQUARTERS: 1828 L Street, Suite 1200, Washington, D.C., 20036.
ALA REPRESENTATIVE: James A. Rizzolo, Information Science and Automation Division (1976–77).

American National Standards Institute: American National Standards Committee on Instructional Audio-Visual Systems Standards (PH 7)
(founded 1968).
PURPOSE: To develop "standards, recommended practices, performance specifications, nomenclature, and test methods for instructional audiovisual systems."
MEMBERSHIP: 17.
CHAIRPERSON: Marvin I. Mindell.
VICE-CHAIRPERSON: Richard G. Nibeck.
SECRETARY: Richard Hittner.
PUBLICATION: *Standards and Recommended Practices* (variable).
HEADQUARTERS: 1430 Broadway, New York, New York, 10018.
ALA REPRESENTATIVE: Howard S. White, *Library Technology Reports* (1975–76).

American National Standards Institute: Sectional Committee on Library Work, Documentation and Related Publishing Practices (Z 39)
(founded 1940).
PURPOSE: "To establish standards for concepts, definitions, terminology, letters and signs, practices, and methods in the field of library work, in the preparation and utilization of documents, and in those aspects of publishing that affect library methods and use."
MEMBERSHIP: 55; *Annual Expenditure*: $40,000 (1976–77).
CHAIRPERSON: Jerrold Orne (June 1975–June 1978).
VICE-CHAIRPERSON: Ben H. Weil.
PUBLICATION: *News about Z39* (quarterly).

HEADQUARTERS: School of Library Science, University of North Carolina, Chapel Hill, North Carolina, 27514.
ALA REPRESENTATIVE: Fred Blum, Resources and Technical Services Division (1975–76).

American National Standards Institute: Sectional Committee on Micrographic Reproduction (PH 5)
(founded 1953).
PURPOSE: "Standardization of terminology, definitions, sizes, format, quality, apparatus, and procedures for the production and use of microform reproduction."
MEMBERSHIP: 41; Annual Expenditure: $62,500.
CHAIRPERSON: Harold J. Fromm (January 1974–June 1977).
VICE-CHAIRPERSON: Lester O. Kruger.
SECRETARY: Don M. Avedon.
HEADQUARTERS: Secretariat, NMA, 8728 Colesville Road, Silver Spring, Maryland, 20910.

American School Counselor Association
(founded 1953).
PURPOSE: Largest division of the American Personnel and Guidance Association, it is "dedicated to . . . [the] advance [of] the broad educational aspect of guidance and counseling in all settings."
MEMBERSHIP: 14,000; Annual Expenditure: $300,000 (July 1976–June 1977).
PRESIDENT: Norman Creange (July 1976–June 1977).
PRESIDENT-ELECT: Louise Forsyth.
PUBLICATIONS: School Counselor (5 issues a year); Elementary School Guidance and Counseling (4 issues a year).
HEADQUARTERS: 1607 New Hampshire Avenue, N.W., Washington, D.C., 20009.
ALA AFFILIATION: Joint Committee, American Association of School Librarians; chairperson, Valerie J. Wilford.

American Vocational Association
(founded 1925).
PURPOSE: "To develop and promote comprehensive programs of vocational education through which individuals are brought to a level of occupational performance commensurate with their innate potential and the needs of society."
MEMBERSHIP: 52,431.
PRESIDENT: James E. (Gene) Bottoms (July 1976–July 1977).
EXECUTIVE DIRECTOR: Lowell Burkett.
ANNUAL CONVENTION: December 3–8, 1976, Houston, Texas.
PUBLICATIONS: American Vocational Journal (monthly except June, July, and August); Yearbook of the American Vocational Association (annual).
HEADQUARTERS: 1510 H Street, N.W., Washington, D.C., 20005.
ALA AFFILIATION: Joint Committee, American Association of School Librarians; chairperson, Joseph Blake.

Association for Asian Studies
(founded 1941).
PURPOSE: "To further interest in and scholarly study of Asia." It publishes scholarly research and other materials designed to promote Asian studies; sponsors research through conferences, fellowships, and programs; and carries on related activities "to encourage cooperation and exchange of information within the field of Asian studies in the United States and Canada and among scholars and scholarly organizations in these and other countries of the world."
MEMBERSHIP: 6,000 (September 1976); Annual Expenditure: $331,450 (1976).
PRESIDENT: Marius B. Jansen (April 1976–March 1977).
VICE-PRESIDENT: John M. Echols.
SECRETARY-TREASURER: Rhoads Murphey.
ANNUAL CONFERENCE: March 19–21, 1976, Toronto, Canada.
PUBLICATIONS: Journal of Asian Studies (quarterly); Bibliography of Asian Studies (annually); Asian Studies Newsletter (5 issues a year); Committee on East Asian Libraries Newsletter (3 issues a year).
HEADQUARTERS: 1 Lane Hall, University of Michigan, Ann Arbor, Michigan, 48109.
ALA AFFILIATION: Committee on East Asian Libraries, Eugene W. Wu, Harvard-Yenching Library, Harvard University.

Association for Childhood Education International
(founded 1892).
PURPOSE: "To work for the education and well-being of all children; to promote desirable conditions, programs and practices for children from infancy through early adolescence; to raise the standard of preparation and to encourage continued professional growth of teachers and others concerned with the care and development of children; to bring into active cooperation all groups concerned with children in the school, the home and the community; to inform the public of the needs of children and the ways in which school program must be adjusted to fit those needs."
MEMBERSHIP: 25,000; Annual Expenditure: $500,000 (estimated 1975–76).
PRESIDENT: Max J. Berryessa (April 1975–April 1977).
EXECUTIVE SECRETARY: Alberta L. Meyer.
ANNUAL STUDY CONFERENCE: April 11–16, 1976, Salt Lake City, Utah.
PUBLICATION: Childhood Education (6 issues a year).
HEADQUARTERS: 3615 Wisconsin Avenue, N.W., Washington, D.C., 20016.
ALA AFFILIATION: Joint Committee, American Association of School Librarians; chairperson, Dorothy S. Heald (1975–76).

Association for Educational Communications and Technology*
(founded 1923).
PURPOSE: "To facilitate humane learning through the systematic development, utilization and management of learning resources, which include people, processes and media in educational settings."
MEMBERSHIP: 7,786 (November 11, 1976); Annual Expenditure: $1,129,000 (1976–77).
PRESIDENT: Richard Gilkey (April 1976–April 1977).
VICE-PRESIDENT/PRESIDENT-ELECT: William F. Grady.
EXECUTIVE DIRECTOR: Howard B. Hitchens.
ANNUAL CONVENTION: March 9–15, 1975, Dallas, Texas.
PUBLICATIONS: AVI (Audiovisual Instruction) (10 issues a year); AVCR (AV Communication Review) (quarterly).
HEADQUARTERS: 1126 16th Street, N.W., Washington, D.C., 20036.
ALA AFFILIATION: Joint Advisory Committee on Nonbook Materials, William Quinly; Resources and Technical Services Division Committee on Catalog Code Revision, William Quinly.

Association of American Colleges
(founded 1915).
PURPOSE: "To enhance and promote humane and liberating learning. To strengthen institutions of higher education as settings for humane and liberating learning."

Organizations and Associations

MEMBERSHIP: 610.
CHAIRPERSON: Theodore D. Lockwood (February 1976–February 1977).
VICE-CHAIRPERSON: Paul F. Sharp.
PRESIDENT (executive officer): Frederic W. Ness.
ANNUAL MEETING: February 8–10, 1976, Philadelphia, Pennsylvania.
PUBLICATION: *Liberal Education* (quarterly).
HEADQUARTERS: 1818 R Street, N.W., Washington, D.C., 20009.
ALA AFFILIATION: Joint Committee on College Problems, Association of College and Research Libraries; ALA staff liaison officer, Beverly P. Lynch (1975–76).

Association of American Library Schools
(founded 1915).
PURPOSE: "To promote excellence in education for library and information science as a means of increasing the effectiveness of library and information services." Affiliated with ALA, Council of National Library Associations, International Federation of Library Associations, and Council of Communication Societies.
MEMBERSHIP: 650 personal; 98 institutional; *Annual Expenditure:* $40,000.
PRESIDENT: Guy Garrison.
VICE-PRESIDENT/PRESIDENT-ELECT: Margaret K. Groggin.
EXECUTIVE SECRETARY: Janet C. Phillips.
ANNUAL CONFERENCE (WITH ALA): January 16–18, 1976, Chicago, Illinois.
PUBLICATION: *Journal of Education for Librarianship* (quarterly).
HEADQUARTERS: 471 Park Lane, State College, Pennsylvania, 16801.
ALA AFFILIATION: Library Education Division, Thomas J. Galvin.

Association of American Publishers
(formed in 1970 by merger of the American Book Publishers Council and the American Educational Publishers Institute).
PURPOSE: To improve the status of intellectual products in the U.S. and to nurture and strengthen the public understanding that books and allied media play a central role in society. The Association provides its members with information on the conditions of the book trade, government policies, and pending legislation on matters such as copyright and censorship. It also provides a framework within which groups comprising the combined general trade and educational publishing industry and interested professional associations can exchange ideas and work together.
MEMBERSHIP: 300; *Annual Expenditure:* $1,000,000.
CHAIRPERSON, BOARD OF DIRECTORS: Joan D. Manley (July 1, 1976–June 30, 1977).
VICE-CHAIRPERSON: Harold T. Miller.
PRESIDENT (EXECUTIVE OFFICER): Townsend Hoopes.
ANNUAL MEETING: May 3–5, 1976, Boca Raton Hotel and Club, Boca Raton, Florida.
PUBLICATIONS: *Washington Newsletter* (monthly); divisional newsletters.
HEADQUARTERS: One Park Avenue, New York, New York, 10016.
ALA AFFILIATION: Joint Committee, Resources and Technical Services Division; chiarman, Connie R. Dunlap; ALA staff liaison officer, Carol R. Kelm (1975–76).

Association of International Libraries*
(founded 1963).
PURPOSE: "To promote cooperation among international libraries, to realize bibliographic control of international documents, and to assist in training international librarians."

MEMBERSHIP: 215; *Annual Expenditure:* $1,500.
PRESIDENT: Theodore Dimitrov, Geneva (August 1976–August 1979).
SECRETARY-GENERAL: O. Cerny.
PUBLICATION: *AIL Journal* (quarterly).
HEADQUARTERS: United Nations Library, Palais des Nations, Geneva, Switzerland, 1211.

Association of Research Libraries
See article in alphabetical order in text.

Atlantic Provinces Library Association*
(founded 1950).
PURPOSE: To promote library service throughout the Atlantic Provinces; to cooperate with other associations on matters of mutual concern; and to serve the professional interests of librarians in the region.
MEMBERSHIP: 225; *Annual Expenditure:* $6,000 (1975–76).
PRESIDENT: Edward Hanus.
VICE-PRESIDENT/PRESIDENT-ELECT: Alan Macdonald.
ANNUAL MEETING: May 16–18, 1976, St. John's, Newfoundland.
PUBLICATION: *A.P.L.A. Bulletin* (4 issues a year).
HEADQUARTERS: c/o School of Library Service, Dalhousie University, Halifax, Nova Scotia, Canada.

Big Brothers of America
(founded as a national organization in 1946, although the movement dates from 1903).
PURPOSE: To promote friendships between mature, male, adult volunteers with social-worker skills and boys and young men from father-absent homes under the guidance and supervision of a professional social worker. An attempt is made to meet the primary needs of the boy through personal friendship between one man and one boy and the knowledge on the part of the boy that somebody cares for him as an individual human being.
MEMBERSHIP: 315; *Annual Expenditure:* $766,306 (1975).
PRESIDENT: Maurice Schwarz, Jr. (June 1976–June 1977).
VICE-PRESIDENT/ADMINISTRATION: Cyrus J. Quinn.
VICE-PRESIDENT/OPERATIONS: John J. Frank.
EXECUTIVE VICE-PRESIDENT: Lewis P. Reade.
ANNUAL CONVENTION: June 16–19, 1976, Indianapolis, Indiana.
PUBLICATIONS: *Communicator* (9 issues a year); *Ambassador* (quarterly).
HEADQUARTERS: 220 Suburban Station Building, Philadelphia, Pennsylvania, 19103.
ALA LIAISON OFFICER: Helen Mullen, Children's Services Division (1975–76).

Boys Clubs of America
(founded 1906).
PURPOSE: "To promote the health, social, educational, vocational and character development of all boys throughout the country, irrespective of race, color, creed or national origin."
MEMBERSHIP: 1,071,414; *Annual Expenditure:* $3,693,612 (September 30, 1975).
PRESIDENT: John L. Burns.
EXECUTIVE DIRECTOR: William R. Bricker.
ANNUAL CONFERENCE: May 30–June 3, 1976, New Orleans, Louisiana; National Boy of the Year Contest, April 1976.
PUBLICATION: *Keynote Magazine* (quarterly).
HEADQUARTERS: 771 First Avenue, New York, New York, 10017.
ALA REPRESENTATIVE: Elga M. Cace, Children's Services Division.

Canadian Association of Music Libraries
(founded 1971).
PURPOSE: "To encourage the development of and cooperation between music libraries; to initiate and/or participate in projects dealing with music and musical resources; to cooperate with other organizations concerned with music; and to act as the Canadian branch of the International Association of Music Libraries."
MEMBERSHIP: 90; *Annual Expenditure:* $2,350 (August 1975).
PRESIDENT: Maria Calderisi.
VICE-PRESIDENT: Kathleen McMorrow.
EXECUTIVE SECRETARY: Lorna Hassell.
ANNUAL MEETING: May 1976, Quebec.
PUBLICATION: *CAML Newsletter* (quarterly).
HEADQUARTERS: c/o Music Division, National Library, Ottawa, Ontario, Canada, K1A 0N4.
ALA AFFILIATION: Joint Advisory Committee on Nonbook Materials.

Chief Officers of State Library Agencies (COSLA)
(founded 1973).
PURPOSE: to provide "a means for cooperative action among its 50 members to strengthen library services to the American people through the work of the state library agencies. Its purpose is to provide a continuing mechanism for dealing with the problems faced by the heads of those state agencies which are responsible for statewide library development."
MEMBERSHIP: 50
CHAIRPERSON: Joseph F. Shubert (November 1976–1978), State Librarian, The State Library of Ohio.
VICE-CHAIRPERSON: John A. Humphry, State Librarian, New York State Education Department.
SECRETARY-TREASURER: Carlton J. Thaxton, Director, Division of Public Library Services, 156 Trinity Avenue S.W., Atlanta, Georgia, 30303.
ALA AFFILIATION: Executive Secretary: Mary Power of ALA; President: Barratt Wilkins of the Association of State Library Agencies.

Child Study Association/Wel-Met, Inc.
(founded 1972, although the movement dates from 1888).
PURPOSE: To operate resident camps for children, teenagers and older adults and to plan and develop demonstration programs for children and families not reached by existing service systems. The Association also publishes books and pamphlets that develop understanding of family life and child development.
MEMBERSHIP: 1,866; *Annual Expenditure:* $1,850,000 (October 31, 1976).
PRESIDENT: Howard Stein (November 1975–October 1976).
FIRST VICE-PRESIDENT/PRESIDENT ELECT: Frank E. Karelson.
EXECUTIVE DIRECTOR: Harriet Dronska.
PUBLICATIONS: Annual bibliographies; Parent education pamphlets (2 to 4 yearly).
HEADQUARTERS: 50 Madison Avenue, New York, New York, 10010.
ALA LIAISON: Augusta Baker, Children's Services Division (1975–76).

Children's Theatre Association of America
(founded 1944 as the Children's Theatre Conference).
PURPOSE: To encourage live theatre for children, to promote communal theatre activities, and to provide a meeting ground for those interested in the Children's Theatre by sponsoring annual meetings and encouraging regional meetings throughout the year.
MEMBERSHIP: 982; *Annual Expenditure:* $6,295 (August 1975–August 1976).
PRESIDENT: Coleman Jennings (August 1975–August 1976).
VICE-PRESIDENT/PRESIDENT-ELECT: Judith Kase.
NATIONAL CONVENTION (WITH AMERICAN THEATRE ASSOCIATION): August 1975, Washington, D.C.
PUBLICATION: *Children's Theatre Review* (quarterly).
HEADQUARTERS: 1029 Vermont Avenue, N.W., Washington, D.C., 20005.
ALA REPRESENTATIVE: Amy E. Spaulding, Children's Services Division (1975–76).

Coalition for Children and Youth
(incorporated as National Council of Organizations for Children and Youth)
(founded 1973).
PURPOSE: "To serve as an umbrella agency for local, state, and national organizations working for and with children and youth; to collect and disseminate information pertinent to public policies, legislation, and program implementation as they relate to children and youth, specifically in our five cluster areas: day care, foster care and adoption, health, juvenile justice, and families and parenting. Primary function is to represent and document the needs of children and youth so that, as a coalition, we can more effectively advocate on their behalf."
MEMBERSHIP: 150 full member organizations, 225 associate member organizations and individuals.
PRESIDENT: Gen. John F. McMahon, Volunteers of America (September 1976–September 1977).
FIRST VICE-PRESIDENT: Clyde E. Shorey, National Foundation for March of Dimes.
EXECUTIVE DIRECTOR: Judith S. Ain.
BICENTENNIAL CONFERENCE: February 1–4, 1976, Washington, D.C.
PUBLICATIONS: *Focus on Children and Youth* (monthly); *America's Children '76; Children's Directory of Government Agencies* (annually).
HEADQUARTERS: Suite 800, 1910 K Street, N.W., Washington, D.C., 20006.
ALA REPRESENTATIVES: Alice E. Fite, American Association of School Librarians; Lyle Eberhardt, Association of State Librarian Agencies; Mary Jane Anderson, Children's Services Division; Dorothy M. Sinclair, Public Library Association.

Coalition of Adult Education Organizations
(founded 1969).
PURPOSE: "To operate on a nonprofit basis for the promotion of social welfare, by developing, maintaining, and improving a balanced system of adult and continuing education."
MEMBERSHIP: 19 organizations.
PRESIDENT: Constance J. McQueen (July 1976–June 1977).
PRESIDENT-ELECT: Robert A. Allen, Jr.
VICE-PRESIDENT: John R. Mackenzie.
SECRETARY/TREASURER: Charles J. Longacre.
ANNUAL MEETING: June 1976, Washington, D.C.
HEADQUARTERS: 810 18th Street, N.W., Washington, D.C., 20006.
ALA REPRESENTATIVES: Andrew M. Hansen, Honore L. Moton, Reference and Adult Service Division.

Continuing Library Education Network and Exchange (CLENE)
(founded 1975).
PURPOSE: To provide equal access to continuing education opportunities and to ensure library and information science personnel and organizations the competency to deliver quality library and information services to all. Also, to create an awareness and a sense of need for continuing education of

Organizations and Associations

library personnel on the part of employers and individuals as a means of responding to societal and technological change.
MEMBERSHIP: 550 (December 1, 1976).
PRESIDENT: Ruth J. Patrick (1976–77).
PRESIDENT-ELECT: Travis Tyer.
EXECUTIVE DIRECTOR: Elizabeth W. Stone.
ANNUAL MEETING: CLENE Assembly II, February 16–17, 1976.
PUBLICATIONS: CLENExchange (quarterly); *Directory of Continuing Education Courses and Programs for Library Personnel, Information and Media Specialists* (annually); *CLENE MEMBERSHIP Directory; Concept Papers, An Annotated Bibliography of Recent Continuing Education Literature; CLENE Proceedings—First Assembly—January 1976; CLENE Proceedings—Second Assembly—July 1976.*
HEADQUARTERS: Box 1228, 620 Michigan Avenue, N.E., Washington, D.C., 20064.
ALA AFFILIATION: Library Education Division; ALA liaison officer, Margaret Myers (1975–76).

See also *Continuing Professional Education.*

Corporation for Public Broadcasting Advisory Council of National Organizations
(founded 1968).
PURPOSE: To "serve in an advisory and consultant capacity to the Board and President of the Corporation for Public Broadcasting." Main functions of the Council include identifying the needs of Corporation members, assisting in the evaluation of programs and providing feedback to the staff and Board, providing a means of communication from Public Broadcasting to the public, and providing an opportunity for member organizations to participate in specific programs and projects undertaken by Public Broadcasting.
MEMBERSHIP: 45 organizations.
CHAIRPERSON: Nancy McMahon (October 1975–September 1977).
VICE-CHAIRPERSON: James Williams.
SECOND VICE-CHAIRPERSON: Harold Wigren.
ANNUAL BOARD MEETING: September 15, 1976, Washington, D.C.
HEADQUARTERS: 1111 16th Street, N.W., Washington, D.C., 20036.
ALA REPRESENTATIVE: Eileen D. Cooke (1975–76).

Council of National Library Associations*
(founded 1942).
PURPOSE: To promote closer relationship among the national library associations of the United States and Canada.
MEMBERSHIP: 16 national associations.
CHAIRPERSON: Robert M. Henderson (1976–77).
SECRETARY-TREASURER: Ruth B. Hilton.
HEADQUARTERS: c/o Matthew R. Wilt, Catholic Library Association, 461 W. Lancaster Avenue, Haverford, Pennsylvania, 19041.

Council of Specialized Accrediting Agencies*
(founded 1971).
PURPOSE: "To strengthen the effectiveness and quality of postsecondary, professional, and specialized education through accreditation and related activities."
MEMBERSHIP: 41; *Annual Expenditure:* $2,500.
CHAIRMAN: Robert Glidden (February 1976–February 1977).
VICE-CHAIRPERSON: Dorothy Ozimek.
SECRETARY-TREASURER: Alfred Stamm.
MEMBERSHIP MEETING: February 1976, Atlanta, Georgia.
HEADQUARTERS: c/o Council on Postsecondary Accreditation, One Dupont Circle, Suite 760, Washington, D.C., 20036.

Council on Postsecondary Accreditation*
(founded 1975).
PURPOSE: "To improve Postsecondary Education through the accreditation process."
MEMBERSHIP: 4,000; *Annual Expenditure:* $275,000 estimate.
CHAIRPERSON OF THE BOARD: Dana B. Hamel (July 1, 1976).
VICE-CHAIRPERSON: Kenneth G. Picha.
PRESIDENT (executive officer): Kenneth E. Young.
EVENTS: National Seminar for Accrediting Executives, February 4–6, 1976, Atlanta, Georgia; August 4–6, 1976, Denver, Colorado.
PUBLICATIONS: *Accreditation* (quarterly); occasional papers on various topics (approximately quarterly).
HEADQUARTERS: One Dupont Circle, Suite 760, Washington, D.C., 20036.

Day Care and Child Development Council of America
(founded 1965).
PURPOSE: "To provide universally available child care to all children who want or need it."
MEMBERSHIP: 4,000; *Annual Expenditure:* $500,000.
CHAIRPERSON OF THE BOARD: John Niemeyer.
PRESIDENT: Andrew W. L. Brown (May 1976–May 1977).
VICE-PRESIDENT: Gwen Morgan.
EXECUTIVE DIRECTOR: Theodore Taylor.
ANNUAL MEETING: May 19–23, 1976, Reston, Virginia.
PUBLICATION: *Voice for Children* (monthly).
HEADQUARTERS: 622 14th Street, N.W., Washington, D.C., 20005.

Educational Film Library Association*
(founded 1943).
PURPOSE: "To stimulate the production, distribution, and utilization of films and other audio-visual materials in libraries, schools, and universities. Also to serve as a clearinghouse of information about nontheatrical film."
MEMBERSHIP: 1,900; *Annual Expenditure:* $198,000 (1975–1976).
PRESIDENT: James Buterbaugh (July 1976–June 1977).
VICE-PRESIDENT: Edward Mason.
EXECUTIVE DIRECTOR: Nadine Covert.
EVENT: 18th Annual American Film Festival, June 1–5, 1976, New York, New York.
PUBLICATIONS: *Sightlines* (quarterly); *EFLA Evaluations* (10 issues a year).
HEADQUARTERS: 46 West 61st Street, New York, New York, 10023.

Girls Clubs of America
(founded 1945).
PURPOSE: "To guide girls for multiple roles in home, work, and civic affairs; to help girls find their own identity, develop potential talents and skills and achieve a sense of responsibility."
MEMBERSHIP: 180,000; *Annual Expenditure:* $889,513 (December 31, 1975).
PRESIDENT: Mrs. J. Michael Prejean.
VICE-PRESIDENT/PRESIDENT-ELECT: Mrs. Harry C. Pratt.
EXECUTIVE DIRECTOR: Edith B. Phelps.
NATIONAL CONFERENCE: April 13–16, 1975, New York, New York.
PUBLICATION: *Girls Club News* (quarterly).
HEADQUARTERS: 133 East 62nd Street, New York, New York, 10021.

Illinois Regional Library Council*
(founded 1971).
PURPOSE: "To serve as a coordinating agency for all types of libraries, information centers, and library agencies in the Chicago metropolitan area with improvement of access to information by all metropolitan area residents being its primary objective."
MEMBERSHIP: 303; *Annual Expenditure:* $77,272.04 (June 30, 1976).
PRESIDENT: William B. Ernst, Jr.
VICE-PRESIDENT: David L. Reich.
EXECUTIVE DIRECTOR: Beth A. Hamilton.
ANNUAL MEETING: April 2, 1976, Chicago.
PUBLICATIONS: *Multitype Library Cooperative News* (monthly); *Libraries and Information Centers in the Chicago Metropolitan Area* (triennially).
HEADQUARTERS: 425 North Michigan Avenue, Chicago, Illinois, 60611.

Illuminating Engineers Society
(founded 1906).
PURPOSE: "To establish scientific lighting standards and recommendations and to develop and communicate this information to all interested parties." Society comprises professionals who are actively engaged in the practice of teaching of illumination.
MEMBERSHIP: 10,000.
PRESIDENT: C. J. Long (July 1, 1976 – June 30, 1977).
PRESIDENT-ELECT: David Patterson.
EXECUTIVE VICE-PRESIDENT: Frank M. Coda.
ANNUAL CONFERENCE: July 13 – 17, 1975, San Francisco, California.
PUBLICATIONS: *Lighting Design and Application* (monthly); *Journal of the Illuminating Engineering Society* (quarterly).
HEADQUARTERS: 345 East 47th Street, New York, New York, 10017.
ALA REPRESENTATIVE: Sub-Committee on Library Lighting, Howard S. White, *Library Technology Reports* (1975 – 76).

International Association of School Librarianship*
(founded 1970).
PURPOSE: To encourage development of school libraries and library programs throughout all countries, to promote the professional preparation of school librarians, to bring about closer collaboration between school librarians in all countries (including loan and exchange), to encourage the development of materials, and to initiate and coordinate activities, conferences, and other projects.
MEMBERSHIP: 450; *Annual Expenditure:* $2,764.00 (1975 – 76).
PRESIDENT: Jean E. Lowrie (August 1975 – July 1977).
VICE-PRESIDENT: Margot Nilson.
EVENT: Annapolis Junction, Maryland, July 30 – August 1, 1976; "Crucial issues in school library development."
PUBLICATIONS: *IASL Newsletter* (quarterly); *Annual Proceedings.*
HEADQUARTERS: Western Michigan University, Kalamazoo, Michigan, 49008.

International Board on Books for Young People
See article in alphabetical order in text.

International Federation for Documentation (FID)
See article in alphabetical order in text.

International Federation of Library Associations (IFLA)
See article in alphabetical order in text.

International Personnel Management Association*
(founded 1973 with the amalgamation of the Society of Personnel Administrators and the Public Personnel Administration).
PURPOSE: "An association of government agencies and officials to advance civil service and personnel practices."
MEMBERSHIP: 6,000 (1,000 agency and 5,000 personal).
PRESIDENT: Muriel M. Morse.
PRESIDENT-ELECT: Robert C. Garnier.
EXECUTIVE DIRECTOR: Donald K. Tichenor.
INTERNATIONAL CONFERENCE: November 28 – December 2, 1976, Washington, D.C.
PUBLICATIONS: *Public Personnel Management* (bimonthly); *IPMA News* (monthly); *IPMA Agency* (monthly).
HEADQUARTERS: 1313 East 60th Street, Chicago, Illinois, 60637.

Joint Council on Educational Telecommunications*
(founded 1950).
PURPOSE: "To advise the educational community regarding educational and social applications of communications technology and implications of telecommunications policy; to assist in experimentation and projects to meet those ends."
MEMBERSHIP: 21.
PRESIDENT: Armand L. Hunter (July 1975 – June 1977).
VICE-PRESIDENT: Harold Wigren.
EXECUTIVE DIRECTOR: Frank W. Norwood.
PUBLICATION: *JCET Monitor* (monthly).
HEADQUARTERS: 1126 16th Street, N.W., Washington, D.C., 20036.
ALA REPRESENTATIVE: Donald P. Hammer, Information Science and Automation Division.

Library Association*
(founded 1877 in London).
PURPOSE: "To unite all persons engaged or interested in library and information work, to promote their generalized and specialised professional interests and to encourage high standards of professional practice. To promote and encourage bibliographic study and research and to publish information of service or interest to members of the Association."
MEMBERSHIP: 23,537; *Annual Expenditure:* £940,000 ($1,600,000).
PRESIDENT: D. J. Foskett (January 1976 – December 1976).
PRESIDENT-ELECT: Sir Frederick Dainton.
SECRETARY: R. P. Hilliard.
1976 CONFERENCES: National Conference, September 6 – 10, Scarborough; Association of Assistant Librarians, April 9 – 11, Hereford; Cataloguing and Indexing Group, April 9 – 12, Exeter; Industrial Group, June 25 – 27, Reading; International and Comparative Librarianship Group, 10th Anniversary Conference, September 23 – 25, Loughborough; Public Libraries Group – Weekend School, April 2 – 5, Lancaster University; Reference, Special and Information Section – Silver Jubilee Conference, April 2 – 5, Cambridge; University, College and Resarch Section, March 26 – 29, Hull; Youth Libraries Group – Weekend School, October 15 – 17, Buxton.
PUBLICATIONS: *Library Association Record* (monthly); *The Library Association Year Book; Journal of Librarianship* (quarterly); *Library & Information*

Science Abstracts (6 issues a year).
HEADQUARTERS: 7 Ridgmount Street, London, WC1E 7AE, England.

Middle East Librarians' Association*
(founded 1972).
PURPOSE: To facilitate communication among members through meetings and publications; to develop standards for the profession and education of Middle East library specialists; to compile and disseminate information concerning Middle East libraries and collections; to encourage cooperation, especially in the acquisition of materials and the development of bibliographic controls; and to promote research in and development of indexing and automated techniques as applied to Middle East libraries.
MEMBERSHIP: 145; Annual Expenditure: $400.
PRESIDENT: Fawzi Khoury (November 1976–November 1977).
VICE-PRESIDENT: Virginia Gibbons.
SECRETARY-TREASURER: Janet Heineck.
EVENT: Annual meeting November 11, 1976, Los Angeles, California.
PUBLICATION: Mela Notes (3 issues a year); James Pollock, editor.
HEADQUARTERS: Regenstein Library, Room 560, University of Chicago, 1100 East 57th Street, Chicago, Illinois, 60637.

National Accreditation Council for Agencies Serving the Blind and Visually Handicapped*
(founded 1967).
PURPOSE: To stimulate improvement of services to persons who are blind or otherwise visually handicapped through developing standards for agencies and schools, which provide specialized services, and by accrediting those agencies and schools which demonstrate effectiveness in applying these standards.
MEMBERSHIP: 63 accredited agencies and schools; Annual Expenditure: $246,347 (June 30, 1976).
PRESIDENT: Louis H. Rives, Jr.
VICE-PRESIDENTS: Huntington Harris; Howard H. Hanson; Jack W. Birch.
EXECUTIVE DIRECTOR: Richard W. Bleecker.
ANNUAL MEETING: November 17, 1976, New York, New York.
PUBLICATIONS: Standard-Bearer (3 issues a year); Annual Report.
HEADQUARTERS: 79 Madison Avenue, Room 1406, New York, New York, 10016.

National Association of Elementary School Principals*
(founded 1921).
PURPOSE: To facilitate positive educational leadership; to serve as an agency for the collection and dissemination of information pertinent to elementary school principalship; to provide services such as publications, conferences, research; to promote the principle of equal rights; and to enhance harmonious relationships between elementary school principals and teachers.
MEMBERSHIP: 23,973; Annual Expenditure: $1,096,348 (August 31, 1976).
PRESIDENT: Bertha G. Maguire (September 1, 1976–August 31, 1977).
VICE-PRESIDENT/PRESIDENT-ELECT: Bill M. Hambrick.
EXECUTIVE DIRECTOR: William L. Pharis.
NATIONAL CONVENTION: April 24–28, 1976, Atlantic City, New Jersey.
PUBLICATIONS: National Elementary Principal (bimonthly); Spectator Newsletter (bimonthly).
HEADQUARTERS: P.O. Box 9114, 1801 North Moore Street, Arlington, Virginia, 22209.

National Association of Exposition Managers*
(founded 1928).
PURPOSE: "To advance the arts and sciences pertaining to education through the use of exhibits, exhibitions and expositions for the dissemination of knowledge and information."
MEMBERSHIP: 500; Annual Expenditure: $150,000.
PRESIDENT: John Rogers (December 1976–November 1977).
VICE-PRESIDENT/PRESIDENT-ELECT: Rudy Lang.
EXECUTIVE DIRECTOR: Thomas J. Sullivan, Jr.
EVENTS: Mid-year Meeting, June 2–6, 1975, Milwaukee, Wisconsin; Annual Meeting, December 2–5, 1975, Phoenix, Arizona.
PUBLICATION: Exposition Managers' News (bimonthly).
HEADQUARTERS: 108 Wilmot Road, Suite 105, Deerfield, Illinois, 60015.
ALA REPRESENTATIVE: Christopher Hoy.

National Council of Teachers of English
(founded 1911).
PURPOSE: "To improve the quality of instruction in English at all educational levels; to encourage research, experimentation, and investigation in the teaching of English; to facilitate professional cooperation of the members; to hold public discussions and programs; to sponsor the publication of desirable articles and reports; and to integrate the efforts of all those who are concerned with the improvement of instruction in English."
MEMBERSHIP: 45,000; Annual Expenditure: $2,000,000.
PRESIDENT: Charlotte K. Brooks.
EXECUTIVE DIRECTOR: Robert F. Hogan.
ANNUAL CONVENTION: November 27–29, 1975, San Diego, California.
PUBLICATIONS: Language Arts (8 issues a year); English Journal (9 issues a year); College English (8 issues a year); College Composition and Communication (quarterly); English Education (quarterly); Abstracts of English Studies (10 issues a year); Research in the Teaching of English (3 issues a year); CSSEDC Newsletter (quarterly); Council-Grams (5 issues a year).
HEADQUARTERS: 1111 Kenyon Road, Urbana, Illinois, 61801.
ALA AFFILIATION: Joint Committee, American Association of School Librarians; chairperson, Thomas W. Downen (1975–76).

National Council of Teachers of Mathematics
(founded 1920).
PURPOSE: "To assist in promoting the interests of mathematics in America . . . and to revitalize and coordinate the work of local organizations of teachers of mathematics."
MEMBERSHIP: 48,000; Annual Expenditure: $1,690,000 (May 31, 1976).
PRESIDENT: John C. Egsgard (April 1976–April 1978).
PAST PRESIDENT: E. Glenadine Gibb.
EXECUTIVE DIRECTOR: James D. Gates.
ANNUAL MEETING: April 1975, Denver, Colorado.
PUBLICATIONS: Mathematics Teacher (8 issues a year); Arithmetic Teacher (8 issues a year).
HEADQUARTERS: 1906 Association Drive, Reston, Virginia, 22091.
ALA AFFILIATION: Joint Committee American Association of School Librarians; cochairperson, Eloise Brown, Public Schools Libraries, Washington, D.C.

National Micrographics Association
(founded 1945).
PURPOSE: "To serve its professional and trade mem-

bers in fostering applications of micrographics, including interfaces with other information-processing technologies that facilitate the effective storage, transfer, and use of information."
MEMBERSHIP: 8,000; *Annual Expenditure:* $1,334,000 (May 1976–May 1977).
PRESIDENT: Thomas P. Anderson (May 1976–May 1977).
VICE-PRESIDENT/PRESIDENT-ELECT: Richard J. Conners.
EXECUTIVE DIRECTOR: O. Gordon Banks. (Address all general correspondence to executive director.)
ANNUAL CONFERENCE AND EXPOSITION: April 27–30, 1976, Chicago, Illinois.
MID-YEAR MEETING: October 13–15, 1976, Denver, Colorado.
PUBLICATIONS: *Journal of Micrographics* (bimonthly); *Micrographics Today* (10 issues annually); *Buyer's Guide to Micrographic Equipment, Products, and Services* (annually); *Proceedings of the Annual Conference and Exposition* (annually); other publications available.
HEADQUARTERS: 8728 Colesville Road, Silver Spring, Maryland, 20910.

National Municipal League*
(founded 1894).
PURPOSE: The League is dedicated to the proposition that "informed, competent citizens participating fully in public affairs in their home communities are the key to good local, state and national government."
MEMBERSHIP: 6,050; *Annual Expenditure:* $418,000 (1975).
PRESIDENT: Carl H. Pforzheimer, Jr.
EXECUTIVE DIRECTOR: William N. Cassella, Jr.
NATIONAL CONFERENCE: November 7–10, 1976, Williamsburg, Virginia.
PUBLICATION: *National Civic Review* (monthly).
HEADQUARTERS: 47 East 68th Street, New York, New York, 10021.

National Story League
(founded 1903).
PURPOSE: To encourage the creation and appreciation of the good and beautiful in life and literature through the art of storytelling.
MEMBERSHIP: 1,300; *Annual Expenditure:* $5,815 (1976–1978).
PRESIDENT: Mrs. James Lea (July 1976–July 1978).
VICE-PRESIDENT: Mrs. J. A. Reynolds.
EDITOR: Marylouise Reighart.
PUBLICATION: *Story Art Magazine* (bimonthly).
HEADQUARTERS: 555 Tod Avenue, N.W., Warren, Ohio, 44485.
ALA REPRESENTATIVE: Linda Oscarson, Children's Services Division.

National University Extension Association
(founded 1915).
PURPOSE: "An association of institutions of higher education which have a commitment to continuing education and extension."
MEMBERSHIP: 230.
PRESIDENT: Paul Hadley (April 1976–March 1977).
VICE-PRESIDENT/PRESIDENT-ELECT: Phillip E. Frandson.
EXECUTIVE DIRECTOR: Lloyd Davis.
ANNUAL CONFERENCE: April 1976, St. Louis, Missouri.
PUBLICATIONS: *Newsletter* (biweekly); *Continuum* (quarterly); *Guide to Independent Study* (biannually); *On-Campus/Off-Campus Degree Programs for Part-time Students.*
HEADQUARTERS: One Dupont Circle, Suite 360, Washington, D.C., 20036.
ALA AFFILIATION: Joint Committee on university library extension services, Association of College and Research Libraries; Barry E. Booth; staff liaison, Frank MacDougall (1976–1977).

National Voluntary Organizations for Independent Living
(founded 1971).
PURPOSE: "To help older persons maintain their independence by staying in their own homes as long as possible through the provision of the in-home services they need."
MEMBERSHIP: 158 (January 1976).
CHAIRPERSON: Peter G. Meek.
VICE-CHAIRPERSON: Rev. Donald F. Clingan.
NCOA ASSOCIATE DIRECTOR: Marjorie A. Collins.
HEADQUARTERS: c/o National Council on the Aging, Inc., 1828 L Street, N.W., Washington, D.C., 20036.
ALA REPRESENTATIVE: John Balkema.

New England Library Information Network (NELINET)
(founded 1966).
PURPOSE: A multistate network of academic, research, public, and other libraries with a mission "to facilitate the sharing of library and information resources and services for the people of New England."
MEMBERSHIP: 50; *Annual Expenditure:* $1,189,394.92 (July 1975–June 1976).
CHAIRPERSON: Gai Carpenter (July 1, 1976–June 30, 1977).
VICE-CHAIRPERSON: Sherrie Bergman.
EXECUTIVE DIRECTOR: Ronald F. Miller.
PUBLICATIONS: *Channel* (newsletter, 5 issues a year); *NELINFO* (technical newsletter, variable).
HEADQUARTERS: 40 Grove Street, Wellesley, Massachusetts, 02181.
ALA REPRESENTATIVE TO NATIONAL ADVISORY PANEL: Henriette Avram, Information Science and Automation Division (1976–77).

New Mexico Book League*
(founded 1971).
PURPOSE: To organize all librarians, booksellers, publishers, and authors in the Southwest into a viable group that can act . . . to further interest in books and reading, knowing that only by collective effort will the scattered and segmented book industries be able to make real progress in an area of sparse population.
MEMBERSHIP: 311; *Annual Expenditure:* $1,200.
PRESIDENT: Justine Thomas (February 1975–March 1977).
VICE-PRESIDENT/PRESIDENT-ELECT: Henry Servatt.
EXECUTIVE DIRECTOR: Dwight A. Myers.
ANNUAL MEETING: March 27, 1976, Socorro, New Mexico.
PUBLICATION: *Book Talk* (bimonthly).
HEADQUARTERS: 8632 Horacio Place, N.E., Albuquerque, New Mexico, 87111.

Parents Without Partners, Inc.
(founded 1957).
PURPOSE: "An international, non-profit, non-sectarian educational organization devoted to the welfare and interests of single parents and their children."
MEMBERSHIP: 145,000; *Annual Expenditure:* $1,000,000
PRESIDENT: Dorothy Gilbert (July 1976–July 1977).
FIRST VICE-PRESIDENT: Freda Mark.
EXECUTIVE DIRECTOR: Virginia Martin.
ANNUAL MEETING: July 1975, Washington, D.C.
PUBLICATION: *The Single Parent* (10 issues a year).
HEADQUARTERS: 7910 Woodmont Avenue, Washington, D.C., 20014.

Organizations and Associations

ALA REPRESENTATIVE: Mary B. Bauer, Children's Services Division (1975–76).

President's Committee on Employment of the Handicapped
(founded 1947).
PURPOSE: "To build an attitude of acceptance in the work force and in all of society for handicapped people who are job ready and qualified. To encourage other handicapped people to become job ready. To mobilize employers . . . and all facets of society in this effort."
MEMBERSHIP: 700; *Annual Expenditure:* $1,300,000 (July 1, 1976).
CHAIRPERSON: Harold Russell.
VICE-CHAIRPERSONS: Jayne Baker Spain, Robert Collier, and Victor Riesel.
EXECUTIVE DIRECTOR: Bernard Posner.
PUBLICATION: *Performance* (monthly).
HEADQUARTERS: 1111 20th Street, N.W., Washington, D.C., 20210.
ALA REPRESENTATIVE ON LIBRARY COMMITTEE: Lelia Saunders.

Puppeteers of America
(founded 1937).
PURPOSE: To raise the standards of the art of puppetry through an educational program of annual conferences, institutes, workshops, lecture programs, exhibitions, publications, and advisory services.
MEMBERSHIP: 2,500; *Annual Expenditure:* $25,000.
PRESIDENT: Nancy Staub (July 1976–June 1977).
VICE-PRESIDENT: John Miller.
EXECUTIVE SECRETARY: Olga Stevens.
ANNUAL NATIONAL PUPPETRY FESTIVAL: June 18–20, 1975, St. Charles, Missouri.
PUBLICATION: *The Puppetry Journal* (bimonthly).
HEADQUARTERS: P.O. Box 1061, Ojai, California, 93023.
ALA REPRESENTATIVE: Donald Reynolds, Children's Services Division (1975–76).

Round Table of National Organizations for Better Education*
(founded 1953 as Round Table for the Support of Public Schools).
PURPOSE: To meet annually and exchange information on major issues in education, to learn what organizations are doing for and in education, and to obtain expert information on trends. Round Table is a clearinghouse, not a decision-making body.
MEMBERSHIP: 45; *Annual Expenditure:* $1,785.
CHAIRPERSON OF THE PLANNING COMMITTEE: Jerry Cordrey (January 1976–December 1976).
SECRETARY-TREASURER: Harold V. Webb.
ANNUAL MEETING: November 14–16, 1976, Harriman, New York.
HEADQUARTERS: 225 Touhy Avenue, Park Ridge, Illinois, 60068.

Salvation Army, The
(founded 1865).
PURPOSE: "Expressed by a spiritual ministry to preach the Gospel, disseminate Christian truths, provide personal counseling, and undertake the spiritual, moral and physical rehabilitation of all persons in need who come within its sphere of influence regardless of race or creed."
MEMBERSHIP: 384,817 (U.S. only, December 1975).
NATIONAL COMMANDER: Commissioner Paul S. Kaiser.
NATIONAL CHIEF SECRETARY: Colonel George Nelting.
PUBLICATIONS: *War Cry* (weekly); *Young Soldier* (monthly); *SAY* (monthly).
HEADQUARTERS: 120-130 West 14th Street, New York, New York, 10011.
ALA REPRESENTATIVE: Marya Hunsicker, Children's Services Division.

Society of American Archivists
(founded 1936).
PURPOSE: To provide a means of contact, communication, and cooperation among archivists and archival institutions through its publication program, annual meetings, symposia and committee activity. The Society also advances professional education and training, offers job placement services, supports research, and represents archivists in areas involving related professions.
MEMBERSHIP: 2,750
PRESIDENT: Robert M. Warner (October 1976–October 1977).
VICE-PRESIDENT/PRESIDENT-ELECT: Walter Rundell, Jr.
EXECUTIVE SECRETARY: Ann Morgan Campbell.
ANNUAL MEETING: September 28–October 1, 1976, Washington, D.C.
PUBLICATIONS: *American Archivist* (quarterly); *SAA Newsletter* (bimonthly).
HEADQUARTERS: P.O. Box 8198, Library, University of Illinois, Chicago, Illinois, 60680.
ALA AFFILIATION: Joint Committee on Library Archives; ALA Staff Liaison Officer, Robert Wedgeworth.

Toy Manufacturers of America
(founded 1916).
PURPOSE: "To coordinate toy manufacturers throughout the U.S. into one group of independent participants to exchange ideas, goals, and show achievements."
MEMBERSHIP: 240.
PRESIDENT: Samuel B. Sherwin.
PUBLIC RELATIONS DIRECTOR: Ted Erickson.
ANNUAL AMERICAN TOY FAIR: February 22–25, 1976, New York, New York.
HEADQUARTERS: 200 5th Avenue, New York, New York, 10010.
ALA REPRESENTATIVE: Anne Hoffman, Children's Services Division.

United States Department of State: Government Advisory Committee on International Book and Library Programs
(formed 1962).
PURPOSE: "To advise the government on policies and operations of its book and library programs and to achieve closer coordination between public and private book and library activities overseas."
MEMBERSHIP: 12.
CHAIRPERSON: Leo Albert.
EXECUTIVE SECRETARY: Carol M. Owens.
HEADQUARTERS: Cu/ALS, Room 420, SA2, Department of State, Washington, D.C., 20520.
ALA REPRESENTATIVES: Vacant, Jean Lowrie, Jane Wilson (official observer).

United States National Commission for UNESCO
(founded 1946).
PURPOSE: "To further within the U.S. the policies and programs of UNESCO; to give advice to the government in matters relating to UNESCO."
MEMBERSHIP: 100.
CHAIRPERSON: Sarah Goddard Power (1976–78).
VICE-CHAIRPERSONS: Shirley Joseph; Robert Garvey; Eugene Lyons.
EXECUTIVE SECRETARY: John E. Upston.
ANNUAL MEETING: December 1976, Warrenton, Virginia.
PUBLICATIONS: *World Population News Service* (variable); *Step/News International* (variable).

HEADQUARTERS: Department of State, Washington, D.C., 20520.
ALA REPRESENTATIVE: Esther J. Walls.

Universal Serials and Book Exchange
See article in alphabetical order in text.

Women's Joint Congressional Committee*
(formed 1920).
PURPOSE: "A coalition-type clearinghouse for the legislative work of national organizations engaged in promoting federal measures pertaining to the general welfare."
MEMBERSHIP: 25.
PRESIDENT: Scottie Foster (October 1976–September 1977).
VICE-PRESIDENT/PRESIDENT-ELECT: Dana Tracy.
ALA REPRESENTATIVES: Eileen D. Cooke, Jane B. Nida (1976–77).

Women's National Book Association
(founded 1917).
PURPOSE: To recognize and honor achievement, the WNBA presents the Constance Lindsay Skinner Award to an American woman.
MEMBERSHIP: 1,100; Annual expenditure: $6,000
PRESIDENT: Ann Heidbreder Eastman
VICE-PRESIDENT: Elizabeth A. Geiser
ANNUAL MEETING: July 1976, Chicago.
PUBLICATIONS: The Bookwoman and "Directory."
HEADQUARTERS: c/o Apt. 5-G, 166 N. Dithridge St., Pittsburgh, Pennsylvania, 15213

Outreach
See Disadvantaged, Library Service to.

People
See Biographies; Obituaries; State Reports. Consult Index.

Personnel and Employment: Affirmative Action

Library affirmative action in 1976 scored few gains over the previous year. Statistical surveys posted little evidence that discrimination against women and minorities in libraries was on the wane. The legal waters were even muddier than before. There was also some evidence of a lack of understanding or interest in equal employment opportunity (EEO) and affirmative action (AA) in libraries. The future does not portend well for affirmative action without persistent effort to make the library community aware of the role that EEO/AA plays in the development of sound, unbiased personnel practices.

STATUS OF WOMEN

Out of a large assortment of salary and other statistical surveys that appeared within the past year, there are few notes of optimism. Kenneth D. Shearer and Ray L. Carpenter in "Public Library Support and Salaries in the Seventies," Library Journal (March 15, 1976) report that the substantial differentials between the pay of male and female public library directors remains virtually unchanged at 28 percent from past years. Carol L. Learmont

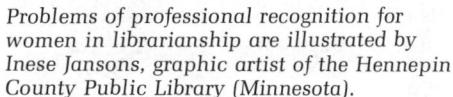
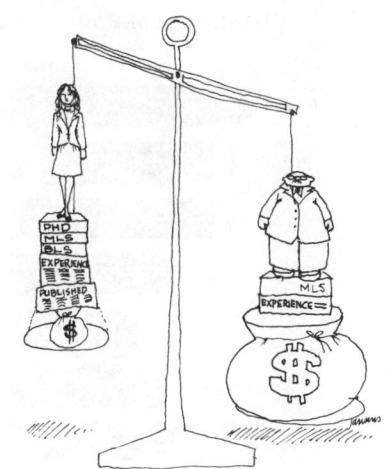

Problems of professional recognition for women in librarianship are illustrated by Inese Jansons, graphic artist of the Hennepin County Public Library (Minnesota).

and Richard L. Darling's survey, "Placements and Salaries 1975" LJ (July 1976), notes that, while the pay differentials for male and female beginning librarians receded some from 1974, there was still a 3.7 percent difference in favor of male first-year professionals.

Academic Scene. The academic library picture is bleak. The Association of College and Research Libraries (ACRL) "Salary Structure of Librarians in Higher Education for the Academic Year 1975–76" (August 1976) substantiated that there were salary differences in every classification—3.2 percent at the entry point to 23.3 percent at the director level—in academic libraries. Though 61.5 percent of all librarians in the 1,208 institutions surveyed by ACRL were women, and they made up 71.5 percent of the bottom professional step, they represented only 35.8 percent of the academic library directorships. Russell Bidlack completed a survey of "Faculty Salaries of 62 Library Schools, 1975–76," Journal of Education for Librarianship (Spring 1976). His data calculated a 5 percent difference in the salaries of all full-time faculty members paid on a fiscal year basis and a 14 percent differential for those paid on the academic year—both figures in favor of male faculty. He reported that 41.5 percent of the full-time faculty and 20 percent of the library school deans are women.

MINORITY STATUS

The ALA Office for Library Personnel Resource's "Survey of Graduates and Faculty from Library Education Programs in the United States Awarding Degrees and Certificates, 1974–75" (published in 1976) is the most comprehensive and up-to-date source of statistical information on the availability of minority librarians. This study showed little change in the number of minorities completing degree and certificate programs—9.8 percent in

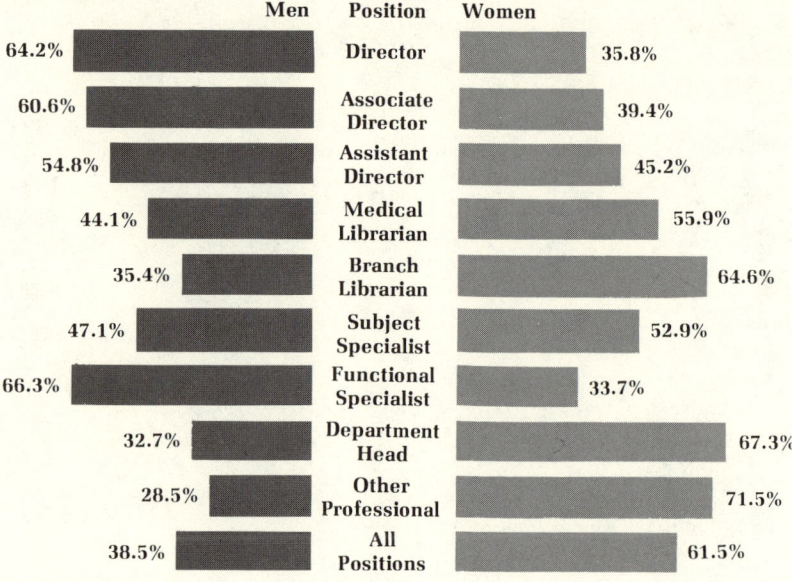

Distribution of Professional Library Staff at Each Position, 1975-76

Men	Position	Women
64.2%	Director	35.8%
60.6%	Associate Director	39.4%
54.8%	Assistant Director	45.2%
44.1%	Medical Librarian	55.9%
35.4%	Branch Librarian	64.6%
47.1%	Subject Specialist	52.9%
66.3%	Functional Specialist	33.7%
32.7%	Department Head	67.3%
28.5%	Other Professional	71.5%
38.5%	All Positions	61.5%

Source: *ACRL Salary Survey, 1975—76*

1974/75 as opposed to 10.8 percent the previous year. About 8.6 percent of those graduated in 1974/75 from ALA accredited master's degree programs are Black, American Indian, Asian-American or Spanish surnamed, a total of 548 individuals (Table 1). Similarly, the ACRL salary survey noted that about 9.6 percent of the total survey population were minorities, which is comparable to the number of minority librarians within the availability pool.

The salary and classification picture, however, was not as bright. According to the ACRL survey, minority librarians were more heavily represented in the lower echelons of library service. The average salaries for the minorities included in the ACRL study "are, at every level, less than those for all staff combined."

Studies indicate that Latinos and Native Americans are not chosen for librarianship in numbers representing their availability in the pool of college graduates. Arnulfo Trejo has confirmed the scarcity of Hispanic librarians. Trejo's directory of Spanish-heritage librarians, *Quien es Quien*, lists only 245 individuals in 28 states, Washington, D.C., and Puerto Rico. (The directory is available for $3 from the University of Arizona, Bureau of School Services, Tucson.) Roberto Cabello-Argandōna further documents the need for stronger recruitment of Spanish-heritage librarians in his *Library Journal* article, "Recruiting Spanish-speaking Library Students" (May 15, 1976). (See also REFORMA.)

LEGAL CONCERNS

A number of legal questions cloud the affirmative action picture. In days of recession and tight budgets the use of seniority rules to determine staff layoffs has come into conflict with affirmative action efforts. The courts have not ruled consistently on whether "last hired, first fired" seniority rules can be applied to individuals who are protected under affirmative action plans.

Henry Garland details in "The M.L.S., Affirmative Action, Equal Employment Opportunity, and Equivalency," *California Librarian* (October 1975) the legal questions surrounding the validity of librarian job requirements. Library affirmative action plans occasionally include career ladder development and equivalency exams in an effort to broaden the selection criteria and increase the chances for hire and promotion of protected class individuals. This is a controversial procedure, since some feel that the development of equivalencies in place of the accredited M.L.S. degree threatens the professionalism and status that librarians have fought so hard to attain. Generally speaking, equivalency development goes back to one of the fundamental aspects of affirmative action, test, or selection procedure, validation. If the M.L.S. degree is proven to be the only valid route to some jobs, then libraries are within legal bounds to require it. If in analyzing certain jobs, however, it is found that individuals with the equivalent in training or experience can do the work acceptably, then equivalency and career ladder development to fit qualified noncredentialed individuals into the professional ranks will become an essential part of library affirmative action plans. This area may also be one to be decided ultimately by the courts—unless libraries are willing to resolve it for themselves through test validation.

"Reverse Discrimination." A California Superior Court ruled that Los Angeles County Public Library erred in selectively certifying and promoting two minority librarians ahead of several others who scored better on a promotional exam. The decision is being appealed. Meanwhile, other courts have taken different interpretations of what constitutes illegal "reverse discrimination." A New York court determined that the Downstate Medical School could waive certain academic credentials on a temporary and limited basis in order to recruit minority students (*LJ*, June 1, 1976, p. 1246). A district court, however, made just the opposite determination against the Georgetown Law Center in Washington, D.C. (*LJ*, September 15, 1976, p. 1822). The Supreme Court chose to avoid ruling on "reverse bias" in 1974 when it judged the *Defunis Case* "moot" on the basis that the plaintiff had gained admittance and had graduated from the University of Washington Law School by the time the case got to the high court. Justice Douglas in that case, however, filed an opinion that "reverse discrimination" may not be tolerated unless the courts have required a "race-conscious" program in order to rectify past discrimination. Again, more guidance is needed from the Supreme Court to resolve the dilemma.

Libraries should not use "reverse discrimination" as an excuse to avoid the development of sound affirmative action programs. There is much that can be done to create workable plans that will never involve an institution in a reverse bias suit. These action programs include the validation of selection, promotion, and performance evaluation procedures to assure that they are bias-free and job-related; widened recruitment efforts to include news media, professional and community groups, and academic programs that are directed toward women and minorities; evaluation of library building design to make sure that there are no barriers to the handicapped; staff workshops which acquaint all levels of staff with affirmative action's purpose and goals; and many other related activities. Karl Nyren concluded in an "LJ Skirmish Line" report on "reverse bias" (April 15, 1976), "the cry of 'reverse discrimination' . . . should never be raised against an affirmative action policy that is properly nurtured and brought to maturity in a community or institution that has given it birth."

ACTIVITIES WITHIN THE PROFESSION

The ALA Office for Library Personnel Resources (OLPR) continues to provide leadership in the area of affirmative action. Its Affirmative Action Packet, available for $1, includes citations from state and federal law pertaining to AA, guidelines on preparing a plan, articles on EEO/AA, and minority and women's group recruitment sources. The Office publishes annually the "Survey of Graduates and Faculty From Library Education Programs in the United States Awarding Degrees and Certificates." In November 1976 OLPR cosponsored with the Institute for Manpower Management a seminar on job analysis techniques. Marilyn Salazar, ALA's Minority Recruitment Specialist, has completed a report of the *Illinois Minorities Manpower Project, May 1972–August 1974* (ALA, 1976). This project is an example of effective minority recruitment through the coordinated efforts of community people, state and local libraries, professional associations, and library schools. It should serve as a model for library education recruitment programs in other states.

The Equal Employment Opportunity Subcommittee of ALA published in the July/August 1976 *American Libraries* a checklist of items that it will watch for in reviewing library affirmative action plans. The same issue contains a republication of the ALA policy that mandates the review of library affirmative action plans by the Association. Through November 1976 the EEO Subcommittee had received only nine plans to evaluate, four from public libraries, three from state units, and two from academic libraries.

ALA Council and membership took up several matters relating to affirmative action. At Midwinter 1976 the Legislative Committee reported on its efforts to monitor EEO/AA legislation through ALA's Washington office. The Association gave testimony during the previous year in support of better funding for the U.S. Health, Education and Welfare Department's affirmative action enforcement efforts. At the Annual Conference, Council approved the inclusion of a check-off for the Minority Scholarship on the membership renewal form. It also passed a resolution (Council Document #83) calling for an action program to "combat racism and sexism in the library profession and in library service" through awareness training surveys and programs and through revisions of sex- or race-biased cataloging practices.

The Public Library Association sponsored workshops on affirmative action during its "Idea Exchange" at the ALA Annual Conference. At least one state group, the Michigan Library Association, also sponsored sessions on affirmative action at its annual conference. Low attendance at affirmative action programs and the scarcity of plans that have been received by the ALA Equal Employment Opportunity Subcommittee are signs that librarians view this as a highly specialized, somewhat mysterious and confusing area that does not directly apply to them. But all *are* affected. Virtually all libraries are covered under the Title VII of the Civil Rights Act as amended that prohibits discrimination on the basis of race, color, sex, religion, national origin, age, or handicap. While not all libraries or their governing institutions are required to write action plans to implement equal employment opportunity, written plans provide a good insurance policy for library administrators and their staffs against discriminatory practices or civil rights suits. — ELIZABETH DICKINSON

Personnel and Employment: Performance Appraisal

If the assumption is made that the performance appraisal system within a library exists to assist in the improvement of individual and organizational performance, then one can point to a number of recent developments that show libraries are making significant progress in this area of personnel management. During the ALA Centennial Conference, the Public Library Association presented a program entitled "Public Libraries and Performance Appraisal." The performance appraisal systems of three major public libraries were reported upon by personnel from each of the three libraries (Prince George's County Memorial Library of Maryland, Brooklyn Public Library, and Baltimore County Public Library).

The system being used at Prince George's County seems to be the most complete and is

Library Director Terence Risko in his office in the new $1,400,000 Bettendorf, Iowa, library. A "flippant remark" to a TV newsman regarding tax money for the new library brought criticism and pressure by an alderman for his dismissal. Under home rule, however, autonomy granted the Library Board left no legal grounds for action by the City Council. An apology by Risko followed, and he retained the support of the Library's Board, whose President noted that Risko had been working day and night to open the library.

worthy of study by all library personnel. Prince George's County library system wanted an appraisal system that was both result and job centered. They wanted to avoid a system that was personality centered with emphasis on effort rather than results. Their system has three main features: (1) a Position Description; (2) Performance Standards; and (3) Delegation of Authority. Each employee working with a supervisor writes a statement relating to his job in each of these three areas. The Position Description is an explanation of what the employee does in performing his duties. The Performance Standards are set and agreed upon by the employee and the supervisor. The Delegation of Authority delineates that area in which the employee is authorized to act without obtaining permission from the superior.

After these three statements have been written and agreed upon, a minimum of two reviews or progress assessments are made each year. During the reviews needed changes in the three statements are assessed. The midyear conference is a formal time set aside for the employee and the supervisor to evaluate together the progress made during the first six months of that year. The results of the year-end review is the only one written up and filed with the Personnel Office.

This system has taken over three years to develop and is reportedly superior to the library's former system. Details on the system with a full example of a Position Description with Performance Standards and the Delegation of Authority are provided in an article prepared for publication by Mary A. Hall.

Performance appraisal systems have been established by academic libraries with results similar to those in public libraries. Such a system is described in a recent publication entitled *Staff Performance Evaluation Program at the McGill University Libraries: A Program Description of a Goals-Based Performance Evaluation Process with Accompanying Supervisor's Manual*. The work was prepared by the Association of Research Libraries, Office of University Library Management Studies, and McGill University Libraries. It is published by the Association of Research Libraries.

Except for Unit Goals and Unit Performance Standards included by McGill, the McGill system is similar to the Prince George's County system in many ways. The standards are developed by each working unit with leadership provided by the unit's supervisor. The Unit Goals are evaluated semiannually. Every individual staff evaluation culminates in the completion of the Annual Performance Evaluation Form. This completed form is the result of the study of a number of worksheets designed for the processes of setting unit and individual goals as well as standards. The form and the worksheets are part of this ARL publication.

The value of these two systems is that they are both excellent models for study and imitation. They are outstanding because, if used correctly, employees will (1) know what is expected of them; (2) know what standards are being used to judge their performance; and (3) will get regular feedback from their supervisors as to their progress toward the goals of the unit and the library. Each employee, further, has a major role in the development of the goals and standards of the library.

NEAL K. KASKE

Personnel and Employment: Staff Development

Library staff development programs are emerging as an important response to the financial pressures faced by libraries. As service needs increase and fiscal resources decline, full use of staff capabilities and potential become essential. Well-trained personnel are needed to exploit technological innovation. The growing complexity of library operations requires more sophisticated managerial techniques. Full use of new media requires special skills. Simultaneously, stable or reduced budgets require that maintenance of current programs or introduction of new training activities result in concrete benefits. In view of these demands, many libraries are cautiously introducing staff development as a critical first step toward improving library performance.

TRENDS

Skill Identification. The dilemma posed by current financial pressures has influenced some of the directions library staff development may take in the future. For example, as a preliminary stage in manpower planning and program design, many libraries are attempting to identify skills needed for library programs. The introduction of machine-based bibliographic search services in libraries is normally preceded by a study of the staff requirements and the availability of particular skills. Resulting staffing patterns and training programs reflect the unique requirements of machine-based information services.

Management Techniques. A second trend is the increasing emphasis on training in human resource management techniques. Behavioral science research demonstrates improvement in library performance is possible through greater involvement of individual staff in library decision-making processes, development of better interpersonal skills, creation of working climates emphasizing mutual trust, shared commitment, and clear goals; sufficient organizational concern with individuals' interest, goals, and needs; and more extensive use of small groups as problem-solving and decision-making bodies.

Experimentation. A third trend is experimentation with contemporary educational methodologies in staff development programs. Training and continuing education programs are adopting adult learning models and instructional laboratory settings in which students become active participants in defining and conducting the learning process. At the Management Skills Institute conducted by the ARL's Office of University Library Management Studies, for example, participants identified problems and then formed task forces to share ideas and develop solutions.

NATIONWIDE EFFORTS

All levels of the library profession appear concerned with improving library staff development activities. A new national organization, CLENE (the Continuing Library Education Network and Exchange), has been established. State agencies are investing resources in the design and operation of training activities. Regional and local groups are working together to deal with common concerns. And individual libraries are establishing formal organizational positions for training officers. The following comments highlight activities within the several levels of the profession.

Efforts on the part of the U.S. Office of Education and various national organizations provide direction, guidelines, and models for staff development programs. In addition, governmental and foundation funding encourage experimentation, innovation, and pluralism in the development of improved programs.

Financial resources for a number of Office of Education training programs were provided through Title II, Part-B of the Higher Education Act or from the Library Services and Construction Act. Special emphases of these grants were on upgrading the skills of minority staff and enhancing skills needed to provide more effective service to the physically handicapped, economically disadvantaged, and the institutionalized.

CLR Programs. The Council on Library Resources, Inc., supports several programs designed to upgrade managerial and professional capabilities. The CLR Fellowship Program, initiated in 1969, allowed over 180 midcareer librarians to pursue self-developed study projects in substantive, administrative, and technical aspects of librarianship. CLR fellows utilized a leave of absence to research a range of topics, including bibliographic control in England, space planning for government documents, and the role of state commissions in the development of libraries. The Council's Academic Library Management Intern Program, initiated in 1969, was designed to assist in the development of skilled managers for academic libraries. In 1976 five interns worked closely with high-level academic library administrators to observe their techniques in dealing with daily managerial problems and to participate in the decision-making processes. The Council, recognizing libraries' need for greater subject expertise, approached this problem in two ways. Its Advanced Study Program, initiated in 1975, enabled five librarians to pursue full-time graduate course work in scholarly programs. The University of Chicago Library Program for Ph.D.'s was initiated in 1974 to encourage nonlibrarians holding doctoral degrees to enter the library profession. It involved CLR's support of a University of Chicago program leading to a master's degree in library science for these specialists.

CLENE. 1976 was the first full year of operation for CLENE. The significance of this new organization lies in its potential to stimulate fresh approaches to continuing education, while coordinating activities throughout the country and assuring quality in the training programs made available to libraries. Its two assemblies and continuing education fairs provided vehicles for librarians to share experiences, ideas, and expert knowledge. CLENE's first year of operation also resulted in the creation of a permanent administrative structure, methods for assessing continuing education needs, and the communication channels necessary to collect and disseminate information. CLENE received funding for projects to design a model recognition system for continuing education and to operate an extended institute to train state library agency personnel. CLENE secures support from almost 500 individual members, 15 organizational members, 15 state agencies, and the U.S. Office of Education.[1]

ARL

Operation of a training program at the Association of Research Libraries' Office of University Library Management Studies (OMS) illustrates the priority that staff development is becoming for the larger library organization. The Management Review and Analysis Program (MRAP), designed to furnish research libraries with guidelines to perform an internal study and evaluation of their management policies and activities, is an example of this training commitment. By the end of 1976 23 libraries had examined organizational, supervisory, and staff development practices within this procedure. In addition, the Office operated three Management Skills Institutes during the year, provided training films and resources to member libraries, and sponsored research to improve library training capabilities.[2]

ALA

The ALA Committee on Staff Development, chaired by John DePew at Florida State University, provided another example of profes-

Personnel and Employment: Staff Development

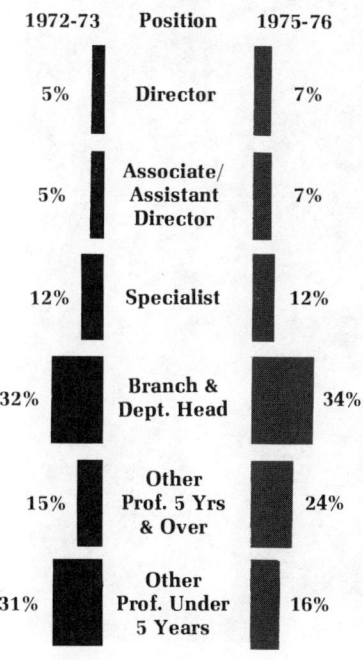

Distribution of Professional Library Staff by Position 1972-73 & 1975-76

1972-73	Position	1975-76
5%	Director	7%
5%	Associate/Assistant Director	7%
12%	Specialist	12%
32%	Branch & Dept. Head	34%
15%	Other Prof. 5 Yrs & Over	24%
31%	Other Prof. Under 5 Years	16%

Source: ARL Annual Salary Survey 1975–76

C. Lamar Wallis, Memphis Public Library Director, introduces speakers at the Library's Staff Institute Day program in November 1976.

sional concern in 1976. This committee advances staff development primarily through the dissemination of information and the provision of workshops. The Committee is re-evaluating its objectives in view of national developments and new continuing education efforts. The Committee prepared a bibliography and a directory of staff development activities. It presents in *Special Libraries* bibliographies of materials relevant to staff development.[3]

The Committee on Staff Development in Large Research Libraries, an informal discussion group, met twice in 1976. Its major interests were on improving methods of needs assessment and in developing a collection of materials describing staff development programs in participating libraries. The Committee, chaired by Sheila Creth (University of Connecticut Library), also distributed a news sheet to participants describing various staff development activities in research libraries. Another important Committee activity was the preparation of a position paper on the role of staff development in academic libraries as a cost-effective dimension of library operations.

REGIONAL EFFORTS

Networks and consortiums frequently serve as liaisons or communication links between national and local efforts. These regional organizations are sensitive to local needs and can translate national resources into activities beneficial to a large portion of their own memberships.

Under Peggy O'Donnell's direction the Southwestern Library Association's (SWLA) Continuing Education for Library Staffs (CELS) produced on-demand workshops throughout the Southwestern Region. An example of these was "Developing Skills in Planning Library Programs." CELS also developed and distributed audio cassettes of journal article abstracts. The Western Interstate Commission for Higher Education's (WICHE) Library Program, now called WILCO (Western Interstate Library Coordinating Organization), completed its Office of Education-Funded "Institute for Training in Staff Development" series and published the project's final report in June 1976.[5] These institutes guided participants through the necessary steps for planning library staff development programs. WILCO is also building a network of training and development personnel in the Western United States. WILCO's Western Continuing Education Exchange (WESTEX) operates in cooperation with CLENE, gathering and exchanging information on continuing education resources.

The Cooperative Information Network (CIN) in California produced a number of workshops and training modules with special emphasis on reference skills. CIN also provided workshops on planning and evaluation in libraries and operated a series of 20 communication workshops for public service staff. Some of CIN's staff development efforts have also been directed toward providing programs specifically for support staff.[6] The New England Library Board, headed by Mary McKenzee, implemented a Library Interchange Program which involves the exchange of staff among participating libraries in that region for a period of two weeks for the purpose of familiarizing staff with alternative practices in other libraries.

STATE EFFORTS

State agencies continued to strengthen their roles as staff development sponsors and catalysts. Libraries frequently consulted with these agencies for advice on developing their own programs and to learn about existing resources in the state. The Illinois State Library Agency worked with library schools, the state association, and system managers to provide staff development programs designed for specific groups of personnel. The State Library also coordinated various state-supported staff development programs and published *Continuations*, a newsletter listing opportunities for library staff and trustee development throughout Illinois and the country. The Missouri State Library built a video tape collection to be used for staff development purposes throughout the state. The Michigan State Library encouraged the use of the continuing education units (C.E.U.). That State Library also provided programs for library trustees and for librarians working in institutional settings.

LOCAL EFFORTS

An emerging role for individual libraries is providing access to training programs developed regionally or nationally and communicating local staff training needs to the designers of programs.

A number of libraries operated some sort of staff development effort, either by collaborating with other organizations or on an individual basis. Columbia University, for example, conducted a staff development needs assessment during the early part of 1976 to define areas requiring development. Joyce Veenstra, Columbia University Libraries' training officer, reported that the assessment would result in a management seminar in early 1977. Faith Harders at the University of Kentucky Library reported a series of monthly programs to introduce staff to new and existing services and operations, such as the on-line bibliographic data base. The library also sponsored a management program developed by the University of Kentucky. The McGill University Libraries, directed by Marianne Scott, collaborated with the Association of Research Libraries' Office of University Library Management Studies in designing a goals-based performance evaluation program. The program included supervisory training designed to facilitate the implementation of the evaluation program.[7]

ISSUES

Library staff development has been widely accepted as a necessary investment. If the investment is to dramatically improve library services, then several issues must be confronted. One issue centers around the development of precise performance objectives. If the purpose of staff development activities is to enhance staffs' performance, these objectives need to be more precisely defined. The identification of desired results is especially useful for evaluating training programs in terms of their value to the library. As libraries increasingly depend upon outside organizations and private consulting firms to supply training materials, assessment of these materials by qualified experts will be needed.

Another issue of concern is coordinating internal staff development activities. Needs assessment, the development of career paths, performance evaluation, and training opportunities should be integrated into a total staff development program. A final issue is expanding support and commitment to staff development from all levels of the library profession. This commitment is needed in the form of financial resources, improved coordination and communication among various groups, and an increased willingness to try new approaches. A first step in gaining this commitment, however, lies in demonstrating the staff training programs contribute to superior library service.

DUANE E. WEBSTER;
NANCY I. ZEIDNER

REFERENCES

1. Elizabeth W. Stone, "Final Report on Planning for the Continuing Education Network and Exchange (CLENE)" (Washington, D.C.: Graduate Department of Library Science, The Catholic University of America, 1976), pp. 1-6.
2. Duane E. Webster, "The Management Review and Analysis Program: An Assisted Self-Study to Secure Constructive Change in the Management of Research Libraries," *College & Research Libraries* (March 1974), pp. 114-125.
3. "Staff Development" is the name of the column under which the bibliographies appear in *Special Libraries* on a quarterly basis.
4. Association of Research Libraries, Office of University Library Management Studies, "Fifth Annual Report" (Washington, D.C.: Association of Research Libraries, Office of University Library Management Studies, 1975).
5. Final Report of WICHE/USOE Institute for Training in Staff Development (Boulder: Western Interstate Commission for Higher Education, June 1976).
6. Esta Lee Albright, "CIN Staff Development Project: Summary" (Stanford: Stanford University, 1976).
7. McGill University Libraries and Association of Research Libraries, Office of University Library Management Studies, "Staff Performance Evaluation Program at the McGill University Libraries" (Washington, D.C.: Association of Research Libraries, Office of University Library Management Studies, 1976).

Personnel and Employment: Job Market

The job market for professional librarians continued to tighten in 1976. While there was growth in employment, it was not sufficient to compensate for major reductions in staff caused by budgetary constraints. Major public libraries such as Detroit, Queens Borough (New York), and Brooklyn were forced to lay off both professional and support staff during 1976. Others handled cutbacks through attrition, freezing positions as they became vacant.

One major employer, the Chicago Public Library, was forced to impose a freeze for a unique reason. The city's revenue sharing funds, including the library's share, were tied up in federal court because of alleged discriminatory hiring practices in the police department. Regardless of the cause, the result was no money for jobs.

Public libraries were not the only ones hit. Trenton State College in New Jersey reduced its professional librarian staff by two-thirds when its book budget was cut in half. The University of Denver lost 10 of its 24 librarians. Many school districts presented voters a choice of increased taxes or the elimination of "extras" such as athletics, band programs, and libraries. In many of these communities, residents felt they could not absorb the additional taxes. The result, then, is a greater burden on an already strained public library.

Supply. There are indications that the supply of librarians is not increasing as rapidly as anticipated. In the annual survey of placements and salaries of graduates of ALA-accredited programs ("Placements & Salaries 1975: A Difficult Year." *Library Journal*, July 1976) Carol Learmont and Richard Darling noted that

Source: ARL Annual Salary Survey, 1975-76

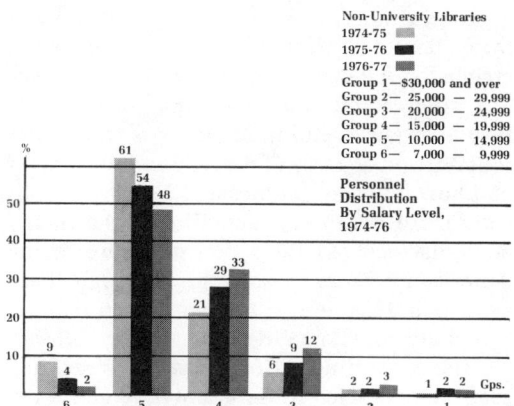

Personnel and Employment: Job Market

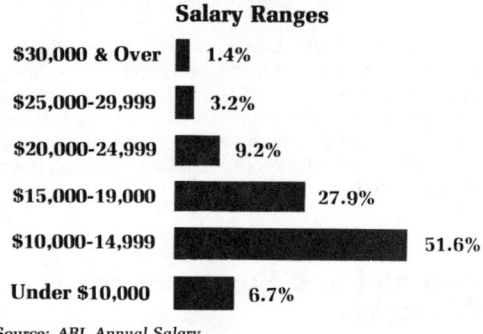

Salary Ranges
- $30,000 & Over — 1.4%
- $25,000-29,999 — 3.2%
- $20,000-24,999 — 9.2%
- $15,000-19,000 — 27.9%
- $10,000-14,999 — 51.6%
- Under $10,000 — 6.7%

Source: ARL Annual Salary Survey 1975–76

there were fewer graduates in 1975 than in the previous year. The average number of graduates per class had dropped from 123 in 1974 to 120.

Library schools are now practicing truth in advertising. Catalogs almost always explain that the job market is anywhere from tight to uncertain and that employment requires flexibility and mobility. Some schools have been using a statement prepared by ALA's Office for Library Personnel Resources based upon the Bureau of Labor Statistics study issued in 1975. Although it is now required of all professional schools participating in the federal guaranteed student loan program, only a few catalogs have actual placement figures for previous classes. (See also Education, Library.)

In an attempt to resolve the tightness of the job market from the job seeker's view, the District of Columbia Library Association considered a resolution calling for a moratorium in the granting of accreditation to library science programs. Such a proposal has not been considered by the ALA. It is the position of the ALA Committee on Accreditation that it is not a proper function of an accrediting agency to attempt to control entry into a profession by denying accreditation to programs which meet established standards. It is the prerogative of the school to determine the number of students admitted to a program. The school, however, has a responsibility to provide job market information to prospective students. (See also Accreditation.)

Placement Programs. To assist library schools to meet their placement obligations, the staff of the ALA Office for Library Personnel Resources (OLPR) participated in placement programs in approximately 10 schools throughout the United States. The programs enabled students to obtain comprehensive information about the library job market and how to be successful in it. Students were given literature on sources of placement information and how to write resumes and letters of application. An additional benefit was that many students received their first exposure to the American Library Association through these programs. This helped to assure them that the profession was concerned about their welfare.

After examining various modes of providing placement service to librarians, the OLPR developed a prototype of a computerized service. The model was based upon the service being offered as a U.S. Department of Labor demonstration by the National Registry for Agricultural Economists, a companion service of the National Registry for Librarians. At its fall meeting in 1976, the ALA Executive Board voted to ask the Department of Labor to consider the development of the National Registry for Librarians into such a computerized placement service.

Professionalism Issues. Fear of a declining job market led a group of middle management librarians in Los Angeles and Orange Counties in California to form Concerned Librarians Opposing Unprofessional Trends (CLOUT). CLOUT charges that volunteers and clerical workers are taking over library tasks that require the advanced training of a master's degree. They claim that this practice is both detrimental to library service and dangerous to the professional interests of degreed librarians.

At the same time, libraries are boasting of how they are saving money using volunteers. While most volunteers are limited to serving at library functions, pushing book carts, and clipping newspapers, others are performing professional duties such as reader advisory service.

Libraries also continued the trend toward promoting paraprofessional employees into librarian positions. While no major libraries announced changes in selection criteria as they had in 1975, the West Virginia Library Commission began a two-week, 70-hour course to upgrade the skills of non-degreed librarians. Originally designed for librarians in small and isolated rural communities, the program was expanded to accommodate all unqualified librarians.

There continues to be pressure upon the American Library Association to step into this situation. Attempts to create a division dealing strictly with the needs of professional librarians failed at the 1976 Midwinter Meeting. Other than editing out sexist language, the Council agreed with the OLPR Advisory Committee that the Library Education and Manpower Policy did not need substantive change.

Meanwhile, discussion continues on the subject of certifying librarians through equivalency or proficiency testing. Certification is already in use by the Medical Library Association and the American Association of Law Libraries. To have any significant impact, such a program would have to be developed by the ALA on a national level.

It is, perhaps, ironic that at a workshop conducted by the Council on Library Technical Assistants, LTAs were concerned about nonprofessional clerical employees assuming responsibilities which require the specialized training that LTAs have. They were also afraid that their jobs were jeopardized by employees who would work for less money.

Court Decisions. The U.S. Supreme Court played a major role in personnel administration in 1976. Hearing several cases pertaining to the discharge of public employees, the Court held that permanent employees have no constitutional right to pretermination hearings (*Bishop* v. *Wood*); it was not unconstitutional to require the retirement of state police officers at age 50 (*Massachusetts Board of Retirement* v. *Murgia*); and that a sheriff may be enjoined from firing patronage employees who were not affiliated or sponsored by a particular political party (*Elrod* v. *Burns*). In another discharge case (*McDonald* v. *Santa Fe Trail Transportation Co.*), the Court held that both Title VII of the 1964 Civil Rights Act and Section 1981 of the Civil Rights Act of 1866 protect white persons as well as nonwhites, thereby allowing suits alleging "reverse discrimination."

After already deciding that state and local governments could not deprive persons of jobs on the basis of their lack of U.S. citizenship, the Court extended that protection to employment with the federal government (*Hampton* v. *Mow Sun Wong*). The Court held that the Civil Service Commission lacked the authority to impose such a restriction, reserving it only to Congress and the President. The effect of this decision was short lived, however, as President Ford, within a matter of weeks, ordered the Civil Service Commission to hire only U.S. citizens.

The decision with the greatest effect upon public employment concerned the 1974 amendment to the Fair Labor Standards Act (*National League of Cities* v. *Usery*). The amendment extended minimum-wage and overtime protection to virtually all employees of government agencies. The greatest effect would be upon student pages in public libraries and all student employees in college and university libraries, who would now be eligible for the minimum wage. In striking down this amendment, the Court ruled that the states' rights doctrine precluded federal involvement in this area. It is expected that this same argument will be used to defeat any federal legislation in the area of public employee collective bargaining or pensions.

Another Supreme Court decision affecting many library employees is the controversial determination that employers who offer medical insurance to employees may exclude coverage for pregnancy without being guilty of sex discrimination (*Gilbert* v. *General Electric*). While employers were spared the decision of adding maternity coverage at greatly increased premiums or terminating their insurance programs altogether, various women's and civil rights groups were mobilized to seek legislation that would void the Court's action.

BARRY E. SIMON

Preservation of Library Materials

The ever increasing awareness by librarians of their responsibilities for the physical care of books and that preservation of collections is an inseparable part of library management continued in 1976. In July at the Centennial Conference of the American Library Association, the Preservation of Library Materials Committee sponsored a program on "Preserving the National Heritage: The Administration of Library Conservation Activities," at which a large and enthusiastic attendance testified to the growing awareness within the profession of this important area. The ALA Preservation Committee's meetings have become an important forum for the exchange of information on preservation and for stimulating interest in the subject as a whole.

Preservation Conferences. In April the library schools of Columbia and Rutgers Universities jointly sponsored one-day conferences (given on successive days at each school) entitled "Books in Peril: A Conference on the Preservation of Library Materials" and covering the causes of deterioration and preventive measures and strategies for organizing and administering a comprehensive preservation program within a library.

In December in Chicago, the Newberry Library and the American Association for State and Local History jointly sponsored a seminar on the conservation of paper. Investigated in depth were the philosophy and management aspects of preservation as well as treatment of materials.

Courses in conservation administration are now a regular part of the curricula at the graduate schools of library science at the University of Chicago (conducted by Richard D. Smith) and at the University of Rhode Island (conducted by Robert Morrison, Director of Education, New England Document Conservation Center). The University of Hawaii's Graduate School of Library Studies offered for the first time in 1976 a course, "Introduction to Library Conservation," conducted by Gerald Lundeen. Other courses are offered at Wayne State University, Department of Library Science (Ed Gilbert); Columbia University School of Library Service taught alternately by Susan Thompson and Paul Banks); and at the University of Illinois, Graduate School of Library Science (every other summer, Banks).

Since 1970 it has been a requirement for successful completion of Josephine Fang's course in library technical services at Simmons College School of Library Science for students to spend at least one day in the preservation workshops at the New England Document Conservation Center to become aware of some of the problems of book preservation and their solutions.

The Association of Law Librarians at their

Preservation of Library Materials

annual meeting in Cambridge, Massachusetts, in June devoted part of their program to the preservation and conservation of legal materials. The paper presented on that subject (*Preservation and Conservation of Legal Materials*) was published in the *Law Library Journal*, vol. 69, no. 3, in August 1976.

LC Preservation Conference. The highlight of the year in library conservation was the planning conference convened by the Library of Congress December 16–17. There for two days representatives from all categories of libraries and library associations, the scientific community, professional conservators, and representatives from public and private foundations reviewed with the Librarian of Congress and his principal assistants for perservation the scope of the problem and proposed solutions. The consensus of the meeting was that there is an urgent requirement for a national library conservation program under the direction of the Library of Congress and administered through regional cooperative conservation centers strategically located about the country. As the next step, Frazer Poole, the Assistant Director for Preservation, designated by the Librarian of Congress to coordinate the effort, was to establish steering committees to initiate action along the lines agreed upon by the conference participants.

The 1976 Professional Enhancement Seminar for the Case Western Reserve Libraries staffs on June 3, 4, and 5 in Cambridge, Ohio, was devoted solely to the study of the management aspects of library conservation. Under the direction of conservators and technicians from the New England Document Conservation Center, professional and non-professional staff members of that university's several libraries studied the causes and effects of deterioration; measures to prevent damage by improving environmental and storage conditions; and investigated those repair and restoration techniques considered suitable for in-house treatment.

In September consecutive two-day seminars on conservation administration were sponsored by the Western Interstate Library Coordinating Organization (WILCO) in Burlingame, California, and Denver. Although intended primarily for the enlightenment of WILCO's membership, these meetings, again conducted by the New England Document Conservation Center conservators, drew participants from the Midwest, the Southeastern U.S., and the Gulf Coast. Based on the interest of the attendees in cooperative conservation, the Executive Director of WILCO initiated action to investigate further the feasibility of the establishment of regional conservation centers to serve the needs of public and private libraries in the Mountain States and on the West Coast. Similarly, the Director of Libraries at Case Western Reserve created a task force to examine the practicability of a conservation center for the CWR libraries that would also serve as a regional center for states bordering Ohio.

OAS Activities. The Organization of American States is supporting a regional workshop for library and archives conservation to serve the needs of the Central American countries and the Caribbean Islands. The Centro Taller Regional de Restauracion y Microfilmacion de Documentos para El Caribe y Centro America, located in the Archives of the Dominican Republic in Santo Domingo, in the beginning is emphasizing the training of technicians from member countries in modern methods for book and document repair as a first step in a long-range program.

During the Third Brazilian Congress on Archival Sciences in Rio de Janeiro from October 17–22, the Social Sciences Documentation Group's Subgroup on Preservation and Restoration sponsored a two-day seminar on the preservation of books and documents. The sponsors hope that this will be only the first step in what will ultimately become a national program for library and archives conservation in Brazil.

Other Activities. The Cellulose, Paper and Textile Division of the American Chemical Society at the Society's annual meeting in San Francisco in late August addressed itself to the problems of paper preservation. Panels discussed the permanence of paper of historic and artistic value, the stabilization of paper, and paper repair and support. The lectures by experts in each of these fields, scheduled to be published as a book by the American Chemical Society in mid-1977, will be of interest to library administrators and others concerned with the care of books and documents.

The University of California Libraries have established a task force to examine all aspects of library administration including the management aspects of conservation. Current thinking by members of that task force is that two conservation centers will be established to meet the needs of the libraries on the nine campuses of that university.

In March the Library Binding Institute sponsored a conservation workshop at Osgood Hill, Boston University's Study Center in North Andover, Massachusetts. The meeting, conducted for LBI by the New England Document Conservation Center, was attended by librarians and library binders from throughout the eastern half of the United States. Other conservation workshops with emphasis on quality book production and rebinding were sponsored by LBI in May in Greensboro, North Carolina, and by the LBI and the Art Libraries Society/Southern California Chapter in Pico Rivera, California. These three production workshops were examples of the growing awareness of the need for more understanding by library management of the mechanics of book production and other structural factors influencing the life of a book. It is important to note that the Library Binding Institute in 1976 established a Book Testing Laboratory at the Rochester Institute of Technology's School of Printing. This laboratory will be used to educate graphic arts students on how books, particularly library bound volumes, are bound. The laboratory will also be used in connection with LBI's research and quality control programs and workshops for bindery employees and others interested in prolonging the useful life of books. The laboratory, the property of RIT, will also establish a library on binding techniques and materials and with funds provided by the binding industry, set up a program of lectures on binding and related subjects. (See *also* Binding.)

Deacidification Experiments. While the benefits of "conventional" aqueous deacidification methods using calcium or magnesium bicarbonates are well established, aqueous methods require disassembly of bound books and thus are not economically feasible for mass treatment. The W. J. Barrow Research Laboratory in Richmond, Virginia, developed a morpholene process for the deacidification of whole books; a pilot program was in operation in 1976 at the Virginia State Library in Richmond. Development in this vapor-phase treatment, which can neutralize acid in books placed 30 at one time in a vacuum chamber designed for that purpose, is being followed with much interest by professional conservators. Followed with equal interest is the development at the Library of Congress of a mass method for deacidification of books using the chemical diethyl zinc. Although highly toxic, flammable, and explosive, only safe to use in vacuum chambers operated by highly skilled technicians, the use of this vapor phase technique will be warranted if it is possible to someday deacidify large numbers of books at one time.

A less exotic method and less efficient but still effective process for deacidifying whole books is by spray deacidification using the chemical methyl magnesium carbonate developed and patented by the Research Laboratory at the Library of Congress. This chemical reacts with acid in paper as do sprayable magnesium methoxide solutions (Wei T'o) increasing the pH to a neutral or slightly alkaline state and at the same time depositing buffering carbonates to inhibit new acid contamination at a later date.

The Library of Congress has also patented and released for general use an aqueous deacidification technique based on the use of solutions of calcium and ammonium carbonates to deacidify and buffer paper that can be immersed in water for treatment.

Strengthening Brittle Pages. Next in importance to methods for the mass deacidification

At Dallas Public Library, Helen Barbour hangs magazines for drying after a broken water pipe damaged books and periodicals on five levels of the building in 1976.

of books is the requirement for a process for the mass treatment of books to increase the folding strength of pages embrittled by acid. During 1976, Richard Smith continued his work on that problem as part of his work for the Public Archives of Canada on the development of a non-aqueous method for mass deacidification.

Barrow Preservation Research, Inc., is presently working on a project for strengthening brittle book pages with cellulose-reactive dialdehydes or monomers such as butadiene or acrylonitrile. BPRI has in the laboratory increased the fold strength of single pages (one-at-a-time) as much as ten times (1–5 folds to 20–50 folds) for an estimated additional lifetime of 10–50 years. BPRI considers it possible to accomplish a comparable improvement on whole books (five or more at a time) by a vapor-phase application to paper of the cellulose-reactive chemicals in chambers designed originally for mass deacidification of whole books. The ultimate objective of BPRI is to be able to load a vacuum chamber with 75 to 100 books and in a single operation (or two separate operations in close sequence) deacidify and buffer the acid pages and at the same time significantly increase the strength of the acid-embrittled paper.

PUBLICATIONS

There still remains an urgent requirement for a library and archives conservation journal or bulletin that will publish regularly, frequently, and accurately the results of investigations and developments in the nature of library materials; the causes and effects of damage to these materials; new and improved methods of environment control; and advances in repair and restoration techniques, for the information of conservation administrators as well as conservators and conservation technicians. Until that time, workers in the field must be content with having to obtain this information from many sources, often long after the studies leading to the published information are completed. Librarians should be aware of and obtain as they become available, the series of pamphlets and leaflets being prepared by the Preservation Office of the Library of Congress on various aspects of book repair and restoration. Three of these (*Selected References in the Literature of Conservation; Environmental Protection of Books and Related Materials;* and *Preserving Leather Bookbindings*) were available at year's end.

Extensive Topic Coverage. *Library Security Newsletter* (Haworth Press) expanded its coverage to include many preservation topics and added a very useful "abstracts" section alerting LSN readers to useful articles on preservation in other periodicals. *Microform Review* (April 1976) published an article by Pamela Darling (Head of the Preservation Department at Columbia University Libraries) on "Microforms in Libraries; Preservation and Storage" discussing the criteria for the conversion of printed library materials to microforms as an alternative to preservation by other means. Every issue of *Library Scene* published by the Library Binding Institute has informative articles on bookbinding for conservation. Volume 5, no. 2 (June 1976), for instance, has an important article on "The Physical Protection of Brittle and Deteriorating Documents" by Frazer Poole. Poole's article is only one of five significant discussions in that issue.

Two issues of *Art Dealer and Framer* (November and December 1976) contain articles by Richard Smith on paper deacidification. Although written primarily for those concerned with works of art on paper, they are of much interest to librarians.

The January 1976 *Journal of Academic Librarianship* contains an article by Karen Lee Shelley, "The Future of Conservation in Research Libraries," which describes the need for conservation programs directed by professional librarians.

The special section on conservation in *Library Journal* (November 15, 1976) entitled "Books in Peril" should be required reading for every member of every library staff. Pamela Darling's article, "A Local Preservation Program: Where to Start," is an excellent step-by-step guide for the establishment of effective conservation programs in-house. Paul Banks in "Cooperative Approaches to Conservation," in the same minisymposium, discusses the pros and cons of regional centers, and Frazer Poole presents a general outline of "The Proposed National Preservation Program of the Library of Congress." Pamela Darling's "Call to Action" expresses the sense of urgency: ". . . if we are going to save most of what we now have, we've got to get moving fast. . . . We cannot afford to do nothing until that glorious day when we know how to do everything perfectly. . . . Preservation . . . is not a field that we can leave to the experts, if we are to rescue the millions of books and other library materials quietly rotting on our shelves" (p. 2343). GEORGE M. CUNHA; STAFF

Principal Libraries of the World

The libraries included in the following listing have been selected on the basis of size, comprehensiveness of collection, and provision of outstanding resources for a particular location.

Biblioteca Apostolica Vaticana
Vatican City State, founded 1475
TYPE: serves Vatican
NUMBER OF ITEMS IN COLLECTION: 65,000 ms.; 130,000 archival files; 100,000 engravings; 7,000 incunabula; 900,000 other vols.
SPECIAL COLLECTIONS: Dukes of Urbino (1690); Queen Christina of Sweden (1690); Florentine Marquis Capponi (1745); Barberini (1902); Chigi (1923); Greek Bible of 4th c.; Vergils of 4th and 6th c.; 4–5 copies of palimpsest of Cicero's *Republic*; autographs of St. Thomas Aquinas, Tasso, Petrarch, Boccaccio, Poliziano, Michaelangelo and Luther
PUBLICATIONS: *Studi e Testi; Edizioni Illustrate Cataloghi*

Biblioteca Nacionale
Madrid, Spain, founded 1712
TYPE: national library
NUMBER OF ITEMS IN COLLECTION: 2,173,000 vols.; 26,122 vols. of mss.; 3,000 incunabula; 45,000 rare books, prints, music, maps, reviews
SPECIAL COLLECTIONS: Theology; cannon law; history

Aerial view and reading room, Biblioteca Nacionale, Madrid.

Bibliotheca Nazionale Centrale
Florence, Italy, founded 1747

TYPE: state library; copyright library

NUMBER OF ITEMS IN COLLECTION: 4,000,000 vols. and pamphlets; 24,000 mss.; 4,000 incunabula

SPECIAL COLLECTIONS: Codes of Dante and other Italian authors; Galileo collection of more than 300 mss.; autographs of Boccaccio. Machiavelli; Alfieri; Leopardi, and others

PUBLICATIONS: *Bibliografia Nazionale Italiano; Catalogo Alfabetico Annuale*

Bibliothèque Nationale
Paris, France, founded 1480

TYPE: national library; copyright library

NUMBER OF ITEMS IN COLLECTION: 7,000,000 vols.; 155,000 mss.; 450,000 medals and coins; 940,000 musical documents; 6,000,000 prints and engravings; 500,000 titles of periodicals; 800,000 maps

SPECIAL COLLECTIONS: Art; bibliography; biography; directories and address books; encyclopedias and dictionaries; history; law and jurisprudence; literature; philogy and linguistics; music; philosophy; poetry; psychology; religion; travel; geography; maps

PUBLICATIONS: *Bibliographie de la France; Bulletin des Bibliothèques de France,* containing the *Bulletin de Documentation bibliographique*

Bibliotheque Royale Albert I
Brussels, Belgium, founded 1837

TYPE: national library; copyright library

NUMBER OF ITEMS IN COLLECTION: 3,000,000 vols.; 18,000 periodicals; 35,000 mss.; 35,650 rare printed books; 700,000 prints, 100,000 maps; 160,100 coins and medals

PUBLICATIONS: *Bibliographie de Belgique; Belgica Selecta*

British Library
London, England, founded 1753

TYPE: national library; copyright library

NUMBER OF ITEMS IN COLLECTION: 9,500,000 printed books; 75,000 Western mss.; 30,000 Oriental mss.; 100,000 charters and rolls; 18,000 seals and casts of seals; 3,000 Greek and Latin papyri

SPECIAL COLLECTIONS: *Codex Alexandrinus; Codex Sinaiticuss* of the Bible; collection of Greek papyri from Egypt; manuscript collections (Sir Robert Cotton and Robert Harley); Lindisfarne Gospels; illuminated mss.; Sanskrit mss.; Hebrew mss.

SPECIAL CAPABILITIES: Combines comprehensive library with museum of antiquities

PUBLICATIONS: *British National Bibliography; British Museum; Department of Printed Books; General Catalogue of Printed Books; The British Library Journal*

Chicago Public Library
Chicago, Illinois, founded 1872

TYPE: public library

NUMBER OF ITEMS IN COLLECTION: 5,579,128 vols.

SPECIAL COLLECTIONS: Civil War; early English and American periodicals; Franco-German war proclamations and broadsides; North American Indian; Western travel; World's Columbian Exposition, Chicago, 1893; Aaron Montgomery Ward Environmental and Ecology Collection; patent collection; Vivian G. Harsh Collection on Afro-American History and Literature

Columbia University Libraries
New York, New York, founded 1754

TYPE: university library

NUMBER OF ITEMS IN COLLECTION: 4,500,000 vols.

SPECIAL COLLECTIONS: Architecture; East Asian collection; Columbiana

SPECIAL CAPABILITIES: Participates in New York State Interlibrary Loan Network and METRO (Metropolitan Reference and Research Library Agency)

Cornell University Libraries
Ithaca, New York, founded 1865

TYPE: university library

NUMBER OF ITEMS IN COLLECTION: 4,300,000 vols.

SPECIAL COLLECTIONS: American Civil War; American history; Assyriology; Botany; Brazil; China and Southeast Asia (Wason); Cornelliana; Fiske Dante Collection; dramatic literature; Egyptology; English and French Revolutions; Freemasonry; German-American relations (Faust); German literature and philogy (Zarnache); history of superstition and witchcraft; human relations area files; Fiske Icelandic Collection; Joyce; Kipling; Marquis de Lafayette (10,000 letters, mss., and documents); languages and literature; Lavoisier; legal trials; Lewis; Napoleon; Nathan; ornithology; Hamilton Wyndham Pascal Collection; Fiske Petrarch Collection; philosophy; Réformation; Fiske Rhaeto-Romantic Collection; Theodore Roosevelt; Bernard Shaw; May Antislavery Collection; Spinoza; Tarkington; Wordsworth

Deutsche Staatsbibliothek
Berlin, German Democratic Republic, founded 1661

TYPE: national library

NUMBER OF ITEMS IN COLLECTION: 5,237,679 vols.; 37,212 periodicals

PUBLICATIONS: *Berliner Titeldrucke; Jahresberichte der Deutschen Staatsbibliothek; Zeitschriften bestandsverzeichnisse; Gesamtkatalog de Wiegendrucke; Zentralkatalog der DDR; Zeitschriften und Serien des Auslands*

Harvard University Library
Cambridge, Massachusetts, founded 1638

TYPE: university library

NUMBER OF ITEMS IN COLLECTION: 9,028,385 vols.

SPECIAL COLLECTIONS: John Keats and his circle (Keats Memorial Collection); theatre collection; printing and graphic arts; Theodore Roosevelt Collection; Windsor Memorial Map Room; Woodberry Poetry Room; Harry Elkins Widener Memorial Collection; Trotsky Archive; Farnsworth (recreational reading) Room; Author collections of note include: Aristophanes, Bacon, Byron, Caldecott, Carlyle, Cervantes, Chaucer, Coleridge, E. E. Cummings, T. S. Eliot, Emerson, Faulkner, Galsworthy, Goethe, William James, Kipling, Longfellow, Milton, Moliere, Petrarch, Alexander Pope, Rousseau, Schiller, Shakespeare, Shelley, Stevenson, Thackery, Thomas Wolfe, and others

SPECIAL CAPABILITIES: Numerous major research

Exterior and reading room, Bibliothèque Nationale, Paris.

Principal Libraries of the World

units and libraries of Harvard provide specialized information

PUBLICATIONS: *Harvard Library Bulletin*

Jewish National and University Library

Jerusalem, Israel, founded 1892

TYPE: national library; university library

NUMBER OF ITEMS IN COLLECTION: 2,000,000 vols.; 10,000 mss.; 200 incunabula; 17,000 current periodicals

SPECIAL COLLECTIONS: Dr. Abraham Schwadron Collection of Jewish autographs and protraits; Yakuda Collection; Dr. Harry Friedenwald Collection on the History of Medicine; the Professor M. Buber Archives; the National Sound Archives; and the Jacob Michael Collection of Jewish music

SPECIAL CAPABILITIES: Laboratory for the preservation and restoration of books and manuscripts

PUBLICATIONS: *Kirjath Sepher; Index of Articles on Jewish Studies*

Library of Congress

Washington, D.C., founded 1800

TYPE: national library; copyright library; serves U.S. Congress

NUMBER OF ITEMS IN COLLECTION: (72,466,926 items); 16,466,899 vols.; 111,014 bound newspapers; 31,031,504 mss.; 3,502,101 maps; 394,111 microopaques; 904,292 microfiche; 645,733 microfilms; 183,202 motion picture films; 3,384,178 music; 342,574 recordings on discs; 41,168 recordings on tapes and wires; 1,214,567 books for blind and physically handicapped; 4,146 books in large type; 2,784,505 talking books; 264,159 talking books on tapes; 174,412 prints and drawings; 983,032 broadsides, photocopies; 42,040 posters; 8,-448,437 photographic negatives, prints and slides

SPECIAL COLLECTIONS: Books for the blind and physically handicapped; Cartographic materials; Law Library; Manuscripts; Microfilm; Motion Picture Film; Music; Orientalia; Prints and Photographs; Rare Books; Serials, Technical Reports

SPECIAL CAPABILITIES: MARC (machine-readable catalog information) tapes; printed catalog cards; talking books program; NPAC (National Program for Acquisitions and Cataloging); Congressional Information Service; American Folklife Center; Cataloging in Publication program

PUBLICATIONS: *National Union Catalog; Register of Microform Masters; National Union Catalog of Manuscript Collections; Catalog of Copyright Entries; Monthly Checklist of State Publications; L.C. Publications in Print;* and others

Library of the USSR Academy of Sciences

Leningrad, USSR, founded 1714

TYPE: acts as enquiry, loan and reference center for the 136 libraries in the academy's departments and institutes

NUMBER OF ITEMS IN COLLECTION: 13,800,000 vols.

Los Angeles Public Library

Los Angeles, California, founded 1872

TYPE: public library

NUMBER OF ITEMS IN COLLECTION: 4,161,905 vols.; 35,404 microreels; 267 microfilms

SPECIAL COLLECTIONS: Accounting; American Indians; California in fiction; California and Southwest; cookbooks; crime and criminal methods; Dreiser; early voyages and travels; foreign language dictionaries; genealogy [Monnette]; maps; shorthand history [Clark]; telephone and city directories; theatre [Dobinson]; World War I and II [Treanor]

National Agricultural Library

Beltsville, Maryland, founded 1862

TYPE: national library for collection and dissemination of agricultural information

NUMBER OF ITEMS IN COLLECTION: 1,500,000 vols.; 616 microcards; 13,170 microfiche; 928 microfilms; 45,708 microsheets

SPECIAL CAPABILITIES: CAIN (on-line bibliographic data base); STAR (Serial Titles Automated Record)

PUBLICATIONS: *Agricultural Libraries Information Notes*

National Diet Library

Tokyo, Japan, founded 1948

TYPE: national library

NUMBER OF ITEMS IN COLLECTION: 2,957,594 vols.; 27,757 periodicals

SPECIAL COLLECTIONS: Deposit library for Japanese publications and publications of the U.S. government, U.N., UNESCO, ILO, WHO, ICAO, and GATT

PUBLICATIONS: *Japanese National Bibliography; Japanese Periodicals Index; Current Publications; National Diet Library Monthly Bulletin*

National Library of Australia

Canberra, Australia, founded 1902

TYPE: national library; copyright library

NUMBER OF ITEMS IN COLLECTION: 1,000,000 vols.; 35,000 serials; 170,000 maps; 40,000 pictures and prints; 500,000 photographs; 20,000 microfilms; 8,000 educational and documentary films; 2,000 historical films

SPECIAL COLLECTIONS: Australiana including Pethrick, Ferguson and Nan Kivell collections; Mathews ornithological collection; English literature, American history, and publications in Asian languages

PUBLICATIONS: *Australian Books; Australian Films; Australian Government Publications; Australian Maps; Australian National Bibliography; Australian Public Affairs Information Service*

National Library of Egypt

Cairo, Egypt, founded 1870

TYPE: national library; legal depository

NUMBER OF ITEMS IN COLLECTION: 1,500,000 vols.

SPECIAL CAPABILITIES: Fine arts library

PUBLICATIONS: *Egyptian Publications Bulletin*

National Library of Medicine

Bethesda, Maryland, founded 1836

TYPE: national library for collection and dissemination of information important to progress of medicine and public health

NUMBER OF ITEMS IN COLLECTION: 1,500,000 vols.

SPECIAL CAPABILITIES: CANCERLINE (on-line bibliographic retrieval system on cancer); MEDLINE (on-line data base available to libraries around the country); TOXLINE (on-line data base on toxicology); CHEMLINE (on-line data base for chemical

Central reading room, Library of Congress, Washington, D.C.

nomenclature information); AVLINE (audiovisuals on-line)

PUBLICATIONS: *Index Medicus; Bibliography of Medical Reviews; Bibliography of the History of Medicine; NLM Current Catalog; Toxicology Bibliography; Current Bibliography of Epidemiology*

National Library of Nigeria
Lagos, Nigeria, founded 1962

TYPE: national library

NUMBER OF ITEMS IN COLLECTION: 60,000 vols.

SPECIAL COLLECTIONS: Special collections of Nigerian and U.K. government publications; U.N. documents; newspapers

PUBLICATIONS: *Special Libraries in Nigeria; The Arts in Nigeria A Selective Bibliography; 18th and 19th Century Africana in the National Library of Nigeria; The National Library of Nigeria: A Guide to Its Use; Index to Selected Nigerian Publications;* and others

National Library of Peking
Peking, Peoples Republic of China, founded 1912

TYPE: government library

NUMBER OF ITEMS IN COLLECTION: 4,400,000 vols.

SPECIAL COLLECTIONS: Imperial collections of the Southern Sung (13th c.), Ming (1368–1644), and Ching (Manchu) (1644–1911) dynasties; 5th c. mss.; 9th c. woodblock prints

New York Public Library
New York, New York, founded 1895

TYPE: public library

NUMBER OF ITEMS IN COLLECTION: 8,500,000 vols.

SPECIAL COLLECTIONS: Berg collection of English and American literature; Arents collection of books on tobacco; Spencer collection of illustrated books and books on fine bindings; Performing Arts Research Center (Lincoln Center) with its dance, music, and theater collections; Schomburg Center for Research in Black Culture (over 55,000 vols.)

Österreichische Nationalbibliothek
Vienna, Austria, founded 1526

TYPE: national library

NUMBER OF ITEMS IN COLLECTION: 2,130,000 vols.; 13,000 periodicals; 30,088 mss.; 7,874 incunabula; 155,384 autographs; 35,241 music mss.; 86,202 vols. of printed music; 197,051 maps; 167,990 geographical and topographical pictures; 520,000 photographic negatives; 1,202,000 items including drama texts, autographs, costume and stage designs, prints, photographs

SPECIAL COLLECTIONS: Papyri collection; theater and motion picture collection; mss. from Austrian monasteries and library of Matthias Corvinus, after capture of his capital "Buda" by Turks in 1526; printed works rich in German and Slavonic literature

SPECIAL CAPABILITIES: Institut für Restaurierung for restoration of books is one of the library's departments. The Internationales Esperantomuseum is attached to the library.

Oxford University's Bodleian Library
Oxford, England, founded 1602

TYPE: university library; copyright library

NUMBER OF ITEMS IN COLLECTION: 3,500,000 vols.; 50,000 mss.

SPECIAL COLLECTIONS: Oriental mss.; English literary and local history; early printing; particularly strong in early books and mss.

PUBLICATIONS: *The Bodleian Library Record*

Pahlavi National Library
Tehran, Iran, founded 1935

Exterior, State V.I. Lenin Library, Old Building, Moscow.

TYPE: national library

NUMBER OF ITEMS IN COLLECTION: 100,000 vols.

SPECIAL COLLECTIONS: Rare Persian and Arabic mss.

PUBLICATIONS: *National Bibliography*

Stanford University Libraries
Stanford, California, founded 1885

TYPE: university library

NUMBER OF ITEMS IN COLLECTION: 4,000,000 vols.

SPECIAL COLLECTIONS: Transportation; Sir Isaac Newton; typography; music; English and American literature; technical information service for business and industry

SPECIAL CAPABILITIES: Hoover Institution on War, Revolution, and Peace

State Library of South Africa
Pretoria, South Africa, founded 1887

TYPE: national library; legal depository

NUMBER OF ITEMS IN COLLECTION: 700,000 vols.

SPECIAL CAPABILITIES: Responsible for the Joint Catalogue of Books in South African Libraries; depository library for U.S. government and U.N. publications

PUBLICATIONS: *South African National Bibliography; State Library Bibliographies; State Library Contributions to Library Science; African Reprint Series; Annual Report*

State V. I. Lenin Library
Moscow, USSR, founded 1862

TYPE: national library; copyright library

NUMBER OF ITEMS IN COLLECTION: 27,000,000 vols.; 2,500,000 mss.

SPECIAL COLLECTIONS: Complete files of newspapers in all 90 languages of the Soviet Union and 120 foreign languages. Department of rare books includes: incunabula, Aldines, palaeotypes, Elzevirs, specimens of earliest Slavonik printing, rare editions of Russian secular works, and others

Universiteitsbibliotheek von Amsterdam
Amsterdam, The Netherlands, founded 1578

TYPE: university library

NUMBER OF ITEMS IN COLLECTION: 2,000,000 vols.; 45,000 maps; 5,000 mss.; 40,000 letters

SPECIAL COLLECTIONS: Hebrew section and rich collection of Amsterdam imprints and atlases

SPECIAL CAPABILITIES: Includes Biblioteca Rosenthaliana; Reveil-Archieves; Albert Verwey Archives; Provo Archives; Jetterode Library; Vondel Museum; Frederik von Eden Museum

PUBLICATIONS: Publishes monthly lists of new acquisitions and a special catalogues series

The British Library

Negotiations continued smoothly in 1976 for the acquisition of a new site for the British Library at Somers Town, west of St. Pancras railway station in London. It was hoped that building would begin in 1979–80. Two main Reference Division reading rooms (for humanities and science) would be provided, linked by a central catalog hall. Meanwhile, some reorganization was taking place at the Science Reference Library, Holborn, London, to make it more convenient during the years preceding the move to Somers Town. In 1976 the BL's Newspaper Library's comprehensive catalog became available to the public. The BL Lending Division at Boston Spa in Lincolnshire announced that its telex room for receipt of requests had proved more than 80 percent successful; failure occurred when askers provided insufficient information about the items required.

As new statutory owners of the British Museum's former archive and manuscript collection as well as of its printed books, the BL issued in 1976 a leaflet entitled "What to see in the British Library," which provided a plan of the display rooms and showcases in the British Museum building where famous treasures such as Magna Carta and the Codex Sinaiticus could be seen. Exhibitions held by the BL during 1976 included one on the Qur'an and one on the quincentenary of the printer William Caxton. Shown in the Caxton exhibition was the MS of Sir Thomas Malory's *Morte D'Arthur*, acquired in 1976 by the BL from Winchester College for £ 150,000. The MS dated from a few years before Caxton's 1485 version of Malory. The BL also acquired in 1976 a collection of autographed music manuscripts by 32 living British composers. (*See further* feature article on the British Library in this *Yearbook* by Harry T. Hookway.)

University of California, Berkeley, Library
Berkeley, California, founded 1868
TYPE: university library
NUMBER OF ITEMS IN COLLECTION: 4,649,533 vols.
SPECIAL COLLECTIONS: History of Western North America, especially California and Mexico; Mark Twain collection; rare books collection; regional oral history collection

University of Illinois at Urbana-Champaign Library
Urbana, Illinois, founded 1867
TYPE: university library
NUMBER OF ITEMS IN COLLECTION: 4,920,173 vols. and periodicals; 536,793 pamphlets
SPECIAL COLLECTIONS: Special collections in classical literature and history; English literature including Milton and Shakespeare; Western U.S. history; Lincolniana; Italian history; music; architecture; science and technology

Yale University Library
New Haven, Connecticut, founded 1701
TYPE: university library
NUMBER OF ITEMS IN COLLECTION: 6,175,168 vols. and pamphlets
SPECIAL COLLECTIONS: Matthew Arnold; Asch; Berkeley; Benet; Carlyle; Coleridge; Cooper; Conrad; Defoe; Dickens; Dryden; George Eliot; Fielding; Goethe; Goldsmith; Hardy; Langston Hughes; Samuel Johnson; Kafka; Kipling; Sinclair Lewis; Ezra Pound; Napoleon; Rilke; Shakespeare; Steiglitz; Thackery; Twain; Edith Wharton; Wordsworth; Elinor Wylie
PUBLICATIONS: *Gazette*

Private Libraries

See *Independent Research Libraries*.

Processing Centers

The processing center handles the technical function of the library, starting with the material order placing, checking in, presearching and cataloging, making book and catalog cards and final preparation for use in the library service unit. Processing centers in operation in 1976 were associated with large municipal or county libraries, regional libraries, major universities, state libraries, and commercial enterprises. Large city libraries such as those in Chicago, Los Angeles, and New York operate centers. State examples were the North Carolina State Library Processing Center, Raleigh, and the Maryland Materials Center, Salisbury. Commercial processor examples included Blackwell North America, Bro-Dart, and Josten's.

In local city processing centers annual items handled ran upward from 100,000 with 20 staff members or more. Job classified titles were clerical and paraprofessional with catalogers and supervisors kept to a minimum. In large cities the assessment of local processing centers was under active review since public service priorities tended to be rated higher because of limited staff and escalating costs. Despite the position freeze in the New York City libraries, Queens Borough Public in 1975–76 cataloged 20,381 items and processed 248,756 volumes with a core of 9 professional and 47 clerks; Brooklyn Public cataloged 26,984 items and processed 200,698 volumes with 37 clerks and 10 librarians. In Brooklyn the staff loss accentuated commercial processing usage. Record keeping and presearching of new and replacement titles, however, remained heavy. The outside processing of new materials and replacement items, Adult and Juvenile, was proving successful, and unit costs were well below the last estimated in-house cost of $1.75. The control of the work for the processors was in the Cataloging Department, and the processors who are nearby may be phoned or visited easily. The use of Library of Congress copy expedites the cataloging aspect of this cooperative arrangement. Processing center operations give varying degrees of preparation to paperback materials and handle audiovisual items in ways similar to those for monographs.

State Centers. State processing centers operate as a department of the state library or as an affiliated agency. They assist libraries in the state with purchase, cataloging, and processing of materials at a set unit cost. Some centers, such as North Carolina's, have been given a state subsidy to keep the unit cost down ($1.20 per volume, 1975–76). Maryland has a materials center which catalogs and processes materials for 19 of the county library systems and for the State Library of Delaware. Low costs encourage use ($1.25, fiction; $1.80, non-fiction). The Illinois Library Materials Processing Center has a unit charge of $1.75 per volume. The Florida State Library stopped its centralized book processing service on June 30 because it could not compete with commercial processors nor was the use made by its member libraries considered adequate.

In addition, many states have regional library systems which may render member processing services. The Centralized Processing Center of the Central Kansas Library System, Great Bend, serves 50 member libraries with full processing, using Telemarc cards. The Four County Library System, Binghamton, processes materials for its members, as do certain systems in New York State. The Northeast Texas Library System, at its Dallas headquarters, does centralized ordering and contracts for the degree of cataloging/processing desired by the 46 member libraries. In 1977 these system members were to begin selecting cassette tapes and phonodiscs from education funds (card sets, $1.30). Special funding and legislation recently have helped processing operations develop in regional libraries.

Commercial processing operations are generally controlled with unit charges varying from under one dollar to several depending on customization. These use cataloging copy or MARC tapes. The quality of service depends upon the details of the contract. Libraries purchasing processing commercially should be able to circulate such items upon receipt without alteration. Some users of commercial services make additions to the processed materials. Various items added, such as labels, plastic covers, "check point" labels, and ownership stamping, can often be included in the commercial agreement at no additional cost. Some commercial processors have book-lease arrangements.

During 1976 processing centers continued to grow because of larger materials budgets, but manpower use queries were surfacing. Libraries continued to take all possible shortcuts in cataloging and processing to get materials to their readers. The regional libraries were developing an increasingly important role as processing centers. It was found that many more libraries were using networks for cataloging copy or cards while only a minority tended to use full commercial processing service. Some college and public libraries were using more than one commercial processor. Local centers were using, or considering, not only computer-based LC copy, but also the place of commercial services in their in-house processing.

DALLAS R. SHAWKEY

Public Broadcasting

See *Telecommunications and Public Broadcasting*.

Public Libraries

Money was the big topic. The Bicentennial year for public libraries saw much activity with networks, microfilm catalogs, independent learners, information and referral programs, multi-type systems, mini-computers, and cooperative ventures with other government agencies; but the problem of library support was still the number one concern. If the matter of finances was not quite so critical as it had been during the preceding year, it was, nevertheless, still the most important subject to the major city libraries, and, to a lesser degree, to a number of small libraries as well.

THE CITIES

New York, predictably enough, had the most grief, just as in 1975. The NYPL branch system, Brooklyn, and Queensborough again were the hardest hit by cutbacks. The NYPL branch system shut down eight branches until CETA and Title X staffing gave some relief. After the cuts the remaining staff were shared among units of paired branches with service hours down 50 percent from 1972. Brooklyn took a 26 percent cut in staff (310) and a 45 percent reduction in hours (1,187). Queensborough was rocked with a $5,000,000 reduction, affecting staffing of bookmobiles and building programs, and limiting branch service to three days a week.

Cutbacks. Detroit, which had suffered greatly in 1975 reductions, faced heavy city cutbacks until the state came through with $5,500,000 for the central library. Buffalo and Erie County saw the prospect of losing all county funding, laid off 87 staffers, and closed a branch and its Young Adult Department. Denver appeared headed for as much as 15 percent less than in the year before and prepared to drop as many as 40 administrative and public service positions while slashing the book funds and cutting the jail and bookmobile services.

In Pittsburgh the county appropriation was down by $511,000, or 8 percent of the total budget; in Phoenix the new mayor said libraries and museums were "amenities" that would receive only "small donations" from the city. Toledo found it necessary to drop 30 staffers,

An Ad Hoc Committee to Save Our Library successfully protested the closing of the Columbia branch of the New York Public Library. Round-the-clock sit-ins, read-ins, and sleep-ins were organized in January 1976. Laid-off clerks and librarians reopened the library in February after CETA funds were provided.

cut Main's evening hours, and stagger branch schedules. San Francisco continued its downward slide with a $273,583 reduction; Riverside, California, cut 85 hours of service and $57,391 from books, and dropped seven staff positions. With a $330,000 deficit Rochester froze 14 positions (including that of associate director), closed its Teen Lounge, and reduced hours for the Local History department.

Down in Memphis the budget hearings began with plans for a $580,000 slash but wound up three months later with only an $83,000 loss in the materials fund; two months later all 32 CETA positions were lost. Minneapolis, facing a $200,000 deficit, cut back branch hours. New Haven described 1976 as "a year of survival and consolidation."

Prosperous Few. But while most cities were fighting the wolf from the door, a few were enjoying library prosperity. Cleveland was way out in front. Its successful tax levy campaign at the end of 1975 brought its library a whopping $18 per capita. And Texas, as usual, had big money in Dallas and Houston, the latter receiving a 32 percent increase, mainly for staffing and operating its new building.

It was apparent from election results in late 1975 and in 1976 that the voters were more willing to support library services than politicians seem to believe. Most city and county govening bodies tended to discourage anything that would cause a rise in the tax rate, yet the voters in Atlanta, Houston, Austin, Cleveland, and Youngstown went to the polls and approved bond issues and tax levies. Columbus, Ohio, won a tremendous victory at the polls and practically doubled its budget in just over a year with the new .6-mill tax levy. Voters all the way from Vicksburg, Mississippi, to Multnomah County, Oregon, showed their willingness to pay for libraries. In Cabell County, West Virginia, Vigo County, Indiana, Durham, North Carolina, Roswell, New Mexico, and Arlington Heights, Illinois, the taxpayers also voted to tax themselves for new or renovated buildings. But in jurisdictions where the decisions are made without going to a popular vote, politicians generally decided that the electorate would be unwilling to pay the bill.

STATE AID

While the year started off with threatened reductions in state aid to public libraries in a number of states, by late fall it was clear that almost no states actually showed a net reduction. Colorado reduced its general aid by 7 percent, but it increased its aid to cooperative ventures, to the Colorado Reference Center, and to Denver's Bibliographic Center.

Appropriation Increases. On the plus side Indiana took the top prize with aid to public libraries for the first time in its history when it voted $800,000 for the year. Alabama and West Virginia ran a close second for doubling their state aid budgets. In Alabama a citizens' lobby called "Libraries PLUS" did the trick. In West Virginia a citizens' campaign not only got the 1975 appropriation doubled but nailed down a guaranteed minimum for future years. Rhode Island jumped its assistance from a pitiful $.05 per capita to a more respectable $.30, while South Carolina was promised the introduction of a bill that would increase library aid from $.35 cents to $1 per capita.

New York State's legislature boosted its aid by $4,000,000, and Michigan picked up the $5,500,000 tab for Detroit's central library. Illinois went from $.70 to $1 per capita and now will offer equalization grants to its public libraries; Kentucky set aside $3,407,000 for state aid; and the citizens of Oklahoma voted to raise the allowable library tax support in the general election.

TOWNS, COUNTIES, REGIONALS, CO-OPS

As in 1975 the gains far outnumbered the losses in the budgets of small and medium-sized libraries and of systems. Starting with the largest county system, the Los Angeles County Library managed some budget boosts in addition to $450,000 in LSCA grant funds, but inflation and salary raises nullified part of the gains. Upstart Broward County, Florida, continued to soar with a 29 percent increase of $600,000, and Cumberland County, North Carolina, came close behind with a 28 percent increase, tripling its budget since 1973. Other county systems made less spectacular but comfortable gains: Contra Costa, 11.2 percent; Multnomah County, Oregon, up $300,000; Baltimore County and Hennepin County, Minnesota, 9 percent each; Oklahoma County, 4.5 percent. Fairboult County, Minnesota, won a referendum authorizing funding for a new countywide library system.

Budget Slashes. A few fell upon hard times. The voters in Salem, Oregon, approved a $159,000 cut, and in Jackson and Josephine Counties, Oregon, budgets were also slashed. Oil tax revenue losses were blamed in Natrona County, Wyoming, where staffs had to be reduced in special services and in the bookmobile and AV departments. Utica, New York, took a 28 percent loss and withdrew from the Mid-York system, while the town of Burlington, Vermont, cut salaries by 26 percent and shut down to 42 hours per week.

NEW TECHNOLOGY

Next to the crucial matter of money the subjects most often heard among public librarians during the year were networks, computers, and microfilm catalogs. Up to now public libraries had been content to stand by and let the academic library staffs wrestle with the new technology. More than one public library director had been heard at conventions to say, "I'm waiting until the academic people work all the bugs out, and when they finally get something that works at a reasonable cost, I'll move in and buy a tried and true product." Tight budgets were at the root of such caution—not unwillingness to experiment. Few public libraries had access to computers and trained data processing staffs as did their university counterparts, and the nature of their popular book service did not exert the pressure for rapid and in-depth information that academic librarians experienced.

Turning Tide. By 1976, however, the tide was turning. Information was becoming the watchword of most alert public libraries. Filling the "need to know" was taxing small staffs and impoverished book collections, so it was a natural reaction to begin looking seriously at sharing resources through networks, which meant that the public librarian had to embrace computers, ready or not. The finest tool for sharing a system's resources, the printed book catalog, had rapidly become too expensive and bulky to perpetuate, and along came the new technology with "computer output microfilm" and reading machines that made possible the finding of a catalog entry in a matter of seconds; the result—a rush to COM catalogs in public libraries in 1976.

The mini-computer came in for a share of attention in the bicentennial year also, as public libraries began purchasing or leasing them for circulation control and a host of other in-house operations. Orlando began developing full-service data processing applications on a mini-computer: acquisitions, payroll, personnel records, circulation control, statistical reports, and surveys. St. Louis Public drew up specifications for a small computer that would not only handle circulation but also keep up with additions to a union list of serials, its index to newspapers, make film bookings, perform routines for service to the blind, and keep up with financial accounts. In Illinois, the State Library, three systems, and some individual libraries have all linked their mini-computer circulation control systems for dial-up access to each other's data bases for interlibrary loan purposes. Utah will ask the next legislature for funds to provide its major public libraries with mini-computers for circulation control and other in-house uses.

Networking Emphasis. The newest emphasis on networking and multistate sharing of resources seemed to come from the West, where several states under the aegis of WICHE (Western Interstate Commission on Higher Education) are joining together to share data bases and computerized holdings records and to do centralized planning. The Washington Library Network includes eight public libraries, the State Library, and one academic library and provides cataloging data and cards, location data, customized book and microfilm catalogs, acquisition data, and accounting control. Circulation and serials control are scheduled for 1977. Kansas and Iowa joined Colorado, South Dakota, Utah, and Wyoming in Denver's Bibliographic Center for Research with access to OCLC, BALLOTS, Lockheed, SDC, and *The New York Times* information systems.

Networking in other parts of the country included, in addition to the ever present OCLC, Western New York State's Nioga, Buffalo, and Chautauqua-Cattarangus systems which not only double as major research centers but tie in to the State Library data bank at Albany. Two facsimile transmission networks operate in Michigan, one to 19 public library systems (350 libraries) and the other to 22 regional educational media centers, transmitting 600 interloan requests daily. Facsimile has reached the speed of two minutes for letter size going coast to coast, and 60 seconds is often clocked. In Ohio the State Library granted $550,000 to OCLC to convert to machine readable form the retrospective catalogs of its seven major public libraries.

The biggest rush to any of the new technology in 1976 appeared to be in the field of the COM catalog. Fairfax County, Virginia, claimed to be the largest public library to reach the goal first of converting its book catalog to microfilm. Its COMCAT was installed in March at a cost of $36,025 for the microfilm and $73,840 for 130 readers. The largest system to announce plans to convert from book to microfilm was Los Angeles County, which made history with the early book catalog printed with the old accounting style computer printout. Every week news came of more public libraries going to microfilm. A small controversy began to brew as to whether roll film or microfiche was the better choice for format. As the year came to an end the list of COM catalogs included: St. Louis County; Clark County (Las Vegas); Salt Lake County; Palm Beach County; Black Gold Region, California; Enoch Pratt, Baltimore, Hartford, Prince George's Counties, Maryland; Monroe and Lenawee Counties, Michigan; Forsyth County, N.C.; and Chesapeake, Virginia. St. Paul and Minneapolis received a grant of $230,000 for a systems de-

Public Libraries

The Houston Public Library received a 32 percent increase in funds in 1976 for staffing and operating its new central library building. Below, floor to ceiling windows are special features of the building. A Claes Oldenberg sculpture is in the library's plaza (bottom).

Public Libraries

Urban Library Services

By the mid-1970's, two-thirds of all Americans lived in the 243 Standard Metropolitan Statistical Areas, according to the U.S. Bureau of Census. Public libraries in these urban centers have acted as primary service units for the immediate population and as secondary resource points for those living in adjacent regions. Urban public libraries have long served the needs of a changing population, and the present decade is no exception. Each major library system has a broad constituency that ranges from the specialist to the undereducated, and beyond, to the non-user. Services are provided for the young and old, for the student at whatever age, for the business community, for industry, and for the municipal government.

Major public library systems in urban areas have developed sizable material collections and specialized resources in numerous subject areas. They presently serve as vital links in existing interlibrary loan networks and will become even more important as national resource sharing programs emerge in the near future. Urban public libraries have frequently pioneered new services and set trends both in the United States and abroad.

Financial Problems. Juxtaposed against the picture of the urban public library as a resource center for information and service is the crisis of the cities. Financial problems trouble most American cities to a greater or lesser degree. Even cities in the so-called boom areas of the "sun belt" felt the financial crunch in 1976. More prosperous suburban counties that surround the core cities began to experience financial problems in the Bicentennial year. Recession, inflation, and unemployment took their toll not only in industrial centers but also in many other cities across the country.

Nowhere in 1976 was the relationship of municipal crisis and public library service cuts more dramatically illustrated than in New York City. The New York Public Library, the Brooklyn Public Library, and the Queens Borough Public Library absorbed massive cuts in personnel and material budgets. The Denver Public Library reported a 10 percent cut in funds for the year. Memphis-Shelby County Public Library and Information Center absorbed a 16 percent slash. Public libraries in San Francisco, Detroit, St. Louis, Baltimore, Los Angeles, Philadelphia, to name but a few, experienced no-growth budgets or actual cuts. (*See further* accompanying article.)

Funding Sources. Urban public libraries look to local governmental units for their primary funding. This basic local support is supplemented in many libraries with state funds of varying per capita amounts. Federal Library Services and Construction Act funds have been available for short term programs. Citizen groups in many cities have rallied around the public library to seek increased support, only to find that local funds were not available. The Urban Library Council, which was organized in 1971 by directors and trustees of urban public libraries, continued to work for special and direct federal support for urban libraries. In 1976 the ULC worked closely with ALA to add a new Title V to LSCA which would benefit urban public libraries.

Urban public library administrators, like others across the nation, have been aware of a need to match services to user requirements during an era of major social and technological change. In this connection, many have turned to the Public Libraries Association publication by Allie Beth Martin, *Strategy for Public Library Change* (ALA, 1972), for new directions. Many others are vitally concerned about measurement of service since financial cuts usually mean service cuts. Clearly, unless librarians devise new measurements of urban library performance, it will become increasingly difficult to compete effectively for adequate operating funds within an urban framework where scarcity of resources is the rule of the day. Consequently 1976 was a year when urban librarians awaited the results of the special PLA study on "Performance Measures for Public Libraries."

Shifting Services. The 70's have seen a renewed interest in reference services, including the reference interview, computerized data banks, and community information service. The national discussion of reference service has extended well beyond public libraries and is of equal concern to college and academic librarians. Financial restrictions have forced many urban public librarians to place a high priority on reference and information service.

Neighborhood or Community Information Services have replaced emphasis on outreach services in a growing number of libraries. While community information and referral service is growing on one hand, more large urban libraries in 1976 were exploring computerized data based services. Some libraries provided the computerized services through their own resources while others were able to offer access to the data banks through interlibrary cooperatives. Although not new, the concept of an "Information Broker" who may work within the framework of an existing library, or operate as an independent consulting company, surfaced in 1976. The question of user fees for a whole range of services that extend from duplication of library materials to specialized reference service was being asked more frequently in 1976.

Another of the basic services stressed by urban public libraries in the past decade has been adult education activities. Directed to a variety of special users, adult education ranges from Adult Basic Education programs, General Education Development (GED) preparation, Independent Study Projects, College Level Examination Program (CLEP), to Educational Counseling. Adult education also includes a range of formal and informal cultural programs.

Cultural Programs. The National Endowment for the Humanities has funded NEH Learning Libraries at the Boston

Public Library, The District of Columbia Public Library, and the Chicago Public Library. The public library in this program becomes an educational and cultural center which offers lectures, films, and discussion sessions. In some projects, the participants may obtain college credit. Much in evidence in 1976 were cultural programs that were planned to celebrate the Bicentennial.

Lifelong Learning was given considerable emphasis when new federal legislation was introduced in 1976 to support Lifelong Learning Centers. Also new during 1976 were a number of educational brokerage centers. Most were organized with federal monies from the Fund for the Improvement of Post-Secondary Education. Public libraries are viewed in the legislation as one of the natural settings for neutral educational brokerage services. The Free Library of Philadelphia, with funding from the Pennsylvania Department of Education, is implementing a Lifelong Learning Center to provide educational, career, and vocational guidance in five libraries and two state employment security offices. The Houston Public Library reported that 15 branches serve as adult learning centers and announced that all future branches will include space for learning centers.

Services to Handicapped. Under the leadership of the Library of Congress, urban public libraries have had a long history of service to the blind and, in more recent years, with some categories of the physically handicapped. Although the Rehabilitation Act of 1973 guarantees open access and affirmative action protection for the handicapped, only limited funds have been provided to implement the Act. Public libraries will, no doubt, be called upon for provision of additional services and more open access to facilities in the future.

During 1975 and 1976, urban public libraries initiated special programs to serve the deaf. The District of Columbia Public Library has been one of several urban public libraries to take the lead with this special group of library users. In addition to providing books and interpreted programs, many large public libraries are also installing teletype communication units so that deaf patrons may receive information services in their own homes.

Radio Services. The Huntsville-Madison County (Alabama) Public Library has launched a 100,000 watt radio station reaching 500,000 people. This is the third major library radio station to become operational. The others are located in Nashville, Tennessee, and Louisville, Kentucky. Programming for the Huntsville station will include 70 percent music of all types, local and syndicated news and will provide special programming on a separate channel for blind patrons.

Although urban public libraries reported a number of new projects during the year, 1976 was not noteworthy for innovation of new services. It is quite unlikely that urban library services can be expected to improve until substantial amounts of additional funding can be channeled into the large and medium-sized cities.

KEITH DOMS

---

sign to convert their catalogs back to 1968 to machine readable form.

Explanations for the soaring activity in microfilm catalogs included (1) the lost cost, as compared to book catalogs, which made possible frequent accumulations of new entries; (2) the development of satisfactory images directly from computer tape; (3) the development of reliable and durable reading machines; and (4) the rising cost of paper and the increasing bulk of book catalogs. (See *further* Automation; Networks.)

INFORMATION AND THE
INDEPENDENT LEARNER

"Adult education," as it was called in its heyday in public libraries in the 50's and 60's, came in for its full share of attention in 1976, but it was generally referred to under such terms as "continuing education," "self-directed learning," "independent learning," and so on. Closely allied with it were college-level courses that were open to the young of college age as well, who might pursue learning in public libraries outside the campus with halls of ivy or the more modern classrooms of community colleges.

A consortium of public libraries was at work with the CEEB's national self-educative program: Tulsa, Portland (Maine), St. Louis, Denver, Atlanta, Miami-Dade, Enoch Pratt, Salt Lake City, Woodbridge, and Minneapolis. Dorchester County, Maryland, and Salisburg State College cooperated in CLEP courses, as did Oklahoma County and the local junior college. More than 20 of the Nassau Library System's libraries offered off-campus centers for work toward both the bachelor's and the master's degrees. In Houston 15 branches (and each new one) have learning centers and offer GED tutoring. Monroe County and Wayne State University cooperate in lifelong learning courses. St. Louis Public makes available cassettes to those wishing to pursue college courses.

I and R Services. The increasing emphasis upon information led to a growing number of public library information and referral services on a regular basis. Detroit and Houston continued to report excellent results from their established I and R services. Memphis had a highly successful first year with its new service, reporting a file of more than 600 human service agencies and organizations and cooperation from all. Rochester's Monroe County Library System had its "Human Services Directory"

Noted photographer, author, and filmmaker Gordon Parks (right) reads his poetry during the Denver Public Library's "Frame Work" program. Director of the library's community services, Graham H. Sadler, looks on at left.

data base chosen as the data base for Monroe County's I and R system. In Maryland, Baltimore County's AID service was working well, and Enoch Pratt began anew on I and R with its INFER (Information for Every Resident) program. The Kentucky State Library reported I and R installed formally in four public libraries and informally in many more. One less than enthusiastic note came from St. Louis Public, where the city government and a major TV station seem to get most of the I and R business. (See further Information and Referral Services.)

BUILDINGS

At year's end the 11-floor design for Dallas' spectacular Central Research Library was given the go-ahead for development of working drawings with completion time predicted for 1981 at the earliest. Estimated to cost $44,000,000 it is expected to store 2,300,000 volumes and seat 2,800 readers. The Dallas city manager told the newspapers that the old downtown library would probably be sold to private interests to help pay for the new structure, which will face the new Dallas Municipal Center.

Atlanta went full speed ahead with drawings for its $18,000,000 plus central library, while San Francisco called off its bond issue campaign in March and rescheduled it for 1978. The AIA-LAD award winner in 1976 was a public library for Pekin, Illinois, a town of 35,000, where the Everett M. Dirksen Congressional Leadership Research Center is also a part of the new structure. First honors in the same competition went to the Jefferson Market Branch of NYPL, a Greenwich Village landmark first renovated in 1967.

Around the nation new buildings and renovations were planned, underway, or already completed in Sacramento, Stamford, Vigo County, Indiana, Arlington Heights, Illinois, Salt Lake County (an addition to the 1974 building experiencing "wall to wall people"), Pelham Bay and Hamilton Granger Branches of NYPL, and Vicksburg, Mississippi. Kentucky reported 12 new buildings and renovations; South Carolina reported on buildings in Marion, Fairfield, and Florence Counties and in the Abbeville-Greenwood Region; Maryland saw new buildings in Anne Arundel, Baltimore and Prince George's Counties; Connecticut reported buildings in Millford, Wilton, Groton, New London (addition), Westbrook and Guilford.

Awards. AIA-LAD Awards of Merit went to Hapeville, Georgia; Novato Branch, Marin County, California; Rockford Road Branch, Hennepin County, Minnesota; and Corning, New York. Arkansas received bids at last on its new State Library building, and Hawaii was busy with planning for a new State Library building, also.

An interesting sidelight on buildings this year was the increasing number of joint-use structures, a complete turnaround from the Wheeler dicta of former years. Memphis opened its Hollywood Branch with a community health center sharing part of the total building and had plans for two more which would share with the recreation, health and human services agencies. Baltimore County shared its new Woodlawn Library with the health department; Arlington County, Virginia, shared its Aurora Hills Branch with a recreation center and a fire station; and Cokato, Minnesota (Great River Regional) shared its building with a museum. (See also Buildings.)

MULTI-TYPE SYSTEMS, OUTREACH, VIDEO

Other public library news told of increasing cooperation among types of libraries in forming systems—in fact, systems have grown so fast in recent years that the Public Library Association Board saw fit to create a Systems Section at its summer conference meetings. A few of the many instances of multi-type cooperation: Illinois offered affiliate membership in public library systems to school, special and academic libraries; Colorado reported an increase in multi-type co-ops from 123 to 279 libraries; and the Utah State Library purchased and processed books for both public and school libraries.

Ardor for outreach may have cooled somewhat in '76. The Baltimore County staff and public ranked it pretty low in their priorities, and St. Louis Public bluntly stated that its efforts to reach non-users had not been effective as a substitute for traditional methods. Outreach to foreign language groups proved more successful than outreach to the poor and disadvantaged English-speaking population. Memphis, Nashville, and Hennepin County reported successful work with Vietnamese refugees, while the New Mexico State Library developed successful libraries for the Pueblos. In eight participating Chicago suburbs the Palatine Public Library operated a successful program for 6,000 Spanish-speaking residents.

Videotape and cable TV projects sailed along with quality improving as experience widened. San Jose, Dearborn, Memphis, Tuc-

The "Green Earth Forum" program of the Public Library of Cincinnati and Hamilton County in October 1976 provided 16 free lectures on horticulture, including talks on house plants (left) and growing orchids (right).

son, Monroe County, Indiana, and numerous other public libraries attracted special attention with their video accomplishments. The Chicago Public Library made history by becoming the first organization other than a radio or TV station to win the Broadcaster's Promotion Association's first place award for a Bicentennial series, "Happy Birthday America," two-minute vignettes on the nation's history.

ALLIE BETH MARTIN, 1914–1976

The story of public libraries in the Bicentennial year ends on a sad note. Allie Beth Martin, ALA President and Director of the Tulsa City-County Library, died on April 11, 1976. Referring to her *Strategy for Public Library Change* (ALA, 1972), she spoke of the satisfactions of "seeing public libraries move with the times . . . having the public library recognized in the community as an important agency. . . ." Public librarianship's loss was the entire profession's loss. Her biography and a statement *In Memoriam* by Clara Stanton Jones, appear in the first and Centennial edition of this *Yearbook* (page vi), which was dedicated to her. C. LAMAR WALLIS

Public Library Association

1976 was a year of change for PLA. Changes at ALA Headquarters began in January when Executive Secretary Gerald Born announced his resignation effective April 1. It was decided that, instead of employing an Executive Secretary who would work exclusively with PLA, the Division would join with the American Library Trustee Association (ALTA) and the Reference and Adult Services Division (RASD) in an administrative arrangement new to the ALA: a joint secretariat would be established to serve the three Divisions. The office would be staffed by an Executive Secretary, an Associate Executive Secretary, an administrative assistant and two secretaries; all five would work with the three Divisions.

This new arrangement seemed to offer several advantages. Instead of one top-level person who was thoroughly familiar with the work of one Division only, ALTA, PLA, and RASD would have two staff officers — an Executive Secretary and an Associate Executive Secretary. These two would share responsibility for the work of the three Divisions and each would contribute a unique perspective to the conduct of the secretariat. If one were traveling or away from the office for other reasons, the other could see to it that the Divisional business was continued. The Administrative Assistant would hold a post of considerable responsibility and would supervise the other two members of the support staff.

From April through June, when the new secretariat was not yet established, Ruth Tarbox served on a part-time basis as Interim Executive Secretary of PLA. In July, Andrew Hansen, previously Executive Secretary for ALTA and RASD, became Executive Secretary of the new joint secretariat. Mary Jo Lynch joined the unit in September as Associate Executive Secretary.

Projects. Work on PLA projects continued while services at headquarters were being rearranged. The most ambitious project was a research proposal prepared by the Goals, Guidelines and Standards Committee with the assistance of the Public Research Institute of Arlington, Virginia. The proposal which the PLA Executive Board approved in March is based on a new approach to standards for public libraries which had been evolving within the committee for a number of years. The document outlines a 15-month research effort "to develop and test a process that library managers and others can use to set standards of performance for community library service." The proposal was approved by the ALA Executive Board at its April meeting, and the Executive Director was authorized to seek outside funding.

Publications. The Public Library Reporter series was augmented by the publication of No. 17, *Planning Library Workshops and Institutes* written by Ruth Warncke. This is a practical volume "addressed to the people who are called upon to organize and conduct workshops and institutes on any of the myriad aspects of library service and operation, either in their roles as staff members, or as members of organizations. It is concerned with principles and practices applicable to any subject matter but illustrates these principles and practices with examples related to library concerns covering many types of libraries and many kinds of library activity."

New Directions. The 1976 Annual Conference saw PLA experimenting with a new program format. Instead of a single major program meeting, PLA, through the efforts of its Activities Committee, presented an "Idea Exchange." Eight concurrent mini-sessions were offered and repeated at four different times on eight topics such as "Public Libraries and Community Analysis" and "Public Libraries and Performance Appraisal." Included in each 50-minute session were brief presentations by practitioners. Further contact information — people and readings — was provided in handouts.

When the Executive Board of PLA met at Conference it voted to establish two new Sections within the association. The Alternative Education Programs Section was given responsibility for non-traditional literacy and learning programs in public libraries. It will serve as a forum on resources and problems in this field and as a liaison with other groups both within ALA and outside the association. Patri-

Public Relations

cia Gaven of the Englewood (N.J.) Public Library and Travis Tyer of the Illinois State Library were asked to co-chair the Organizing Committee of the section.

The Public Library Systems Section was also established at the Annual Conference. The objectives of this section are to encourage improved library service through the organization and strengthening of public library systems; to provide a forum for discussion of problems distinctive to public library systems; to provide continuing education to members of public library systems; to interpret public library systems to the American public and to relate public library systems to cooperative ventures of a multitype nature. Barry Booth of the Illinois Valley Library System was asked to chair the Organizing Committee of this Section.

Finally, the 1976 Conference saw the inauguration of "Project Survival," which was to be a year-long effort centered in the Standard Metropolitan Statistical Areas of the nation. The project would dramatize and disseminate information on the importance of libraries to the quality of American life, document the deterioration of library support in many parts of the country, and encourage regional planning of library service. Daniel Boorstin, Librarian of Congress, spoke at the PLA Membership meeting and encouraged "Project Survival" in his remarks on the need for a "Library Renaissance."

Genevieve Casey, PLA President, appointed Ronald Dubberly to chair an ad hoc Interdivisional Steering Committee to plan "Project Survival." ACRL, ALTA, AASL, and ASLA appointed representatives to the Committee, which met in the Seattle area in the early autumn 1976. At that time the Committee drafted a plan and requested funds from the ALA Executive Board. Although the request for funds was denied, the Executive Board endorsed the concept of "Project Survival" and made several suggestions as to how the committee might improve and implement plans for the project.

MARY JO LYNCH

PLA Officers

PRESIDENT (July 1976–July 1978):
Genevieve Casey, Division of Library Science, Wayne State University, Detroit

VICE-PRESIDENT/PRESIDENT-ELECT (July 1976–July 1978):
Ronald Dubberly, Director, Seattle Public Library

EXECUTIVE SECRETARY:
Andrew Hansen

ASSOCIATE EXECUTIVE SECRETARY:
Mary Jo Lynch

Membership (August 31, 1976): 4,177 (2,631 personal and 1,546 organizational)

Public Relations

One-third of the U.S. population has never used a library, 37 percent have no idea how public libraries are funded, and a majority of nonusers are totally ignorant of the wide range of services and facilities available beyond books. These facts, released early in 1976 in a Gallup Poll conducted on behalf of 16 state library agencies and the American Library Association, were reported in the first edition of this *Yearbook*.

The library world was not particularly startled by the Gallup findings, as the results follow the pattern of similar research conducted in 1967 for the National Advisory Commission on Libraries and in 1949 for the Public Library Inquiry. Yet as inflation and recession increase the competition for limited public funds, the library's need to attract users and citizen and government support has somewhat increased the interest in public relations or planned communication programs.

PIO Promotional Activity. At the national level, the ALA's Public Information Office (PIO) continued to expand its public service advertising program for libraries. The program began in 1975 when the ALA inherited responsibility for National Library Week (NLW) from the National Book Committee.

Although long recognized as the national voice for libraries, the ALA had not previously been active in generating national media coverage. Yet both need and media interest were great, and the first full-fledged ALA effort—the 1975 NLW campaign—was awarded the Silver Anvil by the Public Relations Society of America and the Golden Trumpet by the Chicago Publicity Club.

Building on the press interest generated in 1975, PIO, with the support and advice of the NLW Committee chaired by Alice Norton, continued to place feature stories and radio and television spots with the national media. Although NLW remains a major focus, the income generated from the sale of NLW posters and other graphics has been used to support a year-round publicity program for libraries.

During 1976 PIO placed 15 national wire service stories, 13 national magazine articles, and 10 television interviews, all with a combined reader/viewer total estimated in the millions. Public service ads were used over a period of nine months in seven national magazines, including *Time*, *Newsweek*, and the *New Yorker*. The value of the contributed magazine ad space calculated for the months of April and May alone totaled over $28,000. ALA public service radio announcements were accepted by all three radio networks and receive continuous play. A television spot accepted by CBS is also frequently aired.

What was the message communicated by this national publicity? The feature and news stories ranged in subject from literacy training programs to school media centers. All types of libraries were featured, the purpose being to let the public know that libraries are information centers, vital to the quality of life in America. The national publicity also provides an effective backdrop for the many state and local NLW activities—both because it serves as a stimulus for librarians to approach local media with library-related stories and because local editors often pick up on a national story and explore the local angles.

The 1976 NLW graphics were prepared with the assistance of the Chicago agency office of N.W. Ayer ABH International and were displayed in 3,000 libraries. The NLW theme was again "Information Power." The posters illustrated many nontraditional library services and were taglined "At the Library? At the Library! Come see what's new besides books."

Grolier Grant. The NLW Committee also administers the $1,000 annual Grolier National Library Week Grant. The goal of the grant is to stimulate public relations activities, thereby increasing library visibility and state association interest in NLW. The 1976 grant was presented to the Illinois Library Association for implementation of its "Librarians to the People" project. The proposal called for establishment of a statewide speakers' bureau with volunteers tapped from among the Association's members. In the second year of the Grolier Grant project, 10 proposals were submitted by state library associations. Nine were submitted for the 1975 grant.

"About Books." The ALA PIO also added a weekly syndicated book review and library "best-seller" list to its year-round publicity effort. The "About Books" column is distributed by Newspaper Enterprise Association to its over 700 subscribing papers nationwide, at no cost to ALA. The reviews, written by ALA staffers, cover three to five recent titles on a related theme and resemble a newspaper feature article in length and style. Attached to each column is a survey of "What Americans Are Reading," compiled from tabulations of most-requested books submitted by 150 participating libraries. This national poll is the first ever to measure titles people are checking out of libraries rather than titles they are buying at bookstores. It provides weekly attention for ALA and for libraries and reminds users that their library lends best-sellers as well as older books and classics. Local libraries have also used it successfully to highlight their collections and services.

ALA Centennial. The occasion of the ALA's Centennial in July 1976 stimulated much library publicity. The ALA Centennial Conference in Chicago, with its many special programs and events, generated national as well as heavy Chicago coverage. The Association later commemorated ALA's actual founding date (Oct. 6, 1876) with a 16-page supplement to the Sunday *New York Times* (October 3, 1976). The "Great American Library Success Story" included features on the progress, people, services, and problems of American libraries. Completely paid for by advertisers, it reached an estimated 4,500,000 *Times* readers.

While the ALA's national public service advertising campaign increases library visibility, promoting good library public relations takes more than national media coverage. The real work must be done at the local level.

Public Relations Section (LAD). The Public Relations Section (PRS) of ALA's Library Administration Division brings together people concerned with developing public relations skills and sharing resources. Under the leadership of chairperson Sue Fontaine, the 1,728 member Section jumped to the front lines of Association activity by sponsoring a preconference institute prior to the Centennial Conference in Chicago. The "Public Relations Panorama" had an attendance of 157—a good indication of the growing interest in public relations. In his keynote speech, James Fox, Past President of the Public Relations Society of America, confronted conferees with certain cold realities. Librarians, he charged, are responsible for insufficient funding and low visibility through failure to explain themselves to the public. He urged librarians to recognize that public relations is a legitimate management tool and to become more aware of political organizing techniques. The same call for political awareness and action was the final word of the Conference in a strong speech by Major Owens, New York state senator. Between those messages were two days of skill development and information exchange.

Similar continuing education activities are the concern of a PRS committee that creates packaged workshops designed to train people in the use of public relations materials and methods.

The PRS also jointly sponsors the annual John Cotton Dana Public Relations Awards Contest with the H. W. Wilson Company. The 31st annual contest broke all records for the number of entries received. Over 155 scrapbooks and nonprint materials from various types of libraries all over the world were entered, and 61 programs were recognized with awards or honorable mentions. The PRS awarded a certificate to the H. W. Wilson Company in appreciation of its sponsorship.

Project Survival. Another Division of ALA, the Public Library Association, ventured into the national public relations scene by launching "Project Survival." The year-long project calls for collection of data on the deterioration of library support. The data will be used to awaken the public to the importance of libraries to the quality of life and to encourage regional planning for library service. This ambi-

National Library Week 1976 stressed the wide range of information services available at libraries.

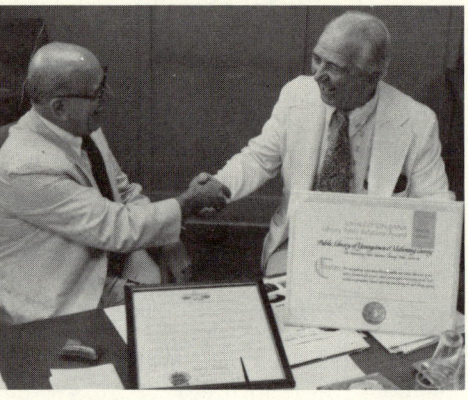

Above left, H. W. Wilson Company President Leo Weins (left) accepts a 1976 citation from Paxton P. Price, President of ALA's Library Administration Division, for the company's 31-year sponsorship of the John Cotton Dana Public Relations Awards. Above right, Director David W. Griffith of the Public Library of Youngstown and Mahoning County receives a special John Cotton Dana Award from Ohio Congressman Thomas P. Gilmartin for promoting outstanding cooperation between schools and public libraries in a Bicentennial project to create permanent murals depicting local library history.

tious campaign was announced during the ALA Centennial Conference and encouraged by Daniel Boorstin, Librarian of Congress, who said, "Our aim should not be merely resuscitation of public libraries but a library renaissance. How can we accomplish this? First we must collect the facts about libraries, about the increase of readers' needs, and about our ability—or inability—to satisfy and stimulate those needs. Of course, we at the Library of Congress will do everything to help. Then we must awaken the minds and conscience of the community to the uses of libraries and especially to the interfusing of interests, activities and purposes with those of our other institutions—educational and recreational."

Project Survival was approved in principle by the ALA Executive Board; plans for funding were being developed at year's end.

Citizens Committee. Survival of public libraries is also the concern of an independent committee that was formed during 1976. The National Citizens Emergency Committee to Save Our Public Libraries, organized by Whitney North Seymour, has 73 national committee members from 38 states and is headquartered in Washington, D.C. The committee's honorary co-chairpersons are Isaac Asimov, Terrence Cardinal Cooke, Margaret Truman Daniel, Ralph W. Ellison, George Meany, and Leonard Woodcock. The group has already become much more than a letterhead list of notables through its development of carefully researched fact sheets on such topics as the role of public libraries in helping the elderly and in helping people find jobs. Such reports have been distributed to all members of Congress and to many state and local officials. The Citizens Emergency Committee produced a 25-page fact sheet entitled "Public Libraries and the Public's Right to Know," outlining how libraries aid the flow of information in news media, books and periodicals. It includes testimonials from newspapers across the country on the importance of free public libraries, and is introduced by Theodore H. White.

STATE PROGRAMS

Wisconsin. In order for librarians to live up to the claims made by NLW, Project Survival or the National Citizens Emergency Committee, they need guidance, inspiration and practical help. Wisconsin's Coordinated Library Information Program (CLIP) has been meeting this need for libraries across the country. Headed by Marian Edsall, the service was developed with LSCA funds by the Wisconsin Division for Library Services. Among its many activities, CLIP provides public relations materials and training to Wisconsin's public librarians and has extended these services nationally. CLIP now has 3,500 subscribers in 50 states and five countries to its semimonthly newsletter, "Tips from CLIP." Although suffering from funding deficiencies in 1976, CLIP still managed to produce posters and other library promotional materials, make "Tips from CLIP" more indispensable than ever, produce television and radio spot announcements, and circulate packets of sample publicity and public relations materials.

Other state level public relations programs continued in 1976 and some new ones emerged.

Texas. A $18,500 LSCA Title II grant to the Texas Library Association was used to develop a statewide information program scheduled to begin in January 1977. The program theme is "Texas Libraries = Information." The Dallas public relations firm of Tracy-Locke has been retained to help develop public service radio and TV announcements as well as magazine and newspaper articles on public, school and academic library service.

Pennsylvania. The Pennsylvania Library Association received a $75,000 LSCA grant from the state library to carry out a statewide publicity campaign for libraries. The funds were received in March, 1975, and have been used to create radio, television and print public service advertisements, as well as a button campaign and training workshops. The project theme is "I'm a KNOWbody," and the distribution of publicity materials was planned to continue through 1977.

West Virginia. As usual, the energetic West Virginia State Librarian, Fred Glazer, led the way in creating clever, carefully executed and delicious programs designed to focus public and legislative attention on libraries. West Virginia librarians served homemade apple pies to their legislators on Library Appreciation Day in February with a message that a "library pie requires state dough." The pies were accompanied by a recipe book listing all the ingredients necessary for providing library services to the 1,744,237 West Virginia residents. Libraries around the state also held open houses to share pie, coffee and ideas with the lawmakers.

Other States. The Illinois State Library was awarded a $408,000 LSCA grant for the Illinet Public Information Program in 1975. The program will begin in 1977.

The Michigan Library Association sent Ben Franklin (a convincing local actor) to the state legislature to tell the library story, and followed up by using Ben in TV spots.

Similar programs, coupled with effective use of NLW ideas and materials, are on the increase in many states. A survey by Kathleen Rummel of the Illinois State Library indicates that many state agencies now employ public relations or public information specialists.

Bond Issues. Successful passage of bond issues in several cities is further proof of a growing awareness of the importance of effective planned communication. In Atlanta, an advertising agency and Friends of the Library group combined forces and won a bond issue campaign that provides $19,000,000 for a new central library. Residents of Youngstown and of Mahoning County (Ohio) voted for the first increase in library support since 1961. The library staff and supporters waged a strong campaign using direct mail to all families, resulting in a tremendous two-to-one victory. The vote was 79,985 for the library and 39,176 against.

Training. Training in public relations that makes such victories possible is given in ALA workshops or state and regional library association conferences. Such programs have become a regular feature of most library association meetings.

Several library schools have also sponsored special one- or two-week workshops in public relations. Few full courses are offered, however, in ALA-accredited graduate library education programs. A survey taken in the spring of 1976 by ALA's Library Education Division, found only 11 of the 64 accredited programs listing course work in public relations. A perusal of the catalogs of those 11 schools turned up only four course descriptions, although some focus on public relations may be included in administration or public library courses.

Unless economic conditions improve substantially, libraries will continue to be affected by two trends: the demand for services will swell as the funds necessary to provide those services shrink. Solid and creative public relations programs will prove to be the best tool toward bridging the gap.

PEGGY BARBER

Publishing, ALA

The long-awaited ninth edition of ALA's *Guide to Reference Books* appeared in September 1976. Prepared by Eugene P. Sheehy of Columbia, assisted by Rita G. Keckeissen and Eileen McIlvaine, it draws on the eighth edition (1967), edited by Constance Winchell. Because Isadore G. Mudge's introduction to the sixth edition (1936) is still useful as a succinct statement of essential points for reference work, Sheehy reprints it in the ninth. Delays in publication of the ninth, in part caused by revision of the format of the index, led to a disappointing fourth quarter financially for Books and Pamphlets. That department of ALA's Publishing Services showed a deficit of $20,000 for the fiscal year ending August 31. Brisk sales of the ninth edition in the last four months of 1976 reversed the picture. One-third of the way into the new fiscal year, sales revenue, thanks largely to *Guide to Reference Books*, was 69 percent ahead of the previous year's.

Books and Pamphlets. ALA strengthened its list of professional tools in 1976: Ruth Warncke's *Planning Library Workshops and Institutes* (Public Library Reporter no. 17) is a practical handbook at a time of increasing interest in continuing education. Jerrold Orne's *Language of the Foreign Book Trade*, which gives abbreviations, terms, and phrases in 14 languages of the Western world and the U.S.S.R., was brought out in its third edition, and P. William Filby's *American and British Genealogy and Heraldry: A Selected List of Books* in its second. The 496-page Filby revision increases the number of annotated titles from 2,000 to 5,000. A new work by Richard Sweeney Halsey is based on his application of comprehensive statistical analysis to 42,900 different recorded versions of musical works issued on LP's. His purpose is "to ease the way for those who want to build, enlarge, or upgrade their collections." The statistical methods he uses in *Classical Music Recordings for Home and Library* stimulated lively response from critics who question their valid-

Table 1. Booklist (1976)

Books reviewed	**4,781**
Adult	2,900
Young Adult	319
Children's	1,147
RSBR reviews	151
RSBR notes	264
Nonprint materials reviewed	**1,912**
16mm films	318
Filmstrips	1,200
Recordings	116
Slides	21
Videocassettes	107
Multimedia kits	106
Exhibits	44
Books and galleys received	**17,383**
Adult	13,854
Children's & Young Adult	3,529

Table 2. Reference and Subscription Books Reviews (1976)

Books and sets received	906
Rejected	290
Reviews published	151
General encyclopedias	3
Other forms	148
Notes published	264
Special lists and articles	22

ALA Publishing Services moved to this building at 716 Rush Street, Chicago, in June.

Table 3. ALA Periodicals (1976)

Periodical	Editor(s)	Publication Frequency	Subscription*	Circulation
American Libraries	Arthur Plotnik, Editor ALA, Chicago	11 issues a year; July/August combined	Free to ALA members; available to institutions at $20 per year.	39,000
Booklist	Paul Brawley, Editor ALA, Chicago	23 issues a year	$24 per year.	39,000
CHOICE (ACRL)	Richard Gardner, Editor Middletown, Connecticut	11 issues a year; July/August combined	$35 per year.	6,000
College & Research Libraries (ACRL)	Richard D. Johnson, *Journal* Editor State University of New York, College at Oneonta Mary Frances Collins *News* Editor State University of New York at Albany	17 times a year (6 bimonthly journal and 11 monthly news issues; July/August combined)	Free to Division members; subscription $15 per year; single journal issues $1.50; news issues $1.	12,000
Documents to the People (GODORT)	Jaia Heymann, Editor Drew University Library, Madison, New Jersey	Bimonthly	Free to Round Table members; otherwise by a contribution of $10 per year.	1,400
Exhibit Newsletter (ERT)	Paul E. Rafferty, Editor Field Enterprises Educational Corp., Merchandise Mart Plaza, Chicago, Illinois	Quarterly	Free to Exhibits Round Table members.*	350
Financial Assistance for Library Education, Academic Year 1977–78	Margaret Myers, Editor ALA, Chicago	Annually	50¢ a copy.*	10,000
FLIRT Newsletter (FLIRT)	Robert Lane, Editor Air University Library, Maxwell Air Force Base, Alabama	Quarterly	Free to Federal Librarians Round Table Members.*	500
Footnotes (JMRT)	Ann Scott, Editor Virginia Beach, Virginia	Quarterly	Free to Junior Members Round Table members.*	1,000
HRLSD Journal (HRLSD)	Robert F. Ensley, Editor State Library, Springfield, Illinois	2 issues a year	Free to Division members.*	1,600
HRLSD Newsletter (HRLSD)	Mary Power ALA, Chicago	Irregular	Free to Division members.*	1,600
IFRT Report (IFRT)	Ione Pierron, Editor Eugene, Oregon	Irregular	Free to Intellectual Freedom Round Table members.*	950
Journal of Library Automation (ISAD)	Susan K. Martin, Editor University of California, Berkeley	Quarterly	Free to Division members; subscription $15 per year; single issues $4.	5,500
LAD Newsletter (LAD)	John F. Harvey, Editor St. Johnsbury, Vermont	Quarterly	Free to Division members.*	5,000
Leads (IRRT)	Edward Moffat, Editor Palmer Graduate Library School, C. W. Post Center, Long Island University, Greenvale, New York	Quarterly	Free to International Relations Round Table members; subscription $10 per volume.	600
LED Newsletter (LED)	Margaret Myers, Editor ALA, Chicago	Quarterly	Free to Division members.*	2,200
Library Resources & Technical Services (RTSD)	Wesley Simonton, Editor University of Minnesota, Minneapolis	Quarterly	Free to Division members; subscription $15 per year; single issues $4.	9,500
Library Technology Reports	Howard S. White, Editor ALA, Chicago	6 issues a year	$125 per year.	1,500
Newsletter on Intellectual (IFC)	Coeditors: Judith F. Krug, Roger L. Funk ALA, Chicago	6 issues a year	$8 per year.	2,700
PLA Newsletter (PLA)	Nancy Doyle, Editor Winston-Salem, North Carolina	4 times a year	Free to Division members.*	4,200
ASLA President's Newsletter (ASLA)	Irma R. Bostian, Editor State Library, Springfield, Illinois	4 times a year	Free to Division members.*	1,300

Public Library Trustee (ALTA)	Robert L. Faherty, Editor Algonac, Michigan	Periodically	Free to Division members.*	2,700
RQ (RASD)	Geraldine King, Editor Ramsey County Public Library, St. Paul, Minnesota	Quarterly	Free to Division members; subscription $15 per year; single issues $4.	7,000
RTSD Newsletter (RTSD)	Mary Pound, Editor University of Texas, Austin	Quarterly	Free to Division members and *Library Resources & Technical Services* subscribers.	9,500
School Media Quarterly (AASL)	Glenn Estes, Editor Graduate School of Library and Information Science, University of Tennessee, Knoxville	Quarterly	Free to Division members; subscription $15 per year; single issues $4.	7,500
SORT Bulletin (SORT)	Marywave Godfrey, Editor Pierce County Library, Tacoma, Washington	Semiannually	Free to Staff Organizations Round Table members.*	300
SRRT Newsletter (SRRT)	Linda Katz, Editor Wolfson Library, King of Prussia, Pennsylvania	3 issues a year	Free to Social Responsibilities Round Table members; $3 to individuals; $20 to institutions.	1,200
Top of the News (CSD/YASD)	Coeditors: Caroline Coughlin, Simmons College, Boston, Massachusetts, and Shirley Fitzgibbons, College of Library and Information Service, University of Maryland	Quarterly	Free to Division members; subscription $15 per year.	11,000
Washington Newsletter	Eileen Cooke, Editor Director of ALA Washington Office	Irregular (minimum of 12 issues)	$8 per year.	2,200

*Asterisk indicates not available by subscription (December 1976).

A selection of new titles published by ALA in 1976.

At the ALA Centennial Conference the Publishing Committee (George Bobinski, right foreground, chair) hears Mary Jane Anderson of Children's Services Division, right. Members at her right are Carol Nemeyer and Travis Tyer.

From left, the ALA Sales Manager, Robert Hershman, Associate Executive Director for Publishing, Donald E. Stewart, and Director of Marketing, Guy Marsh, plan promotion of the first edition of The ALA Yearbook, published in 1976.

ity in selecting music; others welcomed the new reference source.

Manfred Kochen and Joseph C. Donohue, editors of *Information for the Community*, take account of the "need for everyday information" and cover various aspects of Information and Referral (I & R) Centers. I & R on a direct level is provided by another new ALA book, *Information for Everyday Survival: What You Need and Where to Get It*, prepared by the Appalachian Adult Education Center at Morehead State University (Kentucky). In a five-column format, the nonconventional book in size and content lists items, annotations, sources, reading levels, and costs. It covers "everyday" interests, among them aging, children, community, education, free time, health, and jobs.

A Century of Service: Librarianship in the United States and Canada, edited by Sidney L. Jackson of Kent State University, Eleanor B. Herling of the University of Houston, and E. J. Josey of the New York State Education Department, helped mark ALA's Centennial. Twenty-one contributors honor a profession—and the people in it—by reviewing advances, failures, and prospects. *An Architectural Strategy for Change*, on public libraries, edited by Raymond M. Holt, appeared as the revised proceedings of a Library Administration Division institute in New York (1974). It gives the keynote address by the late Allie Beth Martin. Contributors include Milton S. Byam, David R. Smith, Charles A. Ward, Carolyn J. Else, and James W. White.

Commitment to provide service to those in need of it was reflected in 1976 in other new titles: *Reading and the Adult New Reader*, by Helen H. Lyman, whose five-year study had led to the publication of *Library Materials in Service to the Adult New Reader* (ALA, 1973); *The Special Child in the Library*, Barbara Holland Baskin and Karen H. Harris, editors, providing ideas on extending the right to read to all children, including the exceptional; and *Start Early for an Early Start: You and the Young Child*, Ferne Johnson, editor, for "all those interested in the intellectual growth and development of young children." Many besides children's and YA librarians will enjoy the charm of "Interviews at Home"—with writers and illustrators—in *British Children's Authors* by Cornelia Jones and Olivia R. Way.

The first edition of this *Yearbook* was introduced at the Centennial Conference. The response to the direct-mail sales promotion was exceptional (5 percent v. industry average of 2 percent). Three thousand copies were sold by the end of 1976, and editorial work was well along at year's end toward publication of the second edition in late spring 1977.

Pamphlets. Pamphlets in 1976, as in previous years, continued to be among the most popular items ALA offers. Tens of thousands are sold and distributed. In 1976 the profession continued its high demand for *Notable Children's Books 1975* (selected by the Book Evaluation Committee of the Children's Services Division), *Newbery Medal Books* (awarded annually by CSD), and *Caldecott Medal Books* (awarded annually by CSD to the artist of the most distinguished American picture book for children). A list of 72 titles published between 1960 and 1974 that were still being read by young adults in the mid-1970's was issued as *Still Alive: The Best of the Best 1960–1974* by the Young Adult Services Division. YASD also sponsored *Best Books for Young Adults 1975* and a series of five pamphlets for "the college bound" on fiction, nonfiction, biographies, theatre, and the "current scene." *Notable Notables 1944–1974* is a list selected from 31 annual Notable Books lists prepared by members of ALA from 1944 to

1974 (Reference and Adult Services Division). One of Publishing's shortest items in 1976 had the longest title: *My old books: What are they worth? What shall I do with them?*

Publishing Services *Third Annual Report* was issued in July 1976. It reported the move of Books and Pamphlets and of Marketing from 50 E. Huron into a four-story brownstone at 716 Rush Street, Chicago. (The mailing address for all publishing offices continues to be 50 E. Huron Street.)

Periodicals. Tables 1 and 2 give statistics on *Booklist.* (For other publications, including ALA newsletters and journals, see Table 3.) *Booklist* continued to build a strong financial record in 1976. In the fiscal year ending August 31, it earned a margin of $58,900 after paying for all overhead and central services. It introduced a new, crisp design, featuring lowercase heads, in September 1976. Its policy statement on selection appeared in the same issue.

American Libraries announced rules for its Prize Article Competition in the December issue: eight prizes of $1,000 each are to be awarded for outstanding articles over a two-year period. The competition is sponsored by the J. Morris Jones–Bailey K. Howard–World Book Encyclopedia–ALA Goals Award. *American Libraries* featured a series of paintings, "Great American Libraries," on its covers from January through May. The issue of June 1976—the Centennial special—presented a national profile of the American librarian. It undertook to answer, with statistics, in interviews, with pictures: "Who We Are."

"The Great American Library Success Story," edited by Arthur Plotnik, Editor of *American Libraries,* was published as a 16-page insert in the *New York Times* on October 3, 1976.

At its fall meeting, the Executive Board of ALA accepted the recommendation of an ad hoc committee, chaired by Thomas Galvin of the University of Pittsburgh, on the place of *Choice* in the ALA administrative structure: *Choice* will continue to be administered by the Association of College and Research Libraries, an ALA Division. *Choice* published (vol. 12, March 1975–February 1976) 6,466 reviews, selected from more than 17,000 titles received during the year from publishers in the U.S. and Canada.

LTR. The November issue of *Library Technology Reports* was devoted to an updating of a survey of theft detection systems by Nancy H. Knight, a subject in which interest continued to be high. Other subjects covered in 1976 include book trucks, OCLC, microform readers, office furniture and steel shelving, and audio and video tape recorders. The November issue went to 1,500 subscribers, an increase of more than 100 over the previous year.

DONALD E. STEWART

Publishing, Book

The book publishing industry was in a relatively healthy economic state in 1976, at the same time enjoying some important legislative successes in the areas of copyright, postal affairs, taxation, and education appropriations. Book publishers' annual sales for 1976 approached $4,000,000,000, according to preliminary figures reported in the Association of American Publishers (AAP) *Annual Industry Statistics.* The industry earned more than in 1975, but the number of units sold did not keep pace because of continuing inflation.

Mergers and Acquisitions. Mergers and acquisitions of and by major book publishing houses continue with several important paperback firms purchased by hardcover houses in 1976: Doubleday & Co., Inc., purchased Dell (Dial, Delacorte, Delta), CBS put the final touches on the purchase of Fawcett, and Grosset & Dunlap acquired Ace. Among other mergers and acquisitions, Crown Publishers acquired Julian Press and the Ingram Book Company, a relatively small regional book wholesaler several years ago, greatly expanded its business by acquiring a West Coast wholesaler, Raymar Book Company. Time-Life Books moved to Washington, D.C., and the electorate made similar plans for Jimmy Carter, a book reader and one-time library trustee. Harper & Row moved its Religious Books Department to San Francisco to join its college text subsidiary, Canfield Press, while Simon & Schuster, on the other hand, publicized the signing of a long-term lease in New York City. Rolling Stone announced that it is moving East.

Will the consolidation of some big publishing houses create the need to extract more *Jaws* from the publishing output? That is, will there be more common-denominator publishing for mass appeal? Probably, given the burdens of the high cost of money, walloping increases in the cost of labor (publishing is a labor-intensive industry) and materials. Representatives of all sectors of the industry (publishers, suppliers, wholesalers, the library world) joined in forming the Book Industry Study Group, Inc., a not-for-profit corporation chaired by Andrew H. Neilly, Jr., President of John Wiley & Sons, to assist in the exchange of ideas among members of the book industry and to facilitate research into related subjects. The Group has reported on paper capacity and the future of library acquisitions.

Sales. Sales gains were posted for most book publishing categories in 1976, with a noticeable shift in distribution channels from dependence on the institutional market to increased emphasis in the retail sector. Adult trade hardbound books increased 5.5 percent, book clubs jumped ahead 12.5 percent, and mail order publications were up a whopping 62 percent. Juvenile hardbounds, highly dependent on the

Alex Haley, author of Roots, *being interviewed in October by Chicago Public Library's Broadcasting Director, Barbara Moro, on the library's weekly radio program, "Your Library Notebook."*

Text/Fiche published by the University of Chicago Press enables microfiche images to be viewed on a console reader or a hand viewer in a lighted room. An alternative to the high cost of reproducing color artwork, the system allows 84 images per 4 x 6 inch card keyed to the printed text.

library market, were down 1.7 percent. El-Hi and college sales were flat, largely a reflection of dropping enrollments and continuing budget stringencies. University press books recouped, with sales up 15.5 percent in hardcover sales and 7.1 percent in paperbound. Mass market paperback books gained 11.6 percent in sales dollars, and technical, scientific, and medical books increased 10 percent.

New life is being given to books through media tie-ins with TV series and movies. While mass marketers are not expected to desert their traditional role as reprinters, virtually each title that made the 1976 hardcover bestseller lists will come out in paper in 1977, in most cases 12 months after original publication date. The bidding figure for reprint rights appears to be scaled down some, with only three books sold for more than $1,000,000 in 1976: "The Final Days," "Your Erroneous Zones" (both Avon) and "Sleeping Murder" (Bantam). Publishers were also issuing many original novels in paperback and more trade paperbacks, whose publishers are seeking both educational and retail markets.

Bestsellers still warranted very large printings and much brouhaha. In his August 1976 Nichols Lecture at the University of Denver, Simon Michael Bessie, Senior Vice President at Harper & Row, reported little change in the characteristics of American readers, based on his comparison of 1950 and 1975 bestseller lists. While fiction, juvenile, and religious books dominated the industry in 1950, he noted, sociology, economics, fiction, and science subjects are the current forerunners. Paperbacks in all categories, trade and mass market, are finding willing audiences, with a noticeable increase in paperback books for children and young adults in 1976. Poetry has suffered a severe decline in the last quarter century due, in part, to the decrease in number of independent, personal book stores, to diminished library purchases of the genre, and to strong pulls from other media on uses of leisure time. Two newsmaking books in 1976 were a part of the literary fallout of the Nixon era: Spiro T. Agnew's "The Canfield Decision" and John Ehrlichman's "The Company." Playboy Press reported wholesaling 60,000 copies of the Agnew book with paperback rights to Berkeley Publishing, and Simon & Schuster reported heavy distribution in sales of the Ehrlichman book which debuted in May 1976, with paperback rights to Pocket Books and film rights to Paramount.

Distribution. The industry has long recognized book distribution as a difficult area in need of improvement. In 1976 the AAP formed a Book Distribution Task Force to explore the efficiencies of data transmission for handling book orders and invoices, the more efficient use of international standard book numbers (ISBN) and other standardized systems. The committee is chaired by Harold Miller, President of Houghton Mifflin and incoming Chairman of the AAP Board. The industry continues to participate actively in the Cataloging in Publication Program administered by the Library of Congress. At the year's end, some 1,100 publishers were participants in the Program. The industry also maintains its active interest in committees of the American National Standards Institute Z-39 Subcommittee, especially those working on Standard Account Numbers, Standard Order Forms, and Book Publishing Statistics.

At Christmastime, the industry, through the AAP, experimented with its first institutional advertising campaign, using the slogan "A Book Is a Loving Gift." Three television commercials were tested in New York and Minneapolis/St. Paul. If test results are satisfactory, the industry will broaden its base of contributors and mount a major campaign next year.

Copyright. The end of a long wait for a new copyright law came on October 20, 1976, when President Ford signed the bill which will become law on January 1, 1978. Following more than two decades of tense consideration and negotiation by legislative and special interest groups, the extensive lead time allows the Copyright Office to revise its regulations, the President to appoint a Copyright Royalty Commission, and the education of concerned groups about implementing the new law. (*See further* Copyright.)

International Activities. Publishers are attentive to the rapid growth of the international book trade, to the need for indigenous publishing in developing countries, to changes in international and national laws including the 1976 termination of the British Traditional Trade Agreement. In 1976 the United States imported 25 percent of Great Britain's output of books, 10.5 percent of the German publishers' output and 23 percent of Italy's book production. The need for freely open channels and for government's awareness of the cultural, political, and commercial aspects of books and other media publishing is vital and must be the concern of national and international library, education, and publishing organizations, as W. Bradford Wiley emphasized in his talk on the International Flow of Books Program on July 18, 1976, at ALA's Annual Conference. Industry representatives participated in a publishing seminar in Nigeria in 1976, bringing together publishers, booksellers, and librarians in common cause. AAP's President, Townsend Hoopes, led a group of publishers to the USSR in 1976 to explain U.S. book publishing in a seminar there.

Publishing Education. Education for, in, and about publishing became the subject of intense study by a new AAP committee, chaired by Samuel S. Vaughan, Publisher of Doubleday Books. In cooperation with the Publishing Division of the Special Libraries Association, institutions of higher learning across the country were surveyed to discover what book publishing courses are offered. A total of 86 pertinent courses came to light and are reported in a directory of the "Education For Publishing Survey Report" distributed by the AAP. In November 1976, 46 educators and publishers convened for a first Education for Publishing Colloquium, a meeting that served as a catalyst drawing people with common interests together for the first time. Plans were under way for educators and publishers to stay informed about relevant trends in the industry, employment opportunities, special courses, and more. Educators were considering ways to improve coordination of their efforts to track students who have taken publishing courses at Radcliffe, the University of Denver, New York University, and Stanford, for example. The Committee, to report to the AAP Board in the spring of 1977, will include recommendations for the future of education for publishing.

The AAP continued to manifest concern for the freedom to express and disseminate ideas, domestically through the education, litigative, and legislative activities of its Freedom to Read Committee, and internationally through the Committee on International Freedom to Publish, which concerned itself with the oppression of writers and publishers abroad and with other inhibitions on freedom of expression of the international scene.

ASSOCIATION OF AMERICAN PUBLISHERS

Publishing, Magazine

The proverb what is good for the periodical publisher may be bad for the librarian proved itself once again in 1976. Romping happily up the economic comeback trail, general magazine publishers in 1976 reported average increases of 20 to 30 percent in ad revenues over 1975. At the same time, the annual periodical price index (*Library Journal*, August 1976, pp. 1600–05) indicated that the cost of an American periodical in 1976 was $2.58 more than in 1975. The average 1976 subscription price of $22.52 was up 12.9 percent.

Increases were due to two basic causes: (1) scholarly, scientific, and specialized publishers, who make up almost 95 percent of the source of large library titles, had continuing higher production costs in 1976 and had to increase cover prices to meet economic ends; (2) general magazine publishers who traditionally keep subscription prices down to boost circulation had begun to reverse the formula—they now counted as much upon revenue from readers as from advertisers. *Good Housekeeping* was among several women's magazines (others were *Ms* and *Ladies' Home Journal*) who for the first time in memory reported circulation revenues exceeded advertising profits. Precisely what this trend may mean to editorial policy was uncertain, but there were at least two indicators in 1976.

Alternatives for Revenue. The first was seen at *Esquire*. A plan was devised to have a company sponsor a magazine article much along the same lines as commercials on television support programs. Xerox paid Harrison Salisbury $55,000 for an article in the magazine's Bicentennial issue. In return he mentioned the sponsor at the beginning and the end of the article. Two more projects were planned. Dependent as much on the goodwill of readers as on advertising income, the publisher cancelled the other company sponsored articles when readers raised a furor. *New Yorker* writer E.B. White summarized the winning argument against the new method of underwriting magazine costs: "I don't want IBM or the National Rifle Association providing me with a funded spectacular when I open my paper. I want to read what the editor and publisher dig up on their own—and paid for out of the till" (*The New York Times*, June 10, 1976, p. 15).

Perhaps more reliance on readers than on advertisers will improve commercial magazines, but the same philosophy is seeping down to some of the specialized titles. For example, the otherwise stodgy alumni *Harvard Magazine* developed a new theory for limited circulation titles. Reach out for readers who want to be associated, no matter how tenuously, with the University. How to do this? Provide them with a general magazine with wider appeal than to the "old boy" circuit. And this is precisely what the editors have done. The result: the magazine is almost out of the red, and as one critic put it, the title is pushing *The National Geographic* as *the* magazine to have on display in waiting rooms of corporations, doctors' offices, and law firms. Actually, this formula may work for some specialized titles, although for esoteric journals in chemistry, physics, philosophy, and others, the only immediate defense against disaster seems to be raising subscription prices.

TRENDS

CONSER's Promise. Faced with rising subscription costs, libraries have had to seek savings by cutting administrative and clerical serials tasks. One hope was offered by the cooperative national project to establish basic serial records for American and Canadian libraries which was well under way in 1976. CONSER, a file-building project at the Ohio College Library Center, will establish machine readable bibliographic records for approximately 250,000 current serials. Later responsibility for the records will shift to the Library of Congress and an effort will be made to include retrospective titles. The purpose is, according to the CONSER manual, "to establish a file which will be accessible via past, present, and future bibliographic, descriptive or other iden-

Publishing, Magazine

"The January issue comes out in October, the April issue comes out in January, the July issue comes out in April, and the October issue comes out in July, but I don't have any of them."

tifying approaches." CONSER may be working for the impossible—a unified, national method of cataloging serials which should save labor and costs (*see also* Automation).

In the never ending estimates of how many people read what, one of the more interesting approaches was supplied by the *Media Industry Newsletter* for advertisers and magazine publishers. In its June 7 issue MIN reported: "in a sample of 1200 respondents in the top 50 markets, 19.3 percent bought hardcover books or paperbacks in the last month. However, only 1.7 percent bought a book which they had first read as a condensation in a magazine or newspaper." And: "Of those that read condensation . . . only 8.6 percent found it 'well written' and the *Reader's Digest* was the only publication consistently cited for its abridged books. Faith in the most widely circulated magazine in the world is not only shared by readers but also by many advertisers. In March the *Reader's Digest* won a place in *Guinness Book of Records* for running the most expensive print advertisement in history—$1,280,000 for a 48-page insert to advertise the Bicentennial in Pennsylvania.

Acquisition of Comics. If reader antipathy to popular titles condensed in magazines might be an excuse for libraries to avoid excessive purchase of ephemeral books, the librarian could find little encouragement for continuing exclusion of at least the better comic magazines. Along with other popular culture materials, the comic received a final heavy nod of approval by none less than literary critic Leslie A. Fiedler. Reviewing the impressive 785-page *World Encyclopedia of Comics* (New York: Chelsea House, 1976), the distinguished English professor admitted to being "hooked" on some comics, "though I scarcely confessed the fact even to myself" (*New York Times Book Review*, September 5, 1976).

Censorship. Even censorship took some unorthodox twists. Along with the "standard" cases reported in the *Index on Censorship* and *Newsletter on Intellectual Freedom*, there were less obvious problems. For example, in the March issue of *Atlantic Monthly* there was a 5,000 word article on "Rip-Off at the Supermarket." While denying the company actually banned the magazine from its numerous supermarket newsstands, executives of one chain reportedly sent out a memo alerting stores to the issue. The result was that the staid *Atlantic* disappeared from many racks. The magazine's publisher said it was the chain's right to sell what it pleased, but it was depressing to think that ideas may be treated as if they were bottles of catsup.

A more serious, lasting check on the press came with the Supreme Court's denial of *Time* magazine's appeal to reverse a lower court ruling. The court had awarded a Palm Beach woman damages for a story in *Time* regarding her divorce. The magazine pleaded the woman was a "public figure," and as such she had to prove *Time* guilty of "actual malice," as well as inaccuracy. Not so said the Supreme Court, and in so doing may have indicated to publishers that the Court had become less sympathetic toward First Amendment privileges.

New Magazines. While *McCall's* celebrated its 100th anniversary with a 304-page April issue, a number of new general titles appeared in 1976. Those of special interest to libraries: *Working Woman*, a no-nonsense magazine for working women; *L'Officiel/USA*, an English language version of the French high fashion magazine; *Travel & Fashion*, for "the beautiful people who enjoy life"; *American Business*, from the not to be repressed Ralph Ginzburg, who spent time in jail after issuing his now defunct *Eros*; and *Children's Express*, a commercial venture along the line of *Kids* in that all of the writers and the editor are under 21 years of age. Then there was *Firehouse*, for both fire fighters and fire buffs—almost sure of success because its editor is the author of the best-selling *Report From Engine Co. 82*. Along with the annual crop of 75 to 100 new general magazines, there were the usual specialized journals which seem to defy economic laws by existing primarily on membership dues and library subscriptions. Among more intriguing titles were *The De-Acquisitions Librarian*, dedicated to weeding of books; and *Spirit*, the magazine of Black arts and culture. Some idea of the still exploding information scene was provided by the 1975–76 edition of *Ulrich's International Periodical Directory*. It identified 60,000 titles, or 5,000 more than in the 1973–74 edition.

Controversy. If one sought the most controversial magazine of the year it would be *Counter-Spy*, a Washington quarterly along the line of the old *Ramparts*. (The *Village Voice*, treated in many libraries as a newspaper, won the controversy award hands down with publication of the U.S. House committee report on intelligence activities.) When CIA station chief Richard Welch was gunned down in Athens, *Counter-Spy* was the target of criticism because it had identified the agent in an earlier issue. Although admitting discomfort, but not blame, the editors countered with a new list of names in a subsequent issue. A magazine which appeals to a diametrically opposed audience to that of *Counter-Spy* is *Soldier of Fortune*. In its second year, *Soldier of Fortune* enjoyed continuing and growing readership by extolling the virtues of mercenary soldiers. It, too, looks to the CIA for ways to attract readership. For example, a major article in 1976 concerned spy devices employed by the CIA.

BILL KATZ

Publishing, Newspaper

Although affected by the declining economy in 1975–76, newspaper advertising reached a new high of $8,430,000,000 in 1975 (the latest year for which statistics were available). The American Newspaper Publishers Association (ANPA) reported that with 378,500 employees, the industry ranked behind only the steel and auto industries as an employer. There continued to be a slight decline, however, from the industry high of 385,500 recorded in 1973.

The share of total advertising revenue claimed by newspapers was 29.8 percent, more than the combined shares of radio and television. Advertising revenues steadily increased despite the economy's sluggish performance, but at a slower rate. Television claimed 18.8 percent of the nation's advertising budget; radio 7.1 percent and all other media 39.1. Other major earners were magazines with 5.6 percent and direct mail with 14.9.

Declining Numbers. The number of newspapers declines at a slight rate each year; that trend is more noticeable among weeklies than among the daily publications. The total number of dailies in 1975 was 1,756, down 12 from the previous year. Morning papers decreased by one to 339 and evening papers declined from 1,449 to 1,436. Nineteen daily newspapers publish both morning and evening and were counted in each category, a decrease in that category from 21 for the previous year.

Daily circulation has declined at a slow rate since an all-time high of 63,147,000 in 1973 and stood at 60,655,000 at the end of 1975.

Sunday circulation slipped to 51,096,000 from the all-time high two years earlier of 51,717,000. Some publishers have deliberately reduced their circulation to conserve newsprint but other reductions were laid to changing reader habits and to increased retail prices of the product. A combination of factors including inflation, recession, buyer habits, and conservation measures reduced newsprint consumption from 10,206,500 tons in 1974 to 9,090,500 tons in 1975.

Weekly newspapers showed somewhat more effect of the soft economy than dailies although gross income was up $100,000,000 to $1,700,000,000 in 1975. Weekly circulation declined by 1.7 percent to 35,176,130 and the number of weeklies was down 126 to 7,486 in 1975. The total weekly circulation declined for the first time in 10 years to 35,176,000.

Canadian Papers. Canadian newspapers remained financially sound. As did their American counterparts, Canadian newspapers led all other media in advertising revenue approaching $527,000,000 for 29.3 percent of the total Canadian expenditure.

Daily circulation dropped from a high in 1974 of 4,985,382 to 4,885,782 or 2 percent. The number of dailies in Canada decreased by one to 114 in 1975, that one loss being in the morning category, which decreased to 22 while evening papers stood at 92.

STAFF

Publishing, Newspaper

Newspapers and the First Amendment

Throughout the Bicentennial year newspapermen and other journalists fought to preserve the Founding Fathers' conception of freedom of the press against an increasing number of judges and public officials who sought to abridge it.

All of the traditional, generally conservative journalistic organizations became aroused, held seminars, passed resolutions and appointed committees. Most active in the defensive effort, however, was the three-year-old Reporters' Committee for Freedom of the Press. It issued newsletters and reports on the status of the legal struggles and lobbied for legislation previously considered unnecessary, to protect newsgatherers and the people's right to know.

Despite open meetings and open records (sunshine) laws, reporters increasingly were barred from meetings of city councils, school boards and similar public groups and were denied access to public records. In DeKalb, Illinois, the *Northern Star*, student publication, sued the administration of the school, Northern Illinois University, for violating the Illinois open meeting law. Similarly the *Call-Chronicle* sued Allentown, Pennsylvania, officials for withholding the transcript of a four-hour police hearing.

The Ohio Supreme Court reversed lower court decisions to permit the Dayton *Daily News* to check the list of city jail inmates. However, the Texas Supreme Court refused to allow the Houston *Chronicle* to see all police records, including "offense records" and "rap sheets."

Mandel Case. Most publicized case of a judge's attempt to conceal court records involved the corruption trial of Maryland Governor Marvin Mandel. The U.S. Court of Appeals for the Fourth District ruled that sealing all records indiscriminately abridged press freedom. In Philadelphia an article critical of Mayor Frank L. Rizzo was ripped out of 40,000 copies of *Hustler* magazine. It assailed Rizzo for reputedly calling for a ten-hour blockade of the *Inquirer* building by the Philadelphia Building and Construction Trades Council. Rizzo unsuccessfully sought a court injunction to prevent distribution of an *Inquirer* issue which contained a satirical piece about him. He then sued the paper for $6,000,000.

There were scores, perhaps hundreds of cases of judges barring reporters from their courtrooms during preliminary hearings or parts of trials. Contempt citations followed journalistic violations of gag orders and appellate court decisions were inconsistent. Typical cases included the following:

The Minnesota Supreme Court unanimously reversed Jackson County Judge Harvey Holton, who had excluded the public and press during the selection of a jury to try James Stewart, 18, for first-degree murder and aggravated robbery of an Iranian student at Oregon State University.

The California Supreme Court refused to hear an appeal by KPFK, cited for contempt for refusing to surrender a purported communiqué from the Symbionese Liberation Army.

Le Mistral, a New York French restaurant, won $1,200 compensatory and $250,000 punitive damages from CBS on a trespassing charge growing out of a CBS-TV news team's filming of patrons.

A federal judge in Brooklyn was reversed by the U.S. Court of Appeals of the Second Circuit for excluding the public and press from a $5,000,000 negligence suit by Connie Francis against the Howard Johnson Motor Lodge where the singer was raped.

Judith Exner was refused an injunction to prevent *Star*, a national weekly, from publishing details of an affair she allegedly had with President John F. Kennedy.

Lt. William Calley, imprisoned for his participation in the My Lai massacre during the Vietnam war, failed to persuade the United States Supreme Court that excessive publicity had jeopardized his chances for a fair trial. The U.S. Court of Appeals for the Fifth Circuit had previously decided in favor of Calley.

The Ohio Supreme Court ruled for the Akron *Beacon-Journal* and the Dayton newspapers after lower court judges had excluded reporters from criminal trials.

Gag Orders. Gag orders in important cases attracted attention. For instance, the federal judge in the trial of Patricia Hearst for bank robbery barred reporters while he questioned prospective jurors. In Denver the press was barred from the preliminary hearing of singer Claudine Longets, former wife of Andy Williams, charged with manslaughter in the death of a professional ski champion, Vladimir (Spider) Sabich.

San Mateo, California, County Municipal Court Judge Wilbur Johnson tried to prevent press coverage of the search of the Frederick Woods estate in connection with the kidnapping of a school bus with 26 children and the driver, later found buried in an abandoned quarry. The sheriff had already released the news, however, before he heard of the judge's order.

Some of these acts of judicial editorship occurred even after a 9-0 United States Supreme Court decision in late June which the press hoped would be respected by other judges. The case arose in Lincoln County, Nebraska, where Judge Ruff ordered a gag on news of the preliminary hearing into mass murder charges against Erwin Simants, charged with killing six members of the Henry Kellie family at Sutherland, Nebraska. The Nebraska Supreme Court upheld the gag order as did United States Supreme Court Justice Harry A. Blackmun, who, however, changed his mind when the full court acted. The press's jubilation over the decision was blunted by Chief Justice Warren E. Burger's statement that the court did not rule out the possibility that such orders might be issued to protect an individual's right to a fair trial under other circumstances which, however, he did not enumerate.

Prior Restraint. For about two centuries journalists had also believed they were constitutionally protected against prior restraint in news gathering and fact publishing. Throughout the years there were occasional incidents of reporters and editors being jailed for refusing to reveal their news sources, but the victims always emerged as heroes to their colleagues and readers. Then, in June, 1972, came the United States Supreme Court's 5 to 4 decision that a New York *Times* reporter, Earl Caldwell, could be held in contempt for refusing to tell a grand jury where he obtained information concerning the Black Panthers.

Although the case against Caldwell has not been pursued, in the wake of the precedent-making decision, there have been hundreds of reporters who were cited for contempt and either fined or jailed or both for refusing to reveal sources of confidential information. About half the states have passed shield laws to grant journalists the same privilege to be silent that lawyers, doctors and clergymen enjoy. Despite these laws numerous judges have disregarded the legislation. This is especially true in California, where the Fresno *Bee* case occurred and where William Farr has served several jail terms totalling at least 45 days for refusing to reveal where, when he was a Los Angeles *Herald-Examiner* reporter, he learned of the future plans of the Charles Manson family, which murdered Sharon Tate. In 1976, at the same time it struck down the Nebraska gag law, the United States Supreme Court refused to review Farr's case.

News-Source Protection. Another case that gave journalists good cheer was in a different category: confidentiality, or the right of the newsgatherer to refuse to reveal his news sources. At Fresno a California Superior Court judge finally gave up after two editors and two reporters for the Fresno *Bee* spent 15 days in jail and seemed willing to remain there indefinitely rather than tell anyone how they learned about testimony before a grand jury investigating a bribery charge against a public official who, incidentally, was tried and acquitted. Commented Judge Hollis Best when he finally released the four:

"I am persuaded that the newsman's ethic is a moral principle."

During 1976 several appellate courts reversed lower courts that had cited newsmen for contempt for refusing to violate confidentiality. One such case concerned Frank Mayo of the Denver *Rocky Mountain News* who had obtained a transcript of secret grand jury testimony about a murder. The Florida Supreme Court overturned a contempt citation against Lucy Ware Morgan of the St. Petersburg *Times* who obtained the contents of a sealed grand jury report. A U.S. Court of Appeals vacated citations against two Charleston *Gazette* (W. Va.) reporters in a similar case. In Chicago a federal appellate court struck down a district court rule barring lawyers from talking to reporters.

Schorr Case. The most important confidentiality case of 1976 involved Daniel Schorr, veteran reporter for Columbia Broadcasting Company. The Ethics Committee of the House of Representatives spent $150,000 in the vain attempt to learn where Schorr obtained a copy of the report of the House Select Committee on Intelligence which the House had voted not to make public. The House's action did not come until after *The New York Times* had published the highlights of the report, highly critical of the Central Intelligence Agency, the Associated Press had distributed much of the same information, and Schorr had broadcast it over the CBS network. Nevertheless, Schorr was cited for giving a copy of the report to *Village Voice*, a New York weekly.

At least 385 persons testified before the Ethics Committee, and it became apparent that probably at least 170 copies of the report had been in circulation. After Schorr firmly refused to tell how he obtained his copy, a motion to recommend a contempt citation to the House as a whole failed, but by only one vote, 6 to 5. Schorr, who had been suspended by CBS during the many months the issue was pending, resigned from CBS. He accepted appointment as a journalism professor on the West Coast. Since there was no clearcut or one sided verdict no precedent was established by the historic case.

Other Issues. An important change in judicial interpretation of libel laws occurred when the United States Supreme Court upheld the $100,000 judgment against *Time* magazine awarded Mary Alice Sullivan, who lost a 17-month divorce countersuit to Russell Firestone. He had sued charging "extreme cruelty and adultery," but the verdict omitted mention of adultery which, if proved, would have made it impossible for her to receive alimony. *Time* reported that Firestone had won the case and cited his original grounds. Until the decision in this case, courts had considered honest errors where there was no malice as a defense.

Revision of the federal criminal code was postponed as civil liberties and journalistic groups vigorously opposed the proposed legislation in Congress. The omnibus 1975 bill, S. 1, dubbed "Nixon's Revenge," was broken into several separate bills, but the objectionable features were retained: secrecy and penalties for both public employees and publications for violations of what was deemed not fit for the public to know.

Still unsolved at year's end was the murder of Don Bolles, investigative reporter for the Phoenix *Arizona Republic*. Bolles lived 11 days after a bomb exploded in his automobile. He had been lured to a restaurant presumably to obtain information on underworld activities in real estate. The Investigative Reporters and Editors, which held its first conference in Indianapolis in June 1976 with about 300 members, undertook the task of continuing the crusading work that Bolles was killed to prevent. (*See also* Intellectual Freedom.)

Most journalists probably agree with the *Cincinnati Enquirer's* editorial comment that "the battle for freedom of the press is a battle never fully, permanently won."

CURTIS MACDOUGALL

Realia

Standards for cataloging nonprint materials; an interpretation and practical application by Alma M. Tillin and William J. Quinby, 4th edition, was published by the Association for Educational Communications and Technology in 1976. Though definition of realia was broad, "things as they are, without alteration," it did exclude replicas. Communication with libraries around the country revealed that public librarians tend to include games, toys, art prints, sculpture, equipment, and tools as realia.

A sampling of current practice follows: The Elk Grove Village (Illinois) Public Library has a multiplicity of materials other than books, Administrative Librarian Janet Steiner reported: sculpture, toys, hand puppets, art prints, cassette players, and a pattern exchange, and especially games. Games remain on the shelves very little time, even in multiple copies. The use of "Baggies" for small pieces helps reduce loss.

Crutches, walkers, and wheelchairs loaned to those in need for unlimited lengths of time are a part of the service at the E. Jack Sharpe Public Library, White Cloud, Michigan (Nancy Harper).

Winskill Elementary School Instructional Materials Center (Cecelia Zellinger, Director) in Lancaster, Wisconsin, follows the state Department of Public Instruction's *Cataloging, processing, administering AV materials* for an extensive collection of curriculum-related realia, excepting audiovisual equipment, framed art prints, games, phonics kits, and other materials. All material in the I.M.C. circulates to students, teachers and the general public.

Quality learning toys are featured at the Maude Preston Palenske Memorial Library, St. Joseph, Michigan, reported Alice Thornycroft, Children's Librarian. The toys are circulated in colorful denim drawstring bags; and games and puzzles have been added for older children. The program has grown rapidly in its first year and has experienced only minor problems of loss, damage, or theft. Cataloging has been minimal.

In academia, realia finds use as display materials. Texas Tech University Librarian Grace E. Lee reported recent exhibits of Japanese items with the Admiral Perry report of his expedition to Japan; Australian aboriginal artifacts; and several student displays on a variety of topics, all using realia as enchantment.

A leader in public library use of realia, Joseph Eisner's Plainedge Public Library, Massepequa, New York, added auto ramps, jack stands, a jack and a heavy-duty buffer to its dwell meters and auto timing lights. They have also added an appliance truck, furniture dollies, saws, a small engine repair kit, a miter box and saw to their list of equipment for loan; other items include a typewriter, sewing machine, rototiller, posthole digger, 8 mm projector, cassette player, electronic calculator, belt sander, saber saw, router, and extension ladder.

Patterns, table games, and various small art works, in many cases donated, are checked out or given away as need and supply dictate, reported Darlene Van Zuilen, Librarian at Mendon (Michigan) Public Library.

Music, toys and kids playing on the floor help Trish Gwyn create a warm, relaxing atmosphere for the children's room at Rockingham County Public Library in Eden, North Carolina. Her use of realia to illustrate the theme of a story hour (an aquarium with *Swimmy*, for instance) demonstrates another imaginative use of things in support of books.

The Canal Fulton (Ohio) Public Library in 1976 added 7-10X zoom binoculars, a 35mm single lens reflex camera, a metal-mineral detector, and an audio synthesizer to its growing list of realia.

An Early Learning Materials Center utilizing games, toys, and objects available to teachers for use with 4- to 7-year-old children is a feature of the Grosse Pointe (Michigan) Public Library. Another aspect reported by Director William T. Peters is the collection of hand and power tools provided and maintained by the local Rotary Club. The range of tools is wide (from goggles to tin snips) and a note on their literature encourages suggestions for new additions to the collection.

These scattered reports, signaling imagination, enthusiasm, innovation and, perhaps most of all, success, underscore the need for a forum on the use of realia in libraries of all kinds.

THOMAS BROWNFIELD

Recordings, Sound

Ideally, the libraries of the United States should have essentially the same sorts of cultural, economic, and social relationships to sound recordings that they have to books and other sources of printed information. If this premise is accepted, then no one who knows much about sound recordings and their role in American culture would seriously suggest that the profession has come even close to this ideal. For one thing, the librarian's use of sound recordings remains largely a local phenomenon. By this is meant that the vast systems of manual and automated bibliographic control and access which have been structured to deal with printed information have not been supplemented by similar systems to control and provide access to sound recordings. Such projects as these seldom include sound recordings: systems of retrospective collection building, systems of interlibrary loan, copying services, union catalogs, cooperative acquisitions programs, or programs for resources sharing. This melancholy assessment of the state of the art is necessary if one is to fully appreciate the advances made during 1976.

Discographic Control. The most notable accomplishments were in the area of discographic control ("discographic control" being for sound recordings exactly what bibliographic control is for printed materials: one of the foundations of library service). Richard S. Halsey's *Classical Music Recordings for Home and Library* (ALA, 1976) filled a long-standing and serious gap in the library literature, and should quickly be accepted as the standard guide to the recorded repertory. In addition to an extensive discography of in-print items, which may be considered a standard catalog of classical recordings, Halsey includes much information on selection, acquisitions, and organization. G.K. Hall & Co. published in 1976 the *Catalog of Phonorecordings of Music and Oral Data Held by the Archives of Traditional Music,* thus providing access to the unique holdings of Indiana University's magnificent collection. The same publisher also announced plans to issue the massive catalog of the sound recordings in the Eastman School of Music's Sibley Music Library. These two publications are examples of the sorts of tools which are needed if librarians are to begin to provide access to discographic data and the contents of major historical, archival, and reference collections. One hopes that they are but the first of a long series of special library catalogs.

Cataloging. Librarians seemed to respond favorably to the new version of Chapter 14 of the *Anglo-American Cataloging Rules* (ALA, 1976). In 1976 the Cataloging Code Revision Committee of the ALA approved further revisions of this section of the rules, which will be incorporated into the Second Edition of AACR. The revisions are generally extensions of traditional library policies with the addition of principles of International Standard Bibliographic Description. Fundamental questions of special forms of entry for sound recordings have not been dealt with, nor have the new rules incorporated standard discographic practice. Though some librarians may be happy with the new rules, discographers and other specialists who have never approved of library-style cataloging will continue to complain about AACR.

ARSC. The Association for Recorded Sound Collections (ARSC) continued to move ahead, albeit slowly and cautiously, on several important projects. Gerald D. Gibson, who became President of ARSC in 1976, resigned as Editor of the *ARSC Journal* and was replaced by Michael H. Gray. Among several outstanding pieces published in the *ARSC Journal,* Steve Smolian's "Standards for the Review of Discographic Works" (*ARSC Journal,* 7, no. 3, 1976, pp. 47–55) is the most coherent statement of standards for discography yet issued.

Other ARSC projects still in progress at the end of 1976 include the initiation of a publications program, a series of discographic monographs, and a syllabus for the education of sound archivists and record librarians. Plans for a union catalog of the holdings of several major archives, under discussion for several years, seem to have materialized into a firm project. The collections involved are those with strong collections of early commercial recordings of classical music (e.g., the Stanford University Archive of Recorded Sound). ARSC has set up the apparatus to develop discographic standards to serve as the cataloging code for this project.

New Archives. The preservation and organization of sound recordings to document 20th-century culture and provide resources for research seem to present problems which preclude their being integrated with either circulating collections of sound recordings or with collections of printed materials. Hardly a year passes without several announcements of new archival collections to deal with some dimension of this historico-cultural aspect of sound recordings. To the list of institutions already interested in recordings of jazz, one can now add the National Ragtime and Jazz Archive at Southern Illinois University.

Attempts to preserve recordings of the early days of radio broadcasting with a few notable exceptions have been the work of private collectors. This important cultural assignment has now been taken over by the Museum of Broadcasting in New York City. Founded and financed (through 1980) with a donation from William S. Paley, the Museum will document the history of radio and television broadcasting and is assembling a reference collection of audio and visual tapes going back to the earliest days of radio broadcasting.

More and more libraries were involved in local oral history projects during 1976. A tremendous amount of data is available and more will be inventoried and indexed.

Notable Publications. Both the Smithsonian Institution and the Library of Congress Music Division's Recorded Sound Section issued important LP recordings in 1976. These included both reissues of historical 78 rpm sources and new material never before released. For the Library of Congress Richard Spottswood compiled and edited a monumentally important series of LP recordings, "Folk Music in America" (five LPs were issued in 1976, and there are more to come). The Smithsonian Institution continued its series of LP recordings of classic jazz. With the appointment of Alan Jabbour to head the Smithsonian's Folk Life Division, librarians can expect recorded material of the uniqueness and high

Recordings, Sound

quality of the work Jabbour did with Carl Fleischhauer for LC's Archive of Folk Song ("The Hammons Family: A Study of a West Virginia Family's Traditions," 12-inch LP recording AFS L65-L66, Library of Congress, 1973).

The Industry. More than one critic compiling lists of "best recordings of the year" noted that current American music is characterized by a rich diversity of styles. The audiences which provide the economic base for the recording industry, however, consist of young people between the ages of 14 and 24. These listeners purchase recordings of popular music. Within the industry there was much concern about the decline in the size of this age group and its economic impact on the industry. Manufacturers were urged to begin to actively cultivate audiences (i.e., "markets") of people who have passed the ripe old age of 24. The modest increases in the sales of jazz recordings (a genre now largely supported by adults) and recordings of classical music seem to indicate beginnings of a change in patterns of production and sales that had been stable for more than a decade.

In summary, school, public, and academic libraries serving traditional educational and entertainment functions did not report any spectacular innovations during 1976. But scholars and researchers, who have been poorly served in the past, saw improved professional services. The cultural elitism, which for many decades limited most library collections to forms of classical music, was a thing of the past. Public libraries acquired large quantities of popular recordings. Academic libraries were faced with younger scholars working in areas of popular culture research and teaching which required not only recordings of popular music, but also recordings of radio and television broadcasts. The performance of academic libraries in serving the burgeoning interest in popular culture research has not yet been formally surveyed or evaluated. As to serious interest in the scholarship of recorded sound, optimism should be tempered by the knowledge that only some 140 libraries subscribed to the *ARSC Journal* last year.

GORDON STEVENSON

Reference and Adult Services Division

A highpoint of 1976 for the Reference and Adult Services Division (RASD) of the American Library Association was the adoption of "A Commitment to Information Services: Developmental Guidelines" [RQ 15:327–330 (Summer 1976)] by the RASD Board of Directors, Midwinter 1976. These guidelines, prepared by the RASD Standards Committee, were the focus of one of the Division's ALA Centennial Conference programs.

The wide range of other topics considered in the numerous programs presented by the Division and its units during the 1976 ALA Centennial Conference served to suggest the even wider range of the Division's interests, concerns, and activities of its units during the year. A preconference workshop, "Teaching Design—Interlibrary Loan Basics," at Rosary College, July 16–17, was planned to assist those who must themselves conduct interlibrary loan workshops. Other Conference programs included consideration of on-line bibliographic services (Information Retrieval Committee); experiences in the translation of the third edition of the *Great Soviet Encyclopedia* (Division program in cooperation with the Macmillan Company, the American publisher); an information exchange on bibliographic data bases for business reference (Business Reference Services Committee); and the heritage of the genealogical collections in the growth of the Newberry Library (History Section Genealogy Committee). A tour of some of the ethnic museums and repositories in Chicago was arranged by the History Section.

The Library Services to an Aging Population Committee compiled a directory of state and regional agencies working with the aging and set up an Older American Program Idea Exchange now available on loan for use at conferences and seminars.

A sampling of the RASD membership participated in a survey conducted for the Information Retrieval Committee, "Attitudes Toward Automated Information Retrieval Services Among RASD members" [RQ 16:133–141 (Winter 1976)]. Not many RASD members have been involved in automated information retrieval services, but those surveyed generally agreed that libraries should be involved with such services. Preliminary results of the survey aided the Committee in planning its Conference program. Membership interest in the topic was further evidenced by the establishment of a discussion group on Machine-Assisted Reference Services (MARS) and the distribution in September of an occasional newsletter, *Messages from MARS*, by that group.

Notable Books. The Notable Books Council was responsible for compiling and annotating two lists in 1976: *Notable Books 1975* and *Notable Notables*, both published in leaflet form by ALA Publishing Services. The former is the 32nd such list compiled for the general adult reader and for librarians who work with adult readers. (For a complete list of Notable Books, 1944–1975, see the first edition of this *Yearbook, 1976 Centennial Edition*.) *Notable Notables*, compiled by a subcommittee of the Notable Books Council, is a selection from the 31 annual lists, 1944–74, based on the current criteria for Notable Books: literary merit, inspiration or pleasure, knowledge comprehensible to the nonspecialist, or promise of a contribution toward the solution of a contemporary problem. Several books which the passage of time has marked as outstanding were also included even though they were not selected for the earlier annual listings.

Outstanding Reference Books. The annual list of Outstanding Reference Books was again compiled for publication in the *Library Journal* (April 15, 1976). This list is aimed at the small and medium-sized library and adheres to the conventional definition of a reference source compiled specifically to supply ready information on a certain subject or group of subjects in a form that will facilitate its easy use. Copies of the titles on the list were solicited from the publishers for exhibit during the ALA 1976 Centennial Conference and at various library conferences and continuing education workshops for library staff members.

RQ. *RQ*, the official quarterly journal of the Division, continued as a perquisite of membership in the Division and was also made available to nonmembers by subscription. In addition to "A Commitment to Information Services: Developmental Guidelines," other items prepared by RASD committees and published in *RQ* are: "Indian Materials and Services Committee [*RQ* 15:215–218 (Spring 1976)], "The State of the Art of Bibliography and Indexing of American History," History Section Bibliography and Indexes Committee [*RQ* 15:219–221 (Spring 1976)], and "History Section News" [*RQ* 16:68–69 (Fall 1976)].

1976 Mudge Citation. The Isadore Gilbert Mudge Citation for 1976 was awarded posthumously to John Neal Waddell, "an outstanding reference specialist, a gifted teacher of reference work, and a librarian who carried forward the scholarship and the concept of service exemplified by Isadore Gilbert Mudge and Constance M. Winchell." No recipient was named for the Dartmouth Medal Award.

Indexes. The Committee on Wilson Indexes completed the study of the periodical coverage of *Applied Science and Technology Index* and initiated studies of the periodical coverage of *Education Index* and *Readers' Guide to Periodical Literature,* all indexes published by the H.W. Wilson Company. Final decisions on inclusion of specific titles in each index are made by a vote of the subscribers but this is greatly facilitated by the work of this RASD Committee in developing the voting lists.

Catalog Use. The Catalog Use Committee's report of its study of the Library of Congress *Subject Catalog* was submitted to the Library of Congress in June. Although the survey suggested that the *Subject Catalog* is of primary importance to technical services departments, it also revealed that it is an important tool in library public services and is commonly used for literature searches and for checking materials available in specific disciplines.

History. The History Section of RASD represents the subject interests of librarians and others engaged in history reference and in historical research with users of library collections. The Section's Local History Committee initiated a project of collecting information about local history collections in libraries with the objective of identifying criteria for establishing guidelines for local history services and materials in libraries.

Labor Service. The American Federation of Labor/Congress of Industrial Organizations–ALA (RASD) Joint Committee on Library Service to Labor Groups was another committee conducting a survey in 1976. The findings of this survey to ascertain the status of existing labor collections and services in public libraries throughout the country will be used by the Joint Committee to expand and clarify its service to libraries and labor organizations.

ANDREW M. HANSEN

RASD Officers

PRESIDENT: (July 1976–June 1977):
Ruth White Ormston, University of Georgia, Athens

VICE-PRESIDENT/PRESIDENT-ELECT:
Virginia Boucher, University of Colorado Libraries, Boulder

SECRETARY:
Barbara J. Brown, Pennsylvania State Library, Harrisburg

EXECUTIVE SECRETARY:
Andrew M. Hansen

ASSOCIATE EXECUTIVE SECRETARY:
Mary Jo Lynch

Membership (August 31, 1976): 5,502 (3,396 personal and 2,106 organizational)

Reference Services

In compiling the reference happenings for 1976, and in view of the American Library Association's centennial celebration this year, it is interesting to compare reference concerns of 1876 with those of today. Samuel S. Green of the Worcester Free Public Library is considered to be one of the first advocates of reference service in libraries as we know it today.

I paraphrase what Green said at the 1876 conference in Philadelphia:[1] (1) There are certain types of patrons who need to be asked if they can be helped; (2) caution should be taken by the librarian in recommending resources for medical and legal questions; (3) people have to be instructed to use a catalog; (4) mingle freely with patrons and help them, find out what they need, and after this policy is pursued for a series of years, the community will realize that it cannot dispense with its library and will see that there are more funds for books and staff; (5) a "reference" librarian should have sympathy, cheerfulness, and patience; (6) a librarian should be unwilling to have an inquirer leave

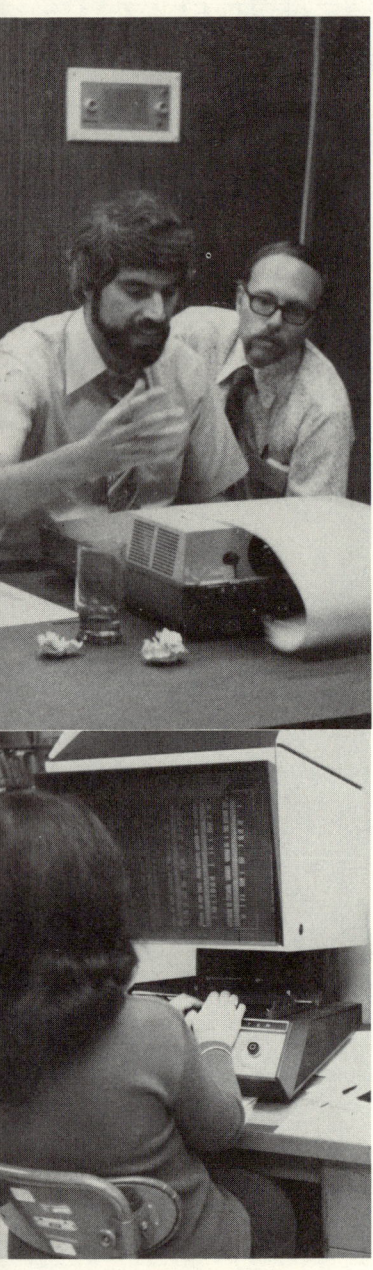

(Top) A representative of Lockheed Information Systems instructing reference librarians in a 1976 workshop on techniques of on-line searching sponsored by the Arizona State Library Extension Service. The Extension Service also developed the Arizona Numeric Register on microfiche (above) to aid statewide interlibrary loans.

the library with his question unanswered.

The concerns in 1876 were the same as those in 1976. One could agree, at least, that when reference librarians get together they still discuss the same things.

New Guidelines. After 100 years, then, reference librarians are just now getting something that may be called "reference service guidelines." These new guidelines prepared by the Standards Committee of the Reference and Adult Services Division, "A Commitment to Information Services: Developmental Guidelines," were approved by the RASD Board in January. Many of these guidelines reflect Green's ideas. The complete document appears in many places. *LJ*, April 15, 1976, has it on pages 973–4. This same issue has a discussion of the guidelines by Bernard Vavrek, who also refers to Samuel Green.[2]

The year 1976 can be considered, then, a milestone because of these guidelines, and whether or not one feels they are "naive" and a "disappointment," as does Archie Rugh of Wichita (KS) State University,[3] they are the only ones we have.

California Reference Plan. As reported last year, California librarians were disturbed about poor reference service and the fact that reference questions were increasing each year by 20 percent. The library community could not come up with a draft plan for additional state funding in 1975 based on the systems study by the Peat, Marwick, Mitchell & Company; however, the California Library Association did approve in December a legislative package which is based largely on library cooperation, both loans and reference service. The plan provides for reference grants at the system level and for two or more statewide reference centers. Of major importance, some reference funds must be used at the systems level for materials, for reference specialists, and for training staff for more effective service to the underserved. Other funds are earmarked for system-wide staff training in reference skills. The plan also provides that one or more of the state reference centers shall be designated as a repository for ethnic minority collections. California librarians hope that this plan will become law in 1977.

With regard to staff in-service reference training, the Bay Area Reference Center (BARC) at the San Francisco Public Library still advocates continuing education as a basic part of any reference referral program. A needs survey was conducted in 1976 to ascertain the type of subject material library workers were most interested in and needed for training. The highest priorities for public reference librarians were: (1) public relations, (2) information and referral, (3) collecting local history, (4) adults with poor reading skills, and (5) business reference. (Rare books came in last—number 23.) Special librarians, on the other hand, voted for: (1) information and referral, (2) business reference, tying with automation and government documents, (3) public relations, (4) rare books, and (5) energy. (Genealogy and music reference rated the least priority.)

Of major importance this year was BARC's workshop on "How to Give a Workshop."[4] Librarians from California and Nevada attended. As a result 221 librarians can now conduct their own reference training using BARC's basic guidelines and tailoring them to the needs of their own target group.

Lack Standards. The lack of standards and the difficulty in codifying definitions for the gathering of statistics on reference service hinder the progress of reference measurement, and was a major topic at ALA's Centennial Conference. The Library Administration Division, ALA, this year was given permission to seek outside funding for a study of reference service measurement. The results will be invaluable for planning on all levels and very important to use in better funding support of local libraries.

Cooperative reference networks, formal and informal, were again news in 1976. More and more reference librarians are going out of the four walls of their immediate library to answer reference queries. Carl Orgren, Professor at the School of Library Science, University of Iowa,[5] reported a unique service using library school reference students to answer questions referred to them by the general library public. There is also successful use of student assistants at the reference desk at California State University, Fresno.

Retrieval Use Studied. Orgren has not found it necessary to establish an information retrieval system for oft-asked questions. The Southern California Answering Network (SCAN) and BARC, on the other hand, find that some queries tend to be asked so many times that some sort of automated retrieval system may be found feasible and indeed necessary in the near future. The Pierce Library, University of Wisconsin-Stout, uses a KWOC Index to reference questions, but evaluation of its use has not yet been made.

Regarding reference networks, Beverly Lynch points out that reference librarians lack the basic knowledge of the needs of their users and to what use information is put. She also has discovered that librarians who know their clients well give better reference service.[6] This is, of course, impossible in a reference referral (network) situation, since the answering librarian never sees the patron. BARC has found that there has to be constant attention paid to training, particularly in conducting the reference interview.

One of the biggest reference network events of this year was the establishment of the National Telephone Reference Service pilot project.[7] Participants can call the Library of Congress on a free "hotline" for help with certain reference requests after their own resources are exhausted. Replies are transmitted by telephone or teletype, usually within 24 hours. The 10 libraries and information network participants already offer a similar reference service on a state or regional basis. They were chosen to provide a balance by type of library and by geographical region. They are: (1) the Research Libraries Group, New Haven; (2) the Georgia Library Information Network; (3) the Indiana State Library; (4) the Bibliographical Center for Research, Denver; (5) the Southern California Answering Network, Los Angeles; (6) the Illinois State Library; (7) the New Jersey State Library; (8) the North Carolina State Library; (9) the University of Texas, Austin; and (10) the Bay Area Reference Center, San Francisco.

This network is a pilot project. The participants are delighted with the service and think of it as the beginning of a national reference network.

Last year this report devoted some space to libraries that were providing "Information and Referral" services. BARC presented another workshop on the subject this year at California librarians' request. Many new I&R services were added all over the country in 1976. A list of these services in 26 states is contained in *American Education*, November 1976.[8] And a new book on the subject by Clara Jones is expected in 1977.

The use of automated, on-line data banks in reference work, particularly in academic libraries, seems to dominate the literature and probably provides the most interesting programs and exhibits at library conferences. The program at the annual meeting of the American Society for Information Science (ASIS) was crowded with the "biggies" in the field relating their computer experiences.

Computer Studies. Many studies are currently being made on computer use and the reference librarian. Rhoda Garoogian, Pratt Institute, in a survey on the use of the N.Y. Times Information Bank by libraries,[9] gives an interesting rationale for subscribing to the service: (1) the enhancement of reference service; (2) interest in greater use of computerized information retrieval; and (3) advancement of the library's image. (There is no doubt about the public relations potential for any type of library!)

Another study was reported on at the 1976 conference of the American Library Association by Danuta Nitecki of the University of Tennessee at Knoxville, who pointed out a need for a great deal more education in the field. Costs and staff overload have been major barriers to more computer use, and she reported that even though many libraries have computerized reference, there is still a great deal of reluctance to divert funds from other purposes.

Pauline Atherton, from Syracuse University, reported at ALA that automation had certainly changed academic libraries in that reference service is now being changed from a walk-in one to one that features office hours and appointments. She also pointed out that automation use has led to the overuse of collections, the overworking of staff, and the mutilation of journals.

Interest in the subject at the ALA conference in July was so high that out of it came a new discussion group – MARS, Machine Assisted Reference Service. It is designed for those library workers who are involved in planning, performing, managing, or the teaching of computer-assisted form of reference service in libraries. The group promises to be an active one. They will meet at ALA conferences and are planning a newsletter.

Question of Fees. Although, as previously stated, costs have always been a deterrent to reference automation use in libraries, there is strong evidence by librarians of opposition to charging user fees for the service. This opposition seems to be growing, and fast. The cover for *LJ*, September 15, displayed this quote on a cathode ray tube screen: "Online search services currently . . . benefit only a few and are effectively denied to the majority . . ."[10] Prices seem to vary from library to library, depending on the data being searched, the difficulty of the subject, and the skill of the searcher.

Elaine Clough, Business Librarian of Ventura County, California, compiled a bibliography[11] about fees for public library reference service for the Reference and Information Service Chapter at the 1976 conference of the California Library Association.

By mail vote, membership of the CLA voted against "Fee Charges for Information and Referral." The main concern expressed is the charging by tax-supported libraries for access to data bases which in many cases were developed with tax funds, and that charges are an obstacle to the free flow of information. The same resolution was expected to be considered also by the Council of the American Library Association at its midwinter meeting in 1977.

Video and Cable. With regard to the use of video and cable communication in reference – the pioneer was, and still is, Wyoming's Natrona County. Its activities were reported in this column last year. *LJ*'s issue for October 1 contains a complete survey of library video art. Natrona, *LJ* says, is now investigating a high speed information retrieval system using cable TV for distribution.

Video is also valuable for library PR purposes. Another use is for staff training. Orlando (Florida) Public Library conducted a study of the reference interview with the use of videotape in actual library situations to find out how librarians react at the reference desk and how they could improve.

Handicapped Service. Although in its infancy at many libraries, reference service to the physically handicapped is rightfully taking its place with so-called normal service. The White House Conference on the Physically Handicapped, to take place in 1977, will surely bring much-needed changes in traditional library services. Some states conducted conferences on the handicapped in 1976, and it seems that the physically handicapped will be demanding in the future that they get the kind of library service they deserve.

Some work has been done in libraries with regard to reference service to the deaf, particularly at the Akron-Summit County Public Library in Ohio, and the Metropolitan Cooperative Library System in California offers 24-hour, toll-free telephone/TTY service, handling research and general reference questions.[12]

Miscellany. *RQ* is still the best source for reference tips and news for the on-the-desk reference librarian. It is now available on subscription at $15 a year, beginning with the Fall, 1976, issue. Its Government Publications column was enlarged this year to include local, state, and international, as well as the United States Government.

The National Center for Education Statistics is beginning to include data on reference service in its federal library survey. Questionnaires were sent to college and university libraries in 1976, and it is planned to include public, school and state library agencies in 1977.

The *Reference Service Policy Manual*, written by the Reference Department of the University of Massachusetts, is now available from ERIC, one of the few "Reference Service Policies" in existence.

For map reference librarians, the Wilson Indexes will now note articles that contain maps as well as illustrations and portraits.

The changes made in the *Monthly Catalog* in August, using MARC tapes and LC Subject Headings, at the request of librarians and others, make for much easier retrieval of federal government documents.

For better access to government documents, look into the new CIS *U.S. Serial Set Index*, and although not a 1976 event, the *Cumulative Subject Index to the Monthly Catalog*.

In 1976 reference librarians had the same interests as Samuel Green in 1876—service to the patron. The year's review shows they are doing something about it.   GIL MCNAMEE

REFERENCES

1. Green, Samuel S. "Personal Relations between Librarians and Readers," *American Library Journal*, Nov. 30, 1876, pp. 74–81.
2. Vavrek, Bernard, "Bless You Samuel Green! A Discussion of RASD's New Information Guidelines," *Library Journal*, April 15, 1976, pp. 971–975.
3. Rugh, Archie G. "Reference Standards & Reference Work," *Library Journal*, July, 1976, pp. 1497–1500.
4. Bay Area Reference Center. "An Outline of How to Plan a Workshop," revised edition 8/76; and "Proceedings of the Workshop on How to Give Workshops." (ERIC issues both of these documents.)
5. Orgren, Carl F., and Barbara J. Olson. "Statewide Teletype Reference Service," *RQ*, Spring, 1976, pp. 203–209.
6. Lynch, Beverly P. "Networks and Other Cooperative Enterprises: Their Effect on the Function of Reference," *RQ*, Spring, 1976, pp. 197–202.
7. *Library of Congress Information Bulletin*, November 5, 1976, pp. 675–676.
8. Smith, Eleanor Touhey, and Pauline Winnick. "Your Library: Neighborhood Ombudsman," *American Education*, November, 1976, pp. 7–11.
9. Garoogian, Rhoda. "Library Use of the New York Times Information Bank: a Preliminary Survey," *RQ*, Fall, 1976, pp. 59–64.
10. Gardner, Jeffrey J., and David M. Wax. "Online Bibliographic Services," *Library Journal*, September 15, 1976, pp. 1827–1832.
11. Clough, Elaine B., comp. "Public Library Reference Service—What is it worth$$$$$."
12. DaRold, Joe, and Betty Bray. "Service to the Deaf," *News Notes of California Libraries*, Vol. 71, No. 1, 1976, pp. 15–20.

REFORMA

REFORMA celebrated the Bicentennial and its fifth year of existence in July with the theme "Cuatro siglos de lo nuestro"—a 400-year review of Hispanic peoples in America, history and contributions. Rudolph Acuña presented a controversial but revealing slide presentation and keynote speech.

The past fiscal year has been primarily dedicated to the establishment of viable chapters. The birth of the Pacific Coast and Texas Chapters is a harbinger of more to follow in Massachusetts, New York, Miami, and Chicago, which are still embryonic. REFORMA's *Newsletter* is maintaining a strong sense of national identity and keeping members appraised of needs, opportunities, and developments.

"Standards in serving Hispanics in public libraries" is the selected theme for the Detroit conference in June 1977. The committee is working on the draft for this two-day-session workshop. Attendants will be asked to consider the draft, section by section, offering their recommendations as they go. Membership meeting, workshop I and the George Sanchez award dinner June 20, and workshop II on June 21 will be open to all friends of REFORMA.

Newly elected officers are Roberto Cabello-Argandoña, a Chilean who heads UCLA's Chicano Research Library, President-elect, and Iliana L. Sonntag, an Argentinean who is Library Science Head Librarian, University of Arizona,

Secretary. Four new members were elected to the rotating Executive Board. They are Marta Ayala, Arizona; Luis Herrera, Texas; M'Liss Garza, and Violet Vallin, California.

The largest concentration of members is found in California. Many of these have had a background of experience working through The Committee on Recruitment of Mexican American Librarians. REFORMA's activities in California include the procurement of a Spanish Speaking consultant at the State Library Office; securing verbal commitment for a Minority Services Coordinator at a large system; working to correct minority service disparities found at another large system; and helping to reschedule a Senior Librarian's Civil Service examination which all Spanish surnamed failed to pass. Much of this same kind of action will be undertaken by chapters as they develop in other areas of the country.

An ALA affiliate, REFORMA has also explored affiliation with a number of library and librarian organizations interested in promoting top library services to the nation's 17,000,000 Hispanic Americans. — JOSÉ TAYLOR

REFORMA Officers

PRESIDENT (July 1976 – June 1977):
José Taylor, Los Angeles Public Library, California

VICE-PRESIDENT/PRESIDENT-ELECT:
Roberto Cabello, Argandoña, UCLA

SECRETARY:
Iliana Sonntag, University of Arizona at Tucson

Headquarters: 2093 N. Medina Avenue, Simi Valley, California 93063 (temporary)

Regional Library Associations

MOUNTAIN PLAINS LIBRARY ASSOCIATION

The Mountain Plains Library Association is a regional library association of approximately 600 personal and 150 institutional members from the states of Colorado, Kansas, Nebraska, Nevada, North Dakota, South Dakota, Utah, and Wyoming. The association has several purposes including regional exchange of information through a bimonthly newsletter, sponsorship of an annual convention, and support of the professional development of librarians through continuing education activities and scholarships for graduate study.

In recent years MPLA has established the policy of holding its annual convention jointly with other state or regional associations. The 1976 convention was November 10–13 in Albuquerque with the Southwestern Library Association. The convention's theme, "The Net Worth of Networking," was supported by general addresses by Al Trezza, Executive Director, National Commission of Library and Information Science; Clara Jones, President, American Library Association; and Roderick Swartz, State Librarian, Washington. Preconference workshops were sponsored by the various sections of the two associations.

Members at the convention established a Trustees' Section in MPLA and elected Peg Wood of Hays, Kansas, Chairperson. The purpose of the Trustees' Section is to provide a forum for trustees in the region. The combining of the association's constitution and bylaws into a single document called the Bylaws was approved by the membership.

August (Gus) Hanniball, University of Utah Libraries, Salt Lake City, resigned as President in 1976. Hanniball had provided impetus to MPLA through his forward-looking leadership and strong personal drive. He received the first MPLA Distinguished Service Award in appreciation of his contributions to the association.

Continuing Education. Perhaps the most significant activity of MPLA during 1976 was the establishment of a continuing education program. The Ad Hoc Continuing Education Committee, chaired by Virginia Boucher, University of Colorado Libraries, Boulder, established two continuing education programs and laid the groundwork for further developments. The "One-to-One" program provided $200 stipends to five individuals to help defray expenses while they visited a learning site for one week. The goal of the program was to provide an opportunity for observation, informal discussion, and work experience for the participants in libraries related to their interests. Eligibility requirements included membership in MPLA, at least three years of library experience, and relevance to current position. The initial programs, learning sites, and participants included:

Program	Participant	Learning Site
Educational Media for a Community College	Sister Collette Crone Donnelly Community College Kansas City, Kansas	Learning Materials Center, Community College of Denver, Red Rocks Campus, Golden, Colorado Muriel Woods, Director
Public Library System Management	James L. Dertien Bellevue Public Library Bellevue, Nebraska	Central Kansas Library System, Great Bend, Kansas James B. Soester, Director
Story Hours for Children	Lola Harens Yankton Community Library Yankton, South Dakota	Sheridan County Fulmer Public Library, Sheridan, Wyoming Georgia Shovlain, Director
Outreach Services for the Blind and Physically Handicapped	Hilde L. Hobbs Ft. Collins Public Library Ft. Collins, Colorado	Utah State Library, Salt Lake City, Utah Russell Davis, Director
Community Information Referral Service	Mary F. Petterson Weber County Library Ogden, Utah	Minot Public Library, Minot, North Dakota Janeice Hiatt, Acting Director

Regional Library Associations

The committee also produced a 16-minute slide/tape presentation, "Affirmative Action for Libraries," focusing on the role of the library as employer. Special emphasis was placed upon the needs of smaller libraries which do not employ personnel directors. The presentation is available from the Executive Secretary. The committee has been made a standing committee of MPLA.

The enrichment of libraries in the region is supported by a scholarship program for graduate library education. This year's recipient was Richard Van Orden of Salt Lake City, Utah.

Future directions of the association include continued emphasis on the development of continuing education opportunities for librarians of the region, continued exchange of information, educational opportunities, and job vacancies through the newsletter, and sponsorship of students through scholarships.

CHARLES BOLLES

MPLA Officers

PRESIDENT (1976–1977):
Vern West, Jefferson County Public Library, Colorado

VICE-PRESIDENT/PRESIDENT-ELECT:
H. Robert Malinowsky, University of Kansas Libraries

SECRETARY:
Dorothy Middleton, Cheyenne East High School Library

EXECUTIVE SECRETARY:
Joseph R. Edelen, University of South Dakota Library

PACIFIC NORTHWEST LIBRARY ASSOCIATION

The Pacific Northwest Library Association has approximately 1,000 members from Alaska, British Columbia, Idaho, Montana, Oregon, and Washington as well as a few loyal followers from other states.

During 1976 the organization worked under the direction of Norman Alexander, then Director of the Southern Oregon State College Library. The culmination of the year's activities came at the Eugene, Oregon, Annual Conference, August 18–20 with workshops and business sessions.

The conference workshops were five and one-half hours in length. Each workshop developed an overview of its respective topics with enough detail to ensure some information carry-back on the part of the participant. Enrollment in the workshops ranged from 45 to almost 160. The workshops were "Management and Leadership Skills" by Gerald Jacobson of the Training and Development Section, Human Resources Department for the State of Oregon; "Cataloging and the Anglo-American Cataloging Rules" by Professor Ronald Hagler, School of Librarianship, University of British Columbia and Canadian Representative to the AACR Committee on Rules Revision; "Freedom to Read is Freedom to Think" by Paulette Thompson, Reference Librarian, University of Oregon; "Public Information and Public Relations," a panel coordinated by Mike Sheafe, Public Information Coordinator, King County Library System; "On-Line Reference Searching Techniques" by Frances Spigai, Library Representative, Western Sales Division, Lockheed Information System; and "Serials: Problems and Changes" by Dorothy Glasby, Head of the Catalog Section, Serials Record Division, Library of Congress.

Guest speaker for one session was Vaughn Davis Bornet, historian and author, speaking on "Presidential Papers—Problem for Self-Governing Society." At a subsequent session the Young Reader's Choice award was given to John D. Fitzgerald for *The Great Brain Reform*. Caroline Feller Bauer, of the University of Oregon, School of Librarianship, was the Association's guest speaker. A workshop titled "WILCO Forum for Resources Sharing and Networking" was conducted by Eleanor Montague, Director of WILCO.

The PNLA Conference concluded August 20 with a reception for John Dean III and first time attendees at the Conference. Dean, former White House counsel, spoke on The American Gospel of Success.

The *PNLA Quarterly* is one of the organization's primary ways to keep the membership aware of activities taking place in the states and province. Richard Moore, Library Director of Southern Oregon State College, turned the editorship of the *Quarterly* over to Jerold Nelson of the University of Washington, continuing a publication that won the ALA H.W. Wilson Library Periodical Award in 1964 and 1974.

FLORENCE M. FRAY

PNLA Officers

PRESIDENT (October 1976–October 1977):
Florence M. Fray, Spokane Public Library

FIRST VICE-PRESIDENT:
Mary L. Bates, Blue Mountain Community College, Pendleton, Oregon

SECOND VICE-PRESIDENT:
Edward G. Linkhart, Lewiston-Nez Perce County Library, Idaho

TREASURER:
Gary E. Strong, Washington State Library, Olympia

EDITOR:
Jerold Nelson, University of Washington, Seattle

SOUTHEASTERN LIBRARY ASSOCIATION

The Southeastern Library Association was organized in 1920 "to promote library interests and services in the Southeastern states." In addition to its original objective, the Association has for a number of years endeavored "to cooperate with regional and national agencies with related interests, and to stimulate research in library and related problems in the region."

Until 1972, when West Virginia joined the Association, the nine constituent states of SELA were Alabama, Florida, Georgia, Kentucky, Mississippi, North Carolina, South Carolina, Tennessee, and Virginia. The membership is approximately 3,000.

For more than 50 years the Association has served not only as a medium for the discussion and solution of regional library problems, but also as a unifying force, strong enough to influence legislation and to attract foundation and, later, federal funds for regional library projects. The success of SELA's early programs resulted in the organization of state library agencies in the area, the establishment of the position of school library supervisor in the southern states, the nation's first regional library survey (1946–47), and the upgrading of library education and the sponsoring of practical library workshops throughout the Southeast.

The second Southeastern States Cooperative Library Survey, 1972–74, sponsored by the Southeastern Library Association under the direction of Mary Edna Anders, is serving as an effective springboard for present associational advances.

In implementing the recommendations of the survey the Association initially secured the services of an interim executive director and later employed a permanent executive director. The Association established a headquarters office in the Atlanta area and received a grant of $100,000 from the Tennessee Valley Authority to assist in the support of the office of Executive Director as a demonstration project in regional development.

SELA is comprised of eight Sections: Library Education, Public Librarians, School and Children's Librarians, Reference and Adult Services, Resources and Technical Services, Special Libraries, Trustees and Friends, and the University and College Section.

The Southeastern Librarian has been published quarterly by SELA since 1951. The journal is currently edited by Leland M. Park, director of the Library of Davidson College. A membership directory is published biennially with supplements during the alternate years.

The Southeastern Library Association holds biennial conferences in the cities of the South. The third Joint Conference with the Southwestern Library Association is scheduled for 1978 in New Orleans. — J. B. HOWELL

SOUTHWESTERN LIBRARY ASSOCIATION

The first priority of the Southwestern Library Association in 1976 was the development of a regional continuing education program, following the master plan contained in *Continuing Education for Library Staffs in the Southwest*, by Allie Beth Martin and Maryann Duggan.[1]

SWLA's major work projects are administered by its Southwestern Library Interstate Cooperative Endeavor (SLICE) Office. Continuing Education for Library Staffs in the southwest (CELS) is a project of SLICE. Peggy O'Donnell serves as Director of the SLICE Office and as CELS Coordinator. In 1976 funding of SLICE projects was provided by SWLA, the six state library agencies in the SWLA region, and the National Endowment for the Humanities.

CELS Project. SWLA in 1976 officially adopted an SWLA/CELS Position Paper on Continuing Education, which specified the main functions of the SWLA/CELS Office as (1) long-range planning for the continuing education needs of the southwestern region, (2) the production of programs and packages that can most appropriately be produced at the regional level, (3) serving as a clearinghouse for programs developed both within and without the region so that quality continuing education activities can be shared across state lines, (4) providing consultation to state library associations, state library agencies, and other groups, (5) maintaining a state-of-the-art survey of continuing education activities, and (6) responding to the specific needs of the SWLA membership by planning special programs, preconferences, and institutes.

One of the first steps in SWLA's plan for a regional continuing education program is "training the trainers," that is, training a select group in the process of planning continuing education programs, with the trainees becoming, in turn, the trainers of other groups throughout the region. The CELS Coordinator developed a workshop, "How to Plan and Implement Continuing Education Programs," which has been offered in Arizona, New Mexico, Oklahoma and Texas and is available on contract from the SWLA Office.

SELA Officers

PRESIDENT (November 1976–October 1978):
J. B. Howell, Mississippi College, Clinton

VICE-PRESIDENT:
Helen D. Lockhart, Memphis Public Library, Tennessee

SECRETARY:
Larry T. Nix, Greenville County Library, South Carolina

TREASURER:
William H. Roberts, Forsyth County Library, Winston-Salem, North Carolina

EXECUTIVE DIRECTOR:
Johnnie Givens

Headquarters: Box 987, Tucker, Georgia 30084

Regional Library Associations

Also available on contract within the SWLA region are workshops on grantsmanship, consulting skills, computer applications in libraries, and the planning and production of library humanities programs for the adult public. From mid-1975 through 1976, the CELS Coordinator developed and participated in 17 workshops which reached a total audience of 1,000 in the SWLA region.

SWLA's continuing education plan calls for the provision of the opportunity for self-education. In March 1976 the CELS Project initiated a bimonthly audio cassette current awareness service, available by subscription, providing abstracts of selected articles from 22 library periodicals.

Continuing Education Network. In July 1976 the SWLA Board approved the "Design for a Regional and Statewide Continuing Education Network" prepared by a task force of the Continuing Education Interest Group. The network will provide the mechanism for the identification and evaluation of continuing education programs in the region. State library agencies and associations will establish a clearinghouse of continuing education activities within each state, with the CELS Office serving as the regional clearinghouse. Partial implementation of the network had been accomplished by year's end, and full implementation was expected within a year.

Humanities Project. In 1974 SWLA received a planning grant from the National Endowment for the Humanities to develop a project that would encourage public libraries in the six-state region to sponsor humanities programs for the out-of-school adult public. During this six-month planning project, representatives from both the library and the academic communities in the region began an inventory of humanities resources in the southwest and devised a regional plan to stimulate library involvement in NEH programs. The proposal which resulted from this planning grant, "The Southwestern Mosaic: Living in a Land of Extremes," was funded by the Endowment and began operation in February 1976.

The goal of the project was to stimulate the use of the public library as a medium for relating academic humanists to the current concerns of the general adult public through the development of library humanities programs. This goal was to be accomplished by creating materials that could be used to develop humanities programs and by promoting project activities and the NEH state-based programs through library publications and workshops.

In its initial year, the project produced three sets of kit materials based on three general topics: natural resources, political institutions, and the multicultural heritage of the southwest. Materials in the kits included an essay on the topic by an academic humanist, reading lists, programming suggestions, and a manual on program planning. Publication was planned for 1977.

User Education. In July 1975 the SWLA Board created a Task Force on Library Instruction in the Southwest, which proposed a four-phase program involving (1) the production of a directory of library instruction programs offered by academic libraries in the SWLA region, (2) a distribution center for the collection and dissemination of instructional materials produced by academic libraries in the region, (3) development of demonstration materials and workshops intended to help librarians initiate and improve instructional programs in their libraries, and (4) expansion of the project to include public, school, and special libraries in the region.

In 1976 the Task Force completed the first phase of its program with the publication of *Academic Library Instruction in the Southwest*, a directory of user education programs in 216 academic libraries in the six-state SWLA region.[2]

Bibliographic Networking. In January 1976 the SWLA Board created a task force to compile a directory of networks and consortia in the region. The task force proposal recognized the emerging communication pattern in interlibrary loan as network to network rather than library to library. The directory will identify local, state, and multistate networks in the region as the first step toward the development of a regional resource-sharing network. A preliminary draft of the directory was completed in 1976, with use of the data to be determined by the SLICE Council.

Joint Conference. SWLA and the Mountain Plains Library Association brought together librarians from 14 states at a joint conference at Albuquerque, November 11–13.

In implementation of the continuing education programs of both associations, six preconference institutes, with a total attendance of 276, were held on November 10–11. Institute topics were bibliotherapy, grantsmanship, professional effectiveness, public relations, state documents, and budgeting.

"The Net Worth of Networking" was the theme of the conference, which the associations dedicated to the late Allie Beth Martin, ALA President who died in April 1976. Principal speakers were Clara Stanton Jones, ALA President; Alphonse F. Trezza, Executive Director of the National Commission on Libraries and Information Science; and Roderick Swartz, State Librarian of Washington.

HEARTSILL H. YOUNG

REFERENCES
1. Allie Beth Martin and Maryann Duggan, *Continuing Education for Library Staffs in the Southwest* (Austin, Published for the Southwestern Library Association by the Graduate School of Library Science, The University of Texas at Austin, 1975).

2. Southwestern Library Association, Task Force on Library Instruction in the Southwest, *Academic Library Instruction in the Southwest* (Southwestern Library Association, 1976).

SWLA Officers

PRESIDENT (November 1976–October 1978):
John F. Anderson, Tucson Public Library, Arizona

VICE PRESIDENT/PRESIDENT-ELECT:
Sam A. Dwyson, Prescott Memorial Library, Louisiana Technical University, Ruston 71270

EXECUTIVE SECRETARY:
Marion Mitchell, 7371 Paldao Drive, Dallas, Texas 75240

Research

Research played an increasingly important role in library and information science during 1976. In the first ten months of the year, 59 doctoral degrees in library and information science were awarded by U.S. library education programs; new research projects were funded by the U.S. Office of Education, the National Library of Medicine, and the National Science Foundation. Several important research projects were completed and an ongoing research project conducted three studies. Surveys conducted and published during the year added to the fund of information about librarians and libraries in the United States. Two new research groups were established during the year, and Conference programs on various aspects of research in library and information science proved to be some of the best-attended programs held during the Centennial Conference of the ALA in Chicago.

From January through October 1976, library education programs in the United States awarded 59 doctoral degrees; it is likely that several more degrees were granted during the final two months of the year. Since the doctoral degree is a research degree, the number awarded and the institutions that awarded them are of special interest to the community of researchers in library and information science.

Case Western Reserve University awarded the greatest number of degrees (nine) and Indiana University and the University of Pittsburgh awarded the next greatest number with eight degrees each. Three library education programs (Columbia University, the University of Illinois, and Rutgers University) awarded five doctoral degrees each; and two programs (Florida State University and the University of Southern California) awarded four degrees each. Two schools (University of California at Berkeley and Southern Illinois University) awarded two doctorates each; and seven schools (the Universities of Maryland, Michigan, and Minnesota, Syracuse University, the University of Texas, Texas Woman's University, and the University of Wisconsin) awarded one doctoral degree each (Data supplied by C. H. Davis, ed., "Research Record," *Journal of Education for Librarianship.*)

RESEARCH GRANTS

During 1976 the U.S. Office of Education, the National Library of Medicine, and the National Science Foundation were among the federal agencies that funded research projects in library and information science.

The Office of Education funded 19 projects with money appropriated under the Higher Education Act, Title II-B, Library Research and Demonstration. The total funds awarded in fiscal year 1976 ($999,918) was almost exactly the same as the amount awarded in FY 1975 ($999,514.) The downward trend in funding for library research appears to have been checked, at least temporarily, at the $1,000,000 level, which was less than one third of the amount ($3,555,000) appropriated in FY 1967, the first year money was available for library research under the Higher Education Act, Title II-B.

NLM Grants. The National Library of Medicine administers a program of grants to assist medical libraries in developing better health information services, particularly services that relate to the development of biomedical information networks. The grants are authorized by the Medical Library Assistance Act (1965) and its extensions.

The NLM research grants are for basic and applied research projects that support investigations into more effective methods for disseminating health knowledge. Research demonstration grants are awarded to support innovative pilot projects that translate experimental results into actual operation. The general areas of research support include biomedical librarianship and information science, application of new technologies, biomedical communications, and information activities relating to continuing education.

NSF. In FY 1976, as in other years, the National Science Foundation had a much larger amount of money (approximately $5,253,700) for funding research than the Office of Education. The Division of Science Information, NSF, funded projects in the following categories: research, user requirements, economics of information, access improvement, and national/international coordination. Only the projects funded under the research program are shown in Table 3.

RESEARCH STUDIES

Of the research studies completed in 1976, three are of special interest. They are Gallup

Research

Table 1: Projects Funded under the Higher Education Act, Title II-B, Library Research and Demonstration, FY 1976

Organization	Principal Investigator	Project Title	Funding
Arizona, University of	Helen M. Gothberg	Training Library Communication Skills: Development of 3 Video Tape Workshops	$ 26,111
Arizona State University	Norman C. Higgins	Improving Library Education for Selected Minorities	23,394
Catholic University, Washington, D.C.	Elizabeth W. Stone	A Proposal to Develop a Model for a Continuing Education Recognition System in Library and Information Science Including Provision for Non-traditional Studies and the Development of a Prototype of Home Study Programs	81,800
Cleveland Library Council of Greater Cleveland	Dorothy Sinclair	Design and Testing of a Cleveland Method for Reaching an Agreement for Shared Responsibilities in Collection Building Among Academic and Public Libraries in a Metropolitan Area.	35,779
Denver, University of	Ruth M. Katz	Serving Senior Patrons: Integrated Media Library Staff Training Package	84,677
Maryland State Department of Education	Mary L. Eidleman	Information and Referral Service for Residents of Maryland's Eastern Shore	66,299
National Indian Education Association	Loretta V. Ellis	Indian Library Services Technical Assistance Center (ILSTAC)	62,027
New England Board of Higher Education	Ronald F. Miller	Demonstration and Evaluation of the Effects of Incentives on Resource Sharing Using a Computerized Interlibrary Communications System	75,953
New Mexico, University of	Lotsee Smith	American Indian Community Library Demonstration Project	87,900
North Carolina, University of, Greensboro	Theodore C. Hines	Computer Based Systems for Increasing Information Access to School Media Center Materials: Research, Demonstration, Education	52,623
Pittsburgh, University of	Patrick Penland	Individual Self-Planned Learning in America	81,876
Southern California, University of	Martha Boaz	Library Education Program Without Walls	44,900
SUNY–Albany	Glyn T. Evans	Collection Development Analysis Using OCLC Archival Tapes	42,415
Virgin Islands, Department of Conservation and Cultural Affairs	Henry C. Chang	Virgin Islands Demonstration Library Network Study	29,590
Washington, University of	Brenda Dervin	The Development of Strategies for Dealing with the Information Needs of Urban Residents: Phase III – Survey of Information Practitioners	77,122
WICHE, Boulder, Colorado	Eleanor Montague	A Proposal to Develop and Demonstrate a Statistical Data Base System for Library and Network Planning and Evaluation	59,000
Wisconsin, University of, Madison	Margaret Monroe	Relationship of Social Participation to Use of Media among Mexican American Urban Poor	18,002
Yadkin Valley Economic Development District	Jimmie R. Hutchens	Yadkin Valley Early Childhood Creative Library Program	30,000
Operations Research, Inc.	Ted Brandhorst	Preparation of Two Directories of OE-Funded Research in Library and Information Science	20,450
		Total	$999,918

Table 2: Research Grants Awarded by the National Library of Medicine under the Medical Library Assistance Act (1965), FY 1976

Organization	Principal Investigator	Project Title	Funding
Beth Israel Hospital, Boston	Warner V. Slack	Counseling in Nutrition by Computer	$280,073
Lehigh University	John J. O'Connor	Retrieval of Answer-Passages from Biomedical Papers	134,600
Missouri, University of, Medical School	Richardson K. Noback	Developing Clinical Information Needs and Systems	108,565
New York University	Naomi Sager	Computer Structuring of Medical Narrative	165,478
Tufts University, School of Medicine	Norman S. Stearns	Documented Reading for Improved Patient Care and CME Credit	170,365
		Total	$859,081

Organization, Inc., *Use of and Attitudes Toward Libraries in New Jersey;* Western Interstate Library Coordinating Organization, Western Interstate Commission on Higher Education, *Cost and Funding Studies of the Proposed Western Interstate Bibliographic Network;* and University of North Carolina at Charlotte, *The Academic Library Development Program.*

New Jersey Study. The Gallup study was designed to collect information about public attitudes as they affect the state's need for libraries, with a special focus on public libraries. The data will allow an assessment of current needs and will provide a base point for tracking changes. The State Library plans to use the data in the development of its long-range state plan.

The study goes beyond an examination of the stable relationship between demographic characteristics and library use and analyzes qualitative attitudinal variables that affect library use. The two-phase study consists of an initial series of group discussions with citizens. From these conversations, the areas of inquiry for the second phase of the study were refined to focus on five areas: extent of library use, reasons for use, interest in specific library services, attitudes relating to accessibility and availability of libraries, and leisure and lifestyle patterns.

Cost and Funding Studies. To provide a basis for the empirical study of the economic issues of network technical support services, the Western Interstate Library Coordinating Organization Study concentrated on three areas: collection of cost data in western libraries; the impact of network services on libraries; and identification of economic issues confronting network development. The major achievements of the study include the analysis of data from 100 libraries; the preparation of a librarian's handbook on network cost considerations; and the development of instruments for the cost analysis of technical services and interlibrary loan.

Academic Library Program. The purpose of the *Academic Library Development Program* was to adapt and modify the Management Review and Analysis Program (MRAP) developed by the Association of Research Libraries' Office of University Library Management Studies for the use of smaller academic libraries. MRAP was designed for large university and research libraries to use in self-study programs of their management. In the belief that small and medium-sized academic libraries needed a method for conducting the same type of self-evaluations of their management structure, a modification of the successful MRAP system was selected as the most efficient means of developing the needed plan. Under the direction of P. Grady Morein, the necessary modifications in MRAP were made and then tested at the University of North Carolina at Charlotte Library. (*See also* Management, Library.)

SPEC Studies. The Office of University Library Management Studies of the Association of Research Libraries (q.v.) continues to conduct an important on going research program in its Systems and Procedures Exchange Center (SPEC). The program is devoted to the exchange of information relating to specific areas of academic and research library management. The Center was created in 1973 in response to the expressed need of ARL member libraries for a streamlined method of exchanging management information. The objectives of the Center are (1) to collect information and documentation regarding current practices in specific areas of library management; (2) to provide access to academic libraries' original documentation and the Center's analyses for the use of the library community; (3) to publish analytical state-of-the-art reviews on management topics; (4) to identify library management expertise and facilitate its exchange; (5) to promote experimentation and innovation on the basis of what has succeeded elsewhere.

During 1976 the Systems and Procedures Exchange Center conducted three studies: User Services Survey; Organization, Staffing

Table 3: Research Programs Funded by the Division of Science Information, National Science Foundation, FY 1976

Organization	Principal Investigator	Project Title	Funding
Illinois, University of, Urbana	Martha E. Williams	Data Base Selector for Network Use—A Feasibility Study	$ 63,000
Case Western Reserve University	William Goffman	An Integrated Theory of Information Transfer	45,700
Institute for Scientific Information, Philadelphia	Morton V. Malin	Bibliometric Study of the Characteristics of Review Literature	53,100
Ohio State University	Thomas G. DeLutis	Performance Measures for the Design and Analysis of Information Systems	99,800
Massachusetts Institute of Technology	J. F. Reintjes	Research in the Coupling of Interactive Information Systems	140,700
New York University	Naomi Sager	Information Structures in the Language of Science	153,400
IIT Research Institute	Peter B. Schipma	Enhancing the Retrieval Effectiveness of Large Information Systems	47,100
		Total	$602,800

Research

and Operation of the Gifts and Exchange Functions; and Management of Fiscal Spending Activities. The results of the first two studies were tabulated and published in six SPEC Kits and Flyers. Responses from the third survey were yet to be received and tabulated at year's end.

NATIONAL SURVEYS: ALA, ARL, AND NCES

Among the surveys completed during 1976 were those sponsored by the American Library Association, the Association of Research Libraries, and the National Center for Education Statistics.

Library Association Surveys. The ALA Association for College and Research Libraries sponsored the survey *Salary Structures of Librarians in Higher Education for the Academic Year 1975–76;* Richard J. Talbot and Ann von der Lippe, University of Massachusetts Library, conducted the survey, which continues the earlier surveys by Cameron and Heim.

The purpose of the survey was to examine the salary structures of librarians in post-secondary education, to collect data on the percentages of women and minorities in the professional work force in academic libraries, and to make comparisons between the salaries of academic librarians and faculty members.

The authors reported that the salaries of academic librarians have failed to rise significantly since 1972–73, and the pyramidal structure of librarians remained substantially unchanged. The authors found that women comprise 61.5 percent of the total professional work force in college and university libraries; in every category and at every level, men earn more than women. In gross terms, the percentage difference was 3.2 at the entry level, rising to 23.3 at the director level.

Minorities made up 9.6 percent of the academic librarians surveyed, and were distributed across all positions. Few librarians, the study found, are paid as well as associate professors in the institutions in which they work; their salaries compare more nearly with those of assistant professors.

In the Introduction to the Association of Research Libraries *Annual Salary Survey, 1975–76,* Suzanne Frankie, compiler, notes that ARL university librarians may experience a slight gain of 3.8 percent in purchasing power for the first time in four years. The apparent economic recovery, Frankie notes, was achieved at the cost of staff reduction; in the past year 86 ARL university libraries reduced by a total of 110 the number of professional positions in their libraries. An encouraging finding of the survey is that in the last three years, the proportion of ARL university librarians receiving $15,000 or more increased from 30 to 50 percent, while those receiving less than $15,000 has decreased from 70 to 50 percent. (*See further* Association of College and Research Libraries; Association of Research Libraries.)

Federal. The National Center for Education Statistics in 1976 published the *College and University Library Statistics, 1973,* a supplement to Phase I of the Library General Information Survey (LIBGIS). Data from public libraries and school libraries/media centers, 1974/75, constitute LIBGIS I.

NEW RESEARCH GROUPS: TORONTO AND BOOK INDUSTRY

Two research groups began operation. The Centre for Research in Librarianship, of the Faculty of Library Science at the University of Toronto, which was founded in November 1975, began operation in 1976. The Book Industry Study Group was organized and formally incorporated in 1976.

Centre for Research in Librarianship. The only installation in Canada devoted to research in library science, the Centre for Research in Librarianship, was founded to facilitate research both in librarianship and allied fields. John P. Wilkinson became the Centre's first director.

The stated goals of the Centre are to (1) further an understanding of the nature of librarianship and of information interfaces in general by adding to the body of relevant specialized data, particularly as it pertains to Canada; (2) increase the visibility of librarianship and cognate disciplines in Canada in terms of political and fiscal support; (3) provide a research and intellectual focus for library educators, graduate students, and librarians throughout Canada, as well as for interested researchers from other countries. On an irregular basis, the Centre publishes a *Newsletter* to inform the field of its activities.

In its first year of operation, the Centre received support for three major projects. The first was with the Canadian Library Association for the development of the research design for a Canadian Association of Public Libraries inquiry into public library needs in Canada; the second with the Regina Public Library Board for a study of children's services in the Regina Public Library; and the third with the Metropolitan Toronto Library Board for the development of a standard catalogue of Canadian materials.

Book Industry Study Group. A voluntary association, the Book Industry Study Group (BISG) is made up of individuals and firms from the various sectors of the book industry: publishers, manufacturers, suppliers, wholesalers, retailers, librarians, and others engaged professionally in the development, production, and dissemination of books. The Group's immediate purpose is to promote and support research in and about the industry, so that the various sectors will be better able to realize their professional and business plans. The Group's ultimate goal is to increase readership, improve the distribution of books of all kinds, and expand the market for books. Andrew H. Neilly, Jr., President of John Wiley & Sons, chairs BISG.

BISG contracted with John P. Dessauer, Inc., to conduct its first project, a survey of the various industry sectors to identify information needs and priorities and to recommend a long-range plan of action for the Group. The report of the survey appeared in April.

A second project undertaken by BISG was the *Paper Availability Study* prepared under the supervision of E. Wayne Nordberg, General Partner, Prescott, Ball, and Turben. The project was completed and the report published late in 1976. The Group's third project was *Library Acquisitions: A Look Into the Future*, by John P. Dessauer. Dessauer did the survey in 1974–75 and the report, published in November 1976, updates the information in the first survey.

Two long-term projects are being developed by BISG. The first is the *Book Manufacturing Loading/Capacity Study*, which will attempt to determine if the industry can be made more productive by increased standardization and changes in seasonal scheduling. The second projected study is the *Consumer Marketing Survey* covering such topics as consumer demographics, reading tastes, buying habits, and satisfaction or dissatisfaction with specific products and outlets. In addition, BISG plans to compile a bibliography updated regularly that lists research studies of interest to the different sectors of the industry.

ANNUAL CONFERENCE PROGRAMS

Programs on research and research-related topics drew standing room only audiences at the 1976 Annual Conference of the ALA in Chicago. Interest in research was especially evident in the large numbers of persons who attended the programs on research sponsored by the Library Research Round Table, the American Association of School Librarians Research Committee, and the Reference Services Statistics Committee, LOMS/LAD.

LRRT Programs. In 1975 the Library Research Round Table began a series of Research Forums which were attended by crowds that strained the capacity of the meeting rooms. The 1976 Forums again drew large audiences and covered a variety of topics ranging from operations research to historical research. Robert W. Burns, Jr., directed the 1976 Research Forum Series. The 1976 Forums were "Operations Research Techniques and Their Uses in Libraries," Michael K. Buckland; "The Impact of Networks on Libraries—Directions for Future Research," Mary Jane Reed; "Books and Empires: The Rise of Bibliography in Nineteenth-Century Russia, Germany, and England," Marianna Tax Choldin; "SPSS as a Library Research Tool," Maurice Marchant; "Style and Substance in American Librarianship: Case Studies of Twentieth Century Leadership Roles," Phyllis Dain.

In addition to the Forums, the LRRT presented a program by information scientist Manfred Kochen of the University of Michigan Mental Health Research Institute.

The LRRT also sponsored the LRRT Research Competition for reports of completed research. Two awards of $400 each were presented to the winners of the 1976 Competition.

The winners of the 1976 LRRT Research Competition were James C. Baughman, Simmons College School of Library Science, for his paper entitled "Toward a Structural Approach to Collection Development;" and Ruth Wender, Esther Fruehauf, Marilyn Vent, and Connie Wilson, University of Oklahoma Health Sciences Center, for their report, "The Determination of Clinician Continuing Education Needs from a Literature Search Study."

AASL "Forum for Research." The "Forum for Research" was sponsored by the American Association of School Librarians Research Committee. David V. Loertscher, chairperson, introduced the speakers who reviewed their current research project: Dennis P. Leeper, "A Comparative Study of Open Space and Self-Contained Elementary School Library-Media Centers;" Phyllis F. Cantor, "Role Expectations for Library Media Services Held by Library Media Specialists, School Administrators, and Teachers;" Fred C. Pfister, "Actual and Ideal Roles and Functions of Texas School Librarians;" Marilyn L. Miller and Alida G. Geppert, "Student Accessibility to School Library Media Center Resources in Southwestern Michigan Secondary Schools;" and Rull Bell, "Evaluation of Three Different Library Security Systems."

Reference Measurement. A program on statistics of reference service sponsored jointly by the Statistics for Reference Services Committee, LAD/LOMS, the Library Research Round Table, and the Reference and Adult Services Division attracted a large audience of conferees. Katherine Emerson, Chairperson of the Reference Services Statistics Committee, presided over the two-part program on "Purposes of Reference Measurement." Part one of the program posed the question, "After Statistics—Then What? The Application of Reference Service Statistics." Cynthia Duncan gave the keynote speech which was discussed by panelists Kathryn Gesterfield, Ben E. Grimm, Vern M. Pings, and Ronald Billings. Part two of the program was titled, "Apples, Oranges, or Fruit? What to Count—Definitions and Discussion." Featured speaker was Theodore Drews of the National Center for Education Statistics who reported on the Library General Information Survey. —BARBARA O. SLANKER

Resources and Technical Services Division

Research Libraries

See under type of library—*Academic, Public, School, Special*; See also *Independent Research Libraries, Association of Research Libraries; Association of College and Research Libraries.*

Resources and Technical Services Division

Though 1976 was both a year of Centennial and Bicentennial observance, the Resources and Technical Services Division (RTSD) of ALA took comparatively little time from its current efforts and activities to celebrate those occasions or to reflect on its past history. At its annual meeting, members paused briefly to hear a series of papers commemorating the Dewey and Cutter Centennials. The program included Phyllis A. Richmond (Case Western Reserve School of Library Service), who read a paper entitled "Mr. Dewey's Classification, Mr. Cutter's Catalog, and Dr. Hitchcock's Chickens"; Richard Sealock (Forest Press) and Benjamin Custer (Library of Congress) spoke on the Dewey Decimal Classification—its history, and its relation to international efforts. Aside from this commemorative program, RTSD and its four sections (Resources, Serials, Reproduction of Library Materials, and Cataloging and Classification) spent the year being intensely and immediately involved in a broad spectrum of issues, problems, and concerns. Perhaps the two most important concerns revolved around the issues of survival and standardization.

Because of the revised ALA dues schedule and a reduction in the number of personal RTSD members, RTSD was forced to look critically at its resources in attempting to match them to its programs. Though drastic or radical changes in program were not actually made during the year, considerable effort was expended by Divisional Officers and the Executive Secretary attending and participating in meetings of the Divisional Interest Special Committee (DISC) at the regularly scheduled ALA meetings and in attending a special meeting of Division Vice Presidents held in Chicago on March 26, 1976. In an attempt to begin to deal with the basic problem, the RTSD Board at its annual meeting took positive action by establishing a standing membership committee charging it with the responsibility to develop and pursue a continuous campaign to recruit and retain members for RTSD from among existing and potential ALA members and to provide a liaison between ALA membership services and RTSD members. Francis Spreitzer (University of Southern California) was appointed Chairperson of the Membership Committee. Earlier the RTSD Board had approved and voted funds for a Divisional newsletter. Regular publication of the RTSD *Newsletter* began in January 1976.

Standards and Standardization. The issues of standards and standardization once again loomed large in the Division's priorities and consumed a major portion of its time and energy on all levels. The Catalog Code Revision Committee (CCRC) continued its work of soliciting input from the library community and revising *Anglo-American Cataloging Rules (AACR)*. A number of special program meetings and open hearings were conducted by CCRC at the Midwinter and Annual Meetings. A major development in this area was a decision taken by the Joint Steering Committee (JSC) of CCRC to have the revised AACR conform to the emerging International Standard Bibliographic Description (General) [ISBD(G)]. In effect this decision meant that uniform treatment for the description of all library materials would be required in the revised AACR. The ISBD(G) is sponsored by the International Federation of Library Associations (IFLA) as a standard and is based upon the previously developed and promulgated ISBD(M) (Monographs) standard, which was used as the basis for the revision of the *AACR Chapter 6, Separately Published Monographs,* published by ALA. By the end of the year the drafting of rules for the revised AACR was well under way and CCRC reported that a 1977 publication deadline would be met for the revised AACR.

The RTSD Board, anticipating the need for greater involvement and participation in international catalog code efforts in the future on the part of the American Library Association, approved the establishment of a Special Committee on International Cataloging Consultation. It is to study procedures involved in the development of international cataloging policies by international organizations and to propose methods to establish communication and ensure adequate consultation between these international organizations and RTSD. John Byrum (Library of Congress), who chairs CCRC, was appointed chairperson of this newly established Special Committee.

Preoccupation with standards and standardization is also reflected in a large number of the activities of the Sections of the Division. The following examples show the range and diversity of RTSD's concerns and activities in this area during the year. The Resources Section prepared and submitted for approval for publication "Guidelines for Handling Library Orders for Published And Available Microforms" and "Guidelines For the Formulation of Collection Development Policies." The Council of Regional Groups (CRG) sponsored a program at the annual meeting devoted to the RTSD role in standardization; speakers at this CRG program included Howard Pasternak (Booz, Allen & Hamilton), who discussed the role of RTSD in developing standards; Carl Spaulding (Council on Library Resources), who described the development of the American National Standards Institute (ANSI) standard for advertising micropublications; and John Byrum (Library of Congress), who addressed the problem of standardization in national and international cataloging activities. The Preservation of Library Materials Committee was drafting at year's end a statement on the quality of book papers. The Subcommittee on Subject Analysis of Audiovisual Materials drafted and issued guidelines on subject headings. The Reproduction of Library Materials Section (through its Standards Committee) continued to press for the development of standards for evaluating the permanence and stability of nonsilver films such as diazo and vesicular films. The Representation in Machine-Readable Form of Bibliographic Information Committee (MARBI), a joint committee of RTSD, the Information Science and Automation Division, and the Reference and Adult Service Division, are evaluating among a number of other proposals a Hebrew character set adequate for machine input. The units of RTSD during 1976 were concerned not only with identifying issues and problems but also with seeking and influencing solutions.

Awards. Aware that recognition fosters and encourages new work and also promotes quality and excellence, the Division supports an active program of awards given annually to mark and draw attention to major contributions in the field of technical services. The 1976 Margaret Mann Citation, sponsored by the Cataloging and Classification Section, and given for outstanding achievement in cataloging and classification, was awarded to Dr. Eva Verona in recognition of her publication entitled *Corporate Headings* (IFLA, 1975). The Esther J. Piercy Award, given for outstanding achievement and promise in technical services to a person who has been in the profession fewer than 10 years, was given to Ruth Tighe (National Commission for Libraries and Information Science, Washington, D.C.). The Resources Section Scholarship Award to acknowledge creative and innovative research in the form of an article or book in the field of acquisitions, collection development, and related developments in libraries was presented for the first time. Recipients were Hendrik Edelman (Cornell University), Carol Nemeyer (Association of American Publishers, New York), and Sandra Paul (Random House, New York) for their article "The Library Market: a Special *Publishers Weekly* Survey" (*Publishers Weekly*, June 16, 1975). In a lighter vein, LUTFCUSTIC (Librarians United to Fight Costly, Unnecessary Serial Title Changes), a group informally sponsored by the Serials Section, gave their "worst serial title change of the year" award to the *Mountain Plains Library Association Quarterly*, which changed its name to the *MPLA Newsletter*.

RTSD is a "now" organization, human in scale, involved in current issues and future planning. Its major and overreaching objective is to play a positive, active role in molding and influencing developments within the field of technical services on both a national and international level. (*See also* Acquisitions; Anglo-American Cataloging Rules; Cataloging and Classification; Serials; Standards; and other articles on technical services and related professional interests.)

PAUL J. FASANA

RTSD Officers

PRESIDENT (July 1976–June 1977):
Paul Fasana, New York Public Library

VICE-PRESIDENT/PRESIDENT-ELECT:
Norman Dudley, University of California

EXECUTIVE SECRETARY:
Carol R. Kelm

Membership (August 31, 1976): 6,029
(3,850 personal and 2,179 organizational)

Right to Read

See *Literacy Programs, Library.*

School Libraries and Media Centers

Budget cuts, declining enrollments, and the accountability movement had an impact on school libraries and media centers in the Bicentennial year. In the midst of the "back to the basics" rallying cry to remove all "frills" from school programs, at least one librarian was urging schools to emphasize books and reading by separating them from other media in the school library.[7] At the same time the unified media program concept was growing as schools continued their task of developing educational programs for a generation of children raised on television.

ACCOUNTABILITY IN SCHOOL MEDIA PROGRAMS

Taxpayers become increasingly critical of growing local expenditures, one place in which they could exert influence on governmental budgets, and school media programs were affected as administrators searched for ways to hold down costs in inflationary times. Oak Park, Illinois, was one community which froze the position of school media supervisor when the position became vacant. Elsewhere some professional positions, particularly in elementary schools, were downgraded to aides as a cost-cutting tactic. Hawaii, with a statewide school system, threatened to convert its professional elementary school media specialist positions to 12-month civil service status on a par with public librarians, which would

School Libraries and Media Centers

mean the posts would no longer require teacher certification.

There were bright spots in the picture as communities increased media staff positions. Birmingham, Alabama, whose superintendent, Wilmer S. Cody, was honored with the AASL Library Service Award for School Administrators, passed a special bond issue to bring its elementary school libraries up to the accrediting standards of the Southern Association. This meant placing a full-time professional librarian in each school.

North Haven, Connecticut, was one of a number of communities which retained media specialist positions in the wake of elementary school closings to make it possible for other schools to replace part-time staff with full-time people. This method of upgrading educational programs to gain parent support for closing neighborhood schools could provide a boost to school media programs if adopted in other school districts. Declining enrollments also permitted use of remodeled classroom space for providing or enlarging school media center facilities in a period when new school construction was greatly reduced.

Support for school media programs from organized teacher associations and unions proved crucial in a number of situations in 1976. In Buffalo, where the Vice-President of the Buffalo Teachers Federation is an elementary school librarian, a three-week teacher strike saved elementary school library positions which the Board of Education had planned to eliminate. Ironically, the fine money levied against the teacher association was used to pay part of the costs of the program. New York City's Library Media Committee of the United Federation of Teachers secured a stay order from the State Education Commissioner, Ewald B. Nyquist, that prevents library media specialists in high schools from assignment to teach regular subject classes in addition to their media center duties. New York State requires one certified library media specialist per 1,000 students in high schools with enrollments up to 3,000 students. Some New York City schools were trying to alleviate teacher reductions by reassigning library media specialists to teaching duties in spite of a city-drafted plan that would appear to preclude this action. The union was monitoring the interpretation of the plan in the light of the Commissioner's ruling. With strong teacher bargaining groups and wider contract provisions in many states, media programs which are backed by teachers have powerful allies in the fight to maintain professional positions.

Louisville: Case Study. School systems in which media programs are an integral part of the curriculum can muster the active support of teachers, administrators, and the public to ward off threatened program reductions. Strong leadership at the district level with media coordinators working closely with other administrative and curriculum supervisors is another factor in developing and maintaining a high-level media program, and a good public information program builds community support. The Jefferson County Public Schools of Louisville, Kentucky, served as a case study of these points in 1976.

When the Board of Education suggested elimination of all elementary school librarians in the recently merged city-county district, many forces went to work to prevent the action. The Jefferson County School Media Association, affiliated with both the state library association and the state teachers association, was able to mobilize the Jefferson County Teachers Association to an advocacy role for the media program. A carefully developed fiscal study of the estimated value of the collections in the elementary school media centers and the probable loss rate if they went unstaffed was prepared by the school librarians. An hour-long television show on threatened sections of the school budget, featuring scenes from the school media centers, explained to the public the ways in which the media program served the schools. The elementary school principals, convinced of the value of the media professionals to their educational programs, set the retention of the elementary school librarians as their top priority. Faced with all this testimony of the importance of the media professionals, the Board of Education decided to make budget cuts elsewhere. Later in the fall one of the issues in a teacher strike was restoration of a portion of the extended year for school librarians in Jefferson County. The county continued its fine record of integrating media in the instructional program as Rebecca T. Bingham, Director of Media Services, was named to a new task force to explore the need for curriculum change in the Jefferson County Schools.

Systems Approaches. The accountability movement in schools in 1976 affected school media programs as local education agencies adopted management by objectives, program budgeting, and other systems approaches to education. Although some school systems, such as Greenwich, Connecticut, reported sizeable increases in media allocations under PPBS, other communities felt the standard PPBS delineation of the media budget as a support function rather than as a part of the instructional program would make it difficult to maintain or increase appropriations.

Security. Accountability also led to an increased interest in security systems in school media centers. The need for mechanized security systems in secondary schools was debated by school media specialists—some claiming that open access to all materials and equipment by students was the solution and others convinced that the security system would protect the serious student. One high school girl, inspecting her school media center's new security system commented, "Now we won't have to steal to get the materials we need for our school work."

Evaluation. Evaluation of program and personnel received emphasis in 1976 as media specialists searched for objective measures of the value of media programs in education as an answer to critics of media budget requests. Media specialists concerned about the evaluation of school media programs could find help in two 1976 publications: ALA's publication of James Liesener's *A System for Planning and Communicating School Media Programs* and AECT's draft edition of *Evaluating Media Programs: District and School*. Utah was one state which offered annual evaluations of school district programs done by a team from the State Board of Education, and several state departments of education published program evaluation guides.

Some states embarked on programs of teacher evaluation that were causing a fresh look at the role of the media professionals in the schools. New techniques of performance evaluation were being employed to supplement traditional checklist rating sheets. At least one school, Dixie High School in St. George, Utah, evaluated teachers on their effectiveness in using media in their teaching.[4]

Certification and Competency Training. Although there is some indication that state departments of education are moving away from their earlier interest in competency-based training and certification,[10] several publications in the media field featured competency-based training and certification of media professionals. AASL and AECT each published competency-based certification guidelines for media professionals in 1976; a reaction from some practitioners was that a joint project in this field would have been more valuable.

As more states moved toward new certification requirements for media specialists with a unified media background, continuing education programs gained new importance. While professionals trained in either library science or audiovisual education were protected by grandfather clauses, most people in the field could see the advantage of developing broader competencies. State library and media associations were playing a key role in continuing education efforts.

With the number of states where school library and audiovisual associations have merged or consolidated approaching the halfway mark, there was an upsurge in pressure for merged efforts at the national level. As the year closed AASL and AECT were responding to this grassroots sentiment from members by increased mutual cooperative efforts.

Margaret Chisholm and Donald Ely in 1976 published an important book on a competency approach to media personnel in schools which met with mixed reaction from the field.[5] Highly praised by some media specialists, it was criticized by others because it did not give sufficient attention to the future of educational technology. It was also criticized for the use of terminology that was at variance with both *Media Programs: District and School* and AECT's *Educational Technology. Definitions and Glossary of Terms*. The Chisholm-Ely book continued the functional approach to media programs used in earlier studies by AASL and AECT, but described the 10 functions of integrated media centers as organization, personnel management, design, information retrieval, logistics, production, instruction, evaluation, research, and utilization.

Differentiated staffing in school media programs gained in prominence, as school systems searched for the most cost-effective ways to deploy staff. Written job descriptions were prepared in many districts. Mountain View Intermediate School (Beaverton, Oregon) provided one model for differentiated staffing with paraprofessionals handling such jobs as independent study facilitator and community resource coordinator.[4]

MEDIA PROGRAMS AND SCHOOL CURRICULUM

The arguments between book-centered librarians and media specialists in schools surfaced again during the year when Leonard Freiser, Chairperson of the AASL Video Communications Committee, used a portion of the time at the AASL Preconference on Children and Television to urge a return to the books-only school library of the past, albeit with carpeting on the floor.[7] Rebuttals at the meeting stressed the importance of meeting the learning needs of all students with a variety of media. The debate continued with publication of part of Freiser's speech in *School Library Journal*.

Learning Resources Center of the Laura Ingalls Wilder Elementary School, Littleton, Colorado. The Littleton District Public Schools won first place in the 1976 School Library Media Program of the Year sponsored by AASL and Encyclopaedia Britannica.

School Libraries and Media Centers

While a minority of educators claimed that use of multimedia in schools was responsible for the drop in reading scores, most recognized that this is a simplistic explanation of the vast changes in society's use of information sources. The unified media concept continued to grow in schools; media specialists maintained that reading is more important than ever but that all media must be used in educational programs. There were increased expenditures for audiovisual materials with media kits on book-related topics a popular purchase. School media specialists provided reading guidance as part of a learner-oriented media program, but they did not slight efforts to teach media literacy and a critical analysis of television viewing to students.

In a state of the art survey of audiovisual programs for youth published in *Top of the News,* Elizabeth Fast described activities in six categories: (1) media as a mode of presentation, (2) media as part of the circulating collection, (3) media as a source of reference information, (4) media as a means of creative expression by patrons, and programs with (5) media literacy or (6) media appreciation as the major goal.[6] In developing curriculum-related programs using nonprint materials, media specialists have not forgotten books as an important form of media. Recognizing the broad spectrum of learning styles, however, media specialists recommend a variety of media to accomplish educational objectives.

Student production of media as a learning experience or method of reporting or both was popular although budget cuts sometimes meant that students were forced to purchase their own film or tape. There appeared to be a growing emphasis on student production to meet carefully specified objectives rather than merely exercising the equipment because it was available in the school. Some high schools gave credit to students for courses in producing and using media.

Although some television programming fell victim to budget cuts, in other places television was able to show cost-effective education. Middletown High School (Maryland) was one school that used video cassettes, developed by the State Department of Education, for a consumer education program integrated into the school curriculum.[4] Cable television's public channels provided a means of disseminating student and teacher productions as communities tried to prove the value of the trial channels for educational purposes.

Career education programs enabled some schools to build closer relationships between guidance and media departments. Library-based career information centers, such as the exemplary one at Putnam High School in Oklahoma City, Oklahoma, were developed to integrate career education into the secondary school curriculum.[4] Many schools prepared media to show local career possibilities to supplement the plethora of commercially available material.

The Bicentennial celebration involved many school libraries and media centers in special projects. Although some of the activity was geared to media production, many of the schools emphasized reading drawn from the rich heritage of older books and newly published materials aimed at capturing Bicentennial interest. The Lakewood, Ohio, schools had a noteworthy program called "Passport to Freedom" developed by the school system's library media staff in cooperation with the public libraries. Local history projects were popular in many communities.

Instruction in the use of libraries and media, a topic of hot interest in libraries as witnessed by the sizeable number of petitioners for a new round table in ALA to deal with the topic, remains a controversial subject in school media programs. While some media specialists regarded the pressing need for basic instruction on the college level as a reflection of the poor design of traditional programs of library skills study in the schools, others felt that more emphasis on skills teaching was the answer.

School systems revised lists of library skills to add items about the operation of equipment and the production of media; in some cases sequences of skills were geared to reading ability rather than to grade level. Schools with flexible scheduling leaned toward small group or individualized instruction designed to teach those skills required for an immediate purpose in the instructional program. Media specialists could use a mounting list of commercially developed media for group or self instruction in skills although variations in different school media centers sparked local production of materials in this area. Some schools, such as J. C. Mitchell Elementary School in Boca Raton, Florida, employed a media center skill learning station approach, while the Buchanan Elementary School in Livonia, Michigan, was one of a number of schools to utilize a prescribed learning program for all skills including reference and study skills.[4] Most schools did not have sufficient personnel to take on complete responsibility for student searching even if the media staff agreed with the philosophy stressing the importance of using rather than locating information.

FEDERAL LEGISLATION AND SPECIAL EDUCATION

School libraries and media centers were affected by federal legislation during the year. Mandates for special education programs had an impact on the media program, while Title IV-B funding replaced Title II as a source of

Student browsing in the Demonstration Library Media Center of the Shawnee Mission North High School Library, Kansas. The Center was remodeled in 1976 under ESEA Title II funds.

school library materials. The revised copyright law caused rumblings in the schools.

Although most states had legislation or programs for special education or both, Congress' recent Education for All Handicapped Children Act regarding the right of all handicapped children to education required most states to increase the scope of their efforts in the field. The emphasis on "mainstreaming" made individualization of instruction a necessity, and media programs offered valuable assistance to the classroom teacher in the development of curriculum and teaching techniques to meet this need. Nonprint materials were especially helpful for students whose problems made reading difficult.

Nationally there was increased attention to the gifted child, and media programs had a part to play here, too. Traditionally, school library resources have been important in meeting the needs of the gifted student. A number of states make extra funding available for gifted as well as handicapped students; the problem in both cases is determining an equitable way of channeling some of the funds into the media program. (*See also* Health and Rehabilitative Library Services; Disadvantaged, Library Service to the.)

Title IV-B. FY 1976 marked the end of Title II of the Elementary and Secondary Education Act (ESEA) and the beginning of Title IV, Part B, established as the Libraries and Learning Resources Program under Public Law 93-380. In FY 1977 Title IV-B, which consolidated the school library materials component of ESEA, Title II, the equipment and minor remodeling funded under the National Defense Education Act, Title III, and the guidance, counseling, and testing previously part of ESEA, Title III, was under full-scale operation.

Although funds are allocated to local education agencies on a noncompetitive basis with a distribution formula which allots substantial funds to districts with greater than average tax effort for education but lower per pupil expenditures than the state average and to those districts with a higher number of students whose education is more costly than average, the decision about spending the funds is made at the local level. As long as funds distributed on the basis of the high-cost students are spent in the schools these students attend, the money may be spent on one or more of the three categories consolidated in the legislation. In other words, there is no automatic allotment of funds for school library materials.

Federal legislation did not mandate school library media representation on state Title-IV advisory councils, but most states did have such representation, and an early survey showed that 9.6 percent of the advisory council members had this background.[9] In some school districts local advisory councils were established to work out the distribution of the funds. Limited data showed that a sizeable share of the first year's Title IV-B funds had gone into media, but some states predicted that more would go into guidance, counseling, and testing in FY 1977 when full funding was available to school districts.

Although state plans attempted to keep paperwork to a minimum, Title IV-B, with its requirement that school media materials and equipment requests be part of a program with stated objectives and evaluation plan, did require a way of looking at the acquisition of media different from Title II. It was another example of the need for media specialists to view materials in the context of their role in the instructional program rather than merely counting items added to collections.

Title IV-B includes a maintenance of effort stipulation so that federal funds are not used to supplant local or state expenditures. Many communities are having difficulty with this clause, especially where declining enrollments made dollar amounts decrease even if per pupil expenditures remained constant. New York State was permitted to waive maintenance of effort in financially dependent cities and in districts where voters rejected increased educational spending in FY 1976, and FY 1977 brought a new interpretation of maintenance of effort from Washington that should allow most local education agencies to qualify for Title IV-B funds.

It was too soon to tell if school libraries and media centers would gain more benefit under the consolidated Title IV-B than they had from categorical aid. As with revenue sharing, decision making at the local levels leads to a varied record of spending; some communities report increased funds for media programs, while in others guidance programs received the major share of the money. Federal funds continue to be an important source of revenue for school media programs.

Other Laws. Although Title IV-B is the principal funding legislation, some school media programs benefitted under Title IV-C with innovative or exemplary programs involving media. Funding under Title IV-C, like ESEA Title III which it replaced, required increasing local contributions over a three-year period. In addition to special programs in media, media specialists were working to add media components to Title IV-C proposals in various curriculum areas.

Even though the new copyright law does not take effect until January 1978, school media personnel were studying its provisions and examining their own practices in the light of the new legislation. Better definition of "fair use" and inclusion of media personnel in the same category as teachers will be helpful in school media programs. Although some schools provide copying machines for student use and utilize photocopying in interlibrary loans, the major impact of the revised law in schools will probably come in the area of reproduction of materials, both print and nonprint, for teaching and learning. (See also Copyright.)

SELECTION AND CENSORSHIP

Selection of media for school collections continued to provoke controversy as a few school librarians and media specialists rejected the frankness found in some materials, especially books for young adults. The concept of quality of writing as a criterion for selection continued to be challenged by some professionals who were willing to purchase anything in print as long as the students would read it. On the other hand, media specialists applauded a growing improvement in the caliber of audiovisual materials although a vast quantity of mediocre media was still being marketed.

Censorship attempts continued to make the news throughout the U.S., usually aimed at familiar titles. The *American Heritage Dictionary*, however, was banned in Cedar Lake, Indiana, and Anchorage, Alaska. It was criticized for obscene words. A picture book by John Steptoe, *My Special Best Words*, was removed from the Quincy (Massachusetts) schools. Both sex education materials and sexist media were criticized in Montgomery County, Maryland.

The most newsworthy censorship problem of the year occurred in the Island Trees School District in Levittown, Long Island (New York). There the Board of Education removed a long list of books from the high school library, catalog cards and all. In spite of criticism of the action by a citizens' review committee and the United Teachers Union of Island Trees, the Board maintained that the books, including works by Bernard Malamud, Kurt Vonnegut, Jr., and Eldridge Cleaver, were "educationally unsound" for high school students.

Hope for school systems came from a court action of the U.S. Court of Appeals for the Sixth Circuit (Kentucky, Michigan, Ohio, and Tennessee). The Court held school officials cannot arbitrarily remove books from the school library because the subject matter is considered distasteful. In overturning a lower court action, the decision cited the students' right to find and read books. Although not binding on other courts, the action will certainly be cited as precedent in future cases and may prevent boards of education elsewhere in the country from censorship attempts. (See also Intellectual Freedom.)

THE LOOK AHEAD

It seems likely that budget problems will cause continued careful scrutiny of the value of school media programs. In school districts where media professionals can demonstrate the effectiveness of the media program in relationship to the instructional program of the school, the media budget can expect support from teachers, administrators, and the general public.

The interest in the incorporation of school libraries and media centers in library systems or networks should grow. In Illinois school libraries have become part of the library systems, which previously emphasized public and academic libraries. As the year ended the National Commission on Libraries and Information Science had appointed a task force to explore the ways in which school media programs could tie into a national network as a prelude to further activity in this field.

ELIZABETH T. FAST

REFERENCES
1. American Association of School Librarians, Certification of School Media Specialists Committee, *Certification Model for Professional School Media Personnel* (Chicago: American Library Association, 1976).
2. Association for Educational Communications and Technology, *Certification and Accreditation Guidelines* (Washington, D.C.: Association for Educational Communications and Technology, 1976).
3. Association for Educational Communications and Technology, Committee on Evaluation of Media Programs, *Evaluating Media Programs: District and School, a Method and an Instrument*. Draft edition. (Washington, D.C.: Association for Educational Communications and Technology, 1976).
4. D. Philip Baker, *School and Public Library Media Programs for Children and Young Adults* (Syracuse, N.Y.: Gaylord Professional Publications, 1977).
5. Margaret E. Chisholm and Donald P. Ely, *Media Personnel in Education: A Competency Approach* (Englewood Cliffs, N.J.: Prentice-Hall, 1976).
6. Elizabeth T. Fast, "MEDIA: The Language of the Young," *Top of the News*, 33 (Fall 1976), pp. 50-63.
7. Leonard Freiser, "The Media Jargon Joyride: Progress Backwards," *School Library Journal*, 23 (October 1976) pp. 80-81.
8. James W. Liesener, *A System for Planning and Communicating School Media Programs* (Chicago: American Library Association, 1976).
9. Sharon McKee, *Libraries and Learning Resources: Results of the 50-State Survey of the ESEA IV-B Program* (National Association of State Educational Media Professionals and National Audio-Visual Association, 1976).
10. Melvin G. Villeme, "The Decline of Competency-Based Teacher Certification," *Phi Delta Kappan*, 58 (January 1977), pp. 428-9.

Science Information, Division of

The Division of Science Information (DSI), formerly the Office of Science Information Service (OSIS), National Science Foundation, supports research and coordination activities designed to increase effective use of available scientific information. Both basic and applied research are supported. Investigations of conceptual and theoretical problems help expand knowledge for future improvements in science information services and may contribute to development of radically new systems. Applied research covers information transfer: the recording of new information, means for more effectively processing and distributing literature and data, and ways of increasing the use of available information. At the applied level, DSI has consistently supported research on problems of libraries, particularly those of research libraries. Examples include support for development of library and information service standards, improvements in interlibrary loan operations, cost/benefit analyses of libraries' operations, development of experimental computer-based retrieval systems, and research to provide guidelines for developing networking arrangements among libraries and information centers.

Funding Projects. The DSI research program showed considerable vigor during the federal fiscal year 1976—the 12 months ending June 30, 1976. During that period DSI processed 227 research proposals, of which 93 or 36 percent were funded. Put another way, all proposals received totaled more than $18,000,000, while funds awarded totaled $5,900,000, the amount of funds allocated to DSI for fiscal year 1976. The estimated budget for the 1977 fiscal year is $4,800,000. At this level, approximately 65 research projects will probably be supported. Guidelines for submitting proposals and summaries of awards made annually are available free from DSI.

Communication. DSI also acts as a focal point for communication among federal and private scientific and technical information programs. Activities include addressing common problems and preparation of an annual report of federal scientific and technical information programs. The most recent report at year's end, "Federal Scientific and Technical Communication Activities: 1975 Progress Report," is available from the National Technical Information Service (NTIS), Springfield, Virginia, 22161. It provides a chapter on trends in federal scientific and technical information activities and highlights for more than 60 federal programs. A similar report for 1976 should be available early in 1977.

DSI also serves as a focal point for international scientific and technical information activities. U.S. participation in the UNISIST program of UNESCO, in information activities of the Organization for Economic Cooperation and Development (OECD), and participation in nongovernmental, international scientific information organizations are carried out through DSI. In addition, DSI is responsible for scientific information projects included in U.S. bilateral scientific and technical information agreements with the Soviet Union, Japan, Egypt, Mexico, India, and other countries.

Finally, DSI actively pursues dissemination of research results from supported projects. In addition to publications, DSI arranges seminars and symposia in which project investigators report results. These are frequently arranged in conjunction with national professional meetings. Others are held as separate meetings at NSF and elsewhere. Further information is available from the Division of Science Information, National Science Foundation, 1800 G Street, NW, Washington, D.C. 20550. — LEE G. BURCHINAL

SCMAI
See Mediation, Arbitration, and Inquiry.

Security Systems

Security systems to prevent the unauthorized removal of library materials continue to attract the attention of librarians. They offer a partial solution to high loss rates and patrons disgruntled about not finding library materials that have "disappeared"—partial because no system is entirely foolproof. Security systems in 1976 represented a sizable investment for libraries ranging from approximately $5,000 to $9,000 for a single exit system exclusive of turnstile and sensor costs. Once a library selects a particular system, it then is locked into purchasing sensors for its library materials from that company. Competition among companies offering security systems for libraries is great.

Systems Available. During 1976 six companies were actively competing for the library market. They included: Checkpoint Systems, Inc. (Checkpoint Mark II); Gaylord Brothers, Inc. (Gaylord/Magnavox); General Nucleonics (Sentronic models S-76 Scanscope and S-64); Knogo Corporation (Knogo Mark II); Library Bureau (Book Mark); 3M Company (Tattle-Tape and Spartan). Several of the companies have sold systems to libraries for a number of years, notably General Nucleonics, Checkpoint, and 3M. Knogo entered the library market after experience in retail stores. The Gaylord/Magnavox system is one of the newest systems.

The companies selling security systems reported changes in the systems they sell. Checkpoint Systems concentrated its efforts on the Checkpoint Mark II system. Although Checkpoint stated it would continue to service and supply the Checkpoint I systems, it no longer sold them.

Gaylord Library Systems reported it had approximately 35 installations by the end of 1976. Introduced in early 1975, the Gaylord system was a newcomer to the field but was attracting considerable attention.

General Nucleonics introduced a new system, the S-76 Scanscope, at the ALA Centenni-

Optical scanner, part of system which monitors over 300,000 books annually checked in and out of the University of Illinois undergraduate library at Urbana.

Drawings published by the Library Security Newsletter (from top down) portrayed library losses from arson, medieval punishment by religious authorities for book theft, and continued concern over purloined library materials.

Disasters

The year 1976 reflected a continued concern by librarians over the protection of library materials from theft, fire, and other natural or unnatural calamities.

The first month of the year, in fact, saw the gathering of almost 100 librarians to a METRO-sponsored Conference on Library Security, where attendees were advised on the practicality of purchasing space-age security hardware from closed-circuit TV systems to ultrasonic motion detectors. Speakers from the insurance industry intoned long lists of "do's and don'ts" for fire protection and safety hazard precautions, while other speakers argued that the historical resistance to sprinkler systems in libraries may cause disaster.

Library Fires

The 1976 library press reported a $275,000 loss at Smith College's Library from a fire that broke out in the reference room. Elsewhere, the New England Deposit Library was the victim of a vicious arson attack, begun by perpetrators who stuffed burning papers through the letter slot of the front door. Arsonists caused $175,000 in reported damage to library books in Kern County's (California) school library, where eight out of nine of the library's rooms were destroyed causing damage of over $1,000,000.

An important new fire protection manual for librarians, *Managing the Library Fire Risk* by John Morris (University of California, Berkeley), began wide distribution in 1976. The first comprehensive guidebook on the subject in recent years, the manual covered disaster preparedness, automatic fire protection systems, the arson danger, and alternatives for protecting the library collection.

"Protecting Federal Record Centers from Fire: A Summary Report" was issued in 1976 from the General Services Administration, Washington, D.C. The new report repeated the standard but important rules for document-storage facility protection.

Finally, the National Fire Protection Association (NFPA) added a "self-inspection blank" in 1976 as an appendix to its pamphlet NFPA #910, "Protection of Library Collections." This pamphlet and its new 1976 appendix is prepared by NFPA's Committee on Libraries, Museums, and Historic Buildings. (*See also* Insurance for Libraries.)

Flood Damage

When the massive Teton Dam in Idaho gave way in 1976, it virtually wiped out the City of Rexburg (pop. 10,000) and with it, the city's only public library.

The stormy flood waters swamped about 30,000 books, leaving only the top two shelves in the adult department untouched. The flood waters swirled also to the neighboring town of Sugar City, where the School Community Library lost its collection of several thousand books. Because the Teton Dam is a federal facility, funds from the Federal Disaster Assistance Administration were to be used to rebuild both libraries.

Internal Theft

Two stories of major library embezzlement reached the library press in 1976. Jack W. Bryant, formerly Director of the Wilmington Institute (now the Wilmington and New Castle County Libraries) was sentenced to serve 18 months behind bars for using $75,000 in library funds to upgrade his own personal collection of Oriental art. In Lexington, Virginia, Lt. Col. George Davis, Head Librarian at the Virginia Military Institute, pleaded guilty to stealing over 7,500 books from the library's collection, valued at more than $34,000.

Defenses

Electronic Security Systems

The year 1976 saw a continued interest in electronic security systems in libraries, despite widespread budget slashes. Among the major manufacturers, Checkpoint reported a sales rate increase of 57 percent in 1976.

In a new development, Baker and Taylor began in 1976 to offer a new service of installing the "sensitized strips" in whatever books they processed for libraries. Indications were that this service would be imitated by other jobbers, and would involve all the major electronic security systems on the market.

In November *Library Technology Reports*, the ALA subscription service, issued a major revision of its 1974 survey of electronic security systems by Nancy Knight. The update included new information on the Gaylord/Magnavox Book Security System, which came on the market in 1975.

National Register

The Archival Security Project of the American Association of Archivists established its National Register of Lost or Stolen Archival Materials in July. Sent out to over 800 manuscript dealers, libraries, and archival institutions on a bimonthly basis, the Register has resulted in the recovery of six items so far. The Archival Security Project has also begun final preparations for its Security Consultant Program, in which security consultants will be made available to rare book and manuscript libraries and archival institutions. Half the cost of consultation will be absorbed by the Project and half by the host institution.

One of the most important events in 1976 in regard to the security of rare document materials was the successful prosecution of Ronald Ellis Wade, who was sentenced to a year in the Los Angeles County Jail for the theft of 45 historical documents from the Special Collections Department of UCLA's University Research Library. In the sentencing Judge Pierce Young cited a statement from the UCLA Archivist, emphasizing the seriousness of rare document theft, and thus setting a precedent for legal activity.

Model Library Laws

A benchmark activity in 1976 for library security was the continuing development of model legislation by Alex Ladenson of the Chicago Public Library (and also associated with the Archival Security Project). The model legislation represents an effort to recommend changes in state statutes: library theft under its provisions becomes a distinct crime, and the statute offers specific advantages for non-law enforcement personnel who attempt to deter it. Specifically, proof of concealment of library materials would become *prima facie* evidence of intended theft, and library employees may legally detain suspects if probable cause of book or manuscript theft is evident. Librarians would be given legal safeguards in their attempts to detain or question suspects without fear of suit for false arrest—a right long established in many states for defense against shoplifting and most clearly established in Virginia's current library laws.

Industrial Security Involvement

The year 1976 saw the first activity on the part of industrial security specialists to become involved with library security. The American Society for Industrial Security (ASIS) established a standing committee on Museum, Library, and Archival Security. Chaired by Ralph Ward, a security consultant, the Committee intends to "plan and provide programs designed to assist those assigned to the security of museums, libraries and archives to carry out their responsibilities, and to plan and promote programs and activities to aid museums, libraries, and archives from external and internal threat of theft and vandalism."

BILL COHEN;
JAN REBER

---

al Conference. It featured the Scanscope console, which depicted in graphic form the area of the body that triggered the alarm. The older system, S-64, was also still available.

Knogo Corporation offered the Knogo Mark II system, an electromagnetic system introduced in late 1975-early 1976.

Library Bureau, which underwent ownership changes, continued to market Book Mark, a magnetic system similar to the Sentronic S-64 system.

3M Company, offering the Tattle-Tape and Spartan systems, celebrated the installation of its 1,000th worldwide book detection system at the ALA Centennial Conference.

Details about each of these systems as well as reports on user experience with them are published in "Theft Detection Systems for Libraries" in *Library Technology Reports* (November 1976).

Health Hazards. During 1975 concern was expressed at a public hearing of the Food and Drug Administration regarding the adverse effect some antitheft systems might have on heart pacemakers. FDA announced it was "made aware of two incidents when pacemakers may have been interfered with by antitheft devices." The meeting concluded with the suggestion that manufacturers of pacemakers and antitheft devices should work together to establish a test program to determine what hazards, if any, exist. As a result of that meeting test results were received by FDA from the manufacturers. James Veale, Bureau of Medical Devices and Diagnostic Products, FDA, and moderator of the 1975 public meeting, reported that in most cases no interference was experienced. In the case of a pulse-type system, however, a pacemaker may be interfered with for a brief instant during the time the wearer passes through the sensing columns, possibly causing one missed heart beat. Veale noted that some manufacturers of this type of system have made modifications to allow their system to pulse a signal only when a patron passes through the sensing columns, thus reducing the chances of affecting a lingering bystander. However, the overall findings of the test results, according to Veale, did not indicate that antitheft devices presented a significant hazard to cardiac pacemakers and the issue will probably be dropped.

Questions regarding other possible health hazards to people from electromagnetic systems have been raised. (Not all of the systems available to libraries are electromagnetic. Those that are include Gaylord/Magnavox, Knogo Mark II, 3M's Tattle-Tape and Spartan.) In the United States no federal regulations and no formal standards cover electromagnetic radiation in the amounts transmitted by security systems. An official from the Bureau of Radiological Health, FDA, reported that the amount of radiation emitted is significantly less than, for example, a microwave oven and, consequently, development of possible standards is not considered a priority item. No specific tests have been conducted to determine possible hazards. Thus, although security system manufacturers deny any possible radiation hazard, no definitive study has been made of possible effects of electromagnetic systems.

FCC Ruling. Of significance to security system manufacturers is the anticipated ruling of the Federal Communications Commission on Part 15 of the FCC rules. The Checkpoint Mark II system operates on a radio frequency subject to FCC regulations. The FCC assigns and regulates the use of radio frequencies when the power output of a system exceeds certain levels. The Checkpoint Mark II system reportedly did not meet all the technical requirements under Part 15 of the FCC rules. However, the FCC granted Checkpoint a temporary waiver to continue to operate and sell its systems pending action on the Checkpoint petition for a rule change. Final action on the rule change was expected by the end of the year.

The number of libraries utilizing security systems continues to grow. Improvements and refinements in the systems available to libraries continue to make such systems more attractive then ever.

NANCY H. KNIGHT

Serials

The year 1976 was extremely active for serials at all levels, local, regional, national, and international. The International Serials Data System (ISDS) moved through its fifth year of operation and expansion. It was confronted with problems of standards and those of the general bibliographical management of serials. Subscription prices rose again and outdistanced most budget allocations. New copyright regulations relative to "fair use" for the reproduction of serials were codified and made law (See Copyright). The continuing concerns over interlibrary cooperation coupled with the need for sharing resources received increased scrutiny regarding national responsibilities and control.

In fact, one of the most frequently used words in 1976 relative to serials—both directly and indirectly—was that of "national," which appeared in numerous frames of reference. Phrases such as "national serial system," "OCLC goes national," and "RLG [Research Libraries Group] goes national" peppered the literature. The word "networking" also dominated the scene as the complexities of handling serials efficiently became more evident while the number of network proposals and developments increased. The CONversion of SERials Project (CONSER) moved steadily forward as new bibliographical refinements were developed and a change in management contemplated.

Cost of Serials. The battered subject of the cost of serial subscriptions was once again a matter of extreme importance during the year as prices continued to rise. Although there was some stabilization of book budgets in many libraries around the country, the inflationary factors which have haunted the profession continued to haunt and served to keep serial ordering in check. The "order-one/cancel-one" syndrome gained wider acceptance in serial circles.

Cost index figures presented an uneven profile depending upon the index consulted and the way in which one wished to use such figures. The August 1976 issue of Library Journal carried "Price Indexes for '76: U.S. Periodicals and Serial Services" compiled by Norman B. Brown. His examination of 3,151 American periodical subscription prices for 1976 revealed that periodical prices had increased by 12.9 percent—or what cost $19.94 the previous year could be had in 1976 for $22.52. An examination of 1,382 American serial services showed that there was an increase of 9.7 percent—or the item invoiced in the previous year at $118.03 required an outlay of $129.47 from the serial budget.

F. F. Clasquin's comparative studies of subscription prices for periodicals in the October 1976 issue of the Library Journal provided an example of the trend toward a growing need for complex cost information regarding serials. His "Authority Groups of Titles," set up in 29 broad classifications, were derived from the titles covered by specific subject-oriented indexing and abstracting services. The result is a variety of tabulations presenting "average" prices for one year subscriptions, long-term subscription rates, rates to types of institutions, and a comparison of rates for foreign and domestic titles.

Attention is directed to the part that the CONSER Project might possibly play in evolving standards through the use of the Library of Congress (LC) Subject Classification scheme in the event that a national or central authority is established for serial information. Serials budget control is pointing in the direction of making possible a computerized examination of titles in each category that might be made annually. Rate information would be produced in terms of the above mentioned elements as an aid in developing more realistic serial budgets and handling more effectively the devastating drain the annualization of serials can be on any allocation for library materials.

CONSER. The two-year CONversion of SERials (CONSER) Project which began in 1974 to develop a serials data base of 200,000 to 300,000 records moved forward. The July 9 issue of the Library of Congress Information Bulletin cited the following figures regarding records now included in the CONSER data base: from LC's MARC serial record approximately 28,700; the Minnesota Union List of Serials (MULS) about 85,000; and another 3,000 from the National Library of Canada. In addition, the initial data base included the input of science and technology titles from the National Serials Data Program (NSDP) in cooperation with the National Federation of Abstracting and Indexing Services.

In June LC reached full operational status in the CONSER Project. LC's records input to the CONSER data base is on-line utilizing CRT terminals. These records were distributed monthly to libraries through the MARC Distri-

Average Cost of Periodicals and Serial Services

	1970–71	1971–72	1972–73	1973–74	1974–75	1975–76
U.S. Periodicals	$11.66	$13.23	$16.20	$17.71	$19.94	$22.52
U.S. Serial Services	90.05	95.38	103.45	109.31	118.03	129.47

Source: Library Journal, July issue of each year except for 1976 (August).

bution Service—Serials. Additional input was coming at year's end from Boston Theological Institute, Cornell, the National Agricultural Library, the National Library of Medicine, New York State Library, the State University of New York, the University of California, Yale, and Florida's Union List of Serials. Participation in CONSER is still on a limited basis.

Library of Congress. The *LC Information Bulletin* for September 10 indicated the data base contained 140,000 records and added 3,000 each month. The Project was managed in 1976 by the Council on Library Resources (CLR), but the responsibility was slated for transfer to LC by November 1977. To facilitate the change, a grant of $165,800 by CLR to LC was made during the year to support the necessary programming and systems design for the integration of the functions of CONSER with a variety of technical processing activities that will comprise LC's projected national bibliographic service. In addition to the management responsibility, LC will also be charged, according to proposals at year's end, with the permanent maintenance of this national serials data base including the distribution of resulting products. To facilitate these changes, the CONSER Continuation Team comprised of Richard Anable, Pamela Bacher of the MARC Development Office, George Parsons of CLR, and Mary E. Sauer of NSDP will function as the primary group working on the details involved in taking CONSER to LC.

National Serials Data Program. The National Serials Data Program (NSDP) continued to expand. A grant of $132,000 for a two-year period was received by LC from the National Science Foundation to develop a standardized and compatible central automated data base for serials in science and technology. Under the direction of Joseph W. Price, the project is handled through NSDP. The results of this work would provide the library community and publishers, it was planned, with bibliographical data on the world's serials in this subject area. It was intended that 30,000 to 40,000 sci/tech serials would be added to the NSDP data base during the period of the grant. The National Federation of Abstracting and Indexing Services was cooperating by providing the necessary documentation on science and technical serials.

As the result of a grant from CLR, the Boston Theological Institute is working with NSDP to encourage the use of International Standard Serial Numbers by publishers of religious serials. Boston Theological Institute is also supplying bibliographic documentation and data to the CONSER Project.

NSDP assumed new responsibilities during the year with the expansion of its services relative to the development and implementation of the CONSER Project. In conjunction with ISDS/Canada, NSDP now provides bibliographical data in machine readable form to the International Centre (IC) in Paris at the Bibliothéque Nationale. NSDP serves as a national source of input into the International Serials Data System as does ISDS/Canada for that country. The ISDS network now has grown to 22 national or regional centers. In addition to the U.S. and Canada they included Australia, Argentina, Finland, France, Italy, Japan, Nigeria, Sweden, Tunisia, United Kingdom, West Germany, Yugoslavia, and the Moscow Regional Center comprised of eight national centers (Bulgaria, Cuba, Czechoslovakia, East Germany, Hungary, Mongolia, Poland, and Russia).

As a result of programs which have evolved from the MARC Development Office, the bibliographic records of authenticated International Standard Serial Number (ISSN) and key titles are replicated from the CONSER tapes received from the Ohio College Library Center. These are converted into the ISDS exchange format from the MARC Serials format and sent on a regular basis to the International Centre by both NSDP and ISDS/Canada.

During the year, NSDP distributed a series of brochures in a stepped-up effort to encourage more wide-spread use of ISSN. The brochures outlining the uses and advantages of ISSN were: *ISSN: A Brief Guide*; *ISSN: Publisher's Guide*; and *ISSN: Procedures for Requesting Assignment.* NSDP has also put together a new reference work, *ISSN-Key Title Register,* which contains full bibliographic description and the ISSN for each title processed by NDSP between January 1973 and March 1975. In addition to the ISSN, the publication also provides access through corporate authors, key titles, and variant titles.

National Periodicals Lending Library. To promote a national periodical library and to review the major issues concerning the establishment of such a library, the Association of Research Libraries (ARL) and Center for Research Libraries (CRL) formed a joint committee on the establishment of a National Periodicals Lending Library. At the ARL meeting in May in Seattle, the membership was advised that a progress report had been forwarded to the NCLIS Task Force on a National Periodical System. It recommended that CRL be assigned the responsibility for the development of a national periodicals lending library as one component in the national periodicals system. The National Commission on Libraries and Information Science Task Force was examining various alternatives relative to the implementation and design of such a periodicals library.

The groundwork on which the development of such a library evolves is the study commissioned by ARL and financed by the National Science Foundation (NSF). The publication, *Access to Periodicals: a National Plan* by Ver-

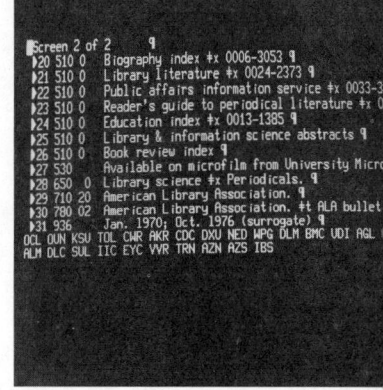

A search of CONSER (Conversion of Serials Project) records elicits on-line detailed bibliographic information for American Libraries.

non E. Palmour and others, was published in February 1974 by ARL. The basic configurations considered in the report are:
1. A single new facility with a comprehensive collection, a National Periodical Resources Center modelled after the British Library Lending Division.
2. A new multi-location national system based on a number of satellite resource centers with dedicated collections of the most heavily used titles, and a single new national center serving as the major resource in the system.
3. A regional resource network based on designated existing library collections.

The responsibility of handling the growing demands on library resources for serials has taken the natural course of seeking the strongest support, both from managerial and financial points of view. The Library of Congress, the U.S. national library, although not designated as such officially, is being looked to as the organization which will shoulder the main burden of finding support for cooperative library programs, particularly in the area of serials.

With this in mind, NCLIS feels strongly that the role of LC should include, among other items:
1. Operation of a comprehensive National Serials Service.
2. Expansion of its lending function to that of a National Lending Library of final resort.
3. Expansion of coverage under the National Program for Acquisitions and Cataloging (NPAC).
4. The on-line distribution of the bibliographic data base to the various nodes of the national network.

In line with this, NCLIS supports the position of establishing " . . . a national periodical bank, and machine-readable data banks of articles and abstracts in the fields of language, literature or musicology."

Thus the Journal Access Program in operation at the Center for Research Libraries (Chicago), referred to in the first edition of this *Yearbook* (1976) as an example of cooperative use of library resources, has, as a concept, been expanded into thinking which involves a National Serials Lending Library.

National Center. A report from Gene Palmour, who heads up the NCLIS Task Force on a National Periodicals System, indicates that a single national center for handling serials would be best, augmented by hierarchical components comprised of local and regional centers that would carry the responsibility of providing the high-use periodicals. It is estimated that this would be about 2,000 titles at the local level which would accommodate 50 percent of the need. At the regional level, an additional 6,000 titles would be required, for a total of 8,000 titles which would meet 90 percent of the need. An additional 37,000 titles held by the national center, or 45,000 in all, would be able to meet the needs for serials not held at the local or regional level.

Palmour observed that this approach is compatible with the goals of NCLIS to improve access and delivery of periodicals so that a few large research libraries would not be saddled with the burden. It was intended that this national approach would not interfere with the growth of serial collecting at the local level or preclude the necessity for state and regional cooperative networks. A nationwide system would handle an estimated 1,000,000 loans and photocopies a year.

Microforms. There is an increasing concern among librarians over the amount of space required to house serial collections. The growth in the number of serial publications, in addition to the problems of cost and control, has produced a need to reexamine the wisdom of maintaining back files in hard-copy form. In addition to the cost factors in binding and housing, there is the replacement of missing issues prior to binding. On the other side is the financial outlay for equipment to handle microforms and the continued maintenance cost of such hardware. The cost of building new stack units and the general lack of space in many libraries during 1976 made the problems of microform maintenance more palatable for handling retrospective files of serials, particularly in science and technology, for which usage levels are not as intense as in the social sciences and humanities. "Cost Comparison of Periodicals in Hard Copy and on Microform", in the July issue of *Microform Review* by J. R. Reed, analyzes the economics and special problems of these two forms of serials under purchasing costs, servicing, maintenance, and housing.

Serials and Networking. In addition to the major role OCLC is playing with the CONSER Project, other phases of serial management are also being developed. In August Ann Ekstrom (OCLC) issued revisions to the *Serials Control Subsystem: Users' Manual, December 1975*, which documented modifications to the subsystem including the implementation of new search techniques. At that point the program for the automatic check-in features had been tested by the OCLC staff. Plans to install these programs in the on-line system in September/October proceeded as did the scheduling of training sessions for Ohio and independent libraries and the network offices. Plans were to have broader availability of this subsystem in 1977.

Networking and serials form a fascinating duo, and the investment of time, energies, and money in this area continues to accelerate. The Research Libraries Group, a consortium comprised of Columbia, Harvard, New York Public

Library, and Yale, are developing into a major force in the exploration on a national level of the capabilities U.S. libraries provide in network organization. A grant from the Carnegie Corporation of New York of $197,000 was given to fund the work of developing remote online access to serials and other library material maintained in the Library of Congress' data base.

However, not everything has been left to the tender care of automation. The RTSD Serials Section Ad Hoc Committee to Study Manually Maintained Serial Records completed the first phase of its study. A 415-page report, *Manually Maintained Serials Records,* presented the tabulation of data received from 89 libraries in the U.S. and Canada dealing with checking-in, claiming, and related matters. A second part to this report was in preparation. Work also continued on the development of a standardized serials claim form. A special subcommittee was set up by the American National Standards Institute (ANSI Z39) charged with the responsibility "to create a standard serials claim form." Requests for suggestions and/or examples of claim forms may be forwarded to the ANSI Subcommittee Z39.42.S-33.

Cataloging and Serials. The Monthly Catalog of United States Government Publications with the July issue began utilizing main entries as established by the *Anglo-American Cataloging Rules* and the Library of Congress. Subject entries are derived from the *Library Of Congress Subject Headings,* 8th Edition, and its supplements. All of this is tied into a neat package via MARC format and the OCLC network.

Another tidy arrangement was worked out relative to MARC Serials. The commitment by the Library of Congress to the CONSER Project prompted the bringing of production activities involving "the project" together. As a result the MARC Serials editing and input operations of the MARC Development Office were transferred to LC's Serial Record Division. This section authenticates selected CONSER records to ensure conformity to AACR rules as well as LC practice.

Opposing points of view remained regarding the meeting of "standards" and the sorting out and dovetailing of such "standards" so as to provide a logical answer when the question is asked, "Where does it all lead?"

Several articles appeared in 1976 relative to ISBD(S), ISSN, NSDP, CONSER, ISDS, and other areas in serials represented by familiar acronyms, abbreviations, and initials. "Automated Serials Control: Cataloging Considerations" by Mary Sauer (NSDP–LC) examined developments in serials bibliographic control at both the national and international levels (*Journal of Library Automation,* 9:8–18, March 1976). An article by Paul Fasana, "Serials Data Control: Current Problems and Prospects" (*Journal of Library Automation,* 9:19–33, March 1976), sits back to back with the first citation and outlines some of the untidy matters in the world of acronyms wherein standards have been ignored, misinterpreted, or are in conflict.

A positive momentum has developed toward organizing serial resources at a national level. In addition to this nationalization of efforts to handle library materials in a more effective manner there is the growing need to gain bibliographical control through standardization at the national and international levels. The handwriting was on the library wall at the end of 1976. One hopes we will be able to interpret it so that the meaning is clear.

(*See also* Automation; Cataloging and Classification; Networks; Micrographics.)

WILLIAM H. HUFF

REFERENCES
1. Association of Research Libraries, *The Library of Congress as the National Bibliographical Center* (Washington, D.C., Association of Research Libraries, 1976).
2. Association of Research Libraries, *Minutes of the Eighty-Eighth Meeting, May 6–7, 1976, Seattle, Washington* (Washington, D.C., Association of Research Libraries, 1976).
3. Bernard M., Fry, et al., *Economics and Interaction of the Publisher-Library Relationship in the Production and Use of Scholarly and Research Journals* (Washington, D.C.: U.S. National Science Foundation, Office of Science Information Services, 1975).
4. National Commission on Libraries and Information Science. *Annual Report '74/'75* (Washington, D.C.: U.S. Government Printing Office, 1976).
5. Vernon E. Palmour, *Access to Periodicals: a National Plan.* (Washington, D.C.: Association of Research Libraries, 1974).

Social Responsibilities

Viewed from a distance the astonishing thing about social responsibility is that it was very much alive and well in 1976. The year 1976 was a presidential election year, and hundreds of public libraries throughout the country participated in this event by cooperating with the League of Women Voters and providing information on candidates of the major parties; many libraries provided citizens the opportunity to register to vote. Librarians, library school students, and faculty continued the trend, which began in the late '60's and early '70's to no longer spend their lives cloistered in isolation. They were busy, engaged in many undertakings and projects of unprecedented variety and complexity that would enhance the quality of life.

THE PUBLIC LIBRARY

The public library sector of librarianship seems to provide a large number of examples of responsiveness to those needs of its constituencies, which place the public library in the vanguard of social responsibility activities.

Social Responsibilities

One of the most noteworthy and heartwarming accomplishments in 1976 was the high priority placed upon social responsibility as reflected in the Montclair (New Jersey) Public Library's mission statement adopted in September. The statement indicates that "As a service agency conscious of its social responsibility, the mission of the Montclair Public Library is to participate actively in the improvement of the quality of life of Montclair's citizens regardless of age, educational level, ethnic background, financial status, physical ability or personal philosophy." Betty Turock, director of MPL, declared that "the introductory sentence . . . in the mission statement makes it clear to our community and our profession that we believe library service and social responsibility are synonymous."

Service to Institutions. Several major public libraries instituted and/or strengthened service to correctional facilities. Hardy R. Franklin, director of the District of Columbia Public Library, reported that the special bookmobile weekly service to five correctional institutions "makes it possible for residents to request specific materials which are supplied either from central library collections or from paperback purchases made locally, with minimum delay . . . ." The Chautauqua-Cattaraugus Library System (New York) initiated a program for residents of correctional institutions as well as materials deposits at county jails. While numerous libraries provided service to prison populations, one of the most ambitious was reported by Jane Hale Morgan, deputy director, Detroit Public Library. "A grant from the State of Michigan permitted the upgrading of service at the Detroit House of Correction. A regularly rotated collection of books deposited at the institution was replaced by an enlarged, permanent collection of circulating fiction and non-fiction as well as basic reference materials; periodicals and newspapers; and a wide-ranging occupational file. The grant money paid the salary of a full-time librarian whose background was in prison librarianship. Activities include a weekly film discussion program with lively participation on the part of the inmates. Special selections of books are delivered to the cell block every week for those prisoners who do not have the freedom to visit the library. The State plans to move a 450-volume collection of legal materials into the library for the use of men interested in the application of the law to their individual cases."

Bilingual Programs. Several libraries instituted bilingual programs for Spanish-speaking citizens and for Vietnamese immigrants. The Nashville (Tennessee) Public Library has a program for English as a second language for families. The New York Public Library and the Memphis/Shelby County Public Library and Information Center had similar programs. The Memphis project was funded in 1976 for a second year to reach Vietnamese people to aid them in learning English as a second language. A major bilingual program initiated by the Rochester (New York) Public Library is the establishment of Biblioteca Manuel Alonso, a library designed especially for Puerto Ricans and other Spanish-speaking residents of Monroe County. Books, magazines, recordings and films in Spanish, as well as story hours and puppet shows in Spanish are provided. The staff is Spanish speaking.

Community information and referral service programs were not only uninterrupted but grew steadily in all parts of the country. Memphis' LINC (Library Information Center) is now established in all branches of the library system. The Montclair Public Library boasts of "the most comprehensive information and referral service in a medium-sized public library in the United States." The program was known as NICHE (Neighborhood Information Center Helps Everyone) and was directed by Cheryl Marshall, urban information specialist. The year 1976 was a "banner year." Staffed with specialists in communication, community research and referral networks, the facility was open six days a week. Information was available through video banks, agency referral, microforms, newspaper indexing sources, photo essays, in-house produced flyers, posters, and bulletins. They offered information that included, but was not limited to, consumer goods and services, housing, transportation, educational opportunities available for training, retraining, medical and health services, and recreation. The Monroe County Library System in 1976 agreed to conversion of its computer-assisted paper directory to an on-line data base to support an information and referral service recently established jointly by Monroe County and the United Community Chest. MCLS is the sole agency to expand, update, and refine this data base. In 1976, Detroit's information and referral service (TIP) contracted with the Senior Citizens' Department to develop an in-depth list of resources most used by seniors.

OTHER LIBRARIES

Academic Libraries. College and university libraries in 1976 continued their efforts to make their libraries more responsive to the instructional and research needs of students and faculty. A growing number of academic libraries added data base services. John Brewster Smith, director of the State University of New York at Stony Brook Library, outlined a unique program, Environmental Information Service, an extensive and well-indexed file of materials relating to every aspect of the Long Island and New York metropolitan area environment. The program was used heavily by university researchers, agencies of local government, area industrial researchers and members of the general public. The most visible aspect of social responsibility seen at work in the nation's academic libraries is the unrestricted use made by noncampus groups such as on-site access by the general public to all library facilities, an active interlibrary loan program with other types of libraries (public, school, and special), and service to special groups in the community such as teachers and health professional personnel. Another example of social responsibility is reflected in the work of the State University of New York at Cortland Library. Selby U. Gration, director, explained, "We have in a small way, assisted the local jail and hospital by the donation of materials and serving as consultants in the development of such collections on a volunteer basis." Community use is made of academic libraries in every state of the union. In 1976 conferences and institutes on resource sharing and interlibrary loan signal that the academic library is continuing to be a socially responsible institution.

School Libraries. School library media specialists marched in the social responsibility procession in 1976. Several reports from around the country provided data that dramatically displayed the rising consciousness, among school library media specialists, of confirmed and suspected needs of students to become more familiar with the election process. Using the 1976 presidential election year as a springboard, several school library media centers actively participated in student-run presidential elections and provided vital information on the two presidential candidates, President Ford and Governor Carter.

Social Responsibility and Women. The commitment of the profession to upgrade the status of women received increased attention during 1976. Women library workers in Oakland, California, forced the city administration to utilize affirmative action principles in the hiring of a new Oakland Public Library Director. Their efforts included a presentation of a WLW statement to the City Council on March 2 resulting in the appointment of Leila White, the first woman to be appointed in 102 years. The Bay Area chapter of Women Library Workers urged the appointment of a woman director of the San Francisco Public Library, but was unsuccessful. WIRS' (Women Information and Referral Service) of the Montclair (New Jersey) Public Library was one of the founders of the Rape Coalition of Montclair, and its program. Virginia E. Parker, assistant director of the Port Washington (New York) Public Library, organized a "Consciousness Raising Group." The highlight of the program was a month-long "Celebration of Women," a series of events of, by, and for Port Washington women.

The Detroit Public Library continued its support of Detroit Women Writers, who maintain their headquarters at DPL. This group was organized because women were denied access to the all-male Press Club. Hundreds of libraries participated in the Women's Equality Day on August 26, the anniversary of the 19th Amendment, which gave women the right to vote. Finally, the ALA Council in 1976 established a Standing Council Committee on the Status of Women in Librarianship.

Publications and Exhibitions. The obligation of librarians to provide alternative publications to their users and to provide a mechanism to exhibit these materials in order that they will have the widest possible distribution was stronger in 1976 than ever before. The periodicals and newsletters reported in 1975 were continuing to be published and were joined by several new titles. *The Hennepin County Library Cataloging Bulletin,* edited by Sanford Berman, received the coveted H.W. Wilson Library Periodicals Award. Steve Johnson, of *Rain,* Portland, Oregon, cites several new information resource periodicals: *Acorn* (Governors State University, Park Forest South, Illinois), *Co-Evolution* Quarterly (Sausalito, California), *Edcentric* (Eugene, Oregon), *Ganglia* (University of Toledo, Toledo, Ohio), MAKARU (Vancouver, B.C.), *New Age Journal* (Brookline Village, Massachusetts), *Resources* (Cambridge, Massachusetts), *Self Reliance Newsletter* (Institute for Local Self Reliance, Washington, D.C.), *Workbook* (SW Research and Information Center, Albuquerque, New Mexico). *The Task Force Newsletter* (SRRT) provided attendees at the 1976 ALA Conference with a gay materials collection list *SHARE Directory* (Sisters Have Resources Everywhere) was issued by Women Library Workers in a second edition. The Office for Library Service to the Disadvantaged published several annotated bibliographies on ethnic groups as part of its Bicentennial Reading Series.

Exhibits constitute a unique way of communicating information on library resources. Multicultural Resources, Stanford, California, provided 8,000 books, pamphlets, pictures, and periodicals on Asian, Black, Native and Spanish-speaking Americans. In 1976 this unique resource was purchased by the Office of Child Development/H.E.W., Region IX.

Temple University's Contemporary Culture Collection of the Samuel Paley Library hosted a small presses conference and book fair in Philadelphia for COSMEP East in April. The Detroit Public Library made space available to groups with no other facilities available for displays or activities. Over 30 small presses were represented in Adam Strohm Hall where publishers and poets autographed and sold the hard-to-find, limited editions of their work. During and after the open house itself, the exhibit of "Alternative Library Publications" was displayed at the First Annual Midwestern Writers' Festival and Book Fair, held in October at the College of St. Catherine in St. Paul, Minnesota.

Social Responsibilities

Library Education. A sample of activities of the students and faculty of five library schools provides evidence that supports the view that library school students by and large are committed to social responsibility. At the Graduate Library School, the University of Arizona, Arnulfo Trejo reported a one-year program to train more Spanish-speaking librarians which came to a close in September. Trejo reported that there are only 244 Spanish-heritage librarians to serve a population of at least 10,577,000 Spanish speaking citizens. Several library schools have started programs to recruit Spanish-speaking and other minorities.

Librarians are urging library schools to take more emboldened steps in the recruitment of minorities. At the University of Pittsburgh, Thomas J. Galvin, Dean, Graduate School of Library and Information Sciences, added to the staff a half-time minority woman for special responsibility for recruitment, admissions and financial aid for minority students. In the area of curriculum, Galvin cited special courses such as Library Service for the Underserved and Community Communications Services that are particularly responsive to concerns in the library and information science curricula. Students earned academic credit for supervised work in community agencies, hospitals and volunteer organizations such as the Three Rivers Council of American Indians, Information and Volunteer Services for Allegheny County.

A strong sense of social responsibility caused the faculty of the North Carolina Central University School of Library Science to develop its Early Childhood Specialist Program. The program was planned to help parents who do not have the income or knowledge to help their children to develop learning skills which they should have when they enter school. Funds were acquired from the Xerox and Carnegie Corporations to establish a "Play 'n' Learn" center in a branch of the Durham County Library. The Dean of the School and another faculty member served with the Coalition in Action for a new Durham Library, visiting churches to enlist support of the bond issue. During the summer and fall Libraries and Legislation classes planned and participated in a variety of activities which they believe helped in the four to one passage of the bond referendum to build a new main library in downtown Durham.

At the University of California at Berkeley, Fay Blake reported that library school students worked on a field project at the San Francisco jail in cooperation with a librarian at the San Francisco Public Library. Two Berkeley students worked on a field study at a home for battered and abused wives and their children, establishing a small library for their use with information services on legal, economic, and consumer matters.

Fighting the Budget Crunch. Columbia University students joined community residents in a six-week around the clock sit-in, read-in, sleep-in, to protest the closing of the Columbia branch and seven other branches of the New York Public Library in a city budget-cutting move. Their efforts were rewarded, when the city found federal funds in the CETA program to reopen the eight branches and rehire 30 librarians and clerks.

Coalition groups of citizens gathered at the New York Tremont Branch and the Columbia Branch and engaged in protest for six weeks. Articles appeared in major newspapers as well as such ethnic papers as the *New York Amsterdam News, El Vocero, El Diaro-La Prensa*. As a result library branches in the Bronx, Manhattan, and Staten Island were reopened. In New York State's second largest city, the Buffalo and Erie County Public Library also faced a crisis financial situation. Services were curtailed, staff fired, and branches closed. Citizens of this community rallied in support of the library. The *Buffalo Courier-Express* of September 29 indicated that citizens "displayed their strength . . . when an estimated 1,000 of them jammed the auditorium of Daeman" College to protest the plight of their public library. Newspapers and political leaders joined hands with citizen groups to protest the severe library cutbacks.

The American Library Association. The quest for an organization that responds positively to social responsibility was a major thrust of ALA members in 1976. At the 1976 ALA Midwinter Meeting, Council adopted the following resolutions: (1) recommending libraries' support of part-time employment with full benefits for the employee, pro-rated to the proportion of the work week; (2) approving the preparation of guidelines on the use of nonsexist terminology in ALA publications; (3) accepting establishment of an Ad Hoc Committee on the Status of Women in Librarianship, as proposed by the SRRT Task Force on Women; (4) authorizing ALA to assist public libraries in extending their services to local jails and detention facilities; (5) extending the ALA Equal Employment Opportunity Policy to cover handicapped persons.

Two important actions were taken by ALA Council in July 1976: (1) A Standing Council Committee on the Status of Women in Librarianship was authorized and funded by Council; and (2) A resolution strongly supported by the Council on Interracial Books for Children was passed, urging a greater awareness of the profession to racism and sexism, and providing that library schools be surveyed for their courses in training librarians to such awareness, and that a model training program be developed by the Library Administration Division.

At the ALA Centennial Conference in July

ACRL joined with Johnson Publications and the Black Caucus of ALA in sponsoring a reception for incoming President Clara S. Jones and Georgia State Senator Julian Bond. Invited to address the main ACRL meeting on the theme, "Let's Celebrate Ethnicity!," Bond spoke of the plight of the poor and disadvantaged throughout the country and of the professional person's continuing responsibility to change the imbalance in the national economic picture. — E. J. JOSEY

Social Responsibilities Round Table

The Social Responsibilities Round Table (SRRT) formed two new task forces in 1976. The Strategies on Facing Financial Crisis Task Force will work on short-term and long-term solutions to the financial problems of urban libraries. The Task Force on Library Service of Language Collections will tackle the problems of multi-lingual collections and service to non-English speaking patrons.

SRRT Officers

COORDINATOR:
Barbara Ford, 436 Surf, Apt 16, Chicago Illinois 60657

ASSISTANT COORDINATOR:
Mary Biblo

SECRETARY:
Lillian L. Shapiro

TREASURER:
Shirley Edsall

Membership (August 31, 1976): 866

In an effort to become more effective within the association, SRRT endorsed the successful candidacy of Eric Moon for ALA President in 1976 and saw several of its members elected to ALA Council. SRRT also played an active part in three major ALA issues in 1976, introducing the successful resolution supporting Permanent Part-Time Employment, the less successful but controversial resolution urging the use of private or corporate funds to maintain services and personnel in those libraries facing budget reductions, and supporting the resolution introduced by Brad Chambers of the Council on Interracial Books for Children (and a SRRT member) calling for ALA to actively combat racism and sexism in the library profession. This resolution, passed by SRRT Action Council, then by Membership and Council, proved to be the only issue fully discussed at the ALA membership meeting.

The Alternatives in Print Task Force completed the 1976-77 edition of *Alternatives in Print*. The Gay Liberation and Ethnic Materials Task Forces each held provocative programs and issued new publications, including a *Gay Materials Core Collection List*, and a *1976 Supplement to A Gay Bibliography*, both available from the Gay Task Force, *A Directory of Ethnic Librarians* and *A Directory of Ethnic Publishers and Resource Organizations*, both compiled by Beth Shapiro. The Task Force on the Status of Women realized one of its major goals in 1976—the establishment of an official ALA Committee on the Status of Women in Librarianship. It held an all-day workshop at the Annual Conference, and continued to publish both *Women in Libraries,* a bi-monthly newsletter, and *Bulletin Board,* a listing of positions. — NANCY KELLUM-ROSE

Sociedad de Bibliotecarios de Puerto Rico

The Sociedad de Bibliotecarios de Puerto Rico (Society of Librarians of Puerto Rico) was founded in 1961 with four goals: (1) to promote library work and the recognition of the profession in Puerto Rico, (2) to promote the establishment of a graduate library school at the University of Puerto Rico, (3) to provide opportunities for continuing education within the profession, and (4) to expand and improve library services throughout the Island. In 1969 the Río Piedras campus of the University of Puerto Rico established the Graduate School of Librarianship. It had graduated 303 librarians with the MLS degree by December 1976.

The Society met in April 1976 for its annual meeting. The theme was "The Library Responds to the Needs of Puerto Rican Society." Various professional activities during the year included the semi-annual meeting and several lectures for the Society's members. During the year a new constitution was drawn up and approved.

The Society publishes both a bulletin and a

SBPR Officers

PRESIDENT (April 1976–April 1977):
Edison Irizarry, Inter-American University, San Germán, Puerto Rico

PRESIDENT-ELECT (April 1977–April 1978):
Arturo Fernández-Ortiz, University of Puerto Rico
Río Piedras Campus

VICE-PRESIDENT:
Gladys Henríquez, Inter-American University San Juan Campus

SECRETARY:
Tomasita Hernández, University of Puerto Rico
Mayagüez Campus

TREASURER:
Luis Concepción, University of Puerto Rico
Río Piedras Campus

Headquarters: P.O. Box 22898
University of Puerto Rico Station
Río Piedras, Puerto Rico 00931

---

newsletter on an irregular basis. *Cuadernos Bibliotecológicos,* devoted to library studies, surveys, and bibliographies, is also published. Membership dues is $15.00 annually.

ARTURO FERNÁNDEZ-ORTIZ

Special Libraries

Special libraries are, almost by definition, so diverse that it is impossible to report on them with any degree of accuracy over a year. In fact, an attempt to define a special library has exercised special librarians for the past half century, and 1976 was no exception. As a by-product of cooperation with NCLIS, Special Libraries Association has had a series of committees on definition but their products have not been entirely satisfactory. One definition can be found in an article by Shirley Echelman, now President-elect of SLA in which she says:

"A physical collection of information, knowledge, and/or opinion limited to a single subject or a group of related subjects or to a single format of information product or a group of related formats; organized under the aegis of an institution which provides funds for its continuance; administered by a librarian or a specialist in the subject or subjects covered; and carrying the mission of acquiring, organizing, and providing access to information and knowledge in furtherance of the goals of the parent institution."

A modification of this definition has been used by Special Libraries Association as a basis for publishing a directory of special libraries serving commerce and industry in collaboration with the National Centre for Educational Statistics.

Many people believe, however, that the special library goes far beyond these narrow limits and beyond even the walls of a library per se. Perhaps it is the special librarian that should be defined rather than the special library because the special librarian is the key. It is the service that matters in the special library rather than the collection and the special librarian can function with a computer terminal, a thesaurus, and a telephone in very much the same way we used to say he or she could function with a World Almanac, a Columbia Encyclopedia, and a telephone. The data files of the information broker may be today as much a special library as the best specialized collection of a large industrial corporation, the data base of the New York Times, or the scholarly collection of the special department of a university library. The special library is a dynamic entity, not a static collection or place, and we may continue to try to capture its essence in a definition for a long time to come.

1976 Activities. If we think in terms of the special librarian rather than of the special library, certain activities and trends can be reported for 1976. It is difficult to discuss them without referring constantly to Special Libraries Association which reflects their activities and interests in the most effective way. To point up the varied activities of special librarians, a quote from Jean Deuss's report to the annual meeting of SLA will suffice.

"Nothing can answer better the question, 'What is so special about special libraries?' than to look at the activities of SLA members.

They meet at waxworks, prisons, apple farms, battlefields, Walt Disney World, Playboy Clubs, and restaurants called the Pickle Jar of Red Geranium. Their interests range from genealogy to medical malpractice, to the double helix, to Summer Olympics, to Transaction Analysis, and to the Loch Ness Monster. They participate, cooperate, and sponsor any number of workshops, seminars, colloquiums and just plain meetings, singly, together, or with state and local library associations or other professional associations. And if they do not have enough to do, they undertake projects ranging from publishing directories and union lists to giving aid to worthwhile causes at home and abroad."

In 1976 the Bicentennial played its part in the activities of special librarians as it did in the activities of all Americans. This has given them an opportunity to reexamine their own role in the light of probable future developments as well as to celebrate with parties, open houses, and displays.

Special librarians, as never before, are struggling to learn up-to-date management skills. Every day one hears of courses on skills of management and workshops on personnel and budgeting. As they turn more to the outside for help in running libraries, they realize that there is greater and greater need for research in special librarianship and the needs which can be filled by special libraries. It is a field in which research has heretofore been somewhat neglected and SLA has been publishing "State of the Art" reviews suggesting fields in which research would be welcome. The SLA Research Committee has taken some initiative in this area and is trying to define needs. SLA also has a research-grants-in-aid fund which provides funding for research into special librarianship.

Networking. New developments in librarianship have, of course, interested the special librarian, just as they have done every other librarian. Indeed special librarians are frequently in the lead in promoting and developing improved techniques. Special libraries are becoming more and more involved in micrographics, and in the use, management, and construction of data bases.

The most exciting and important development in this field is networking. Special librarians now realize that they can no longer go it alone, and, with the high cost of obtaining information and even of interlibrary loans, the network seems to be the best route for libraries, special libraries included. At the SLA winter meeting in 1975, a Networking Committee was established and prepared a manual entitled "Getting into Networking: A Guide for Special Libraries," a step-by-step manual to assist special librarians to overcome the legal, psychological and confidentiality barriers of getting involved in networking, as well as to provide practical, down-to-earth know-how on what to do to get a network going.

Some of the difficulties which have been faced by special librarians have been legal, since networks are frequently subsidized by governments. There is a certain reluctance to subsidize those libraries in for-profit organizations which make up a large portion of existing special libraries. This barrier, however, is being overcome in certain areas and will no doubt be resolved in due course. In several areas these problems have been resolved and special libraries are moving into networking. One of these areas is in Southern California where a CLASS (California Library Authority for Systems and Services) has come formally into existence formed by a joint powers agreement. It is unique in that it is a public agency which includes in its charter libraries in the private sector. Membership is a prerequisite for CLASS service which will include a computerized listing of publications in California libraries, for cataloguing, interlibrary loan, and reference. Special librarians were involved in the planning and are eligible to become members. Transportation libraries have had considerable experience with TRIS and many special libraries are involved in this subject network.

Copyright. Copyright was perhaps the subject of the greatest interest to special librarians in 1976, many of whom were deeply involved in revision of the Copyright Act. Early in 1976, when the Senate passed the copyright law and published its report, it was clear that there were problems for all librarians, but special problems for special librarians. Libraries, for example, in profit-making organizations were precluded from making photocopies for employees engaged in the organizations' profit-making business. Libraries in not-for-profit organizations were penalized if they made photocopies for the profit-making sector. This effectively cut off many special libraries from photocopying of any kind. In view of the seriousness of the situation, SLA's Executive Director Frank McKenna, who was monitoring developments, discussed the problems at length with members of the SLA Board and with its Chapter and Division Cabinets in Cincinnati in January and a letter was sent to all members suggesting that they alert their management to the problems and raise the con-

sciousness of the legislators so that this deleterious bill would not go through. Many members of the Association responded not only by writing letters to their Congressmen but by alerting their management who also wrote letters of protest.

All major library associations were involved in the work on the copyright bill but none more involved than SLA, whose executive director took a leading role in pointing out to Congress just what problems would arise for librarians if the bill went through. It is to a large extent due to work done by McKenna and other association executive directors that the final bill was revised so that the library photocopying can continue to take place and that the needs of scholars will not be jeopardized.

Special Libraries Association. One cannot report on special libraries without reporting on Special Libraries Association itself. As of December 31 the membership stood at 9,600, an increase over last year of 175. During the year three Provisional Chapters were granted full Chapter status: Sierra Nevada Chapter; Mid-South Chapter; and Mid-Missouri Chapter. Two new Provisional Divisions have been formed: Environmental Information Provisional Division; and Library Management Provisional Division. In addition, there are a number of new student groups which are becoming one of the new strong areas of SLA. Students who are introduced to the Association become valuable members to the Association with the minimum delay.

Publications. The Association carried on its continuing programs of professional activities. In addition to developing networking guidelines, two other pamphlets have been prepared, designed to assist librarians or would-be librarians. One, entitled "Equal Pay for Equal Work! Women in Special Libraries," was a well researched and presented guide to assist women, who often work as the only librarian in their organization, to take advantage of the U.S. and Canadian laws in their favor and to better present their work, their training and their skills to management in order to gain better salaries and conditions of employment. The other, produced by the Positive Action Committee on Minority Groups, entitled "Be a Special Librarian: Get it Together," was de-

The Source, in Darien, Connecticut, is a current affairs library specializing in political periodicals and publications of political organizations. (Above) Mrs. Benjamin D. Gilbert, President of the Library.

309

signed to bring the profession of special librarian to the attention of members of minority groups.

Government Printing Office. A problem which troubles all librarians, namely the difficulties of getting good service from the Government Printing Office, was addressed with vigor by the Government Services Information Committee. In cooperation with other associations including ALA's GODORT, U.S. Depository libraries, and the American Association of Law Libraries, the committee is working with the GPO to improve service. The recent changes in the index to GPO's catalog can be attributed to the pressure of these groups.

Salaries. SLA's triennial salary survey shows some improvement in salaries since 1973. The median salary is up 17 percent and the mean, now $16,300, up 16 percent. Bias based on sex shows a drop: the median for women in 1976 was 19 percent below the median for men as compared to 24 percent in 1973. The full results were published in the December issue of "Special Libraries."

Conference Activities. SLA's annual conference was held a mile high in Denver, from June 6 to 10. Many SLA records were broken at this conference including number of attendees (2,694), number of exhibitors, and number of sessions. Poster sessions were tried for the first time and were a tremendous success. A speakers' clinic was available for those who wished to upgrade their skills, and a mailing service for those who hate to go home laden down with conference papers. The most provocative subject on the business agenda was the question of future involvement of Chapters in conference planning. Between those who want to get involved and those who hope to wash their hands of everything but program planning there was lively, even bitter, debate. SLA's 28 Divisions jointly and severally ran some 60 sessions at the Conference, including updates, workshops, speakers, panel discussions, tours, and business meetings. "Information, the unlimited resources" was the theme of the conference. Russell Ackoff, in his keynote address, addressed the problem of information pollution and attracted many members by his invitation to participate in his SCATT system.

Awards. SLA's Professional Award was given to Jacqueline D. Sisson, Fine Arts Library, Ohio State University, Columbus, in recognition of her two-volume index to Adolfo Venturi's "Storia dell'Arte Haliana." Named to SLA's Hall of Fame were Ruth M. Nielander and the late Phoebe Hayes, both of whom have made continuing valuable contributions to the Association.

Looking Outward. In last year's article in the ALA Yearbook, Edward G. Strable stressed that SLA had perhaps reached a turning point in its history in that it had begun to recognize the importance to it of other library communities. In 1976 as perhaps never before SLA has looked outward.

Cooperating with other library associations has led to valuable contributions vis-à-vis copyright and the GPO. Involvement in networking with other types of libraries is on the increase. In addition SLA is taking more part in activities with other associations both national and international.

Sponsored programs at the conferences of American Society for Information Science and American Federation of Information Processing Societies have continued, as well as cooperation at the local level with ASIS, with the Canadian Association of Special Libraries and Information Services, and with the Canadian Association of Information Science. SLA is participating actively in CLENE. One of its members served on the Library Advisory Group to the Library of Congress Task Force on Goals, Organization and Planning. A representative to the President's Committee on Employment of the Physically Handicapped has taken an active role and encouraged the Board to endorse a resolution urging a national network and central information center on vocational rehabilitation literature.

At an international level, SLA has begun to participate heavily in the Special Libraries Division of IFLA and with other international library associations.

Special librarians like other librarians tend to suffer from an image which is outdated now if in fact it ever was true. President Mark H. Baer, in his inaugural address to the Annual Meeting in Denver stressed that:

"We are our image. Considering the importance of the work we do, why has our professional image remained so dim? Why has the recognition I know we should have apparently been denied us?

"I believe that this is because we, each of us, are still tied to the old passive image we loathe so much. We tie ourselves to this image to a greater extent than we realize. We have not yet really grasped the importance of the work we do. We have not made our expertise sufficiently apparent to others. We speak of the importance of the special librarian very courageously to each other; but diffidently to others. Apparently we have not sufficiently convinced ourselves. How can we hope to convince others?. . . . Each of us is ultimately responsible for the progress librarians are going to make. No unspecified 'they' out there are going to do the job for you or for me. Each of us must contribute positively.

"If you are not part of the solution you are truly part of the problem!"

Special librarians in 1976 were still struggling with the old problems: how to serve the client better, how to get GPO publications, how to upgrade status, how to manage staff, how to find obscure information. They are better trained than ever, have better tools than ever, are aware of their own importance and better recognized as key information specialists than ever. Mark Baer raised some challenging questions which need to be addressed in 1977.　　　　　　　　　　　　MIRIAM TEES

Staff Organizations Round Table

The Staff Organizations Round Table (SORT) celebrated its 40th anniversary by hosting a hospitality suite for two days during the 1976 ALA Conference. A number of people interested in the Round Table had an opportunity to talk leisurely among themselves and with current and past members of the SORT Steering Committee. Two resource persons were invited to join discussions—one each afternoon—to serve as springboards for conversation and ideas. Irwin Klass, a labor and public relations consultant, and Albert Herling, Director of Public Relations for the Bakery and Confectionery Workers International Union, were greeted. Many spheres of concern were explored, including, but not limited to, the role of unions in various types of organizations and the relationship of public library staffs to their governing boards.

The Committee's request for suggestions elicited hearty response, and the ideas received will serve as the basis for future SORT programming. As a result of the enthusiasm of the response and the nature of the ideas garnered during the course of the week, the Steering Committee left the Conference with the encouragement that SORT can play a valuable role in ALA and that there is potential for increasing the core of active participants in its programs.

A development of major import was the departure from ALA of SORT's staff liaison, Barry E. Simon. During the year a revised constitution was presented to the membership with the final vote pending at year's end. Under the guidance of its editor, Marywave Godfrey, two issues of the *SORT Bulletin* were published. The members of the 1976–77 Steering Committee were Frances M. Jones (chairperson), Lee Ash, Patrick Ashley (past-chairperson), Margaret Hudak (secretary), Margaret Jones, Ruth Leek, Jack Siggins (programs), and Martha Van Horn.

　　　　　　　　　　　　PATRICK ASHLEY

Standards

Recognition and awareness of national and international standards in 1976 increased proportionately with the exuberant expansion of cooperative and networking groups in the information community. In the U.S. the initiatives of NCLIS, the Committee on Coordination of National Bibliographic Control, the CONSER Project, and many others led to more acute understanding of the critical place of standards in these activities. Abroad, 1976 witnessed a rapid expansion of standardizing developments in UNISIST, the International Federation of Library Associations (IFLA), UNESCO, the Committee on Universal Bibliographic Control (UBC), the International Council of Scientific Unions—Abstracting Board (ICSU-AB), and many others. A considerable change was evident in recognition of the need to carry products of these varied organisms through to final acceptance and publication by official national and international standards agencies.

Though there was an enormous amount of work in ALA Divisions in 1976, primarily in areas of cataloging practice, it was not a notable year for the production of finished standards. The *Handbook of Organization* lists no fewer than 15 standards committees in ALA. Some have recently completed their primary assignments; some have ongoing projects; others serve simply to monitor current developments with a view to developing needed standards.

RASD Guidelines. The most noteworthy product of ALA's standards groups in 1976 is the document *A Commitment to Information Services: Developmental Guidelines,*[1] produced by the Standards Committee of the Reference and Adult Services Division. The guidelines were accepted by RASD on January 20, 1976, and now constitute an approved professional statement of reference (or information) service.

Nonprint. Two recent standards products in fields of nonprint materials derive from joint efforts by ALA and the Association for Educational Communications and Technology (AECT). The first of these, *Media Programs, District and School,* is a joint production of AASL and AECT combining all previous efforts of both organizations in a definitive collection of guidelines for this very complex field. The second is the fourth edition of *Standards for Cataloging Non-Print Materials,* published by AECT in 1976. Of particular importance to standards is the general and specific designator code, a two-letter alpha code which, for lack of better methods, provides at least a basic classification of media types. It should be noted that the *Guidelines for Audio-Visual Materials and Services for Large Public Libraries* (Chicago, ALA, 1975), developed by the Audio-Visual Committee of the Public Library Association of ALA, also provides a list of definitions and bibliography.

Some of the recent work of GODORT's State Documents Task Force Committee on Standards for State Documents, begun in 1974, the *Guidelines for State Servicing of State Documents,* now constitute a significant contribu-

ACRL Statements. The Association of College and Research Libraries,[2] following the notable conclusion of their standards committee's work on the revision of *Standards for College Libraries* in 1975, appointed a new subcommittee to revise its *Guidelines for Two-Year College Learning Resources Programs.* ACRL also published two newly composed statements on recurrent problem areas, reproduction and access to special types of library materials. *Statement on the Reproduction of Manuscripts and Archives for Non-Commercial Purposes* was approved in July 1976. *Statement on Access to Original Research Materials in Libraries, Archives, and Manuscript Repositories* was also approved in July 1976. A draft statement on the *Reproduction of Manuscripts and Archives for Commercial Purposes* was published for review in 1976 and was to be fully reworked in 1977.

ANSI/Z39 Standards. Probably the most important production of ANSI/Z39 in 1976 was the new standard *Identification of Countries of the World* (Z39.27-1976). This standard has an international counterpart (ISO 3166), *Codes for the Representation of Names of Countries.* The code is well on the way to becoming an integral part of world-wide information transfer systems. Additional codes for smaller geographic entities are now being developed in many countries.

Significant progress was made with a U.S. standard for *Bibliographic References.* Following prodigious efforts by three successive committees, this proposed standard was finally approved in July and was being prepared for publication by ANSI at year's end. The final draft will also appear in a forthcoming issue of *JASIS.* Another standard which was subject to prolonged discussion, the *Romanization of Slavic Cyrillic Characters* (Z39.24), was finally approved in 1976 and went into preparation for publication. Also in publication is a new standard *Format for Scientific and Technical Translations.* The final draft of a standard for *Bibliographic Code Design* (Z39.33) was approved in 1976 and will be published in 1977. This standard will provide direction for all future code development for bibliographic systems. Each of these new standards has been submitted to the International Standards Organization for consideration as an international standard.

One proposed standard, *Code Identification of Serial Articles,* proposed in 1976, failed to meet a number of cogent objections in balloting. A new committee was organized, and is now preparing its own draft for circulation.

Ongoing work in Z39 includes modifications of *Bibliographic Information Interchange on Magnetic Tape* (Z39.2-1971) in the area of the *Technique for Dynamic Definition.*

A final draft of a proposed standard for *Microfiche Headers* met serious opposition in balloting and will be resubmitted in 1977. The proposal for a *Standard Order Form (Monographs)* was being recast in 1976 in view of comments received during membership review. Two revised standards resulted from the mandatory five-year review for *Periodicals: Format and Arrangement* (Z39.1-1967) and *Book Publishing Statistics* (Z39.8-1968). The former was being voted at year's end and will likely be published in its completely revised form in 1977. Drafting of the latter was delayed until completion of the definitive glossary of the definitions. This also should appear in the 1977 list. Working committees in drafting stages at year's end included the revisions of *Basic Criteria for Indexes* (Z39.4-1968), the *Standard Account Number, Microform Publishing Statistics, Synoptics, Serials Holdings Data, Book Spine Layout, Serial Claim Form,* and *Newspaper and Journal Publishing Statistics.*[3]

ANSI/Z39 continues to receive urgent expressions of the need for national standards for refereeing of journal articles and for a media code; unfortunately, the proponents of these endeavors appear to be still not well enough organized or motivated to achieve national standardization.

Other ANSI Committees. Among other relevant ANSI committees, X3: Computers and Information Processing, has one subcommittee, X3L8: Data Elements and Coded Representations, especially important to evolving library networking activities.[4] The 1976 progress report of X3L8 includes a number of published standards and ongoing standards work of considerable interest to the now rapidly mechanizing library systems. A basic document is the *Guidelines for the Development of Standard Representations of Data Elements,* now published as *Federal Information Processing Standard 45* (FIPS 45) by the National Bureau of Standards. NBS has also published as *Letter Circular 1067* (April 1976) the full text of *Codes for the Names of Countries,* which is identical with ISO 3166 and ANSI/Z39.27, a joint committee product of X3L8 and Z39.

X3L8 has continued its work in furthering the specificity of the Country Code, with a proposed *Code for Continents and Water Areas* now being voted. It has subcommittees working on *Codes for Cities, Towns and Places of the U.S.* and *Codes for Subdivisions of Countries.* A proposed *Code for Point Locations* has been approved by X3L8 and is now moving to upper level approval channels. A Canadian draft on this area is also being circulated. Completed work of X3L8 in this area is represented by *Codes for States of the U.S.* (X3.38) and *Codes for Counties of States of the U.S.* (X3.31).

Problems and experiences of X3L8 in what is known as Author Authority have foundered on the rocks of privacy and security. After some years of effort to develop a standard for *Identifiers for Individuals*, the work was withdrawn. Work is continuing on *Identifiers for Organizations*; it may be useful for future library work on corporate entry. Of potentially great interest is a new project of this committee, the *Use of Separators in Data Representation*. This study may lead to standardization of separators used in library systems.

Micrographics. The Place of ANSI/PH5 (Microcopying) in the development of standards of importance to the library community increases each year, as new formats and projects evolve. The year 1976 was not as notable for new standards as it was for broadening of the PH5 program of activities. A basic and notable historical record of micrographics standards development appeared in 1976.[5] An informative article, it provides a definitive statement of progress. One new standard, *Format and Coding for Computer Output Microfilm* (PH5.18-1976), brings to 15 the number of standards now available in this field. Other work of the year has contributed to the production of a draft international standard (DIS 5126) *Computer Output Microfiche*, by ISO/TC46/SC1 Working Group 1. These two standards provide a clear signal of future directions in micrographics and its computer interrelations. Also of interest to librarians is a definitive statement on permanent film recorded in correspondence by the Archivist of the U.S., James B. Rhoads.

The National Micrographics Association, which holds the Secretariat of ANSI/PH5, had 12 standards committees meeting in 1976. Of particular interest to librarians is work now proceeding on a standard for *Recommended Practice for Inspection and Quality Control of Non-Silver Films*. Their Information Storage and Retrieval Committee is working on a revision of ANSI/PH5.3 covering image orientation and is studying the possibility of developing standard bar codes on 16mm film. The Public Records and Archives Committee, a joint committee of the NMA and The Society of American Archivists, has completed its work on a proposed standard.

INTERNATIONAL STANDARDS

A new British Standards Institution product, the *Draft Standard Specification for Microfilm Jackets* (January 1976), will certainly influence a parallel development in the U.S.

The international counterpart of ANSI/Z39 is the International Standards Organization Technical Committee 46: Libraries and Documentation; 1976 saw the initiation of a quarterly newsletter *News About TC46* available upon request from the Secretariat. The following list represents the principal publications and activities of TC46 in 1976.

Brussels Meeting. ISO/TC 46 held its 16th Plenary session at Brussels, Belgium, in May 1976.[6] In the course of this meeting its *Subcommittee 1: Documentary Reproduction* issued a lengthy status report, but produced no new standards. *Subcommittee 2: Conversion of Written Languages* drafted a new introduction on the "General Principles of Script Conversion" to serve for all future conversion standards work. It also set forth its program of activities, to be led by the newly assigned Secretariat in France, including a review of the Romanization of Japanese (DIS 3602), the Conversion of Non-Slavic Cyrillic letter languages (DIS 2805), of Slavic Cyrillic letter languages (DIS 9), of Hebrew (DIS 259), of Arabic (DIS 233), and of Greek (DIS 843). *Subcommittee 3* is developing a *Vocabulary of Information and Documentation* (VID), of which Chapter 1: *Basic Concepts for Information and Documentation* was to be published as ISO/DIS 5127/I. It was reported that the International Council on Archives had decided to join the work by preparing a list of terms concerning *Storage and Preservation of Documents* as Chapter V of the VID. Other chapter drafts were reviewed. *Subcommittee 4* acted on an extended Latin alphabet character set (DP 5427) and the Greek alphabet character set (DP 5428). They also considered for future action an African character set, a mathematical character set, and a set for bibliographical control characters. UNIMARC was reworked; filing rules and some suggestions for the amplification or clarification of ISO 2709 were considered.

A number of new subjects for standardization were proposed to TC 46 during the Plenary session, notably the presentation of bibliographies, drafting of titles, criteria for price indexes, and a revision of ISO 832, *Abbreviations of Typical Words*. The establishment of a Steering Committee, in which the U.S. will have one representative, was also approved at this meeting.

ISO Standards—Published and in Preparation (1976)

ISO/DIS 8   Documentation—Presentation of Publications (submitted to ISO Council)
ISO 214 Documentation—Abstracts for publication and documentation (published in March 1976)
ISO/DIS 2384.2 Presentation of translations (submitted to ISO Council)
ISO/DIS 2707 Microcopying—Transparent A6 size microfiche of uniform division—Image arrangements No. 1 and No. 2 (submitted to ISO Council after the insertion of ISO 3273 concerning the charac-

Standards

terestics of microfilms)

ISO/DIS 2708 Microcopying—Transparent A6 size microfiche of variable division—Image arrangements A and B

ISO 3334 Microcopying—ISO Test Chart No. 2—Description and use in photographic documentary reproduction (published in September 1976)

ISO/DIS 3388 Patent documents—Bibliographic references—Essential and complementary elements (submitted to ISO Council)

ISO/DIS 4087 Microcopying of newspapers on 35mm unperforated microfilm for archival purposes (submitted for publication as DIS)

ISO/DIS 5122 Documentation—Abstract sheets in serial publications (a second version is in preparation)

ISO/DIS 5126 Computer output microfiche (a second version is in preparation)

ISO/DIS 5127/I Documentation—Vocabulary of Information and Documentation (VID). Chapter 1. (submitted for publication as DIS)

The following Draft International Standards concerning transliteration were discussed at the recent meeting of SC 2 of ISO/TC 46 in Brussels, May 1976.

ISO/DIS 9 Transliteration of Slavic Cyrillic characters into Latin characters (final version in preparation)

ISO/DIS 233 Transliteration of Arabic characters into Latin characters (comments from TC 46 Member Bodies to be circulated among SC 2 members)

ISO/DIS 259 Transliteration of Hebrew characters into Latin characters (comments from TC 46 Member Bodies to be circulated among SC 2 members)

ISO/DIS 843 Transliteration of Greek characters into Latin characters (final version in preparation)

ISO/DIS 2805 Transliteration of alphabets of non-Slavic languages using Cyrillic characters (final version in preparation)

ISO/DIS 3602 Romanization of Japanese (a new version is in preparation)

Drafts (DIS) and proposals (DP) circulated by ISO/TC 46 in 1976 included *Presentation of Translations* (DIS 2384.2), *Presentation of Periodicals* (DIS 8), *Outline ISBD(M)* (DP 1168), and *Abstract Sheets in Serial Publications* (DIS 5122).

Bibliographic Control: Progress Reports. Two notable progress reports, one written by Henriette Avram[7] and the other by Elizabeth Tate,[8] provide an excellent introduction to the status of both international and national standards work on UBC and the interchange of bibliographic records in machine-readable form. Their articles will aid the reader, whether novice or expert, in following the intricate network of competing agencies and organizations now deeply involved in solving the complex problem of bibliographic control.

As noted initially, the activities of IFLA, NCLIS, CONSER, UNISIST and others are ever more specifically oriented to standards. Each of these has broader scope than the standards which evolve from their work, however, and each is reported on in other places in this *Yearbook*. (Consult those articles and the *Index* for references to various programs.) It is useful to note here again the increased sense of awareness that the standards, whether formulated before or after the fact, are fundamental to any application of information management.   JERROLD ORNE

REFERENCES
1. Bernard Vavrek, "Bless You Samuel Green!" in *Library Journal* 101:971–74 (April 15, 1976).
2. *College and Research Library News* 37:10 (November 1976), p. 271–73.
3. *Status Report-1976*. American National Standards Committee Z39 on Library Work, Documentation and Related Publishing Practices (Chapel Hill, N.C.: University of North Carolina, 1976), 38 pp.
4. *Minutes of the Forty-ninth Meeting*, ANSI/X3L8 (June 11, 1976); Doc. no. X3L8/206 (July 22, 1976).
5. Carl E. Nelson, "The Evolution of NMA Standards Work," *Journal of Micrographics* 9:5 (May–June 1976), p. 223–34.
6. Report and Resolution, 16th Plenary Meeting of ISO/TC46—Documentation, Brussels (May 1976); Doc. no. ISO/TC46/N 1171 (July 1976).
7. H. D. Avram, "International Standards for the Interchange of Bibliographic Records in Machine-Readable Form," *LRTS* 20:1 (Winter 1976), p. 25–35.
8. E. L. Tate, "International Standards: The Road to Universal Bibliographic Control," *LRTS* 20:1 (Winter, 1976), p. 16–24.

State Library Agencies

Budget and fiscal problems continued to be of major concern in 1976 as a number of states suffered losses of operating or state aid funds while others were required to adhere to "hold-the-line" formulas that were imposed on state agencies. New York won a significant legislative victory that saw $8,000,000 added in state library aid, a gain that was partially offset by the loss of the Assistant Commissioner for Libraries title when the Governor's budget eliminated funds for that and for five other assistant commissioners. John A. Humphry retained his basic title of State Librarian and a complete administrative restructuring of the State Library took place. The former Library Development Bureau, for example, was split into two separate units: (1) the Bureau of Regional Library Services headed by Robert Flores and (2) the Bureau of Specialist Library Services headed by E. J. Josey. The "in-house" functions of the State Library were reorganized, and under the supervision of Director Peter J. Paulson the State Library was completing plans for the move to the new building on the Albany Mall. The card catalog will be replaced by a completely computerized operation in the new facility.

Somewhat the reverse fiscal situation happened in New Jersey which saw its state aid cut from $7,500,000 to $6,500,000 at the same time the State Library was being strengthened through the addition of seven new positions, $85,000 in book funds, and a new office in the legislative chambers to serve as a small legislative reference branch at such times as the legislature is in session.

In Ohio, after two years of wrangling, the Ohio State Library Board was sustained by the State Controlling Board (a legislative agency) in its position that formerly impounded LSCA funds should be used for library purposes, and not be paid into the State General Fund as proposed by the Ohio Office of Budget and Management. The $1,000,000 involved was used for automation and two new statewide resources programs in grants made between the June 21 decision and the June 30 deadline for expenditure of the contested funds. The dispute apparently did not affect the basically good relations that existed between the State Library and the Executive Budget Office, which on August 27 issued a three-page memorandum explaining the State Library's important role in state government and urging all agencies to "understand and use the services available. . . ."

A significant restructuring of the law library facilities available to the bench and bar of Connecticut was achieved through legislation that abolished the former county law libraries and made the State Library responsible for operating a three-tiered system of law library opportunity. The enabling act establishing the new system became effective on July 1, 1976, and provided $400,000 for the 14 staff members added to the State Library payroll and for the legal materials to be centrally purchased and processed for the 13 outlets. With typical Yankee ingenuity (Connecticut variety), the program will be funded by increases in court filing fees.

Surveys, Studies, and Cooperative Endeavors. Two major surveys of state-supported libraries were under way: a study of state library agencies conducted for the National Center for Education Statistics (NCES) by the State Library of Florida, with Barratt Wilkins as project director, and a survey of special libraries serving state governments, conducted by the State Library of Ohio with Joseph Shubert as project director. Both were scheduled for completion in late 1977. In addition, state librarians were involved in the planning for a survey of library cooperatives and consortia, and indicated their support for a survey of special libraries in commerce and industry by the Special Libraries Association.

State library agencies became increasingly involved in continuing education and at least 15 agencies were members of CLENE (the Continuing Education Network and Exchange). CLENE (q.v.) was established in 1975 with the help of a number of state library agencies. Continuing education planning staff from 25 state library agencies participated in a CLENE institute held at the Illinois State Library in Springfield in October to do advanced work on statewide continuing education.

In December a number of state library agency heads participated in a seminar at the University of Pittsburgh, the first step in a continuing education program initiated by the NCLIS. The seminar was conducted by Frank A. Sessa and Brooke Sheldon of the University of Pittsburgh Library School.

State library agency membership in OCLC is growing rapidly, largely as a result of staff participation in such regional networks as NELINET, SOLINET, and similar consortia. Several state libraries, including New York, Pennsylvania, Illinois, and Ohio, were entering state documents into the OCLC on-line data base to improve bibliographic control and access to state publications.

New Buildings. New state library buildings opened in Alabama, Florida, West Virginia, and South Dakota, and the Ohio State Library completed its first year in expanded quarters. The Hawaii State Library was making plans for a new headquarters building in the government complex in downtown Honolulu.

New Agency Heads. Several top-level administrative changes were made during the year. David McKay was appointed North Carolina State Librarian to succeed the late Philip Ogilvie. Marian Leith, who had served as Acting State Librarian for much of 1976, was appointed by President Ford to the National Commission on Libraries and Information Science. Anthony Miele was named as Head of the Alabama Public Library Service and Robert L. Clark, Jr., was appointed head of the Department of Libraries in Oklahoma. Jack C. Mulvey succeeded Mary E. Love as Director of the Mississippi Library Commission. In New Hampshire, Avis M. Duckworth was appointed State Librarian to succeed the late Emil L. Allen, Jr. In Oregon, Marcia Lowell was selected to succeed Eloise Ebert, who retired in June after 27 years in the Oregon State Library.

LSCA Extension. The Chief Officers of State Library Agencies meeting in Austin, Texas, on November 16 adopted a resolution urging Congress to pass the LSCA extension prior to March 15, 1977 and suggested a limitation of not more than 20 percent but not less than 10 percent for state administration of LSCA and requirements precluding the use of federal funds to reduce or replace state monies. COSLA also endorsed the proposed Title V for urban libraries provided that state or regional access to the urban library collections or both is guaranteed.   ROGER H. MCDONOUGH

State Library Agencies

Marguerite B. Cooley, of the Arizona Library, Archives, and Public Records Division, Joseph J. Anderson, Nevada State Librarian, at the COSLA (Chief Officers of State Library Agencies) meeting in Austin, Texas, in November.

Telecommunications and Public Broadcasting

On Capitol Hill 1976 saw the end of the public service of two long-time leaders in the field of communications policy making. Torbert Macdonald (D. Mass.) stepped down from the chairmanship of the House Subcommittee on Communications in April, only weeks before his death. On the Senate side his opposite number, John O. Pastore of Rhode Island, public broadcasting's oldest and closest friend, announced his intention to retire at the session's end.

Macdonald was succeeded by Lionel Van Deerlin, (D. Calif.) former California TV newsman, whose first act was to initiate hearings on cable television which his predecessor had planned. Intended to shed light on the complex questions of cable regulation rather than to deal with specific legislative proposals, the cable hearings clearly contributed to Van Deerlin's announced determination to place high on the subcommittee's agenda for the next session a total and complete rewriting of the Communications Act of 1934. No one who understands the situation believes that that process will be any less complex nor any speedier than revision of the Copyright Act. The stage is set for a lengthy debate on the shape of telecommunications in America for the remainder of the 20th century—not only broadcasting, cable, and satellites, but telephone, telegraph, computer teleprocessing, and the communications technologies present and future.

As early as February 1976 a Consumer Communications Reform Act was introduced which would essentially end the FCC's power to encourage competition in the interstate common carrier business. Its proponents argue that competition undercuts the ability to minimize user costs through economies of scale; its enemies see it as promoting a Bell System monopoly. The "Bell Bill" never came to hearings during 1976, but it is sure to reappear in 1977 and will not be disposed of, one way or the other, without extensive and heated Congressional debate.

Pastore's Impact. Senator Pastore's departure came after long service, including important leadership in the 1962 Educational Television Facilities Act, which has provided Federal matching grants for construction of public television (later radio and television) stations, the All Channel bill which mandated that TV receivers be equipped for UHF as well as VHF reception, and, most important for noncommercial radio and television, the Public Broadcasting Act of 1967.

Pastore stayed to see enactment of the "missing" piece of public broadcasting legislation, long-range funding for the Corporation for Public Broadcasting. The final version of the appropriations bill provided $103,000,000 for fiscal year 1977, and up to $107,150,000 for FY 78 and $120,200,000 for the final year of the present authorization—a marked increase over the $78,500,000 CPB got for FY 76. Each year the Congress is to make the appropriation for two years hence. How much money public broadcasting gets will depend upon a matching formula with $1 of federal funds allocated for each $2.50 the entire public broadcasting community has raised from non-federal sources.

Videodiscs and Cassettes. Those who thought that 1976 would be the Year of the Videodisc were doomed to disappointment. The major contenders, MCA-Phillips and RCA, failed to bring the videodisc to the American consumer market. MCA-Phillips promised a late 1977 debut, and at year's end RCA was silent on the subject. The portents from Europe have not been good. Introduction of the British-German Teldec combine's TeD system was greeted with applause from the engineers and apathy from the buying public. Back in the U.S., a small California company, i/o Metrics, continued to be bullish about its photo-optical videodisc system, and it reported that it plans to market it first as a still-frame information retrieval device, then for off-line computer memory applications, and leave to later the prospects and problems of color television programs in the home. The i/o Metrics approach promised interesting potentials for the library and information science field.

In contrast, 1976 saw growing consumer acceptance of Sony's ½-inch Betamax videocassette format, the home-oriented offshoot of the highly successful ¾-inch U-Matic cassette system. As the year ended, however, a new cloud loomed in the sky: a lawsuit by Universal City Studios and Walt Disney Productions to challenge the legality of off-air videotape copying at home. That is a reminder that passage of the Copyright Revision Act of 1976 was as notable an event in the field of telecommunications as it was in print publishing and other areas. The way was cleared for passage of the long-awaited bill by resolution of the vexing cable issue through a payment formula agreed to in April by the National Cable Television Association and the Motion Picture Association of America.

Access Rules. On April 1, 1976, the FCC amended its cable television access rules, deleting the requirement that all new systems in the 100 largest television markets provide four access channels but substituting the following provisions: *all* cable systems having more than 3,500 subscribers must now provide at least one composite access channel (up to four if the demand is sufficient and the system can provide them). Where a dedicated access channel is not available, cable systems must provide access time on channels blacked out when distant stations carry network programs available locally. According to an analysis by the Joint Council on Educational Telecommunications, the net result is a reduction in the number of systems required to provide access, but that will be reversed as newer systems grow above the 3,500 subscriber mark. By extending access requirements to large systems outside the top 100 markets the new rules substantially increase the number of cable subscribers who may be reached.

SATELLITES

If developments in the videodisc field were disappointing, news about communications satellites was plentiful and encouraging. The nation's third domestic satellite system got under way with the launch of Comstar I in May and Comstar II in July. Operated by the Communications Satellite Corporation's subsidiary, Comsat General, the new system will, for the first years of its life, serve the "long lines" needs of AT&T, GTE (America's second largest phone company), and the Hawaiian Telephone Company. Existing domestic satellite systems are those of Western Union and RCA.

Public Broadcasting. The Corporation for Public Broadcasting and the Public Broadcasting Service unveiled their plans for interconnecting the nation's noncommercial television stations via three (later four) leased channels on Western Union's domestic satellite system. The estimated annual operating cost, including financing and debt service, is a bit over $10,000,000 a year—a figure that is only marginally greater than that presently spent by public television for a single channel of terrestrial distribution.

The satellite interconnection for public television will be fully operational in 1979 and its multiple channels will permit local stations to chose among program options. The satellite interconnection will bring live network service for the first time to stations in Puerto Rico, Hawaii, Alaska, and the Virgin Islands.

Of considerable interest to the public service community is the question of access by others to the satellite system for national closed-circuit professional meetings, data transmission, and other possible uses. CPB and PBS have indicated that they will turn to their colleagues in the Public Service Satellite Consortium to explore such questions after the FCC gives its approval to the first-step, "lead" application which is now before it.

Network for Education. The Public Service Satellite Consortium, a nonprofit group whose 60-plus members include ALA and the Joint Council on Educational Telecommunications, has announced its intention to explore ways of developing a satellite-based national network for continuing education. Sharing time on Public Broadcasting's Satellite Interconnection System represents one option, but a still more exciting long-term prospect is a proto-operational satellite designed specifically for public service needs to be built by Hughes Aircraft and launched on the National Aeronautics and Space Administration's space shuttle some time in 1979. Negotiations were underway as the year ended.

The proposed satellite would represent a follow-on to the experimental NASA satellites which have already demonstrated the feasibility and applicability of high power satellites and small and relatively inexpensive earth stations. Opportunities for experimentation continue to be offered by NASA on ATS-6 (sixth in the Applications Technology Satellite series) and the joint U.S.-Canadian Communications Technology Satellite (CTS).

Experiments. The Communications Technology Satellite, the most powerful ever launched, was successfully orbited from Cape Canaveral in January and since that time a wide variety of education, health and social experiments by both U.S. and Canadian users have been in progress. In the meantime, ATS-6, which served India for a year for the highly successful Satellite Instructional Television Experiment (SITE), has been put into a slow orbital drift that will bring it back to its new parking space from which it will be available during 1977 for another year of experiments in the U.S. and other Western Hemisphere and Pacific locations. During its journey home, ATS-6 was used to demonstrate high-powered satellite technology to interested nations in Asia, Africa and Latin America.

Conference Plans. Less glamorous, but no less important, were the continuing preparations for the 1977 and 1979 World Administrative Radio Conferences to be held in Geneva by the International Telecommunications Union. ITU is a UN agency, and its agreements have treaty force. The 1977 WARC will deal with broadcasting satellites in the new 12 GHz band pioneered by CTS. The 1979 meeting will be a plenary session, reexamining all communications regulations and, like the proposed rewrite of the U.S. Communications Act, designed to set the shape of communications for the remainder of the century.

FRANK W. NORWOOD

Theatre Library Association

The yearly "activities" of the Theatre Library Association generally occur as three distinct events. In the spring, the George Freedley Memorial Award for a distinguished book on live theatre and the Theatre Library Association Award honoring a book in the field of recorded performance are presented. In 1976 the presentation was made in New York at the Gotham Book Mart Gallery on May 17. The Freedley Award was presented to Mrs. Donald

Theatre Library Association

Oenslager, whose husband's book *Stage Design: Four Centuries of Scenic Invention* (Studio-Viking) was published shortly before his death. The TLA Award was presented to Robert Sklar for *Movie-Made America: A Social History of American Movies* (Random House). There were no honorable mentions in either category.

In the summer the Annual Theatre Library Association program meeting is held during American Library Association Conference in the conference city. In 1976 "TLA Day" was Thursday, July 22, in Chicago. On the afternoon before, TLA had a booth at the Fair-in-the-Park, where many ALA Conference attendees heard about TLA for the first time.

The Thursday events began with a tour of the Auditorium Theatre and the Chicago Theatre. Seventy-five people took advantage of the chance for a behind-the-scenes glimpse of these two superb examples of Chicago theatre architecture—the one a fully restored Louis Sullivan-Dankmar Adler masterpiece and the other a survivor of the colossal movie palace architecture of the golden era of the American cinema. The afternoon program meeting was held in the main auditorium of the Goodman Theatre. A multipart presentation included a panel on alternative theatre in Chicago, a performance by one of the alternative theatre groups, a provocative reminiscence by Claudia Cassidy on Chicago's theatre history, and a hair-raising presentation by Barnhard Hooks on the great Iroquois Theatre fire in Chicago.

That evening, the Shaw Society of Chicago performed a dramatic reading of Act One of *Back to Methuselah* at the splendidly renovated Cultural Center of the Chicago Public Library. This was open to all ALA Conference attendees, as are all of TLA's program meetings. It was the only chance that most ALA members had to have a formal look at the magnificent room designed by Tiffany; it once again glows in jewel-like magnificence with all the marble and mosaic restored.

Board Election. In the fall of each year, the annual business meeting of the Theatre Library Association is held, usually in New York City. The 1976 meeting was on October 29, in the Vincent Astor Gallery of The New York Public Library at Lincoln Center. Four members were elected to three-year terms on the Board of Directors. Four members are elected each year. The board for 1976–77 is as follows:

- Hobart F. Berolzheimer, Free Library of Philadelphia.
- Richard M. Buck, Performing Arts Research Center, New York.
- Mrs. Robin Craven, private collector, New York.
- Ford E. Curtis, Curtis Theatre Collection, University of Pittsburgh.
- William Green, Department of English, Queens College, Flushing, N.Y.
- Robert M. Henderson, Library & Museum of the Performing Arts, New York.
- Frank C. P. McGlinn, private collector, Philadelphia.
- Paul Myers, Curator, Theatre Collection, The New York Public Library at Lincoln Center.
- Mrs. Jeanne T. Newlin, Curator, Harvard Theatre Collection, Harvard College Library, Cambridge.
- Paul R. Palmer, Curator, Columbiana Library, Columbia University.
- Mrs. Sally Thomas Pavetti, Eugene O'Neill Memorial Theatre Center, Inc., Waterford, Conn.
- Mrs. John F. Wharton, Theatre Collection, The New York Public Library at Lincoln Center.

Under the by-laws of Theatre Library Association, the Board elects the Executive Committee (officers). The officers for 1977–78, were elected at the Board meeting of December, 3, 1976. The term of office of Executive Committee members is two years.

Publications. Dr. Mary C. Henderson, the new Editor of *Performing Arts Resources*, reported that volume four would be an international issue featuring European activities and collections. She requested suggestions for articles. Communication may be addressed to her at the organization headquarters. *Performing Arts Resources*, an annual, first appeared in 1975. It discusses "the contents and locations of theatre collections, both public and private." It is hoped that it will contribute to "easier accessibility and higher standards of scholarship."

The Theatre Library Association is responsible also for the publication of a quarterly newsletter, *Broadside* (not to be confused with the folk music publication of the same name).

Membership. Individuals or institutions interested in the aims and activities of the organization may become a member. Dues are $15 annually for personal members and $20 for institutional, based on the calendar year, January to December. As of October 15, 1976, TLA

TLA Officers

PRESIDENT (December 1976–November 1977):
Brooks McNamara, Graduate Drama Department, School of the Arts, New York University

VICE-PRESIDENT:
Louis A. Rachow, The Walter Hampden–Edwin Booth Theatre Collection and Library, The Players

SECRETARY-TREASURER:
Richard M. Buck, Performing Arts Research Center, New York Public Library at Lincoln Center (acts as Executive Director)

Headquarters: 111 Amsterdam Ave., New York, NY 10023

had 248 personal and 212 institutional members. The expenditures of TLA from November 1975 to October 1976 were $7,100, including $3,850 for *Performing Arts Resources II,* which was shipped to all members as part of their annual dues.   RICHARD M. BUCK

Toys and Games

A Library Services and Construction Act grant for $25,900 to the Franklin Lakes, New Jersey, Public Library to establish a Demonstration Center for Preschool Services, called "Parents and Children Learning Together" and which includes toys and games, resulted in a town vote for a new public library—a building of their own.

Greenville County Library, Greenville, South Carolina, in September received a federal grant to develop a national model to demonstrate the role of the public library in meeting the learning needs of children up to age three, and the related needs of parents and child care personnel. Titled "Project Little Kids," it is conceived as a three-year, $46,167 project.

The Oklahoma Department of Libraries instituted a confirmation of their "Gentle Nudge" project involving eight more libraries, making a total of 15, beginning programs of toys and games with lectures, workshops, and discussions about early childhood development for parents.

Developments in Connecticut include Target Children: Urban Five (Bridgeport, Hartford, New Britain, New Haven, Stamford), an LSCA grant focused on the needs of some 147,000 children either not interested in reading, or reluctant readers. Toys, games, realia, plus the development of Heritage Boxes (including realia), are bringing new life into the library environment. The project is thought to be the first such cooperative venture among sizable autonomous libraries without geographic affinity or system membership. Twenty-four public libraries are participating in a demonstration loan of toys and games for The Special Child as part of another LSCA grant. This follows a September Hands-On Realia Demonstration with resource leaders and a rotating schedule so participants could experience working with the objects at each table designed for construction; coordination; verbal, visual, and auditory discrimination; language acquisition; social and imaginative play. A small training grant enables videotaping of parent support programs on Choosing Toys, Reading Relationships with Toys and Games (for in-state continuing education), and other ideas.

Prince George's County Public Library has developed special kits for the hearing impaired child that include toys. "Mainstreaming" the special child in the local community offers new opportunities for library services and programs. Support for this project appears in the Fall 1976 Public Library Association Newsletter in an article titled *An Adventure In Sensitivity* by Diana Young, Children's Consultant, North Carolina State Library.

The first list of recommended toys, games, and realia done by the ALA/Children's Services Division Toys Games and Realia Committee will appear in the January 1977 Booklist. The ALA has taken over publication of "Toys to Go" by the Connecticut Realia Committee. The 1976 U.S. Office of Education publication *Library Programs Worth Knowing About* includes information on the Clovis, New Mexico, "Parent/Child Toy Lending Library and Family Center" and on Albuquerque's "Pre-School Readiness Program."
    FAITH H. HEKTOEN

Trustees

"For the trustees of public libraries in the U.S., 1975 was a year of sharing problems brought on by depressed economic conditions and reduced financial resources of libraries." So went the opening sentence in this article in the 1975 *Yearbook*. It is a true and accurate summary for 1976. But if the conditions did not change, attitudes did, and there was considerable activity in 1976 of a more visible level. Faced with more uncomfortable seats on local boards or cooperative governing units, trustees began to respond to the need to find funds and to make libraries more worthy in the eyes of the dispensers of money, including the electorate.

Unfortunately, statistics of activity and direction by trustees are not easy to assemble. Activities of the Urban Libraries Council received the attention and effective national publicity naturally generated by a spotlight on the plight of the larger cities. Hundreds of small libraries labored just as hard in more restricted settings to push for libraries as necessary resources needing support.

The best evidence of activity is in the programs developed for conferences of the state library associations. Most of the leadership in the associations is vested in librarians, and public libraries are usually dominant. When that leadership chooses to devote time and attention to programs for trustees, that state's efforts are rewarded. Where there are active trustee associations or sections in the state association, there are trustees who can join in legislative programs or be stimulated to greater efforts in home communities. Programs for state conferences seem to show a trend toward better programming for trustees and more recognition of trustee talent. Several state associations have elected trustees to presidencies; most have a spot for trustee participation in the form of an automatic position on the board.

Jimmy Carter, then campaigning for the Democratic Party presidential nomination, speaking at the dedication of the Lake Blackshear Regional Library, Americus, Georgia, on March 21. He noted that his first elective office was as a trustee of that library in 1961.

Problems of Trustee Participation. Trustees (called directors in some states) are usually lay persons, attached to libraries by appointment (by election in some states) through the local political process. Most hold career positions of their own and, when asked, opt for limited meetings not requiring overnight stays—a limiting factor on their participation in association activities. (Ohio surveyed its trustees in 1976 and found that 101 out of 353 replying had attended a state conference; 239 reported they could not afford the time required, and 243 wanted to avoid trustee activities on Saturday and 86 on weekdays.) Without contact with a library association, trustees lose valuable learning opportunities, and, while trustees may organize effectively within a community, their influence may be lost at the legislative level.

Many state associations offer area workshops for trustees—one-day affairs within easy driving distance. Subjects for such workshops indicate a knowledge of local problems: censorship, book selection, personnel manuals, legal responsibilities of a trustee, using volunteers, public relations, central purchasing, standards, library law, building services, budgeting, board-staff relationships, library objectives, collective bargaining, cooperation, and construction. Few associations have done much in the way of publications. Generally, there is a state manual for trustees. Sometimes there are newsletters. In the states with active systems, there are organized efforts to teach and serve trustees. But continuity is difficult to achieve, requiring more attention than normally is available from volunteers in the state association or from the generally depleted staff in state library agencies.

Response to 1976 Issues. With or without help from library leadership in associations and cooperatives, trustees in 1976 were forced to cope with the major problems of funding and performance of their local public libraries. In many communities, the age of library expansion had cooled; it was no longer possible to count on a successful referendum or a leap in valuation to indulge in interesting new services. Communities which voted more taxes found themselves being analyzed to isolate reasons for their success. Yet there were many cases of voters' supporting libraries. In Illinois, for example, carefully planned "Projects Plus" consisting of funded services to non-served areas won public support in 13 out of 15 library district votes in fiscal 1975. In each case, citizen action was emphasized, good public relations planned, and cooperation with political leadership pursued. Common elements of success in the business of getting more money for libraries or establishing new libraries have not been assembled scientifically, but they seem to involve following the best practice recommended by earlier efforts. A good deal of sharing of techniques took place.

Libraries in 1976 were emphasizing services and talking to people about the losses and changes made necessary by less money and more inflation. Libraries which had ridden the bandwagon of the new and different generally benefited from the experience of reaching new users and providing different services. Smaller libraries particularly found it difficult to drop the art print service or curtail the lending of films in favor of the "basics," now defined more broadly by the users. Where cost cutting became absolutely mandatory, trustees were torn among dropping a popular program, reducing book purchases or curtailing hours. In most cases, hours lost.

The process of decision making was an interesting one. As trustees had participated in building more sophisticated services, they hated to retreat. Cutting back became an involved procedure. What are the basics? What does the community want? What solution is least damaging to our new image as a resource? Why does the library have to suffer when we have done such a good job? These were among questions debated as the difficult decisions were made. This is not to imply that all library boards and staffs approached cost cutting with a user orientation, but it is refreshing to note that many did. The message of service has cut through, and many trustees were angered by having to retreat.

Revenue Sharing. One result of the starvation diet for many libraries was grim and effective action by trustees to cut their libraries in on revenue sharing funds given to municipalities, townships and counties. The total obtained by aggressive local action was not much as a percentage of the whole, but it was a source libraries were learning to tap. Worth Township in Cook County, Illinois, shared with all the libraries in its area, giving in visibly to concerted action and a considerable outpouring of supporters of the library service.

Expectations from revenue sharing funds were unreliable at best, and libraries began to look at their traditional base of support—the property tax. Despite some approving referenda for construction funds or a tax hike, voters were generally able to muster an outcry against adding to the property tax. Especially in communities with many single-family homes (where tax assessments reflect the inflated value of the home), libraries began to look elsewhere for future funding. In most cases, this meant to the revenue of the state. Techniques varied. Some states asked for funding of systems—to share the funds through cooperative services; some pursued per capita allotments; some sought permission to raise ceilings on the local tax; many sought better support for the state library agency. No one discovered any "new" money. It was evident that libraries would need to compete for funds in the state legislature just as at home. And to do so meant more sophisticated efforts by the state library associations.

Lobbying for Libraries. State library associations found trustees well suited to lobbying. They were usually active in local politics, served on many committees in their home areas, were converts or pioneers in good library service, and enjoyed the ability to deny any personal monetary interest in a piece of legislation. In lobbying, librarians and trustees found a common ground, and the pace in most states elevated in 1976. A number of state associations hired paid lobbyists to guide their efforts. Networks of home front lobbyists were set up or improved. The very word "lobbying" began to win acceptance. A healthy interest in the welfare of libraries was translated into insistence that legislators give libraries their due. Citizen persuasion was effective in many states—and in city councils and county buildings as well. A benefit of 1976 was the improved assertiveness of the library community in demanding support for libraries.

ALTA, ALA, and Trustees. A natural source of impetus for funding for libraries was the American Library Association, itself maintaining an active legislative staff in Washington, D.C. The trustee unit of ALA, the American Library Trustee Association (ALTA), was active at national meetings involving its leadership and trustees in lobbying at the national level—for the extension of Library Services and Construction Act funding, on the landmark copyright bill with its implications for photocopying, and for a White House Conference on Library and Information Services. But ALTA was uneasy about its role in ALA. Dues increases had taken a toll of membership, since many trustees paid their own dues and found a $50 base questionable. ALTA persuaded ALA into a bylaws change establishing a base of $20 for a trustee membership in ALA, plus $15 for ALTA as a division. At the end of 1976 ALTA was holding on as a viable unit, partly because its overhead was reduced when a troika of divisions combined at ALA headquarters under one program secretary. ALTA leadership was still concerned about the number of trustees (300) attracted to the ALA Conference. The number was small in comparison to the potential, and the faces were familiar. Still, ALTA continued to generate leadership willing to travel, to speak, and to write. The unit was fighting to maintain its independence but had small success in one area, that of trustees elected to the ALA Council. In 1976 only one lay person served on Council, despite a nominating committee which did select noted trustees to run. ALTA itself went to the single slate method to avoid the waste of talent in elections with no issues other than survival of ALTA. (See also American Library Trustee Association.)

Urban Trustees. Although the Urban Libraries Council is organized independently, it meets with ALA and generally works with ALTA on a Conference program. In 1976 it managed an important change of direction for the ALA legislative program. The ALA Legislation Committee voted to pursue a new title for urban libraries. Allocation of funds would be on a per capita basis to libraries in communities of a certain size, estimated at 100,000 to ensure that every state will get some of the funds, which will be sought in the 1977 Congress. The urban group has been an aggressive force in recognizing the decline of libraries in the cities.

Another entrant in the battle by the layman to get funds for libraries is the National Citizens Emergency Committee to Save Our Public Libraries, headed by Whitney North Seymour, Jr., of New York City. The Committee seeks to promote federal support for libraries through contacts with Congressmen by key persons, primarily library trustees, in each state. Research from the committee, headquartered at 1666 K Street, N.W., Washington, D.C., has focused on the role of libraries in the economy, from providing jobs to helping others to prepare for jobs and advancement.

Issues of 1976. While finding funds to develop, promote, and continue good library services was clearly the most common and important of the issues facing trustees in 1976, other concerns surfaced with regularity across the country.

Staff Relationships. A number of "cases" handled by SCAMI (Staff Committee on Arbitration, Mediation and Inquiry) centered on how library boards deal with firings. Several boards were censored for their procedures and for the absence of written policies. Without regard to the merits of individual situations, there is evidence that boards have been accustomed to considerable autonomy in dealing with staff and defend their right to fire, while the victims of firing ask for clearer procedures, due process, and appeals. A few state library associations are establishing limited mechanisms to assist both boards and staff in this area (Illinois and California, for example). The issue of the board's control, at least over the head librarian, is growing as more activist librarians encounter traditional policies and as communities are more aware of the library and its collections, programs and policies.

Censorship. Although most public libraries profess adherence to intellectual freedom statements issued by ALA, many do not have policies for dealing with censorship and the increase in community concern over pornography, which has replaced political expression as the censor's chief target. Few boards pursue the concept of wide choice in controversial reading, just as few librarians order extensively in certain areas. When the censorship of book selection breaks down, boards and librarians can expect community reaction. The area is an uneasy one for trustees, who have their roots and futures in the community and often anticipate considerable damage to their reputations if they stand up to censors who may reflect substantial opinion in the community. Trustees who have experienced censorship episodes report that the best weapon is the prepared defense of written policies affirming the right to read and providing a complaint procedure that gives them time to marshal support.

Collective Bargaining, Salaries. Except in larger cities and in communities where the library may be a department of municipal government, collective bargaining by library employees grew slowly in the mid-1970's. Trustees are surprised at the slow pace, having begun to prepare themselves somewhat in advance of librarian interest in unionization. Recent workshops on this issue have discovered little activity in the small libraries, probably because they are too small to maintain a drive for recognition. Trustees still face the problem of moving librarians from the "dedicated but underpaid" category to the "competitive with business" class. Boards have usually leaned on state salary surveys for guidance in hiring head librarians and on head librarians for recommendations below that level. The result is a generally rising level for new heads, even in a surplus market, but slow increases for other staff. Trustees are, more and more, requiring a master's degree for top positions and hoping for "professional" education in newly hired personnel. Except in small libraries, job descriptions commonly call for the MLS. Entry level positions command slightly better salaries now than five years ago, but often lag behind inflationary pressures. Trustees often reflect the community's opinion that library work is clean and enjoyable, and thus sought even at moderate wages. A few state trustee groups (New Jersey is an example) have been actively urging higher salaries for librarians.

Trustee Skills. Most state library associations and the state library agencies are involved in setting standards, grappling with planning, sponsoring continuing education and pursuing networking. The trustee often feels that the professional is making the demands, frequently without trustee input. Trustees ask that they be involved in developing the skills that will improve library service. In many cases library boards feel they are being pressured into technological experiments when they need better interlibrary loan delivery. They try to follow dictates for orderly planning, often without help. They budget for continuing education but see few results. A detachment between trustees and the profession occurs when the profession pursues goals and objectives exceeding the preparation of the trustee. Despite many workshops and programs for trustees, many feel that they are on the sidelines, as do many of the librarians tied to their jobs without the opportunity to participate in association work or attend lengthy workshops. Public librarians need to remember their base in the community and bring trustees along in the preparation for coming breakthroughs in library service and importance.

In summary, little was new to trustees in 1976. They continue to oversee their libraries, sell them to the community, plan for their futures and hope for their growth. In 1976 and in all other years, the job of librarian and trustee will be to take in and turn over new classes of trustees, administering much the same short courses, and hoping that the inoculation will preserve the continuity of the tradition of lay involvement in the libraries they use.

ALICE B. IHRIG

UNESCO

Implementation of the NATIS (National Information System) program increased in momentum in 1976. The advantages to be derived from that cooperative action at the national level became more apparent to policymakers and professionals throughout the world. The NATIS program aims, through a series of 12 objectives at national level, to create or improve national information systems so as to enable all countries, whatever their stage of development, to participate in international information systems.

Networks. Emphasis in the NATIS program has been placed on developing library networks based on modern methods and using innovative technology and cooperative schemes, for example, the computer-based university library network in Malaysia, the data base for policymakers in Tunisia. Computerization has also been used in compiling union catalogs at the National Library of Thailand and the National Information and Documentation Centre at Cairo (Egypt). At the same time, public and school library networks have been developed in different regions of the world often in conjunction with projects for the eradication of illiteracy, for example, in the village libraries system in Tanzania, or the public and school library networks in Brazil, El Salvador and Indonesia. In other countries, such as the Cameroon, Togo, and the Seychelles, plans have been made for establishing an overall national information system. Information about NATIS projects is published regularly in *NATIS News*. Reports on these projects are available from the UNESCO Division of Documentation, Libraries, Archives, and Book Promotion in Paris, France.

The planning and development of national information systems was also discussed at regional meetings of experts at Brazzaville, Congo, in Africa, at Rabat, Morocco, in the Arab States and at Bogota, Colombia, in Latin America. The latter meeting studied the development of national archives within the NATIS context. An important intergovernmental conference on communication policies in Costa Rica recommended the inclusion of NATIS as an integral part of national communication policies.

Professional Education. One of the NATIS objectives deals with supplying manpower at various levels to operate the national information system. Emphasis has also been placed, therefore, on professional education and training. Twelve refresher courses, seminars, and workshops were held in different parts of the world. The training of teachers of library science and documentation was carried on in specially designed courses offered in the United States and the United Kingdom; formal education programs including information science subjects were established at a library school for the Maghreb countries created at Rabat, Morocco, with UNESCO assistance, and at the two regional library schools also created in previous years with UNESCO assistance, at Dakar, Senegal, and Kampala, Uganda. Fellowships were awarded to enable students from developing countries to attend these and numerous other courses. In addition, revision of curricula to keep pace with modern library and documentation techniques was studied at regional symposia for supervisors of library and documentation schools in Baghdad, Iraq, Bangalore, India, and Bogota, Colombia, which resulted in exchanges of experience and recommendations for future action. *Preliminary Survey of Education and Training Programmes at University Level in Information and Library Science* by D. J. Foskett was issued during 1976.

Guidelines. To assist planners in implementing the NATIS objectives in their countries, UNESCO issued three guidelines: *National Information Policy*, by D. J. Urquhart; *Design and Planning of National Information Systems*, by Björn Tell, and *Establishing a Legislative Framework for NATIS*, by P. Sewell, A. W. Mabbs and E. M. Broome. Two further guidelines were also prepared for publication in 1977.

UBC. Universal Bibliographic Control (UBC), a cooperative venture for the pooling of national contributions to make a total international network, has been designed to help solve the problem of the control of bibliographic information. UBC has been adopted as a major NATIS objective, and during 1976 a Planning Committee was set up to plan and start preparation for the International Congress on National Bibliographies which UNESCO will organize in cooperation with IFLA in Paris from September 12–15, 1977. This will be a working congress of those responsible for the compilation, preparation and publication of national bibliographies, and the aim will be to reach agreement on minimum standards and acceptable practices, i.e., ISBDs for monographs, serials, non-book materials, cartographic materials, music, and relevant ISO and other standards, for the production of national bibliographies to facilitate the international exchange of bibliographic records and data and the sharing of resources.

Projects continued actively during 1976 included International Information System on Research in Documentation, the information received from the co-operating National Information Transfer Centres in over 70 countries being processed by the UNESCO Computerized Documentation Service and published regularly in the bimonthly bulletin *Bibliography, Documentation, Terminology* (appearing in four language editions); the annual bibliography of translations throughout the world, entitled *Index translationum*, of which volume 26 covering 1973 appeared; the information exchange network of the International Bureau of Education in Geneva; and the International Data Bank for the Social Sciences (DARE). The *UNESCO Bulletin for Libraries*, a bimonthly periodical appearing in five languages, continued to report on all UNESCO activities and to carry original contributions from leading librarians and documentalists from all over the world.

Other Activities. Because of the interdependence of the activities for the development of library services resulting from the establishment of NATIS and those to improve the distribution of books and to promote the reading habit, these activities were closely integrated, especially at the operational level. Several meetings and symposia were held on children's literature in the service of international understanding and peaceful cooperation at Tehran, Iran, on promotion of the reading habit at New Paltz, N.Y. and on publication of books in the various languages of multilingual countries at Moscow and Alma Ata, USSR. The Regional Book Development Centres for Africa South of the Sahara, Latin America, and the Arab States were all active in holding training courses on printing and publishing management, on book publishing and production, and on the graphic arts and publishing. Information about the book promotion program continued to appear in *Book Promotion News*, which appears irregularly in English and French.

Toward the end of 1976, the UNESCO General Conference held its 19th session at Nairobi, Kenya. A resolution was adopted which will give UNESCO one general information program covering activities in the fields of documentation, libraries, and archives in general and of scientific and technological information that formerly were carried out independently. The general information program will have two main drives: one aimed at achieving UNISIST goals for a world scientific information system, the other at creating or improving the documentation, library, and archives infrastructure or national information system (NATIS), without which UNISIST cannot become a reality.

Guiding the planning and implementation of the program will be an Intergovernmental Council (superseding the UNISIST Steering Committee), composed of representatives of 30 member states, and an International Advisory Committee of experts and specialists (merging the International Advisory Committee on Documentation, Libraries and Archives and the International Advisory Committee for UNISIST).   I. BETTEMBOURG

Universal Bibliographic Control

The basis for IFLA's long-term program of Universal Bibliographic Control (UBC) — which is accepted as Objective 14 under the NATIS (National Information Systems) program of UNESCO — is twofold: the recognition that each country is best qualified to identify and record the publications of its national authors, and the acceptance by all countries of international standards in making the descriptive record.[1] The activities of the IFLA International Office for UBC are determined by this philosophy and its consequent establishment of priorities for action. The major role of the IFLA UBC Office is in promoting and assisting projects which will aid the international standardization of bibliographic records and in supporting national plans and projects for the improvement of national bibliographic control. In pursuit of these objectives IFLA carries out a number of functions: the provision of services to working groups; the collection and dissemination of information; liaison and coordination among national and international cataloging and bibliographic organizations; and an editorial and publishing program, including the journal *International Cataloguing*.[2]

A number of meetings related to UBC and IFLA's program of International Standard Bibliographic Descriptions (ISBDs) took place late in 1975 and during 1976: of major significance was the establishment of the framework of a general international standard bibliographic description [ISBD (G)] with which the specialized ISBDs will conform. Various projects reached next-to-final stages after working group meetings and provisional drafts were discussed in open sessions at the IFLA General Council, Lausanne, August 1976. It was anticipated at year's end that various working groups would complete their recommendations in 1977, including UNIMARC, the international communications format. Publications prepared by the IFLA UBC Office during 1976 included *Examples of ISBD(M) Usage in European Languages, Standardization Activities of Concern to Libraries and National Bibliographies*, and a revised and enlarged version of the 1967 edition of *Names of Persons*. A work of considerable importance published late in 1975 was Eva Verona's *Corporate Headings*, for which she received the ALA Margaret Mann Citation for 1976. Publications of the IFLA UBC Office are available in North America from the Canadian Library Association.

UBC is as much a national as an international program, and every country in improving its national bibliographic control is advancing the progress of UBC. Hence emphasis was placed on the establishment and improvement of national bibliographies which will be examined in depth at an international congress organized by UNESCO in close association with IFLA, planned for September 1977. Much background work in preparation for that congress was undertaken during 1976. (*See also* IFLA; UNESCO.)   DOROTHY ANDERSON

REFERENCES
1. For the background of IFLA's UBC program, see the papers of the IFLA 39th General Council Meeting, Grenoble, 1973, including the statement of the IFLA President in *IFLA Annual 1973*, pp. 28–30. See also Dorothy Anderson, "IFLA's programme for UBC: the background and the basis" in *IFLA Journal* 1(1) (1975), 4–7.
2. *International Cataloguing*, quarterly, available from the Longman Group Limited, Journals Division, Edinburgh, includes a section in each issue reporting on national and international UBC projects.

Universal Serials and Book Exchange

Resource sharing among libraries of all kinds continued to be USBE's principal concern during 1976, as it has been since 1948. By the end of the year USBE had a membership of 1,635 libraries and 10 library centers throughout the world, ranging from 1,294 institutions in the United States to single libraries in some other countries. Some 820 academic institutions worked with 50 public libraries, 10 cooperatives, and 765 special libraries of government, profit-making, and nonprofit agencies, to contribute the publications which form the USBE clearinghouse collection of 4,000,000 periodical issues, books, and documents.

Member libraries selected 365,000 publications during 1976 from the stocks organized and maintained by USBE, at an average cost to each library of $2.20 per item from standard fees assessed by USBE to cover the average cost of processing each type of request or kind of publication. Members' acquisitions averaged 223 items in the year for each library. The actual range was from one out-of-print find for each of several institutions to 73,000 journal issues provided to a new medical library abroad.

The size, flexibility, and present and potential riches of USBE as the depository of resource-sharing libraries led to its being discussed during 1976 as one of the possible components of a national serials system, by a Task Force of the National Commission on Libraries and Information Science. The recommendations of the Task Force will be made public in 1977.

In the meantime USBE is broadening and diversifying the method and aims of its distribution of publications, beyond the principal purpose of giving libraries an effective and economical source for collection development and for replacement of missing items. Interlibrary loan departments of member libraries now use the USBE resource as a substitute for more costly interlibrary loan services. Special libraries in particular are using USBE as a source for articles listed by on-line information services, and for publications needed for personal use by individuals on their staffs. USBE is also serving non-member institutions and individuals, at a higher fee than members.

In 1976, under the presidency of Warren B. Kuhn, Dean of Library Services at Iowa State University, USBE brought out two new information leaflets: "Your best first source—USBE" and "Your Guide to USBE Services." These publications are distributed on request. The monthly newsletter changed title from *Newsletter* to *USBE/NEWS*. ALICE D. BALL

Washington Report

The nation's Bicentennial was the year of the second session of the 94th Congress (notable among other things for a Capitol Hill sex scandal) and the year of the presidential election that marked an end to eight years of Republican administration under Presidents Nixon and Ford.

In Congress the House passed a five-year extension of the Library Services and Construction Act (HR 11233), but the measure died for lack of action in the Senate Education Subcommittee. (LSCA extension will be an early agenda item in the 95th Congress.) Funding for library and education programs was increased somewhat during the year (see Table), and although President Ford vetoed the appropriations bill that provided funds for libraries along with other education, health, and welfare programs, Congress promptly overrode the veto and the measure became law (PL 94-439).

In addition, a number of bills made their way through the legislative process, several of which have implications for libraries. They include a new copyright law, a new program of federal grants for major research libraries, a new federal commitment to expand opportunities for lifelong learning, a new program of "challenge grants" to assist cultural institutions (including libraries) in great need, a very small telecommunications demonstration program, tax amendments, and a new infusion of public works construction funds. Each is briefly discussed here.

Copyright. On October 19 the bill for general revision of the copyright law (S. 22) was signed by the President and became Public Law 94-553. This marked the first major revision of the laws governing intellectual property in the United States since 1909. Title 17 of the United States Code is amended in its entirety by PL 94-553. With a few exceptions, the provisions of the new copyright law become effective January 1, 1978.

The new law extends the duration of copyright to the life of the author plus 50 years. This brings U.S. law into conformity with international practice and represents a fundamental change from the maximum 56-year duration of present U.S. law which is based on a system enacted by the English Parliament in 1710. Under the new law, 50 years after an author's death all his or her works copyrighted after 1977 fall into the public domain at once. The Register of Copyrights is to maintain current records relating to the death of authors of copyrighted works.

Of major significance to educators, librarians, and users is the provision of the new law that gives statutory recognition to the fair-use doctrine. Fair use is a concept that does not lend itself to exact definition, but generally speaking has been described by the Register of Copyrights as allowing "copying without permission from, or payment to, the copyright owner where the use is reasonable and not harmful to the rights of the copyright owner."

The new law codifies the fair-use doctrine in general terms. The statute refers to purposes such as criticism, comment, news reporting, teaching, scholarship, or research, and it specifies four criteria to be considered in determining whether or not a particular instance of copying or other reproduction is fair. The statutory criteria (set forth in Section 107) are (1) the purpose and character of the use, including whether such use is of a commercial nature or is for nonprofit education purposes; (2) the nature of the copyrighted work; (3) the amount and substantiality of the portion used in relation to the copyrighted work as a whole; and (4) the effect of the use upon the potential market for or value of the copyrighted work.

Another section of the new copyright law of importance to libraries authorizes libraries and archives to make single copies of works under certain circumstances which may not be fair use. Section 108 authorizes, for example, archival reproduction of an unpublished work, copying to replace a damaged or stolen copy, copying an out-of-print work, and making a

Washington Report

single copy of a single article or small excerpt of a work for a user—but each of these provisions carries with it special rules and requirements that must be understood by the librarian wishing to make a copy as authorized by Section 108. (See *ALA Washington Newsletter*, November 15, 1976, vol. 28, no. 13, for more information on the new copyright law as it affects libraries.)

Research Libraries. The Education Amendments of 1976 (PL 94-482) include as Sec. 107 a new Title II, Part C, to the Higher Education Act authorizing grants to major research libraries: $10,000,000 for fiscal year 1977, $15,000,000 for 1978, and $20,000,000 for 1979, with a statutory limitation of not more than 150 research libraries that are to receive grants under this program. The Commissioner of Education is directed to establish criteria designed to achieve reasonable regional balance in the allocation of funds, and is expected to publish draft regulations in the *Federal Register* early in 1977. *See also* Independent Research Libraries.

In general, the new law defines a major research library as a "public or private nonprofit institution, including the library resources of an institution of higher education, an independent research library, or a State or other public library, having library collections, which are available to qualified users and which—(1) make a significant contribution to higher education and research; (2) are broadly based and are recognized as having national or international significance for scholarly research; (3) are of a unique nature, and contain material not widely available; and (4) are in substantial demand by researchers and scholars not connected with that institution."

The Education Amendments of 1976 were signed into law after Congress had adjourned for the year, so appropriating funds for the new research library program is a task that fell to the new Congress convening in January 1977. Whether or not Congress would decide in 1977 to appropriate funds for the new HEA II-C would depend at least in part on how effectively research libraries communicated their needs to Senators and Representatives on Capitol Hill.

Lifelong Learning. The Education Amendments of 1976 (PL 94-482) include a federal commitment to expand opportunities for lifelong learning. Title I, Part B, of the Higher Education Act authorizes $90,000,000 over a three-year period to improve coordination of federal support for life-long learning and review lifelong learning opportunities provided through employers, unions, the media, libraries, museums, schools, and other organizations to determine means by which they can be made more effective.

The statute enters the bureaucratic jungle by requiring that the Assistant Secretary of Education assume responsibility for implementing the new program in cooperation with other federal agencies and bureaus "to the extent practicable" including the National Institute of Education, Fund for the Improvement of Postsecondary Education, National Center for Education Statistics, the U.S. Office of Education's Bureau of Postsecondary Education, and others, including the National Commission on Libraries and Information Science.

The Ford Administration did not show interest in a new federal lifelong learning program and consequently it was left to the new Administration to implement Title I-B of the Higher Education Act. Support is likely to be forthcoming from the new Administration because Walter Mondale was one of the chief sponsors of lifelong learning legislation during the 94th Congress. As Vice-President he is expected to continue his interest in education generally, and in lifelong learning particularly.

Challenge Grants. Legislation extending for four years the authorizations for the National Endowments for the Arts and the Humanities was signed into law on October 8 (PL 94-462). Included as Title III of this law is a program of

Congressional Appropriations and President's Budget FY 1977 Compared with FY 1976 Appropriations

	FY 1976 Congressional Appropriation	FY 1977 President's Budget	FY 1977 Congressional Appropriation
Library Services & Construction Act	$ 51,749,000	$ 51,749,000	$ 60,237,000
Title I Library Services	49,155,000	41,749,000	56,900,000
II Public Library Construction	-0-	-0-	-0-
III Interlibrary Cooperation	2,594,000	10,000,000	3,337,000
Elementary & Secondary Education Act (ESEA)			
Title IV-B Libraries & Learning Resources	147,330,000*	137,330,000*	154,330,000*
Higher Education Act (HEA) Title II	11,475,000	9,975,000	
Title II-A College Library Resources	9,975,000	9,975,000	deferred
II-B Library Training	500,000	-0-	"
II-B Library Research/ Demonstrations	1,000,000	-0-	"
II-C Research Libraries	-0-	-0-	"
Title VI-A Undergraduate Educational Equipment	7,500,000	-0-	"
Library of Congress (LC)	119,125,400	142,938,200	137,895,200
LC National Prog. Acquis. & Cataloging	10,173,391	11,474,749	10,767,497
National Library of Medicine (NLM)	22,632,000	27,234,000	27,234,000
Medical Library Assistance Act	6,433,000	8,000,000	8,000,000
Nat'l. Comm. Libs. & Inf. Science (NCLIS)	468,000	517,000	492,575
GPO Superintendent of Documents	44,364,700	47,476,000	47,188,400

*advance funded program

"challenge grants" to be administered by each of the Endowments. The aim of the challenge grants, which authorize one federal dollar to match three dollars from nonfederal sources, is to assist cultural institutions in great need to increase levels of support, provide administrative and management improvements, and increase public participation and greater citizen involvement in planning. Libraries are specifically mentioned in the legislative history as eligible for the challenge-grant program to be administered by the National Endowment for the Humanities.

Telecommunications. The Educational Broadcasting Facilities and Telecommunications Demonstration Act (PL 94-309) authorizes a new $1,000,000 program to promote the development of nonbroadcast telecommunications facilities and services for the delivery of health, education, and public or social service information. The 95th Congress convening in January 1977 was expected to review and extend this program which was initially created for one year only. Telecommunications legislation has great potential impact on library service, and should be watched closely by librarians of all types. (See also feature article on Telecommunications.)

Taxation. A product of many compromises, the so-called Tax Reform Act of 1976 (PL 94-455) provides a host of new tax amendments including one that establishes a new elective set of standards for determining whether a tax-exempt charity has engaged in so much lobbying that it loses its exempt status and can no longer receive deductible charitable contributions. This amendment was intended to provide a more definite test based upon a nonprofit organization's expenditures, plus less harsh sanctions for violations, than exist under the old law which simply states that to qualify as charitable, an organization must devote "no substantial part" of its activities to lobbying. Whether the new law will assist library organizations depends to some extent on the regulations issued by the Internal Revenue Service; they were not available at the end of 1976.

Public Works. Before adjourning to campaign for the November elections, Congress passed a public works employment act (PL 94-369) and appropriated $2,000,000,000 to carry out its construction provisions. Library buildings were among construction projects eligible for the grants being administered by the Department of Commerce's Economic Development Administration (EDA). By year's end it was reported that EDA had received applications totaling about $24,000,000,000 for the $2,000,000,000 available. Congress was expected to continue and expand the program in 1977 to combat continuing recession and high unemployment. SARA CASE

White House Conference

Both President Gerald Ford and Democratic candidate Jimmy Carter sent statements supporting the White House Conference on Library and Information Services to the ALA Centennial Conference in Chicago in July.

President Ford announced his intention to convene the conference, to request the necessary appropriations to fund it, and to make his appointments to the advisory committee. He said:

> The challenge confronting those who provide information services to the public is one of harnessing modern technology. Telecommunications, computers, and micrographics must be further employed to reduce the costs of making information more widely accessible and improving the speed and accuracy with which source materials can be supplied.
>
> It is my hope that the White House Conference on Library and Information Services will, through its State, territorial, and national assemblies, provide the impetus for advancing the quality of America's informational services.

At the same time, President-elect Carter said:

> I believe that the public should have more input into the decisions concerning the role of their local libraries. A nationwide series of library conferences culminating in a White House Conference is one method of implementing this process.
>
> Libraries are a national resource, and all of the nation must share in their upkeep. By the same token all of the nation must have access to the information contained in our many and diverse libraries. The strength of our system of government is the collective wisdom of our people. Our libraries are one crucial foundation of that wisdom.

On August 30 President Ford transmitted a budget request to Congress, asking for a supplemental appropriation for fiscal year 1977 in the amount of $3,500,000 for the National Commission on Libraries and Information Science to carry out the conference. The document stated that the conference "will develop recommendations for the improvement of services provided by the Nation's libraries and information service centers. It was authorized by Public Law 93-568. These funds will be used for financial assistance to the States in preparation for the national conference and for staff for the Commission."

Unfortunately the budget request came after Congress had already set an adjournment timetable and had decided to defer a supplemental money bill until early 1977. So by December 31—the second anniversary of its signing into law—the White House Conference had been moved only a couple of steps toward implementation. Still pending was President Ford's pledge to appoint 15 members to the advisory committee to carry out the conference. This would round out the 28-member panel called for in the law; 13 were named last year—10 by Congress and three by the National Commission. EILEEN D. COOKE

Women in Librarianship, Status of

Data on the status of women in librarianship in 1976 is available only on a scattered basis: for a type of library, a particular institution, a region, or a level of position. No current overview of the status of women in the profession exists, and there is almost no data on the status of women in the technical, paraprofessional, and clerical levels of librarianship. The results of surveys released during the year show little change in the disparities between position and salary of men and women librarians reported in 1975.

Salary Surveys. The annual survey of American Library Association accredited library school graduates' initial placements and salaries continues to show progress for beginning women librarians in the higher salary ranges (C. L. Learmont and R. L. Darling, "Placements and Salaries 1975," *Library Journal* 101, July 1976). The 1975 median high salary for women was $750 above that of men. In the low salary ranges, however, women continue to fall below men; the difference between the median low salary for men and for women graduates was $1,257. Of the 49 schools reporting 42 recorded higher low salaries for men than women. The median salary for all 1975 women graduates ($9,980) was 96.4 percent of the men's ($10,350). The salary differential, 3.6 percent, is 2.4 percent less than that reported for 1974 graduates, but approximately the same as in 1973.

Progress is not so apparent in academic libraries. The ALA Association of College and Research Libraries reports that women make up 61.5 percent of the professional staff; are the majority in every position except director, associate and assistant director; and earn less than men at every level (*Salary Structures of Librarians in Higher Education for the Academic Year 1975–76*, ALA, August 1976). The salary percentage difference at the early level is 3.2 percent, close to the difference for all graduates in the 1975 salary survey, but rises to 23.3 percent for directors. The salary gap is greatest (29.8 percent) for medical and law librarians. This pattern for women is much the same in all academic libraries: universities, colleges and two-year institutions.

At Stanford University 18 women librarians were awarded $50,000 in back pay and benefits as the result of a salary difference grievance filed 25 months earlier. A University survey of library working conditions and salaries showed inexplicable differences in salaries of men and women senior librarians. Inequities were not found in the lower professional levels where there are fewer male librarians ("Woman Librarian Protests Job Bias—with Results," *Christian Science Monitor*, December 1, 1976, p. 38).

Age Factor. The 1976 Special Libraries Association salary survey reports that 79 percent of the respondents are women ("SLA Salary Survey 1976," *Special Libraries 67*, December 1976). Data, cross-correlated by age and sex, reveals a salary gap in favor of men which widens with age. In the 20–29 year old age group the percentage difference is 1.6 percent; in the 60 and above age group the difference is 24 percent. Median salaries for women librarians have increased by 18 percent since 1973, the date of the last SLA salary survey; men's salaries have risen by 10 percent. The actual dollar increase in women's median salaries is also higher than men's by $600. While the 1976 data shows a narrowing gap, the median salary of women special librarians was still $3,400 (18.8 percent) less than that of the men.

In an update of their 1971 and 1973 analysis of public libraries serving areas of 100,000 or more, K. D. Shearer and R. L. Carpenter report a drop in the number of women library directors from 34 percent to 28 percent ("Public Library Salaries and Support in the Seventies," *Library Journal 100*, March 15, 1976). Women directors tended to be in the smaller libraries and in the South. The median salary reported for male directors was $24,000, for women, $18,750. Even when population size and region are controlled the differences remain significant. The salary percentage difference, 28 percent, has changed only by 2 percent since 1971. In the area of equatable support for public libraries women directors remain behind men, $5.96 per capita as opposed to $5.04. The difference, however, narrowed from 23 percent in 1973 to 19 percent in 1975. Whether this difference is a result of the library, sex, region, women directors themselves, or some combination is uncertain. Differences between salaries offered to beginning librarians by men and women directors changed dramatically from 1973 to 1975. Salaries paid by male directors were 6 percent ($500) higher in 1973; in 1975 they were only 2 percent ($180) higher than those paid by women directors. While the number of women directors and their salaries have not improved since 1973, financial support and initial salaries for librarians employed by women directors of public libraries serving areas of more than 100,000 has improved.

Disparities Noted. Deans and directors of 12 (20 percent) of the library schools included in the 1975–76 survey of faculty salaries conducted by R. E. Bidlack, are women; 49 (80 percent) are men ("Faculty Salaries of 62 Library Schools, 1975–76," *Journal of Education for Librarianship* 16, Spring 1976). The median salary of the ten women deans and directors with fiscal year appointments is $29,707; the median for the 45 men with similar appointments is $31,250. Of the 697 full-time faculty members reported by the 62 participating schools, 408 are men (58.5 percent)

See also Canadian Correspondent's Report

and 289 are women (41.5 percent). Of the 146 full professors 39.8 percent (43) are women; 84.3 percent of the associate professors (91) and 85.1 percent of the assistant professors (114) are women. Women outnumber men three to one in the instructor ranks and make up 72.7 percent of the full-time lecturers. At all levels and appointments, except lecturers with fiscal year appointments, the salaries of full-time male faculty are higher than women of the same rank and appointment.

Gains in 1976. In the organizational spheres of librarianship women made noticeable gains in 1976. Building on existing structures in the American Library Association and expanding the year-old national network, Women Library Workers, women in librarianship moved to formalize and solidify political power and to develop new action fronts.

At its 1976 Centennial Conference the American Library Association established a Standing Committee of Council on the Status of Women in Librarianship. Establishment of the committee was the culmination of a two year campaign within the association to create a policy level body to address women's issues. Membership and Council also passed a resolution on sexism and racism at the 1976 conference which charges the Association with combatting sexism and racism in library education, staff development, cataloging procedures, and amongst library users. A report at the 1977 annual conference is expected.

Within the ALA's Social Responsibility Roundtable Task Force on Women, a women in library administration discussion group was organized and a study group formed to review the five-year-old structure and goals of the Task Force.

Active discussion groups on sexism in materials continued in ALA's Children's Services Division and Young Adult Services Division.

An interest Group on Women in Librarianship was established within the American Association of Library Schools during the fall of 1976. The first meeting is planned for the 1977 AALS conference.

Women Library Workers, a U.S. and Canadian organization of professional, technical, clerical, and administrative library personnel, sent a national organizer on a seven-month tour of North America. Membership in WLW grew from 250 to 650. The number of local chapters rose from four to 23. Local chapter actions ranged from a letter campaign on Library of Congress subject headings to efforts responsible for the appointment of the first woman director of the Oakland, California, public library in 103 years.

Trends are difficult to determine, but if one can be identified for 1976, it is that a small but growing number of the women who make up 84 percent of the profession are becoming more actively concerned with their situation.

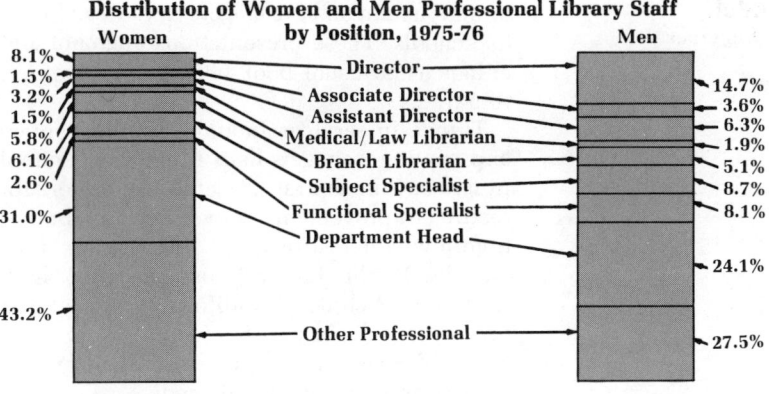

It is not clear whether improvement in salary differential at the entry level will continue for those librarians or whether isolated victories, such as those at Stanford and Oakland, will affect other libraries. An in-depth analysis of the status of women at all levels of librarianship is badly needed to identify not only trends but barriers to the equalization of women's position.   KATHLEEN WEIBEL

Young Adult Library Services

Young Adult library services continued in 1976 to be a growing specialization as locally, regionally, and nationally librarians working with youth are rediscovering the benefits of cooperation, joint sharing of information, and the importance of administrative training.

YA Activities. Young Adult librarians sponsored a wide variety of activities in 1976 aimed at their young adult audience, ranging from a special Science Fiction Video Club organized and produced by young adults themselves (with a little help from Sara Jean Marks, former YA Librarian, Wilmot Branch, Tucson, Arizona, they publish a triannual booklet called *The Alien Quack*) to the more traditional book discussion club organized at Pasadena, California, by YA Librarian Elaine Zorbas. A number of different libraries (Alameda County, California; King County, Washington; Santa Clara County, California; Fresno, California) are sponsoring hand-decorated clothing contests, with prizes, even some fashion shows. Queensborough, New York, sponsored a "Dynomite 1976—Creative Arts Contest" with prizes for the best creative piece on the Bicentennial theme. Many libraries are experimenting and showcasing student-made film festivals, with or without prizes. Craft programs, sports, music, poetry, and career information are high on the list of favorite and most successful programs. Attendance is not always primarily young adult and that continues to provide soul-searching questions.

A number of different libraries (Enoch Pratt Free Library, Baltimore; Free Library of Philadelphia; Queensborough Public Library, New York) are producing elaborate, sophisticated and effective audiovisual slide shows for pre-

Young Adult Library Services

sentations aimed at teenagers in the local public schools. These presentations augment and enhance the usual book-talking efforts of YA Librarians.

Trends in services include drop-in centers and moving teenagers back into formal school programs (Enoch Pratt), "Catch-Up Center" for reading improvement (Denver Public Library), high/low interest/reading information (Los Angeles Public Library), use of video with teenagers (Richmond, California), appeal and use of photography in bookmobile service in New Mexico, setting up Advisory Youth Boards, and organizational needs.

Regional and National Organizational News. A number of states did hard organizational work in 1976. Foremost is Ohio, where YA librarians organized a YA round table, edited a special edition of the *Ohio Library Association Bulletin* and completed a statistical survey of needs and existing status. Wisconsin's Division for Library Service started a YA reviewing section on a state level. Alabama University Library School sponsored a workshop on "The Library and the Young Adult" which featured Margaret Edwards and Lillian Gerhardt, Editor of *SLJ*, plus role-playing, programming, and book-talking information. Arizona State Library sponsored a YA workshop in February featuring Patty Campbell, Lillian Gerhardt, and Richard Peck. In July Arizona University (Tucson) had a week-long summer workshop on YA services featuring Carol Starr, Blossum Elfman, and Phyllis Anderson Woods. Mary Kay Chelton was a guest lecturer specializing in YA consultation for Dalhousie University Library School in the spring of 1976. The New York Library Association (fall, 1976) focused on intellectual freedom—"Should Youth Be Allowed To Know?"

The Maryland Library Association Adultand YA Services Division passed four resolutions which were sent to and endorsed by the MLA Board of Directors calling for (1) establishment of a YA consultant post in the state level and the formation of statewide guidelines; (2) the appointment of a YA Coordinator in each public library system in the state; (3) annual course work in YA services and adolescent psychology in every ALA-accredited school; and (4) allowance for input from YA Librarians on library design and decoration.

YA Service Programs. The state aid scene continued to have an effect on YA service programs as Rochester, New York, abolished the YA Room to save money and a huge struggle to combine the three age level specialist positions at Nassau County, N. Y., into one position almost succeeded. Meanwhile federal money was helping establish YA services in small western towns like Mesa, Arizona, and Boulder City, Nevada. Santa Fe Public Library planned a new branch with a special YA section developed by YA Librarian Valarie Brooker and a local group of young adults. And prestigious Los Angeles County Library reestablished YA services because, according to County Librarian Carol Moss, "the demands on Adult Services resulting from heightened interest in consumerism, ecology and senior citizens preclude adequate attention to the young adult population, as a subunit of Adult Services." (CLA NEWSLETTER, April 1976, page 2; Volume XV, No. 4). San Jose Public Library (California) also established a formal YA services program, organized and led by YA coordinator Virginia Carpio. Member libraries of the South Bay Cooperative Library System (California) pooled their resources for programming and book talking plus sharing resources and information. A survey of staff and public done by Baltimore County Public Library on priorities for the library system showed YA services as one of the top three priorities (*LJ/SLJ Hotline*, October 18, 1976, p. 1).

Communication and Training. The in-house newsletter is becoming a popular form of information exchange, as *The Flying YA Newsletter* from San Jose Public Library (California) and *The Yarns* (Joan Atkinson, editor, temporarily published under the auspices of Alabama University Library School) join other established system and regional newsletters. The newly established YA Coordinators, Consultants Discussion Group of YASD (Bob Smith, Chairperson, Cuyahoga County, Ohio) hopes to bring YA leaders together for more information exchange and sharing. The four Bay Area (California) YA coordinators have produced the first in a planned series of YA training videotapes (Hassle-Free YA Programming available for $45 from Mike Ferrero, CATVO Project, San Jose, California).

Survey. To celebrate the ALA Centennial, YASD published an in-house pamphlet, *Personality Profile—YASD*, in July, giving capsule summaries of 32 YA librarians influential in current development of YA librarianship. As an analysis of where YA services were coming from and going to, a survey indicated that contact with teenagers, book talking, and programming were the strongest job motivational factors, followed quickly by the challenges of establishing a YA department, presenting effective workshops, reviewing, regional and national organizational efforts, and the effects of serving as a meaningful catalyst for social change. In response to a question on assessed needs, the respondents asked for survival and expansion justifications for budget-minded administrators, reported the need to work with library educators to develop YA library school curriculum, and asked for needed research. Areas identified for research included assessment of YA library service effectiveness in influencing the lives of young adults, investigation of ways of creating a body of professional literature and of establishing a YA literature award, and testing for reading effectiveness.

Trends. The use of paperbacks in libraries, both public and school, is receiving renewed attention—focusing on reviewing of original publications, reprinting from hardbacks, technical processing and distribution. Mary Kay Chelton, YASD President, addressed the Education Paperback Association at the ALA Conference in 1976 and stressed the need for more communication, more attention to library institutional needs, and consumer relationships. Meanwhile, a recent issue of *School Library Journal* called for the national organizations to bring forth leadership in this area. A related subject is the unknown future effect of computerized circulation control of paperbacks and the new technology's effects on traditional public service goals. Also of concern to YA Librarians are the current crisis centers, Information and Referral centers, government funding (based on the National Commission on Libraries and Information Science priorities), cable television, and the implications of accreditation procedures on existing library school education.   CAROL STARR

Young Adult Literature

Writers and publishers of young adult books continued to follow every twist and turn of adolescent fancy in 1976, and some works of real originality and imagination were produced—at least in nonfiction. Unfortunately YA fiction was not as good in 1976 as it had been in the recent past; novels written for young adults were unusually meager and ordinary.

The Standouts. The few YA fiction titles with any quality or popular appeal stood out by default. Patricia Windsor again produced a sensitive work in *Diving for Roses* (Harper & Row). Sonia Levitin's clever *Mark of Conte* (Atheneum) had young adults everywhere asking for "the book about the kid that the computer got his name mixed up." Another book with a welcome dollop of humor was Barbara Wersba's *Tunes for a Small Harmonica* (Harper & Row), in which a gutsy young girl shocks her elegant Park Avenue parents by playing the harmonica for money on street corners. Two books that received much critical acclaim were *Home Before Dark* by Sue Ellen Bridgers (Knopf) and *Father's Arcane Daughter* by E. L. Konigsburg (Atheneum). But the real winner in realistic YA novels for 1976 came from an unexpected source—Ursula Le Guin, the great science fiction writer. YA librarians were overjoyed with her small perfect jewel of a love story, *Very Far Away From Anywhere Else* (Atheneum). Another deceptively simple book with great poignancy and power was *Dear Bill, Remember Me?* by Norma Fox Mazer (Delacorte), a collection of short stories in the YA style.

Many writers from the YA stable were not heard from at all this year, and several others produced disappointing works: Paul Zindel's preposterous *Pardon Me, You're Stepping on My Eyeball* (Harper & Row) and Barbara Corcoran's insipid *Cabin in the Sky* (Atheneum), for example. Kin Platt's male teenage sex fantasy, *The Terrible Love Life of Dudley Cornflower* (Bradbury), was found by many librarians to be possibly honest but certainly pornographic—and undeniably insulting to women.

The "Problem" Book. The didactic "problem" novel still flourishes, but teenagers in these books in 1976 got drunk instead of pregnant and were victims of rape rather than homosexual innuendo. Teenage alcoholism was the theme of Sandra Scoppetone's *The Late Great Me* (Putnam), a subject also explored in nonfiction (*Questions and Answers about Alcoholism* by Robert Curtis (Prentice-Hall) and *Teen-age Alcoholism* by Jim Haskins (Hawthorn). Following the lead set by Patricia Dizenzo in the paperback original *Why Me?* (Avon), Richard Peck wrote a psychologically accurate novel of the aftereffects of rape on a sensitive adolescent girl, *Are You in the House Alone?* (Viking). A nonfiction counterpart was *Speak Out on Rape* by Margaret Hyde (McGraw Hill). James Trivers, in his novel *Hamburger Heaven* (Prentice Hall), explored a problem area of more immediate concern to most teenagers—work.

As is often the case, the landmark books in YA fiction were written for adults. Judith Guest's extraordinary *Ordinary People* (Viking) described the anguish of reentry from a suicide attempt, a more common teenage problem than many are willing to admit. *Ruby* by Rosa Guy (Viking), a work of complexity and depth, depicted a lesbian relationship with warmth and subtlety. A new Kurt Vonnegut title, *Slapstick* (Delacorte), was maligned by critics but snatched joyfully off the shelves by young adults. And Alex Haley's almost-novel, *Roots*, was a blockbuster for the entire nation.

Science Fiction. Science fiction, once the province of the lonely intellectual adolescent male, continued to gain a broader readership. The phenomenal popularity of anything Star Trek was reflected in the publication of a *Concordance* (Bjo Trimble, Ballantine), a *Puzzle Manual* (Jim Razzi, Bantam), *Star Trek Logs* up to number eight (Alan Dean Foster, Ballantine), and *The Star Trek Reader* (James Blish, Dutton). Other most popular science fiction titles with young adults were *Imperial Earth* by Arthur Clarke (Harcourt Brace), *Children of Dune* by Frank Herbert (Putnam), and the fourth book in Roger Zelazny's Amber series, *Hand of Oberon* (Doubleday).

Movie and TV Sources. Tie-ins with movies or TV were responsible for the popularity of many YA books. Screenplay adaptations were often careless trash, such as *Dawn, Portrait of a*

Richard Peck, author of Are You In the House Alone? *published by Viking.*

Sandra Scoppettone, author of The Late Great Me, *published by Putnam.*

Andrea Eagan, author of Why Am I So Miserable If These Are the Best Years of My Life? *published by Lippincott.*

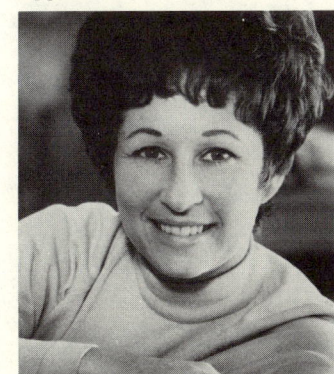

Sonia Levitin, author of Mark of Conte, *published by Atheneum.*

Young Adult Literature

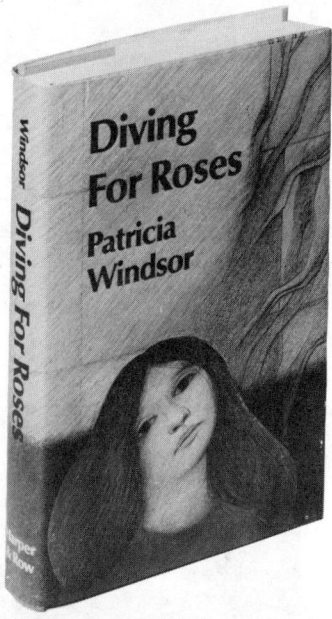

Patricia Windsor, author of Diving For Roses, *published by Harper & Row.*

Teenage Runaway by Julia Sorel (Ballantine), but occasionally YA librarians had cause to rejoice when film or TV brought a work of real value to the attention of young readers: *One Flew Over the Cuckoo's Nest* by Ken Kesey (Viking, New American Library) was very much in demand. As the year ended, librarians stocked up on books by and about Woody Guthrie in happy anticipation of a wave of interest created by the film "Bound for Glory."

Horror and disaster films continued to inspire a lush crop of horror and disaster books. Mostly pictorials, these gore-filled volumes began to alarm some YA librarians by their profusion and popularity and a tendency to increasing ghastliness. A related interest, parapsychology and the occult, was much better served; Doubleday's *Library of the Supernatural*, a richly illustrated 21-volume series edited by Colin Wilson, struck a nice balance between the sensational and the serious.

Psychological Self-Help. Perhaps the most exciting development in YA publishing this year was the emergence of a new genre: the psychological self-help book written by a mental health professional to guide teenagers through the agonies of adolescence. Teen advice books in the past often had been written by motherly ladies or magazine editors and had seldom dealt with problems any deeper than acne or the first kiss. The new books wrestled seriously with the crises of identity and self-worth which our society imposes on young people. Titles asked questions such as *Why Am I So Miserable If These Are the Best Years of My Life?* (Andrea Eagan, Lippincott), *If You Really Knew Me, Would You Still Like Me?* (Eugene Kennedy, Argus), and *Can I Help How I Feel?* (Carl Morrison, Atheneum). For the young adult who needs to go further, a sound and useful source was *Help; A Guide to Counseling and Therapy Without a Hassle* by Jane Marks (Messner).

Perhaps the best book of this type was Sol

Marcy Heidish, author of A Woman Called Moses, *based on the life of Harriet Tubman, published by Houghton Mifflin.*

Norma Fox Mazer, author of Dear Bill, Remember Me? *published by Delacorte Press.*

Sue Ellen Bridges, author of Home Before Dark, *published by Knopf.*

Gordon's *You! : The Psychology of Surviving and Enhancing Your Social Life, Love Life, Sex Life, School Life, Home Life, Work Life, Emotional Life, Creative Life, Spiritual Life, Style of Life, Life* (Quadrangle). This offered wisdom and comfort in a joyful and slightly raunchy free-form style. The author is a national authority on adolescent sexuality who has mastered, or maybe never lost, the ability to talk to kids. Unfortunately, the distribution and promotion of this superb book were so mangled that it inadvertently became the best kept publishing secret of the year.

Sports. Sports interests in 1976, of course, were dominated by the Olympics, and YA librarians found themselves needing multiple copies of every book on women's gymnastics after the stunning success of Nadia Comenici. Pele was another new (to the U.S.) sports hero; three biographies and many soccer books reflect his popularity. Several skateboard books were received with enthusiasm. Kiting, a surprise fad possibly related to 1975's hang-gliding enthusiasm, resulted in a number of beautiful books, notably *The Complete Book of Kites and Kite-flying* by Will Yolen (Simon and Schuster). The Oriental martial arts are still with us, but not quite as popular as last year. Sports biographies and technique and pictorial books on the standards—baseball, football, and basketball—were less in evidence.

Biographies. Biography written for YAs has never really found its stride; writers seem to be unable to reduce a life to the size and vocabulary supposedly acceptable to young adults without squeezing all the juice out of it. However, earnest efforts continue to be made and the year saw a few successes. *A Woman Called Moses* by Marcy Heidish (Houghton Mifflin) brought Harriet Tubman to life with uncommon skill. *Free Woman, The Life and Times of Victoria Woodhull* (Marion Meade, Knopf) was praised. *A Special Kind of Courage* by Geraldo Rivera (Simon and Schuster) harked back to the old "inspirational" biography. Three excellent collections of the lives of outstanding women were *Different Drummers* by Antoinette May (Les Femmes), *Enterprising Women* by Caroline Bird (Norton), and *Women of Courage* by Margaret Truman (Morrow). But the biography that young adults really were reading was *The Fonz* by Charles Pike (Pocket Books).

Rock. Books on rock music were excellent and plentiful, and English publishing houses also produced a number of spectacular and relatively inexpensive pictorials. The big rock music title of the year was Rolling Stone's magnificent *Illustrated History of Rock and Roll*. The same editors also produced *Dancing Madness* earlier in the year, which showed kids (if they did not already know) how to do the Hustle and the Bump. Two titles for would-be superstars were *Making Music for Money* by James Lincoln Collier (Watts) and *So You Want To Be a Rock and Roll Star* by Sharon Lawrence (Dell). Rock biographies improved in quality—for example, *The Led Zeppelin Biography* by Ritchie Yorke (Methuen/Two Continents). Folk rock had a thoughtful overview in *Electric Children* by Jacques Vassal (Taplinger). Picture books of country music stars were popular in some parts of the country. And young adults were enthusiastic about the collection by Elton John's lyricist, Bernie Taupin—*The One Who Writes the Words* (Knopf).

Other Interests. Other young adult interests reflected in books were magic, CB radio, and comics as a literary form. A unique book which was a center of controversy among young adult librarians was *Gramp* by Mark and Dan Jury (Viking), a photo essay by two young men on the senile decay and death of their grandfather as he is cared for lovingly at home by his large family. Some librarians praised the book for its honesty and beauty; others were offended by its unblinking look at the undignified and ugly details of death.

Two important YA reading needs have not yet been met by publishers. High interest/easy reading is still created only accidentally. That elusive skill of producing irresistible appeal in a text which is not a deterrent to reluctant readers has not yet been mastered. An even more serious publishing gap is the nearly total lack of books that reflect with any authenticity the lives of the teenagers of Chicano and Latino cultures in the United States.

PATRICIA J. CAMPBELL

Young Adult Services Division

During 1976 the Young Adult Services Division (YASD), a Division of the American Library Association, focused much of its efforts and attention on financial issues facing the Division. The new dues schedule, put into effect in September 1975, enabled YASD to establish its own office and staff. And at the end of 1976 YASD had survived its first year on its own. A drop in membership, though, meant that the Division's income was not as much as had been anticipated. Consequently, at the end of 1976 the YASD executive secretary, hired on a part-time basis ($4/5$ time) in October 1975, was not yet able to go to full-time status. In addition, funding for various committee activites and projects was kept at a minimal level and several hoped for projects (a quarterly newsletter and a brochure on programming methods and ideas) were postponed until funds were available.

Programs. At the Centennial Conference in Chicago YASD held several programs "Celebrating Young Adults and Library Media Services to Them." A panel, moderated by Rick

Grimm of the Prince George's County Memorial Library System, included as members: Cecil Beach, Florida State Librarian; Nathaniel Blackman, principal of an alternative high school; Ruth Kutz, president of a library youth advisory council; Bill Moyes, an 18-year-old library trustee; Jane Botham, director of library promotion for a publishing house; Mark Rogovin, a muralist for the Chicago Public Art Workshop; and Donna Adrian, President of the Canadian School Library Association. Members outlined how the particular agency they represented paid special attention to the needs of young adults. The "Second Chance Sociable" allowed advocates to present a case for a young adult book which they felt had been neglected or forgotten too soon. The author luncheon featured guest speaker M. E. Kerr (whose real name is Marijane Meaker), author of many young adult books including *Dinky Hocker Shoots Smack, Love Is a Missing Person* and *Is That You, Miss Blue?* Almost 100 young adult guests who had been sponsored by local business and civic groups were recognized for their outstanding community contributions and were encouraged to actively participate in the post-luncheon program by questioning the guest author. A sampling of films from the annually produced list, Selected Films for Young Adults 1976, was also shown during the Conference week.

Projects. Among the on-going projects continued in 1976 by YASD Committees were development of a philosophical statement defining young adult services in public, school and institutional libraries; preparation of bibliographies for *Teachers' Guide to Television* and other related publications; development of an annual award for two books, fiction and nonfiction, with strong appeal to young adults; development of a position paper outlining the need for training in library schools in the areas of young adult services; circulation of *Living Library Patterns*, a collection of YA programming ideas; preparation of an information sheet on how to use effectively the *Best Books for Young Adults* list; selection of the *Best Books for Young Adults–1975*, and *Selected Films for Young Adults 1976*; development of three information packets on library services to young adults who are blind, physically handicapped, and shut-ins; preparation of mediographic essays on "Basic Sources for Young Adult Workers' Training" and "The Homosexual Experience," and compilation of an annotated list of magazines that young adults are reading. The Joint CSD/YASD Advisory Committee to the Editors of *Top Of The News* continued to work on a proposed policy statement for the journal.

Several YASD committee projects resulted in new resources to aid librarians who work with young adults. The YASD Survival Kit (available for $2.25 pre-paid from the YASD Office, 50 E. Huron, Chicago, Illinois) provides information and materials to promote and justify the existence of young adult services as part of any total public library program. Included in the kit are items from libraries around the country, selected because they demonstrate the purpose and methods of providing services to young adults. Two new information packets were produced by the Library Service to Young Adults in Institutions Committee: "Juvenile Correctional Institution Library Service" and "Juvenile Mental Health and Mental Retardation Library Services."

Additional committee activities during 1976 resulted in the selection of a logo design for the Young Adult Services Division. Heidi Kearns submitted the award-winning design in a contest that drew entries from all over the country. To aid in the promotion of young adult services and membership in the Young Adult Services Division a brochure, "If You Work With Young Adults. . . ," was produced and widely distributed.

New Committees. During the year the YASD Board authorized several new committees: YASD Intellectual Freedom Committee; Task Force on Personal Crisis Information; Sexism in Adolescent Literature Committee, and a High-Interest/Low-Ability Level Materials Evaluation Committee. A CSD/YASD interdivisional committee was also formed to revise the pamphlet "Selecting Materials for Children and Young Adults" (ALA, 1967).

Publications. In 1976 complete revisions were produced of all five of the YASD "Outstanding" lists for the college bound: biographies, current scene, fiction, nonfiction and theatre. *Still Alive: The Best of The Best 1960–1974*, the result of the 1975 YASD San Francisco preconference, was an annotated list of titles still being read by young adults. Other publications included the annual brochures, *Best Books For Young Adults* and *Selected Films For Young Adults*. The Division also made available *Booktalking: You Can Do It* by Mary K. Chelton, reprinted from the April *School Library Journal*. *Top Of The News* continued as the quarterly journal of both Children's Services Division and YASD.

EVELYN SHAEVEL

YASD Officers

PRESIDENT (July 1976–June 1977):
Mary K. Chelton, Westchester Library System, Hartsdale, New York

VICE-PRESIDENT/PRESIDENT-ELECT:
Rosemary Young, Denver Public Library

EXECUTIVE SECRETARY:
Evelyn Shaevel

Membership (August 31, 1976): 4,022 (1,847 personal and 2,175 organizational)

Canadian Correspondent's Report

During 1976, Canadian libraries, in common with other tax-supported institutions, functioned in an economic environment characterized by inflation, slow growth, and federal government price and wage controls. As a consequence, library budgets were severely strained and there were few reports of expansion of library services and facilities.

Some of the highlights of the year included the closing by the University of Toronto Library of its card catalog; the initiation by the National Library of a comprehensive review of its organization and services; the imposition by several academic libraries of charges for interlibrary loans; the publication of two major studies of public library services, one for Ontario and the other for the Island of Montreal; the completion of a research design for Project Progress, a project proposing a comprehensive study of public library services in Canada; acquisition by two academic libraries of their one millionth volume; and resolution between the Canadian Library Association and the Canadian writing community of the question of a public lending "right" for authors.

Academic Libraries

Three libraries—McMaster University, Hamilton, Queen's University at Kingston, Ontario, and the University of Western Ontario, London—recently became members of the Association of Research Libraries (ARL). Other Canadian members are Toronto, McGill, Alberta, and British Columbia. According to the rank under tables for 1973–74 published by ARL (which then had 82 member institutions), the University of Toronto ranked first in six of the ten categories: number of professional staff (full-time equivalent), number of nonprofessional staff (FTE), total staff (FTE), total expenditure for materials and binding, total salaries and wages, and total operating expenditures. Toronto ranked second in total number of volumes in the library, tenth in current periodicals and sixteenth in total microform holdings. British Columbia ranked first in total microform holdings and sixth in number of nonprofessional staff (FTE).

The revised draft of guidelines on academic status for university librarians prepared by a joint committee of the Canadian Association of University Teachers (CAUT) and the Canadian Association of College and University Libraries (CACUL) was brought before the respective meetings of the two associations for approval. CAUT approved the guidelines as drafted while CACUL approved them with minor modifications in the section dealing with salaries and benefits. Other topics covered included appointments, dismissals, grievance procedures, and university and library governance. The basic premise enunciated in the guidelines is that "the professional staff of university libraries are partners with faculty members in contributing to the scholarly and intellectual functions of the university and should be accorded academic status."

Accreditation

M.L.S. programs in four more Canadian library schools—Western Ontario, British Columbia, Montreal and Dalhousie—were accredited under ALA's 1972 *Standards for Accreditation*, bringing the total number of accredited programs in Canada to six. The two M.L.S. programs previously accredited are at McGill and Toronto.

Acquisitions

The University of Manitoba Libraries marked the acquisition of its millionth volume. That volume, purchased by the Alumni Association, is a 1784 holograph from the North West Traders addressed to Governor Frederick Haldimand and deals with the discovery of a new route from Lake Superior to the River Ouinipique (Winnipeg).

In late 1975 the University of Waterloo added the millionth volume to its collection, *Hundreds and Thousands: The Journals of Emily Carr*, a special limited edition with a portfolio of color plates.

The National Library of Canada added about 1,000 titles to its collection by purchasing part of the library of the Olivier family of Joliette, Quebec. The purchase consists mostly of Canadiana. Among the more interesting titles are those on Frédéric-Alexandre Baillargé, the versatile Canadian writer, and his family, and those on Université Laval's dispute in Montreal. There was also much useful material on religious affairs in French Canada, and on education in Quebec and the Laurentian region.

Automation

The National Library of Canada and the Canada Institute for Scientific and Technical Information (CISTI) are jointly evaluating a computer-based library management system called DOBIS which is being developed by the University of Dortmund in Germany. Late in 1975 the DOBIS system was selected by the National Library as having the greatest potential for managing a bibliographic data base of the magnitude and complexity required to support the present and planned national programs. At the same time, plans were being made for the application of library operations to CISTI and, on March 30, 1976, CISTI and the National Library signed an agreement to evaluate the DOBIS system jointly. The Ontario/Quebec-based library consortium, UNICAT/TELECAT, through the Council of Ontario Universities, is also participating in the evaluation project and contributing resources.

The DOBIS system is still being developed and contracts have been negotiated to acquire program materials as they become available. The cataloging, cataloging search, and circulation modules had been completed by the end of 1976. Depending on the results of Phase One evaluation, decisions will be made, subject to availability of funds, as to whether to proceed with Phase Two, which would include the modification program and testing, or to consider alternative solutions. Implementation would be a later phase.

Awards and Prizes

LOUISE AYLWIN was awarded the Canada Council Children's Literature Prize (French) for *Raminagradu* (Montreal, Editions du Jour).

GARTH BLUE, Chief Librarian, Prairie Farm Rehabilitation Administration Library, Regina, received a Public Service Merit Award of $2,500 in recognition of his leadership in the development of a program for the sharing of information resources and library services among federal libraries in his region.

BRANT COUNTY (Ontario) Board of Education and YORKTON (Saskatchewan) School Unit No. 36 each received an award from Encyclopaedia Britannica for their contributions to school librarianship in Canada.

BILL FREEMAN received the Canada Council Children's Literature Prize (English) for *Shantyman of Cache Lake* (Toronto, James Lorimer & Company).

Glück, poetry by Claude Haeffely, photographs by Francisco Olaechea, designed and illustrated by Henri Paul Bronsard, and published by L'Hexagone, Montreal, was chosen best of show at the third annual Design Canada "Look of Books."

CLEMENT J. HARRISON, Professor, School of Library Service, Dalhousie University, was elected President of the Commonwealth Library Association at its meeting in Kingston, Jamaica.

PATRICIA HART of Richmond Hill (Ontario) Public Library received the Ontario Library Trustees Award.

KEN HAYCOCK, formerly Educational Media Consultant for the Wellington County (Ontario) Board of Education, was awarded the University of Michigan School of Library Science Beta Phi Mu Award.

WILLIAM KURELEK received the Amelia Frances Howard-Gibbon Medal for his illustrations in *Prairie Boy's Summer* (Montreal, Tundra Books).

LARRY MOORE, Professor of Education, School Librarianship Program, Queen's University, Kingston, Ontario, received the

1976 Award of Merit presented by the Ontario Library Association. THE REV. AUGUSTE-M. MORISSET, Professor Emeritus and Director Emeritus, University of Ottawa Library School, was named a Member of the Order of Canada by the Governor General. FRED PILE received the Merit Award from the Canadian Library Trustees Association for his contributions as a trustee of the North York (Ontario) Public Library and as the Association's former president.

MORDECAI RICHLER received the English Medal Award for the most outstanding children's book of the year in English, *Jacob Two-Two Meets the Hooded Fang* (Toronto: McClelland & Stewart).

EILEEN TRAVIS, Regional Librarian of the Saint John (New Brunswick) Regional Library, was awarded an honorary degree at the Spring Convocation of St. Thomas University in Fredericton, N.B. MARIE TREMAINE was awarded the degree of Doctor of Letters by Trent University, Peterborough, Ontario, for her contribution to librarianship and bibliography.

JOHN WRIGHT, Professor, Faculty of Library Science, University of Alberta, received the Margaret B. Scott Award (formerly the Merit Award) given by the Canadian School Libraries Association.

Book and Periodical Development Council

The Book and Periodical Development Council (BPDC), the body formed in 1975 to bring together all the major English-language non-governmental organizations concerned with book and periodical use in Canada, underwent changes in its membership during 1976. The League of Canadian Poets joined the Council while the Canadian Book Publishers Council, composed mainly of foreign-owned publishers in Canada, decided not to renew its membership, indicating that the BPDC's method of operation made it difficult for member associations to work effectively together. The BPDC elected Henry C. Campbell, Chief Librarian, Toronto Public Library, as its chairman.

Cataloging and Classification

One of the year's most significant events was the closing by the University of Toronto Library of its card catalog on June 30. It was the culmination of a file-conversion project which began in 1965, and followed a full year of intensive planning and preparation. The first phase of preparation called for the translation of all machine-readable files in their progression of formats evolved over the past ten years into a consistent MARC format, and for their integration into one file which could receive all future catalog records and be available for updating and for use. As a result the University of Toronto Library began its new academic year with an automated catalog file of about 1,200,000 records covering the collection back to its foundation in 1890.

The second phase of preparation at Toronto involved the planning and production from this data base of alternative forms of access which would permit the library to stop adding to the card catalogs. Though the long-range objective is for the principal access to be on-line through computer terminals, the alternative at the beginning is COM (Computer Output Microform) in both film and fiche. Unlike other large libraries which are closing their card catalogs and producing supplements by computer, the Toronto COM catalog will replace the card catalog as the fullest source of information. The main file, which contains the full bibliographic records, is arranged in shelf order and so gives the library user a bibliographic access point not previously available. The three index files (author, title, and subject) are briefer but all contain information about holdings and location and are sufficient in themselves for most purposes. The COM files are updated monthly by cumulated supplements on fiche. As on-line operation becomes more economical, Toronto plans to shift its emphasis from COM to on-line access.

The National Library's MARC Records Distribution Service has been fully operational since April 1, 1976. At present, three options are offered subscribers: CAN/MARC (Canadian MARC) weekly tapes; CAN/MARC and LC (Library of Congress) MARC records for monographs converted to CAN/MARC on one tape (weekly); user selected records on tapes and/or unit card output. Through exchange or purchase agreements or both, current tapes are being received from the National Library of Australia, the Library of Congress, Bibliothèque Nationale (Paris), and the British Library. Conversion specifications and programs are being written, when possible, to allow additional tape service options and expansion of the MARC Records Distribution Service source file.

The National Library has begun a Computer Output Microfilm (COM) service for a Canadian corporate names authority file. The base authority file contains approximately 15,000 records, of which 8,000 are main entries and 7,000 associated references. History notes are included. Personal name authorities are also included but the major content is Canadian government corporate names. The file is currently growing at the rate of about 100 records per week, and a bi-weekly cumulated supplement is planned to update the base file.

The Canadian Committee on MARC (CCM) was formed during the year to act as an advisory body to the National Library. The Committee includes two representatives appointed by the Canadian Library Association, two by ASTED (L'Association pour l'avancement des sciences et des techniques de la documentation), and two by the National Library which provides the secretariat. The terms of reference for the Committee are to act as the Canadian MARC Advisory Committee to the National Library by examining the MARC communications formats and making recommendations on them; to examine CAN/MARC formats as a medium for the exchange of machine-readable bibliographic information in Canada; to establish a procedure for receiving, evaluating, and making recommendations on proposed national and international standards for the representation in machine-readable form of bibliographic information and other related standards; and to maintain liaison between its constituent organizations and relevant outside agencies.

During 1976 the Blackwell North America Computerized Library Catalog Support System, initiated by the Association of Atlantic Universities, was installed at the Computing Centre of the University of New Brunswick, Fredericton. The system is designed to provide computer cataloging to participating libraries in the Atlantic Region and will operate for two years, at which times a decision will be made as to whether it meets the needs of the region. The data base consists of Library of Congress MARC records and contributed cataloguing from libraries participating in the system. Other national data bases will be added later.

Children's Literature

More than 800 persons attended the Pacific Rim Conference on Children's Literature in Vancouver, May 10–15. Sheila Egoff, coordinator of the conference and Professor, School of Librarianship, University of British Columbia, reminded the registrants that Canadian children's literature is still facing enormous problems such as the vast geography and small population of the country, its pervasive regionalism and diverse cultural heritages, the competition from the international scene, "a rising nationalism that could become chauvinism," writers who say they are producing good manuscripts but cannot get published, and publishers who say they cannot get good manuscripts and that, even if they do, they do not sell well.

A six-month promotional project for the establishment of a Canadian children's book center ended in October. The project, under the auspices of the Book and Periodical Development Council and the directorship of Irma McDonough, Coordinator of Children's Library Services for the Provincial Library Service of Ontario, was funded by a $37,000 grant from the Canada Council. The project had two priorities: to publicize the benefits of the proposed center, and to promote Canadian children's books and their authors, illustrators and publishers across Canada. The center would be a primary source of information and promotion for Canadian children's books, and the collection of current books together with a retrospective collection of important out-of-print books, would furnish a reference resource for writers, teachers and librarians. A report of the project, including a recommendation for the establishment of the center, has been made to the Canada Council.

Continuing Professional Education
Ever since the University of Ottawa ended its courses in library science in 1972, there has been no local graduate program in librarianship in the National Capital Area for those persons interested in improving their qualifications. In July 1976, the Ottawa-Hull Committee on Continuing Education in Librarianship was formed to determine what the wants and needs were for local access to library science courses. The Committee mailed out questionnaires to local librarians and received 328 completed replies. The responses were gathered together in a report which indicated a desire for library science courses in the area for degree credit as well as for professional development. In December the deans and directors of three library schools —McGill, Toronto and Western—met together with the Committee to discuss the possibilities and prospects for initiating courses in the Ottawa-Hull area.

Films
The Lethbridge Public School Board approved the establishment of a regional film library to serve Southern Alberta. The provincial government will provide $100,000 to begin the program with the purchase of films, equipment, and supplies for the library.

Government Publications
Information Canada, the distribution and sales agency for federal government publications, was discontinued in 1976 and the Canadian Government Bookstores in six Canadian cities were closed as an economy measure. The distribution and sales functions are now carried on by the Publishing Centre, Department of Supply and Services, Ottawa, which continues to issue the *Daily Checklist* and monthly and annual catalogues of Canadian government publications. In addition, federal government publications are also being sold to the public by certain commercial booksellers authorized as sales agents.

A brief about distribution of Canadian federal government publications and the right of the public to information concerning the public business (freedom of information) was presented to the Standing Joint Committee of the Senate and House of Commons of Canada on Regulations and Other Statutory Instruments by the Canadian Library Association. The brief made specific recommendations for improvements in the listing and distribution of federal government publications and for facilitating access to unpublished studies, reports, and data.

For many years staff members of the Alberta Legislative Library, Edmonton, have clipped newspaper articles concerning the debates of the Legislative Assembly and organized them chronologically in scrapbooks. The collection known as the "Alberta Scrapbook Hansard" has now been microfilmed for the period 1906–1974 and copies are available for purchase.

The Ontario Ministry of Government Services published two major bibliographies of Ontario government publications. *Publications of the Government of Ontario, 1867–1900*, by Olga B. Bishop, covers the period from Confederation to the beginning of the 20th century and complements her *Publications of the Government of the Province of Canada, 1841–1867*. *Publications of the Government of Ontario, 1956–1971*, by Hazel I. MacTaggart, assisted by Kenneth Sundquist, continues her bibliography of Ontario government publications for the period 1901–55.

The Canadian Library Association published *Access to Canadian Government Publications in Canadian Academic and Public Libraries* by Edith Jarvi, Associate Professor, Faculty of Library Science University of Toronto. The study deals with bibliographical control of government publications, distribution, processing and organization of government publications in the library, as well as data about use and users. The report makes recommendations for action and for further study.

The National Library completed a survey of official publications in Canada with a view to describing holdings significant for research purposes. The survey found that parliamentary publications of the Canadian federal and provincial governments are, on the whole, well represented in libraries in all parts of Canada, both currently and retrospectively. In general, documents from other countries are not so well represented. Official publications from Australia, Belgium, France, Great Britain, and the United States are more readily available than those from the rest of the world. In particular, South America and the Arab countries of North Africa and the Middle East are poorly covered. Of the Asian countries, only India and Sri Lanka seem to be fairly well covered.

Intellectual Freedom
Two high schools in Peterborough (Ontario) County banned *The Diviners*, by Margaret Laurence, and *The Lives of Girls and Women*, by Alice Munro, because of four-letter words and explicit sexual references. Both authors have won Governor General's awards for their work.

After a trial in Toronto, MacMillan Company of Canada was acquitted of charges of distributing an obscene book, *Show Me!*, a picture book of sex for children and parents. In giving his decision, Judge Graburn stated, "I cannot find any undueness in the exploration of sex in *Show Me!* considered in the light of contemporary Canadian standards."

A resolution requesting the Government of Canada to remove the section on the distribution of obscene material from the Criminal Code was passed by the Canadian Library Association at its annual conference. The resolution pointed out that, at present, obscenity is legally defined as the undue exploitation of sex which may be variously and ambiguously interpreted because of differing and changing community standards.

Interlibrary Lending
A survey report entitled *Interlibrary Lending in Canada*, by B. Stuart-Stubbs and others (Ottawa: National Library, 1975), documented the extent of such service, its rate of increase over the past few years, and the burden borne by "net lenders," i.e., those libraries that lend considerably more items than they borrow. On January 1, 1976, one of the largest net lenders, the University of Toronto Library, began (with certain exceptions) to charge a fee of $8 for each filled request. The fee represents the cost of salaries and supplies for the loan of a document or provision of a photocopy in lieu of the original. Other university libraries followed the lead of Toronto in charging a fee; by the end of the year they included British Columbia, Victoria, Alberta, Calgary, and Guelph.

Because the imposition of interlibrary loan charges created hardships for many libraries and library users, especially in those regions of Canada not well served by libraries, the Canadian Library Association presented a brief to the federal government making three major recommendations aimed at rectifying the situation: that the federal government assume permanent financial responsibility for the cost of out-of-province loans made by libraries other than national or federal government libraries; that the federal government assume financial responsibility for loans made to federal government libraries other than to the national libraries or to federal government personnel; and that the federal government offer incentives for the development of local and provincial interlibrary lending systems, and subsidize the continuing operation of such systems as necessary to ensure acceptable standards of library service throughout Canada. The brief was referred to an interdepartmental committee of the federal government, chaired by the National Librarian, Guy Sylvestre, which will make a report to the Ministers concerned.

Library Associations
Since 1970, the chief librarians and directors of the major academic research libraries in Canada have been organized as the

Canadian Academic Research Libraries (CARL), and have formed a section within the Canadian Association of College and University Libraries (CACUL), a divison of the Canadian Library Association (CLA). Concerned on the one hand with the need to speak more directly on behalf of their institutions to governmental and other bodies, and on the other hand with their diminishing influence within CACUL, members of CARL voted to withdraw from CACUL and CLA to form an independent organization known as the Canadian Association of Research Libraries. The new organization came into being in June at the time of the CACUL/CARL annual meetings.

The Library Association of Alberta and the Alberta Library Trustees Association submitted two briefs to the Alberta government: one a report on Alberta public libraries to the 1980's; the other a report recommending standards for public libraries, increased provincial grants, creation of a Library Development Board to coordinate the development of regional public library systems, and the establishment of a provincial library.

Library trustees in the British Columbia Library Association decided to leave BCLA to form the British Columbia Library Trustees Association.

A new association, the Joint Regional Library Boards Association of Nova Scotia, was formed in October to present a united front to the provincial government. All regional library trustees are to be members of the Association, with chief librarians as exofficio nonvoting members. One of the first tasks facing the Association is to present its views to the newly established Provincial Committee charged with reviewing existing legislation for regional public libraries in Nova Scotia.

The Libraries in Crisis Committee of the Manitoba Library Association released figures showing that financial support for library service in that province still has a long way to go. Despite modifications in provincial grants to public libraries resulting from MLA's 1975 campaign for better funding, the government has failed to develop and support a library system for the rural areas of the province, particularly in the north.

The Ontario Library Association, the oldest library association in Canada, celebrated its 75th anniversary at its annual conference in Toronto, October 28–31, 1976. The OLA also adopted a new constitution restructuring the OLA Council and its relationship to the Association's four divisions. During the year OLA introduced two new publications: *Expression*, a semi-annual, and *Focus*, a monthly superseding the *Newsletter*.

The Institute of Professional Librarians of Ontario (IPLO), founded in 1958, and probably the first major library association in North America whose membership was restricted to professional librarians, ceased operations in June. Dedicated to furthering the welfare and status of professional librarians, IPLO had found it increasingly difficult in recent years to attract and retain new members and to finance its continuing education and publications programs. A similar body in British Columbia, the Association of British Columbia Librarians, ceased operations in 1975, leaving the Corporation of Professional Librarians of Quebec as the only remaining province-wide professional library association in Canada.

As one Ontario association died, another was created—the Administrators of Medium Public Libraries of Ontario composed of chief librarians of public libraries serving populations of less than 100,000. The body became the fifth public library organization formed in the province since 1968 when the Directors of Ontario Regional Library Systems began. The others are County and Regional Municipal Libraries (1970), Chief Executives of Large Public Libraries of Ontario (1975), and the Ontario Public Libraries Advisory Committee (1975). The latter body consists of representatives from the other four groups and was formed to deal with issues common to all groups.

The Quebec Library Association and ASTED (Association pour l'avancement des sciences et techniques de la documentation) presented a joint brief to the Quebec Minister of Cultural Affairs and Recreation protesting the Ministry's Green Paper proposal for an "alternative public library system" in Quebec. The Green Paper, which has been published in French only, proposes local depots to sell or rent books for approximately every 5,000 people, and a union catalog for each depot to be maintained by volunteers.

Legislation is being prepared in Saskatchewan as a result of a campaign by the Saskatchewan Library Association and the Saskatchewan Library Trustees' Association to make support of public library systems mandatory for all municipalities, including those in rural areas.

Library Education
The School of Library Science of the University of Alberta, renamed the Faculty of Library Science, dropped its one-year postgraduate program leading to the degree of Bachelor of Library Science and initiated a two-year program leading to the degree of Master of Library Science. As a result, all seven graduate library schools in Canada now offer the M.L.S. degree only, a departure from the traditional B.L.S. program that was discontinued first by McGill in 1964. The new Dean of the Faculty of Library Science at Alberta is Charles H. Davis from the University of Michigan. He succeeded Mary E.P. Henderson, who remained on the teaching staff.

Vivian S. Sessions, formerly Director of the Center for the Advancement of Library-Information Science at the City University of New York, assumed the post of Director of the Graduate School of Library Science, McGill University, succeeding Professor Effie Astbury, who remained on the teaching staff.

During the academic year 1974–75, Canadian library schools awarded a total of 565 degrees as follows: Alberta 60; British Columbia 59; Dalhousie 29; McGill 64; Montreal 70; Toronto 142; and Western Ontario 141.

The total part-time and full enrollment for the Fall of 1974 was as follows: Alberta 45; British Columbia 131; Dalhousie 73; McGill 133; Montreal 160; Toronto 298; Western Ontario 126.

According to a survey of library technician training programs for 1973–74 conducted by Professor John Marshall of the Faculty of Library Science, University of Toronto, and published in 1976, there were 23 such programs in Canada. They were: Alberta 2; British Columbia 1; Manitoba 1; Ontario 8; Quebec 10; Saskatchewan 1. In general, library technician training programs in Canada require completion of grade 12 for admission and are of two academic years' duration. Typically, these programs consisted of approximately 50 percent academic studies and 50 percent technical subjects. About 600 students graduated from library technician programs during the 1973–74 academic year.

Library Service to Shut-Ins
The Greater Victoria Public Library received a gift of a new station wagon from the Kiwanis Club of Victoria to improve service to library patrons who are house bound. Some 480 people in the Greater Victoria area confined to their homes due to disability or age received regular visits and selections of reading and listening materials from library staff and volunteers. Books in regular and in large print, talking books, records, and cassettes were chosen to meet the individual needs of each shut-in patron.

Library Service to the Handicapped
The report of the National Library Task Group on Library Service to the Handicapped was published during 1976. It recommended that the National Library continue to gather information about library services to the handicapped, with a view to eventual compilation of directories of such services in Canada. It also recommended that the National Library collect information and statistics on the eligible handicapped population to be served in Canada. The report stressed the need for explicit reference in future Canadian copyright legislation to the noncommercial production and provision of reading materials for the handicapped in order to secure exemption from infringement for the non-

profit transcription of reading materials into special media for the use of the visually, physically, and perceptually handicapped. The report recommends that the National Library form a national production standards committee and that it establish a union catalog of media materials for the handicapped.

The report proposes the establishment of a national program of library science to the handicapped with shared responsibility among the national, provincial, and local levels of government and with the Canadian National Institute for the Blind as one of the major production facilities. It further proposes that the provincial educational authorities be responsible for the establishment, administration, and coordination of a program for handicapped students and for the selection, production, and distribution of educational reading materials.

In addition to establishing the Task Group on Library Service to the Handicapped, the National Library has also created a Division for the Visually and Physically Handicapped. However, the current spending restraints of the federal government will slow the development of the Division and delay implementation of those Task Group recommendations that require substantial funds.

Library Statistics

A summary of the state of libraries in Canada may be gained from statistics issued by the federal agency, Statistics Canada, in 1976.

Libraries in Canada

Type of library and report year	Number reporting	Full-time enrollment or population	Total holdings	Total operating expenditures	Total staff
University (1972–73)	184	316,140	28,935,000	$90,608,000	7,230
College (1972–73)	135	156,414	4,258,000	$13,287,000	1,382
Centralized School Libraries (1972–73)	7,064	3,236,000	34,974,000	$5.73[1]	2,844
Public (1974)	702	22,446,000	32,770,000	$107,914,000	5,500
Special (1970)	761[2]	—	—	—	—

[1]Per-pupil expenditure for all library materials.
[2]Based on figures in Canadian Association of Special Libraries and Information Services, *Special Libraries and Information Centres in Canada*, rev. ed. (Ottawa, Canadian Library Association, 1970).

National Library

In September the National Library began a comprehensive review of its goals, objectives, organization, and services. The review is important because of the rapid growth of the Library during its first 23 years of existence and because of the increased demand for services and funding being made on it. Other factors which led to a reexamination of the National Library's role were the increased complexity of Canadian library systems services, and networks, especially the developments in automated networks, and the growing need for national and international library cooperation. The National Library Advisory Board, The Council of Federal Libraries, the national library associations, and certain other national organizations concerned with library services in Canada have been invited to present their views. Senior staff of the Library will meet with the National Librarian, Guy Sylvestre, and H. A. Shepherd, a management consultant, to institute the review while other staff members will hold similar meetings with the Planning Office which is responsible for coordinating the input to the review from both staff and users. The study will take at least a year to complete and final recommendations should be published by October 1978, the National Library's 25th anniversary.

People

Major appointments during 1976 included that of CLAUDE AUBRY, Director, Ottawa Public Library, as Chairman, Ontario Provincial Library Council, Toronto; GROVER C. BURGIS as Chief Librarian of Thunder Bay (Ontario) Public Library, succeeding Peter Mutchler who resigned; CHARLES H. DAVIS as Dean of the Faculty of Library Science, University of Alberta, succeeding Mary E. P. Henderson, who remains on the teaching staff; JEAN DE CHANTAL as Librarian, International Development Resource Centre, Ottawa, succeeding H. Arthur Vespry who was posted to the IDRC Singapore Office; JOHN E. DUTTON as Chief Librarian, Winnipeg Public Library, effective April 1, 1977, succeeding Nettie J. Siemans who retired; KATHLEEN M. FOY as Head of the Montreal Children's Library, succeeding Kathleen Jensen who retired; ANNE M. GALLER as Coordinator, Library Science Program, Concordia University, Montreal, succeeding Melba Wilson who died; MICHELLE GAUTHIER as Librarian of the Resource Centre, Huronia Historical Parks, Midland, Ont.; GERTRUDE GUNN, Chief Librarian, University of New Brunswick, to the National Library Advisory Board, Ottawa; GREG HAYTON as Chief Librarian of the Fort Erie (Ontario) Public Library; FRANÇOISE HÉBERT as Director of National Library Services for the Canadian National Institute for the Blind, Toronto; RONALD L. LEWIS as Head Librarian at St. Mary's University, Halifax.

SARA MALEY, Chief Librarian of the Barrie (Ontario) Public Library, succeeded Constance Hardy who retired; FRED MATHEWS, Professor, School of Library Service, Dalhousie University, was appointed to another term on the Advisory Board on Scientific and Technical Information, National Research Council, Ottawa; JUDITH S. RUAN, Director of Library Services of the City of Brampton Public Library and Art Gallery, named to the Ontario Provincial Library Council; DEBORAH C. SAWYER was named Editor of the *Canadian Education Index*, Toronto; VIVIAN S. SESSIONS, Director of the Graduate School of Library Science, McGill University, succeeded Professor Effie Astbury, who remains on the teaching staff; DAN SUDAR, Director of the Lake Erie Regional Library System, London, Ontario, succeeded C. Deane Kent, who retired; DOROTHY TEMPLIN, Director of the Central Ontario Regional Library System, Richmond Hill, succeeded Colin Robertson who retired, and JOHN TOOTH was named Chief Librarian of the Manitoba Department of Education Library, Winnipeg.

Canadians who died during the year 1976 included CLARE BICE, illustrator and author of children's books and retired Director of the London (Ontario) Art Gallery and Museum; IRENE DAWSON, Programs Officer, Canadian Library Association and former staff member of the London (Ontario) Public Library and Lakehead University Library, Thunder Bay, Ontario; BEATRICE M. EVANS, retired Chief Librarian, Provincial Library Service, Ontario Department of Education, Toronto; MARGARET B. SCOTT, Professor, School Librarianship, Faculty of Education, University of Toronto, and a Past President of the Canadian School Libraries Association, and ELIZABETH WILLIAMSON, head of the Cataloguing Department, University of Windsor Library.

Personnel and Employment: Collective Bargaining

Librarians employed by the National Library of Canada and the Public Archives of Canada organized a separate local union during 1976 within the Public Service Alliance of Canada after having voted to switch their bargaining agent from the Professional Institute of the Public Service of Canada. The move to change bargaining agents was initiated by the Library Science Group consisting of approximately 375 librarians employed by the Treasury Board in federal government libraries across Canada.

Public Lending Right

The continuing debate between librarians and the Canadian writing community over a proposed public lending "right" ended in Halifax in June when the Canadian Library Association passed a compromise resolution satisfactory to both sides. The CLA resolution recognized the cultural importance of the contribution of Canadian writers and sympathized with the financial difficulties in which many authors find themselves. CLA urged the federal government to develop and fund a system of increased financial rewards to writers and indicated CLA's readiness to support the use of library holdings data in the development of such a system. CLA made these recommendations "in recognition of the cultural contribution of Canadian writers and *not* in recognition of any legal entitlement to recompense for the library use, i.e., a public lending 'right'."

Public Libraries

During the year *The Ontario Public Library: Review and Reorganization*, by Albert Bowron, library consultant, was published by the Ontario Provincial Library Council, which had obtained a $25,000 grant for the study from the Ontario Government. The report deals with the most important issues faced by Ontario's public libraries such as the relationships between public libraries and municipal and provincial governments, regional libraries and regional government, county libraries, the future of library boards, bibliographic networks, financial support, and the quality and quantity of service to the public.

The Bowron report makes 43 specific recommendations including reconstitution of the Provincial Library Service Branch as the Public Library and Community Information Services Branch, establishment of an Ontario Public Library Board to supersede the Ontario Provincial Library Council, appointment by municipal council of each municipal library board to be composed of nine members, development by regional library systems and the new provincial library board of program budgeting techniques as a top priority, encouragement of the formation of county public library systems, monitoring by the provincial library board of the development of electronic data processing in order to ensure a coordinated approach to library automation, development by the OPLB of qualitative and quantitative standards for public libraries in Ontario, and further study of library service to Franco-Ontarians and native peoples. Reactions to the Bowron report from the library community were conveyed to the Ontario Provincial Library Council for consideration. In late November the Council met to agree on a final response to the report which was forwarded to the Ministry of Culture and Recreation for possible implementation.

A study of public libraries in 30 municipalities on the Island of Montreal was undertaken by Claude Aubry, Chief Librarian, Ottawa Public Library, and Laurent Denis, of the University of Toronto. Objectives of the study, which was financed and published by the Quebec Ministry of Cultural Affairs, the provincial agency responsible for public libraries, were to analyze existing conditions, to identify community needs, to set objectives and priorities to meet the needs, and to determine the appropriate means of achieving the objectives. The surveyors found that many citizens had no library service whatsoever, collections were scanty, that most libraries were understaffed and housed in inadequate facilities, that financial support varied widely and was inadequate, and that specialized services in many cases did not exist. Lack of any inter-municipal coordination was the chief obstacle to improved library services.

The principal recommendation of the Aubry-Denis study was for the creation of a new library agency to be financed by the provincial government to coordinate public library service in the Montreal region (rather than to serve the public directly). This agency, which would be a private corporation administered by a board made up of representatives from each library involved, would help to enrich and enlarge present services, assist in offering new ones, and supply consultative and public relations services. Several recommendations related specifically to the Montreal Public Library, which the surveyors found to be understaffed, underfinanced and failing to play a leadership role in the region. Another set of recommendations dealt with an extensive program of library construction. The report was the first official one on Montreal libraries since public libraries came under the jurisdiction of the provincial Ministry of Cultural Affairs.

Reference Services

The library of the Ontario Institute for Studies in Education (OISE), Toronto, in 1976 began offering an extended reference service to provide in-depth literature searches for teachers, administrators, school boards, and community groups. The library had offered a similar service in the past at no charge but there was a limit to the time given to requests. Beginning July 1 the library offered a coordinated information service at an hourly fee that covered staff time necessary to complete the research. The service drew on OISE library's extensive collection of educational materials including a complete run of the ERIC microfiche system, as well as more obscure items such as local school board reports and curriculum materials.

The National Research Council of Canada is jointly sponsoring with the Ontario Ministry of Industry and Tourism a referral service for scientific and technical information. ASK (Access to Scientific Information), based in Toronto, handled inquiries from anywhere in Metropolitan Toronto and the four surrounding counties. Opened in December 1975, ASK could become, if successful, the prototype for a series of regional referral centers across Canada. ASK is based on two principles: (1) that oral communication is the most important source of information and (2) that use of information services is determined by ease of access. ASK does not handle information itself but directs the user to a source such as a library, a data base center, a government department or agency, an association, a company, or an individual expert in science and technology willing to share knowledge with potential users. Subject experts are listed in a confidential Knowledge Source Index with details regarding their area of expertise. The National Research Council has solicited support for ASK from special librarians in the region served by inviting them to join the group of organizations willing to accept referrals.

School Libraries

In the first study ever undertaken of the availability of Canadian books in schools, a Work Group of the Toronto Board of Education concluded that Toronto students could gain only a "stunted, inadequate knowledge of Canada and Canadians," from current classroom and library materials. The report of the two-year study stated that "students are being denied access to a substantial amount of useful information about Canada, Canadians, and the community in which they live." The study isolated three causes for the inadequacy of Canadian content in the available learning materials: lack of funds, lack of suitable material to purchase, and the failure to establish Canadian content as a high priority in the selection of materials.

Young Adult Literature

Canadian Juvenile Fiction and the Library Market, the report of a study to "explore the relationship between the marketing practices of Canadian publishers of children's books and the selection policies of Canadian elementary school libraries and children's departments in public libraries," was published in 1976 by the Canadian Library Association.

The study, prepared by John Wilkinson, Director of the Centre for Research in Librarianship, University of Toronto, indicates a mean figure of 16 percent as the proportion of elementary school libraries which held a copy of any given Canadian award-winning juvenile title. For public libraries, the percentage was 66. One of the main problems is that "while publishers assume that libraries can be reached through marketing techniques directed at an audience that is literate and well informed about publishing practice . . . library personnel are all too frequently hampered by a lack of knowledge of publishing and authorship in Canada."

R. BRIAN LAND

Women in Canadian Librarianship

While the status of women in Canadian librarianship may not have improved over the last five years, an awareness of the issues concerning women in the profession has grown through the library media, national and provincial status of women committees, and library association programs.

The latest statistics available (Statistics Canada: Public Libraries in Canada 1973, August, 1976) show that in 36 municipal libraries with population centers of 100,000 and over, 16 of the chief librarians were male and five female. (Breakdown by sex was not available for some positions.) In 214 reporting public libraries in Canada there were 1,002 female full-time professional librarians and 276 male full-time professional librarians. Female librarians were not represented in management roles in proportion to their representation in the public library field.

The national library group which is trying to redress some of these imbalances within the profession and increase women's access to information in the community is the Canadian Library Association's Status of Women Committee. This group began its fourth year of work in 1976 under the leadership of its convenor, Anne Smart of Saskatoon, Saskatchewan. A workshop at the annual Canadian Library Association Conference in Halifax in June 1976 concentrated on the rights of Native women and the role librarians could play in providing information to women on the Reserves. The Committee put forth a resolution on the Indian Act to be presented to the CLA membership asking that CLA communicate to the Department of Indian Affairs and Northern Development and to the Native peoples' groups the necessity to remove from the Indian Act Section 12 (1) (b) (that Indian women who marry non-Indians lose their Indian status; hence, their children also lose Indian status). Because of the political implications involving both Native people and women, the resolutions committee ruled the resolution out of order. A revised resolution changed to include the suggestion that individual Indian bands were losing their per capita grants due to such a law, hence their library funding, passed in a standing vote of 95 to 61.

Budget cuts within CLA during 1976 affected this committee and drastically reduced their budget to $50. Without funds for travel or research, the possible effectiveness of the Committee has been minimized; consequently, members are concentrating on creating an awareness of the issues and keeping these issues alive through the Canadian library print media. They plan to keep in touch with other concerned feminists by sending a representative to the National Action Committee on the Status of Women meeting and approaching the Canadian Research Institute for the Advancement of Women for their support.

Both Saskatchewan and Manitoba library associations have active Status of Women committees and the Atlantic Provinces Library Association planned to establish such a committee.

Because of the work of these organizational committees, the CLA as a whole, was responsive to some of the issues and concerns of the feminist community within the profession. The CLA released a four-page "Guidelines on non-sexist language" in June of 1976 to be used in all CLA publications, reports, letters, and other public documents. The guidelines were prepared as a result of a resolution initiated by the Status of Women Committee and passed at the 1975 CLA conference, approved by the Editorial Publications and Policy Committee, the Status of Women Committee, and the Editorial Board of the Canadian Library Journal.

Outside the CLA, a major study of the "Career Paths of Librarians," begun in 1974 by Linda Fischer, Waterloo University, Waterloo, Ontario, and Sherrill Cheda and Phyllis Yaffe, librarians at Seneca College of Applied Arts and Technology, Willowdale, Ontario, was completed in 1976. It had been funded with a $30,000 grant from the Canada Council. The raw data, taken from a scientifically selected sample with over 80 percent response, is now on computer tape for analysis by the researchers. It is the first study of librarians to attempt to determine attitudes toward work, promotion, salary, responsibility and management positions. This study is the outgrowth of the projects of the first Canadian Library Association Status of Women Committee in 1973.

The "nonprofessional" library workers in Canada (Library Technicians, Library Assistants and clerical staff) are also in a female-dominated four-fifths minority position and are struggling through their provincial and local organizations and unions to increase their status within the library community. Within the Ontario Community Colleges of Applied Arts and Technology, library technicians (female-dominated) have a salary scale lower than technicians (male-dominated) (Jennifer Singh, "Library Technicians/Mysteries?" Emergency Librarian, vol. 4, no. 1, September/October 1976, p. 3–8).

Female library workers in Canada find strong support in the alternative Canadian library magazine, Emergency Librarian (46 Gormley Avenue, Toronto M4V 1Z1, Ontario, Canada). The magazine consistently publishes articles, bibliographies, and news of feminist interest. In 1976 the April issue was devoted to "Women in Prison" and the September issue was on the theme of women library workers. Reviews and columns, "Books for Liberated Kids," and "Notes from the Other Side of the Irony Curtain" stress feminist resources.

Library schools in Canada have been slow to respond to the changing library profession; consequently, their curriculum has not formally reflected material on the status of women within the field at any of the five schools. Nevertheless, extensive planning began in 1976 for the first course on feminist resources to be taught at the Dalhousie School of Library Service in the summer semester, 1977. — SHERRILL CHEDA

London Correspondent's Report

Academic Libraries

During 1976 alarm was aroused by the *Report* of a working party set up by the University Grants Committee (UGC) on the size of university libraries. It had been estimated that 11 university libraries were already full to capacity, that a further 26 would become so by 1985, and that the building of extensions was largely impracticable. The report based its recommendations on an assumed allowance of an unchanging 3.8 metres of books per student. In order to maintain it, older books would have to be removed annually from "current" shelves for the accommodation of new acquisitions. It was envisaged that a reserve store, carrying up to five years' worth of discards, could be held in each library. Beyond that, books would have to be dispersed or lodged with the British Library Lending Division (BLLD), and, if required, borrowed either through local networks or directly from the BLLD.

Criticism of the report was widespread, but perhaps most notably expressed by the Standing Conference of National and University Libraries (SCONUL), which asserted that the plan encouraged excessive centralization and reliance on the BLLD, and might even represent a threat to democracy and academic freedom. Libraries of the most recently established universities were likely to be the hardest hit. The working party's suggestion that serials were especially good candidates for rapid removal was criticised on the ground that it was likely to penalize research, thus diminishing the academic status of universities. While the working party had used the term "self-renewing library" to describe their concept, senior members of Aberdeen University denounced it as planning to impose "self-destroying" libraries.

In view of current spending cuts, the report was perhaps not entirely realistic. Some university libraries remained understocked—such as that at Cardiff where, in an incident, students hammered on the library windows in protest against the emptiness of the shelves within. Another result of cutbacks was reduction of opening hours, against which undergraduates at Cambridge staged a mass sit-in.

Archives

The major current activity in the British archive world was preparation for the move of the Public Record Office from Chancery Lane in the City of London to Kew in West London, to be carried out between January and July 1977. Fully automated user-access and archive requisitioning procedures were being prepared. There was debate in Parliament and in the General Synod of the Church of England on the care of local archives; parochial registers and administrative records were to be moved to diocesan offices should storage facilities in their place of origin be judged inadequate. The General Advisory Committee of the British Broadcasting Corporation set up a subcommittee to advise on the proper storage of the BBC's unique archive collection and the creation of an efficient retrieval system.

The County of Tyne and Wear (established 1974) set up an Archives Users' Consultative Council, aimed at coordinating the interests of archivists and the public. Its members were representatives from Newcastle University, the polytechnics of Newcastle and Sunderland, the local colleges of education, and various publishers and lawyers.

Provision for good storage and trained care of archives remained distinctly haphazard, as was demonstrated by a survey of Scottish archive custody given by Richard F. Dell, of Strathclyde Regional Archives, to the Society of Archivists' annual conference. While local patriotism had inspired Orkney to maintain an archivist since 1973, and Shetland had appointed one in 1976, the new region of Grampian (established 1975) was less well provided for than one of its constituent districts, Moray and Nairu, which boated two archivists. In Strathclyde itself, an enormous region, local interests resented the transfer of material to Glasgow, but in 17 districts records were being held without adequate storage facilities. In Liverpool City Libraries unemployed graduates were taken on to catalog crew lists and cemetery records, and a large collection of photographic negatives was indexed.

Automation

Despite savage cuts in other areas of library and information services, some progress in automation seems to have continued in British libraries, probably because projects were fairly long-term and not easy to jettison. Acceptance of the importance of automation was shown by the BL Research and Development Department's grant of £5,000 to the Department of Library and Information Services at Manchester Polytechnic to evaluate a proposed course on library automation. Already all post-graduate librarianship students at Manchester studied automation for one full term, and the project was to assess their reaction and the effect on their performance.

Throughout 1976 the BL continued its work to provide by 1977 short-term on-line services for its MARC bibliographic file that covered most British copyright material since 1950 and the LC MARC records, and had links with the Bibliographic Services Division's Local Cataloguing Service (LOCAS). Meanwhile, the BL was also working on the MERLIN (Machine Readable Library Information) system devised ultimately to combine all existing BL computer-based services, including the production of the British National Bibliography (BNB), a complete catalog service using Library Software Package (LSP), and distribution of MARC tapes. MERLIN was planned as a central data base that would also serve the entire United Kingdom library network. Programming of the first stage began in 1976 and it was hoped that tests could be made by the end of the year.

Another BL achievement was the production by its Music Bibliography Group of a MARC format for scores that could become the center of a national music cataloging system.

A major event in 1976 was the first-time production by computer programs of the Library Association's *Library and Information Science Abstracts (LISA)*. An important feature of the scheme was that, in future, cumulative indexes would be made by merging the tapes of the six individual issues produced in one year. The 1976 *LISA* was to be offered through the major on-line vendors in Europe and the U.S. Magnetic tapes of *LISA* back numbers (from its first publication in 1969) were to be marketed through Learned Information (Europe) Limited.

Yorkshire public and academic libraries advanced rapidly in automation. Six branches of the North Yorkshire County Libraries started the first phase of a partially on-line computer system for the ordering, receipt, cataloging, and location of stock. In the field of issue, a land line established between Sheffield Central Library and its Stockbridge branch would allow issues from both to be recorded, while Sheffield Polytechnic in September inaugurated a £14,000 system covering the issue and return of books, having converted its Bookamatic System into an Incoterm on-line operation. Hertfordshire's Technical Book Service went on-line to the Lockheed Dialog Information Retrieval System, and the London and South-Eastern (Library) Region (LASER) ordered a minicomputer-based on-line system to maintain its regional catalog and internal networks.

Biographical Notes

RUSSELL BOWDEN, former Lecturer in the Department of Library and Information Studies at Loughborough University of Technology, was appointed Deputy Secretary of the LA in 1976. He had become a librarian almost by accident. Born in Manchester in 1934, he worked briefly on the stage, set sail for India but on the way called at the British Council's establishment in Baghdad and remained there as its librarian. From 1957 to 1973 he worked in various British Council libraries, qualifying as a librarian in 1963. At Loughborough he was tutor for the M.A. course in archives, library, and information studies.

GEORGE ARTHUR CARTER, who retired in 1976 from the post of Deputy Director of Libraries and Museums for Cheshire, was an authority on local history, and revised (1973) J. L. Hobbs' *Local History and the Librarian*. Appointed to Warrington Library (1926), he became Deputy Librarian (1936) and later Chief Librarian. From 1958 he was publications officer for the Lancashire Bibliography. He took up his last post at the local government reorganization in 1974.

FRED CORNELL, who retired in April 1976 from the post of the LA's Editor of General Publications, had been the longest serving member of its headquarters staff. He was Assistant Editor of the *Library Association Record* from 1936, becoming also Publications Officer (1946) and Assistant Editor of the *Journal of Librarianship* from 1969. He was in charge of the administration of the LA's Carnegie, Kate Greenaway, and Wheatley medals.

JEREMY DIGGER, a member of the systems development branch of the BL, at 32 became Editor of the LA's *Library and Information Science Abstracts (LISA)*. He had held a three-year research job with Information Science Index Languages Test (ILSIT) at the College of Librarianship, Wales, and later he worked on the PRECIS research project of the BNB, applying it to one issue of *LISA* and making it available for MARC users.

DOUGLAS JOHN FOSKETT, Librarian since 1957 of London University's Institute of Education, was President of the LA for 1976. Born in London in 1918 and educated at London University, he served in Ilford Public Library from 1940 to 1948, and in the Metal Box Company's library until 1957. An LA council member from 1952 (Chairman 1962-63), he was an instigator of its Classification Research Group, and as chairman of the LA's Education Committee (1968-72) foresaw and encouraged the development of librarianship as a graduate profession. Among his many books were *Creed of a Librarian* (1962) and *Library Systems and Information* (1970).

LORNA VINCENT PAULIN, who retired as County Librarian of Hertfordshire, the first woman to hold office as the President of the LA, by her zest remained a legendary figure in British librarianship. Born in Bexley, Kent, in 1914 and educated at London University, where she later took the diploma in librarianship, she worked in Kent County Libraries from 1936 and became deputy County Librarian in 1944. County Librarian of Nottinghamshire from 1948, she moved to Hertfordshire in 1952. She contributed sections to a number of books on librarianship and was awarded the OBE (Order of the British Empire) in 1970.

DOUGLAS HAROLD VARLEY, who retired in 1976 as Librarian of Liverpool University, a post he had held since 1966, had behind him a distinguished career in pioneering library techniques in Africa. Born in London in 1911, he was deputy librarian at the Royal Empire Society from 1934 to 1938, when he became Secretary and later Chief Librarian of South Africa's National Library at Cape Town, where he helped to found a School of Librarianship. In 1961 he resigned to become librarian of the multiracial University College in Salisbury, Rhodesia. In 1964 he organized the Leverhulme Conference in Salisbury, which led to the establishment of the Standing Conference of African University Libraries (SCAUL). At Liverpool he encouraged the centralization of the university's library services. He was author of several books on librarianship in Africa.

Bookselling

For the British book trade, and particularly for booksellers, 1976 was a year of problems, but also of plans to solve them.

Steeply rising costs had eroded profit margins; and of 376 booksellers surveyed early in 1976, 91 had made no profit in 1975. During 1976 costs continued to rise, the biggest single increase being in wages, resulting from the effect of the Equal Pay Act upon booksellers, who employed mainly women. Post, telephone, heating, and lighting had all risen again. Cuts in local authority spending reduced sales to schools and libraries; and bookshops were threatened by competition from supermarkets and chain stores, whose nationwide networks enabled them to buy books in bulk at higher discounts.

The most acute problem created for booksellers by publishers was caused by publishers' imposing surcharges or reducing discounts on low-value orders—a practice likely in 1976-77 to cut profits by a further 2 percent. Smaller booksellers were hardest hit.

Low profit margins added bite to booksellers' complaints of publishers' order handling and distribution. Time lapse on orders averaged 14 days, and might be several weeks. Complaints also included frequent discrepancies between order, invoice, and parcel.

Lack of nationally organized, in-depth wholesaling was another difficulty. To small booksellers especially, wholesaling offered great advantages: cutting costs and postal and administrative delays by providing a single order, invoice, delivery, and payment system; widening stock range; and ensuring quick deliveries. Many publishers opposed it, however, because traditional pricing systems left no margins for wholesalers' discounts, and because of heavy investment in computerized order handling and distribution.

Because some problems confronting booksellers were shared by publishers, they joined in trying to solve them. Considered the most revolutionary long-term answer to poor order handling, postal and delivery delays, and low-value orders (troublesome to publishers as well as booksellers) was the Litos tele-ordering terminal, developed by the West German book wholesalers, Libri, and offered for sale in London in late 1976. Orders, numerically coded and fed into it by the bookseller, would be transmitted by telephone into publishers' computers. Delivery time would be cut by up to a third and errors virtually eliminated, it was claimed. The main computer-using publishers promised financial backing if booksellers would promise large-scale participation and if a tele-ordering clearinghouse could be set up. To make ISBNs, used to identify titles, readily available to booksellers, a monthly updated supplement to the annual *British Books in Print* would be produced on microfiche—a valuable bibliographical aid.

Religious publishers and booksellers joined to organize a successful first U.K. "Christian Book Week" in October. They also initiated an important new venture, the Religious Book Foundation, to promote "flow . . . of Christian literature" and to carry religious books out into a secular society.

Despite problems, new bookshops opened. One with an assured future was the Bernard Shaw Bookshop at the British Museum, started with money left by Shaw, and expecting sales to top £600,000 a year. The opening of Collet's International Bookshop, incorporating Collet's Russian Bookshop, was celebrated as a landmark in East-West relations. The first Collet bookshop was founded in 1934 by Eva Collet (who died, aged 86, two days after the new shop's official opening), and Collet shops became internationally famous as centers of East-West trade. In striking contrast was the Bookshop Near the Top of the World on Sanday, one of the most northerly of the Orkney Islands; it was to become the islanders' only source of books when the library service by boat from Orkney was stopped.

A book business seeming not to feel the prevailing pinch was W. H. Smith. Newsagent, bookseller, stationer selling a wide range of leisure goods, owner of bookshops and bookstalls throughout the U.K. and in Canada, France, Belgium, and the Netherlands, of a book wholesale and distributing business and, with the U.S. publisher

Doubleday, of the flourishing Book Club Associates, W. H. Smith reported record turnover and profits for 1975–76, and planned a £9,000,000 expansion program for 1976–77. During 1976 the U.K. retail division encouraged hardcover books with a "Book of the Month" promotion.

Diversification and powerful backing helped to keep some bookshops profitable. The Hammick Group, owned by Associated Book Publishers (A.B.P.), with six shops by 1976, opened a "cash-and-carry" service during the year. Charles Hammick, the group's founder, and A.B.P. regarded bookselling and publishing as a single trade: an attitude perhaps promising the best solution of booksellers' and publishers' problems.

Buildings, Furniture, and Equipment

The Concrete Society commended the Arts and Social Studies Library of University College, Cardiff. The building, for which Ore Arup and Partners were structural consultants, had four floors, supported by only six internal columns.

The new development for the Radcliffe Science Library at Oxford achieved mention in *The Guiness Book of Records* as the world's largest underground library. Its new reading room had 13,000 feet of open shelving, and on a floor below were more than 83,000 feet, most in hand-cranked Montamobil Shelving by Bruynzeel Storage Systems of Aylesbury, Buckinghamshire. In 1968 the estimated cost was £500,000, and inflation had added another £14,000 to the overall bill.

In a time of financial stringency, many library authorities attempted conversion rather than new building, often very successfully. Glasgow City Libraries converted a bank to provide a new library for Hutchesontown; the floor space measured 2,000 square feet and a stock of 10,000 books was to be carried. A particularly attractive conversion was that of the former town hall at Camelford in Cornwall. The first floor was prepared as an exhibition and meeting center, while the library stock was established on the second. About 5,000 books were provided and the county authority expected readership to double. The work was carried out with the financial aid of the Historic Buildings Council, and Camelford Town Trust agreed to demand only a nominal rent.

A permanent exhibition and design center for library furniture and equipment was established at the College of Librarianship, Wales. Equipment on view included a wide variety of material for filing systems, book repair, and audio-visuals.

Cataloging and Classification

The Joint Steering Committee for Revision of the Anglo American Cataloging Rules (JCAACR) announced that a new standard bibliographic description, ISBD(G), would be adopted. Its advantage was that it provided for inclusion of all types of media. The need for such integration in the catalogs of British public libraries and schools was emphasized at a LA conference held on nonbook sources in February 1976. Bernard Chibnall, Director of the Media Services unit at Sussex University, argued that the BNB could be adapted so that each entry provided information not only on content of the item but on its form, e.g., book, slide, filmstrip, and other materials. It was announced that the LA, working with the National Council for Educational Technology, had produced a code of cataloging rules (LANCET) that provided unified coverage for all media.

An international bibliographic service for medicine, chemistry, zoology, and veterinary science, already established on the continent of Europe, was introduced to Britain by Information and Library Services. Books, serials, and conference proceedings in all languages were covered, the data being supplied weekly on cards providing all normal bibliographic information together with a brief precis of an item's content. The cards, which could be used as catalog cards, were to be backed up periodically by the issue of a consolidated printed catalog.

Children's Literature

If numbers and range of new series and activities were criteria, 1976 was a year of growth for children's literature in the U.K. Even in titles published—1,891 during January–December, only 50 below 1975's September total—there was little sign of cutback, although children's publishers had been hit by lower library and school spending.

Straws showed the wind's direction. Several new series were in paperback; some replaced color with black and white illustration. The number of illustrated series suggested concern to sell overseas rights. At the Frankfurt International Book Fair, Dent sold co-edition rights in three photographic color series; Macmillan followed its *Our World Encyclopaedia* (published in 12 languages in 1975–76) with *Look It Up*, an international reference project for younger children; and Methuen sold rights in Focus, a series on interrelationship of world resources, to 11 countries.

Best-sellers at home and abroad were Hamlyn's wide-ranging paperback Beaver Books, with Charles Causley's narrative poem *The Tail of the Trinosaur* and Raymond Briggs's *Midnight Adventure* among first titles. Other new paperback series included Penguin's Practical Puffins—things to make and do; Armada Dandelions, topic books for young children; Dent Dolphins (Dent's Children's Illustrated Classics also came out in paperback); Longman Tadpoles, stories for the 6–8 age group, illustrated by Quentin Blake; and, from Macdonald Educational, Quizz Books and Readabouts. Two of many new hardcover fiction series were Pelham's Young Mermaids, for the under 10s, and Collins' Young Fiction for the 7–11 age group. Usborne, a new children's publisher with an adventurous approach to rousing interest and imparting knowledge, launched several series—Nature Trail Books, Time Travellers, Children's Guides (to the physical world), Young Scientist—with big printings in eight or more languages.

In announcing its Information Book Awards, *The Times Educational Supplement* praised the greater integration of text and illustration in 1976 entries. The Senior Award went to Macdonald Educational's dazzling *Encyclopaedia of Africa*, a triumph of teamwork; the Junior Award to Eleanor Allen's *Wash and Brush Up*, a history of personal hygiene and the influence on it of changing social attitudes.

New attitudes were seen in fiction. Hodder's "Olly Sees It Through" series for the 4–9 age group, adapted from Swedish, treated childhood's traumatic experiences —going to the hospital, birth of a brother, divorce, death—with unusual honesty and understanding. Robert Westall's *The Machine-Gunners*, a first novel that won the Carnegie Medal and was runner-up for *The Guardian*'s children's fiction award, had as its themes the power struggle between children and adults, the gang structure of children's society, deception, violence, and how people control it. In *The Borribles* Michael de Larrabeiti, reacting against the cosiness of much children's fiction, produced a sadistic, antiheroic gang-warfare fantasy.

New Children's Rights Workshop "Other Awards" for unbiased books of high merit were won by Bernard Ashley's *The Trouble with Donovan Croft*, a novel exploring the problems of life in a multiracial society; Louise Fitzhugh's *Nobody's Family Is Going to Change*, and Shirley Hughes's picture-storybook *The Helpers*, a Kate Greenaway Medal runner-up.

Many writers developed more traditional genres. The Whitbread children's fiction award was revived and won by Penelope Lively's subtle time fantasy, *A Stitch in Time*; *The Guardian*'s children's fiction award went to Nina Bawden's *The Peppermint Pig*, a sensitive account of a child's depth of feeling. A runner-up for the Carnegie Medal (and winner of the Newbery Medal) was Susan Cooper's *The Grey King*, fourth novel in her fantasy sequence *The Dark Is Rising*.

National Children's Book Week, extended to make July National Children's Book Month, was widely celebrated. Hitchin Library organized a competition for making or painting a bookworm incorporating

"National Children's Book Week 3–10 July." Knight Books (Hodder's children's paperback imprint), their authors, and characters from them invaded Newcastle-upon-Tyne; authors were interviewed on radio and television and, with the characters, promenaded to bookshops and libraries. During the week 50,000 Knight Books were sold.

In July the Children's Books of the Year exhibition at the National Book League was opened, with more than 300 books displayed; and the Children's Book Fair and Seminar—on "Are Publishers Producing the Right Children's Books?"—was held, for the first time open to librarians and teachers as well as booksellers.

Pooh's birthday (October 14) was a national occasion, with tributes and special programs on radio and television, and articles in newspapers. Bookshops and libraries gave parties; Methuen (Pooh's publisher) organized an outing to Cotchford Farm, Sussex, where Pooh, Christopher Robin, and A. A. Milne lived and where *Winnie-the-Pooh* and *The House at Pooh Corner* were written. Methuen's plans began in January, with a "Hum with Pooh" competition, Pooh posters, and 1977 honeypot-shaped Pooh calendars. Celebrations were so numerous and widespread that the BBC television 11 p.m. news program ended on October 14 with "and that's the end of tonight's news from Pooh." (See Biographies.)

Education, Library

Discussion on library education during 1976 centered on two main topics: the move toward librarianship as a graduate profession and the controversy about the relative importance, in training, of theoretical and practical studies. Although it was thought inevitable that eventually all librarians would be graduates, as was already required in the other EEC countries, there was a considerable backlash from some, perhaps the older, chartered librarians, who felt their hard-won status was being undermined. The LA itself was obliged to stress that it had never suggested that existing chartered librarians would need to do further study. Nevertheless, a questionnaire sent by its education secretary to a 10-percent sample of newly qualified nongraduate associates of the LA showed that 71 percent of respondents expected to continue their studies, perhaps with the Open University. As a compromise, many chartered librarians were applying to attend the part-time M.A. course available at Leeds Polytechnic.

Many librarians expressed doubts about the orientation of training. Most felt that it was at present too theoretical. At the LA's RSIS (Reference Section of Information Services) May conference, L. G. Lovell, Director of Cultural Services at Manchester, urged librarians to become active information officers; he thought professional library education should be a four-year degree course and that half of the time should be spent in a "teaching" library.

Law and Legislation

After 25 years of agitation by authors, a bill to set up machinery to administer Public Lending Right (to benefit authors) was introduced in Parliament in March and seemed set to become law. Criticism of the bill's terms were many: it covered books only, excluding other media; it assigned PLR only on books loaned, thus excluding reference library stock; and it offered no right in cases of multiple authorship. The bill survived a gamut of parliamentary hazards only to be "talked out" at the very end of the 1975–76 session, its subject being insufficiently emotive or political to attract dedicated support. Because it had been expected to pass, no official provision was made for a new bill in the 1976–77 session; and PLR advocates had to consider whether to try to introduce a private member's bill or one in the House of Lords.

An issue not dissimilar was the infringement of copyright that improved reproduction or photocopying of book materials had made an everyday occurrence, especially in schools. The Publishers' Association had already planned to set up a blanket license system whereby education authorities could purchase limited rights to book reproduction, and further discussions were held in 1976.

"Booksellers" charged under the Obscene Publications Acts of 1959 and 1964 had put forward the defense that pornographic material served the "public good" in that it might divert from anti-social activity persons with special sexual tensions. However, both in the Court of Appeal (March) and the House of Lords (November) it was pointed out that section 4 of the 1959 act, on which the defense was based, had been framed to protect works relevant to "the interests of science, literature . . . or of other objects of general concern". It was also held that the admissible "evidence of experts" was to establish the value of such works and did not cover evidence by psychiatrists or others about the possible therapeutic value of pornographic material.

Library Association

Preparations were going ahead for celebration of the Centenary in 1977; it was announced that Queen Elizabeth II would become the LA's patron from the date the Centenary began. President of the LA during the Centenary year would be Sir Frederick Dainton, Chairman of the University Grants Committee, and the first non-librarian to be President since Sir Charles (now Lord) Snow in 1961. Dainton had been chairman of the National Libraries Committee, the Report of which preceded the establishment of the BL.

Douglas Foskett, President of the LA for 1976, and other council members met Lord Donaldson, new minister for the arts, in June 1976. The LA's national conference was held at Scarborough, Yorkshire, in September.

An issue that caused dissension throughout the year was a proposed increase in subscription fees. Chartered librarians were especially resentful, because membership in the LA remained for them an essential professional qualification. It was argued that as more librarians emerged from the library schools with CNAA (Council for National Academic Awards) degrees, the numbers needing to keep up Associate (A.L.A.) status would decline, and the LA's membership would be affected. However, it was stated that membership had in fact risen by 20 percent over the last five years and stood at well over 23,000. The LA's newly founded public libraries' group was growing rapidly and at year's end had more than 4,000 members.

Obituary Notes

EVA ASTBURY (d. Feb. 14, 1976) was from 1962 to 1974 County Children's Librarian of the East Riding of Yorkshire, based at Hull. As Children's Librarian at Surbiton in Surrey she had pioneered the development of a readers' club, a story hour, and a puppet theatre. Soon after her marriage in 1950 she and her husband moved to Leeds and later to Hull, where she started family reading groups. She had reviewed books for *Junior Bookshelf*.

LIONEL GEORGE MCCOLVIN (d. Jan. 16, 1976), City Librarian at Westminster from 1938 until his retirement in 1961, was a prominent member of the LA, editing the *Library Association Record* from 1941 to 1945 and serving as President in 1952. As a contributor to the 1959 Roberts Report on the updating of the 1892 and 1919 Public Library Acts, he was an architect of the 1964 Public Libraries and Museums Act. At Westminster he founded the Central Music Library and established the invaluable Central Reference Library, the largest in Southeast England apart from the British Museum (now the BL's Reference Division). He was chairman of IFLA's public libraries section, and spoke extensively for the British Council and UNESCO.

JOHN B. PURDIE (d. Feb. 12, 1976), former County Librarian of Renfrewshire, and a lifelong member of the Scottish LA, was notable for his reorganization of Bristol and later Clydebank Central Libraries after damage and disarray caused by bombing during World War II. In Renfrewshire he established a number of school libraries.

Personnel and Employment: Performance Appraisal

In 1976 the Local Authorities Management Services and Computer Committee (LAMSAC) published a three-volume report, *The Staffing of Public Libraries*. Based on research done in 1972–73, when more than 220 library staff of all grades, working for a wide variety of local authorities, were interviewed, the report was an attempt to establish guidelines for the staffing of public libraries. The work of both professional and nonprofessional librarians was measured in terms of decimal hours spent on each group of tasks. For professionals it was found that 31 percent of their time was devoted to maintenance and cataloging of stock, 33 percent to readers' enquiries and needs, 24 percent to management, 8 percent to servicing (planning staff timetables, keeping accounts) 2 percent to staff development, and 2 percent to planning for the future. On average, the services of 1.51 professional grade librarians were required for every 1,000 items of stock; it was found that the returns for no authority sampled deviated more than 11 percent from this mean. In service to hospitals and housebound readers it was found that 4 hours' work (not necessarily skilled) was required for every 100 readers.

Personnel and Employment: Supply, Salaries, Collective Bargaining

Owing to severe retrenchment in all areas, the job prospects for librarians was not reassuring. Early in 1976, when local authorities planned their budgets, it was admitted that a number of posts would be phased out. For instance, Surrey expected to lose about 33 full-time and 300 part-time jobs, Cumbria 2½, Redbridge 4½, and Bedfordshire 2. Glasgow and Cheshire expected a 10 percent run-down of staff. The shortfall of jobs was increased by the widespread shelving of plans for appointing qualified librarians to run school libraries.

There was also frustration at the apparent dilatoriness of the National and Local Government Officers' Association (NALGO) in negotiating an arbitration award for chartered librarians in public libraries.

A payment scale had been proposed and a job evaluation study projected by the Advisory Conciliation and Arbitration Service in May 1975, but nothing further had been done and by November 1976 the Library Association wondered whether the union was serving its librarian members adequately.

In the public sector another trouble was the tendency, especially noticeable in London boroughs since an administrative reorganization in 1973, for chief librarians' posts to be downgraded, a practice that would adversely affect the salary scales of their subordinates. Examples occurred in 1976 in Berkshire and in the London borough of Tower Hamlets. The LA, NALGO, and the Society of Metropolitan and County Chief Librarians usually boycotted such posts.

Personnel and Employment: Staff Development

Serious concern was voiced at the absence of provision of short-term management training courses for librarians. It was established that there were about 10,000 librarians in Britain on career grades and that of those only about 800 a year received any management training, whereas industrial and business executives went on courses frequently. Of some 54 centers where courses of interest to librarians were organized, only 14 included management in their schedules, and then only at random. The LA and the BL's Research and Development Department set up a joint project to investigate this serious omission. One useful course for senior librarians given during 1976 was on interviewing. Held at the School of Management, Ealing Technical College, in London, it was followed by a series of similar courses organized by the London and Home Counties branch of the LA.

Public Libraries

In 1976 the main preoccupation was financial cuts in the library service and their effect on staff and public. Building programs were cancelled or delayed, and some jobs were lost; inconvenience to the public was caused by shorter hours (many libraries closing on Saturday afternoons), the closure of small branch libraries, and by the sudden disappearance of newspapers, magazines, and serials from library shelves. The reduction likely to have the most serious long-term effect was that in book funds. Statistics compiled for the Library and Book Trade Relations (LIBTRAD) working party on estimated book funds for 1976–77 showed that increases over figures for 1975–76 were 14–18 percent for London and the counties, 9 percent for metropolitan districts, and 5 percent for Scottish districts. But these averages concealed very great variations. Some local authorities had actually reduced their book funds, one by as much as £70,000; and several planned to spend only sums equal to those spent in 1975–76, which, because of inflation, now represented a reduction in real terms. The full significance of LIBTRAD's figures could not be appreciated except in relation to those for 1974–75 and 1975–76; Buckinghamshire, for instance, might seem to have done well to show in its 1976–77 appropriation an increase of £68,000 until it were seen that in 1975–76 it had cut its fund by 77 percent.

The main reason for these cuts or standstills was the government's reduction of the rate support grant, an annual payment made from central to local funds. The cuts were severely criticized by the LA and other interested bodies; it was even suggested in *The Sunday Times* in April that many of the proposed reductions in book funds contravened the Public Libraries and Museums Act, 1964, which had laid down guidelines for a minimum ratio of book acquisitions to the local area's population figures.

In these circumstances some libraries sought to raise money by other means. Following the precedent set by Somerset's successful sale of redundant bookstock in 1975, Dudley Libraries in 1976 sold 9,000 books for £800, Bradford sold 9,800 for a net profit of £900, and Staffordshire County Libraries sold 6,700 books and 1,000 records and cassettes for £1,200. Other sales took place and were planned. However, this practice evoked some criticism. Normally secondhand bookshops had refused to buy books stamped as public library property, but now some members of the public would, perfectly legally, be owners of ex-library books which it was difficult to mark as genuinely sold in a way that could not be fraudently copied.

Despite the severe retrenchment, some developments occurred. A few new libraries were completed and opened. Among them were the Portsmouth's new Central Library which was claimed as the largest in the South of England, and the new extension at the Langside branch library at Glasgow.

Even if there were fewer books to borrow, overall use of public libraries increased. In East Kilbride, a growing "new town", the rise was 20 percent during 1975–76; more significant, perhaps, was the 4.7 percent (including 5.4 percent children) rise recorded by Kensington and Chelsea, London. William Davies, Librarian of Bradford, in a speech at the LA conference, noted that in the U.S. during the depression years 1930–35 the graph of public library book issues had correlated very closely with that of unemployment. He claimed that a similar parallel existed in the Britain of 1976.

Publishing, Book

The year was one of challenge and change for UK book publishers. New problems stimulated initiative, and new methods were used to overcome existing problems: rising costs, distribution delays, a market depressed at home and threatened abroad.

Predictions of a dramatic fall in titles published were unfulfilled. Publishers' 1975 cutbacks caused a 25 percent drop in first-quarter totals, but by September, with 24,599 titles, only 8.35 percent below 1975's September total, the decline had slowed. Higher book prices were eroding profits: although total sales value rose, fewer books were sold. High prices made UK books less competitive in world markets; but falling value of sterling helped to offset them.

Home sales declined as library and education cuts took effect. The home market was also threatened by importation from other EEC countries of U.S. remaindered paperback editions of books in which UK publishers held copyright—a consequence of conflict between EEC open market regulations and UK copyright law.

The main challenge came from opening to competition traditional UK overseas markets. Planning was directed toward raising exports. A fall in 1975's export figure to just under 41 percent was less serious than it seemed: many publishers had avoided inflationary pressures at home by establishing overseas companies, whose results contributed over half their 1975–76 turnover.

Overseas activities were strengthened. Faber, Elek, and Granada opened U.S. companies; Associated Book Publishers (ABP) reorganized for greater international expansion and arranged U.S. marketing through its Canadian company. Longman acquired from the Xerox Corporation the Australian educational Cheshire Publishing Pty. Sphere Books, a Thomson organization subsidiary, extended its new tele-ordering system to Australia.

Concern to develop foreign markets and to protect copyright combined to turn UK publishers into EEC publishers. The copyright problem was decisively tackled. John Calder, who saw U.S. editions of his firm's copyrighted titles in a London bookshop, took legal actions. The court ordered the shop to return the books to the importer and the importer to pay costs and compensation. This, with warnings of further legal action from Calder, and from Penguin, which would prevent such imports, even of UK copyright titles in which its U.S. associate, Viking Penguin, held rights, deterred others.

To offset reduced library buying, publishers promoted hardcover sales to the public. A series launched with a £100,000 promotion campaign by Heinemann, its associate Secker, and Octopus, a Hamlyn subsidiary, under a new Heinemann/Octopus imprint, was outstandingly successful. Ten handsomely produced, low-priced volumes, each containing major novels by such bestselling Heinemann/Secker authors as Galsworthy, D. H. Lawrence, Kafka, Steinbeck, and Erle Stanley Gardner, published in September, had sold out a 50,000,000-copy printing by October.

Rising paperback sales and anxiety to ensure full authors' royalties, rights, and market coverage inspired other diversifications. Futura, a British Printing Corporation (BPC) paperback subsidiary, joined Macdonald and Jane's, BPC's general hardcover company, in launching hardcover Macdonald Raven Books; Macdonald and Jane's, with Futura, started a Futura/Macdonald paperback list. New Futura imprints included Troubadour (quality romance fiction) and Orbit (science fiction). The Cape-Chatto-Bodley Head and Granada groups founded Triad Books, a new paperback company; and ABP created a new general paperback imprint, Magnum Books.

New independent companies included Open Books, concentrating on books for student teachers and social workers, with an annual sales booster—in 1976, *Love's Mysteries: a Guide to the Psychology of Sexual Attraction*; Oresko Books, announcing a scholarly artbook list; and Pierrot Publications, launching an illustrated softcover list with a winner, *Fitness the Footballers' Way*.

The independent Quartet Books was acquired by the Namara Group, headed by a Palestinian Arab financier; its subsidiary, the feminist Virago, became independent. Longman took over UK and other distribution rights for Webster's dictionaries, agreeing with their U.S. publisher, Merriam, to join in developing them.

New methods of cutting production costs and distribution delays were developed by book manufacturers, notably Billings, and Redwood Burn, offering budget book plans, and by publishers, who introduced tele-ordering (*see* Bookselling) and extended micro-publishing. Already used in the UK for learned journals, library catalogs, and, by the Pergamon Press, for simultaneous book and microfiche publication of new titles, microfiche was adopted by the Oxford University Press and Longman for out-of-print titles, so saving short-run production and storage costs.

Publishing, Magazine

Vitality, shown by determination to survive despite difficulties and by new ventures, distinguished UK magazine publishing in 1976. Costs were still rising, pushing cover prices up; higher postal charges hit many magazines; and many were threatened by reduced library spending. For most, circulation had fallen, yet magazines, harder-hit highbrow periodicals, and learned journals managed to survive. Newcomers, undeterred by the problems confronting UK publishing, plugged small holes in market coverage or aimed at specialized readership: a sign that magazine publishing remained a buoyant section of the industry.

Hi-Fi Weekly, *Classical Music Weekly*, *Prima*, and *Woman's World* entered highly competitive markets. The two weeklies faced competition from successful, established monthlies. *Prima*, a monthly for middlebrow younger women, attracted them by a well-tried blend of romantic fiction and features on health, home, and beauty, and took a less extreme line on controversial issues than *Cosmopolitan* and *She*, its closest rivals. *Woman's World*, another monthly for the same age group, launched by the International Publishing Corporation (IPC), first announced for 1973, twice postponed, then cancelled, was due early in 1977 after a £250,000 promotion: another sign of optimism in the magazine world.

A new socio-political comic for adults, *Ally Sloper*, resurrected as its title and "hero" a cartoon character created in 1867 and killed off in 1922. *Captain Britain* was a weekly comic for boys; *Oh Boy!*, a weekly magazine for girls. Another weekly, *Events*, backed by £100,000,000 from the Saudi Arabian royal family aimed at providing the western world an objective view of the Arab world.

The *Economist*, *Listener*, *New Statesman* (with circulation down to about 40,000), *Tatler and Bystander*, and *Spectator* (struggling to raise circulation from the all-time low of 12,000 to which it fell after 1975's ownership change) raised cover prices. *Bananas*, a literary quarterly in tabloid newspaper format, publishing short stories, started in January 1975 by the novelist Emma Tennant "to encourage people to read and enjoy . . . fiction and to encourage imaginative writers", in September 1976 persuaded the bookseller and newsagent W. H. Smith chain to sell it at shops and bookstalls, so raising its sales from about 1,000 to around 13,000 two months later.

Publishing, Newspaper

A year that began with improved performance and prospects for most UK newspapers ended with gloom again prevailing.

In 1975 sales of most national papers fell by 8 percent; for some, by much more. Even the *Sun*, shining more brightly each year since its 1969 takeover by Rupert Murdoch, reported only a minimal circulation rise; and the *Daily Mail* was the only other national daily to keep sales up. Signs of economic recovery early in 1976, however, raised advertising revenues and sales; and most papers reported higher profits for January–June.

By November, the situation had changed. Return of national economic crisis renewed crises for newspapers. Costs rose; advertisers and readers withdrew. The main single problem was the price of imported newsprint, rising as sterling's value fell. Between August and early November devaluation of the pound had added 14 percent to its price. *The Observer*, which had barely survived 1975's crisis, stated that a rise of up to 30 percent in production costs resulting from devaluation had caused the difficulties that by late October threatened closure. Early in November Mirror Group Newspapers (MGN; *Daily Mirror, Sunday Mirror, The People*) announced that a profit rise expected by 1977-78 would have vanished in rising costs; and Sir Richard Marsh, new Chairman of the Newspaper Publishers' Association (NPA), warned national papers that in 1977 they would be paying an extra £30,000,000 for newsprint, with other costs also higher. Another rise in cover prices, with consequent circulation losses, was inevitable.

The first to press for the rise was Associated Newspapers, for which gloom had never lifted. Its only profit-maker was the *Sunday Express*. Sales of the *Daily Express* had fallen by 176,000 in July 1975–July 1976, and group profits by £1,800,000, with further losses expected for July–December.

Also in November, an independent report on the newspaper industry, by Dataquest, predicted closures if financial help were not soon forthcoming. Provincial dailies would merge with their evening sisters. Either the *Daily Express* or the *Daily Mail* would go; and so would either the London *Evening Standard* or *Evening News*. So would *The Observer* and, eventually, *The Times* (still, after Lord Thomson's death in August, backed by a Thomson family trust).

By late November *The Observer* had been saved. Need for a £1,000,000, long-term capital investment had caused its trustees to suggest takeover by Murdoch's News International. When this fell through, various backers came forward, among them a Hong Kong newspaper group, the millionaire financier Sir James Goldsmith, and Associated Newspapers, planning to popularize the paper and move it politically from left-of-center to center. Possible loss of another radical paper, with the *Daily Mirror*'s massive sales being overtaken by the rising *Sun*, created anxiety. Last-minute rescue by the U.S. Atlantic Richfield oil group, headed by Robert O. Anderson, also head of the Aspen Institute for Humanistic Studies, ensured its financial stability and continued editorial independence.

In March the interim report of the Royal Commission on the Press had proposed help for newspapers which, it stated, could only bridge the gap between revenue and costs by reducing manpower and investing in new technological production methods. It estimated investment costs at about £20,000,000 for national newspapers, with £30,000,000 – £35,000,000 more needed for "socially acceptable" redundancy payments. The changes would eventually bring in an annual £35,000,000. With leaders of the industry, it rejected government subsidy; it proposed that loans be provided by the private-sector Finance for Industry (FFI), with up to 4 percent government interest relief for their first two years.

Serials

The future for academic journals, especially for those concerned with science or technology, seemed grim. The annual survey of periodical prices commissioned by the LA showed that prices had risen steeply since 1970, with a corresponding decline in subscriptions. It was expected that some valuable serials would cease publication, with an adverse effect on research. Statistics issued in June 1976 showed that the prices of journals concerned with the humanities had risen by an average of 26.4 percent since 1975, those of scientific and technological journals by 26.7 percent, and those of medical journals by 31.2 percent. The average cost of an annual subscription to a learned journal was now £30.11. Although the price increase since 1970 had been sharper in Britain than in Canada and the U.S., the average cost of journals was still marginally less in Britain than in North America (see Acquisitions for U.S. prices).

Despite appalling difficulties, some new serials were launched. Ruskin College, Oxford, started its twice-yearly *History Workshop*; a quarterly, *Inter-Disciplinary Science Reviews*, had its first issue in March 1976. *Art Libraries Journal*, successor of the ARLIS *Newsletter*, appeared in April 1976. A more commercially biased publication was *Development Sheffield*, produced by Sheffield City council's promotion committee to encourage local industry.

Special User, Services to

Awareness of the needs of adult illiterates or slow readers increased rapidly, and was shown particularly in attempts to provide for them simple reading matter that was also suitable to their interests. The Adult Literacy Resource Agency offered *Guidelines for Publishers in Producing Reading Material for Adults with Reading or Writing Difficulties;* in Manchester a tabloid newspaper, *This Month*, specifically produced for this group, sold 10,000 copies of its first issue in April 1976. The second edition of the LA's *New Readers Start Here* (August 1976) gave useful guidelines on suitable material, commenting that publishers unfortunately seemed still unwilling seriously to cater to this market. The Adult Literacy Resource Agency gave £500 to the College of Librarianship, Wales, to set up a collection of books suitable for loan to adult new readers, and at Nene College, Northampton's language center, a new base was provided for adult literacy instruction.

The Schools Library Association's booklet, *Each According to his Need*, by Margaret Marshall of Leeds Polytechnic's School of Librarianship, disclosed that there were 150,000 children in Britain's Special Schools whose handicap in some way prevented their making normal use of books.

The library at the Henshaw Residential School for the Blind and Partially Sighted at Harrogate, Yorkshire, contained a high proportion of large print books, together with fiction, nonfiction, reference works, and serials in braille. The problems of those unable to hold books (assessed at around 500,000) were stressed by Graham Hennessy, Appeals Director of the National Listening Library, which had 600 titles available for loan. The Library's work had been increasingly hampered by high postal charges. Although registered blind persons were exempt from the charges, those temporarily blind or in other ways prevented from handling ordinary books received no concessions. Of the Listening Library's 1,400 members, only some 20 were libraries, and it was felt that librarians needed to improve their service to this section of the public.

A Library Advisory Council working party collected evidence from the National Bureau of Handicapped Students on difficulties persons in wheelchairs experienced in public buildings. It was discovered that library facilities were less satisfactory than those in theatres or shops. It was found that 51.5 percent of the libraries sampled were accessible, but only in 32 percent of the libraries could upper floors (where records, cassettes, and other materials were often kept) be reached in wheelchairs.

The Disabled Living Foundation named Brompton Library in London as providing exceptionally good access and facilities for the disabled. North Kensington was planning to install a ramp and an elevator.

STEPHANIE MULLINS;
DOROTHY PARTINGTON

State Reports

State correspondents report here on events of general interest during 1976. They provide systematic coverage on state library associations and state agencies. Data are given as of the end of 1976 unless otherwise indicated. ALA membership is given for state associations reporting it.

ALABAMA

Public Libraries. A serious effort was made in 1976 to improve public library services in the State. The budget for the Alabama Public Library Service was increased 62.5 percent from $178,000 to $300,000; and at a time when many state agencies suffered reduced budgets, state aid for local libraries remained at $650,000 or $.18 per capita. There seemed to be a growing concern among key members of the Alabama legislature about library service in the state. This was a result, at least in part, of an active campaign by interested citizens to improve state support of library services. One group, Libraries PLUS (People for Libraries Urging Support), organized an influential lobbying activity.

The voters of Tuscaloosa approved by a 5 to 1 margin a bond issue for a new library building. In March the Alabama Public Library Service opened its new building on Monticello Drive in Montgomery. Other new library buildings occupied during the year were the Carl Elliott Regional Library in Jasper and the H. Grady Bradshaw Chambers County Library donated by the West Point Pepperell Foundation. New library construction was also completed at Gardendale, Selma, Opelika, Arab and Wetumpka.

In October Governor George Wallace approved the transfer of the administration of library services for the blind and physically handicapped from the Special Technical Facility at Talladega to the Alabama Public Library Service in Montgomery. A new building adjacent to the new APLS facility is being planned to house this library service program.

Alabama Library Association (founded 1904)

Membership: 1,547; *Annual Expenditure:* $12,000.
President: George R. Stewart, Birmingham Public Library (April 1976 – March 1977).
Vice-President/President-elect: Mozelle Cummings, Alabama Public Library Service, Montgomery.
Second Vice-President: Sandra King, Lurleen Wallace State Junior College, Jasper.
Secretary: Julia Rotenberry, University of Montevallo.
Treasurer: Neil Snider, Livingston University.
Annual Meeting: April 7–9, 1976, Topeka.
Publication: The Alabama Librarian (bimonthly).

Alabama Public Library Service
Anthony Miele, Director
6030 Monticello Drive
Montgomery, Alabama 35130

Union Catalog. The Alabama Public Library Service announced plans to establish a cooperative union catalog for the libraries in Alabama. A grant will support the conversion to machine-readable form of the catalog records of Birmingham Public Library, the largest public library in the State. To this will be added the OCLC records used by the college and university libraries in the State who are members of SOLINET. From these tapes COM catalogs will be produced and deposited in a number of libraries throughout the State. The COM catalogs will be updated quarterly, and retroactive records from other libraries will continue to be added as they become available in machine-readable form.

WLRH-FM Public Radio, operated by the Huntsville-Madison County Public Library, began operation on October 13. It was the first of its kind in Alabama and will broadcast 18 hours a day within a prime radius of 75 miles.

School Libraries. A five-mill property tax passed by the citizens of Birmingham made possible the establishment of centralized libraries in all the system's elementary schools. In recognition of his successful efforts to upgrade the Birmingham school system, and particularly library service in the schools, Wilmer Cody, Superintendent of the Birmingham City School System, was awarded the Distinguished Library Service Award for School Administrators at the annual convention of the American Library Association.

In Montgomery a one-half cent sales tax aimed at supporting the accrediting of elementary and junior high schools has resulted in the employment of librarians for every school and the establishment of libraries in each school.

Efforts continued during the year to draft revised standards for school library certification. General agreement was reached on major issues by representatives of the Alabama Library Association and the Alabama Instructional Media Association who prepared a draft of suggested standards which has been presented to the deans of schools of education for approval.

College and University Libraries. For libraries in the state institutions of higher education it was a year of entrenchment, as state appropriations to higher education were reduced.

Six libraries completed their first year of use of the OCLC cataloging data base

State Reports—Alaska

through the Southeastern Library Network: the University of Alabama, the University of Alabama in Birmingham, Auburn University, the University of South Alabama, Troy State University, and Jacksonville State University. During the year Spring Hill College received a grant from the Kellogg Foundation to fund membership in SOLINET and purchase an OCLC cathode-ray-tube terminal.

Cooperation between college and public libraries was formalized by the agreement of SOLINET members to cooperate in the state union catalog sponsored by the Alabama Public Library Service.

Birmingham-Southern College dedicated in October the new Charles Andrew Rush Learning Center. Construction was underway at year's end for a new library for Miles College to be occupied sometime in the spring of 1977.

Library Education. The emphasis during the year 1976 definitely was on continuing education for librarians. Several conferences and workshops were well attended. Two of particular interest, sponsored by the Graduate School of Library Service at the University of Alabama, created considerable continuing education interest in the state. On April 30–May 1, a conference on the Library and the Young Adult featured Margaret Edwards, formerly Young Adult Coordinator at the Enoch Pratt Free Library. On May 10–11, the Graduate School of Library Service sponsored a Symposium on the Book Arts. Representatives from private presses, mostly in the southeastern United States, were featured speakers, and there were demonstrations of bookbinding, woodcutting, type design, calligraphy, and marbleizing. The Symposium was followed by a two-week Typographic Workshop giving instruction in typesetting and hand printing.

The School of Library Media at Alabama A & M University became the first single-purpose library school to be accredited by the ALA. It specializes in training school librarians.　　　　　PAUL H. SPENCE

ALASKA

Highlights. Library development by the end of 1976 included consolidation of several film collections in one statewide system operated from two centers; design of a program to produce a single union list of serials for the state; publication of the *Alaska Resources Directory;* concentrated effort to resolve the newspaper index problem, and significant improvement of library programs through grants for materials and facilities.

Alaska Library Association. Through its second Task Force on Library Development and Legislative priorities, the Association recommended greater use of micro-

Alaska Library Association
(founded 1960)

Membership: 299 (73 ALA members); Annual *Expenditure:* $5,000 (est.).
President: Marilyn Scott, Anchorage School District (March 1976–March 1977).
Vice-President/President-elect: Margie Thomas, West Valley High School, Fairbanks.
Secretary: Beverlee Weston (Anchorage Public Library), 777 Elm, Apt. 666, Anchorage, Alaska 99509.
Publication: The Sourdough (bimonthly).

Division of State Libraries
Richard B. Engen, Director
Pouch G. Capitol
Juneau, Alaska 99801

forms to decrease costs and increase access to resources; more support for local and regional libraries; standards, financial support and coordination for school libraries; access via satellite to data banks and other facets of on-line networking; establishment of a clearinghouse for media produced in and about Alaska; reaffirmation of the principle of statewide interlibrary cooperation; and a reemphasis on continuing education for library personnel. Many of the ensuing activities of the Association directly supported the recommendations. The annual conference in Juneau helped meet an identified continuing education need by offering as its program a government documents course for credit. *Cache for Alaska Reading,* 3rd edition, was published and distributed by the Association as a Bicentennial project. An honorary membership was awarded to Frosty Johnson upon her retirement from 30 years of service with the public library in Kodiak.

Advisory Council for Libraries. The Council undertook a study of problems connected with local or other funding support for library programs in new facilities and the possibility of a Governor's Conference on Libraries and Information Science. The Council also reviewed construction applicants under the general obligation bond program for community libraries and for Regional Resource Libraries, as well as overall planning and development of the statewide library program in its various parts.

Networking. The big effort in networking in 1976 was the publication of the *Alaska Resources Directory,* a computer produced catalog of the University of Alaska's Alaska collection produced in cooperation with the Washington Library Network. The *Directory* will be distributed in microfiche format to libraries in the state. Active planning took place in 1976, looking toward Alaska's libraries to go on-line to the WLN in 1977. Using networking in

the sense of using new technology for cooperative library services, other activities in the state included the installation of the state's first computer-based circulation system in the Fairbanks North Star Borough Library, the launching of the University of Alaska's statewide computer system with potential for libraries to be on-line to the main computer, a serious pursuit for satellite time for information transfer, and computer production of a state-wide union list of serials.

Networking in its broader sense of working together has seen an emphasis on continuing education needs, on the recommendations of the Governor's Committee on Management and Efficiency, on the orientation needs of new regional school boards and local school committees, and on strengthening of collections and services.

Construction. A major regional resource center in Fairbanks and some 18 community libraries were ready to be constructed at year's end thanks to the general obligation bond passed in 1974. Several more probably would be approved. The Fairbanks facility will be a 40,000-square-foot building housing a combined library system for the North Star Borough and the northern region of Alaska. A small auditorium, a skylight entrance with five 17-foot mature fig trees, an Alaska room with pegged oak floors, a rolled tin ceiling, and a large stone fireplace in the informal reading room are some of the special features. Communities receiving grants are as small as Eagle (1970 population of 34) and as large as Kodiak (approximately 4,000 population).

Continuing Education. Continuing education was reestablished as a priority by the Alaska Library Association and the Alaska State Library. The Association sent out 700 comprehensive forms to attempt a broad survey of Continuing Education needs in the state from beginning to postgraduate level. Results were being compiled at year's end and will provide the focus for Continuing Education efforts in the state both by the AkLA and Alaska State Library. The University of Alaska, Anchorage, and the Media Services Department offered graduate level courses in media development in 1976. The Rasmuson Library staff at the University of Alaska, Fairbanks, drafted plans for a two-year course for Library Technical Assistants. The first course was scheduled for the spring semester in 1977.

Media and Film Services. The Media Services Department at the University of Alaska's Anchorage branch was funded for the first time by the state legislature. The staff includes three professionals and clerical support. The U.A. Anchorage Library is producing videotape courses, among them courses in drafting and technology, in cooperation with the instructional facility. 16mm films in the state have been coordinated in collections for statewide use through the University of Alaska system and the Alaska State Library. The University's major center is at the Fairbanks campus; the Alaska State Film Library's two centers are in Anchorage and Juneau. The State Film Library has a combined total of 12,000 films, videotapes and videocassettes. Individuals, community libraries, and schools are eligible to use the film collection.

Rural School Reorganization. A major reorganization and redirection of education in the state occurred when the centralized state-operated rural school system was decentralized into 21 new rural school districts. The State Board of Education decided that local communities, regardless of size, would have local high schools if desired. The library community, aware of the almost complete lack of library and media materials and staff in the new school districts and new high schools, was working on that new area of concern in 1976.

Northern Libraries Colloquy. The 6th Northern Libraries Colloquy was held in July in Fairbanks. The Colloquy is an international meeting of librarians, administrators, and researchers whose library collections are either in the north or serve clientel with primary interest in the north. Approximately 70 participants from the U.S., Canada (Northwest Territory, Yukon Territory, Alberta, Ottawa, Newfoundland), Norway, Finland, and France attended the four-day meeting which focused on libraries and research in Alaska. In addition to formal sessions, participants toured a pipeline pump station, a musk ox farm, and a permafrost tunnel.

MARY MATTHEWS

ARIZONA

Visions '76. A major event of the year was the Arizona State Library Association's 50th anniversary celebration. ASLA was conceived on November 12, 1926, by a group of 24 interested persons who met in the Supreme Court Chamber of the Capitol Building in Phoenix to discuss library service for Arizona. In the Association's constitution adopted at a meeting the following May, the purpose of the organization was stated: "To extend the usefulness of libraries throughout the state, to work for state-wide library service, and to consider the problems of librarians within the state." ASLA celebrated the anniversary at the state conference held in Tucson. The theme of the conference, "Visions '76; A Look into the Past with a View to the Future," reflected Arizona librarians' contin-

Arizona State Library Association (founded 1926)

Membership: 958 (319 ALA members); Annual Expenditure: $20,000 (1975–76).
President: Coralie (Parsil) Wolf, Tucson Public Library (October 1976–September 1977).
Vice-President/President-elect: Sharon Womack, Maricopa County Library.
Secretary: Jane Julien, Northern Arizona University, 507 N. James, Flagstaff, Arizona 86001.
Annual Conference: September 30–October 3, 1976, Tucson.
Publication: ASLA Newsletter (monthly).

State Library, Archives, and Public Records Division

Marguerite B. Cooley, Assistant Director
3d Floor, State Capitol
Phoenix, Arizona 85007

ued interest in preserving the rich cultural heritage of the southwest and at the same time seeking new ways of improving library service throughout the state. Members of the Rio Grande Chapter of the Special Libraries Association joined ASLA members as conferees from Arizona, New Mexico, and California gathered for the occasion—which was designated a state Bicentennial event.

The conference program focused on the past with such noted writers as Alex Haley, author of *Roots* (1976) and Lawrence Clark Powell, well known expert on southwest literature and history. Looking to the future, conference participants heard discussions regarding video applications in libraries and current problems in library service faced by publishers, and attended programs on censorship in schools and libraries. Workshops dealt with continuing education, government documents, children's literature, young adult services, automated bibliographical control, employment, lobbying, indexing and abstracting, games and simulation, and multicultural perspectives in literature for children and young adults. At the close of the conference the outgoing ASLA President, Mary Choncoff, announced that her goal of 1,000 ASLA members had been reached.

Continuing Education. If it can be said that two main themes characterized activities throughout the state during the year, they were extending library services and promoting library education. Many organizations were active in the support of continuing education for librarians. The faculty and staff of the Graduate Library School of the University of Arizona made a serious effort to support continuing education through a series of workshops, colloquiums, and conferences. These efforts were directed to professionals in the southwest as well as to enrolled graduate students of the University of Arizona.

Donald C. Dickinson, Director of the Library School in Tucson, noted, "Since the Graduate Library School is the only accredited program in a wide geographical area, continuing education is an obligation which we must continue to pursue." In addition to the workshops, which covered diverse topics, including television in libraries and proposal writing, the Library School sponsored notable colloquium speakers. They included Edwin Castagna, former Director of the U.C.L.A. Library; Bozo Tezak, Director of the Center of Documentation of the University of Zagreb; Robert Hayes, Dean of the U.C.L.A. Library School; Joseph Becker, author and member of the National Commission on Libraries; Paul Janaske, U.S. Office of Education; John Ayala, President of REFORMA, and Bessie Moore, member of NCLIS. The School created a new Continuing Education committee headed by Helen Gothberg, a faculty member. Committee members represent various areas of librarianship from within the southeast corner of the state. It will act as an advisory committee to the school and will coordinate efforts with other state and regional continuing education committees.

The Arizona State Library and its active arm, Library Extension Service (LES), also worked hard in 1976 to provide a large number of educational workshops throughout the state. Workshops covered a variety of library skills and attitude-related topics—among them were interlibrary loan, young adult services, adult services, cataloging, Indian services and materials, and planning a public relations program.

The School Library Divisions of the State Association had a busy year under the leadership of the SLD president, Jo Nell Roberts. Guest speakers cosponsored by the Division and the Arizona State Department of Education included Theodore Taylor, author of the *Cay*, and Gerald McDermott, winner of the 1975 Caldecott Award for *Arrow to the Sun*. In February the Division sponsored an idea exchange and community resources demonstration in Phoenix. That workshop included everything from snake handlers to puppeteers. In April a three-day conference on The Artist Within You was held in Tucson and represented the cooperative efforts of the Arizona Commission on the Arts and Humanities, the Department of Education, and the Graduate Library School with the School Libraries Division. The purpose of the creative arts forum was to help stimulate creativity in the schools through the library media center. Participating artists included Betty Baker, western writer; Christopher Cerf, Children's Television Workshop and author; Pamela Douglas, filmmaker and television producer; Richard Howard, poet and Pulitzer prize winner; Charles Loloma, Hopi artist and Indian philosopher; Robin Sandefur, Radio-TV-Film Bureau, University of Arizona; Ramona Weeks, co-publisher and co-editor of the Baleen Press; and participants from the Invisible Theater of Tucson.

Other committees and round tables of the Association also sponsored workshops throughout the year including the Government Documents Round Table and the Continuing Education Committee.

Extended Services. Networking and cooperative programs which have extended library materials and services were also emphasized during the year in Arizona due in part to the encouragement of both state and federal grants. With the assistance of LES of the State Library, six libraries in the state became actively involved with the Community Reading Development Project. This project involved each library's working hand in hand with the community's Right-To-Read Coordinator and training volunteer teachers to work with adult non-readers in the library. Marguerite Cooley, State Librarian, reported that the program, along with one which involved locating homebound library patrons, met with so much interest and success that they would be continued for another year.

Adult and children's services have long been the mainstay of public libraries in Arizona; however, the young adult reader became the target of some much deserved interest and new programming in 1976. A number of young adult librarians have been added to public library staffs, including Mesa Public Library, which along with hiring a YA librarian through a federal LSCA Transition Quarter grant added a YA "People Pit." Tucson Public Library continued to lead the way with an impressive NEH-funded program called "Childhood's End? Growing up in the 70's." The showpiece of this effort was a video production featuring candid interviews with young adults across the spectrum of economic and social backgrounds. Topics on which these young people sounded off included education, sex, morality, and authority. Libraries in Casa Grande, Phoenix, and Yuma are also providing improved young adult services.

Worthy of note is the cooperation of many libraries to improve services and extend information in Region I of the state, which includes the Phoenix area. In this region plans are developing toward the possibility of a county-wide borrowers' card and shared cataloging or a possible regional transportation system for purposes of interlibrary loan or both. In the southwest corner of the state with its sparse population, Yuma City-County Library is finding lots of business coming its way through the year-old Books by Mail program. A second project of this library is its telephone stories—one in English and one in Spanish. Yuma has been granted permission to serve not only Arizona residents but also those in nearby California. It is the first library in Arizona—and possibly the southwest—to cross a state line to improve its service patterns. Finally, the Arizona Numeric Register (ANR) is starting to take shape as some 25 libraries begin to use this fiche-produced union list of materials entered by LC number. With the addition of all of Tucson Public Library's holdings, ANR currently provides union cataloging and locations for most of the public libraries in the state. Next to be entered in this list are the holdings of the three major Arizona university libraries.

Buildings. The year 1976 brought some good results in facility improvement for the State Library. The Library Extension Service moved to leased new quarters. The space for the Library for the Blind and the Physically Handicapped was doubled. In addition, Arizona finally saw the completion of its regional library system with the final building and staffing of the Greenlee County Library. Also completed for public libraries during 1976 was the addition of 61,500 feet to the main library of Phoenix Public. The major building event of the year, however, was the new library of the University of Arizona. The old library building, constructed in 1923, opened its doors for the last time on December 18. It has been replaced by a library over three times its size. The new $12,000,000 building had been under construction for three and one-half years. Although called the University Library, it is essentially the social sciences and humanities library. The older Science Library and some other collections such as the Graduate Library School Library will remain as separately housed collections. In addition to the library materials in the social sciences and humanities, the new library will also include space for government documents, nonbook media, special collections, and the technical services and administrative offices of the library system. Features of the building include a central reference area, current periodical reading room, individual carrels, and private and small group study rooms.

Grants. In addition to state and federally funded projects mentioned, the Graduate Library School of the University of Arizona received two grants from the U.S. Office of Education. The first was for a year-long Graduate Institute for Spanish-speaking American students. This highly successful project, tagged the GLISA Program, was under the direction of Arnulfo Trejo and Robert Johnson. A second grant was received by the School for a research study which developed and tested an audio-tutorial program for a course in basic reference.

Legislation. The most significant legislation passed at the state level in Arizona was State Library Bill HB 2356. The result of this law was to change the administrative control of the Arizona Department of Library, Archives and Public Records from the Governor back to the legislature. Included in this law was a section establishing a state-wide library depository system. Arizona librarians have, in addition, been actively working through the State Library to obtain state legislative funding for the provision of qualified staffing for its seven correctional institutions. Although these institutions have some minimal library service, either directly or indirectly through the state interlibrary loan network, effective service remained wanting at year-end.

Arizona and other southwest librarians indicated that they intend to take on Ma Bell. The telephone company announced its decision to discontinue the practice allowing public libraries to list their service hours in the white pages of the telephone directory. The decision would affect public libraries in seven states.

White House Conference. As in many other states, Arizona is laying the ground work for the long awaited White House Conference on Libraries and Information services by establishing a blue-ribbon panel to organize and stage a Governor's Conference. Arizona librarians stood ready at year's end to meet with neighbors and colleagues to play their own role: to extend the usefulness of libraries throughout the nation, to work for nation-wide library service, and to consider the problems of librarians throughout the nation.

HELEN GOTHBERG

ARKANSAS

Personnel Certification. As in other parts of the country, a growing area of concern in Arkansas is that of certification of school media personnel. Because of this concern an implementation workshop on certification was held in September, directed by three members of the national certification committee of the American Association of School Librarians. The purpose was to evaluate existing librarian and media specialist certification in Arkansas by comparing it to national and regional trends and emphases in certification. The group reached consensus on the following points: (1) certification in Arkansas needs revision; (2) certification should represent a unified library science educational media concept; (3) multiple levels of entry should be designed to allow for beginning, intermediate, and advanced competency levels; (4) certification should

Arkansas Library Association
(founded 1911)

Membership: 1,085; *Annual Expenditure:* $23,000 (1976).
President: Richard Reid, University of Arkansas at Fayetteville (January 1, 1976–December 31, 1976).
Vice-President/President-elect: Cassie (Mrs. Bill) Brothers, Helena-West Helena Public Schools.
Executive Secretary: Katherine Stanick, 701 North McAdoo Street, Little Rock, Arkansas 72205.
Annual Conference: September 26–28, 1976, Hot Springs.
Publication: Arkansas Libraries (quarterly).

Arkansas Library Commission
Frances Neal, Librarian
506½ Center Street
Little Rock, Arkansas 72201

be at least partially competency based.

A task force has been formed to continue to develop a proposal for revised certification standards.

The Southwestern Library Association continues to be of importance to Arkansas Librarians. More than 40 attended the Biennial Conference in Albuquerque in November. Richard Reid, assistant librarian, University of Arkansas, Fayetteville, was elected president of the SLICE council.

Years of effort by many people to secure a state library building culminated November 16 when construction of a new building to house the Arkansas Library Commission, history and archives, began. Occupancy is promised for August 1978.

ALA Activities. The Arkansas Library Association in 1976 opened a headquarters office for the first time in the 65-year history of the organization. The office was dedicated March 1 in the Little Rock Public Library.

A memorial scholarship fund was established during 1976 to honor Allie Beth Martin, President of the American Library Association, and Constance Mitchell, retired librarian at Arkansas State Teachers College. Both died during 1976.

The Public Library Division of the Arkansas Library Association, cooperating with the Arkansas Library Commission and the University of Central Arkansas, sponsored a Government Documents in Public Libraries workshop in August. Gladys Sachse was Director.

Edward Holley, Past President of the American Library Association, was featured speaker at the annual conference of the Arkansas Library Association September 26–28. William D. North, attorney and counsel for the Freedom to Read Foundation, spoke at the opening general session on "Copyright Legislation and Its Effect on Libraries." The conference was in Hot Springs.

People. Frances Nix, Hendrix College Librarian, was named Deputy Director of the Arkansas Library Commission June 1. Betty Jean Morgan of North Little Rock has been named Supervisor of school library programs for the State Department of Education.

Sue Morgan, immediate Past President of the Arkansas Library Association, became media specialist for the Pulaski County Special School District July 1. Three Arkansas Library Association members serve on the Woman's National Book Association: Jane Cazort, Little Rock; Mary Sue Shepherd, Central Arkansas Library System; and Mary Gaver, President.

Guy DiBenedetto resigned as Chairman of the Reference Division to accept a position at Auburn University. Juana Young assumed the responsibility for the Association. She is a member of the library system at the University of Arkansas, Fayetteville.

Lauren D. Carter was named to succeed Verna Evans, who retired as Supervisor of Libraries for Little Rock Public Schools.

Velma Lee Adams retired as head librarian at Southern State College in June. She was succeeded by Bruce D. Robinson.

George M. Zumwalt assumed the position of Chief of Library Service at the Little Rock and North Little Rock VA Hospitals. Mary Virginia Taylor was named Medical Librarian. Mary Elizabeth Upton retired as Chief of Library Services at the Veterans Administration Hospital Library in April. Blanche Miller, Medical Librarian at the institution, retired in July.

Deaths. Adolphine Fletcher Terry, long a member of the Arkansas Library Commission, died July 25.

Hester Smith, trustee of Hot Spring County Library, died at Malvern, Arkansas. Rogers Moore, trustee of Faulkner–Van Buren Regional Library, died January 2. Norma Cecilia Gitelman of Fayetteville, a librarian at the University of Arkansas, died February 10. Margaret Moore Jacobs, a life member of the Arkansas Library Association, and a contributor to the construction of the Clarendon Library named for her, died February 16.

ALICE GRAY

CALIFORNIA

The Past Is Prologue. As in every year, the achievements, the hopes, the programs, the efforts made or attempted grew out of earlier achievements, hopes, programs, or efforts made or attempted. In California during 1976 three or four major efforts were made by the California Library Association and the California State Library. Some of these were cooperative efforts, others working in parallel, obeying, it was hoped, the laws of perspective by converging in the distance on a prescribed goal.

Public Library Services Act. The major effort by both organizations was a rewriting of the time-honored and now time-serving Public Library Services Act. The basic benefits of this program were the distribution of parsimonious state funds granted to public library jurisdictions that had formed cooperative systems with other public libraries.

For some time the California Department of Finance had been less than happy with the automatic per capita funding which the act prescribed as the sole distribution formula. The hard-headed and light-handed Department of Finance has kept the annual funding at about $1,000,000 even though the original legislation had a built-in formula that would have allowed an amount of almost ten times that amount (based on growing matching percentages of local public library expenditures).

In an effort to insure more adequate state funding and to allieviate some diverse opinions about the distribution of these funds to California Libraries, the State Library under an HEW grant sponsored a one-week Library Planning Institute in San Francisco just before the Annual ALA Conference in 1975. About one hundred participants representing a cross-section of librarians of all types of libraries, trustees, friends, and government officials discussed the present state funding and tried to devise a consensus formula or proposal that might receive more sympathetic state legislative attention and be widely accepted by the California library community.

During the early part of 1976 a draft document was developed by an augment-

California Library Association
(founded 1895)

Membership 3,400; *Annual Expenditure:* $215,000 (1976).
President: Gilbert W. McNamee, Bay Area Reference Center, San Francisco Public Library (1976).
Vice-President/President-elect; June D. Fleming, Palo Alto Public Library (1976).
Executive Secretary: Stefan B. Moses, Suite 300, 717 K St., Sacramento, California 95814.
Annual Conference: December 2–6, 1976, Los Angeles.
Publications: California Librarian (quarterly); *CLA Newsletter* (monthly).

California State Library
Ethel S. Crockett, State Librarian
P.O. Box 2037,
Sacramento, California 95809

State Reports—California

ed Government Relations Committee of CLA. During July and August six widely publicized meetings were held throughout the state to give the public a chance to express opinions on the document.

Basically the new proposals would bring in the possibility of funding for other types of publicly supported libraries. A basic per capita formula for municipal and county public library systems remains but additional funding would be provided for each filled interlibrary loan within the system and grants to libraries would be available if they were burdened by over-the-counter borrowing by citizens of other system members. In addition cooperative systems would have advisory boards of lay persons with minority representation guaranteed in those service areas having such minority groups. Finally, the new proposal provided for statewide services through two state reference centers: one at the Los Angeles Public Library, called SCAN (Southern California Answering Network), and one at the San Francisco Public Library, called BARC (Bay Area Reference Center). The state centers were to be charged with making reciprocal or contractual agreements with all types of libraries to make available interlibrary exchange of information for the benefit of the state's population. The proposed plan recognized that full contemporary library service requires that individual libraries need to be able to call on a vast array of resources and services if their constituency is to be properly served. This recognition requires a universal sense of vision, a Picasso-like ability to look at a flat frame of reference and see full-sided figures. It is not, perhaps, an easy angle of vision to acquire.

The consensus, as reported from these meetings, was presented to the Council (the governing body) of the California Library Association at a September meeting. Council well represented membership in not being able to come to entire agreement at that meeting. A special committee had to be formed to report "recommendations on certain portions of the draft plan" at a November Council meeting. Basically the crucial unresolved question was funding for single-member systems. Under the PLSA funding in 1976 there were five single-member systems (Kern County, Long Beach, Los Angeles City, Los Angeles County, and the City and County of San Francisco). The original draft document dropped any proposed funding for these single-member systems believing that cooperation meant cooperating with someone other than oneself. Los Angeles City in particular spoke of actively opposing any proposals that did not recognize its uniqueness and have prescribed funding. The special committee as a compromise recommended "grandfathering" these systems into the new proposals and the November meeting of Council accepted the amended draft document.

All this work was preliminary to the forwarding of the proposal to the 1977 California Legislature meeting in January.

CLASS. A major effort reaching fruition during 1976 was the California Library Authority for Systems and Services (CLASS). Persons attending the 1975 ALA San Francisco Conference might have noticed buttons proclaiming, "California Has CLASS." It didn't have CLASS—yet. The progress of this authority, slouching around Sacramento waiting to be born, could be followed through memos in various numbers of a California State Library publication, *From the State Librarian's Desk*. The basic document covering CLASS is a joint powers agreement. It was signed on June 17 in Los Angeles after over two years of planning. The signatories were Wilson Riles, California Superintendent of Public Instruction (represented at the ceremony by Ethel S. Crockett, California State Librarian), David Saxon, President of the University of California, Mayor Tom Bradley of the City of Los Angeles, Supervisor Dan McCorquodale of the County of Santa Clara (represented at the ceremony by Supervisor Rodney Diridon), and Robert Burnham, Superintendent of the Grossmont Community College, Mayor Bradley said on the occasion of the signing, "We are all here celebrating this morning but the people who should really celebrate are the users." It was announced at the CLA annual conference that Richard Miller, formerly of NELINET, had been appointed Director of CLASS starting early in 1977.

This newly formed entity is nowhere mentioned in the proposed draft legislation for new state library support. Its concurrent development gave some librarians great hope and some librarians great fear. CLASS is designed as a service organization for libraries of all types, academic, public, business and institutional. Eventual financing is to be on a fee basis for services supplied but there is a possibility of the necessity for interim financing from public fund sources. If the fees do not raise the necessary monies, possible future additional financing from public funds might also be required. Hopes are generated because such an overall authority might actually develop a real state-wide system of consortia that would bring all the bibliographic resources of the state to all the libraries of the state. Fears are generated because the already totally inadequate state funding of public library systems might be further diluted and federal LSCA funds might possibly be diverted.

Studies. Two studies undertaken during 1976 have potential importance to libraries and librarianship—not only in California but also throughout the United States. One was begun through the auspices of the California State Library, which has signed with the Sacramento-based Selection Consulting Center to develop guidelines on the position of beginning librarian. The Center is to undertake a task analysis of the duties outlined by various participating library jurisdictions in describing the routines performed in a beginning librarian position. Some 15 public libraries including the California State Library are taking part in the study. Some libraries have voiced reservations about the validity and reliablity of the study. The basic question is of paramount importance when the profession hears of "alternative career ladders" (*i.e.*, non-M.L.S. requirements) for beginning professional positions. One such alternative was developed by the Sacramento City-County Library System, which now has an "equivalency of experience or other education" as sufficient for possible promotion into the professional ranks. Harold Martelle, City-County Librarian, explained this development as an answer to a particular population growth in a service area originally served by two separate governmental jurisdictions. It was formulated on an equivalency examination to give some persons who have had years of service an equal opportunity to compete for beginning professional positions. A new organization, Concerned Librarians Opposed to Unprofessional Trends (CLOUT), has appeared and is vocal in insisting that the 5th year graduate degree in library science is the only viable road for entrance into the profession. In view of the general library job shortage as well as demands associated with Title VII of the Civil Rights Act of 1964, with Executive Order 11246 of 1965, and with the resulting affirmative action programs pushing for alternative career ladders, the matter is a convoluted one. An article in the *California Librarian*, October 1975, by Henry Garland is an excellent introduction into the complexities.

Professional Standards. Concurrent with the Center's study is the report of the Committee on Professional Standards of the California Society of Librarians, a constituent organization of CLA. The report proposes a method of activation of legislation already in the laws of the State of California allowing for the development of a certified list of librarians. Reservations about this document were expressed at the annual Conference of CLA and further action is still pending. CLA membership did take action on a draft Statement of Professional Responsibility for Librarians accepting only the principles stated in the document.

Continuing Education. One aspect of

librarianship in California should be mentioned (recognizing that it is not unique to the state): the many, many opportunities offered for continuing education. It would require pages to list the many opportunities that are available in almost all regions of the state throughout the year for attendance at seminars, symposia, colloquies, workshops, and minicourses. Librarians wishing to take advantage of some of these programs at whatever their staff level need, of course, the encouragement and recognition of their administration and governing bodies if good to excellent library service in the state is to become the norm.

So the nation's Bicentennial year saw those concerned with library service in California cooperating, studying, planning, pleading, seeking, fighting and working together, sometimes simultaneously, over and with and for the limited available funds to bring the best possible service to their constituents. The year 1976 also saw important efforts and proposals inching along to bring all the library resources and services that are available in the state—and in the nation—to all the library users of the state.

WILLIAM L. EMERSON

COLORADO

Statewide Library Program. *Libraries Colorado: A Plan for Development,* approved by the State Board of Education in 1975, was printed and distributed in 1976. The State Library began implementation of this long-range plan by guiding the growth of regional library service systems from public library cooperatives to legally established systems with membership of school districts, academic, public, and special libraries. In one year, the number of members of the seven systems increased from 112 to 279.

A key strategy in the implementation of *Libraries Colorado* is the formulation of a networking plan for Colorado. A network coordinator was hired for the first time by the State Library. Virginia Boucher, Interlibrary Loan Librarian at the University of Colorado, took a one-year leave of absence to draft the networking plan and monitor on-going networking projects. The integration of on-going projects into a structure was a principal focus for the networking plan. Two current Colorado Library Network projects include Payment for Lending and the Information and Communication Network. Payment for Lending was funded for $114,000 for 1976–77 by the Colorado General Assembly to reimburse libraries for interlibrary loan. Information and Communication Network is an $85,000 LSCA I project administered by the Colorado State Library and the Bibliographical Center for Research. Using com-

Colorado Library Association
(founded 1892)

Membership: 800; *Annual Expenditure:* $35,000.
President: Harriet Lute, Englewood Public Library
Vice-President/President-elect: Ron Stump, High Plains Regional Library System, Greeley.
Executive Secretary: Eleanor Baker, 1727 S. Nile Court, Aurora, Colorado 80012.
Annual Conference: October 17–21, 1976, Colorado Springs.
Publication: Colorado Libraries (quarterly).

Colorado State Library

Anne Marie Falsone, Assistant Commissioner, Office of Library Services
1362 Lincoln
Denver, Colorado 80203

puter terminals in six locations in the state, the libraries can offer computerized information retrieval at a low cost to their patrons. The terminals are also used to communicate interlibrary loan requests. A major portion of the project was a series of 10 workshops throughout the state to demonstrate to over 200 library personnel how computers could be used to improve reference services.

Another key project begun in 1976 is the Colorado Index Project. Funded with LSCA, Title I, an indexed checklist to Colorado State Publications is being produced quarterly, providing the first index to Colorado state documents. The long-range plan called for the development of guidelines for public libraries. These are currently being drafted by the State Library.

People. Anne Marie Falsone, formerly Supervisor of Title IV-B of the Elementary and Secondary Education Act of the Colorado Department of Education, was named Assistant Commissioner, Office of Library Services. Falsone is the first woman to be appointed to an assistant commissioner position in the Department of Education. She assumed her position as head of the State Library in September 1976.

Several library directors were appointed for Colorado's academic libraries. They included Claude J. Johns, Jr., at the University of Northern Colorado in Greeley; Donald E. Riggs at the Auraria Higher Education Center; Ray Anderton at the Auraria Media Center; Beverly Moore at the University of Southern Colorado in Pueblo; and Major Benjaman C. Glidden at the Air Force Academy.

New Facilities. Three major new libraries were dedicated in 1976. The Learning Resources Center of the Auraria Higher Education Center opened to serve the students and faculty of the University of Colorado at Denver, the Community College of Denver-Auraria, and Metropolitan State College. The building covers one entire city block and covers 185,000 square feet. The new public library in Fort Collins was built at a cost of $1,600,000 and opened in the fall of 1976.

Jefferson County opened a new public library headquarters and branch in Lakewood. The $1,650,000 facility houses the administration and processing departments of the county operation as well as serving Lakewood patrons with over 150,000 library materials.

New buildings or additions were also opened by the Sterling, Douglas County, Jackson County, La Veta, and Adams County Public Libraries.

Professional Associations. The Colorado Association of School Librarians and the Colorado Audio-Visual Association joined forces in 1976 to form the Colorado Educational Media Association. Bettie Helser of the University of Colorado at Denver became the Association's first President.

The Colorado Library Association assumed a more active role in legislative action by retaining a legislative advocate to help carry out the CLA legislative program.

The Colorado Chapter of the Special Library Association hosted the 67th Annual Conference of the Special Libraries Association. Approximately 2,500 librarians and information specialists attended the national conference.

Joint School/Public Libraries. Increased interest in combining school and public libraries was expressed in Colorado's rural areas. Cripple Creek and Fort Lupton opened new facilities that combined the high school and public libraries in new high school buildings. Several other communities are exploring the idea as a way to get maximum benefit from limited resources in communities of low population density.

Encyclopaedia Britannica Award. Arapahoe County School District 6 in Littleton was awarded the Encyclopaedia Britannica–American Association of School Librarians Award for excellence in media centers. The district completed a long-range plan of improvement in media which included having a professional librarian/media specialist in each elementary school.

ANNE MARIE FALSONE

CONNECTICUT

Advisory Groups. The State Library Board's two citizen advisory groups continued their work during 1976. One of these groups, created by state legislation in 1975, is the interagency library planning committee, of not more than 25 persons, to "aid the State Library Board in planning for statewide library service, other than

State Reports—Connecticut

Connecticut Library Association
(founded 1891)

Membership: 902 (170 ALA members); *Annual Expenditure:* $35,000.
President: Dency Sargent, Capitol Region Library Council, Hartford. (July 1, 1976–June 30, 1977).
Vice-President/President-elect: Virginia Dowell, New Britain Public Library.
Association Secretary: Patti Bandolin, Colebrook Stage, Winsted, Connecticut 06098.
Annual Meeting: April 29–30, 1976, New Haven.
Publications: CLA Memo (10 issues a year); *Connecticut Libraries* (quarterly).

Connecticut State Library

Charles Funk, Jr., State Librarian
231 Capitol Avenue
Hartford, Connecticut 06115

for school libraries, by discussing, comparing, evaluating, and recommending plans and courses of action." School libraries are excepted because they are under jurisdiction of the Department of Education in Connecticut.

The second state advisory body is the Cooperating Library Service Units Review Board (CLSURB). Members are appointed by the State Librarian to "establish criteria for and promote development of a system of cooperating library service units," according to the 1975 legislation that created the body. The Review Board submitted a grant proposal, "Program for the Development of Regional Library Service Units and the Initiation of Planning for a Connecticut Library Network," calling for use of LSCA Funds ($600,000) to establish the units and to fund them for three years.

The law describes the Unit and its purpose: "Library Service Unit: an entity providing library and information service from an organized body of recorded knowledge which may be in the form of books, periodicals, audio or video recordings on film, disc or tape; machine-stored information or knowledge preserved in any other recorded form, and which service was created and continues to exist for the purpose of transmitting such knowledge to mankind." The Review Board has also recommended that "the interagency library planning committee undertake the design of a statewide planning effort."

Residency Requirement. One of the state's largest public libraries, Bridgeport, was threatened by a residency requirement that would have forced 14 library employees to move into the city of Bridgeport or quit. The issue went to the courts, and was still in litigation at year's end. In New Haven the library board adopted a policy giving preference to residents; and the Hartford city government moved to require all city employees to live in the city. The policy had not yet been adopted by the public library, however. The library is an association, not a city department.

The state's county law libraries were transferred to the State Library in July. Because of budget cutbacks, the State Library was forced in October to reduce hours of service of its state-wide telephone information service, *Library Line,* from six days a week to five, and from 68 hours a week to 40. The State Library's reciprocal borrowing plan ("Connecticard") showed an increase in the flow of materials among libraries during the year.

Budget Problems. The larger public libraries continued to be plagued by budget problems. In Hartford the allocation was approximately $200,000 more than in 1975, but the level was still not back to what it was in 1974. The Hartford Library is still on a restricted schedule: 56 hours a week for the main library and an average of 28 hours for branches, compared with the normal 68 and 44.

The Bridgeport library had only about $13,000 more than in the previous year's budget and continued to have a number of vacancies. The New Haven library lost seven positions in its budget, but has been allowed to fill those in the budget in contrast with prior years when as many as 25 percent of the jobs were frozen or laid off.

Buildings. Several new buildings were completed in 1976. The library on the campus of Connecticut College in New London was moved into a new 100,000-square-foot building during the summer. Designed by the firm of Kitham Beder and Chu of New York, the building cost $6,217,000, has a book capacity of 550,000 volumes, and seats 565 readers. The Librarian is Brian Rogers. Kurt Vonnegut spoke at the dedication in September.

The new Milford Public Library building was opened in July, concluding a ten-year campaign to replace an 80-year-old building. The new library has 39,000 square feet and cost $2,040,000. The book capacity is 158,000 and there are seats for 291 readers. Book use increased 64 percent during the first four months in the new quarters, compared with the same four months in the old building. The Librarian, Stanley Carman, noted that this record was made with the same book collection; "people just could not find the books in the overcrowded stacks in the old building," he said.

When the new building for the Windsor Public Library was opened in January, hundreds of local residents turned out on a Saturday to move the library's 35,000 volumes from the nearby temporary library "in a manner reminiscent of the British bucket brigades to put out fires," according to the local news account.

The event was under the direction of the Town Manager, who commented: "I can't believe it! It's working!" Governor Ella T. Grasso, a resident of nearby Windsor Locks, turned up for the move, and members of the town council and the town clerk were part of the human chain that transported books from one building to another. The highest temperature recorded during the day was 12°F. A local fast-food restaurant gave out more than 1,000 free meal tickets to volunteers, in addition to hundreds of gallons of coffee and other beverages. The new Windsor building cost $1,500,000 and occupies 23,000 square feet.

Construction of a library at the University of Connecticut in Storrs, begun in the summer of 1975, continued in 1976; completion was expected in 1977. Planned space of 400,000 square feet will make the largest building on campus. Total book capacity will be two million volumes with reader seats for 3,000. Estimated project cost was $19,000,000.

Other new buildings under construction in 1976 were the following: Groton, 24,600 square feet, construction cost $988,990, completion date May 1977; Westbrook, 12,000 square feet, $395,000, spring 1977; and Guilford, 15,000-square-foot addition, $754,000, 1977.

The public library in Stamford, the Ferguson Library, hired Warner, Burns, Tome and Lunde of New York City to design an addition of 41,000 square feet and to renovate the library's present 40,000 square feet. Proposed cost was estimated at $5,750,000.

A 20,000-square-foot addition to the New London public library was completed at a cost of about $1,000,000 and in neighboring Waterford an addition of 7500 square feet was completed at a cost of $679,015.

An 8,000-square-foot addition to the Terryville Public Library was dedicated in February. Residents contributed more than $500,000 toward the cost of the structure, connected to the 2,700-square-foot original building.

People. Elinor M. Hashim, Director of the Welles-Turner Memorial Library in Glastonbury, was elected in July to succeed Judge Raymond E. Baldwin as Chairperson of the State Library Board. Judge Baldwin, a former United States Senator, Governor, and Chief Justice of the State Supreme Court, has chaired the Board since it had been organized in 1965. Hashim was formerly a reference librarian in the Manchester and New Britain public libraries. She is a member of the Manchester board of education.

Degi Jennings became the first "female chairperson in the history of the library committee of the New Britain Institute" in March, according to the *New Britain Herald*. She is a teacher in the New Britain schools, and is active in other community organizations.

Leanor Wexler was elected President of the New Haven Board of Library Directors in 1975, becoming that Board's first woman to hold the post.

Nina T. Cohen, Associate Director of Libraries for Public Services at the University of Washington, was named Caleb T. Winchester Librarian at Weslyan University in July. She succeeded Wyman W. Parker, who has retired. Cohen had held her former position since 1973. For six years beginning in 1967, she was Director of the Western New York Library Resources Council in Buffalo and was an adjunct faculty member at the State University of New York (Buffalo) School of Information and Library Studies. She was previously associated with university and public libraries in Buffalo and Tonawanda, N. Y.

Marie V. Hurley retired in August after 22 years in the Ferguson (public) Library of Stamford; the past 11 years as director of the library. She is a Past-President of the Connecticut Library Association and former member of the ALA Council. She was active in many state and community projects.

Ernest Di Mattia, formerly Director of the Half Hollow Hills Library in Long Island, became Ferguson Library (Stamford) Director in October.

Joyce Hubbard, former Southington Public Library Director, sued that town in July for $180,000 in damages, and sought instatement as head of the library. She claimed that she was dismissed from her position in 1975, "wrongfully and improperly." She seeks back pay and $150,000 punitive damages. The suit had not been tried as of year's end. — MEREDITH BLOSS

DELAWARE

State Conventions. The Delaware Library Association and the Delaware Learning Resources Association convened jointly at Rehoboth Beach during the weekend of October 9, 1976. The two groups, in which several individuals have dual membership, had met together occasionally in one-day meetings. The longer convention was planned in response to suggestions from the members. Delaware's size makes overnight stays unnecessary, and the change may be a sign of professional growth.

Alice B. Ihrig, Chairperson of the White House Conference Planning Committee for ALA, was the keynote speaker at the dinner meeting opening the convention. The program included a visit to the College of Marine Studies at Lewes with a tour of the outdoor marine study station and the

Delaware Library Association
(founded 1934)

Membership: 167; *Annual Expenditure:* $1900.

President: John C. Painter, Delaware Technical and Community College, Georgetown, Delaware (April 1976 – March 1977).

Vice-President/President-elect: Daniel Coons, Delaware State College.

Secretary: Barbara Weeks, Newcastle Public Library System; 2306 Jamica Drive, Kingsridge, Wilmington, Delaware 19810.

Annual Conference: April 1976, Dover, Delaware.

Publication: Delaware Library Association Bulletin (quarterly).

Division of Libraries
Mrs. Rusby, Office Manager
P.O. Box 635
W. Loockerman Street
Dover, Delaware 19901

seagoing research ship. Melvin Zisfein, Deputy Director of the new National Air and Space Museum of the Smithsonian Institution, described the planning and offerings of the museum.

Both DLA and DLRA held separate meetings in Dover in the spring of 1976. Fran Andrews, Coordinator of Community Relations, Delaware Technical and Community College, instructed the DLA group in ways to improve public relations. Congressman Pierre duPont, who later was elected governor of Delaware, also addressed the meeting and pledged his support for libraries.

At the spring meeting of DLRA, Nancy Nelson, director of a project at Newark High School on cable utilization, presented a program titled "The Single Television System in the Educational Environment." Techniques of television production in schools were demonstrated with a videotape player. A reading specialist demonstrated an innovative reading program for secondary schools that utilizes video cassettes of current TV shows to motivate and develop reading skills. Students in the project manage, produce programs, form crews, and publicize their own cable TV station.

DLA and Brandywine College cosponsored a Learner's Advisory Seminar held at the college in June for the College Entrance Examination Board. Approximately 25 directors or key decision makers of small or medium sized libraries attended. The Library Study Project of CEEB aims to identify and describe services for adult independent learners, to encourage participation by public libraries, and to provide libraries with training in planning, implementing, and evaluating these programs.

Continuing Education. In addition to the workshops of the library associations, DLA and Delaware Technical and Community College sponsored a series of Saturday programs. The workshops were directed by Helen Barnett, Librarian at the Stanton campus of the college. The first program, "Coping with the Economic Crunch," was led by Ernest DeProspo of the Graduate School of Library Service, Rutgers University. His presentation focused on the application of business techniques to library management. The second program, "Improving Communications between Library Staff, Clientele and Administration," was conducted by Sarah Fine and James Williams of the Graduate School of Library and Information Science, University of Pittsburgh. They discussed barriers to effective communication and the means of overcoming them. "Inter-Library Cooperation" was the subject of the address by Elizabeth Hoffman, Dean of the Library School at Villanova University, given at the final workshop in the series. Discussion centered on matters of interlibrary cooperation relevant to Delaware.

Encouraged by the interest in these workshops, the Library Development Committee of DLA planned to hold another seminar in 1977.

Public Relations. Steps have been taken in local libraries to improve public relations through better communication. The New Castle County libraries provided timely information on the busing issue which arose over the court ordered desegregation plan for the Wilmington city schools. Information centers with retrospective and current newspaper clippings, copies of proposed desegregation plans, directories of involved community groups and government officials, private school catalogs and other pertinent materials were made available in each of the six libraries in the system.

The Milford Public Library developed radio spot announcements advertising library services. Effective publicity resulted from the distribution of paper place mats to local area restaurants and snack bars.

A survey had indicated that only 25 to 29 percent of the state's population use public libraries (*The Library Listens – Delaware Library Association Survey, 1973*, Division of Urban Affairs, University of Delaware, Newark, Delaware, 1974). DLA undertook a public awareness campaign beginning with an exhibit at the Delaware State Fair. Major support for the project came from the Division of Libraries; and was supplemented by the Association. Librarians volunteered to man the exhibit. The three counties in the state furnished bookmobiles used for displays. The exhibit made the general public aware of the various programs and activities to fill personal needs offered by 15 libraries. Handouts

State Reports—Delaware

included buttons, shopping bags, bumper stickers, and descriptive brochures on library services. Presentations included puppet shows, storytelling, and silent movies. Demonstrations covered the use of reference services for business, ERIC, interlibrary loans, and talking books. Letters were sent to all state legislators inviting them to visit the exhibit.

Library Development and Services. The Library Services and Construction Act (LSCA) awarded a grant to make available a library and library services at the Sussex Correctional Institute at Georgetown. Completion of a new minimum security building and plans to renovate an old maximum security building have released space for the library. Resources and services will make it possible to comply with the court order to give inmates access to legal resources.

The State Division of Handicapped Services provided a certified Braillist to teach a 12-week course in Braille writing at Wesley College in Dover. A class of six formed the nucleus for a volunteer system to make Braille translations of materials needed for the clientele of handicapped services.

The library law of 1975, creating county library districts, posed a problem for libraries with service areas crossing county lines. To erase the difficulty for the Milford library, the Kent County Levy Court created the Milford Library District to raise funds in Kent County to share the expense of the Milford library which is in Sussex County.

The Wilmington Institute Library and the Dover Public Library sponsored notable "outreach" programs. In Wilmington the library extended services to the Spanish-speaking population through depository collections at the Latin American Community Center and at the Roberto Clemente Center. Juvenile and adult books in Spanish and in English, recordings and bilingual filmstrips emphasizing self-help and recreational materials were provided.

The Dover Public Library contracted with the Kent County Levy Court to give outreach services to preschool children and the elderly. Special programs included interpretative dramatics, story hours, puppetry and films. The handicapped and migrants also benefited and use was made of playgrounds and parks throughout the county. A grant from the Division of Aging added titles to support the program and LSCA funds were used to increase reference sources and Delawareana.

Resources. *Bibliography of Delaware, 1960–1974*, was compiled by the Reference Department of the Hugh M. Morris Library, University of Delaware, to supplement Reed's *Bibliography of Delaware Through 1960* (University of Delaware Press, 1966). The University of Delaware Bicentennial Committee sponsored the publication of the new work. More than 2,000 entries on all aspects of Delaware life were included and indexed. The bibliography may be purchased from the University Bookstore, Newark, Delaware, 19711 for $5 plus a mailing charge of 50 cents.

A union list of serials at the four campuses of the Delaware Technical and Community College and the Delaware State College Library has been computerized in the President's office of DTCC.

The Eleutherian Mills-Hagley Foundation received a grant from the National Historical Publications and Records Commission to conduct a regional survey and make recommendations for preserving and using the historical records of the seven railroads that were combined to form the Conrail System.

State of the Economy. A new regulation which combined federal funds for library resources with certain other educational components caused needless apprehension that school libraries would be disadvantaged by its implementation. The supervisor of library/media services in the state Department of Public Instruction reported that about 71 percent of funds available in Delaware under ESEA-Title IV-B was spent on library resources. The balance was used for instructional equipment, guidance services, testing, and counseling. About a third of the school districts, however, decreased local support for library resources. The cause may be attributed to a decrease of 4 percent in enrollments, transfer of funds due to inflation, and/or state mandated cuts of 4 percent in expenditures.

The number of certified full-time and part-time school librarians employed decreased in 1976 by slightly over 2 percent; library aides increased in about the same number. The decrease in librarians may be partly explained by the closing of two elementary schools.

Awards. Two scholarships for pursuing library education are offered annually in the state. DLA presents the G. Estelle Wheeless scholarship, given in memory of a former president of the association, to the applicant accepted or enrolled in an accredited library school who shows the greatest potential and need. DLRA awards the Helen H. Bennett scholarship, given in honor of the first state supervisor of school libraries in Delaware, to a person working in Delaware schools. This stipend may be used for registration or tuition while preparing for state certification as a librarian/media specialist or while working for a master's degree in a media field.

Citation for the outstanding librarian of the year was presented by DLRA to Irene Faucett Larrimore, who had served "both school and public libraries with distinction for many years." The award was presented posthumously.

People. Irene Faucett Larrimore, Chairperson and Director-coordinator of the Seaford School District Libraries and President of the Delaware Library Association 1974–75, died in September. She had been a member of the Seaford Board of Education and served as President in 1963. She had been President of the Delaware Library Trustees Association, the Sussex County Library Commission, and the Seaford Public Library Commission. She was a charter member of the Sussex County Vocational-Technical School Board.

Walter A. Young, Jr., Librarian at New Castle Middle School, was elected President of the Delaware State Education Association for a term of two years. He served as President of the New Castle-Gunning Bedford Education Association for two years.

Sam Douglas, first New Castle County Librarian, appointed in 1975, resigned in September 1976. Ralph Cryder, Director of Parks and Recreation for New Castle County, was named Acting Director.

Jack W. Bryant, convicted of misappropriating funds of the Wilmington Institute Library, of which he was Director, was sentenced to 18 months in jail, to be suspended after a year for two years' probation, in Superior Court.

The case of Patricia Chalfant Trivits, dismissed by Bryant from the staff of the Wilmington Institute Library in 1972, was denied by the Court. Trivits sought reinstatement and $180,000 in damages. ALA's Committee on Mediation, Arbitration and Inquiry concluded that the employee was fired without due process, but did not enter the court case.   HELEN H. BENNETT

DISTRICT OF COLUMBIA

Organizational Changes. Along with recollections of numerous Bicentennial observances, 1976 may well be remembered by District of Columbia librarians as a year of significant organizational changes. Foremost of these, perhaps, was the creation of the Metropolitan Washington Library Council. The Council, an outgrowth of the nine-year-old Librarians' Technical Committee of the Metropolitan Washington Council of Governments (COG), is a multitype, interjurisdictional library cooperative open to all libraries. Unlike its predecessor, the Library Council will be governed on an institutional member-one vote basis. A combined working body/board of trustees, the Librarians' Committee, will be elected on a representative basis by members of the Library Council. The new organization will continue to benefit from its affiliation with COG.

District of Columbia Library Association
(founded 1894)

Membership: 839; *Annual Expenditure:* $7,800.

President: Marilyn Gell, Council of Governments of the Washington Metropolitan Area (June 1976–May 1977).

Vice-President/President-elect: Catherine A. Jones, George Washington University.

Secretary: Monteria Hightower, Martin Luther King Library; 901 G Street, N.W., Washington, D.C. 20001.

Annual Meeting (banquet): May 1976, Washington, D.C.

Publication: Intercom (monthly).

During 1976 Marilyn Gell, Chief of Library Programs, and the Librarians' Technical Committee established draft bylaws and a dues schedule, issued publicity, and made preparations for the initial meeting of the Library Council January 21, 1977. At the end of 1976 it appeared that membership support would be excellent and that the new organization should be able to augment services while moving gradually toward financial independence.

Another significant organizational change was the appointment and first sessions of the Board of Trustees of the new University of the District of Columbia. Although implementation of the consolidation of three public institutions—District of Columbia Teachers College, Federal City College, Washington Technical Institute—was delayed beyond the June 30, 1976, date established by the District of Columbia Postsecondary Education Reorganization Act, the formation and actions of the Board were nearly certain to lead to an institutional merger during 1977. The long legislative and consolidation process had been disruptive for the three institutional libraries.

The third organizational change was the extension of the OCLC-affiliated Capital Consortium Network (CAPCON) from the libraries of the Consortium of Universities to non-Consortium institutions in Maryland, Virginia, and the District of Columbia. By the end of the year, Dumbarton Oaks Research Library, the Georgetown University Medical Center, Virginia Theological Seminary, Towson State University, and the University of Baltimore were operational. Three institutions were under contract and awaiting terminals; and another half-dozen libraries were in advanced planning stages. In addition, the network established policies and fee schedules for full and terminal sharing libraries, planned for expanded telecommunication needs, and voted to acquire OCLC-MARC archive tapes on both retrospective and current subscription bases. A major concern at the end of the year was the indefinite status of the Maryland Library Center for Automated Processing (MALCAP) which had effectively handled CAPCON activity within that state.

District Public Library. Although events were somewhat less dramatic at the District of Columbia Public Library, the system undertook an imposing array of programs while continuing its struggle with budget reductions, shortened service hours in branches, and a District of Columbia hiring freeze which prevented the library from filling 80 authorized positions, nearly 15 percent of its allotment of 550. As reported by Lawrence Molumby, the Bicentennial year began with a flurry of activities. The Martin Luther King Memorial Library was designated the official city center for ceremonies honoring his birthday. Three days of concerts, exhibits, films, and official ceremonies included a visit by Betty Ford. In March the library was also the site for "Memphis Revisited," a moving memorial service which included a reenactment of Dr. King's last speech by Federal Communication Commissioner Benjamin Hooks.

The library embarked on two major automation projects during the year: the installation of OCLC terminals through participation in FEDLINK, and the receipt of a CLSI minicomputer, initially programmed for registration and circulation control and for film booking. Both projects were supported by federal funding under Title I of the Library Services and Construction Act. Other notable projects were a special photocopying project designed to preserve the fragile and irreplaceable clipping files of the Washingtoniana Division, financed by a grant from the National Endowment for the Humanities; the appointment of staff for a new Community Information Service; and the appointment of a Video Librarian who will develop resources and use of this medium.

The library continued its leadership in services to the deaf by appointing Alice Hagemeyer as its Librarian for the Deaf. A special handbook for deaf Bicentennial visitors was one of her first projects, followed by staff training to serve deaf needs. During the summer three Kiosk libraries were opened in Anacostia. The small, mostly glass, 1,000-book installations stirred great community interest and were heavily used. Through donations from the Peabody Library Association, the stately Georgetown branch was renovated.

Under the leadership of 1975–76 Chairperson William Whitesides and 1976–77 Chairperson Mary Jo Detweiler, the COG Librarians' Technical Committee continued or expanded existing programs while working toward its reorganized status. The highly successful continuing education workshops, directed by Library Planner Mary Sage, were retained on a self-supported basis after the termination of a one-year U.S.O.E. grant in June. Among the useful offerings were supervision, management by objectives, space planning, and zero based budgeting. A study prepared by the information systems task force chaired by Ray Price was entitled *A Feasibility Study for Providing On-Line Bibliographic Data Base Access to the Public Through the Libraries of the Metropolitan Washington Area*. Specific recommendations will be considered by the Librarians' Committee in 1977. Other task forces negotiated new cooperative purchasing contracts, explored a cooperative contract for film services, and developed publicity for area libraries including radio and television public service spots. Significant publications included two newsletters, *Bicentennial Briefs* and *Axis*, a report of cooperative library activities; *MAGS*, a union list of 7,000 periodicals held by public libraries, and an annual report. The well established jobline averaged more than 450 calls a week and the Metropolitan Area Interlibrary Loan Service (MAILS) handled more than 5,000 items a month.

Consortium Activities. It was also an active year for the Consortium of Universities of the Metropolitan Area. In addition to the management of CAPCON, the eight-member consortium issued a 10,000 title supplement to its *Union List of Serials* (3rd edition, 1974), adopted common policies for special collections and interlibrary loan photocopying, conducted workshops and tours, and completed a study of scientific serial subscriptions. The popular direct borrowing program for faculty and graduate students totalled more than 50,000 loans. A 25-page compilation of library statistics covering 1974–75 was issued in March and a similar report for 1975–76 was issued in December. These compilations are interesting for their reporting of main campus, law, medical and total institution statistics and for their inclusion of support and activity ratios based on full-time equivalency data.

Academic Libraries. Several of the academic libraries completed sizable projects during the year. George Washington University finished a large-scale self-analysis including one of the largest and most sophisticated user studies that has been done by an academic library. Progress was also made by the library in its efforts to establish a comprehensive set of policies. Gallaudet College likewise undertook a critical evaluation of its services. The handsome Founders Library at Howard University was extensively renovated. Under its Director of Libraries, Binford Conley, Howard also designed and implemented an automated acquisitions system,

State Reports—Florida

restructured its organization, and finished most of the planning for a sizable addition to the main library. On the negative side, American University and Catholic University encountered further obstacles to the construction of needed facilities.

The Department of Library Science at the Catholic University of America continued to develop new and distinctive programs for the post-master's level as well as offering a wide range of courses for the M.S. in L.S. degree. Among the new specialized programs first offered in 1976 were: (1) oral history, (2) federal library administration, (3) a joint degree program in educational technology leading to a joint master's degree or an M.S. in L.S. and an Ed.D. degree, and (4) a joint program with George Washington University leading to a Ph.D. in American Studies and a master's degree in library science, with a special emphasis on Americana at the Library of Congress.

DCLA. The District of Columbia Library Association was most visible for its lead sponsorship of the Joint Spring Workshop, chaired by Courtney Funn; for its cohosting with the ALA Washington office of the annual Legislative Day chaired by Charmaine Yochim, successfully aimed at the appropriations and education/library committees; for its role as cohost with seven other associations of a reception in April honoring Daniel Boorstin; for the popular new-member reception held at the Folger Shakespeare Library; and for its annual banquet featuring political humorist Mark Russell. As Presidents William Whitesides and Marilyn Gell noted, most of the organization's success was due to its hard working interest groups and standing committees. The work of the Executive Board was focused on administrative reforms and the further definition of intraorganizational relationships.

SLA. The Washington Chapter of the Special Libraries Association made a significant improvement in its financial condition and stimulated membership interest through its workshop series which culminated in a Bicentennial Special Meeting at Valley Forge in May. The all-day program was cosponsored by seven chapters, but owed its success largely to D.C. Chapter President F. Kurt Cylke and Sarah Thomas Kadek. Not content with its active 1975–76 year, the Chapter began its fall activities with an open house at the spectacular new Smithsonian Air and Space Museum (cosponsored by DCLA, ASIS, the Baltimore Chapter of SLA and arranged by Librarian Catherine Scott), a three-day conference on maps and map librarianship and a book fair cosponsored with the Baltimore Chapter.

Publications. Publications of special interest in addition to those previously noted were DCLA's sprightly and informative newsletter *Intercom* edited by Mary Feldman and Joseph Judy, SLA's *Chapter Notes*, and union lists covering legal periodical holdings, serial holdings of the Washington Theological Consortium, and journal holdings of 65 specialized libraries jointly issued by the Interlibrary Users Association and Sigma Data Computing Corporation.

People. Jack Ellenberger, Librarian at Covington and Burling, was elected 1976–77 President of the American Association of Law Libraries. Two District librarians, Lee Putman (1975–76) and Stanton Biddle (1976–77), were awarded management internships by the Council on Library Resources. Elizabeth Stone, Chairperson of the Catholic University Department of Library Science, received a Certificate of Distinction from the ALA Library Education Division for her work in continuing education and the development of CLENE.

Notable retirees were Elizabeth Hage, Director of the Prince George's County Memorial Library System for 19 years and an active participant in District library activities; Mildred Helvestine, Director of the Department of Transportation Library; Elizabeth Tate, Chief of the Descriptive Cataloging Division, Processing Department, Library of Congress; Walter Williams, Head Librarian, District of Columbia Teacher's College; and Elva Van Winkle, Deputy Coordinator of Children's Services, District of Columbia Public Library. Keith Wright resigned his position as Librarian, Gallaudet College, to join the faculty of the Catholic University of America on a full-time basis. —DARRELL LEMKE

FLORIDA

Services to the Handicapped. The Florida Regional Library for the Blind and Physically Handicapped, in Daytona Beach, observed its 25th year of service during 1976. In that anniversary year, the following significant program developments were realized: establishment of Florida's sixth Subregional Library (a branch of the Miami–Dade Public Library System); implementation of an automated inventory and circulation system, funded by a LSCA research and development grant; completion of a comprehensive census of Florida's certified braillists and braille proofreaders; inauguration of a centralized circulating film service on the subject of blindness, other handicapping conditions, and rehabilitation; establishment of the first radio (audio) reading network in the state.

At the request of the Association of Southern Librarians for the Blind and

Florida Library Association
(founded 1920)

Membership: 1,248 (687 ALA members);
Annual Expenditure: $42,044 (includes $21,043 grant administered for State Library).
President: Eloise L. Harbeson, Tallahassee Community College (May 1976–April 1977).
Vice-President/President-elect: Glen Miller, Orlando Public Library.
Executive Secretary: Verna Nistendirk, 2862 W.W. Kelly Road, Tallahassee, Florida 32301.
Annual Meeting: April 21–24, 1976, Hollywood, Florida.
Publication: Florida Libraries (6 issues a year).

State Library of Florida
Cecil Beach, Director (1976)
R. A. Gray Building
Tallahassee, Florida 32304

Physically Handicapped, the Florida Regional Library accepted publishing responsibility for *Dikta*, the Association's new quarterly official organ and the first professional journal concerned with subjects relating to librarianship for the handicapped.

Success of the Multistate Center networking concept was documented during October when the Library of Congress, Division for the Blind and Physically Handicapped, extended contractual agreements for the Multistate Center for the South (MSCS), Daytona Beach, and the Multistate Center for the West (MSCW), Salt Lake City, and began negotiations for the establishment of two additional Multistate Centers in the country. The MSCS affords interlibrary loan and other support services to regional libraries for the blind and physically handicapped in the Southern Conference: Alabama, Florida, Georgia, Louisiana, Kentucky, Mississippi, North Carolina, Puerto Rico, South Carolina, Tennessee, Texas, Virginia, and the Virgin Islands.

Adult Services. Adult service programming in Florida libraries is expanding and indicates clearly how much public libraries are doing in the area of community education.

Added to the old standbys—the film series, the books discussion groups and hobby classes—are seminars and programs and service support in many areas of vital concern to today's adult. Literacy classes in the library, programming and resource provision for the adult new reader, services aimed specifically at the older American (which include, in several instances, free income tax clinics), and seminars for and about women are providing a broad spectrum of continuing educational opportunities for Florida residents. Small business and investment seminars are popular, as are nutrition programs.

Two regional library systems are actively involved in assisting handicapped adults: the Northwest Regional Library System and the Suwannee River Regional Library. The Northwest Regional Library System has an extensive program of programming and resource delivery for illiterate adults in its six-county region. The Library System is also providing continuing captioned film programs for deaf patrons. The Suwannee River Regional Library provides literacy instruction by staff members, using the Laubach literacy method. This System also provides instruction in braille transcription for those sighted adults wishing to assist blind patrons in its seven-county region.

Another innovative program for adults is the program begun by the Children's Department of the Orlando Public Library. Its "Sharing Literature with Children" program is being shared with libraries throughout the state and is proving popular, particularly with older adults who are grandparents, or who are involved in the Foster Grandparent programs in various communities.

The Miami-Dade Public Library System's Artmobile is traveling throughout Dade County with art exhibits.

Bilingual education has been in demand, particularly with the influx of the Vietnamese refugees. Leon-Jefferson Library System has an active program which includes the development of Vietnamese-English cassette tapes for pronunciation practice and a textbook-workbook for use with the tapes. This System has also started a branch library in a rural Leon County community school. The Volusia County Library System has been involved in providing Vietnamese-English instruction in its Deland branch, as well as instruction in Spanish, French and German in both the Deland and the New Smyrna Beach libraries.

Mentioned here are only a few of the many ongoing programs that public libraries are providing in the area of adult services. Other activities concern small boat handling, body language courses, mental health seminars, dancing for senior citizens, apple-head doll making and baby sitting clinics, ham-radio licensing classes and even a "Sunday in the Library" of traditional gospel singing by community choirs. Public library adult services were alive and thriving in Florida in 1976.

Children's Services. Is there anything new under the sun? Under Florida's hot, almost straight overhead sun, new enthusiasm has been sparked by the annual series of Regional Workshops to help plan for the Statewide Reading Motivation Summer Program. Summer Reading Programs are not new, as is well known; creation of new enthusiasm each year assumes the proportions of a miracle. In 1976 Florida tried to make the planning more participatory than ever, by including new members, on the statewide advisory committee, by enlisting two working children's libraries to conduct the workshops, and by their including in the workshop format a program segment for the local host library.

Publicity materials in Florida get more professional and effective. For the first time, a 30-second singing commercial was distributed for radio stations, as well as 30-second and 60-second TV spots, advertising the possibility of a "Book Trek into New Worlds" through the local libraries.

Attention focuses in the program on (1) reaching the non-user; (2) reaching the pre-schooler; and (3) parent education. Though these were not new ideas, new emphases marked statewide efforts to achieve from idealized objectives concrete results in hundreds of local communities.   BARRATT WILKINS

GEORGIA

Library developments in Georgia in 1976 concerned primarily completion of building projects, personnel changes, steady growth in funding for school and public libraries, and the many and various kinds of programs continued or implemented in the libraries across the state. Since the Georgia Library Association holds its conferences biennially in odd-numbered years, the Association's principal activity was planning for the 1977 conference and for institutes to be held in the winter and spring of 1977. The Association provided strong representation at the Washington

Georgia Library Association
(founded 1898)

Membership: 1095; *Annual Expenditure:* $15,016.
President: A. Ray Rowland, Augusta College (October 1975–September 1977).
Vice-President/President-elect: Barbara C. Cade, Atlanta Public Schools.
Executive Secretary: Ann W. Morton, P.O. Box 833, Tucker, Georgia 30084.
Biennial Conference: October 22–25, 1975, Atlanta (no meeting in 1976).
Publication: Georgia Librarian (May and November).

Division of Public Library Services
Carlton J. Thaxton, Director
156 Trinity Avenue, SW
Atlanta, Georgia 30303

Legislative Day. Eight prominent members of the Association participated and fruitful contact was continued with the state's senators and several congressmen.

Buildings. Several major public library building projects were completed during fiscal year 1976; the aggregate cost was just over $6,000,000, of which almost $2,000,000 came from state funds to supplement the local resources. The projects added about 175,000 square feet to public library facilities. They also reflected passage of several local referenda to generate the needed local funds. In cost, the most extensive were at Columbus, Brunswick, Warner Robins, Americus, LaGrange, Carrollton, and in Atlanta (branches of the Public Library).

New library buildings were also completed at Augusta and Shorter colleges, and an addition was completed at Berry College. The Theology Library at Emory University underwent extensive renovation and an addition to house the Hartford Collection was acquired during the year at a cost of $1,750,000. The first phase of renovation of the library at Agnes Scott College in Decatur was completed.

Public Library Funding. Per capita expenditure for public libraries continued to increase in 1976. A total of $22,555,106 was expended for services and operations in the 158 counties (out of 159) which qualified for state and federal funds by virtue of constituting a library system or being affiliated with a system. Of the total, $15,784,084 came from local funds, $5,833,476 from state funds, and $937,546 from federal funds.

School Library/Media Centers. A statewide committee has been appointed by the Department of Education to work toward a criterion-reference test to be used as a basis for determining eligibility for certification as library media specialist. The committee comprises school administrators, classroom teachers, library media specialists at the building level, and system level library media personnel. It is expected that the committee will review requirements for basic, entry-level certification, as well as requirements for fifth-year certification. A competency based examination is projected as a requirement for newly certificated library media specialists and for in-service specialists seeking certificate renewal.

A recent tabulation showed that there were 1,886 full-time library media specialists in the state's school systems. Of these, approximately 7 percent held sixth-year certificates and 40 percent held fifth-year certificates; almost half of all school library media specialists held a master's degree. More than 500 schools had either a half-time or full-time media center aide. Seventy percent of the schools had the benefits of a system or shared services lev-

State Reports—Hawaii

el supervision for coordination of the library media programs.

Reports showed that approximately $5,700,000 were expended annually for school library resources, or $5.76 per pupil. Per pupil expenditure was increased by some 7 percent over the previous year. Resources included almost 13 books and two nonprint items per student.

People. Retirements during the year included those of Grace Hightower, head of Media Field Services, Georgia Department of Education; Edith Foster, Director, West Georgia Regional Library in Carrollton; Sarah Maret, Director, Athens Regional Library; and Anna Schinkel, Director, Colquitt-Thomas Regional Library in Moultrie. All had served extensively and with distinction.

Ella Gaines Yates was appointed in late November as Director of the Atlanta Public Library. Hoyt Galvin served for several months as Interim Director following the resignation of Carlton C. Rochell to accept the deanship of libraries at New York University. Galvin's attention was given primarily to completing building plans for the new central library, approved in a 1975 referendum.

Other new directors were appointed at the following libraries: Athens Regional Library, Roxanna Austin; Berry College Library, Ondina Gonzales; Colquitt-Thomas Regional Library, Melody Stinson; Houston County Library, Judith Golden; Ohoopee Regional Library, Edward McCabe; Uncle Remus Regional Library, Jane Lake, and West Georgia Regional Library, LeRoy Childs. JOHN CLEMONS

HAWAII

New Construction. Hawaii ended 1976 with two major new library facilities, a new State Centralized Processing Center and a $13,000,000 addition to Hamilton Library at the University of Hawaii. The Center, which services the state's 266 public and public school libraries, processes over 300,000 volumes annually. The building, 17,620 square feet in area, was constructed at a cost of $653,000. With the opening of the new Center, Hawaii State Library was well on its way to an automated acquisition system, but was still operating automated and manual systems in tandem. Automated cataloging records are being generated for all new acquisitions although the microform catalog, which was projected for fall 1976, was delayed.

Construction of Phase II of Hamilton Library was ahead of schedule and part of the building was occupied in December. Phase I of the Library, built in 1968, consisted of four floors with 106,000 square feet of space and a capacity for 800,000 volumes. Phase II adds 174,000 square feet of space, features a periodical reading room, and will increase the number of reader stations to 3,500. When Phase II is fully occupied, it will house all the special collections, the main collection and the Graduate School of Library Studies. The combined capacity of the two major libraries on the campus, Hamilton and Sinclair, will be 1,700,000 volumes.

The University filled the position of Dean of the Graduate School of Library Studies, appointing Ira Harris, Acting Dean, to the position. Harris had served on the faculty at the University since 1965.

Reorganization Controversy. In reviewing Hawaii library activities in the last edition of this *Yearbook*, it was reported that the library community in the state awaited the release of a comprehensive audit of the management and organization of the Office of Library Services. Many anticipated that the report would provide an unbiased view of, and perhaps suggest some solutions to, the complex organization of Hawaii's library system, which had generated much comment and controversy over the last decade. The report was not made public and it appeared at year's end that it never would be. It was hoped it would be made available to persons involved in the reorganization proposals reported here.

The organization controversy accelerated during 1976. In February a bill was introduced in the legislature that would establish a State Department of Public Libraries, but it died with the end of the session. In June an experimental reorganization plan was implemented which downgraded the heretofore back-up Hawaii State Library in downtown Honolulu to the status of a branch.

Hawaii Library Association
(founded 1922)

Membership: 434; *Annual Expenditure:* $11,000.
President: Katherine Knight, Waikiki-Kapahulu Library, Honolulu (April 1976–March 1977).
Vice-President/President-elect: Harry Uyehara, University of Hawaii, Graduate School of Library Studies.
Secretary: Mary Lu T. Kipilii, Hawaii State Library; c/o HLA, P.O. Box 4441, Honolulu, 96813.
Annual Conference: March 26–27, 1976, Honolulu.
Publications: HLA Newsletter (bimonthly); *HLA Journal* (annually).

Office of Library Services, Department of Education
Mae Chun, Assistant Superintendent for Library Services/State Librarian
P.O. Box 2360
Honolulu, Hawaii 96804

In the fall Pandora's Box was opened with the release of the Government Organization Commission's proposal for the reorganization of the Hawaii State Library. The general charge to the Commission was to address the twin problems of responsiveness and cost in state government. It sought to establish through its recommendations, clear-cut accountability for government services through both structural and administrative changes. Carrying out its intent to emphasize the growing importance of life-long education for all, the Commission proposed a "Life Long Learning System," at the University of Hawaii, headed by a chancellor. The State libraries (in Hawaii this includes all public libraries) would be one wing of the system, responsible for service delivery. Public librarians would hold appointments through the University Board of Regents. The other wing of the system would be responsible for adult education, open university programs, early childhood education, and all educational activities not directly under the jurisdiction of the State Department of Education and the University System. The former wing would be headed by a vice-chancellor for libraries and the latter by a vice-chancellor for cultural and community affairs. The proposal, in effect, moves the public libraries from the Department of Education and places them in the University of Hawaii System.

Since the state of Hawaii is the only public education agency serving the state's 870,000 inhabitants (there are no municipally supported educational institutions or libraries), the proposal had considerable support. Although seen by some as a creative approach to an educational objective, the proposal drew fire from the library and educational communities because of the implications of implementation.

Though the primary opposition came from the school library and teacher community, there were wide ranging implications in the proposal for all librarians who work in the state system libraries. Concern was primarily caused by the recommendation of the Commission "that all librarians be put into one category: public librarians, school librarians and University of Hawaii librarians."

The school library community, supported by school teachers, vigorously opposed the proposal that school librarians would either become part of the librarians group or return to teaching. Testimony to the Commission was overwhelmingly opposed to the concept of removing school librarians from control of the school principals and placing them under control of the Life Long Learning Chancellor at the University. Through the efforts of numerous groups, among them the Hawaii State

Teachers Association, the Hawaii Association of School Librarians, and the Hawaii Library Association, the Commission appears to have been persuaded to reverse the school library decision and leave the school librarians and school libraries under the jurisdiction of the Department of Education. Community/school libraries would be an exception and would be operated as public libraries and staffed by public librarians.

The revised proposal, not yet official, would establish a new state department, independent of the Department of Education and the University of Hawaii. In this department would be grouped public libraries and all other life-long learning and cultural activities that were to have been included under the initial proposal under the Life-Long Learning Chancellor at the University of Hawaii System. The new department would have no teaching staff as the proposal calls for the department to contract for services at every level and field of learning.

The initial proposal would have placed all librarians as administrative professional and technical employees of the University of Hawaii. At present school librarians, public librarians, and university librarians are included in three different units of the State Collective Bargaining System. The bargaining unit for public librarians in the proposed new department has not been clarified.

Having previously reported that there were no municipally supported libraries in the state, a report may now be given on the establishment of the first of its kind, a quasi-municipally supported library on the island of Oahu. Early in 1976 there were rumblings about the delay in getting a library from the Makiki community. More than $1,000,000 had been appropriated for land acquisition for a library but the money had not been released by the Governor. In the meantime the State Department of Education, the agency that has jurisdiction over all public libraries in Hawaii, recommended against the establishment of a public library in Makiki and submitted that recommendation to the Board of Education in September. The DOE pointed out that there were seven public libraries within a five-mile radius of the proposed site, and they suggested that priority for new libraries be accorded those neighborhoods that did not have this kind of proximity to any library services.

On Septembr 14, the Mayor of Honolulu announced that the city would help establish a library in Makiki and that it would be stocked with donated books. It would be manned initially with city employees from the Parks and Recreation Department, along with community residents who had volunteered to manage the facility. Community associations launched a drive to gather material for the library.

On September 15 the Board of Education voted against the DOE recommendation that no library be built in Makiki and voted to ask the Governor to establish a library at the site that the city proposed to use.

On September 17 the city, in conjunction with community volunteers, opened a Makiki library in a building that had once contained the Hawaii Sugar Planters Association Library. Supervising the volunteers was a recent graduate of the University of Hawaii Graduate School of Library Studies who is also a volunteer. ROSE MYERS

IDAHO

In 1976 Idaho libraries and librarians continued to pursue their interests in continuing education, networking, and regional systems development. Construction on major library buildings continued and smaller buildings were begun. The formation of several library districts throughout the state increased the percentage of the state offering library services to its citizens, and increased state aid freed the State Library from dependence upon federal monies for its operations and allowed larger grants to the regional library systems. The darkest day of the year came June 5 when the flood caused by the failure of the Teton Dam totally demolished the Madison County and Sugar-Salem School Community libraries.

Continuing Education. In 1976 Idaho maintained its membership in CLENE (Continuing Library Education Network and Exchange), with Helen Miller, State Librarian, elected to the Board of Directors.

The Idaho Library Association conference, May 2–4 in Burley, further emphasized continuing education through its program format of numerous concurrent workshops. Workshop topics included networking, budgeting, audiovisual equipment and materials, and public relations. Conferees were asked to participate in a continuing education needs assessment, as were librarians and trustees who had not been able to attend the conference, and a statewide continuing education program was formulated. A direct result of this needs assessment was the employment by the State Library of its first professional staff member, Richard Wilson, to coordinate the continuing education program. Wilson attended the CLENE Institute on Statewide Planning for Continuing Education at the Illinois State Library, in November.

The System Clinic in organizational development begun in 1975 under the direction of Lawrence Allen of the University of Kentucky and the University of Hawaii library schools and Edwin Olson, University of Maryland library school, was concluded in 1976. During the course of the year-long clinic, representatives of the six regional library systems and the State Library analyzed the roles of the component participants in the statewide public library system, learned and polished management and planning skills, examined and streamlined the state interlibrary loan system, and sought to broaden the base of statewide library planning. The clinic culminated with the November Trustee Workshops, conducted by Allen in the six library regions. Librarians and trustees worked together to develop local action plans.

Additional workshops were conducted throughout the state under regional and State Library sponsorship. Marjorie Fairchild, Emeritus Professor of Library Science at Boise State University, presented a series of two-day workshops on materials selection in the six regions.

Network Activities. The Idaho State Library continued to pay full membership fees for all libraries using the Pacific Northwest Bibliographic Center (PNBC) at the University of Washington. In 1976, however, Idaho was instrumental in effecting a change in the fee structure, basing it on usage rather than on total population of a member state. This is more advantageous for Idaho, where the interlibrary loan structure has been formalized for many years. In June of 1976 Idaho's regional systems agreed that an experimental period of using the mail rather than the LITTY (Libraries of Idaho Teletype) dataphone did not adversely affect service, and did save staff time and money. The dataphones were removed from the six system headquarters libraries and the State Library. The three universities and Ricks College Library are retaining their LITTY dataphone linkages, however, for fast inter-

Idaho Library Association
(founded 1915)

Membership: 402; *Annual Expenditure:* $13,619 (July 1, 1976).
President: Ruth Seydel, State Department of Education, Boise (June 1976–June 1977).
Vice-President/President-elect: Milo Nelson, University of Idaho Library, Moscow.
Secretary: Mabelle Wallan, 801 E. Jefferson St., Boise, Idaho 83702
Annual Meeting: May 2–4, 1976, Burley, Idaho.
Publication: The Idaho Librarian (quarterly).

Idaho State Library
Helen M. Miller, State Librarian
325 W. State Street
Boise, Idaho 83702

State Reports—Illinois

communication and sending requests to PNBC and to the Pacific Northwest Health Sciences Library (PNHSL), also at Seattle.

Idaho's health information program received two boosts in 1976. The State Legislature appropriated $30,000 to the State Library to provide continuation funding for the MEDLINE search center called HIRC (Health Information Retrieval Center) at the Mountain States Tumor Institute. This fund provided shared staff with the Institute and with St. Lukes Hospital Library, in-coming and out-going communcation costs for any health professional in Idaho. The State Library submitted a Medical Library Resources Project Grant proposal to the National Library of Medicine, and received first-year funding of $43,675 to develop an Idaho Health Libraries Network (IDA-HEAL-NET). Judy Romans, an Idahoan with master's degrees in librarianship and in chemistry, a 1975-76 Postgraduate Assistant at the National Library of Medicine, heads the new developmental program. Total funding for the three-year period of the grant is expected to be $113,175. As Idaho has no medical school, and permanent library staff in only 10 of its 52 hospitals, the project will focus on the setting up of local libraries, the coordination of resources in hospitals, and in academic libraries, the in-service training of staff.

Funding. The 1975 Idaho legislature provided sufficient state general funds so that the full operation of the State Library's services could be carried by state rather than federal monies. All Library Services and Construction Act (LSCA) funds were thus available in FY 1976 for grants. The 1976 Legislature continued this full operational funding, and boosted the state aid appropriation for FY 1977 to $357,000. The appropriation is approximately 50 cents per capita and includes $154,000 for library construction, $183,000 for grants to regional library systems, $5,000 for continuing education grants, and $15,000 for establishment grants to new library districts.

The 1976 legislature also provided a supplemental FY76 appropriation of $50,000 to assist in current library construction projects, and $500,000 to the State Library for a phase-two addition to the State Library and Archives building. Ground breaking on the addition was expected early in 1977. The addition will provide approximately 12,000 square feet, half as much as in the phase-one portion of the building.

The legislature also provided $10,000 and authorization to initiate a Radio Reading Service for the blind and physically handicapped in southwestern Idaho. The SCA station, utilizing a sub-channel of KBOI-FM, was to be ready to begin broadcasting four hours a day in January 1977, when the first 150 receivers were to be delivered. Lions Clubs are raising funds to buy the needed receivers.

1976 was a good year for the establishment of new library districts: Kootenai County was formed March 16, to cover all the rural areas outside the existing municipalities with libraries; the Valley of the Tetons District was expanded to include all of Teton County, on October 13, and Clark County formed a district, at the instigation of Dubois citizens, on December 13.

The six regional library systems moved forward confidently, with greater participation by member libraries and trustees in the decision-making process. Increased state grants went toward the purchase of books, equipment, building renovation, and additional personnel. Needed library materials were purchased with regional funds, rather than being indiscriminately forwarded on into the interlibrary loan system.

Construction. Midvale, Cambridge, Caldwell, and Mountain Home completed new buildings in 1976. Renovation or additions were carried out in Jerome, Burley, Aberdeen, Carey, and Athol. Grandview and Bear Lake moved into new quarters. New buildings were started in Salmon and Sun Valley. The state's largest projects, the $2,700,000 public library in Idaho Falls and the $5,000,000 Idaho State University Library in Pocatello, were expected to be completed in 1977.

The Flood. A librarian's nightmare became reality on June 5 as the Teton Dam, 40 miles northeast of Idaho Falls, gave way, releasing 80,000,000,000 gallons of water on the residents of the Upper Snake River Valley. The libraries in Rexburg and Sugar City, two communities which felt the full thrust of the floodwaters, were destroyed. Together, the libraries had served all the residents of Madison County. Sugar City lost a collection of approximately 15,000 books and Madison County lost most of its 25,000-volume collection. Floodwater reached a height of five feet in the Rexburg library. The Children's Department, in the basement of the building, was inundated. The Sugar City Library, a school-community library located in the local high school, felt the brunt of the 30-foot-high wall of water that washed away that small community.

Both libraries are busily rebuilding. The Sugar City High School was rebuilt over the summer and with it, the Library. Scoured shelving awaited the arrival of materials at year's end. The Rexburg Library operated out of temporary quarters in the newly rebuilt City Hall building, and planned to begin construction of a new building in 1977. Both libraries received tremendous amounts of help from other libraries, people from across the country, numerous local and national service clubs, and other organizations. The Ricks College Library provided assistance through the loan of equipment and furniture, storage space, temporary quarters immediately after the flood, and hours of encouragement and advice during the involved claiming procedure.

Awards. Notable among Idaho notables in 1976 was Eli M. Oboler, Idaho State University Librarian, who received the 1976 Robert B. Downs Award for outstanding contributions to the cause of intellectual freedom in libraries. Oboler was selected for the honor by the faculty of the Graduate School of Library Science at the University of Illinois at Urbana-Champaign. The award includes a citation and $500.

Honored as Trustee of the Year by the Idaho Library Association was Doris Lyman, trustee for the Portneuf Library District in Pocatello. Lyman has served on the Portneuf board for many years and has been instrumental in the development of the Gateway Regional Library System as Chair of the system's Board of Directors. —JEANNE GOODRICH

ILLINOIS

Bicentennial, budget, and interlibrary cooperation were predominant library themes in 1976. In addition to celebrating the nation's 200th anniversary, Illinois and the nation's librarians also celebrated the 100th anniversary of the American Library Association and the Dewey Decimal Classification System. Bicentennial and centennial themes, exhibits, displays, and programs were visible everywhere, particularly for the first half of the year. This cheerful atmosphere, however, had its more somber side. The hard facts of inflation, personnel cutbacks, and the increasing information needs of the community affected every type of library. Belts were

Illinois Library Association
(founded 1896)
Membership: 3,815 (1,100 ALA members); *Annual Expenditure:* $100,000.
President: Melvin R. George, Northeastern Illinois University, Chicago.
Vice-President/President-elect: Frank Dempsey, Arlington Heights Memorial Library.
Executive Secretary: John Coyne.
Annual Conference: November 3-5, 1976, Chicago.
Publication: ILA Reporter (quarterly).

Illinois State Library
Kathryn Gesterfield, Director
209 Centennial Building
Springfield, Illinois 62756

State Reports—Illinois

tightened for the second and third years as libraries examined the efficiency of their operations and sought appropriate economies.

Bicentennial, Centennial Events. Some future historian undoubtedly will record all of the events of the year 1976. Innumerable Bicentennial programs, displays, and exhibits were in evidence throughout the state emphasizing not only America's past accomplishments but looking toward the future. The topic for the Allerton Institute at the University of Illinois, for instance, was Changing Times–Changing Libraries; it was held, appropriately, at Century 21.

Within the space limits of this report, it is possible to list only a few of the many types of programs sponsored by libraries. The American Library Association opened the 95th annual conference with its 100th birthday celebration Celebrate-A-Century dinner at the Conrad Hilton and Chicago Art Institute. Forest Press, Publisher of the Dewey Decimal Classification, celebrated the Dewey Decimal Classification Centennial by giving a centennial certificate to continuous users of Dewey.

Many libraries launched local and oral history programs. The Newberry Library and the Chicago Historical Society prepared a series of eight workshops to enable participants to develop skills in local history research. The Starved Rock Library System completed a progress report on its local history project; and the Bur Oak Library System opened the Morris Grundy Local History Room. The State Librarian announced the establishment of IRAD—the Illinois Regional Archives Depository System for storing local government records throughout the state. IRAD has been financed by a grant from the National Endowment for the Humanities to the State Archives Division and is effective through June 30, 1978. The six state universities designated as depositories are Northern Illinois, Southern Illinois, Eastern Illinois, Western Illinois, Sangamon State, and Illinois State Universities.

A number of public libraries and library systems prepared histories of library members (Cumberland Library System, Starved Rock and Lewis and Clark Library Systems, for instance) and several are preparing taped oral histories of their communities. The Shawnee Library System received an Illinois State Library improvement grant to make its genealogical collection available to libraries throughout the state; and the University of Illinois was awarded a $5,300 LSCA grant by the State Library to produce a map bibliography entitled *The American Revolution: Maps in the University of Illinois Library, 1750–1800.*

The largest on-going Bicentennial project in the state was the Illinois State Historical Library's "Sound and Light Show at the Old State Capitol," a 45-minute long electronic recreation of the story of Lincoln's relationship with the Old State Capitol.

Finances. Continuing escalation of costs coupled with many zero-growth budgets presented a bleak outlook for the future. Libraries, however, were somewhat encouraged by the passage of federal library aid bills and substantial increases for public libraries and public library appropriations by the Illinois State Legislature. The 1977 LSCA Title I funds were increased by $7,745,000 over 1976 and Title III funds increased by $743,000. The Illinois System act was amended to authorize a boost in the system funding formula; raised from $.70 to $1 per capita and from $25 to $35 per square mile; and the passage of House Bill 3612 increased equilization grants for public libraries. A total of $163,787 was awarded to 72 libraries in Illinois. (Eligible libraries are those taxing not less than .06 percent and whose per capita yields less than $1.50.) The passage of this legislation may be partially attributed to the efforts of the ALA and its sponsorship of Library Legislation Days in Washington, D.C., April 5–6; and the efforts of the Illinois Library Association's four-point legislation program—increased equalization grants to public libraries with an inadequate tax base; a program of state grants for public library construction; the increased system funding cited above; and (a non-financial program) continued opposition to censorship of all library materials. For the third year, the Illinois State Library offered $1,300,000 to systems for the purchase of books and nonbook materials through the Library Resources Enrichment Program.

Several libraries applied for and received additional aid from revenue sharing funds. Local libraries received a total of $62,694,704 from local tax support (total expenditures amounted to $77,053,807).

Despite federal and state increases, David Reich, Director of the Chicago Public Library System, and Lester Stoffel, Executive Director of the Suburban Library System, still predicted financial difficulties that could be counteracted only by reduction in staff and services. Peter Niemi, Director of the Champaign Public Library, urged re-thinking of the concept of free public libraries and consideration of the imposition of registration and rental fees to help supplement library income derived from local property taxes.

In an attempt to find some solution to the financial predicament of libraries, the Urban Library Council authorized a $12,000 study of state support for public libraries. Rodney Lane, author of the NCLIS *Report on Alternatives for Financing the Public Library*, will examine the legal obligations of the states to aid public libraries and suggest strategies to raise the level of state financial support.

Interlibrary Cooperation. Kay Gesterfield, Director of the Illinois State Library, emphasized the state's financial and moral support of multitype library systems in her report to the Management Institute for State Library Agency Directors at the University of Pittsburgh Graduate Library School. In a *Hotline Report* (December 13, 1976) Gesterfield was reported to have said that academic, special, and school libraries were encouraged to affiliate with the public library systems and were "eager" to share their resources with the public libraries. Listings of new academic, school, and special library affiliates in public library system newsletters reinforced Gesterfield's general statement and reflected the interest of all types of libraries in multitype cooperation. In 1976, for instance, four school libraries and a medical library became affiliates of the Corn Belt Library System. Three hospital medical libraries (Delnor, Elgin, and St. Joseph) affiliated with the DuPage Library System and the Carle, Bush Lincoln, Mercy, Burnham, and University of Illinois-Health Sciences medical libraries joined the Lincoln Trails Library System. The Lewis and Clark Library System reported that the Lovejoy Library and Biomedical Libraries of Southern Illinois University, Blackburn, and Principia College among others had joined the system. These libraries all look forward to the benefits that can be received from cooperative reference and interlibrary loan programs, access to ILLINET, cooperative collection development, and sharing resources.

In a six-month experiment dealing with direct access, nine academic libraries (Concordia Teachers College, Elmhurst College Library, George Williams College, Illinois Benedictine College, Prairie State College, Rosary College, Thornton Community College, Trinity Christian, and Triton College Libraries) will permit patrons with a Suburban Library System borrower's card to borrow materials without charge. The program will be evaluated.

Another type of access program, the Courtesy Pass Program, will allow Rolling Prairie System Libraries to access its affiliate libraries.

As part of the continuing program to encourage interlibrary cooperation, the Illinois State Library awarded a $25,000 LSCA grant to the Northern Illinois Library System to implement the Illinet Data Base Interconnect Project. Funds will be used to determine the effectiveness of the LIBS 100-System for interlibrary loan searching and communication; the costs of using the LIBS 100 over dial-up telephone lines for

State Reports—Indiana

the purpose; and the effectiveness of the input standards now in use as an aid in facilitating proper identification of materials.

New Buildings. 1976 appeared to be a remarkable year for the dedication of new buildings, building additions, and ground breaking for new libraries. The University of Illinois at DeKalb, Sangamon State University at Springfield, and Western Illinois University have new library buildings. Additions and renovations were started at Wheaton College.

New public libraries were dedicated in Columbia, Murphysboro, Lansing, Geneseo, Dundee, Lake Bluff, Mascoutah, Palatine, and Tinley Park. Among the public libraries that noted additions, renovations and remodeling were the libraries in Bellwood, Creve Coeur, Deerfield, Harvey, Highland Park, Hoffman Estates, Marshall, Moline, Mundelein, Northbrook, South Beloit, and Eureka. Ground breaking took place for the new Bloomington Public Library, the result of a vigorous drive on the part of the citizens of the community to obtain a new library for the city.

Awards And Grants. Professor Martha E. Williams, Director of the Information Retrieval Research Laboratory at the University of Illinois, received $57,289 from the Illinois State Library to study the feasibility of generating a statewide union catalog based on the holdings of the Illinois libraries that have machine-readable catalogs. The Suburban Library System received $66,661 to support a children's services/school service liaison consultant. The Illinois Library Association, was presented the Grolier National Library Week Grant for the best public relations proposal for 1976. The Chicago Public Library was awarded first place by the Broadcasters Promotion Association for its Bicentennial series, "Happy Birthday America."

Twenty-five college libraries received $8,000 grants from the W. K. Kellogg Foundation enabling them to become part of the Illinois OCLC Bibliographic Data Base.

ILA Annual Meeting. Theme of the conference, November 3–5, was Communicate/Celebrate. Gerald R. Miller, of the Department of Communications, Michigan State University, Richard Calabrese, Department of Communications, Rosary College, and Peggy Sullivan, University of Chicago Graduate Library School, were among those who discussed "The Communication Process." Michael Killian, of the *Chicago Tribune*, spoke on the election. The varied program included a symposium on the futuristic views of information systems and a workshop on workshops.

Appointments. Appointments during 1976 included Patricia S. Breivik, Librarian, Sangamon State University; Lila Brady, Director, Northern Illinois Library System; Joanne Cox, Librarian, Marquette Heights Public Library; Alex Crossman, Director, Peoria Public Library; Neil C. Flynn, Director, Lewis and Clark Library System; Ann M. Garrett, Librarian, Mount Vernon Public Library; Mary Gerber, Librarian, Bradford Public Library; Rita Hoyt, Librarian, Mount Vernon Public Library; Brinda Matherly, Librarian, West Salem Public Library; Arden Perkins, Librarian, Fountaindale Public Library District; and Amy Wolf, Business Library, Caterpillar Tractor Company.

Retirements. Retirements included Helen Haney, founding Librarian of the Fountaindale Public Library; and Ellanor Sewell, Assistant Director and Head of Processing, Lewis and Clark Library System (since 1966).

Deaths. Deaths in 1976 included those of Elizabeth Johnson, Librarian, Business Library, Caterpillar Tractor Company, and Fred Donnelly, Librarian, Eisenhower Public Library. — SYLVIA G. FAIBISOFF

INDIANA

First Aid. For the first time ever, the Indiana Legislature appropriated funds for the support of the state's 240 tax-supported public libraries. The State Budget Bill, signed by Governor Otis Bowen on February 25, included an allocation of $800,000 to the State Auditor for distribution.

The amount received by each public library was based on the library's 1976 operating budget as a percentage of all public library budgets in the state. For comparison with other states, Indiana's 240 public libraries serve a population of 4,703,705 (9.5% of the state's population does not have library service), so the state funding amounted to $.17 per capita.

Indiana Library Association
(founded 1891)

Membership: 771; *Annual Expenditure:* $23,500 (1976).
President: Mary McMillan, Plainfield Public Library (December 1976– November 1977).
Vice-President/President-elect: Robert Trinkle, Monroe County Public Library, Bloomington.
Executive Director: Susan Cady, 1100 West 42nd St., Indianapolis, Indiana 46208.
Annual Meeting: April 22–24, 1976, Indianapolis.
Publication: Focus on Indiana Libraries (bimonthly).

Indiana State Library
Marcelle K. Foote, Director
140 North Senate Avenue
Indianapolis, Indiana 46204

Leadership for this milestone achievement was provided by the Indiana Library Association—Indiana Library Trustee Association Joint Legislative Committee chaired by Ray Gnat, Director of the Indianapolis-Marion County Public Library.

Executive Office. The Indiana Library Association (ILA) and the Indiana Library Trustee Association (ILTA) joined forces to establish a joint Executive Office on April 1. The newly created Joint Governing Board, comprised of incumbent President, President-elect, and two Past-Presidents from both associations, appointed Susan Cady to the position of Executive Director. Cady had served as coordinator of the Central Indiana Area Library Services Authority since its formation in 1974.

Changing Focus. The quarterly journal of ILA, *Focus on Indiana Libraries*, has given up its journal status in favor of faster, fresher news at less expense.

Beginning in July 1947 as a two-page newssheet, it became a letterpress quarterly in 1951. Toward the end of the 60's, *Focus on Indiana Libraries* peaked in size (48 to 56 pages per issue) if not in quality. Conversion to offset in the early 70's provided a more attractive format that endured until the ILA membership reordered the priority of expenditures by establishing an executive office with ILTA.

With the publication of volume 30, no. 1, January/February 1976, Focus appeared as a four-page foldover carrying the subtitle "Newsletter of the Indiana Library Association," and has been published bimonthly during the year.

ILA Business. The annual meeting of ILA was held November 6 at the Airport Hilton in Indianapolis. Officers elected were Jasper H. Wright, President (South Bend Public Library), Mary McMillan, Vice-President/President-elect (Plainfield P.L.), Robert Logsdon, Secretary (Evansville P. L.), and Ellen Sedlack, director-at-large (Greencastle-Putnam County P. L.). In December the ILA Executive Board accepted with regret the resignation of Jasper Wright from the office of President for reasons of health, appointed Mary McMillan to fulfill the unexpired term of that office, and named Robert Trinkle Vice-President (Monroe County P. L., Bloomington).

Several amendments to the constitution and bylaws were approved: requirements for appointments to and funding of the Scholarship and Loan Fund Committee were eliminated, the ILA Executive Director and the Director of the State Library became nonvoting ex-officio members of the ILA Executive Board, and the 1976 surcharge on the dues structure that had been in effect since 1967 was incorporated into a new scale effective in 1977.

The cost of active personal membership in ILA under the new dues is $1 per $1,000 annual salary up to $7,999 with minimum dues of $6; for annual salaries of $8,000 and over, $2 per $1,000 with a maximum of $50. Institutional memberships range from $10 to $100 according to size of annual operating budget.

Two new round tables were established: Government Documents and Community Services. A name change for the Library Education Round Table was approved—it became Continuing Education.

ILTA Business. The annual meeting of the Indiana Library Trustee Association was held concurrently with ILA. Elected for the 1976-77 year were Winifred Pettee, President (Indianapolis-Marion County Public Library), William Laramore, vice president/president-elect (Plymouth P. L.), Carolyn Henson, secretary (Vigo County P. L.), Ralph Burress, treasurer (Jefferson County P. L.), Alice Swartz (Crown Point P. L.) and Lila Milford (Marion P. L.), directors-at-large, and Joseph Sawyer, past president (Union County P. L.)

School Media Centers. The primary concerns of school media personnel are encouraging students to read for pleasure, implications of PL 93-380 Title IV-B for school media programs, ways to elicit support for the media program from administrators and teachers, and the use of games and realia in media centers, according to the responses to a survey conducted by the Division of Instructional Media of the Indiana Department of Public Instruction.

Transition from categorical federal funding of school library resources under ESEA Title II to consolidated program funding under ESEA Title IV-B Libraries and Learning Resources occurred during the year. Statewide expenditures in round dollar figures for each of the eligible program areas were as follows:

School Library Resources, $900,000 (includes $57,000 for guidance materials placed in media centers); Instructional Equipment, $515,000; Guidance, Counseling, Testing, $36,000; Processing and Installation, $40,000; and Minor Remodeling, $3,000.

A state conference on visual literacy was held with nationally known authorities conducting sessions. Another conference examined the national guidelines in *Media Programs: District and School* (ALA, AECT, 1975).

Special Libraries. The Indiana Chapter of the Special Libraries Association had 136 members at year end with representation from all varieties and types of libraries in the state. Virginia Humnicky, Indiana University School of Medicine Library, was elected President for 1976-77, and Miriam Drake, Purdue University Libraries, President-elect.

Joint Conference. Billed as the "Spirit of '76: A Revolutionary Convention," ILA and ILTA joined the Indiana School Librarians Association (ISLA) and the Indiana Association for Educational Communications and Technology (IAECT) in co-sponsoring a conference at the Indianapolis Convention Center, April 22-24. Evaluations by the 1,399 attendees rated the conference a success and indicated considerable interest in another within a few years

This first of its kind in Indiana drew 91 exhibitors and attracted several nationally known speakers, including Jack Frymier, Harry Mark Petrakis, Robert Marx, Alice Ihrig, Al Trezza, and Dorothy Sinclair.

Humanities Grant. A grant of $36,100 was awarded to ILA-ILTA for a one-year project, "Public Library Services and the Humanities," to begin January 1977. The project will investigate the potential role of academic humanists in public library services, particularly in the areas of collection development, public programs, and continuing education.

Governor's Conference. In preparation for a White House Conference on Library and Information Services, a Core Committee has been actively planning for an Indiana Governor's Conference. Seven librarians, representing all major state associations and types of libraries, began work in April. Alice Ihrig, Chairperson of ALA's White House Conference Committee, attended the first meeting.

Chaired by Alice Wert, Vigo County Public Library, the Core Committee submitted funding proposals to private foundations and gained the support of Governor Bowen's office. It was expected that some funding for the conference would be included in the Governor's Executive Budget to be acted on by the Indiana Legislature in April 1977. A Citizens' Planning Committee would then be organized for a conference tentatively scheduled to meet in 1978.

Networks: INCOLSA. Under the continued leadership of Barbara Markuson, Executive Director, the Indiana Cooperative Library Services Authority (INCOLSA) was rapidly becoming an efficient statewide network of coordinated bibliographic information service. The 121 member libraries in 1976 included 63 public, 27 academic, 20 school systems, and 11 special libraries. Most of the large public libraries and all but a few of the academic libraries were inputting data, as well as the Indiana State Library, the Indiana University School of Medicine, and other special libraries.

Current programs include activities in the areas of continuation of the Indiana Union List of Serials, initiation of MARC-based cataloging for both small and large libraries, a pilot project union catalog of books, and MARC cataloging workshops.

In mid-1976 INCOLSA was given a boost when 14 of Indiana's smaller academic libraries received grants of $8,000 each from the W. K. Kellogg Foundation for INCOLSA terminal installation and start-up costs.

By the end of 1976, the first full year of operation, the Indiana data base contained nearly 100,000 records. It is expected to reach 500,000 in 1978, not including titles in the Indiana Union List of Serials.

Networks: Teletype. The Indiana library teletype network, the state's oldest LSCA network project, officially known as the Interlibrary Communication Project (TWX), continues to be a reliable means of communication and information sharing.

During the fiscal year ending June 30, 1976, the TWX network's 14 public libraries, 4 state university libraries, the State Library, and Indiana University School of Medicine Library originated a total of 17,367 teletype messages. In addition, 5,288 telephone credit card calls were originated by small public libraries that are assigned as "satellites" to the 14 public libraries, which serve as TWX centers for the geographic areas of the state.

The teletype machines, formerly leased, were purchased in 1976 with LSCA funds, and under the agreement current in 1976 each participating TWX library paid only the Western Union monthly usage fee. In-state toll charges and credit card calls, which amounted to $27,903 in fiscal 1975-76, were paid from LSCA funds.

Networks: ALSA's. An Area Library Service Authority (ALSA), a voluntary municipal corporation of member libraries of all types in a prescribed geographic area, has been established in ten of the state's fourteen regions and planning at year's end was in progress in two of the remaining four.

ALSA's have been dependent on federal funding under LSCA Title I, with typical third-year operating grants in the $50,000 to $60,000 range. A bill for state funding for ALSA's is included in the 1977 ILA-ILTA legislative package. [For further information on ALSAs and other Indiana networks see "Indiana Report" in *The ALA Yearbook* (1976); See also Joseph M. Dagnese and Michael K. Buckland, "The Hoosier Way to Synergism," *Special Libraries* 67:382-85 (August 1976).]

Legislative Activity. Aggressive grass roots efforts to gain the support of legislators were made during the year by many librarians and trustees. Mary Barrickman, Lake County Public Library, reports the following activity. A press conference was called in May by the Public Relations Committee of the seven public libraries in Lake County to explain the critical need for more funding for libraries. State legislators and representatives of area newspa-

State Reports—Iowa

pers and radio and television stations were invited to hear firsthand from library users and board members how the lack of adequate funding was affecting services.

Legislators and newsmen were reminded that public libraries, which in Indiana are supported almost entirely by property taxes, had been operating on frozen property tax rates since 1973, and that the law in Indiana had been interpreted to exclude libraries from receiving Revenue Sharing funds.

Public libraries received state funding for the first time in 1976, and ILA-ILTA requested $1,2000,000 for the 1977 fiscal year. In addition, $781,057 was requested for funding ASLAs and $146,832 for INCOLSA.

Construction. The Alexander M. Bracken Library at Ball State University, Muncie, was dedicated on March 26. During the program, honorary degrees of doctor of laws were awarded to Frederick H. Burkhardt, Clara Stanton Jones, and Jesse Hauk Shera (see Biographies). The five-story building has a gross area of 321,800 square feet, an open shelf capacity of 950,000 volumes, seating for 2,878 users, and cost $14,900,000.

The New Castle-Henry County Public Library opened its new building to public use on May 7. Construction project costs of $756,000 provided 16,353 square feet on two levels with a book capacity of 88,000.

Dedication of the addition to the Indiana State Library and Historical Building took place on October 22. Principal speaker was Governor Otis R. Bowen. He noted that the State Library was in its 151st year and that the $4,900,000 new addition will nearly double the usable space of the original building. Sources of funds were the Indiana State Historical Society (nearly half), the state General Assembly ($2,600,000) and federal sources ($340,000).

EDWARD N. HOWARD

IOWA

During 1976 many Iowa libraries underwent changes, some for the better and some that were drastic disappointments to those providing library services to Iowans.

Library lovers in Richland have a brand new building and part of the credit goes to a $94 bullfrog. The frog, along with seedcorn, a hand-made quilt, a $127 pair of geese, and many other items, sold at a library fund-raising auction that netted over $5,000. Richland is one of 53 small communities in Iowa that undertook building, remodeling, or relocating projects during the year. Twenty-three libraries planned to build new facilities, ten completed or planned remodeling additions, and ten relocated or planned to relocate in existing buildings.

Iowa Library Association
(founded 1896)

Membership: 1700; *Annual Expenditure:* $21,000.
President: Judith A. Ellis, Director, Davenport Public Library.
Vice-President/President-elect: Douglas M. Hieber, Head, Circulation Department, University of Northern Iowa Library, Cedar Falls.
Secretary/Treasurer: Gayle Burdick.
Annual Conference: October 14–15, 1976, Conway Center, Waterloo.
Publication: The Catalyst (bimonthly).

State Library Commission of Iowa

Barry L. Porter, Director
Historical Building
Des Moines, Iowa 50319

Financial Belt Tightening. Some of the larger public libraries suffered setbacks as financial belt tightening took its toll. Fiscal year 1977 was a bleak year for the Waterloo Public Library. The City Council reduced rather than increased its support in the face of inflation, forcing staff layoffs and reducing the operating schedule. The Main Library reluctantly reduced its schedule from 72½ to 51½ hours per week; branches cut their hours from 68½ to 41½ hours per week; some bookmobile stops were eliminated. In addition, the library lost 60 percent of its materials budget and discontinued many special programs and services.

The Council Bluffs City Council informed all departments that the city would not fund the capital expenditures account for FY 1976–77. By law that account includes the Free Public Library's materials budget. The council agreed to grant $20,000 revenue sharing money to the library to purchase books, but the previous years's book budget had totaled over $50,000. This step necessitated cutbacks in both staff and services.

When the City Council in Cedar Rapids mandated severe cuts in the Public Library budget, council members also proposed that the library's Board of Trustees impose a one-dollar resident user fee. The Board voted unanimously against the fee. The council urged reconsideration, but the board adamantly reaffirmed its position, with the Board's President stating, ". . . it is the principle involved. Whatever the gain in revenue, it could not offset the incalculable loss of the advantages of our open-to-all institution."

Regional Systems. While existing libraries both suffered and prospered, some areas of Iowa did not have local libraries to serve them. The regional library systems have encouraged local financial support; they stimulated the public libraries within each county to seek funds for the support of library services to residents of the unincorporated areas and incorporated areas without libraries. This effort won legislative support at the state level in 1976 when the legislature mandated a specific minimal tax or its equivalent for library services for all governmental units in Iowa.

The Iowa legislature also appropriates monies for the state's seven regional library systems. The State Library Commission distributes the combination of state and federal funds to the systems, which serve 493 public libraries and through those libraries, a total Iowa population of 2,825,041. Each region elects its own board of trustees to represent specific geographic areas within the region. The board sets policies for the region and appoints a librarian with a professional recognized degree as a regional administrator.

Mandated by Iowa law to "provide supportive library services to existing public libraries and to encourage local financial support of public library service," the regional systems have developed a variety of programs directed toward achieving these goals.

Services to existing libraries include interlibrary loan of books and some audiovisual materials and a reference service. Through interlibrary loan, all levels of libraries throughout the state exchange materials, from the smallest public library to the three state university libraries, as well as private colleges, community colleges and special libraries. The regional libraries contract with a major library agency within each region to use its collection, to maintain regional union files, and to access I-LITE, the statewide teletype network.

Rotating collections of materials made available to public libraries include book collections, large-print materials, audiovisual aids, framed art works, records, and cassettes. Contracts with a public library film cooperative make available for loan a collection of 16mm films. Book lease programs meet the demands for current literature during peak demand periods.

Regional staff members consult with local libraries through in-library contact as well as by telephone and written communication. Consultation covers the whole range of library management, including the aesthetics and practical considerations of library design and layout, collection management, development of library policies, and advising in-library personnel, library boards, local government, and social organizations.

Supportive library services have also included the development of statewide continuing education courses in librarianship offered at the regional level. Though directed especially to those presently working as librarians or serving as library trustees, anyone who is interested in improving library-oriented skills may attend the courses.

State Library. The State Library sponsors the Iowa Library Information Teletype Exchange. I-LITE offers high-volume, rapid reference, and interlibrary loan service to Iowans through 20 public, college, and university teletype stations. During FY 1976, I-LITE filled 71 percent of its 57,929 materials and information requests. Each request that circulated on I-LITE cost $1.48; each filled request cost $2.09.

ILA. The Iowa Library Association (ILA) sponsors seven district meetings each spring, and in 1976 the theme "Reaching Out" provided information about State Library programs that reach out to serve all Iowa libraries and examples of local library programs that reach out to serve the libraries' communities.

In October at the annual conference more exhibits than at any prior ILA conference filled the ample exhibit hall at Conway Center in Waterloo. Dick Gregory, *Administrators' Digest* Editor Robert Alvarez, and William Siarny of the Illinois Health Libraries Consortium spoke to the conference theme, "Iowans Like Action," and charged that librarians must continue to take action. Aware of the budget cutbacks in Iowa libraries and libraries throughout the country, Gregory stated that as cities are forced to trim their budgets, they would decide that they cannot survive without police protection, fire protection, sewer systems, and streets. But they might very well decide that cities can survive without libraries, and he emphasized that cities without libraries have no need for librarians, adding, "Those are *your jobs* I'm talking about!" Alvarez prodded librarians to always question *why* things are done. He warned that librarians who practice such questioning will upset many people, but he urged questioning as a means to evolve more efficient library service. Siarny discussed problems posed for libraries by the new copyright legislation.

The ILA Executive Assistant Relations Committee revamped the job of Executive Assistant, which includes the positions of Secretary, Treasurer and Editor, and established a new pay scale and benefits. The Employer/Employee Rights and Responsibilities Committee established a Board of Inquiry to investigate complaints of employer-employee relations within the state. The Board of Directors established an Iowa Library Association/Iowa Educational Media Association Cooperative Planning Committee to examine the possibilities of cooperation between the two organizations. Most school librarians belong to IEMA and not to ILA, but the two share common interests and goals.

The Intellectual Freedom Committee monitored the progress of the case of *Jerry Lee Smith* v. *U.S.* from an Iowa district court to the U.S. Supreme Court, which heard the opening oral arguments in December. ILA and ALA have filed *amici curei* (friends of the court) briefs at all stages of the appeal. The case involves the distribution of allegedly obscene materials *within* the state, whose legislature has "decriminalized" such materials for adults. The decision will determine whether or not state obscenity rulings are binding under federal prosecution and whether or not libraries and/or librarians might be prosecuted for transporting as a part of central processing, interlibrary loan, or acquisition of such materials.

The College and University Section of ILA established itself as the Iowa Chapter of ACRL in 1976. In 1975, the Iowa Private Academic Librarians voiced concern that such a chapter should exist and hoped that it could strengthen interest in and the programs of the Section. At the 1975 Annual Conference, Section members voted to affiliate with the national organization to take advantage of the benefits they could gain as an ACRL chapter. The required petition quickly gathered many signatures, and the group became the Iowa Chapter of ACRL. The chapter then held its first spring workshop with the Iowa Private Academic Librarians Conference as co-sponsor. The program included several mini-workshops on bibliographic instruction and a general session. The 57 librarians who attended represented universities and four-year and two-year colleges.

GAYLE BURDICK;
REBECCA CHRISTIAN

KANSAS

Libraries in Transition. The Kansas Library Association 1976 conference theme, Libraries in Transition, proved prophetic. The "transition" moved sunflower state libraries more surely into the world of computerization, microfilming of catalogs, and direct contact with data banks. With the help of a $100,000 federal grant, three of the state's seven systems and the State Library began transferring their union catalogs to machine readable form for computer storage and microfilming. The process is expected to take at least a year, according to Ernestine Gilliland, State Librarian, but eventually the combined catalog data will be available on microfilm. Systems involved in this initial step are Central, North Central, and South Central. Library leaders hope to include all other libraries in the state eventually.

Also with federal funding assistance, the State Library initiated installation of video

Kansas Library Association
(founded 1900)

Membership: 589; *Annual Expenditure:* approx. $10,000.
President: Marty Tucker, Kansas State Library (July 1976 – June 1977).
Vice-President/President-elect: Charles Bolles, Kansas State Library.
Secretary: Helen Suellentrop, Central Kansas Library System; 1409 Williams, Great Bend, Kansas 67530.
Annual Conference: April 4 – 6, 1976, Topeka.
Publication: KLA Newsletter (quarterly).

Kansas State Library
Ernestine Gilliland, State Librarian
3d Floor, Statehouse
Topeka, Kansas 66612

display terminals, operating on telephone lines, in the major public libraries, system headquarters, and the State Library, for more efficient interlibrary loan communication and as a plug-in to data banks around the country.

It was an experimental first year in the automation field. The extent of the benefit of the transition to the average patron is not yet clear, but new mechanization is geared toward quicker, more convenient service, and more sharing of books and services.

State aid for Kansas libraries and systems in 1976 was increased to $872,411, or $.33 per capita, from $600,000 ($.23 per capita) for the previous year. Although the State Library, backed by a resolution from the Public Libraries Division of KLA, asked for a 10 percent increase, the state aid figure for 1977 was held at a plateau figure of $875,000.

KLA Activities. Leadership of KLA passed from John Glinka, Director of the University of Kansas Libraries, to Marty Tucker, Assistant State Librarian. At the annual conference in Topeka in April, special speakers were John J. McAleer, Boston, biographer of Rex Stout, a Kansas native, and Herman Lujan, Director of the Institute for Social and Environmental Studies at the University of Kansas.

The state association continued to support legal counsel which represented library interests in the legislature. Annual expenditures of the organization ran to approximately $12,000. Membership was 589 individual and 110 institutional, and interest in KLA membership was reported increasing among the state's librarians.

Buildings. With emphasis on the dollar crunch and mechanized tools for better service, building was at a minimum during 1976. Concordia, in north central Kansas, built a new $350,000 library, however. It contains a Carlson Room, housing papers and memorabilia of Senator Frank Carlson.

State Reports—Kentucky

The city collected $100,000 on a one-mill levy over 10 years and $134,000 came from federal Library Services and Construction Act funds. Additional money was donated. The library, with 9,475 square feet and capacity for 40,000 volumes, was occupied in May at ceremonies at which Art Linkletter was the principal speaker.

A 2½-year building project at the Topeka Public Library, completed in 1976, turned the main building around from north to south and added 30,000 square feet of space. The trick was in designing the enormous increase in space so that it could be handled by available staff, since money was not provided for more staffing, according to James Marvin, the Librarian.

The new area contains a sculpture court, story hour patio, drive-up service window, art gallery, Topeka Room, and auditorium to seat 200. A separate building, closer to the main building front door than the main building back door, has space for bookmobiles and other vehicles on the lower level and the technical processing department upstairs. Exterior of the addition and the new building is of Kansas limestone from the same quarry as that of the original building. A mill a year was accumulated for five years for the building project, which cost $1,700,000.

MARY ANNE CRABB

KENTUCKY

Louisville Public Library. A subregional Branch for the Blind and Physically Handicapped opened in the main library of the Louisville Free Public Library November 1. Supported by state and federal funds, the library serves the residents of Louisville and Jefferson County who qualify for service as victims of disabling diseases or visual handicaps. Materials available for circulation are Talking Books, cassettes, and braille books.

The Library's two noncommercial educational FM radio stations increased their power to 100,000 watts each. WFPK, the Library's classical music station, broadcasts in full stereo. WFPL is the Library's talk and information station. Both stations are members of the National Public Radio Network, broadcasting 18 hours a day the year round.

The Children's Department, located in the Main Library, is experimenting with a new format for its programs for school-age children. The programs, called KALEIDOSCOPE, are presented on Saturdays and have resulted in a reversal in the declining attendance figures of previous years. Half of each hourly program is devoted to a featured presentation which may be puppet shows or audience participation theatre put on by the Children's Department staff,

Kentucky Library Association
(founded 1907)

Membership: 1,159; *Annual Expenditure:* $25,000.
President: (Ms.) Vivian Hall, Geology Library, University of Kentucky (October 1976 – October 1977).
Vice-President/President-elect: Edwin Strohecker, Murray State University, Murray, Kentucky.
Executive Secretary: Thomas A. Sutherland, Paducah Public Library, 555 Washington Street, Paducah, Kentucky 42001.
Annual Conference: October 7 – 9, 1976, Louisville.
Publication: Kentucky Library Association Bulletin (quarterly).

Department of Library and Archives

Charles F. Hinds, State Librarian
Box 537
Frankfort, 40601

but more often is the unique contribution of talented individuals from the community.

State Library. During 1976 the Kentucky Department of Library and Archives showed continued progress in support of public library services to citizens of the commonwealth. While all six divisions of the agency maintained their previous level of program performance, additional areas of service and programming were developed.

The Audiovisual Section expanded its services to include 8mm films. In FY 1975 – 76, 8mm projectors were purchased for all county libraries. A beginning collection of 8mm films was also provided.

In FY 1975 – 76, KENCLIP (Kentucky Cooperative Library Information Project), a network of the state, public, and university libraries, handled more than 10,000 requests for information. Future projections indicate at least a 10 percent increase in this figure.

Early in the year the state library became the initial library to contract for the *Courier Journal* and *Louisville Times* retrieval system that enables the Reference Staff to access much of the newspapers' files and provide service to public libraries throughout the state. In June the newspaper conducted the first of a series of seminars in the use of the information that will be available. The newspaper clippings are on microfilm and michrofiche and are retrievable through a computer terminal.

Direct state financial aid grants totaling $245,300 were distributed to county public libraries based on a population per capita income formula—FY 1976. Professional salary increments were provided to encourage employment of trained personnel as heads of Kentucky's local public libraries. Thirty-six grants (totaling $97,500) were possible during FY 1976. A special appropriation was granted by the Kentucky General Assembly to purchase bookmobiles necessary to bring the 110-vehicle fleet's replacements up to date.

Establishment and accomplishment cash grants plus technical-consultative assistance from KDLA brought countywide library service to several Kentucky counties. Establishment grants were made to Knott and Campbell Counties. Such a grant permits a demonstration of countywide library services. Accomplishment grants were made to communities which have established library service and obtained adequate local financial support through creation of a library taxing district. Counties recently achieving this goal include Casey, Grayson, and McCreary.

A move into an expanded leased facility and the addition of a tape technician to the staff have increased the service capability of the Kentucky Regional Library for the Blind and Physically Handicapped. The first sub-regional program for Kentucky's blind and physically handicapped is being established in Louisville. This library will serve Jefferson County clients, who make up 20 percent of the state's total.

Correctional institutions in Kentucky will have an added sum of money ($39,509) to build up a collection of vocational and guidance materials during 1977.

Eleven library construction projects held dedication ceremonies during 1976. Renovated or new facilities were opened in 10 counties: Tremble, Crittenden, Mercer, Warren, Marshall (Hardin Branch), Boone, Calloway, Franklin, Greenup (Flatwoods), and Fayette (Lansdowne Branch).

The Technical Service Division's service of centralized purchasing, cataloging, and processing produced approximately 229,000 books and materials during FY 1976. Of the total over 223,000 were distributed to county public libraries with the remaining 6,000 added to the State Library collection.

Public Library Certification. Public Library Certification has been radically changed to ensure by 1980 that member county libraries are headed by certified librarians. In 1973 only 15 percent of the head librarians were certified under Kentucky standards. It was up to 48 percent by 1976, and by 1980 it was anticipated that 100 percent would be certified. At the same time the professional standards were raised to require a degree including 21 hours in library science or a comprehensive examination in library science and academic subjects.

Oral History Commission. The Kentucky Bicentennial Oral History Commission was established by the 1976 Kentucky

State Reports—Kentucky

General Assembly and placed in the Kentucky Department of Library and Archives for administration of the project. The program consists of two levels. Level I, a grants program to existing institutions, is administered by the Executive Committee of the Commission which includes the State Librarian, Charles F. Hinds, Historical Society Director William Buster, and Forest Pogue, nationally known oral historian. Kentucky newspapermen Al Smith, Commission Chairman, and John Ed Pierce, Vice-Chairman, were instrumental in the original organization and proposal of the project. At-large members are Al Shands, film producer; Robert Martin, former Eastern Kentucky University President and President of the Kentucky Historical Society; and Thomas D. Clark, noted Kentucky historian. Level II has been organized through the public libraries acting as coordinators for formation of a committee in each community.

Continuing Education. Change is implicit in the very concept of Continuing Education and Kentucky evidenced this throughout 1976. The Kentucky Library Association named an ad hoc committee to investigate what its membership felt would be the most appropriate focus for the Association on statewide continuing library education. The result was a call for a committee on "Professional Development" to be named representing all sections of the Association with an ex-officio status for the Office for Continuing Education. The Executive Board agreed and members of this committee were to be named in 1977.

The Office for Continuing Education initiated new efforts at strengthening its statewide effort through the publication of a *Directory of Human Resources in Kentucky* and the development of a series of learning packages aimed at improving "the reference process" in local public libraries throughout the state. The *Directory* gives names of persons in Kentucky who have the ability and desire to make a contribution to the statewide continuing education effort.

More short-term learning activities have been developed for librarians in the state. The Office for Continuing Education is initiating a new series of symposia on issues critical to the profession beginning in spring 1977, with a symposium on copyright. Proceedings of the symposia will be published for broader distribution to the profession.

Kentucky librarians also initiated an effort toward greater cooperation with other agencies in the state involved with adult and continuing education through the Kentucky Association for Continuing Education (KACE). Staff from the state library were on the fall KACE convention program and the Director of the Office for Continuing Education was elected Vice-President and President-elect of KACE.

Awards. Mrs. Hunter A. Adams was honored by the University of Kentucky in 1976 in two singular ways. First, the President approved the College of Architecture faculty's motion to give her name to the Architecture Library she headed until retiring in 1976. Second, Mrs. Adams was awarded, on the faculty's and students' petition, the Algernon Sydney Sullivan Medallion at University commencement exercises in May.

Susan D. Csaky received three special honors for 1976-77. She received a grant from the International Research and Exchange Board (IREX), was appointed Council of Library Resources Fellow, and obtained a scholarship from the American Association of Law Libraries.

SLA. The Kentucky Chapter of the Special Libraries Association began 1976 with a meeting in Lexington. Giles Frappier, Assistant Librarian of the Library of Parliament, Ontario, and Past President of the International Special Libraries Association, was the guest speaker. Frappier spoke on copyright and its implications for libraries in both the United States and Canada.

The chapter also sponsored a spring workshop in Berea on April 29–30: Computer Based Library Networks and Bibliographic Data Base Search Services. Forty participants attended.

Of significance was the formation of a Kentucky Student Chapter at the University of Kentucky under the guidance of Katherine Cveljo, a Professor in the College of Library Science.

Central Area. The Bluegrass Librarians Association, a new organization for Kentucky, is made up of all types of librarians in the central area of the state. Charles Hinds served as the interim President.

KLA. The Kentucky Library Association held its annual meeting in Louisville, October 7–9. Highlight of the conference was a panel on "The Closing of LC's Card Catalog." Lois Chann, College of Library Science, University of Kentucky, chaired the meeting and panel participants were David Remington of the Library of Congress; Gail Kennedy, SOLINET, University of Kentucky; Ann Exstrom, Director of Library Systems, OCLC, Ohio State University; and Bill Caddell, Frankfort (Indiana) Public Library.

Other outstanding programs included "Collection Development in Academic Libraries," Jo Ann Harrar, Director, University of Maryland Libraries; "The Value of Professional Societies, Pro and Con," Ann Hamilton, moderator with Bess Clotfelter, University of Kentucky taking opposing views; "The British Lending Library, a First Resort," Patricia Renfro, Reference Department, University of Kentucky.

University of Kentucky. Rosemary DuMont and Wayne Wiegand accepted the offers of the University of Kentucky College of Library Science to become assistant professors.

Timothy W. Sineath was appointed Professor of Library Science and Dean of the College of Library Science, effective July 1, 1977. Thomas Waldhart served as Acting Dean in 1976.

Charles Williams, who had been at the Lexington College since 1974, left the College of Library Science on July 1 to accept a position at Centenary College in Shreveport, Louisiana, as Director of the Library.

Robert E. Cazden was promoted from Associate to Full Professor at the UK College of Library Science. Cazden had been with the College since 1966.

Retirements. C. R. Graham, Director of the Louisville Free Public Library, will retire on July 1, 1977, it was announced in 1976. Graham, known as "Skip," during his more than 35 years of dedicated service brought national recognition to the Library.

Margaret Willis, former State Librarian, retired from the position of Director of Field Services on March 31. Willis had served in that position since July 1, 1973. The "First Lady of Kentucky Public Libraries" remained active in library service by assisting the Kentucky Department of Library and Archives and Friends of Kentucky Libraries, Inc.

She was succeeded as Director of Field Services by Ellen Hellard. Hellard had been associated with KDLA for 10 years as a regional librarian/district library director.

Six University of Kentucky librarians retired in 1976 with a total of more than 150 years combined experience. They were: Jacquline P. Bull, founder and Head of Special Collections; Kate Irvine, Head of Reference; Mary Ada Sullivan, organizer and Head of the Newspaper/Microtext Department; Lucille Keating, Serials Librarian in the Law Library; Hunter A. Adams, Head of the Architecture Library; and Carolyn Hammer, Curator of Rare Books.

Assistant State Librarian. Barbara Williams assumed the position of Assistant State Librarian on September 1. She was Director of the Kentucky Department of Finance and Administration Library from 1968 to 1975. She was previously on the staff of KDLA. — BARBARA S. MILLER

State Reports—Louisiana

LOUISIANA

Legislation. State government reorganization mandated by the new Louisiana Constitution was effected by Act 513 of 1976. It places the State Library in the Department of Culture, Recreation, and Tourism with the State Librarian as an Assistant Secretary, but preserves the authority of the State Library Board to appoint the State Librarian and the State Board of Library Examiners. Sandra Thompson was named Secretary of the Department, which, in addition to the State Library, includes the State Museum; the Parks and Recreation Commission; the Art, Historical, and Cultural Preservation Agency; and the Tourist Development Commission.

Of real benefit to librarians interested in public employment at various levels of government is Act 416, which permits a person who has been a member of any state, municipal, or parochial retirement system for at least three years to transfer membership service credit of at least three years from any other state, municipal, or parochial retirement system. It also provides for repaying a refund, plus 5 percent interest to reestablish credited service of at least three years.

Of major significance in 1976 to public libraries in the state, most of which are supported by an ad valorem tax, were opinions from the Attorney General indicating that the Constitution of 1974 does not provide limitations on either millage rates or the duration of a tax which may be approved by the electorate for special purposes such as public library maintenance. Formerly the millage rate was limited to five mills and the duration of the tax to ten years.

Also of importance to public libraries is Act 689 of 1976 which does away with the long-established system of deducting commissions for the sheriffs from the revenues collected for local taxing authorities, including the library. A mandatory rollback is provided to keep the library and other taxing entities from realizing an increase in ad valorem revenues, but this will put an end to increasing sheriffs' commissions resulting in decreasing library incomes.

New Buildings. Two public library branches and one new main library building were dedicated during the year. The West Baton Rouge Parish Library central building in Port Allen was dedicated with an open house April 11. The 9,000-square-foot building was constructed at a cost of some $362,300, most of which came from a bond issue. Federal revenue sharing funds from the local governing body made up $140,000.

The Epps Memorial Branch of the Calcasieu Parish Library was dedicated April 4. This neighborhood branch in north Lake Charles was named in memory of the late Rochelle P. Epps, a library board member and teacher. The 3,400-square-foot building was constructed at a cost of $134,098. The entire project, including purchase of property, building, furnishings, books, and other library materials, was made possible by a grant by the local governing body from federal revenue sharing funds.

The Berwick Branch of the St. Mary Parish Library was dedicated October 31. Cost of the 4,500-square-foot building was $165,950. Of that amount, $106,650 was appropriated by the local governing body, and $59,400 was received from the State Highway Department, which purchased the old building for right-of-way purposes.

LLA Awards. Margaret T. Lane, who retired as recorder of state documents, received the Essae M. Culver Distinguished Service Award presented annually to a professional member of the Association whose service and achievements have been of particular value to Louisiana librarianship.

The Louisiana Library Association Modisette Awards were presented to Murphy A. Tannehill as the outstanding public library trustee and to the Byrd High School, Shreveport; the St. Martinville Primary School, St. Martinville; and the Concordia Parish Library, Ferriday. The Modisette Awards pay tribute to the late James Oliver Modisette, who for 15 years chaired the Louisiana Library Commission.

Tannehill, of Urania, was honored for his 23 years of service on the LaSalle Parish Library Board, six years of which he served as Board Chairman; his five years as a member of the Louisiana State Library Board of Commissioners, one year of which he served as Chairman.

Librarian Lucile A. Tindol accepted the award for the Byrd High School Library, which was cited for its cooperative efforts with faculty and students in the sponsorship of special programs and research projects to enliven the school's courses. The St. Martinville Primary School Library, with Claire F. Dunbar as librarian, was recognized for its media program.

The winner of the 1975 Louisiana Literary Award was Joe Gray Taylor, Professor of History and Head of the History Department at McNeese State University, for *Louisiana Reconstructed, 1863–1877*. The book was cited for its coverage of economic conditions in Louisiana during the period.

George Fuller, Superintendent of Iberia Parish Schools, was awarded the annual Educator's Award by the Louisiana Association of School Librarians. He was recognized for his awareness of the need for good school libraries.

The Sue Hefley Award was presented by the Louisiana Association of School Librarians to William Armstrong for his book *Sounder*. The award in the form of a plaque is awarded to the author whose book has been chosen from a master list by Louisiana students in grades four through eight.

Other Awards. Lynda Netherland, Librarian of the Bossier and Red River Parish libraries in Benton and Coushatta, was named the Outstanding Young Woman of the year in Bossier Parish by the Junior Chamber of Commerce.

John B. Richard, Librarian of the Louisiana State University in Alexandria, was named the 1975 winner of the *Alexandria Daily Town Talk*'s Civic Oscar. He was cited for his many civic achievements.

Bronislaw "Mike" Janowski, Librarian of the Evangeline Parish Library in Ville Platte, received the Louisiana Farm Bureau's Freedom Award. The award is given to a person who has espoused the cause of freedom, particularly through speeches, letters, and editorials.

Pearl Rhymes, a 41-year member of the Richland Parish Library Board, received distinguished service awards from both the Rayville Kiwanis Club and the Town of Rayville.

Beth Barnett, a staunch library supporter of Crowley, was honored as that city's Outstanding Citizen of the Year 1975 and cited for her leadership in the passage of a $1,300,000 bond issue for the expansion of the Acadia Parish Library.

Adele M. Jackson, of the Southern University Library staff in Baton Rouge, was one of 10 selected to participate in the internship program sponsored by the ACRL for administrators of predominately Black college and university libraries.

Two Louisiana libraries, the Iberville Parish Library in Plaquemine and the

Louisiana Library Association
(founded 1926)

Membership: 1,236; *Annual Expenditure:* $20,050.
President: M. Eugene Wright, Jr., New Orleans Public Library (July 1976–June 1977).
Vice-President/President-elect: Agnes Harris, Union Parish Library.
Acting Executive Secretary: Sharilynn Aucoin, P. O. Box 131, Baton Rouge, Louisiana 70821.
Annual Meeting: March 31–April 2, 1976, Lafayette.
Publication: L. L. A. Bulletin (quarterly).

Louisiana State Library

Thomas F. Jacques, State Librarian
P. O. Box 131
Baton Rouge, Louisiana 70821

State Reports—Louisiana

Barksdale Air Force Base Library in Bossier City, were recipients of John Cotton Dana awards.

The New Orleans Public Library received an honorable mention for its 1974 annual report in the ALA Library Public Relations Council PR Awards Contest.

The Milton H. Latter branch of the New Orleans Public Library, in the Williams Mansion, was added to the National Register of Historic Places.

The Cammie G. Henry Louisiana Room and Archives in the Eugene P. Watson Memorial Library at Northwestern State University in Natchitoches was designated a national attraction by the American Revolution Bicentennial Administration in Washington, D.C.

Continuing Education. An institute on "Continuing Library and Information Science Education Program Planning for State Library Agency Personnel" was held at Louisiana State University in Baton Rouge March 14–21, 1976. The Institute was sponsored by the Graduate School of Library Science in cooperation with the Chief Officers of State Library Agencies and funded by a HEA Title II-B grant. Thirty-two representatives from 29 states attended, including Sandra Cooper, Public Library Consultant from the Louisiana State Library. Donald D. Foos, Dean of the Graduate School of Library Science, served as Institute Director and John C. Sanderlin, Associate Director of Libraries, Florida Technological University, as Administrative Assistant. Program participants included Wayne L. Schroeder, Martha Jane Zachert, Harold Goldstein, Mary Neiball, Cheryl Metoyer, Thomas Sutherland, and Gwen Cruzat.

State Librarian Thomas F. Jaques appointed a task force to advise the State Library on continuing education. The task force will assist the State Library in carrying out the objective in its long-range plan which calls for the development of "a state plan for the organization and structure of a coordinated program of continuing education for library personnel in Louisiana, working in cooperation with representatives of the various types of library activity, by September 30, 1977." The 26-member group, which includes librarians, trustees, and library educators, is chaired by D. W. Schneider, Associate Director of the Louisiana State University Library at Baton Rouge.

Public Library Programs. Five Louisiana libraries were selected to participate in the national Films Plus program: Bossier Parish Library, Caldwell Parish Library, Iberville Parish Library, Catahoula Parish Library, and the East New Orleans Branch of the New Orleans Public Library. This experimental program, sponsored by the Modern Language Association and the National Endowment for the Humanities, is designed to stimulate more effective use of the library as a humanities resource by encouraging the reading of library books related to the project's film series.

The Iberville Parish Library in Plaquemine received an anonymous gift of $1,500 to fund a Personal Development Series, planned in cooperation with the local mental health clinic, with programs such as "Be Your Own Person," conducted by a family counselor. The Parish Library also received a grant of $600 from the Louisiana Tourist Commission to develop a sound slide program and museum display on the Atchafalaya River Basin.

The Jackson Parish Library in Jonesboro sponsored art workshops in watercolor and the dry brush technique by Ronnie Wells, a local artist who has become nationally known for his paintings of Southern scenes.

Special Libraries. The Health Sciences Library Association of Louisiana (HSLAL) was organized to encourage and promote interaction and educational programs that will further the objectives of health-related libraries. At an organizational meeting Jane Lambremont, of the Earl K. Long Hospital Library, Baton Rouge, was elected President; Cheryl Jordan, Lafayette Charity Hospital, Vice-President; and B. Carol McGee, Central Louisiana State Hospital, Secretary-Treasurer. Anne Pascarelli of Xavier University in New Orleans spoke on "Basic Reference Sources in Pharmacology."

Retirements. Marilla Lay Warner, Librarian of the Huey P. Long Law Library, a unit of the Attorney General's office, retired in early April. During the last two years before her retirement, after 32 years of service, she compiled an index to the reported opinions of the attorneys general of Louisiana from 1950 through 1970.

After 35 years of service, Patricia Catlett retired as Reference Librarian of the Southeastern Louisiana University Library in Hammond. During a University award convocation, Catlett was honored by the Division of Student Affairs for her years of service at Southeastern, especially her extracurricular contributions.

Tillie Schenker, Librarian of the East Baton Rouge Parish Library, retired at the end of the year after serving in the position since 1947. She was Assistant Librarian from 1936 to 1947, and also worked with the State Library prior to that. In 1962–63 she served as President of the Louisiana Library Association.

Virginia Wilkins, Librarian of the Acadia Parish Library in Crowley since it was established in 1946, retired on October 1.

Anne Jane Dyson, Head of the Humanities Division, and Helen Palmer, Head of the Science Division at the Louisiana State University Library in Baton Rouge, retired on September 1. Dyson had been on the staff since 1935 and Palmer since 1961. They were co-compilers of several bibliographies of literary criticisms: *American Drama Criticism, European Drama Criticism* and *English Novel Explication*, published by the Shoe String Press.

Elizabeth Casellas retired as Director of the Norman Mayer Library, Graduate School of Business Administration, Tulane University, after 22 years of varied experience in business librarianship, business research, and university teaching.

Roby H. Sparr, Assistant Library Administrator for the Jefferson Parish Library from 1967, retired November 1. He had been with the library since 1958, having held positions in the acquisitions and cataloging departments.

Appointments. Charles B. Williams was appointed Director of the Centenary College Library in Shreveport. Williams, who holds four degrees from the University of Oklahoma, was formerly Assistant Professor of Library Science at the University of Kentucky.

John B. Richard was named City Parish Librarian of the East Baton Rouge Parish Library effective January 1, 1977. He had been Director of the Library at Louisiana State University in Alexandria from 1960 and was formerly with the Louisiana State University in Baton Rouge. He served as President of the Louisiana Library Association in 1969–70.

Carla Klapper was appointed Director of the Bayouland Library System in Lafayette. She was formerly reference librarian for the system.

Lyle Johnson was appointed Librarian of the Acadia Parish Library in Crowley effective October 1. He was formerly Assistant Librarian of the Pike-Amite County Library in McComb, Mississippi.

Deaths. Miss Marjorie Ledoux, Librarian of the Middle American Research Institute Library, at Tulane University in New Orleans, died July 1, 1976.

Shirley Knowles Stephenson, Louisiana State University Professor Emeritus of Library Science, died September 13. Professor Stephenson was a member of the Graduate School of Library Science faculty from 1943 to 1972. In 1975 she received the Essae M. Culver Award for her outstanding contribution to Louisiana librarianship.

A. Otis Hebert, Director of the Center for Acadian Studies at the University of Southwestern Louisiana, died on October 9. Hebert was Director of the Louisiana Department of Archives and Records from 1966 to 1974, a member of the Region 7 Advisory Council of the National Archives and Records Service, and a founder of the Society of Southwest Archivists. Widely

State Reports—Maine

published in the field of archives and history, he had served as Executive Secretary of the Louisiana Historical Association for seven years.

Sister Mary Aquin Lorio, O.P., former Librarian at St. Mary's Dominican High School in New Orleans, died September 20.
VIVIAN CAZAYOUX

MAINE

Regional System. Three library districts were created in Maine by enactment of Public Law 626, an act of the Maine State Legislature to create a regional library system. Central Maine Library District (CMLD), Southern Maine Library District (SMLD), and Northeastern Maine Library District (NMLD) have been in operation for approximately two years. Each district has a district consultant and an area reference and resource center. The district consultant is hired by the Executive Board of the district council and acts as an adviser in all library related areas for school and public libraries within each district. The position requires a person with a broad background in all areas of library work and also an understanding of Maine communities and their fiscal conditions. The area reference and resource center is responsible for providing a supplementary collection of books, periodicals, and reference materials. Local libraries use the reference and resource center for interlibrary loan, photo duplication of periodical materials, and answers to reference questions. The district consultant is closely allied with the resource center. The Maine State Library with Lewiston Public Library as a fiction center, Portland Public Library, and Bangor Public Library serve as the three area reference and resource centers.

Each of the three districts has focused on different aspects of librarianship. The Central District funded a reference book project for public libraries, district book selection meetings, and joint meetings for children's librarians on a regular basis. The Southern District held a series of workshops dealing with the role of the library trustee and is currently supporting a cooperative cataloging project. The Northeastern District is involved with a common borrowing system among the libraries in its district.

State Library. Since the advent of the regional library system in Maine, the role of the Maine State Library has changed to some extent. It continues to serve as the nonfiction resource center for the Central Maine Library District. Emphasis is being placed on such special services as bookmobile libraries, library services to the handicapped, special libraries, and the film cooperative. Government reorganization at the state level has resulted in closer contacts with school librarians and media specialists. Several State Library staff members are members of a media team that works for the benefit of both school and public libraries.

Maine State Library staff also includes a regional library system consultant who is responsible for the supervision of the three district consultants and their district councils. This position is primarily concerned with budget matters and with long-range plans for future library development.

Buildings. Two major building programs were completed in Maine during 1976. Fogler Library at the University of Maine at Orono increased its floor space by 57,200 square feet with its $2,500,000 addition. As the leading research library in the state, Fogler Library was in desperate need of more space.

Waterville Public Library made a significant addition to its floor space with a multi-floor construction. The addition will contain new stack areas, a new circulation area, and a community meeting room, and provide access for the physically handicapped. Some of the support was from LSCA federal funds.

MLA Conferences and Publications. The annual conference of MLA was held May 13–14 in Rockport. The conference began with a video tape produced by librarians at the Bangor Public Library. The tape both shocked and amused the audience as interviewees on the street told why they do not use the library. A panel discussion on "How Libraries May Better Respond to the Needs of Maine People" elicited discussion among representatives from several Maine organizations on what their members wanted to see in their libraries. The report of the Continuing Education Committee, "Report and Recommendations of the Continuing Education Committee," was edited by Mary Elizabeth Dudman. The report polled people in the field and made concrete recommendations. Mary McKenzie from the New England Library Board spoke on the interest of her Board in continuing education. She stated that it was one of the top priorities of NELB, which had created a Task Force for further recommendations from all six New England states. The Health Services Network held a panel discussion on "Information Needs for Nurses," and pinpointed deficiencies in library services to nurses in many areas. Principal speaker at the conference was Edward D. (Sandy) Ives, Director of the Northeast Archives of Folklore and Oral History. The report of the Legislative Committee, "Legislative Handbook of the Maine Library Association," was edited by Frederick von Lang. It discusses lobbying techniques and a communications network covering the whole state so that legislators can be contacted when and if necessary. Stephen King, author of "Carrie" and "Salem's Lot," reminisced about his experiences from early childhood, in his hometown, school and college libraries.

The MLA fall conference was held on October 15, 1976, at the Bangor Community College. The Attorney General of Maine, Joseph Brennan, discussed the conflict between the right to privacy and the public's right to know. Presently there is no privacy act legislation in Maine. Jack Short, Past President of the Library Trustee Association of ALA, spoke on the role of the trustee as outlined in ALA guidelines. Nancy Dikeman, of the Maine Office on Volunteerism, Augusta, outlined ten steps in developing a volunteer program. The Franco-American Session, opened with a videotape segment of "La Bonne Aventure," a series of 20 programs produced by the Maine Public Broadcasting Network to raise the self-esteem of Franco-American children ages 3 to 7 in Maine and New England.

An Intellectual Freedom Committee was made a standing committee of MLA. A major publications of MLA, compiled by the Bicentennial Committee, is *Bibliography of Maine, 1960–1975*. It was edited by Eric S. Flower.

People. Appointments made during 1976 included Richard Sibley, formerly with Millinocket Public Library, appointed Director of Waterville Public Library. He replaced Norman Moore, a Past President of the Maine Library Association.

Margaret Thibeault became Director of the Louis B. Goodall Memorial Library in Sanford. Susan Anderson was named Head Librarian at the York Public Library. The new Librarian at Millinocket Public Library is Carl Beizer. Jean Houle retired as Librarian of the Madison Public Library. New Head Librarian at Bridgton Public Library is Sally MacAuslan.

Maine Library Association
(founded 1893)

Membership: 716; *Annual Expenditure:* $5,200.
President: Richard F. Gross, Director, Lewiston Public Library.
Vice-President: Benita Davis, Bangor Public Library.
Secretary: Richard Sibley, Director, Waterville Public Library.
Annual Meeting: May 13–14, 1976, Rockland.
Publication: Downeast Libraries (five issues per year).

Maine State Library

J. Gary Nichols, State Librarian
Cultural Building
Maine State Library
Augusta, Maine 04333

Enid M. Crooker, Librarian of the B. H. Bartol Library at Freeport, died in early November. Ann Westervelt was appointed the new Librarian. FREDERICK VON LANG

MARYLAND

1976 Status Report. With the publication of *Master Plan for the Development of Library Services in the State of Maryland* in December 1974, organized development of library services gained new momentum at all levels of operation. The *1976 Status Report* published in June describes the remarkable progress that was realized during calendar 1975.

The following findings are felt to be of major significance in pointing up the status of library service in Maryland at the end of 1976:

Three county library systems and the three regional resource centers (comprised of 17 of Maryland's 24 jurisdictions) have begun systematic planning, developing annual and long-range plans based on an analysis of community information and service needs and evaluation of present services. Recommendations call for all public libraries to formulate plans.

Task Force for Long-Range Planning for Media Technology in Maryland, published in 1976, provided a plan of action to direct and accelerate the "corporation, adoption, and use of instructional technology within the educational programs being provided to and by the 24 local educational agencies in Maryland." Recommendations speak directly to the provision of a full range of information services to students, school personnel, and the school community.

The Division of Library Development

Maryland Library Association, Inc.
(founded 1923)

Membership: 1100; *Annual Expenditure:* $30,000.
President: Lance C. Finney, Maryland State Department of Education, Division of Library Development and Services (May 1976–April 1977).
Vice-President/President-elect: Ruth Almeida, Annapolis and Anne Arundel County Library.
Executive Secretary: Christine M. Johnson, 115 West Franklin Street, Baltimore, Maryland 21201.
Annual Meeting: April 29–30, 1976, Baltimore.
Publication: The *CRAB* (bimonthly).

Maryland State Department of Education

Nettie B. Taylor, Assistant State Superintendent for Libraries and Director
P.O. Box 8717, Baltimore-Washington International Airport
Baltimore, Maryland 21240

and Services, Maryland State Department of Education, continued to assist local public library units in meeting staff training needs. These efforts emphasized planning and evaluation of library services (immediate, short- and long-range), associate library program, services to disadvantaged persons, principles of good management, information and referral services, and materials in specialized subject areas. Simultaneously, a concerted effort was made to provide training (preservice and inservice) opportunities for library media personnel at all levels of operation in Maryland's 24 education subdivisions.

Library Services Growth. Progress continued in the reduction of barriers to statewide media services. Of the state's 1,339 public elementary and secondary schools, only 50 were without school media centers; all academic institutions in the state maintained campus-based libraries; and all 23 counties and Baltimore City, which comprise the 24 local jurisdictions in Maryland, supported a public library system.

A wide variety of resources, services, and personnel existed. Per capita support for public libraries ranged from $9.42 down to $2.42. As of June 30, 1976, per capita support averaged $7.23.

Support for schools also showed a wide range in per capita support for textbooks, varying from a high of $11.94 to a low of $4.72. In the purchase of nontextbook library resources, the range was even broader, from $20.19 to $0.53, in the local jurisdictions.

Funding Enoch Pratt. The Central Library of the Enoch Pratt Free Library of Baltimore City was designated the State Library Resource Center in 1971. The equitable sharing of operating costs between city and state raises many questions for which answers are not readily available. In view of the state's continuing responsibility for the provision of library and information services, the General Assembly passed Senate Joint Resolution 13 in early 1976 requesting the Governor to appoint a committee to study the funding of the State Library Resource Center. This group would also be charged with devising a method of fairly allocating costs of the Enoch Pratt Free Library system to the State Library Resource Center. The report of the Governor's Committee on Funding the State Library Resource Center was forwarded to the Governor in November 1976. The library community is hopeful that affirmative action on the recommendations will be forthcoming.

The development and use of a union catalog on microfilm continues. Now comprised of the collections of the Enoch Pratt Free Library of Baltimore City, four county public library systems, one community college, and three university collections, the two 1000-foot film reels carry in excess of 800,000 titles.

MILO. At the heart of statewide library service one observes the vital role played by Maryland Interlibrary Organization. Shortened to MILO, MILO-Central refers to the central send-receive headquarters of the statewide teletype network housed within the Central Library of the Enoch Pratt Free Library in Baltimore. Increasing network traffic led the Division of Library Development and Services to call in a consultant to evaluate the contract services of MILO-Central and to analyze present procedures and record-keeping. Submitted in September, *Maryland Interlibrary Organization: MILO-Central* by Dana L. Alessi is presently being reviewed by appropriate administrators as a basis for planning.

Information and Referral Services are now available in 19 of Maryland's 24 subdivisions. Structured I & R services implies a fully developed file directory of agencies and organizations within the community manipulated by a specially trained staff. While 15 I & R services are administered by public library systems, four are independent of libraries.

A desired trend persists: more schools are being equipped with television receivers and an increasing number of teachers are participating through the use of the telecasts in their classrooms.

Production of four reading series (print and nonprint for age levels from 4 to 13) was completed this year and all four series are being telecast over the four activated public television channels.

All four series were nominated for "Emmy" awards. Unfortunately, each was in competition with the others. The series "Once Upon a Town" won and an "Emmy" was awarded to the State Department of Education by the National Academy of Television Arts and Sciences.

These series brought other awards, one of them being a John Cotton Dana Library Public Relations Award presented at the annual American Library Association conference in Chicago. The citation: "For top quality video presentation introducing four new instructional television reading series productions for grades PreK-8."

Construction. The number of library buildings completed in the United States during 1976 was greater than in any one of the prior four years, and Maryland enjoyed a good share of the activity:

Frostburg State College opened an exceptionally functional 112,000 square-foot library in April. The Learning Resources Center of the Dundalk Community College began a wide range of services in new quarters in October. The Annapolis and Anne Arundel County Library moved into a new, 18,000 square-foot headquarters facility. The same system opened a long-awaited branch in Crofton. Carroll County Public Library occupied its Mount Airy Branch. The Hillcrest Heights Branch of Prince George's County Memorial Library and the Bethesda Library of the Montgomery County Library system brought major agencies to densely populated communities. Howard County Library opened a branch in Long Reach, and the Enoch Pratt Free Library of Baltimore dedicated its Fort Worthington Library Center.

The Division of Library Development and Services, Maryland State Department of Education, continued to exercise its responsibility to communicate ideas and information to the library community. In addition to the previously mentioned publications, titles of major importance include *Facts About Maryland's School Media Programs 1975–76*, *Humanizing School Media Facilities*, *Issues in Media Management 1976*, and *Services of a School Media Program*.

Maryland Library Association. The Annual Conference held at the Baltimore Hilton Inn in Pikesville on April 28–30 drew more than 500 registrants. A one-day preconference dealt with "Networking: From Theory to Practice." Responding to problems and criticisms voiced at prior conferences, the program focused on practical considerations of networking as applied to both cataloging operations and reference services. The first day of the conference featured a program addressing "Compression and Crunch: Job Security and Outlook" and brought speakers from the U.S. Department of Labor, a graduate library school, and library administrations.

Other programs addressed coordination among academic libraries; library trustee roles in planning; the intricacies of censorship, racism, and sexism, media selection problems; children's services idea exchange; and the pros and cons of security systems.

Many of the issues being debated within the American Library Association are of course being addressed at the state level. Sexist terminology is being removed from the Association's Constitution and Bylaws. Dues schedules, membership categories, other-than-calendar-year operations, and personal liability insurance for librarians have come under scrutiny.

A poll conducted in August indicated that the Maryland Library Association, District of Columbia Library Association, and Virginia Library Association members favor a combined annual conference in 1978. A special committee, with representatives from each of the three groups, is at work on the shared program.

In addition to 13 standing committees, there are four ad hoc committees addressing special charges set by the Executive Board.

Both the Federal Relations Committee, instrumental in the passage of Senate Bill S2657 extending and amending HEA and ESEA, and the Legislative and Planning Committee have had a busy year. In addition to Senate Joint Resolution 13 mentioned earlier, legislation redefining the law concerning funding of current operating expenses of public libraries met with approval in 1976. Two House of Delegate bills concerning public library trustees were enacted. The first of these required members of the boards of trustees to reside in the county that the member's board serves; the second states that a member of the boards of library trustees who fails to attend at least 50 percent of that board's scheduled meetings during any one calendar year shall be considered to have resigned from the board. The bill makes provision for replacing such members.

Now, at the end of calendar 1976, a bill has been drafted to increase State Library aid to $4 per capita (presently $3). This bill combines the current operating expenses with public library incentive fund monies. The legislation requires that no less than 80 percent of the state aid be used for operating expenses and no more than 20 percent be used for capital improvements.

People. In public libraries, 1976 saw the retirement of Elizabeth B. Hage as Director of the Prince George's County Memorial Library and the appointment of Walter Shih as Acting Director. Anna Curry was named Assistant Director of the Enoch Pratt Free Library in Baltimore. Vaughn Simon was appointed Chief, Processing Division, in the same system.

Elliot Shelkrot became Chief, Public Services, Baltimore County Public Library.

Linda Mielke was named Specialist in Community Services, Division of Library Development and Services, Maryland State Department of Education.

H. Thomas Walker, Jr., was appointed Supervisor of Media Services, Howard County Public School System. Rose R. Cardamone assumed responsibilities as Media Specialist, Review and Evaluation Center, Anne Arundel County Public Schools and Maryland State Department of Education.

Cora Kenney left the Anne Arundel County Board of Education where she served as Coordinator of Library and Media Services to accept an appointment as Director, Department of Defense Dependents School of Europe.

The library community was grieved by the untimely passing of Desmond P. Wedberg on May 27, 1976. Des, as he was affectionately known, was a leader in audiovisual education and a professor in the College of Education at the University of Maryland. A native of Redlands, California, Dr. Wedberg also taught at the University of Southern California, the California State Polytechnic College, New York University, and Columbia University. LANCE C. FINNEY

MASSACHUSETTS

Financial Support. Although the regional public library systems and direct state aid grant support level was maintained for fiscal 1977, the state agency, the Bureau of Library Extension, saw its budget cut by approximately $63,000 for the same period. The Massachusetts Library Association (MLA) had submitted legislation to increase the state support for the regional public library systems and the direct state aid grant which was not passed by the legislature.

In Massachusetts, the dog tax is used in most communities for the local school system or the public library. Efforts were made in the spring of 1976 to have those funds allocated for animal control. No final report had been filed as of year's end about the outcome of a study committee's efforts to resolve the issue.

Intertype Library Cooperation. A report was filed during the year with the Board of Library Commissioners on its conference held in November 1975. At year's end, the Board was expected to release a summary of the report to the library community. Participants at the conference received a copy of the complete report.

Board of Library Commissioners. The term of one member expired in the early summer and thereafter two other members of the five-person Board resigned. Solomon Rosenbaum, recommended by both the Massachusetts Library Association and the Massachusetts Library Trustee Association, was appointed a Commissioner. The lack of a full Board adversely affected the

---

Massachusetts Library Association
(founded 1890)

Membership: 1,100 (200 ALA members); *Annual Expenditure:* $23,500.
President: Joseph S. Hopkins, Worcester Public Library (July 1975–June 1977).
Vice-President: Margaret Brown, Charlestown Branch, Boston Public Library.
Executive Secretary: Patricia A. Demit, Box 7, Nahant, Massachusetts, 01908.
Annual Conference: May 10–11, 1976, North Falmouth.
Publication: Bay State Librarian (5 issues a year).

Bureau of Library Extension

Charles Joyce, Director
648 Beacon Street
Boston, Massachusetts 02215

work of the Board. Meetings were cancelled and postponed several times because of the lack of a quorum.

Regional Public Library Systems. The Bureau staff conducted a study of the regions in 1975 and presented a report referred to as a "Data Summary." This document did not contain any recommendations. Dissatisfaction on the part of many librarians was expressed in a series of public meetings conducted by the Board of Library Commissioners early in 1976. Many complained about the use made of the questionnaire and the application of certain statistics in the Data Summary. Although it was generally agreed that the regions were not perfect, they were effective, had extended library service, and until something better could be implemented, no one wanted to limit the development of regional service. In April the recommendations of the Bureau staff concerning the regions were released to directors and trustees of the contracting libraries, the regional administrators, and at the same time to the Board of Library Commissioners. Trustees and librarians were prepared for the meeting with the Board of Library Commissioners and the Board found itself in an embarrassing position. It was finally agreed that the Bureau staff recommendations would be withdrawn and no further distribution made.

At the same meeting a discussion on the Plan of Service for the Eastern Massachusetts Regional Library System resulted in agreement that a committee of librarians and trustees would be appointed to study the documents and procedures relative to the regional systems.

A committee known as the Ad Hoc Committee to Study the Regional Library Systems was appointed. Although it lacks representation from the Plan of Service Committee and includes librarians from all types of libraries, the regional systems were willing to wait for conclusions and recommendations.

Library Services and Construction Act. The administration of LSCA had been satisfactory from the viewpoints of both the regional systems and many libraries until 1975–76. During 1975–76, the regional systems did not receive the supplementary LSCA funds which they had been receiving. LSCA grants were allocated to smaller libraries in a very pronounced effort to spread the funds over a larger number of communities. In some cases, projects were funded without any consultation with the LSCA Advisory Committee.

During 1976 that Committee adopted bylaws approved by the Board of Library Commissioners to provide for all grant proposals—even those prepared by Bureau staff—to be submitted to the Committee. The size of the Committee will probably be increased and provisions have been made for continuity, if the increased size is approved.

LSCA is a matter of concern because it appears substantial amounts are being used to fund positions at the Bureau of Library Extension.

Library Service. Throughout Massachusetts many libraries—public, school, and academic—face funding problems. In spite of the funding situations, a number of libraries either alone or in groups have developed interesting programs of service. Bibliographical tools such as union lists of periodicals are available in both public and academic libraries. Union catalogs are functioning in several of the sub-regions. John Cotton Dana Awards were received by the public libraries in Cambridge, Concord, and Watertown while Memorial Hall Library in Andover received an award from the Public Relations Council.

Public, academic, and special libraries continue to explore and implement cooperative computer programs using OCLC and other data-base services. Individual libraries such as the Worcester Public Library and the Boston Public Library are using either in-house computers or municipal facilities to develop systems in a number of different activities. Mini-computers are being installed by commercial services in public libraries. All libraries are working for compatibility so that a library can use parts of different systems to develop their total program.

Future. The Massachusetts Library Association planned to file another bill requesting additional funding for public libraries and the regional systems. The Board of Library Commissioners in 1976 intended to file a bill to provide for the reorganization of the Board. In essence the bill provides for the transfer of the Board and Bureau from the Massachusetts Department of Education to the Office of the Secretary of Educational Affairs. The proposed bill will probably provide for other changes which had not been worked out at year's end. The reports of the Ad Hoc Committee to Study the Regions, the appointment of two Commissioners to the Board of Library Commissioners, the changes in the LSCA Advisory Committee, and the results of legislative activity will all be important in the development of library service.

Appointments. Thomas F. O'Connell was named Director of Libraries at Boston College. Suzanne Noonan was named Director of Massachusetts Educational Television, formerly the Bureau of Media Services. Louis L. Tucker was named Director of the Massachusetts Historical Association succeeding Stephen T. Riley, who retired.

MARY A. HENEGHAN

MICHIGAN

Networks and Grants. A $1,500,000 grant from the W. K. Kellogg Foundation of Battle Creek to develop a statewide computer-based library information network in Michigan provided the real breakthrough for networking in 1976. Computer terminals in each of Michigan's 24 library systems will allow individual libraries to rapidly obtain research and bibliographic information and library materials not available locally. The State Library of Michigan received $85,000 of the grant; and the Michigan Library Consortium, a 50-member organization of all types of libraries that coordinates the members' OCLC services, received $145,000 to continue coordination and to provide staff in-service training. Each public library system and the 488 public and academic libraries in the state may apply for a grant ranging from $500 to $8,000, dependent upon the size of library and the services provided. The Kellogg Foundation sought to encourage libraries to share their resources by utilizing existing technology and support the continuing education of library personnel.

Other network developments included the installation of telefacsimile copiers in each of the 22 Regional Educational Media Centers (REMC's) providing daily communication with the State Library, the public library systems, the University of Michigan Library, and the Michigan State University Library. The Michigan Bibliographic Network involving the Wayne Oakland Federated Library System and the Josten Library Services Division's Telemarc was expanded with other library systems in Michigan. This growth in networking based upon certain agreed conditions including the use of the MARC II format

Michigan Library Association
(founded 1891)

Membership: 2495 (875 ALA members); *Annual Expenditure:* $66,739.
President: Robert G. Gaylor, Kresge Library, Oakland University, Rochester (November 1, 1976–October 31, 1977).
Vice-President/President-elect: Joann L. Wilcox, Ortonville Library trustee.
Executive Secretary: Frances H. Pletz, 226 W. Washtenaw, Lansing, Michigan 48933.
Annual Conference: October 27–29, 1976, Grand Rapids, Michigan.
Publications: Michigan Librarian (quarterly); *Michigan Librarian Newsletter* (6 issues a year).

Michigan Department of Education
Francis X. Scannell, State Librarian
735 E. Michigan Avenue
Lansing, Michigan 48913

State Reports—Michigan

when converting catalog data to computers and the involvement of all sizes and types of libraries could enable Michigan to become a prototype for implementing the recommendations of the National Commission on Libraries and Information Science.

Legislation. Appropriation of $5,500,000 in state aid funds by the Michigan Legislature to the Detroit Public Library in the midsummer extended the services of the main library to any resident of Michigan who presents appropriate identification of name and address. Passage of the legislation officially designates the Detroit Public Library as a state resource.

The second annual legislative day sponsored by the Legislation Committee of the Michigan Library Association and held in Lansing on September 15 concentrated on the members of the Senate, where legislation to organize the state into library regions and increase state funding of library service was held at year's end in the Appropriations Committee after passage by the Michigan House of Representatives. "Ben Franklin" paid a visit to the Senate during National Library Week (see below) and a deluge of mailgrams was addressed in early November to legislative leaders.

Lobbying efforts were again successful in blocking passage of legislation concerning alleged pornography and changes in the penal fine laws which would further reduce local support funds for many public libraries in the state.

New Library Construction. Innovative and aesthetically pleasing design linked with well integrated site planning marked the new library construction completed in 1976. Included in the list of new buildings and additions is the new public library at Portage which cost $1,760,500; the 20,000-square-foot addition to the Avon Township Public Library at Rochester costing $1,480,000; the Maryville Public Library Branch of the St. Clair County Library System which cost $360,000; and the Kentwood Branch of the Kent County Library for a cost of $638,000. Imaginative additions to older Carnegie public library buildings were completed at Albion and Allegan, where the new addition's exterior exactly matched the original building. While most of the new construction was financed by a combination of local and federal funds, the 3,090-square-foot Township Public Library in Leland was unique in that individuals in this small community contributed the total $190,000 needed for its construction. The chairman of the fund drive was Harlan B. Hatcher, President Emeritus of the University of Michigan.

National Library Week. Highlight of National Library Week in Michigan was the appearance of Ben Franklin before a session of the Michigan Senate; important library legislation was stalled in the Education Committee. Ben, portrayed by Ralph Archbold, a Detroit actor, spoke on behalf of Michigan libraries and received statewide media coverage. Prior to this event two 30-second TV spots produced by the Public Relations Committee of the Michigan Library Association and Judy Anderson Associates of Battle Creek featuring Ben Franklin touring the Henry Ford Public Library in Dearborn were sold to libraries throughout the state.

Other National Library Week activities included the East Detroit Public Library's production, "Literary Kicks of '76," a modern dance tour of the library, choreographed by a professional dancer and dedicated library fan. For the County Library System in Monroe a troupe of live costumed storybook characters visited each branch library during the week, and for the Port Huron Public Library a local radio station broadcasted all week from the library's lobby.

Bicentennial Activities. Parades, portraits, programs, time capsules, and booklists were utilized by libraries in Michigan to celebrate the Bicentennial Year. Activities included the Niles Public Library's "We Were Here in 1976," with library borrowers standing behind painted cardboard historical costumes to have their picture snapped and enclosed in a special folder, and the appearance of Verna Aardema Vugteveen, local resident and author of the 1976 Caldecott Award book, *Why Mosquitoes Buzz in People's Ears*, on the Norton Shores Branch of the Muskegon County Library's prizewinning float in the Seaway Festival Parade.

Children in the 40-member Wayne Oakland Federated Library System in southeastern Michigan participated in a "Happy Birthday to Us" summer reading program, while the Mid-Peninsula Library Federation headquartered in Iron Mountain issued place mats depicting local historical scenes to all the libraries in the system to use as promotional materials in local restaurants. A time capsule filled with 1976 memorabilia and to be opened in 2076 was buried in the lawn of the Ferndale Public Library.

A two-day "Library Street Fair" in July sponsored and coordinated by the Grand Rapids Public Library featuring demonstrations of early American crafts, carnival rides, games, and a book sale attracted several thousand people. The Grand Rapids library also sponsored a year-long series of programs on the theme "One Month Is Not Enough," featuring both local and internationally famous Black artists, poets, musicians, and performing artists, among them the Alvin Ailey Dancers, Mary Helen Washington, and Maya Angelou.

Publishing activities included *Bicentennial Broadside*, a bibliography of materials and resources dealing with America's development, past, present, and future, compiled by the Michigan Association of Media Educators (MAME) and a catalog of 100 titles on Michigan history recorded and issued by the Library for the Blind and Handicapped, State Library of Michigan.

Michigan Library Association. Clara S. Jones, President of the American Library Association and Director of the Detroit Public Library, was the keynote speaker at the Michigan Library Association's 84th annual conference October 27–29 in Grand Rapids. President Jones reviewed the significant events in the history of ALA from 1876 to 1976.

The 750 conferees spent Thursday in four mini workshops repeated twice on various aspects of management and libraries under the direction of David Berlo, President of the Center for Communication Analysis, Washington, D.C., and were enthralled by Maya Angelou, poet, author, singer, and dancer, who spoke at the evening's banquet.

Awards were presented at the President's luncheon on Wednesday to honor the achievements of Kenneth King, Director of the Mt. Clemens Public Library, as Librarian of the Year for successfully transforming the library into a community-oriented institution in three years; to Robert G. Gaylor, Associate Dean, Oakland University Library and Trustee of the Avon Township Library, Rochester, who received the Trustee Citation of Merit for his notable contribution to the state library legislation program; to Carol Woodruff, member of the Roseville Public Library Friends, who received the Walter Kaiser Memorial Award for initiating an innovative public relations program and organizing a library friends group; and to Eileen Thornton, Librarian, Nottawa Township Library, Centreville, who received the Loleta Fyan Award given annually to a young librarian who has served as a professional librarian fewer than five years.

A first-time award was presented to Caswell and Caswell, Inc., of Troy for the best designed exhibit booth that carried through the Conference theme, "Those Were the Days."

A Continuing Education Committee was added to the list of standing committees in changes in the Association's bylaws approved at the Friday business meeting. David McKee, Chairperson of the Membership Committee, reported a 30 percent gain in membership in the Association for the year for a total of over 2,400 members. "Watch birds" have agreed to watch for nonmembers or members who have forgotten to renew their memberships. Names of "watch birds" and new members were published in the *Michigan Librarian* or the *Newsletter* on a regular basis.

Michigan Association of Law Libraries. Law librarians in Michigan meeting in conjunction with the Michigan State Bar annual meeting in September 1976 formally created the Michigan Association of Law Libraries with a steering committee to plan a spring meeting. Promoting service to the law libraries, and members of the bar in Michigan, the group anticipates a statewide distribution of Michigan legal publications; interlibrary loan services; computerization of bibliographic records of journal holdings in the law libraries; cooperative placement of qualified library personnel, and consulting with law firms who need help with library matters.

People. Martin Cohn, of the School of Librarianship of Western Michigan University, received a Teaching Excellence Award of $1,000 at the annual alumni homecoming luncheon held at the University on October 16.

Richard Vogt of Mason was named the "Volunteer Tape Reader of the Year" by the Library for the Blind and Physically Handicapped, State Library of Michigan. Vogt, the first person among the 125 volunteer readers so honored, had logged over 2,000 hours of reading time since March 1967. Over 10 years, volunteer readers put 3,300 books into audio form.

Retirements in 1976 included Mary Daume, Director of the Raisin Valley Library System, Monroe, and Past President of the Michigan Library Association, in January; Robert Armstrong, Assistant Director of the Detroit Public Library and Past President of the Michigan Library Association, January 16; Virginia Savery, Director of the Royal Oak Public Library, in January; the Rev. Robert J. Kearns, S. J., Director of the University of Detroit Libraries, June 30; Kathleen J. Uniechowski, Associate Director of the University of Detroit Libraries, also on June 30; Lawrence Ebbing, formerly Library Director, recently Public Service Librarian, Macomb County Community College, May 14, and four members of the Willard library, Battle Creek, who retired June 30. They were Marie Dusenberg, Assistant Director; Jean Hunter, Head, Children's Room; Corrine Wascher, Head, Cataloging and Processing; and Rachel Childs, Assistant, Circulation Department; together they had contributed over 106 years of combined service to Willard Public Library.

Margaret B. Duffield, trustee for many years of the Avon Township Public Library, Rochester, died on September 18 in an automobile accident. She founded the Friends of the Avon Township Library and worked diligently for library legislation at the state level.

Merlin Young, trustee of the Branch County Library, Coldwater, and Chairperson-elect of the Trustee Division of the Michigan Library Association, died on January 14.   ELIZABETH HAYDEN

MINNESOTA

For the Minnesota Library Community, 1976 was a year in which the structure, funding, and delivery of library and information resources were brought into sharper focus. 1975 had been a transitional year. Librarians developed a clearer recognition that while libraries have primary responsibility to their clientele, the total information needs of their users can be met only through the cooperative utilization of resources at the local, state, regional, and national levels. Accomplishment of such cooperation requires rethinking organizational relationships, establishing adequate local, state and federal funding levels, and improving the mechanism for delivery of increasing numbers of library and information resources to users.

In the past year, countless hours of debate were spent struggling with these issues. Many different approaches were espoused and although there were few definitive answers, patterns appear to be emerging. Coordinated activity encourages local initiative. National bibliographic, communication, and automation standards enhance individual efforts by allowing their integration into state, regional, and national systems. With appropriate local collections and access to broader resources, users are well served. Demonstrated activity hints at the potential of cooperation for improving user access to needed information sources. Improved library and information services for all Minnesota residents strongly suggest increased state funding.

Minnesota Library Association
(founded 1896)

Membership: 1,191; *Annual Expenditure:* $20,658.
President: Jan Schroeder, Duluth Public Library (October 1976–October 1977).
Vice-President/President-elect: Mary Heiges, Hopkins Public Library.
Secretary: Darlene Weston, Minneapolis Public Library–Franklin Branch.
Annual Meeting: October 7–9, 1976, Minneapolis.
Publication: MLA Newsletter (9 issues a year).

Department of Education, Office of Public Libraries and Interlibrary Cooperation

William G. Asp, Director
301 Hanover Building
480 Cedar Street
St. Paul, Minnesota 55101

Three developments of the past year deserve special note. First, the State Advisory Board on Library Services was restructured. In a stepped process, the 38 members were reduced to 15. It is expected that this will prove to be a stronger and more efficient working group. One-third of its membership consists of Minnesota citizens who are not librarians, a federal requirement, and it includes constituents from each Congressional District. Along this same line, the Minnesota Library Association (MLA) Library Futures Task Force continued the initial steps taken by the Minnesota Council of Academic Library Directors in their "Draft Plan for a Minnesota Library Network." After that document was endorsed by MLA at its annual conference, the Executive Board appointed the Task Force and named as Chair Robert Rohlf, Director of the Hennepin County Library. The Task Force submitted its final report to the MLA Executive Board and the general membership at the fall 1976 Conference. The report, including its recommendations, stimulated considerable debate.

Legislative Committee. The second significant item is the work of the MLA Legislative Committee chaired by Joel Rosenfeld, Executive Director of MELSA (Metropolitan Library Service Agency). The Committee spearheaded the jointly sponsored MLA and MASL (Minnesota Association of School Librarians) Legislative Workshop, August 6 and 7. Much of the success of the workshop must be credited to the inimitable Alice Ihrig of Illinois, who injected her enthusiasm and know-how. The Legislative Committee has assumed much of the responsibility for working with the Office of Public Libraries and Interlibrary Cooperation (OPLIC) and their parent body, the Minnesota State Department of Education, to increase State funding for public libraries on a formula basis similar to that used to fund elementary and secondary education. They were successful in getting State Department of Education support for a $10,946,734 budget request to the Legislature. The 1975–76 appropriation was $4,500,000. The Committee is busy laying the groundwork for an active grass roots approach to local legislators to insure its final passage.

Cooperation. The third significant item is that Minnesota has demonstrated that cooperative activity is possible and mutually beneficial. During 1975–76, 356,464 items were shared among Minnesota libraries. This volume is especially remarkable considering that available statistics suggest that in 1967–68 there were 20,000 comparable interlibrary loan transactions.

Minnesota, as have other states, saw the emergence of regional and subject consortia, cooperatives, networks, and systems.

State Reports—Minnesota

In 1976, for the first time, more items were shared locally than centrally through MINITEX.

Most of the regional or subject consortia use the MINITEX communication system, bibliographic data base, and/or delivery system. The one-third-million-plus shared items represent only library-to-library transactions. They do not begin to tabulate the many transactions in which individuals, because of reciprocal borrowing agreements and book or union catalogs, have gone directly to a holding library for needed materials.

Library resource sharing in Minnesota has been a continuing process, developed in many places and given leadership by countless individuals. The contributing factors are the development of regional public library systems with reciprocal agreements and delivery systems, with establishment of subject consortia and multitype library networks with union catalogs and delivery systems, and book catalog production by several MELSA libraries. It is interesting to note that CLIC is able to fill 67.75 percent of its requests with resources available within the consortium. In addition, CLIC was able to provide 5,902 items to other libraries through MINITEX. Another activity of the regional systems, networks, and consortia is publication of newsletters. Currently over 25 are published regularly.

Periodical Exchange. Special note should be made of the periodical exchange. Libraries and individuals in Minnesota contribute their duplicate and discarded periodical issues by the thousands. By using the existing delivery system and checking want lists of libraries, over 25,000 needed issues or volumes were provided to participating libraries at little or no cost.

Regional Libraries. A new regional library, West Central Regional, was formed by Ottertail, Grant, Douglas, and Stearns Counties. Robert Hemmingson is the Director. During 1976, seven new counties were added to systems, making a total of 66 counties (of 87) that provide library services to their citizens. This represents 3,523,932 persons, or 93 percent of the state population.

Bibliographic Access. Bibliographic access was greatly enhanced in 1976 by publication of the Anoka County Library Book Catalog, a supplement to the Hennepin County Library Catalog, a microfiche edition of the *Minnesota Union List of Serials* (MULS), and the retrospective conversion projects of Tri-College University (Concordia College, Moorhead State University, and North Dakota State University), 80,000 titles, and CLIC (Cooperating Libraries in Consortium), 160,000 titles in the preliminary catalogs. Both these systems contracted with Brodart and use COM microfilm on ROM readers.

In August 1975 the Minnesota Council of Academic Library Directors began serious discussions and identified two urgent needs which they believed must be met to insure effective and efficient delivery of library services within their institutions and the state: (1) the development of a machine-readable bibliographic data base for monographs and (2) the implementation of a systematic cataloging process to reduce costs and improve processing time. After thorough investigation of the available options, the Council requested that the Minnesota Higher Education Coordinating Board (MHECB) and MINITEX negotiate a contract with OCLC (Ohio College Library Center) and seek foundation funding to support the initial costs.

This corporate and cooperative decision making was indeed exciting. The librarians chose to function as one body instead of 30, each proceeding individually at his own pace in his own direction. But the directors persevered. As part of the assessment process, they imposed uniform cost analysis on their cataloging practices starting with 1974–75 in order to monitor and evaluate the new system. Having determined their current costs, they can give careful attention to providing improved service and to gaining maximum efficiency from the automated system. A MHECB/MINITEX-OCLC contract was negotiated. The Bush Foundation of St. Paul granted MHECB $216,066 and the Kellogg Foundation granted $88,000 for a total of $304,066. Bibliographic access is the key to physical access.

Interlibrary Loan Study. A major event occurred in June when the National Commission on Libraries and Information Science (NCLIS) announced its Interlibrary Loan and Photocopying Study. The project, funded by the National Science Foundation and National Commission on New Technological Uses of Copyrighted Works (CONTU), was awarded to King Research. For the study, King Research will conduct national surveys and also analyze calendar 1976 MINITEX document delivery data.

Preliminary King Research data for early 1976 indicates that MINITEX is able to fill 96 percent of its requests for journal articles. This is made possible by MULS (the data base now includes over 90,000 titles at over 250 locations) and the borrowing arrangements with Wisconsin, North Dakota, the Center for Research Libraries, and the British Library, Lending Division. Approximately 91 percent of these items were available in Minnesota.

New Buildings and Libraries. The new building at Brooklyn Park (Hennepin County) was completed in 1976 and Minnesota Valley Regional at Mankato was under construction. Two new libraries came into being: The Minnesota Energy Agency and the Freshwater Biological Institute. The Institute, an exciting, ultra-modern research center, was the dream of businessman Richard Grey. In December, the $4,200,000, debt-free facilities were turned over to the University of Minnesota. Significant research to preserve freshwater is already under way.

Associations. A brief listing of some of the organizational activity suggests the same pattern of concern with planning and cooperation seen in library activity. Without a doubt the highlight of this activity was the vote by the memberships of the Minnesota Association of School Librarians (MASL) and the Audio Visual Communications Association of Minnesota (AVCAM) to disband and form a combined organization, MEMO (Minnesota Educational Media Association).

The MLA Midwinter Conference presented "Planning the Development of Statewide Library Services" with a panel of local leaders. National and regional perspectives were given by Alphonse Trezza of NCLIS and John Metz of MIDLNET (all of the Minnesota organizations eligible for membership in MIDLNET, OPLIC, the University of Minnesota, and MINITEX are charter members). The Spring Meeting of the Academic and Research Library Division of MLA featured "Networking at the State Level" with Vern Pings from the Michigan Consortium. The Technical Services Division of MLA sponsored a well-attended working session on "Cataloging and Bibliographic Standards."

Minneapolis hosted the 1976 Annual Conference of the Medical Library Association, with Glenn Brudvig in charge of local arrangements. The Minnesota Chapters of ASIS and SLA continue to hold joint meetings and publish a joint newsletter. In April they sponsored Symposium VII, "Ideas for Action, a Symposium on Planning." These two-day symposia continue to be highly successful in program and attendance and financially.

On April 27 MELSA sponsored a one-day workshop on intertype library cooperation with Beth Hamilton from the Illinois Regional Library Council. Fifty-nine librarians from several states attended the OPLIC Building Conference "Planning New Library Buildings" with Ray Holt from California as principal leader. A well-planned one-day workshop "Serving the Visually Handicapped" brought Frank Kurt Cylke, Chief of the LC Division for the Blind and Physically Handicapped, to the state. This was the culmination of a small grants award to Merrilyn Jones to study the library needs of the visually handicapped.

SMILE (South Central Minnesota Interlibrary Exchange) sponsored a booth with the National Library of Agriculture at FARMFEST '76. An OPLIC grant supported production and distribution of an agricultural bibliography.

Awards. Luther Brown, Dean of Learning Resources, St. Cloud State University—MLA Librarian of the Year; Ellef Erlien, Lake Agassiz Regional Library—MLA Trustee of the Year; Gil Johnsson, Nobles County Library—MLA Certificate of Merit. Hennepin County Library and Sanford Berman of the *Hennepin County Library Cataloging Bulletin* received the H.W. Wilson Company Library Periodical Award. Hennepin County Library, Rockford Road Branch in Crystal received a Library Buildings Program Award. Clodaugh Neiderheiser, University of Minnesota, was named Fellow of the Forest History Society.   ALICE WILCOX

MISSISSIPPI

InfoPass. A loosely organized group of central Mississippi libraries has embarked upon the path of intertype library cooperation. Calling itself the Central Mississippi Library Council (CMLC), this group of ten Jackson metropolitan area libraries is composed of four private colleges, one state university, one state-supported junior college, two state special libraries, the state library commission, and one six-county public library system. The initial project of CMLC was the implementation of a pilot project known as InfoPass for a three-month trial period beginning October 1, 1976.

The 10 cooperating libraries included the following: Educational Media Services, State Department of Education; George M. McLendon Library, Hinds Junior College;

Mississippi Library Association (founded 1909)

Membership 1,200; *Annual Expenditure:* $31,400 (1977 budget).
President: Jeannine Laughlin, Meridian Public Schools, Meridian, Mississippi (January–December 1976).
Vice-President/President elect: Jim Anderson, First Regional Library, Hernando, Mississippi.
Secretary: June Breland, Mississippi State University, Mississippi State, Mississippi.
Treasurer: Lyle Johnson, Pike-Amite Library System, McComb, Mississippi.
Annual Conference: October 20–22, 1976, Biloxi.
Publication: Mississippi Library News (quarterly).

Mississippi Library Commission

Jack Mulkey, Director
P.O. Box 3260
Jackson, Mississippi 39207

Henry Thomas Sampson Library, Jackson State University; Information Services, Mississippi Library Commission; Information Services Division, Mississippi Research and Development Center; Jackson Metropolitan Library System (public); L. Zenobia Coleman Library, Tougaloo College; Leland Speed Library, Mississippi College; Millsaps-Wilson Library, Millsaps College; Warren Hood Library, Belhaven College.

InfoPass, or Information Passport, means optimal access to book and other informational materials. It is a procedural control of access between cooperating, intertype library agencies. The referring library screens an informational request to determine a patron need which cannot be satisfied from available in-house resources. The plan called for a comprehensive directory of participant resources which could be consulted for member subject collections and other strengths such as rare, unusual, or prohibitively expensive material.

A delivery service linking participating libraries was considered crucial to the success of the pilot project because it would tie the institutions together, enabling exchanges of photocopied materials, films, records and book materials in a quick, reliable way not previously available. Delivery service between the 10 libraries began on October 14, with running time on the 50-mile loop taking about three and one-half hours.

CLAM. The Consortium for Library Automation in Mississippi (CLAM) was incorporated as a nonprofit organization in the state of Mississippi on February 21, 1975, for the purpose of promoting library automation and to serve as a catalyst for cooperative library activities in the areas of automation and networking in the state. Librarians from across the state have contributed to the accomplishment of these goals with a strategy for better communication and education in the field of library automation. The culmination of these efforts is embodied in the two highly successful conferences sponsored by CLAM, featuring nationally recognized leaders in the library profession, which attracted more than 100 librarians and interested individuals in December 1974, and again in November 1975.

Cooperation with the Mississippi Library Association and the Mississippi Library Commission is an integral component of the CLAM scheme. A CLAM preconference was planned to begin prior to the MLA annual convention on October 20–22, 1977, in Jackson.

Officers and Task Force members of the Consortium for Library Automation in Mississippi for 1976 were George Lewis, President; Gerald Buchanan, Vice-President; Carol West, Secretary/Treasurer; Harold Ard; Frances Coleman; Natelle Isley; Jeannetta Roach; Barbara Carroon; Ellis Tucker; and Billy Scruggs.

MLA Annual Conference. Dorothy Downing, Right to Read Office, HEW, was featured at a workshop sponsored by the Right to Read Committee and the Friends of Mississippi Libraries, October 20–22, in Biloxi. Theme was "Today's Libraries for Tomorrow's Needs."

The Junior Members Round Table spotlighted "Scooter Mouse" and his creator, Mattie Rials of the Pike-Amite Library System, a 1975 winner of a John Cotton Dana Award for Public Relations. CLAM presented Ellsworth Mason on the topic "Library Automation and Its Implication for the Future."

Kathryn Tuckers Windham, popular author of ghost stories, was the speaker at the School Library Section program.

Barry Hannah, author from Mississippi and Professor of Creative Writing at the University of Alabama, read from his works and discussed trends in fiction at the Public Libraries Section program. Ellsworth Mason spoke also at the College and University Section meeting. His topic was "Trends in Academic Libraries."

Benny Lucroy, Director of Education, Mississippi Authority for Educational Television, conducted a workshop on the use of video as it relates to libraries.

A seminar held in conjunction with the meeting featured Peggy Barber, Public Information Office Director for ALA. Other participants were Bob Clark, Director of the Mid-Mississippi Regional Library, Kosciusko; Mrs. Richard Foxworth, Columbia; Mrs. George Hoff, Clinton; and John K. Bettersworth, Mississippi State University.

Another feature of the convention was designed to appeal to public librarians. Edward M. Walters, Archivist and Assistant Professor of History at the University of Mississippi, discussed the topic "Identification of Rare Books."

The keynote speaker at the Book Banquet was Gerald R. Shields. His topic was "One Librarian Facing Tomorrow's Needs."

Awards 1976. The Peggy May Award for outstanding work in library development was given to Mary Love, former Director of the Mississippi Library Commission.

The MLA Award for Outstanding Achievement went to Margarete Peebles, retired Head of Acquisitions, Mississippi State University Library.

The Past Presidents' Award to the Outstanding Young Librarian was awarded to Rush Miller, Director, Delta State University Library.

Regional Meetings. The central theme of the 1976 Regional Meetings was (*see below*) Long-Range Planning and Librarian

State Reports—Missouri

Reaction to the study by Charles Evans. Regional Chairpersons were Central East—Kay Taylor, Meridian Public Library Director, Meridian; Southwest—Kathleen Hutchison, Copiah-Jefferson Davis Regional Library; Southeast—Kathleen McIlwain, Jackson-George County Regional Library; Northeast—June Breland, Mississippi State University; Northwest—Miriam D. Greene, Coahoma Junior College, Clarksdale; and Central West—David Woodburn, Ricks Memorial-Sharkey County Library, Yazoo City

News. The Mississippi Association of Media Educators (MAME) met during the Mississippi Education Association convention and elected Bessie Hollingsworth of Enochs Junior High School in Jackson President. Other officers elected were Paul Pelloquinn, Delta State University, President-elect; Berl Hunt, University of Mississippi, Vice-President; Carolyn Reed, Pearl River Junior College, Secretary; and Barbara Carroon, Library Supervisor, Hinds County Schools, Treasurer.

Twenty-seven public libraries throughout Mississippi participated in DIXIE '76, a Mississippi Library Commission program funded by the Mississippi Committee for the Humanities. The program was designed to bring academic humanists and the general public together to discuss critical issues facing Mississippians and to define common goals important to the future of the state.

Since Mississippi, and the South as a whole, has traditionally been regarded as being "different" in character and tradition from the rest of the nation, DIXIE '76 discussed cultural uniqueness and asked how this trait may enable southerners as Americans to furnish leadership in the continuing pursuit of the American dream of a society based on liberty, equality, and justice for all.

Ninety-four programs were presented by the 27 participating libraries. Those 27 libraries were: Batesville, Clinton, Como, Corinth, Drew, Greenwood-Leflore, Gulfport-Harrison County, Hernando, Holmes County (Durant), Humphreys County (Belzoni), Indianola, Inverness, Lawrence County (Monticello), Lee County (Tupelo), Lowndes County (Columbus), Madison County (Canton), Margaret Reed Crosby (Picayune), Moorhead, Oktibbeha County (Starkville), Oxford, Pike-Amite (McComb), Ricks Memorial (Yazoo City), Ruleville, Sardis, Senatobia, Southaven, and Tunica.

The University of Mississippi School of Library and Information Science sponsored a tour of major European libraries. The tour, which carried three hours credit, included visits in Ireland, England, France, Italy and Spain.

Resolutions memorializing two outstanding librarians were presented during the 1976 Annual Convention of the Mississippi Library Association. The librarians honored were Jeanne Broach of Meridian and Mary Jo Ross of Hattiesburg, both former Presidents of the Association.

The University of Mississippi established the Graduate School of Library and Information Science with Ellis Tucker serving as Director.

The Mississippi Library Commission observed its Fiftieth Anniversary March 18. The goal of 1926, "To Give the People of Mississippi the Best Library Service Possible," is still the goal for the Commission.

The Department of Library Science at the University of Southern Mississippi became the School of Library Services under the leadership of Onva K. Boshears, Dean.

People. Margarete Peebles, Head Acquisition Department, Mississippi State University, retired after 43 years of service on the Library staff.

Mary Love, Director, Mississippi Library Commission, was presented the Outstanding Mississippian Award by former Governor William Waller for her distinguished service in Library Development.

Joe Forsee, Mississippi Library Commission, was promoted from Consultant to Assistant Director for Administration.

June Breland, Mississippi State University, was awarded the Faculty Scholar Award from the Graduate School of Library Service at the University of Alabama. She was also a recipient of a 3M Company JMRT Award to attend the 1976 ALA Convention.

Joellen Ostendorf joined the Mississippi Library Commission Technical Services Staff as Cataloger.

Ernestine Lipscomb, Director, Henry T. Sampson Library, Jackson State University, retired after 19 years of service.

Lelia G. Rhodes was appointed Director of the Jackson State University Library on July 1.

Mary Ellen Guess, Library Supervisor, Jackson Public Schools, retired.

Velma Tillman Champion became Reference Librarian at the Mississippi Library Commission.

Richard Greene was named Director of the Mid-Mississippi Regional Library.

Grover Ashley was named Director of the Joseph Anderson Cook Library, University of Southern Mississippi.

Tricia Hollis joined the Mississippi Library Commission staff as Public Information Representative.

Warren F. Tracy joined the faculty of the School of Library Service, University of Southern Mississippi.

William Majure was named Director of the Kemper-Newton Regional Libraries, Union.

Sid Graves was named Director of Clarksdale-Carnegie Public Library, Clarksdale.

Iola J. Magee, former Director of Lincoln-Lawrence-Franklin Regional Library Brookhaven, retired on December 31, 1976.

Courtney Tannehill became Director of the Neshoba County Library, Philadelphia.

William E. Stant, Jr., was named Director of the South Mississippi Regional Library, Columbia.

Annie Pinson became the Library Supervisor, Jackson Public Schools.

Sharman Smith became Director of the Lincoln-Lawrence-Franklin Regional Library, Brookhaven. GEORGE R. LEWIS

MISSOURI

State Library. Years of effort on the part of Missouri librarians saw reward in 1976 by passage of legislation establishing the Missouri State Library as the official depository for state documents. Governor Christopher S. Bond signed the bill on June 24, providing for a central distribution system for state publications. Regional depositories throughout the state are being set up to receive selected state publications.

Four areas in Missouri prepared proposals and received federal funds through the Missouri State Library to hire local network coordinators to explore cooperation among libraries in their areas. They are Northeast Missouri Library Service, Northwest Missouri Library Network, Southwest Missouri Library Network, and Mid-Missouri Library Network.

The Missouri State Library and the Uni-

Missouri Library Association (founded 1900)

Membership: 1257 (240 ALA members); Annual Expenditure: $45,000.
President: Jane Miller, University City Public Library Trustee (October 1976–September 1977).
Vice-President/President-elect: Harold R. Jenkins, Kansas City Public Library, Kansas City, Missouri.
Executive Secretary: Marilyn Lake, 403 South 6th Street, Columbia, Missouri 65201.
Annual Conference: October 13–15, 1976, Springfield, Missouri.
Publications: Missouri Library Association Newsletter (bimonthly); *MLA Membership Directory* (annually).

Missouri State Library
Charles O'Halloran, State Librarian
308 E. High Street
Jefferson City, Missouri 65101

versity of Missouri School of Library and Informational Science again sponsored a series of week-long summer institutes for librarians. The institute on communications explored human relations, the psychology of communications, language, and different models for analyzing communication efforts. The institute, Evaluating the American Political System, examined the U.S. form of government and such basic issues as elitism vs. populism, equality vs. inequality, trust and suspicion, and the election. Librarians and staffers from all types of libraries as well as public library trustees attended the institutes at Stephens College.

The State Library made available career development scholarships for staff members of Missouri public libraries who desired to attend library school to complete a master's degree program. Three scholarships were granted in 1976. The State Library also granted internships to ten college sophomores and juniors. Students worked in public libraries during the summer of 1976.

Andrea Hawkins, Coordinator of Library Resources at the State Library, represented the Library at meetings of CLENE (Continuing Library Education Network and Exchange) during 1976.

MLA. Beverly Lynch, Executive Secretary of ALA's ACRL, speaker during the MLA Conference in Springfield, Missouri discussed "Faculty Status for Librarians".

MACRL held a spring meeting at Meramec Community College in St. Louis. Louise Giles (see Obituaries), who was President of ACRL in 1976, was a featured speaker along with Nathan Smith of Brigham Young University, and Michael Maguire of St. Louis Community College at Forest Park.

The Public Library Division and Trustees and Citizens Division, Junior members Round Table, and Library Education and Manpower Committee co-sponsored a two-day workshop on "Missouri Laws Affecting Libraries." Topics covered included property taxes, government regulations affecting library employees, audits, and functions of the Office of the Attorney General.

New Services. The first cumulative edition of the *Index to St. Louis Newspapers* was completed in 1976. The extensively cross-referenced index is a monthly listing of news and feature articles and editorials from four St. Louis newspapers.

The Union List of Serials Project in the Greater St. Louis Metropolitan Area neared completion in 1976. Undertaken in 1972, the project includes the serials holdings from all types of libraries in the metropolitan area.

Park College's MAILS service (Mid-America Inter-Library Services) continues to expand its services to libraries in the midwest. MAILS subscribers are in Missouri, Kansas, Nebraska and Iowa. The service provides low-cost printouts, rapid interlibrary loan, and a catalog card service.

The Library Services Center of Missouri is now a member of OCLC. The Center provides cataloging and processing services for libraries throughout Missouri.

On August 10 the restored library at the Governor's Mansion in Jefferson City was unveiled. Books filling the shelves of the library were donated in part by the Missouri Library Association.

Public Libraries. The St. Louis Public Library inaugurated a new service for skiers in 1976. Information on skiing conditions in the New England, middle Atlantic, southern, midwestern, Rocky, and far mountain ski resorts was made available daily through a special hot line to the library's reference center. For downtown residents and workers who are unable to go there during the day, the Library began a drive-up service, complete with red, white, and blue booth. Books ordered by telephone before 3 P.M. may be picked up after 4 P.M. the same day. The Library confirms the availability of the desired items and issues them in advance to the borrower's library card number. The Library also provided help with income tax preparation in ten of the system's branches. Patrons needing assistance phoned the participating libraries for an appointment to work out their tax problems. Help was given by members of the American Association of Retired Persons and the University of Missouri–St. Louis.

The regional library for the blind and physically handicapped, housed in the St. Louis Public Library, was transferring in 1976 a large portion of its existing collection from open-reel tape and talking books to cassettes.

The Cape Girardeau Public Library began a circulating toy collection in 1976. Included in the collection were items for activities dealing with the alphabet, numbers, color perception, telling time, manipulative skills and musical rhythms. Complete instruction sheets are circulated with each item.

The Dunklin County Library conducted a four-part discussion series titled, "You Bet Your Life: An Examination of Health Care, Justice and Agriculture in Southeast Missouri." Each session was taped for television viewing and the local radio station carried live broadcasts of the discussions, along with open lines for questions. The sessions were made possible by the Missouri Committee for the Humanities, Inc., the state-based arm of the National Endowment for the Humanities.

At St. Louis County Library, filing in the card catalog ceased in 1976 and catalog cards are no longer being printed for books received. The library is converting to microfilm for access to its collection of over one million volumes.

The Mid-Continent Public Library opened two Resource Centers containing books and materials concerning the mentally and physically handicapped. A grant from the Missouri State Library provided the impetus for establishment of the Centers, which provide information to parents, educators, and interested citizens. Materials are available for a 28-day loan period to all individuals of the library district, and are available for interlibrary loan between the other branches of the library system. In addition to books, cassettes, filmstrips, educational games, recordings, and educational learning kits are available.

Children's and YA Services. Praise for the efforts of the Children's and Young Adults Book Selection Committee of the Missouri State Library came in 1976 from George A. Woods, Childrens Book Editor of the *New York Times*. The book selection group, composed of children's and young adult librarians, meets three times a year for book reviewing and issues an annotated list of reviews after each session. In a letter addressed to the State Library Woods said, "I think you all do a very incisive job in your criticism of books; you are not awed by the reputations of some authors and you speak forthrightly by saying 'not recommended' or 'marginal purchase'."

Young adult newsletters are going strong at the Barry-Lawrence Regional Library and the Cape Girardeau Public Library. The publications, titled "Bookworm's Dyn-O-Mite" and "The No Name Newsletter," contain information about books, services, programs, current records, jokes, drawings, and contests. They are distributed to high school English classes and school libraries and are also available at the two libraries.

Marcia Hall, regional programmer for Daniel Boone Regional Library, was named film list editor of the 1977 Selected Films for Young Adults. The annotated list of 16mm films is compiled annually by members of the Media Selection and Usage Committee of the ALA Young Adult Division.

The Eighth Annual Children's Literature Festival, sponsored by Central Missouri State University, attracted such authors as Leonard Wibberley, Berniece Rabe, Jacqueline Jackson, Peter Z. Cohen, Alberta Wilson Constant, and many others.

Scott Corbett, author of many children's books, won the Mark Twain Award for *The Home Run Trick*. Boys and girls in grades three through eight are eligible to vote for

State Reports—Montana

their favorite book from a list selected by Missouri librarians and educators. Each year the winning author is honored at the Missouri Association of School Librarians spring conference.

Lincoln Collection. Fred D. Schwengel, Northeast Missouri State University alumnus and President of the U.S. Capitol Historical Society, presented to the University what is believed to be the largest private collection of Lincoln memorabilia. The collection of Lincoln books, papers, slides, and photographs is housed in Pickler Memorial Library. Schwengel also donated $1,000 for the establishment of a Lincoln trust fund to be used for preserving and continuing the collection and to provide for awards for outstanding speeches or writings on Lincoln. He intends to add to the fund by donating half of what he receives for honorariums, with the other half going to the U.S. Capitol Historical Society.

People. Charles O'Halloran, Missouri State Librarian, wrote a challenging article on convention-going in the February 1976 issue of *Show-Me Libraries* that drew response from librarians across the country. He argued that librarians might do well to read a book on a specific subject or by a famous author rather than travel miles to attend a meeting, spending the taxpayer's money. O'Halloran, after Jack Cross, Commissioner of Higher Education for the state, submitted his resignation to the nine-member Coordinating Board for Higher Education, was appointed interim Commissioner.

Robert Lin, Librarian and Assistant Professor of History at Culver-Stockton College, donated to the College the fee he received for an article to show his gratitude for the College's commitment to research. His article, "The Concept of Naturalness in Taoism and Ch'an" (Zen), appeared in the Spring 1976 issue of the *Journal of Asian Culture*.

Sue Reed, Librarian at the Pacific branch of Scenic Regional Library, published her first book, *In Retrospect—A Bicentennial Review of Our Historical Heritage*. It tells the story of Pacific and its surrounding area from early settlement days to the present.

Appointments. Ronald G. Bohley was appointed library director at the University of Missouri-Rolla. He was head librarian for the Purdue University North Central Campus in Westville before going to Missouri.

Carl R. Sandstedt became the new Director of St. Charles City–County Library System. Sandstedt was administrator of Georgia's library program for the blind and physically handicapped.

Walter J. Hartmetz was named Cass County Librarian in 1976. He had directed the Miami (Oklahoma) Public Library prior to accepting the directorship of the county library system.

John Gribben was appointed Director of Libraries at the University of Missouri-Columbia. He succeeded Dwight Tuckwood, who resigned the position in March but remained a member of the library staff. Gribben was Library Director at Tulane University before taking the position in Missouri.

Retirements. Ina Naylor, Director of the Daviess County Library from 1949, retired in 1976. Betty Stanley is the new County Librarian. Betty Powell retired as Mississippi County Librarian after 25 years. Marilyn Grant succeeded Powell.

Death. Charlotte Bass, first Librarian of Lebanon Public Library (now Kinderhook Regional Library), died September 22. She was a member of the Shakespeare Club which founded and organized the library.

MADELINE MATSON

MONTANA

Legislation. Much time was spent by many people to assure passage of Referendum No. 70 to create a one-mill property tax levy for support of public libraries in federations. Regrettably, the measure did not pass in 1976.

Historians, archivists, and librarians from the Montana Historical Society and the units of the Montana University System are working to create a cooperative historical records network. The plan includes cooperative acquisition and processing and inter-unit loans of collections. Bills creating and financing the network will be introduced in the state legislature. Senator Margaret Warden was instrumental in advocating the needs for financing the network.

Montana Library Association
(founded 1906)

Membership: 578; *Annual Expenditure:* $8,416 (April 1, 1975, latest reported).
President: Geneva T. Van Horne, University of Montana, Missoula (June 1, 1976–May 31, 1977).
Vice-President/President-elect: Alene Cooper, Montana State Library.
Secretary: Rita Schmidt, Great Falls Public Schools.
Annual Meeting: May 6–8, 1976, Helena.
Publication: MLA President's Newsletter (4 issues a year).

Montana State Library
Alma S. Jacobs, State Librarian
930 E. Lyndale Avenue
Helena, Montana 59601

Montana Library Association. The Association met in Helena, May 6–8. The theme of the conference was "Beyond the Centennial." The media specialists and the school librarians merged into one Division. Robert Wedgeworth, ALA Executive Director, was a principal speaker, and he assisted with workshops. Norman Alexander, President of the Pacific Northwest Library Association (and a former Montanan), also was a speaker. A panel discussed state funding of public library systems, and there were minisessions on a variety of subject interests.

Workshops continue to be the concern of the Continuing Education Committee. A survey was undertaken among library staff members around the state to determine their areas of interest. It is hoped to set up a series of workshops on library skills and problems.

Jeff Edmunds of Billings Public Library and Ingrid Bergagel of Eastern Montana College Library are working on a uniform list of subject headings to be used when indexing Montana newspapers. When completed this cooperative project is to be in computer print-out form.

State Library Activities. The Montana State Library Commission announced a statewide demonstration program of library service to all public libraries not participating in federations. It was funded through Title I, Library Services and Construction Act. These funds were granted to the Montana State Library to promote library development. This demonstration project, which created six Public Library Federations, ended November 30. Federations will contract for service through their headquarters library. Interlibrary Loan will be offered only through the headquarters libraries. The State Library is financing a TWX in each headquarters library and will screen all reference questions and requests the headquarters library cannot handle.

Public Libraries. Billings Public Library has begun producing a catalog on microfiche. With start-up funds from LSCA, they have their holdings for the last three years. They plan to continue cataloging in this form. The Lewis and Clark Library (Helena) features a microfilm catalog and a computerized circulation system.

Academic Libraries. The Commissioner of Higher Education in 1976 established an Inter-Unit Committee on Libraries for the Montana University System with the Academic Deputy of the Commission as liaison. An organization meeting was held and individual libraries are studying the ALA Standards and determining areas of cooperation.

New Buildings and Additions. There are two new libraries in Blaine County—the

County Library in Chinook and the Harlem Public Library. The Lewis and Clark county Library in Helena was dedicated September 25. The Hearst Free Library, Anaconda, has been declared a national historical site. The library was a gift to the people of Anaconda from Phoebe Hearst, mother of William Randolph Hearst, and was formally dedicated on June 11, 1898. Funding for the restoration will come from the National Park Service and the City of Anaconda.

Networks. Montana can look forward to its first union list of serials to aid in locating serial titles throughout the state. Consequently, libraries will be able to more effectively share their resources, thus avoiding unnecessary duplication and expense. All types of serials will be included: journals, periodicals, annuals and yearbooks, newspapers, proceedings—anything which is published over a long period of time and for which there is no foreseeable end. Because microfiche is the most inexpensive and effective means for listing holdings, each library will have several fiche files. The MINITEX (Minnesota Interlibrary Telecommunication Exchange) programs, at the University of Minnesota, has agreed under contract to produce the list. Twenty-nine special, academic and public libraries in Montana were participating at year's end. Funding was from a LSCA Title I grant from the State Library.

The Biomedical Communication Development program, which had been attached to the Montana State Library, terminated July 1. Pacific Northwest Regional Health Services Library had been supporting this operation and the grant ran out. Librarians from the State Library, Montana State University, and hospitals around the state are organizing a health sciences information network. MSU, with a MEDLINE Center and a large collection of medical journals, will serve as the center of the network.

Awards. Inez Herrig, Librarian at Lincoln County Free Library, Libby, received a plaque from the Montana State Library Commission in recognition of her support for the development of libraries through federations. Herrig organized the first library federation 20 years ago. The commission acknowledged her contributions to the development of Montana Library Federations.

John Stephens was named the Montana Library Association's Trustee of the Year at the 1976 Conference. He is Blaine County Commissioner and was responsible for the two new library buildings in Blaine County.

Richard T. Rate, Superintendent of Fort Benton Elementary Schools, received the School Administrator of the Year Award, also at the MLA 1976 conference.

ALICE MCCLAIN

NEBRASKA

The major activities of Nebraska libraries, librarians, and supporters belie the popular notion that people do not want to be involved. Before, during, between, and after the two chief gatherings of 1976, which were the April 27–28 Governor's Conference on Library Services and the October 21–22 Nebraska Library Association's Annual Conference, citizens, librarians, task forces, committees, and boards blended their ideas and plans to try to improve and extend library services throughout the state.

Governor's Conference. The Governor's Conference planners used 1975 data gathered by the Information Powermobile Program, which had surveyed citizen reaction to Nebraska libraries and analyzed questionnaire data, to determine strengths and weaknesses of current media services and programs. Under the theme "The Citizen's Challenge," keynote speaker Alice B. Ihrig and 250 delegates (75% citizens and 25% librarians) participated in a working conference sponsored by the Nebraska Educational Media Association (NEMA), Nebraska Library Association (NLA), and Nebraska Library Commission (NLC), funded by contributions from individuals and a private foundation, and chaired by Shirley Flack of Scottsbluff Public Library. Fifteen mixed groups of conference participants, each limited to one area of concern, attempted to find practical solutions to library service problems previously identified by citizens, to establish priorities for meeting the needs of all segments of the population, to formulate action programs for support and improvement, and to gather statewide information for incorporation

Nebraska Library Association
(founded 1895)

Membership: 971; *Annual Expenditure:* $10,100.
President: Charles Gardner, Hastings College (October 1976–October 1977).
Vice-President/President-elect: Margery Curtiss, Sidney Public Library Board Member.
Executive Secretary: Louise Boyd Shelledy, 3420 South 27th Street, Lincoln, Nebraska 68506.
Annual Conference: October 21–22, 1976, Lincoln.
Publication: NLA Quarterly.

Nebraska Library Commission
John L. Kopischke, Director
1420 P Street
Lincoln, Nebraska 68508

into a national plan and the White House Conference on Library and Information Services. Follow-up work continued under the chairmanship of Charles Stelling of Wayne State College Library, with emphasis on publicity and cooperation—the two greatest needs articulated by the citizens. A slide-tape presentation was prepared for statewide distribution, and meetings were being held throughout the state to deal with specific problems and solutions.

Program Development. State and federal funding continued to assist with support of the library development programs within the six networks into which Nebraska is divided. An appropriation of $150,000 was provided by the state to 202 public libraries, LSCA funded applications were approved for basic and incentive grants to the 16 correctional and service institutions for handicapped and other minority groups, and applications were received for nearly $205,000 for 1977 LSCA grants for network projects to meet deficiencies identified in the *Nebraska Long-Range Plan.* Programs supported in 1976 include the preparation of a union list of serials in the Northern Network; a series of continuing education workshops in the Mari Sandoz Network; the Mail-a-Book Project of the Central Network, which consisted of the preparation of a catalog of available paperbacks and free mailing from and to the Holdredge Public Library for any resident in an eight-county rural area or city which does not have minimum library services as defined in the *Nebraska Long-Range Plan,* and free service via collect telephone requests and mail delivery to any visually impaired or physically handicapped resident of the state from the NLC in Lincoln or public libraries of Hastings, Kimball, or North Platte.

Systems Development. NEBASE, the Nebraska Base OCLC Network, established in May and headquartered at NLC, will, when fully installed, bring together the formerly independent OCLC members at Kearney State College, the University of Nebraska-Lincoln (UNL), and NLC, with Chadron State, Concordia Teachers, Doane, Hastings, Union, and Wayne State Colleges, and Nebraska Wesleyan University. Placement of terminals was to continue into 1977, and the addition of members from other academic as well as public and special libraries was anticipated at year's end.

Services from MEDLINE and DIALOG Systems and the Bibliographical Center for Research (BCR) in Denver are also available in some Nebraska libraries.

Academic Library Cooperation. The Postsecondary Educational Library Directors of Nebraska (PELDON) developed a state plan approved and accepted in prin-

State Reports—Nevada

ciple by the administrators of all 32 Nebraska academic institutions and NLC. The document is *Nebraska Plan for the Coordination of Postsecondary Educational Libraries*. It has implemented a system of reciprocal direct borrowing for all Nebraska college and university faculty members and for students at 23 of the institutions. Other features projected in the plan are shared information about print and nonprint holdings, rapid querying and acknowledgment of interlibrary loan requests, a rapid and reliable delivery system, information from on-line citation and data banks, a repository for seldom or lesser used materials, sharing of reference resources and services, sharing of nonprint media production facilities and expertise, continuing education programs for library personnel, and coordination with other state, regional, and national groups or networks.

Regional Activities. Nebraska has joined Iowa, Kansas, and Missouri in an attempt to coordinate and plan Library Education Opportunities for Mid-America (LEOMA). A survey to assess educational needs of library staff members was being planned in 1976 by a task force as an outgrowth of a conference, attended by representatives from the library associations, state library agencies, and library schools, for preliminary discussion of problems, needs, areas for potential cooperation, and future possibilities for action in the four states.

NLA strengthened its involvement in the regional Mountain Plains Library Association (MPLA) by paying a membership fee and providing some support for its Nebraska representative to MPLA's annual conference.

Annual Conference. Attendance at the annual conference of NLA reached 547—more than half of the membership, a figure believed to be the largest number to date. The convention theme was "Lifelong Learning: The Link between Learner and Library Media Center is YOU!" The program included a speech by Louis A. Lerner of NCLIS; a mixed media presentation by Don Roberts of Hennepin County Library in Minneapolis, Minnesota; speeches and autograph sessions by Nebraska authors and illustrators, among them Gail Rock, Peggy A. Volzke Kelley, and Joan I. Tomlinson; a celebration of the 75th anniversary of NLC; and numerous special interest groups on topics such as Poetry and Publishing, Nebraska History, Instructional Television, Intellectual Freedom, Preservation Techniques, Technical Processing, an ALA Caucus, and a session in which children discussed books and their library/media centers.

Awards. The Mari Sandoz Award, given by NLA to an outstanding Nebraskan who has brought recognition to the state by literary or artistic contributions, was presented to Sophus Keith Winther, author of *The Grimsen Trilogy*, which includes the recently reissued immigrant novel, *Take All to Nebraska*. Winther participated in an Immigrant Literature Forum and addressed the Association's convention at the awards banquet.

The Meritorious Service Award was presented to Gwendoline Birky of Lincoln and the Trustee Award to Helen Quirk of Hastings.

Spring Meetings. District meetings, sponsored by the Trustees, School, and Public Library Sections, were held in each of the six Nebraska network areas: Sidney, McCook, Grand Island, Columbus, Beatrice, and Bellevue. The programs emphasized library and media work with children, with program participants from each area. Story-telling demonstrations and reviews of notable children's and adult books were also given.

Buildings and Collections. The $5,000,000 Memorial Library at the University of Nebraska-Omaha was occupied, as were the College of Law Library and the $4,000,000 addition to Love Library at the University of Nebraska-Lincoln.

A library was established at the Center for the Study of Youth Development at Boys Town in Omaha.

The Dawes County Law Library of 5,000 volumes was moved from the county courthouse to Chadron State College Library.

The professional library of Sophus K. Winther, Danish novelist, was presented to Dana College, Blair. With Dana's earlier gift of the Lauritz Melchior collection of phonodiscs, tapes, scores, scrapbooks of press clippings, letters, and personal papers, the C.A. Dana—Life Library now serves as an important source of Danish material for scholars.

People. John L. Kopischke from the Wisconsin Division for Library Services at Madison became the Director of NLC, succeeding Jane P. Geske, who resigned.

John Nelson left his position at Arizona State University, Tempe, to become Law Librarian at the University of Nebraska–Lincoln (UNL).

Jack G. McCarthy, the first professionally trained librarian in the Nebraska Department of Corrections, became Penal Complex Librarian in Lincoln, after three years in the catalog department of UNL's Love Library.

State Legislation. NLA supported retention of Library Service for the Blind and Physically Handicapped under the NLC. The Unicameral's Military and Veterans Affairs Committee had been considering transfer to the Rehabilitation Services for the Visually Impaired of the Department of Public Institutions. Action on the transfer was postponed pending a study to be conducted by the Military and Veterans Affairs Committee. — VIVIAN A. PETERSON

NEVADA

Nevada State Library. The primary direction of the Nevada State Library (NSL) during 1976 was to continue improved access to information resources of the state. During the year the rapid communication system was maintained between the State Library and the regional resource centers in Clark, Elko, and Washoe County Libraries as well as the University system libraries. This resulted in consistently improved interlibrary loan services to the independent and local libraries.

Nevada State Library administered state and federal grant funds through the participation and recommendation of the Nevada State Advisory Council on Libraries. All regions realized increased collections, support of 17 program personnel, additional facilities, and regional extension to rural areas utilizing three additional bookmobiles.

Other projects funded in 1976 include a program for Humboldt County, where Librarian Sharon Allen established a reading center on the Fort McDermitt Indian Reservation and a project conceived by Nancy Cummings, Young Peoples Librarian at the Clark County Library, to provide materials for preschool children and day care centers.

All three correctional institutions supported by the state employ grant-funded professionally qualified librarians. All three indicated intent to seek authorization and future funding of the positions through legislative action. Nevada state prisons were to receive $11,900 in federal funds to purchase additional materials, initiate a program for rotating materials through the three (planned to be four) sep-

Nevada Library Association
(founded 1946)

Membership: 240 (approx. 90 ALA members); *Annual Expenditure:* $0,000.
President: Joyce Ball, Public Services Librarian, University of Nevada Libraries, Reno.
Vice-President/President-elect: Robert G. Anderl, Assistant Director, University of Nevada at Las Vegas Library.
Executive Secretary: Robin Barker, Nevada State Library, Capitol Complex, Carson City, Nevada 89710.
Annual Meeting: October 6–9, 1976, Las Vegas.
Publication: High Roller (9 issues a year).

Nevada State Library
Joseph J. Anderson, State Librarian
Carson City, Nevada 89701

arate facilities, and to train library support staff from the resident population.

Nevada State Library prepared, in cooperation with Lake Tahoe Research Coordination Board, a computer-based Bibliography of Lake Tahoe Research Materials, the first reference tool for material concerning Lake Tahoe. Two publications were released by NSL: *Organizing the State Agency Collection* and *Government Documents in Nevada.*

Annual Convention. The Nevada Library Association (NLA) celebrated its 30th anniversary in Las Vegas, October 6–9, 1976. The year's theme was "The Unconvention." Nevada librarians responsible for the new twist to the annual meeting were Charles Hunsberger, Hal Erikson, Lamar Marchese, and Virginia Mulloy. The opening session wrap-up featured a program on "The Importance of Being Unconventional."

NLA Award. The 1976 NLA special citation was awarded to Helen Luce, who retired as the Library Program Officer for United States Office of Education, Region IX. Luce received the presentation for consistently demonstrating her knowledge of, and sensitivity to, the needs of Nevada. The visible effects of her intelligent advice are to be seen throughout the state.

Programs. Clark County Library District (CCLD) received a $3,700 grant from the Nevada Humanities Committee for a program: "People and Penalties; Marijuana Reconsidered," a four-part program focusing on historical and social impact of marijuana use.

CCLD was also a recipient of the John Cotton Dana Library Public Relations Award for their development of a 60-second television spot, the "Amazing Offer." The public service announcement was created and written by Lamar Marchese, Virginia Mulloy, and Allan Goldberg, of the Clark County Library.

Young Adults. A demonstration project to develop library services to young adults was designed by Carroll Gardner, Director of the Boulder City Library, and Thomas Hollis, Director of the Henderson District Public Library. The project is unique in Nevada—it is the first program funded with a federal grant through the state library in which two independent libraries share one librarian. Previously there were no young adult specialists in the state. Allan Schwartz was hired in April 1976 as the new young adult librarian.

Nevada Serials. Under the direction of Robert Anderl, University of Nevada at Las Vegas, a microfiche edition of the new Nevada Union List of Serials was distributed to every library showing holdings in the list. The complete list contains 17,966 entries and cross-references on seven sheets of 4x6-inch microfiche.

Intellectual Freedom. NLA's Intellectual Freedom Committee formulated a plan and guide for a legislative hot line to monitor any censorship as well as other library-related legislation. Chairperson Martha Gould reported that this would provide a means for calling immediate support for any pertinent legislation being considered. The Committee also produced Nevada's first Intellectual Freedom statement of policy.

Nevada's Union Catalog. The State Network Design Team, under the project director, Robert Anderl of the University of Nevada at Las Vegas, worked during the year to develop improvements in networking in Nevada.

Input from all interested libraries in the form of order slips or extra main-entry cards is matched against bibliographic records stored on the BALLOTS data base at Stanford University. Wherever a Nevada holding matches a computer record, the bibliographic information is entered on a special tape which, at regular intervals, is run off and printed on microfiche as a catalog.

For technical reasons, a separate holdings record is printed with short-title information, Library of Congress card number, and the symbols for Nevada libraries owning the book. Together the two sets of fiche make up a union catalog of current books owned by Nevada Libraries.

As it existed in October 1976, the Union Catalog had approximately 3,300 entries with the bibliographic portion available in either divided or dictionary catalog formats. It can be used to provide cataloging data and also to provide locations for interlibrary loans. Other potential uses of the catalog can be run to reflect the holdings of any particular combination of libraries, for example, all Clark County holdings, or holdings of the community colleges. Libraries can have specialized catalogs made, such as a list of audiovisual material available in a particular school district, or a union list of gambling materials. The Information Nevada Policy Committee directed a limited experiment on using the catalog for Inter-Library Loans.

The Clark County Library District Catalog, which became available in microfilm format in July 1976, and is updated quarterly, lists over 100,000 titles owned by the library. The catalog lists books by author, title, and subject, and gives locations of the books in the district. Thirty microfilm readers were in use in the district libraries and four at other libraries in the county: the University of Nevada at Las Vegas, and the North Las Vegas, Boulder City, and Henderson Public Libraries.

THOMASINE KLEFFEN

NEW HAMPSHIRE

State Librarian Appointed. The appointment of Avis M. Duckworth as State Librarian was announced on February 5 by the State Library Commission. Duckworth, a native of Manchester and Goffstown, New Hampshire, is a graduate of the University of Michigan and of Simmons College School of Library Science and has completed course work as a doctoral candidate in library administration at Columbia University. During her professional career she has held subsequent posts at the Library of Congress, the Queens Borough (New York) Public Library, the Massachusetts College of Arts, and as Director of the South Huntington (New York) Public Library and of Adult Services at the Manchester (New Hampshire) City Library. She became New Hampshire's Assistant State Librarian in 1971. She succeeds Emil W. ("Bill") Allen, State Librarian from 1964 until his death in May of 1975.

New Hampshire Library Council. A half-dozen years ago the various library groups and interests in New Hampshire, seeking a means by which to coordinate certain of their efforts and functions within this relatively small state, established the New Hampshire Library Council, an institution not of individuals but of groups. The Council comprises the chief officers of each statewide group and of the State Library and representatives for the New England Library Association and the American Library Association. It serves to focus attention on library-related matters of interest to public, school, academic, and special (particularly hospital) libraries, library trustees, and Friends of the Library groups. The Council issues, with the State Library, the newsletter *Granite State Libraries,* plans and sponsors the principal

New Hampshire Library Association (founded 1889)

Membership: 250.
President: Bea Jordan, New Hampshire College, Manchester, New Hampshire (May 1976–May 1977).
Vice-President/President-elect: Jean Michie, Richards Library, Newport, New Hampshire.
Secretary: Susan Goodwin, Technical Library, Portsmouth Naval Shipyard.
Annual Meeting: May 17–19, 1976, Farley, Vermont.
Publication: Granite State Libraries (bimonthly).

New Hampshire State Library

Avis M. Duckworth, State Librarian
20 Park Street
Concord, New Hampshire 03301

State Reports—New Hampshire

statewide annual conference, and carries forward the state's scholarship program (awarding a total of $2,100 in 1976).

The New Hampshire Library Council's 1976 Annual Conference, held at Bedford May 17–18, had as its theme "Significant 76." In addition to business and program meetings of particular interest to the constituencies of the member organizations of the Council, the conference featured speakers such as Library Journal's John Berry, political cartoonist Bob Alexander, and Kevin Cash, author of Who the Hell Is William Loeb?, a study of the publisher of the state's largest-circulation daily newspaper.

The following notes some of the 1976 activities of the member organizations of the Council:

NHLA. The state's oldest library-interest group, the New Hampshire Library Association, was incorporated in 1889 by 50 "important men" (including but one librarian, Dartmouth College's Marvin Bisbee). More than fourscore years later the Association continues to seek ways to meet the needs of the people of the state through its libraries. This year in particular has been one of self-examination to determine how it may best function and most efficiently be constituted. To this end a number of special meetings have been held and the membership polled by questionnaire (the results favoring Association activity with the following priority: continuing education, intrastate information exchange, scholarships, intellectual freedom, and employee grievance procedures).

Ever in need of funds in addition to membership income to support its activities, the Association held two simultaneous public auctions (with virtually anything eligible for sale) in two geographically separate locations in the state. Only one was successful (and that rewardingly so), but a selection of the merchandise of the other turned a handsome profit at a "silent auction" at NHLA's fall meeting in November. Significant Association disbursements during the 1975/76 fiscal year included contributions to the New Hampshire Library Council's scholarship efforts ($600) and to the ALA Washington Office ($300).

Academic Librarians. The Academic Librarians of New Hampshire is a small, intentionally informal group which functions as a relatively autonomous section of the state library association. It traditionally holds two meetings each year, one at the New Hampshire Library Council conference in the spring (this year's featured a talk by Sam Ellenport of Boston's Harcourt Bindery) and a fall meeting at a new or expanded academic library facility in the state. Another statewide group taking a consciously introspective look, ALNH this year polled its membership and found itself quite satisfied with its own relaxed and loosely organized nature.

Hospital Librarians. Another small group, newly independent of the state library association (from which—with gratitude for several years' sponsorship—it disassociated in 1975) is the New Hampshire Hospital Librarians Association. It also met twice in 1976: at the May state conference to hear a talk on "The Clinical Librarian" by Gertrude Lamb of the Hartford (Connecticut) Hospital, and in October at the Cheshire County Hospital in Keene.

Trustees Association. The New Hampshire Library Trustees Association is a large and active organization serving public library trustees across the state. It pursues a variety of programs (including meetings, seminars, and workshops) designed to acquaint trustees with the needs of their library and its patrons. At the state library conference it presented a panel discussion entitled "The Significant Trustee," moderated by John T. Short of Avon, Connecticut, President of the American Library Trustee Association. In October more than 80 members gathered in Concord for the Fall Conference to hear special presentations from the chief officers of the State Library and the Historical Society.

School Librarians. In 1976 the Intellectual Freedom Committee of the New Hampshire Educational Media Association issued their report entitled "Plain Rapper," a compilation of materials consisting of a selection of basic statements, interpretations, and writings about intellectual freedom as formulated by the American Library Association, the American Association of School Librarians, and the National Council of Teachers of English, as well as a statement of policies for selection of School Library Media Resources, including suggested policy and procedure for handling challenged materials and a form for requesting reconsideration of such materials. Additionally, NHEMA met in conference on a number of occasions to share concerns common to school librarians in the state.

Awards. Emerson Greenaway of New London was awarded ALA's Special Centennial Citation in July, the presentation noting: "As an ambassador of librarianship to his city, his state, his nation and the world, Emerson Greenaway's efforts have led to greater appreciation of the importance of libraries and librarians." Greenaway, very much active in library affairs in the state, currently serves as State Chairman of the New Hampshire Governor's Conference on Libraries.

In May, Adelaide B. Lockhart, Director of Library Services at Dartmouth College, was presented with Simmons College School of Library Science's Seventh Annual Alumni Achievement Award "for her contributions to librarianship in general as active member and officer of professional organizations and for her distinguished career in academic librarianship and administration." Among her many offices, Lockhart is past-President of the New England Library Association and most recently New Hampshire representative to ALA Council.

The 1976 New Hampshire Library Trustees Association Award for Trustee of the Year was presented jointly to Mrs. Richard Fowler and Maurice C. Aldrich of Hanover for their long and determined efforts toward the building of that town's new library. Donald Mullen of the Dover Public Library received the Association's Librarian of the Year award for work in his town and region and for his service to the state, including his recent chairmanship of the State Advisory Council on Libraries. The Special Library Awards went to Marion Welch of Kensington and to William H. Barkley of Hampton. A special award in recognition of outstanding service was presented to Barbara Cotton, Librarian of the Laconia Public Library.

The Nashua Public Library's Business Information Sessions program was awarded third prize in the national Public Relations Awards Contest sponsored by the Library Public Relations Council. The presentation, made during ALA's centennial conference, was in the category of "best coordinated publicity promoting a library program, service, or resource."

In October the Peterborough Town Library was presented a special centennial certificate by the Forest Press Division of the Lake Placid Education Foundation in recognition of its 19th-century adoption and continued use of the Dewey Decimal Classification.

Governor's Conference. In March Governor Meldrim Thomson, Jr., agreed to support a statewide Governor's Conference on Libraries in preparation for the 1978 White House Conference. Mrs. Richard Fowler, Chairman of the Board of Trustees of Hanover's Howe Library, was appointed Chairman of the Citizen's Planning Committee for the Conference, scheduled to be held at Concord in September 1977. The New Hampshire Library Commission approved a Title III LSCA Grant to help defray conference expenses.

Regional Activity. New England comprises six relatively small states sharing many common concerns and often combining their resources in various regional efforts. The New England Library Board, for instance, sponsors such activities as the New England Serials Service (NESS) and the New England Document Conservation Center. New Hampshire is thoroughly active in such endeavors and well represented in regional professional activities (for example, the past and current presidents of the New England Library Association and the president of ACRL's New England Chapter are all academic librarians in the state). STANLEY W. BROWN

NEW JERSEY

The economic situation continued to be a major concern of libraries and librarians in New Jersey in 1976. Much of the activities of all New Jersey librarians and library trustees were aimed at the state-wide economic problems of which libraries were a small part. The New Jersey Supreme Court stated two years previously that each child in New Jersey should receive a "thorough and efficient" education (wording is from the New Jersey State Constitution) and that reliance upon an inequitable property tax was unconstitutional as it could not provide this thorough and efficient education. In 1975 New Jersey Governor Byrne brought before the State Legislature an income tax proposal five times. Each time it was defeated. In 1976 after many changes and amendments, New Jersey finally passed a new tax law. It is, however, unclear as to what, if any, benefit the income tax will have for public or college and university libraries. School libraries are obviously identified as part of the thorough and efficient education. As such, it is likely that they may receive considerable additional funding in 1977.

Budget Cuts. In the Governor's budget recommendations for the 1976–77 fiscal year additional state aid to library cuts were suggested. The previous year state aid had received a 26.5 percent cut from full funding. Strenuous action on the part of librarians, trustees, and library friends saved even further cuts. For a second year

---

New Jersey Library Association
(founded 1890)

Membership: 1800; *Annual Expenditure:* $52,255 (November 1976).
President: William I. Bunnell, County College of Morris Library, Dover (July 1976–June 1977).
Administrative Secretary: Pauline A. Schear, 221 Blvd., Passaic, New Jersey 07055.
Annual Conference: May 5–9, 1976, Atlantic City.
Publication: New Jersey Libraries (10 issues a year).

Division of State Library, Archives and History, State Department of Education
David C. Palmer, Acting Director and State Librarian
185 W. State Street
Trenton, New Jersey 08625

---

the library community mounted a substantial drive to retain the same amount of monies as had been received the previous year. This was partially successful with approximately $1,500,000 returned to library aid. Nevertheless, state library aid now stands at 66.2 percent of full funding or a total of $6,745,000.

In spite of the uncertainty of what value the income tax would have for libraries and faced with the obvious impact the state aid cuts would have, the entire library community girded for a two-prong battle to support the income tax proposals and to retain or increase the amount of aid. Although it was only partially successful, John H. Livingstone, Jr., President-elect of the New Jersey Library Association, stated that these two years on the economic battle front may have had lasting value for all New Jersey libraries. Livingstone said that for the first time the political community in the state is very much aware of libraries, librarians, and their supporters. The massive campaign of letters, telephone calls, telegrams, and personal contact with legislators by the library community had considerable impact, according to Livingstone, on the politicians of the state.

In many other respects, 1976 was a comparatively quiet year for New Jersey libraries. For a second year no construction funds were made available from the state. The loss of federal and state monies for this purpose coupled with the general economic situation slowed new library construction considerably within the state. Very few new or renovated library buildings came into existence as compared to the boom years of the late 1960's.

Crunch Kills Network. The 1976 *ALA Yearbook* reported on creation of CAPTAIN (Computer Aided Processing and Terminal Access Information Network) for information exchange and retrieval among New Jersey State colleges and universities. Due to financial and technical problems, the CAPTAIN program died in 1976. The colleges and universities involved have found it necessary to turn to other, already established networks for service.

The New Jersey Library Association (NJLA) held successful conferences in Atlantic City and Morristown in conjunction with the New Jersey School Media Association and the New Jersey Library Trustee Association. At the Atlantic City conference, Peggy Barber, Director of the Public Information Office of ALA, was NJLA's guest for the entire conference. Barber was an outstanding representative of ALA and her presence was greatly appreciated by all attending the conference.

NJLA, the School Media Association, and the Trustee Association were in the forefront of the economic battles of the year; and NJLA reorganized its publishing policy and programs for the future.
SCHUYLER MOTT

NEW MEXICO

State Library and State Government Reorganization. New Mexico's chief executive declared that "it is time we called a halt to the senseless and haphazard growth of government in New Mexico . . ." and called for the reorganization of the state's 296 boards, bureaus, commissions, departments, and divisions. Nineteen reorganization bills had been introduced into the 33rd legislative session by the end of 1976, and if successful, the new system would become effective July 1, 1977. Under the Governor's plan, related agencies and services would be brought together within one of 12 departments, each to be headed by a secretary. Combined, the secretaries would form the Governor's cabinet. The State Library would become a division within the Department of Educational Finance and Cultural Affairs, along with the New Mexico Arts Commission, the Museums of New Mexico, and the Public School Finance Division of the Department of Finance and Administration. Essentially, the relationship between the State Library and the libraries in the state would remain the same. The greatest change would be the transferral of powers held by the State Library Commission to the State Librarian (who would continue to hold that title). The State Library Commission and the LSCA mandated Advisory Council on Libraries would be combined to serve as a single advisory body to the State Library.

Buildings, Collections, and Celebrations. On September 7, 1976, after the is-

---

New Mexico Library Association
(founded 1924)

Membership: 601 (110 ALA members); *Annual Expenditure:* $12,000.
President: Elinor McCloskey, Albuquerque Public Schools.
Vice President/President-elect: Vida Hollis, Northeastern Regional Bookmobile, Cimarron.
Secretary: Karen James, State Department of Education, Santa Fe, New Mexico 87501.
Annual Conference: March 31–April 3, 1976, Sante Fe.
Publication: New Mexico Library Association Newsletter (5 or 6 issues a year).

New Mexico State Library
C. Edwin Dowlin, State Librarian
P.O. Box 1629
Santa Fe, New Mexico 87501

State Reports—New York

sue had been on the ballot three times, voters in Roswell passed a $1,200,000 bond issue for a new library building. The vote was 3,367 for; 2,802 against—the largest voter turnout for a city bond issue. Previous bond issues had failed in 1968 and 1970. Plans call for a building with 22,000 square feet, a meeting room, and parking for 50 cars.

The old, pueblo-style main building of the Albuquerque Public Library (vacated when the new building opened in 1975) is to be restored to its original appearance for use as a research facility with its focus being local history, genealogy, and Spanish heritage materials.

The late Senator Clinton P. Anderson of New Mexico bequeathed his personal library, which included Roosevelt, Truman, Eisenhower, and Kennedy memorabilia as well as rare publications, to the University of New Mexico. The collection is housed at the Zimmerman Library. The gift included monies to finance the building of a room to house the collection.

During 1976 the Artesia Public Library celebrated its 70th birthday. The library, started by a group of citizens, received its enabling charter six years before New Mexico became a state.

Film Service to Schools Withdrawn. After consideration of a study and survey of State Library film services, the State Library Commission decided that the Library could no longer provide films to schools. The Commission noted that without additional resources, the film collection was too small to support even the most limited statewide film service for schools; and, that given the present source of funding as well as the Commission's commitment by statute to support public library services, State Library film support efforts must be directed to libraries.

Statewide Inventory Control System. Ten New Mexico librarians representing public, academic, and special libraries in 1976 reviewed a 3M computerized inventory control system. The librarians began to see statewide applications as they discussed desirable applications such as inventory and circulation control, the ability to access the shelf list of other libraries for interlibrary loan purposes, and the immediate generation of statistical and report data. The librarians have sought advice from others and are preparing a statement of needs for a statewide system.

Bus Library. The children of Canjilon (who have a long ride to school each day) have been given a shelfful of books to help fill the time spent on the school bus. Maintenance of the collection is a continuing project of the Rio Grande Chapter of the Special Libraries Association.

PAUL A. AGRIESTI

NEW YORK

As 1976 drew to a close, the state of libraries and librarianship in New York was good. Perhaps this is only because matters could have been worse. Like most other states, New York has had more than its share of branch closings, austerity budgets, excessing of personnel, and attacks against intellectual freedom and due process. But thanks to the courageous dedication of many individual librarians, other friends of libraries, and the zeal of our professional organizations in particular, New York was able to get its message across both to legislators and the public. Accomplishments of 1976 should be the motivation for even more daring and successful endeavors in 1977.

Legislation. During the week of July 19 Governor Hugh Carey signed into law Senate Bill 3587D, Public Library System Aid Increase, and the Supplemental Budget that appropriated $4,000,000 in state aid to the financially hard-pressed public libraries and public library systems. So ended a two-year campaign by NYLA involving widespread grass roots support that grew to over 500 letters and telegrams a day at the height of the action. The new state aid was to be paid out in two payments of $1,000,000 before April 1, 1977, and $3,000,000 in April and May 1977.

All libraries that conform to the Commissioners' standards of registration may qualify for Local Sponsor Incentive Aid. Libraries may receive no less than 75 percent of the LSIA for which they qualified in the prior year, even if the local support does not increase. This brings the state's share of support of public libraries to $29,000,000 annually.

New York Library Association
(founded 1890)

Membership: 4,500 (approx. 1,200 ALA members); *Annual Expenditure:* $130,000.
President: Mary B. Cassata, Department of Speech Communication, SUNY at Buffalo (October 1976–November 1977).
Vice-President/President-elect: Lucille Thomas, Library Supervisor, School District #16, Brooklyn, New York.
Executive Director: Dadie Perlov, 60 East 42 Street, Suite 1342, New York, New York 10017.
Annual Conference: October 14–17, 1976, Lake Placid, New York.
Publication: Bulletin (10 issues a year).

New York State Education Department
John A. Humphry, State Librarian
State Education Building
Albany, 12224

A Legislative Day in Albany on March 30 drew more than 250 public, academic, and school librarians, as well as Trustees and Friends.

The rest of the bills in the NYLA legislative program died in committee. At least two of them were to be reintroduced in the 1977 session with little change. These are bills developed by the State Education Department for the Regents, and endorsed by NYLA, and are concerned with Library Service to Native Americans (public library service on Indian Reservations) and School Contingency Budgets. During the early part of the 1976 session, NYLA chose not to endorse the major library bill supported by the Regents, which attempted a new comprehensive regional approach toward library support. An amended and revised version of that bill has been approved by the Regents for introduction in the 1977 session and has received preliminary endorsement by NYLA.

School Library Media Section. Under the theme of Mediaship Is Leadership, all activities and resources of SLMS for 1975–76 were focused toward leadership development with the membership. Key phrases in the efforts have been increased visibility, concern for individuals, commitment to professional beliefs, and strengthened cooperation.

Affiliation has been a ma'or thrust, both at the local and the national levels. A year-long study to develop a formal affiliation process between SLMS and the statewide local associations has been conducted. As a result a task force is now developing a process for affiliating. Nationally, SLMS reviewed and accepted the AASL/ALA Affiliation Plan and in October formally applied for governance affiliate status.

Various activities at the state level have been significant. Continuing as a member of the New York State Council of Educational Associations, SLMS has maintained strong liaison with other subject area associations. Through this group, an SLMS delegate serves on a major state committee appointed by Commissioner Nyquist: Committee on the Arts and General Education. By request of the State Education Department, SLMS has engaged in discussions leading to a review of the existing New York State curriculum mandates. Leadership responsibilities have also been realized in certification activities, including planning for the future competency-based mode.

In addition to numerous local and regional workshops, SLMS held its 8th Annual Spring Conference for two days in Syracuse. Further, a full program of activities for SLMS members was implemented in October at the NYLA Fall Conference.

State Reports—New York

Scholarship awards were granted to two members. In addition, the Lewiston-Porter Central School District received the John T. Short Award for its outstanding School Library Media Day celebrations. A new award was approved by the Board to recognize a New York State administrator who has contributed significantly to the support or development of an elementary level library media program.

Reference and Adult Services. The RASS continued their interest in developing the skills of reference and adult services librarians throughout New York state. Among the projects carried out in 1976 were the following: Adult services idea packets were circulated to Section members on request. The packets consisted of program fliers, book lists, newsletters and annual reports produced by New York state libraries. A pamphlet, *Do It*, an introduction to information and referral services, written by Kay Adams and Nancy Johmann, will encourage libraries of all sizes to develop information and referral services.

NYLA Activities. The New York Library Association launched its Continuing Education Program in 1976 by sponsoring a one-day long mini course on "Communication Strategies for Librarians." The underlying premise for the "strategies" was two-fold: (1) communication plays a fundamental role in the fusing of the complex and intricate human relationships that are a part of the daily business of living and coping; (2) librarians share a heavy responsibility with other professional communicators as managers and gatekeepers of information.

A team of communication scholars and consultants from various parts of the country led a number of workshops on such areas as interpersonal communication skills; encounters between librarians and their various publics and constituencies; non-verbal skills; symbols of power; role of the mass media; self-evaluation; and libraries as vehicles for the transmission of culture. In addition NYLA made library association history by offering the CEU unit of credit to the more than 200 mini course participants who opted for it.

NYLA's newly formed ad hoc committee on continuing education, headed by New York State Education Department's E. J. Josey, is charged with the continued exploration and development of continuing education opportunities and programs for all New York State librarians and library support staffs, alternative plans for course credit, and proposals for outside funding.

Intellectual Freedom. The Intellectual Freedom Committee increased its membership to 15 in 1976. Meeting three times during the year in New York City, the group consulted with Irene Turin, supervisor of the Island Trees School District Libraries on Long Island, and members of the administration of the teacher's union in their challenge to the School Board's arbitrary removal of previously approved titles from the library shelves. As the year drew to a close, the American Civil Liberties Union was supporting several parents in a suit against the School Board. The NYLA-IFC counseled some students into filing a complaint with the American Library Association under ALA's Action Program in Mediation, Arbitration, and Inquiry. In addition, the IFC worked closely and behind the scenes with librarians fending off attacks on an item in their collection. This action involved two schools and one public library. In all but one case the items remained in the collection. In one school library the items remain in the collection "labelled" and requiring parental permission for use by the student.

Junior Members Round Table. At the annual conference of the New York Library Association in 1976, a Junior Members Round Table affiliate to ALA-JMRT was established within the New York Library Association. Although a JMRT "committee" was created in 1975 to organize Conference Orientation, it was not until a new constitution providing for round tables passed in 1976 that the group could become a Junior Members Round Table in the ideal sense of the term.

Governor's Conference. After more than 10 years, the second New York Governor's Conference is tentatively scheduled for 1978 as a preliminary to the White House Conference in 1979. Responsibility for the Conference is vested in a Commission named by the Governor and chaired by Edwin Newman of the National Broadcasting Corporation. John Mackenzie Cory, Director of the New York Public Library, and Dinah Lindauer, Coordinator of Programs and Services, Nassau Library System, are coordinating the New York Library Association's support and advice for the Conference.

The first meeting of the Governor's Commission on Libraries was held in New York City, June 4. Governor Carey addressed the Commissioners and members of the NYLA Ad Hoc Committee who had been invited to attend.

Book Selection Guidelines. The New York State Board of Regents in October adopted its first set of guidelines that would help local school districts select controversial text and library books—including materials dealing with sex. The inclusion of sexual incidents or profanity should not automatically disqualify a book. Such materials should be "subjected to a test of literary merit and reality," the Board declared.

The regents said district school boards should recognize as a basic principle that parents have a right to determine that individual material in the school library may not be appropriate for their child. The guidelines state that "a parent request that such a book or other item not be given to their child should be honored." The Regents suggested, however, that school boards should not permit "any parent or group of parents to determine what materials may be used for pupils other than their own children."

As a first step, the Regents urged that each local school district develop a materials selection policy that would reflect the thinking of the district and insure a consistent procedure by all school personnel.

NYLA Annual Conference. More than 2,100 librarians, exhibitors, and guests attended NYLA's 83d Annual Conference at Lake Placid, October 14-17, Several actions were approved by the membership. They include a program to provide a retirement option for NYLA staff; approval of a donation of $350 to the Nassau Civil Liberties Union for legal expenses in defense of First Amendment rights in the Island Trees School District after the removal of 11 titles from the school library media center; acceptance and approval of a petition from the Junior Members Round Table Committee for official Round Table status; and approval of five additional continuing education grants for a total of $2,175.

The Conference heard a report on changes in the State Education Department by the legislature. Five assistant commissioner positions were abolished. One was the position of Assistant Commissioner for libraries, held by John A. Humphry. He was reassigned and designated State Librarian. The position of Director, Division of Library Development, was abolished. The Division will now be made up of the Bureau of Regional Library Services, with Robert Flores as Chief, and the Bureau of Specialist Library Services, with E. J. Josey as Chief. Lore Scurrah continued as Chief of the Bureau of School Libraries.

People. Elizabeth Miller, children's librarian at Westbury for 22 years, retired in 1976. Muriel C. Javelin, interagency consultant for the Nassau Library System, retired in March after 49 years in the profession.

Newly elected officers of the New York Black Librarians Caucus are Evelyn Hall, President; Natalia Davis, Vice-President; Phyllis Fisher, Recording Secretary; and Robert Ford, Treasurer.

NYLA Council member Dan Casey has been appointed to the New York State

State Reports—North Carolina

Board of Regents Advisory Council on Libraries. Werner Rebsamen of Rochester Institute of Technology has been named Director of Technology of the Library Binding Institute. Ruth Weber, former Acting Director of the Suffolk Cooperative Library System, is new Director of the Westchester Library System. Robert Sheridan, formerly Director of Levittown Public Library, has been named Director of the Suffolk Cooperative Library system.

Marguerite Yates, Lockport, a strong supporter of public libraries in the state, was given the Velma K. Moore Award at the annual meeting of the New York State Association of Library Boards during the 83d annual NYLA Conference.

Deaths. Daniel R. Newton, Director of the Bryant Library in Roslyn, Long Island, for the past 16 years, died January 1. Edwin K. Tolan, Head Librarian at Union College, died February 1.

Elizabeth Caven Seely, Librarian Emeritus at Sarah Lawrence College, died February 2. Carlyle Frarey, assistant to the Dean at Columbia's School of Library Service, died March 13. He was formerly acting Dean of the North Carolina School of Library Science.

Margaret Hunt Evans, former Assistant Director of the Buffalo Public Library, died March 17. G. Patterson Crandall, associated with the Patterson Library, Westfield, since 1912, died April 1.

MICHAEL G. DERUVO

NORTH CAROLINA

NCLA Activities. 1976 was a non-conference year for the North Carolina Library Association (NCLA) which meets biennially. Many librarians from the state took the opportunity to attend the Southeastern Library Association (SELA) meeting in Knoxville, Tennessee. The numerous sections of NCLA were active, however, sponsoring a variety of workshops including programs on interlibrary loans and "How to Talk to Your Legislator." The North Carolina Association of School Librarians (a division of NCLA) held its biennial meeting October 28–30 in Raleigh.

Public Libraries. Durham County approved a $3,000,000 library bond, September 14, for construction of a new main public library. The 65,000-square-foot building will replace a 5,300-square-foot Carnegie library built in 1921. A four-acre site has been donated to the library by the owners of a local television station. Credit for success of the bond issue, following failures in 1968 and 1972, went to the Coalition in Action for a New Durham Library System composed of representatives from the city's professional and citizens' organizations, and interested individuals. The

North Carolina Library Association (founded 1942)

Membership: 2,000; *Annual Expenditure:* $66,504 (1975).
President: Annette L. Phinazee, North Carolina Central University, School of Library Science, Durham (November 1975–November 1977).
Vice-President/President-elect: Leonard L. Johnson, Greensboro Public Schools.
Executive Secretary: Chrys A. Cranford, Appalachian State University, P. O. Box 212, ASU, Boone, North Carolina 28608.
Publication: North Carolina Libraries (quarterly).

Division of State Library

David N. McKay, Director and State Librarian
109 East Jones Street
Raleigh, North Carolina 27611

Coalition raised over $7,500 for their campaign, distributed brochures, provided speakers for civic groups and telephoned voters. The group is now trying to establish a library endowment and to revitalize the Friends of the Durham Library.

The Cumberland County Public Library received an $88,000 LSCA Special Project Grant from the North Carolina State Library to provide state-wide foreign language public library services. A large concentration of foreign speaking residents live in the library's service area which includes Fayetteville and areas adjacent to Fort Bragg. The library received an earlier $7,500 LSCA grant in order to purchase Vietnamese language materials. Both grants will enable the Cumberland County Public Library to provide bilingual resources for non-English-speaking residents of the state.

The Greensboro Public Library established a continuing education information and reference service known locally as LEO (Lifetime Educational Opportunities). The service lists more than 1,200 different courses, but the coordinator, Reference Librarian Eugene Pfaff, estimates there are 10,000 continuing education opportunities in the local community.

Academic Libraries. North Carolina Agricultural and Technical State University (Greensboro) was awarded a Council on Library Resources Library Enhancement Project grant. The purpose of the CLR grant is to increase faculty and student use of the library.

The library conducted a conference in June on the Multi-cultural Academic Library Services in Predominantly Black Institutions of Higher Education. The program, attended by librarians from five states, was funded by a grant from the Southern Education Foundation.

Perkins Library at Duke University established the Jay B. Hubbell Center for American Literary Historiography. The Center, to be a part of the manuscript department, will collect and preserve correspondence and other primary sources related to American literary history, criticism, and bibliography. Hubbell, who taught American literature at Duke from 1927 to 1955, has been a member of the editorial board of *American Literature* since 1929. His papers and the editorial file of the journal will form the nucleus of the collection.

The Central Piedmont Community College (Charlotte) installed a dial access system of recorded academic, information, and entertainment programs. The system, dubbed DOLLY (Dial Our Listening Library Yourself), is available on public telephone lines enabling callers to listen from telephones outside the library. The weekly schedule of 20 programs is published by two local newspapers with their television listings.

The Wake Forest University Library purchased a 13,000-volume collection of 20th-century English and American authors. The collection was assembled over a period of 40 years by Lynwood Giacomini of Chevy Chase, Maryland. The library received substantial financial assistance for the purchase from Nancy Susan Reynolds of Greenwich, Connecticut.

New Buildings. A new central library building for the Asheville and Buncombe County Libraries, under construction in 1976 in the Asheville business district, was scheduled for completion in fall 1977. The 52,000-square-foot building was expected to cost $2,400,000. The two-story structure will be connected directly to a parking garage constructed separately by the city of Asheville.

Groundbreaking for a 32,000-square-foot Learning Resource Center at Davidson County Community College took place in May. The $1,100,000 Center will house the Library, Individualized Instruction Center, Audiovisual Department, and Television Studio.

A new building housing the Nantahala Regional Library and the Murphy Town Library was dedicated July 3. The 17,000-square-foot building cost $467,000.

Networks and Interlibrary Cooperation. Responsibility for the North Carolina Union Catalog was transferred from the University of North Carolina to the State Library. The State Library will assume the task of receiving and filing cards submitted by participating libraries, searching the card file for libraries seeking locations, and searching SOLINET files for libraries without terminals. For many years the University maintained a card file of holdings from other libraries in the state. In recent years cards for UNC holdings were interfiled and the whole catalog microfilmed and distributed to selected locations throughout the state. Meanwhile the State Library had established an IN-WATS line so that the state's libraries would have telephone access to the State Library Reference Service and interlibrary loan locations. The new arrangment places total responsibility for administration of the interlibrary center with the State Library.

A Centennial. On December 2 librarians and library educators from throughout the country gathered in Chapel Hill to honor Louis Round Wilson, who celebrated his 100th birthday December 27. Wilson was librarian at the University of North Carolina from 1901 to 1932, Dean of the School of Library Science, and Dean of the Graduate School of Library Science at the University of Chicago. Symposia on "Library Education in the South since World War II" (with Jack Dalton, Virginia Lacy Jones, and Mary Edna Anders) and "University Libraries and Change" (featuring Herman Fussler, Robert Downs, Guy Lyle, and Stephen McCarthy) drew large numbers of librarians. The centennial program was sponsored by the University Library and the School of Library Science. See feature article on Louis Round Wilson in this *Yearbook*.

Awards. Lester Asheim, William Rand Kenan, Jr., Professor of Library Science at the University of North Carolina at Chapel Hill, received the American Library Association's Joseph W. Lippincott Award at the ALA Centennial Conference. Asheim has a distinguished record of achievement as a librarian, library educator, and researcher. (See Biographies.)

Appointments. Eugene A. Brunelle was appointed Director of Library Services at East Carolina University. Brunelle was Director of Instructional Resources and Professor of English at St. Mary's College of Maryland. Charles D. Pipes, former Head of the Flint, Michigan, Downtown Branch Public Library, was appointed Director of the Northwestern Regional Library in Elkin. William Gosling, former Program Manager of the Cataloging in Publication Office at the Library of Congress, was named Assistant University Librarian for Technical Services at Duke University.

David McKay became State Librarian September 1. He came to North Carolina from Minnesota, where he had been Director of the Minneapolis–St. Paul Metropolitan Library Service Agency.

Retirements. Aileen and Mable Aderholt retired in 1976 as Librarian and Assistant Librarian from Lenoir-Rhyne College. The Aderholt sisters served a total of 76 years— Aileen since 1934 and Mable since 1942— at Lenoir-Rhyne.

Edna Creech retired after more than 29 years (24 as Librarian) with the Columbus County Public Library. Kathleen Gilleland retired after 16 years as Director of the Northwestern Regional Library in Elkin.

Elizabeth Holder retired from the University of North Carolina at Greensboro. At retirement she was Head Reference Librarian but in her 24 years at the University had served in several capacities including Acting Director. Nancy Clark Fogarty, a member of the reference staff since 1970, will fill the position.

Jerrold Orne retired after almost 20 years as Librarian and Professor of Library Science at the University of North Carolina at Chapel Hill. Orne was Director of the University Libraries from 1957 until 1972 when he was named Professor in the School of Library Science. He received numerous awards including the Award of Merit from the American Society for Information Science (1971), and the Melvil Dewey Award (1972) and Joseph W. Lippincott Award (1974), both from the American Library Association.

Minnie Padgett Schaberg retired after 10 years as Head of Acquisitions for Wilson Library of the University of North Carolina at Chapel Hill. Helen Thompson, Director of the Scotland County Memorial Library since 1954, retired in February.

Deaths. Philip Smythe Ogilvie, North Carolina State Librarian since 1965, died January 24. Ogilvie, a graduate of the Catholic University (D.C.) Library School, had served in libraries in North Carolina, South Carolina, Georgia, Virginia, Mississippi, and Oklahoma before becoming State Librarian. He was a leader in promoting library service for all the state's citizens. State aid to public libraries grew to ninth in the nation under his direction. North Carolinians may look forward with confidence to library development in the state because of Phil Ogilvie's planning and leadership.　　　　DAVID P. JENSEN

NORTH DAKOTA

State Library Commission. During 1976 the State Library Commission participated in three major studies, two of which it commissioned. The first, a study of library service in the Lake Agassiz Region, was prepared by the Library Advisory Council. The second, a study of the Lewis and Clark Region, prepared by that Regional Library, sought to identify the resources of all types of libraries in the region and to define the purpose of the regional library, to serve as a basis for future planning. Both reports have just recently been delivered and their findings and recommendations are not yet known.

A study prepared for the North Dakota Legislative Council by Russell Fridley of

State Reports—North Dakota

North Dakota Library Association
(founded 1906)

Membership: 300; *Annual Expenditure:* $5,000.
President: Dennis M. Page, Grand Forks Public Library (October 1975– September 1977).
Vice-President/President-elect: Dina Butcher, Minot Public Library.
Secretary: Georgie Hager, Minot State College Library.
Treasurer: Ell-Piret Multer, Northern Prairie Wildlife Research Center, Jamestown.
Annual Conference: September 23–25, Bismarck, North Dakota.
Publication: Good Stuff (quarterly).

North Dakota State Library Commission

Richard J. Wolfert, State Librarian
Highway 83 North
Bismarck, North Dakota 58501

the Minnesota Historical Society, on the other hand, takes the State Library Commission as its subject. Its recommendations include elimination of the traveling library program, expansion of MINITEX teletype services, and development of a division within the Library to coordinate statewide library planning and development.

Two projects which had been in process for some time were brought to a successful conclusion during the year. A union catalog in COM format has been produced which makes available in 135 fiches the 120,000 volumes of Mary College, the McLean-Mercer Regional Library, and the State Library. A second project saw public and academic library statistics for the State converted to computer format, also.

The contract with MINITEX was successfully renegotiated under terms which make available to all libraries in North Dakota the resources of Minnesota libraries. Through the State Library, LSCA funds were made available to five county senior citizen projects, all in the Devils Lake area, to assist their attempts to bring library service to rural senior citizens.

Several years ago the Library Commission was removed from the Capitol grounds in Bismarck to a site a mile away. There is now the encouraging word that the State Legislative Council will recommend that the Library be returned to the Capitol grounds in Bismarck. This would provide for greater efficiency in the operation of the Library and would restore it to a state of higher visibility to the people of North Dakota whom it serves.

Governor's Advisory Council. The Governor's Advisory Council on Libraries is an appointed group of librarians and lay persons established by Governor Arthur Link.

State Reports—Ohio

Its purpose is to make possible, through study and recommendation, maximum use of all library resources in the State. In its two years of existence, the Council has assimilated a great deal of information. Reports have been heard from all library groups and minority and/or special groups being served through grants. Several State officials have met with members of the Council to broaden its knowledge of such topics as State revenue sharing proposals, budgetary procedures and priorities, and public instruction concerns.

In the area of accomplishments, Sister Gordon Barnard's study of libraries in institutions has already resulted in changes and improvements, particularly at the State Penitentiary. The Council's report for the two-year period will include a number of recommendations for State Library direction and for the maximum utilization of library services available in the State.

NDLA. The North Dakota Library Association completed its 70th year with a total membership of 300. In 1976 the Association sponsored four regional conferences at which members of the Public and Trustees Sections met with area legislators to discuss library problems. Over 300 registrants attended the "Fabulous '76 Convention" in Bismarck. The program of mini-workshops provided information and an opportunity to discuss such topics as micrographics, MINITEX, children's literature, and genealogy. Highlighting the activities were addresses by Alice Ihrig and Andy Hanson, representing ALA, and Russell Fridley, Director of the Minnesota Historical Society.

Proposed at the Convention was a plan to hold statewide meetings biannually with regional meetings scheduled in the "off" years. Dwindling funds, long distances, and small staffs are problems which might yield to this proposed format. Registrants were receptive to the suggestion, which will be considered again at the next convention. They gave approval in addition to a recommendation of the Executive Board that future editions of The Good Stuff be edited on a rotating basis by the Sections of NDLA.

School Library Section. A review of school library reports for the past five years indicates a trend toward increasing the elementary services and programs in the State and a corresponding growth in the quantity and quality of library materials. However, there is a concern that the elimination of State Title II fund will retard this growth. Provisions for disbursement of funds under the new Title IVB program, it is thought, are inadequate and in some cases discriminatory.

The NDLA convention held in Bismarck was considered the best ever by the school librarians. Donald Reynolds of Princeton, New Jersey, Alice Ihrig, President of the Illinois Library Association, and Darrell Hildebrandt, Bismarck Memorial Library (whose Children's Round-Table was memorable) highlighted a stimulating program.

The *Handbook for Media Centers in North Dakota Schools,* developed by a committee of the School Library Section, was published by the State Department of Public Instruction in 1975. This is a step toward assisting all schools in updating and evaluating their library media center programs.

Ruth McMartin, Director of Instructional Resources for the Fargo Public Schools, coordinated materials for the North Dakota Section of an annotated bibliography on regions of the United States to be published by ALA.

Trustees Section. Public relations, media and legislative contact were the focal point of four highly successful regional workshops held by the Trustees Section. The meetings were held at the same time and place as those of the NDEA School-Media section. After holding separate meetings, the two groups joined forces at luncheons to which local state representatives and government officials were invited. These meetings proved so successful that academic and city/county librarians wish to participate in the future. The Trustees' Convention meetings featured Alice Ihrig at the luncheon and a lively rap session which explored the future alternatives of going-it-alone or cooperating with larger units in NDLA or other organizations.

Academic Section. Academic librarians serving state colleges and universities lost their faculty status this past year. Efforts of a committee established by the Academic Section to counter this threat in the end proved to be ineffective.

The Academic Section's long-standing interest in bibliographical control is at present represented by the work being done in two of its committees. One is engaged in compiling a bibliography of state documents available in libraries throughout the State. Another has undertaken a complete examination of the N.D. State Documents depository system. A preliminary report seeks to establish a working definition of these materials and proposes guidelines for their distribution to and retention by various types of libraries in the State. A complementary project to be undertaken by this same committee in the future will be the production of a manual for processing deposited documents.

Though the Section recognizes its responsibility to provide opportunities for continuing education for librarians throughout the State, several factors, such as the great distances and small number of librarians, make it uncertain how to proceed if, indeed, such an undertaking could be productive. As a preliminary step, therefore, the Section has established a committee to study the feasibility of undertaking a program of continuing education.

Cooperation. The Tri-College University, of which North Dakota State University in Fargo is a member, saw the completion of the initial step toward development of a machine-based union catalog. Typed records of post-1968 holdings have been submitted by the three libraries for processing. The first films containing the merged records were expected in December. At the same time plans are underway for the Tri-College as part of the Minnesota system to join the OCLC system.

Resignations. Ralph Stenstrom resigned as Project Director for the State Library Commission to become Director of Libraries at Hamilton and Kirkland Colleges in Clinton, New York. Before joining the State Library staff, Stenstrom had served as the first TCU Libraries Coordinator in Fargo-Moorhead.

Everett Foster, Director of the Minot Public Library since 1967, resigned to become a rancher in Montana.

Judith Murray, TCU Libraries Coordinator in 1975–76, has been named Vice-President, Library Support Services for Library Interface Systems, Inc., in Minnetonka, Minnesota. While with Tri-College, she was responsible for coordinating the planning and implementing of the computer-based Tri-College Libraries card catalog.   PATRICIA SCHOMMER

OHIO

If one word had to be selected which would best describe 1976 for Ohio libraries, it would have to be "Cooperation." Apparently gaining impetus from the previous year's Interlibrary Cooperation Planning Institute, an increased emphasis was placed on cooperation among all types of libraries. This report contains numerous examples of cooperative ventures between school and public libraries, public and academic libraries, and public and special libraries.

Public Libraries. As predicted in the 1976 *Yearbook,* Ohioans' use of public library materials increased considerably in 1975. The 1976 *Ohio Directory of Libraries* showed that total circulation of all materials for 1975 topped 62,000,000, the highest in six years, and 6.1 percent higher than the previous year. Adult circulation continued to increase at an even greater rate of 7.7 percent. Other vital statistics include the following: the total number of volumes in Ohio public libraries was 27,600,000, a 2.7 percent increase over 1974; volumes

State Reports—Ohio

Ohio Library Association
(founded 1895)

Membership: 2353; *Annual Expenditure:* $94,392.
President: Jane Ann McGregor, Ohio Valley Area Libraries, Wellston (October 1976–September 1977).
Vice-President/President-elect: Charlotte Leonard, Dayton Montgomery County Public Library.
Executive Director: A. Chapman Parsons, 40 South Third Street, Suite 409, Columbus, Ohio 43215.
Annual Conference: October 27–30, 1976, Columbus.
Publications: OLA Bulletin (quarterly); *Ohio Libraries Newsletter* (8 issues a year).

The State Library of Ohio

Joseph F. Shubert, State Librarian
65 South Front Street
Columbus, Ohio 43215

added totaled 1,500,000 in 1975, an 8.8 percent increase over 1974; and total staff in Ohio's public libraries numbered 4,109. A look over four years indicates that there have also been changes in the staffing patterns. In 1975 1,017 of the 5,109 staff were professionals, a 5.8 percent increase from 1971. Fewer Ohio libraries were without professional staff in 1975 than in 1971 and professionals were working in 142 of Ohio's public libraries as compared to 123 libraries in 1971. Receipts from the intangibles tax increased in 1975 but that source still did not provide adequate financial support for many of Ohio's public libraries. Several libraries moved to place tax levies on the ballot.

Academic Libraries. The 1976 *Ohio Directory of Libraries* reported statistics for 120 academic libraries in Ohio. Expenditures in 1975 totaled $37,400,000 with personnel costs accounting for 54.7 percent or $20,300,000 while library materials totaled $10,200,000 or 27.3 percent. Book collections for the 120 libraries totaled 18,400,000 with 884,244 volumes added in 1975. Professional staff accounted for 40.2 percent of the total staff of 1,904.

OLA Activities. Several major accomplishments were achieved by the Ohio Library Association in 1976. A new salary schedule for Academic and Public Libraries and Educational Media Centers for 1977–78 was published as a supplement to "Recommended Job Classifications and Salary Goals for Ohio Academic Public and School Libraries for 1974–75." For the first time the salary schedule included recommendations for Clerk I, II, and III. Also undertaken during the year was an in-depth review of the Ohio Library Development Plan. A major revision to this landmark library plan will be completed in 1977.

The annual conference, was based on the theme "Building On Our Heritage," and was the second largest conference ever held with 1,159 attending. Highlights of the conference included John Berry III, Editor of *Library Journal,* speaking on individual rights for public employees; Phillip Shriver, President of Miami University of Ohio and an Ohio historian, speaking on "Ohio Heritage"; Trustee John T. Short of Avon, Connecticut, discussing "The Role of the Public Library Trustee"; Julia Losinski, YA Coordinator, Prince George's County, Maryland, Library System, addressing "Young Adults Are in Your Future"; Alphonse F. Trezza, Executive Director of NCLIS, explaining "National Planning for Libraries and Information Services," and Milton Byam, Director of the Queens Borough Public Library, putting the final touch on the conference with a practical approach for "Putting It All Together For the User." In a spirited business meeting a resolution was passed instructing OLA to request the General Assembly to appoint a joint bipartisan legislative study committee to work with a committee of librarians and trustees toward the development of an Alternative Funding Program for Ohio public libraries.

OASL + EMCO = OELMA. The Ohio Association of School Librarians and the Educational Media Council of Ohio were consolidated during a joint annual conference in October. Co-presidents were elected for the newly formed Ohio Educational Library Media Association (OELMA). The new Association of over 2,000 members marks the end of several years of planning to combine efforts to achieve goals of both groups.

OELMA, OLA, and OLTA planned to stage a concurrent annual conference October 27–29, 1977, in Dayton.

ALAO. The Academic Library Association of Ohio held its Second Annual Conference in October with the theme "Bicentennial Leap—Futurescope on Libraries." Highlights of the conference were addresses by Sara Case, Associate Director of the ALA Washington office, discussing "Library Future in Governmental Affairs"; Rosemary Magrill, University of Michigan School of Library Science, exploring the "Future of Library Education"; Hal Schell, Dean of Library Administration, University of Cincinnati, pondering the "Future of the Card Catalog," and Leonard Everett Fisher, painter, illustrator, and author, speaking on "Reflections of an American Artist - 1776."

State Library. After more than two years of dispute between the Ohio State Library Board and the Ohio Office of Budget and Management, the State Controlling Board refused to take action on an OBM request to transfer $1,000,000 in LSCA funds from the State Library to the state's general fund, thus assuring use of these funds for Ohio's libraries. The Controlling Board action came just nine days before the June 30 deadline for expenditure of the funds. The contested $1,000,000 had been held in the U.S. Treasury pending the outcome of an HEW audit requested by the State Library Board and Controlling Board action. In accordance with State Library Board policy and the advice of the Advisory Council on Federal Library Programs, the $1,000,000 will be expended for new resources and automation which will yield both immediate and long term results without incurring unrealistic commitments for the state or local libraries. The three projects being funded include: (1) A retrospective conversion of adult nonfiction catalog data from seven major public libraries and the State Library to machine readable form in the OCLC data base. The project will enlarge the data base by approximately 1,500,000 titles and 4,000 locations. (2) An Ohio areawide coordinated book-sharing program under which 20 multicounty library systems will receive a total of $250,000 for purchase of books in specific subject fields which they identify as critical. (3) An Ohio-Midwest History and Government Resources statewide program under which main libraries, branch libraries, and institution libraries will choose from among options in adult and children's books, maps, films and filmstrips.

The State Library continues to provide an excellent backstopping service for Ohio's libraries. Some 22,846 books and periodical articles were loaned to readers and other information seekers in their own communities through their local public libraries. Another 9,928 books were located for Ohio libraries through the Union Catalog and teletype interlibrary loan network.

In 1976 the Library published the *Ohio Documents Classification Scheme,* an important guide for those who organize or manage document collections.

Interlibrary Cooperation. As a follow-up to the Interlibrary Cooperation Planning Institute held in 1975 and sponsored by the Ohio Library Association, Ohio State University, and the State Library of Ohio, *Focus on the Future* was published; it contains the major addresses of the Institute as well as the recommendations that came out of the Institute. The publication will be the major document for discussion on interlibrary cooperation in the state. To complement *Focus on the Future,* the State Library also prepared a 30-minute videotape, *Interlibrary Cooperation: An Opportunity for the Future Growth of Ohio Li-*

State Reports—Oklahoma

braries, which reports on the institute and is designed to promote further discussion. An Ad Hoc Ohio Multitype Interlibrary Cooperation Committee was formed to insure that the momentum established at the October meeting continues. Members of the Committee were appointed by seven Ohio professional and trustee library organizations, the State Department of Education, the Board of Regents, and the State Library of Ohio.

Further cooperation took place with the "Spirit of 76 Caravan," which brought together more than 800 school and public children's librarians for 12 day-long workshops to plan Bicentennial Cooperative reading programs. Staff from the State Library and the State Department of Education, with a grant from the Ohio American Revolution Bicentennial Advisory Commission, put it all together. Visits were made to Ohio's 12 Right to Read Areas in order for public and school libraries and multi-county cooperatives to coordinate the reading improvement aims of the State Department of Education.

OCLC Activities. OCLC doubled its performance in 1976 when participating libraries cataloged over 5,000,000 books and produced 39,600,000 catalog cards. OCLC also moved into new quarters during the year, thus consolidating its computer facility. New functions added included the capability of cataloging films, serials control, and a new authorization level identifying operators engaged in re-classification of a collection. Work also began on the Acquisitions System which is being supported by a grant from the Council on Library Resources and which will be tested in early 1977. An important step was taken with the appointment of an Advisory Council to help shape OCLC's future directions including OCLC's role relative to any national on-line network to be developed.

Intellectual Freedom. The U.S. Court of Appeals for the Sixth Circuit ruled in August that school officials may not arbitrarily remove books from a school library. In a unanimous decision the court overturned a 1974 ruling by a U.S. District Court that upheld the withdrawal of *Cat's Cradle* and *Catch 22* from the school library shelves in Strongsville, Ohio. The court, in its opinion, stated that "a library is a storehouse of knowledge" and "when created for a public school, it is an important privilege created by the state for the benefit of the students in the school. That privilege is not subject to being withdrawn by succeeding school boards whose members might desire to winnow the library for books, the content of which occasioned their displeasure or disapproval." The court said that ordering the books off the shelves would seriously impair the student's ability to find them. This, the court said, would run counter to the First Amendment guarantee of free speech and press. (*See further* Intellectual Freedom.)

Awards. Several librarians and trustees were honored for their achievements. Jessie Hall of the Mansfield Public Library was the first recipient of the Supportive Staff Award. Elfreda Chatman of the Youngstown and Mahoning County Public Library received the Diana Vescelius Memorial Award; Lee Howley, Jr., President of the Board of Trustees of the Cleveland Public Library, was recognized as Trustee of the Year; A. Robert Rogers of the School of Library Science at Kent State University was honored as Librarian of the Year; Constance Koehn of the Cleveland Public Library received the *OLA Bulletin* Best Article of the Year Award. The OLA Hall of Fame Awards were presented to Jean M. Coleman, Vice President of the Dayton and Montgomery County Public Library Board of Trustees, and to Ruth Hess, who retired from the State Library. The first Ohio Library Trustee Association Award of Achievement went to the Troy-Miami County Public Library Board of Trustees.

Martha Driver, Ilo Fisher, Robert Donahugh, and A. Robert Rogers, retiring Directors of the Ohio Library Association, were presented awards of appreciation for their service.

Fourteen notable Ohio Librarians were elected to the Ohio Library Association Hall of Fame during the OLA Annual Conference. They were William Howard Brett, Electra C. Doren, Linda A. Eastman, James C. Foutts, Charles B. Galbreath, Thirza E. Grant, Chalmers Hadley, Herbert S. Hirshberg, Julia Wright Merrill, Paul A. T. Noon, Azariah S. Root, Burton E. Stevenson, Alice S. Tyler, and Joseph L. Wheeler. A keepsake pamphlet, *Notable Ohio Librarians*, was published in their memory and distributed during the conference.

JOHN S. WALLACH

OKLAHOMA

Legislation. Election day, 1976, found Oklahomans at the polls in record numbers, and one of the State Questions, SQ 507, held special meaning for the future development of Oklahoma libraries. State Question 507 provided for a constitutional change which increased the maximum mill levy ceiling from two mills to four mills. It was approved by the voters by more than 29,000 votes. It will be of direct benefit only to those libraries which operate as part of a system, and it allows the voters in individual counties the option of increasing the millage support of their libraries, should they

Oklahoma Library Association
(founded 1907)

Membership: 825; *Annual Expenditure:* $26,800.
President: Alfreda Hanna, Bethany Nazarene College, Bethany, Oklahoma (July 1976–June 1977).
Vice-President/President-elect: Sheila Alexander, Oklahoma State Department of Education.
Secretary: Sheryl Anspaugh, Tulsa City-County Library; 400 Civic Center, Tulsa, Oklahoma 74103
Annual Conference: March 25–27, 1976, Oklahoma City.
Publication: Oklahoma Librarian (quarterly).

Department of Libraries
Robert L. Clark, Director
200 North East 18th
Oklahoma City, Oklahoma 73105

wish to do so. Provisions were also made to alter the constitution to allow Oklahoma's two largest counties, Oklahoma and Tulsa, to form multicounty library systems. The success of SQ 507 was due primarily to excellent planning and dedicated effort on the part of librarians, trustees, library users, students, and many others. Some of the groundwork was laid in early April at a State Legislative Day when librarians met at the Capitol to confer with legislators, and later held a reception for members of the state legislature. The Oklahoma House of Representatives, through the effort of Representative Hannah Atkins, presented a citation to the President of the Oklahoma Library Association, which commended librarians for their contributions to the state and for their "tireless efforts in promoting and improving libraries."

Pottowatomie County voters on November 2 approved a levy which allows the county to join the Pioneer Multi-county Library, after a short demonstration funded by state and federal funds. Earlier in the year, citizens of Woodward County approved a two-mill library tax, and thus became the first county in Oklahoma to vote a library tax without a multi-county library demonstration.

Buildings, Gifts. The Law Library of the University of Oklahoma moved in May into its new space in the recently completed Law Center. The new library can accommodate approximately 166,000 volumes.

The Allie Beth Martin East Regional Library in Tulsa was dedicated on August 1. It is the first library in Tulsa to be named for an individual and was so designated to honor the late Director of the Tulsa City-County Library who was, at the time of her death on April 11, 1976, President of ALA.

State Reports—Oregon

Hard work by Lawton citizens resulted in the 55-year-old Carnegie Library Building in Lawton being designated as a national monument. It will be listed in the National Register of Historic Places.

Seminole Junior College dedicated its new David Lyle Boren Library in September. The $500,000 library is named in honor of Governor David Boren.

The University of Tulsa McFarlin Library received an anonymous contribution of $1,000,000 to be used toward a planned $3,000,000 addition to the library. The expansion is necessary because of the many special collections added to the library during the past year. The collections include nearly a thousand foreign translations of the works of Graham Greene, a fine D. H. Lawrence collection, including first editions, manuscripts, letters, and art works. One of the most outstanding is the Sheppley Collection of approximately 6,000 items concerning the American Indian and Oklahoma. It includes books, manuscripts, photographs, maps, and government documents and provides a major research source for history, language and literature, and law of the American Indian.

OLA. The Oklahoma Library Association's Executive Board selected 20 librarians, representing all types of libraries in Oklahoma, to serve as the first Visiting Committee for the School of Library Science at the University. The Director of the School requested the formation of the Advisory Committee to work with the faculty to improve communication between librarians in the field and library educators and to discuss and recommend improvements tion with the Oklahoma Department of Libraries and the School of Library Science, presented the "Most Important Employees" intended primarily for the paraprofessional staff. Featured participants were Zahea Nappa and James Alsip discussing "hands on" information for A-V maintenance. Oklahoma University Library School students acted as guides for small groups.

Early in December the Reference Division and Social Responsibilities Round Table held workshops in Oklahoma City, Tulsa, and Lawton on "Information and Referral Programs." Carolyn Luck and Robert Croneberger, who have established I&R Services in Detroit and in Memphis, discussed their work in public libraries.

The School Librarians Association has a new name, Oklahoma Association of School Library Media Specialists (OASLMS). The Association met during the Oklahoma Education Association meeting in Tulsa in October. Keynote speaker was Leroy Lindeman, Curriculum Division of the Utah Department of Education.

Oklahoma now has its own interlibrary loan code, which was formulated by the Interlibrary Loan Code Committee of OLA. The code was correlated with the ALA National Interlibrary Loan Code, but is more liberal in meeting the needs of libraries in Oklahoma. The code was approved by the Executive Board in January and by the OLA membership in March.

National Library Week was celebrated in one of Oklahoma City's largest shopping centers. Gary England, Chief Meteorologist of an Oklahoma City television station, served as state chairperson. At the shopping center thousands of shoppers saw puppet shows, magic shows, storytelling sessions, participated in book drawings, and met Oklahoma authors in "Author Alley." It was a tremendous success, because of the cooperation and generosity of the merchants, librarians, authors, and many friends and helpers.

Oklahoma librarians celebrated the Bicentennial year at their annual meeting in Oklahoma City, March 25–27. Theme of the conference was "The Spirit of '76: a view of the past, a vision of the future." Speakers included Clara Jones, President of ALA; Frances Neel Cheney, author and faculty member of the Library School at Peabody; Barbara Markuson, Director of the Indiana Cooperative Library Service Authority, and others.

A special OLA Bicentennial Writer's Award went to Angie Debo, Oklahoma author and historian; the Citizen's Award to L. G. Hyden, legal counsel for the State Examiner's and Inspector's Office, and the Distinguished Service Award to Irma Tomberlin, Professor of Library Science at the University of Oklahoma. The second Social Responsibilities Round Table Citation of Merit for an outstanding Outreach Program was presented to the McAlester Public Library for its PALS (People Aiding Library Services) project. Staffed by volunteers, the program offered service to nursing homes and the homebound. The 1976 Sequoyah Children's Book Award was presented to Thomas Rockwell for his delightful work, *How to Eat Fried Worms*. More than 18,000 Oklahoma boys and girls in grades three through six voted in the 1976 program.

SLA. The Oklahoma Chapter of the Special Libraries Association published *Directory of Special Libraries and Information Centers in Oklahoma*.

People. Robert L. Clark, Jr., was appointed Director of the Oklahoma Department of Libraries, assuming the position in September.

Esther M. Henke, Associate Director for Library Services at the Oklahoma Department of Libraries, was appointed by Speaker of the U.S. House of Representatives, Carl Albert, a member of the White House Conference on Library and Information Services.

Frances Kennedy, Executive Secretary of OLA and Director Emeritus of the Library at Oklahoma City University was honored by the University with the honorary degree Doctor of Humane Letters.

Gene Hodges, Director of Central State University Library and a past president of OLA, retired in June.

Pat Woodrum was named Director of the Tulsa City-County Library System. She had served as the Associate Director of the System. John Walker was appointed Director of the East Central University Library after the retirement of Casper Duffer.

Richard Bradberry became Head of the Library Department at Langston University. He had held the position of Humanities Librarian at Auburn University.

Deaths. The death of Allie Beth Martin, Director of the Tulsa City-County Library System and President of the American Library Association, on April 11, 1976, was a deep loss to the people and libraries of the state and nation, for she was universally loved and respected. Her biography and a statement in memoriam appear in the first edition of this *Yearbook* (1976), p. vi, which was dedicated to her memory.

Carl McFall, father of Ruth Frame, Deputy Executive Director of ALA, died after a traffic accident. The Oklahoma Library Association had honored Mr. McFall in 1975 with its Citizen's Award for his many contributions to libraries in Oklahoma.

IRMA R. TOMBERLIN

OREGON

Financial Problems. In her last "Letter to Libraries," retiring State Librarian Eloise Ebert wrote: "Never has the budget crisis been so widespread nor so alarming. Alternatives are being explored in units of local government throughout the state and more elections will be held. Mandated services and their rising costs are pushing out the optional services, and there are no easy solutions. Property taxes may have reached the limit for the support of local public services."

Inflation plus Oregon's 6 percent limitation on annual property tax increases is endangering basic services including library services.

Faced with curtailed budgets that would decimate systems many libraries or their governing bodies turned to the voter with special library levies. Multnomah County faced elimination of all services except one branch and the Central Library. Led by former Governor Tom McCall, the Friends of the Library Campaign Committee waged a vigorous campaign that led to passage of a three-year serial levy of $2,200,000 each

397

State Reports—Pennsylvania

Oregon Library Association
(founded 1940)

Membership: 629 (approx. 200 ALA members); *Annual Expenditure:* $10,000.
President: Carol Hildebrand, Lake Oswego Public Library (April 1976–April 1977).
Vice-President/President-elect: Richard E. Moore, Southern Oregon State College Library.
Secretary: Carol Jenkins, Dental Library, University of Oregon Health Sciences Center; 611 S.W. Campus Dr., Portland, Oregon 97201.
Annual Conference: April 29–May 1, 1976, Lincoln City.
Publication: Oregon Library News (bi-monthly).

Oregon State Library

Marcia Lowell, State Librarian
State Library Bldg.
Salem, Oregon 97310

year, by an overwhelming majority. A contiguous county, Washington, which had been operating on LSCA demonstration grants, also received voter support, benefiting from the active citizen and media support from Multnomah County. Having the same ballot measure number obviously helped it along. Many Washington County residents, it was said, may have thought they were voting to save the Multnomah County Library!

Two other LSCA demonstration systems had to go to the polls the second time before receiving support from the voters.

County and City libraries that were not supported by voters at the polls curtailed their staff and services. One small library was voted money for staff, utilities, and supplies but no money for books!

As city libraries have had to curtail services to their own constituencies, many of them, formerly part of a network or county system, have found it necessary to charge out-of-city residents fees for services formerly given without charge.

During the non-legislative year of 1976 the Oregon Library Association and the State Library Board of Trustees prepared a measure to be submitted to the 1977 legislature. It would establish financial assistance programs to provide public library services. At its spring conference a workshop was held on Legislative Techniques. Alice Ihrig led a workshop for trustees and was guest speaker at the banquet.

State Catalog. A new Oregon State Library Book catalog supplement lists all works of adult nonfiction and adult fiction in foreign languages added to the Oregon State Library collection from July 1974–December 1975 as well as all English language and adult fiction titles added since January 1975. This is a supplement to the previously published eight-volume *Book Catalog of Adult Non-fiction,* December 1965–74, and replaces previous supplements.

Changes. Librarians serving city and county jails met to set minimum standards for jail libraries in the state.

To better use its funds and book collection the Multnomah County Library was converting its Central Library collection and that of its 16 branches to CLSI computer. In the future books will be charged and borrowers registered by the computer system.

To become more effective in providing library services in a systematic way to the citizens of Oregon, 30 librarians from school, special, academic, and public libraries met in October 1976 at a State Library sponsored workshop to discuss the sharing of Oregon Library resources and to develop short and long term goals. This was the first of a series of workshops to be held throughout the state in the following year.

Higher Education. The year 1976 in Oregon was marked by an effort to share resources. Several projects were completed, others initiated. Foremost was the completion of the Oregon Union List of Serials (ORULS), composed of the serials holdings from 52 libraries in the Northwest. This four-volume set was distributed in early fall. It was expanded by a 60-microfiche edition which included state and federal serial documents as well as the cataloged serials available in the printed edition.

In late summer a microfiche copy of the eight card catalogs of the Oregon State System of Higher Education (OSSHE) libraries was delivered to each of the system libraries. This 16,300-microfiche catalog was developed to facilitate interlibrary lending. To complement the fiche catalog, the eight OSSHE libraries began depositing main-entry catalog cards with the Chairman of the OSSHE Interinstitutional Library Council for the purpose of developing a union catalog to supplement the basic microfiche catalog. The supplementary union catalog is in process of being converted to machine-readable form by a commercial firm in an effort to periodically produce a system-wide union catalog on microfiche.

The Library On-Line Information and Text Access (LOLITA) program at Oregon State University (OSU) is in process of being expanded to include the acquisitions records at the University of Oregon, Portland State University, and Oregon College of Education. Eventually all eight libraries of OSSHE will be incorporated and become one module of the commercial catalog mentioned above.

The trend in higher education in Oregon is toward a basic index to resources in the academic libraries for the purpose of sharing those resources. This was being done at minimum cost to the libraries, yet in such a manner that the records could be merged with developing library networks in the West.

People. Eloise Ebert retired as State Librarian August 30. She went to the State Library as Assistant State Librarian in 1949 from Europe, where she had been Chief Librarian in charge of U.S. Army and Air Force post libraries after World War II in American occupation zones. Prior to going overseas she had been Librarian at Fort Francis E. Warren, Wyoming, and was a librarian in Falls City, Nebraska; Sauk Centre, Minnesota; and in Council Bluffs, Iowa. She has held offices in state, regional and national library associations. During her 17-year tenure the population of Oregon doubled. Public library expenditures increased 840 percent, volumes in public libraries increased 131 percent and the State Library collection 64 percent. Per capita support for library services more than doubled.

Marcia Lowell, who headed the city library in Wayland, Massachusetts, became Oregon's new State Librarian September 1, 1976.

Rodney K. Waldron, Director of the William Jasper Kerr Library at Oregon State University, was elected Chairman of the Interinstitutional Library Council. He succeeds Norman D. Alexander, who resigned as Director of the Southern Oregon State College Library to accept the directorship of the California Polytechnic State University Library.

Nina Greig, Children's Librarian with the Multnomah County Library since 1956, died February 19. She had served as a member of the Newbery-Caldecott Committee and as a director of the Children's Services Division of ALA. She had also been active in the Pacific Northwest Library Association and had served as a children's librarian in Corvallis, Oregon, and Tacoma, Washington. MARY DOWNEY; RICHARD MOORE

PENNSYLVANIA

PLA Conference. "We've honored the past . . . Our Challenge is the future" served as the theme for the 75th Diamond Jubilee conference of the Association. Past presidents were honored at the banquet which featured Richard Adams, author of *Watership Down,* commenting on the importance of literature in shaping reading habits of children. An opening debate by Reid Buckley and Max Lerner provided an intellectually stimulating introduction to three days of programs. Continuing educa-

Pennsylvania Library Association
(founded 1901)

Membership: 2,600 (660 ALA members); *Annual Expenditure:* $112,019.
President: Donald C. Potter, Carnegie Library of Pittsburgh.
Vice-President/President-elect: Richard Fitzsimmons, Worthington—Scranton Campus Library, Pennsylvania State University.
Executive Secretary: Nancy L. Blundon, 100 Woodland Road, Pittsburgh, 15232.
Annual Conference: September 26–29, 1976.
Publication: PLA Bulletin (bimonthly).

State Library of Pennsylvania
Ernest E. Doerschuk, Jr., State Librarian
Box 1601
Harrisburg, Pennsylvania 17126

tion led the list of topics under discussion by the group.

Affirmative action, resource sharing, and the question "How Big Is Big Enough?" with Daniel Gore left participants something to ponder on their way home from Pittsburgh.

Two resolutions were passed. One directed the Board to make the passage of a public library retirement bill its number one priority for the next legislative year. The other enjoined the Board to appoint a committee to identify minority librarians, recruit minority candidates for professional librarianship, and provide or seek funds for the support of library education for minority candidates. An additional $1,000 was added to the scholarship budget.

PLA Action. Much discussion surrounded the study by the Organization and Bylaws Committee in regard to the distinction between standing and special committees, and by implication the voting rights and meeting expense reimbursement of members of the PLA Board.

The legislative adviser, Evelyn Henzel Crawford, resigned as of October 1, leaving the organization to search for a new advocate. Crawford had served for seven years in the position after having formerly served in the Pennsylvania House of Representatives for three terms.

An *Organizational Handbook* was developed by the New Librarian's Round Table and the Publications and Public Relations Committee and published as a pull out in the *Bulletin*.

In 1977 a *Trustee Manual* will be published under a $10,650 grant from the State Library to the Trustee Division.

Fiscal Problems. As in most states, fiscal issues were high on the list of priorities in Pennsylvania in 1976. The State Library itself lost eight staff positions, while legislative mix-ups actually put the $800,000 operating funds in limbo for most of the year.

During the year much effort was put into the support of SB 1189. The legislature had already appropriated $600,000 in new money for partial support of the bill if passed. When fully funded it would have given county governments sharply increased incentive to support countywide libraries. Local libraries would have been able to earn $.75 per capita state aid; libraries where market values of real estate was low would qualify for more equalization aid and the four regional libraries would have their grants increased by half. The Senate passed the bill unanimously, but it died in committee in the House when amendments were added. The Department of Education has placed a priority on the reintroduction of the bill in the new session of the legislature.

Individual libraries with problems included Dauphin County with a $116,000 deficit budget and Altoona with a 56 percent cut. The Montgomery County-Norristown Library had not received its $50,000 from the borough fathers by August and so closed its walk-in service for two weeks until public outcry encouraged the delivery of funds. But at year's end only a partial payment had been received. The Carnegie Library of Pittsburgh had a $500,000 budget cut and had to reduce hours of opening.

Wilkes-Barre's Ousterhout Library was completely eliminated from the School Board budget. Eventually $40,000, only half of the previous year's allocation, was given. Next the School Board submitted a 3-mill tax levy for the November ballot. Under state law any question submitted must state the tax is exclusively for library use. So the Ousterhout Board had no option but to go to court and ask for a removal of the question. At the hearing the Board of Education withdrew and both sides were meeting to settle the matter at year's end.

School Libraries and Media. Educational Media and School Library Advisory Councils were combined by the Department of Education into a new joint council chaired by the Rev. Lewis A. Rongione, O.S.A., of Villanova University.

Early in the year a memo from the Secretary of Education, John Pittenger, requested statewide hearings "concerning merging the current separate certifications for school librarians and media specialists into one standard combining both specialties."

Pennsylvania Guidelines for Media Programs were approved, guided by the *ALA-AECT Media Guidelines*. The document was introduced at the PLA conference.

Building. New library buildings were dedicated in Blossburg, Tredyffrin, Marple, Harrisburg, Lykens, and Allegheny College. Gound was broken for California State College Library, and Montgomery County—Norristown's new headquarters was scheduled for a January 1977 opening. In Philadelphia two new branches were added to bring the total number of Philadelphia Free Library branches to 48.

Standards. During the summer a series of public hearings across the state were held by the (Governor's) Advisory Council on Library Development on proposed systems standards for Pennsylvania libraries. A survey is under way to measure the gap between proposed district standards and current practices. The actual cost of bridging the gap will be established. Now that local standards have been applied, the state is placing the most emphasis on developing the system and district guidelines.

State Library. Publications by the State Library included *General Library Research Manual*, a revised catalog of *Recordings of the Spoken Word, Abstracting and Indexing Services*, and bibliographies on *Mental Health and Retardation* and *Women in Higher Education*. A union list of microforms in state college libraries and *Year's Work in Pennsylvania 1972–73* were to be published in 1977.

A *Bicentennial Information Newsletter* edited by Don Brown of the State Library was an aid to libraries concerned with providing information on materials and programs for the 200th anniversary of the nation's birth.

Governor's Conference. Work began under conference planning chairperson Diane Katz of Pittsburgh, a member of the Advisory Council on Library Development, on the Governor's Conference to be held at the Host Inn, Harrisburg, on October 31 through November 1, 1977. Names of professionals, trustees and lay persons were submitted to the Governor and the 28-member planning committee. The theme developed for the conference is "The Future is K-NOW."

Richard C. Torbert was named to succeed Richard Thomson who resigned after serving as chairman of the council for seven years. Diane Katz was appointed lay member succeeding J.T. DeWeese. Two trustee appointments were Gary Bechtel of the Adams County Library Board and William Crum, a trustee of Abington Community Library, Clarks Summit. They replaced Thomson and Howard E. Thorne. Torbert resigned in December; Bechtel is serving as acting chairman.

Grants. The Drexel University Graduate School of Library Service, under a grant from the Bureau of Library Development of the State Library of Pennsylvania, produced a plan for interlibrary cooperation in the Commonwealth of Pennsylvania. The plan was submitted to the State Library and was being printed at year's end for general distribution.

State Reports—Pennsylvania

The report, *A Plan for Library Cooperation in Pennsylvania*, is supported by a State Library grant. Project director was Charles Meadow and the State Library coordinator David R. Hoffman.

Scott Bruntjen, Madelyn Valunas, and Signe Kelker, all on the library faculty at Shippensburg State College, have been awarded a National Science Foundation Institutional Grant to develop a pilot program for the searching of on-line data bases.

The merger of the Erie City and County Libraries was assisted by a LSCA Title I grant, making the system the third largest in the state. Other Title I fundings included the Free Library of Philadelphia's development of library services to the deaf ($44,560), and the integration of these services into the ongoing library operation.

The University of Pennsylvania Library received $100,000 from the William Penn Foundation. This is a portion of the $8,000,000 being sought as part of the University of Pennsylvania Library's capital development campaign.

An Office of Education Grant from HEW for $81,876 to the GSLIS of the University of Pittsburgh will be used to study self-learning patterns of persons who use community resources in independent learning projects.

PALINET and ULC. For the first year the Pennsylvania Library Information Network (PALINET) and the Union Library Catalog were under joint direction. While the number of libraries participating in the OCLC system has grown, the use of ULC location services has declined markedly. The expansion of the OCLC and the microfilming of the ULC, both supported with LSCA grants, have been the major factors in the change. The microfilm has effectively decentralized the service. Seventy-four libraries currently participate in the OCLC through PALINET, a big jump over the four users in 1973.

PRLC Grants. The Pittsburgh Regional Library Center (PRLC) in 1976 was awarded two LSCA-I grants for support of OCLC on-line services to western Pennsylvania District Library Centers. The Union Library Catalogue of Pennsylvania was added on microfilm to the other film and book catalogs of the PRLC Clearinghouse for Interlibrary Loan. The Clearinghouse has grown to be the largest resource bank for interlibrary loan locations in the state.

The *PRLC Newspaper List* was expanded to include 42 libraries and published in a new edition. The *Western Pennsylvania Resources Directory* was revised and expanded. An excellent slide-tape instruction module was published—*The Monthly Catalog: Your Key to U.S. Government Publications*. Initial conversion of the PRLC/University of Pittsburgh serials data base was completed and the records added to the OCLC on-line data base. The Center's cooperative efforts extended to continuing education in co-sponsoring, with the University of Pittsburgh Graduate School of Library and Information Sciences and the Pittsburgh chapters of SLA and ASIS, a heavily attended workshop—On-line Literature Searching for Reference Librarians.

Awards. Keith Doms, Director of the Free Library of Philadelphia from 1969, received in 1976 the 15th distinguished service award presented by the PLA in recognition of "exceptionally meritorious statewide service" to libraries.

PLA Certificates of Merit were presented to Nancy L. Blundon—for her exceptional service to officers and members of the Pennsylvania Library Association; Margaret Darken—for her leadership in improvement of public library services to the citizens of Pennsylvania in her role as trustee; John Phillip Immroth (posthumous presentation) for his contributions to the library profession in Pennsylvania as an educator, author and scholar (*see* Obituaries); Joyce B. Scholl—for her contributions to the development of school library service in Pennsylvania as School Library Development Advisor for the Pennsylvania Division of School Libraries; Nicholas Stevens—for his accomplishments in raising the standards of librarianship in the state as an educator and as a member of the (Governor's) Advisory Council on Library Development. Daniel Boorstin, the 12th Librarian of Congress, was the 18th recipient of the Drexel University Distinguished Achievement Award.

People. Divinia Astraquillo was appointed Business and Administration Librarian at Drexel University. Margaret Clark became the Librarian of the new Northwest Area Examination Center at Edinboro. Laurabelle Eakin was named Director of the University of Pittsburgh's Falk Library of the Health Professions. She had served as Assistant Director and Head of Readers Services there. Loretta Farris, Chairperson of PLA's Northeast Chapter and Director of the Hoyt Library in Kingston, succeeded Joan Diana as Head of the Northeast Area Examination Center at the Luzerne Intermediate Unit in Kingston. Frances Hopkins became Reference Librarian at Franklin and Marshall College. Adele Patterson is the new Librarian of the Western Area Examination Center in Pittsburgh. Gregor Preston joined the Catalog Department of Pennsylvania State University Libraries. He formerly headed the Catalog Department of Butler University Library, Indianapolis.

Bonnie K. Sherman will fill the newly-created position of Program Development Librarian for the Cheltenham Township School and Public Libraries System. Frederick Smith, who was assistant Librarian at Westminster College, was named Librarian upon the retirement of Mabel C. Kocher in August 1975. Andrea Angelo joined the staff of Peoples Library, New Kensington, as Adult Services Librarian. Ligonier Valley Library named Joanne Vance Muchoney Library Director and M. Janet Hudson the new Children's Librarian.

William L. Beck was appointed Director of Library Services at California State College, California, Pennsylvania. Clifford P. Crowers assumed the duties of Head of the Government Publications Department at the Free Library of Philadelphia. Martha Manheimer was named Professor at the University of Pittsburgh Graduate School of Library and Information Sciences. Appointed to the GSLIS faculty in 1969, she had been Associate Professor since 1972. Brooke E. Sheldon was appointed Lecturer for the 1976-77 academic year at the Graduate School of Library and Information Sciences, University of Pittsburgh.

Thomas J. Galvin, Dean of GSLIS, University of Pittsburgh, was appointed External Examiner for the Department of Library Studies, University of Ibadan, Nigeria. A PLA Past President, Sister M. Constance Melvin, I.H.M., was named Dean of the Marywood College Graduate School. Sister Constance, who became Professor and Chairperson of the Department of Librarianship at the School, began her duties August 9. Blane K. Dessy assumed the position of Director of Library Services at the Juniata County Library on August 1.

Allen Kent was named Distinguished Service Professor at the University of Pittsburgh.

Marjorie M. Quigley was presented the Award for Outstanding Contribution to the Pennsylvania State University Libraries. Quigley is an Associate Librarian and head of the Altoona branch of the Pennsylvania State University Libraries.

Retirements. Ruth Rhen retired from Carnegie Library of Pittsburgh on June 30. Eleanor Este Campion, Director of the Union Library Catalogue of Pennsylvania since 1948, retired at the end of May.

Deaths. John Phillip Immroth, Associate Professor in the Graduate School of Library and Information Sciences of the University of Pittsburgh, died in Scranton, Pennsylvania, on April 2, 1976, while attending a meeting of the Board of Directors of the Pennsylvania Library Association. (*See* Obituaries.)

Helen-Jean Moore, Library Director of Point Park College, Pittsburgh, died on March 8, Moore, PPC Library Director since 1962, had also served as an English Professor, and Acting Dean at the College.

PAT REDMOND

RHODE ISLAND

Incentive Grants. Limitations on funding in the fiscal year 1976 resulted in the small total sum of $11,500 in state monies allotted for Incentive Grants by the Rhode Island Department of State Library Services. Proposals in the amount of $21,644 were submitted and awards were in the amount of $8,398 plus the special grant to the Providence Public Library for a multi-agency project of $3,100.

Public Libraries and Special Funding. With library budgets shrinking and costs on the rise, many public libraries in Rhode Island used additional funding sources in 1976 to initiate needed programs, expand services, and add special items to the collection. A survey conducted by the Rhode Island Department of State Library Services in January revealed that about 50 percent of the public libraries in Rhode Island reported receiving small grants from private citizens and such community service organizations as garden clubs, and Friends of the Library groups. Many gifts were used for the purchase of furniture or special materials, such as large print books.

During 1976 public libraries in Rhode Island successfully applied to the following agencies or programs (among others): Revenue Sharing, Rhode Island State Council on the Arts, Rhode Island Foundation, United Way, Department of State Library Services Incentive Grant Program, and federal programs such as Community Development (HUD) and Community Action (OEO). For example, the Providence Community Action Program provided funds through August for several programs at the Providence Public Library: Child Learning Center (Smith Hill Branch), pilot Child Learning Center projects (Wanskuck and Olneyville branches), and the Learning Outreach Center (South Providence Branch). The Rhode Island Library Film Cooperative will be able to purchase new films with funds awarded by the Rhode Island Foundation to the Warwick Public Library ($10,000) and by the Rhode Island Department of Community Affairs, Division on Aging, to the Rhode Island Department of State Library Services ($5,000).

Legislation. As in 1975, four bills were supported in the state legislature by the Rhode Island Library Association. One would have made Providence College and Bryant College libraries special research centers, joining the ranks of the Brown University, Rhode Island College, and the University of Rhode Island Libraries in receiving compensation for the service. A second would increase per capita funding to city and town public libraries to $.40, up from $.25. A third proposed the increase of per capita funding to regional centers to $.45, up from $.25. The fourth would raise the level of funding to the Providence Public Library, serving as principal public library, from $223,000 to $300,000.

Robert Persson, Development Officer for Providence Public Library, was named official RILA lobbyist. Through the work of the Government Relations Subcommittee of the RILA and its many supporters and the work of Robert Persson in particular, Governor Philip W. Noel signed into law bill 75-H. 5668 as amended, "State Aid to Libraries." The new law will increase per capita state aid to public libraries from $.25 to $.30. It is thought to be the first library legislation in Rhode Island since the enabling legislation of 1964–67.

In other legislation affecting libraries in Rhode Island, a bill that would prohibit certain specific depictions of sexual conduct slipped through both houses of the Assembly and was signed by the Governor.

The Rhode Island Library Association Intellectual Freedom Committee opposed the bill.

In legislation to be introduced during the 1977 session of the R.I. General Assembly, the RILA Government Relations Sub-Committee was preparing to introduce a bill to increase per capita funding to regional centers to $.45 from $.25, a bill to raise the level of funding to the Principal Public Library (Providence Public Library) from $223,000 to $300,000, a bill to provide the Rhode Island Film Cooperative (which purchases 16mm films for the use of most libraries in Rhode Island) with an additional $25,000, a bill to create a Legislation Study Committee on Library Service in Rhode Island, a bill to increase per capita funding to city and town public libraries from $.30 per capita to $.40 per capita, and a bill to make Providence College and Bryant College libraries special research centers.

RILA. The Rhode Island Library Association Spring Conference was held in May at the Kingston Free Library and the University of Rhode Island. Travis Tyer of the Illinois State Library and Secretary of the Advisory Committee to CLENE (the Continuing Library Education Network and Exchange) delivered the keynote address on the Conference theme: "Can Libraries Accept the Challenge of Continuing Education?"

President Jim Giles explained that while dues were increased in 1975, a loss of several hundred members meant only about $1,500 in additional revenues, not $8,000 as previously expected, and made it impossible to implement some Long Range Plan recommendations such as hiring a publicist.

Informative workshops were held on extending traditional library school education and on management's role in continuing education. In the first workshop Evelyn Daniel discussed the challenges facing the University of Rhode Island Graduate Library School, including expansion of the internship program in libraries for graduate students. Bette Holley, of URI's Division of University Extension, explained the Continuing Education Unit (CEU), a measurement of an individual's experience in a noncredit program. Mary MacKenzie, Director of the New England Library Board, spoke on coordinating continuing education efforts in New England and the need to distinguish different kinds of education for librarians and support staff.

In the second workshop Vincent Igliozzi of the State Equal Employment Office stated that the Governor's Executive Order Number 14 demanded equal employment opportunity in all agencies receiving state grants.

Five concurrent workshops covered prominent foreign language collections in the state. (Portuguese at the Fox Point Branch of the Providence Public Library by Phylis Pacheco, Polish at the Pawtucket Public Library by Wanda Moskwa, Spanish at the Central Falls Free Public Library by Emil A. Ciallella, Jr., Italian at the Westerly Public Library by Helen Giles, and French at the Woonsocket Public Library by Doris Chapdelaine).

ACRL. In April the Association of College and Research Libraries, New England Chapter, held a conference on "People Power, Management of Human Resources Development," at Newport. Speakers included William Hunzeker, Assistant Professor of Management Information Science, New Hampshire College; Sheila Creth, Assistant Director for Personnel,

---

Rhode Island Library Association (founded 1903)

Membership: 510 (est. 250 ALA members); *Annual Expenditure:* $13,050 (July 1976).
President: Dan Bergen, University of Rhode Island Graduate Library School, Kingston (May 1976–November 1977).
Vice-President/President-elect: Ardis Holliday, Westerly (R.I.) Public Library.
Secretary: Margaret Caldwell, University of Rhode Island; 104 Longview Drive, Warwick, Rhode Island 02888.
Annual Conference: November 4–5, 1976, Newport.
Publication: RILA Bulletin (monthly).

Rhode Island Department of State Library Service
Jewel Drickamer, Director
95 Davis Street
Providence, Rhode Island 02908

State Reports—Rhode Island

University of Connecticut Library, Storrs, Connecticut; Mary Chatfield, Associate Librarian, Baker Library, Harvard Business School; E. J. Josey, Chief, Bureau of Academic and Research Libraries, New York State Education Department; and Eric Moon, President of Scarecrow Press and President-elect of ALA.

RILA held its annual Fall Conference in November in Newport. Conference seminars and workshops included everything from community analysis, communication skills, catalogers' status, children's films, computerized catalogs and creative dramatics through legislation, the local library school and library buildings to puppets, publishing, serials, taxes, and technical assistants. Members unanimously approved a revised dues structure allowing for a wider range of membership fees.

Buildings. The year 1976 in Rhode Island saw the completion and beginning of a number of building programs. In Kingston work was completed on a 70,000-square-foot, $4,000,000 addition to the main library at the University of Rhode Island. The Arnolds Mills and Sherman Le Clerc branches of the Cumberland Public Library were closed upon completion of the renovation of the former Monastery off Diamond Hill Road. The renovated building will function as the central library for the town.

The Warwick Public Library began a $750,000 renovation project in July to remodel the existing main library building to include an expanded children's room, a more efficient circulation center, and a more modern reference area.

October saw the completion of plans for an addition to the Narragansett Pier Free Library that will nearly quadruple the size of the present building. The library addition will be built with $274,000 in Federal Community Development Funds and is scheduled to be completed in July 1978.

Five public libraries in Rhode Island (Barrington, Central Falls, Coventry, Lincoln, and Middletown) sought funds through the Public Works Act for library construction in 1977. None of the libraries received any funds at the first allocation in December.

Networks and Interlibrary Cooperation. During 1976 the Rhode Island Department of State Library Services and the public libraries in Rhode Island conducted a series of demonstrations of computerized circulation systems. The aim of the demonstration was to begin a series of informative studies that would eventually lead to a computerized circulation system to be used statewide. Among the circulation systems studied were the Gaylord Circulation Control System, the Computer Library Services, Inc., system LIBS 100, Information Dynamics Corporation's BIBNET System and the 3M Company's computerized circulation system.

URI Graduate School. A team appointed by the American Library Association's Committee on Accreditation evaluated the University of Rhode Island Graduate Library School program leading to the master of library science degree and voted not to accredit the program under the 1972 standards. Nancy Potter, Acting Dean of the School, said that the University and the Graduate Library School will not appeal the decision of COA. The school responded by concentrating on faculty recruitment, strengthening library science holdings in the University Library, developing an active Advisory Committee, reviewing the curriculum, publishing student newsletters, and studying goals and objectives. The School intended to make sufficient progress to again receive accreditation within two years.

Brown University Strike. By far the biggest news on the collective bargaining scene during past years in Rhode Island was the strike by library clerical workers at Brown University. Library clerical workers walked out on August 24 after failing to reach agreement on a wage reopener clause in their contract.

On November 14 the clerical workers ratified an agreement with the school to end their three-month strike. Forty-nine of the 54 library clerical strikers agreed by a two-to-one margin to a six percent across-the-board increase plus a $100 lump sum payment to each worker. As of November 22, the strikers from Local 134 of the Service Employees International Union were back to work. Its effects will probably be felt for a long time to come.

Awards. RILA's annual award for distinguished contributions to librarianship was presented to Edward Judson Humeston, retiring Dean of the University of Rhode Island's Graduate Library School.

At the RILA Fall Conference letters of commendation for distinguished service were presented to Doris Chapdelaine, Director of the Woonsocket-Harris Public Library for many years, and to Jim McCann from the Department of State Library Services.

Appointments and Resignations. The Senate in January confirmed the appointment of Jewel Drickamer as Director of the Department of State Library Services.

Norman Tilles, Chairperson of the Pawtucket Public Library Board of Trustees, announced his retirement after 10 years of service on the Board. He was replaced as chairperson by the Rev. Donald F. Belt. January also saw Gail Sonneman Davidson appointed Fine Arts Librarian at the Woonsocket-Harris Public Library. Rob Maier of the Cranston Public Library resigned his post to become Director of the Bedford Public Library in Massachusetts.

William D. Goyette, Jr., formerly Associate Director of the Holyoke, Massachusetts, Public Library, was named the first Director of the South Kingstown Municipal Library System. Connie Wentzel left the cataloging department at the University of Rhode Island Library to become Administrative Assistant for the Society for Values in Higher Education in New Haven, Connecticut. At the Pawtucket Public Library, Thomas Viti, Head of the Reference Department, resigned to become Head of Public Relations in the Somerset, Massachusetts, Public Library.

Tobi Geberer, Pawtucket Public Library's Community Services Coordinator, resigned to become a Library Director in the Broward County Library System (Ft. Lauderdale, Fla.). At the same time, James Aylward, Director of the Middletown Free Library, announced his resignation to become Director of the Naval Education and Training Center Library in Newport, R.I. Charles Moore, formerly Director of the Auburn, Massachusetts, Public Library, was appointed Director of the Woonsocket-Harris Public Library, and Nancy Peace, Librarian of the R.I. Historical Society Library, resigned to pursue doctoral studies at Columbia University. She was succeeded by Nancy Chudacoff, also of the Historical Society.

Edward J. Humeston, Jr., retired in June as Dean of the University of Rhode Island's Graduate Library School. He was succeeded by Nancy Potter, who will be Acting Director while a search is conducted for a permanent replacement.

Curt Bohling, Director of the Pawtucket Public Library, and his wife, Lynn Bohling, Director of the Johnston (R.I.) Mohr Library, announced their resignations effective August 1 to open an antiquarian book store. Lee Flanagan was named Acting Director at Pawtucket Public Library, and Robert Burford resigned as Head of Reference at Pawtucket Public Library to become the new Director of the Mohr Library in Johnston.

William Bergeron became the new Head Librarian at the Oaklawn Branch of the Cranston Public Library. He formerly worked at the main library for the Cranston system. At the R.I. Department of State Library Services, Beverly Jones was appointed Chief Planning and Development Officer. She formerly headed the State Processing Center, which was closed in 1975.

Death. Sally E. Coy, former Librarian of the Westerly Public Library, died October 17. She had been Head Librarian at the library for many years and had done much to promote the library's development prior to the time it was designated a Regional Center in 1964. —EMIL A. CIALLELLA, JR.

SOUTH CAROLINA

SCLA Activities. The South Carolina Library Association held its 50th Annual Conference in October. The conference, held in the State Capitol, Columbia, was attended by 510 librarians and trustees. Its theme was "From Chapbook to Data Bank; Libraries - Past and Present."

SCLA awarded its first Friends of the Library Award to Jean Galloway Bissell, Chairperson, Richland County Public Library Board (Columbia) and former member of the Greenville County Library Board. The award seeks to recognize a non-librarian who has made significant contributions to the development of libraries and librarianship in the state. Bissell has long been an effective spokesperson for public libraries in South Carolina. The award was presented by Ilene Nelson, Chairperson of the Public Relations Committee.

Upon recommendation of the Ad Hoc Scholarship Committee, a $500 scholarship fund was established to provide opportunities for continuing education for practicing librarians and library employees. Applications for the grant are made to SCLA Executive Board. Recipients must agree to remain and work in South Carolina for one year.

Sue Hardin, Chairperson of the Planning Committee, introduced a motion to appoint a Continuing Education Committee to oversee projects such as workshops and institutes. The Committee will disburse funds to groups who wish to conduct workships or programs. Funds remaining or profits will be returned to the Committee for future projects.

The members of the Public Library Sec-

South Carolina Library Association (founded 1915)

Membership: 914; *Annual Expenditure:* $10,745.
President: Margaret W. Ehrhardt, South Carolina Department of Education (January 1976 – December 1977).
Vice-President/President-elect: Lennart Pearson, James H. Thomason Library, Presbyterian College, Clinton, South Carolina.
Secretary: Margaret F. Huff, Orangeburg-Calhoun Technical College, Orangeburg, South Carolina 29115.
Annual Conference: October 1976, Charleston.
Publication: The South Carolina Librarian (semiannually).

South Carolina State Library

Estellene P. Walker, State Librarian
P. O. Box 11469
Columbia, South Carolina 29211

tion accepted proposals to revise the official classification and salary schedule and suggested reference guidelines. Catherine Lewis, Standards Committee Chairperson, presented the revised schedule which reflected a 10 percent increase in salaries over the 1975 level.

The Committee on Reference Statistics, including John Landrum, Chairman, Jan Buvinger, Marion Mangion, and Joan Sorenson, presented a list of recommended procedures for Public Libraries compiling reference statistics. The guidelines seek to provide uniformity to the statistics compiled. Many of the recommendations were based on definitions proposed by Library Administration Division, ALA and the reporting of reference statistics in the annual report of South Carolina State Library. Copies may be obtained from John Landrum, Director of Reader Services, South Carolina State Library.

State Aid. Public libraries in South Carolina receive $.35 per capita support from the state. Eligible libraries must be county systems or larger. Therefore all but four systems are county systems. The four exceptions serve two or more counties. State Aid is administered through the budget of the South Carolina State Library and distributed on the basis of the 1970 census in each county or region. This money may be used to supplement professional and pre-professional salaries up to 40 percent, purchase materials, and certain types of equipment.

Because of inflation, rising salary costs at all levels, and some confusion at the local level because of a shift in powers of local government (until 1975 all county budgets had to be approved by the state legislature) the public library section of the South Carolina Library Association made an increase of state aid to $1 per capita a major goal for the next two or three years.

The drive for this increase was spearheaded by the Legislative Committee of the Public Library Section. SCLA. Under the Committee Chair, Dennis Bruce of the Spartanburg County Library, public library directors and trustees met twice to formulate plans. The members voted to request the Board of the State Library to include the request in its budget proposal. A second motion directed the Legislative Committee to develop a plan of action and report on it no later than the SCLA annual conference in October. Those in attendance also heard Margie Herron, South Carolina State Library, on the background of State Aid. F. William Summers, then Assistant Dean of the College of Librarianship, University of South Carolina, spoke on a successful State Aid campaign in Rhode Island; State Senator Richard Riley and State Representative Nick Theodore, both of Greenville County, spoke on the

political and legislative process in South Carolina.

Verena Bryson, Chairperson of the Public Library Section, and Jean Galloway Bissell, Chairperson of the Richland County Public Library Board, appeared before the Board of the State Library and the State Budget and Control Board to present the request.

Thomas Cooper Library. The University of South Carolina completed construction on the Thomas Cooper Library. The 285,000-square-foot building is the result of nine years of effort by Kenneth Toombs, Director of Libraries. The library was designed by Edward Durrell Stone and Lyles, Bissett, Carlisle and Wolfe as an adaptation and expansion of Stone's award-winning Undergraduate Library (1961). The seven-story library includes several innovative features. The four underground floors require no heating system as they are heated by the lights. The Education Library and the Science Library each are incorporated into the building as separate entities. Cost of the building and furnishings was $8,097,320. The library was accepted as a member of the Association of Research Libraries for the first time in its history.

Committee for the Humanities. The South Carolina State Library and the South Carolina Wildlife Federation, a private, non-profit organization, have been awarded a grant from the South Carolina Committee for the Humanities to produce a documentary film on the Richard B. Russell Dam Project.

The dam is to be constructed on the Savannah River, which forms the state line between South Carolina and Georgia. The site is to be between the Hartwell Reservoir and the Clark Hill Reservoir on the same river.

The film is planned to produce factual information on what has become a controversial topic. Jacqueline E. Jacobs, Wildlife Executive Secretary, will produce and direct the film. The State Library will provide research information and coordinate screenings at major public library buildings throughout the state.

Tentatively titled "The Russell Dam, A Question of Values," the film will explore the many facets of South Carolina life that will be affected by a decision to construct or not construct the dam. When completed, the film will be available for groups and organizations to view at local public libraries. The Wildlife Federation will provide moderators for each presentation.

The Humanities Committee also sponsored programs in several public libraries in conjunction with the Institute for Southern Studies of the University of South Carolina. The Anderson County Library, the Spartanburg County Library, and the Beau-

State Reports—South Dakota

fort County Library presented seminars based on "Figures of the Revolution in South Carolina." Stephen E. Meats, Associate Professor of English and Chairman of the Humanities Division at the University of Tampa, and visiting professor in the Southern Studies Program, served as program moderator.

The Anderson, Charleston, and Greenville County Libraries hosted a series of programs focusing on Faulkner, Welty, Peterkin, and Chestnut. Noel Polk was program director.

Children's Book Award. The South Carolina Association of School Librarians initiated the Children's Book Award program in 1976 in one pilot school from each of South Carolina's judicial districts. A master list of 20 children's books was chosen by a panel composed of school librarians, library consultants, teachers, and administrators. Students from grades 4 to 8 voted for their favorite. The 1976 winner was *How To Eat Fried Worms* by Thomas Rockwell.

Awards For the fourth time, the Greenville County Library won a John Cotton Dana Award for an outstanding public relations program. A special award was given to the Library for its promotion of the library as an "Information Place."

The promotional effort was part of the library's Area Reference Resource Center Project, which is funded by an LSCA grant administered by the South Carolina State Library. The campaign, which stretched across a seven-county area, included billboards, book bags, and television in addition to target public relations efforts. Pat Shufeldt is the Regional Reference Librarian in charge of the Area Reference Resource Program.

The Greenville County Library also picked up the first prize for Best Radio Spot in the 1976 PR Awards Contest sponsored by the Library Public Relations Council. The public service announcement was sponsored by Radio Station WFBC (Greenville) in cooperation with Verena Bryson, Community Relations Coordinator for the library.

The Lineberger Memorial Library of the Lutheran Theological Southern Seminary in Columbia received the Award of Merit from the Buildings Award Program for 1976. The program is jointly sponsored by the American Institute of Architects and the American Library Association. The library was designed by Walter D. Ramberg, Professor of Architecture at Georgetown University. The building which cost $1,000,000 was a gift of the Lineberger Foundation in the neighboring state of North Carolina.

Grants. The Council on Library Resources recently announced recipients of grants under its Library Service Enhancement Program. The University of South Carolina and Presbyterian College (Clinton) were among the 12 academic libraries selected to receive grants for the 1976-77 academic year.

The grant is given to develop programs aimed at "integrating the library more fully into the teaching/learning process." Directors and project librarians of the recipients are Kenneth Toombs (Director) and Ilene Nelson, University of South Carolina; Lennart Pearson (Director) and Joane Pressau, Presbyterian College.

Elspeth Pope, Associate Professor of the College of Librarianship, University of South Carolina, was awarded a fellowship from the Council of Library Resources for the academic year 1976-77. Pope will use the grant to study bibliographic control and use of bibliographic data for books published in England.

Appointments. F. William Summers, Assistant Dean and Professor of the College of Librarianship, University of South Carolina, was named Dean on July 1, 1976. Summers succeeds Wayne S. Yenawine, who had been dean of the college since its inception.

Summers has also accepted an invitation by Daniel Boorstin, Librarian of Congress, to serve on the LC Advisory Group on Libraries.

Carlanna Hendrick, Chairman of the South Carolina State Library Board and Lecturer in History at Francis Marion College, was named to a two-year term to the Region IV Archives Advisory Council. The Council promotes cooperation between the National Archives and Records Services and the public.

Elections. Betty Callaham, Deputy Director of the South Carolina State Library, was elected as Chapter Councilor to the American Library Association. She succeeds Carl Stone, Director, Anderson County Library.

Two South Carolinians have been elected to positions in the Southeastern Library Association. Gerda Belknap, Extension Librarian, Richland County Public Library, has been elected as South Carolina Representative to the regional organization and Larry Nix, Director, Greenville County Library, has been elected to serve as SELA Secretary.

Shirley M. Tarlton, Librarian, Winthrop College, was elected to a three-year term on the Board of Directors of SOLINET (Southeastern Library Network).

CARL STONE

SOUTH DAKOTA

The year 1976 was marked by a revision of the state public library law, completion of the new state library building and the new public library for the citizens of

---

South Dakota Library Association
(founded 1907)

Membership: 647 (97 ALA members); Annual Expenditure: $3,000.
President: Jan Olsen, Mitchell Public Library (October 1976-September 1977).
Vice-President/President-elect: Dorothy Liegl, South Dakota State Library, Pierre.
Secretary: Martha Schaer, Yankton Community Library.
Annual Conference: September 22-24, 1976, Pierre.
Publication: Book Marks (bimonthly).

South Dakota State Library
Herschel V. Anderson, State Librarian
State Library Building
Pierre, South Dakota 57501

Brookings, the growth of new services, and increased cooperation among libraries of all types.

After a year and a half of preparation and discussion by trustees and librarians, the proposed revision of the state's public library law was ready for presentation to the 1976 legislature. Many librarians and trustees worked long and hard to acquaint their legislators with the ramifications of the measure; consequently, the bill passed without trouble. The revised public library law went into effect in July. It places all public libraries under one set of regulations and allows a community to levy a special tax up to 3 mills for support of a local library. The revised law was designed to facilitate cooperative activity among various types of libraries and to encourage growth of regional systems.

State Association. Two main efforts which the South Dakota State Association completed in 1976 were an interlibrary loan code and a voluntary certification program for public librarians. The interlibrary loan code which was approved at the convention is intended to promote a more liberalized policy among the libraries adopting it. It is based on the premise that it is the responsibility of the total library community to provide every South Dakotan with access to whatever library materials that person needs.

The Certification and Accreditation Committee of SDLA was divided into two subcommittees—one to work on upgrading school standards concerning libraries and the other to work on standards for public libraries. The work of the first committee was still pending at year's end; the work of the second was approved at the convention and South Dakota now has a voluntary certification program for public librarians.

The SDLA annual convention was in the capital city, Pierre; its theme was "Exploring South Dakota." John R. Milton of the University of South Dakota dealt with "What Matters Literature in South Dako-

State Reports—South Dakota

ta?" A special feature of the Convention was an opportunity for participants to elect to earn one continuing education unit or one hour of credit by attending workshop sessions in one of three sequences: Library Administration, Selection and Use of Library Materials, or Improving Library Services.

State Library. The South Dakota legislature approved a budget of $735,400 for the State Library, with $479,100 from state resources, $225,500 from federal sources and $30,000 from other funds.

The highlight of the year was the completion of the new state library building in the Capitol Complex. The two-story modular construction contains 52,000 square feet and was built at a cost of $2,131,000. All formerly separate services of the state library agency moved into the new building by early November.

The State Library continued to fund the TWX network of 13 libraries by means of LSCA grants. In addition, it offered a new service—the METRO Program of BCR—to all citizens of the state. Access to the computerized data bases of System Development Corporation (SDC), BALLOTS, DIALOG, and the New York Times Information Bank was available to all citizens in 1976. Transaction fees are covered by the State Library through tax revenues. South Dakota became the first state to offer such service.

Public Libraries. New or improved library facilities for citizens of Avon, Corsica, and Lemmon were completed during 1976; they are communities with populations under 2,000. Brookings, a city of 14,000, replaced its 1915 Carnegie building with a one-story structure of 16,600 square feet. It includes stack areas for 60,000 volumes, seating capacity for 106, and a meeting room for 88. Cost was $582,000. Formal dedication ceremonies were held on November 21. Planning for the new facility began in 1969. After two unsuccessful attempts to pass a bond issue, the residents of Brookings voted to replace their library building in April 1975.

Other communities working toward new buildings were Belle Fourche, Sturgis, Madison, and Grant County.

With approval at the annual convention, South Dakota public librarians now have a voluntary certification program. The provisions for type of certificate to be given are based on the amount of education in librarianship one has achieved. Certificates will be issued for a three-year period to SDLA members and may be renewed upon completion of certain professional requirements. Connected to the certification program for librarians is a provision for accreditation of public libraries as well. The major requirement as to type of certificate needed is based on the size of the population served. They range from libraries serving 2,500 or less to libraries serving 25,000 or more.

School Libraries. In the town of Salem (population 1,400), the public library had closed several years ago, but the Salem Public School Library in 1976 made its services available to the town as a whole. Elsewhere, school libraries in Dupree and Ipswich opened their doors to the public for the first time with special summer programs.

The School Library Media Section of SDLA continues to gain members and to work for the improvement of school libraries. Concerted efforts to upgrade the school accreditation rules resulted in meetings with governmental decision-making bodies. Proposed changes involve a raise in annual expenditures for materials, additional educational requirements for media specialists, and an increase in the number of support staff. Ardis Ruark, newly-appointed Library Consultant for the State Division of Elementary and Secondary Education, aided the Section. As the end of the year approached, the rule changes were still under consideration by the State Board of Education.

Academic Libraries. The state-supported colleges and universities again felt the budget crunch. College library budgets were suggested for the bulk of budget cuts by some advisers, but the Board of Regents refused that recommendation and left the cuts to each campus. All the schools chose to cut the library budgets some, with Black Hills State College losing the least. The three largest institutions, USD, SDSU, and South Dakota School of Mines and Technology had to cut their acquisitions budgets. Financial prospects for 1977 budgets were not good because of poor economic conditions brought on by a devastating year-long drought in the state of South Dakota.

The first institutions in the state to formally join the OCLC system were Mount Marty College, Yankton; Sioux Falls College; and Augustana College, Sioux Falls. These small private liberal arts colleges were among several hundred throughout the nation awarded $8,000 grants by the W. K. Kellogg Foundation. The Foundation which is interested in networks and computer technology for libraries provided the funds for purchase of computer terminals and training of library personnel.

The Dr. Leland Case Library Collection of Western Historical Studies was dedicated in formal ceremonies at Black Hills State College, Spearfish, on April 30. The collection contains many rare items of Western lore.

In 1976 the Academic Section of SDLA began gathering and organizing the data for the fourth edition of the South Dakota *Union List of Serials*. The last edition was published in 1973. This list is of vital importance for interlibrary loans in the state.

Work continued on the new H. M. Briggs Library for South Dakota State University. The $3,800,000 structure has 121,000 square feet on three floors. It will nearly triple the size of the old library and will provide reader space for approximately 1,000; May 1, 1977, was the scheduled completion date.

Intellectual Freedom. Efforts to pass an obscenity ordinance in Rapid City were watched carefully by the librarians of that community. When the final ordinance passed, the local librarians, led by Phil McCauley, had seen to it that school, college, university, public museum or public libraries would not be subject to prosecution for possession, dissemination, or display of materials considered obscene.

Awards. Trustee of the year was Charles Burke, Pierre banker, in honor of his 26 years of leadership as a trustee of the Rawlins Public Library, Pierre.

Librarian of the year was Betty Siedschlaw, State Library Consultant to Institutions, for her work as a public library consultant, her work with special libraries throughout the state, and the publication of her book *Play and Learn With Toys*, a bibliography of toys for teaching retarded children.

The Carl Gaumer Annual Awards for most improved reference collections went to St. Mary's School for Indian Girls, Linda Juhnke, librarian; Huron Senior High School, Margaret Moxon, librarian; and Tripp County Library, Winner, Nadine Nelson, librarian.

The University of South Dakota Distinguished Service Award was given to Ruth Bergman for 42 years of service in the University Library. Bergman was twice President of the South Dakota Library Association.

People. Following are appointments made in 1976: David Barton, Assistant Director, Alexander Mitchell Public Library, Aberdeen: Mary Busby, Children's Librarian, Alexander Mitchell Public Library, Aberdeen; David Calloway, Director, Madison Public Library; Dorothy Liegl, Library Consultant, S.D. State Library; Mary Modica, Librarian, S.D. School for the Deaf; Alan Ogden, Law Librarian, USD Law Library; Stephen K. Ooton, Director, Huron Public Library; Cherryi Povey, Assistant Director, USD School of Medicine Health Science Library; Robert Precoda, Director, Vermillion Public Library; John Vincent, Handicapped Service Librarian, S.D. State Library; Sidney Wang, Catalog Librarian, Rapid City Public Library; Barbara Bates Wince, Reference Librarian and

State Reports—Tennessee

Assistant Professor, Augustana College, Sioux Falls, and Cynthia Winn, Young Adult Librarian, Sioux Falls Public Library. — EMILY K. GUHIN

TENNESSEE

Buildings. The Chattanooga-Hamilton County Bicentennial Library (formerly Chattanooga Public Library) commenced moving to the new $4,500,000 library building on September 27. The old library, on the periphery of the campus of the University of Tennessee at Chattanooga, is being purchased by the University. At one time the building housed the public library and University library. The University library has already occupied its new building.

The Knoxville-Knox County Public Library has captured the use of a unique building for an East Tennessee Historical Center. The use of the Custom House, an all-marble and iron (fireproof) building in Knoxville's center city, was won only after three years, countless meetings, letters and contacts, numerous reports and estimates, many friends, and the power of political persuasion.

The Hollywood Branch of the Memphis/Shelby County Public Library system opened its doors on June 21. The 6,250-square-foot building occupies one wing of a building which also houses the Memphis/Shelby County Health Department Community Clinic. The joint occupancy, the first of its kind for the Library, is proving to be a successful venture and is resulting in additional plans for future cooperative buildings.

At the end of 1976 the George Peabody College for Teachers, School of Library Science, moved into facilities in the Industrial Arts Building on the Peabody campus, more than quadrupling the space originally available to the School. Facilities are available for all classrooms, administrative and faculty offices, secretarial support, and a student commons. In the same building is the remodeled and redesigned Media Center, with which the School of Library Science will be working more closely. This is the first move of the School in over 40 years.

On December 8 the Public Library of Nashville and Davidson County opened the Z. Alexander Looby Library and Recreation Center. The Center combines for the first time in such a joint venture the resources of the Public Library and the Department of Parks and Recreation. Through its presence the residents of North Nashville have access to a library, a museum, and a theatre, as well as a gymnasium, a craft and game room, and, by 1977, an olympic-sized outdoor swimming pool. This facility, funded by Model Cities at a cost of $1,000,000 and housed in 24,359 square feet, is architecturally consistent with the nearby Metro Center, a private enterprise venture along the banks of Nashville's Cumberland River.

The Lexington-Henderson County Library has moved to new quarters in the Lexington Civic Center Building. The Mt. Juliet Branch of the Lebanon-Wilson County Library opened in January. The library board and staff of Fayetteville—Lincoln County Public Library hosted an open house at their new building on June 13. Eagleville Bicentennial Library was opened in the late fall.

Grants. The Memphis/Shelby County Public Library and Information Center is operating the "International Project," a federally-funded grant to assist foreign persons in the Memphis area who speak English as a second language.

The Title II-B program on race relations information continued at George Peabody College for Teachers, School of Library Science, for the third year, with three fellows during the 1975–76 year and six fellows during the 1976–77 year. This has been one of the successful programs for the training of information specialists to work with race relations information in libraries and other information agencies in the community.

Gifts. The Memphis Chapter of Links, Inc., under the cosponsorhip of the Tennessee American Revolution Bicentennial Commission, donated five oral history tapes and over 40 photographs to Memphis/Shelby County Public Library and Information System. The tapes and photos are on aspects of Memphis Black history.

The Galston-Busoni Archives and the Galston Music Collection, a collection including 2,000 pieces of music for piano, manuscripts, letters, and memorabilia, have been donated to the University of Tennessee Library at Knoxville.

The Knoxville-Knox County Public Library was a prime beneficiary in the estate of the late Mary U. Rothrock's personal library of books on librarianship and the library profession and on Tennessee and the South. The residual share of Miss Rothrock's estate, estmated at between $200,000 and $250,000, was left to the Department of Local and Regional History in the Knoxville-Knox County Public Library. In addition to these bequests, Miss Rothrock left $10,000 to the Southeastern Library Association to be used for an annual award to an individual making an outstanding contribution to librarianship in the Southeast.

The University of Tennessee's Knoxville Special Collections Library has been given the papers of Robert S. Hartman, philosopher, author, and scholar, by his widow, Rita Hartman, and son, Jan S. Hartman. Professor Hartman, author of several books and many scholarly articles concerned with axiology, was a member of the UTK Philosophy Department in the 1960's and 1970's.

Friends of the Library. The Mayne Williams Public Library in Johnson City organized a Friends of the Library group in 1976. The organization published a quarterly newsletter, sponsored a two-day fiber and needlepoint exhibit, and began an evening lecture series.

In late summer the Friends of the Knoxville-Knox County Public Library invited members of the Knoxville City Council, the Knox County Court, and the Knox County Commission, as well as the Mayor and the County Judge to a catered dinner held at Lawson McGhee Library. Members of the Boards of Directors of the Friends and of the Library, as well as the library director and the department heads talked informally with the officials. Following the meal, a slide-tape presentation, purchased by the Friends, was shown. This presentation focused on services offered by the Library.

Friends of Memphis and Shelby County Libraries held its first annual Book and Author Dinner on October 24. Well-known authors, including John Toland, Mary Hemingway, Mary MacCracken, and Nancy Dickerson, attracted an enthusiastic public response. More than 400 attended.

Programs. The Knoxville-Knox County Public Library System held a "Children's Favorite Book Election" throughout the system during the presidential election week and the week preceding. More than 840 children participated.

The Public Library of Nashville and Davidson County established a program of Library Service designed especially for persons whose native language is not English and who have difficulty speaking and understanding English. The program is

---

Tennessee Library Association
(founded 1902)

Membership: 1,532 (473 ALA members);
Annual Expenditure: $23,489 (July 1, 1976).
President: Frank Gresham, Joint University Libraries, Nashville, Tennessee.
Vice-President/President-elect: Gary R. Purcell, University of Tennessee.
Executive Secretary: Betty Nance, P.O. Box 12085, Nashville, Tennessee 37212.
Publication: Tennessee Librarian (quarterly).

Tennessee State Library and Archives

Katheryn C. Culbertson, State Librarian and Archivist
403 Seventh Avenue North
Nashville, Tennessee 37219

designed to serve all nationalities and age groups from the pre-school child to the senior citizen.

As a Bicentennial project, the Mayne Williams Public Library, Johnson City, sponsored a program of "rededication" for city and county residents. Scrolls pledging rededication to the United States Declaration of Independence were made available at the Library for persons wishing to sign them and 7,272 signatures were collected. These scrolls, along with memorabilia of 1976 gathered by other organizations, were placed in a time capsule to be opened in the year 2076. The Library also opened a new "drive-in window" service. Patrons call in their book order, then drive by to pick them up.

TLA Activities. The Tennessee Library Association prepared a Legislative Program in 1976 reflecting the service goals of Tennessee libraries in order to acquaint the State's legislators, government officials, and citizens of library needs and opportunities. This has been published in an issue of the *Tennessee Librarian* and was to be issued in pamphlet form for wide distribution. The material will also be used for discussion at the Legislative Day in Washington, D.C., on February 3, 1977, and at legislative breakfasts to be held in Nashville early in 1977. Plans are also being made to reactivate the Tennessee Libraries Legislative Network.

The Junior Members Round Table was approved as a new section for the Tennessee Library Association. The purpose of this new section is to orient new members to the library profession, to encourage participation in professional organizations, and to promote a sense of responsibility for the development of the library profession.

Julius Jay Marke, Law Librarian and Professor of Law at New York University, delivered the 28th annual University of Tennessee Library Lecture on April 27. Professor Marke, an expert on copyright law and a participant in Congressional hearings on the present copyright bill, discussed "Copyright v. Intellectual Property."

Video. The activities of the Community Video Center of the Memphis/Shelby County Public Library were diversified during 1976. A continuing series, the American Issues Forum, was committed to videotape during the year. Related programs included the visit of the Bicentennial Wagon Train to the city of Memphis. In August the library began cablecasting on CATV channel 9, the first local organization to begin programming on cable.

Media Program. In the fall of 1976 the George Peabody College for Teachers, School of Library Science, introduced a new school library media program featuring a number of new courses, including production and design of nonprint media and options for short courses in video production, sound production, film production, and photography. In addition, short courses such as storytelling and cataloging of nonprint media helped to strengthen a program which is designed to be very much in harmony with the new ALA Standards (*Media Programs: District and School*).

People. Frances Neel Cheney, Professor Emeritus, George Peabody College for Teachers, School of Library Science, received the Constance Lindsay Skinner Award during the ALA Conference in 1976 for an enduring and unique contribution to the world of books and to the larger society through books.

Donald R. Hunt, formerly Director of the Library at San Jose State University, was appointed Director of Libraries and Professor in Library Science, University of Tennessee, Knoxville, May 1.

Diane Cofer was appointed Head of Extension Services and Betty Conaway Head of Cataloging for the Memphis/Shelby County Public Library and Information Center. Willye Neal was appointed Head of the new Hollywood Branch Library in Memphis.

Hugo F. Sandoval, Coordinator of Instruction Media/Assistant Professor of Library Science, and Teresa Gayle Poston, Assistant Professor of Library Science, joined the staff of the George Peabody College for Teachers, School of Library Science.

Rene Jordan, former Head of the Clinch-Powell Regional Library, was appointed Head of the Extension Department, Knoxville-Knox County Public Library. Connie G. Battle was appointed Director of the Oak Ridge Public Library. Don Craig was named University Librarian, Middle Tennessee State University, Murfreesboro. Virginia O. Harman, School Library Media Specialist, George Peabody College for Teachers, retired in 1976.

Deaths. Mary Utopia Rothrock, Secretary-Treasurer of TLA, 1916–18, and President 1919–20, 1927–28, died January 30. Her importance in the history of librarianship goes far beyond her role in this state. Her contributions were felt by the profession of the entire country over a period of 50 years. For her "outstanding contributions to librarianship" in 1935–36 she received the first Lippincott Award of the American Library Association for her "rare vision and intelligence shown in organizing regional library service and related adult education activities." Active in many professional library associations, she was a founder and the first President of the Southeastern Library Association. She was also President of the American Library Association 1946–47. (See Obituaries.)

Carl T. Cox, Professor of Library Science at the Graduate School of Library and Information Science, the University of Tennessee, Knoxville, died September 1. Dr. Cox had an important impact on the library profession through his teaching and his activities in professional associations. He chaired ALA's Outstanding Reference Books Committee and was also a former President of the Tennessee Library Association and the East Tennessee Library Association. A memorial scholarship fund was established in his name by the Graduate School of Library and Information Science. (See Obituaries.) ROBERT F. PLOTZKE

TEXAS

Budget Boost. At the beginning of fiscal year 1976, when governments elsewhere were facing severe budget cutbacks—and Texas was trying to maintain its fiscal integrity by funding no new programs—the Texas State Library received a 195 percent increase in budget. Much of this was directed toward the regional public library systems and the service to the blind and physically handicapped.

Significant state funding for regional public library systems organized under provisions of the Texas Library Systems Act of 1969 made possible a variety of programs in the 10 systems. All took over responsibility for workshops and technical assistance within their areas. Since the legislation gives each system considerable leeway in determining what programs are most needed for its area, the programs included diverse activities: System-wide film collections, books-by-mail for unserved areas, a reference backup that goes beyond the interlibrary loan network in one area, and collection development.

Texas Library Association (founded 1902)

Membership: 3,405; *Annual Expenditure:* $70,136 (1975–76).
President: Paul M. Parham, Texas Christian University, Fort Worth (April 1976–April 1977).
Vice-President/President-Elect: Shelah A. Bell, Director, Irving Public Library System.
Executive Secretary: Jerre Hetherington, 8989 Westheimer, Suite 108, Houston, Texas 77001.
Annual Conference: April 7–9, 1976, Houston.
Publications: Texas Library Journal (quarterly); *Added Entries* (3 issues a year).

Texas State Library

Dorman H. Winfrey, Director and Librarian
Box 12927, Capitol Station
Austin, Texas 78711

State Reports—Texas

Although 1976 was the first year for significant state funding, the legislation itself dates to 1969. In an effort to determine areas in which changes could be made to strengthen the systems and also to solve certain administrative problems, a contract was signed by the State Library with the Public Administration Service to study the governance of the systems. The state's library community decided that the changes suggested would be premature in view of the limited experience with systems. However, the in-depth study of systems and attitudes toward them is providing valuable information on possible future directions for systems activity in the state.

Texana Projects. Of interest outside Texas are current efforts to make information on printed and manuscript material on Texas more accessible. During the past year information on state documents has been added to the Ohio College Library Center (OCLC) data base by the State Library's cataloging unit. In a second program the State Library, Waco-McLennan County Library, Dallas Public Library, Houston Public Library, Stephen F. Austin State University Library, are adding data on Texana in their collections to the OCLC data base. A microform union list of these titles will be produced.

A third program of much interest to researchers is the production of inventories of records now in counties. Under the supervision of the Center for Community Services at North Texas State University (NTSU), students at Texas colleges and universities are producing these inventories. They are being edited at NTSU and printed and distributed by the State Library's Archives Division. As a result of the microfilming program now being carried out by the Church of Jesus Christ of the Latter Day Saints, copies of many of these records are now being produced. Under the State Library's Regional Historical Resources Depository Program, inactive records of historic interest are being deposited in designated depository collections.

An agreement signed late in the year between the Division for the Blind and Physically Handicapped, Texas State Library, and the Midland Free Tape Lending Library will make Texana more accessible to the Division's patrons. Master tapes of Texana and materials in Spanish will be reproduced on the State Library's duplicating equipment for circulation. Among the titles to be produced initially is *Texas Monthly*.

The Texas Numeric Register, a computer-generated list of Library of Congress catalog card numbers published four times a year on microfiche, is speeding interlibrary loan requests both in the public library community served by the Texas State Library Communications Network and in the academic library network, Texas Information Exchange. Some 4,500,000 volumes (1,500,000 titles) appeared on the November 1976 edition.

Efforts to use automation effectively continue in the Archives Division, Texas State Library. The current high interest in genealogical research is resulting in great numbers of name searches. The first activity of this kind was an alphabetical list of all persons who received Texas Confederate Pensions.

Physical Facilities. The Houston Public Library's downtown central library, an eight-story, $10,500,000 center for an expanding library system was dedicated January 17. An octagon-sided building, it contains 333,620 square feet and will enable the library ultimately to enlarge its collection to 2,000,000 volumes.

The Houston Academy of Medicine-Texas Medical Center Library was devastated by flood on June 15. Substantial damage was done to the area in which rare books and the soon-to-be opened Audiovisual Services were located. A primary casualty was "death by drowning" of the computer in a Medical Center computer service facility which caused the automated circulation system to collapse.

Design plans for the Central Research Library, Dallas Public Library, have been approved and funding possibilities are under study. The 11-story facility carries an estimated price tag of $44,000,000.

Special ceremonies marked the opening of a new central building for the Amarillo Public Library November 28. With a book capacity of 400,000 volumes, the library will seat 300. Construction costs including site acquisition and development were $2,050,000; furniture and equipment, $350,000; size: 60,000 square feet.

Of special interest to the General Libraries of the University of Texas at Austin was the December awarding of the general construction contract for the Fine Arts Complex, a segment of which includes a 49,000 square foot Fine Arts library. Nearing completion (with moves expected late summer 1977) are both the Perry-Castañeda Library and the Chemistry Library. With seating for 2,800 readers and a book storage capacity of 3,250,000 volumes, the Perry-Castañeda Library will be the third largest academic library building on the continent.

University of Houston library patrons were able in 1976 to make use of the new John H. Freeman Wing, an addition to the M.D. Anderson Library building. Dedication is scheduled for January 28, 1977.

Projects and Services. MARCIVE, a San Antonio cooperative with over 200 members, began offering a new SDI (Selective Dissemination of Information) service providing weekly printouts of all bibliographic information within a specific subject or subject area with data derived from MARC (Machine-Readable Cataloging Copy) tapes.

Community services are easier for Dallasites to locate due to the use of APL/CAT (A Programmed Language Community Access Tool). The CAT, a computer, is maintained by the Dallas Public Library in cooperation with the North Texas Council of Governments. Selected information from it has been published in the second edition of *Open Dallas*, which lists services, clubs, organizations, groups interested in various social activities, etc.

CarAVan is the audiovisual bookmobile added to the El Paso Public Library system in 1976. Films are shown at community stops—viewed on a screen installed in the side of the bookmobile.

Publications. *Microforms in Texas Libraries: A Selected Union List* compiled by Lois Bebout, sponsored by the Texas Information Exchange, and produced by the General Libraries, the University of Texas at Austin, lists holdings of 44 major library collections in Texas.

Using the format of the Pathfinder series published by Massachusetts Institute of Technology, librarians of the Reference Subcommittee of the InterUniversity Council of the North Texas area have prepared *Southwest Trailblazers*. Each list includes basic research tools on Texas and Southwest topics.

A fascimile edition of the manuscript of Valentine Overton King's *Index to Books about Texas before 1889* was printed under auspices of the Archives Division, Texas State Library, as a Bicentennial publication.

For an expenditure of just over $100 to print and distribute 75,000 letters, the Dallas Public Library system promoted its summer reading program by enclosing a short letter in each elementary school report card on the last school day.

Beginning March 1976 was a continuing education service for Texas librarians: the *SWLA/CELS* (Southwestern Library Association, Continuing Education for Library Staffs) *Audio Cassette Journal*. Sixty minutes of reviews of articles from recent library journals are prepared for tape presentation by professional librarians in the Southwest, several of whom are Texans.

Academic Libraries. Daniel J. Boorstin, Librarian of Congress, delivered the commencement address at the University of Texas at Austin May 22.

In support of the developing Shepherd School of Music curriculum, Fondren Library, Rice University made substantial additions to the music collection. The Music Library underwent reorganization and an extensive reserve collection was opened to support the music school's courses.

Prose and Poetry of the Live Stock Industry of the United States (Denver, Kansas City: National Livestock Historical Association, 1905) was added to the Texas A&M University Sterling C. Evans Library November 20 as the library's one millionth volume. It will be added to the Jeff Dykes Range Livestock Collection.

School Libraries. In May 1976 the Texas State Board of Education established criteria for two new programs: Learning Resources Specialist (LRS) Certificate Program (36 semester hours) and the Learning Resources Endorsement (21 semester hours). The programs emphasize graduate-level work and represent competencies in both library science and educational technology. All those who currently hold the Provisional or the Professional Librarian Certificate, or who complete such programs by August 31, 1979, will be deemed automatically to have, for assignment purposes as a librarian under the Texas Public School Finance Plan, the equivalent of the Endorsement or the LRS Certificate.

Public Libraries. A staffing procedure for the San Antonio Public Library now allows this facility to remain open 361 days per year. The library is open except for four special occasions (Christmas, Thanksgiving, Easter, and San Jacinto Day). Staffing is done by volunteers with time and a half pay for those working over the regular 40-hour workweek.

The 75th anniversary of the Dallas Public Library was celebrated in superior style November 6–14. "The Arts—Who Pays?" was the subject of a symposium on the interrelationship of the arts, business, and government in today's society. "Urban Libraries and Librarians: Future Prospects" were discussed at the Librarians' Dinner program. Publication of *An Illustrated 75-Year History of the Dallas Public Library* by Larry Grove was supported by the Friends of the Dallas Public Library, as was a 16-page miniature volume *Why Miniature Books*, by Stanley Marcus and Marvin Stone. Branch library programs and receptions honored community leaders.

The Dallas Public Library has purchased an important collection of over 75,000 photographs and negatives depicting the history of Dallas from 1929 to 1976.

Cataloging of the Charles Reimers "Rare and Old Children's Book Collection" and preparation of a printed guide (publication expected early 1977) was completed by staff of the Fort Worth Public Library. Approximately 330 English and American imprints comprise the collection which will be on permanent exhibit in the new central library (expected construction date: April 1978).

Texas Library Association. This was a year of major activity for the Texas Library Association (TLA). At the spring annual conference, the TLA Council approved the adoption of new by-laws. The Council also gave preliminary approval to rescind the Constitution (the document which had previously governed the Association) subject to ratification by membership vote. Following a mail vote, the Constitution was indeed rescinded and TLA has a new governing document. Major changes include a more comprehensive statement of objectives which affirm the Association's status as a nonprofit organization, a change in term of office for officers, and the addition of Interest Groups as units.

The Annual Assembly, held in September, was a working session for all TLA committees. Special attention was paid to the programs of all TLA units and the fiscal affairs of the Association, with an effort made to relate priorities and work programs to fiscal resources.

All units received in November a statement from the TLA Executive Board reaffirming TLA's appreciation of library trustees and the Friends of Texas Libraries. In December the TLA Legislative Committee and others urged action to inform Texas legislators of the need to provide the services of at least one full-time Learning Resources Specialist in each public school building. Districts of less than 500 average daily attendance will be served by a multi-district librarian.

TLA will develop and implement a statewide public information program to inform Texans of services available to them through their local library through the Texas Major Resource System. To be funded by a $21,620 grant under Title III, Library Services and Construction Act, the program will be developed with the aid of a professional public relations firm.

By-laws were approved during the year for the Institutional Interest Group which will carry the acronym JAILS (Juvenile & Adult Institutional Library Service) and will be available for write-in selection on 1977 TLA membership forms.

College and university librarians at state-supported schools will monitor the progress of the proposed Texas Higher Education Personnel Act which leaves vague the status of librarians. The exclusion of college and university librarians from coverage of the Act was formally supported by TLA by resolution passed at the Annual Assembly.

Texas Reference Sources, 1975–76 published in November 1976 *Texas Library Journal* updated *Texas Reference Sources* published in 1975. Projects of the TLA Reference Round Table, the bibliographies list recent reference materials about Texas of interest to librarians.

Awards. The Siddie Joe Johnson Award was initiated in 1976 to honor outstanding achievement in the area of children's library services. It will be presented to a public or school librarian who serves preschool through eighth-grade children, with the first presentation to occur at the 1977 TLA annual conference.

Awards presented at the 1976 annual conference were: Texas Librarian of the Year, David M. Henington, Director, Houston Public Library; and Texas Library Trustee of the Year, Norma Jean Stanton, Irving.

Looking forward, TLA will celebrate its 75th anniversary in joint conference with the New Mexico Library Association in El Paso, April 13–16, 1977.

Deaths. C. Everett Taylor, Assistant Librarian, Abilene Christian University, died September 9.

Harry H. Ransom, Chancellor Emeritus, University of Texas System, died April 19.

MARY POUND

UTAH

Add them together—1976, Bicentennial Year, the elections—and a true pyramid of events becomes evident. Utah was abustle and quickened with an involvement in everything and anything historical, whether it was dinosaurs, archaeological diggings, the geology of the great mountains that surround and protect each valley, tales of Indians or pioneers, one's own genealogy, or the gathering of the folklore that may partially explain the intellectual vigor of the friendly people—all this meant an upsurge in the use of libraries in 1976.

From the time of its settlement to the present, Utahns have followed the admo-

Utah Library Association
(founded 1912)

Membership: 660 (75 ALA members); Annual Expenditure: $8,000.
President: Lucile Thorne, Library School, Brigham Young University (April 1976–March 1977).
Vice-President/President-elect: E. Dale Cluff, Marriott Library, University of Utah, Salt Lake City.
Executive Secretary: Gerald A. Buttars, Utah State Library Commission; 2150 South 300 West, Suite #16, Salt Lake City, Utah 84115.
Annual Conference: March 31–April 2, 1976, Salt Lake City.
Publications: Utah Libraries (semiannually); *ULA Newsletter* (irregular).

Utah State Library Commission
Russell L. Davis, Director
2150 South 300 West
Salt Lake City, 84115

State Reports—Utah

nition to "seek wisdom out of the best of books." When the territory of Utah was created in 1850, its first public library was established, and it has been said that at the time of the Chicago fire in 1871, there were more books in Utah than in Chicago—people from all over having sent books, being distressed over Utah's distance from civilization and feeling that books would help Utahns to become good citizens.

By 1976 librarians realized their expanded roles and through the Bicentennial attention many projects were funded that ordinarily could not have gotten off the ground. Summer reading programs, puppet shows, quilt contests, commissioned paintings, story hours, folklore fests, Bicentennial bookmobile, special displays and exhibits—all had been used.

Expanding Services. Typically, the year 1976 saw a continuation of the struggle for funds but even so, several of the smaller libraries were going ahead with plans for remodeling, expanding, or acquiring a new building. A small branch of the Weber County library system was dedicated in Roy early in the year. Whitmore Library, Salt Lake County, noted for its achievements, started an extensive remodeling program in June. Before the year's end the catalog department there and the interlibrary loan staff were using OCLC, and the information center was searching the New York Times Data bank as well as ERIC, DIALOG, and other data bases provided by the Bibliographic Center for Research in Denver. Installing terminals in Whitmore was the beginning of computerized information and referral services for the general public. The microfilm catalog from Autographics provided a union catalog, updated every two months, in every branch. The last phase of becoming totally computerized in certain operations will take place in 1977 when CLSI, an automated circulation control system, including film bookings, will be in use at Whitmore and several key branches.

Mountain Bell Telephone Company complied with a request to expedite communication between Whitmore and the ten branches by providing the equipment that allows the press of one button to make the connection. This capability, along with the telecopier that can be found in the four key branches and Whitmore, ties the System much more closely together. With 764 square miles for a service area, Salt Lake County Library System needs all the help it can get for the rapid transmittal of information. Guy Schuurman, Director of the System, has guided the plan that saw Whitmore built in 1974 as the headquarters and center of the System. Registration of borrowers has peaked at 70 percent of the population.

The spirit of service is keen in all Utah's public librarians even though their facilities do not compare with those of the Salt Lake County Library System. Under the direction of Mary Petterson, the Public Library Section (PLS) of ULA has continued to hold regional workshop programs—one being held in Springville with 15 small public libraries represented from that central Utah area. Because most of the public libraries of Utah are small, and some very isolated, the PLS hopes to bridge the communication gap and to help the small library staff find an answer to some of their problems.

Genealogical Treasure House. As part of an active acquisition policy, the Genealogical Library of the Church of Jesus Christ of Latter-day Saints (Mormon) acquires 36,000 100-foot reels of microfilm and 7,000 printed volumes annually. On January 1, 1976, 875,914 reels of microfilm and 144,208 printed volumes were among the holdings of this unique library—the largest genealogical library of its kind in the world. Its collection represents the equivalent of more than 4,000,000 printed volumes of 300 pages each.

Beginning with a modest microfilming program in 1938, 75 microfilm cameras are operated by the Genealogical Department filming genealogically valuable material worldwide. This material includes original manuscript records such as church registers, land, census, vital, military, tax and court records, family Bibles, newspapers and similar records of particular value to genealogists and historians.

The Library has a massive Computer File Index (on microfiche) containing approximately 28,000,000 names. Other special collections include a voluminous collection of more than 7,000,000 alphabetized family group records and a three-by-five card index containing 30,000,000 names. These three sources include names from all countries of the world and for all time periods.

LDS Church Library. This library was founded on the admonition to collect all works by or about members of the Church and the Church itself as a tremendous Library-Archives at the headquarters of The Church of Jesus Christ of Latter-day Saints. It acquired a highly sophisticated computer software package to expand its indexing and abstracting service capabilities. Beginning in 1976 the Library produced the *Index to Mormonism* in *Periodical Literature* to serve the needs of the research community. This has proven to be the most complete index to periodical literature about Mormonism available and fills a major information void. In addition to its coverage of current material, the library has initiated a far-reaching program for indexing literature retrospectively, including periodicals, newspapers, and monographs. Related services such as abstracting, computerized retrieval (SDI), and information retrieval to facilitate retrospective searches are also being implemented.

In 1976 the LDS Church Library also created or expanded several specialized resource files, including the "Historic Sites File," folders containing pertinent information about buildings, early trails, monuments and markers, and other sites of particular relevance to Mormon history; the "Bibliography Card File," a record of each reference request handled by the library staff which entailed a significant effort to compile sources, or which otherwise resulted in a collection of the most informative references on a given subject; and a "Biographical File of Prominent Living Mormons." The staff of the library includes one of the leading conservators of the world, Paul Foulger.

State Historical Society Library. This Library of the Division of State History began a Japanese-American Archives to document the history of that group's experiences in Utah. Oral histories were gathered along with a great many photographs. The Utah Oral History Consortium is making great strides in collecting and coordinating statewide oral histories, and a manuscripts processing manual has been prepared under the direction of Jay Haymond. A number of registers were prepared by Ann Hinckley to assist patrons in their use of the Society's Manuscript collections.

State Library. In May 1974 the Division for the Blind and Physically Handicapped of the Library of Congress designated the Utah State Library Commission, Division for the Blind and Physically Handicapped, as the Multi-State Center to serve the 14 western states. It is one of two such centers in operation, the other being in Florida. The Utah Multi-State Center is under the direction of Gerald Buttars. Although in operation for only two years, it has already proved a tremendous asset to the regional libraries in the West—over 4,000 blind people currently were taking advantage of these service in the mid-1970's.

Also available are the talking books on records. Special record players designed for operation by the blind are loaned to readers.

Bookmobile Services. The Utah State Library Commission dispatched a Bicentennial Bookmobile into every town in every county of Utah. It stopped at all public, college, university and school libraries and in the first four months of 1976 had been visited by 45,000 people. It included rare first editions of books of the Revolutionary Period from the Special Collections of the University of Utah. The Bookmobile was furnished by the State

Library and it was staffed by librarians from throughout the state. Another bookmobile began its coverage of the State with a special exhibit of the travels of Dominguez-Escalante (August–October 1776).

The State Library has 19 bookmobiles in operation 52 weeks of the year. Those with facilities for showing movies and slides are sent to the small isolated communities or areas far removed from easy access to such services. Over two million books were loaned from the bookmobiles in 1976. The demand rose over a third in the Uinta Basin area, where there is an oil boom.

Richard Rademacher, the Chair of the planned Governor's Conference and Director of the Salt Lake City Public Library, resigned in 1976 to accept the Directorship of the Wichita Public Library in Kansas. Dennis Day from Troy, Ohio, became the new director of the Library.

ULA. 1976 was a year of methodically shoring up the hopes and goals of the Utah Library Association. The challenge was given to the librarians of Utah at the annual convention held in April, the theme of which was "Utah Libraries: Heritage and Horizons". Bobbee M. Hepworth and Yvonne D. Clement presented two aspects in formal papers. Preconvention workshops were held prior to the convention and were well attended. They included a Documents workshop, one on personal time management, one on small public libraries, and the organization of the Junior Members Round Table. President Guy Schuurman presented the gavel to incoming president Lucile M. Thorne.

The University and College Section held two workshops on the similar theme of making a total learning package for the members. The 1975–76 theme was "Identity for Academic Librarians/Professionalism, Status, and Research." The 1976–77 theme was "Emphasizing the Undergraduate/Instruction, Orientation and Collection Development."

Utah State University Library. The State University Library entered into a cooperative agreement to participate in the program of the United States Department of Agriculture Regional Document Delivery System to deliver library materials to the employees of the U.S.D.A. and also provide for them on-line searches as well as current awareness services. Beginning in January of 1976, 20 requests were received, and by July the number had mounted to 316 for the month, and each month continues to escalate, proving that a great need is being met. In addition, the library received a grant from the National Agricultural Library to microfilm and put on fiche all back issues of the Experiment Station and Extension Service publications.

The Center for Outlaw and Lawman History is at the Utah State University Library, the official repository for the materials collected by the National Association and its members. A Newsletter also issues from the University campus. Utah State University has several growing Western Americana programs related to the outlaw and lawman subject. An important purpose of the program is to promote a scholarly approach to the study of the outlaw of the American West.

The Utah State University Library and its collection was combined with other educational media programs and services to make a single administrative organization: The Merrill Library and Learning Resources Program.

Weber State College Library. Weber State College dedicated in 1976 a new library addition that doubled the amount of available library space. It completed a building project begun over ten years earlier. On the day of the dedication, it was announced that the Library was the recipient of a $1,000,000 gift. The deferred gift will enable the Library to develop an outstanding undergraduate collection. At nearly the same time an important book collection was given by a local donor. Other important collections given recently are the Laurence J. Burton Congressional Collection and the Paul Bransom Art Collection.

University of Utah Libraries. A library instruction package was designed in cooperation with the teaching faculty, funded by a CRL-NEH grant; an active promotion and training was given in the use of on-line data bases in engineering, the physical and social sciences; and the Special Collections Department completed the fifth and sixth books in its published series entitled, "Utah, the Mormons and the West." 1976 saw the installation of a turn-key, minicomputer circulation control system. The system will go on-line with a file of 320,000 machine-readable records available for use. The manual catalog operation was converted to OCLC, and the Library's union list of serials saw publication as a COM edition. 1976 saw too the completion of a year-long MRAP study and the beginning of the implementation of related organizational changes. In-house personnel as well as outside experts participated in an active staff development and training program as part of the University Libraries' endeavor to extend the scope of their collections and expand their services to match the academic and research needs of the University.

Brigham Young University Harold B. Lee Library. This Library completed a 225,000-square-foot addition that more than doubles the size of the library facilities. The total facility is now 430,000 square feet. It provides stacking space for over 2,000,000 volumes; seating for 4,800 students; 140 faculty members can be served in its expanded faculty research rooms. It provides over 40 group study rooms of various sizes ranging from five-person to twenty-person accommodations. There is an expanded Learning Resource Center, which accommodates 260 people besides the regular carrel-viewing stations and four large group viewing rooms. The Special Collections Library houses a large and rare collection of materials on Utah, Mormon Americana, Hafen, Clark, Victorian Literature, Melville, Whitman, and Wordsworth, to name only a few. There is a large music score collection which includes, among other collections, the Bruning collections of early American sheet music, manuscripts of music recorded by Capitol records and the Bonime collection of broadcast scores from the big band era.

State in Summary. To make a quick generalization about the 1976 state of libraries in Utah, one would take a somewhat conservative attitude that characterizes life in Utah—the ups are less dramatic, the recessions less drastic. Add all the reports together and the sum total is that libraries have always played an important role in the history of Utah for they have always, in so many ways, reached out to people. George Herbert (1593–1633) in *Jacula Prudentum* expressed the true sense in his preface: "The best of the sport is to do the deed and say nothing." Why say more?

IDA-MARIE JENSEN

VERMONT

In all sections of the library field in Vermont, 1976 has seen a renewed solidarity for support of the concepts of intellectual freedom, continuing education, and the public library as a vital part of the community. Perhaps the budget crunch everywhere has revived the old Yankee spirit of self-reliance and making-do. The tiny hamlets and small cities (the largest,

---

Vermont Library Association (founded 1892)

Membership: 500; *Annual Expenditure:* $4,595.
President: Douglas W. Durkee, Green Mountain College, Poultney, (January–December, 1976).
Vice-President/President-elect: Joseph Popecki, St. Michael's College, Winooski (January–December, 1977).
Annual Meeting: May 26–28, 1976, Poultney.
Publications: Vermont Libraries (bimonthly).

Vermont Department of Libraries
John McCrossan, Commissioner and State Librarian
Montpelier, Vermont 05602

State Reports—Vermont

Burlington, is not 50,000, and it is twice as large as Rutland, second largest) showed a marked Bicentennial spirit of pride and desire to effect self-improvement, and their libraries have fared well in the endeavor. The pastoral beauty of mountains, valleys, and rolling pastures in a sparsely settled northern State does not allow for vast development in educational and library technology, but proportionately, progress in human terms is heartwarming and always lively.

Vermont Library Association. Featured for the third consecutive year was an annual conference at Green Mountain College in Poultney, sponsored by VLA, the Vermont Educational Media Association, and the Vermont Library Trustees Association. A rousing preconference on women, titled, "If We're So Smart, Why Ain't We Rich?", concluded with an address by Virginia Clark, President of the American Association of University Professors. The general conference, on "Alternative Goals for the Vermont Library Community," featured children's illustrators Tomie DePaola and Trina S. Hyman, architect Robert Burley, Executive Director of the Association for Educational Communications and Technology, Howard Hitchins, and the Editor of *Library Journal*, John Berry, among several others. The conference concluded with a party in the College Library for some 18 Vermont authors and artists.

A first for VLA in 1976 was the Association's establishment of a part-time position of Executive Secretary. The position was to be filled in 1977.

The five VLA district meetings of 1976 continued discussions of intellectual freedom and the potential change in the state Obscenity Law. Work sessions were held at every district meeting on "What I Expect of VLA in 1977." Discussions resulted in serious deliberations pointing toward a new Association newsletter, to appear as frequently as once a month and as supplement to the present *Vermont Libraries*, which is a joint, bimonthly publication of the Department of Libraries, VLA, and VLTA.

Department of Libraries. The year saw several areas of development and notable activity at the Department of Libraries (DOL). Since Vermont is a small, rural state, a very large portion of leadership and services emanate to every community from the Department. Among such services are the five large Regional Libraries, the State Law Library, Bibliographic and Reference Services, Children's Services, Books by Mail Service, and, new in 1976, The Vermont Library for the Blind and Physically Handicapped.

On August 1, by designation of the Library of Congress, the Vermont Department of Libraries assumed full responsibility as The Vermont Library for the Blind and Physically Handicapped. Previously, the New York State Library provided a portion of that service to Vermont. On September 17, the Department held an Open House in honor of the new library service.

The Children's Services Consultant, Caroline Heilmann, designed and implemented an ambitious and successful summer program. She wrote a 62-page manual, *Creative Summer Programming*, which is available for purchase from the Department of Libraries. Then, with two assistants, she arranged a caravan of children's summer programs, visiting 62 Vermont communities in less than two months. To top this program attended by hundreds of Vermont children, Heilmann produced a film in cooperation with Kim Worden of the Film Department of the University of Vermont. Entitled *Stories in Motion: Alternative Techniques to Storytelling*, the 16mm film is in color and runs for 26 minutes. Inquiries about the film should be sent to the Department.

The Books-by-Mail program, completed its fifth year of operation, serving a great need of the elderly and the most rural residents, who account for 50 per cent of its use. A Department workshop on Oral History, led by Janice Rushworth, and another on Volunteers, led by Sally Roberts, proved outstanding.

Patty Klinck, Assistant State Librarian, attended the workshop on Continuing Education in Springfield, Illinois, in November. Sponsored by NCLIS to seek development of State Plans for Continuing Education, Vermont was one of 27 states invited to participate.

In cooperation with the College/Special Libraries Section of VLA, the Union List of Periodicals of the Department, under the direction of Fred Lerner, was under consideration as the data base of a statewide Union List of Serials.

Public Libraries. Two communities honored their librarians for many years of service. Bradford honored Laura Dickey after 40 years as librarian, and Craftsbury saw the retirement of their librarian, Mary Dustin, who had served that library for 60 years.

The Thetford Library Federation library and historical building was completed as the first Bicentennial community project designated by the Vermont Bicentennial Commission. It represents the combined efforts of some nine library organizations and other educational agencies for a town of 1,400.

Baldwin Memorial Library in Wells River held an open house on April 6 to mark completion of a new addition which doubled the size of the library. The construction, interior decoration, and furnishings were all contributed as donations and volunteer labor by members of the little town and its library staff. The results are a warm, friendly community center.

The Pierson Library in Shelburne opened an audio room, initiated by an LSCA incentive grant. Interior decoration and furnishings were contributed by the trustees, the Jaycees, the Friends of the Library and the Shelburne Craft School.

School Libraries. Aiding and encouraging the works of school libraries and media centers in Vermont is the Vermont Educational Media Association. It has been a vital organization in the development of State Certification of School Media Personnel, guidelines for Materials Selection Policies, and the publication of the *Vermont Handbook for School Media Centers*. VEMA was founded in 1971, as a merger of the Vermont School Library Association and the old Vermont Educational Media Association. Its membership numbered 120 in 1976. Its publication is the quarterly *VEMA News*.

In cooperation with the School for International Training in Brattleboro, and the Vermont Council of Teachers of English, VEMA sponsored one of its most successful workshops on the techniques of producing media for classroom and library use. Direct positive photography, filmmaking, creative television production, and programs of original sound-slide synchronization were featured.

The VEMA portion of the Annual Conference of VLA, VLTA, and VEMA, held at Green Mountain College in Poultney, featured Howard Hitchins, Executive Director of AECT, on copyright. Hitchins presentation drew the largest crowd at a conference meeting.

Because Vermont is so small, VEMA finds it vital to cooperate with other Associations. VEMA in 1976 was seeking nongovernance affiliation with AASL and AECT; it cooperates on a representational basis with the New England Educational Media Association. VEMA is an affiliate of the Vermont Education Association and thus in touch directly with the National Education Association.

Academic and Special Libraries. The outlet for news and activities of academic and special libraries in Vermont is the fast-growing College/Special Libraries Section of VLA. A major achievement of this Section of the Association in 1976 was the work begun on the Vermont Union List of Serials. Many decisions have yet to be made, but, with the data base of the *Union List of Periodicals* of DOL, organization was under way. Such a statewide list would allow Vermont to take part in the New England Library Board's interest in a Regional Union List of Serials.

Awards. The 1976 Elva Sophronia Smith Grants were given to Marianne Worden,

Librarian at Waters Memorial Library in Underhill; Judith McAlpine, Librarian of the Sheldon Public Library; and Alice Bayles, Librarian of the Dover Free Library. Under the terms of the will of Elva Sophronia Smith, the Smith Grant Awards are made each year by the Vermont Department of Libraries. Miss Smith, of Burke, was a teacher, librarian, and author. She died in 1965 at the age of 94, stipulating that a portion of the income from her legacy be used "to aid in the development and maintenance, or either of them, of library service to the children of Vermont."

People. Four major appointments for positions within the state were made in 1976. Frank Woods was appointed Library Consultant for Audio-Visual Services with the Department of Libraries on March 23, succeeding Barbara Eniti.

Sally Roberts began her post as Southeast Regional Librarian on March 30, succeeding Mary Barter, who retired from her job and from her office as ALA Chapter Councilor after eight years of service in both.

Dorothy Allen was appointed Director of Library Users Services Division of DOL, succeeding Henry O. Marcy IV. Allen had been head of DOL Special Services unit since 1968.

Ronald Rucker assumed the position of Librarian at Middlebury College on July 1, succeeding John R. McKenna, who died in September 1975. — JOSETTE ANNE BOISSE

VIRGINIA

Bicentennial Reprise. In most communities throughout the Old Dominion the observance of the Bicentennial was a "time to celebrate and a time to remember." The picture emerges of many libraries and archival groups digging into their own resources to uncover little-known as well as important facts about their communities. Arlington County Historical Society, for example, produced a book entitled *Arlington County, Virginia: a History* by Cornelia B. Rose, Jr.

The resurgence of feeling for local history was one of the most significant results of Bicentennial activities. Across Virginia libraries sponsored historical displays, exhibits, and demonstrations, both within the library and in the communities. Prince William County Public Library cooperated with other community agencies in sponsoring a two-day Bicentennial Craft Festival at the County Fair Grounds. The Portsmouth Public Library, under a grant from the Virginia Foundation for the Humanities and Public Policy, provided speakers for the American Issues Forum, promoted by the American Library Association.

Bibliographies of local holdings on Bi-

Virginia Library Association
(founded 1905)

Membership: 1,465; *Annual Expenditure:* $24,105.
President: Maurice Leach, Washington and Lee University (December 1975–November 1976).
Vice-President/President-elect: Janet E. Minnerath, Virginia Medical Information Service, Virginia Commonwealth University.
Secretary: Gladys R. Caywood, Newport News Public Schools, 12465 Warwick Boulevard, Newport News, Virginia 23606.
Executive Secretary: Roberta Miller, Henrico County Public Library, Box 27032, Richmond, Virginia 23261.
Annual Conference: November 18–20, 1976, Roanoke.
Publication: Virginia Librarian Newsletter (6 issues a year).

Virginia State Library
Donald R. Haynes, State Librarian
Richmond, Virginia 23219

centennial subjects proliferated in Virginia libraries of all types. One of the most elaborate was produced by the Newport News Public Library System entitled: *A Call to Arms: a Checklist of Materials on the American Revolution in Libraries on the Lower Virginia Peninsula.* The City of Norfolk prepared a carefully planned packet, extolling the virtues and facilities (including the Library) of the city.

Many state, county and municipal agencies cooperated with libraries in Bicentennial promotions. Ray Williams, consultant from the State Library, chaired a Bicentennial Task Force of the Librarians' Technical Committee of the Metropolitan Washington Council of Governments; the committee circulated *Bicentennial Briefs*, a monthly newsletter of Bicentennial activities.

VLA. The Virginia Library Association was confronted with several crises during the year. Inadequate income seemed to top the list in view of membership demands for an executive secretary, better and more frequent section programs, and reorganization for geographic representation and increased involvement in Association affairs. Another problem was revolt by some vendor/exhibitors over conference location, exhibit management, and exhibit fees. There was also considerable concern about the proliferation of nonaccredited librarian training courses overlapping ALA-accredited and other nonaccredited programs throughout the state. The Executive Board employed Roberta Miller, Director of Henrico County Public Library, as the Association's first Executive Secretary.

The Executive Board appointed Marilyn Norstedt of Virginia Polytechnic Institute and State University *Virginia Librarian* Editor, replacing Henry James, Librarian of Sweetbriar College, who departed on sabbatical for research and writing at Harvard.

Membership dues were increased from $5 a year to a salary-based range of $7.50 to $30 for personal membership and $20 to $50 for institutional members. A reorganization resulted from a two-year study of an ad hoc Development Committee which determined that membership wanted regional meetings and representation on the official policy body and also state-level sections by type of library. Short-term interest can be recognized and discussed via Forums. The Regional Chairman, the Section Chairmen, Standing Committee Chairmen, ALA and Southeastern Library Association (SELA) elected representatives, the Editor of the *Virginia Librarian*, Chairmen of Forums, the Executive Director, and Officers of the Association form the Council as the policymaking body. An Executive Committee composed of the Officers and the Executive Director transacts business between annual meetings.

The Trustees' Section inaugurated its first Annual Trustee Award and named the Section Chairman, Pat Pfeifer of the Newport News Library Board, as the first recipient. She had served as Chair for two years and had led the move for maximum state aid funding for public libraries.

The membership bestowed Honorary Life Membership on Virginia Ruff of the Bedford County Public Schools, Margaret Hopkins of the Lynchburg College Library, and Arthur Kirkby of the Norfolk Public Library. All honorees have retired from their positions.

Interlibrary Cooperation. Interlibrary cooperation was fostered by the State Library through continued grants to the Librarians' Technical Committee of the Washington Council of Governments, Project TIMES (*New York Times* Information Bank) for Tidewater Area libraries, Virginia Interlibrary Communication, and updating of the *Virginia Union List of Serials.*

The Washington Council of Governments is supported basically by federal and local jurisdictional funding, but the library program has been overwhelmingly augmented through the participation of the three state librarians involved — Nettie Taylor, Maryland Department of Education, Hardy Franklin, Director of the District of Columbia Public Library, and Donald Haynes, Virginia State Librarian. The Council of Governments framework completes a network of interlibrary cooperation involving libraries from Manassas, Virginia, to Enoch Pratt in Baltimore. The network is being expanded into a Council of libraries on a paid institutional membership basis which will include public, col-

State Reports—Washington

lege, university, school, special, federal and national libraries.

Buildings. New public library building have been opened in Bon Air (8,000 square feet), Ettrick-Matoaca (8,000 square feet), and La Prade (8,000 square feet), branches of the Chesterfield County Public Library. The Woodrow Wilson Library expansion (12,800 square feet) of the Fairfax County System opened in 1976.

The Petersburg Public Library received a former Jewish Reform temple as a gift from the disbanded congregation and converted it into the Rodof Sholom Branch (3,500 square feet).

The Henrico County Public Library opened the new Fairfield Area Library (24,000 square feet) which includes the system administrative offices (8,000 square feet), Dumbarton Library (22,500 square feet), and Tuckahoe Library (32,000 square feet).

The Lonesome Pine Regional Library opened a new branch in Dickenson County, Clintwood, and the Roanoke City Library relocated its Melrose Branch in a new building. The Great Neck Branch was dedicated by the Virginia Beach Department of Public Libraries and Information.

Two libraries were severely damaged by fires. The Slemp Memorial Branch of Lonesome Pine Regional suffered $200,000 damage plus destruction of 20,000 volumes. Several thousand items were lost when fire caused $25,000 damage to the Fauquier County Public Library, Warrenton.

New community college libraries listed in the *Library Journal* architectural issue are Central Virginia (25,080 square feet), J. Sargeant Reynolds (10,271 square feet), John Tyler (32,000 square feet), Northern Virginia Manassas Campus (57,988 square feet), Thomas Nelson (70,000 square feet), and Tidewater (24,300 square feet).

Academic library buildings were occupied at Old Dominion University, Norfolk (130,696 square feet) with an addition at the University of Richmond (89,250 square feet, 53,520 new).

State Library. As of midyear, the State Library announced that 95 percent of the population has access to public library service, a large increase since 1966 when only 81 percent was served. There were 88 libraries compared to 76 ten years ago, but most of the new ones are in small cities or sparsely populated counties. It is apparent that existing regional libraries have been strengthened by the addition of counties or cities, but state support has been inadequate to the task of encouraging more regionalization. The State Library augmented its staff with four area consultants: Donna Brown, Southwest, Area 1; Hanna McLay, Southside, Area 2; William Chamberlain, Southeast, Area 3, and Raymond E. Williams, Northern Area 4.

Much of the momentum for jail and institutional service has been from the State Library's Institutional Consultant, Reed Coats in 1976.

School Libraries. Perhaps the most significant development in the area of school libraries has been the formation of the Virginia Educational Media Association. The Association represents all librarians and media specialists and merges the School Librarians Department and the Virginia Association for Educational Communication and Technology of the Virginia Education Association.

Academic Libraries. The Library Advisory Committee of the State Council of Higher Education for Virginia has been actively engaged in developing ways in which to improve library services in the Commonwealth through increased cooperation among Virginia's academic libraries. Library activities offering potential for cooperative action were identified and Task Forces were appointed to study four of these: the coordinated development of library resources; serials service; interlibrary loan service; and the housing of infrequently used research materials.

Two useful publications were issued from Task Force investigations in 1976. The analysis of library resources in Virginia libraries resulted in the *Directory of Virginia Library Resources*, and data gathered during the study of interlibrary loan practices in Virginia has been compiled in the *Manual of Interlibrary Loan Policies of Virginia Libraries*. Both publications will greatly assist all libraries in identification of and access to library collections in Virginia. John Molnar coordinates Library Planning for the State Council.

The 1976 General Assembly appropriated $60,000 for each year of the 1976–78 Biennium to support the development of plans for total library resource utilization within consortium regions. Up to $10,000 per year will be available to each Consortium of Continuing Higher Education to support cooperative library projects of an innovative experimental nature.

People. Notable retirements and resignations from Virginia libraries in 1976 were: Brewster E. Peabody as Director of the Old Dominion University Library; Philip C. Wei as Director of the Mary Baldwin College Library; Annie Louise Bowman and Ruby Dickerson, Catalogers at the Library of VPI&SU.

Lillian M. Burch retired as Chairperson of the Appomattox Regional Library Board, Hopewell, after 20 years in that position; Robert Whitesides, Director of the Appomattox Regional Library resigned to attend a linguistics school for translating the *Bible* for tribes who have no written language; Edith M. Farley, Head Librarian of the Tazewell County Public Library; Lizzie Mae Cutchin, Head Librarian of the Franklin Public Library after 45 years; Sam Clay, Director of the Virginia Beach Public Library and City Information Officer became Assistant City Manager; Hannah Breckinridge was named a lifetime honorary member of the Botetourt-Rockbridge Regional Library Board after 23 years on that Board; Caroline Knapp, Librarian, Pulaski County Library.

James Samuel Miller, Librarian of the Norfolk State College, died in 1976. New appointments to Virginia libraries included: Connor Tjarks, Head of Central Processing, Virginia Commonwealth University Libraries, Richmond; Gertrude Coddington Davis, Head Librarian, Mary Baldwin College, Staunton; Kendon L. Stubbs, Associate University Librarian, University of Virginia, Charlottesville; Mrs. Edward F. Hufstedler, Librarian, Rappahannock County Public Library, Washington; S. Nelson Worley, Director, Appomattox Regional Library, Hopewell; Marcy Sims, Director, Virginia Beach Public Library, promoted from Assistant Director; Cathy Rainer, Director, Radford Public Library; Zelda Schiffenbauer, Director of Montgomery-Floyd Regional Library, Christiansburg, promoted from Assistant Director; Stephen L. Matthews, Director, Loudoun County Public Library, Leesburg; Jean Heath, Librarian, Pulaski County Public Library; Clare DeCleene, Librarian, Tazewell County Public Library, Tazewell; Martha W. Vasquez, Librarian, Williamsburg Public Library; Barbara Rice, Librarian, Augusta County Public Library, Staunton.

The American Theological Library Association elected John B. Trotti as its Vice-President/President-elect. Trotti is Librarian and Associate Professor of Bibliography at the Union Theological Seminary, Richmond, Virginia.

Howard Ogden, Director of the Hampton Public Library, was elected Vice-President of the Tidewater Genealogical Society.

WILLIAM L. WHITESIDES

WASHINGTON

Washington Library Network. The Washington Library Network was established by the legislature in early 1976 with four systems components identified: interlibrary systems, reference/referral, telecommunications, and computer systems. The purposes of the Network include the sharing of resources of all types, including human expertise, and the processing, storing, and sharing of information. The Interlibrary System will allow cooperation and coordination among all types of libraries in new patterns of service. A study by an out-

Washington Library Association
(founded 1905)

Membership: 1,117 (293 ALA members); Annual expenditure: $22,865 (1976–77).
President: Malcolm Alexander, Central Washington State College, Ellensburg (August 1975–July 1977).
Vice-President/President-elect: Betty Bender, Spokane Public Library.
Executive Secretary: Ellen Fawcett, 11819 19th Avenue, S.W., Seattle, Washington 98146.
Annual Meeting: May 5–8, 1976, Spokane.
Publications: CAYAS Newsletter (quarterly); *OPEN Newsletter* (irregular); *Conference Planning Handbook*, 1976.

Washington State Library
Roderick G. Swartz, State Librarian and Executive Director of the Washington Library Network
Olympia, Washington 98504

side consulting firm validated the necessity and the cost effectiveness of a Centralized Storage and Lending Center. All types of libraries are anticipated to participate in the facility. The State Library planned to request the 1977 legislation for construction funds.

Augmentation of the Reference/Referral System will begin with the designation of major Resource Centers. A request for supplemental funding to reimburse these libraries for performing statewide services was to be submitted to the 1977 Legislature as part of the State Library's budget.

The telecommunications and computer systems are described as the "utilities" of the Network. The Telecommunications System was limited in 1976 to an in-WATS telephone network called SCAN (State Controlled Area Network) in which libraries participated. This interconnects the State Library, public and private academic institutions, and the larger public libraries. The feasibility and cost effectiveness of adding other libraries was being examined. Washington Library Network computer system had as participants eight district libraries, the State Library, a four-year college and the two universities as the developmental phase neared completion at year's end.

The rules and regulations for the Network accommodate libraries of all types and sizes through the three categories of membership and the organizational structure. Basic membership entails participation in interlibrary loan and reference/referral. The cooperative membership allows the purchase of products and requires contributions to the data base. A principal member, in addition to the basic agreement to participate in interlibrary loan and reference/referral, contributes cataloging and holdings information to the data base by on-line access, plus has use of other computer-based services.

The *Resource Directory*, a union catalog of eight district libraries, the State Library, and a four-year college, was converted from a book catalog to microfiche format. The fiche catalog will be cumulated quarterly, and may be purchased by subscription. Over 300 readers were placed in publicly-supported libraries in the state.

School Library Standards. A law passed in late 1975 provided for the adoption and implementation of standards for integrating school libraries and media services into Learning Resource Centers. A survey of all school districts was conducted to determine what did exist at the building level, the district level, and what other sources were used to access learning materials. The data were compiled to show where standards were met and to determine the cost necessary to achieve minimum standards in school districts of the state. The results of the K-12 survey were to be reported to the 1977 legislature. Practical descriptors to use in measuring attainment of the standards were developed by involvement of representatives from all levels of K-12 administration and representatives from other types of libraries.

Buildings. Plans were underway in 1976 for a new headquarters building for the Kitsap Regional Library to be constructed in Bremerton in 1977 following the successful passage of a bond issue levy for the $1,900,000 facility.

Construction of a new service center for the North Central Regional Library in Wenatchee began in late 1976 and plans had been made for a new Timberland Regional Library service center.

The King County Library System dedicated three new libraries during the year. Kenmore and White Center were funded in part by funds remaining in the $6,000,000 bond issue passed in 1966, while Federal Way's new building replaced that lost through fire.

Ten libraries submitted requests in October 1976 for funding of library construction projects under the Public Works Employment Act of 1976.

Funding and Legislation. A committee of public library directors and State Library staff met during the summer and fall 1976 to develop proposed legislation to provide supplementary state funding for public libraries and to provide funds designed to encourage the establishment and development of services and to encourage cooperation.

People. Allene F. Schnaitter succeeded G. Donald Smith as Director of Libraries at Washington State University, Pullman. Smith retired June 30 after 30 years of service to the University, 26 of which had been as Director of Libraries. Schnaitter was Director of Libraries and Professor of Human Learning and Development at Governor's State University, Park Forest South, Illinois.

Belinda K. Pearson, an economist at Sea-First Corporation, Seattle, was appointed by the Governor to the State Library Commission to succeed Mrs. Bruce A. (C'Ceal) Coombs. C'Ceal Coombs has been an effective voice for libraries in the Pacific Northwest and the nation for over 20 years. Between 1954 and 1960 she served as the first paid lobbyist for the Washington Library Association. In 1960 she was appointed to the State Library Commission by the Governor for two four-year terms, followed by appointment by the next Governor for two four-year terms. During her years of service she reactivated the Washington Library Trustee Association, was instrumental in establishing a trustee section in the Pacific Northwest Library Association, was active in ALA, and served as President in its Trustee Association, receiving the ALA International Trustee Award.

DOROTHY CUTLER

WEST VIRGINIA

Construction, programs, education, and finances were given major consideration in the libraries of West Virginia during the 1976 year. Progress was made in all areas.

Finances. While many other states have had to contend with decreasing library support from state and local governments, West Virginia has experienced a new awareness of the value of libraries to its citizenry. The state legislature, under the active leadership of Frederic Glazer, Executive Secretary of the West Virginia Library Commission (state library), increased funding for library grant-in-aid and construction. An attempt was made to bring to the voters of the state a constitu-

West Virginia Library Association
(founded 1914)

Membership: 900; *Annual Expenditure:* $10,000.
President: Barbara Bonfili, Librarian, Morgantown High School.
Vice-President/President-elect: Ruth Ann Powell, Acquisitions Librarian, Fairmont State College.
Secretary: Karen Golf, Reference Librarian, WVLC Science and Cultural Center, Charleston.
Annual Conference: October 11–13, 1976.
Publication: West Virginia Libraries (quarterly).

West Virginia Library Commission
Frederic J. Glazer, Executive Secretary
Science and Cultural Center
Charleston, West Virginia 25305

State Reports—Wisconsin

tional amendment that would have earmarked a percentage of certain revenue for library support. Although the attempt failed in 1976, the publicity given libraries and the active participation of library patrons did influence the Legislature to vote additional revenue for library support. The Governor of West Virginia, Arch A. Moore, Jr., has been a strong supporter of funding and construction of libraries.

Construction. In 1972 a long-range state program for library development was conceived. It had as one of its major goals the construction of libraries in remote areas of the state so as to put a public library facility within easy reach of every citizen. This goal, nearing the end of the five-year program was becoming a reality in 1976. An innovative building design, an octagonal shaped, prefab building called the Instant Carousel Library, has become a popular shape in West Virginia. With a federal grant to aid communities with little funds of their own, 13 instant library projects were approved during 1976. Other library construction has been increasing also. Five major construction projects were completed during the year—libraries were opened in Raleigh County, Harrison County, Putnam County, Kanawha County, and Roane County. Several smaller storefront libraries were opened during the year.

A major construction project was completed during the year. The West Virginia Science and Cultural Center, built next door to the state Capitol, opened in July. The event was greeted with loud cheers from state librarians as the State Library Commission moved into the new quarters. For the first time all services offered by the state library would be housed in one location.

Programs. What good are buildings without good library programs? With additional funds from state and local sources, and with special project grants from the federal government, new programs and services have been promoted. Grants for books, audiovisuals, Bicentennial, and other programs were given to many state libraries. A total of $506,497 in special grants was given during 1976. A film lending library, operated out of the state library headquarters opened in November of 1976. Librarians were invited to view films in October, to learn the rules and regulations governing the use of the films, and to sign agreements with the Library Commission. Several small libraries that could not afford them were given projectors purchased with special grant money. A training session for those who would be operating the projectors was a requirement to get one. A catalog with annotations was given to each librarian present for the training. An initial collection of 1,500 16 mm sound, black and white, and color films was made available for use in libraries throughout the state. This is a first for such a program in West Virginia. Steve Christo of the State Library Commission staff headed the program.

Awards. Members of the "Exposure" team of the State Library Commission won recognition for their promotional ideas in 1976. For the second consecutive year the agency's "Exposure" Division, staffed by Steve Boggess, Carol Bryan, Lee Soard, and Ross Taylor, received the John Cotton Dana Award for the excellence of its image-building services for public libraries. The West Virginia Library Commission was the only state library in the nation to achieve winning status in this competition. The publicity was first used during the state's Annual Library Appreciation Sunday activities and "Library Pie" participants were happy to know that the PR experts considered the efforts well done as opposed to half baked. The "Library Pie Requires State Dough" campaign received a second award, presented by the Library Public Relations Council. The PR plan to gain legislative funding for libraries was cooked up by public librarians throughout the state in the form of home baked pies and presented to all Senate and House members when they attended activites at their local libraries on Library Appreciation Sunday. A message at the bottom of the pie plate asked the legislators for a larger slice of the pie for state libraries.

Public Library Activities. In an effort to create continuity in the organization of the Public Library section, a committee appointed by the Chairperson wrote by-laws for the section, establishing a legal basis for the election of officers and of other procedures. A document, "Minimum Recommended Salaries and Fringe Benefits for Employees of West Virginia Public Libraries," was researched and written after two years of study. Both documents were presented at the general meeting of the West Virginia Library Association during the annual conference and were accepted almost unaminously. These documents will serve as working papers to new librarians and new Library Boards in the future. The Minimum Standards, although only recommendations, will serve as a negotiating point for salaries and benefits.

Academic Libraries. Academic librarians attended an Archives Workshop conducted by Curator George Parkinson and assistant curators Harold Forbes and Rodney Pyles of the West Virginia Collection at WVU. The workshop included presentations on special collections, aural materials, and archives and manuscripts.

An Instructional Technology Symposium was held at WVU on March 12. The Symposium was chaired by Mary Novak, AV Librarian at WVU. She was assisted by Linda Jacknowitz, Medical Center AV Librarian. The symposium was attended by faculty and staff members of state institutions.

School Libraries. Monongalia County School Libraries held a Media May Day on the first day of May. Elementary and Secondary school students were invited to design Media teaching devices. There were over 200 entries from students of all ages. Entries ranged from Mock-ups, Video Tapes, Movies, Cassettes, Dioramas from elementary school children, and Film Strips to a Model Globe Theater and Costumes. Projects were judged according to grade level and prizes were given in each group. The prizes were donated by exhibitors of Library-related materials. A second one was planned for larger quarters in 1977.

Special Libraries. The directory of *Special Libraries and Their Librarians* was updated in 1976. A subject index was added to the directory. LUELLA I. DYE

WISCONSIN

Cooperative Efforts. The theme of the 85th Annual Conference of the Wisconsin Library Association was "Cooperation Not Competition." The conference represented both a culmination and a beginning for a wide range of cooperative efforts and other activities of the library and information community in Wisconsin. It represented, for example, the culmination of one phase of an exploration of affiliation between WLA and the Wisconsin Audiovisual Association (WAVA). The conference was a joint one, with both associations involved fully in planning and conference participation. Also, reports and discussions at sev-

Wisconsin Library Association
(founded 1891)

Membership: 2,425 (754 ALA members); *Annual Expenditure:* $37,770 (October 1975–September 1976).
President: Wayne R. Bassett, Marathon County Public Library (January–December 1976).
Vice-President/President-elect: Marianna Markowetz, University of Wisconsin-Milwaukee Library.
Administrative Secretary: Elizabeth S. Bohmrich, 201 West Mifflin Street, Madison, Wisconsin 53703.
Annual Conference: October 27–29, 1976, Oconomowoc.
Publication: WLA Newsletter (bimonthly).

Wisconsin Department of Public Instruction, Division for Library Services

W. Lyle Eberhart, Administrator
126 Langdon Street
Madison, Wisconsin 53702

eral program meetings represented the end of the work of the Task Force on Interlibrary Cooperation and Resource Sharing, a broadly based group of some 45 members which had prepared a recommended plan for enhancing cooperation in the state.

And yet, as the following paragraphs are intended to illustrate, the conference was at the beginning of many important developments that promise to improve library and information services in the state. The programs dealing with the recommendations of the Task Force on Interlibrary Cooperation and Resource Sharing initiated study and discussion by many persons and groups, as the recommendations are translated into legislation or are otherwise implemented. The joint annual conference was only one step in continued exploration of the appropriate relationship between WLA and WAVA. And among the last meetings held at the conference was one called by W. Lyle Eberhart, Administrator of the state library agency, to begin the planning for Wisconsin's participation in the White House Conference on Libraries and Information Services.

Task Forces. The year of 1976 in Wisconsin librarianship might have been called the year of the task force. With LSCA funding through the Division for Library Services, University of Wisconsin–Extension began to implement the recommendations of the Task Force on Library Manpower and Education, which had completed its work during 1975. The Continuing Library Education Planning and Coordination Project, COLEPAC, under the direction of Kathleen Weibel, was set up to serve as a clearinghouse and planning agency for Wisconsin library and media personnel. In addition, the State Council on Public Library Certificates and Standards began the process of rewriting the regulations for public librarian certification, as recommended by the task force.

School Library Media Centers. Also fitting in with the work of the Task Force on Library Manpower and Education was the School Media Certification Task Force. This group of state agency staff and media personnel from throughout the state produced a final draft proposal for revised certification standards for school media personnel, based on the concepts of unified media and competency based certification. After discussion began at the WLA-WAVA conference, the proposal was to be started through the route of hearings and other steps toward adoption as a part of the State Administrative Code. Two other task forces in the school media field were active in 1976. The Long-Range Plan Task Force completed its work, and a long-range plan for school library media program development was published in the September–October 1976 issue of *Wisconsin Library Bulletin* (along with the annual revision of the state's Comprehensive Long-Range Program for Library Service). The task force to revise the state school library media standards continued its work through 1976, hoping to issue a proposal for revised standards during 1977.

Public Libraries. For public librarianship, 1976 was a year of working to maintain and extend past gains in state-aided system development. At the beginning of the year, 11 county or multi-county systems served the citizens of 42 of Wisconsin's 72 counties. At the end of the year, a new system had been added and others had expanded, so that 47 counties were served. The biennial budget for the state contained much lower funding for state aid to systems than was called for by the statutory formula. A special bill to raise funding to 75 percent of the formula was passed by the legislature but vetoed by the Governor. After concerted political activity by the library community, the veto was overridden, and funding for 1977 was set at the 75 percent level.

Academic Libraries. Two groups serving academic librarians were particularly active in 1976. The Wisconsin Association of Academic Librarians, a division of WLA, had a year-long series of continuing education programs entitled "Librarianship–New Patterns." Programs held in various parts of the state included explorations of new patterns related to networking, library administration, legislation, and women in librarianship. The Council of Wisconsin Librarians, Inc. (COWL), an organization of private and public college and university libraries in the state, brought the services of OCLC into the state. COWL set up the Wisconsin Library Consortium (including, in addition to academic libraries, some of the state's larger public libraries) to provide liaison and interaction with OCLC. Nancy H. Marshall was appointed Director of the consortium. As of October 1976, nine libraries were on line with OCLC, with 11 more to be brought on line during 1976–77.

Other Library and Information Services. Special libraries and information services were active and visible in Wisconsin in 1976. The Wisconsin Chapter of the American Society for Information Science (chartered in 1974) provided several programs for its members, as did the Wisconsin Chapter of SLA. Both groups cooperated with other associations, including providing representatives on the Task Force on Interlibrary Cooperation and Resource Sharing and in the initial planning group for the White House Conference. The year saw particular interest in the expansion of access to computerized data bases. For example, funding from the state library agency brought the state access to the New York Times Information Bank through Milwaukee Public Library. The University of Wisconsin–Madison signed a contract with a data-base broker to provide access to a number of data bases through the university library system (in addition to those that had been available through individual campus libraries for several years). And many other libraries and information services continued or added data base services during the year.

Multi-type Activities. The year 1976 saw the continuation of cooperative activities that cut across types of library lines. The area multi-type library councils, organizations of libraries and information services of all types, were an important force in this regard. Two of these councils undertook long-range planning efforts during the year. Both the Madison Area Library Council and the Library Council of Metropolitan Milwaukee adopted recommendations of long-range planning committees that charted important directions and priorities for cooperative activities in their areas. MIDLNET, the Midwest Region Library Network, sponsored planning and information exchange meetings during the year and undertook other activities to help the libraries in the area work with each other and within developments at the national level.

Milestones. A second master's degree program in Wisconsin was accredited by ALA in 1976—that of the University of Wisconsin-Milwaukee.

New buildings occupied during 1976 include one for the Southwest Wisconsin Library System (the first new headquarters building for a multi-county system), the Eau Claire Public Library, and the Engineering and Physical Sciences Library of the University of Wisconsin-Madison.

People. Among those who retired during the year were Helen Wahoski and George Earley, after long and fruitful service at the University of Wisconsin–Oshkosh and Kenosha Public libraries, respectively. Peter Draz was appointed Head Librarian of the State Historical Society Library in Madison, effective October 11.

Bernard Franckowiak left the position of Director of the Bureau of School Library Media Programs in the Division for Library Services to become Associate Professor at the University of Washington School of Librarianship (See Awards). John Kopischke resigned as Director of the Bureau for Reference and Loan Services in the same agency to assume the position of Executive Director of the Nebraska Library Commission. The Wisconsin Library community was saddened by the death of Ione Nelson, who had been a public library consultant with the state agency for more than 20 years, and that of Louis A. Lange,

State Reports—Wyoming

who had been an active public library trustee at the local and state levels.

Awards. Peter G. Hamon was appointed Director of the Bureau for Reference and Loan Services in October. The WLA Annual Conference was the occasion for several awards. Leah Gruber, of Prairie du Sac, was presented the Trustee of the Year Award. The Clarence B. Lester Award for the Library of the Year went to the Southwest Wisconsin Library System. William D. Grindeland, Director of the school library media programs for the Racine school district, won the Librarian of the Year honor. A Special Service Award was given to Bernard Franckowiak. Ben Logan's book, *The Land Remembers*, was chosen for the Banta Award, WLA's literary award. —CHARLES A. BUNGE

WYOMING

The Coal Rush Continues. During 1976 it became increasingly obvious that one of the keys to U.S. energy independence was Western coal, some of the largest and richest deposits of which lie in Wyoming. While politicians and energy officials continued to squabble over whether the coal would be delivered to eastern furnaces by rail or by a yet-to-be built slurry pipeline, several law suits brought by environmentalists were settled, allowing strip mining to begin. People continued to move into the state in search of energy related jobs to the extent that no one has the vaguest idea how many people live in the state. New towns have cropped up like mushrooms, creating heavy demands on public libraries.

State Library. The State Library completed an extensive reorganization which was part of a larger reorganization creating the State Library, Archives and Historical Department. The Department consists of four major divisions: Museum, Archives, Historical Research, and State Library, with a deputy responsible for each division. Other aspects of the reorganization would allow the State Library to cope with an increase of 119 percent in requests for information from around the state.

The State Library sponsored workshops for the continuing education of Wyoming librarians, orientations for new library directors, began planning for a new building, and began a state-wide study of library needs. Further developments included the beginning of participation in a program of on-line bibliographic searching through the METRO program sponsored by the Bibliographic Center for Research (Denver), and the beginning of an automated Union Catalog for Wyoming Libraries.

Advisory Council on Libraries. The Wyoming Advisory Council on Libraries held a two-day meeting in Lander to consider goals and objectives for state-wide library development. The purpose of the meeting was to establish priorities in light of heavy population impact and static budgeting. Major priorities were (1) the continuing and strengthening of the State Library's role as back-up book collection and reference center serving all tax-supported libraries of the State; (2) the strengthening of continuing education programs for Wyoming library personnel and (3) the establishment of a union catalog of Wyoming libraries.

USOE Institute. One of the major happenings in the state was the State Library's sponsorship of the USOE Institute called "Education of Prospective State Library Agency Professional Personnel," directed by Jane Robbins. This program brought together 12 graduate library school students for ten weeks' extensive training in state librarianship. Guest lecturers included Joseph Shubert, State Librarian of Ohio, Frederick Glazer, State Librarian of West Virginia, and William Summers, Dean of the Graduate Library School at the University of South Carolina.

Other Developments. The Coe Library of the University of Wyoming, the only four-year institution in the state, under the leadership of newly appointed Director Bob Patterson, began to explore and define its future role and responsibilities to the state as a whole. The new Fremont County Library was dedicated. This beautiful building is virtually unique in its creative presentation of the old Carnegie building adjoining a new structure. Georgia Shovlain, Director of the Sheridan County Library and winner of several national awards, was named Outstanding Wyoming Librarian for 1976. —JOHN M. CARTER

Wyoming Library Association (founded 1914)

Membership: 400 (70 ALA Members); Annual Expenditure: $7,720
President: Wayne H. Johnson, Wyoming Library, Cheyenne.
Executive Secretary: Irene Nakako, Rock Springs Public Library.
Annual Meeting: April 25–27, 1976, Cheyenne.
Publication: Wyoming Library Roundup (quarterly).

Wyoming State Library
William H. Williams, Director
Wyoming Library
Archives and Historical Department
Cheyenne, Wyoming 82002

CORRECTIONS

In *The ALA Yearbook* (1976), p. 15–16, *for:* first and only non-U.S. librarian to serve as President: George H. Locke *read:* second non-U.S. librarian....

In *The ALA Yearbook* (1976), p. 16, caption, George H. Locke: the same correction.

In *The ALA Yearbook* (1976), p. 460, *for:* 1975, Virginia Haviland for *M.C. Higgins, the Great read:* 1975, Virginia Hamilton.... (compare p. 104 for biography of Virginia Hamilton, 1975 Newbery Medal winner).

In *The ALA Yearbook* (1976), p. 479, *Index, for:* Abstracting: See Indexing and Subtracting Services *read:* Abstracting: See Indexing and Abstracting Services.

INDEX

Abbreviations and acronyms, VIII
Abell, Millicent D., 7, 31
"About Books" column, 261
Abstracting: See Indexing and Abstracting Services
Abstracts, reuse of, 108
Academic Libraries, 1-7 (also 76 ed.)
  administration survey, 190
  audiovisual materials, 31, 209
  budget problems, 1, 32, 68
  building projects, 69, 70, 72, 75
  Canada, 335, 339
  circulation systems, 39, 40
  COM catalogs, 207
  HEA funding, 188, 326
  independent research libraries, 153-156
  interlibrary cooperation, 172, 173
  John Cotton Dana Awards, 44
  London report, 342
  management self-study, 287
  performance appraisal, 240
  salaries, 5, 31, 32, 237, 288, 328
  social responsibilities, 304, 305
  user education program, 284
  See also Association of College and Research Libraries; Association of Research Libraries; Principal Libraries of the World
Academic Library Development Program, 4, 5, 287
Access to Periodicals: A National Plan, 301, 302
Accounting: See Budgeting, Accounting, and Cost Control
Accreditation, 7-11 (also 76 ed.)
  blind and visually handicapped people, agencies for, 234
  Canada, Great Britain, and Australia, XXXIX-XLIII, 335
  Council of Specialized Accrediting Agencies, 232
  Council on Postsecondary Accreditation, XXXIX, 8, 232
  graduate programs, 8, 9, 112
  job market squeeze, 244
  standards, 7-11, 112
  See also Committee on Accreditation; Education, Library
Ackoff, Russell, 310
Acquisitions, 11-13 (also 76 ed.)
  academic libraries, 2, 5
  book publishers, 267
  British Library policy, XXVII, XXVIII
  Canadian libraries, 335
  comics, 270
  cooperative programs, 217
  independent research libraries, 155, 156
  survey, 289
  See also Collection Development; Gifts, Bequests, Endowments; Special Collections
ACRL: See Association of College and Research Libraries
Adams, Mrs. Hunter A., 371
Adams, Velma Lee, 353
Administration: See Management, Library
Adrian, Donna, 334
Adult Education Association of the United States of America, 226, 227
Adults Library Service to, 13-15 (also 76 ed.)
  public library programs, 256-258
  See also Independent Study in Public Libraries; Reference and Adult Services Division
Advertising: See Public Relations, Library
AFL/CIO-ALA Joint Committee on Library Service to Labor Groups, 182, 228
AG ECON (Agricultural Economics) data base, 210
Aging, Library Service to: See Older Adults, Library Service to
Agnon, Shmuel Yosef, 122
AGRICOLA, 110, 210
Agricultural Library: See National Agricultural Library
AIA-ALA library building awards, 69, 70, 75, 190, 258
Aids to a Theological Library, 25
Air Force libraries: See Armed Forces Libraries
ALA Council: See Council, ALA
ALA Datebook, XIX
ALA Goals Award, 42
ALA Publishing Services, 264-266 (photos)
ALA Yearbook, XIX, 266
Alabama report, 349, 350
Alaska report, 350, 351
Albert J. Beveridge Award, 46
Alexander, Malcolm, 415
Alexander, Mary Louise, **221**
Alexander, Norman, 282
Alexander, Sheila, 396
Allain, Alex P., 10 (also Biographies 76 ed.)
Allen, Emil L., 315
Allen, Lawrence, 363
Alliance for Information and Referral Services (AIRS), 112
Alliance of Associations for the Advancement of Education, 227
Almeida, Ruth, 375
Alsmeyer, Henry, 135
ALTA Honor Award, 42
Alternatives in Print, 307
Aman, Mohammed M., 115, 180
Amelia Frances Howard-Gibbon Medal, 46
American Antiquarian Society, 142, 155
American Association for Gifted Children, 227
American Association for the Advancement of Science, 227
American Association of Archivists, 298
American Association of Community and Junior Colleges, 227
American Association of Law Libraries (AALL), 16, 17, 185, 186 (also 76 ed.)
American Association of Library Schools, 329
American Association of Publishers, 176
American Association of School Librarians (AASL), XXI, 17-19 (also 76 ed.)
  Forum for Research, 289
  international relations, 179
American Association of University Professors, 227
American Book Publishing Record, 50, 51
American Booksellers Association, 67, 176, 227
American Chemical Society, 246
American Civil Liberties Union, 227, 228
American Correctional Association, 228
American Council of Learned Societies, 92
American Council on Education, 228
American Documentation Institute: See American Society for Information Science
American Federation of Labor, 228, 277
American Film Festival, 126-128
American Historical Association, 30
American Indian Libraries Newsletter, 112, 123
American Indians and libraries, 123, 124
  Canadian report, 341
  library career training, 188, 238
  projects, current, 112, 187, 305
  See also 76 ed.
American Jewish Historical Society, 122
American Libraries, XX, XXI, 20, 196, 197, 264, 267
American Library Association
  awards and prizes, 42-46
  Book Week USA, 176
  Centennial activities, XIV-XXI, 78, 119, 196, 261, 266
  Centennial Citations, 49, 104
    See also: Anderson, Florence; Greenaway, Emerson; Haycraft, Howard; Henne, Frances; McKenna, Frank; Stevenson, Grace; Thorpe, Frederick; Van Jackson, Wallace; Waller, Theodore
  Centennial guests, 174, 175, 177, 178
  ethics, 116
  highlights and organization, *facing title page*
  history, XIV, XXI, 19, 20
  Honorary Members 49
    See also: Downs, Robert; Gaver, Mary; Jones, Virginia Lacy; Liebaers, Herman; Melcher, Daniel; Shera, Jesse; Rothrock, Mary; Martin, Allie Beth
  international activities, 179
  Notable Books, 220
  publishing, 263-267
  social responsibility, 306
  standards committees, 311
  Yearbook, 1976, 266
  See also ALA entries
American Library Association: See also specific headings
  Divisions (Listed under the following titles)
    American Association of School Librarians
    American Library Trustee Association
    Association of College and Research Libraries
    Association of State Library Agencies
    Children's Services Division
    Health and Rehabilitative Library Services
    Information Science and Automation Division
    Library Administration Division
    Library Education Division
    Public Library Association
    Reference and Adult Services Division
    Resources and Technical Services Division
    Young Adult Services Division
  Offices (Listed under the following titles)
    Disadvantaged, Library Service to the
    Intellectual Freedom
    Personnel and Employment Research
    Washington Report
  Round Tables (Listed under the following titles)
    American Library History Round Table
    Exhibits Round Table
    Federal Librarians Round Table
    Government Documents Round Table
    Intellectual Freedom Round Table
    International Relations Round Table
    Junior Members Round Table
    Library Research Round Table
    Social Responsibilities Round Table
    Staff Organization Round Table
American Library History, 19, 20 (also 76 ed.)
American Library History Round Table, XVIII, 20 (also 76 ed.)
American Library Society, 20-22 (also 76 ed.)
American Library Trustees Association (ALTA), 22, 23, 259, 321 (also 76 ed.)
American National Red Cross, 228
American National Standards Institute committees, 164, 228, 229, 303, 312, 313
American Newspaper Publishers Association, 271
American Political Science Association archives, 140
American School Counselor Association, 229
American Society for Industrial Security (AUIS.) 299
American Society for Information Science (ASIS), 23, 24 (also 76 ed.)
American Theological Library Association (ATLA), 24-26 (also 76 ed.)
American Vocational Association, 229
AMIGOS, 218, 225
Amos, Virginia, 124
Anable, Richard 301
Anderl, Robert G., 386, 387
Anders, Mary Edna, XXXI, 283
Anderson, Florence, 49, **53,** 104
Anderson, Herschel V., 404
Anderson, Jim, 381
Anderson, John F., 285
Anderson, Joseph J., 315 (photo)
Anderson, Le Moyne W., 30
Anderson, Mary Jane, 87, 89, 174, 179, 231, 266 (photo)
Anderson, Susan, 374
Anderson, Thomas P., 215
Anderton, Ray, 355
Andrew W. Mellon Foundation, 3, 32
Andrews, Charles, 7
Anglo-American Cataloging Rules, 26, 179, 275, 290, 303 (also 76 ed.)
  London usage, 344
  revision, 78, 79
ANSI: See American National Standards Institute committees; Standards
Anspaugh, Sheryl, 396
Appalachian people, library services for, 112, 187, 199
Arbitration: See Mediation, Arbitration, and Inquiry
Architectural Strategy for Change, An, 266
Architecture: See Buildings

419

Archives, 27, 28 (also 76 ed.)
  copyright issue, 325, 326
  gifts, 140, 141
  London report, 342
  music collections, 275
  Register of Lost or Stolen Archival Materials, 298
  research, access to, 30, 31
  Security Project, 298, 299
  Society of American Archivists, 28, 236
Area Library Service Authority (ALSA), 367
Arizona report, 187, 184, 351, 352
Arkansas report, 352, 353
Armed Forces Libraries, 28, 29 (also 76 ed.)
  John Cotton Dana Awards, 45
  Librarians Achievement Citation, 42
Armstrong, William, 372
Army libraries: See Armed Forces Libraries
ARPANET, XXXVII
Arson: See Fires, loss from

Arundel, Anne, 375, 376
Ash, Lee, 311
Asheim, Lester, 45, **53**, 116, 192, 393
Ashley, Patrick, 311
Asian Americans and libraries, 118
  Asian American Librarian Caucus (AALC), 118
  Association for Asian Studies, 229
  Chinese research materials, 34
  Japan exhibit, 118 (photo)
  librarians, 238
  library services, current, 112, 304, 305, 361
  See also 76 ed.
ASLA Report on Interlibrary Cooperation, 35
Asp, William G., 379
Association for Asian Studies, 229
Association for Childhood Education International, 229
Association for Educational Communications and Technology, 212, 229
Association of American Colleges, 229, 230
Association of American Library Schools (AALS), XXXIX, 112, 113, 230
Association of American Publishers (AAP), 67, 171, 230, 267-269
Association of American University Presses, 176
Association of College and Research Libraries (ACRL), 30-33 (also 76 ed.)
  College and Research Libraries, XXI, 20, 264
  community colleges, 179
  salary survey, 237, 328
  standards committee work, 312
Association of International Libraries, 230
Association of Jewish Libraries, 122
Association of Media Producers, 130
Association of Recorded Sound Collections (ARSC), 275
Association of Research Libraries, 33, 34 (also 76 ed.)
  Annual Salary Survey, 288
  Canadian members, 335
  collection analysis, 1, 92
  management studies, 4, 241, 287
  national periodicals library, 301, 302
Association of State Library Agencies (ASLA), 34-36, 148 (also 76 ed.)
Associations: See Organizations and Associations
Astbury, Effie, 338, 339
Astbury, Eva, 345
Atherton, Pauline, 279
Atkinson, Hugh, 7
Atkinson, Joan, 330
Atlantic Provinces Library Association, 230
Aubry, Claude, 339, 340
Aucoin, Sharilynn, 372
Audiovisual media
  ANSI committee, 228
  PLA committee, 127-129
  See also Films; Filmstrips; Multimedia Materials; Realia; Recordings, Sound; School Libraries and Media Centers; Television in libraries
Augustus Long Health Sciences Library, 205 (photo)
Austin, Derek, 175
Australian Council on Awards, XLII
Australian library schools, XXXIX-XLIII
Automation, 37-41 (also 76 ed.)
  academic libraries, 4, 279
  Canada, 335
  circulation systems, 90-92
  London report, 342
  micrographics used with, 207
  See also Circulation Systems; Information Science and Automation Division
Avedon, Don M., 215, 229
Avram, Henriette, 37, 125, 165, 194, 235, 314
Awards and Prizes, 42-49 (also 76 ed.)
  ALA, 42-46
  Centennial Citations, 49, 104
  bibliographic aids, 186
  buildings, 190, 258
  Canadian recipients, 335, 336
  children's literature, 87-89, 174
  classification research, 175
  conference attendance, 182, 192
  documents, 143
  films, 127-129
  information science, 24, 162
  intellectual freedom, 167, 172
  library education, 192, 197
  reference specialist, 277
  school library programs, 19
  special libraries, 310
  technical services, 291
  See also specific names of awards and recipients and state reports
Aylwin, Louise, 335

Babbitt, Natalie, 80
Bacher, Pamela, 301
Bader, Barbara, 87
Baer, Mark H. **53**, **54**, 310, 311
Baker, Augusta, 174, 231 (also Biographies 76 ed.)
Baker, Dale Burdette: See Biographies 76 ed.
Baker, Eleanor, 355
Baker, Harold E., 173
Baker, Philip, 18
Baker and Taylor, 298
Balkema, John, 235
Ball, Joyce, 386
BALLOTS, 40, 219
Bancroft Prizes, 46
Bandolin, Patti, 356
Banks, O. Gordon, 215
Banks, Paul, 245, 248
Bar-coded labels, 4, 40, 91
Barber, Lynn, 1
Barber, Peggy, 125
Barbour, Helen, 247 (photo)
BARC: See Bay Area Reference Center
Barnett, Beth, 372
Barron, Margaret, 107
Barrow Preservation Research, Inc., 140, 247
Baskin, Barbara, 266
Bassett, Wayne R., 416
Bates, Mary L., 282
Batsel, John D., 25
Batty, C. David, 37
Bauer, Mary B., 236
Baughman, James C., 45, 198, 289
Bay Area Reference Center (BARC), 218, 278, 279, 353
Beach, Cecil, 334, 360
Beattie, James L., 33
Beatty, Samuel, 23 (photo), 24
Beaumont, Dennis, 37
Beckman, Margaret, 25
Bell, Shelah A., 407
Bell and Howell, 140
Bellow, Saul, 122
Bender, Betty, 415
Bender, David R., 19
Benson, Nettie Lee, 33
Bequests: See Gifts, Bequests, and Endowments
Bergen, Dan, 401
Berman, Sanford, 43, 197, 305
Berolzheimer, Hobart, 318
Bessie, Simon Michael, 268
Best Books for Young Adults 1975, 266, 334
Best of the Best, The, 1960-1974, 266, 334
Besterman Medal, 46
Bestseller lists, 261, 268
Beta Phi Mu,, 42, 50, 116, 169, 192
Bettelheim, Bruno, 87
Bibliographic aids and services
  Anglo-American Cataloguing Rules, 26
  ANSI standards, 312, 313
  Bibliographic Center for Research (BCR), 40, 172, 218, 255
  Bibliographic Retrieval Service (BRS), 38, 108
  British Library, XXVIII, XXIX
  data-base reference service, 109, 161
  indexing and abstracting services, 158
  instruction, 3, 30
  International Standard Bibliographic Description, 153, 290, 324, 344
  serials, 37
  technical reports, 215
  terms defined, 218, 219
  See also Cataloging and Classification; Data Bases; Indexing and Abstracting Services; Networks
Bibliographic Automation of Large Library Operations Using a Time-Sharing System: See BALLOTS
Bibliographic control
  AECT project, 212, 213
  bibliographies published, 50, 51
  CoCoNaBiC, 212
  international work, 153, 314
  national network, 219
  nonbook materials, 209
  Universal Bibliographic Control, 79, 153, 323, 324
Bibliography and Indexes, 50, 51 (also 76 ed.)
  See also Indexing and Abstracting Services
Bibliography of Agriculture, 110
Biblioteca Apostolica Vaticana, 248
Biblioteca Nacionale, Spain, 248
Biblioteca Nazionale Centrale, Italy, 249
Bibliotheque Nationale, 249, 301
Bibliotheque Royale Albert I, Belgium, 249
Biblo, Mary, 307
BIBNET, 41
Bice, Clare, 339
Bicentennial, U.S., 27
  bookmobile, 94
  Chicago Public Library series, 259
  children's services, 83
  Library of Congress, 196
  "76 United Statesiana," 34
Biddle, Stanton, 120, 360
Bidlack, Russell E., 10, 237, 328
Big Brothers of America, 230
Bilingual projects, 106, 111, 304, 361
Binder, Lucia, 174
Binding, 52
  Book Testing Laboratory, 52, 247
  independent research library statistics, 155
  See also Preservation of Library Materials
Bingham, Rebecca T., 292
Biographies, 53-65 (also 76 ed.)
  Canadian report, 339
  London report, 342, 343
  Biographies, young adult, 333
Birmingham International Education Film Festival, 4th, 129
Blackman, Nathaniel, 334
Blacks and libraries, 118-120 (also 76 ed.)
  Black Caucus, ALA, 119, 307
  film series, 189
  librarians, 6, 119, 120, 238
  projects, current, 305
  See also Discrimination; Ethnic Groups, Library Service to
Blake, Dorothy W., 18
Blake, Fay, 306
Blake, Joseph, 229
Blanco, Hugo, 170
Blatt, Burton, 147
Blind and Physically Handicapped, Library Service for the, 66 (also 76 ed.)
  Canadian services, 338, 339
  London report, 348
  LSCA funding, 186, 187
  National Accreditation Council, 234
  outreach programs, 84, 94
  services, 145-148, 257, 280, 334, 360
  vocational rehabilitation, 310
  See also Health and Rehabilitative Library Services
Blue, Garth, 335
Blum, Fred, 229
Blundon, Nancy L., 399
Board of Education for Librarianship: See Committee on Accreditation
Bobinski, George, XVIII, XX, 20, 266 (photo)
Bobker, Lee, 169
Bock, Joleen, 6
Bødker, Cecil, 88, 174
Bohmrich, Elizabeth S., 416
Bokum, Fanny, 135 (photo)
Bolles, Charles, 369
Bolles, John S., 70, 190
Bond issues, 263
Bone, Larry Earl, 15
Bonfili, Barbara, 415
Book and Periodical Development Council, 336
Book card, 90
Book Industry Study Group, 13, 267, 288, 289
Book Manufacturing Loading/Capacity Study, 289
Book Mark system, 297, 299
Book Testing Laboratory, 50, 247

Book Week, 80, 176
Bookbird, 174
Booker Prize for Fiction, 46
Booklist, 89, 263, 264, 267
Bookmobile: See Community Delivery Service; See also 76 ed.
Books for Religious Education, 79
Bookselling, 67, 68
  ALA publishing, 263, 266, 267
  bestseller lists, 261, 268
  binding, 52
  photocopying issue, 101
  "problem" novels, 331
  purchase statistic, 270
  reviews, 261, 263
  See also Awards and Prizes; Children's Literature; Paperbacks; Publishing, books; Young Adult Literature
Boorstin, Daniel J., XV, XVIII, 19, 37, 153, 192, 260, 262, 360
  photos, XVIII, 195
  See also Biographies 76 ed.
Booth, Barry E., 235, 260
Borden, Gail, 43
Born, Gerald, 259
Bostian, Irma R., 36, 264
Boston Globe–Horn Book Awards, 46
Boucher, Virginia, 277, 281, 355
Boutwell, Wendell, 203, 204
Bowen, Judith, 157
Bowron, Albert, 340
Boys Clubs of America, 230
Bracewell, R. Grant, 25
Brademas, John, 183
Bradley, Lynne, 165
Braille books, 66
Branch libraries, 93
Bratislava International Biennial (BIB) of Illustrations, 46, 47
Braverman, Charles, 126
Brawley, Paul, 264
Breland, June, 381
Bridgegam, Willis, 32
Bridges, Sue Ellen, 331, 332 (photo)
Brinberg, Herbert R., 161
British Library, XXII-XXX, 249, 252
British Library Act, XXV, XXX
British Library and Information Science Abstracts (LISA), 108
British Library Lending Division, 217, 252
British library services: See London report
British Museum Library, XXIII, XXIV
British National Bibliography, XXIII, XXVI
British Traditional Trade Agreement, 268
Brittle pages, 247, 248
Broadside (TLA), 318
Bro-dart, 41, 90
Brooker, Valarie, 330
Brookhart, Robert, 27
Brothers, Cassie, 353
Brown, Barbara J., 277
Brown, Eloise, 234
Brown, Margaret, 376
Brown, Norman B., 300
Brown, Russell, 342, 343
Brownridge, Ina C., 7
Brudage, Avery, 140, 141
Bryant, Jack W., 298, 358
Bryum, Jr., John D., 179
Buck, Richard M., 318
Budgeting, Accounting, and Cost Bostian, 68, 69 (also 76 ed.)
  academic library trouble, 1, 32, 68
  adults, services for, 14
  British Library, XXVI
  Canadian library expenditures, 339
  children's services, 84
  federal appropriations: See Federal funding for libraries
  fees: See Fees, use of
  Independent Research Libraries, 155 (table)
  journal prices, 93
  periodicals and serials, 300
  public library total, 131, 190, 253, 254
  state library agency survey, 35, 36
Budington, William S., 154
Buildings, 69-76 (also 76 ed.)
  academic libraries, 6
  grants, 133, 327
  insurance, 166
  LAD projects, 190, 191
  Library Buildings Award Program, 45
  local projects, 185
  London report, 343
  LSCA funding, 187
  public libraries, 258
  state libraries, 315
  See also Furniture and Equipment; specific state reports
Buildings and Equipment Section (LAD), 72, 73, 75, 190
Bulletin Board, 307
Bunnell, William I., 389
Burdick, Gayle, 368
Bureau of Indian Affairs (BIA), 123
Burgis, Grover, 37, 339
Burk, Leslie, 165
Burke, Jane, 125
Burkhardt, Frederick Henry: See Biographies 76 ed., 368
Burns, Jr., Robert W., 289
Burroughs, Jr., John J., 42
Butcher, Dina, 393
Buttars, Gerald A., 409, 410
Byrum, John, 290, 291

Cabello-Argandona, Roberto, 238, 280
Cable, Mary, 89
Cable TV: See Telecommunications and Public Broadcasting; Television in libraries
Cace, Elga, 230
Cade, Barbara C., 361
Cady, Susan, 366
CAIN (Cataloging and Indexing) 210
Calabrese, Richard, 147, 225, 366
Caldecott awards: See Randolph J. Caldecott awards
Calder, John, 347
Caldwell, Margaret, 401
California Library Authority for Systems and Service (CLASS), 2, 173, 185, 218, 309, 354
California report, 185, 278, 279, 353-355
CALL, 197
Cameron, Donald F., 5
Campbell, Henry C., 336
Campion Award, 47
Canadian Association of Music Libraries, 231
Canadian Institute for Scientific and Technical Information, 139
Canadian Library Association, XXXIX, XLIII, 76-78 (also 76 ed.)
  Book of the Year for Children Medal, 47
Canadian report and activities, 335-341 (also 76 ed.)
  Centre for Research in Librarianship, 288
  children's literature awards, 88
  library schools and accreditation, XXXIX-XLIII, 7, 10
  newspaper statistics, 271
CANCERPROJ, 214
Canelas, Dale, 189
Capital Consortium Network (CAPCON), 359
CAPTAIN, 40
Card catalog: See Cataloging and Classification
Carey-Thomas Award, 47
Carnegie awards, 47, 88
Carnegie Corporation Library Programs, 53
Carnovsky, Leon: See Obituaries 76 ed.
Carpenter, Ray L., 237, 328
Carpio, Virginia, 330
Carrasco, Alys, 42
Carroll, F. Laverne, 181
Carroll, Hardy, 7
Carter, George Arthur, 343
Carter, Jimmy, 27, 106, 319 (photo), 327
Carter, John M., 171
Carter, John W.: See Obituaries 76 ed.
Carter, Lauren D., 353
Carter, G. Woodson Book Award, 47
Carter G. Woodson Regional Library, 208, 209
Case Western Reserve Libraries, 246
Casellas, Elizabeth, 373
Casey, Genevieve, 260
Cassata, Mary B., 390
Cassettes, 130, 140, 316
Cataloging and Classification, 78, 79 (also 76 ed.)
  British Library, XXVI
  Canada, 336
  card catalogs, 3, 78, 139
  Catalog Code Revision Committee (RTSD), 26, 179
  Cataloging and Indexing (CAIN), 210
  Cataloging Distribution Service (CDS), 78
  Cataloging in Publication (CIP) program, 78
  ethics statement, 21
  international activities, 179, 194
  London report, 344
  processing centers, 252, 253
  sound recordings, 275
  theological libraries, 25
  See also Anglo-American Cataloging Rules; National Union Catalog
Catholic Library Association (CLA), 79. 80 (also 76 ed.)
Catholic University, 188, 360
Catlett, Patricia, 373
Caywood, Gladys R., 413
Cazort, Jane, 353
Censorship: See Intellectual Freedom
Centennial, ALA: See American Library Association
Centennial Citations, ALA, 49, 104
Center for Documentation and Communication Research, 63
Center for Research Libraries, xxviii, 1, 217, 301, 302
Centre for Research in Librarianship (Toronto), 288
Century of Service, A, 266
Certification Model for Professional School Media Personnel, 17, 19
Certification programs, 201, 244, 293
Challenge-grant program, 326, 327
Chambers, Brad, 307
Chang, Roy, 118
Chaplan, Margaret, 5
Charges, library: See Fees, use of
Charles Scribner's Sons Award, 42
Check-A-Book system, 39
Checkpoint Plessey, 39
Checkpoint Systems, 139 (photo), 297-299
Cheda, Sherrill, 341
Chelton, Mary Kay, 330, 331, 334
Cheney, Frances Neel, **54**, 62, 407
Chibnall, Bernard, 344
Chicago Academic Library Council, 2
Chicago Public Library, 15, 135, 208, 209, 249
Chief Officers of State Library Agencies (COSLA), 36, 231, 315
Child Study Association of America/Wel-Met, Inc., 47, 231
Children's Book Council (CBC) 80-82 (also 76 ed.)
  Book Week, 80, 176
  gift certificates, 86
  IBBY, 173, 174
  poetry program 87
  Showcase, 80, 82
Children's Book Week: See Children's Book Council
Children's Library Services 82-86 (also 76 ed.)
  ALA books, 266
  book awards, 174
  early training program, 306
  exceptional, services for, 145-147, 295
  realia, use of, 274
  toys and games, 319
  See also Films, Children's; School Libraries and Media Centers
Children's Literature, 86-88 (also 76 ed.)
  awards and prizes, 87-88, 174
  Canada, 336, 337, 340
  London report, 344, 345
  notable books, 82, 266
  See also International Board on Books for Youth; Young Adult Literature
Children's Services Division (CSD), XXI, 88, 89 (also 76 ed.)
  children's films, 128
  international activities, 173, 174, 179
Children's Television Workshop, 189
Children's Theatre Association of America, 231
Chinese, services for: See Asian-Americans and Libraries
Chisholm, Margaret, 293 (See also Biographies 76 ed.)
Choice magazine, 30, 32, 264, 267
Choncoff, Mary, 351
Christian Gauss Award, 47
Chun, Mae, 362
Church of Jesus Christ of Latter-day Saints, 410, 411
Churchwell, Charles D., 10, 195 (photo)
Cincinnati Electronics Corporation, 91, 92
CINE (Council on International Non-Theatrical Events), 129
Circulation Systems 90-92 (also 76 ed.)
  automation, 39-41
  bar-encoded labels, 4, 40, 91
  See also Automation; Information Science and Automation Division
CIRT (Career Interests Region Two), 187
Citizen Advice Bureau, 159
City University of New York (CUNY), 1
Civil liberties issues, 169, 227, 228, 239, 245
CL Systems Incorporated, 41
Clark, Mary E., XX (photo)
Clark, Robert L., 315, 396

421

CLASS: See California Library Authority for Systems and Service
Clausman, Gilbert J., 206
Cleland, Margaret, 165
CLENE (Continuing Library Education Network and Exchange), 95-97, 112-114, 116, 211, 212, 231, 232, 241, 315
Cleveland Area Metropolitan Library System (CAMLS), 172
Clift, David H., XV
Cline, Nancy, 143
Clough, Elaine, 279
CLSI system, 39, 41
Cluff, E. Dale, 409
Coalition for Children and Youth, 231
Coalition of Adult Education Organizations, 231
Coco, Alfred J., 17
Co Co Na Bi C, 212
Code of Ethics Committee, 116
Cody, Wilmer, 18, 19, 42, 292, 349
Coe, Rev. Chalmers, 21
Cole, Fred Carrington, 54, 104
Cole, John Y., XX
Coleman, Jean, 118
Collection Development, 92 93, (also 76 ed.)
　academic libraries, 30, 31
　AIA-ALA awards, 75
　British Library, XXVI, XXVII
　British Museum Library, XXIII
　Canadian holdings, 339
　Judaica research, 121, 122
　Library of Congress, 196
　music, 275
　principal libraries of the world, 248-252
　Slavic, 124
　See also Acquisitions; Gifts, Bequests, Endowments
Collective bargaining: See Unions, library
College and Research Libraries (ACRL), XXI, 20, 264
College Level Examination Program (CLEP), 199, 209
College libraries: See Academic libraries; Association of College and Research Libraries
Collins, Mary Frances, 31, 264
Colorado Report, 355
COLT: See Council on Library Technical Assistants
Columbia University Libraries, 249
COM process, 3, 78, 207, 214, 215, 255, 336
COMARC, 38, 194
Committee for Archives and Research Libraries in Jewish Studies, 122
Committee on Accreditation (COA), XXXIX, XLII, 7-11, 112
Committee on Education for Health and Rehabilitation, 192
Committee on Professional Ethics, 117
Committee on Staff Development, 241, 242
Committee on the Coordination of National Bibliographic Control (CoCoNaBiC), 212
Communications Act, 188, 316, 317
Communications satellite, XXXVI, XXXVIII, 317
Community Antenna Television (CATV), XXXVI
Community Delivery Service, 93-95
　bookmobiles, 93, 94 and 183 (photos), 304
Community Education and Consumers Education, 112
Comprehensive Employment Training Act, 68, 185

Computer Library Service, Inc., 91
Computer Output Microfilm: See COM process
Computer-Readable Bibliographic Data Bases sourcebook, 109, 110
Computers, library use of
　ANSI committee, 228
　British Library, XXIX
　circulation systems, 91, 92
　copyright issue, 97, 98
　data interchange, 164
　mini-computer systems, 255, 256
　NCLIS coordination efforts, 212
　on-line terminals, 3, 4, 107-110, 120, 160-162
　See also Data Bases, Computer Readable
Comsat General, 317
CONACYT, 225, 226
Concepción, Luis, 307
Concerned Librarians Opposing Unprofessional Trends (CLOUT), 201, 244, 354
Conferences: See State report articles
Congressional papers: See Documents, government
Congressional Research Service, 194, 195
Conley, Binford, 359
Conmy, Peter T., XX
Connecticut College Library, 6 (photo)
Connecticut report, 315, 355-357
Conners, Richard J., 215
CONSER: See Conversion of Serials project
Conservation administration, 245-248
"Consortium," defined, 219
Consortium for Public Library Innovation, 156, 157
Consortium of Universities of the Metropolitan Area, 359
Constance Lindsay Skinner Award 47, 61, 63, 237
Construction: See Buildings
Consumer Communications Reform Act, 316
Continuing Education for Library Staffs in the Southwest (CELS), 283, 284
Continuing Library Education Network and Exchange: See CLENE
Continuing Professional Education, 95-97 (also 76 ed.)
　Adult Education Association, 226, 227
　Canada, 337
　CLENE, role of, 211-213
　data-base use, 110
　information science course, 23
　law librarians, 16
　literacy programs, 199
　media specialists, 293
　MPLA program, 281
　satellite-based network, 317
　staff development, 241-243
　state library agencies, 315
　SWLA project, 283, 284
　See also CLENE; Education, Library; Personnel and Employment
Control Data Corporation, 107
CONTU (National Commission on New Technological Uses of Copyrighted Works), 97, 98, 193, 194 (also 76 ed.)
　CONTU Guidelines, 99-104
　information products, 163
　See also Copyright
Conversion of Serials (CONSER) project, 37, 194, 211, 212, 269, 270, 300-303
　See also Automation; Serials

Cooke, Eileen, 177, 232, 237, 265
Cooke, Michael, 181
Cooley, Marguerite B., 315 (photo), 351, 352
Coons, Daniel, 357
Cooper, Alene, 384
Cooper, Michael, 38
Cooper, Susan, 45, **55**, 87, 89
"Cooperative," defined, 219
Cooperative Information Network (CIN), 242
Cooperative Library Systems: See Interlibrary Cooperation
Copernicus Award, 47
Copyright, 13, 98-104, 325, 326 (also 76 ed.)
　academic libraries, effect on, 6,7
　adult services, 14
　American Association of Law Libraries, 16
　automation applications, 41
　collection development, 93
　GODORT, 143
　implementation, 268
　information products, 163
　interlibrary copies, 184
　Library of Congress, 193, 194
　London report, 345, 347
　medical libraries, effect on, 204, 205
　photocopying, study of, 213
　Register of Copyrights, 193, 325
　school media centers, 295, 296
　special libraries, 309
　videotape copying, 316
　Wainwright v. Wall Street Transcripts 198
　See also CONTU; Fair use issue
Corbett, Elizabeth M., XX
Corcoran, Barbara, 331
Coretta Scott King Award, 47
Cornell, Fred, 343
Cornell University Libraries, 249
Corporate Headings (Verona), 44, 79, 291, 324
Corporation for Public Broadcasting, 232, 316, 317
Correctional facilities, service to, 16, 106, 146-148, 186, 304
　American Correctional Association, 228
　women in Canada, 341
　YA programs, 334
COSLA: See Chief Officers of State Libbrary Agencies
Cossar, Bruce, 78
Cost control: See Budgeting, Accounting, and Cost Control
Coughlan, Margaret, 89
Coughlin, Caroline, 265
Council, ALA, 104-106 (also 76 ed.)
Council of National Library Associations (CNLA), 232
Council of Specialized Accrediting Agencies, 232
Council on Library Resources, 4-6, 132-134, 241
　Cole, Fred, 54
　CONSER project, 38, 301
　See also Federal funding; Foundations and Funding Agencies
Council on Library Technical Assistants (COLT), 106, 107, 113, 201, 244
Council on National Academic Awards, XL, XLI
Council on Postsecondary Accreditation (COPA), XXXIX, 8, 232
Council Resolutions Committee, 105
Covert, Nadine, 127 (photo)
Cox, Carl Raymond, **221**
Cox, Carl Thomas, 116, **221**, 407
Cox, James C., 80
Coyne, John, 364

Cranford, Chrys A., 392
Craven, Robin, 318
Cretsos, James M., 24
Crockett, Ethel S., 353
Crowley, John, 31
Csaky, Susan D., 371
Culbertson, Katheryn C., 406
Culkin, John, 127
Cummings, Mozelle, 349
Curran, Donald C., 193
Curtis, Ford E., 318
Curtis, Robert, 331
Curtiss, Margery, 385
Custer, Arline (Kern): See Obituaries 76 ed.
Custer, Benjamin, 290
Cutter, Charles Ammi, 78
Cylke, F. Kurt, 360

Dahm, Helmut, 28
Daily, Jay E., 21
Dain, Phyllis, 197, 289
Dainton, Sir Frederick, 345
Dale, Doris C., XVIII, XXI
Dalton, Jack, XXXI, 179
Damaged books, treatment of, 247
Daniel Boone Regional Library, 94
Darling, Pamela, 248
Darling, Richard, 237, 243, 244, 328
Dartmouth College, 207
Dartmouth Medal Award, 42, 277
Data Bases, Computer Readable, 107-110 (also 76 ed.)
　academic libraries, 3
　agricultural, 210
　biomedical, 205
　copyright issue, 97, 98
　indexing and abstracting services, 158
　international, 161
　Library of Congress, 37, 38
　medical, 214
　on-line reference services, 160, 161
　serials, 300
　technical information, 215
　update service, 23
　See also specific names of data bases; Networks
Data Gathering and Instructional Manual for Performance Measures in Public Libraries, A, 200, 202
Daume, Mary, 124
David H. Clift Scholarship, 42, 192
Davies, William, 346
Davis, Benita, 374
Davis, Charles, 37, 338, 339
Davis, Donald, 20
Davis, George, 298
Davis, Malcolm, 186
Davis, Russell L., 409
Day, Melvin, 23 (photo), 24, **55**
Day Care and Child Development Council, 232
Dayton, Donald, 25
Deacidification process, 247, 248
Deaf, urban services to, 257, 280, 359
Dean, Frances C., 19
De Chantal, Jean, 339
De Gennaro, Richard: See Biographies 76 ed.
Degrees, library education, 10, 113, 115, 241, 285
　Australia, Canada, and Great Britain, XXXIX-XLIII
　doctoral degrees awarded, 285
　minority graduates, 238
Deininger, Dorothy, 114
Delaware report, 357, 358
Dell, Richard F., 342
Delougaz, Nathalie, 179
De Marco, Michael C., 121
Demit, Patricia A., 376
Dempsey, Frank, 364
Denis, Laurent, 340

Dennis, Willye, 119
de Paola, Ron, 121
DePew, John, 241
Deposit stations, 95
Depository Library System: *See* Government Publications and Depository System
De Prospo, Ernest, 156, 202, 357
Dessauer, John P., 13, 289
Deterioration: *See* Preservation of Library Materials
Detroit Public Library, 68, 184, 185, 305
Detweiler, Mary Jo, 359
Deuss, Jean, 308
Deutsche Staatsbibliothek, 249
De Wath, Nancy, 38
Dewey, Melvil XVIII, XIX
Dewey's Decimal Classification, XVIII, 78
Dial-a-story services, 84
DIALIB project, 38
DiBenedetto, Guy, 353
Dickerson, G. Fay, 25
Dickinson, Donald C., 351
Digger, Jeremy, 343
DIKTA, 66
Dillon, Leo and Diane, 46, **55, 56,** 87-89, 119
Di Mattia, Ernest, 125, 191, 357
Diodati, Carmine M., 121 (photo)
Disadvantaged, Library Service to, 110-112, (*also* 76 ed.)
 bookmobile usage, 93, 94, 183, 304
 Canadian programs, 338
 LSCA funding, 186, 187
 outreach, 84, 110-112, 186, 256, 258
 volunteers, usage of, 14, 15
 See also Blind and Physically Handicapped; Community Delivery Service
Disasters, 166, 298, 299, 363, 364, 408
Discographic control, 275
Discrimination issues, 237-239
 reverse, 238, 239, 245
 sex-bial issue: *See* Women, status of
 See also Black Americans and Libraries; Disadvantaged, Library Service to; Ethnic Groups
Distinguished Achievement Award, 47
Distinguished Library Service Award for School Administrators, 42
Distribution Conference, 127
District of Columbia report, 187, 358-360
Dix, William S.: *See Biographies 76 ed.*
DOBIS system, 335
Doctor's degree: *See* Degrees, library education
Documentation: *See* International Federation for Documentation
Documents, government
 access to, 280
 federal officials, 27, 141
 "format copyright," 163
 fulfillment services, 161
 Government Documents Round Table, 143
 historical interest, 27, 28, 140
 preservation: *See* Preservation of Library Materials
 presidential papers issue, 27, 140
 publications and depository system, 144, 145
 technical research, 215, 216
Documents to the People Award, 143, 264
Doerschuk, Jr., Ernest E., 399
Dolgikh, F. I., 28

Donald W. Kohlstedt award, 124, 125
Donato, Raffaele, 121
Donohue, Joseph C., 266
Donovan, David, 179
Dorothy Canfield Fisher Memorial Children's Book Award, 47
Douglas, Sam, 358
Douglas, William O.: *See Biographies 76 ed.*
Dowell, Virginia, 356
Dowlin, C. Edwin, 389
Downen, Thomas W., 234
Downs, Robert, 49, **56,** 116
Doyle, Nancy, 182, 264
Drake, Miriam, 367
Drew, Sally, 172
Drickamer, Jewel, 401, 402
Drive-in library services, 95
Drucker, Peter, 200
Dubberly, Ronald, 260
Duckworth, Avis, 315, 387
Dudley, Norman, 291
Duggan, Maryann, 37, 283
Dunbar, Claire F., 372
Dunkin, Paul Shaner: *See Obituaries 76 ed.*
Dunlap, Connie R., 32, 230
Duplica, Moya M., 147
Durkee, Douglas W., 411
Dutton, John E., 339
Duvall, Betty, 107
Dyson, Anne Jane, 373

Eagan, Andrea, 331 (photo)
Earnshaw, Donald C., 23
Eastman, Ann Heidbreder, 237
Eberhart, W. Lyle, 35, 231, 416, 417
Ebert, Eloise, 315, 397, 398
Echelman, Shirley, 308
Edelen, Joseph R., 282
Edelman, Henrik, 31, 46, 291
Edelman, Judith, 70, 190
Edgar Allen Poe Awards, 47
Edsall, Marian, 262, 307
Education, independent: *See* Independent Study in Public Libraries
Education, Library, 112 (*also* 76 ed.)
 AALS: *See* Association of American Library Schools
 awareness training, 105
 Beta Phi Mu, 50, 169
 bilingual needs, 106
 book publishing courses, 268, 269
 Canada, Great Britain, and Australia, XXXIX-XLIII, 335, 338
 data-base use, 110
 degrees: *See* Degrees, library education
 equivalency tests, 238, 244
 faculty salaries, 328, 329
 HEA funding, 188
 job market, 243-245
 London report, 345
 management training, 201
 media specialists, 293
 minority librarian survey, 237, 238
 national information system, 323
 public relations, 263
 social responsibility, 306
 SWLA program, 284
 See also Accreditation; Library Education Division; Standards
Education Amendments, 326
Education of All Handicapped Children Act (1975), 145, 295
Educational broadcasting: *See* Telecommunications and Public Broadcasting
Educational Broadcasting Facili-

ties and Telecommunications Act, 327
Educational Film Library Association, 126-128, 232
Egoff, Sheila, 336
Ehrhardt, Margaret W., 403
Ekstrom, Ann, 302
Elderly: *See* Older Adults, Library Service to
Eleanor Farjeon Award, 47
Elementary and Secondary Education Act (ESEA), 134, 184, 185
 Title IV-B, 169, 170, 187, 295, 326
 Title IV-C, 295
Ellenberger, Jack, 17, **56,** 186, 360
Ellis, Judith A., 368
Ely, Donald, 293
Emanuel, Shirley P., 210
Emerson, Katherine, 289
Emily Award, 127
Employment practices: *See* Personnel and Employment
Encyclopaedia Britannica Award, 355
Endowments: *See* Gifts, Bequests, and Endowments
Engen, Richard B., 350
Engineering Index (Ei), 215
Ensley, Robert, 147, 264
EPILEPSYLINE, 214
Epstein, Rheda, 182
Equal employment opportunity, 237-239
Equipment: *See* Furniture and Equipment
Erie County Public Library, 306
ESEA: *See* Elementary and Secondary Education Act
Estes, Glenn, 265
Esteves, Roberto, 166
Esther J. Piercy Award, 42, 291
Ethics 21, 116, 117 (*also* 76 ed.)
Ethnic Groups, Library Service to, 118-124 (*also* 76 ed.: Minorities, library service to)
 academic librarian survey, 288
 affirmative action, 237-239, 307
 exhibits, 305
 librarian salaries, 5
 library career training, 188, 281, 306, 309, 310
 LSCA funding, 186, 187
 reverse discrimination, 238, 239
 See also specific groups; Discrimination
Eunice Rockwell Oberly Memorial Award, 42
EURONET, 161
Evaluation: *See* Measurement and Evaluation
Evans, Beatrice M., 339
Everly, Joe, 125
Exceptional Service Award, 146, 147
Exhibit Newsletter (ERT), 264
Exhibits, 234, 305 (*See also* 76 ed.)
Exhibits Round Table, 124, 125 (*also* 76 ed.)
Exhibits Round Table Award, 45
Expenditures, library: *See* Budgeting, Accounting and Cost Control

Fadero, Joseph, 181
Faherty, Robert L., 265
Faibisoff, Sylvia, 172
Fair employment practices, 204
Fair Labor Standards Act, 245
"Fair use" issue, 13, 99, 101, 102, 168, 193, 325
Falsone, Anne Marie, 355
Fancher, 136
Fardell, Joyce, 181
Farley, Richard A., 125, 211
Fasana, Paul, 291, 303
Fast, Elizabeth T., 189, 294

FAUL (Five Associated University Libraries), 218
Faunce, Maria and Stephen, 225
Faust, Clarence Henry: *See Obituaries 76 ed.*
Fawcett, Ellen, 415
Federal agencies: *See specific names*
Federal Communications Commission, XXXVIII, 168, 299, 316
Federal Criminal Code, 169
Federal documents: *See* Documents, government
Federal funding for libraries
 agencies, 134
 archival projects, 28
 bookmobiles, 93
 building projects, 69, 73
 Canada, 76
 Comprehensive Employment Training Act, 68
 demonstration programs, 112
 DSI research program, 297
 effectiveness study, 213
 ESEA: *See* Elementary and Secondary Education Act
 Ford's administration, 12, 183
 HEA: *See* Higher Education Act
 independent learning, 157, 158
 independent research libraries, 154, 156
 legislation summary, 325-327
 Libraries and Learning Resources, Office of, 186-189
 library education, 114
 Lifelong Learning Centers, 257
 National Commission on Libraries and Information Science, 327
 National Endowment for the Humanities, 213, 214
 non-sex-biased materials, 169, 170
 public broadcasting, 316
 public works, 184
 research grants, 285-287
 revenue sharing, 184
 special education, 145
 trustees, role of, 321
 urban public libraries, 256
 See also Council on Library Resources; Financing the Public Library
Federal Librarians Round Table (FLIRT), 125 (*also* 76 ed.)
Federal libraries: *See* Armed Forces Libraries; Principal Libraries of the World; *also* 76 ed.
Federal Trade Commission, 186
Fees, use of, 3, 4, 14, 190, 191
 Canada, 337
 charging machines, 90
 communication networks, 108
 information access, 38
 medical libraries, 205
 photocopies, 102
 punchcards, 131 (photo)
 reference automation, 279
Fennell, Doris, 181
Fernandez-Ortiz, Arturo, 307
Ferrero, Mike, 330
FID: *See* International Federation for Documentation
Fiedler, Leslie, 270
Field Enterprises, 197
Filby, P. William, 263
Film Library Administration Institute, 127
Films, 125-128 (*also* 76 ed.)
 Canada, 337
 foreign agent issue, 168, 169
Films, Children's, 128, 129 (*also* 76 ed.)
 Educational Film Library Association, 232
 young adults, 334
Filmstrips, 130 (*also* 76 ed.)

423

Financial Assistance for Library Education, 192, 264
Financial support for Libraries: See Federal Funding for Libraries; Financing the Public Library; Foundations and Funding Agencies
Financing the Public Library, 130-132
Fineman, Charles S., 153
Finney, Lance C., 375
Fires, loss from, 166, 298, 299
First Amendment freedoms, 50, 167-171, 185, 272, 273
Fischer, Linda, 341
Fischer, Margaret T., 23 (photo), 24
Fiske, Marjorie, 85, 86
Fite, Alice E., 19, 132
Fitzgerald, John D., 282
Fitzgibbons, Shirley, 265
Fitzsimmons, Richard, 399
Fleming, June D., 353
Fleming, Lois D., 112
FLIRT Newsletter, 125, 264
Flood damage, 298
Flore, Robert, 314
Florida report, 360, 361
Folklife Center, 195
Fontaine, Everett O., **221**
Fontaine, Sue, 135, 261
Food and Nutrition Information and Educational Materials Center (FNIC), 210
Foote, Marcelle, 21, 366
Footnotes (JMRT) magazine, 264
Ford, Barbara, 307
Ford, Gerald R., 12, 13, 27, 98, 99, 106
   appropriations, 183, 184
   legislation, 245, 268, 325-327
   presidential papers, 140
Ford Foundation, 134
Foreign Agents Registration Act, 168, 169
Foskett, D. J., 323, 343
Foundation Center, 132
Foundations and Funding Agencies, 132-134 (also 76 ed.)
   See also Council on Library Resources; Federal funding; Gifts, Bequests, and Endowments
Fox, James, 261
Francis Joseph Campbell Citation, 42, 146, 148
Francis Parkman Prize, 47
Frankie, Suzanne, 33, 288
Franklin, Cathryne, 18
Franklin, Hardy R., 141 (photo), 304
Franklin, John Hope, XV (See also Biographies 76 ed.)
Franklin, Ralph, 37
Frantz, Jr., Ray, 34
Frarey, Carlyle, 116, **221, 222**
Fray, Florence M., 282
Frederic G. Melcher awards, 42, 47, 88
Freedman, Maurice, 79, 165
Freedom of Information Act: See Intellectual Freedom; See also 76 ed.
Freedom to Read Committee (AAP), 269
Freedom to Read Foundation, 134, 135, 172 (also 76 ed.)
Freeman, Bill, 335
Freiser, Leonard, 18, 293
"Friends of IBBY," 87, 174, 191
Friends of Libraries, 135, 136 (also 76 ed.)
Fritz, Jean, **56, 57,** 87, 89
Fruehauf, Esther, 198, 289
Fruehauf, Missi, 45
Fry, Bernard M., 1, 10, 93
Fulla, Ludovit, 88
Fuller, George, 372

Funding: See Federal Funding for Libraries; Foundations and Funding Agencies; Financing the Public Library
Funk, Jr., Charles, 356
Furniture and Equipment 136-140 (also 76 ed.)
   London report, 343
   See also Buildings
Fussler, Herman, XXXI, 46, **57**

Gaffner, Haines B., 161
Galler, Anne M., 339
Gallozzi, Charles, 42, 146, 148
Gallup Organization, Inc., 285, 287
Galvin, Thomas J., XIX (photo), 32, 191, 230, 267, 306
Gambee, Budd, 20
Games: See Toys and Games
Gardner, Charles, 385
Gardner, Richard, 32, 264
Garoogian, Rhoda, 279
Gauthier, Michelle, 339
Gavel Award, 47
Gaven, Patricia, 157, 198, 260
Gaver, Mary V., 49, **57, 58,** 116, 353
Gay liberation activities, 305, 307, 331
Gaylor, Robert G., 377, 378
Gaylord Company, 39, 90, 91, 139, 297-299
Geiser, Elizabeth A., 237
Gelb, Ignace J., 143
Gell, Marilyn, 359, 360
Geller, Evelyn, XX
Gendron, Michele, 42
Genealogical Library (Mormon), 410, 411
General Education Provisions Act, 170, 183
General Educational Development program, 209
General Nucleonics, 297
General Revenue Sharing, 131, 132
General Services Administration, 215, 216
Gentle Nudge project, 84, 319
George, Melvin R., 364
George Freedley Memorial Award, 317, 318
Georgia report, 131, 361, 362
Gesterfield, Kathryn, 364, 365
Giblin, James, 82
Gibson, Gerald D., 275
Gift certificates, book, 86
Gifts, Bequests, and Endowments, 140-143 (also 76 ed.)
   benefactor award, 22
   collection development, 92, 93
   endowment decline, 156
   Independent Research Libraries, 155 (chart)
   National Agricultural Library, 211
   national exchange centers, 13
   See also Acquisitions; Collection Development
Gilbert, Mrs. Benjamin D., 309 (photo)
Giles, Louise, 32, 120, **222,** 228
Gill, Sue, 107
Gilliland, Ernestine, 369
Girl Scout Materials, 89
Girls Clubs of America, 232
"Give-a-Book Certificates," 86
Givens, Johnnie, 283
Glasby, Dorothy, 282
Glazer, Fred, 262, 415
Gleason, Eliza Atkins, 120
Gleaves, Edwin S., XX
Glidden, Benjamin C., 355
GODART: See Government Documents Round Table
Godet, Marcel, 151, 152
Godfrey, Marywave, 265, 311
Golden Eagle Awards, 129
Goldstein, Samuel, 197

Golf, Karen, 415
Goodall, John, 80, 165
Goode, William J., 116, 117
Goodwin, Susan, 387
Gore, Daniel, 2
Gosling, Jean O., 6
Gosnell, Charles F., 166
Govan, James, XXXI
Government activities
   agencies: See specific names
   data bases, 109
   documents: See Documents, government
   funding: See Federal funding
   information industry, 161-164
   personnel legislation, 245
   telecommunications, XXXVIII
Government Advisory Committee on International Book and Library Programs (GAC), 176
Government Documents Round Table (GODORT), 143 (also 76 ed.)
Government Printing Office (GPO), 13, 144, 145, 207, 208, 310, 326
Government Publications and Depository System, 144, 145 (also 76 ed.)
   See also Documents, Government; Government Printing Office
Graham, C. R., 371
Graham, Earl C., 43, 146, 147
Graham, Robert, 18
Grants: See Foundations and Funding Agencies; Federal funding
Gration, Selby U., 305
Gray, Michael H., 275
Great Britain: See London Report; British entries
Green, Samuel S., 277, 280
Green, William, 318
Greenaway, Emerson, 49, **58,** 104
Greenaway Award, 88
Gresham, Frank, 406
Gribbin, John H., 7
Grierson Award, 127 (photo)
Griffin, Linda, 42, 192
Griffis, Joan, 18
Griffith, David W., 262 (photo)
Grimm, Rick, 333, 334
Grolier Foundation awards, 42, 43, 261
Grosch, Audrey N., 24
Gross, Richard F., 374
Gude, Gilbert, 195
Guest, Judith, 331
Guide to Reference Books, 263
Guidelines for Audio-Visual Materials and Services, 311
Guides for the Law Book Industry, 186
Gunlocke Chair Co., 136, 138
Guy, Rosa, 331
Gwyn, Trish, 274

Haeffely, Claude, 335
Hage, Elizabeth, 360
Hager, Georgie, 393
Hagler, Ronald, 282
Halbey, Hans, 87, 174
Haley, Alex, 118, 267, (photo), 331, 351
Hall, Mary A., 240
Hall, Vivian, 370
Hallowell, 136
Halsey, Richard Sweeney, 263, 275
Hamada, Miles, 118
Hamilton, Beth, XVI
Hajklton, Virginia, 174 (See also Biographies 76 ed.)
Hammer, Donald P., 136, 165, 191, 233
Hammond, Jane Laura: See Biographies 76 ed.

Hammond Incorporated Library Award, 43
Handicapped people: See Blind and Physically Handicapped, Library Service for the
Hanna, Alfreda, 396
Hanniball, August (Gus), 281
Hannigan, Jane Anne, 105, 191
Hans Christian Andersen Medal, 47, 88, 174, 179
Hansen, Andrew M., 23, 157, 231, 259, 260, 277
Hapeville Branch Library, Georgia, 74 (photo)
Harbeson, Eloise L., 360
Hardy, Constance, 339
Harkins, Arthur M., 36
Harlan, Donna B., 22
Harlan, John B., 22
Harmful Matters Statute, 134
Harris, Agnes, 372
Harris, Anita, 203, 204
Harris, Ira, 362
Harris, Karen H., 266
Harris, Michael H., XX
Harrison, Clement J., 335
Harry Kalven Freedom of Expression Award, 167
Hart, Patricia, 335
Hartray, Jr., John H., 70, 73, 190
Harvard Magazine, 269
Harvard University Library, 141, 249
Harvey, Bruce, 166
Harvey, John F., 264
Haskin, Susan M., 148
Haskins, Jim, 331
Haskins Medal, 48
Havard-Williams, Peter, 176
Haviland, Virginia, 43, **58, 59,** 174
Hawaii report, 362, 363
Hawken, William R., 208
Haycock, Ken, 78, 335
Haycraft, Howard, 49, **59,** 104
Hayden, Robert, 196
Hayes, Pheobe, 310
Haynes, Donald R., 413
Hays, Dick, 186
Hayton, Greg, 339
HEA: See Higher Education Act
Heald, Dorothy S., 229
Health and Rehabilitative Library Services, 145, 146, 192 (also 76 ed.)
   Exceptional Service Award, 43
Health and Rehabilitative Library Services Division, 146-148, 179, 225 (also 76 ed.)
Health sciences research, 96, 97
Hebert, A. Otis, 373
Hébert, Françoise, 339
Hefley, Sue, 372
Heidish, Marcy, 332 (photo)
Heiges, Mary, 379
Heilprin, Laurence B., 24
Heim, Peggy, 5
Heins, Paul, 179
Hellard, Ellen, 371
Helvestine, Mildred, 360
Hemingway, Mary, 135 (photo)
Henderson, Mary C., 318
Henderson, Mary E. P., 338, 339
Henderson, Robert M., 318
Heneghan, Mary A., 189
Henne, Frances, 49, **59,** 104
Hennessy, Graham, 348
Henríquez, Gladys, 307
Henry Z. Walck Publishers, Inc., 89
Herbert Baxter Adams Prize, 48
Herbert Putnam Honor Fund Award, 43
Herling, Eleanor B., 266
Hernández, Tomasita, 307
Hershman, Robert, 266 (photo)
Hess, James A., 22, 46
Hetherington, Jerre, 407

HEW appropriations bill, 183, 188
Heymann, Jaia, 264
Hickey, Doralyn, 24, 25
Hieber, Douglas M., 268
Higher Education Act (HEA), 134
  appropriations for, 12, 183, 186, 188, 326
  Title I-B, 157
  Title II-B, 114, 216, 285, 286
  Title II-C, 7, 34, 93, 154
Hightower, Monteria, 359
Hildebrand, Carol, 398
Hilles, Frederich W., 142
Hinds, Charles F., 370, 371
Hinshaw, Marilyn, 182
Hinton, Frances, 179
Historical records: See Archives; Documents, government
History: See American Library History; American Library History Round Table
Ho Leo C., 118
Hoadley, Irene B., 10
Hoagland, Sister Mary Arthur, 80
Hoffberg, Judith, 52
Hoffman, Alexander C., 102
Hoffman, Anne, 236
Hoffman, William J., 227
Hogemeyer, Alice, XIX (photo)
Hogrogrian, Nonny, 124
Holley, Edward G., XV, XVIII, XXI, 18, 20, 105, 353
  photos, XVII, XIX
  See also Biographies 76 ed.
Holliday, Ardis, 401
Hollis, Vida, 389
Holmes, Jeanne M., 211
Holt, Raymond M., 70, 189, 190, 191, 266
Home delivery: See Community Delivery Service
Hookway, Harry T., XXV (photo)
Hooper, Rea E., 140
Hoopes, Townsend, 268
Hope, Tom, 130
Hopkins, Joseph S., 376
Horn, Zoia, 106
Horrocks, Norman, 21
Houston Public Library, 255 (photo)
Howard-Gibbon Medal, 88
Howell, J. B., 283
Howells Medal, 48
Hoy, Christopher, 234
HRLSD Journal and *Newsletter*, 264
Hubbard, Joyce, 357
Hudak, Margaret B., 311
Huff, Margaret F., 403
Humnicky, Virginia, 367
Humphrey, John A., 314, 390
Hunsicker, Marya, 236
Hunt, Donald R., 7
Hunt, Mary Alice, 50
Hunter, Mollie: See *Biographies 76 ed.*
Hurlimann, Bettina, 174
Hurwitz, Neal H., 111
H. W. Wilson Company, 16, 43, 115, 191, 197, 261, 277
Hyde, Margaret, 331

I and R Services: See Information and Referral Centers
IASL Newsletter, 181
IBBY: See Friends of IBBY; International Board on Books for Young People
IBBY Honor Books, 174
Idaho report, 363, 364
IFLA (International Federation of Library Associations and Institutions), 148-153, 324 (*also 76 ed.*)
  ALA involvement, 176
  FID, 175
  IASL, 180, 181
IFRT Report 264

Ihrig, Alice, XIV, 18, 357, 367
ILLINET, 91, 216
Illinois Library and Information Network: See ILLINET
Illinois Minorities Manpower Project, 239
Illinois report, 364-366
  funding, 184, 185, 320
  multitype system, 172, 216
  Regional Library Council, 233
  State Library Agency, 242
Illuminating Engineers Society, 233
Immroth, John Phillip, 116, 172, **222, 223,** 400
InCoLSA, 218
Independent Libraries: See *76 ed.*
Independent Research Libraries, 153-156, 326
Independent Research Library Association, (IRLA) 154-156
Independent Study in Public Libraries, 156-158 (*also 76 ed.*)
  adult services, 15, 257, 258, 326
  Woodson Regional Library example, 208, 209
Index for Religious Periodical Literature, 25
Index to Foreign Periodicals, 16, 17
Indexing and Abstracting Services, 158 (*also 76 ed.*)
  CAIN (Cataloging and Indexing), 210
  Committee on Wilson Indexes, 277
  information industry, 160, 161
  PRECIS system, XXVII, 78, 175
  See also Bibliography and Indexes
Indian Library Services Technical Assistance Center, 123
Indiana Cooperative Library Services Authority (InCoLSA), 218
Indiana report, 366-368
Indiana State Library, 173
Indians: See American Indians and libraries
Individualized education: See Independent Study in Public Libraries
INFO/Speed, 161
Information and Referral Centers, 158-160, (*also 76 ed.*), 279
  AIRS, 112
  disadvantaged, services to, 111, 304
  public library examples, 256-258
  reference books, 266
Information Dynamics Cooperation, 41
Information Industry, 160-163
Information Science: See Automation; Circulation Systems; Data Bases; Networks; Processing Centers; Serials; Telecommunications
Information Science Abstracts, 108
Information Science and Automation Division (ISAD), 163-166 (*also 76 ed.*)
  telecommunications, 212
  See also American Society for Information Science; National Commission on Libraries and Information Science
Inovar Corporation, 41
Institute for Computer Sciences and Technology, 212
Institutionalized persons: See Correctional facilities, service to
Insurance for Libraries, 166, 190, 298 ,*also 76 ed.*.
Intellectual Freedom, 167-171,

369, (*also 76 ed.*)
  AASL committee, 19
  ALA Office for, 167, 170
  ALS involvement, 21
  Canada, 337
  children's materials, 17, 85, 296, 396
  ethics statement, 21
  Harmful Matters Statute, 134
  magazine cases, 270
  Newsletter, 264, 270
  school systems, 85, 86
  trustees, role of, 321, 322
  newspapers and the First Amendment, 272, 273
  See also First Amendment freedoms; Obscenity issues; Privacy, right to
Intellectual Freedom Committee, 168-172
Intellectual Freedom Round Table, 171, 172 (*also 76 ed.*)
Intergovernmental Council, 324
Interlibrary Communication Project (TWX), 367
Interlibrary Cooperation, 172, 173 (*also 76 ed.*)
  academic libraries, 1-3
  British Library, XXVIII, XXX
  Canadian report, 337
  children's libraries, 86
  fees, use of, 4
  international: See IFLA
  LSCA funds, 187, 326
  National Library Resource Centers, 217, 218
  networks, 216-219
  photocopying issue, 100, 101, 184, 193
  RAL file, 38
  state library agencies, 34, 35
  telecommunications, XXXIV
  USBE resource, 325
  See also Copyright; Networks
International Animation Film Festival, 129
International Association of School Librarianship, 180, 181, 233
International Board on Books for Young People (IBBY), 89, 173, 174, 179 (*also 76 ed.*)
International Children's Film Festival, 129
International Congress on Archives, 28
International Congress on National Bibliographies, 323
International Federation for Documentation (FID), 61, 174, 175, 228, 323 (*also 76 ed.*)
International Federation of Archival Associations, 28
International Federation of Library Associations and Institutions: See IFLA
International Lending, office for, 153
International libraries: See Principal Libraries of the World
International library activities
  Association of International Libraries, 230
  book publishing, 268
  cataloging, 290
  Government's Advisory Committee, 236
  IFLA, 148-153
  information industry, 161
  Library of Congress, 194
  Organization of American States, 225, 226, 246
  scientific and technical information, 297
  serials projects, 301
  special librarians, 310
  standards, 312-314
  See also UNESCO

International Organization for Standardization, 175
International Personnel Management Association, 233
International Reading Association Children's Book Award, 48
International Relations, 175-179 (*also 76 ed.*)
  intellectual freedom issues, 170
  MARC distribution service, 37
International Relations Round Table, 180 (*also 76 ed.*)
International School Librarianship, 180, 181
International Serials Data System, 300
International Standard Bibliographic Description (ISBD), 153, 290, 324, 344
International Standard Serial Number (ISSN), 301
International Standards Organization Technical Committee 46, 313, 314
International Telecommunications Union, 317
i/o Metrics Co., 316
Iowa report, 368, 369
Irita Van Doren Award, 167
Irizarry, Edison, 307
Isadore Gilbert Mudge Citation, 43, 277
Ishimoto, Carol, 32
Israel issue, 170, 177
Italian Americans and libraries, 120, 121 (See also *76 ed.*)
Izard, Anne, 84

J. Morris Jones World Book ALA Goals Award, 42, 197
Jabbour, Alan, 196, 275
Jackson, Adele M., 372
Jackson, Miles M., 50
Jackson, Sidney, XX, 266
Jackson, Wallace Van, 104, 119
Jacobs, Alma S., 384
Jacobs, Nina, 29
Jacobson, Gerald, 282
Jacques, Thomas F., 372, 373
Jails: See Correctional facilities, service in
James, Karen, 389
James A. Hamilton–Hospital Administrator's Award, 48
James Bennett Childs Award, 43, 143
James Russell Lowell Prize, 48
Janaske, Paul, 186
Jane Addams Children's Book Award, 48, 88
Janowski, Bronislaw "Mike," 372
Japanese: See Asian Americans and libraries
Jarvi, Edith, 337
Jay, Donald, 179
Jenkins, Carol, 398
Jenkins, Harold R., 382
Jensen, Kathleen, 339
Jewish Americans and libraries, 121-123
Jewish Book Council, 122
Jewish Caucus, ALA, 122 (See also *76 ed.*)
Jewish National and University Library, 250
Jimpie, Babetta, 19
JMRT 3M Company Professional Development Grant, 43
Joachim, Linda, 107
Jobline, 23
John Burroughs Medal, 48
John Cotton Dana Public Relations Awards, 43-45, 190, 191, 261, 262 (photo)
John Gilmary Shea Prize, 48
John Grierson Award, 127
John Newbery awards, 45, 87-89, 266

425

John Phillip Immroth Memorial Award, 172
John R. Rowe Memorial Award, 45
Johns, Jr., Claude J., 355
Johnson, Barbara Coe: See Biographies 76 ed.
Johnson, Christine M., 375
Johnson, Ferne, 89, 266
Johnson, Frosty, 350
Johnson, John, 107
Johnson, Leonard L., 392
Johnson, Lyle, 373, 381
Johnson, Margaret, 37
Johnson, Richard D., XXI, 32, 264
(See also Biographies 76 ed.)
Johnson, Robert, 352
Johnson, Stephen, 127 (photo), 305
Johnson, Wayne H., 418
Joint Council on Educational Telecommunications: See Telecommunications; See also 76 ed.
Joint Steering Committee for Revision of AACR (JSCAACR), 26
Jones, Catherine, 359
Jones, Clara Stanton, XVI-XVIII, XXXI, 95, 106, 119, 120, 259, 279, 281, 284, 307, 368
photos, XVII, XVIII, 195
See also Biographies 76 ed.
Jones, Cornelia, 266
Jones, Frances M., 311
Jones, Margaret, 311
Jones, Virginia Lacy, XXXI, 49, **59, 60,** 116, 119, 120
Jordan, Bea, 387
Joseph L. Andrews Bibliographical Award, 48, 186
Joseph W. Lippincott Award, 45
Josey, E. J., 266, 314
Journal Access Program, 302
Journal of Library Automation (JOLA), 164, 165, 264
Journal of Library History, 19, 20
Journals: See Library Press; Publishing, Magazine; Periodicals
Joyce, Charles, 376
Julien, Jane, 351
Junior Members Round Table, 181, 182 (also 76 ed.)
Jurgemeyer, Frederick H., XVIII
J. W. Lippincott Award, 116

Kadek, Sarah Thomas, 360
Kahn, Herman: See Obituaries 76 ed.
Kansas report, 369, 370
Kantor, Paul B., 202
Karp, Irwin, 102
Kaser, David, XVIII, 50
Kastenmeier, Robert, 99, 102, 103, 169
Kate Greenaway Award, 48
Katz, Linda, 265
Keaney, Kevin, 29, 125
Kegan, Elizabeth Hamer, 28, 193
Keller, Daniel, 127 (photo)
Keller, Richard, 127
Kellman, Amy, 84, 179
Kellogg Foundation, 40, 41
Kelm, Carol R., 230, 291
Kent, C. Deane, 339
Kent, George, 120 (photo)
Kentucky report, 292, 370, 371
Kerker, Ann E., **60,** 206
Kerr, M. E., 334
Kilgour, Frederick G.: See Biographies 76 ed.
Kimbrough, Joseph, 189
King, Geraldine, 265
King, Sandra, 349
Kipilii, Mary Lu T., 362
Kirkegaard, Preben: See Biographies 76 ed.
Kissinger, Henry A., 142
Kitchen, Paul, 78 (See also Biographies 76 ed.)

Klapper, Carla, 373
Klein, Fannie J., 186
Knight, Katherine, 362
Knight, Nancy H., 4, 267, 298
Knogo Corporation, 297, 299
Kobayashi, Vivian, 118
Kochen, Manfred, 197, 266, 289
Kochoff, Stephen, 135 (photo)
Kohlstedt Exhibit Award, 45
Konigsburg, E. L., 331
Kopischke, John L., 385
Krug, Judith, **60,** 167, 264
Krupsak, Mary Ann, 138
Kuhn, Warren B., 325
Kunitz, Stanley, 196
Kurelek, William, 335
Kurzweil Computer Products, 66
Kusche, Lawrence David: See Biographies 76 ed.
Kutz, Ruth, 334

Labor Groups, Library Service to, 182, 183, 277 (also 76 ed.)
See also Unions, library
La Comb, Denis J., 95
Lacy, Dan, XV, XVIII (See also Biographies 76 ed.)
LAD Newsletter, 264
Ladenson, Alex, 28, 298
Lake, Marilyn, 382
Lam, Errol, 118
Land, Brian, 76, 176 (See also Biographies 76 ed.)
Lane, Margaret T., 372
Lane, Robert, 264
Lane, Rodney, 365
Lathem, Edward C., 34
Latinos: See REFORMA; Spanish-Speaking People, library service to
Laughlin, Jeannine, 381
Laura Ingalls Wilder Medal, 45
Law and Legislation, 183-185 (also 76 ed.)
affirmative action, 238
copyright issues: See Copyright
FCC fairness doctrine, 168
films, 168, 169
gifts, deductions for, 93
health and rehabilitative services, 145, 146
independent learning, 157, 257
intellectual freedom issues, 169, 170
Libraries and Learning Resources, Office of, 186-189
library personnel decisions, 245
library security, 298, 299
London report, 345
magazine censorship, 270
medical libraries, 204
presidential papers, 27
press, freedom of the, 272, 273
public broadcasting, 316
public library financing, 130-132
reverse discrimination, 238, 239
school libraries and media centers, 19, 171, 294-296
summary, 325-327
See also: Federal funding for libraries; Washington Report; specific names of Acts; specific state reports
Law Libraries, 185, 186, 315, 328, (also 76 ed.)
Law Library Journal, 16, 17
Leach, Maurice, 413
Leader, Herbert, 176
LEADS (IRRT) magazine, 180, 264
Learmont, Carol, 237, 243, 244, 328
Learned Society Libraries: See Independent Research Libraries
LED Newsletter, 264
Ledoux, Majorie, 373
Lee, Mollie Houston, 120
Lee, Rohama, 127

Leek, Ruth, 311
Legislative activities, federal: See Law and Legislation; Washington Report
Le Guin, Ursula, 331
Leith, Marian, 315
Leo Baeck Institute, 122
Leonard, Charlotte, 395
Lepman, Jella, 173
Leroy C. Merritt Humanitarian Fund: See 76 ed.
Letsinger, Judith, 18
Levitin, Sonia, 331
Lewis, Ronald L., 339
Li, Tze Chung, 112, 118, 180
Librarians
Asian Americans, 118, 238
Black, 6, 119, 120, 238
ethics statement, 21
Italian Americans, 121
Jewish Americans, 122
job market, 243-245
library science, 111
mediation, 203, 204
placement problems, 114, 115
salaries: See Personnel and Employment
social responsibilities, 303-307
Spanish speaking, XXXIX, 106, 238, 281, 306
special libraries, 308
"Who We Are," 196, 267
World Congress of Librarians, 153
See also Education, Library; Personnel and Employment; Social Responsibilities; Women in Librarianship
Libraries and Learning Resources, Office of, 186-189 (also 76 ed.)
Library Administration Division 189-191, 278 (also 76 ed.)
Library and Information Service Needs of the Nation, 15
Library and Statutory Distribution Service, 144
Library Association, Australia, XXXIX, XL, XLIII
Library Association, British, XXXIX-XLIII, 233, 345
Library Association, Canadian, 337, 338
Library Binding Institute, 52, 246-248
Library boards: See Trustees
Library Buildings Award Program, 45
Library Bureau, 136-139, 297, 299
Library Education and Manpower, 53
Library Education Division, 113, 179, 191, 192 (also 76 ed.)
Library Environment Resources Office, 193
Library History Seminar V, 19, 20, 50
Library Journal, XX, 196, 200, 219, 248
Library of Congress, 192-196, 250 (also 76 ed.)
acquisition and cataloging programs, 78, 79, 183, 268
appropriations, 326
automation, 37, 38
blind and physically handicapped services, 66
COM fiche usage, 207
CONSER project, 301
interlibrary cooperation, 173
Madison Annex, 72, 193
Music Division, 275
National Periodicals System, 212, 213, 301-303
networks, 40, 219
preservation efforts, 246-248
reference requests project, 279
serials, 269

Subject Catalog, 277
Thomas Jefferson Building, XVIII
Library of the USSR Academy of Sciences, 250
Library Personnel Interchange (LPI), 35
Library Press, 196, 197 (also 76 ed.)
Library Research and Demonstration program, 188
Library Research Round Table, 197, 198, 289 (also 76 ed.)
Library Research Round Table Research Award, 45
Library Resources & Technical Services (RTSD), 264
Library schools: See Education, Library
Library Science: See specific topics such as Automation; Research; Serials
Library Security Newsletter, 248
Library Service Enhancement Program, 4
Library Services and Construction Act (LSCA), 131, 134, 315
appropriations for, 12, 183, 186, 187, 325, 326
Title II, 73, 154
Title III, 216
Title V, 68
Library Technology Reports, 264, 267
Library Trends, 20, 196
LIBS 100 System, 91
Liebaers, Herman, XV, 49, **60,** 152, 176
Lieberman, Irving, 176
Liebert, Robert M., 19
Liegl, Dorothy, 404, 405
Liesener, James, 293
Life of the Mind lectures, XV
Linkhart, Edward G., 282
Lippincott, Joseph Wharton, **223**
Literacy and the Nation's Libraries, 111, 199
Literacy Programs, Library, 199-200 (also 76 ed.)
adult services, 15
disadvantaged, services for, 111
London report, 348
Literacy Volunteers of America, 111, 199
Little, William, XXXI
Livsey, John D. (Jim), 125, 144
Lobbying, 327
Lockhart, Helen D., 283
Lockheed data bases, 38, 39
Lockheed Retrieval Service, 108
Loertscher, David V., 289
London Report and British activities, 342-348 (also 76 ed.)
children's literature awards, 88
Citizen Advice Bureau, 159
library schools, XXXIX-XLIII
See also British headings
Long, Philip, 164
Lorenz, John G., 7, 33 (See also Biographies 76 ed.)
Lorio, Sister Mary Aquin, 374
Los Angeles Public Library, 250
LoSasso, John S., 206
Louis Round Wilson Scholarship, XXXI
Louisiana report, 187, 372-374
Love, Mary, 315
Lovell, L. G., 345
Low, Edmon: See Biographies 76 ed.
Lowell, Marcia, 315, 398
Lowrie, Jean E., 21, 176, 179, 181, 233, 236
Luehrmann, Jr., Arthur W., 207
Lundeen, Gerald, 245
Lunin, Lois F., 24
Luntz, Jerome D., 161
Luster, Arlene, 29

Lute, Harriet, 355
Lyman, Doris, 364
Lyman, Helen H., 15, 266
Lynch, Beverly P., 7, 32, 230, 278
Lynch, Mary Jo, 23, 259, 260, 277

McBee Key-Sort cards, 90
McClaughry, Helen, 29
McCloskey, Elinor, 389
McColvin, Lionel George, 345
McColvin Medal, 48
McCormick, Thomas F., 144, 145
McCrossan, John, 411
McDermott, Gerald: *See Biographies 76 ed.*
McDonald, John P., 7, 33
Macdonald, Torbert, 316
McDonough, Irma, 174, 336
MacDougall, Frank, 235
McElderry, Margaret K.: *See Biographies 76 ed.*
McGill University Libraries, 240, 242
McGlinn, Frank C. P., 318
McGregor, Jane Ann, 395
McGuire, Alice Brooks: *See Obituaries 76 ed.*
McKay, David, 315, 392, 393
McKenna, Frank, 25, 49, **61**, 104, 309
McKenzee, Mary, 242
McLain, Elmer W., 118
McMahon, Nathalie, 29
McMillan, Mary, 366
McNamara, Brooks, 318
McNamara, Margaret Craig: *See Biographies 76 ed.*
McNamee, Gilbert W., 353
McSweeney, Josephine, 50
Mabel Smith Douglass Library, 4 (photo)
Machine-readable data bases: *See Data Bases, Computer Readable*
Machlup, Fritz, 5, 92
Macy, Francis U., 157
Magazines: *See Publishing, Magazine; Periodicals; Serials*
Magazines, flexible disc, 66
Magna Design, 136
Maier, Joan, XXXVIII, 125
Mail-order-delivery (MOD), 93, 94
Maine report, 374, 375
Majer, Diance, 82
Malamud, Bernard, 122
Malinowsky, H. Robert, 282
Management, Library, 200, 201 *(also 76 ed.)*
  academic, 4, 5
  British Library, XXX
  ethics statement, 21
  International Personnel Management Association, 233
  MRAP, 241, 287
  performance improvement, 240, 241
Management Review and Analysis Program (MRAP), 241, 287
Managing the Library Fire Risk, 166, 298
Manning, Dale, 182
Manuscripts
  access to, 30, 31
  British Library, XXVII
  collections: *See Principal Libraries of the World article; Collections*
  gifts of, 140, 141
  Judaica research, 121, 122
  See also Documents, government; Archives
Map reference, 280
MARC data base, 194
  Canadian use of, 336
  expansion, 37, 38
  London report, 342
  MARC Development Office, 37
  music format, 210

serial record, 300, 301, 303
MARCAL format, 225, 226
Marcia C. Noyes Award, 48
Margaret Mann Citation, 45, 79, 291, 324
Marine Corps libraries: *See Armed Forces Libraries*
Marke, Julius J., 16
Markowetz, Marianna, 416
Marks, Sara Jean, 329
Markuson, Barbara, 3, 197
MARS (Machine Assisted Reference Service), 279
Marsh, Guy, 266 (photo)
Marshall, Cheryl, 304
Marshall, John, 338
Marshall, Margaret, 348
Martelle, Harold, 354
Martin, Allie Beth, 75, 97, 169, 179, 256, 259, 266, 353, 396, 397
  centennial conference, XV, XVI, XXI, 49
  continuing education, 283
  See also 76 ed.
Martin, Miles, 112
Martin, Susan K., 179, 219, 264
Marvin, James, 370
Maryland report, 375, 376
Massachusetts Institute of Technology visual collection, 209, (photo)
Massachusetts report, 376, 377
Master's degree: *See Degrees, library education*
Mathews, Virginia, 214
Mathis, Sharon Bell, 88, 119
Mavor, Anne S., 156
Mawrina, Tatiana, 174
Maxey, Charles, 5
Maxiwagon, 95
Maxwell, Margaret, 20
May Hill Arbuthnot Honor Lecture, 87, 89
Mazer, Norma Fox, 331, 332 (photo)
Measurement and Evaluation, 201, 202 *(also 76 ed.)*
  library management, 200, 201
  media centers, 293
  reference service, 278, 289
Media: *See Multimedia Materials; School Libraries and Media Centers*
Media Centers: *See School Libraries and Media Centers*
Media Industry Newsletter, 270
Media Programs: District and School (1975), 311
Media specialist, 17, 291-293, 361
Mediation, Arbitration, and Inquiry, 203, 204, 321 *(also 76 ed.)*
Medical insurance issue, 245
Medical Libraries, 204-206, 328 *(also 76 ed.)*
  See also National Library of Medicine
Medical Library Assistance Act, 204, 205, 285, 286
Medical Library Association 96, 206, 207 *(also 76 ed.)*
MEDLARS (Medical Literature Analysis and Retrieval System), 214
MEDLINE, 38, 214
Meem, John Gaw, 141
Melcher, Daniel, 45, 46, 49, **61**
Melsens, J., 176
Melvil Dewey awards, XXXI, 45, 46
Menninger, Walter, 146
Meredith, Louise: *See Obituaries 76 ed.*
MERLIN system, 342
Mester, Jean, 124
Metcalf, Keyes D., XV, **61**, 73, 190
Metoyer, Cheryl, 112

Metropolitan Library Systems, 172, 173
Metzdorf, Robert Frederic: *See Obituaries 76 ed.*
Mexican-Americans: *See Spanish speaking people, library service to*
Meyer, Helen Honig, **61, 62**
Michie, Jean, 387
Michigan report, 377-379
  Detroit Public library, 68, 184, 185, 305
  networks, 255
Microfiche: *See Micrographics*
Microfilm: *See Micrographics*
Microform: *See Micrographics*
Microform Review and *Microform Equipment Review,* 208
Micrographics, 207, 208
  ANSI committee, 229
  color artwork, 267 (photo)
  computer output microfilm: *See COM process*
  deposit documents, 144
  Independent Research Libraries, 155 (chart)
  microfilm, conversion to, 255, 257
  microfilm, preservation of, 248
  microfilm reader systems, 140, 207
  Micrographics Catalog Retrieval System, 41
  National Micrographics Association, 214, 215, 234, 235, 313
  Register of Additional Locations, 38, 194, 207
  serials, 302
  standards, 313
  theological literature, 25
Micropublications, standards for, 208
Middle East Librarians' Association, 234
Middleton, Dorothy, 282
MIDLNET (Midwest Region Library Network), 40, 172
Midwest Film Conference, 126
Miele, Anthony, 38 (photo), 315, 349
Mikva, Abner, 169
Milam, Carl H., XXI
Milczewski, Marion A., XXXIII
Mildred Batchelder Award, 46, 88, 89, 179
Military libraries: *See Armed Forces Libraries*
Miller, Arthur, 24
Miller, Barbara, 89
Miller, Gerald R., 366
Miller, Glen, 360
Miller, Harold, 268
Miller, Helen M., 363
Miller, Jane, 382
Miller, Richard, 354
Miller, Roberta, 413
Miller, Ronald, 2, 37, 173, 235
Miller v. California, 134, 135, 167
Mills, Lois, 143
Milne, A. A., 86, 87, 345
Milstead, Agnes, 18
Minarcini, et al. v. Strongsville City School District, et al., 171
Minick, Evelyn C., 42
Minimum-wage protection, 245
Minnerath, Janet E., 413
Minnesota report, 379-381
Minnesota Union List of Serials: *See MULS*
Minority groups: *See Ethnic Groups, Library Service to; Women; specific names of groups*
Minority Scholarship, 46
Mississippi report, 133 (photo), 381, 382
Missouri report, 382-384

Mitchell, Constance, 353
Mitchell, Marion, 285
Mitchem, Teresa, 125
Mitre Corporation, 66
MLA Exchange, 206
Modisette, James Oliver, 372
Modra, Helen, 112
Moffat, Edward, 264
Molumby, Larry, 166, 359
Molz, Kathleen, XV, XIX (photo) (*See also Biographies 76 ed.*)
Mondale, Walter, 157, 326
Monography publications, 20
Monroe County Library System, 304
Montague, Eleanor A., 7, 37, 282
Montana report, 384, 385
Montclair Public Library, 304, 305
Moon, Eric, XIX (photo), **62**, 307
Moore, Beverly, 355
Moore, Everett Thomson: *See Biographies 76 ed.*
Moore, Larry, 335
Moore, Richard, 282, 398
Moore v. Younger case, 134
Morein, P. Grady, 5, 287
Morgan, Jane H., 10, 304
Morgan, Sue, 353
Morisset, Auguste M., 336
Moro, Barbara, 267 (photo)
Morris, John, 166, 298
Morton, Ann W., 361
Moses, Stefan B., 353
Moss, Carol, 330
Moton, Honore, 231
Mountain Plains Library Association, 281, 282
Mudge, Isadore Gilbert, 263
Mulkey, Jack, 381
Mullen, Helen, 89, 230
MULS (Minnesota Union List of Serials), 300
Multer, Ell-Piret, 393
Multicultural Resources, 305
Multimedia Materials, 208, 209 *(also 76 ed.)*
  bibliographic control, 212
  nonprint materials reviewed, 263
  realia, 274
  standards, 311
  See also: Films; Filmstrips; Realia; Recordings, Sound; School Libraries and Media Centers; Television in libraries; Toys and Games
Multitype systems, 172, 173
Mulvey, Jack C., 315
Mumford, L. Quincy: *See Biographies 76 ed.*
Munn, Ralph: *See Obituaries 76 ed.*
Munthe, W., 151
Murphy, Elizabeth, 228
Museum of Broadcasting, 275
Music: *See Recordings, Sound*
Music libraries, 231
Music Library Association 210 *(also 76 ed.)*
Mutchler, Peter, 339
Mutschler, Herbert F., 189
Myers, Margaret, 192, 232, 264
Myers, Paul, 318

Nakako, Irene, 418
Nance, Betty, 406
Nasri, William Z., 21
Nathan Marsh Pusey Library, 71 (photo)
National Accreditation Council for Agencies Serving the Blind and Visually Handicapped, 234
National Agricultural Library 210, 211, 250 *(also 76 ed.)*
National Archives, 27, 28
National Archives and Records Service, 140

427

National Association for Public and Continuing Adult Education (NAPCAE), 112
National Association of Elementary School Principals, 234
National Association of Exposition Managers, 234
National Association of Spanish Speaking People: See REFORMA
National Book Award, 48, 88
National Bureau of Standards, 212
National Center for Education Statistics, 5, 131, 218, 280, 288
National Center for Educational Brokering, 157
National Center on Educational Media and Materials for the Handicapped, 146
National Central Library, Britain, XXIII
National Citizens Emergency Committee, 262, 321
National Coalition Against Censorship, 167, 168
National Commission on Libraries and Information Science, 131, 132, 211-213, 217 (also 76 ed.)
  federal funding, 326, 327
  lifelong learning, 158
  national information policy, 162, 163
  network planning, XXXVIII, 216
  periodicals library, 301, 302
  report, 14, 15
  serials, 325
National Commission on New Technological Uses of Copyrighted Works: See CONTU
National Community Education Association, 112
National Council of Organizations for Children and Youth, 231
National Council of Teachers of English, 167, 234
National Council of Teachers of Mathematics, 234
National Diet Library, Japan, 250
National Endowment for the Humanities, 213, 214 (also 76 ed.)
  American Antiquarian Society, 142
  enhancement programs, 4
  grants, 154, 156, 256, 257, 326, 327
National Federation of Abstracting and Indexing Services, 300, 301
National Foundation for the Arts, 154
National Historical Publications and Records Commission (NHPRC), 28
National Indian Education Association, 123
National Information System (NATIS), 322-324
National Labor Relations Board, 5
National League of Cities v. *Usery*, 245
National Lending Library for Science and Technology, XXIII
National Libraries: See Principal Libraries of the World; See also 76 ed
National Library Associations, Council of, 232
National library network, 40, 41
National Library of Australia, 250
National Library of Canada, 300, 335-340
National Library of Egypt, 250
National Library of Medicine, 214, 250 (also 76 ed.)
  appropriations, 285, 286, 326
  British Library usage, XXVIII
  communications satellite, XXXVIII
  medical library issues, 204-206
  medical literature access, 38, 108
  See also Medical Libraries
National Library of Nigeria, 251
National Library of Peking, 251
National Library Resource Centers, 217, 218
National Library Week: See Public Relations, Library
National Medal for Literature, 48
National Micrographics Association, 214, 215, 234, 235, 313 (also 76 ed.)
National Municipal League, 235
National Periodicals system, 1, 93, 212, 217, 218, 301, 302
National Program for Acquisitions and Cataloging (NPAC), 302
National Reference Library of Science and Invention, XXIII, XXIV
National Register of Last or Stolen Archival Materials, 28
National Registry for Librarians, 244
National Science Foundation, 213, 285, 287, 301
National serials system, 300-302, 325
National Story League, 235
National Study Commission on Records and Documents of Federal Officials, 27
National Technical Information Service (NTIS), 99, 163, 215, 216 (also 76 ed.)
National Telephone Reference Service, 278, 279
National Union Catalog, 207 (See also 76 ed.)
National University Extension Association, 235
National Voluntary Organizations for Independent Living for the Aging (NVOILA), 225, 235
NATIS: See National Information System
Navy libraries: See Armed Forces Libraries
Naylor, Alice, 107
NCLIS: See National Commission on Libraries and Information Science
Neal, Frances, 353
Nebehay, Elisabeth, 180
Nebraska report, 385, 386
Neilly, Andrew H., 267, 289
NELINET (New England Library Information Network), 218, 235
Nelso, Jerold, 282
Nelson, Milo, 363
Nemeyer, Carol, 46, 266 (photo), 291 (See also Biographies 76 ed.)
Netherland, Lynda, 372
Networks, 216-219 (also 76 ed.)
  academic libraries, 3
  bibliographic, 79
  children's libraries, 86
  circulation systems, 40
  cost analysis study, 287
  data interchange, 164
  inter-American, 225, 226
  interlibrary cooperation, 172, 173
  law libraries, 185, 186
  Library of Congress, role of, 194
  LIBS 100 System, 91
  LSCA funds, 187
  national library network, 40, 41
  NATIS program, 322, 323
  public libraries, 255, 257
  reference usage, 278, 279
  satellite based, 317
  search charges, 108
  serials, 302, 303
  special libraries, 308, 309
  staff development, 242
  state legislation, 184, 185
  SWLA directory, 284
  telecommunications usage, XXXVII, XXXVIII
  See also specific networks such as: AMIGOS; CLENE; OCLC; WILCO
Nevada report, 386, 387
New England Document Conservation Center, 245, 246
New England Library Association, 35
New England Library Board, 35, 242
New England Library Information Network: See NELINET
New Hampshire report, 387-389
New Jersey report, 314, 389
New Mexico Book League, 235
New Mexico report, 389, 390
New York Public Library, 73 (photo), 140, 143, 155, 251, 253, 254 (photo), 256, 306
New York report, 131, 184, 314, 390-392
New York Times, library supplement, XIX, 196, 261
New York Times Information Bank, 279
Newbery awards: See John Newbery awards
Newberry Library, 143, 155
Newlin, Mrs. Jeanne T., 318
Newman, Ralph: See Biographies 76 ed.
News media, control of, 170
Newsletter on Intellectual Freedom, 264, 270
Newspaper: See Publishing, Newspaper
NICHE, 304
Nichols, J. Gary, 374
Nida, Jane B., 297
Nielander, Ruth M., 310
Niemi, Peter, 365
Nigeria, library activities in, 176, 181
Nistendirk, Verna, 360
Nitecki, Danuta, 279
Nix, Larry T., 283
Nixon, Richard, 27, 156
Nobel Prize for Literature, 48
Non-English Speaking, Library Service to: See 76 ed.; specific groups; Literacy Programs
Nonprint materials: See Multimedia Materials
North Carolina report, 96, 392, 393
North Dakota report, 393, 394
Norton, Alice, 260
Notable Books, 220, 276 (also 76 ed.)
Notable Children's Books, 82, 266
Notable Notables 1944-1974, 266, 276
Notes, 210
Novak, Gloria J., 191
Novato Branch Library (Calif.), 74 (photo)
Noyes, Naomi, 227
NTIS: See National Technical Information Service
Nyquist, Ewald B., 292
Nyren, Karl, 2, 15, 239

Oberlin College, learning center, 139
Obituaries, 221-224 (also 76 ed.)
Oboler, Eli M., 364
O'Brien, Gael M., 4
Obscenity issues, 134, 135, 169, 296, 337, 345, 369
OCLC (Ohio College Library Center)
  authority control, 41
  CONSER, 269, 270, 300-303
  expansion, 3, 78, 172, 173, 187, 395, 396
  machine-readable form conversion, 255
  medical usage, 204-206
  National Agricultural Library, 211
  retrieval system grant, 41
  role of, 40
  serials data, 37, 301, 302
  state library agencies, 315
  utility defined, 218
  See also Automation; Cataloging and Classification; Networks; State reports
O'Donnell, Peggy, 242, 283
Oenslager, Mrs. Donald, 317, 318
Ofek, Uriel, 174
Office for Library Personnel Resources (OLPR), 237-239, 244
Office for Library Services to the Disadvantaged, 112
Office for Scientific and Technical Information, XXIV
Office of Education, U.S., 134, 285
Office of Information Policy, 162
Office of Management and Budget (OMB), 162
Office of Science Information Service: See Science Information, Division of
Office of University Library Management Studies, 1, 241, 243, 287
Ogilvie, Philip, 315, 393
O'Halloran, Charles, 382
Ohio College Library Center: See OCLC
Ohio report, 172, 173, 315, 394-396
Ohio State University, 146
Oklahoma City University, 188
Oklahoma report, 84, 396, 397
Olafson, Shirley, 182
Olafson Memorial Award, 182
Older Adults, Library Service to, 225 (also 76 ed.)
  agency directory, 276
  home delivery, 94
  LSCA funding, 186
  National Voluntary Organizations for Independent Living, 235
  programs, 304
  volunteer utilization, 85, 225, 235
  workshop, 146-148
Olsen, Jan, 404
Olsen, Wallace C., 211
Olson, Edwin, 363
Online, 108
On-line computer terminals: See Computers, library use of
On-Line Review, 108
Optical scanner, 297 (photo)
Opticon reader, 146
Optiscope Enlarger, 146
Oregon report, 184, 397, 398
Organization of American States, 225, 226, 246 (also 76 ed.)
Organizations and Associations, 226-237 (also 76 ed.)
Orgren, Carl, 278
Ormston, Ruth White, 277
Orne, Jerrold, 6, 116, 228, 263, 393
Oscarson, Linda, 235
Österreichische Nationalbibliothek, Austria, 251
Ostrove, Geraldine, 210
Otto Kinkeldey Award, 48
Outreach: See Disadvantaged, Library Service to
Owens, Major, III, 25
Oxford University's Bodleian Library, 251

Pacific Northwest Library Associa-

tion, 282
Page, Dennis M., 393
Pahlavi National Library, 251
Painter, John C., 357
Palmer, David C., 389
Palmer, Helen, 373
Palmer, Leland M., 283
Palmer, Paul R., 318
Palmour, Gene, 302
Palmour, Vernon E., 301, 302
Pan, Elizabeth, 37
Panizzi, Antonio, XXIII, XXVI
Paper Availability Study, 289
Paperback books, 13, 86, 268, 331, 347
Paraprofessionals, use of, 201, 244
Parents Without Partners, Inc., 235
Parham, Paul M., 407
Park, Leland M., 283
Parker, Virginia E., 305
Parks, George, 32
Parks, Gordon, 258 (photo)
Parks, Lethene, 148
Parsons, A. Chapman, 395
Parsons, George, 301
Parton, James, 193
Pastore, John O., 316
Patent information, 175
Patrick, Ruth, 113, 232
Patterns of Education and Accreditation for Librarianship: Canada, Great Britain, and Australia, XXXIX-XLIII
Patterson, Flora E., 78
Paul, Sandra, 46, 291
Paulin, Lorna Vincent, 343
Paulson, Peter J., 314
Pavetti, Sally Thomas, 318
Pearson, Karl, 37
Pearson, Lennart, 403
Pearson, Lois R., 197
Peck, Richard, 331
Peel, Bruce, 10
Pekin Public Library, Illinois, 72 (photo)
Peltola, Bette, 89
Pemberton, Jeff, 108
P.E.N. Translation Prize, 48
Penland, Patrick R., 157
Pennsylvania report, 188, 262, 398-400
People: *See* Biographies; Obituaries; State reports; *specific names*
Percy, Charles, 169
Performance appraisal: *See* Personnel and Employment: Performance Appraisal
Performance Measures for Public Libraries, 200, 202
Performing Arts Resources, 318
Periodicals
 ALA, 264, 265, 267
 copies made, 161
 cost of, 13, 300, 348
 information resource, 305
 national system, need for, 1, 93, 212, 217, 218, 301, 302
 photocopying issue, 100, 101
 vocational-technical, 30
 See also Publishing, Magazine; Serials
Periodicals for Religious Education Centers and Parish Libraries, 79
Perkins, Carl Dewey: *See* Biographies 76 ed.
Perlov, Dadie, 390
Personnel and Employment: Affirmative Action, 237-239 (also 76 ed.)
 slide-tape program, 282
Personnel and Employment: Job Market, 243-245
Personnel and Employment: Performance Appraisal, 239, 240, 346 (also 76 ed.)
Personnel and Employment: Salaries

academic libraries, 5, 31, 32, 237, 288
 faculty, 115
 Independent Research Libraries, 155
 London report, 346
 special libraries, 310
 trustees, role of, 322
 women, 5, 31, 237, 288, 310, 328, 329
Personnel and Employment: Staff Development, 240-243, 346 (also 76 ed.)
Peters, William T., 274
Peterson, Axel, 181
Peterson, Kenneth G., 7
Pfeiffer, Peggy L., 19
Phi Beta Kappa awards, 48, 49
Phinazee, Annette, 120, 392
Phonorecords, 100
Photocopying: *See* Copyright
Physically handicapped: *See* Blind and Physically Handicapped, Library Service for the
Picache, Ursula, 181
Pierce, Chester M., 19
Pierron, Ione, 171, 264
Pile, Fred, 336
Pilpel, Harriet, XV, **62**
Piternick, Anne B., **62**, 76-78
Pitts Theology Library, 25 (photo)
Piturro, Frank, 121
PLA Newsletter, 264
Platt, Kin, 331
Pletz, Frances H., 377
Plotnik, Arthur, XIX, 196, 197, 264, 267
Poetry projects, 80, 100, 101, 196, 268
Polacheck, Demarest L., 228
Policies and Procedures for Selection of Instructional Materials, 18, 19
Polish Americans and libraries, 124
Poole, Frazer, 195, 246, 248
Popecki, Joseph, 411
Porter, Barry L., 368
Post, Mrs. Ruden W., 141
Postal rates, 12, 208
Potash, Dr. and Mrs. Joe, 140
Potter, Donald C., 399
Pound, Mary, 265
Powell, Anne, 114
Powell, Ruth Ann, 415
Power, Eugene B., 162
Power, Mary R., 36, 148, 231, 264
PRECIS system, XXVII, 78, 175
Preservation of Library Materials, 245-248 (also 76 ed.)
 deacidification process, 140
 national program, 195
 sound recordings, 275
 See also Binding
Presidential papers, ownership of, 27, 140
President's Committee on Employment of the Handicapped, 236
President's Newsletter (ASLA), 264
Price, Douglas S., 24
Price, Joseph, 37, 301
Price, Paxton P., 262 (photo)
Price, Ray, 359
Prince George's County library system, 240
Princeton University, 4
Principal Libraries of the World, 248-252 (also 76 ed.)
 Association of International Libraries, 230
Prints and Posters: *See* 76 ed.
Prisons: *See* Correctional facilities, service to
Privacy, right to, 13, 14, 213
Prizes: *See* Awards and Prizes
Processing Centers, 252, 253 (also 76 ed.)

Program of Action, ALA, 204
Proxmire, William, 168
Public broadcasting: *See* Telecommunications and Public Broadcasting; Television in Libraries; *See also* 76 ed.
Public Broadcasting Act, 316
Public Broadcasting Service, 165, 317
Public Information Office, 260, 261
Public Interest Satellite Association, XXXVIII
Public Lending Right issue, 76, 77, 339, 340
Public Libraries, 253-259 (also 76 ed.)
 building projects, 69, 70, 72, 75
 Canadian, 77, 339-341
 children's services, 82-86, 319
 citizens committee, 262
 community delivery service, 93
 federal funding, 68, 130-132, 186-189
 humanities programs, 284
 independent study in, 156-158
 John Cotton Dana awards, 43, 44
 London report, 346
 multimedia service, 208
 performance measures, 200, 202, 239, 240
 public access statistics, 186, 187, 260
 salaries, 328
 social responsibility activities, 303, 304
 Urban Library Services, 256, 257
 See also Adults, Library Service to; Children's Library Services; Financing the Public Library; Independent Study in Public Libraries
Public Library Association, 259, 260 (also 76 ed.)
 alternative education programs, 157, 198
 performance appraisal, 202
 "Project Survival," 69, 261, 262
 Systems Section, 258
Public Library Reporter series, 259
Public Library Services Act, 353
Public Relations, Library, 260-263 (also 76 ed.)
 AAP campaign, 268
 John Cotton Dana Award winners, 43-45
 LAD projects, 190, 191, 261
 National Library Week, 260, 261 (*See also* 76 ed.)
 publicity, library, 260, 261
 video usage, 279, 280
Public Service Satellite Consortium, XXXVIII, 165, 317
Public works legislation, 73, 184, 187, 327
Published Search program, 215
Publishing, ALA, 263-267 (also 76 ed.)
Publishing, Book, 267-269 (also 76 ed.)
 bibliographies compared, 50, 51
 children's literature 86, 87
 information industry, 160, 161
 London report, 343, 344, 347
 paperbacks, 13, 86, 268, 331
 sales statistics, 13
 See also American Booksellers Association; Bookselling; Copyright
Publishing, Magazine, 269-271 (also 76 ed.)
 library journals: *See* Library Press
 London report, 347
 See also Periodicals; Serials
Publishing, Newspapers, 271 ,also 76 ed..
 braille, 66

First Amendment issues, 272, 273
London report, 347
photocopying, 101
Puerto Rico, Society of Librarians of, 307, 308
Pulitzer Prizes, 49
Puppeteers of America, 236
Purcell, Gary R., 406
Purdie, John B., 345, 346
Putnam, Herbert, XVIII
Putnam, Lee, 147, 360

Quackenbush, Robert, 80
Quad Retone process, 86
Quien es Quien, 238
Quinby, William J., 274
Quinly, William, 229

Rachow, Louis A., 318
Racism issue, 105, 329
Radcliffe Science Library (Oxford), 343
Radio, library usage of
 advertising, library, 260, 261
 broadcasting defined, XXXV
 fairness doctrine, 168
 federal funding, 186-189
 Library of Congress, 194
 library stations, 257
 reference collection, 275
 World Administrative Radio Conferences, 317
Radnitz, Robert, 127, 128
Rafferty, Paul, 125, 264
Railsback, Tom, 99, 104
Ralph R. Shaw Award for Library Literature, 46
Randall, David A., *See* Obituaries 76 ed.
Randall, Gordon, 29, 125
Randall Memorial Library, 74 (photo)
Randolph J. Caldecott awards, 46, 87-89, 266
Ranganathan Award for Classification Research, 49, 175
Ransom, Harry Huntt, **223**
Rape, books about, 331
Rare books and manuscripts, 140-143, 298
 government: *See* Documents, government
Rare Books and Manuscripts Section, 33
Rather, Lucia, 37
Ray, Gordon N., 34
Reader's Digest, 270
Readers Services Department, 194, 195
Reading centers, 95
Reading machines, 66
Realia, 274 (also 76 ed.)
 toys and games, 319
 See also School Libraries and Media Centers; Multimedia Materials
Rebsamen, Werner, 52
Recordings, Sound, 274-276 (also 76 ed.)
 British Library collection, XXVIII
 copyright issue, 99, 102, 103
 gifts, 141, 142
 reference source, 263
 rock music books, 333
 See also Music Library Association
Red Cross, American National, 228
Redding, Harold T., 161
Reed, J. R., 302
Reed, Nancy Ann, 42, 192
Reed, Sarah Rebecca, 111
Reese, Ernest J., 4
Reference and Adult Services Division (RASD), 276, 277 (also 76 ed.)
 Public Library Association, 259

Reference and Adult Services Division *(cont.)*
  reference service guidelines, 278
  Standards Committee, 311
Reference Service Policy Manual, 280
Reference Services, 277-280 *(also 76 ed.)*
  books, list of, 277
  British Library, science, XXVII
  Canadian service, 340
  ethics statement, 21
  Library of Congress, 194
  machine-based, 38, 39
  measurement, 190
  urban public libraries, 256
Referral centers: *See* Information and Referral Centers
REFORMA, 280, 281 *(also 76 ed.)*
  library education, bilingual, 106, 111, 304
  See also Spanish-speaking people, library service to
Regina Medal, 49
Regional Library Associations, 281-285
Regional networks, defined, 218
Register of Additional Locations (RAL), 38, 194, 207
Register of Copyrights, 193, 325
Register of Lost or Stolen Archival Materials, 298
Rehabilitation Act, 257
Rehabilitative services: *See* Health and Rehabilitative Library Services
Rehnberg, Marilyn, 165
Reich, David, 365
Reid, Marion T., 1
Reid, Richard, 353
Reilly, Jane A., 157
Reiniger, Lotte, 128 *(photo)* 129
Religious education aids, 79
Remington, David, 37
Repair and restoration: *See* Preservation of Library Materials
  See also Association of College and Research Libraries; Association of Research Libraries;
  Independent Research Libraries;
  Library Research Round Table; *specific types of libraries*
Research Libraries Group (RLG), 2, 3, 40, 173, 194
Research (and statistics), 285-289 *(also 76 ed.)*
  academic libraries, 5
  access to, 30, 31, 186, 187
  acquisition costs, 13
  British Library, XXIX
  continuing library education, 96
  independent learning statistics, 156
  independent research libraries, 155 (table), 156
  information activities, 160
  Italian census, 120, 121
  library usage statistics, 260
  literacy, 192
  minority librarians, 237, 238
  NEH grants, 213, 214
  photocopying, 101, 103
  science information, 297
  special librarianship, 308
  technical reports, 215, 216
Research and Technical Services Division, XVIII
Research libraries
  Center for Research Libraries, XXVIII, 1, 217, 301, 302
  conservation programs, 248
  federal funding, 7, 93, 183, 326
  staff development, 242
  Marc usage, 37
  network organization, 78, 302, 303

Resource sharing: *See* Interlibrary cooperation
Resources and Technical Services Division, 290, 291 *(also 76 ed.)*
Resources and Technical Services Division Resources Scholarship Award, 46, 291
Revenue Sharing, general, 131, 132, 184, 320
Reverse discrimination: *See* Discrimination
Reynolds, Donald, 236
Rheta A. Clark awards, 49
Rhoads, James B., 28, 313
Rhode Island report, 401, 402
Rhymes, R. R., 372
Richard, John B., 372, 373
Richler, Mordecai, 87, 336
Richmond, Phyllis A., 290
Rifenburgh, Richard, 137, 138
Riggs, Donald E., 355
Right to Read: *See* Literacy Programs, Library
Riley, Robert H., 161
Ringer, Barbara, 62 *(See also Biographies 76 ed.)*
Risko, Terence, 240 *(photo*
Risom Inc., 136, 138
Rizzolo, James, 228
Robart, Fran W., 26
Robbins, Jane, 114
Robert B. Downs Intellectual Freedom Award, 56
Roberts, Jo Nell, 351
Roberts, William H., 283
Robertson, Amy, 181
Robertson, Colin, 339
Robertson, Don, 118
Robinson, Bruce D., 353
Rochell, Carlton C., 7, 362
Rochester Institute of Technology School of Printing laboratory, 52, 247
Rockford Road Branch Library, Minn., 74 *(photo)*
Rogers, Brian, 356
Romani, Nina N., 210
Romans, Judy, 364
Roots, 118, 331
Rosenthal, Joseph A., 165
Ross, Patricia, 82
Rossell, Beatrice Sawyer, **223, 224**
Rotenberry, Julia, 349
Rothrock, Mary U. (Topey), 49, **224,** 406, 407
Rothstein, Samuel, 77
Round Table of National Organizations for Better Education, 236
Round Tables, dues for, 104, 105
Rouse, Roscoe, 70, 190
Rouse, Sandra H., 107
Rowland, A. Ray, 361
Royalty payments, photocopying, 103, 104
RQ (RASD) magazine, 265, 277, 280
RTSD Newsletter, 265
Ruan, Judith S., 339
Ruffner, Elizabeth, 22, 46
Rummel, Kathleen, 263
Rusby, Mrs., 357
Russo, Antonette, 17
Ryan, Mary, 94

Sjostrom, 136, 138
Sklar, Robert, 318
SLICE: *See* Southwestern Interstate Cooperative Endeavor
Sloan, Brenda D., 120
Slocum, Hester B., 50
Smart, Anne, 341
Smith, Bob, 330
Smith, Dorothy, 107
Smith, Eldred R., 7, 30, 32
Smith, Jessie Carney, 50
Smith, John Brewster, 304
Smith, Joshua, 37
Smith, Richard D., 245, 247, 248

Smith v. *United States,* 134, 369
Smolian, Steve, 275
Snider, Neil, 349
Snyder, Nancy, 42
Social Responsibilities, 304-307 *(also 76 ed.)*
Social Responsibilities Round Table, 307, 329 *(also 76 ed.)*
Sociedad de Bibliotecarios de Puerto Rico, 307, 308 *(also 76 ed.)*
Society of American Archivists, 28, 236
Software, 215, 216
SOLINET (Southeastern Library Network), 40, 172, 218
Sonntag, Iliana L. 280
Sony, 140, 316
Sophar, Gerald J., 24, 211
SORT Bulletin, 265
Sound: *See* Recordings, Sound
Source Library, The, 309 (photo)
Sourcebook of Library Technology, 208
South Carolina report, 403, 404
South Dakota report, 184, 404-406
Southeastern Library Association (SELA), 172, 282, 283
Southeastern Library Network: *See* SOLINET
Southern California Answering Network (SCAN), 278, 279, 354
Southern Regional Educational Board (SREB), 40
Southwest Wisconsin Library System, 132 (photo)
Southwestern Library Association (SWLA), 242, 283-285, 353
Southwestern Library Interstate Cooperative Endeavor (SLICE), 283, 284
Spalding, C. Sumner: *See* Biographies 76 ed.
Spanish speaking people, library service to
  Latin America, FID role with, 175
  librarians, XXXIX, 238, 281, 306
  library education, 106
  Organization of American States, 225, 226, 246
  programs for, 187, 304, 305
  REFORMA, 280, 281
  Sociedad de Bibliotecarios de Puerto Rico, 307, 308
Sparr, Roby H., 373
Spaulding, Amy, 231
Spaulding, Carl, 290, 291
Special Collections: *See* Acquisitions; Collection Development; Gifts, Bequests, and Endowments; Principal Libraries of the World; *See also* 76 ed.
Special Libraries, 308-311 *(also 76 ed.)*
  John Cotton Dana awards, 44
  reference priorities, 278
  survey, 315
Special Libraries Association, 308-310
  Hall of Fame, 49
  Professional Award, 49
Special Projects Act, 189
Sperry-Rand, 136-138
Spigai, Frances, 37, 282
Sports books, 333
Spottswood, Richard, 275
Spreitzer, Francis, 290
Spyers-Duran, Peter, 7
SRRT Newsletter, 265
Staff Committee on Arbitration, Mediation and Inquiry: *See* Mediation, Arbitration and Inquiry
Staff Organizations Round Table (SORT), 311 *(also 76 ed.)*

Standards, 311-314 *(also 76 ed.)*
  academic libraries, 30
  accreditation, 7-11, 112
  ANSI committees, 164, 228, 229, 303, 312, 313
  bibliographic records, 212
  correctional institutions, 146
  discography, 275
  ethics, 116, 117
  measurement, 202
  micropublications, 208
  nonprint materials, 274
  public libraries, 259
  RTSD committee work, 290, 291
  serials claim form, 303
  state level, 35
  trustees, 322
  UBC program, 324
  See also Accreditation; Education, Library
Standards for Accreditation, 7, 112
Standards for Cataloging Non-Print Materials, 311
Stanford University, 3, 41, 133, 251, 328
Stanick, Katherine, 353
Starr, Cecile, 127
State activities
  aid, changes in, 314, 315
  documents, standards for, 311, 312
  instructional equipment grants, 188
  John Cotton Dana awards, 44
  law and legislation, 184, 185
  public libraries, 254
  study committee, 36, 131
  See also specific State reports
State and Local Fiscal Assistance Act, 73
State Library Agencies 314, 315 *(also 76 ed.)*
  continuing education, 95, 96
  cooperatives, 172, 173
  COSLA, 36, 231, 315
  networks, 218
  staff development, 242
  trustees, 320-322
  See also Association of State Library Agencies; *specific State Reports*
State Library of South Africa, 251
State processing centers, 253
State V. I. Lenin Library, 251
Statement on Professional Ethics, 116, 117
Statistics: *See* Research
Stearns, Shirley, 135
Steinbach, Sheldon Elliott, 102
Steiner, Janet, 274
Steinitz, Kate Trauman: *See* Obituaries 76 ed.
Stephen B. Luce Library, 71 (photo)
Stephenson, Shirley K., 373
Steuermann, Clara, 210 (See also Biographies 76 ed.)
Stevens, Norman D., 6
Stevenson, Grace T., 49, **63,** 104, 225
Stewart, Donald E., 266 (photo)
Stewart, George R., 349
Stoffel, Lester, 365
Stone, Elizabeth W., 50, **63,** 116, 192, 232, 360
Stone, I. F., 171
Storytelling, 83-85, 235
Stovel, Madeleine, 37
Strable, Edward G., 310
Strader, Helen, 111
Strategy for Public Library Change, 256, 259
Strohecker, Edwin, 370
Strong, Bernard, 29
Strong, Gary E., 282
Studer, William J., 7
Stueart, Robert D., 192

Stump, Ron, 355
Subject Catalog, 277
Sudar, Dan, 339
Suellentrop, Helen, 369
Sullivan, Peggy, XXI, 89, 179, 197, 366
SUNY-Albany, 38, 188
Surridge, Ronald, 157
Surveys, 288
Sutherland, Thomas A., 370
Sutherland, Zena, 174, 179
Suzuki, Janet, 118
Swanson, Ken, XVII
Swartz, Roderick, 172, 173, 281, 284, 415
Sylvestre, Guy, 337, 339
Sysdac system, 90
System Development Corporation, 38, 39, 41, 108
Systems and Procedures Exchange Center (SPEC), 287, 288
Systems Control Incorporated, 39
Szabo, Charlotte, 84
Sachs, Nelly, 122
Sadler, Graham H., 258 (photo)
Sage, Mary, 359
Salaries: See Personnel and Employment
Salary Structures of Librarians in Higher Education survey, 5, 31, 288, 328
Salazar, Marilyn, 239
Salvation Army, 236
Sargent, Dency, 356
Satellite communication: See Telecommunications and Public Broadcasting
Sauer, Mary E., 301, 303
Saunders, Lelia, 236
Sayre, Edward C., 50
SCAMI: See Mediation, Arbitration, and Inquiry
SCAN: See Southern California Answering Network
Scannell, Francis X., 377
Schaaf, Robert, 143
Schaer, Martha, 404
Schear, Pauline A., 389
Schenker, Tillie, 373
Schmidt, C. James, 5
Schmidt, Rita, 384
Schmidt, Susan, 112
Schnaitter, Allene F., 7
Scholz, William, 37
School Libraries and Media Centers, 291-296 (*also 76 ed.*)
 budget restrictions, 68, 69
 Canadian report, 340
 construction, 69
 "Cooperation Game, The," 173
 copyright issue, 99-103
 exemplary schools, file of, 179
 federal funding, 186-188
 First Amendment issue, 170, 171, 185
 international school librarianship, 180, 181, 233
 John Cotton Dana Awards, 45
 media selection and specialists, 17-19, 130, 208, 209
 networks for, 86
 outreach services, 84
 social responsibilities, 305
 See also American Association of School Librarians; Children's Library Services
School Library Journal, 196
School Library Media Award, 49
School Media Quarterly, XXI, 265
Schools, library: See Education, library
Schroeder, Jan, 379
Schultz, Erich R. W., 25
Science fiction books, 331
Science Information, Division of (DSI), 296, 297 (*also 76 ed.*)
SCMAI: See Mediation, Arbitration, and Inquiry

Scoppetone, Sandra, 331
SCORPIO, 195
Scott, Ann, 182, 264
Scott, Margaret B., 339
Scott, Marianne, 242, 243
Scott, Marilyn, 350
Scoville, Maxine, 23
Scribes Award, 49
Sealock, Richard, 290
Security Systems, 139, 297-299 (*also 76 ed.*)
 academic libraries, 4
 archival property, 28
 collection development, 93
 ethics statement, 21
 fire prevention, 166
 school media centers, 292, 293
 theft detection survey, 267
 See also disasters
Seeley G. Mudd Library, 3 (photo)
Self-help books, 332, 333
Serials, 300-303 (*also 76 ed.*)
 ANSI work, 312
 CONSER, 194, 269, 270
 cost of, 13
 London report, 348
 LUTFCUSTIC, 291
 OCLC data base, 37
 Universal Serials and Book Exchange, 324, 325
 See also Conversion of Serials (CONSER) project; Periodicals; Publishing, Magazine
Serials Control Subsystem, 302
Sessa, Frank B., 50, 315
Sessions, Vivian, 115, 338, 339
Sevensma, T. P., 151
Sex discrimination: See Women, Status of
Seydel, Ruth, 363
Seymour, Whitney North, 321
Shaevel, Evelyn, 334
Shank, Russell, 227
Shapiro, Beth, 112, 307
Shapiro, Lillian L., 307
Shared Cataloging and Regional Acquisitions Program: See National Program for Acquisitions and Cataloging
Shaw, Spencer, 82 (photo), 120
Shaw, Thomas Shuler: See Obituaries 76 ed.
Sheafe, Mike, 282
Shearer, Kenneth D., 237, 328
Sheehy, Eugene P., 263
Sheldon, Brooke, 315
Shelledy, Louise Boyd, 385
Shelley, Karen Lee, 248
Shelley, Laura, 135
Shepard, E. H., 65
Shepherd, Mary Sue, 353
Shera, Jesse, 49, **62, 63**, 116, 368
Shirley Olofson Memorial Award, 46
Short, John T., 22
Shubert, Joseph, 315, 395
Shulevitz, Uri, 80, 174
Sibley, Richard, 374
Siemans, Nettie J., 339
Siggins, Jack, 311
Silver Slate Pencil Award, 88
Simon, Barry E., 311
Simonton, Wesley, 264
Simpson, Donald B., 35, 36, 218
Sinclair, Dorothy, 172, 231
Singh, Jennifer, 341
Sisson, Jacqueline D., 310

Talbot, Richard J., 5, 31, 288
Talking-books, 66
Talking Calculator, 146
Tannehill, Murphy, 372
Tarbox, Ruth, 259
Tate, Elizabeth, 314, 360
Tauber, Maurice F., XXXI, XXXIII
Tax Reform Act (1976), 327
Taxes, 41, 93
Taylor, Ferebee, XXXI

Taylor, Jennifer L., 119
Taylor, Joe Gray, 372
Taylor, Nettie B., 375
Taylor, Richard, 107
Technical assistants: See Council on Library Technical Assistants
Technical information, 215, 216, 297
Technotec service, 107
Tees, Miriam H.: See Biographies 76 ed.
Telecommunications and Public Broadcasting, XXXIV-XXXVIII, 41, 316, 317
 cable television, 95, 316, 317
 Corporation for Public Broadcasting, 232, 316, 317
 costs, 39
 educational television, 327
 fairness doctrine, 168
 federal funding, 186-189
 Information Science and Automation Division committees, 165, 166, 212
 Joint Council on Educational Telecommunications, XXXVIII, 233
 legislation, 327
 networks, 218
 satellites, 317
 video usage, 279, 280
 See also 76 ed.: Public Broadcasting and Satellite Communication
TELENET, 108
Telephone usage, XXXIV, XXXV
Television, educational: See Telecommunications and Public Broadcasting
Television in libraries
 effects on children, 18, 19, 82
 examples, 258, 259
 fairness doctrine, 168
 federal funding, 186
 films for, 129
 Library of Congress, 194
 library promotion, 260, 261
 media centers, usage, 294
 network news, 101
 reference collection, 275
 telecommunication explained, XXXIV-XXXVIII
 See also 76 ed.
Television-related books, 331, 332
Tennessee report, 406, 407
Terhune, Joy, 19
Tests, photocopies of, 102, 103
Texas A and M University Library, 12 (photo)
Texas report, 262, 407-409
Thaxton, Carlton J., 361
Theatre Libraries: See 76 ed.
Theatre Library Association, 317-319 (*also 76 ed.*)
Theatre Library Association Award, 317
Theft: See Security Systems
Theological libraries: See American Theological Library Association
Thomas, Lucille, 390
Thomas, Margie, 350
Thomison, Dennis, XX
Thompson, Paulette, 282
Thompson, Sandra, 372
Thompson, Susan, 20, 245
Thorne, Lucile, 409
Thornton, Eileen, 1
Thornycroft, Alice, 274
Thorpe, Frederick, A., 49, **63, 64**, 104
3M Company system, 39, 41, 297, 299
3M-JMRT Professional Development Grant, 43
Thurber, Mariana J., 42
Tibbe, Helen Galston, 141

Tiffany, Burton C.: See Biographies 76 ed.
Tighe, Ruth, 37, 42, 291
Tillin, Alma M., 274
Tindol, Lucile A., 372
Tomaino, Mary Y., 50
Tomberg, Alex, 109
Top of the News, XXI, 265, 334
Toro, Jose Orlando, 156
Totten, Herman L., 50, 120
Toward a National Program for Library and Information Services, 14, 131, 194, 211
TOXLINE, 109
Toy Manufacturers of America, 236
Toys and Games, 319 (*also 76 ed.*)
Transliteration, 314
Travis, Eileen, 336
Trejo, Arnulfo, 238, 306, 352
Trejo, Tamiye, 118
Tremaine, Marie, 336
Trezza, Alphonse, 39 (photo), 281, 284 (*See also Biographies 76 ed.*)
Tricontinental Film Center, 168, 169
Trivers, James, 331
Trivits, Patricia C., 358
Trotti, John B., 25, 414
Trustee Citations, 46
Turstees, 319-322 (*also 76 ed.*)
 See also American Library Trustees Association
Tsuneishi, David, 118
Tucker, Marty, 369
Turock, Betty, 304
Two-year college programs, 6, 31, 69
Tyer, Travis, 157, 232, 260, 266 (photo)
Tyner, Sue, 37

Ulrich's International Periodicals Directory, 270
UNESCO, 322-324 (*also 76 ed.*)
 conferences, 153
 FID, 175
 Florence Agreement, 106
 IASL gift coupons, 181
 Israel issue, 170, 177
 NATIS, 322-324
 programs, 177, 179
 UNISIST, 297
 U. S. National Commission for, 236
UNIMARC, 324
Unions, library, 203, 204, 292
 AFL-CIO, 182, 228
 Canada, 339
 collective bargaining, 5, 31
 National Labor Relations Board, 5
 relationship with, 201
 See also Labor Groups, Library Service to
UNISIST: See UNESCO; See also 76 ed.
United States Department of State: Government Advisory Committee on International Book and Library Programs, 236
United States National Commission for UNESCO, 236
Universal Availability of Publications (UAP), 153
Universal Bibliographic Control (UBC), 79, 153, 323, 324 (*also 76 ed.*)
Universal Serials and Book Exchange, 324, 325 (*also 76 ed.*)
Universalist Historical Society, 141
Universiteitsbibliotheek von Amsterdam, 251
University libraries: See Academic Libraries; Association of College and Research Libraries

431

University of California, Berkeley, 3, 41, 252
University of Chicago, circulation system, 39
University of Illinois at Urbana-Champaign Library, 252
University of Pittsburgh's Graduate School of Library and Information Science, 157
Urban Growth and New Community Development Act, 187
Urban Library Council, 131, 183, 256, 319, 321
Urban Library Services, 256, 257
Urban Professionals, Library Service to: See 76 ed.
U.S. Children's Books of International Interest, 89, 179
U.S. Information Agency, 161
U.S. Office of Education, 241
U.S.S.R., exchange programs, 179
USSR Academy of Sciences, Library of the, 250
Utah report, 409-411
Uyehara, Harry, 362

Vaidyanath, Chandra, 118
Vainstein, Rose, 50
Van Deerlin, Lionel, 316
Van Horn, Martha, 311
Van Horne, Geneva T., 384
Van Jackson, Wallace, 49, **64**
Van Orden, Richard, 282
Van Winkle, Elva, 360
Van Zuilen, Darlene, 274
Vance, Kenneth, 181
Varieur, Normand, 125
Varley, Douglas Harold, 343
Vaughan, Samuel S., 268
Veale, James, 299
Velasquez, Marta, 144 (photo)
Vent, Marilyn, 45, 198, 289
Vermont report, 411-413
Verona, Eva, 46, 79, 291, 324
Vespry, H. Arthur, 339
Video and Cable Communications Section committees, 165, 166
Videodiscs, 316, 317
Vietnamese, library services for: See Asian-Americans and Libraries
Virginia Metal Products, 136, 138
Virginia report, 187, 413, 414
Visitoner reading machine, 66
Vocoder, 146
Vogel, Amos, 127 (photo)
Voight, Melvin, 191 (photo)
Volunteers, usage of, 14, 85, 94, 111, 199
von der Lippe, Ann, 5, 288
Vonnegut, Kurt, 331
Vosper, Robert, 153

Waddell, John Neal, 43, 277 (See also Obituaries 76 ed.)
Wade, Ronald Ellis, 298
Wainwright v. Wall Street Transcripts, 108
Waldrop, Ruth W., 18, 19
Walker, Estellene P., 403
Wallace, James O., 107

Wallace, Sarah Leslie, 135
Wallan, Mabelle, 363
Waller, Theodore, 49, **64**, 104
Wallis, C. Lamar, 242 (photo)
Walls, Esther J., 176, 179, 237
Wanger, Cuadra, and Fishburn study, 108
Ward, Ralph, 299
Warncke, Ruth, 259, 263
Warner, Marilla Lay, 373
Warner, Robert M., 28
Wartluft, David J., 26
Washington Library Network, 173, 184, 219, 255, 414, 415
Washington Newsletter, 102, 265
Washington Report, 325-327 (also 76 ed.)
See also Law and Legislation
Washington state report, 184, 414, 415
Waters, Richard L., 191
Waters, Samuel T., 211
Watts, Franklin, 86
Wax, David M., 3
Wax, Olivia N., 266
Weatherford, John W., 5
Weaver, Frances A., XXXI
Webster, Duane, 125
Wedgeworth, Robert, XIX, 21, 176, 179, 204, 236
Weeks, Barbara, 357
Weiner, Karl, 171
Weins, Leo, 262 (photo)
Weisman, Jody, 135 (photo)
Welsh, William J., 2, 193
Wender, Ruth, 45, 198, 289
Wentroth, Mary Ann, 84
Wersba, Barbara, 331
Wert, Alice, 367
West, Vern, 282
West Virginia report, 207 (photo), 262, 415, 416
Westall, Robert, 87 (photo)
Western Continuing Education Exchange (WESTEX), 242
Western Heritage Awards, 49
Western Interstate Library Coordinating Organization Study, 287
Weston, Beverlee, 350
Weston, Darlene, 379
W. H. Smith & Son Literary Award, 49
Whalen, Lucille, 10
Wharton, Mrs. John F., 318
Wheatley Medal, 49
Whisenton, Andre Carl, 119
White, E. B., 88, 174, 269
White, Herbert S., 1, 24
White, Howard, 228, 264
White, Leila, 305
White, Lucien W.: See Obituaries 76 ed.
White House Conference, 123, 131, 184, 213, 327 (also 76 ed.)
White House Conference on Handicapped Individuals, 146, 280
Whitenack, Carolyn I., 42, 50, **64, 65**, 116, 192
Whitesides, William, 359, 360

Whitman, Kathryn A., 22
Whitmore, Marilyn P., 50
Whitney, Virginia P., **65**
WICHE: See WILCO
Wijnstroom, Margreet, **65**, 176
WILCO (Western Interstate Library Cooperative), 218, 242, 246, 255
Wilcox, Alice E.: See Biographies 76 ed.
Wilcox, Joann L., 377
Wiley, W. Bradford, 268
Wilford, Valerie J., 229
Wilkins, Barratt, 36, 231, 315
Wilkins, John, 119
Wilkins, Virginia, 373
Wilkinson, John, 288, 340
Willard, Charles, 25
William H. Welch Medal, 49
Williams, Barbara, 371
Williams, Charles B., 373
Williams, Edward Christopher, 120
Williams, James, 119, 357
Williams, Martha E., 109, 366
Williams, Walter, 360
Williams, William H., 418
Willis, Margaret, 371
Wilson, Connie, 45, 198, 289
Wilson, Jane, 175-177, 179, 236 (See also Biographies 76 ed.)
Wilson, Louis Round, XXXI-XXXIII, 7, 46, 393
Wilson, Richard, 363
Wilson Library Bulletin, 196
Wilt, Matthew R., 80, 232
Windsor, Patricia, 331, 332 (photo)
Winfrey, Dorman H., 407
Winger, Howard W., XVIII, XX, 20, 50, 196
Winkler, Paul, 25 (See also Biographies 76 ed.)
Winnie-the-Pooh celebration, **65**, 86-88, 345
Winslow, Mildred, 181
Wisconsin report, 172, 216, 262, 416-418
Wiseman, Frederick, 126
W. J. Barrow Research Laboratory, 247
W. K. Kellogg Foundation, 3
Wolf, Coralie (Parsil), 351
Wolf, Edwin, 33
Wolfert, Richard J., 393
Womack, Sharon, 351
Women, status of, 305, 306
  Canadian report, 341
  filmstrips, 130
  history study project, 28
  maternity coverage, 245
  rape, books about, 331
  sexism issue, 105, 106, 169, 170, 184, 237-239, 307, 310, 329
Women in Librarianship, Status of, 328, 329 (also 76 ed.)
  affirmative action, 237-239
  Canadian report, 341
  salaries, 5, 31, 237, 288, 310, 328, 329
  social responsibility for, 306, 307

special libraries, 309
Women Library Workers, 329
Women's Joint Congressional Committee, 237
Women's National Book Association, 47, 237
Wong, Elsie, 118
Wood, Johanna, 18
Wood, Peg, 281
Woodrow Wilson Foundation Award, 49
Woodson Regional Library workshop, 120 (photo)
Worcester Area Cooperating Libraries (WACL), 218
Worden, 138, 139
Workbooks, photocopying, 102, 103
World Administrative Radio Conferences, 317
World Confederation of Organizations of the Teaching Profession (WCOTP), 180
World Congress of Librarians, 153
Wouk, Herman, 122
W. R. Hewlett Foundation, 133
Wright, Donald E., 189
Wright, Jasper H., 366
Wright, John, 336
Wright, Keith, 360
Wright, Jr., M. Eugene, 372
Wu, Eugene W., 229
Wyoming report, 279, 418

Xerox Corporation, 41

Yaffe, Phyllis, 341
Yale University Library, 252
Yates, Ella G., 119, 171, 362
Yee, Margaret, 118
Yivo Institute for Jewish Research, 121, 122
Yeh, Irene, 118
Young, Diana, 319
Young, Juana, 353
Young, Kenneth E., 232
Young, Rosemary, 334
Young, Walter A., 358
Young Adult Library Services, 329-331 (also 76 ed.)
  films, 128
  LED activities, 192
Young Adult Literature, 331-333 (also 76 ed.)
  Canadian report, 340
  See also Children's Literature; International Board on Books for Young People
Young Adult Services Division, 333, 334 (also 76 ed.)
Yungmeyer, Elinor, 10

Zambia, library acitvities in, 181
Zealberg, Catherine, 125
Zeh, Louis J., 215
Zindel, Paul, 86, 331
Zorbas, Elaine, 329
Zumwalt, George M., 353
Zurkowski, Paul G., 161

SEP 12 1977

Z
721
A525
1977